THE COMMON LAW LIBRARY

Number 7

THE LAW OF AGENCY

OTHER VOLUMES IN THE COMMON LAW LIBRARY

AUSTRALIA
The Law Book Company
Brisbane · Sydney · Melbourne · Perth

CANADA
Carswell
Ottawa · Toronto · Calgary · Montreal · Vancouver

AGENTS
Steimatzky's Agency Ltd., Tel Aviv;
N.M. Tripathi (Private) Ltd., Bombay;
Eastern Law House (Private) Ltd., Calcutta;
M.P.P. House, Bangalore;
Universal Book Traders, Delhi;
Aditya Books, Delhi;
MacMillan Shuppan KK Tokyo;
Pakistan Law House, Karachi, Lahore

THE COMMON LAW LIBRARY

NUMBER 7

BOWSTEAD AND REYNOLDS

ON

AGENCY

SIXTEENTH EDITION

BY

F. M. B. Reynolds, Q.C.(Hon.), D.C.L., F.B.A.

Honorary Bencher of the Inner Temple;
Fellow of Worcester College
and Professor of Law in the University of Oxford

WITH THE ASSISTANCE OF

Dr Michele Graziadei

Ricercatore, Faculty of Law, University of Trento

LONDON
SWEET & MAXWELL
1996

First Edition	(1896)	By William Bowstead.
Second Edition	(1898)	,, ,, ,,
Third Edition	(1907)	,, ,, ,,
Fourth Edition	(1909)	,, ,, ,,
Fifth Edition	(1912)	,, ,, ,,
Sixth Edition	(1919)	,, ,, ,,
Seventh Edition	(1924)	,, ,, ,,
Eighth Edition	(1932)	,, ,, ,,
Ninth Edition	(1938)	By Arthur H. Forbes.
Tenth Edition	(1944)	,, ,, ,, ,,
Eleventh Edition	(1951)	By Peter Allsop.
Twelfth Edition	(1959)	By E. J. Griew.
Thirteen Edition	(1968)	By F. M. B. Reynolds and B. J. Davenport.
Fourteenth Edition	(1976)	,, ,, ,,
Fifteenth Edition	(1985)	By F. M. B. Reynolds.
Sixteenth Edition	(1996)	,, ,, ,,

Published in 1996 by Sweet & Maxwell Limited of
100 Avenue Road, Swiss Cottage,
London NW3 3PF
Computerset by PB Computer Typesetting,
Pickering, N. Yorks
Printed and bound in Great Britain by
Athenæum Press Ltd, Gateshead, Tyne & Wear

Reprinted 1996, 1998, and 1999

No natural forests were destroyed to make this product;
only farmed timber was used and replanted

A CIP catalogue record for this book is available from the British Library

ISBN   0 421 537 809

©
Sweet & Maxwell
1996

PREFACE

It is now 10 years since the last edition of this work, and this edition is, in a sense, overdue. However, for several years from the publication of the last edition there were not many significant developments in agency law, apart from the enactment of the Enduring Powers of Attorney Act, which was a Bill at the time of the last edition, statutory modification of the *ultra vires* rules in company law, and a relentless accrual of diverse material on fiduciary duties from all over the common law world. The coming into effect of the Commercial Agents (Council Directive) Regulations 1994 on January 1 of that year, however, made a new edition imperative; and during 1994 and 1995 a surprising number of leading cases appeared, some while the text was in proof. These include *Attorney-General for Hong Kong v. Reid* on bribes, the speech of Lord Lloyd of Berwick in *Siu Yin Kwan v. Eastern Insurance Co. Ltd* on the undisclosed principal doctrine, a recent succession of English cases on fiduciary duties (*Kelly v. Cooper, Henderson v. Merrett Syndicates Ltd* and *Target Holdings Ltd v. Redferns*, with some help from *White v. Jones*), in which significant views are expressed by Lord Browne-Wilkinson, and the landmark judgment, at any rate for English law, of Lord Nicholls of Birkenhead on accessory liability (formerly "knowing assistance") (*Royal Brunei Airlines Sdn.Bhd. v. Tan*). The effect of the decision of the Court of Appeal on apparent authority in *First Energy (U.K.) Ltd v. Hungarian International Bank Ltd* remains to be seen. There has also been a decision of the Court of Appeal (*Presentaciones Musicales SA v. Secunda*) and two significant judgments by Colman J. and Waller J. (*National Oilwell U.K. Ltd v. Davy Offshore Ltd* and *Suncorp Insurance and Finance v. Milano Assecurazioni SpA*) on ratification. Most recently there have been two judgments of Lord Hoffmann on agency and the notion of primary representative in company law (*El Ajou Dollar Land Holdings Plc* in the Court of Appeal and *Meridian Global Funds Asia Ltd v. Securities Commission* in the Privy Council). In addition, of course, the whole text has required reconsideration, and I have tried to provide or extend discussion of various points which came to my attention in connection with actual disputes — often the best source of new ideas. A particular example is the doctrine of agency of necessity, where *The Choko Star* prompted me to suggest that the law may need rethinking.

The Commercial Agents Directive provides a significant problem for English lawyers, who are accustomed neither to the notion of a commercial agent, nor to categorisation of agents in general, nor to protection of agents as opposed to principals. Since it represents a type of regulation that is well known in continental European countries, it

v

seemed to me that common lawyers would need help in respect of the ways in which such rules have been and are understood in other jurisdictions. I was fortunate in enlisting the help of Dr Michele Graziadei of the University of Trento, who has enabled the book to contain a much fuller exposition than I could have provided myself using traditional common law methods of interpretation, and we hope that this new and (to some) unfamiliar material may prove of use. The Regulations which implement the directive are printed as an appendix.

I have for some time been considering adding a chapter on the Conflict of Laws. In the end, however, I came to the conclusion that I could not improve on what has already been written on the subject; so I have contented myself with a brief note drawing attention to the difficulties which are encountered in this area.

Although for most purposes the Statute of Frauds is dead since the Law of Property (Miscellaneous Provisions) Act 1989, the Act and its *travaux préparatoires* are almost silent on how the law of agency is to apply in respect of it: I have therefore thought it prudent to retain, with cautionary comments, a lot of the (quite rich) material on agency under the Statute of Frauds and its subsequent manifestations.

As Mr Brian Davenport and I said in the preface to the 13th edition, the first which we undertook, this book was originally called "A Digest of the Law of Agency" and was written as a code at a time when codification had been in fashion. Revising it for this edition I have been more aware than I was before of the extent to which it must when first published in 1896 have been a more or less complete digest of the agency cases. I have in this edition, as in previous editions, eliminated some of the Victorian case law, especially that in specialised contexts such as bankruptcy; but many of the old cases contain surprisingly clear and succinct statements of principle which form the foundation of the modern law, and I have hesitated to remove too many: it seems to me that it is still not yet the time to kill off these roots altogether and that if this store of material should be preserved anywhere it is in this book. I have again retained the Articles as statements of principle: it seems to me that agency is a subject which lends itself to formulations of general principle as starting points for dispute resolution, even though their application in practice may prove far from straightforward. Readers will note that the old format of Article, Comment and Illustration, which is still used in other textbooks, is now accompanied by numbering of the paragraphs — this is to facilitate eventual handling of the material by computer.

I am grateful to many colleagues and practitioners who have asked me stimulating questions and given me valuable advice: they are, over the last 10 years, too many to list. I am, however, specifically grateful to Mr I. D. D____, Fellow of St Catherine's College, Oxford, Mr Simon ___ow of Lincoln College, Oxford, and Associate Professor

Peter Watts of the University of Auckland, for substantial guidance in the area of equity; and to Professor Dan Prentice, Fellow of Pembroke College, Oxford and Allen & Overy Professor of Corporate Law in the University of Oxford, for similar help in the area of company law. My debt to the writings of Professor (now Justice) Paul Finn will be apparent; at one point I have even ventured to adopt his terminology verbatim. As his formal retirement nears, it is also right that I should again thank Professor G. H. Treitel, Q.C., Fellow of All Souls College, Oxford and Vinerian Professor of English Law, for help with the first edition of the book which I undertook, help which went far beyond what one has any right to expect from a friend and colleague, and much of which still shows in the present text. I also still owe much, as does the book, to my former collaborator Mr Brian Davenport, Q.C., a commentator who does not allow one to err unwarned.

I must acknowledge also patient and cheerful help from the staffs of the law libraries of the National University of Singapore, the University of Otago, the University of Auckland, and my own home library, the Bodleian Law Library at Oxford, at which libraries virtually all the work has been done: and, as with the last edition, the tolerance of students of the National University of Singapore, the only students on whom my ideas have been regularly tried out. I am most grateful also to the editorial staff of the publishers for handling what became a very complex manuscript with patience and efficiency, and for permitting an unusually high number of changes in proof, mostly made necessary by the developments occurring in the first part of 1995. They have borne the burden of numbering the paragraphs and footnotes, and preparing the table of cases.

Finally, I ought to apologise to those who are concerned by the use of the masculine pronouns "he" and "him" as words of indeterminate reference. To circumvent the immense amount of occasions in this book where the words "principal" "agent" and "third party" require such referents would have required an exercise in editing almost as extensive as that as to substance. While I have made some obvious modifications (and missed some) I have not faced up to going further. Very many of the usages of these words, and of other terms such as "warehouseman", are in fact accurate reportage of the cases.

I originally sought to state the law as at January 1, 1995; but I have been able to insert references to what I see as the most important developments up to July 31, 1995.

F.M.B.R.
University of Auckland
and Worcester College, Oxford

September, 1995

vii

CONTENTS

ix

CONTENTS

CONTENTS

xiii

CONTENTS

STANDARD ABBREVIATIONS

The following standard works on the law of agency are referred to throughout this book without further description.

Powell	Raphael Powell, *The Law of Agency*, 2nd edition, 1961.
Fridman	G. H. L. Fridman, *The Law of Agency*, 6th edition, 1990.
Stoljar	S. J. Stoljar, *The Law of Agency*, 1961.
Restatement	Restatement, Second, Agency (American Law Institute) 1958.

TABLE OF CASES

Paragraph numbers in bold denote where the facts of a case appear as one of the illustrations.

UNITED KINGDOM

RX

xxiii

xli

xlviii

c

ci

Canada

Hong Kong

India

Ireland

Malaysia

New Zealand

Singapore

South Africa

United States of America

TABLE OF STATUTES

CHAPTER 1

NATURE OF THE SUBJECT

Article 1

AGENCY AND AUTHORITY

(1) Agency is the fiduciary relationship which exists between two **1–001**
persons, one of whom expressly or impliedly consents that the
other should act on his behalf so as to affect his relations with
third parties, and the other of whom similarly consents so to
act or so acts. The one on whose behalf the act or acts are to
be done is called the principal. The one who is to act is called
the agent. Any person other than the principal and the agent
may be referred to as a third party.[1]

(2) In respect of the acts which the principal expressly or impliedly
consents that the agent shall so do on the principal's behalf,
the agent is said to have authority to act; and this authority
constitutes a power to affect the principal's legal relations with
third parties.[2]

(3) Where the agent's authority results from a manifestation of
consent that he should represent or act for the principal
expressly or impliedly made by the principal to the agent
himself, the authority is called actual authority, express or
implied. But the agent may also have authority resulting from
such a manifestation made by the principal to a third party;
such authority is called apparent authority.[3]

(4) A person may have the same fiduciary relationship with a
principal where he acts on behalf of that principal but has no
authority and hence no power to affect the principal's relations
with third parties. Because of the fiduciary relationship such a
person may also be called an agent.[4]

Comment

1. Theoretical basis of agency in the common law

Purpose of definition. It is customary to begin a systematic treatise **1–002**
with some sort of definition of its subject-matter. The definition given

---

[1] *Restatement*, §1.
[2] *Restatement*, §§6, 7.
[3] *Restatement*, §§8, 15, 26, 27. And see in general Conant, "Proposed Code of Agency
Contracts" (1971) 13 Mal. L.R. 98.
[4] Below, para. 1–017.

here is based on that in the American *Restatement*, and it is hoped that it may provide a useful starting point to an area of law where concepts have been "particularly troublesome".[5]

Definitions such as that above serve two purposes. They may, first, simply form an introduction to the subject-matter following. But recourse may also be had to such a definition when general words such as (in this context) "agent" and "agency" appear in propositions of law, particularly in statutes and other formal documents. What meaning should be attributed to these terms in such contexts is discussed later.[6] A major problem in the application of the law in this area is that questions are frequently asked in forms such as "Is A an agent?", "Is A B's agent or C's agent?", as if a clear answer could be given for the purposes of resolving a dispute. Any useful answer has to be couched in a much more restricted form, for agency is a relative notion and there are many acceptable uses of the term which do not always coincide with each other.

It must be stressed at the outset therefore that the definition given above is intended to be read as a whole. No single sentence should be treated as encapsulating the whole notion of agency. The first of the above propositions, (1), is no more than the first of four. Taken by itself it is very wide, as Woolf J. noted in a case involving the distinction between sale and agency for the purpose of a taxing statute.[7] For the purposes of most legal usage, (2) and (3) provide an essential restriction, in limiting the central use of the term to cases where the agent has authority to affect the principal's legal position. The proposition in (4) adds for completeness another situation where the terms "agent" and "agency" may be not inappropriately used.

1–003　　**Limits on definition.** But in any case definitions are, however commonplace, of limited utility in law as elsewhere: in particular, reasoning based on initial definitions is often suspect. A longer explanation is usually required than can be encapsulated in the definitional form. No one has the monopoly of the "correct" use of this or any other term. The word "agency", to a common lawyer, refers in general to a branch of the law under which one person, the agent, may directly affect the legal relations of another person, the principal, as regards yet other persons, called third parties, by acts which the agent is said to have the principal's authority to perform on his behalf and which

---

[5] Müller-Freienfels, in *Civil Law in the Modern World* (Yiannopoulos ed. 1965), pp. 77, 79.

[6] Below, para. 1–020.

[7] *Customs and Excise Commissioners v. Johnson* [1980] S.T.C. 624, 629 (though the formulation there referred to is that of the 15th edition of this work: the present formulation is narrower).

when done are in some respects treated as the principal's acts. These acts are probably thought of as most likely to occur in connection with the formation and discharge of contracts and in the disposition of property, but the same idea appears in many other parts of the law. Even in this context, the term "agency" may be used to refer to the relationship between the principal and the agent; to the function of the agent with respect to the outside world; or to the sum total of all legal relations involving principal, agent and third parties arising in such situations.[8] But these are only some possibilities: even in legal terminology the term may be used in other senses, and lay usage of the words "agency" and "agent" provides further variations. The definition given in (1) above selects as the initial referent of the term "agency" the relationship between principal and agent which, since it involves special trust, is a fiduciary one. In view of the other relationships which are also involved this selection may appear somewhat arbitrary. But in what follows it will be argued that that relationship is fundamental to this whole branch of the law, since it provides the paradigm situation and justification for the application of the typical rules regarding the agent's power to affect the principal's legal position *vis-à-vis* third parties, which in fact then dominate the subject.

Fundamental role of agency by agreement. The basic notion behind the common law of agency can be explained along the following lines. The mature law recognises that a person need not always do things that change his legal relations himself: he may utilise the services of another to change them, or to do something during the course of which they may be changed. Thus where one person, the principal, requests or authorises another, the agent, to act on his behalf, and the other agrees or does so, the law recognises that the agent has power to affect the principal's legal position by acts which, though performed by the agent, are to be treated in certain respects as if they were acts of the principal. This result is not confined to cases where the agent simply has specific instructions to do one thing, *e.g.* to sign a document. A person who acts in such a way (sometimes called a *nuntius* or messenger) performs no more than a ministerial function, which is attributable to the person for whom he acts without much stretching of elemental notions. Any developed system must also recognise the more advanced notion of permitting a person to give to another a general authority to act according to his own discretion within certain limits. 1–004

Basis in unilateral manifestation of will. The basic justification for the agent's power as so far explained seems to be the idea of a unilateral manifestation by the principal of willingness to have his legal position 1–005

---

[8] Powell, pp. 31–32.

changed by the agent.[9] In this respect the word "agreement" is slightly misleading, though convenient. There is certainly no conceptual reason which requires a contract between principal and agent to achieve this creation of power, and it is indeed clear that no contract is necessary, for a person without juristic capacity may be an agent.[10] Further, if only the relations between principal and third party are in issue, it may not be necessary for the agent to have agreed to, or even perhaps to have knowledge of, the conferring of authority at all, if it can be established that the principal had conferred it[11]; though such a situation would be an unusual one.

1–006   **Extensions of reasoning.** The basic idea is extended to cases where the words and conduct of one person towards another are such that the law treats that other as entitled to regard himself as authorised in certain respects, even though the first person cannot be shown to have had, and may indeed not have had, a specific intention of conferring authority; and to cases where the first person subsequently approves an act done by another on his behalf though he had not previously authorised it. The paradigm situation, in which the principal intends to confer authority, is in this book referred to as agency by express agreement.[12] The first extension set out above is called agency by implied agreement[13]; and the second is dealt with under the heading of ratification.[14]

1–007   **No requirement that agent purport to act for principal.** In some legal systems such reasoning would normally only be accepted in the case of an agent who when acting purported, or at least was understood, to do so on behalf of, or "in the name of", a principal, though the principal need not actually be named.[15] The common law, however, has no such requirement: if there is preceding authority to act for the principal, the rules so far set out, other than those as to ratification, will apply despite the fact that the existence of the principal, or his connection with the transaction, is unknown to the third party. Where his existence or connection with the transaction is not known, the principal is referred to

---

[9] Montrose (1938) 16 Can.B.R. 757, 779; Müller-Freienfels (1964) 13 Am.J.Comp.L. 193, 203. See also *Sinfra A-G. v. Sinfra Ltd* [1939] 2 All E.R. 675, 682 (power of attorney a "one-sided instrument").

[10] See Article 5; *Restatement*, §26, note *a*; the *Yasuda* case [1995] Q.B. 174.

[11] See Comment to Article 8.

[12] Articles 7, 24–26.

[13] Articles 8, 27–32.

[14] Articles 13–20.

[15] See, *e.g.* French CC, arts. 1119, 1984; BGB, para. 164(1). There may be exceptions in some systems for situations where the agent is a "man of straw."

as undisclosed,[16] and the rules then applicable are referred to as the doctrine of the undisclosed principal, which can be regarded as a unique feature of common law (though some civil law systems now approach some of its results, and such results were earlier known to the *ius commune*). In addition to the exclusion of ratification, however, the doctrine is limited by other safeguards appropriate to the fact that it in substance involves intervention on a contract by one not contemplated as a party to it.

No requirement that agent pursue recognised commercial function. 1–008
Although the main operation of agency principles is in the commercial sphere, they are in fact absolutely general and may apply to domestic and other non-commercial situations. There is no requirement that the agent pursue a commercial function at all, and certainly none that he pursue a commercial function of a recognised type.

Agency by estoppel and apparent authority. By a further extension, 1–009
the law may treat a third party dealing with a person who appears to have authority from a principal as entitled, by virtue of the principal's words or conduct manifested to him, to assume that the person in question has such authority, regardless of whether anything has occurred from which the law would draw that conclusion if the matter were in issue only between the supposed agent and the supposed principal. This reasoning takes effect in two related doctrines, the doctrine of agency by estoppel and that of apparent authority. The first applies where the supposed agent is not authorised to act for a principal at all, but is allowed by the principal to appear as if he is; the second applies where an agent is allowed to appear to have a greater authority than he has had conferred on him. Both doctrines operate regardless of whether the agent himself believed that he was authorised, provided that he reasonably appeared to the third party to be authorised. But the basis of the doctrines makes it essential in both cases that he has purported to act on the principal's behalf. Because the full consequences of the basic agency relationship are not applicable, the main doctrine of apparent authority is not fully discussed until the section dealing with the relations between the principal and third parties,[17] though agency by estoppel is briefly treated at an earlier stage[18] in Chapter 2.

Agency by agreement as paradigm case. By this explanation, the basic 1–010
situation of agency is treated as being that in which the principal agrees that the agent should act for him and (normally) the agent agrees to do

---

[16] See Article 78.
[17] Articles 74, 85.
[18] Article 21.

so. This is the paradigm, and it is from their similarity in various respects to this situation that the others derive their legal force. It is for this reason that the term "agency" is assigned to this relationship in the wording of Article 1(1). The other cases may fairly be regarded as derivatives. Ratification cases can, but only with difficulty, be assimilated into the paradigm situation; and agency by estoppel and apparent authority cases only affect third parties in the first instance, so do not give rise to the full range of results flowing from the paradigm situation.

This account conforms with the approach taken by the English cases. In 1863 Lord Cranworth said that "No one can become the agent of another person except by the will of that other person"[19]; more than 100 years later the same starting point was selected by Lord Pearson when he said: "The relationship of principal and agent can only be established by the consent of the principal and the agent."[20] Although the notions of "will" and "consent" are objectively determined, they clearly remain fundamental.

1–011   **Authority as the basis of power.** The technical description of the results which the law puts on the agency situations described is however to say that in all of them the agent has a power to affect the principal's legal relations[21]: and this terminology has already been used above. It is nevertheless more commonly said that the agent has authority. When examined, this authority amounts to no more than a power of a special sort, a power by doing an act to affect the principal's legal relations as if he had done the act himself. But the notions of authority and power are different.[22] Where such a power is voluntarily conferred by one person on another (the paradigm case), the person on whom it is conferred is said to "be authorised" by the other, or to "have his authority". But, as can be seen from what is said above, the power may exist in a person upon whom it cannot be said to have been voluntarily conferred. In the common law, such cases seem exceptional, and it is said that there is only "agency by estoppel" or "apparent authority". Yet the power is the same: there is no temptation to talk of "apparent power". "Authority", like "possession", carries the image of a paradigm case

---

[19] *Pole v. Leask* (1863) 33 L.J. Ch. 155, 161 (a dissenting speech).
[20] *Garnac Grain Co. Inc. v. H.M.F. Faure & Fairclough Ltd* [1968] A.C. 1130n., 1137; see also *Atlas Maritime Co. S.A. v. Avalon Maritime Ltd (The Coral Rose) (No. 1)* [1991] 4 All E.R. 769, 774–775, 779.
[21] Hohfeld, *Fundamental Legal Conceptions as Applied in Judicial Reasoning* (4th printing, 1966), p. 52; Montrose (1938) 16 Can.B.R. 757.
[22] Powell, p. 6; Corbin (1925) 34 Yale L.J. 788, 794; Montrose, *op. cit.* n. 9 above at p. 763; Falconbridge (1939) 17 Can.B.R. 248, 251–252; Dowrick (1954) 17 M.L.R. 24, 37.

justifying a legal result: "power" is neutral and simply states the result regardless of the justifications for it.

Actual and apparent authority. The placing of actual and apparent authority together in the definition in Article 1(3) can therefore be criticised, for actual authority arises where the principal agrees that the agent shall act for him (the paradigm case), whereas apparent authority can be said to be no authority at all, in that the principal has not authorised the agent to act, even if a third party is entitled to assume that he has. But the two types of authority are frequently spoken of together, and have certain common consequences; it seems important therefore, to reflect this usage at the outset. This scheme can also be justified on the basis that in both cases the authority stems from the principal's objectively determined consent, the difference being that in one case the consent is manifested to the agent and in the other to the third party. The wording of Article 1(3) (which is derived from the *Restatement*[23]) reflects this reasoning, though the notion of manifestation to the third party is frequently an artificial one.[24]

1–012

Fiduciary relationship between agent and principal. Since the agent has conferred on him special powers which enable him to change the legal position of another, the law also imposes on him special duties of a fiduciary nature towards that other.[25] These duties are not necessarily contractual (though of course they may be) for it is not necessary that there be any contract between principal and agent. Rather, they originate from equity, and are some of the duties imposed by equity on express trustees. Consequently, their application is not confined to agents.[26] It has recently been said in the Privy Council that "agency is a contract made between principal and agent ... like every other contract, the rights and duties of the principal and agent are dependent upon the terms of the contract between them, whether express or implied."[27] This approach is discussed later,[28] where it is submitted that the statement should be treated with reserve. For the present it is sufficient to say that though the fiduciary duties can be modified by contract, they are nevertheless a sufficiently prominent part of the agent's position to be incorporated within the original definition and noted at the outset.

1–013

---

[23] §§ 26, 27; and see Abbott (1896) 9 Harvard L.R. 507; Montrose, *op. cit.* n. 9 above.
[24] Below, para. 8–029.
[25] Articles 45–55; Dowrick (1954) 17 M.L.R. 24; *Guerin v. R.* [1984] 2 S.C.R. 335, 383–385, 394; (1984) 13 D.L.R. (4th) 321, 339–341, 348–349. This is primarily true of situations other than those of agency by estoppel and apparent authority.
[26] See *Guerin v. R.*, n. 25 above.
[27] *Kelly v. Cooper* [1993] A.C. 205, 213–214 *per* Lord Browne-Wilkinson.
[28] Below, para. 6–034.

1–014   **Other features: remuneration on commission.** The fiduciary duties lead to another feature of agency. It is inconsistent with those duties that an agent should act in respect of his relationship with the principal for his own profit (unless he discloses this to the principal and the principal consents). His relationship with his principal is commercially related rather than commercially adverse. Thus he should be remunerated by commission in respect of the services he has rendered, and not take his own undisclosed profit as an independent intermediary.[29]

1–015   **Duty of due diligence.** There is a further feature of the relationship between principal and agent which may be taken as typical. It is that the agent owes to the principal, unless there are other indications, only a duty to use due diligence, or, if appropriate, his best endeavours to achieve the result required. He does not owe the strict duties customarily imposed on, for instance, a seller, who has an adverse commercial relationship with his buyer.[30] To some extent this is of course a feature of contracts for services, as opposed to contracts for the transfer of property, in general; but although no doubt an agent *can* undertake strict liability, the duty of due diligence is, when combined with the features already referred to, also a typical indication of agency.

1–016   **Internal and external aspects of agency.** The full reasoning above has been developed to meet the case of a person who may be called an agent in a strict sense, who has the power to affect his principal's legal relations. To such an agent legal rules attach which require the drawing of a distinction between what may be called the internal and external aspects of agency. The *external* aspect is that under which the agent has powers to affect the principal's legal position in relation to third parties. The *internal* aspect is the relationship between principal and agent, which imposes on the agent (subject to any contract) special duties vis-à-vis the principal, appropriate to the powers which he can exercise on the principal's behalf. These are some of the duties owed by an express trustee to his beneficiary. To an agent in the fullest sense, both aspects are applicable. Some persons may, however, be described as agents by virtue of the internal relationship but have no external powers.

1–017   **Incomplete agency: internal relationship only. The "canvassing" or "introducing" agent.** Article 1(4) seeks to achieve completeness by taking in a well-established type of intermediary who makes no contracts and disposes of no property, but simply introduces two parties desirous

---

[29] Articles 47, 48. The commission need not be related to the value of the transaction: its essence is that it is not an independent profit taken by the agent, but rather a fee paid to him by the principal.
[30] Below, para. 1–030.

of contracting and leaves them to contract between themselves. In effecting such introductions he is remunerated by commission, which he may sometimes take from both parties. Such a person is a common figure in most western legal systems and may well be referred to as an agent. The most obvious example of such an intermediary in the English cases is the estate agent, who introduces purchasers to vendors and tenants to lessors of houses and vice versa.[31] Such persons are sometimes also referred to as brokers, and indeed in some English-speaking countries the estate agent is referred to as a "real estate broker": but this may be misleading since the current practice, at any rate in England, is to use the term "broker" for persons who go beyond introductions and certainly do make contracts for their principals, *e.g.* commodity brokers, insurance brokers and stockbrokers. Canvassing agents are on the fringe of the central agency principles used by the common law, since their powers to alter their principals' legal relations are at best extremely limited.[32] They do, however, act for their principals in a capacity which may involve the repose of trust and confidence, and hence are subject in some respects to the fiduciary duties of agents towards their principals.[33] They are also subject of typical rules, largely developed in estate agent cases, as to entitlement to commission, which are normally regarded as part of agency law and are relied on also by agents who have greater powers to bind their principals.[34] They may sometimes hold money for their principals.[35] The rules applicable to the internal relationship between principal and agent will therefore apply as appropriate, and for this reason such persons should certainly be treated in a work on agency even though they lack the external powers of the agent. It is an advantage of the formulation of basic agency principle in Article 1, which selects the internal relationship between principal and agent as a distinguishing feature of agency, that it can be taken to cover such persons. Canvassing agents are persons to whom the internal parts of agency law may apply, but who, because of the limited nature of their external powers to affect their principals' legal positions, are not agents in the full sense of the word.[36] They may therefore be said to provide an example of "incomplete agency".

---

[31] There is an elaborate discussion of a statutory definition of a "real estate agent" in *Freehold Land Investments Ltd v. Queensland Estates Pty. Ltd* (1970) 123 C.L.R. 418.

[32] See Article 30, Illustration 6.

[33] See Article 47, Illustrations 16, 17.

[34] Articles 58–60.

[35] See Comment to Article 54.

[36] For a useful general survey see Yiannopoulos (1959) 19 La.L.Rev. 777 esp. at pp. 799 *et seq.* In *Vogel v. R. & A. Kohnstamm Ltd* [1973] Q.B. 133 an introducer of business was held not to be an agent: see pp. 136–137, 147. See also *Okura & Co. Ltd v. Forsbacka Jernverks A/B* [1914] 1 K.B. 715.

1–018   **Indirect representation: the "commission agent".** There is another situation which can be said to amount to "incomplete agency": that of what may be called indirect representation. In commercial spheres a method of representation can be adopted whereby a principal appoints a person, who may be called an agent, to deal (especially to buy[37]) on his behalf, on the understanding that when dealing with any third party the agent will deal in his own name as principal. As between principal and agent, however, the relationship is one of agency[38]; *viz.* the agent does not promise to achieve a result but only to use his best endeavours, he does not answer to his principal on the strict basis appropriate to seller or buyer[39] (though he may have some of the rights of a seller, *e.g.* a lien[40]), he is normally remunerated by commission, he is a fiduciary and thus may not without disclosure take commission from the other party. Here again the internal aspect of agency is found but not the external. This arrangement is sometimes referred to in civil law countries as indirect representation, and representatives dealing on such a basis may in particular circumstances be referred to as operating under the contract of *commission* (the title referring to the task entrusted to the agent rather than to the method of remuneration).[41] Its recognition can lead to a method of expounding agency law on the basis that a principal wishing to appoint a representative has the choice of two methods,

---

[37] For analogous arrangements regarding selling, see *Kirkham v. Peel* (1880) 44 L.T. 195; *New Zealand and Australian Land Co. v. Watson* (1881) 7 Q.B.D. 374; and cases on factors generally (below, para. 1–040); *Bosanquet v. Mofflin* (1906) S.R. (N.S.W.) 617; *Benmag Ltd v. Barda* [1955] 2 Lloyd's Rep. 354; *Fleming v. London Produce Co. Ltd* [1968] 1 W.L.R. 1013.

[38] See *Ireland v. Livingston* (1872) L.R. 5 H.L. 395, 407–409; *Armstrong v. Stokes* (1872) L.R. 7 Q.B. 598; *Robinson v. Mollett* (1875) L.R. 7 H.L. 802, 809–810; *Cassaboglou v. Gibb* (1883) 11 Q.B.D. 797, 803–804; *Montgomerie v. U.K. Mutual S.S. Assn.* [1891] 1 Q.B. 370, 372; *Butlers (London) Ltd v. Roope* [1922] N.Z.L.R. 549; *Downie Bros. v. Henry Oakley & Sons* [1923] N.Z.L.R. 734; *Bolus & Co. Ltd v. Inglis Bros. Ltd* [1924] N.Z.L.R. 164, 175; *Sopwith Aviation & Engineering Co. Ltd v. Magnus Motors Ltd* [1928] G.L.R. (N.Z.) 380; *Isaac Gundle v. Mohanlal Sunderji* (1939) 18 Kenya L.R. 137; *Witt & Scott Ltd v. Blumenreich* [1949] N.Z.L.R. 806; *Rusholme & Bolton & Roberts Hadfield Ltd v. S.G. Read & Co.* [1955] 1 W.L.R. 146, 152; *J.S. Robertson (Australia) Pty. Ltd v. Martin* (1956) 94 C.L.R. 30; *Teheran-Europe Co. Ltd v. S.T. Belton (Tractors) Ltd* [1968] 2 Q.B. 53, 59–60; affd. [1968] 2 Q.B. 545; Hill [1964] J.B.L. 304; [1967] J.B.L. 122; (1968) 31 M.L.R. 623; (1972) 3 J. Maritime Law & Commerce 307; Schmitthoff, 1970 I Hague *Recueil des Cours* 115, 151–154; Lando [1965] J.B.L. 179, 374; [1966] J.B.L. 82. Many of the best cases on the relationship between principal and agent are to be found in Commonwealth jurisdictions, where the principals who used English agents were based.

[39] Below, para. 1–030.

[40] See the important material collected in Article 71.

[41] See, *e.g.* Hamel, *Le Contrat de Commission* (Paris, 1949); Cohn, *Manual of German Law* (2nd ed.), Vol. 2, pp. 40 *et seq.*; Horn, Kötz and Leser, *German Private and Commercial Law* (1982), pp. 232–234; Schmitthoff, 1970 I Hague *Recueil des Cours* 115, 122–125; Müller-Freienfels (1955) 18 M.L.R. 33, 36–38.

direct or indirect representation.[42] The principal of such an agent in civil law countries will not usually be liable, though he may be able to sue and hence to intervene in the agent's bankruptcy.

Is indirect representation accepted at common law? This dichotomy   1–019
between direct and indirect representation is unlikely to be attractive to common law systems, which tend to reach the result of direct representation with more facility than the civil law. But this apart, it is difficult to see any doctrinal objection at common law to the setting up of indirect representation. Indeed something like this seems to have been the mode of operation of the nineteenth century factor,[43] who received goods on consignment and sold them without making clear whether he sold his own goods or those of another. A commercial intermediary operating on this basis is sometimes even referred to in nineteenth century cases as a "commission agent" or "commission merchant".[44] But by a unique development of the common law the factor's principal was held entitled to intervene not only to sue, but also to be liable on the factor's contracts: this is said to be the origin of the common law doctrine of the undisclosed principal.[45] Such an intermediary may therefore sometimes in English law be regarded as creating *direct* representation, at least where he gives no indication that he is acting for a principal and perhaps on occasion even where he does give such indication.[46] This seems to have led to an assimilation of this special arrangement with normal agency. The majority of the cases seem therefore to assume, without the point being properly argued, one of two possible interpretations to such a situation. The first is that the intermediary is a normal agent of an undisclosed principal, and that the undisclosed principal rules therefore apply with the result that the principal is liable and entitled whatever the intentions of the parties.[47] The second is that because the agent in such a situation has no external authority to create privity of contract between his principal and the third

---

[42] See Schmitthoff, *op. cit.* n. 41 above at pp. 136–137; Hill (1968) 31 M.L.R. 623.
[43] Below, para. 1–040.
[44] As to commission agents, see the leading case of *Ireland v. Livingston* (1872) L.R. 5 H.L. 395, 408; *Armstrong v. Stokes* (1872) L.R. 7 Q.B. 598; Story, *Commentaries on the Law of Agency* (1839), § 33. The term "commission agent" appears in *Cassaboglou v. Gibb*, n. 38 above, at p. 804; *J.N. Lyon & Co. Ltd v. N. Fuchs* (1920) 2 Ll.Rep. 333. See also *Fleming v. London Produce Co. Ltd* [1968] 1 W.L.R. 1013 as to the term "general commission agent" in connection with tax legislation. See in general Munday (1977) 6 Anglo-Am. L.Rev. 221, esp. at pp. 232 *et seq.*
[45] See Comment to Article 78.
[46] *e.g. Maspons y Hermano v. Mildred, Goyeneche & Co.* (1882) 9 Q.B.D. 530 (affd. on other grounds (1883) 8 App.Cas. 874).
[47] *e.g.* the *Maspons* case, n. 46 above; and see *Brown & Gracie Ltd v. F.W. Green & Co. Pty. Ltd* [1960] 1 Lloyd's Rep. 289; Reynolds [1983] *Current Legal Problems* 119.

party, the undisclosed principal rules do not apply at all and the agent must himself alone be a party to the contract of sale, carriage, or whatever transaction he has performed for the principal, and deal with his principal as principal.[48]

There is a certain amount of judicial authority for the intermediate position of indirect agency. It was most clearly enunciated by Blackburn J. when he said:

> "Any person, if he chooses, may give an order to an agent to buy as his agent, not only with an express dispensation from any obligation to establish privity of contract between him and the person from whom the agent buys, but even expressly refusing authority to the agent to establish such privity.
>
> This is the ordinary authority given to a foreign commission merchant who (on account of the great inconvenience which would result from establishing privity of contract between the foreign producer and the home merchant) is not allowed (far less required) to establish privity of contract between them ... This, however, in no way interferes with the existence of a fiduciary relation.[49]

If the approach to be derived from the majority of the cases is correct, however, this is an area where the breadth of common law agency principles, which normally produce a more flexible result, act as a limiting factor and exclude the recognition of such an arrangement.[50] There seems no obvious reason why this should be so, unless it be thought undesirable that a principal should be able by agreement with the agent to determine his liability to third parties.[51]

1–020   **Meaning of term "agent" in the abstract.** When it is necessary, as in statutory interpretation, to attribute a meaning to the word "agent", it may be said that the central significance of the term agent refers to a person who attracts both the external and internal aspects of agency, for it is here that the complete complex of rules is most fully worked out,

---

[48] See, e.g. the dissenting judgment of Diplock L.J. in *Anglo-African Shipping Co. of New York Inc. v. J. Mortner Ltd* [1962] 1 Lloyd's Rep. 610 (which, it is respectfully submitted, presents an analysis which does not accord with commercial reality). See also the same judge in *Garnac Grain Co. Inc. v. H.M.F. Faure & Fairclough Ltd* [1966] 1 Q.B. 650, 684 (affd. [1968] A.C. 1130n.), and *Limako B.V. v. Hentz & Co. Inc.* [1979] 2 Lloyd's Rep. 23. See further *B. & M. Readers' Service Ltd v. Anglo Canadian Publishers Ltd* [1950] O.R. 159 (subscription to magazine).

[49] *Robinson v. Mollett* (1875) L.R. 7 H.L. 802, 809–810 (a dissenting judgment). See also his famous judgment in *Ireland v. Livingston* (1872) L.R. 5 H.L. 395.

[50] It is possible to identify situations of a different type where a person who may be called a representative acts as principal but accounts on an agency basis: e.g. the position of an issuing and correspondent bank in documentary credits (as to which see e.g. *Benjamin's Sale of Goods* (4th ed.), §§ 23–132 et seq). But this does not involve an act which the principal could do himself, and hence is not easily regarded as agency.

[51] And even this point could be met if the doctrine of the undisclosed principal applies to such a situation: below, para. 8–072.

and it is because of the external powers that the internal duties are imposed. And where the term agent is used in a statute or formal document, it has been said that it may be presumed that the word is used in this, its proper legal connotation, unless there are strong contrary indications.[52]

Essence of agency. Should the essence of agency then be regarded as   **1–021** the internal or external aspect of the concept, or as both? In the fullest sense it requires both; and the internal aspect follows the external, *i.e.* as stated above, it is because the agent has the power to alter the principal's position that the fiduciary duties are imposed on him. In another sense, however, it is the internal conferring of the power that justifies that power, which would make the internal aspect primary. However this question is viewed, it is useful to note the typical features of the internal position which distinguish agency from other relationships: the agent undertakes to use due diligence on behalf of another, rather than undertakes strict duties to another in a situation commercially adverse to that other; he is subject to fiduciary duties; and is remunerated by commission rather than by taking his own profit. Though any of these three features can be modified in an appropriate case, they nevertheless remain typical.

Companies: agent and organ.[53] A company can only act by agents,   **1–022** and in general the rules of agency and vicarious liability enable a company to be held liable and entitled in respect of acts performed on its behalf when this is appropriate. But there are situations where a particular state of mind is required, not of the agent but of the principal himself. It may be held that the relevant rule does not apply to companies. But if it does, it may be necessary to make a distinction between "mere" agents of a company, and agents so centrally concerned with its operations, or with the relevant part of its operations,[54] that their acts may be deemed to be not those of the agent but rather those of the company itself. Thus, for example, it may be necessary by the use of such reasoning to determine whether a company has knowledge of breach of fiduciary duty,[55] whether there is "actual fault or privity" in

---

[52] *Shell Co. of Australia Ltd v. Nat Shipping and Bagging Services Ltd (The Kilmun)* [1988] 2 Lloyd's Rep. 1, 16 *per* Sir Denys Buckley (in a dissenting judgment).

[53] See Müller-Freienfels in *Civil Law in the Modern World* (Yiannopoulos ed. 1965), 77, 90–92; Gower, *Modern Company Law* (5th ed.), pp. 193 *et seq.*

[54] *El Ajou v. Dollar Land Holdings Plc.* [1994] 2 All E.R. 685; *Meridian Global Funds Management Asia Ltd v. Securities Commission* [1995] 3 W.L.R. 513.

[55] See cases cited above, n. 54. In the *Meridian* case it is said that "It is a question of construction in each case as to whether the particular rule requires that the knowledge ... should be attributed to the company": *per* Lord Hoffmann. This observation is plainly of general significance, and is not confined to knowledge.

the company itself[56]; and in criminal law it may be necessary to attribute *mens rea* to the company itself.[57] The distinction manifests itself in other ways also: thus it has been held that a signature may be effected for a company by an agent; but equally the signature, though affixed by an agent, may purport to be that of the company itself.[58]

1–023   **"Externalised" theories.** The explanation of the common law of agency offered above can, however, be subjected to fundamental criticisms. A simple version of such criticisms is to say that it is the law that imposes certain consequences on the facts in all these cases; thus all agency arises by operation of law, and the insistence on consent in the internal relationship as the ground base of agency is misplaced.[59] This view can fairly easily be said to fail to attach sufficient importance to the paradigm case, the degree of similarity to which renders appropriate or inappropriate the use of the sort of reasoning to which that situation gives rise. The controversy is similar to that as to whether there is a distinction between "possession in fact" and "possession in law", or whether all possession, being attributed by the law, should be treated as possession in law.[60] Admittedly there are few limits on the situations where the law can regard someone as possessing: but the paradigm case where there is physical control or something very near to it nevertheless regulates to some extent what are thought to be acceptable uses of the term "possession", in whatever context. Hence the notion of "possession in fact." The same is true of the notion of authority as opposed to that of power.

More elaborately, but to similar effect, it may be argued that cases of genuine express conferring of authority are in fact the exception rather than the rule, at least where disputes arise, and that the external power conferred by the law on the agent, which applies also in situations of

---

[56] *Lennard's Carrying Co. v. Asiatic Petroleum Co. Ltd* [1915] A.C. 705 (on Merchant Shipping Act 1894, s. 502); *The Lady Gwendolen* [1965] P. 294; *The Marion* [1984] A.C. 563.

[57] *e.g. D.P.P. v. Kent & Sussex Contractors Ltd* [1944] K.B. 146; *R. v. I.C.R. Haulage Ltd* [1944] K.B. 551; *Moore v. Bresler Ltd* [1944] 2 All E.R. 515; *Tesco Supermarkets Ltd v. Nattrass* [1972] A.C. 153; *Seaboard Offshore Ltd v. Secretary of State for Transport* [1994] 1 W.L.R. 541, H.L.

[58] *Newborne v. Sensolid (Great Britain) Ltd* [1954] 1 Q.B. 45: below, para. 9–081. But this distinction has no significance in connection with s. 9(2) of the European Communities Act 1972, now s. 36C of the Companies Act 1985 (see below, para. 9–080): *Phonogram Ltd v. Lane* [1982] Q.B. 938 (a case which casts some doubt on the distinction in general). See further below, paras. 8–185, 8–194.

[59] *e.g.* Salmond and Winfield, *Law of Contracts* (1927), p. 340: "An agent may be defined as a person who is authorised by law to exercise on behalf of another person ... any power possessed by that other person of entering into a contract or other agreement, or of doing any other act in law"; Dowrick, *op. cit.* n. 25 above at pp. 35–38.

[60] See Salmond, *Jurisprudence* (12th ed.), Chap. 9.

apparent authority, is so clearly predominant that it, and not subjective consent, should be emphasised and analysed as the connecting link between cases of agency.[61] Agency situations should therefore be viewed in the first place from the point of view of the third party, and apparent authority should, again, be an application of the normal rules rather than an exception accommodated by elaborate explanations. In some continental European legal systems a sharp distinction is therefore made between the internal relationship of principal and agent and the general external power of the agent. This is particularly so in German law, and systems influenced by it, where the distinction achieved prominence following a famous article by Paul Laband published in 1866.[62] It leads to greater emphasis on the external aspect of agency situations than the approach set out in Article 1: the conferring of power may in all cases be regarded as a unilateral act in the law directed from the principal not to the agent, but rather to the third party.

The contrast between such an approach and that of the common law as here explained can be likened to the conflict of principle frequently recognised in the law of property between security of title and security of transactions. In some jurisdictions the approach which prefers the value of protecting apparently valid transactions predominates. At common law, or at any rate in the English common law, the predominant principle is, however, that a person does not lose his ownership except by his own voluntary act. Significant exceptions are created only by statute (principally the Factors Act 1889[63]) and under the doctrine of estoppel.[64] The same is true of contractual obligations: a person cannot be subjected to a contractual obligation through another except by his own volition. Exceptions can in general only be created by statute (the most obvious being the Partnership Act 1890[65]) and under the doctrine of apparent authority, which may itself be based on estoppel.[66]

---

[61] Seavey (1920) 29 Yale L.J. 859, 872 *et seq.*; Fridman (1968) 84 L.Q.R. 224, 228–231.

[62] *Die Stellvertretung bei dem Abschluss von Rechtsgeschäften nach dem Allgemeinen Deutschen Handelsgesetzbuch* (1866) 10 *Zeitschrift für Handelsrecht* 183. See Müller-Freienfels (1964) 13 Am.J.Comp.L. 193, 197–202: Schmitthoff 1970 I Hague *Recueil des Cours* 115, 120 *et seq.*; Schlesinger, *Comparative Law* (5th ed.), pp. 769 *et seq.*

[63] Article 89; see also Sale of Goods Act 1979, ss. 24, 25 (derived from the Factors Act).

[64] Articles 85, 87; see also Sale of Goods Act 1979, s. 21.

[65] ss. 5, 10.

[66] Articles 21, 74. It may be noted that the requirements for an estoppel are less stringent in the area of obligations than in that of property to such an extent that it can be doubted whether estoppel is in truth the basis of the results reached in the law of obligations. This is not surprising, for it has long been established that obligations can be imposed on the basis of objective appearances: but it perhaps indicates that the rules protecting against loss of ownership are too severe.

It seems that common law unaided is almost bound to arrive at this particular balance, since it must proceed by the use of commonly accepted principles. The principles concerning loss of property or imposition of obligations seems an inevitable starting point, even if their results are later to be modified by secondary doctrines. With one possible exception, to be discussed below, no other reasoning seems readily available for initial use. Therefore agency depends on the consent of the principal except where corrective (estoppel or similar) reasoning can be found or the result is modified by statute, as in the Factors Act. To achieve a completely different emphasis would require a general statute, or at least the acceptance of a technique of judicial reasoning which can derive general policies from particular statutes. The German doctrinal separation referred to above was in fact derived from the *Prokura*, a general authority in commercial matters created by the Commercial Code of 1861.[67] Reasoning from statutes has not been a feature of the common law.[68]

But even the most extreme externalised theories are in fact likely to derive the agent's power ultimately from such an internal starting point, for example, creation of *Prokura*, or appointment to a specific position, which the principal need not have made, and may, with appropriate publicity, cancel.[69] Indeed, on one view his main protection lies in this possibility of cancelling the authority completely by removing the agent.

When this is borne in mind, common law is not so different as may appear. It has been said that its approach to agency, as outlined above, fails to make the proper distinction between the internal relation between principal and agent and the external relation between the agent and third parties, but simply derives the one from the other.[70] But it has already been pointed out[71] that at common law the authority of an agent stems not from any contract between principal and agent (for

---

[67] HGB, para. 49; see Müller-Freienfels (1964) 13 Am.J.Comp.L. 193, 207 *et seq.*, 341–346.

[68] But see *Beverley Acceptances Ltd v. Oakley* [1982] R.T.R. 417, 426 *per* Lord Denning M.R. (dissenting); "This means that we need no longer interpret the Factors Acts by the letter. We can go by spirit which lies behind them. Modern law has made them a particular application of general principle."

[69] See Grönfors (1962) 6 *Scandinavian Studies in Law* 95 (in English), referring to s. 10(2) of the Uniform Scandinavian Contracts Act of 1915. The same writer's *Ställningsfullmakt och Bulvanskap* (Stockholm, 1961) contains an exhaustive international bibliography to that date. It was reviewed by Müller-Freienfels (1963) 12 Am.J.Comp.L. 272 (together with Stoljar's *Law of Agency* (1961)).

[70] See Müller-Freienfels (1957) 6 Am.J.Comp.L. 165, 170–173; *cf.* the same writer in *Civil Law in the Modern World*, (Yiannopoulos ed. 1965), 77, 86–89. A similar point can be made of French law: see Müller-Freienfels (1964) 13 Am.J.Comp.L. 341, 346–349. The internal and external aspects are clearly distinguished in *Waugh v. H.B. Clifford & Sons Ltd* [1982] Ch. 374.

[71] Above, para. 1–005.

indeed there need not be one) but from the unilateral grant of authority. This *may* occur in pursuance of a contractual relationship; but the conferring of authority is a separate event which may occur also in other circumstances. Parallels to the civil law notion of grant of general authority to a person in a specific position can also be found in the controversial common law notion of usual authority.[72] The contrast may therefore lie rather in the nature and extent of the conclusions drawn from the initial reasoning than in that reasoning itself. In any case, each approach generates its own difficulties. The common law approach has considerable difficulty in completely explaining the basis of apparent authority[73]: but its concentration on the conferring of authority enables it (for better or worse) to accommodate the rights and liabilities of the undisclosed principal.[74] The "external" approach certainly protects innocent third parties. But the protection can perhaps be excessive: for it can (unless other, corrective doctrines can be invoked) lead to the conclusion that third parties are entitled to rely on the appearance of agency even though they have reason to know that the agent was not in fact authorised.[75] It appears also to be associated with a tendency to isolate numerous different types of agent, each with its own special rules; though this is probably a legacy of the Romanistic notion of nominate contracts.[76]

The tort approach. From time to time a different approach to agency   **1–024** problems has been urged by common law writers, an approach quite separate from the "externalised" theories referred to above. It has been argued that traditional agency reasoning, which requires authority or its appearance for one person to alter the legal position of another, is inadequate, and that recourse should be had to a line of reasoning which seeks more generally to place responsibility on the instigator or beneficiary of the enterprise in relation to which a person acts.[77] Sometimes it has been suggested that a principle similar to that of vicarious liability in the law of torts should be adopted in place of normal agency reasoning.[78] A suggestion for the adoption of such an approach was comparatively recently put forward by Lord Wilberforce:

"It may be that some wider conception of vicarious responsibility other than that of agency, as normally understood, may have to be recognised in order to

---

[72] See Comment to Article 22.
[73] See Comment to Article 74.
[74] Above, para. 1–007; Article 78.
[75] Müller-Freienfels, (1964) 13 Am.J.Comp.L. 193, 211 *et seq.*
[76] See Schmitthoff, 1970 I Hague *Recueil des Cours* 115, 123–124 (listing 13 types of intermediary known to German law); Bonnell [1984] Uniform L.Rev. 52.
[77] Seavey (1920) 29 Yale L.J. 859, esp. at pp. 883–885.
[78] *e.g.* Wright (1936) 1 U.Toronto L.J. 17, 40 *et seq.*; Mearns (1962) 48 Va.L.Rev. 50.

accommodate some of the more elaborate cases which now arise when there are two persons who become mutually involved or associated in one side of a transaction."[79]

The case itself involved the potential liability of a finance company for the representations of a car dealer who assisted his buyers in obtaining finance from the company for their purchases from him—a common enough situation. If it was sought to generalise on this situation alone, it might perhaps be possible to develop a doctrine that where two parties are in a business association of some sort, the nature of which is unclear to the outside world, the burden should rather be on the party who appears to be the instigator of, or possibly even merely a participator in, the combined business to show that there was not and would not reasonably be expected to have been authority in the other party, rather than the reverse. Lord Wilberforce had earlier said:

"Thus there are two rival views as to the manner in which a typical hire purchase transaction should be regarded. That expressed by Holroyd Pearce L.J. and by Pearson L.J. involves an analysis without any initial presumption of each individual transaction, on the available documents and evidence, in order to see whether, in any respect, the finance company (or, if that is relevant, the hirer) should be held to have conferred authority (actual or apparent) upon the dealer to act as his agent. That of Lord Denning M.R. and Donovan L.J. takes as a starting point the established mercantile background of hire-purchase transactions, as known to and accepted by all three parties, takes that as establishing in general the basis for an agency relationship, and finally considers, against that background, any individual features of the particular case to see whether they confirm or weaken the agency inference.

My Lords, for my part I think that the latter approach is now to be preferred."[80]

This was however a dissenting speech; the majority of the House of Lords decided the question in issue against liability by the application of normal agency principles, and Lord Wilberforce himself was able also to justify the (minority) result which he reached in favour of liability on the basis of orthodox doctrine. Subsequently it was held that a person employing the services of an estate agent to sell his house was not liable when the agent without authority took deposits from a number of people, who were thereby defrauded[81]; that a finance company was not bound by the representations of a hire-purchase information service, set up by finance companies as a non-profit-making organisation, as to

---

[79] *Branwhite v. Worcester Works Finance Ltd* [1969] 1 A.C. 552, 587. See also *First Energy (U.K.) Ltd v. Hungarian International Bank Ltd* [1993] 2 Lloyd's Rep. 194, 196, 204 *per* Steyn L.J.

[80] At pp. 585–586.

[81] *Sorrell v. Finch* [1977] A.C. 728, Illustration 4 to Article 94: see Articles 94, 113.

whether a particular vehicle was the subject of a hire-purchase agreement[82]; that an insurance company was not liable for representations made by a branch manager (an employee who was more or less a canvassing agent or a controller of canvassing agents[83]) which were neither actually nor apparently authorised[84]; and that a company was not liable in tort for fraudulent misrepresentations by a manager not within the scope of his apparent authority.[85] All these decisions tend against any generalised approach of the sort mentioned,[86] which is in any case directed towards the principal's *duties*. Orthodox agency law gives him rights also.

A more drastic use of such reasoning might seek to make the principal liable regardless even of whether he was known by the third parties to be connected with the transaction. This, which is again a liability doctrine only, would be an extension of the undisclosed principal doctrine[87] and would more obviously require to be based on reasoning similar to that used in tort cases, where a person vicariously liable need not of course have been known to exist at the time of the incident in question. In the speech of Lord Wilberforce quoted above it was later suggested[88] that this was the true matter in issue in *Garnac Grain Co. Inc. v. H.M.F. Faure & Fairclough Ltd*,[89] where it was sought to say that a commercial concern which sold goods and at the same time secretly contracted to repurchase them from a sub-sub-buyer was liable to the sub-buyer as an undisclosed principal of the sub-sub-buyer. The argument in that case was unsuccessful, however; and more recently a company was held not liable for the act of an employee (a true agent) who caused the loss to third parties by a negligent valuation set out on the principal's notepaper, effected contrary to his instructions and in such a way that the third parties did not know who had prepared the valuation.[90] Recent decisions again suggest, therefore, that the

---

[82] *Moorgate Mercantile Co. v. Twitchings* [1977] A.C. 890, Illustration 8 to Article 86. Both the above two cases are criticised by Fridman (1982) 20 U. of W.Ont.L.Rev. 23.

[83] As to canvassing agents see above, para. 1–017.

[84] *British Bank of the Middle East v. Sun Life Assurance Co. of Canada (U.K.) Ltd* [1983] 2 Lloyd's Rep. 9, Illustration 10 to Article 77 (noted [1982] J.B.L. 496; [1983] J.B.L. 409).

[85] *Armagas Ltd v. Mundogas S.A. (The Ocean Frost)* [1986] A.C. 717.

[86] See Fridman (1983) 13 Manitoba L.J. 1. But see the observations in the difficult and specialised case of *Heatons Transport (St Helens) Ltd v. Transport and General Workers' Union* [1973] A.C. 15, 99–100, which suggests a similarity between authority and scope of employment; *Re Supply of Ready Mixed Concrete* [1992] Q.B. 213; *First Energy (U.K.) Ltd v. Hungarian International Bank Ltd* [1993] 2 Lloyd's Rep. 194, Illustration 12 to Article 74.

[87] See Comment to Article 22; Montrose (1937) 17 Can.B.R. 224.

[88] At p. 587.

[89] [1968] A.C. 1130n.

[90] *Kooragang Investments Pty. Ltd v. Richardson & Wrench Ltd* [1982] A.C. 462.

orthodox basis of agency law, which requires some indication of authority or of the appearance of it, will still be followed. That is not to say, however, that the use made of agency doctrine may not vary from time to time, and case to case, for the doctrine is a flexible one.[91]

Vicarious liability is indeed connected with agency law historically, and in practice governs certain of the principal's tort liabilities, which cannot necessarily be readily separated from his contractual position. The doctrines of agency by estoppel and apparent authority are also in some ways similar to vicarious liability in tort, since they involve liability only. In the United States it was at one time fashionable to seek to link agency reasoning in contract and property with vicarious liability in tort with a view to the development of more general principles.[92] But it seems that such schemes are no longer in fashion, and if this is so it is with good reason.[93] For a tort situation is in general not one voluntarily entered into by the aggrieved party, whereas an agency situation is. This means that the duty to compensate in tort may be more readily imposed than a similar duty in contractual situations. Although it is now recognised that the boundary between contract and tort is more fluid than may sometimes have been thought in the past, the distinction between the two types of obligation still seems a valid one and no satisfactory organising technique based on different notions has yet been propounded. Furthermore, a major reason for the imposition of liability on one person for the torts of another is the degree of control exercised over him: the main instance of vicarious liability is that of a master for the torts of his servant. But, although an agent may be an employee, the typical agent is not, and acts in an independent manner. Finally, in agency disputes the question is not, as it is usually in tort, merely one of liability of the instigator of an enterprise: a person designated as principal to a transaction will also be able to sue, except in situations of pure apparent authority—and even here there may be ratification. Agency is therefore more instructively viewed as a notion facilitating commerce rather than as part of a generalised area of law providing compensation for the acts of others; and for these reasons it is submitted that the traditional approach remains correct.

1–025   **Diverse use of agency reasoning.** The ruling notion of agency law may be said to be that the acts of a person (the agent) authorised, or to be treated as authorised, by another are in certain circumstances to be

---

[91] This, it is suggested, is the answer to the points made by Fridman in (1982) 20 U. of W.Ont.L.Rev. 23.

[92] See Conard (1949) 1 J. Legal Ed. 540; Mechem (1949) 2 J. Legal Ed. 203; Street, *Foundations of Legal Liability* (1906), Vol.2, Pt. IV; and *Restatement*. See also Wyse (1979) 40 Mont. L.Rev. 31.

[93] See Ferson (1951) 4 Vand.L.Rev. 260; Müller-Freienfels in *Civil Law in the Modern World* (Yiannopoulos ed. 1965), 77, 107–108, 117–120.

treated as having the same legal effect as if they had been done by that other (the principal). This is sometimes expressed by the idea that the agent's acts *are* those of the principal: *qui facit per alium facit per se.* Reasoning along these lines may be found in the spheres of contract, property, tort, restitution, criminal law, evidence, administrative law, taxation,[94] labour law and elsewhere. But though this approach has value in imposing some unity on the law applicable to situations where one party represents or acts for another, it should not be taken too literally. It is misleading to assume that a single set of principles, valid for the whole law, relating to the representation of one person by another can be evolved under the title of agency.[95] The main application of such reasoning is in the law of contract, where it is obviously desirable for rules to exist under which a person may make a contract for another, and such reasoning was necessary to render the principle liable in *assumpsit*. Different policies may regulate the considerations applicable in the law of property, of tort and elsewhere. Nor is it possible exhaustively to analyse agency principles separately in each branch of the law, since the boundaries between the branches are too fluid. Finally, agency principles in English law evolve from disparate sources: from common law as to master and servant, from Admiralty cases concerned with shipmasters, from equity and the law of trusts, from cases on deeds, and from the action of account.[96] Agency reasoning should therefore be regarded as a tool to be picked up as and when it may be useful.[97] The study, and separate treatment of agency as a subject is valuable, but no hidden key is to be found thereby. Indeed in the vast majority of cases problems of agency arise as questions of fact only: and perhaps the majority of cases on agency are useful not as laying down rules, but as providing examples of views that may be taken of facts.

---

[94] Some interesting reasoning can be found in *Conservative and Unionist Central Office v. Burrell* [1982] 1 W.L.R. 522; see Emery, (1983) 133 N.L.J. 87.

[95] See the *Restatement* criticised on these grounds by Miller (1936) 20 Marquette L.Rev. 141.

[96] Holdsworth, *H.E.L.* VIII, pp. 222–229, 248–254; Pollock and Maitland, *H.E.L.*, Vol. 2, pp. 225 *et seq.*; Holmes, 3 *Select Essays in Anglo-American Legal History* (1909), p. 368; Stoljar, pp. 14–17; Simpson, *History of the Common Law of Contract* (1975), pp. 552–557.

[97] *cf.* the difficulties put forward by Fridman (1968) 84 L.Q.R. 224; (1982) 20 U.W.Ont. L.Rev. 23. A recent example of unilluminating use of agency reasoning as a tool is to be found in cases on mortgages and guarantees executed by persons under undue influence from third parties to the transaction: *e.g. Coldunell Ltd v. Gallon* [1986] Q.B. 1184; *King's North Trust Ltd v. Bell* [1986] 1 W.L.R. 119: in *Contractors Bonding Ltd v. Smee* [1992] 2 N.Z.L.R. 157, 167 the reasoning of apparent authority was also referred to. Since *Barclays Bank Plc. v. O'Brien* [1994] 1 A.C. 180 it has not been necessary to stretch agency reasoning in this way. The application of agency reasoning in "*Romalpa*" clauses (below para. 8–162) may also prove inappropriate.

2. Agency distinguished from other relationships

The nature of agency is sometimes further elucidated by comparing it with other legal relationships.

1–026 **Agent and trustee.**[98] Agents and trustees have many similarities, for both are persons who act on behalf of others and, though agency is essentially a common law notion much of the law of agency is derived from, or is connected with, the law of trusts, which is of course equitable.[99] But the two functions, though they have considerable overlap, are conceptually different. An agent acts for another; but a trustee holds property for another.

Thus a *trustee* holds money or property for another, to which he has the legal title, but which belongs in equity to the beneficiary, whose rights are largely enforceable on a proprietary rather than on a personal basis.[1] As such, a trustee may have no agency functions at all. Furthermore, a trustee's duty is to carry out the terms of the trust; he is not normally subject to control by the beneficiary, nor to revocation by him of the trust. Lastly, the position of express trustee is a well-recognised and specialised one to which various forms of statutory regulation apply.[2]

An *agent*, on the other hand, may often hold no money or property for his principal at all; if he does receive money from or for his principal, he may merely be in the position of debtor to his principal in respect of it[3] and if he receives goods he may hold them as bailee only.[4] As such, therefore, an agent may have no trustee functions or liabilities at all. He may well be subject to some degree of control by his principal, and his authority can normally be revoked.[5] His function is far too varied in the many spheres in which it may operate to be the subject of general statutory regulation, though statutes may affect particular types of agent or agency situation.[6]

But of course a trustee *may* also in appropriate circumstances have agency powers. And an agent *may* hold money or property as trustee: the principal may well seek to secure this in order to achieve protection should the agent become insolvent.[7] Sometimes agents hold as bare

---

[98] Street (1892) 8 L.Q.R. 220; *Restatement*, § 14B and comment; *Restatement, Second, Trusts*, § 8 and comment; *Scott on Trusts* (4th ed.), § 8.
[99] See Dowrick (1954) 17 M.L.R. 24, 28–32.
[1] Subject to the special difficulties caused by the proposition "Equity acts *in personam*."
[2] *e.g.* Trustee Act 1925.
[3] *e.g. Neste Oy v. Lloyd's Bank Plc* [1983] 2 Lloyd's Rep. 658: below, para. 6–043.
[4] *e.g.* a factor: below, para. 1–040.
[5] Article 122.
[6] *e.g.* Powers of Attorney Act 1971; Estate Agents Act 1979.
[7] See Comment to Article 45; Articles 51, 54.

trustees: in such cases the agency function predominates.[8] And an agent is subject to fiduciary duties which usually lead also to money which he receives improperly being regarded as money of the principal held upon constructive trust, and hence subject to a proprietary claim.[9]

Thus the two functions, though conceptually distinct, may be difficult to differentiate: one person may have both capacities in relation to another.[10]

Agent and bailee.[11] Like a trustee, a bailee holds for another, but he   **1–027** only holds as possessor, and ownership remains in the bailor. The notion of bailment is moreover restricted to chattels. An agent may hold no property for his principal at all; or he may hold property as trustee. Equally, a bailee as such may have no agency powers.[12] However, an agent *may* hold his principal's chattels as bailee: this was the practice, for example, of the nineteenth century factor.[13] And a bailee *may* sometimes be regarded as having agency powers to do such things as are reasonably incidental to his use of the goods which he holds, *e.g.* have them repaired, in which connection an artificer's lien created by him may be valid against his principal.[14] The authority may, in accordance with normal principles, be actual, express or implied,[15] or apparent[16]: in the latter case limitations on authority may be ineffective against a third party who did not know of them.[17] Again, the categories are not mutually exclusive: one person may have both capacities in relation to another, and indeed that of trustee also. Thus a commercial intermediary may be a bailee of goods, an agent to sell them and a trustee of the proceeds of sale.

---

[8] *e.g. Trident Holdings Ltd v. Danand Investments Ltd* (1988) 49 D.L.R. (4th) 1, where it was held that a bare trustee subject to the control of beneficiaries was their agent and could bind them by contract.

[9] Articles 45–55.

[10] For other differences see Fridman, pp. 20–23. See also *Pople v. Evans* [1969] 2 Ch. 255, where it was held that an agent who sued on behalf of an undisclosed principal was not a trustee for the purposes of estoppel *per rem judicatam*.

[11] Fridman (1964) 114 L.J. 265.

[12] See *Buxton v. Baughan* (1834) 6 C. & P. 674; *Cassils & Co. v. Holden Wood Bleaching Co.* (1914) 112 L.T. 373; *Pennington v. Reliance Motor Works Ltd* [1923] 1 K.B. 127; *cf. Smith v. General Motor Cab Co. Ltd* [1911] A.C. 188. See also *Bart v. British West Indian Airways Ltd* [1967] 1 Lloyd's Rep. 239 (person collecting and forwarding football pool coupons not agent of investors to make contract with carrier).

[13] Below, para. 1–040. Another example is an auctioneer.

[14] *Tappenden v. Artus* [1964] 2 Q.B. 185. See also *Coldman v. Hill* [1919] 1 K.B. 443, 456. *cf. Gallimore v. Moore* (1867) 6 S.C.R. (N.S.W.) 388.

[15] *Singer Mfg. Co. v. L. & S.W. Ry. Co.* [1894] 1 Q.B. 833; *Keene v. Thomas* [1905] 1 K.B. 136; *Greene v. All Motors Ltd* [1917] 1 K.B. 625. See Articles 24 *et seq.*

[16] *Albemarle Supply Co. Ltd v. Hind & Co.* [1928] 1 K.B. 307; *Bowmaker Ltd v. Wycombe Motors Ltd* [1946] 1 K.B. 505, 509.

[17] See cases cited above, n. 14; Articles 74, 85.

1-028   **Agent and servant; agent and independent contractor.** The dichotomy of servant (or employee) and independent contractor stems from the law of tort: a person is more readily liable for the torts of his servants than for those of his independent contractors. The difference turns on the degree of control exercised. A servant has been defined as a "person employed by another to do work for him on terms that he, the servant, is to be under the control and directions of his employer in respect of the manner in which his work is to be done."[18] An independent contractor has been defined as "one who undertakes to produce a given result, but so that in the actual execution of the work he is not under the orders or control of the person for whom he does it, and may use his discretion in things not specified beforehand."[19] Much space has been devoted in books to considering the relationship between these figures and the agent.[20] It is submitted that the controversy is somewhat sterile. Some employees have agency powers, and these may be (as in the case of a manager) very wide; in other cases (*e.g.* a domestic employee) they may be very limited. Others have no agency powers. Many agents (*e.g.* brokers) could be called independent contractors; other independent contractors (*e.g.* repairers) are unlikely to have agency powers. To some extent the matter turns on whether the principal has a degree of control over the independent contractor's commercial acts, *e.g.* contracts.[20a] Persons may exercise agency powers who fall into neither category: an obvious example is a gratuitous agent. Though there are interactions, both historical and practical, it is unlikely that the terminology can be reduced to a satisfactory scheme.

1-029   **Distributors, concessionnaires or franchisees.**[21] A supplier of the goods of a manufacturer, whether on a retail or whosesale basis, who has some form of concession as a regular stockist, distributor or

---

[18] Salmond and Heuston, *Torts* (19th ed.), p. 511; wording approved in *Hewitt v. Bonvin* [1940] 1 K.B. 188, 191. See also *Ready Mixed Concrete (South East) Ltd v. Minister of Pensions and National Insurance* [1968] 2 Q.B. 497. The substance overrides the form: a person who purports to be, or to be employed as, "labour only sub-contractor" may be a servant or employee: see *Ferguson v. John Dawson & Partners (Construction) Ltd* [1976] 1 W.L.R. 1213; *O'Kelly v. Trusthouse Forte Plc.* [1984] Q.B. 90. See also *Australian Mutual Provident Society v. Chaplin* (1978) 18 A.L.R. 385.

[19] Pollock, *Torts* (15th ed.), p. 63. See also *Honeywill & Stein Ltd v. Larkin Bros. Ltd* [1934] 1 K.B. 191, 196.

[20] Powell, pp. 7–24; Fridman, pp. 27–32; Stoljar, pp. 3–5; *Restatement*, §§ 1, 2 and comments. See also *Lower Hutt City v. Att.-Gen.* [1965] N.Z.L.R. 65.

[20a] See *CFTG-TV Ltd v. Mr Submarine Ltd* (1994) 108 D.L.R. (4th) 517 (advertising agency); *Restatement*, § 14.

[21] The topic of franchising is a specialised one. See, *e.g.* Adams and Prichard Jones, *Franchising* (3rd ed.); Prest, *Franchising: Law and Practice* (1990); (1979) 39 Maryland L.Rev. 264; Sandrock (1979) 48 U.Cincinnati L.Rev. 699. For a case where a franchising company was held to have ordered goods as agent for its franchisee, see *Toycorp Ltd v. Miltan Bradley Australia Pty. Ltd* [1992] 2 V.R. 572.

franchisee is often described as "agent", "selling agent", "main agent" and the like, for the manufacturer of the goods which he supplies. Although it is possible that he is an agent in the common law sense,[22] it is nowadays much more likely that he actually buys from the manufacturer and resells to his own customer. In one case his typical position was made very clear by a clause reading: "The term 'agent' is used in a complimentary sense only, and those firms whom we style our agents are not authorised to advertise, incur any debts, or transact any business whatever on our account, other than the sale of goods which they may purchase from us; nor are they authorised to give any warranty or make any representation on our behalf other than those contained in the above guarantee."[23] Such a person or concern may have limited agency functions such as those of guarantee referred to, or as to transmission of complaints and rectification of faults. But in general the relationship is an adverse commercial relationship quite different from agency and is therefore not treated in this book except for the purpose of distinguishing it from agency. In continental European countries and elsewhere, the protection given to commercial agents[24] may sometimes be extended to distributors and the like. The E.C. Directive on this subject is, however, confined to commercial agents, and in the United Kingdom there is therefore no reason to extend it further. The analogy of agency is not normally followed where a purchase for resale is identified: the contract is one of sale. Any additional relationship between the parties to a distributorship agreement turns on the terms of the particular contract and such contracts therefore require careful drafting.

There is however overlap between such distributors and true agents in that the contracts under which both act may be affected by mandatory general rules such as those of EC competition law[25] and those relating to restraint of trade.[26] Indeed, the restrictions contractually imposed on distributors, such as requirements not to compete, sometimes place them under the manufacturer's control in a way that makes the analogy

---

[22] This seems to have been a practice more favoured some time ago. See *Williamson v. Rover Cycle Co. Ltd* [1901] 2 I.R. 189, 615; *Sproule v. Triumph Cycle Co. Ltd* [1927] N.I. 83.

[23] *Sproule v. Triumph Cycle Co. Ltd*, n. 22 above (where the distributor was nevertheless held an agent). Such clauses are not uncommon. In *Vogel v. R. & A. Kohnstamm Ltd* [1973] Q.B. 133, 136 such a concern was said to be "in no legal sense of the word an agent at all." See also *The Kronprinzessin Cecilie* (1917) 33 T.L.R. 292; *W.T. Lamb & Son v. Goring Brick Co. Ltd* [1932] 1 K.B. 710; *B. Davis Ltd v. Tooth & Co. Ltd* [1937] 4 All E.R. 118; *Martin-Baker Aircraft Co. Ltd v. Canadian Flight Equipment Ltd* [1955] 2 Q.B. 556 ("selling agents").

[24] See Chap. 11.

[25] See, *e.g.* Bellamy and Child, *The Common Market Law of Competition* (4th ed.), esp. Chap 7.

[26] See *e.g.* Chitty, *Contracts* (27th ed.), Vol. 1, §§ 16–066 *et seq.*

of agency not inappropriate. Thus in an important case the High Court of Australia were split by 3 to 2 on the question whether a particular distributorship contract gave rise to fiduciary duties.[27] Such distributors may also hold goods as bailees only, and in general their contracts may contain reservation of title clauses, so called *"Romalpa"* clauses,[28] which in authorising the distributor to resell goods on which the seller has reserved title may use expressly or by implication the terminology of agency. The question whether a power of resale is exercised as agent would affect the liability and rights on that sale of the original seller and/or his right to the proceeds of sale. But the matter has not yet arisen for decision.[29]

1–030   **Agent and seller; agent and buyer.** The above discussion raises the distinction between agency and sale. These relationships, unlike the others dealt with above, are mutually exclusive: in respect of a particular transaction a person cannot be acting as agent if he is a buyer or seller to his principal and vice versa.[30] Sale is a commercially adverse relationship; agency involves a fiduciary relationship of trust and confidence. The solution to commercial disputes may frequently turn on whether the parties are to be regarded as parties to one or the other relationship. Thus a manufacturer may contract not to market his goods through anyone but a particular supplier, who is said to be "sole" or "exclusive agent". If the supplier is on the true construction of the agreement a buyer from the manufacturer, the manufacturer may be in breach of contract if he sells the goods himself[31]; but if the supplier is a true agent the manufacturer will usually be entitled to sell personally as well.[32] If the supplier buys from the manufacturer and resells, it is he

---

[27] *Hospital Products Ltd. v. U.S. Surgical Corp.* (1984) 156 C.L.R. 41.

[28] See *Aluminium Industrie Vaassen B.V. v. Romalpa Aluminium Ltd* [1976] 1 W.L.R. 676: *Re Bond Worth Ltd* [1980] Ch. 228; *Borden (U.K.) Ltd v. Scottish Timber Products Ltd* [1981] Ch. 25; *Re Peachdart Ltd* [1984] Ch. 131; *Clough Mill Ltd v. Martin* [1985] 1 W.L.R. 111; Chitty, *Contracts* (27th ed.), Vol. 1, §§ 41–135 *et seq.*; para. 8–162, below.

[29] Reynolds (1978) 94 L.Q.R. 224, 235–238.

[30] The question has arisen in the specialised context of value added tax. See *Customs and Excise Commissioners v. Johnson* [1980] S.T.C. 624 (provision of educational courses); *Potter v. Customs and Excise Commissioners* [1985] S.T.C. 45 ("Tupperware" sold at specially convened functions); *Hill v. Customs and Excise Commissioners* [1989] S.T.C. 424 (craft pottery); *Customs and Excise Commissioners v. Paget* [1989] S.T.C. 773 (school photographs sold to parents); *Cornhill Management Ltd v. Commissioners of Customs and Excise* [1991] 1 V.A.T.T.R.1 (fund managers); *Customs and Excise Commissioners v. Music and Video Exchange Ltd* [1992] S.T.C. 220 (profit on resale as commission).

[31] *W.T. Lamb & Sons v. Goring Brick Co.* [1932] 1 K.B. 710. It may, however, be that today the question might turn on whether the word "exclusive" had been used rather than "sole". See below, para. 7–036.

[32] See *Bentall, Horsley & Baldry v. Vicary* [1931] 1 K.B. 253 (an estate agent case); Article 60.

who answers to the ultimate buyer for the quality of the goods, and the manufacturer is liable, in the absence of other indications, in tort or by statute only.[33] If the supplier is the manufacturer's agent, his liability to the ultimate buyer may turn on whether or not he is what is above described as a commission agent.[34] If he is, he may likewise answer as seller for quality, but will have the agent's rights of reimbursement and indemnity against his principal. If he is not, it is the manufacturer who is the seller and he, and not (normally[35]) the agent, must answer for quality of the goods.[36] If the supplier buys from the manufacturer and resells, money paid or due to him from the ultimate buyer may be part of his assets in bankruptcy: if he is an agent, it may not.[37]

The distinction between agent and buyer for resale normally turns on whether the person concerned acts for himself to make such profit as he can, or is remunerated by pre-arranged commission.[38] A supplier who himself fixes the resale price is likely to be a buyer for resale[39]: but the fact that the resale price is fixed by the manufacturer does not necessarily make the supplier an agent,[40] for resale prices are frequently fixed by manufacturers. Exceptionally a buyer for resale may also be paid commission,[41] or an agent remunerated by being allowed to keep the excess over and above a stipulated price.[42] But the making of such a profit by an agent would normally be improper.[43]

Conversely, there may be difficulty in deciding whether a person who has agreed to procure goods for another is acting as that other's agent or selling to him. Again, the first question is to ask whether he takes a

---

[33] *Sproule v. Triumph Motor Cycle Co.* [1927] N.I. 83; *International Harvester Co. of Australia Pty. Ltd v. Carrigan's Hazeldene Pastoral Co.* (1958) 100 C.L.R. 644; and see *Wheeler & Wilson Mfg. Co. v. Shakespear* (1869) 39 L.J.Ch. 36; *Pearlson Enterprises Ltd v. Hong Leong Co. Ltd* [1968] 1 Malaya L.J. 24 (where agent buys for resale, price increase imposed by manufacturer subsequent to resale contract may not be passed on). The statutory liability could be under the Consumer Protection Act 1987.

[34] Above, para. 1–018.

[35] But see Article 100: the agent may sometimes be liable in addition.

[36] *e.g. Parkar's Music & Sports House v. Motorex Ltd* [1959] E. Africa L.Rep. 534.

[37] *Ex p. White, re Neville* (1871) L.R. 6 Ch.App. 397, affd. *sub. nom. John Towle & Co. v. White* (1873) 29 L.T. 78 (a case on *del credere* agency: below, para. 1–036).

[38] See *Weiner v. Harris* [1910] 1 K.B. 285; *Restatement*, § 14 J (listing relevant factors); *Bosanquet v. Mofflin* (1906) 6 S.R. (N.S.W.) 617. *cf.* above, para. 1–014.

[39] *Ex p. White, re Neville*, n. 37 above.

[40] *Michelin Tyre Co. Ltd v. McFarlane (Glasgow) Ltd* (1917) 55 Sc.L.Rep. 35 (a House of Lords case containing a full review of the authorities, and again on *del credere* agency: below, para. 1–036).

[41] *Kelly v. Enderton* [1913] A.C. 191; *Gannow Engineering Co. Ltd v. Richardson* [1930] N.Z.L.R. 361. *cf. Kitson v. P.S. King & Son Ltd* (1919) 36 T.L.R. 162 (publishing).

[42] *Ex p. Bright, re Smith* (1879) 10 Ch.D. 566, 570.

[43] Articles 47–50.

27

profit on the resale which will make him a seller, or a commission, in which case he is likely to be an agent and indeed the making of any further profit would usually be improper. But here another criterion also is relevant. If he is selling, he normally undertakes absolutely to supply the goods on the terms agreed: but an agent prima facie only binds himself to use his best endeavours to make a contract or procure the goods, depending on whether he is a genuine agent or what is above described as a commission agent. [44] Thus a seller answers for defects in description and quality: an agent may not do so at all, because he is not a party to the contract, [45] or if he is a commission agent may only answer for failure to carry out his instructions as closely as is practicable. [46]

There may also in either situation be repercussions as regards the damages obtainable: the measure of damages appropriate to a breach of a contract of sale may not be applicable to breach of the agent's duty. [47] Questions of the passing of property also may depend on how the case is analysed. [48]

Each transaction must be examined on its facts, considering the extent to which an agent's duties are appropriate. Much turns on the extent to which the principal can call for an account, for the duty to account is a typical feature of the agent's position. [49] The ways in which the parties describe themselves are not conclusive. "There is no magic in the word 'agency.' It is often used in commercial matters where the real relationship is that of vendor and purchaser." [50] There may indeed be reasons for principal and agent adopting the relationship of vendor and purchaser, for example, to avoid tax, exchange control rules or trade embargoes. It is also the case that the trading functions of intermediaries may imperceptibly alter over a period. [51]

---

[44] See *Anglo-African Shipping Co. of New York Inc. v. J. Mortner Ltd* [1962] 1 Lloyd's Rep. 610; above, para. 1–019.
[45] See *Ireland v. Livingston* (1872) L.R. 5 H.L. 395; *Brown & Gracie v. F.W. Greene & Co. Pty. Ltd* [1960] 1 Lloyd's Rep. 289.
[46] See *Johnston v. Kershaw* (1867) L.R. 2 Ex. 82; *Butlers (London) Ltd v. Roope* [1922] N.Z.L.R. 549; *Downie Bros. v. Henry Oakley & Sons* [1923] N.Z.L.R. 734.
[47] *Cassaboglou v. Gibb* (1883) 1 Q.B.D. 797, Illustration 4 to Article 71. See further *Restatement*, § 14 K (listing relevant factors).
[48] See Article 71.
[49] *Michelin Tyre Co. Ltd v. McFarlane (Glasgow) Ltd* (1917) 55 Sc.L.Rep. 35; Article 52.
[50] *Ex p. White, re Neville* (1871) L.R. 6 Ch.App. 397, 399 (see n. 37 above). *cf. Weiner v. Harris* [1910] 1 K.B. 285, where a person buying on sale or return was held an agent. See also *Livingstone v. Ross* [1901] A.C. 327; *Garnac Grain Co. Inc. v. H.M.F. Faure & Fairclough Ltd* [1968] A.C. 1130n.
[51] See Hill, "The Broker and the Commodity Markets" in *New Directions in International Trade Law* (Unidroit, 1977), Vol. 2, pp. 523 *et seq.*

Agent and borrower. A person may act as agent and as such use   **1–031**
money stemming from his principal: this money he may hold on trust for
the principal, or receive it as his own subject to a duty to return or
account for it.[52] Alternatively, he may borrow from another on a
commercial basis and hence receive money not as agent at all, even
though he may appear to be conducting business for that other. This
distinction may be important in the case of subsidiary companies.[53]
Questions can also arise as to whether a person providing finance for
another has a charge over that other's property or whether he buys it
from that other, who then resells as his agent.[54]

Agent and person supplying services. An agent obviously supplies   **1–032**
services. Some persons supplying services, however, do so on a
commercially adverse basis: that is to say, as in the case of sellers,
they supply their services for the best price that they can obtain. This
is true of, for example, a repairer or a portrait painter. Such a
person normally owes a duty of best endeavours only, but he is not
remunerated on commission and owes no fiduciary duties. An agent
offers services of a personal and confidential type: as such he is
subject to fiduciary duties also. There is, however, an intermediate
category. Some persons offering personal services, such as solicitors,
charge fees rather than commission (though their fees may in some
way be controlled); but they are under fiduciary duties not as regards
profits made from the exercise of their profession, but in respect of
information held and profits made from their positions *vis-à-vis* their
clients.[55] This is true also of others, who if their work is directed
towards a fixed target which may be valued may actually be
remunerated by commission also, such as patent agents,[56] travel
agents,[57] or even persons assisting in the preparation of a contractual
offer or bid. All these, other than those who render commercial
services on a purely commercial basis, may attract some, but not all,
of the features of agency law.

---

[52] See below, para. 6–043.

[53] For an example of the second situation, see *Atlas Maritime Corp. v. Avalon Maritime
Ltd (The Coral Rose) (No. 1)* [1991] 4 All E.R. 796.

[54] See *Welsh Development Agency v. Export Finance Co. Ltd* [1992] B.C.L.C. 148.

[55] Articles 46–50.

[56] See *Re Frazer's Patent* [1981] R.P.C.53, where a solicitor failed to pay the renewal
fee for a patent, with the result that it lapsed. The solicitor may have been negligent, but
it was held that the proprietor of the patent was not: the solicitor was merely the system
set up by him for renewal, which was reasonable even though it had failed.

[57] See Wassermann (1974) 74 Col. L. Rev. 983; *Pitzel v. Saskatchewan Motor Club
Travel Agency Ltd* (1983) 149 D.L.R. (3d) 122; J. Nelson-Jones and P. Stewart, *A
Practical Guide to Package Holiday Law and Contracts* (2nd ed.).

Article 2

Further Definitions

1–033

(1) A disclosed principal, for the purposes of this book, is a principal, whether named or unnamed, whose interest in the transaction as principal is known to the third party at the time of the transaction in question.[58]

(2) A named principal, for the purposes of this book, is a disclosed principal whose name is known to the third party at that time.[59]

(3) An unnamed principal, for the purposes of this book, is a disclosed principal whose name is not known at that time.[60]

(4) An undisclosed principal, for the purposes of this book, is a principal whose existence as such is not known to the third party at the time of the transaction in question.[61]

(5) A *del credere* agent is an agent who, in consideration of extra remuneration, called a *del credere* commission, guarantees to his principal that third parties with whom he enters into contracts on behalf of the principal will duly pay any sums becoming due under those contracts.[62]

(6) A commercial agent is a self-employed intermediary who has continuing authority to negotiate the sale or purchase of goods on behalf of another person (the "principal"), or to negotiate and conclude the sale or purchase of goods on behalf of and in the name of that principal.[63]

(7) A general agent is an agent who has authority to act for his principal in all matters concerning a particular trade or business, or of a particular nature; or to do some act in the ordinary course of his trade, profession or business as an agent, on behalf of his principal.[64]

(8) A special agent is an agent who has only authority to do some particular act, or to represent his principal in some particular transaction, such act or transaction not being in the ordinary course of his trade, profession or business as an agent.[65]

---

[58] See Comment.
[59] See Comment.
[60] See Comment.
[61] See Comment.
[62] *Morris v. Cleasby* (1816) 4 M. & S. 566; *Hornby v. Lacy* (1817) 6 M. & S. 166: see Comment.
[63] Commercial Agents (Council Directive) Regulations 1993, reg. 2(1): see Comment and Chap. 11.
[64] See Comment; Articles 29, 30.
[65] See Comment.

(9) A factor is an agent whose ordinary course of business is to sell or dispose of goods, of which he is entrusted with the possession or control by his principal.[66]

(10) A broker is an agent whose ordinary course of business is to negotiate and make contracts for the sale and purchase of goods and other property, of which he is not entrusted with the possession or control.[67]

Comment

The terms here defined are terms of art and are found in legal sources. But only the first six, (1)—(6), are of contemporary significance; the others are presented for explanatory purposes only.   1–034

Disclosed principal (named or unnamed), undisclosed principal. It should be noted that the usage in this book does not entirely accord with that found in the cases. As stated, a principal is referred to in this book as disclosed in all situations where the third party knows that there is a principal involved, and it does not matter whether the principal is named to, or even identifiable by, the third party so long as the third party realises that there is a principal involved and does not at the time of the transaction in question think that he is dealing with the agent alone. The term "disclosed principal" therefore includes both named and unnamed[68] principals; these are referred to in the *Restatement*[69] as disclosed and partially disclosed principals. The term "undisclosed principal" is reserved for cases where the third party does not intend to deal with a principal at all and intends to deal with the agent personally: these cases are regulated by special rules, and raise different equities.   1–035

There are however difficult marginal cases where the existence of a principal was suspected or even known, but because the third party intended to deal with the agent, the undisclosed principal rules have been applied; and there are also cases which clearly involve unnamed but disclosed principals, where the term "undisclosed" has been used.[70]

---

[66] *Baring v. Corrie* (1818) 2 B. & A. 137, 143; *Stevens v. Biller* (1883) 25 Ch.D. 31, 37: *Rolls Razor Ltd v. Cox* [1967] 1 Q.B. 552, 568. See Comment.

[67] *Baring v. Corrie*, n. 66 above; *Fowler v. Hollins* (1872) L.R. 7 Q.B. 616. See Comment.

[68] *i.e.*, principals whose identity is known to the third party at the time of the transaction, and principals whose identities are not known, though it is known that there is a principal involved.

[69] § 4. But the Reporter, Professor Seavey, preferred "identified" and "unidentified": see (1929) 7 Proc.Am.Law Inst. 258.

[70] See *e.g. Benton v. Campbell, Parker & Co.* [1925] 2 K.B. 410, 414; *Thornton v. Fehr & Co.* (1935) 51 Ll.Rep. 330; *Hersom v. Bernett* [1955] 1 Q.B. 98; *Teheran-Europe Co. Ltd v. S.T. Belton (Tractors) Ltd* [1968] 2 Q.B. 545; *Marsh & McLennan Pty. Ltd v. Stanyers Transport Pty. Ltd* [1994] 2 V.R. 232.

The matter is discussed under the heading of undisclosed principal,[71] where it will be seen that it is in fact not clear in exactly what circumstances a person may rank as an "undisclosed principal".

1–036 *Del credere* **agent.**[71a] A *del credere* agent is an agent who for a special commission undertakes in effect the liability of a surety to his principal for the due performance, by the persons with whom he deals, of contracts made by him with them on his principal's behalf.[71b] His obligation is confined to answering for the failure of the other contracting parties, owing to insolvency or the like, to pay any ascertained sums which may become due from them as debts (largely in respect of the price of goods bought).[72] The principal is therefore not entitled to litigate with a *del credere* agent any disputes arising out of contracts made by him, nor is such an agent responsible to the third party for the due performance of the principal's contract.[73] In this respect the *del credere* agent is the antithesis of the commission agent, whose function is effectively the reverse.[74]

A *del credere* agency may in principal be inferred from the course of conduct between the parties,[75] though such inference would nowadays be rare.[76] An agreement by an agent to act on a *del credere* commission is not a promise to answer for the debt, default or miscarriage of another person within the meaning of section 4 of the Statute of Frauds but a contract of indemnity, and it is therefore not necessary that such an agreement should be evidenced in writing.[77]

Del credere agency would often in modern conditions involve liabilities which an ordinary commercial agent acting for commission

---

[71] See Article 78.

[71a] Chorley (1929) 45 L.Q.R. 221; (1930) 46 L.Q.R. 11. See also Schmitthoff, 1970 I Hague *Recueil des Cours* 115, 162–165; Hill (1968) 31 M.L.R. 623, 639, n. 64; below, para. 9–020.

[71b] See cases cited at n. 62 above. He cannot sue for advances made to his principal which are covered by sums due to the principal the payment of which he has guaranteed: *Graham v. Ackroyd* (1853) 10 Hare 192. See also *Bramwell v. Spiller* (1870) 21 L.T. 672.

[72] *Thomas Gabriel & Sons v. Churchill & Sim* [1914] 3 K.B. 1272; *Rusholme & Bolton & Roberts Hadfield v. S.G. Read & Co.* [1955] 1 W.L.R. 146. Indeed, the principal would have to sue the third party to quantify the damages arising from the third party's insolvency: see at p. 151. The execution of a deed of assignment does not establish a loss: *Montague Stanley & Co. v. J.C. Solomon Ltd* [1932] 2 K.B. 287.

[73] *Churchill & Sim v. Goddard* [1937] 1 K.B. 92.

[74] Above, para. 1–018.

[75] *Shaw v. Woodcock* (1827) 7 B. & C. 73.

[76] *Nouvelles Huileries Anversoises S.A. v. H.C. Mann & Co.* (1924) 40 T.L.R. 804 (mere description in contract of agents as *del credere* agents did not constitute them such): *J.M. Wotherspoon & Co. Ltd v. Henry Agency House* (1961) 28 Malaya L.J. 86 (no *del credere* agency where no special commission paid).

[77] *Couturier v. Hastie* (1852) 8 Exch. 40; *Wickham* (1855) 2 K. & J. 478; *Sutton & Co. v. Grey* [1894] 1 Q.B. 285.

would be reluctant to undertake, and has been largely superseded by documentary credits, credit guarantees, confirmations and similar methods of securing payment from overseas buyers undertaken by institutions with special expertise.[78] But it seems that such arrangements are still made in certain contexts, for example dealings with numerous and unknown buyers, or with underdeveloped countries.

Distinction between del credere agent and buyer. Problems as to the distinction between agent and buyer arise conspicuously in the case of *del credere* agents. The general topic is discussed above,[79] but it should be noted that some of the leading cases have involved this type of agent.[80]   **1–037**

Commercial agent. The term "commercial agent" stems from continental European legal systems and is not known to the common law. It is significant in English law now because of the E.C. Directive on Self-Employed Commercial Agents,[81] which regulates the relations between commercial agents and their principals, and in particular gives them special rights on termination of their agency. Such rights have long been known to continental legal systems, but were unknown to the common law. The Directive was implemented in Great Britain[82] by the Commercial Agents (Council Directive) Regulations 1993,[83] made under section 2(2) of the European Communities Act 1972 and effective on January 1, 1994. The rules for commercial agents as defined are therefore somewhat different from the general rules of agency law described in this book. They are dealt with together as a unit in Chapter 11, where the definition given above is further expanded. They are also referred to at the relevant points in the description of the general rules of English law.   **1–038**

The remaining distinctions are mainly significant in the understanding of old cases.

General agent, special agent. This distinction, an obvious and commonsense one, is relevant to the question of the nature and extent of the authority conferred on the agent, and was principally significant in the early development of the doctrine of apparent authority. It was a general agent who had such authority and might bind his principal by an   **1–039**

---

[78] See further below, para. 9–020.
[79] See Comment to Article 1.
[80] *Ex p. White, re Neville* (1871) L.R. 6 Ch.App. 397, affd. *sub nom. John Towle & Co. v. White* (1873) 29 L.T. 78; *Michelin Tyre Co. Ltd v. Macfarlane (Glasgow) Ltd* (1917) 55 Sc.L.Rep. 35.
[81] Dir. 86/653: [1986] O.J. L382/17.
[82] As to Northern Ireland, see Commercial Agents (Council Directive) Regulations (Northern Ireland), S.R. 1993 No. 483 (effective January 13, 1994).
[83] S.I. 1993 No. 3053, as amended by S.I. 1993 No. 3173.

act which he had been forbidden to do.[84] Similar reasoning appears to have been used in the civil law to fix the principal with liability for the agent's unauthorised acts.[85] The distinction is maintained by the *Restatement* in this connection,[86] and also in connection with the doctrine of "inherent agency power"[87] though the Reporter, Professor Seavey, would have liked to abolish it.[88] But the doctrine of apparent authority is nowadays in England normally explained without reference to the distinction, but rather by invocation of the notion of estoppel or similar reasoning.[89] Such case law as exists comparable to the notion of "inherent agency power" is also explained in other ways.[90] Therefore, though the distinction between general and special agents is a well-established one, it is doubtful whether it is of much utility in English law at the present day.[91]

1–040   **Factor, broker.**[92] The distinction between these was again of great importance in the nineteenth century, when many of the cases from which our present rules are derived were decided.[93] Some knowledge of the commercial practices of that time helps in understanding those cases. The distinction concerned commercial sales, but within that area of activity was general and not confined to particular trades. A factor was an agent for sale, often of goods sent from another country which he held on consignment: he had possession or control of the goods he sold and usually sold in his own name without disclosing the name of his

---

[84] See *Smith v. M'Guire* (1858) 3 H. & N. 554; *Brady v. Todd* (1861) 9 C.B. (N.S.) 592; *Butler v. Maples* 76 U.S. 822 (1869). A dramatic example is *Hatch v. Taylor* 10 N.H. 538 (1840) (complicated instructions regarding sale of a team of horses). See also Stoljar, pp. 77–80. The meaning of "general agent" in the context of an insurance policy is considered in *Excess Life Assurance Co. Ltd v. Fireman's Insurance Co. Ltd* [1982] 2 Lloyd's Rep. 599. In *Barrett v. Irvine* [1907] 2 I.R. 462 it was held that a multiplicity of separately authorised transactions does not constitute a general agency (as to which also see *Pole v. Leask* (1863) 33 L.J. Ch. 155, 162).

[85] Müller-Freienfels (1964) 13 Am.J.Comp.L. 193, 341; Schmitthoff, 1970 I Hague *Recueil des Cours* 115.

[86] See §§ 3, 127–132, 161, 161A.

[87] See §§ 194, 195, 195A; Comment to Article 22.

[88] (1929) 7 Proc.Am.Law. Inst. 240. But *cf.* (1955) 1 Howard L.J. 79, where he approves the distinction on the ground that it facilitates the wider liability of an undisciplined principal; he had expressed a similar view in (1920) 29 Yale L.J. 859, 882.

[89] See Comment to Article 74. The notion of usual authority can however be related to the concept of the general agent.

[90] See Comment to Article 22.

[91] See also Müller-Freienfels (1964) 13 Am.J.Comp.L. 193, 341: Comment to Article 29. "The most useful thing that can be said about a special agent is that he is one who falls outside the ambit of any useful generalisation": Mechem, *Outlines of Agency* (4th ed.), p. 46.

[92] See in general Munday (1977) 6 Anglo-Am.L.Rev. 221 (a valuable survey).

[93] See Stoljar, pp. 242–247.

principal.[94] Indeed, he might not indicate whether he was dealing on behalf of a principal or on his own account. Such a person would readily be held to have apparent authority to sell the goods, or even to have apparent ownership of them, so that his dispositions might be valid even if unauthorised. Payment to a factor was a good discharge even to a buyer who knew of the agency, and where he sold in his own name the factor had the right to sue for the price.[95] The broker is a figure who emerges later than the factor, a person who negotiates and makes contracts between buyers and sellers of goods which he may never see: of him the above propositions are not therefore necessarily true. He should not sell in his own name,[96] and payment to him would not be a good discharge,[97] though these were only prima facie rules. The distinction was far from clear. Thus a factor might act also as an independent merchant; and one person might act as both factor and broker. An understanding of the distinction is however essential for the reading of many nineteenth century cases: for example, several decisions are based on the notion that a person dealing with a broker must have known that he had a principal whether he said so or not, but would not necessarily know this of a factor.[98] But the term "factor" is little used in the above sense today (indeed it is used in other senses, e.g. that of credit factoring[99]); and the term "broker" has been applied to many more types of activity than the commodity broker referred to above, and is often applied to intermediaries whom the definition given does not fit at all, e.g. insurance brokers, mortgage brokers, shipbrokers. Further, the Factors Act 1889, the culmination of legislation formulating and extending the special rules applicable to unauthorised dispositions by factors and protecting those who dealt with them, introduced a new term for its purposes, that of "mercantile agent": this is discussed elsewhere.[1] The general distinction is therefore out of date, but important for the comprehension of early case law.

---

[94] *Baring v. Corrie* (1818) 2 B. & A. 137, 143; *Rolls Razor Ltd v. Cox* [1967] 1 Q.B. 552, 568. But he may do: *cf. Stevens v. Biller* (1883) 25 Ch.D. 31. An interesting explanation is given in *The Matchless* (1822) 1 Hagg. 97. As to his discretion, see *Smart v. Sandars* (1846) 3 C.B. 380 (see also (1848) 5 C.B. 895). See as to the general trade background Miller (1957) 24 U.Chi.L.Rev. 256.

[95] *Drinkwater v. Goodwin* (1775) 1 Cowp. 251, 255–256. As to the ways in which this could be explained in modern terminology see below, para. 9–009.

[96] *Baring v. Corrie*, n. 94 above.

[97] *Linck, Moeller & Co. v. Jameson & Co.* (1885) 2 T.L.R. 206.

[98] *e.g. Baring v. Corrie*, n. 94 above; *Armstrong v. Stokes* (1872) L.R. 7 Q.B. 598, 610. For a modern example see *N. & J. Vlassopulos Ltd v. Ney Shipping Ltd (The Santa Carina)* [1977] 1 Lloyd's Rep. 478.

[99] See Biscoe, *Credit Factoring* (1975): Salinger [1977] L.M.L.Q. 184. See also Steffen and Danziger, "The Rebirth of the Commercial Factor" (1936) 36 Col.L.Rev. 745.

[1] Article 89.

CHAPTER 2

CREATION OF AGENCY

1.—GENERAL

Article 3

HOW AGENCY ARISES

2–001　(1)　The relationship of principal and agent may be constituted—

(a) by agreement, whether contractual or not, between principal and agent, which may be express, or implied from the conduct or situation of the parties[1];

(b) retrospectively, by subsequent ratification by the principal of acts done on his behalf.[2]

(2) A person may sometimes be estopped from denying that another person is his agent, or that an unauthorised transaction purportedly entered into on his behalf was valid.[3]

Comment

2–002　This general statement seeks only to give an indication of the ways in which the relationship of principal and agent can arise in the full sense, creating internal rights and duties between principal and agent and giving the agent external authority to affect the principal's legal relations with third parties. Sometimes however the issue may be entirely an internal one between principal and agent; and sometimes, when only agency by estoppel or apparent authority is relevant, the issue may, at least initially, be an external one only.

2–003　**Agency arising by agreement.** It has been explained in Chapter 1 that the basic way in which the agency relationship arises is by agreement, and it should be noted that this need not be contractual. As between

---

[1] Section 2 of this chapter.
[2] Section 3.
[3] Section 4.

36

principal and agent some form of agreement would normally be necessary, however, to impose duties on the agent. It is, however, possible that the agent might bind the principal as regards third parties if the principal was in fact willing for the agent to do so, though the agent did not know this.[4]

Ratification. In a second group of cases, a principal may ratify the   2–004
unauthorised acts of a person who purported to act for him while having no actual authority. This in general retrospectively creates the relationship of principal and agent, and the full consequences of such relationship, but although the analogy of authority having been initially conferred is in many respects followed, the relationship cannot easily be said to arise by agreement. Further, certain special rules are found in this area to prevent the retroactivity from operating unfairly.[5] This, therefore, must be treated as a separate type of case. The doctrine of ratification applies also, and perhaps more commonly, to situations where the person who acts is already an agent, but exceeds his authority. Since however it can also create agency it is most conveniently taken in this chapter.

Agency by estoppel. There is also a way in which *some* of the   2–005
consequences of agency can arise, under the doctrine of agency by estoppel. Under this, the principal may be estopped as against a third party from denying that a person is or was his agent. The principal is here bound by the acts of his apparent agent: but the full relationship of principal and agent does not arise between him and such person, the legal position between them being governed by rules which start from the assumption that there is no agreement between them, at least in respect of the transaction in question. "It is ... necessary to bear in mind the difference between this agency by estoppel ... and a real agency, however constituted."[6] Agency by estoppel is therefore introduced in a separate section at the end of this chapter[7]; but since its operation is related to the relationship between principal and third party, full discussion is deferred till Chapter 8, which deals with that relationship. Reference is also made to a somewhat different application of estoppel: cases where a person is estopped by subsequent conduct from disputing the validity of an unauthorised transaction entered into on his behalf.

---

[4] Below, para. 2–032.
[5] Articles 16–19.
[6] *Pole v. Leask* (1863) 33 L.J.Ch. 155, 162, *per* Lord Cranworth.
[7] Article 21.

Article 4

CAPACITY TO ACT AS PRINCIPAL

2–006   Capacity to contract or do any other act by means of an agent is co-extensive with the capacity of the principal himself to make the contract or do the act which the agent is authorised to make or do.

Comment

2–007   "It would seem that the proper view should be that anyone may be a principal who has the mental power to act at all, and that if he is a person of no, or limited, contractual power, his incapacity should be reflected solely in the contract made for him by his agent, which contract would stand on the same footing as if he had made it in person."[8] Such a simple approach, which is also formulated in this Article, cannot however be left without further comment, for where, as often, incapacity leads to voidable transactions, a more complex analysis may be necessary.

2–008   **Minors.** In old cases it is suggested that minors cannot appoint agents at all.[9] The dicta were wider than was necessary for the decisions in connection with which they were uttered,[10] and are nowadays interpreted restrictively. The following judicial statement may provide a better guide: "Whenever a minor can lawfully do an act on his own behalf, so as to bind himself, he can instead appoint an agent to do it for him."[11] This to some extent follows from the general principle that whatever a person may himself do he may do through an agent.[12] Thus a minor may by an agent enter into a contract that binds him in accordance with the general law[13]; and it has been held that a minor may authorise another to make admissions, even contrary to his interest.[14] On the other hand, contracts which would not otherwise bind

---

[8] Mechem, *Outlines of Agency* (4th ed.), p. 9.

[9] *Zouch* d. *Abbot and Hallett v. Parsons* (1765) 3 Burr. 1794, 1804; *Doe* d. *Thomas v. Robert* (1847) 16 M. & W. 778.

[10] See *Chaplin v. Leslie Frewin (Publishers) Ltd* [1966] Ch. 71, 96–97.

[11] *G. (A.) v. G. (T.)* [1970] 2 Q.B. 643, 652, *per* Lord Denning M.R., limiting earlier dicta of his own in *Shephard v. Cartwright* [1953] Ch. 728, 735 (affd. on another point [1955] A.C. 431).

[12] Article 6.

[13] See *R. v. Longnor (Inhabitants)* (1833) 4 B. & Ad. 647; *Doyle v. White City Stadium Ltd* [1935] 1 K.B. 110.

[14] *G. (A.) v. G. (T.)*, n. 11 above (where it was held that in the event there had been no authority).

a minor will not do so merely because made through an adult agent; and a minor cannot by an agent, any more than he can personally, make an irrevocable disposition taking effect by deed, for such a disposition is avoidable by the minor within a reasonable time of coming of age,[15] and the interposition of an agent should make no difference. This latter proposition probably does not, however, extend to dispositions of property taking effect otherwise than by deed, e.g. by writing or delivery, though the matter is not clear.[16]

It is frequently said that a minor cannot execute a power of attorney appointing an agent, and this is supported by the position as to mentally incapable principals, explained below. The cases cited, however, mostly concern warranty of attorney in litigation,[17] where a minor is only permitted to act by his next friend or guardian *ad litem*. The true proposition may rather be that any deed disposing of a minor's property executed by an agent appointed by means of such a power would be voidable by the minor as if he had executed it himself: "an infant cannot appoint an agent to make a disposition of his property so as to bind him irrevocably."[18] But where the power of attorney is executed under seal, which is now requisite,[19] it may be possible to argue that the deed itself is caught by this rule: that not only is the power revocable for the future, but the deed itself is also voidable. It seems that the contract (if there is a contract) with the agent is to be treated like a contract of service, and binding on the minor if it is for his benefit:[20] the effect of this contract is of course a separate question from that of the validity of the agent's acts.[21]

Mentally incapable persons. The normal rule is that the contracts of a   2–009
mentally incapable person are voidable if that person can show that he was at the time of contracting incapable of knowing what he was doing, and that the other party was aware of the incapacity: this is often

---

[15] *Edwards v. Carter* [1893] A.C. 360; *Paget v. Paget* (1882) 11 L.R.Ir. 26; *Burnaby v. Equitable Reversionary Interest Society* (1885) 28 Ch.D. 416, 424; unless, presumably, the disposition is in pursuance of a contract which is in law binding on him. See also *Carnell v. Harrison* [1916] 1 Ch. 328.

[16] See *Chaplin v. Leslie Frewin (Publishers) Ltd.* [1966] 1 Ch. 71, 90, 93, 94, 97. Somtimes of course the disposition may be in pursuance of a contract which is itself voidable: *ibid.*

[17] e.g. *Oliver v. Woodroffe* (1839) 4 M. & W. 650. See also *Zouch d. Abbot and Hallett v. Parsons* (1765) 3 Burr. 1794; *Gibbons v. Wright* (1904) 91 C.L.R. 423, 447; Alcock, *Powers of Attorney* (1935), pp. 63–64; Aldridge, *Powers of Attorney* (8th ed.), pp. 23–24.

[18] *G. (A.) v. G. (T.)*, n. 11 above, at p. 652, *per* Lord Denning M.R.

[19] Powers of Attorney Act 1971, s. 1.

[20] *Chaplin v. Leslie Frewin (Publishers) Ltd*, n. 16 above. See further Webb (1955) 18 M.L.R. 461; *McLaughlin v. Darcy* (1918) 18 S.R.(N.S.W.) 585.

[21] See O'Hare (1970) 3 U.Tas.L.Rev. 312.

referred to as the rule in *Imperial Loan Co. v. Stone*.[22] It might seem that this rule could apply not only to the contract (if any) of agency itself, but also to contracts made by such person through an agent. But it has been held that a power of attorney executed by such a person is void, and that a deed of transfer of shares executed in pursuance of it is void also[23]; and the reasoning seems wide enough to cover simple agency without power of attorney.[24] Further, it has been held that supervening incapacity of the principal terminates the agent's authority and makes the agent liable for breach of warranty of authority.[25] It seems therefore that as regards actual authority the normal rule for relief is not applied as between principal and third party, and the transaction is simply void on the ground that authority was never granted, regardless of the third party's knowledge.[26] It is possible that the same analysis is to be applied to the position between principal and agent[27]: but in so far as this relationship is contractual, it seems in principle that it should be differentiated from the grant of authority and the rule in *Imperial Loan Co. v. Stone*[28] applied. As to apparent authority, there is a decision that the principal may be bound in the case of supervening mental incapacity.[29] The reasoning is at least in part based on the notion that the initial representation of authority was valid.[30] That is not the case discussed. Where the principal was mentally incapable at the time of the initial representation as to authority it is submitted that he would not be held liable even against a person who did not know of the incapacity.

2–010   **Alien enemies.** An alien enemy probably cannot appoint an agent, at any rate if the transaction involved would be of benefit to the enemy country.[31]

---

[22] [1892] 1 Q.B. 599. See also *O'Connor v. Hart* [1985] A.C. 1000. The contracts of a person found to be of unsound mind by inquisition were void even if made during a lucid interval: *Re Walker* [1905] 1 Ch. 160. The same rule presumably applies where a person's property is, under present legislation (Mental Health Act 1983), under the control of the court. But it is not clear whether the principle applies only to contracts relating to property. See Treitel, *Law of Contract* (9th ed.), p. 514.

[23] *Daily Telegraph Newspaper Co. Ltd v. McLaughlin* (1904) 1 C.L.R. 243, affd. [1904] A.C. 776; but *cf. Gibbons v. Wright* (1954) 91 C.L.R. 423. See also *Stead v. Thornton* (1832) 3 B. & Ad. 357n.; *Tarbuck v. Bispham* (1836) 2 M. & W. 2, 8; *Gore v. Gibson* (1845) 13 M. & W. 623; *Elliott v. Ince* (1857) 7 De G.M. & G. 475; but *cf. Ex p. Bradbury, re Walden* (1839) Mont. & C. 625.

[24] See *Gibbons v. Wright*, n. 23 above at pp. 444–445.

[25] *Yonge v. Toynbee* [1910] 1 K.B. 215.

[26] Hudson (1959) 37 Can.B.R. 497. *Contra, Taylor v. Walker* [1958] 1 Lloyd's Rep. 490, 514.

[27] See Powell, pp. 390–391.

[28] [1892] 1 Q.B. 599; above, n. 22.

[29] *Drew v. Nunn* (1879) 4 Q.B.D. 661; see Article 123.

[30] See p. 666.

[31] *Stevenson & Sons Ltd v. Aktiengesellschaft für Cartonnagen-Industrie* [1918] A.C. 239; *Ottoman Bank v. Jebara* [1928] A.C. 269; *Sovfracht, etc. v. Van Udens* [1943] A.C. 203;

Article 5

CAPACITY TO ACT AS AGENT

(1) All persons of sound mind, including minors and other persons   **2–011**
with limited or no capacity to contract on their own behalf, are
competent to act or contract as agents.

(2) But the personal liability of the agent upon any contract of
agency, and upon any contract entered into by him with a
third party, is dependent on his capacity to contract on his own
behalf.[32]

Comment

Rule (1). The rationale of this seems to be that the agent is a mere   **2–012**
instrument and that it is the principal who bears the risk of inadequate
representation.[33] An early example was the married woman, who could
act as agent, though she had no contractual capacity till 1882: indeed it
was her lack of capacity that led to her being held to be an agent for her
husband.[34] Thus a minor may act as agent provided that he has
sufficient understanding to consent to the agency and to do the act
required.[35] A person who cannot read may be an agent to sign a written
contract.[36] But a person incapable of understanding the nature of what
he is doing cannot act as agent.[37] Agency by an alien enemy would
often be void on grounds of public policy.[38]

Statutes sometimes require certain qualifications in persons who act as
agents, *e.g.* solicitors. When this is so, persons who act without such

---

Nordisk Insulinlaboratorium v. Gorgate Products Ltd [1953] Ch. 430 (on termination of
agency); *Boston Deep Sea Fishing & Ice Co. v. Farnham* [1957] 1 W.L.R. 1051 (on
ratification). *Cf. Lepage v. San Paulo Copper Estates Ltd* (1917) 33 T.L.R. 457
(administrator-sequestrator appointed by French court to act for enemy alien may claim
dividends due to alien); *Hangkam Kwingtong Woo v. Liu Lan Fong* [1951] A.C. 707
(application of rule when territory occupied by enemy). See also Article 119.

[32] *Smally v. Smally* (1700) 1 Eq.Ca.Abr. 6.

[33] Müller-Freienfels (1957) 6 Am.J. Comp.L. 165, 180–181; (1964) 13 Am.J.Comp.L.
193, 204; *Norwich and Peterborough B.S. v. Steed* [1993] Ch. 116, 128.

[34] See below, para. 3–039.

[35] *Smally v. Smally*, n. 32 above; *Re D'Angibau* (1880) 15 Ch.D. 228, 246; *Restatement*,
§ 21.

[36] Illustration 1.

[37] *i.e.* cannot affect the position of his principal. But as between himself and his
principal, the rule in *Imperial Loan Co. Ltd v. Stone* [1892] 1 Q.B. 599 applies; see
Comment to Article 4. See also *Norwich and Peterborough B.S. v. Steed*, n. 33 above.

[38] See Article 4 and Article 119; *Kuenigl v. Donnersmarck* [1955] 1 Q.B. 515; *Rayner v.
Sturges* (1916) 33 T.L.R. 87; *Schostall v. Johnson* (1919) 36 T.L.R. 75 (friendly enemy
aliens resident in England).

qualifications may commit offences by doing so, and may not be entitled to remuneration, reimbursement or indemnity; the matter is discussed under Articles 63 and 65. But they will nevertheless bind their principals unless the statute also invalidates their acts.

2–013   **Agent acting for both parties to a transaction.** The agent of one party is not incompetent to act as agent of the other. Thus solicitors frequently act for both the buyer and the seller of a house, though there are many judicial warnings as to the dangers of this practice.[39] It is perhaps more likely that an agent can acceptably acquire the second capacity after the conclusion of the contract negotiated.[40] Where there is no conflict of interest, the matter is straightforward. But an agent who does act in this way runs grave risks of finding himself in a position in which his duty to one party is consistent with his duty to the other, for example as regards information coming into his possession. In such a case he will be in breach of his duty to his first principal, and liable accordingly, unless that principal has given his informed consent to the transaction with the other principal.[41] Where the agent's acts result in a transaction with a third party who knew of the agent's dual capacity, that transaction may be voidable.[42] But in other cases the act of the agent may be valid in itself, though wrongful.[43]

2–014   **One party to a transaction as agent of the other.** Similarly, one party is not in principle incompetent to act as agent for the other party to a transaction. He will however be in breach of his duty if while an agent he fails to disclose his interest,[44] and the transaction is in such a case likely to be voidable.[45] Cases where his act is valid, though a breach of duty, can similarly arise. And in the case of the Statute of Frauds, there

---

[39] See *Moody v. Cox and Hatt* [1917] 2 Ch. 71, 91; *Spector v. Ageda* [1973] 1 Ch. 30, 47; *Mortgage Express Ltd. v. Bowerman & Partners, The Times*, August 1, 1995. For other examples of agents acting for both parties see *Emmerson v. Heelis* (1809) 2 Taunt. 38 (auctioneer); *Newsholme v. Road Transport Insurance Co.*, Illustration 2 to Article 97 (insurance agent); *Briess v. Woolley* [1954] A.C. 333 (director); *The Giancarlo Zeta* [1966] 2 Lloyd's Rep. 317 (freight broker) (Can.).

[40] See Story. *Agency* (6th ed.), § 31, and *Royal Securities Corp. Ltd v. Montreal Trust Co.* (1966) 59 D.L.R. (2d) 666, affd. (1967) 63 D.L.R. (2d) 15.

[41] *Fullwood v. Hurley* [1928] 1 K.B. 498, 502; *Anglo-African Merchants Ltd v. Bayley* [1970] 1 Q.B. 311 (insurance broker); *Eagle Star Insurance Co. Ltd v. Spratt* [1971] 2 Lloyd's Rep. 116, 133; *Richard Ellis Ltd v. Van Hong-tuan* [1988] 1 H.K.L.R. 169. See further below, paras. 6–047, 6–060; Article 50.

[42] *Re a Debtor* [1927] 2 Ch. 367; *Taylor v. Walker* [1958] 1 Lloyd's Rep. 490; *North and South Trust Co. v. Berkeley* [1971] 1 W.L.R. 470, 485. See further Article 98.

[43] See Illustration 3.

[44] See Article 47.

[45] *e.g. Moody v. Cox and Hatt* [1917] 2 Ch. 71; *Spector v. Ageda* [1973] Ch. 30 (solicitors).

is a rule of actual competence: it has long been established that a party to a contract is not competent to sign a contract or a note or memorandum thereof, as agent of the other party.[46] The reasoning is based on the purpose of the statute, and it is submitted that it should also be applied to section 2 of the Law of Property (Miscellaneous Provisions) Act 1989, which now requires the actual contract to be in writing. However, one party can authorise the *agent* of the other party to sign, though it may be difficult to establish that he has in fact given such authority[47]: thus the signature of an auctioneer to a contemporary memorandum or contract of sale operated as the signature of both parties within section 40 of the Law of Property Act 1925,[48] provided that the auctioneer was not himself plaintiff.[49] If he was plaintiff, however, he was suing on a contract made with himself and could not claim to have signed as agent for the other party. But the signature of his clerk (if authorised) might suffice[50]; or even in one case the signature of the employee, himself a licensed auctioneer, who conducted the auction (and who had prima facie authority to sign).[51] Contracts made in the course of public actions are exempted from section 2 of the 1989 Act referred to above, with the result that these cases may on their facts be no longer relevant. They are, however, retained as examples of general principle, and as being still relevant to contracts of guarantee, the only type of contract still covered by the Statute of Frauds.

Rule (2). A minor's liability to his principal, or on the contract which   2–014A
he has made with a third party (where this involves his personal liability[52]) is regulated by his capacity to contract. Where the agency is not contractual, the minor may nevertheless be subject to the non-contractual rights and duties of an agent.[53] The extent to which an agent who is a minor would be subject to fiduciary duties is beyond the scope of this book. A minor cannot be an express trustee[54]: but it has been held that a minor can be a resulting trustee of personalty,[55] and

---

[46] *Wright v. Dannah* (1809) 2 Camp. 203; *Farebrother v. Simmons* (1882) 5 B. & A. 333; *Sharman v. Brandt* (1871) L.R. 6 Q.B. 720.
[47] *Bird v. Boulter* (1833) 4 B. & Ad. 443; *Durrell v. Evans* (1862) 1 H. & C. 174; *cf. Murphy v. Boese* (1875) L.R. 10 Ex. 126.
[48] *Emmerson v. Heelis* (1809) 2 Taunt. 38; *White v. Proctor* (1811) 4 Taunt. 209; *Chaney v. Maclow* [1929] 1 Ch. 461.
[49] *Farebrother v. Simmons*, n. 46 above.
[50] *Bird v. Boulter*, n. 47 above; *Sims v. Landray* [1894] 2 Ch. 318. But an auctioneer's clerk had no prima facie authority to sign; *Bell v. Balls* [1897] 1 Ch. 663. And see Article 8, Illustration 1.
[51] *Wilson & Sons v. Pike* [1949] 1 K.B. 176.
[52] See Article 100.
[53] Article 44.
[54] Law of Property Act 1925, s. 20.
[55] *Re Vinogradoff* [1935] W.N. 68.

there seems no reason why he should not be a constructive trustee. It has been held that a restitutionary claim against a minor is controlled by his contractual capacity[56]: whether this is good law or not, an equitable claim, whether *in rem* or *in personam*, may not be so controlled,[57] and there is also a statutory jurisdication to order the minor to transfer property where it is just and equitable to do so.[58] A minor is liable in tort provided that the tortious action is not merely a way of evading a contractual immunity.[59]

Illustrations

2–015   (1)   A farmer sends cattle by rail: his drover, who cannot read, signs a consignment note containing contractual terms. The farmer is bound.[60]

(2)   The buyer and seller of a house sign a printed form of contract which covers all details except date of completion. The seller's solicitor is instructed to act for the buyer. The seller tells the solicitor the date subsequently agreed for completion, and being asked by the solicitor to confirm this the buyer does so. The solicitor is authorised to create an additional memorandum binding the buyer.[61]

(3)   Lloyd's brokers, who act as agents for the assured, are instructed by the underwriters to obtain an assessor's report in connection with a claim made by the brokers' principals. The brokers obtain such a report and in the course of litigation refuse to show it to their principals. This custom of Lloyd's by which brokers act also for the underwriters is unreasonable[62] and the brokers are in breach of duty to their principals: but their principals are nevertheless not entitled to see the report, which the brokers obtained while acting for the underwriters.[63]

Article 6

ACTS WHICH MAY BE DONE BY MEANS OF AN AGENT

2–016   An agent may be appointed for the purpose of executing a deed, or doing any other act on behalf of the principal, which the principal

---

[56] *Cowern v. Nield* [1912] 2 K.B. 419; criticised, Goff and Jones, *Law of Restitution* (4th ed.), pp. 531–532, 737–738.

[57] But see *R. Leslie Ltd. v. Sheill* [1914] 3 K.B. 607; criticised, Goff and Jones, *op. cit.* n. 56 above, pp. 530–538.

[58] Minors' Contracts Act 1987, s. 3(1).

[59] See Treitel, *Law of Contract* (9th ed.), pp. 506–507.

[60] *Foreman v. G.W. Ry. Co.* (1878) 38 L.T. 851.

[61] *Gavaghan v. Edwards* [1961] 2 Q.B. 220. The analysis of this situation would now be different by virtue of s. 2 of the Law of Property (Miscellaneous Provisions) Act 1989, but the reasoning still seems valid.

[62] See Article 31.

[63] *North and South Trust Co. v. Berkeley* [1971] 1 W.L.R. 470. See (1972) 35 M.L.R. 78. But *cf. Stockton v. Mason* [1978] 2 Lloyd's Rep. 430, where a broker was held to have

might himself execute, make or do; except for the purpose of executing a right, privilege or power conferred, or of performing a duty imposed, on the principal personally, the exercise or performance of which requires discretion or special personal skill, or for the purpose of doing an act which the principal is required, by or pursuant to any statute, to do in person.[64]

Comment

The authorities cited for the proposition contained in this Article **2–017**
indicate that it is a general rule of common law which will apply unless displaced. Similar considerations operate in the reverse situation, *viz.* where it is sought to use the rule *against* a principal. Thus it has been held that a notice to quit may be served on an agent[65]; but that a memorandum under the Moneylenders Act may not be.[66]

Contract. In general a person may make any contract through an **2–018**
agent. He can also perform a contract through an agent unless it is a contract that involves his own personal attributes or otherwise expressly or impliedly excludes vicarious performance.[67] But this is not an assignment of the burden of the contract and the principal remains liable personally.[68] An agent may sign a memorandum of a guarantee in his own name within the requirements of the Statute of Frauds, s. 4,[69] since it refers to a person "thereunto lawfully authorised"[70]: there is no requirement that he state for whom he acts, and he need not be specifically authorised, nor (necessarily) intend to bind his principal by

---

authority to issue temporary cover. It is also arguable that he in many cases has authority to receive premiums on behalf of the underwriter.

[64] *R. v. Kent JJ.* (1873) L.R. 8 Q.B. 305; *Re Whitley Partners Ltd.* (1886) 32 Ch.D. 337; *Jackson & Co. v. Napper* (1886) 35 Ch.D. 162, 172; *R. v. Assessment Committee of St Mary Abbotts, Kensington* [1891] 1 Q.B. 389; *Bevan v. Webb* [1901] 2 Ch. 59, 77; *McRae v. Coulton* (1986) 7 N.S.W.L.R. 644, 663–664; *Restatement*, § 17.

[65] *Doe* d. *Prior v. Ongley* (1850) 10 C.B. 25, 34; and statutes frequently provide for service on agents, *e.g.* Rent Act 1977, ss. 41(2), 151(1).

[66] *John W. Grahame (English Financiers) Ltd. v. Ingram* [1955] 1 W.L.R. 563. The Moneylenders Act 1927 was repealed by the Consumer Credit Act 1974.

[67] See *Davies v. Collins* [1945] 1 All E.R. 247; Chitty, *Contracts* (27th ed.), Vol. 1, §§ 19–046 *et seq.*

[68] *Stewart v. Reavell's Garage* [1952] 2 Q.B. 545. Nor can the agent be sued in contract by the other party to the contract, unless, of course, the principal has acted as agent for the purpose of setting up contractual relations between his agent and the other party.

[69] As amended by the Law Reform (Enforcement of Contracts) Act 1954.

[70] It seems that he can sign his own name or his principal's name: *Graham v. Musson* (1839) 5 Bing.N.C. 603. But as to forms of signature see below, para. 2–024.

contract.[71] An agent may likewise sign a contract for the sale or other disposition of an interest in land for the purposes of the Law of Property (Miscellaneous Provisions) Act 1989; but here, since the document constitutes the contract, an intention to bind by contract is required.

2–019   **Deeds.** A deed may be executed through an agent provided that the agent is duly authorised by deed.[72] An individual authorised to act by power of attorney may execute an instrument in his own name.[73]

2–020   **Agency: delegation.** The rules as to delegation of authority by an agent, which stem from the same principles, are treated separately: see Chapter 5. But in general it is plain that a person or corporation may agree through an agent to act as agent, or may appoint an agent through an agent.

2–021   **Discretionary powers.** A person who is given a power of a discretionary nature must as a rule exercise it in person. Thus where the consent of a particular person was required for the execution of a power of appointment, it was held that he had no power to appoint an agent to consent for him[74]; it has been held that an affidavit verifying documents cannot be sworn by the holder of a power of attorney[75]; and where Chitty J. delegated the appointment of the official liquidator of a company to his chief clerk, the appointment was held invalid.[76]

2–022   **Trustees.** Trustees are in general in the same position and cannot delegate their duties: *delegatus non potest delegare*. But there were exceptions to this[77] and they have been extended and modified by statute.[78]

---

[71] *Griffiths Cycle Corp. Ltd v. Humber & Co. Ltd* [1899] 2 Q.B. 414; *Daniels v. Trefusis* [1914] 1 Ch. 788; *North v. Loomes* [1919] 1 Ch. 378; *Grindell v. Bass* [1920] 2 Ch. 487; *Wright v. Pepin* [1954] 1 W.L.R. 635. Liability for representations as to credit under s. 6 of the Statute of Frauds Amendment Act 1828 does not arise if the representation is merely signed by an agent, except in the case of a limited company: see Article 93.

[72] See Article 10.

[73] Powers of Attorney Act 1971, s. 7(1); below, para. 2–038.

[74] *Hawkins v. Kemp* (1803) 3 East 410. See also *Ingram v. Ingram* (1740) 2 Atk. 88 (special power of appointment). *Aliter*, if the duty is merely ministerial: *L.C.C. v. Hobbis* (1897) 75 L.T. 688.

[75] *Clauss v. Pir* [1988] Ch. 267.

[76] *Re Great Southern Mysore Gold Mining Co.* (1882) 48 L.T. 11.

[77] *Speight v. Gaunt* (1883) 9 App.Cas. 1; *Fry v. Tapson* (1884) 28 Ch.D. 268; *Learoyd v. Whiteley* (1887) 12 App.Cas. 727.

[78] Trustee Act 1925, ss. 23, 25, as amended by Powers of Attorney Act 1971, s. 9. See *Re Vickery, Vickery v. Stevens* [1931] 1 Ch. 572; Jones (1959) 22 M.L.R. 381; Snell, *Equity* (29th ed.), pp. 265 *et seq.*; Article 36, Illustration 8.

Signature by proxy. As a general rule, "at common law a person   2–023
sufficiently 'signs' a document if it is signed in his name and with his
authority by somebody else."[79] An indication that the signature is *per
procurationem* is desirable but not essential.[80] Thus it was held that an
agent might subscribe the name of his principal to the memorandum of
association of a company,[81] or the instrument of dissolution of a
building society,[82] and such a signature still seems sufficient compliance
with the similar wording of the present Companies Act 1985, s. 2, and
the Building Societies Act 1986, s. 87(1), respectively. But there may be
cases where a statute requires personal signature: thus it was held that
an agent could not sign a proposal for a scheme of composition under
the Bankruptcy Act 1914, s. 16(1).[83] There is conflicting authority as to
whether a statute requiring signature "under the hand of" a person
permits signature by an agent.[84] The better view seems to be that it
does not.

Form of signature. The reference above to signature "in his name"   2–024
can be taken to suggest that the agent should write the principal's name
first, adding, if he desires, his own signature below, and there is further
support for such a requirement in the case cited.[84] "On this view if
Richard Roe wished to sign as agent for John Doe he can sign John
Doe by his agent Richard Roe, but he cannot sign Richard Roe as agent
for John Doe."[85] This would be the rule unless there was an indication
in the relevant wording that the agent could sign his own name first,
indicating if desired the person for whom he had signed. The latter
procedure is justified, for example, in the case of the Statute of Frauds,
which contemplated signature by an agent "thereunto lawfully authorised"[86] and by the Powers of Attorney Act 1971,[87] which refers in

---

[79] *L.C.C. v. Agricultural Foods Products Ltd* [1955] 2 Q.B. 218, 223–224, *per* Romer
L.J. See also *R. v. Kent JJ.* (1873) L.R. 8 Q.B. 305 (notice of appeal); *France v. Dutton*
[1891] 2 Q.B. 208 (solicitor's claim for costs); Bills of Exchange Act 1882, s.91(1); *Tennant
v. L.C.C.* (1957) 121 J.P.Jo. 428 (notice to terminate tenancy).
[80] *L.C.C. v. Agricultural Food Products Ltd*, n. 79 above at p. 223.
[81] *Re Whitley Partners Ltd* (1886) 32 Ch.D. 337.
[82] *Dennison v. Jeffs* [1896] 1 Ch. 611.
[83] *Re Prince Blücher, ex p. Debtor* [1931] 2 Ch. 70. (See now Insolvency Act 1985,
s. 111(2).) This case seems to adopt a position somewhat contrary to the rule given in *R.
v. Kent JJ.*, n. 79 supra, as does Denning L.J. in *L.C.C. v. Agricultural Food Products
Ltd*, n. 79 above, at p. 222. However, in *Tennant v. L.C.C.*, n. 79 above, *Re Prince
Blücher* was treated as turning on the special provisions of the Bankruptcy Act 1914; and
see *McRae v. Coulton* (1986) 7 N.S.W.L.R. 644, 663–664.
[84] *Wilson v. Wallani* (1880) 5 Ex.D. 155; but *cf. Re Diptford Parish Lands* [1934]
Ch. 151.
[85] *McRae v. Coulton* (1989) 7 N.S.W.L.R. 644, 664 *per* Hope J.A. (C.A., N.S.W.). See
also *U.B.A.F. Ltd v. European American Banking Corp.* [1982] Q.B. 713; Article 93.
[86] *Graham v. Musson* (1839) 5 Bing. N.C. 603.
[87] As amended by Law of Property (Miscellaneous Provisions) Act 1989, Scheds. 1, 2.

section 7 to signature and other acts by the agent "in his own name". However, despite the above dicta, the inflexibility of such reasoning (the burden of which would be quite unknown to most signers who had not taken legal advice and to many who had) may be doubted: it has been said in the Court of Appeal of New South Wales[88] that such requisites for ordinary signature by an agent should not be rigidly insisted on, at least unless the wording of the enabling provision appears to require it.[89] The crucial question must surely be whether signature by an agent is permissible: so long as the purport of such a signature is clear, it is difficult to see that the form should be of particular consequence.

2–025   **Administrative law: right to be represented before tribunals.** Difficulties can occur in connection with this principle where a person seeks to use it to demand the right to be legally (or otherwise) represented before a domestic or statutory tribunal before which he is entitled or bound to appear, but which by its rules, or in the exercise of its discretion to control its own proceedings, does not wish to permit representation. There is authority for applying the general private law principles of agency to such cases.[90] Viewed from the standpoint of public law, on the other hand, it may be said that the requirement of natural justice do not often demand professional representation or even representation at all[91] and that a tribunal may have perfectly good reasons for seeking to exclude such representation (though exclusion of professional representation is easier to justify than exclusion of all representation). It may be suggested that agency reasoning is not really relevant: the matter is one of contract and natural justice.[92] In the case of a domestic tribunal, although contractual terms contrary to the requirements of natural justice are probably unenforceable,[93] a clear contractual provision or rule excluding representation would normally not contravene those requirements and so would be valid[94]: but in the

---

[88] See *McRae v. Coulton*, n. 85 above, at p. 666.

[89] See p. 664. An example is s. 91 of the Bills of Exchange Act 1882, which provides that it is "sufficient if his signature is written thereon by some other person or under his authority."

[90] *R. v. Assessment Committee of St Mary Abbotts, Kensington* [1891] 1 Q.B. 378; *R. v. Board of Appeal, ex p. Kay* (1916) 22 C.L.R. 183; *Pett v. Greyhound Racing Association Ltd* [1969] 1 Q.B. 125.

[91] *Pett v. Greyhound Racing Association Ltd* (No. 2) [1970] 1 Q.B. 46; *Enderby Town Football Club Ltd v. Football Association Ltd* [1971] Ch. 591.

[92] See *Kok Seng Chong v. Bukit Turf Club* [1993] 2 Singapore L.R. 388.

[93] See *Faramus v. Film Artistes Association* [1964] A.C. 925, 941; *Edwards v. S.O.G.A.T.* [1971] Ch. 354, 376, 381; *Enderby Town Football Club Ltd v. Football Association Ltd*, n. 91 above, at p. 606.

[94] *Enderby Town Football Club Ltd v. Football Association*, n. 91 above. But Lord Denning M.R. thought that an absolute exclusion without the possibility of exceptions might be invalid: at p. 607.

control of its own proceedings the tribunal may not adopt an absolute rule of no representation[95] and should retain a discretion to allow or disallow representation for good reason.[96] In the case of a statutory tribunal the matter is frequently settled by statute or delegated legislation.[97] In the absence of such guidance, it seems again that general agency reasoning is not relevant, and that there is no right to representation even where the facts under investigation may constitute a crime.[98]

Illustrations

(1)   A foreign corporation by a contract submits to the jurisdiction of the English courts. It may appoint a person as its agent to accept service of the writ on its behalf, and service on such agent is valid.[99]   **2–026**

(2)   A bill of sale may be executed by an attorney on behalf of the grantor, and the grantee of the bill of sale is not necessarily incapable of acting as such attorney.[1]

(3)   An agent may be appointed to execute a deed of arrangement.[2]

(4)   A partner may exercise his right to inspect and take copies from partnership books under section 24(9) of the Partnership Act 1890 by means of an agent to whom no reasonable objection could be taken by his co-partners.[3]

(5)   Where the rules of a trade union provided that its books should be open to the inspection of all the members, the members might inspect the books by means of an accountant, the accountant

---

[95] Save for obvious cases such as representation by a "manifestly improper person": see *R. v. Assessment Committee of St Mary Abbotts, Kensington* [1891] 1 Q.B. 378.

[96] See *Enderby Town Football Club Ltd v. Football Association Ltd*, n. 91 above, at pp. 605–606, suggesting that where serious consequences are in issue, representation may be more appropriate; *R. v. Visiting Justice at H.M. Prison, Pentridge* [1975] V.R. 883.

[97] *e.g.* Police (Discipline) Regulations 1965, reg. 8(3)(6), considered in *Maynard v. Osmond* [1977] Q.B. 240.

[98] *R. v. Board of Visitors of H.M. Prison, The Maze* [1988] A.C. 379, following *Fraser v. Mudge* [1975] 1 W.L.R. 1132 and *R. v. Secretary of State for the Home Department, ex p. Tarrant* [1985] Q.B. 251. See also *R. v. Visiting Justice of H.M. Prison, Pentridge* [1975] V.R. 883; *Kok Seng Chong v. Bukit Turf Club* [1993] 2 Singapore L.R. 388; Craig, *Administrative Law* (3rd ed.), pp. 309–310.

[99] R.S.C., Ord. 10, rr. 2, 3; *Tharsis Sulphur & Copper Co. v. Société Industrielle et Commerciale des Metaux* (1889) 58 L.J.Q.B. 435; *Montgomery, Jones & Co. v. Liebenthal & Co.* [1898] 1 Q.B. 487; *British Controlled Oilfields Ltd v. Stagg* (1921) 127 L.T. 209; *Reversionary Interest Society v. Locking* [1928] W.N. 227.

[1] *Furnivall v. Hudson* [1893] 1 Ch. 335.

[2] *Re Wilson* [1916] 1 K.B. 382.

[3] *Bevan v. Webb* [1901] 2 Ch. 59; *Dodd v. Amalgamated Marine Workers' Union* [1923] 2 Ch. 236, affd. [1924] 1 Ch. 116.

undertaking to use the information obtained only to inform his clients of the results of the inspection.[4] Similarly a "person interested" under the Public Health Act 1875, s. 247(4), was entitled to inspect the books and accounts of a local authority by means of an accountant.[5]

(6) A tenancy agreement provided that if the landlords, the L.C.C., wished to determine the tenancy, it must be by "a written notice signed by the valuer to the council." The name of the valuer to the council appeared as signatory to a notice to quit, but his name had been written on the document by an assistant valuer, and there was no indication that the signature was by proxy. Held, the signature was valid provided the valuer had authorised the signature.[6]

(7) A "sampling officer" under Food and Drugs legislation may purchase or take a sample by means of an agent, and lay an information in his own name in respect of an analysis of the sample so procured.[7]

(8) An acknowledgment or part payment under the Limitation Act may be made by or to an agent duly authorised[8]; a right of action may be concealed by fraud for the purposes of the same Act where the fraud is that of an agent[9]; and land may be adversely possessed through an agent.[10]

(9) A notice to quit may be given by and served on an agent.[11]

(10) A declaration under the Law of Distress (Amendment) Act 1908 may be signed by an agent.[12]

---

[4] *Norey v. Keep* [1909] 1 Ch. 561; *Dodd v. Amalgamated &c. Union*, n. 3 above.

[5] *R. v. Bedwelty U.D.C., ex p. Price* [1934] 1 K.B. 333. See now Local Government Finance Act 1982, s. 17 as amended.

[6] *L.C.C. v. Agricultural Food Products Ltd* [1955] 2 Q.B. 218. See also *Harmond Properties Ltd v. Gajdzis* [1968] 1 W.L.R. 1858.

[7] See *Tyler v. Dairy Supply Co.* (1908) 98 L.T. 867; *Garforth v. Esam* (1892) 56 J.P. 521; *Horder v. Scott* (1880) 5 Q.B.D. 552. The relevant provision is now s.78 of the Food Act 1984. And see *Foster v. Fyfe* [1896] 2 Q.B. 104, a case on the Metalliferous Mines Regulation Act 1872.

[8] Limitation Act 1980, s. 30(2); see *Wright v. Pepin* [1954] 1 W.L.R. 635 (solicitor: authorised); *Re Transplanters (Holding Co.) Ltd* [1958] 1 W.L.R. 822 (auditor: not authorised). See also below, para. 8–201, n. 12.

[9] Limitation Act 1980, s. 32(1); see *Applegate v. Moss* [1971] 1 Q.B. 406 (concealment by builder acting as independent contractor to developer); *King v. Victor Parsons & Co.* [1973] 1 W.L.R. 29; *Lewisham L.B. v. Leslie & Co. Ltd* (1978) 250 EG 1289; *cf. Thorne v. Heard* [1895] A.C. 495.

[10] *Lyell v. Kennedy* (1899) 14 App.Cas. 437. See in general Preston and Newsom, *Limitation of Actions* (4th ed.), Chap. 9.

[11] *Jones v. Phipps* (1868) L.R. 3 Q.B. 567; *Townsends Carriers Ltd v. Pfizer Ltd* (1977) 33 P. & C.R. 361; *Tanham v. Nicholson* (1872) L.R. 5 H.L. 561; *Galinski v. McHugh* [1989] 1 EGLR 109.

[12] *Lawrence Chemical Co Ltd v. Rubinstein* [1982] 1 W.L.R. 284.

2.—Agency Arising by Agreement

Article 7

Express Agreement

Where there is an express agreement, whether contractual or not, **2–027** between principal and agent, this will constitute the relationship of principal and agent and the consent of both parties will be contained in it.

Comment

The simplest way in which agency arises, both between principal and **2–028** agent and as regards third parties, is by an express appointment whether written or oral, by the principal,[13] and acquiescence by the agent, or person similarly empowered to act for him. "An 'actual' authority is a legal relationship between principal and agent created by a consensual agreement to which they alone are parties. Its scope is to be ascertained by applying ordinary principles of construction of contracts, including any proper implications from the express words used, the usages of the trade, or the course of business between the parties."[14]

The agreement may be contractual, in which case the normal rules as to offer and acceptance, consideration, mistake, misrepresentation, duress, illegality, etc., apply, and the relations between principal and agent are regulated by the normal law of contract. But it may be not contractual, *e.g.* because there is no consideration, or because one or both of the parties lacks contractual capacity.[15]

Many illustrations will be found in Chapter 3, which deals with the agent's authority, for, as throughout the law of agency, there is much overlap between the question whether a person is agent of another, and whether he has the authority of that other.

Article 8

Implied Agreement

Agreement between principal and agent may be implied in a case **2–029** where each has conducted himself towards the other in such a way that it is reasonable for that other to infer from that conduct consent to the agency relationship.

---

[13] See Article 9 as to formalities.
[14] *Freeman & Lockyer v. Buckhurst Park Properties (Mangal) Ltd* [1964] 2 Q.B. 480, 502, *per* Diplock L.J.
[15] See Articles 4, 5 as to capacity; Article 44 as to gratuitous agents.

Comment

2–030   No special rules of law peculiar to agency are involved here: this Article simply represents, in the sphere of agency, the obvious proposition that contracts are not always expressly made, but often inferred by the court from the circumstances.[16] The same principle applies to non-contractual liability. "While agency must ultimately derive from consent, the consent need not necessarily be to the relationship of principal and agent itself (indeed the existence of it may be denied) but it may be to a state of fact upon which the law imposes the consequences which result from agency."[17]

The principle stated in this Article must not be confused with the notions of agency by estoppel and apparent authority, whereby a *third party* is in certain cases entitled to assume, from the conduct of the principal, that the agent has authority, even where this is not so.[18] The reasonable interpretation must in the present case be applied to determine whether it is reasonable for the agent to think that he has been appointed or authorised, and likewise as regards the principal in respect of the agent: not, as in the case mentioned above, whether the third party is entitled to assume that the agent has authority. In some cases, of course, the court is not considering whether relations exist between principal and agent, nor even whether relations exist between principal and third party, but merely whether a person is an "agent" for the purpose of some statute: in this inquiry the two considerations mentioned may, but need not, be relevant.

2–031   **Consent of the principal.** This may be implied when he places another in such a situation that, according to ordinary usage, that person would understand himself to have the principal's authority to act on his behalf[19]: or where the principal's words or conduct, coming to the knowledge of the agent, are such as to lead to the reasonable inference that he is authorising the agent to act for him.[20] But where one person purports to act on behalf of another, the assent of that other will not be presumed merely from his silence, unless there is further indication that

---

[16] See *Garnac Grain Co. Inc. v. H.M.F. Faure and Fairclough Ltd* [1968] A.C. 1130n; 1137; *Ashford Shire Council v. Dependable Motors Pty. Ltd* [1961] A.C. 336, 349–350; *Reynell v. Lewis* (1846) 15 M. & W. 517. The distinction between express contract and implied contract is of doubtful utility. "A contract implied in fact is like any other contract in legal effect: it differs from an express contract only in that the promise is expressed, wholly or in part, by conduct rather than by words": Mechem, *Outlines of Agency* (4th ed.), p. 28.

[17] *Branwhite v. Worcester Works Finance Ltd.* [1969] 1 A.C. 552, 587, *per* Lord Wilberforce (dissenting). See further Fridman (1968) 84 L.Q.R. 224.

[18] Articles 21, 74.

[19] See *Pole v. Leask* (1863) 33 L.J.Ch. 155, 161–162.

[20] *Little v. Spreadbury* [1910] 2 K.B. 658; *Ashford Shire Council v. Dependable Motors Pty. Ltd*, n. 16 above, at p. 349; *cf. Restatement*, § 15.

he acquiesces in the agency.[21] The substance of the matter is more important than the form: a contract describing the parties as principal and agent is not conclusive that they are such,[22] and conversely there may be an agency relationship though the agreement creating it purports to exclude the possibility.[23] A statement in a contract negotiated by an agent between one party and another that the agent acts for one of the parties is not conclusive that he only does so, if in some respects he in fact acts for the other.[24] The fact that commission is paid by one party is not necessarily inconsistent with the agent's acting for the other party: the source of commission or payments is relevant but not conclusive in determining an agency relationship.[25]

Consent of the agent. It is traditional to state that the agent's consent   **2–032** is required,[26] and to discuss the ways in which this can be implied from acts or waived by the principal. Consent is certainly relevant to the relationship between principal and agent: only mutual consent will give rise to a contract, rendering the agent liable for non-performance of what he has undertaken; and the duties arising in non-contractual agency would normally only do so if there was consent to the relationship. But as regards the position between principal and third party, the relevant act is the conferring of authority.[27] It is earlier suggested that the basis of agency is a unilateral manifestation of will: a power of attorney, for instance, does not require acceptance by the donee of the power.[28] When all that is in issue is whether the supposed agent's act was authorised, it may not be necessary that the agent's consent should have been manifested at all, provided the authority has clearly been conferred. Thus when the principal confers authority on the agent, and the agent purports to act on the principal's behalf, he is not permitted to deny that it was on the principal's behalf that he acted.[29] On the other hand the agent must have purported to act for the

---

[21] *Dixon v. Broomfield* (1814) 2 Chit. 205; *Burnside v. Dayrell* (1849) 3 Exch. 224.
[22] *Nouvelles Huileries Anversoises S.A. v. H.C. Mann & Co.* (1924) 40 T.L.R. 804; *Motor Union Insurance Co. Ltd v. Mannheimer Versicherungs Gesellschaft* [1933] 1 K.B. 812; *Kennedy v. De Trafford* [1897] A.C. 180, 188. See also above, para. 1–030.
[23] *Re Megevand, ex p. Delhasse* (1878) 7 Ch.D. 511.
[24] *Commissioners of Customs & Excise v. Pools Finance Ltd* [1952] 1 All E.R. 775.
[25] *Royal Securities Corp. v. Montreal Trust Co.* (1967) D.L.R. (2d) 666, affd. (1967) 63 D.L.R. (2d) 15; *cf. Les Affréteurs, etc. v. Leopold Walford (London) Ltd* [1919] A.C. 801.
[26] See *e.g. Garnac Grain Co. Inc. v. H.M.F. Faure and Fairclough Ltd* [1968] A.C. 1130n., 1137; *Freeman & Lockyer v. Buckhurst Park Properties (Mangal) Ltd* [1964] 2 Q.B. 480, 501; *Restatement*, § 15 and Comment.
[27] *cf.* Müller-Freienfels (1964) 13 Am.J.Comp.L. 193, 203.
[28] Above, para. 1–005. This is not, however, true of an Enduring Power of Attorney under the Enduring Powers of Attorney Act 1985, which requires execution by donor and attorney (s. 2(1)).
[29] See *Roberts v. Ogilby* (1821) 9 Price 269; *Moore v. Peachey* (1891) 7 T.L.R. 748 (receipt of money by agent).

principal: he will not be regarded as doing so merely because he does what was authorised or requested without other indications. [30]

It is usually possibly to say that an agent who acts as authorised without having indicated consent to the principal is thereby consenting, and that the principal has waived notice of consent. Thus the question of consent will rarely have practical significance. But where a principal grants authority (*e.g.* by renewing an old authority) and the agent acts on his behalf without knowing of the grant, perhaps because he takes a risk, it will be difficult to find consent by the agent: yet it is arguable that his act should bind or entitle the principal. [31] The doctrines of ratification [32] and apparent authority [33] would of course frequently solve such a situation in practice.

Illustrations

2–033   (1)   A called at B's office and orally agreed to be responsible for the price of certain goods to be supplied by B to a third person. B's clerk, in A's presence, made and signed a memorandum of the agreement. Held, that the clerk had no implied authority to sign as A's agent, and that there was not a sufficient memorandum in writing of the agreement to satisfy section 4 of the Statute of Frauds. [34]

(2)   Property is sold under a decree. The solicitor having the management of the sale is, in the conduct of it, deemed to be the agent of all the parties to the suit, as between them and the purchaser. [35]

(3)   Where a letter of credit is opened, the instructing bank and the confirming bank are in the positions, at any rate in some respects, of principal and agent respectively. [36]

(4)   Auditors are not agents of the company whose accounts they audit for the purposes of making an acknowledgment under the Limitation Act. [37]

(5)   A dealer selling goods on credit may by statute act in the capacity of agent of the finance company which finances the arrangement, as regards antecedent negotiations [38] and for the purpose

---

[30] See *Kennedy v. De Trafford* [1897] A.C. 180; Powell, p. 297.

[31] See *Ruggles v. American Central Insurance Co. of St. Louis*, 114 N.Y. 415, 76 N.Y. Supp. 787 (1889) (letter giving agent authority had been posted but not arrived). But *cf. Freeman & Lockyer v. Buckhurst Park Properties (Mangal) Ltd* [1964] 2 Q.B. 480, 501.

[32] Articles 13–20.

[33] Article 74.

[34] *Dixon v. Broomfield* (1814) 2 Chit. 205.

[35] *Dalby v. Pullen* (1830) 1 Russ. & M. 296.

[36] *Bank Melli Iran v. Barclays Bank* [1951] 2 T.L.R. 1057. See further *Benjamin's Sale of Goods* (4th ed.), 23–132 *et seq.*

[37] *Re Transplanters (Holding Co.) Ltd* [1958] 1 W.L.R. 822.

[38] Consumer Credit Act 1974, s. 56.

of receiving notice of withdrawal, cancellation and rescission.[39] He may sometimes be its agent in other respects at common law, *e.g.* to deliver the goods,[40] and to receive notice of revocation of an offer in circumstances where the statutory regulation does not apply.[41] To some extent the question may turn on whether the payments are to be collected directly by the company, or whether the dealer is to collect them. But while he may be agent for certain purposes, there is no general agency relationship and he acts primarily on his own behalf.[42]

(6) Agents of insurance companies frequently act as agents for persons making insurance proposals to such companies by filling in the forms for them.[43]

(7) A car is damaged in an accident. The insurers instruct a garage to effect repairs. It is a question of fact whether they do so on their own account or as agent of the assured. Similar rules apply where the assured orders the repairs. The normal interpretation of such a situation seems to be that the repairers contract with the insurers.[44]

(8) Shop stewards may act as agents for a trade union in negotiation, and in taking industrial action, even contrary to the advice of union officials, provided that they act within union rules or policy.[45] This authority derives from all the members: thus the union also may sometimes act as agent for the members in doing the same.[46] But an official of a trade union who expels a member does not act as that member's agent so as to prevent the member suing for wrongful expulsion.[47]

Article 9

FORMALITIES FOR APPOINTMENT

Subject to the provisions of Article 10, and except where otherwise   **2–034**
expressly provided by or pursuant to any statute, or by the terms of

---

[39] Consumer Credit Act 1974, ss. 57, 69, 102.

[40] *Branwhite v. Worcester Works Finance Ltd*, n. 42 below, at p. 573.

[41] *Financings Ltd. v. Stimson* [1962] 1 W.L.R. 1184.

[42] *Branwhite v. Worcester Works Finance Ltd* [1969] 1 A.C. 552; but the dissenting opinion (on this point) of Lord Wilberforce repays study.

[43] See Article 97, Illustration 11.

[44] See *Bowers (Maghull) Ltd. v. Morton* (1940) 67 Ll.Rep. 1; *Godfrey Davis Ltd. v. Culling & Hecht* [1962] 2 Lloyd's Rep. 349; *Cooter & Green Ltd. v. Tyrrell* [1962] 2 Lloyd's Rep. 377.

[45] *Heaton's Transport (St Helens) Ltd v. Transport and General Workers' Union* [1973] A.C. 15; *Howitt Transport Ltd v. T.G.W.U.* [1973] I.C.R. 1; *cf. General Aviation Service (U.K.) Ltd. v. T.G.W.U.* [1976] I.R.L.R. 224.

[46] See *Chappell v. Times Newspapers Ltd* [1975] 1 W.L.R. 482, 500.

[47] *Bonsor v. Musicians' Union* [1956] A.C. 104. These cases, which were famous when decided, are retained as illustrations of ways in which agency reasoning can be deployed in the area of labour law, and because the general dicta in some of them might on occasion

—cont. on next page

the power or authority (if any) under which the agent is appointed, an agent may be appointed by deed, by writing, or by word of mouth.

Comment

2–035   In general no formalities are required for the creation of agency. This is normally so even where the agent is authorised to enter into a contract that is required to be in writing or evidenced in writing, or to sign a memorandum of such a contract.[48] The approach of English law contrasts with that of some other countries, which may require the same form for authorisation as that necessary for the act authorised, or special forms for powers of a general nature.[49] Thus authority to subscribe the name of the principal to the memorandum of association of a company, or to the instrument of dissolution of a building society, may be given orally.[50] But some appointments are required by statute to be in writing,[51] and some must be by deed.[52] The most conspicuous example of the latter requirement is a power of attorney.[53]

2–036   **Agent for the purchase of land.** A contract for the purchase of land made by an agent as such (whether his principal is disclosed or undisclosed) vests the equitable estate in the principal, and the contract may be enforced by the principal against both the vendor and the agent, even if the agent was appointed orally, provided that the legal estate has not been conveyed to the agent.[54] When the land has actually been conveyed to the agent so as to vest the legal estate in him, he is trustee for the principal and is not entitled to take advantage of the Law of

---

—cont. from previous page

be of use. They should not, however, be regarded as significant authorities on general agency principle; and as to the law now governing the contexts in which they were decided, reference should be made to up-to-date works on labour law.

[48] *Coles v. Trecothick* (1804) 9 Ves. 234, 250; *Deverell v. Lord Bolton* (1812) 18 Ves. 505, 509; *Heard v. Pilley* (1869) L.R. 4 Ch.App. 548. Assuming that the writing can be executed through an agent: see Article 6.

[49] See Müller-Freienfels in *Civil Law in the Modern World* (Yiannopoulos ed. 1965), 77, 108–111 (citing comparative material). See also below para. 11–022 as to commercial agents.

[50] *Re Whitley Partners Ltd* (1886) 32 Ch.D. 337; *Dennison v. Jeffs* [1896] 1 Ch. 611; above, para. 2–023.

[51] *e.g.* Law of Property Act 1925, ss. 53, 54, which require an agent signing certain types of instrument relating to land to be "lawfully authorised in writing," with certain alternatives. See *Richardson v. Landecker* (1950) 50 S.R. (N.S.W.) 250, where it was held in connection with a section similar to s. 53 that a company manager had signed as the company, not as its agent, and did not therefore require written authorisation.

[52] *e.g.* Trustee Act 1925, s. 25, as amended by Powers of Attorney Act 1971, s. 9.

[53] See below.

[54] *Heard v. Pilley* (1869) L.R. 4 Ch.App. 548; *Cave v. Mackenzie* (1877) 46 L.J.Ch. 564.

Property Act 1925, s. 53, which provides that a declaration of trust respecting land or any interest therein must be evidenced by writing, because to allow this would be to permit the statute to be used as an instrument of fraud.[55]

Appointment by corporations. Until 1960 the basic rule was that a **2–037** corporation must contract under seal[56]: thus a corporation could only contract with agent under seal. But the rule had many exceptions and was abolished completely by the Corporation Bodies Contracts Act 1960, whereby a corporation can make contracts by means of any person acting under its authority, express or implied, in the same manner as a private person.[57] Thus a corporation can appoint an agent by parol where a private person could do so, by means of any person acting under its authority, express or implied.[58] Corporations governed by the Companies Act 1985 are in any case provided for under that Act[59]: the two sets of provisions are substantially similar but not identical.

Powers of attorney. A power of attorney is "a formal instrument by **2–038** which one person empowers another to represent him, or act in his stead for certain purposes."[60] It may confer general or particular powers. Before 1971 it was not necessary that such an instrument be a deed, though an unsealed document might not be called a power of attorney[61] and if the authority to execute deeds was to be conferred it would require to be conferred by deed under the rule stated in the next Article. Now, however, the Powers of Attorney Act 1971, s. 1(1), as amended by the Law of Property (Miscellaneous Provisions) Act 1989, requires that instruments creating powers of attorney be executed as deeds: the requirements are given in the next Article. The Act does not define the term "power of attorney": presumably what is referred to is a formal grant of power, especially of general power to represent a person

---

[55] *Rochefoucauld v. Boustead* [1897] 1 Ch. 196; disapproving the earlier view shown in *Bartlett v. Pickersgill* (1785) 4 East 577n. and *James v. Smith* [1891] 1 Ch. 384; *Heard v. Pilley*, n. 54 above, at p. 553; *Du Boulay v. Raggett* (1988) 58 P. & C.R. 138. In any case, the trust may be implied, resulting or constructive, and not covered by s. 53: see *Hodgson v. Marks* [1971] Ch. 892, 933. On the other hand, it is arguable that it is claims of this type that the statute was intended to prevent. See also Article 55.

[56] *Kidderminster Corp. v. Hardwicke* (1873) L.R. 9 Ex. 13; *Cape v. Thames Haven Dock, etc., Co.* (1849) 3 Exch. 841; *A.R. Wright & Son Ltd v. Romford B.C.* [1957] 1 Q.B. 431.

[57] See s. 1(1).

[58] This person is presumably not to be regarded as an agent, but as acting as the company itself. Otherwise complex circular reasoning could arise, especially as regards s. 1(5).

[59] See s. 36 (substituted by s. 113 of the Companies Act 1989).

[60] Jowitt, *Dictionary of English Law* (1959). See also below, para. 3–011.

[61] See Alcock, *Powers of Attorney* (1935), pp. 1–2.

in all matters. It is difficult to believe that it is intended to affect any conferring of authority which could previously have been effected without a deed. Nor does the Act state what is to happen if a power of attorney is executed other than by deed. But where an appointment purports to be by deed, and the document is for some reason ineffective as a deed, the appointment may sometimes be valid as an appointment in writing.[62]

Article 10

AUTHORITY TO EXECUTE A DEED

2–039   Where an agent is authorised to execute a deed on behalf of his principal, his authority must be given in a deed,[63] except where the deed is signed at the direction and in the presence of the principal and of two witnesses who each attest the signature.[64]

Comment

2–040   Certain acts must by law be performed by deed, notably conveyances and many leases. In these cases authority to an agent to execute such a deed must itself be given by deed, usually called a power of attorney. This formerly applied not only to authority to execute a deed, but also to authority to fill up a deed partly executed,[65] or to deliver a deed already sealed,[66] for it was "well-known law that an agent cannot execute a deed, or do any part of the execution which makes it a deed, unless he is appointed under seal."[67] It is not, however, now necessary that deeds be *sealed* at all; and authority (given, *e.g.* to a solicitor) to *deliver* a deed need no longer be given by deed.[68] It has long been established also that a deed may be executed for another in his presence by an amanuensis[69]; and this practice now has statutory authority, requiring the attestation of two witnesses instead of the one normally required.[70]

---

[62] See cases cited at 75, below.
[63] *Steiglitz v. Eglinton* (1815) Holt N.P. 141; *Berkeley v. Hardy* (1826) 5 B. & C. 355; Powers of Attorney Act, 1971, ss. 1, 7.
[64] Law of Property (Miscellaneous Provisions) Act 1989, s. 1(3).
[65] *Hibblewhite v. M'Morine* (1840) 6 M. & W. 200.
[66] *Windsor Refrigerator Co. v. Branch Nominees Ltd* [1961] Ch. 88.
[67] *Powell v. London and Provincial Bank* [1893] 2 Ch. 555, 563, *per* Bowen L.J. See also *Phoenix Properties Ltd v. Wimpole Street Nominees Ltd* [1992] B.C.L.C. 737.
[68] Law of Property (Miscellaneous Provisions) Act 1989, s.1(1).
[69] *R. v. Longnor (Inhabitants)* (1833) 4 B. & Ad. 647; *Ball v. Dunsterville* (1791) 4 T.R. 313.
[70] Law of Property (Miscellaneous Provisions) Act 1989, s. 1(3).

Powers of attorney. By virtue of the Powers of Attorney Act 1971 as   **2–041**
amended,[71] s. 1, an instrument creating a power of attorney[72] must be
executed as a deed by, or by direction and in the presence of, the donor
of the power; in the first case one and in the latter two witnesses are
required to attest the instrument. Under section 9[73] where a trustee,
personal representative, tenant for life or statutory owner delegates his
powers by power of attorney the power of attorney itself still requires at
least one witness.[74]

Where an agent not appointed by deed purports to execute a deed,
the document may be taken to have a lesser effect if the intended result
could in fact be achieved without a deed: thus an invalid appointment
by deed may take effect as an appointment in writing.[75] It was held that
a party might be estopped from denying that a document was sealed;[76]
but now that sealing is no longer required a similar estoppel would be
more difficult to establish, except perhaps as to delivery.

Article 11

CO-AGENTS

(1)   Where an authority is given to two or more persons, it is   **2–042**
      presumed to be given to them jointly,[77] unless a contrary
      intention appears from the nature or terms of the authority, or
      from the circumstances of the particular case.[78]

(2)   Where an authority is given to two or more persons severally,
      or jointly and severally, any one or more of them may execute
      it without the concurence of the others.[79]

---

[71] By Law of Property (Miscellaneous Provisions) Act 1989, Sched. 1.
[72] As to the meaning of this term, see Comment to Article 9.
[73] Amending Trustee Act 1925, s. 25.
[74] The Act also makes provision for proof of powers of attorney (s. 3), and provides a
form of general power of attorney (s. 10 and Sched. 1). Depositing or filing of instruments
creating powers of attorney is not necessary: s. 2. The donee may normally execute any
instrument, sign or do any act in his own name; s. 7. See in general Law Com. No. 30,
Cmnd. 4473 (1970); (1971) New L.J. 746, 751, 764, 771, 795; (1971) 115 S.J. 596; (1971)
35 Conv.(N.S.) 310; (1971) 68 L.S.Gaz. 434, 437; Land Registration (Powers of Attorney)
Rules 1986 (S.I. 1986 No. 1537); Aldridge, *Powers of Attorney* (8th ed.).
[75] *Windsor Refrigerator Co. Ltd v. Branch Nominees Ltd* [1961] Ch. 375; *Hunter v.
Parker* (1840) 7 M. & W. 322, 343–344 (sale of ship); *Marchant v. Morton, Down & Co.*
[1901] 2 K.B. 829 (assignment); *Butler v. Duckett* (1891) 17 V.L.R. 439.
[76] *T.C.B. Ltd. v. Gray* [1986] Ch. 821 (and see [1987] Ch. 458n).
[77] Illustrations 1 to 3.
[78] See *Moore v. Ullcoats Mining Co. Ltd* (1907) 97 L.T. 845 (power to inspect a mine).
For the statutory form of power of attorney conferring joint and several authority see
Powers of Attorney Act 1971, s. 10(1), Sched. 1. As to joint and joint and several
authority under the Enduring Powers of Attorney Act 1985, see s. 11 and Sched. 3.
[79] Illustration 4.

(3)   All the co-agents must concur in the execution of a joint authority in order to bind the principal, unless there is a provision that a certain number shall form a quorum[80]: but where the authority is of a public nature, and the matter to be determined is of public concern, and the persons in whom it is invested meet for the purpose of executing it, the act of the majority is for this purpose deemed to be the act of the whole body, unless a contrary intention is to be collected from the nature of the power and the duty to be performed under it.[81]

Illustrations

2–043   (1)   A provisional committee appointed eight specified persons to act as a managing committee on their behalf. Six of such persons gave an order within the scope of the authority conferred. Held, that the provisional committee were not bound by the order.[82]

(2)   Two persons filled the office of clerk to the trustees of a road. Held, that they must contract jointly in order to bind the trustees.[83]

(3)   The directors of a company, being duly authorised in that behalf, resolved that all their powers, except their power to make calls, should be delegated to three of their number as a committee. Held, that at a meeting of the committee for the purpose of exercising such powers, all the members of the committee must be present.[84]

(4)   A power of attorney was given to 15 persons, "jointly or severally to execute such policies as they or any of them should jointly or severally think proper." Held, that a policy executed by four of such persons was binding on the principal.[85]

Article 12

CO-PRINCIPALS

2–044   Where two or more persons give authority to an agent, it is presumed that the authority is to act for their joint account only,

---

[80] *Brown v. Andrew* (1849) 18 L.J.Q.B. 153, Illustration 1. This is commonly provided in the case of companies.

[81] *Grindley v. Barker* (1798) 1 B. & P. 229; *Cortis v. Kent Waterworks Co.* (1827) 7 B. & C. 314; Judicial Committee of the Privy Council's Report on the Irish Boundary Commission (1924) 59 L.J. 517; *Atkinson v. Brown* [1963] N.Z.L.R. 755; *Picea Holdings Ltd v. London Rent Assessment Panel* [1971] 2 Q.B. 216.

[82] *Brown v. Andrew* (1849) 18 L.J.Q.B. 153.

[83] *Bell and Head v. Nixon and Davison* (1832) 9 Bing. 393.

[84] *Re Liverpool Household Stores* (1890) 59 L.J.Ch. 616. But the articles will usually deal with this problem.

[85] *Guthrie v. Armstrong* (1822) 5 B. & A. 628.

unless a contrary intention appears from the nature of the terms of the authority, or from the circumstances of the particular case.[86]

Comment

The prima facie rule is that the obligation arising from a contract   **2–045** made by two or more persons on one side is joint.[87] Thus where two or more persons give authority to an agent, the presumption is that they are authorising him to act only in such matters as concern them jointly, *e.g.* their joint property, and not in matters concerning one or the other alone.[88] But there may be indications to the contrary: and of course the contractual liability (if there is a contract) of the co-principals may be held to be joint and several rather than joint, in appropriate cases.[89] An agent acting for joint principals is not bound to account to one alone.[90] Payment to or release by one of joint creditors may however discharge a debt under the rules for joint obligations, even where the person concerned is not authorised to receive payment or release the debt[91]: but these rules have exceptions.[92]

3.—Ratification

Article 13

General Principle

Where an act is done purportedly in the name or on behalf of   **2–046** another by a person who has no authority so to do that act, the person in whose name or on whose behalf the act is done may, by ratifying the act, make it as valid and effectual, subject to the provisions of Articles 14 to 20, as if it had been originally done by his authority, whether the person doing the act was an agent exceeding his authority, or was a person having no authority to act for him at all.[93]

---

[86] *cf. Restatement*, § 41; Partnership Act 1890, s. 9; Glanville Williams, *Joint Obligations* (1949), pp. 35–37; see also Treitel, *Law of Contract* (9th ed.), Chap. 14.

[87] See above, n. 86.

[88] *e.g. Keay v. Fenwick* (1876) 1 C.P.D. 745.

[89] Glanville Williams, *op. cit.* n. 86 above, at pp. 38–39.

[90] *Hatsall v. Griffith* (1834) 2 Cr. & M. 679. See also below, para. 6–098.

[91] *Wallace v. Kelsall* (1840) 7 M. & W. 264, 274; *Husband v. Davis* (1851) 10 C.B. 645; *Powell v. Brodhurst* [1901] 2 Ch. 160, 164.

[92] *e.g.* joint banking accounts: *Husband v. Davis*, n. 91 above, at p. 650. See also *Lee v. Sankey* (1873) L.R. 15 Eq. 204 (trustees).

[93] *Wilson v. Tunman and Fretson* (1843) 6 M. & G. 236, 242; *Bird v. Brown* (1850) 4 Exch. 786, 798; *Firth v. Staines* [1897] 2 Q.B. 70; *Restatement*, §§ 82, 83. As to the distinction between agency doctrine and use of the term "ratification" in connection with the release of directors from liability in company law, see Partridge [1987] C.L.J. 122.

Comment

2-047   This Article sets out by way of introduction the general principle of ratification, which is that it is "equivalent to an antecedent authority".[94] The whole notion is much criticised and is often treated as exceptional,[95] mainly in the context of contract because of the lack of reciprocity: the third party is in the power of the principal while the latter decides whether or not to ratify. It is submitted, however, that this is in typical contract situations not correct. The primary application of the doctrine is indeed in the law of contract, where it fills a practical need in validating the acts of agents who act outside their authority in circumstances where it appears advisable to do so. As the comment to the *Restatement* says, "It operates normally to cure minor defects in an agent's authority, minimising technical defences and preventing unnecessary lawsuits."[96] In such a case, as between principal and third party, where the principal seeks to intervene and enforce the contract, the third party is getting exactly what he bargained for. Where the third party seeks to enforce the contract against a ratifying principal he cannot possibly be prejudiced, and the principal is simply held to the transaction which he chose to adopt. Since a master can be liable even for forbidden acts done by an employee in the scope of his employment, it is not surprising that a principal can sometimes be liable for what he has actually ratified.[97] It would seem that ratification should be regarded as providing a normal case of agency, but one where the intention of the parties is given effect to retrospectively.

The position between principal and agent requires slightly more careful formulation. In many cases it is possible to say that the agent, by purporting to act on the principal's behalf, makes an offer to the principal to act as his agent (though not necessarily as his contractual agent), or (where he is already an agent) as his agent in respect of the act concerned, which the principal accepts by ratifying. But the acting outside authority may be a breach of contract; and it seems that there may be cases where the principal ratifies but nevertheless reserves his right to treat the agent as liable to him for the cost of so doing.[98]

---

[94] *Koenigsblatt v. Sweet* [1923] 2 Ch. 314, 325, *per* Lord Sterndale M.R.

[95] Powell, pp. 121–122, 138–139; Seavey (1920) 29 Yale L.J. 859, esp. at p. 891; (1954) 21 U.Chi.L.Rev. 248; *Restatement*, § 82, comment *c*.

[96] § 82, comment *d*. Lord Macnaghten called the doctrine "a wholesome and convenient fiction.": *Keighley, Maxsted & Co. v. Durant* [1901] A.C. 240, 247. An obvious case is where acts are done on the principal's behalf which the agent thinks commercially necessary, but which are not justified under the strict requirements of the doctrine of agency of necessity. Such acts may be regarded as authorised (see below, para. 4–008); but if they are ratified the matter may be put beyond argument.

[97] Fridman, pp. 96–97, Stoljar, pp. 177–178; Twerski (1968) 42 Temple L.Q. 1.

[98] Below, para. 2–092.

Overall it is also true that the retrospective nature of the doctrine of ratification requires special rules to prevent its application having oppressive results, and this makes it a topic requiring special treatment. It does not follow that it is anomalous; and it is certainly convenient.

As stated above, the doctrine is primarily applicable to contract, and the tendency is largely to think of it in this connection. However, the term, and the general notion, are used in other parts of the law also. Different considerations arise in different cases, and it is misleading to think that there is any set of rules for ratification applicable to all parts of the law. [99] Many of the cases where the general notion of ratification is invoked are properly to be classified as involving questions of restitution, conversion, formation of contract, novation, waiver or estoppel. Indeed, it may be that such cases form the majority, and that situations of deliberate ratification of unauthorised acts are rare. [1] Cases where the general notion of ratification is employed should therefore be examined carefully in order to ascertain exactly what is in issue. [2]

Ratification of itself only creates agency in respect of the transaction ratified, though a ratification may sometimes be used as evidence of already existing authority, [3] and a series of ratifications may on the facts be held to confer authority for the future, or to generate apparent authority. [4] For this reason it is to be distinguished from the other examples of creation of agency contained in this chapter. Like apparent authority it can apply where the person whose act is ratified is already an agent, and where he is not an agent at all, though cases of the second type are rarer. [5]

Ratification in advance of act ratified. Powers of attorney and other   2–048
documents frequently contain clauses whereby the principal purports to ratify in advance acts which the attorney may do. Such a clause cannot constitute ratification. It operates, if anything, as a grant of authority; as creating apparent authority; possibly as a contractual offer, whether to agent or third party, which may be accepted by some form of action in

---

[99] *Bird v. Brown* (1850) 4 Exch. 786, 799; *cf.* Stoljar, p. 178.
[1] Mechem, *Outlines of Agency* (4th ed.), §§ 197–198.
[2] See, *e.g. Imperial Bank of Canada Ltd v. Begley* [1936] 2 All E.R. 367, 374–375 (misappropriation of proceeds of cheque); *Banque Jacques Cartier v. Banque d'Epargne de Montreal* (1887) 13 App.Cas. 111 (liquidator acquiescences in false accounts); *De Bussche v. Alt* (1878) 8 Ch.D. 286, 312–315 (sub-delegation by agent); *Royal Albert Hall Corp. v. Winchilsea* (1891) 7 T.L.R. 362 (use of hall justified *quantum meruit*). See also Procaccia (1978) 4 Tel Aviv U. Studies in Law 9; Partridge, *op. cit.* above, n. 93.
[3] See *Hutchings v. Nunes* (1863) 1 Moo.P.C.(N.S.) 243.
[4] *cf. Restatement*, § 43(2). As to apparent authority, see Article 74.
[5] But see *Bird v. Brown*, n. 99 above; also the dissenting judgment of Atkin J. in *R. v. Chapman, ex p. Arlidge* [1918] 2 K.B. 298.

reliance; if consideration can be found, as part of a contract; or as evidence supporting an alleged subsequent ratification.[6]

2–049   **Juristic nature of ratification.**[7] Ratification seems to be a notion *sui generis*. It involves the idea that in certain circumstances a person can by expression of will adopt a transaction on which he is not liable or entitled so as to become liable or entitled in respect of it. It requires no consideration; and a novation would be juristically different.[8] In so far as it depends on the choice of the person concerned, it can be said to be an application of the doctrine of election. But in the case of election to treat a contract as discharged, there is a choice of remedies in respect of a legal relationship already existing: the innocent party to a breach of contract can choose to treat it as discharged, but if he does not do so the contract continues.[9] The other form of election normally cited is that between inconsistent existing rights.[10] In both cases it is usually said that the election must be communicated to the other party involved, and that it is irrevocable once made.[11] It would appear, however, that ratification need not be communicated to anyone if it can be established by probative material[12]; that a party who initially refused to ratify may in some circumstances later do so;[13] and that the doctrine overlaps with restitutionary doctrine and estoppels, especially in the case of ratification by acquiescence or inactivity.[14]

Illustrations

2–050   (1) A entered into and signed a written contract on behalf of B, without authority. A memorandum of the contract was required by statute to be in writing. B subsequently ratified the contract. Not only was the contract itself effective, but A was also deemed to have been B's duly authorised agent to sign the memorandum.[15]

---

[6] See *Midland Bank Ltd v. Reckitt* [1933] A.C. 1, Illustration 8 to Article 24.
[7] See the valuable discussion by Seavey in *Restatement*, Appendix, reporter's notes to § 94 (also printed in (1954) 103 U.Pa. L.Rev. 30).
[8] *Re Portuguese Consolidated Copper Mines Ltd* (1890) 45 Ch.D. 16, 34.
[9] *Photo Production Ltd v. Securicor Transport Ltd* [1980] A.C. 827, 849.
[10] *Scarf v. Jardine* (1882) 7 App.Cas. 345; *United Australia Ltd v. Barclays Bank Ltd* [1941] A.C. 1.
[11] *The Kanchenjunga* [1990] 1 Lloyd's Rep. 391, 397–399; see also *Kammins Ballroom Co. Ltd v. Zenith Investment (Torquay) Ltd* [1971] A.C. 850, 883.
[12] Below, para. 2–072.
[13] Article 18.
[14] *ibid.*
[15] *Maclean v. Dunn* (1828) 4 Bing. 722; *Soames v. Spencer* (1822) 1 D. & R. 32; *Koenigsblatt v. Sweet* [1923] 2 Ch. 314; *Sheridan v. Higgins* [1971] I.R. 291. There seems no reason why the some reasoning should not apply where the contract is required to be in writing, as now under the Law of Property (Miscellaneous Provisions) Act 1989, s. 2.

(2) An agent, without authority, insures goods on behalf of his principal. The principal ratifies the policy. The policy is as valid as if the agent had been expressly authorised to insure the goods.[16]

(3) An agent of the Crown does an act, which would normally be a tort, outside the realm in excess of his authority. The Crown ratifies the act. The act is deemed to be an act of state and the agent is not liable for it.[17]

Article 14

WHAT ACTS MAY BE RATIFIED

Every act, whether lawful or unlawful,[18] which is capable of being done by means of an agent (except an act which is in its inception void[19]) is capable of ratification by the person in whose name or on whose behalf it was purportedly done.[20]   **2–051**

Comment

Lawful or unlawful: contracts. As indicated in the Comment to Article 13, the doctrine, and therefore this Article, applies primarily to contracts. The making of a contract on behalf of another without authority could perhaps be described as unlawful, but such a contract can certainly be ratified. Even a contract induced by a fraudulent, and therefore tortious, profession of agency can be ratified: the fraud is perhaps extinguished in the ratification,[21] but even if this is not so it would be difficult to prove damages. The right to rescind for misrepresentation, whether fraudulent or innocent, is clearly extinguished.[22]   **2–052**

---

[16] *Wolff v. Horncastle* (1798) 1 B. & P. 316; *Williams v. North China Insurance Co.* (1876) 1 C.P.D. 757; *Bedford Insurance Co. Ltd. v. Instituto de Resseguros do Brasil* [1985] Q.B. 966, Illustration 6 to Article 14. See further Article 18.

[17] *Burton v. Denman* (1848) 2 Exch. 167; *Secretary of State for India v. Kamachee Boye Sahaba* (1859) 7 Moo.Ind.App. 476. See further Article 115. In such cases, it may well be said that the doctrine is oppressive to third parties despite the principle of Article 19. As to ratification in public law, which raises special questions, see Lanham (1981) 5 Otago L.Rev. 35.

[18] See para. 2–052, below; Illustrations 1 to 3; *Wilson v. Tunman and Fretson* (1843) 6 M. & G. 236, 242; *Bird v. Brown* (1850) 4 Exch. 786, 799.

[19] See para. 2–054, below.

[20] See Article 15.

[21] *Restatement*, § 360; Powell, p. 140. The same argument would apply to a negligent statement actionable under the principle of *Hedley Byrne & Co. Ltd v. Heller & Partners Ltd* [1964] A.C. 465.

[22] See, *e.g. Bolton Partners v. Lambert* (1889) 41 Ch.D. 295, Illustration 1 to Article 18.

2–052A   **Torts.** The words "lawful or unlawful" are included primarily to indicate that the doctrine can apply to torts. From them it would follow that a principal by ratification may retrospectively turn what was previously an act wrongful against the principal, *e.g.* an unauthorised sale, or against a third party, *e.g.* a wrongful distress, into a legitimate one; or become liable for the tort of another by ratifying. The first proposition is clearly valid: ratification can make an unlawful act lawful *ex post facto.*[23] But as regards liability, the importance of ratification in the law of torts generally is nowadays, except as regards conversion and trespass to goods, open to question.[24] For the cases giving the widest operation to the doctrine of ratification in tort represent an attempt to extend the notion of command to commit a tort, and originate before the establishment of a general doctrine of vicarious liability.[25] Since the acceptance of a general doctrine, these cases will not usually be relevant, save possibly where the act ratified is not within the course of the servant's employment, or where the tortfeasor is not a servant: and even here the doctrine of casual delegation may cover the situation.[26] It may obviously, furthermore, be extremely difficult to determine what constitutes ratification in non-proprietary torts.[27] It may therefore be suggested that the doctrine of ratification, in so far as it makes one person liable for the torts of another (as opposed to providing a defence to an action in tort), normally applies only to conversion, and possibly also to trespass to goods, where the fields of contract, tort and property overlap[28] and liability is strict; and that in torts requiring personal fault it should not be regarded as significant.

Even in the restricted field suggested it will rarely be crucial to the result, since many of the cases can be explained alternatively on the basis of contract, in that they deal with principals who by accepting goods ratify unauthorised contracts[29]; and further, an act said to be a ratification of a conversion may itself be regarded as a conversion.[30]

---

[22] Illustration 3; *Hull v. Pickersgill* (1819) 1 B. & B. 282.

[24] See the valuable discussion in Stoljar, pp. 179–182; Tedeschi (1969) 4 Israel L.Rev. 1.

[25] See 4 Co. Inst 317, referred to in *Eastern Counties Ry. Co. v. Broom* (1851) 6 Exch. 314, Illustration 2.

[26] See below, para. 8–182. If the tortfeasor is not a servant, it may in any case be held that his act cannot be ratified: see *Wilson v. Tunman and Fretson* (1843) 6 M. & G. 236, Illustration 1 to Article 15.

[27] See *Moon v. Towers* (1860) 8 C.B.(N.S.) 611, 614 (a case of trespass and false imprisonment): Stoljar, pp. 179–180. A case often cited in the books is *Novick v. Gouldsberry*, 173 F. 2d 496 (1949) ("If I had been there I would have broke your God damn neck" held ratification of assault). See also *Manduoit v. Ross* (1884) 10 V.L.R. 264.

[28] See, *e.g.* Illustration 1.

[29] *i.e.* the tort ceases to exist. See *United Australia Ltd v. Barclays Bank Ltd* [1941] A.C. 1, 28; *Verschures Creameries Ltd v. Hull & Netherlands S.S. Co. Ltd* [1921] 2 K.B. 608, Illustration 6 to Article 20.

[30] See the explanation of *Hilberry v. Hatton* (1864) 2 H. & C. 822, Illustration 1, given in Powell, p. 122; Stoljar, p. 179.

The cases that depend most obviously on the doctrine of ratification are those envisaging ratification of unlawful distress levied by a bailiff[31]; but most are cases of trespass or conversion, and in many of them liability was denied on the grounds that there was no acting for the supposed principal, or that the supposedly ratifying principal did not know the facts. In some cases the possibility of ratifying other torts has been considered,[32] but the decision has usually been that there was no ratification.

However, other situations can be envisaged where the doctrine of ratification could arise incidentally in a tort case. Thus a coach proprietor might ratify an unauthorised hiring of one of his coaches in order to demand payment for the hire, thereby rendering himself liable for negligence causing damage during the journey: and the owner of a car might ratify unauthorised use of it in order to take advantage of the insurance policy.[33]

Notices. The notion of ratification arises also in other contexts, such   **2–053** as that of the validity of a notice issued by a person who was at the time of issue unauthorised, but whose act was subsequently ratified.[34] Where the notice affects property rights, as in the case of a notice to quit, ratification may not be permitted.[35] Other cases arise in a public law context and may turn on the interpretation of statutes or otherwise raise special considerations.[36]

---

[31] See Powell, p. 122; Article 16, Illustrations 1, 2 and 3; *Haseler v. Lemoyne* (1858) 5 C.B.(N.S.) 530; *Green v. Wroe* [1877] W.N. 130; *Carter v. St Mary Abbotts, Kensington, Vestry* (1900) 64 J.P. 548, Illustration 5 to Article 17; *Becker v. Riebold* (1913) 30 T.L.R. 142; Illustration 3; Clerk and Lindsell, *Torts* (16th ed.), §§ 3–52—3–54; Atiyah, *Vicarious Liability in the Law of Torts* (1967), Chaps. 14, 28.

[32] *e.g.* Illustration 2; *Roe v. Birkenhead, etc. Ry.* (1851) 7 Exch. 36; *Moon v. Towers* (1860) 8 C.B.(N.S.) 611 (trespass and false imprisonment); *Marsh v. Joseph* [1897] 1 Ch. 213; *Briess v. Woolley* [1954] A.C. 333 (fraud); *Edwards v. L. & N.W. Ry.* (1869) L.R. 5 C.P. 445; *Walker v. South Eastern Ry.* (1870) L.R. 5 C.P. 640, 643; *Rowe v. London Pianoforte Co. Ltd* (1876) 34 L.T. 450 (false imprisonment). As to trespass to goods, see *Eastern Construction Co. v. National Trust Co.* [1914] A.C. 197; *Manduoit v. Ross* (1884) 10 V.L.R. 264.

[33] *cf. Dempsey v. Chambers*, 154 Mass. 330, 28 N.E. 279 (1891), cited by Stoljar, pp. 181–182.

[34] See Illustration 4.

[35] See below, para. 2–086; Article 19, Illustration 2.

[36] *St Leonard's Vestry v. Holmes* (1885) 50 J.P. 132; *Firth v. Staines* [1897] 2 Q.B. 70; *R. v. Chapman, ex p. Arlidge* [1918] 2 K.B. 298; *Blackpool Corp. v. Locker* [1948] 1 K.B. 349 (requisitioning); *Warwick R.D.C. v. Miller-Mead* [1962] Ch. 441 (statutory notices to abate nuisances); *Bowyer, Philpott & Payne Ltd. v. Mather* [1919] 1 K.B. 419 (institution of proceedings under Public Health Act); *Ainsworth v. Creeke* (1868) L.R. 4 C.P. 476 (insertion on list of ratepayers); *Re Gloucester Municipal Election Petition, Ford v. Newth* [1901] 1 K.B. 683 (disqualification of councillor); Lanham (1981) 5 Otago L.Rev. 35.

2–054　　**Void acts: companies.** The proposition that a nullity cannot be ratified is in principle uncontroversial. However, much turns on what is meant by "nullity" or "void act". There are in fact few situations where such a principle is significant. The main context for its application was formerly that of *ultra vires* acts of companies. But even if the notion of ratification was relevant in this context, the changes to the *ultra vires* rule made by the Companies Act 1985[37] actually permit ratification,[38] so that the point ceases to require discussion in this context.

2–055　　**Forgeries.** It has been held that a forgery cannot be ratified, and the reason given that a forgery is a nullity. The leading case[39] seeks to make a distinction between voidable acts, which can be ratified, and void acts, such as forgery, which cannot. As a general criterion, however, this is unsatisfactory. It is certainly true that in the case of some voidable acts, *e.g.* the contract of a mentally incapable person, the terminology of ratification has been used.[40] But acts done without authority, *e.g.* the unauthorised issue of a writ, are not appropriately called voidable. If anything, they could be called void; but they can often be regarded as simply suffering from a defect that can be cured.[41] As regards forgery, it is submitted that the true reason why there can normally be no ratification is that the forger who counterfeits a signature or seal makes no profession of being an agent, so that agency doctrines do not apply to him.[42] An unauthorised signature or affixing of a seal for another may also, however, constitute a forgery[43]; and in such a case it seems that there can be ratification.[44]

　　This proposition is sometimes criticised as being over-technical.[45] It is submitted, however, that it is correct: a forger who counterfeits a

---

[37] Companies Act 1985, ss. 35, 35A (substituted by Companies Act 1989, s. 108); see below, paras. 8–033 *et seq.*

[38] *ibid.*, s. 35(3).

[39] *Brook v. Hook* (1871) L.R. 6 Ex. 89, Illustration 5.

[40] Below, para. 2–061.

[41] See the judgments in *Danish Mercantile Co. v. Beaumont* [1951] Ch. 680, Illustration 4; *Pontin v. Wood* [1962] 1 Q.B. 737; *Spackman v. Evans* (1868) L.R. 3 H.L. 171, 244; *Re Portuguese Consolidated Copper Mines Ltd* (1890) 45 Ch.D. 16, 30; above, para. 2–087.

[42] Treitel, *Law of Contract* (9th ed.), p. 641; *Brook v. Hook*, n. 39 above, at p. 100; *Greenwood v. Martins Bank Ltd* [1932] 1 K.B. 371, 378–379 (affd. [1933] A.C. 51); *Imperial Bank of Canada v. Begley* [1936] 2 All E.R. 367, 374–375; *Rowe v. B. & R. Nominees Pty. Ltd* [1964] V.R. 477.

[43] Forgery and Counterfeiting Act 1981, s. 9(1).

[44] See Campbell (1960) 76 L.Q.R. at pp. 130 *et seq.*; *Bank of Ireland v. Evans' Trustees* (1855) 5 H.L.C. 389, 414; *M'Kenzie v. British Linen Co.* (1881) 6 App.Cas. 82, 99–100; *Rowe v. B. & R. Nominees Pty. Ltd*, n. 42 above; *Northside Development Pty. Ltd v. Registrar-General* (1990) 170 C.L.R. 146, 184–185, 200, 207–208.

[45] Stoljar, pp. 185–186; Atiyah, *Vicarious Liability in the Law of Torts* (1967), p. 315.

signature or seal no more professes agency than does a person who disguises himself as another. The reason why the notion of ratification is invoked in these cases is that an adoption of a forgery would often be treated as a promise requiring consideration.[46] Nevertheless, the proper solution to the problem of the adoption of forgeries must, as in many other cases where ideas of ratification, adoption and acquiescence are invoked, lie within the areas of formation of contract, waiver, estoppel, and perhaps the rules as to gifts. Thus it has been held that an estoppel can be raised against a person who induces a third party to believe that a signature is his, if the third party acts on the representation.[47]

Illegality. It has been said that "life cannot be given by ratification to prohibited transactions"[48]; and in that case ratification of a prohibited insurance contract was refused validity. The extent to which it is correct to regard a transaction affected by illegality as actually void will, however, turn on the nature of the illegality, the wording of any relevant statute, and the extent of the illegality. The law is far from clear. It is not appropriate in a book on agency to seek to lay down further propositions.[49]   **2–056**

Illustrations

(1) A, on B's behalf but without his authority, purchases from C a chattel which C has no right to sell, under such circumstances that the purchase of the chattel is a conversion. B ratifies the purchase. B is guilty of converting the chattel.[50]   **2–057**

(2) A, an agent of a corporation, assaults B on its behalf. The corporation ratifies the assault. The corporation is civilly liable to B for the assault. *Sed quaere.*[51]

---

[46] In *Brook v. Hook*, n. 39 above, itself, the consideration was the suppression of a prosecution and so illegal.

[47] *Greenwood v. Martins Bank Ltd* [1933] A.C. 51, Illustration 5 (criticised by Stoljar, pp. 185–186, on the basis that there was no detriment: *sed quaere*); *M'Kenzie v. British Linen Co.*, n. 44 above; *Fung Kai Sun v. Chan Fui Hing* [1951] A.C. 489; *Rowe v. B. & R. Nominees Pty. Ltd*, n. 44 above. See also *Welch v. Bank of England* [1955] Ch. 508; *Spiro v. Lintern* [1973] 1 W.L.R. 1002; *Amalgamated Investment & Property Co. Ltd v. Texas Commerce International Bank Ltd* [1982] Q.B. 84; below, para. 8–030.

[48] *Bedford Insurance Co. Ltd v. Instituto de Resseguros do Brasil* [1985] Q.B. 966, 986 (Illustration 6) *per* Parker J.

[49] See Chitty, *Contracts* (27th ed.), Vol. 1, §§ 16–122 *et seq.*

[50] *Hilberry v. Hatton* (1864) 2 H. & C. 822. And see *Irving v. Motly* (1831) 7 Bing. 543.

[51] *Eastern Counties Ry. v. Broom* (1851) 6 Exch. 314. This proposition might be correct if based on the general rules of vicarious liability, but it seems out of date on the point of ratification, and rests on obiter dicta only, since it was held that there was no ratification. See Clerk and Lindsell, *Torts* (16th ed.), § 3–53.

(3)   A distrains B's goods in the name of B's landlord, but without the landlord's authority. The landlord may ratify the distress, and it is then deemed to have been levied by his authority.[52]

(4)   The managing director of a company, without having authority to do so, instructed solicitors to commence an action in the name of the company. An order for the winding up of the company having been made, the liquidator adopted the action. A motion to strike out the name of the plaintiff company failed; for, although not properly constituted when commenced (so that the defendant acting promptly could have obtained a stay), the action was not a nullity, and the subsequent ratification cured the defect in the proceedings as originally constituted.[53]

(5)   A signs an instrument in B's name without his authority and with intent to defraud. B cannot ratify the signature.[54] But if B, knowing of the forgery, by his conduct induces a third person to believe that the signature is his, and if such third person acts on that belief to his detriment, B will be estopped from denying that it is his signature in any action between him and such third person[55]; as he will be if, knowing of the forgery, he delays in repudiating the signature, so that the third person's chance of recovering from the forger is materially prejudiced.[56]

(6)   B in Hong Kong authorises A in London to write marine insurance risks on his behalf, subject to financial limitations as to the size of the risk. He also has an open cover reinsurance policy. A exceeds the limits in writing risks on B's behalf and declares the risks to the reinsurers. The insurances are void and unenforceable by statute because B is not authorised to carry on insurance business in Great Britain. Claims are made under the insurances. B ratifies the insurances and claims on the reinsurance policy. The original insurances are void

---

[52] *Whitehead v. Taylor* (1839) 10 A. & E. 210. See also *Hull v. Pickersgill* (1819) 1 B. & B. 282 (seizure of bankrupt's property ratified by assignee). For consideration of this problem in connection with liability in tort, see Atiyah, *Vicarious Liability in the Law of Torts* (1967), pp. 314–316.

[53] *Danish Mercantile Co. Ltd v. Beaumont* [1951] Ch. 680. See also *Ancona v. Marks* (1862) 7 H. & N. 686; *Hooper v. Kerr, Stuart & Co. Ltd* (1901) 83 L.T. 729, Illustration 2 to Article 20: *cf. Re State of Wyoming Syndicate* [1901] 2 Ch. 431. And see *Re Portugese Consolidated Copper Mines* (1890) 45 Ch.D. 16 (allotment of shares by irregular meeting); *Warwick R.D.C. v. Miller-Mead* [1962] Ch. 441 (local authority); *Bamford v. Bamford* [1970] Ch. 12 (but may not be on ratification); *Alexander Ward & Co. Ltd. v. Samyang Navigation Co. Ltd* [1975] 1 W.L.R. 673 (arrest of ship in Scotland *ad fundandam jurisdictionem*: see (1976) 39 M.L.R. 327); Article 20, Illustration 10.

[54] *Brook v. Hook* (1871) L.R. 6 Ex. 89; but see Comment, above.

[55] *M'Kenzie v. British Linen Co.* (1881) 6 App.Cas. 82.

[56] *Greenwood v. Martins Bank Ltd* [1933] A.C. 51; *Brown v. Westminster Bank Ltd* [1964] 2 Lloyd's Rep. 187; *Tina Motors Pty. Ltd v. A.N.Z. Banking Group Ltd* [1977] V.R. 205.

whether made with B's authority or not and so cannot be ratified. There is thus no claim on the reinsurance policy.[57]

Article 15

WHO MAY RATIFY

The only person who has power to ratify an act is the person in whose name or on whose behalf the act purported to be done,[58] and it is necessary that he should have been in existence at the time when the act was done,[59] and competent at that time and at the time of ratification to be the principal of the person doing the act[60]; but it is not necessary that at the time the act was done he was known, either personally or by name, to the third party.[61]   2–058

Comment

Person acted for: no ratification by undisclosed principal. It is clear that ratification only applies where the person whose act is in question professed or purported at the time of acting to do so as agent. Although if the agent had authority at that time, an undisclosed principal could take the benefit of the contract and likewise would be liable to be sued,[62] it has been held that an *undisclosed* principal cannot ratify. The reason given in the leading case of *Keighley, Maxsted & Co. v. Durant*[63] is that "civil obligations are not to be created by, or founded upon, undisclosed intentions."[64] It is however difficult to see that this is not exactly what happens under the doctrine of the undisclosed principal. A more general reason sometimes given is that to allow ratification in such a case would be to allow too easy intervention upon a contract by a person not in truth connected with it. In one sense this is obvious: the doctrine of ratification would not be appropriately invoked to allow intervention by a person, uncontemplated by the purported agent, who   2–059

---

[57] *Bedford Insurance Co. Ltd v. Instituto de Resseguros do Brasil* [1985] Q.B. 966, approved on the illegality issue in *Phoenix General Ins. Co. of Greece S.A. v. Halvanon Ins. Co. Ltd* [1988] Q.B. 216. But see now Financial Services Act 1986, s. 132.

[58] Illustrations 1–4; *Watson v. Swann* (1862) 11 C.B.(N.S.) 756; *Smith v. Cox* [1940] 2 K.B. 558 (payment of rent by stranger); *Att.-Gen. v. Wylde* (1946) 47 S.R.(N.S.W.) 99 (ratification of act of Crown agent by another officer of the Crown); *Howard Smith & Co. Ltd v. Varawa* (1907) 5 C.L.R. 68, 82; *Crampsey v. Deveney* [1968] S.C.R. 267, (1968) 2 D.L.R. (3d) 161; *Restatement*, §§ 85, 87.

[59] *Kelner v. Baxter* (1866) L.R. 2 C.P. 174, Illustration 6.

[60] *Firth v. Staines* [1897] 2 Q.B. 70, 75; *Restatement*, §§ 84, 86; and see Illustrations.

[61] See Comment.

[62] Article 78.

[63] [1901] A.C. 240, Illustration 3. See Rochvarg (1989) 34 McGill L.J. 286.

[64] *Per* Lord Macnaghten at p. 247.

simply found it convenient to ratify the transaction. This would, indeed, not be ratification by an undisclosed principal. But *Keighley Maxsted's* case did not involve such a situation. The person whose acts were purportedly ratified was already an agent, and had merely exceeded his authority in respect of the price at which he agreed to buy. Furthermore, the principal chose to ratify and it was the third party who, in suing the principal, sought to rely on the ratification. He was not permitted to do so. It is arguable therefore that at the very least a principal who ratifies should be held liable in the situation where a person who is already an agent exceeds his authority; and possibly should be able to sue in such a case, the third party being adequately protected by the normal restrictions against unfair results of ratification.[65] The decision is however clear that ratification in such a case is ineffective.

Conversely, however, where the agent purports to act for a principal but actually intends to act for himself the principal *can* ratify.[66] And where the agent purports to act for one person, no other person can ratify.[67] "If there is one legal principle better established than another it is this, that nobody can ratify a contract purporting to be made by an agent except the party on whose behalf the agent purported to act."[68] It is under this principle that some forgeries cannot be ratified, for a forger does not usually purport to act *for* someone else but *as* someone else.[69] In tort cases, it is clear that in principle there can be no ratification of a tort unless the tortfeasor has in some way purported to act for the party who subsequently ratifies[70] but exactly what interpretation is to be given to the idea of "purporting to act" is a difficult matter.[71]

2–060   **In existence when act done.** This refers to contracts made on behalf of companies not yet registered.[72] Where the promoters of a prospective company enter into a contract on its behalf before its incorporation, the company cannot after incorporation ratify the contract, because it was not in existence at the time when the contract was made and so could not have made the contract at that time.[73] The company may make a

---

[65] Article 19.
[66] *Re Tiedemann and Ledermann Frères* [1899] 2 Q.B. 66, Illustration 4.
[67] Illustrations 1, 2.
[68] *Jones v. Hope* (1880) 3 T.L.R. 247n., 251 *per* Brett L.J. (Illustration 5)
[69] See above, para. 2–055.
[70] See, *e.g. Wilson v. Barker* (1833) 4 B. & Ad. 614; *Eastern Construction Co. Ltd v. National Trust Co. Ltd* [1914] A.C. 197, 213. See Atiyah, *Vicarious Liability in the Law of Torts* (1967), pp. 314–316.
[71] See Seavey, 21 U.Chi.L.Rev. 248 (1954); *cf.* Twerski, 42 Temple L.Q. 1 (1968).
[72] See Companies Act 1985, s. 117 esp. subs. (8).
[73] *Kelner v. Baxter* (1866) L.R. 2 C.P. 174, Illustration 6; *Re Empress Engineering Co.* (1880) 16 Ch.D. 125; *Re Northumberland Avenue Hotel Co.* (1886) 33 Ch.D. 16; *Melhado v. Porto Alegre, etc., Ry. Co.* (1874) L.R. 9 C.P. 503; *Natal Land, etc., Co. v. Pauline, etc., Syndicate* [1904] A.C. 120.

new contract on the same terms as the old,[74] and this may be proved by part performance,[75] but it cannot ratify the contract. Other remedies have sometimes been found in respect of pre-incorporation contracts[76]; but it has also been held that a company is not bound in equity to pay for work done before its formation, even though it has taken the benefit of the work.[77] Such results have proved inconvenient in practice and in some jurisdictions are changed by statute.[78]

Competent at the time when the act was done. Again, a person   2–061
cannot ratify an act which he was not competent to do at the time it was done: an example appears in Illustration 9. Apart from alien enemies, with whom Illustration 9 is concerned,[79] the main case for considering this requirement is that of minors. Where a contract made for a minor would, if made by the infant himself, be valid,[80] it can presumably be ratified in the normal way. Other contracts are void against the minor but bind the other party: they can be "ratified" by the minor after reaching full age. If entered into through an agent, they can likewise presumably be ratified by the minor personally or through an agent: except that it was long ago held that a penal bond could not be ratified.[81] The distinction between void and voidable acts may regulate the ratification by mentally incapable persons of contracts made on their behalf: they can ratify, when of sound mind, acts which if effected by themselves would have been voidable.[82]

Competent at the time of ratification. A minor clearly cannot ratify a   2–062
contract that would not bind him, while still under age, nor a mentally incapable person while still incapable, nor a person who is an alien enemy, even if he was not such when the act was done.[83]

Unnamed principal. In general, as will be seen from the above rules   2–063
regarding the existence and competence of the principal, the rules for ratification follow those for initial authority: the test is to inquire

---

[74] *Howard v. Patent Ivory Co.* (1888) 38 Ch.D. 156; *cf. Touche v. Metropolitan Ry. Warehousing Co.* (1871) L.R. 6 Ch.App. 671.
[75] *ibid.*
[76] See *Re Empress Engineering Co.*, n. 73 above; *Re Dale & Plant* (1889) 61 L.T. 206; *Rover International Ltd v. Cannon Film Sales Ltd (No. 3)* [1989] 1 W.L.R. 912; Pennington, *Company Law* (6th ed.), p. 89.
[77] *Re English & Colonial Produce Co.* [1906] 2 Ch. 435.
[78] *e.g.* Companies Act 1981 (Australia), s. 81; Companies Act (Singapore), cap. 185, s.35. See Hambrook, (1982) 8 Adelaide L.Rev. 119.
[79] And see *Kuenigl v. Donnersmarck* [1955] 1 Q.B. 515, 539.
[80] *e.g.* a contract for necessaries, or a beneficial contract of service.
[81] *Baylis v. Dineley* (1815) 3 M. & S. 477. It may be regarded as a nullity.
[82] *City Bank of Sydney v. McLaughlin* (1909) 9 C.L.R. 615. See Comment to Article 4. In *Dibbins v. Dibbins* [1896] 2 Ch. 348, Illustration 2 to Article 19, it was assumed that the ratification would have been valid had it been effected in time.
[83] See Comment to Article 119.

whether the principal could have entered into such a transaction at the time when the agent originally acted. If this analogy is followed, since an agent need not always name his principal but may and often does act for a completely unnamed principal (*e.g.* "bought for our principals"), ratification should be possible in such a case also. If the third party is willing to deal on this basis, he should arguably be bound under the doctrine of ratification just as under the normal principles of authority. A number of dicta however suggest that the principal must be known or ascertainable by the third party at the time of contracting. Thus in one case it was said that "The law obviously requires that the person for whom the agent professes to act must be a person capable of being ascertained at the time. It is not necessary that he should be named; but there must be such a description of him as shall amount to a reasonable designation of the person intended to be bound by the contract."[84] An example of the latter category is that of an agent who acts for the heirs of property, whoever they are.[85] Such dicta would, if applied as a rule, restrict the scope of ratification. If there is any policy reason for doing this, it is that the ability to ratify where the principal was completely unnamed and undescribed will depend on the agent having had a particular person in mind; and this may effectively permit him at a later stage to choose the person who is to ratify by declaring that this was the person whom he had originally had in mind. This is not, at least in theory, true in ordinary dealings on behalf of unnamed principals, where actual authority would in the event of dispute need to be proved. Even in such cases however there may be an element of choice, for agents may have identical instructions from several principals and thus be free in practice to choose to which principal a particular contract should be allocated. There is also some possibility of such choice where the question of the intervention or liability of an undisclosed principal arises.[86] Such uncertainties are not therefore unknown to agency law. The dicta quoted come from a nineteenth-century case on insurance, where the difficulty of distinguishing between identifying the person who can sue on the policy as principal and identifying the interests covered by the policy is notorious.[87]

A carefully reasoned judgment at first instance now confirms the above view.[88] It also states (in wording appropriate to its context, that

---

[84] *Watson v. Swann* (1862) 11 C.B.(N.S.) 756, 771, *per* Willes J. See also *Kelner v. Baxter* (1866) L.R. 2 C.P. 174, 184; *Eastern Construction Co. Ltd v. National Trust Co. Ltd* [1914] A.C. 197, 213.

[85] *Lyell v. Kennedy* (1889) 14 App.Cas. 437, Illustration 7.

[86] See Article 78.

[87] See below; Arnould, *Marine Insurance*, 16th ed. (9 and 10 *British Shipping Laws*), §§ 243, 247–250; *cf.* McGillivay and Parkington, *Insurance Law* (8th ed.), § 370. See also *The Albazero* [1977] A.C. 774; and below.

[88] *National Oilwell (U.K.) Ltd v. Davy Offshore Ltd* [1993] 2 Lloyd's Rep. 582; see also *Restatement*, s 87 comment *a*; Powell, pp. 125–126.

of insurance) that "Evidence as to whether in any particular case the principal assured or other contracting party did have the relevant intention may be provided by the terms of the policy itself, by the terms of any contract between the principal assured or other contracting party and the alleged co-assured or by any other admissible material showing what was subjectively intended by the principal assured."[89] Although this decision and these dicta seem, with respect, correct, they do raise considerable problems of evidence, whether within or outside the context of insurance. Where an agent has no principal in mind at the time of the act, but proposes to "allocate" the contract, there can in principle be no ratification. Where he has a principal in mind, there can. The two situations may be difficult to distinguish.

A related point arises from the fact that policies of marine insurance on goods have long been taken out for the benefit of "all those to whom they do, may *or shall* appertain," or similar wording; and it has often been assumed that beneficiaries of such policies may sue on them. It seems that in such a case the understanding is that the agent who procures the insurance need not at the moment have in mind any particular person or persons as the intended principal or principals, provided that there is some general contemplation as to the person or persons intended to benefit.[90] Although there are dicta to the contrary it is submitted that as regards agency reasoning, a person who had no interest at the time of the insurance should not in principle be able to ratify, and therefore should not be able to sue on such a policy as principal. The analogy of authorised contracts should again be followed, and a contract could not be validly made on behalf of a person who might at a future time acquire a particular qualification.[91] Trust reasoning is not so limited. It is possible for a policy on goods to be taken out which covers the interests of such persons; and the person who takes it out may have an insurable interest to do so and be able to recover an indemnity in respect of loss incurred by such persons, which he would hold in trust.[92] Equally such a policy may be assigned; and in an appropriate case such a policy might be held to convey a contractual offer to persons later acquiring the qualification mentioned. It is submitted that it is on this basis that such provisions should be

---

[89] *ibid.* at p. 597 *per* Colman J. The judgment contains authority for this proposition and consideration of such evidence.

[90] See *Boston Fruit Co. v. British & Foreign Marine Insurance Co.* [1906] A.C. 336, 389 (insurance by shipowner could not benefit characterers); *P. Samuel & Co. Ltd v. Dumas* [1923] 1 K.B. 592; [1924] A.C. 431; *Routh v. Thompson* (1811) 13 East 274; *Robinson v. Gleadow* (1835) 2 Bing. N.C. 156; *cf. Watson v. Swann*, n. 84 above; *Byas v. Miller* (1897) 3 Com.Cas. 39.

[91] See *Kelner v. Baxter* (1866) L.R. 2 C.P. 174, 184.

[92] *A. Tomlinson (Hauliers) Ltd v. Hepburn* [1966] A.C. 451. See also *Petrofina (U.K.) Ltd. v. Magnaload Ltd* [1983] 2 Lloyd's Rep. 91.

explained, and that their efficacy in favour of future beneficiaries cannot satisfactorily be based on reasoning that there is agency for a person not at the time ascertainable.[93]

Illustrations

2–064   (1)   A sheriff, acting under a valid writ of execution, wrongfully seizes goods which are not the property of the debtor. The execution creditor does not, by becoming a party to an interpleader issue or otherwise, ratify the act of the sheriff so as to render himself liable for the wrongful seizure, because the act was not done by the sheriff on his behalf, but in performance of a public duty.[94]

(2)   A enters into an agreement professedly on behalf of B's wife and C. B cannot ratify the agreement so as to give himself a right to sue upon it jointly with his wife and C.[95]

(3)   A is authorised to buy wheat on the joint account of himself and B, with a certain limit as to price. A, intending to buy on the joint account of himself and B, and expecting that B will ratify the contract, but not disclosing such intention to the seller, enters into a contract in his own name to buy at a price in excess of the limit. B ratifies, but later refuses to take the wheat. He cannot be sued by the seller.[96]

(4)   A sells wheat to X on P's behalf, and repurchases it himself. He then purports to sell it to Q, R and S on P's behalf, knowing that Q, R and S would not deal with him personally. He really intends to carry through the whole transaction on his own behalf. Q, R and S repudiate the transaction. P may ratify.[97]

(5)   A contracts on behalf of a volunteer corps with B, both parties thinking that the corps as an entity may be bound. The corps as an entity cannot be bound. The contract cannot be ratified by individual members of the corps, because it was not made on their behalf as individuals.[98]

(6)   A contract for the supply of goods is made by "A, B and C on behalf of" a company not yet formed. This company cannot when formed render itself liable by ratification for the price of the goods.[99]

---

[93] This reasoning was accepted in the Court of Appeal of New South Wales in *Trident General Ins. Co. Ltd v. McNiece Bros. Pty. Ltd* (1987) 8 N.S.W.L.R. 270, 276–277, Illustration 8 (affd. on other grounds (1988) 165 C.L.R. 107: but see p. 113).

[94] *Wilson v. Tunman and Fretson* (1843) 6 M. & G. 236; *Woollen v. Wright* (1862) 1 H. & C. 554; *Williams v. Williams and Nathan* [1937] 2 All E.R. 559; *Barclays Bank v. Roberts* [1954] 1 W.L.R. 1212. *cf. Morris v. Salberg* (1889) 22 Q.B.D. 614.

[95] *Saunderson v. Griffiths* (1826) 5 B. & C. 909; *Heath v. Chilton* (1844) 12 M. & W. 632.

[96] *Keighley, Maxsted & Co. v. Durant* [1901] A.C. 240.

[97] *Re Tiedemann & Ledermann Frères* [1899] 2 Q.B. 66.

[98] *Jones v. Hope* (1880) 3 T.L.R. 247n.

[99] *Kelner v. Baxter* (1866) L.R. 2 C.P. 174. See also Article 109.

(7) A person may act on behalf of an heir, or an administrator, or the owner of particular property, whoever he may be, though unascertained and unknown to him, and the person on whose behalf the act was done may ratify it.[1]

(8) A policy of insurance is taken out describing the assured as "X, all its subsidiary associated and related companies, all contractors and subcontractors and/or suppliers." A subcontractor appointed in the following year cannot ratify the contract so as to sue on it as a party to it by virtue of the law of agency.[2]

(9) A trawler owned by a French company is at an English port when, as a result of enemy occupation of France, the company becomes an alien enemy. While this state of affairs continues, A, without the company's authority, acts as manager of the trawler. A's conduct cannot subsequently be ratified by the company, which was not at the time of A's acts competent to be A's principal.[3]

Article 16

Knowledge Necessary for Ratification

In order that a person may be held to have ratified an act done without his authority, it is necessary that, at the time of the ratification, he should have full knowledge of all the material circumstances in which the act was done,[4] unless he intended to ratify the act and take the risk whatever the circumstances may have been.[5] But knowledge of the legal effect of the act may be imputed to him,[6] and it is not necessary that he should have notice of collateral circumstances affecting the nature of the act.[7]

2–065

---

[1] *Lyell v. Kennedy* (1889) 14 App.Cas. 437; *Foster v. Bates* (1843) 1 D. & L. 400. See also *Hull v. Pickersgill* (1819) 1 B. & B. 282.

[2] *Trident General Ins. Co. Ltd v. McNiece Bros. Pty. Ltd* (1987) 8 N.S.W.L.R. 270, 276–277 (affd. on other grounds (1988) 165 C.L.R. 107, but see p. 113).

[3] *Boston Deep Sea Fishing & Ice Co. v. Farnham* [1957] 1 W.L.R. 1051.

[4] Illustrations 1, 2, 6. It seems clear that the knowledge of the agent should not in such a case be imputed to him; see Corbin (1906) 15 Yale L.J. 331. See also *Royal Albert Hall Corp. v. Winchilsea* (1891) 7 T.L.R. 362; *Eastern Construction Co. Ltd. v. National Trust Co. Ltd.* [1914] A.C. 197, 213; *McLean Bros. & Rigg Ltd. v. Grice* (1906) 4 C.L.R. 835; *Taylor v. Smith* (1926) 38 C.L.R. 48; *Bedford Insurance Co. Ltd. v. Instituto de Resseguros do Brasil* [1985] Q.B. 966, 987; *Aotearoa International Ltd. v. Westpac Banking Corp.* [1984] 2 N.Z.L.R. 34; *Restatement*, § 91.

[5] Illustrations 3, 5; *Marsh v. Joseph* [1897] 1 Ch. 213; *Restatement*, § 91, esp. comment e.

[6] *Powell v. Smith* (1872) L.R. 14 Eq. 85: see Comment. See also *Restatement*, § 91, comment c (knowledge could be inferred "when he has such information that a person of ordinary intelligence would infer the existence of the facts in question"); Corbin (1906) 15 Yale L.J. 331.

[7] Illustration 4.

Comment

2–066   This proposition has appeared in all editions of this work, and it is therefore preserved as a general guide. It is obvious that some sort of rule to this effect is appropriate, both for ratification and for situations where similar reasoning is employed.[8] Although most rules relating to ratification are directed towards protecting the third party against unfair result, this rule protects the principal against being too easily treated as having ratified. But it is in fact doubtful whether any satisfactory formulation can in fact be found for all the different circumstances in which such reasoning is encountered.

Many of the clearest cases from which this rule is to be derived concern unlawful distress, and conclude that there was no ratification. It has already been argued that the doctrine of ratification has only limited application to torts.[9] In so far as ratification is applicable to make a person liable in tort, it would seem that the requirement of knowledge should be more strictly interpreted in that branch of the law,[10] whereas in a contractual situation a "blanket ratification" (as by receipt of goods) should be more easily establishable. The objective interpretation of contractual situations, and the related notion that a person may be taken to know matters of which he might be expected to be aware,[11] may obviously allow the inference of ratification where this would not be permissible in a tort case, and it is right that it should.[12] Thus where a person ratified a lease negotiated by an agent under a misapprehension as to its provisions which would not have affected the validity of the contract had the parties made it without an intermediary, he was held bound by it.[13] But where a person to whom a duty of disclosure was owed purported to ratify a transaction (not effected through an agent) which was to his prejudice and voidable as such, this was held inoperative since he did not know that the transaction was voidable.[14]

Illustrations

2–067   (1) An agent wrongfully distrains goods which were neither on the debtor's land nor his property, without the authority of the principal,

---

[8] See above, para. 2–047.

[9] See Comment to Article 14; Atiyah, *Vicarious Liability in the Law of Torts* (1967), pp. 316–318.

[10] *cf. Marsh v. Joseph*, n. 5 *supra*, at pp. 246–247; see also *Edwards v. L. & N.W. Ry. Co.* (1870) L.R. 5 C.P. 445; *Briess v. Woolley* [1954] A.C. 333, 344. But a general ratification of an employer-employee relationship may perhaps involve implied ratification of torts committed by the employee: Atiyah, *op. cit.* n. 9 above, pp. 316–318.

[11] See Comment to Article 75.

[12] Mechem, *Outlines of Agency* (4th ed.), §§ 206–211.

[13] *Powell v. Smith*, n. 6 above. But this may not be an agency case. See also *Hunter v. Parker* (1840) 7 M. & W. 322. Illustration 6.

[14] *Savery v. King* (1856) 5 H.L.Cas. 627. See also *Spackman v. Evans* (1868) L.R. 3 H.L. 171.

and pays over the proceeds to the principal. The principal is not deemed to have ratified the wrongful distress by receiving the proceeds, unless he received them with knowledge of the irregularity, or intended without inquiry to take the risk upon himself. [15]

(2)   An agent, with authority to distrain for rent, wrongfully seized and sold a fixture, and paid the proceeds to the principal, who received them without notice that it was a fixture which had been sold. Held, that the principal had not ratified the trespass. [16]

(3)   An agent, without authority, signed a distress warrant, and, after the distress, informed his principal, who said that he should leave the matter in the agent's hands. Held, that this was a ratification of the whole transaction, though there had been irregularities in levying the distress of which the principal had no knowledge. [17]

(4)   An agent purchased a chattel on his principal's behalf from a person who had no right to sell it, and the principal ratified the purchase. Held, that the principal was guilty of a conversion of the chattel, though he had no knowledge at the time of the ratification that the sale was unlawful. Here, the circumstances rendering the transaction a conversion were collateral to, and did not form part of, the contract ratified. The ratification of the purchase as such was however sufficient to make the principal liable for conversion, liability for which is strict. [18]

(5)   An agent entered into an unauthorised contract for the purchase of land on behalf of his principal. A letter from the principal, saying that he did not know what the agent had agreed to, but that he must support him in all he had done, was held to be sufficient ratification of the agreement, whatever it might be. [19]

(6)   The master of a ship sells it in circumstances where no agency of necessity arises. The owner receives the proceeds of the sale by bills of exchange, believing that a situation of necessity had in fact arisen. On hearing the true facts he arrests the ship, presents the bills for payment and pays the money into court. He has not ratified the sale. [20] But he may be held to have done so if in similar circumstances the only irregularity unknown to him was as to the procedure by which the sale was effected. [21]

---

[15] *Lewis v. Read* (1845) 13 M. & W. 834.

[16] *Freeman v. Rosher* (1849) 13 Q.B. 780.

[17] *Haseler v. Lemoyne* (1858) 5 C.B.(N.S.) 530. See also *Becker v. Riebold* (1913) 30 T.L.R. 142.

[18] *Hilberry v. Hatton* (1864) 2 H. & C. 822. See Powell, p. 122; Stoljar, p. 179. The distinction between these cases and Illustrations 1 and 2 is perhaps that in those Illustrations the principal did not know of the act constituting the conversion at all.

[19] *Fitzmaurice v. Bayley* (1856) 6 E. & B. 868 (see also (1860) 9 H.L.C. 78).

[20] *The Bonita, The Charlotte* (1861) Lush. 252.

[21] *Hunter v. Parker* (1840) 7 M. & W. 322.

(7)   An estate agent makes a contract to sell his principal's land. The principal ratifies, not knowing that the estate agent has subsequently received an inquiry about the land from someone else. The ratification is effective. [22]

Article 17

2–068   WHAT CONSTITUTES RATIFICATION

(1)   Ratification may be express or by conduct.
(2)   An express ratification is a clear manifestation by one on whose behalf an unauthorised act has been done that he treats the act as authorised and becomes a party to the transaction in question. [23]
(3)   Ratification will be implied whenever the conduct of the person in whose name or on whose behalf the act or transaction is done or entered into is such as to show that he adopts or recognises such act or transaction in whole or in part[24]: and may be implied from the mere acquiescence or inactivity of the principal. [25]
(4)   The adoption of part of a transaction operates as a ratification of the whole. [26]
(5)   It is not necessary that the ratification of a written contract should be in writing, [27] but the execution of a deed can only be ratified by deed. [28]

Comment

2–069   **Rule (1).** Just as a grant of authority may be express or implied, so may ratification. Thus suing on a transaction, or basing a defence on it,

---

[22] *Brennan v. O'Connell* [1980] I.R. 13.
[23] See *Restatement*, §§ 83, 93 (which distinguishes between the situation of "affirmance", which is what is here referred to, and the full notion of ratification, which requires the affirmance to be of a ratifiable act, under the proper circumstances and in a proper manner).
[24] Illustrations 1 to 7; Illustration 12; *Waiwera Co-operative Dairy Co. Ltd v. Wright, Stephenson & Co. Ltd* [1917] N.Z.L.R. 178 (ratification of contract by sending goods forward); *Akel v. Turner* [1926] G.L.R. 574 (N.Z.) (ratification of sale of partnership business to company by acting as manager of company); *Restatement*, §§ 93, 99; Atiyah, *Vicarious Liability in the Law of Torts* (1967), pp. 318 *et seq.*
[25] Illustration 9; and see Comment.
[26] Illustrations 2, 3, 10, 11; see also *Bristow v. Whitimore* (1861) 9 H.L.Cas. 391; *Republic of Peru v. Peruvian Guano Co.* (1887) 36 Ch.D. 489; *Re Mawcon Ltd* [1969] 1 W.L.R. 78; *Restatement*, § 96.
[27] *Maclean v. Dunn* (1828) 4 Bing. 722; *Soames v. Spencer* (1822) 1 D. & R. 32; *Koenigsblatt v. Sweet* [1923] 2 Ch. 314; *Sheridan v. Higgins* [1971] I.R. 291.
[28] See *Hunter v. Parker* (1840) 7 M. & W. 322; *Kidderminster Corp. v. Hardwicke* (1873) L.R. 9 Ex. 13; *Oxford Corp. v. Crow* [1893] 3 Ch. 535; *Athy Guardians v. Murphy* [1986] 1 I.R. 65. But see Comment.

will (subject to any rules as to ratifications which come too late[29]) often amount to an implied ratification of it.[30] So also receipt or retention of money with knowledge of the circumstances of a contract under which it is paid will normally constitute ratification of that contract,[31] as will use or disposal of goods received under it,[32] unless the supposed principal did not assent to the transaction and had no alternative but to receive them and use them as they were, *e.g.* where they were already his own.[33] It is clear therefore that ratification of an executed contract will be easier to establish than ratification of an executory contract, for there are few cases where a person can keep another's property, or benefit otherwise at the expense of another, without paying, unless he is unaware of the circumstances.[34] Such cases have a restitutionary basis: as an alternative to a possible claim in rescission or conversion, the courts impose liability as upon the transaction under which the money or goods came into the principal's hands.[35] In a sense, therefore, they are different from those in which inactivity is no more than evidence of a voluntary ratification.[36]

Rule (2). Express ratification. This needs no explanation: it is obvious that if the principal of ratification is accepted at all, an express statement will constitute its prime example. It would seem that a *conditional* ratification would, if the condition was as to a future event, take effect only as a promise to ratify, and only bind if supported by consideration or the requirements of estoppel.

2–070

Rule (3). Implied ratification. Express ratification will however be comparatively rare, and a ratification will more often be implied from words or conduct. Such words or conduct must be unequivocal: they

2–071

---

[29] Article 19.

[30] *e.g.* Illustration 6; *Verschures Creameries Ltd v. Hull & Netherlands S.S. Co. Ltd* [1921] 2 K.B. 608, Illustration 6 to Article 20; *Celthene Pty. Ltd v. W.J.K. Hauliers Pty. Ltd* [1981] 1 N.S.W.L.R. 606, 615; *Life Savers (Aust.) Pty. Ltd. v. Frigmobile Pty. Ltd* [1983] 1 N.S.W.L.R. 431; 438; *Trident General Ins. Co. Ltd. v. McNiece Bros. Pty. Ltd.* (1987) 8 N.S.W.L.R. 270, 280, Illustration 8 to Article 15 (affd. on other grounds (1988) 165 C.L.R. 107).

[31] Illustrations 1, 3. See in general *Restatement*, §§ 94, 98, 99.

[32] Illustrations 2, 4, 7.

[33] Illustration 8.

[34] See, *e.g. Royal Albert Hall Corp. v. Winchilsea* (1891) 7 T.L.R. 362. But the situation may be otherwise where the principal does not use the goods personally, *e.g.* in a husband and wife case like *Morel Bros. & Co. Ltd v. Earl of Westmorland* [1904] A.C. 11.

[35] *Restatement*, Appendix, p. 179; Goff and Jones, *Law of Restitution* (4th ed.), Chap. 38.

[36] *Restatement*, Appendix, Reporter's note to § 94 at pp. 178–180 (also printed in (1954) 103 U. Pa. L.Rev. 30).

must not be such that they could be accounted for by other interpretations,[37] *e.g.* that the principal is simply resuming possession of his own property.[38] Such reasoning is necessary to protect the principal against too easily being held liable as having ratified.

2–072   **Ratification by inactivity or acquiescence.**[39] There is however in principle no necessity for the ratification to be communicated to the other party: it is submitted that it operates, if proved, as a unilateral manifestation of will[40] in the same way as a grant of preceding authority.[41] It will normally be communicated, or at least manifested, to the agent, or sometimes to the third party only: but in principle it would seem that it need not be communicated at all so long as it is manifested in some way.[42] This is largely a problem of executory contracts, since in the cases of executed contracts it will be difficult to remain totally inactive, except in the case of unasked-for improvements to one's own property.[43]

This means that if inactivity of the principal can be taken as manifesting assent, it may constitute ratification.[44] Several cases involving executory contracts can be explained in this way.[45] Indeed, past inactivity in respect of what was done by agents may also be held to confer actual or apparent authority[46]: a person who acts by

---

[37] *Petersen v. Moloney* (1951) 84 C.L.R. 91, 101; *McLauchlan-Troup v. Peters* [1983] V.R. 53 (receipt of rent through agent whose authority was withdrawn, explicable on basis that he acted as agent for payer).

[38] *Forman & Co. Pty. Ltd v. The Liddesdale* [1900] A.C. 190, Illustration 8.

[39] *Restatement*, Appendix, Reporter's note to § 94 (also printed in (1954) 103 U.Pa.L.Rev. 30).

[40] See *Harrisons & Crosfield Ltd v. L. & N.W. Ry. Co. Ltd* [1917] 2 K.B. 755, 758; *Pagnan S.p.A. v. Feed Products Ltd* [1987] 2 Lloyd's Rep. 601, 613; *Shell Co. of Australia Ltd v. Nat Shipping and Bagging Services Ltd (The Kilmun)* [1988] 2 Lloyd's Rep. 1, 11, 14. In the case of a contract made "subject to ratification", however, the situation is different, for what is in issue is formation of the contract, not ratification of it. Hence notice would normally be required unless the offeror had waived notice of acceptance. See *Warehousing and Fowarding Co. of East Africa Ltd v. Jafferali* [1964] A.C. 1, 9–10.

[41] *cf.* above, para. 2–032.

[42] Mechem, *Principles of Agency* (4th ed.), § 216; *Restatement*, §§ 92(*g*), 93(1), 95.

[43] *Forman & Co. Pty. v. The Liddesdale* [1900] A.C. 190, Illustration 8; *Prince v. Clark* (1823) 1 B. & C. 186, Illustration 9; *Rodmell v. Eden* (1859) 1 F. & F. 542; *The Australia* (1859) 13 Moo. P.C. 132; *City Bank of Sydney v. McLaughlin* (1909) 9 C.L.R. 615; *Bamk Melli Iran v. Barclays Bank Ltd* [1951] 2 T.L.R. 1057; *cf. Taylor v. Smith* (1926) 38 C.L.R. 48.

[44] *Bank Melli Iran v. Barclays Bank Ltd*, n. 43 above, at p. 1063.

[45] *Robinson v. Gleadow* (1835) 2 Bing. N.C. 156; *Bigg v. Strong* (1858) 4 Jur.(N.S.) 983; *Phillips v. Homfray* (1871) L.R. 6 Ch.App. 770; *Scots Church Adelaide Inc. v. Fead* [1951] S.A.S.R. 41. See also below, para. 2–076.

[46] *City Bank of Sydney v. McLaughlin* (1909) 9 C.L.R. 615, 625. This could also be relevant if other requirements for ratification were not present, *e.g.* capacity or form. See *Restatement*, § 103, comments *a* and *b*; below, paras. 8–045, 8–047.

representative runs risks in doing so, and may owe a duty to make his position clear where a person acting alone would not. In all these cases, the principal is more likely to be bound where the person concerned is already an agent than when he is not. [47]

Estoppel. When the silence or inactivity is known to and relied on by the third party, an estoppel may in appropriate cases arise against the principal, who may be estopped from saying that he has not ratified. [48] This will be different from an implied ratification if it comes as later and unrelated conduct, or if there is some difficulty as to the ratification, *e.g.* in respect of form or capacity. [49] Conversely, an estoppel may arise if the principal leads the agent to believe that he will not ratify, or does not do so within a reasonable time. [50]   2–073

Torts. Ratification of torts other than conversion and trespass to goods is rare and is most unlikely to be inferred from silence or acquiescence. [51]   2–074

Ratification by agents. Ratification can clearly be effected by an agent, subject to the normal principles of authority. [52] The agent who ratifies requires only authority to ratify, not authority to have performed the act ratified. [53]   2–075

Ratification by companies. An act or transaction done or entered into on behalf of a company may be ratified by the directors, if they have power to do or enter into such an act or transaction on behalf of the company[54]: and a ratification by the directors may be implied from part performance made or permitted by the company. [55] Where an act or transaction is beyond the powers of the directors, it can only be effectively ratified by the shareholders. [56] An act done by the directors   2–076

---

[47] As with apparent authority: see Comment to Article 21.
[48] *cf. Spiro v. Lintern* [1973] 1 W.L.R. 1002, Illustration 34 to Article 74; *Worboys v. Carter* [1987] 2 EGLR 1; below, para. 8–030.
[49] See *Restatement*, § 103; Appendix, p. 166.
[50] Article 19.
[51] *Moon v. Towers* (1860) 8 C.B.(N.S.) 611. But *cf. Barns v. Guardians of St Mary, Islington* (1911) 76 J.P. 11. See above, para. 2–052A.
[52] *e.g. Lawson v. Hosemaster Co. Ltd.* [1966] 1 W.L.R. 1300; see also *Restatement*, § 93(3) and comment.
[53] *Re Portuguese Consolidated Copper Mines Ltd* (1890) 45 Ch.D. 16.
[54] *Reuter v. Electric Telegraph Co.* (1856) 6 E. & B. 341; *Wilson v. West Hartlepool Ry. & Harbour Co.* (1865) 2 De G.J. & S. 475; *Hopper v. Kerr, Stuart & Co. Ltd* (1901) 83 L.T. 729.
[55] *Reuter v. Electric Telegraph Co.*, n. 54 above; *Wilson v. West Hartlepool etc. Co.*, n. 54 above; Illustration 7.
[56] *Spackman v. Evans* (1868) L.R. 3 H.L. 171.

in excess of their powers, but within the scope of the memorandum of association, may be ratified by ordinary resolution of the shareholders,[57] or by an informal meeting of all the shareholders.[58] A number of cases go further and indicate that a ratification by the shareholders may be implied if they can be regarded as having acquiesced in such an act with knowledge of the circumstances, even in the absence of a formal meeting.[59] But it is unlikely that problems will arise in the agency contract, as the third party is protected by statute against unauthorised acts of directors.[60]

2–077   **Rule (4).** The principal cannot adopt the favourable parts of a transaction and disaffirm the rest: he cannot approbate and reprobate, for this would enable him to effect a transaction into which the third party had never intended to enter.[61] He must therefore adopt or reject the transaction *in toto* (though where an agent has effected several separate transactions, the principal may ratify certain transactions individually and refuse to ratify others[62]). This does not, however, mean that there are no circumstances whatever where he may ratify a transaction for one purpose while rejecting it for another. Thus in *Harrisons & Crossfield Ltd v. London and North Western Ry. Co.*[63] a principal whose servant had, while on sick leave, stolen, before the commencement of transit, consignments which the principal had been employed to carry, ratified the transaction to the extent of laying the possession in himself for the purpose of the law of larceny. It was held that he had not ratified so as to vest possession in himself under the contract of carriage, so as to make him liable as a common carrier for non-delivery.

2–078   **Rule (5).** Since authority to execute a contract required to be in writing or to be evidenced in writing need not be in writing,[64] it follows that ratification need not be in writing either.[65] But authority to execute

---

[57] *Grant v. U.K. Switchback Ry. Co.* (1888) 40 Ch.D. 135. *Cf. Boschoek Pty. Co. Ltd etc. v. Fuke* [1906] 1 Ch. 148.

[58] *Re Express Engineering Works Ltd* [1920] 1 Ch. 466; *Re Oxted Motor Co.* [1921] 3 K.B. 32.

[59] See Gower, *Modern Company Law* (5th ed.), pp. 134–138, 175–177.

[60] Companies Act 1985, ss. 35, 35A (substituted by Companies Act 1989, s. 110): below, paras. 8–038 *et seq.*

[61] See Illustration 10; cases cited at n. 26 above. But *cf. Langlands Foundry Co. Ltd v. Worthington Pumping Engine Co.* (1896) 22 V.L.R. 144.

[62] See *Fitzmaurice v. Bayley* (1860) 9 H.L.Cas. 78, 112; Illustration 10.

[63] [1917] 2 K.B. 755. See also *Kinsella v. Hamilton* (1890) 26 L.R.Ir. 671 (ratification of distress does not ratify homicide committed in course of it).

[64] Article 9.

[65] *Soames v. Spencer* (1822) 1 D. & R. 32; *Maclean v. Dunn* (1828) 4 Bing. 722; *Sheridan v. Higgins* [1971] I.R. 291.

a deed must be conferred by deed,[66] and hence ratification of such an action must equally be by deed.[67] But what appears to be a parol ratification may in fact amount to a second delivery[68]; and if a deed was not necessary for the transaction, the document executed may, be treated as a written instrument so that a parol ratification of it is valid.[69]

Illustrations

(1)   A shipmaster without authority of the owner sells his ship. The owners receive the purchase-money with full knowledge of the circumstances in which the ship was sold. The receipt of the purchase-money is a ratification of the sale.[70]

(2)   A is a bankrupt. B, at the request of A's wife, purchases certain bonds with A's money, and hands them to her. The trustee in bankruptcy seizes some of the bonds as part of A's estate. The trustee in bankruptcy has ratified the act of B, and thereby discharged him from liability in respect of money used for purchasing the other bonds.[71]

(3)   A is a bankrupt. B wrongfully sells part of A's property. The trustee in bankruptcy accepts the proceeds or part of them, or otherwise recognises B as his agent in the transaction. B is deemed to have been duly authorised by the trustee to sell the property.[72]

(4)   An agent purchases goods on behalf of his principal at a price exceeding his limit. The principal objects to the contract, but disposes of some of the goods as his own. He is deemed to have ratified the contract, and is bound by it.[73]

(5)   A employs a broker to execute a distress warrant. The broker, in executing the warrant, illegally seizes goods belonging to B. In answer to a letter from B demanding compensation, A writes that he is at a loss to understand the threat of proceedings, but that his solicitor will accept service of any process B thinks proper to issue. This reply is evidence of a ratification by A of the wrongful seizure.[74]

2–079

---

[66] Article 10. But authority to *deliver* a deed need no longer be given by deed: Law of Property (Miscellaneous Provisions) Act 1989, s. 1(c).

[67] See cases cited at n.27 above. They are not conclusive, but the proposition seems correct in principle.

[68] *Tupper v. Foulkes* (1861) 9 C.B.(N.S.) 797.

[69] *Hunter v. Parker* (1840) 7 M. & W. 322; *cf.* above, para. 2–041.

[70] *Hunter v. Parker*, n. 69 above; *cf. The Bonita, The Charlotte* (1861) Lush. 252, Illustration 6 to Article 16.

[71] *Wilson v. Poulter* (1724) 2 Str. 859.

[72] *Brewer v. Sparrow* (1827) 7 B. & C. 310; *Smith v. Baker* (1873) L.R. 8 C.P. 350; *cf. Valpy v. Sanders* (1848) 5 C.B. 887. See also *Gardiner v. Grigg* (1938) 38 S.R.(N.S.W.) 524 (adoption of sale by auctioneer with unauthorised warranty renders principal liable on warranty unless it was collateral).

[73] *Cornwal v. Wilson* (1750) 1 Ves. 510.

[74] *Carter v. St Mary Abbotts, Kensington, Vestry* (1900) 64 J.P. 548. *cf. Barrett v. Irvine* [1907] 2 I.R. 462 (negotiation for a compromise does not amount to ratification).

(6)   A receives the rents of certain property for many years without the authority of the owner (who is unknown, it not being clear who inherited the land on the death of the previous owners). The owner sues A for possession, and for an account of the rents and profits. The action is a sufficient ratification to render A the agent of the owner from the commencement.[75]

(7)   The chairman and deputy-chairman of directors, and the secretary, of a manufacturing company, respectively, ordered goods which were necessary for the purposes of the business of the company, and the goods were supplied and used therein. Held, that though the goods were ordered without authority, the directors must be taken to have known that they had been supplied and used in the business, and that therefore the company was liable for the price.[76]

(8)   A contracts to do certain specified repairs to a ship. An agent of the shipowner, whose authority is to the knowledge of A limited to the repairs so specified, sanctions certain variations in the work, and the repairs are executed according to the contract as varied. The shipowner sells the ship as repaired. The sale is not a ratification of the unauthorised variations.[77]

(9)   A ships goods to Calcutta and entrusts them to the captain of the ship to dispose of them as best he can in the interest of A, and to invest the proceeds in certain specified articles, or in bills at the exchange of the day. The captain sells the goods and invests the proceeds in unauthorised goods. A, on hearing of this, does nothing for 10 weeks, after which he attempts to repudiate the captain's act. A is bound by the sale.[78]

(10)   D, the managing owner of a ship, sells it, through a broker, without authority. The other owners formally ratify the sale and receive their shares of the purchase money. They are liable to the selling agent for commission, the employment of a broker being an essential part of the whole transaction.[79] But ratification by a joint owner of the sale of a house may not constitute ratification of the contract with the estate agent who effects the sale, for the house need not have been sold through such an agent and there is therefore no need to regard the acquiescence in one contract as covering the other.[80]

(11)   A, who was B's manager, fraudulently and without authority obtained from B's bankers, in exchange for cheques drawn by B upon

---

[75] *Lyell v. Kennedy* (1889) 14 App.Cas. 437.
[76] *Smith v. Hull Glass Co.* (1852) 11 C.B. 897; *Allard v. Bourne* (1863) 15 C.B.(N.S.) 468.
[77] *Forman & Co. Pty. Ltd v. The Liddesdale* [1900] A.C. 190.
[78] *Prince v. Clark* (1823) 1 B. & C. 186.
[79] *Keay v. Fenwick* (1876) 1 C.P.D. 745.
[80] *Hughes v. Hughes* (1971) 115 S.J. 911.

the bankers, drafts drawn by the bankers upon themselves, payable to bearer and crossed "not negotiable." A paid these drafts into an account which he had with the C Bank, and the C Bank collected the amounts. In an action by B against the C Bank for conversion of the drafts, held, that B must, in order to have a title to sue, ratify A's act in obtaining the drafts; but that B could not ratify this act without also ratifying A's payment of the drafts into his account with the C Bank, for the form of the drafts necessitated payment into some bank for collection; and that the action therefore failed.[81]

(12)   D instructs an estate agent to act in the sale of a house, no. 17. No. 7 is also on the agent's books. A purchaser wishing to acquire no. 7 is persuaded to sign a contract relating to no. 17 and to pay a deposit, on the agent's representation that the properties are the same. D objects to some of the terms of the contract and refuses to sign it. The agent refuses to return the deposit without an order from D. D by letter requests the agent to return the deposit but the agent again refuses. There is evidence from which it could be determined that D has ratified the agent's receipt of it and may be liable to repay it.[82]

Article 18

EVENTS NOT PREVENTING RATIFICATION

Ratification is effective—   **2–080**

(1)   although the person ratifying had refused at first to recognise the act,[83] unless to allow ratification would unfairly prejudice the third party[84];

(2)   although proceedings have been commenced against the person purporting to act as agent[85];

(3)   of a contract, notwithstanding that the third party has given notice to the principal of his withdrawal from it,[86] unless the contract was made by the agent expressly or impliedly subject

---

[81] *Union Bank of Australia v. McClintock* [1922] 1 A.C. 240: *Commercial Banking Co. of Sydney v. Mann* [1961] A.C. 1. But see Hornby (1961) 24 M.L.R. 271; Megrah [1961] J.B.L. 35; *Canadian Laboratory Supplies Ltd v. Englehard Industries of Canada Ltd* (1977) 78 D.L.R. (3d) 232, 236–237, 247; [1979] 2 S.C.R. 787, 801–804; (1979) 97 D.L.R. (3d) 1, 11–14.

[82] *Benham v. Batty* (1865) 12 L.T. 266.

[83] *Soames v. Spencer* (1822) 1 D. & R. 32; *Simpson v. Eggington* (1855) 10 Exch. 845; see Comment.

[84] See Comment; *cf. Restatement*, § 92(b).

[85] Illustration 4.

[86] *Bolton Partners v. Lambert* (1889) 41 Ch.D. 295, Illustration 1; *Re Tiedemann & Ledermann Frères* [1899] 2 Q.B. 66, Illustration 4 to Article 15.

to ratification, in which case the offer or purported acceptance may be withdrawn at any time before ratification. [87]

Comment

2–081   **Rule (1).** It has been held that where the principal refused to ratify, but, being nevertheless urged to do so, eventually did, he could sue the third party[88]: but that where he indicated that he would not do so, and the third party acted to his prejudice on that basis, the principal could not subsequently ratify.[89] It has also been held that an *uncommunicated* refusal to ratify can be reversed, so that the principal can take advantage of the act ratified.[90] In general it seems, therefore, that the rule is correctly expressed as above: a ratification may be effective against the principal though originally he refused to ratify, and also in his favour unless the third party has relied on a previous refusal in a way that would make a subsequent ratification unfairly prejudical. These conclusions seem better based on the rules as to limits on ratification than an estoppel, since there may be difficulties concerning representations of intention as founding estoppel. This reasoning seems best based on an analogy with the grant of preceding authority, which cannot be withdrawn as regards the transaction authorised once acted on: since the agent's action has already taken place, a ratification cannot without the consent of the other party be withdrawn. A refusal to ratify, on the other hand, is merely equivalent to a refusal to grant authority: this does not prevent a subsequent grant of authority, subject to the doctrine of estoppel. The other limitations on the power to ratify are of course also applicable.[91]

2–082   **Rule (2).** This proposition covers cases where ratification renders lawful an act which was initially a tort, notwithstanding that proceedings have been instituted against the agent prior to ratification: an example appears in Illustration 4. In the case of contract, there is authority that where proceedings have been commenced against a *principal*, he may ratify thereafter and so render himself liable.[92] But a purported

---

[87] *Watson v. Davies* [1931] 1 Ch. 455, Illustration 3; *Warehousing & Forwarding Co. of East Africa v. Jafferadi & Sons* [1964] A.C. 1: see Comment.

[88] *Soames v. Spencer* (1822) 1 D. & R. 32. See also *Akel v. Turner* [1926] G.L.R. 574 (N.Z.).

[89] See *McEvoy v. Belfast Banking Co. Ltd.* [1935] A.C. 24, 45.

[90] *Simpson v. Eggington* (1855) 10 Exch. 845.

[91] *e.g.* that the ratification must be within a reasonable time: though this may also be based in estoppel. See in general Comment to Article 19.

[92] *Richardson v. Oxford* (1861) 2 F. & F. 449.

ratification by the principal after the commencement of proceedings against the *agent* would sometimes not be within a reasonable time[93] and so inoperative against a third party who did not wish to take advantage of it.[94]

Rule (3). This proposition is an application of the technical notion **2–083** that ratification is retroactive and relates back to the time of the act ratified. *Omnis ratificatio retrotrahitur ac priori mandato aequiparatur.* It is often called the rule in *Bolton Partners v. Lambert*,[95] a leading case which appears as Illustration 1. Such a rule is rejected in the *Restatement*,[96] and the case has been criticised as giving an inappropriately full effect to the doctrine of relation back.[97] The third party is in the power of the principal, not merely as to whether he had made a contract, but also as to whether he must already answer for breach of it. Furthermore, when the third party discovers before any ratification that the agent is unauthorised, it may well be argued that he should be able to escape from the transaction rather than have to wait, if only for a reasonable time, to see if he has a contract. In *Fleming v. Bank of New Zealand*[98] the Privy Council reserved the right to reconsider the case. It is certainly true that the judgments in *Bolton Partners v. Lambert* itself consist largely of assertion. It is also true that the rule can only work fairly if it is made the subject of exceptions which are extremely difficult to formulate. This difficulty perhaps casts some doubt on the initial rule.

It is in any case clear that where a contract is made expressly or impliedly subject to ratification, it is not binding at all and there is nothing to ratify.[99] Such an interpretation can be put on most cases where the third party is aware of the lack of authority, whatever the reasons for it. The purported ratification, would in fact simply create the contract, unless the other party had previously withdrawn. The case is

---

[93] See Article 19.

[94] Except as regards the rules relating to mitigation of damages.

[95] (1889) 41 Ch.D. 295, Illustration 1. See also *Re Portuguese Consolidated Copper Mines Ltd* (1890) 45 Ch.D. 16, Illustration 4 to Article 19; *Hooper v. Kerr, Stuart & Co. Ltd* (1901) 83 L.T. 729, Illustration 2 to Article 20; *Koenigsblatt v. Sweet* [1923] 2 Ch. 314.

[96] § 88.

[97] Wambaugh (1895) 9 Harvard L.Rev. 60; Fry, *Specific Performance* (6th ed.), Additional Note A; Seavey (1920) 29 Yale L.J. 859, 890–891; Tamaki (1941) 19 Can.B.R. 733; Pappas (1948) 2 Vand.L.Rev. 100; Hambrook (1982) 8 Adelaide. L.Rev. 119, 134–140; *Restatement,* reporter's note to § 88.

[98] [1900] A.C. 577, 587. See the elaborate dissenting judgment of Isaacs J. in *Davison v. Vickery's Motors Ltd* (1925) 37 C.L.R. 1 and cases and dicta there cited.

[99] *Watson v. Davies* [1931] 1 Ch. 455, Illustration 3; *Warehousing and Forwarding Co. of East Africa v. Jafferali & Sons* [1964] A.C. 1. The judgment in the latter case is not easy to follow. It distinguishes between negotiating subject to approval and contracting subject to ratification. Obviously in the first case the details of the proposed agreement may be vaguer, but in neither case is there any transaction binding the third party.

the same as that where the agent does not purport to have authority.[1] The third party's promise is simply one to keep an offer open and unless there is independent consideration does not bind him. Although it is possible to enter into a contract which binds in the sense that neither party may withdraw from the moment of agreement, but the main obligation does not come into operation unless certain events occur,[2] it is difficult to see that such a contract can be found to exist where the condition relates to the question whether one purported party is bound at all.

It seems also that the rule in *Bolton Partners v. Lambert* is one of agency law only and to be restricted to cases of lack of authority. If the original agreement is ineffective for any other reason (*e.g.* lack of a deed) there is no contract to withdraw from and the doctrine of relation back does not apply.[3]

It has further been held that where the act the subject of purported ratification ceases to be operative before ratification, there is nothing to ratify.[4] The case in question involved unauthorised payment of a debt, and it was said that in such a case the party to whom the debt was paid was entitled to return the money on discovering that the payment had been unauthorised, and apply to his debtor for payment.[5]

Illustrations

2–084   (1)   A made an offer to B, the managing director of a company, and it was accepted by him on the company's behalf. B has no authority to accept the offer. A then gave the company notice that he withdrew his offer, and the company subsequently ratified B's unauthorised acceptance. Held, that the ratification dated back to the time of the acceptance, rendering the withdrawal of the other inoperative. Specific performance was decreed against A.[6]

(2)   A, without B's authority, pays a debt owing by B. The creditor, upon discovering that A was not authorised to pay the debt, returns the

---

[1] *Contra*, Seavey, (1954) 21 U.Chi.L.Rev. 248; *Restatement*, § 85, comment *e*; *cf.* Twerski (1948) 42 Temple L.Q. 1. See *Goodison Thresher Co. v. Doyle* (1925) 57 O.L.R. 300.

[2] See Treitel, *Law of Contract* (9th ed.), pp. 58 *et seq.*

[3] *Kidderminster Corp. v. Hardwick* (1873) L.R. 9 Ex. 13, 22 (followed in *Oxford v. Crow* [1893] 3 Ch. 535) as explained in *Athy Guardians v. Murphy* [1896] 1 I.R. 65. However, *Kidderminster Corp. v. Hardwick* was not referred to in *Bolton Partners v. Lambert* and the approaches of the two cases are not easily reconciled. If the reasoning in *Athy Guardians v. Murphy* is correct, it could also be used to explain *Metropolitan Asylums Board v. Kingham & Sons*, below, Illustration 5 to Article 19.

[4] *Walter v. James* (1871) L.R. 6 Ex. 124, Illustration 2; see Birks and Beatson (1976) 92 L.Q.R. 188 esp. at pp. 190 *et seq.*

[5] At p. 127.

[6] *Bolton Partners v. Lambert* (1889) 41 Ch.D. 295.

money to him. B cannot subsequently ratify, or take advantage of, the payment.[7]

(3) A offers land to a charity at a certain price. The chairman and 14 of the 18 members of the board of the charity visit the property. They tell A that they have all made up their minds to purchase it and that a board meeting to be summoned to approve the purchase will be a mere formality. A may withdraw before the meeting, and a purported ratification by the meeting is ineffective, there being no initial agreement which can be ratified.[8]

(4) An agent, after the death of his principal, distrained in the principal's name for rent due. Held, that the executor might ratify the distress, and so justify the agent, although an action was at the time of the ratification pending against the agent for the trespass, and although the distress was levied before probate.[9]

Article 19

LIMITS ON RATIFICATION

Ratification is not effective where to permit it would unfairly prejudice a third party, and in particular—   **2–085**

(1) where it is essential to the validity of an act that it should be done within a certain time, the act cannot be ratified after the expiration of that time, to the prejudice of any third party[10];

(2) the ratification of a contract can only be relied on by the principal if effected within a time after the act ratified was done which is reasonable in all the circumstances.[11]

Comment

Rule (1): property rights. The clearest cases that can be cited for this proposition are based on property reasoning: that "an estate once vested cannot be divested ... by the application of the doctrine of   **2–086**

---

[7] *Walter v. James*, n. 4 above. But see as to this case Birks and Beatson (1976) 92 L.Q.R. 188, esp. at pp. 190 *et seq.*

[8] *Watson v. Davies* [1931] 1 Ch. 455.

[9] *Whitehead v. Taylor* (1839) 10 A. & E. 210; see also *Foster v. Bates* (1843) 12 M. & W. 226; *Hull v. Pickersgill* (1819) 1 B. & B. 282.

[10] Illustrations 1–3; *Lord Audley v. Pollard* (1597) Cro.Eliz. 561; *Restatement,* § 90.

[11] *Re Portuguese Consolidated Copper Mines Ltd* (1890) 45 Ch.D. 16, Illustration 4; *Celthene Pty. Ltd v. W.K.J. Hauliers Pty. Ltd* [1981] 1 N.S.W.L.R. 606, 615; *Life Savers (Australasia) Ltd v. Frigmobile Pty. Ltd* [1983] 1 N.S.W.L.R. 431, 438; *Trident General Insurance Co. v. McNiece Bros. Pty. Ltd* (1987) 8 N.S.W.L.R. 270, 282 (affd. on other grounds (1988) 165 C.L.R. 107).

ratification."[12] Perhaps it could be said more generally that the location of property interests should not be uncertain. Examples of its operation appear in the Illustrations. To take some of these *seriatim*, it may indeed be desirable that lessees should know where they stand as regards notice to quit, and that landlords should not be able to affect their tenure by ratifying unauthorised and so invalid notices after the time has expired, the situation in Illustration 1; and that a surviving partner who has three months to decide whether or not to exercise an option to buy a deceased partner's share should not be able to extend that period by considering whether to ratify an unauthorised act by his agent, as in Illustration 2. These cases concern the status of interests in land. But it has been argued that the validity of stoppage in transit effected during the transit, but ratified after the transit, should not be covered by the rule in *Bolton Partners v. Lambert*, since commercial expectations in a situation like *Bird v. Brown*,[13] Illustration 3, would surely be that the goods would be stopped pending receipt of authority.[14] *Bird v. Brown* is, however, a leading case, and also involves property reasoning, though in respect of chattels, in that exercise of the right affected the property of the insolvent debtor and hence his creditors. Despite animadversions on some of the reasoning in it,[15] *Bird v. Brown* it is usually in fact cited as the main source of this exception.[16] It will often, no doubt, be possible to establish that there was existing authority in such a case,[17] and it is probably by the implication of pre-existing authority that difficult cases are likely to be solved.

2–087   **Rule as to time limits?** The question then arises whether the exception prohibiting ratification after the expiry of a time limit applies in situations other than those where the ratification would, if permitted, affect property rights. There is considerable authority that it does, and in the recent case of *Presentaciones Musicales S.A. v. Secunda*[18] this

---

[12] *Bolton Partners v. Lambert* (1889) 41 Ch.D. 295, 307 *per* Cotton L.J.; *Bird v. Brown* (1850) 4 Exch. 786.
[13] Above, n. 12.
[14] Stoljar, pp. 195–196.
[15] *Keighley, Maxsted & Co. v. Durant* [1901] A.C. 240, 247, 248.
[16] See *Bolton Partners v. Lambert*, n. 12 above; *Dibbins v. Dibbins* [1896] 2 Ch. 348, 352.
[17] See *Hutchings v. Nunes* (1863) 1 Moo.P.C.(N.S.) 243, where the court apparently held that an agent already had general authority, despite the fact that his acts were ratified after the end of transit.
[18] [1994] Ch. 271, Illustration 6. See Brown, (1994) 110 L.Q.R. 531. In addition to the cases there cited, see *Shaw Savill & Albion Co. v. Timaru Harbour Board* (1888) 6 N.Z.L.R. 456, affd. on other grounds (1890) 15 App.Cas. 429 (see argument).

view was taken by two members of the Court of Appeal,[19] though the third[20] restricted the exception to cases involving property reasoning. The view preferred by the majority has quite frequently been justified by an assertion that the principal can only ratify an act if he could have performed that act at the time of ratification.[21] This, however, does not fit situations such as that where the principal is permitted to ratify a contract of insurance after loss,[22] which would therefore require to be regarded as exceptions based on commercial practice. As a rule, it seems unsatisfactory: and it is moreover not easy to square with *Bolton Partners v. Lambert*[23] itself, where it was not referred to. It seems better therefore to speak in terms of a "time limits" rule, which directs attention towards the purpose of the limit in question; and to abandon the rule regarding the time of ratification, which does not fit the insurance cases.[24]

A viable "time limits" rule seems to require reference to the purpose of the limit in question, and in this context reference to validity has been found useful.[25] It can be said that where it is essential to the *validity* of an act that it should be done within a certain time it cannot be ratified after that time to the prejudice of the third party (for if the third party actually wishes to accept the ratification there can be no objection to it). It can then be said that the making of a contract for another without authority is not a totally invalid act and so can be ratified, as in *Bolton Partners v. Lambert* itself[26]; and in *Presentaciones Musicales S.A. v. Secunda*[27] it was held that since an unauthorised issue of a writ was, like other cases where there is a defect in a writ, not a complete nullity,[28] it could be ratified after the expiration of the limitation period applicable to the cause of action so as to make the period run from the date of the issue.

Another factor that could be borne in mind in this connection is the extent to which the third party is put into a state of uncertainty as to

---

[19] Dillon and Nolan L.JJ.; particular reliance was placed on *Ainsworth v. Creeke* (1868) L.R. 4 C.P. 476, a case on a borough poor-rate.

[20] Roch L.J.

[21] *Bird v. Brown* (1850) 4 Exch. 786, 799; *Ainsworth v. Creeke* (1868) L.R. 4 C.P. 476, 486, 487; *Williams v. North China Insurance Co.* (1876) 1 C.P.D. 757, 764 (*arguendo*), 766. But the argument was rejected in *Hooper v. Kerr, Stuart & Co. Ltd* (1900) 83 L.T. 729.

[22] Below, para. 2–089.

[23] Above, para. 2–083.

[24] Para. 2–089.

[25] See *Presentaciones Musicales S.A. v. Secunda*, n. 18 above, at pp. 279–280.

[26] See *Bolton Partners v. Lambert* (1889) 41 Ch.D. 295, 309.

[27] n. 18 above.

[28] *Danish Mercantile Co. Ltd v. Beaumont* [1951] Ch. 680; *Alexander Ward & Co. Ltd v. Samyang Navigation Co. Ltd* [1975] 1 W.L.R. 673; and see *Pontin v. Wood* [1962] 1 Q.B. 594.

whether the principal will ratify by the unauthorised act, which may lead to his prejudice. If there is such uncertainty, this would be a reason for regarding the act as invalid and hence disallowing ratification as against the third party. This point is much discussed in the old cases on notices to quit,[29] though, as has been said, these can be explained on the basis of property reasoning, in that the leasehold terminates on the expiry of the period set by a valid notice.[30]

If this reasoning is developed, it can be seen that in the case of an unauthorised contract, the third party is protected by the agent's warranty of authority[31] on which he can sue if the principal does not ratify: hence allowing ratification is not unduly prejudicial. In the case of unauthorised legal proceedings, he is protected by the fact that costs would be awarded against a person initiating proceedings without authority.[32] But in the case of unauthorised notices to quit, an alternative remedy against the agent is not easily justifiable. Although in a leading case on unauthorised legal proceedings, *Yonge v. Toynbee*[33] (which in fact concerned unauthorised defence of proceedings) the reasoning for the solicitor's liability proceeded on the basis of warranty of authority reasoning, this was for the purpose of establishing that he was liable though innocent, and the award of costs was made under the court's jurisdiction over solicitors: it is not easy what consideration could be found for a *contractual* promise toward the defendant by a person issuing a writ or defending proceedings. It seems equally difficult to apply breach of warranty of authority reasoning to unauthorised notices to quit. However, this argument does not justify the retrospective operation of ratification in connection with the statutes of limitation either, and it may be noted that the result of *Presentaciones Musicales S.A. v. Secunda* is contrary to that advocated by the *Restatement*.[34]

2–088   **Rule (2): reasonable time.** There is a dictum by Fry L.J. that "if the ratification is to bind it must be made within a reasonable time after acceptance by an unauthorised person."[35] Fry L.J. went on, however, to say that "such a reasonable time can never extend after the time at which the contract is to commence." This part of the dictum has been

---

[29] See esp. *Right* d. *Fisher, Nash and Hyrons v. Cuthell* (1804) 5 East 491; and the argument of Coleridge in *Doe* d. *Mann v. Walters* (1830) 10 B. & C. 626, 627–631; *Doe* d. *Lyster v. Goldwin* (1841) 2 Q.B. 143.

[30] See *Acona v. Marks* (1862) 7 H. & N. 686, 697.

[31] Article 107.

[32] See Cordery, *Solicitors* (8th ed.), pp. 93–94.

[33] [1910] 1 K.B. 215, Illustration 12 to Article 107. See also below, para. 10–026.

[34] See § 91 comment c.

[35] *Metropolitan Asylums Board v. Kingham & Sons* (1890) 6 T.L.R. 217, 218 (Illustration 5).

disapproved[36] and cannot now be regarded as valid.[37] The first part of the dictum seems, however, an appropriate restriction on ratification. It is proably best based on a wider principle, such as that suggested in the *Restatement*,[38] that "If the affirmance of a transaction occurs at a time when the situation has so materially changed that it would be inequitable to subject the other party to liability thereon, the other party has an election to avoid liability." In different words, the rule is one for the protection of the third party against whom the ratification might be invoked. If the principal ratifies and the third party actually wishes to rely on this, he should be entitled to do so. Where the third party wishes to resist ratification, the mere lapse of time may often make it inequitable[39]; but there may be other circumstances which do so. For a start, the third party who discovers that the agent was unauthorised may be put in a state of uncertainty in which a rapid indication by the principal of his position is required: it would then behove the principal to ratify quickly or not at all. And it is sometimes said that if an agent contracts without authority to sell property to another, and the property is then destroyed without anyone's fault, the principal can no longer ratify.[40]

Ratification of policies of insurance after loss. It has, however, long 2–089
been established that a policy of marine insurance may be ratified after loss[41]: this was justified on the basis that "where an agent effects an insurance subject to ratification, the loss insured against is very likely to happen before ratification, and it must be taken that the insurance so effected involves that possibility as the basis of the contract."[42] It has been controversial whether this principle applies to other insurances also, but it has recently been held that it does,[43] and this seems correct.

---

[36] *Celthene Pty. Ltd v. W.K.J. Hauliers Pty. Ltd* [1981] 1 N.S.W.L.R. 606, 615; *Life Savers (Aust.) Pty. Ltd v. Frigmobile Pty. Ltd* [1983] 1 N.S.W.L.R. 431, 438; *Bedford Insurance Co. Ltd v. Instituto de Resseguros do Brasil* [1983] Q.B. 966, 987. See also *Morrell v. Studd and Millington* [1913] 2 Ch. 648.
[37] It is extremely difficult to reconcile with *Bolton Partners v. Lambert* itself. Fry L.J. was a declared opponent of the rule in any case: see Fry, *Specific Performance* (6th ed.), Additional Note A.
[38] § 89.
[39] In *Trident General Insurance Co. Ltd. v. McNiece Bros. Pty. Ltd* (1987) 8 N.S.W.L.R. 270, 282–283 it was held that ratification *against* an insurer was not valid seven years after the making of the policy. The case was affirmed on other grounds, (1988) 165 C.L.R. 107.
[40] See *Williams v. North China Insurance Co.* (1876) 1 C.P.D. 757, 770; *Restatement*, § 98; but *cf.* Stoljar, p. 196.
[41] *Routh v. Thompson* (1811) 13 East 275; *Hagedorn v. Oliverson* (1814) 2 M. & S. 485; *Jardine v. Leathley* (1863) 3 B. & S. 700.
[42] At pp. 764–765; see also p. 770.
[43] *Trident General Insurance Co. v. McNiece Bros. Pty. Ltd* (1987) 8 N.S.W.L.R. 270, 280–281; (decision affirmed on other grounds (1988) 165 C.L.R. 107); *National Oilwell (U.K.) Ltd v. Davy Offshore Ltd* [1993] 2 Lloyd's Rep. 582.

If the commercial background dictates that if policies are entered into on this basis, it is not inequitable to hold the insurer liable. [44]

Illustrations

2–090   (1)   A, without the authority of the landlord, gives a tenant notice to quit. The notice cannot be made binding on the tenant by the landlord's ratification after the time for giving notice has expired. [45]

(2)   It is agreed between A and B, who are partners, that on the death of either of them the survivor shall have the option of purchasing the share of the deceased upon giving notice to the executors within three months after the death. A dies, and within three months after his death, C, on B's behalf, but without his authority, gives notice to the executors of B's intention to exercise the option. Such notice cannot be ratified after the expiration of the three months so as to bind the executors. [46]

(3)   The agent of a consignor of goods, without the authority of his principal, gave notice of stoppage in transit on the principal's behalf. The goods afterwards arrived at their destination, and were formally demanded by the trustee in bankruptcy of the consignee. It was held that the consignor could not subsequently ratify the stoppage in transit and so divest the property in the goods, which had in the meantime vested in the consignee's trustee in bankruptcy. [47]

(4)   Directors of a company purport to allot shares by procedures which are not valid. The allottees complain but do not repudiate the allotments. In the circumstances, ratification of the allotments by the company several months later may be valid. [48]

(5)   A corporation advertises for tenders for the supply of eggs for six months from September 30. K puts in a tender, and on September 22 the board of the corporation resolves to accept it and notifies K. On September 24 K writes that he had made a mistake in drawing up his tender and inserted the wrong price. On October 6 the corporation ratifies the acceptance by affixing its common seal. The ratification is ineffective. [49]

(6)   A solicitor issues a writ without authority, within the period of limitation applicable for the proceedings in question. The person on

---

[44] *cf. Restatement*, § 89 comment *c*.

[45] *Doe* d. *Mann v. Walters* (1830) 10 B. & C. 626; *Doe* d. *Lyster v. Goldwin* (1841) 2 Q.B. 143; *Right* d. *Fisher, Nash and Hyrons v. Cuthell* (1804) 5 East 491.

[46] *Dibbins v. Dibbins* [1896] 2 Ch. 348; *Hughes v. NM Superannuation Pty. Ltd* (1993) 29 N.S.W.L.R. 653. See also *Holland v. King* (1848) 6 C.B. 727.

[47] *Bird v. Brown* (1850) 4 Exch. 786; see Comment.

[48] *Re Portuguese Consolidated Copper Mines* (1890) 45 Ch.D. 16.

[49] *Metropolitan Asylums Board v. Kingham & Sons* (1890) 6 T.L.R. 217; see Comment.

whose behalf the writ was issued ratifies the issue of the writ after the period of limitation has expired. The ratification is effective.[50]

Article 20

EFFECT OF RATIFICATION

(1) The effect of ratification is to invest the person on whose behalf the act ratified was done, the person who did the act, and third parties, with the same rights, duties, immunities and liabilities in all respects as if the act had been done with the previous authority of the person on whose behalf it was done[51]; subject to the agent's liability to the third party for any loss caused by this breach of the warranty of authority, and to his principal for loss caused by his breach of duty except in so far as this has been waived as between them.[52] **2–091**

(2) But the doctrine of ratification may not be invoked to divest or affect prejudicially any proprietary or possessory right vested in any third party at the time of the ratification.[53]

(3) Ratification does not of itself give any new authority to the person whose act is ratified.[54]

(4) A ratification once effected cannot be withdrawn without the consent of the third party.[55]

Comment

Rule (1) is a general statement of the effect of a valid ratification and to a certain extent overlaps with the introductory Article 13. Thus where A, on behalf of P, but without authority, makes a contract with T, and P ratifies the contract, the normal effects of such ratification will be as follows: **2–092**

(i) P and T can enforce the contract against each other as though it had been originally authorised, even though T has meanwhile purported to withdraw from the contract.[56]

(ii) Although in general A remains liable to T for any breach of warranty of authority, it will not normally be possible for T to

---

[50] *Presentaciones Musicales S.A. v. Secunda* [1994] Ch. 271; see Comment.
[51] See *Wilson v. Tunman and Fretson* (1843) 6 M. & G. 236; *Bird v. Brown* (1850) 4 Exch. 786; Illustrations 1 to 5.
[52] See Comment.
[53] Above, para. 2–086; Illustration 9; *Re Gloucester Municipal Election Petition, 1900, Ford v. Newth* [1901] 1 K.B. 683; *Restatement*, § 101(a).
[54] Illustration 10; but *cf. Restatement*, § 43(2).
[55] *cf. Restatement*, § 102.
[56] See above, para. 2–083.

prove damages[57]: A is thus no longer liable to T unless he contracted personally.[58] If, however, he has caused loss to the third party, *e.g.* because the third party has taken advice as to, or even instituted proceedings against him, A might be liable to that extent, subject to the possible duty of the third party to mitigate his damages on ratification,[59] if the ratification was not too late.[60]

(iii) In general it may be said that A is not liable to P for exceeding his authority,[61] for the doctrine of ratification normally contemplates a principal who is glad to waive the technical irregularity and adopt the transaction. This may however not always be so; a principal may ratify a transaction for convenience, or to preserve his commercial reputation, or even from commercial necessity. It is necessary therefore "to consider the matter in two stages. First, is there ratification of the contract which the agent purported to make. Secondly, has the principal waived the breach of duty if any *vis-à-vis* the agent. Often the facts will lead to ratification and exoneration, but not always."[62]

(iv) Equally, in many cases, by ratifying, P may be regarded as accepting an offer by the agent to act as his agent in a manner not previously authorised, on the normal basis as to remuneration, reimbursement and indemnity. Hence P may be liable to pay A such sum in respect of remuneration as A would have been entitled to had the contract been authorised[63] and must reimburse and indemnify A in respect of the transaction.[64] Conversely, A also becomes a fiduciary retrospectively if he was not previously so. But again, where P's ratification is not voluntary, it is submitted that he may ratify but not waive the agent's breach or accept any offer by the agent. In such a case

---

[57] Article 108.

[58] See Article 100.

[59] The proposition contained in *Restatement* § 338, Illustration 2, depends on the supposition that ratification after breach is not permitted: see § 88. This is not so in English law: see above and McGregor, *Damages* (15th ed.), §§ 682, 695.

[60] Article 19.

[61] *Smith v. Cologan* (1788) 2 T.R. 188n.; Illustrations 6, 7; *Union Bank of Australia Ltd v. Rudder* (1911) 13 C.L.R. 152.

[62] *Suncorp Insurance and Finance v. Milano Assicurazion: SpA* [1993] 2 Lloyd's Rep. 225, 234–235 *per* Waller J. See also *Restatement*, § 416; Mechem, *Treatise on the Law of Agency*, (2nd ed.), §§ 492–493; *Mineworkers' Union v. Brodrick* 1948 (2) S.A.L.R. 959, 979; *Delco Australia Pty. Ltd v. Darlington Futures Ltd* (1986) 43 S.A.S.R. 519, revsd. on other grounds (1986) 161 C.L.R. 500.

[63] *Keay v. Fenwick* (1876) 1 C.P.D. 745, Illustration 10 to Article 17; *Mason v. Clifton* (1863) 3 F. & F. 899.

[64] Illustrations 3, 7, 8; *Hartas v. Ribbons* (1889) 22 Q.B.D. 254; Article 64.

the agent may by virtue of the terms of his contract or because of the gravity of his breach be entitled to no payments at all, and the principal may have a valid claim in damages.

(v) Any title acquired by P relates back to the moment of ratification.[65]

Rule (2) has already been considered in connection with time limits. **2–093**
Where an act to be effective must be done within a certain time (*e.g.* the exercise of an option, or of the right of stoppage in transit), to allow a ratification to operate after that time would be to prejudice rights vested in the other party, or in third parties. But the principle as stated here is wider and can apply to proprietary rights vested in persons not connected with the instant transaction at all,[66] or cases where the right is hardly of a proprietary nature, such as the interests of electors or candidates in avoiding corruption in local elections.[67] Such cases will, however, be rare.

Rule (3) may seem obvious: it confines ratification to the act done, **2–094**
though doubtless ratification may be evidence of some other authority.[68]
It is this rule which makes it difficult to say loosely that ratification creates agency, for it is clear that if it did, an authority would be set up that might thereafter need revocation.

Rule (4). Once a contract is validly ratified, it is binding. The third **2–095**
party may agree to rescind it, but the ratifying principal has no unilateral power to dissolve the contract once he has affirmed it. But it may be that where the ratification has been induced by a misrepresentation by the third party, the contract may be rescinded.[69] Similar reasoning will apply in other situations of ratification.

Illustrations

(1) A, on B's behalf, but without his authority, distrains goods **2–096**
belonging to C. B ratifies the distress. If B had a right to distrain, A is discharged from liability, then the ratification having a retroactive effect, and rendering the distress lawful *ab initio*.[70] If B had no right to distrain, A and B are jointly and severally liable as trespassers.[71]

---

[65] *Lawson v. Hosemaster Co. Ltd* [1966] 1 W.L.R. 1300, 1314.
[66] Illustration 9.
[67] *Re Gloucester Municipal Election Petition, 1900, Ford v. Newth* [1901] 1 K.B. 683; this is perhaps a doubtful case.
[68] See above, para. 2–047.
[69] See *Restatement*, § 100, comment *c*.
[70] *Whitehead v. Taylor* (1839) 10 A. & E. 210; *Hull v. Pickersgill* (1819) 1 B. & B. 282.
[71] See *Bird v. Brown* (1850) 4 Exch. 786, 799.

(2) The secretary of a company, without the authority of the directors, sends out a notice purporting to have been issued by order of the board, convening an extraordinary general meeting, a requisition for such meeting having been duly served on the company in accordance with the articles of association. At a board meeting held two days before the date for which the general meeting is called, the directors resolve to ratify and confirm the issuing of the notice by the secretary. The notice is thereby rendered valid, and the meeting is duly summoned. [72]

(3) A insures goods, in which he has no insurable interest, on behalf of B. B, who has an insurable interest in goods, ratifies the insurance. The insurable interest of B is sufficient to support an action by A on the policy, [73] and B is liable for the premium. [74]

(4) A factor contracts to purchase goods on his principal's behalf at a price exceeding his limit. The principal ratifies the contract by disposing of the goods. He must pay the factor the full price. [75]

(5) A buys goods from T on behalf of P without authority. P pays A and ratifies the transaction. It turns out that the goods had been fraudulently disposed of prior to the transaction by the captain of the ship on which they had been. P may not sue A. [76]

(6) A firm of carriers, employed to deliver goods to A, delivers them to B. The senders invoice the goods to B, sue him for the price, recover judgment and take bankruptcy proceedings against him. They may not subsequently sue the carriers for misdelivery. [77]

(7) A shipmaster entered into contracts with the Admiralty for the transport of troops, and paid and incurred various sums and liabilities to enable him to perform the contracts, the shipowner being bankrupt and having mortgaged the vessel. Held, that the master had a right to be repaid the expenses and indemnified against the liabilities, out of the freight due from the Admiralty, the assignees in bankruptcy and mortgagees not being entitled to take the benefit of the contract, unless they also adopted the burdens connected therewith. [78]

(8) An agent who is personally liable unsuccessfully defends an action brought against him for breach of an unauthorised contract

---

[72] *Hooper v. Kerr, Stuart & Co. Ltd* (1901) 83 L.T. 729.

[73] *Wolff v. Horncastle* (1798) 1 B. & P. 316.

[74] *New Zealand Insurance Co. Ltd v. Tyneside Pty. Ltd* [1917] N.Z.L.R. 569.

[75] *Cornwal v. Wilson* (1750) 1 Ves. Sen. 510. And see *Brice v. Wilson* (1834) 8 A. & E. 349 (relatives of deceased order extravagant funeral: ratifying executor personally liable); *cf. Lucy v. Walrond* (1837) 3 Bing. N.C. 841.

[76] *Risbourg v. Bruckner* (1858) 3 C.B.(N.S.) 812. The case is complicated by the foreign principal rule (below, para. 9–018); and there may have been prior authority.

[77] *Verschures Creameries Ltd. v. Hull & Netherlands S.S. Co.* [1921] 2 K.B. 608; see explanation in *United Australia Ltd v. Barclays Bank Ltd* [1941] A.C. 1, 31 and criticism in Goff and Jones, *Law of Restitution* (4th ed.) p. 733, n. 38.

[78] *Bristow v. Whitmore* (1861) 9 H.L.Cas. 391.

entered into by him on behalf of his principal. The principal ratifies what he has done. The principal must indemnify the agent against the damages and costs recovered by the plaintiff in the action.[79] So, where a person is made a party to an action without his authority, he cannot avail himself of the benefit of the action, unless he pays the costs of conducting it.[80]

(9) A commodore in the navy, without authority to do so, appointed a captain. Held, that even if the Crown ratified the appointment, that would not give the commodore the right to share as a commodore with a captain under him, in prizes taken before the date of the ratification, because the rights to the various shares in those prizes would then be already vested.[81]

(10) The directors of a company borrow money in excess of the amount which they have power to borrow. This may be ratified by a simple majority of the shareholders at an extraordinary meeting. But such a ratification confers no further power to borrow in excess of the directors' powers: such power would require a vote of one-half of the shareholders in accordance with the terms of the articles.[82]

4.—AGENCY BY ESTOPPEL

Article 21

AGENCY BY ESTOPPEL

Where a person, by words or conduct, represents or permits it to   **2–097**
be represented that another person is his agent, he will not be permitted to deny the agency with respect to anyone dealing, on the faith of such representation, with the person so held out as agent, even if the relationship of principal and agent has not arisen in one of the ways specified in Article 3.[83]

Comment

Agency by estoppel. The salient feature of agency by estoppel is that   **2–098**
no agency, in the sense in which the word is used in this book, is actually created thereby: complete agency arises by agreement only. The

---

[79] *Frixione v. Tagliaferro & Sons* (1856) 10 Moo.P.C. 175. But in this case there may be have been prior authority. *Quaere* as to the extent to which this result would apply where the principal ratified a contract in respect of which the agent had already incurred expenditure in defending an action for breach of warranty of authority. There seems no reason why it should unless the principal was in some way in breach of his duty to the agent in not ratifying earlier.

[80] *Hall v. Laver* (1842) 1 Hare 571.

[81] *Donelly v. Popham* (1807) 1 Taunt. 1.

[82] *Irvine v. Union Bank of Australia* (1877) 2 App.Cas. 366. Though the third party lender would normally be protected by s. 35A of the Companies Act 1985 (added by Companies Act 1989, s. 108). See below, para. 8–038.

[83] *cf.* Article 74: see Comment.

principal may be estopped from denying that another is his agent, and his relationship with third parties may be affected by the acts of that other: but without more, *e.g.* ratification, the relationship of principal and agent does not arise between him and his apparent agent.

Cases do arise where a person not hitherto an agent for another may bind that other under the doctrine of estoppel. They are comparatively rare in contract situations, though one leading case concerning a managing director who acted as such without having been properly appointed is actually a case of this type.[84] The situation is more likely to arise in connection with dispositions of property by persons holding documents of title or other documents indicating a power to dispose of goods. But the cases mostly concern persons who already have some authority; and since the doctrine only affects the position between principal and third party they are dealt with in Chapter 8, which deals with that relationship, and are to some extent separated in accordance with whether the issue is one of contract[85] or property.[86] This Article therefore only appears here for the sake of completeness of exposition. The principles applicable are the same whether the situation is one of imposing liability in respect of acts of a person not an agent, or of the unauthorised acts of an agent. There may be one reservation: it may be that stronger evidence is sometimes required to establish a complete agency by estoppel, for a person who appoints an agent thereby puts himself on risk as to that agent's acts and owes a duty to others to prevent false and unauthorised acts. The duty to prevent an unauthorised person from purporting to act as one's agent may sometimes be a weaker one.

2–099   **Estoppel by subsequent conduct.** It is possible to have situations where a person is estopped by conduct from proving that a contract purportedly made on his behalf by a person who had no authority, actual or apparent, does not bind him.[87] This would be a more general application of estoppel doctrine and would not be appropriately described as creating agency by estoppel.

---

[84] *Freeman & Lockyer v. Buckhurst Park Properties (Mangal) Ltd* [1964] 2 Q.B. 480, Illustration 31 to Article 74.

[85] Article 74.

[86] Articles 85, 89.

[87] See *Spiro v. Lintern* [1973] 1 W.L.R. 1002, Illustration 34 to Article 74; *Worboys v. Carter* [1987] 2 EGLR 1; *Lease Management Services Ltd v. Purnell Secretarial Services Ltd* (1994) Tr.L.Rep. 337. See below, para. 8–030.

CHAPTER 3

AUTHORITY OF AGENTS

1.—ACTUAL AND APPARENT AUTHORITY

Article 22

TYPES OF AUTHORITY

(1) The authority of an agent may be   **3–001**

    (a) actual (express or implied) where it results from a manifestation of consent that he should represent or act for the principal expressly or impliedly made by the principal to the agent himself; or

    (b) apparent, where it results from such a manifestation made by the principal to third parties.[1]

(2) The propositions contained in Articles 23 to 32 relate directly to actual authority only; but they may also be relevant to the ascertainment of apparent authority.

Comment

The notion of authority is explained in Article 1 and this Article follows   **3–002**
the scheme there adopted. It has already been pointed out that the placing together of these very different types of authority can easily be criticised,[2] and this point is now due for further discussion.

Actual authority. Actual authority is the authority which the principal   **3–003**
has given the agent wholly or in part by means of words or writing (called here express authority) or is regarded by the law as having given him because of the interpretation put by the law on the relationship and dealings of the two parties (called here implied authority).

---

[1] See Comment and Article 1. As to apparent authority, see especially Articles 74, 85.
[2] Para. 1–012, above. See Falconbridge (1939) 17 Can.B.R. 248, 251–252. See also Seavey (1920) 29 Yale L.J. 859; Corbin (1934) 34 Yale L.J. 788.

"An 'actual' authority is a legal relationship between principal and agent created by a consensual agreement to which they alone are parties. Its scope is to be ascertained by applying ordinary principles of construction of contracts, including any proper implications from the express words used, the usages of the trade, or the course of business between the parties. To this agreement the contractor is a stranger: he may be totally ignorant of the existence of any authority on the part of the agent. Nevertheless, if the agent does enter into a contract pursuant to the 'actual' authority, it does create contractual rights and liabilities between the principal and the contractor."[3]

It is common to distinguish express actual authority from implied actual authority. The most obvious case of express authority is a power of attorney. In a commercial setting, express authority can also arise when the principal authorises the agent to do something "by express words, such as when a board of directors pass a resolution which authorises two of their members to sign cheques."[4] Letters conferring authority are also common. The most obvious cases of implied authority arise in the forms of incidental authority (implied authority to do whatever is necessarily or normally incidental to the activity expressly authorised[5]), usual authority (implied authority to do whatever an agent of the type concerned would usually have authority to do[6]) and customary authority (implied authority to act in accordance with such applicable business customs as are reasonable[7]); there is a further general category of implied authority arising from the course of dealing between the parties and the circumstances of the case.[8] But where the express authority is not clear the court will interpret it, and in this and other situations, whether the authority is to be regarded as express or implied is obviously a question susceptible of argument.

3–004   **Scope of this chapter.** This chapter deals primarily with actual authority, and the rules for determining what is and what is not to be regarded as actually authorised. The scope of an agent's authority may require to be investigated from the point of view of any of three relationships: (i) that of principal and third party dealing with the agent, (ii) that of principal and agent, and (iii) that of agent and third party. Thus where there is actual authority, the principal will prima facie be liable to, and entitled to sue, the third party on the agent's transactions, the principal may be liable to indemnify and reimburse the agent and/or

---

[3] *Freeman & Lockyer v. Buckhurst Park Properties (Mangal) Ltd* [1964] 2 Q.B. 480, 502, *per* Diplock L.J.
[4] *Hely-Hutchinson v. Brayhead Ltd* [1968] 1 Q.B. 549, 583.
[5] Article 27.
[6] Articles 29, 30.
[7] Article 31.
[8] Article 32.

entitled to proceeds received by the agent, and the agent will be free from liability for breach of warranty of authority to the third party. In this chapter no distinction is expressly made between these three relationships, to all of which the agent's actual authority may be relevant.

Apparent authority. The placing of apparent authority beside actual authority in this rule can easily be criticised, for the reasoning behind the doctrine of apparent authority involves the assumption that there is in fact no authority at all. Under this doctrine, where a principal represents, or is regarded by the law as representing, that another has authority, he may be bound as against a third party by the acts of that other person within the authority which that person appears to have, though he had not in fact given that person such authority or had limited the authority by instructions not made known to the third party.[9] "Ostensible or apparent authority is the authority of an agent as it *appears* to others."[10]

3–005

On the other hand, the term "apparent authority" is very frequently used, and a chapter on authority that did not mention it alongside actual authority would be misleading. It should, however, be remembered that, at any rate on the approach taken in the English cases,[11] the idea is significantly different from that of actual authority.

The notion of apparent authority is essentially confined to the relationship between principal and third party: the principal may under it be bound by unauthorised acts of the agent. He cannot sue unless he ratifies; and consideration of the other two relationships in cases where there is apparent authority proceeds from the starting-point that there is no actual authority. Therefore apparent authority is primarily dealt with in Chapter 8 on the relationship between principal and third party. The cases cited in this chapter are nevertheless relevant, as the authority which the third party is entitled to assume the agent has is in most situations the authority which would normally be implied between principal and agent in the circumstances. The actual and apparent authority will therefore normally coincide,[12] and it will often not matter which of the two notions is relied on: indeed, some of the cases cited in this chapter are decisions on apparent authority. In many nineteenth century cases, it is not possible to tell upon which doctrine the court bases its

---

[9] Article 74; *Freeman & Lockyer v. Buckhurst Park Properties (Mangal) Ltd* [1964] 2 Q.B. 480, 503.

[10] *Hely-Hutchinson v. Brayhead Ltd* [1968] 1 Q.B. 549, 583 *per* Lord Denning M.R. "Apparent authority, which negatives the existence of actual authority" (*Rama Corp v. Proved Tin & General Investments* [1952] 2 Q.B. 147, 149 *per* Slade J.) is, however, too extreme a statement. So, but in the other direction, is "The apparent authority is the real authority" (*Pickering v. Busk* (1812) 15 East 38, 43 *per* Lord Ellenborough C.J.).

[11] See below, para. 8–029.

[12] *Freeman & Lockyer v. Buckhurst Park Properties (Mangal) Ltd* [1964] 2 Q.B. 480, 502.

decision, and even in the cases that are clearly based on what is now called apparent authority, the authority is sometimes referred to as implied.[13] The isolation of the doctrine of apparent authority is not of long standing: it is only comparatively recently that a sharp distinction has been made in the English cases.[14]

The difference between them occurs in two main situations. First, there may be cases where there is an actual manifestation by the principal to the third party upon which the apparent authority is based, which may indicate something different from the authority which the agent would on general criteria impliedly have. Secondly, there may be apparent authority even though in fact as between principal and agent the agent does not have the implied authority which would be normal in the circumstances, either because the principal has, unknown to the third party, forbidden the act in question, or because of facts known to the agent which negate such authority. Thus a solicitor normally has implied authority to compromise a suit,[15] and hence apparent authority to do so. It could be offensive on the part of the other party's solicitor to demand evidence of authority: yet the first solicitor may have been told specifically not to act in this way, or may have knowledge of his clients's finances which would negate any possibility of his having implied authority to act in this way.[16]

3–006   **Usual authority.** A case can be made out for adding a third type of authority, usual authority.[17] This has been defined by one writer as "the authority which a person normally possesses in certain circumstances to act on behalf of another person, whether or not he is actually authorised so to act."[18]

Although there is no direct judicial support for the use of the term,[19] the idea referred to is found in three roles:

(i) *As a type of implied authority.* Many cases show that where an agent is put in a position which normally carried with it certain authority, he impliedly has such authority unless it is withdrawn from him.[20] Examples appear below. A person can in such circumstances be said to have "usual authority".

---

[13] *e.g. Brooks v. Hassall* (1883) 49 L.T. 569.
[14] See, *e.g. Ryan v. Pilkington* [1959] 1 W.L.R. 403, criticised by Powell, pp. 51–52 and finally disapproved by the House of Lords in *Sorrell v. Finch* [1977] A.C. 728.
[15] *Waugh v. H.B. Clifford & Sons Ltd* [1982] Ch. 374; and see Article 30, Illustration 5.
[16] *Waugh v. H.B. Clifford & Sons Ltd*, n. 15 above, at p. 387.
[17] See esp. Powell, Chap. II; Treitel, *Law of Contract* (9th ed.), pp. 633–635.
[18] Powell, p. 37.
[19] But see the cases cited by Powell at p. 41, n. 2. In none of them, however, does the term "usual authority" appear.
[20] Articles 29, 30.

(ii) *As a type of apparent authority*. Apparent authority seems to involve two types of case[21]: cases where there can be said to be something like a specific representation by the principal of the agent's authority, on which the third party relied, which could be called cases of "genuine apparent authority" and more easily based on estoppel; and cases where the only representation made by the principal is in putting the agent in a position carrying with it a usual authority as described above, where estoppel seems a somewhat less appropriate basis for the principal's liability. In both cases the principal is liable despite reservations in the authority uncommunicated to the third party: but the two could be differentiated as "apparent" and "usual" authority respectively. In this sense usual authority would have affinities with the "externalised" theories of civil law discussed earlier, under which the principal may be liable simply because he has permitted another to assume a recognised type of position in regard to him.[22]

(iii) *As an independent type of authority*. There is a small number of cases in which an *undisclosed* principal has been held liable on a contract made by his agent within such powers as would usually be possessed by a person in such a position, where that authority had in fact been withdrawn. The leading case is *Watteau v. Fenwick*,[23] where Wills J. said "The principal is liable for all the acts of his agent which are within the authority usually confided to an agent of that character, notwithstanding limitations, as between the principal and the agent, put upon such authority. It is said that this is only so where there has been a holding out of authority. ... But I do not think so." In view of the fact that the agent's authority was limited, these cases cannot be treated as based on actual authority: but since the principal was undisclosed, he can have made no representation to the third party, therefore the authority could not have been apparent. The cases can simply be criticised as incorrect[24] and may well be so. If however, they are to be supported on agency grounds they must either be treated as exceptional or as indicating an independent notion which could be called "usual authority".

It might then be possible to build on these cases to erect such a third type of authority, and to say that a principal is bound by the acts of his agent when that agent acts, not only within his actual or his apparent authority, but also when he acts within his usual authority.[25] This would provide perhaps the readiest framework for seeking to emancipate the principal's liability from notions of authorisation and reliance, a matter

---

[21] See Comment to Article 74.
[22] Above, para. 1–023.
[23] [1893] 1 Q.B. 346, discussed below, para. 8–078.
[24] Below, para. 8–078.
[25] *cf.* Powell, pp. 73 *et seq.*; Montrose (1939) 17 Can.B.R. 693; Treitel, *op. cit.* above, n. 17.

discussed earlier.[26] The extension would largely be in the area of undisclosed principals, but cases where the liability of a disclosed principal could be extended can be envisaged. "P appoints A as his general manager for the purchase of houses in Leeds, instructing A, however, not to disclose the existence of the agency and not to purchase except on a surveyor's report. A discloses his position to T, withholding, however, the requirement of a surveyor's report, and purchases houses in Leeds from T as agent for P without a surveyor's report."[27] Under this extended doctrine, but not readily otherwise, P might be bound.

The *Restatement* provides us in a somewhat vaguer way for the liability of a principal beyond the actual and apparent authority: "The liability of a principal to a third person upon a transaction conducted by an agent, or the transfer of his interests by an agent, may be based upon the fact that: (a) the agent was authorised; (b) the agent was apparently authorised; or (c) the agent had a power arising from the agency relation and not dependent upon authority or apparent authority."[28] The notion referred to under (c) is elsewhere described as "inherent agency power" and explained as follows[29]: "Inherent agency power is a term used in the restatement of this subject to indicate the power of an agent which is derived not from authority, apparent authority or estoppel, but solely from the agency relation and exists for the protection of persons harmed by or dealing with a servant or other agent."[30] This approach would accommodate not only the supposed doctrine of *Watteau v. Fenwick*[31] but also other intractable cases which a doctrine of usual authority would not, *viz.* cases where an agent has actual authority to effect a disposition of property but does so in a manner different from that authorised,[32] cases where the agent acts within his authority but for his own benefit,[33] and cases of apparent ownership.[34] But though this approach has been welcomed and approved by writers[35] and may provide a convenient

---

[26] Above, para. 1–024.

[27] Montrose, *op. cit.* n. 25 above at p. 711.

[28] § 140.

[29] § 8A.

[30] See comments to these sections and Reporter's notes to § 161; Seavey (1948) 1 U.Okla.L. Rev. 1 (1948); *Studies in Agency* (1949), p. 181.

[31] n. 23, above. Seavey said that the case was "based upon the theory that the principal is the principal and that because the agent is doing his work the principal ought to be liable": (1933) 13 Nebraska L. Bull. 55, 63.

[32] The supposed doctrine of *Brocklesby v. Temperance Building Society* [1895] A.C. 173: see Article 87 and Comment.

[33] See *Hambro v. Burnand* [1904] 2 K.B. 10, Illustration 1 to Article 76.

[34] See Article 86. Also the old cases on agency of necessity: see Article 35.

[35] Wright (1936) 1 U. Toronto L.J. 17, 40 *et seq.*; Falconbridge (1939) 17 Can.B.R. 248, 252 *et seq.* (more equivocal); Montrose, *ibid.*, 693; Munro (1958) 20 U. Pittsburgh L. Rev. 33; Mearns (1962) 48 Va.L.Rev. 50; Bester (1972) 89 S.A.L.J. 49.

receptacle into which to consign difficult decisions and fact situations, it is submitted that it is too vague to serve as a systematic basis for the formation and prediction of legal decisions.[36]

On the current trend of English case law,[37] it is clear that there is little support for any liability of the principal beyond the agent's actual or apparent authority except the dictum of Lord Wilberforce referred to in Chapter 1[38] and the dubious decision in *Watteau v. Fenwick*.[39] Recent judicial statements of the basic principles of agency are clearly based on the assumption that the principal is only bound where the agent had actual or apparent authority.[40] References to any notion of usual authority should therefore be made and interpreted with caution. As regards usual authority as a form of implied authority, it covers two different types of situation which, it is submitted, should be distinguished.[41] As to apparent authority, the two types referred to above, of specific and general representations[42] are in the cases both subsumed under the same heading and treated together,[43] being connected in a loose manner with estoppel: the "usual authority" cases are not separated off.[44] Further, to treat a type of actual authority and a type of apparent authority together may cause confusion.[45]

The notion of usual authority is nevertheless one that should be borne in mind; for the distinction between the two types of apparent authority is a significant one which illuminates various points of difficulty in the cases.

Authority of necessity. Emergencies may sometimes enlarge the implied authority of an agent. To some extent cases of such extended authority can be subsumed under the accepted heads of implied authority. But many old cases relating to the authority of an agent to act in an emergency contain reasoning linking them with the special but

3–007

---

[36] *cf.* Conant, (1968) 47 Neb.L.Rev. 678, 686: "so vague it can cause more analytical problems that it can solve."

[37] See above, para. 1–024. Dicta from older cases to a different effect can of course be found, for as in other areas nineteenth-century cases contain many lines of reasoning, not all of which were eventually settled on as being acceptable.

[38] Above, para. 1–024.

[39] n. 23 above.

[40] Above, para. 1–024.

[41] See Articles 29, 30.

[42] And see below, para. 8–018.

[43] *Freeman & Lockyer v. Buckhurst Park Properties (Mangal) Ltd* [1964] 2 Q.B. 480, 502–504; *Hely-Hutchinson v. Brayhead Ltd* [1968] 1 Q.B. 549. The same assumption is made in *Miles v. McIlwraith* (1833) 8 App.Cas. 120; *Att.-Gen. for Ceylon v. Silva* [1953] A.C. 461; and in *Eagle Star Insurance Co. Ltd v. Spratt* [1971] 1 Lloyd's Rep. 295; [1971] 2 Lloyd's Rep. 116.

[44] See below, para. 8-029.

[45] See *Freeman & Lockyer v. Buckhurst Park Properties (Mangal) Ltd*, n. 43 above, at p. 503.

limited doctrine of agency of necessity, whereby a person not previously an agent is by an emergency constituted an agent. The cases are dealt with together under that head in Chapter 4.

Article 23

AUTHORITY CANNOT EXCEED POWERS OF PRINCIPAL

3–008   The authority, express or implied, of every agent is confined within the limits of the powers of his principal.

Comment

3–009   This article is in effect a repetition of Article 4, which states that capacity to act as principal is co-extensive with the capacity of the principal to do the act himself, and reference should be made to the authorities there cited. Problems of capacity in relation to apparent authority are also discussed under Article 123. The proposition is, of course, only directly relevant to true agency situations where the agent brings the principal into relationship with the third party. There may be cases where a principal employs an intermediary to act in his own name without involving the principal directly, in circumstances where the principal could not act, *e.g.* because he was foreign, or lacked professional qualifications, and for that very reason. To such situations this Article is not relevant.

2.—EXPRESS ACTUAL AUTHORITY

Article 24

CONSTRUCTION OF POWERS OF ATTORNEY

3–010   Powers of attorney are strictly construed and are interpreted as giving only such authority as they confer expressly or by necessary implication.[46] The following are the most important rules of construction:

(1)   The operative part of a deed is controlled by the recitals where there is ambiguity.[47]

---

[46] *Bryant, Powis & Bryant v. La Banque du Peuple* [1893] A.C. 170, 177; *Withington v. Herring* (1829) 5 Bing. 442, 458; and see Illustrations. As to execution of deeds under powers of attorney, see Article 79.
[47] Illustration 1.

(2) Where authority is given to do particular acts, followed by general words, the general words are restricted to what is necessary for the proper performance of the particular acts.[48]

(3) General words do not confer general powers, but are limited to the purpose for which the authority is given, and are construed as enlarging the special powers only when necessary for that purpose.[49]

(4) The deed must be construed so as to include all incidental powers necessary for its effective execution.[50]

Comment

The term "power of attorney" is usually applied to a formal grant of **3–011** power to act made by deed or contained in a deed relating also to other matters. There was in fact no rule that agency must be created by deed, except where the agent himself is to be empowered to execute a deed, and it seems that such a power could at common law be granted by simple writing.[51] However the Powers of Attorney Act 1971, s. 1, requires that powers of attorney be executed under seal. The term "power of attorney" is not defined, but presumably means a formal grant of agency powers, often of a general nature. To such deeds the strict rule stated above applies: but to other conferring of authority, even where written, the laxer rules given in the following Articles apply.

It is worth nothing that the basic rule here given for powers of attorney is even contrary to the normal rule for deeds, which is that they are construed against the grantor.[52] A reason given is "because the rights of other persons may be affected",[53] though this does not seem very convincing since the rule will usually operate to the prejudice of those other persons. However, the normal rule favouring the grantee has behind it the idea of non-derogation from grant, a principle of the law of property which is not necessarily appropriate in situations of representation. As such the above rule has parallels with the specific requirements which exist in some countries that there be an express authorising clause for certain acts such as alienation of land, mortgage, etc.[54] The comparison should not however be pressed too far, for these rules may operate on agency powers of potentially greater generality than may be

---

[48] *Perry v. Holl* (1860) 2 De G.F. & J. 38, 48; Illustrations 2, 3.
[49] *Attwood v. Munnings* (1827) 7 B. & C. 278, 284; Illustrations 4–6, 8.
[50] *Howard v. Baillie* (1726) 2 H.Bl. 618, 619; Illustrations 7, 9.
[51] See Articles 9, 10. See also the definition above, para. 2–038
[52] See Stoljar, pp. 91–92.
[53] *Re Dowson and Jenkins' Contract* [1904] 2 Ch. 219, 223.
[54] *e.g.* French CC, art. 1988. See Müller-Freienfels in *Civil Law in the Modern World* (Yiannopoulos ed. 1965), 77, 100–102.

required in common law systems, which can make use of the trust to transfer powers.

In any case, the rule here seems well established in nineteenth-century cases, though the notion of protecting the principal as opposed to the third party, which seems to lie behind it, may be regarded now as being somewhat unfashionable, especially in the commercial sphere. The whole idea of strict construction is, indeed, inconsistent with the doctrine of apparent authority, which is now so prominent in the law of agency. [55] Many powers of attorney are however used in non-commercial situations such as absence abroad, illness or debility of the principal. It may be right in such circumstances to place a duty of inquiry on the third party. [56] And in the commercial sphere, powers of attorney tend to be drawn by lawyers and use technical wording which may be assumed to have been carefully chosen. Where an absolutely general power is required, all doubts can be avoided by using the form provided by section 10 of the Powers of Attorney Act 1971, which confers authority to do on behalf of the donor anything which he can lawfully do by attorney.

Extrinsic evidence that the agent was not intended to have these powers, or to have additional powers, will not normally be accepted. This is the more so since powers of attorney are required to be conferred by deed. Such evidence may however be admissible where the wording is ambiguous, or to prove custom. [57]

Illustrations

Rule (1)

3–012   (1)   A power of attorney recited that the principal was going abroad, and the operative part gave authority in general terms. Held, that the authority subsisted only during the principal's absence abroad. [58] But where the operative words are clear, they will prevail over a recital. [59]

Rule (2)

(2)   Power was given "to demand and receive all moneys due to the principal on any account whatsoever and to use all means for the recovery thereof, to appoint attorneys to bring actions, and to revoke such appointments, and to do all other business." Held, that "all other business" must be construed to mean all other business necessary for the

---

[55] See Stoljar, pp. 92–95.

[56] For a survey of the use of attorney in international practice see Eder (1950) 98 U.Pa.L.Rev. 840, who puts forward the view that "the burden of a badly drafted power of attorney should be cast on the principal, not on the third party" (p. 857).

[57] See Article 31.

[58] *Danby v. Coutts & Co.* (1885) 29 Ch.D. 500.

[59] *Rooke v. Lord Kensington* (1856) 2 K. & J. 753, 769.

recovery of the moneys, or in connection with it; and that the power of attorney gave the agent no authority to indorse a bill of exchange received by him under it. [60]

(3) A, who carried on business in Australia, gave an agent in England a power of attorney to purchase goods in connection with the business, either for cash or on credit, and where necessary in connection with any such purchases, or in connection with the business, to make, draw, sign, accept or indorse for him and on his behalf any bills of exchange or promissory notes which should be requisite or proper. It was held that the power of attorney gave no power to borrow money, and the agent, purporting to act in pursuance of the power, having given bills of exchange in respect of a loan, and misapplied the money, that A was not liable on the bills. [61]

Rule (3)

(4) A power of attorney "to recover and receive all sums of money owing ... by virtue of any security ... and to give, sign, and execute receipts, releases, or other discharges for the same, ... and to sell any real or personal property ... belonging" to the principal, does not authorise the agent to exercise the statutory power of sale of real property vested in the principal as a mortgagee. [62-63]

(5) An executor gave a power of attorney to transact in his name all the affairs of the testator. Held, that the agent had no authority to accept a bill of exchange in the name of the executor so as to bind him personally. [64]

(6) A power of attorney "from time to time to negotiate, make sale, dispose of, assign and transfer" gives no authority to pledge. [65] But a power "to sell, indorse and assign" authorises an indorsement to a bank as security for a loan to the agent; such a power being construed as giving (i) authority to sell, (ii) authority to indorse and (iii) authority to assign. [66]

(7) A power of attorney to manage the principal's affairs while he is abroad, amplified by a letter from the principal to his bankers stating that

---

[60] *Hogg v. Snaith* (1808) 1 Taunt. 347. See also *Esdaile v. La Nauze* (1835) 1 Y. & C.Ex. 394; *Murray v. East India Co.* (1821) 5 B. & A. 204; *Harper v. Godsell* (1870) L.R. 5 Q.B. 422.

[61] *Jacobs v. Morris* [1902] 1 Ch. 816.

[62-63] *Re Dowson and Jenkins' Contract* [1904] 2 Ch. 219. See also *Re Bowles' Mortgage Trust* (1874) 31 L.T. 365; *Lewis v. Ramsdale* (1886) 55 L.T. 179; *Hawkesley v. Outram* [1892] 3 Ch. 359; *Bryant, Powis & Bryant v. La Banque du Peuple* [1893] A.C. 170.

[64] *Gardner v. Baillie* (1795) 6 T.R. 591.

[65] *Jonmenjoy Coondoo v. Watson* (1884) 9 App.Cas. 561; *Tobin v. Broadbent* (1947) 75 C.L.R. 378.

[66] *Bank of Bengal v. Macleod* (1849) 5 Moo.Ind.App. 1; *Bank of Bengal v. Fagan* (1849) 5 Moo.Ind.App. 27.

he wished the power to cover the drawing of cheques upon the bank without restriction, does not authorise the attorney to draw cheques in payment of his own private debts.[67]

(8)   A clause in a power of attorney, whereby the principal agrees to ratify and confirm whatsoever the attorney shall do or purport to do by virtue of the power, does not extend the authority given by the power.[68]

Rule (4)

(9)   A partner gave his son a power of attorney "to act on his behalf in dissolving the partnership, with authority to appoint any other person as he might see fit." Held, this gave the son power to submit the partnership accounts to arbitration.[69]

(10)   A power of attorney "to commence and carry on, or to defend at law or in equity, all actions, suits, or other proceedings touching anything in which the principal or his ships or other personal estate may be in anywise concerned" authorises the attorney to sign on behalf of the principal a bankruptcy petition against a debtor of the principal.[70]

Article 25

CONSTRUCTION OF AUTHORITY NOT GIVEN UNDER SEAL

3–013   Where the authority of an agent is given by an instrument not under seal, or is given orally, it is construed liberally, with regard to the object of the authority and to the usages of trade or business.[71]

Comment

3–014   The rules for the construction of documents other than deeds are clearly very much laxer, and it is was said at first instance in the leading

---

[67] *Reckitt v. Barnett, Pembroke & Slater Ltd* [1929] A.C. 176 (a famous case which is noted at (1929) 45 L.Q.R. 6; (1929) 3 C.L.J. 445; (1929) 17 Calif.L.Rev. 258; (1929) 77 U.Pa.L.Rev. 271); *Midland Bank Ltd v. Reckitt*, below. See also *Morison v. Kemp* (1912) 29 T.L.R. 70; *Hayes v. Standard Bank of Canada* [1928] 2 D.L.R. 898. *cf. Australia and New Zealand Bank Ltd v. Ateliers de Constructions Electriques de Charleroi* [1967] 1 A.C. 86 (authority to indorse principal's cheque and pay into own bank account necessary to give business effect to transactions authorised), distinguished in *Day v. Bank of New South Wales* (1978) 19 A.L.R. 32.

[68] *Midland Bank Ltd v. Reckitt* [1933] A.C. 1. Nor can it amount to ratification, since it comes before the act. See above, para. 2–048.

[69] *Henley v. Soper* (1928) 8 B. & C. 16. See also *Withington v. Herring* (1829) 5 Bing. 442; *Willis v. Palmer* (1859) 7 C.B.(N.S.) 340.

[70] *Re Wallace, ex p. Wallace* (1884) 14 Q.B.D. 22.

[71] *Pole v. Leask* (1860) 28 Beav. 562, 574 (affd. (1863) 33 L.J.Ch. 155); *Ireland v. Livingston* (1872) L.R. 5 H.L. 395; *Freeman and Lockyer v. Buckhurst Park Properties (Mangal) Ltd* [1964] 2 Q.B. 480, 502. See also *Restatement*, § 34, listing factors to be taken into account.

114

case of *Pole v. Leask*[72] that where authority is general it will be construed liberally. It is presumably often, though not necessarily true, that a deed is more carefully drawn than a less formal document, and so should be more strictly construed: and powers of attorney may often be executed to establish an agency against a non-commercial background, which would also make strict interpretation appropriate.[73] Be that as it may, in the commercial sphere the interpretation of documents and correspondence concerning the agency relationship is plainly far more liberal where no formal power of attorney by deed has been executed, as can be seen from the cases cited. Reference should also be made to subsequent Articles, for most of the cases there cited concern instructions given in writing.[74] The rule applies *a fortiori* to authority given orally, and indeed *Pole v. Leask*[75] itself was a case of oral authority. The interpretation of both written and oral authority is a matter of law: but in the latter case questions of fact as to what was said and done may make law and fact difficult to distinguish. Furthermore, in both cases questions of the normal course of business, and of trade customs, may arise, which are questions of fact.[76]

Illustrations

(1) An agent was instructed to sell goods at such a price as would   **3–015** realise 15s. per ton, net cash. He sold them at 15s. 6d. per ton, subject to two months' credit. Held, that the instructions might fairly be construed as meaning 15s. net cash, or such a price as would eventually realise 15s. after allowing for interest, or a *del credere* commission; that the contract might be presumed to have reference to some well-known usage of the coal trade; and that the sale was within his authority.[77]

(2) 100 bales of cotton are ordered by a Liverpool merchant from a merchant at Pernambuco. The Pernambuco merchant buys 94 bales. There is evidence to show that it is not normally possible to purchase 100 bales at Pernambuco. The purchase is authorised.[78]

(3) A is authorised to sell and warrant certain goods. He cannot bind his principal by a warranty given at any other time than at the sale of his goods.[79]

---

[72] n. 71, above. The judgment of Lord Romilly M.R. should, however, be read with caution, as it does not clearly distinguish between (what would now be called) actual and apparent authority: see the case on appeal (1863) 33 L.J.Ch. 155, especially the speech of Lord Cranworth.

[73] Stoljar, pp. 91–92.

[74] See especially Article 26.

[75] n. 71, above.

[76] See Articles 27–32.

[77] *Boden v. French* (1851) 10 C.B. 886.

[78] *Johnston v. Kershaw* (1867) L.R. 2 Ex. 82; *Ireland v. Livingston* (1872) L.R. 5 H.L. 395, Illustration 1 to Article 26.

[79] *Helyear v. Hawke* (1803) 5 Esp. 72.

(4)   On the dissolution of a partnership, authority is given to one of the partners by his co-partners (i) to settle the partnership affairs, [80] or (ii) to receive all debts owing to, and to pay all debts owing by, the firm. [81] In neither case has the authority to draw, accept or indorse bills of exchange in the name of the firm.

Article 26

AUTHORITY GIVEN IN AMBIGUOUS TERMS

3–016   Where the authority of an agent is conferred in such ambiguous terms, or the instructions given to him are so uncertain, as to be fairly capable of more than one construction, an act reasonably done by him in good faith which is justified by any of those constructions is deemed to have been duly authorised, though the construction adopted and acted upon by him was not that intended by the principal. [82]

Illustrations

3–017   (1)   A commission agent in Mauritius was authorised to buy and ship 500 tons of sugar (subject to a certain limit in price, to cover cost, freight and insurance), 50 tons more or less of no moment, if it enabled him to secure a suitable vessel. The principal stated that he would prefer the option of sending the vessel to London, Liverpool or the Clyde, but that if that was not possible the goods might be shipped to Liverpool or London. Held that a shipment of 400 tons in a vessel carrying other cargo direct to London and thus not amenable to orders was a good execution of the authority, it being doubtful what the instructions meant. [83]

(2)   An agent undertook to sell and transfer certain stock when funds should be at 85 or over. Held, that he was bound to sell when the funds

---

[80] *Abel v. Sutton* (1800) 3 Esp. 108. See also *Odell v. Cormack Brothers* (1887) 19 Q.B.D. 223; *cf. Smith v. Winter* (1838) 4 M. & W. 454.

[81] *Kilgour v. Finlyson* (1789) 1 H.Bl. 155.

[82] *Ireland v. Livingston* (1872) L.R. 5 H.L. 395, Illustration 1. See above, para. 1–018. But note that with modern communications it may be possible to obtain clarification of instructions and it may be the agent's duty to do so: *Woodhouse A.C. Israel Cocoa Ltd S.A. v. Nigerian Produce Marketing Co. Ltd* [1972] A.C. 741, 772; *Veljkovic v. Vrybergen* [1985] V.R. 419. See also cases cited under Article 25; Article 40; *Moore v. Mourgue* (1776) 2 Cowp. 479; *Comber v. Anderson* (1808) 1 Camp. 523; *Pariente v. Lubbock* (1856) 8 De G.M. & G. 5; *Miles v. Haslehurst* (1906) 23 T.L.R. 142; *Restatement*, § 44.

[83] *Ireland v. Livingston*, n. 82 above. See also *Loring v. Davis* (1886) 32 Ch.D. 625; *International Paper Co. v. Spicer* (1906) 4 C.L.R. 739; *Gould v. South Eastern and Chatham Ry.* [1920] 2 K.B. 186; *J. Vale & Co. v. Van Oppen & Co. Ltd* (1921) 37 T.L.R. 367; *Brown and Gracie v. F.W. Green & Co. Pty. Ltd* [1960] 1 Lloyd's Rep. 289; and see a useful discussion in *Veljkovic v. Vrybergen*, n. 82 above.

reached 85, and had no discretion to wait until they went higher than that price.[84]

(3) A shipowner by telegram requests shipbrokers to "fix steamer" on certain terms. The brokers take this as an instruction to let out one of the shipowner's vessels, to be named subsequently, on such terms. The owner intended them to obtain a ship on charter. The brokers' interpretation is justified.[85]

3.— IMPLIED ACTUAL AUTHORITY

Article 27

TO DO WHAT IS NECESSARY FOR, OR INCIDENTAL TO, EFFECTIVE EXECUTION OF EXPRESS AUTHORITY (INCIDENTAL AUTHORITY)

An agent has implied authority to do whatever is necessary for, or   **3–018**
ordinarily incidental to, the effective execution of his express authority in the usual way.[86]

Comment

This Article only refers to actual authority. A good statement of the   **3–019**
notion behind it is that "an authority of this nature necessarily includes medium powers, which are not expressed. By medium powers I mean all the means necessary to be used in order to obtain the accomplishment of the object of the principal power. ..."[87] But a similar notion is relevant to apparent authority, and statements of the rule appear in this context[88]: indeed in many cases it is unecessary and even impossible to decide whether the decision rests on implied or on apparent authority.[89] A recurring theme is, however, that authority to do an act does not necessarily involve authority to receive payment in relation to it.[90]

---

[84] *Bertram, Armstrong & Co. v. Godfray* (1830) 1 Knapp. 381. See also *Tallentire v. Ayre* (1884) 1 T.L.R. 143.

[85] *Weigall & Co. v. Runciman & Co.* (1916) 85 L.J.K.B. 1187.

[86] *Pole v. Leask* (1860) 28 Beav. 562, 574–575 (affd. (1863) 33 L.J.Ch. 155); *Bayley v. Wilkins* (1849) 7 C.B. 886; *Collen v. Gardner* (1856) 21 Beav. 540; and see Illustrations.

[87] *Howard v. Baillie* (1796) 2 H.Bl. 618, 619, *per* Eyre C.J.

[88] *e.g. Beaufort v. Neeld* (1845) 12 C. & F. 248; *Dingle v. Hare* (1859) 7 C.B.(N.S.) 145; *Wiltshire v. Sims* (1808) 1 Camp. 258.

[89] *cf.* above, para. 3–005. See *Ryan v. Pilkington* [1959] 1 W.L.R. 403; criticised by Powell, pp. 51–52 and finally disapproved by the House of Lords in *Sorrell v. Finch* [1977] A.C. 728.

[90] See Illustrations 2, 11.

Some cases usually associated with the notion of agency of necessity could also be regarded as examples of incidental authority.[91]

Illustrations

3–020   (1)   A is authorised to enter into a binding contract. He has implied authority to sign a memorandum thereof to satisfy the Law of Property Act 1925, s. 40.[92] But it must relate to the contract authorised; and where solicitors, acting upon instructions, bid for three separate lots of property at an auction and the property was knocked down to them, it was held that they had no authority to sign one indivisible agreement to purchase all the lots.[93]

(2)   An assistant in a shop normally has authority to receive payment for goods sold in the shop, but not necessarily to receive it elsewhere[94] or in other circumstances outside the ordinary course of business.[95] A person delivering goods may have no such authority,[96] and a traveller taking orders for the purchase of goods may have no authority to receive the price,[97] though there may be a course of dealing or of business whereby payment to such a traveller is normal.[98]

(3)   A is authorised to buy certain shares. He has implied authority to do everything in the usual course of business necessary to complete the bargain, *e.g.* reimburse the seller for payment on a call.[99]

(4)   A is employed to get a bill of exchange discounted. He has implied authority to warrant it a good bill, but not to indorse it in the name of the principal.[1]

(5)   An agent is authorised to institute proceedings for liquidation of a company. He has authority to give a notice of demand on behalf of the creditor.[2]

---

[91] *e.g. Gokal Chand-Jagan Nath v. Nand Ram Das-Atma Ram* [1939] A.C. 106; see below, para. 4–007.

[92] *Rosenbaum v. Belson* [1900] 2 Ch. 267; the relevant provision is now s. 2 of the Law of Property (Miscellaneous Provisions) Act 1989. And see *Gavaghan v. Edwards* [1961] 2 Q.B. 220; Article 6.

[93] *Smith v. MacGowan* [1938] 3 All E.R. 447. See also *Smith v. Webster* (1876) 3 Ch.D. 49; *Van Praagh v. Everidge* [1903] 1 Ch. 434. But sales by auction no longer require a memorandum, nor to be in writing: Law of Property (Miscellaneous Provisions) Act 1989, s. 2.

[94] *Kaye v. Brett* (1850) 5 Exch. 269, 274.

[95] See *Sanderson v. Bell* (1833) 2 C. & M. 304.

[96] *Lettice v. Judkins* (1840) 9 L.J.Ex. 142.

[97] *Butwick v. Grant* [1924] 2 K.B. 483, Illustration 1 to Article 83. See also *Drakeford v. Piercy* (1866) 7 B. & S. 515.

[98] *International Sponge Importers Ltd v. Andrew Watt & Sons* [1911] A.C. 279, Illustration 2 to Article 83; *Capel v. Thornton* (1828) 3 C. & P. 352. See further Articles 28, 83.

[99] *Bayley v. Wilkins* (1849) 7 C.B. 886.

[1] *Fenn v. Harrison* (1790) 3 T.R. 757; (1791) 4 T.R. 177.

[2] *Metropolitan Waste Disposal Authority v. Willoughby Waste Disposals Ltd* (1987) 9 N.S.W.L.R. 7. See also *Paget v. Pearson* (1949) 49 S.R. (N.S.W.) 235 (authority to obtain possession of premises included authority to sign notice to quit).

(6) A person is authorised to receive certain rents for his own benefit. He has no implied authority to distrain for the rents.[3]

(7) An agent is employed to obtain payment of a bill of exchange from the acceptor. He has no implied authority to receive payment subject to a condition that the acceptor shall not be liable for the expenses of protesting the bill for non-payment.[4]

(8) An agent is employed to sell a consignment of goods by description while afloat. He has no implied authority to warrant them to be of any particular condition or quality.[5]

(9) An agent authorised to deliver a horse has no authority to give a warranty,[6] and an agent authorised to deliver milk has no authority to sell it to someone other than the person to whom it is being sent.[7] A furniture salesman may have authority to cancel the sale.[8]

(10) A bailee for use may have authority to part with possession of the goods when it is reasonably incidental to the reasonable use of them to do so. Thus if he delivers goods for repair, the repairer may acquire a valid lien over them.[9]

(11) A solicitor handling a conveyancing transaction after "subject to contract" agreement has authority to receive all relevant information from the other party.[10]

(12) A person engaged in freight forwarding, and in particular in preparing documents for presentation under a letter of credit, has no authority to receive the payment under the credit.[11]

Article 28

AUTHORITY TO RECEIVE PAYMENT OF MONEY

An agent who is authorised to receive payment of money has prima facie no authority to receive payment otherwise than in cash, unless it is in the normal course of business to do so, or it is usual or customary in the particular business to receive payment in some   **3–021**

---

[3] *Ward v. Shew* (1833) 9 Bing. 608.
[4] *Bank of Scotland v. Dominion Bank (Toronto)* [1891] A.C. 592.
[5] *Benmag Ltd v. Barda* [1955] 2 Lloyd's Rep. 354, 357 (but on the facts of the case such authority could be inferred from the conduct of the parties); *cf. Abrahams v. Spitz* (1963) 107 S.J. 113 (agent to sell car had authority to warrant that it was insured).
[6] *Woodin v. Burford* (1834) 2 Cr. & M. 391.
[7] *Whittaker v. Forshaw* [1919] 2 K.B. 419.
[8] *Leckenby v. Wolman* [1921] W.N. 100.
[9] *Tappenden v. Artus* [1964] 2 Q.B. 185. See further cases cited above, para. 1–027, n. 14.
[10] *Strover v. Harrington* [1988] Ch. 390, 409–410.
[11] *Cleveland Mfg. Co. Ltd v. Muslim Commercial Bank Ltd* [1981] 1 Lloyd's Rep. 646.

other form, and such usage or custom is reasonable or known to the principal at the time when he confers the authority.[12]

Comment

3–022 Many agents have no authority to receive payment at all. Where they have, nineteenth-century cases reiterate a basic rule that there is normally no authority to accept payment except in cash.[13] Under this rule an agent has prima facie no authority to give credit,[14] nor to accept a cheque. Although business practices have changed, it seems worth retaining the collection of cases and the statement of the rule, for care over payment is plainly to be required of any agent. But the rule is conditioned by the general principles as to the authority of agents, under which agents are normally authorised to do whatever is usual in the course of business.[15] It is thus not necessary to establish an actual custom that the agent need not receive cash, though it is obviously permissible to do so:[16] and this is important because customs are difficult to prove.[17] Therefore it has long been fairly easy to establish implied authority to sell on credit.[18] As to cheques, a cheque is usually regarded not as a separate form of payment but as conditional payment,[19] and no problem arises when it is duly met on presentation, for it is then equivalent to payment in cash even where it is in the agent's favour.[20] Disputes can however arise as to whether a cheque is a valid tender,[21] whether an agent is in breach of his duty in accepting a cheque,[22] and whether an agent has actual or apparent

---

[12] See Comment and Illustrations; *Restatement*, § 72. See also Comment to Article 83; Article 27, Illustration 2; Article 30, Illustrations 6, 7.

[13] *Sweeting v. Pearce* (1859) 7 C.B.(N.S.) 449, 480, 484, affd. (1861) 9 C.B.(N.S.) 534, Illustration 4; *Farrer v. Lacy, Hartland & Co.* (1885) 31 Ch.D. 42; *Papé v. Westacott* [1894] 1 Q.B. 272; *Blumberg v. Life Interests and Reversionary Securities Corp. Ltd* [1897] 1 Ch. 171; [1898] 1 Ch. 27.

[14] Though if he does he may be estopped against the principal from saying that he has not received the money: *Gillard v. Wise* (1826) 5 B. & C. 134.

[15] See Articles 25, 27, 29, 30.

[16] See Article 31.

[17] See Comment to Article 31.

[18] See *Houghton v. Matthews* (1803) 3 B. & P. 485, 489; *Pelham v. Hilder* (1841) 1 Y. & C.C.C. 3; *Boden v. French* (1851) 10 C.B. 886; *Papé v. Westacott*, n. 13 above, at p. 278; *R. & E. Tingey & Co. Ltd v. John Chambers & Co. Ltd* [1967] N.Z.L.R. 785.

[19] *D. & C. Builders Ltd v. Rees* [1966] 2 Q.B. 617.

[20] *Bridges v. Garrett* (1870) L.R. 5 C.P. 451; *International Sponge Importers Ltd v. Andrew Watt & Sons* [1911] A.C. 279; *Papé v. Westacott*, n. 13 above; *Bradford & Sons v. Price Brothers* (1923) 92 L.J.K.B. 871 (authorities reviewed); *Clay Hill Brick & Tile Co. Ltd v. Rawlings* [1938] 4 All E.R. 100.

[21] *Blumberg v. Life Interests and Reversionary Securities Corp. Ltd*, n. 13 above.

[22] *Farrer v. Lacy, Hartland & Co.*, n. 13 above; *Pape v. Westacott*, n. 13 above; *Kearney v. Cullen* [1955] I.R. 18 (solicitor).

authority to transfer property or release goods (which may, for instance, be subject to a lien) against a cheque rather than cash. Though the basic rule doubtless remains, it seems likely that a practice of accepting payment by cheque, whether in favour of agent or principal, will fairly readily be recognised nowadays as being in the normal course of business, and hence within the scope of an agent's authority without proof of special usage.[23] The same is true of payment by credit card, which may rank as absolute payment.[24] It will not however prima facie be within the agent's authority to accept abnormal forms of payment.[25] Here it may be necessary to prove an actual custom permitting such payment, and, if the custom is held unreasonable, knowledge of it.[26] But where the debtor to the principal is financially embarrassed, the agent's duty may be to do his best to collect all that he can in the circumstances, and "the onus is on the [principal] in such a case to prove that the [agent] has failed in that duty."[27] In such a case the agent may have discharged his duty by getting what cash he can and giving credit for the rest.[28]

Illustrations

(1) It is provided by the conditions of a sale by auction that the purchase-money shall be paid to the auctioneer. The auctioneer has no authority to receive a bill of exchange in payment, and if his authority to receive payment is revoked during the currency of the bill, such a payment does not discharge the purchaser.[29] So, an insurance broker has

3–023

---

[23] See *Underwood v. Nicholls* (1855) 17 C.B. 239, 244; *Papé v. Westacott*, n. 13 above, at pp. 278, 283 (estate agent); *Farrer v. Lacy, Hartland & Co.*, n. 13 above (auctioneer). In many transactions the supporting of a cheque by a cheque card or credit card may be normal. As to notification that only certain forms of cheque are acceptable, see *International Sponge Importers Ltd v. Andrew Watt & Sons*, n. 20 above; *Bradford & Sons v. Price Brothers*, n. 20 above. As to payment by cheque under a stipulation for payment in cash, see *Tankexpress A/S v. Cie. Financière Belge des Petroles S.A.* [1949] A.C. 76. Where the delivery of goods has the effect of releasing a lien, it may be held that a mere driver, for instance, is not authorised to deliver against a cheque, which may not be met: see *Esterhuyse v. Selection Cartage (Pty) Ltd* 1965 (1) S.A. 360; *McGraw-Edison (Canada) Ltd v. Direct-Winters Tpt. Ltd* [1969] 1 O.R. 663. See further van Zyl (1974) 91 S.A.L.J. 337 (on South African cases).
[24] *Re Charge Card Services Ltd* [1989] Ch. 497.
[25] See Illustrations.
[26] See Article 31; *Sweeting v. Pearce* (1859) 7 C.B.(N.S.) 449, affd. (1861) 9 C.B.(N.S.) 534, Illustration 4.
[27] *Gokal Chand-jagan Nath v. Nand Ram Das-Atma Ram* [1939] A.C. 106, 113 *per* Lord Wright.
[28] *Ibid.*
[29] *Williams v. Evans* (1866) L.R. 1 Q.B. 352; *Sykes v. Giles* (1839) 5 M. & W. 645. See also *Hogarth v. Wherley* (1875) L.R. 10 C.P. 630; *Howard v. Chapman* (1831) 4 C. & P. 508 (no authority to accept payment in goods). *Cf. Farrer v. Lacy, Hartland & Co.* (1888) 31 Ch.D. 42 (cheque).

no authority to take a bill of exchange in payment of a claim in respect of which he is authorised to receive payment.[30]

(2)   An agent is authorised to receive payment of an account, and to retain part of the amount in discharge of a debt due to him from the principal. He has authority, to the extent of his debt, to settle in his own way with the debtor of his principal.[31]

(3)   A authorises B, a country stockbroker, to receive money due from C, a London stockbroker. B has no authority to settle with C by way of set-off, and a custom permitting such settlement is unreasonable.[32]

(4)   A authorises B, an insurance broker, to receive the amount due from the underwriters under a policy of insurance. The underwriters in good faith settle with B by setting off a debt due to them from him, and their names are struck out of the policy. By a custom at Lloyd's, a set-off is considered equivalent to payment as between broker and underwriter. If A is aware of the custom when he authorises B to receive payment, he is bound by the settlement. Otherwise he is not bound, because the custom is unreasonable.[33]

(5)   An agent authorised to receive money has prima facie no authority to receive payment before it is due, and if his authority is revoked before that time, the debtor is not discharged by such payment;[34] he may have no authority to receive payment after it is due,[35] nor to accept it on terms different in some other respect from those prescribed by the contract.[36]

---

[30] *Hine Brothers v. Steamship Insurance Syndicate Ltd (The Netherholme)* (1895) 72 L.T. 79 (but facts rather special).

[31] *Barker v. Greenwood* (1837) 2 Y. & C. Ex. 414.

[32] *Pearson v. Scott* (1878) 9 Ch.D. 198; *Blackburn v. Mason* (1893) 68 L.T. 510; *Crossley v. Magniac* [1893] 1 Ch. 594; *Anderson v. Sutherland* (1897) 13 T.L.R. 163 (all stockbroker cases). As to custom, see Article 31. See also *Underwood v. Nicholls* (1855) 17 C.B. 239; *Wrout v. Dawes* (1858) 25 Beav. 369; *Coupe v. Collyer* (1890) 62 L.T. 927 (solicitors).

[33] *Sweeting v. Pearce* (1859) 7 C.B.(N.S.) 449; affd. (1861) 9 C.B.(N.S.) 534; *Stewart v. Aberdein* (1838) 4 M. & W. 211; *Legge v. Byas, Mosley & Co.* (1901) 7 Com.Cas. 16; *Matveieff & Co. v. Crosfield* (1903) 51 W.R. 365; *McCowin Lumber and Export Co. v. Pacific Marine Insurance Co.* (1922) 38 T.L.R. 901; *Stolos Cia. S.A. v. Ajax Insurance Co. Ltd (The Admiral C)* [1981] 1 Lloyd's Rep. 9. But see *Trading & General Investment Co. v. Gault Armstrong & Kemble Ltd (The Okeanis)* [1986] 1 Lloyd's Rep. 196, 200 where reference is made to evidence given that certain accounts of the customs of insurance companies were "completely out of date". See in general Hodgin, *Insurance Intermediaries: Law and Practice* (1992).

[34] *Breming v. Mackie* (1862) 3 F. & F. 197. But there may be a custom permitting this: *Catterall v. Hindle* (1867) L.R. 2 C.P. 368; *Heisch v. Carrington* (1833) 5 C. & P. 471; see Article 31.

[35] See Article 29, Illustration 7 (insurance agent); *New Zealand Tenancy Bonds Ltd v. Mooney* [1986] 1 N.Z.L.R. 280 (estate agent); *cf. Jawara v. Gambian Airways* [1992] E.G.C.S. 54, P.C. (lawyer).

[36] *Campbell v. Hassel* (1816) 1 Stark. 233. But a contract can be varied by custom: see Article 31.

Article 29

MANAGERIAL AGENTS: IMPLIED AUTHORITY WHERE EMPLOYED TO
CONDUCT TRADE OR BUSINESS OR ACT GENERALLY IN CERTAIN
MATTERS (USUAL AUTHORITY)

An agent who is authorised to conduct a particular trade or business   3–024
or generally to act for his principal in matters of a particular nature,
or to do a particular class of acts, has implied authority to do
whatever is incidental to the ordinary conduct of such trade or
business,[37] or of matters of that nature, or is within the scope of that
class of acts,[38] and whatever is necessary for the proper and effective
performance of his duties[39]: but not to do anything that is outside
the ordinary scope of his employment and duties.[40]

Comment

The authority referred to here is that which arises from appointment to   3–025
a particular managerial post. When the board of directors appoint one of
their number to be managing director, for example, "they thereby
impliedly authorise him to do all such things as fall within the usual scope
of that office."[41]
Many of the cases refer to an agent of this type as a general agent, as
distinguished from a special agent. Much use is made of the distinction in
nineteenth-century English cases, mainly in the context of what is now
called apparent authority[42]: and it has sometimes been referred to in
more recent times.[43] But it is submitted that the distinction should now
be regarded in England as no more than a rather specific example of the
obvious fact that, from the point of view of implied authority, a person
made agent with general authority to do acts of various types or to
negotiate a number of transactions of the same type is likely to have a
wider authority than one appointed with limited authority to do acts of a
particular class or to negotiate a particular transaction: the borderline
between general and special agents is so indistinct that it is unwise to
regard the test as a definitive one.[44]

---

[37] Illustrations 1, 4.
[38] Illustrations 2, 4, 5, 9.
[39] Illustrations 3, 6, 10, 11.
[40] Illustrations 2, 3, 7, 10.
[41] *Hely-Hutchinson v. Brayhead Ltd* [1968] 1 Q.B. 549, 583, *per* Lord Denning M.R.
[42] *e.g. Smith v. M'Guire* (1858) 3 H.& N. 554; see Article 74.
[43] *e.g. Barrett v. Irvine* [1907] 2 I.R. 462.
[44] See above, para. 1–039.

The authority here discussed is an example of what can be called usual authority.[45] It should be noted, as with other Articles in this chapter, that the principle here cited is relevant not only to actual authority but also to apparent authority, in that in many cases the normal implied authority was negatived as between the parties by the circumstances, yet the third party was held entitled to assume that it existed, since the authority concerned would regularly be implied. The "general agent" cases are in fact, as stated above, in the main relevant to the development of the doctrine of apparent authority. However, they can, of course, support the proposition that implied authority will normally extend thus far.[46]

Many of the examples relate to ways of living and trading which no longer exist; their value is simply as providing examples of the typical reasoning used, and analogies.

Illustrations

3–026   (1) A is the manager of an estate. He has implied authority to contract for the usual and customary leases,[47] and to give and receive notice to quit to and from tenants[48] and to enter into agreements with tenants authorising them to change the mode of cultivation, and providing for the basis on which compensation for improvements shall be payable on the determination of the tenancy.[49]

(2) A rent collector has no implied authority, as such, to receive a notice to quit from a tenant.[50] A steward has such implied authority,[51] but not to grant leases for terms of years.[52]

(3) A is the managing owner of a ship. He has implied authority to pledge the credit of his co-owners for all such things, including repairs, as are necessary for the usual or suitable employment of the ship.[53] But he has no authority as such to insure the vessel on behalf of his co-owners,[54]

---

[45] See above, para. 3–006.
[46] e.g. *Collen v. Gardner* (1856) 21 Beav. 540, Illustration 2; *Wright v. Glyn* [1902] 1 K.B. 745, Illustration 10; *Hely-Hutchinson v. Brayhead Ltd* [1968] 1 Q.B. 549, 583. See also *Brady v. Todd* (1861) 9 C.B.(N.S.) 592; *Howard v. Sheward* (1866) L.R. 2 C.P. 148; *Brooks v. Hassall* (1883) 49 L.T. 560; *Baldry v. Bates* (1885) 52 L.T. 620; cases cited at Article 30, Illustration 2. These are cases where the usual authority of the agent is relied on, and therefore the representation giving rise to apparent authority would be very general indeed: see Comment to Article 74.
[47] *Peers v. Sneyd* (1853) 17 Beav. 151.
[48] *Papillon v. Brunton* (1860) 5 H. & N. 518; *Jones v. Phipps* (1868) L.R. 3 Q.B. 567; *Townsends Carriers Ltd v. Pfizer Ltd* (1977) 33 P. & C.R. 361; *Peel Developments (South) Ltd v. Siemens Plc.* [1992] 2 EGLR 85.
[49] *Re Pearson and I'Anson* [1899] 2 Q.B. 618.
[50] *Pearse v. Boulter* (1860) 2 F. & F. 133.
[51] *Roe d. Rochester (Dean & Chapter) v. Pierce* (1809) 2 Camp. 96.
[52] *Collen v. Gardner* (1856) 21 Beav. 540.
[53] *The Huntsman* [1894] P. 214; *Barker v. Highley* (1863) 15 C.B.(N.S.) 27.
[54] *Robinson v. Gleadow* (1835) 2 Bing. N.C. 156.

or to agree to pay a sum of money for the cancellation of a charterparty made by him on their behalf.[55]

(4)   The managing director of a company has authority (subject to the company's memorandum and articles) to sign cheques and bills of exchange,[56] borrow money and give security over the company's property[57] and guarantee loans made by a subsidiary of the company and agree to indemnify other guarantors.[58] He has no authority to bribe representatives of other companies.[59]

(5)   A company secretary has authority to order cars to meet visitors at airports, and in general to make contracts in connection with the administration of the company's affairs.[60]

(6)   The general manager of a railway company has implied authority to order medical attendance for an employee of the company.[61] But a station-master has no implied authority to pledge the credit of the railway company for medical attendance to an injured passenger.[62]

(7)   A is the agent of an insurance company, and has authority to receive the payment of premiums within 15 days of their becoming due. He has no implied authority to accept payment after the expiration of that time.[63] So, a local agent of an insurance company, employed to introduce business, has as a rule no implied authority to grant, or contract to grant, policies on behalf of the company, that being outside the ordinary scope of his employment and duties,[64] though he may be authorised to grant temporary cover.[65]

(8)   The master of a stranded ship has in the absence of express instructions authority to bind his owners or demise charterers by entering into a reasonable salvage contract.[66]

---

[55] *Thomas v. Lewis* (1878) 4 Ex.D. 18. See Scrutton, *Charterparties* (17th ed.), Article 16 (omitted in 18th and 19th ed.). *Quaere* as to the present day.

[56] *Dey v. Pullinger Engineering Co.* [1921] 1 K.B. 77.

[57] *Biggerstaff v. Rowlatt's Wharf Ltd* [1896] 2 Ch. 93.

[58] *Hely-Hutchinson v. Brayhead Ltd* [1968] 1 Q.B. 549. See further Pennington, *Company Law* (6th ed.), pp. 127–128.

[59] *E. Hannibal & Co. Ltd v. Frost* (1988) 4 B.C.C. 3.

[60] *Panorama Developments (Guildford) Ltd v. Fielis Furnishing Fabrics Ltd* [1971] 2 Q.B. 711, recognising the change in the function of company secretaries since the early years of the century.

[61] *Walker v. Great Western Ry. Co.* (1867) L.R. 2 Ex. 228.

[62] *Cox v. Midland Ry. Co.* (1849) 3 Exch. 268. See also *Houghton v. Pilkington* [1912] 3 K.B. 308; *cf. Langan v. Great Western Ry. Co.* (1873) 30 L.T. 173. See also Article 35.

[63] *Acey v. Fernie* (1840) 7 M. & W. 151. See MacGillivray and Parkington, *Insurance Law* (8th ed.), pp. 160 *et seq.*

[64] *Linford v. Provincial, etc., Ins. Co.* (1864) 34 Beav. 291. See Article 77, Illustrations 8, 9, 100.

[65] *Wilkinson v. General Accident Fire and Life Insurance Co. Ltd* [1967] 2 Lloyd's Rep. 182.

[66] *The Unique Mariner* [1978] 1 Lloyd's Rep. 438; but see below, para. 4–008.

(9) The engineer of a local authority has authority to specify the purpose for which goods are required by the authority, for the purposes of the Sale of Goods Act 1893, s.14.[67]

(10) Authority to arrest or give persons into custody is normally implied when the duties of the agent could not efficiently be performed without such authority. A bank manager has no implied authority to arrest or prosecute supposed offenders on behalf of the bank.[68] The manager of a restaurant has implied authority to give into custody persons behaving in a riotous manner,[69] but not persons who refuse to pay a disputed bill.[70]

(11) *Semble*, an agent has authority, unless there are special circumstances, to disclose the existence of the agency, the identity of his principal, his relationship with his principal,[71] and documents evidencing his authority which his principal might reasonably expect that third parties would wish to see for their own protection.[72]

Article 30

PROFESSIONAL AGENTS: IMPLIED AUTHORITY WHERE EMPLOYED IN THE COURSE OF BUSINESS AS AGENT (USUAL AUTHORITY)

3–027   An agent who is authorised to do any act in the course of his trade, profession or business as an agent has implied authority to do whatever is normally incidental, in the ordinary course of such trade, profession or business, to the execution of his express authority,[73] but not to do anything which is unusual in such trade, profession or business, or which is neither necessary for nor incidental to the execution of his express authority.[74]

Comment

3–028   In this case the implied authority arises, not from the managerial nature of the post to which the agent has been appointed, as in the

---

[67] *Ashford Shire Council v. Dependable Motors Pty. Ltd* [1961] A.C. 336.

[68] *Bank of New South Wales v. Owston* (1879) 4 App.Cas. 270, where there is a full review of the authorities; *Abrahams v. Deakin* [1891] 1 Q.B. 516. But many of the old cases on false imprisonment may be out of date in England at least. Whereas in former times a person was "given in charge", the increased speed of communications today means that police officers are normally able to arrive soon enough to effect arrests on their own responsibility. See Atiyah, *Vicarious Liability in the Law of Torts* (1967), pp. 266–267.

[69] *Ashton v. Spiers & Pond* (1893) 9 T.L.R. 606.

[70] *Stedman v. Baker & Co.* (1896) 12 T.L.R. 451.

[71] *United Bank of Kuwait Ltd v. Hammoud* [1988] 1 W.L.R. 1051, 1066–1067.

[72] *Restatement*, §§ 40, 46; Powell, p. 46.

[73] Illustrations 1, 2, 7.

[74] Illustrations 3–6.

previous Article, but from the nature of the general occupation which he carries on apart from this particular agency. Agents of this type also are sometimes referred to as general agents, though as has already been stated, the utility of this term is doubtful.[75] The examples given here are for illustrative purposes, but more specific information should be sought in specialist works dealing with the authorities of those practising various types of trade and profession. Expert evidence as to current practice is more likely to be relevant than old illustrations: as Staughton L.J. said in connection with the authority of a solicitor, "I prefer to have regard to the expert evidence of today in deciding what is the ordinary authority."[76]

This proposition is again an example of what may be called usual authority.[77] As in the previous Articles, the primary reference is to actual authority, but the reasoning will apply also to apparent authority: indeed many of the cases relate to apparent authority, since the notion of general agency was primarily relevant to what is now called apparent authority.[78]

Illustrations

(1) A bailiff is authorised to distrain for rent. He has implied authority to receive the rent and expenses due, and a tender thereof to him operates as a tender to the landlord.[79]   **3–029**

(2) A horse-dealer is authorised to sell a horse. He has implied authority to warrant it.[80] So also has his employee. But the employee of a private seller has not[81] unless he sells in cirumstances where custom requires a warranty.[82]

(3) An architect was employed to make plans for building certain houses. He instructed a quantity surveyor to take out quantities, and then invited tenders, all of which exceeded the limits of the building-owner's proposed expenditure. The quantity surveyor sued the building-owner for his fees, relying on an alleged custom in the building trade, by which the liability for such fees was thrown on the building-owner where no tender was accepted. The jury having found that there was no custom by which an architect was authorised to employ a surveyor without the sanction of

---

[75] See above, para. 3–025.
[76] *United Bank of Kuwait Ltd v. Hammoud* [1988] 1 W.L.R. 1051, 1063.
[77] See above, para. 3–006.
[78] See above, para. 3–025.
[79] *Hatch v. Hale* (1850) 15 Q.B. 10. Tender to a man left in possession by the bailiff is ineffective: *Boulton v. Reynolds* (1859) 2 E. & E. 369.
[80] *Howard v. Sheward* (1866) L.R. 2 C.P. 148; *Baldry v. Bates* (1885) 52 L.T. 620. See also *Bank of Scotland v. Watson* (1813) 1 Dow. 40, 45. But this question is now of less importance in view of warranties implied by statute.
[81] *Brady v. Todd* (1861) 9 C.B.(N.S.) 592.
[82] *Brooks v. Hassall* (1883) 49 L.T. 569; see Article 31.

the building-owner, and the owner not having expressly authorised the employment, it was held that the defendant was not liable. [83]

(4)   A ship's agent has implied authority to arrange and pay for the stowage of cargo. [84] A loading superintendent employed by a f.o.b. buyer has no authority to waive a term of the contract as to description: but failure by him to object to goods which do not conform with the contract description may be attributed to the buyer for the purpose of the buyer's duty to mitigate damages. [85]

(5)   A solicitor entrusted with the conduct of litigation has authority to agree to a settlement of it provided that the settlement does not concern matters collateral to the action. [86] He has in general no implied authority to accept notices on behalf of his clients. [87]

(6)   An estate agent in England has normally no authority to sell land: even though he is instructed as to the price at which the vendor will sell, his function is to solicit offers and transmit them to his principal. [88] But he may be authorised expressly or impliedly to sell [89] though in such

---

[83] *Antisell v. Doyle* [1899] 2 I.R. 275.

[84] *Blandy Bros. & Co. Ltd v. Nello Simoni Ltd* [1963] 2 Lloyd's Rep. 393. *cf. Sickens v. Irving* (1858) 29 L.J.C.P. 25 (no authority to make substantially new contract); *Lindsay & Son v. Scholefield* (1897) 24 R. (Ct. of Sess.) 530. See in general as to ship's agents Trappe [1978] L.M.C.L.Q. 595; Morris [1982] L.M.C.L.Q. 218; also *Intermediaries in Shipping* (Grönfors ed.) (Gothenburg Maritime Law Association, 1990).

[85] *Toepfer v. Warinco A.G.* [1978] 2 Lloyd's Rep. 569. See further as to authority to waive contract terms *Dawson Line Ltd v. Aktiengesellschaft fur Chemische Industrie* [1932] 1 K.B. 433; *Ismail v. Polish Ocean Lines* [1976] Q.B. 893; *Mardorf Peach & Co. Ltd v. Attica Sea Carriers Corp. (The Laconia)* [1977] A.C. 850 (authority of bank to accept late payment); *Surrey Shipping Co. Ltd v. Cie. Continentale (France) S.A. (The Shackleford)* [1978] 1 W.L.R. 1080 (receiver of goods had authority to waive defects in notice of readiness); *State Rail Authority of N.S.W. v. Heath Outdoor Pty. Ltd* (1986) 7 N.S.W.L.R. 170, 194 (advertising manager had authority to indicate circumstances in which employer would terminate advertising contract, but not to vary contract); *Nowrani Pty Ltd v. Brown* [1989] 2 Qd.R. 582 (solicitor had no authority to insert term into sale of land)

[86] *Waugh v. H.B. Clifford & Sons Ltd* [1982] Ch. 374 (authorities reviewed). See also *Re Newen* [1903] 1 Ch. 812; *Little v. Spreadbury* [1910] 2 K.B. 658; *Thompson v. Howley* [1977] 1 N.Z.L.R. 16; *Holmes v. Kennard & Son* (1984) 44 P. & C.R. 202 (solicitor for purchaser had no authority to cancel notice on land register); *Donnellan v. Watson* (1990) 21 N.S.W.L.R. 335 (no authority to agree to different compromise from that authorised); Cordery, *Solicitors* (8th ed.), p. 80; Fridman (1987) 36 U. Brunswick L.J. 9. *Cf.* above, para. 3–005. It has been held that a Citizens' Advice Bureau worker had a somewhat wider authority: *Freeman v. Sovereign Chicken Ltd* [1991] I.C.R. 853.

[87] *Re Munro, ex p. Singer* [1981] 1 W.L.R. 1358.

[88] *Hamer v. Sharp* (1874) L.R. 19 Eq. 108; *Prior v. Moore* (1887) 3 T.L.R. 624; *Chadburn v. Moore* (1892) 61 L.J.Ch. 674; *Thurman v. Best* (1907) 97 L.T. 239; *Lewcock v. Bromley* (1920) 37 T.L.R. 48; *Keen v. Mear* [1920] 2 Ch. 574; *Wragg v. Lovett* [1948] 2 All E.R. 968; (but *cf. Jawara v. Gambian Airways* [1992] E.G.C.S. 54, P.C.); *Law v. Robert Roberts & Co.* [1964] I.R. 292 (authorities reviewed). He is a "canvassing" or "introducing" agent: above, para. 1–017. This does not exclude the possibility of other usages in other countries *e.g. Powierza v. Daley* [1985] 1 N.Z.L.R. 558.

[89] *Rosenbaum v. Belson* [1900] 2 Ch. 267; *Allen & Co. v. Whiteman* (1920) 89 L.J.Ch. 534; *Wragg v. Lovett*, n. 88 above; *Spiro v. Lintern* [1973] 1 W.L.R. 1002.

circumstances he normally has no authority to sign anything but an open contract.[90] In any case he is prima facie authorised to describe the property and state to an intending purchaser circumstances which may affect its value[91]; but not to accept a deposit on such terms as will make the prospective vendor liable in respect of it,[92] nor to receive payment,[93] nor to warrant that the property may legally be used for a particular purpose.[94]

(7)   An auctioneer has authority not only to sell but also at the time of the sale to sign a contract or memorandum of the sale for both vendor and purchaser.[95] In general there is no authority to receive payment.[96] but authority to describe the property[97] and receive a post-contract deposit may be usual,[98] and, except in the case of land, authority to receive the whole price may likewise be usual.[99] An auctioneer has normally no authority to rescind a sale,[1] to warrant,[2] to negotiate terms[3] or to sell by private contract after the auction, even where the public sale proves abortive and he is offered more than the reserve price.[4]

---

[90] *Keen v. Mear*, n. 88 above; *Wragg v. Lovett*, n. 88 above.

[91] *Mullens v. Miller* (1882) 22 Ch.D. 194. But *cf. Overbrooke Estates Ltd v. Glencombe Properties Ltd* [1974] 1 W.L.R. 1335; *Presser v. Caldwell Estates Pty. Ltd* [1971] 2 N.S.W.L.R. 471.

[92] *Sorrell v. Finch* [1977] A.C. 728. See Articles 94, 113. See also *New Zealand Tenancy Bonds Ltd v. Mooney* [1986] 1 N.Z.L.R. 280 (no authority to accept late payment of deposit); *cf. Kohn v. Devon Mortgage Ltd* (1985) 20 D.L.R. (4th) 480 (mortgage broker had authority to receive capital).

[93] See *Mynn v. Joliffe* (1834) 1 Moo. & Rob. 326; *Peterson v. Moloney* (1951) 84 C.L.R. 91; *cf. Butwick v. Grant* [1924] 2 K.B. 483.

[94] *Hill v. Harris* [1965] 2 Q.B. 601. See in general Murdoch, *Law of Estate Agency and Auctions* (3rd ed.), Chap. 3.

[95] *Emmerson v. Heelis* (1809) 2 Taunt. 38; *White v. Proctor* (1811) 4 Taunt. 209; *Kenneys v. Proctor* (1820) 1 Jac. & W. 350; *Earl of Glengal v. Barton* (1836) 1 Keen 769, 788; *Bell v. Balls* [1897] 1 Ch. 663; *Chaney v. Maclow* [1929] 1 Ch. 461. *cf. Van Praagh v. Everidge* [1903] 1 Ch. 434. By virtue of s. 2 of the Law of Property (Miscellaneous Provisions) Act 1989 the contract must now be in writing; but this does not apply in public auctions, which now require neither writing nor memorandum. *Quaere* whether an auctioneer has authority to sign a written contract. See Murdoch, n. 94 above, pp. 273–274.

[96] See *Mynn v. Joliffe*, n. 93 above; *cf. Butwick v. Grant*, n. 93 above.

[97] *e.g. Smith v. Land and House Property Corp.* (1884) 28 Ch.D. 7. But *cf. Overbrooke Estates Ltd v. Glencombe Properties Ltd* [1974] 1 W.L.R. 1335 and *Collins v. Howell-Jones* (1980) 259 E.G. 331, where this authority was excluded.

[98] See *Sykes v. Giles* (1830) 5 M. & W. 645; Murdoch, *op. cit. Law of Estates Agency and Auctions* (3rd ed.), pp. 276 *et seq.*

[99] *cf.* Factors Act 1889, s. 12(3); *Chelmsford Auctions Ltd v. Poole* [1973] Q.B. 542.

[1] *Nelson v. Aldridge* (1818) 2 Stark. 435.

[2] *Payne v. Lord Leconfield* (1882) 51 L.J.Q.B. 642; *Gardiner v. Grig* (1938) 38 S.R.(N.S.W.) 524.

[3] *Seton v. Slade* (1802) 7 Ves. 265, 276.

[4] *Daniel v. Adams* (1764) Ambl. 495; *Marsh v. Jelf* (1862) 3 F. & F. 234. *cf. Else v. Barnard* (1860) 28 Beav. 228; *Bousfield v. Hodges* (1863) 33 Beav. 90. See in general Murdoch, *Law of Estate Agency and Auctions* (3rd ed.), Chap. 3.

Article 31

AUTHORITY IMPLIED FROM SPECIAL USAGES (CUSTOMARY AUTHORITY)

3–030   (1)   An agent has implied authority to act, in the execution of his express authority, according to the usages and customs of the particular place, market or business in which he is employed.[5]

(2)   But agent has no implied authority to act in accordance with any usage or custom which is unreasonable, unless the principal had actual notice of such usage or custom at the time when he conferred the authority;[6] or to act in accordance with any usage or custom which is unlawful.[7]

(3)   The question whether any usage or custom is unreasonable or unlawful is a question of law. In particular, a usage or custom inconsistent with the intrinsic character of the contract of agency,[8] or a usage or custom whereby an agent who is authorised to receive payment of money may require payment by way of set-off, or by way of settlement of accounts between himself and the person from whom he is authorised to receive payment,[9] is unreasonable.

Comment

3–031   **General rule.** This Article embodies the general rule that an agent is authorised to act in accordance with the commercial customs in the sphere in which he operates, *e.g.* a stock or commodity exchange. The rule is, however, of limited application. The rules concerning proof of custom are strict, for their effect in the general law is to imply terms into contracts, which is not normally permitted unless they are to be derived from the nature of the transaction or essential to give it business efficacy. Accordingly, proof of custom is notoriously difficult. "In the mind of a layman there is often a confusion between custom and that which is customarily done, and he wrongly imagines that the latter amounts to a

---

[5] Illustrations 1–7; *Sutton v. Tatham* (1839) 10 A. & E. 27; *Ex p. Howell, re Williams* (1865) 12 L.T. 785; *cf. Restatement*, § 36. There is a useful discussion of the requirement and effects of custom in Law Com. C.P. No. 124, *Fiduciary Duties and Regulatory Rules* (1992), pp. 63–76.

[6] *Robinson v. Mollett* (1874) L.R. 7 H.L. 802, Illustration 8.

[7] *Harker v. Edwards*, (1887) 57 L.J.Q.B. 147; and see Comment. Rules (1) and (2) were cited with approval in *Anglo Overseas Transport (United Kingdom) Ltd v. Titan Industrial Corporation (United Kingdom) Ltd* [1959] 2 Lloyd's Rep. 152, 160.

[8] Illustrations 8, 9.

[9] Illustration 10.

legal custom."[10] The latter would of course be evidence of what authority is reasonably to be implied, or, in other contexts, of what is reasonably to be expected of principal or agent in the circumstances.[11] This Article therefore only applies to generally recognised and established customs in markets or the like, and not to mere customary courses of dealing between agent and third party, or between agents of the particular type and third parties.[12] Evidence of such courses of dealing may be well relevant to establish some other form of implied authority.

Custom. The burden of proving the existence of a custom or usage is a   **3–032** heavy one. It is not normally one that can be discharged by evidence given on affidavit if that evidence is challenged.[13] In order to establish the existence of a custom or usage the plaintiff must show that the alleged custom is (i) reasonable,[14] (ii) universally accepted by the particular trade or profession or at the particular place, (iii) certain; (iv) not unlawful; (v) not inconsistent with the express or implied terms of the contract.[15] Therefore, even if a custom is proved to exist, the court will ignore it if it is expressly or impliedly excluded. But where the custom does exist and is not excluded, it is "to be considered as part of the agreement: and if the agreement be in writing, though the custom is not written it is to be treated exactly as if that unwritten clause had been written out at length."[16]

---

[10] *Re North Western Rubber Co. Ltd and Hüttenbach & Co.* [1908] 2 K.B. 907, 919 *per* Fletcher Moulton L.J. The case itself was overruled in *Produce Brokers Co. Ltd v. Olympia Oil & Cake Co. Ltd* [1916] 1 A.C. 314, which contains a detailed consideration of much of this topic. See also *Drexel Burnham Lambert International N.V. v. El Nasr* [1986] 1 Lloyd's Rep. 356, 365 *per* Staughton L.J.: "What has to be shown by evidence is that the custom is recognised as imposing a binding obligation."

[11] See Articles 27–30.

[12] See *Hamilton v. Young* (1881) 7 L.R.Ir. 289; *Ex p. Howell, re Williams* (1865) 12 L.T. 785; *Cunliffe-Owen v. Teather & Greenwood* [1967] 1 W.L.R. 1421, 1438; *General Reinsurance Corp. v. Forsakringsaktiebolaget Fenna Patria* [1983] Q.B. 856.

[13] *Stag Line Ltd v. Board of Trade* (1950) 83 Ll.Rep. 356, 360. See also *Blandy Bros. v. Nello Simoni* [1963] 2 Lloyd's Rep. 24, 29; [1963] 2 Lloyd's Rep. 393, 400, 404.

[14] Thus in *Anglo-African Merchants Ltd v. Bayley* [1970] 1 Q.B. 311, 323 Megaw J. said that the court would not uphold a custom which contradicted the principle that an agent might not serve both parties simultaneously. This was followed in *North and South Trust Co. v. Berkeley* [1971] 1 W.L.R. 470, Illustration 3 to Article 5; and see Article 46, Illustration 5.

[15] These well-known principles were accepted in *Oricon Waren-Handels G.m.b.H. v. Intergraan N.V.* [1967] 2 Lloyd's Rep. 82, 96 and in *Cunliffe-Owen v. Teather & Greenwood* [1967] 1 W.L.R. 1421, 1439. See also *Con-Stan Industry of Australia Pty. Ltd v. Norwich Winterthur Insurance (Australia) Ltd* (1986) 160 C.L.R. 226. As to (v) see further *Palgrave, Brown & Son Ltd v. S.S. Turid* [1922] 1 A.C. 397, 406; *London Export Corp. v. Jubilee Coffee Roasting Co.* [1958] 1 W.L.R. 661, 675; *Kum v. Wah Tat Bank* [1971] 1 Lloyd's Rep 437.

[16] *Tucker v. Linger* (1883) 8 App.Cas. 508, 511 *per* Lord Blackburn.

3–033   **Rules.** The position as regards rules, *e.g.* of a market or organisation, as opposed to customs, seems, despite suggestions to the contrary,[17] to be the same.[18] It is however obvious that special problems may arise when rules are changed. It has been held that a resolution of a regulatory body passed after a transaction cannot bind the principal or alter the contract between the parties,[19] though it may validly decide a dispute between the parties.[20]

3–034   **Unreasonable customs.** There was much authority for applying the criterion of reasonableness to usages and customs, and especially to the rules of the Stock Exchange,[21] though the law does not normally protect contracting parties from unreasonable terms with much tenderness. But the situations referred to in Rule (3) of this Article are better regarded as *sui generis* rather than examples of unreasonable arrangements[22]: they were held to be actually inconsistent with the nature of the contract of agency, and were in the first edition of this work treated as in themselves a ground for the non-operation of custom. In all these cases the agent has no authority unless the principal knew of the custom when he gave or confirmed the authority for the particular transaction.

3–035   **Unlawful customs.** Knowledge of an unreasonable custom may import assent to it. But it is difficult to see how the law can permit a principal to assent to a custom which is actually unlawful.[23] Nevertheless, a different conclusion seems to emerge from a group of cases relating to the former custom of the Stock Exchange to disregard Leeman's Act,[24] under which contracts for the sale of shares in banking companies were void if they did not contain certain information. In *Perry v. Barnett*[25] it was held that this

---

[17] *Benjamin v. Barnett* (1903) 19 T.L.R. 564.

[18] *Harker v. Edwards* (1887) 57 L.J.Q.B. 147; *Cunliffe-Owen v. Teather & Greenwood* [1967] 1 W.L.R. 1421. But see *Anderson v. Sutherland* (1897) 13 T.L.R. 163.

[19] *Union Corp. Ltd v. Charrington & Brodrick* (1902) 19 T.L.R. 129; *Benjamin v. Barnett*, n. 17 above. And see, on the changing of rules, *Doyle v. White City Stadium Ltd* [1935] 1 K.B. 110.

[20] *Harker v. Edwards*, n. 18 above; *Reynolds v. Smith* (1893) 9 T.L.R. 474; *Bell Group Ltd v. Herald and Weekly Times* [1985] V.R. 613.

[21] *e.g. Pearson v. Scott* (1878) 9 Ch.D. 198; *Blackburn v. Mason* (1893) 9 T.L.R. 286; *Anderson v. Sutherland* (1897) 13 T.L.R. 163; *Sweeting v. Pearce* (1861) 9 C.B.(N.S.) 534; *Hamilton v. Young* (1881) 7 L.R.Ir. 289; *Harker v. Edwards* (1887) 57 L.J.Q.B. 147; *Benjamin v. Barnett* (1903) 19 T.L.R. 564; *Reynolds v. Smith*, n. 20 above.

[22] The matter is exhaustively discussed in *Robinson v. Mollett* (1874) L.R. 7 H.L. 802. But in *Perry v. Barnett* (1885) 15 Q.B.D. 388 the two grounds are treated as the same: see pp. 393–394.

[23] See *Bailey v. Rawlins* (1829) 7 L.J.(O.S.) K.B. 208; *Josephs v. Pebrer* (1825) 3 B. & C. 639, where it was held that an agent was not entitled to reimbursement for illegal transactions.

[24] Banking Companies (Shares) Act 1867; repealed by Statute Law Revision Act 1966.

[25] (1885) 15 Q.B.D. 388.

custom did not bind persons without notice,[26] but it was implied that it might, like an unreasonable custom, bind someone who had notice.[27] In *Seymour v. Bridge*[28] it had been held that this custom could bind a plaintiff who was at the time unaware of the existence of the Act: the case was explained in *Perry v. Barnett* as referring to a situation where there was notice of the usage, even if not of the Act. *Seymour v. Bridge* followed *Read v. Anderson*,[29] where it was held that a principal might come under an obligation to indemnify an agent for paying lost bets, and could not revoke the authority to do so, though the bets were themselves void.[30] However, the payment of a lost bet is in the nature of a gift, and while there is no reason why an agent should not be employed to make gratuitous payments (though revocation of authority would normally be a simple matter[31]): whether an agent can validly be employed to act in such a way as to contravene a statute is more doubtful. The purpose of the Gaming Act 1845, s. 18, was simply to render void and unenforceable wagering transactions: but that of Leeman's Act was "to make Provision for the Prevention of Contracts for the Sale and Purchase of Shares and Stock in Joint Stock Banking Companies of which the Sellers are not possessed or over which they have no Control."[32] The particular problem is now obsolete, not least because of the repeal of Leeman's Act,[33] but it is submitted that much will turn on the nature of the illegality when it is sought to determine whether a principal can assent to an unlawful custom.

Burden of proof. Although the question is one of fact, it seems that the person alleging that there was knowledge of the custom must establish that fact.[34] There may, however, be occasions when judicial notice is taken of a custom that is very well known.   3–036

Illustrations

(1) A was authorised to sell manure. The jury found that it was customary to sell manure with a warranty. Held, that A had implied authority to give a warranty on a sale of the manure.[35]   3–036A

---

[26] Following *Neilson v. James* (1882) 9 Q.B.D. 546. And see *Coates v. Pacey* (1892) 8 T.L.R. 351.
[27] At pp. 394, 395, 397–398.
[28] (1885) 14 Q.B.D. 460.
[29] (1884) 13 Q.B.D. 779.
[30] This result was reversed by the Gaming Act 1892.
[31] See *Read v. Anderson* (1884) 13 Q.B.D. 779, 783.
[32] Preamble (though this was deleted by the Statute Law Revision Act 1893).
[33] Above, n. 24.
[34] See *Sweeting v. Pearce* (1859) 7 C.B.(N.S.) 449, 481–482, 484, 486; affd. (1861) 9 C.B.(N.S.) 534.
[35] *Dingle v. Hare* (1859) 7 C.B.(N.S.) 145.

(2) An agent buys tallow for a foreign principal, undertaking, in accordance with custom, personal liability. The principal becomes insolvent without having paid the agent, who is liable for the price. The agent sells the tallow. If this is the customary procedure in such a situation, the agent is not liable for doing so. [36]

(3) A stockbroker, employed to transact business at a particular place, has implied authority to act in accordance with the reasonable usages of that place, and if he incurs liability when his principal defaults and the vendor, in accordance with local custom, resells the shares, he can recover from his principal. [37]

(4) A broker, a member of the Stock Exchange, when authorised to sell certain bonds, had implied authority, if it was discovered that the bonds are not genuine, to rescind the sale and repay the purchaser the price, in accordance with the usage of the Stock Exchange. [38]

(5) A stockbroker, authorised to buy or sell or carry over shares or stock, had implied authority, according to usage, to execute the order by means of several contracts, or to execute any portion or portions of it. [39]

(6) A bill-broker in London was entrusted with bills for discounting. The jury found that it was usual for bill-brokers in London to raise money by depositing their customers' bills en bloc, the brokers alone being looked to by the customers, and that the parties contracted in reference to such usage. Held, that the broker had implied authority to pledge their bills together with bills of his own and those of other customers. [40]

(7) A broker is authorised to buy wool in the Liverpool market. By a custom of that market, a broker so authorised may buy either in his own name or in the name of his principal, without giving the principal notice whether he has bought in his own name or not. Such a custom is not unreasonable, and the principal is bound by a contract made in the name of the broker, though he had no notice of the custom or of the fact that the contract was made by the broker in his own name. [41]

(8) A broker is authorised to buy 50 tons of tallow. It is customary in the tallow trade for a broker to make a single contract in his own name for the purchase of a sufficiently large quantity of tallow to supply the orders of several principals, and to parcel it out amongst them. The broker has no implied authority to purchase a larger quantity than 50 tons and allocate 50 tons of it to the principal, unless the principal was aware of the usage at the time when he gave the authority, because the effect of such a usage is to change the intrinsic character of the contract of agency

---

[36] *Lienard v. Dresslar* (1862) 3 F. & F. 212.
[37] *Pollock v. Stables* (1848) 12 Q.B. 765; *Hodgkinson v. Kelly* (1868) L.R. 6 Eq. 496.
[38] *Young v. Cole* (1837) 3 Bing.N.C. 724.
[39] *Benjamin v. Barnett* (1903) 19 T.L.R. 564.
[40] *Foster v. Pearson* (1835) 1 C.M. & R. 849.
[41] *Cropper v. Cook* (1868) L.R. 3 C.P. 194.

by turning the agent into a principal, and thus giving him an interest at variance with his duty.[42]

(9)   A broker is authorised to sell stock. All alleged custom of the Stock Exchange, whereby he is himself permitted to take over the stock at the price of the day, if he is unable to find a purchaser, is unreasonable, and such a transaction is not binding on the principal unless he had notice of the custom.[43]

(10)   An insurance broker is authorised to receive from the underwriters payment of money due under a policy. A custom at Lloyd's whereby the broker may settle with the underwriters by way of set-off is unreasonable, and the principal is not bound by such a settlement unless he was aware of the custom when he authorised the broker to receive payment.[44] The same rule has been applied to stockbrokers settling with country brokers, solicitors or other agents.[45]

Article 32

AUTHORITY IMPLIED FROM COURSE OF DEALING AND CIRCUMSTANCES OF CASE

An agent has, in addition to the forms of authority indicated in Articles 27 to 31, such authority as is to be inferred from the conduct of the parties and the circumstances of the case.[46]   3–037

Comment

The types of authority indicated in Articles 27 to 31 do not exhaust the notion of implied authority, for it is clear that over and above authority to do incidental acts, the acts usually performed by a person holding the   3–038

---

[42] *Robinson v. Mollett* (1874) L.R. 7 H.L. 802 (but the dissenting opinion of Blackburn J. has much force: *cf.* above, para. 1–019. For a case where the principal was held to have accepted a usage of similar effect see *Limako B.V. v. Hentz & Co. Inc.* [1978] 1 Lloyd's Rep. 400. *Robinson v. Mollett* was distinguished in cases concerning the right of stockbrokers to buy quantities of shares in a single contract and allocate quantities to particular clients: *e.g. Scott & Horton v. Godfrey* [1901] 2 K.B. 76; *Consolidated Gold Fields of South Africa v. E. Spiegel & Co.* (1909) 100 L.T. 351. As to "marrying" of buying and selling transactions by a broker, see *Jones v. Canavan* [1972] 2 N.S.W.L.R. 236 (custom to do so in Sydney and Brisbane held reasonable).

[43] *Hamilton v. Young* (1881) 7 L.R.Ir. 289. See also *Thornley v. Tilley* (1925) 36 C.L.R. 1 (custom that broker can deal on his own behalf with shares bought for principal unreasonable).

[44] See Article 28, Illustration 4.

[45] See Article 28, Illustration 3.

[46] *Hely-Hutchinson v. Brayhead Ltd* [1968] 1 Q.B. 549, 583; *Freeman & Lockyer v. Buckhurst Park Properties (Mangal) Ltd* [1964] 2 Q.B. 480, 502. For recent examples see *Brick and Pipe Industries Ltd v. Occidental Life Nominees Pty. Ltd* [1992] 2 V.R. 279, 362; *Equiticorp Finance Ltd v. Bank of New Zealand* (1993) 32 N.S.W.L.R. 50.

position in question, the acts usually performed by a person following the agent's particular profession or occupation, and authority to follow usages customary in the place, market or business concerned, an agent may have an authority peculiar to himself implied from the circumstances of the particular case. The question as to implication does not stop at the matters previously mentioned, but goes on to involve consideration of the whole circumstances of the agent's position. This may lead to the agent's having a wider authority initially, or to his authority being enlarged by his principal's acquiescence in his assuming further powers.[47] Thus in *Hely-Hutchinson v. Brayhead Ltd*[48] the chairman of a company acted as *de facto* managing director and chief executive of it, and entered into larger transactions on its behalf which he would sometimes merely report to the board without seeking prior authority or subsequent ratification. The Board acquiesced in this course of dealing. The chairman was held to have had actual authority equivalent to that of a managing director, though he was acting beyond the normal powers of a chairman.

This type of implied authority corresponds to the implied appointment of an agent dealt with in Article 8. It results from the application of the general rules as to interpretation and construction of contracts and agreements.[49] There may of course also be cases where such facts may merely be taken, as a matter of evidence, to point to the fact that express authority was actually conferred.[50]

4.—PRESUMED AUTHORITY

Introductory Note

3–039   In the 13th edition of this book it was stated that "what is sometimes called presumed authority is not a type of authority at all: the phrase simply refers to the fact that the existence of actual authority may sometimes be presumed subject to rebuttal."[51] The main case of presumed authority is that arising, usually in a wife, from cohabitation, which was in the first 13 editions of this book treated in a special chapter on the agency of married women. Such a chapter was appropriate because the position of a married women for long provided the focus for the intersection of a number of agency rules of different kinds of which the presumed authority arising from cohabitation was only one. Her special position was caused by two factors: her husband's obligation to

---

[47] *Hely-Hutchinson v. Brayhead Ltd*, n. 46 above; *Pole v. Leask* (1860) 28 Beav. 560; affd. (1864) 33 L.J.Ch. 155.
[48] Above, n. 46.
[49] See cases cited above, n. 46.
[50] Mechem, *Outlines of Agency* (4th ed.), pp. 30–31.
[51] (13th ed.), p. 65.

support her, and her inability until the late nineteenth-century to own separate property and thus to be liable on contracts.[52]

The latter inability has been long removed;[53] and the most specialised set of rules involved, those as to the powers of a deserted wife to pledge her husband's credit for necessaries, was abolished by statute in 1970.[54] The law as to the agency of a deserted wife, a full account of which was given in the 13th edition,[55] has therefore been deleted; and consequently the position of a wife in the law of agency no longer requires a separate chapter. On the other hand the rules as to presumed authority in the case of cohabitation had a status of their own, and it seems proper now to place them, and to consider their nature, in the chapter on authority. Therefore, though it is true that the phrase "presumed authority" does not refer so much to a type of authority as to a situation where authority is presumed, the cases are isolated as a category here.

It is obvious that social habits have changed since the various times at which these cases were decided, and will continue to do so. In most consumer transactions today, the supplier will look to the person placing the order rather than to another person with whom that person is living. However, this is not always so, particularly in the case of services rendered at a dwelling-house. The relevance of any of these decisions as precedent nowadays is therefore uncertain: but so are many situations regarding the provision of goods and services to domestic establishments. It is not clear, therefore, that the time has come to omit an account of this group of cases altogether.

Presumed authority. This type of authority could be said to be an   **3–040** example of implied authority: indeed it is sometimes so described in nineteenth-century cases, which contain many attempts to set the doctrines in order in different ways. But the most authoritative statement of the applicable rule suggests that there is a rebuttable presumption of fact,[56] *viz.* that from the mere fact of cohabitation and the absence of

---

[52] See the leading case of *Manby v. Scott* (1660) 1 Lev. 4, 2 Sm.L.C. 417.

[53] The last main statute on this topic was the Law Reform (Married Women and Tortfeasors) Act 1935. See in general Bromley, *Family Law* (8th ed.), pp. 555 *et seq.*

[54] Matrimonial Proceedings and Property Act 1970, s. 41(1). s. 41 of the 1970 Act was repealed by the Matrimonial Causes Act 1973, s. 54 and Sched. 3, but not so as to revive the doctrine: Interpretation Act 1889, s. 38(2). *cf.* (1973) 36 M.L.R. at p. 642. Powers were conferred by the 1970 Act on the court to make orders in cases of divorce, nullity and judicial separation with respect to financial provision for the wife and children of the marriage, and in cases of wilful neglect to maintain: these could be made for the purpose of covering liabilities or expenses reasonably incurred before the making of the application. These powers now derive from Part II of the Matrimonial Causes Act 1973 as amended principally by Matrimonial and Family Proceedings Act 1984).

[55] (1968), Articles 37–41. For a more recent account see Hardingham (1980) 54 A.L.J. 661 (discussing also Commonwealth authorities).

[56] *Debenham v. Mellon* (1880) 6 App.Cas. 24.

contrary indications, the finders of fact may, but need not, draw the inference that authority had actually been granted.[57] This differs from implied authority in four ways. First, the accepted categories of implied authority do not cover this case.[58] Secondly, implied authority affects apparent authority: a third party is normally entitled to assume that a person has such authority as would normally be implied.[59] But it is clear that the presumed agency from cohabitation is quite separate from apparent authority.[60] Thirdly, the presumed authority is confined to necessaries. Fourthly, it is possible to say that *implication* of authority is a question of law.[61] But the difference in practice, especially now that such cases are not tried by jury, is likely to be slight.[62]

It should be borne in mind throughout that a wife may also bind her husband in accordance with all the normal doctrines of agency: she may have actual authority, express or implied, or her act may be ratified, or she may bind her husband under the doctrine of apparent authority. Equally, a husband may be an agent for a wife.

Article 33

PRESUMPTION OF AUTHORITY FROM COHABITATION

3–040A

(1) Where a husband and wife live together and maintain a household establishment, a presumption arises that the wife has authority to pledge the husband's credit for necessaries suitable to the style in which they live, in respect of those matters usually entrusted to the management of the wife.

(2) The presumption is one of fact only and is rebutted by evidence.

    (a) and he has forbidden her to pledge his credit, or

    (b) that she was already adequately provided with necessaries, or

    (c) that her husband had already made her a sufficient and agreed allowance for such necessaries.[63]

---

[57] See in general Phipson, *Evidence* (14th ed.), §§ 1–08, 5–02, 5–04; Cross, *Evidence* (7th ed.), pp. 126 *et seq.*; and Comment to Article 33.

[58] See Articles 27–32.

[59] See above, para. 3–005.

[60] See *Debenham v. Mellon*, n. 56 above, at p. 32.

[61] *cf.* material cited above, n. 57.

[62] It is difficult to agree with Fridman, p. 131, that these rules are to be regarded as creating agency by operation of law.

[63] *Manby v. Scott* (1660) 1 Lev. 4, 2 Sm. L.C. 417; *Jolly v. Rees* (1864) 15 C.B.(N.S.) 628; *Debenham v. Mellon* (1880) 6 App.Cas. 24; *Morel Bros. & Co. Ltd v. Earl of Westmorland* [1904] A.C. 11; *Paquin Ltd v. Beauclerk* [1906] A.C. 148; *Miss Gray Ltd v. Earl Cathcart* (1922) 38 T.L.R. 562 (authorities reviewed). See also Wright (1930) 8 Can.B.R. 722.

Comment

Status of the presumption. The cohabitation has been said to give rise   3–041
to a presumption of fact from which it may be inferred "that the husband
really did give his wife such authority."[64] The question whether the wife
acted as her husband's agent is one of fact, and the question to leave to
the jury, when juries were used in this type of case, was whether the
things were supplied to his credit and with his authority, not merely
whether they were necessaries.[65] The presumption may, of course, be
rebutted, and even if it is not specifically rebutted it is not necessary that
agency be found. The real effect of such a presumption is only that it
prevents the submission that there is no case to answer in a situation
where no proof of agency is offered other than the fact of cohabitation:
the situation has also been referred to as giving rise to "some *prima facie*
evidence."[66] "A person suing the husband has not to give any evidence
of authority or agency except the fact of marriage, which is enough to
launch his case."[67]

Cohabitation. The presumption, despite the reference to spouses,   3–042
arises from cohabitation, and not from marriage.[68] Therefore the person
alleged to have authority need not be married to the person sought to be
held liable as principal, but may be his houskeeper or a woman with
whom he is living—or indeed need not be a woman at all.[69] Equally, the
principal need not be a man. The vast majority of the cases, however,
concern the liability of a husband for debts incurred by his wife, and it is
convenient to retain the exposition on this basis. The presumption will
not normally arise, even between husband and wife, where the cohabitation is not in a domestic establishment, *e.g.* is in a hotel.[70]

Two presumptions. In earlier editions of this book two apparently   3–043
separate presumptions were dealt with in two consecutive Articles: the
presumption from cohabitation, and the presumption of authority as
housekeeper. Since both were stated to be rebuttable in the same way it
is not clear what the difference between them was intended to be, and the
cases treat them as the same. "What the law does infer is, that the wife

---

[64] *Debenham v. Mellon*, n. 63 above, at p. 36 *per* Lord Blackburn.

[65] *Reid v. Teakle* (1853) 13 C.B. 627; *Freestone v. Butcher* (1840) 9 C. & P. 643.

[66] *Debenham v. Mellon*, n. 63 above, at p. 32, *per* Lord Selborne L.C.

[67] *Seymour v. Kingscote* (1922) 38 T.L.R. 586, 587, *per* Rowlatt J.

[68] *Debenham v. Mellon*, n. 63 above, at p. 31. Where the husband is absent on military
service, the parties may still be cohabiting: see *Dennys v. Sargeant* (1834) 6 C. & P. 419;
Travers v. Sen (1917) 33 T.L.R. 202.

[69] *Debenham v. Mellon*, n. 63 above, at p. 33; *Munro v. de Chemant* (1815) 4 Camp. 215;
Blades v. Free (1829) 9 B. & C. 167.

[70] *Debenham v. Mellon*, n. 63 above.

has authority to contract for things that are really necessary and suitable to the style in which the husband chooses to live, in so far as the articles fall fairly within the domestic department which is ordinarily confided to the management of the wife."[71] The only possible distinction between the two seems to be that the first refers to necessaries for the wife and children, the second to necessaries for the household: but the same rules apply to both. The "authority as housekeeper" as a separate notion seems to derive from certain old dicta suggesting that the wife has a usual authority[72] independent of limitations unknown to the supplier[73]; but these are no longer valid, it being clear that the presumption can only arise in accordance with the rules here given, and that the husband can only otherwise be liable under the normal principles of actual and apparent authority.[74]

3–044   **Necessaries.** The word "necessaries" covers "the reasonable supply of goods and services for the use of the husband, his wife, children and household."[75] The presumption has traditionally been stated as being confined to necessaries suitable to the style in which the husband chooses to live,[76] though the matter would hardly be so put today.[77] If things are ordered which are not suited to this style,[78] or of a extravagant nature, or excessive in quantity,[79] there is no presumption of authority. The question whether the goods are necessaries is one of fact, and the burden of proof lies on the supplier[80] (though the question whether the goods are capable of being necessaries is one of law[81]); and if the goods are extravagant he cannot even recover a reduced price for them.[82] There is

---

[71] *Phillipson v. Hayter* (1870) L.R. 6 C.P. 38, 42 *per* Willes J.

[72] See Comment to Article 22.

[73] *Ruddock v. Marsh* (1857) 1 H. & N. 601 (see *Debenham v. Mellon* (1880) 5 Q.B.D. 394, 399); Byles J., dissenting, in *Jolly v. Rees* (1864) 15 C.B.(N.S.) 628; Bramwell L.J. in *Debenham v. Mellon*, above (affd. (1880) 6 App.Cas. 24); *Johnston v. Summer* (1858) 3 H. & N. 261, 266 (as to which see *Debenham v. Mellon* (1880) 6 App.Cas. 24, 32).

[74] *Jolly v. Rees*, n. 73 above; Thesiger L.J. in *Debenham v. Mellon* (1880) 5 Q.B.D. 394 (affd. (1880) 6 App.Cas. 24).

[75] *Miss Gray Ltd v. Earl Cathcart* (1922) 38 T.L.R. 562, 565.

[76] *Shoolbred v. Baker* (1867) 16 L.T. 359; *Phillipson v. Hayter* (1870) L.R. 6 C.P. 38; *Harrison v. Grady* (1865) 13 L.T. 369; *Morgan v. Chetwynd* (1865) 4 F. & F. 451; *Jewsbury v. Newbold* (1857) 26 L.J.Ex. 247; *Goodyear v. Part* (1897) 13 T.L.R. 395; *Callot v. Nash* (1923) 39 T.L.R. 291, 293 ("he is entitled to be his own carver").

[77] The cases, indeed, provide an intriguing slice of social history.

[78] *Phillipson v. Hayter*, n. 76 above; *Harrison v. Grady*, n. 76 above; *Montague v. Benedict* (1825) 3 B. & C. 631.

[79] *Freestone v. Butcher* (1840) 9 C. & P. 643; *Lane v. Ironmonger* (1844) 13 M. & W. 368; *Miss Gray Ltd v. Earl Cathcart* (1922) 38 T.L.R. 562.

[80] *Miss Gray Ltd v. Earl Cathcart*, n. 79 above, at p. 565; *Callot v. Nash* (1923) 39 T.L.R. 291, 293.

[81] *Phillipson v. Hayter*, n. 76 above.

[82] *Walter v. Aldridge* (1884) 1 T.L.R. 138.

ancient and weak authority that where a wife is agent for her husband she has authority to bind him by an acknowledgment under the Limitation Act.[83]

Wife's separate business. In *Phillipson v. Hayter*[84] Bovill C.J. suggested that "if the wife, with the concurrence of her husband, carries on a separate trade, goods supplied to her for the purposes of that trade would fall within the same category." But when this was said, a wife could not own separate property and was not personally liable on her contracts: since the Law Reform (Married Women and Tortfeasors) Act 1935, this suggestion is probably no longer valid.   3–045

Relevance of wife's independent means. It has been said that if the wife has means of her own sufficiently ample to provide for her private necessaries, she has no presumed authority to pledge her husband's credit for such necessaries, as distinct from household necessaries[85]: but this is contrary to earlier authority,[86] and the statement was made in a case on the agency of the deserted wife, now abolished, which had a different basis.[87] The proposition therefore seems doubtful in the light of the general rationale behind the presumption.   3–046

Rebuttal of presumption. The presumption may be rebutted by proof that the wife in fact had no authority. This can be established, for example, by proving that her husband had forbidden her to pledge his credit, whether or not the supplier knew of this,[88] or that she was already supplied with a sufficient fixed[89] allowance[90] or was adequately provided with necessaries.[91]   3–047

---

[83] *Gregory v. Parker* (1808) 1 Camp. 394.

[84] (1870) L.R. 6 C.P. 38, 41.

[85] *Biberfeld v. Berens* [1952] 2 Q.B. 770, 782.

[86] *Callot v. Nash* (1923) 39 T.L.R. 291, 293; *Seymour v. Kingscote* (1922) 38 T.L.R. 586.

[87] See above, para. 3–039.

[88] *Jolly v. Rees* (1864) 15 C.B.(N.S.) 628; *Debenham v. Mellon* (1880) 6 App.Cas. 24; *Miss Gray Ltd v. Earl Cathcart* (1922) 38 T.L.R. 562. *A fortiori* if the supplier had notice. On what constitutes prohibition, see *Morgan v. Chetwynd* (1865) 4 F. & F. 451; *Shoolbred v. Baker* (1867) 16 L.T. 359 (whether "the husband did put a check on his wife beyond that sort of grumbling which is said to be the privilege of every man in this country.")

[89] *Goodyear v. Part* (1897) 13 T.L.R. 395.

[90] *Morel Bros. & Co. Ltd v. Earl of Westmorland* [1904] A.C. 11; *Remmington v. Broadwood* (1902) 18 T.L.R. 270; *Slater v. Parker* (1908) 24 T.L.R. 621; *Miss Gray Ltd v. Earl Cathcart*, n. 88 above. But it must be paid, for the purposes of this rule (*i.e.* where no other factor than the allowance can be adduced); *Morgan v. Chetwynd*, n. 88 above.

[91] *Montague v. Benedict* (1825) 3 B. & C. 631; *Reneaux v. Teakle* (1853) 8 Exch. 680. The necessaries need not become her property: *Rondeau Legrand & Co. v. Marks* [1918] 1 K.B. 75.

3–048   **Joint liability.** There is no presumption that a wife has authority to buy goods as agent for her husband and herself jointly.[92] Under the doctrines dealt with here, if he buys goods, she buys for herself or as agent for her husband.

3–049   **Borrowing money for necessaries.** The presumption of authority from cohabitation does not extend to the borrowing of money for the purchase of necessaries: therefore at law money so borrowed is not recoverable from the husband, even if spent on necessaries.[93] But in equity if the money is actually so spent, the lender is probably subrogated to the rights of the supplier and can recover it.[94]

3–050   **Credit given to the wife.** The presumption does not apply where the third party gives exclusive credit to the wife, *i.e.* contracts with her alone and not with her as agent for her husband.[95] This is a question of fact,[96] and an application of the general principles as to formation of contract.[97] The cases indicate that where a supplier deals in respect of necessaries with a person whom he knows to be a married woman, the burden of proving that he is giving credit to her alone lies on the person alleging it.[98] The fact that the wife has private means may be relevant to the determination of this question,[99] though the fact that the husband accompanies his wife shopping is not.[1] But all these propositions obviously require reappraisal in the light of changed conditions.[2] A supplier

---

[92] *Morel Bros. & Co. Ltd v. Earl of Westmorland*, n. 90 above.

[93] *Earle v. Peale* (1711) 1 Salk. 386. And see *Knox v. Bushell* (1857) 3 C.B.(N.S.) 334; *Harris v. Lee*, n. 94 below.

[94] *Harris v. Lee* (1718) 1 P.Wms. 482 ("baron gives feme the foul distemper"); *Re Wood's Estate, Davidson v. Wood* (1863) 1 De G.J. & Sm. 465; *Re Cook, ex p. Vernall* (1892) 10 Mor. 8. This proposition seems correct in principle but cannot be regarded as settled. There was clear authority in connection with the deserted wife's agency, now abolished (above, para. 3–039): see *Jenner v. Morris* (1861) 3 De G.F. & J. 45; *Deare v. Soutten* (1869) L.R. 9 Eq. 151; *Weingarten v. Engel* [1947] 1 All E.R. 425; *Biberfeld v. Berens* [1952] 2 Q.B. 770.

[95] *Bentley v. Griffin* (1814) 5 Taunt. 356; *Metcalfe v. Shaw* (1811) 3 Camp. 22; *Jewsbury v. Newbold* (1857) 26 L.J.Ex. 247; *Callot v. Nash* (1923) 39 T.L.R. 291; *Miss Gray Ltd v. Earl Cathcart* (1922) 38 T.L.R. 562; *Seymour v. Kingscote* (1922) 38 T.L.R. 586.

[96] *Bentley v. Griffin*, n. 95 above; *Jewsbury v. Newbold*, n. 95 above; *Seymour v. Kingscote*, n. 95 above.

[97] See also Comment to Article 84 as to merger and election.

[98] *Paquin Ltd v. Beauclerk* [1906] A.C. 148; *Easton v. Bartlett* (1903) 47 S.J. 707; *Harvey v. Ottoway* [1915] V.L.R. 520; *Seymour v. Kingscote*, n. 95 above, at p. 588. *Paquin v. Beauclerk* is, however, affected by the terms of the Married Women's Property Act 1893. See Wright (1930) 8 Can.B.R. 722. But *cf. Lea Bridge District Gas Co. v. Malvern* [1917] 1 K.B. 803, where the wife had first entered into the contract before her marriage: the contract was held to be with her.

[99] *Freestone v. Butcher* (1840) 9 C. & P. 643; *Callot v. Nash* (1923) 39 T.L.R. 291, 292.

[1] *Seymour v. Kingscote*, n. 95 above, at p. 588.

[2] See *e.g. Fick & Fick Ltd v. Assimakis* [1958] 1 W.L.R. 1006. But *cf. Gage v. King* [1960] 1 Q.B. 188.

supplying household goods, or more especially services (where cash payment is less normal) may now perhaps be more readily held to contract with the husband than one selling clothes: whereas cases on the purchase of clothes are conspicuous among the authorities normally cited.[3]

Other forms of authority. The husband may of course be liable under normal agency principles if he expressly or impliedly authorises the transaction, or ratifies it.[4] He may also be liable under the doctrine of apparent authority, which may bind him even if he had forbidden his wife to pledge his credit, provided that the third party did not know of the prohibition.[5] This would require some identifiable act of holding out: merely living with his wife does not create an apparent authority in her.[6] There is some support for the proposition that a wife who is separated from her husband by mutual consent and has no means to support herself may be found to have implied authority, under normal principles, to pledge his credit.[7] The social background against which a wife might be assumed to be unable to support herself is now different: but there may doubtless be cases where the implication is justified, both in the case of a separated wife and in the case of a cohabitating wife.[8] Old cases state that where a wife is separated from her husband, the burden of establishing authority lies upon the person seeking to charge the husband,[9] and this proposition is doubtless still correct.

3–051

Article 34

AGENCY OF CHILDREN

Children have no implied or presumed authority, as such, to pledge the credit of their parents, even for the supply of necessaries.[10]

3–052

---

[3] *e.g. Miss Gray Ltd v. Earl Cathcart* (1922) 38 T.L.R. 562; *Callot v. Nash*, n. 95 above (a diverting judgment).
[4] *e.g. Waithman v. Wakefield* (1807) 1 Camp. 120 (see Stoljar, p. 161 n. 69); *Millard v. Harvey* (1864) 34 Beav. 237; *West v. Wheeler* (1849) 2 C. & K. 714.
[5] See Article 74; *Ryan v. Sams* (1848) 12 Q.B. 460; *Jolly v. Rees* (1864) 15 C.B.(N.S.) 628; *Wallis v. Biddick* (1873) 22 W.R. 76; *Drew v. Nunn* (1879) 4 Q.B.D. 661; *Debenham v. Mellon* (1880) 6 App.Cas. 24; *Jetley v. Hill* (1884) C. & E. 239.
[6] *Debenham v. Mellon*, n. 5 above.
[7] See *Johnston v. Sumner* (1858) 3 H. & N. 261; *Hodgkinson v. Fletcher* (1814) 4 Camp. 70; *Dixon v. Hurrell* (1838) 8 C. & P. 717; *Emmett v. Norton* (1838) 8 C. & P. 506; *Biffin v. Bignell* (1862) 7 H. & N. 877, 880; *Eastland v. Burchell* (1878) 3 Q.B.D. 432; *Negus v. Forster* (1882) 46 L.T. 675. But these cases are very difficult to disentangle from the cases on the deserted wife's agency, now abolished: see above, para. 3–039.
[8] See *Miss Gray Ltd v. Earl Cathcart* (1922) 38 T.L.R. 562, 565.
[9] *Ozard v. Darnford* (1779) 1 Selwyn's N.P. (13th ed.) 229; *Mainwaring v. Leslie* (1826) M. & M. 18; *Clifford v. Laton* (1827) M. & M. 101; *Johnston v. Sumner*, n. 7 above.
[10] *Shelton v. Springett* (1851) 11 C.B. 452; *Mortimore v. Wright* (1840) 6 M. & W. 482.

Comment

3–053   In the absence of agency created in one of the normal ways, a parent is no more liable than a stranger for debts incurred by his or her child without authority: and the obligation to maintain children affords no implication of a promise to pay for necessaries supplied to them. To render a person liable for things supplied to his or her child, the person supplying them must give some evidence of authority or ratification[11]: but old cases suggest that slight evidence of authority may be sufficient,[12] and this seems reasonable.

Conversely, a parent or other relative does not become an agent for a child more easily than a person not related.[13]

---

[11] *Rolfe v. Abbott* (1833) 6 C. & P. 286.

[12] *Law v. Wilkin* (1837) 6 A. & E. 718; *Baker v. Keen* (1819) 2 Stark. 501. See also *Cooper v. Phillips* (1831) 4 C. & P. 581.

[13] See *G. (A.) v. G. (T.)* [1970] 2 Q.B. 643, 655; *Crampsey v. Deveney* [1968] S.C.R. 267, (1968) 2 D.L.R. (3d) 161; *Hector v. Lyons* (1988) 58 P. & C.R. 156.

CHAPTER 4

AGENCY OF NECESSITY

Article 35

DOCTRINE OF AGENCY OF NECESSITY

(1)   A person may have authority to act on behalf of another in   **4-001**
certain cases where he is faced with an emergency in which the
property or interests of that other are in imminent jeopardy
and it becomes necessary, in order to preserve the property or
interests, so to act.

(2)   In some cases this authority may entitle him to affect his
principal's legal position by making contracts or disposing of
property. In others it may merely entitle him to reimbursement
of expenses or indemnity against liabilities incurred in so
acting, or to a defence against a claim that what he did was
wrongful as against the person for whose benefit he acted.[1]

Comment

Introduction. The term "agency of necessity" is used to indicate a   **4-002**
general notion derived from a group of cases in which a person is
regarded as justified in taking action for the benefit of another in an
emergency. They are said to create a special category of agency which
arises by operation of law in such situations. In previous editions these
cases were treated in Chapter 2 under the heading of "Creation of
Agency". They cannot, however, be classified entirely as doing this, for
although some can be regarded as recognising agency powers in persons
who had none before the event concerned, many refer to a person who
is already an agent, but is by this doctrine given greater powers. This,
together with the fact that it is highly doubtful whether any coherent

---

[1] See Comment. See also Powell, Chap. IX; Treitel (1954) 3 U.Western Australia
L.Rev. 1; W.B. Williston (1944) 22 Can. Bar R. 492; Wade (1966) 19 Vanderbilt L.Rev.
1183; Birks [1971] *Current Legal Problems* 110; Hunter (1974) 23 U.New Brunswick L.J.5;
Marasinghe (1976) 8 Ottawa L.Rev. 573; McCamus (1979) 11 Ottawa L.Rev. 297;
Matthews [1981] C.L.J. 340; Brown (1992) 55 M.L.R. 414; Goff and Jones, *Law of
Restitution* (4th ed.), Chap. 15; Birks, *Introduction to the Law of Restitution* (1989) pp. 193
et seq.; Burrows, *Law of Restitution* (1993), Chap. 8. But the relevance of discussion in
books and articles on the law of restitution to pure agency issues is doubtful: see
Comment.

doctrine is to be derived from them for the modern law, makes it appropriate now to place the topic apart in its own chapter.

The cases from which the doctrine stems seem to be analytically of two quite different types, and treating these two groups of cases as components of a single doctrine has caused confusion. The two types of case have been treated together because it is said that similar specific rules regarding the emergency requisite to trigger off certain legal results apply to both; and that these are rules which create a special form of agency or authority by operation of law. It is suggested below that the first proposition does not now appear to be true: that the emergency rules do not apply to all the cases. It is also suggested that even if the second proposition has hitherto been regarded as true, the notion of a special type of authority by operation of law is at the present time no longer necessary or appropriate.

4–003   **The traditional cases: the shipmaster and the acceptor for honour.** The two traditional cases from which the concept of agency of necessity derives are those of the shipmaster, who has wide powers to bind by contract his owner, and also sometimes the cargo owners, in situations of emergency[2]; and the person who accepts a bill of exchange for honour and succeeds to the rights of the holder against the person for whom he accepts.[3] The second case appears to originate from the law merchant[4] and is now statutory[5]: it may in effect confer a right to reimbursement on the acceptor but its relation to agency is tenuous from the start. The dissimilarity between these two cases is enough to indicate immediately that a category comprising them both is unlikely to be a satisfactory one.

4–004   **First category: the shipmaster.** The first category, based on the case of the shipmaster, creates full agency in that it involves both the external and the internal aspects of the agency relationship. As to the external aspect, the master can create contracts binding and conferring rights on his principal (usually the shipowner or demise charterer) and make dispositions of his principal's property and receive property for his principal also. He has also the internal entitlement to reimbursement and indemnity against his principal in respect of what he has done; if this is not needed, he has a defence to any action brought against him

---

[2] See below, para 4–004.
[3] Bills of Exchange Act 1882, ss. 65–68; and see *Hawtayne v. Bourne* (1841) 7 M. & W. 595, 599.
[4] See *Hawtayne v. Bourne*, n. 3 above at p. 599.
[5] Above, n. 3.

by his principal in respect of his acts. And the act will be valid where validity is in issue. Thus there is old authority that the master can sell[6] or hypothecate[7] the ship, enter into a salvage agreement regarding it[8] and contract for the cargo to be transhipped and carried forward.[9] He can also sell or hypothecate the cargo, whether together with or separately from the ship,[10] and enter into a salvage agreement regarding it.[11] There are a few cases suggesting that these powers may apply also to land carriers.[12] The actual decisions concerning the latter type of carrier involve only claims to reimbursement and indemnity between principal and agent and so may only be examples of the second category: they are further referred below in that connection. It is there submitted, however, that they should in fact be attributed to the first category if that category can be enlarged and re-explained on a broader basis than that of agency by operation of law.

In respect of the shipmaster selling, hypothecating or contracting for salvage of the ship, this involves the extension of the authority of one who is already an agent in the full sense, for the master obviously has already in many situations actual authority, express or implied, from the shipowner (or demise charterer) to make normal trading contracts. However, where the action taken relates to the *cargo*, the master as such has no legal relationship with the cargo owner, and it can therefore be said that the master is by the emergency created an agent where he was not before. Yet he is still agent for the shipowner, who is bailee of the cargo: and although the shipowner may well have had no agency powers prior to the emergency, his position as bailee means that he has a legal relationship with the cargo owner which is in principle sometimes capable of giving rise to such powers, which can be exercised through the master, who is his agent. So the significance of the distinction is doubtful.

---

[6] *The Glasgow* (1856) Swab. 145; *The Australia* (1859) Swab. 480; *Atlantic Mutual Insurance Co. v. Huth* (1880) 16 Ch.D. 474.
[7] *The Gratitudine* (1801) 3 Ch. Rob. 240; *The Bonaparte* (1853) 8 Moo.P.C. 459; *The Hamburg* (1864) 2 Moo.P.C.(N.S.) 289; *The Onward* (1873) L.R. 4 A. & E. 38; *Kleinwort, Cohen & Co. v. Cassa Maritima of Genoa* (1877) 2 App. Cas. 156 (cases of bottomry, *viz.* hypothecating the cargo also).
[8] *The Renpor* (1883) 8 P.D. 115; *The Unique Mariner* [1978] 1 Lloyd's Rep. 438, Illustration 3, discussed also below.
[9] See *The Soblomsten* (1866) L.R. 1 A. & E. 293; Scrutton, *Charterparties* (19th ed.), Art. 129.
[10] As to sale, see *Tronson v. Dent* (1853) 8 Moo.P.C. 419; *Australasian S.N. Co. v. Morse* (1872) L.R. 4 P.C. 222; *Acatos v. Burns* (1878) 3 Ex. D. 282; *Atlantic Mutual Insurance Co. v. Huth*, n. 6 above. As to hypothecation, see cases cited above, n. 7.
[11] See below, para. 4–008.
[12] *Great Northern Ry. Co. v. Swaffield* (1874) L.R. 9 Ex. 132 (stabling uncollected horse); *Sims & Co. v. Midland Ry. Co.* [1913] 1 K.B. 103 (sale of uncollected goods); *cf. Springer v. Great Western Ry. Co.* [1921] 1 K.B. 257.

4–005   **Rules determining necessity.** The rules applicable to the exercise of this authority may be stated as follows. They derive largely from the shipmaster case, and it will be obvious later that they are in large measure inapplicable to the second category. Indeed in *The Winson*,[13] discussed below, Lord Diplock said that they should be confined to cases of the first category.[14]

(a) It must be impossible, or at any rate impracticable, for the agent to communicate with the principal. Some cases imply that communication must be impossible,[15] but this seems too strict: as long ago as 1851 Parke B. spoke of the principal's being unable to be "conveniently communicated with",[16] and in 1895 Lord Esher M.R. of an "opportunity to consult".[17] In *Springer v. Great Western Railway Co.* Bankes L.J. approved the phrase "practically impossible"[18] and Scrutton L.J. spoke of communication as being "commercially impossible".[19] This would include situations where there are too many principals to consult (*e.g.* owners of cargo shipped under bills of lading on liner terms[20]).

(b) The action taken must be necessary[21] for the benefit of the principal.[22] The agent's opinion as to the necessity is irrelevant. It is, however, sufficient if a reasonable person would think there was a necessity.[23] Mere inconvenience does not create necessity.[24] The necessity must of course be for the protection of the interests of the principal, not of the agent.

(c) The agent must have acted bona fide in the interests of the principal.[25]

---

[13] *China Pacific S.A. v. Food Corp. of India (The Winson)* [1982] A.C. 939, Illustration 1, also discussed below.

[14] At p. 958.

[15] *e.g. Prager v. Blatspiel, Stamp & Heacock Ltd* [1924] 1 K.B. 566, 571.

[16] *Beldon v. Campbell* (1851) 6 Exch. 886, 890. See also *Australasian S.N. Co. v. Morse* (1872) L.R. 4 P.C. 222.

[17] *Gwilliam v. Twist* [1895] 2 Q.B. 84, 87.

[18] [1921] 1 K.B. 257, 265.

[19] *Ibid.* at p. 268. And see *Barker v. Burns, Philip & Co. Ltd* (1944) 45 S.R. (N.S.W.) 1 (communication possible despite wartime conditions); *Sachs v. Miklos* [1948] 2 K.B. 23.

[20] See *The Choko Star* [1990] 1 Lloyd's Rep. 516, Illustration 2, discussed also below.

[21] For the meaning of "necessary" see *Prager v. Blatspiel, Stamp & Heacock Ltd* [1924] 1 K.B. 566, 571–572; *Australasian S.N. Co. v. Morse,* n. 16 above; *The Australia* (1859) Swab. 480. And see *Phelps, James & Co. v. Hill* [1891] 1 Q.B. 605.

[22] See *Burns, Philp & Co. Ltd v. Gillespie Bros Pty. Ltd* (1947) 74 C.L.R. 148 (doctrine inapplicable where measures undertaken (in wartime) for security of ship and cargo considered as one adventure).

[23] *Tetley & Co. v. British Trade Corp.* (1922) 10 Ll. Rep. 678.

[24] *Sachs v. Miklos* [1948] 2 K.B. 23.

[25] *Prager v. Blatspiel, Stamp & Heacock Ltd*, above at p. 570; *Tronson v. Dent* (1853) 8 Moo.P.C. 419, 449–452; *The Winson* [1982] A.C. 959, Illustration 1, discussed also below.

(d) The person in whose interest the agent is acting must be competent: for example, a dissolved corporation,[26] or an alien enemy,[27] cannot be a principal under these rules. This limitation is inevitable if the doctrine is one of agency, but its results can be criticised.[28]

(e) It would also seem that in both types of situation the authority could not prevail against express instructions to the contrary: this follows from the fact that it does not operate where the principal can be consulted.[29] The inference is that the principal could forbid the action at the time: if so, he can do so in advance.[30]

Second category: the acceptor for honour. The second type of case   **4–006** involves situations where a person who acts for another in an emergency seeks only reimbursement or indemnity from the person benefited, or to defend himself in respect of what he has done in an action for breach of contract (if there is a contract) or in tort (usually conversion, which he might otherwise have committed by his dealing with property of the principal). No issue arises as regards third parties: if this is an example of agency reasoning, it involves only the internal relationship between principal and agent. Although in 1841 Parke B. said that the acceptor for honour was, after the shipmaster, the only other example of agency of necessity,[31] it is clear that the second category is not in fact confined to the acceptor for honour. Thus it has been held that a carrier may make a contract for the stabling of an uncollected horse and recover the charges from the consignor[32]; that he is justified in selling perishable goods which remain uncollected and are deteriorating[33]; and that a salvor may warehouse goods on behalf of their owner at the termination of the salvage service and recover the cost of doing so.[34] These cases may in fact be examples of the first category: it may be that these carriers made or could have made contracts binding the goods owners to third parties. The actual decisions, however, relate only to the internal relationship between principal and agent. It has also been held that an

---

[26] *Re Banque des Marchands de Moscou* [1952] 1 T.L.R. 739.

[27] *Jebara v. Ottoman Bank* [1927] 2 K.B. 254 (decision revsd. [1928] A.C. 269).

[28] See Goff and Jones, *Law of Restitution* (4th ed.) at p. 368.

[29] See Illustrations 1, 2. See also *Restatement*, § 47; Goddard [1984] L.M.C.L.Q. 255; but *cf. Great Northern Ry. Co. v. Swaffield* (1874) L.R. 9 Ex. 132.

[30] But in *Graanhandel T. Vink B.V. v. European Grain & Shipping Ltd* [1989] 2 Lloyd's Rep. 531, 533 Evans J. said that there could be circumstances where "it might well be argued that the seller's refusal to acknowledge these facts would not prevent the buyer from alleging that the agency did exist." The deserted wife's agency of necessity, now obsolete, applied even though the principal had forbidden the act: see below, para. 4–011.

[31] *Hawtayne v. Bourne* (1841) 7 M. & W. 595, 597.

[32] *Great Northern Ry. Co. v. Swaffield* (1874) L.R. 9 Ex. 132.

[33] *Sims & Co. v. Midland Ry. Co.* [1913] 1 K.B. 103; *cf. Springer v. Great Western Ry. Co.* [1921] 1 K.B. 257.

[34] *The Winson* [1982] A.C. 939, Illustration 1: see below.

agent for sale was justified in shipping the goods elsewhere, even contrary to instructions, where they were in danger because of potentially hostile conditions.[35] On the other hand it has been held that a bailee of furniture was liable in conversion when he sold it after fruitless attempts to contact the owner: though in this case it appears that necessity, as opposed to inconvenience, had not arisen.[36] It should be noted that in these cases the supposed agent may have no prior relationship with the principal, as in the leading case of the acceptor for honour: but he may already be an agent, and is at any rate likely to have some relationship with the person for whom he acts, such as that of bailee.

Since cases in the second category only give rise to internal rights, duties and defences between the person acting and the person benefited, they are not dissimilar to the *negotiorum gestio* of Roman law, which is a quasi-contractual institution entitling the *gestor*, a person intervening in situations of necessity, to reimbursement and also making him liable for acting inappropriately.[37] As such they seem in the modern law more appropriately dealt with as part of the law of restitution. The category in fact contains a limited number of rather miscellaneous situations where the law of agency was pressed into service long ago to provide a way of dealing with problems which probably ought nowadays to be approached differently. The cases usually involve an inappropriate use of agency reasoning, as in another context does the use of a notion of irrevocable agency to create what are really property or security interests.[38] The problems of this category should nowadays, therefore, be considered against the background not of agency but of a possible general principle of necessitous intervention within the law of restitution.[39]

4–007   **Only first category a true example of agency.** Thus only the first category is a true example of agency reasoning, and only that category is therefore really relevant for discussion in this book. It is also much less significant than it was, for modern communications will normally make

---

[35] *Tetley & Co. v. British Trade Corp.* (1922) 10 Ll. Rep. 678.

[36] *Sachs v. Miklos* [1948] 2 K.B. 23; followed in *Anderson v. Erlanger* [1980] C.L.Y. 133. See also *Munro v. Wilmott* [1949] 1 K.B. 295 (similar facts). In *Ridyard v. Roberts*, unrep., C.A., May 16, 1980 a bailee of ponies was held justified in selling them when the owner in breach of contract failed to remove them. In *Coldman v. Hill* [1919] 1 K.B. 443 at p. 456 Scrutton L.J. suggested that a bailee of cattle from whom they are stolen ought, if he cannot contact the owner, to "act as agent of necessity on behalf of and at the expense of the owner." Sometimes statute gives a power of sale: *e.g.* unpaid seller's right to resell: Sale of Goods Act 1979, s.48(3); Protection of Animals Act 1911, s.7; Unsolicited Goods and Services Act 1981; Torts (Interference with Goods) Act 1977, ss.12, 13.

[37] See Buckland, *Textbook of Roman Law* (3rd ed.), pp. 537–538.

[38] See Article 120.

[39] See Goff and Jones, *op.cit.* n. 1 above; Birks, *op.cit.* n. 1 above.

dramatic actions by shipmasters, or indeed others, unnecessary even in remote places: even in maritime salvage situations a master may often be in touch by radio. Situations can obviously still arise, however, where communication is impossible or impracticable; and as regards cargo, where the ship contains goods covered by many bills of lading it may be impracticable to trace and/or communicate with all the cargo owners. [40] Cases may also arise where the cargo owner does not answer, or does not answer clearly, requests for instructions. [41]

This type of agency of necessity seems in origin to be a primitive example of what would now be regarded as vicarious liability reasoning. To impose liability on the principal in such cases was more important than to think of any correlative rights for him. A justification given in 1808 was that the master "is seldom of ability to make good a loss of any considerable amount": [42] hence the owner should be liable. The idea of authority arising in specified circumstances by operation of law is not, however, so satisfactory as the combination of the more general rules of implied and apparent authority, which (particularly the latter) have been developed subsequently to these old cases. For the old rules require that the third party dealing with the agent take the risk as to whether the circumstances creating authority by operation of law have arisen—whether there is an emergency and whether it is impracticable for the agent to communicate with his principal. Furthermore, if it is correct, as is suggested above, that there is no possibility of authority if the principal has been communicated with and has forbidden the act in question, this also is not easy to reconcile with the idea of authority by operation of law. Yet as the law at present stands, if the full requirements are not complied with, the agency power does not exist, whatever the appearance to the third party. Such an approach is much less sensitive to the merits of the cases than the normal rules of implied and apparent authority. [43] It is true that under the doctrine of apparent authority the third party cannot rely merely on the statement of the agent that he has authority, so that if the requirements for operation of the doctrine have not arisen but the master says that they have, the third party will not on that ground alone be protected. [44] But if there was an appearance of authority, modern doctrine would make the shipowner liable in some cases where old cases would not—for example, where it appeared that the act was justified; where the act had been forbidden by the principal but this was not known to the third party;

---

[40] See *The Choko Star* [1990] 1 Lloyd's Rep. 516, Illustration 2, also discussed below.
[41] As in *The Winson* [1982] A.C. 939, Illustration 1, also discussed below.
[42] Abbott, *Merchant Ships and Seaman* (3rd ed.), cited in Holdsworth, *H.E.L.* VIII, p. 250.
[43] See in general below, para. 4–008.
[44] *Armagas Ltd v. Mundogas S.A. (The Ocean Frost)* [1986] A.C. 717.

and perhaps where the agent gave the impression that the principal could not be consulted.[45]

The old English rules are much more elaborately worked out than the corresponding law in the United States, which refers only to inference of authority to act in emergency.[46] There is, however, some other English case law which approaches the question of emergency powers simply on the basis of implied (and hence in appropriate cases apparent) authority, suggesting that the authority of an agent may be enlarged in situations of emergency. This reasoning has been used to justify delegation by an agent of his powers,[47] lending on unusual terms[48] and giving credit in circumstances where this would not be normal.[49] It is submitted that this is the correct approach. It is necessary, however, to add to it the proposition, to be derived from *Tappenden v. Artus* and *The Winson*, discussed below, that a person already in a legal relationship with the principal which is not one of agency (such as a bailee) may likewise have agency powers in certain situations, some of which may involve emergencies. If such an approach is followed, the supposedly separate notion of agency of necessity, or at any rate much of it, could, and, it is submitted, should be absorbed into the general law relating to implied and apparent authority.

4–008   **Salvage contracts: an opportunity for better analysis.** In the case of salvage agreements, where rapid decisions may be required, the advantages in detaching from the ancient, strict rules and subsuming the problem under the general rules of authority can readily be seen. The first step in doing so was taken by Brandon J. in *The Unique Mariner*,[50] where in a salvage situation he held owners bound by the master's signature on Lloyd's Open Form on the basis of apparent authority, without reference to the old rules (which probably were not satisfied,

---

[45] *cf. United Bank of Kuwait Ltd v. Hammoud* [1988] 1 W.L.R. 1051 (below, para. 8–023) where a solicitor was held liable on an unauthorised and fraudulent transaction by an assistant where the transaction could have been authorised had a certain background of facts existed: the third party was entitled to assume from the conduct of the third party that it did. "The bank, knowing that [X] was a practising solicitor with established firms, were entitled to assume the truth of what he said unless alerted to the fact that the contrary might be the case"—*per* Lord Donaldson of Lymington M.R. at p. 1066. See also *First Energy (U.K.) Ltd v. Hungarian International Bank Ltd* [1993] 2 Lloyd's Rep. 194; below, para. 8–023.

[46] See *Restatement*, s. 47.

[47] *De Bussche v. Alt* (1878) 8 Ch.D. 286, Illustration 7 to Article 36. See also *Walker v. G.W. Ry. Co.* (1867) L.R. 2 Ex. 228; *Langan v. G.W. Ry. Co.* (1873) 30 L.T. 173 (railway officials ordering medical attention for passengers: company liable: but here the emergency is not that of the principal, the company).

[48] *Montaignac v. Shitta* (1890) 5 App. Cas. 357, Illustration 15 to Article 74.

[49] *Gokal Chand-Jagan Nath v. Nand Ram Das-Atma Ram* [1939] A.C. 106.

[50] [1978] 1 Lloyd's Rep. 438, Illustration 3.

because the master had already been in touch with the owners at the time). The case only concerned salvage in respect of the *ship*, for whose owner the master is certainly agent, however: and subsequently in the *The Choko Star*[51] the Court of Appeal applied the ancient case law to hold that the master's signature to a Lloyd's Open Form did not bind *cargo* unless it had been impracticable to consult cargo (which was not so).

The main reason given was that though he is agent of the owner, the master is not an agent for cargo, and so cannot act for it except when the special rules of agency of necessity are complied with. There are certainly abundant old dicta to that effect against the background of shipping operations in the nineteenth century. Against this it may be said, as has been suggested above, that the master acts for the shipowner, and the shipowner as bailee may be regarded as having implied and therefore normally also apparent authority to do what is necessary to preserve the cargo during the voyage. This argument was rejected on the basis that there were no grounds for implying such a power (beyond what the agency of necessity doctrine permits) into the contract of carriage between cargo owner and shipowner. The rules regarding the implication of terms into contracts are of course strict[52]: perhaps too much so. But even if those rules are accepted, despite suggestions that "Agency of necessity is traditionally regarded as part of the law of contract",[53] it is not clear that questions of authority are always to be determined by reference to implied terms of the contract between the supposed principal and the supposed agent. Particular relationships, such as that of bailor and bailee, may carry their own implications of implied, and hence apparent, authority. Implied *authority* is inferred "from the conduct of the parties and the circumstances of the case",[54] which is quite different reasoning from that relating to implied *terms of contracts*.

In one of the two principal recent cases on the doctrine, *The Winson*,[55] a salvor procured the warehousing of the goods salved, after completion of the salvage service, and claimed reimbursement of the cost of so doing. This was therefore a case in the second, not the first, category. The full requirements for the operation of traditional agency of necessity were not operative, for the salvor was able to communicate with the cargo owners (who did not give a clear answer) and was in any

---

[51] [1990] 1 Lloyd's Rep. 516, Illustration 2; noted [1991] L.M.C.Q. 1; (1992) 55 M.L.R. 414.

[52] See *Liverpool City Council v. Irwin* [1977] A.C. 239.

[53] Goff and Jones, *Law of Restitution* (4th ed.), p. 367, citing *Notara v. Henderson* (1872) L.R. 7 Q.B. 225 and *Cargo ex Argos* (1893) L.R. 5 P.C. 134; but in fact rejecting this basis on the following page.

[54] *Hely-Hutchinson v. Brayhead Ltd* [1968] 1 Q.B. 549, 583.

[55] [1982] A.C. 939, Illustration 1.

case acting partly for his own benefit (to preserve his lien). But he was held able to recover, Lord Diplock saying that the strict requirements were inapplicable to the second (*negotiorum gestio*) category.[56] It was said that the salvor was under a duty to the goods owner to care for the goods, and that he had "a correlative right to charge the owner of the goods with the expenses reasonably incurred."[57] But with subsequent development of principle, it may be argued that the strict rules are not needed in the first category either. It can then be argued that the bailment relationship is sufficient to give the bailee authority not only to do things entitling him to reimbursement but also to entitle him to make contracts binding on the principal. On this basis the principal might in an appropriate case have been liable directly to the warehouse proprietor. (Though in this particular situation, if the salvor warehoused to protect his lien, he would be unlikely to do so on behalf of another.) Thus in *Tappenden v. Artus*[58] it was held that the bailee of a car could leave it for repair in circumstances creating a lien against the owner. The case is not directly in point, because the decision was based on the bailee's right to use the goods, and hence to keep them in a usable state: but the reasoning is relevant.

The statement by Lord Diplock in *The Winson* that the strict rules should be eliminated from the assessment of cases of the second category is therefore to be welcomed in so far as it provides support for the detachment of the second category from the first. But it does not follow that all the cases where the only questions that have arisen were as to the internal relationship between principal and agent, and in particular the case of the bailee who makes a contract in respect of the goods bailed, are really no more than examples of the second category. Some may be real agency cases, attributable to the first category, and now to be explained on the basis of implied or apparent authority. It has already been suggested that this is true of the land carrier decisions. It is submitted therefore that the old strict rules should no longer have any part to play in cases of the first category any more than in the second; and that the substance of the cases in the first category should be assimilated to the general rules as to implied and apparent authority. On this basis a master may be held to have a general implied authority to sign a salvage agreement for ship and (because of the bailment reasoning above) cargo, perhaps except where consultation is practicable and expected, and hence apparent authority even in some circumstances where the implied authority is not applicable (*e.g.* because the owner has forbidden the contract, or could easily have been consulted). As for the more drastic acts of selling or hypothecating ship or cargo, this

---

[56] At p. 958.
[57] At p. 960.
[58] [1964] 2 Q.B. 185.

would normally require consultation, and it may be that the third party's belief that the master's act is justified is less likely to appear reasonable under the doctrine of apparent authority.

The present law as to the first category. Nevertheless, as the law at present stands, while the ordinary principles of actual and apparent authority apply to determine whether a master has authority to sign a salvage agreement on behalf of the shipowner, the ancient rules set out above are still to be deployed to decide whether he has authority to sign for cargo,[59] and doubtless (if such cases can still arise) whether he has authority to sell or hypothecate ship or cargo. That this may be no longer an appropriate attitude is shown by the fact that Article 6 of the International Convention on Salvage of 1989 gives the master wide powers, including the power to sign a salvage contract for cargo. Although the Court of Appeal in *The Choko Star*[60] thought this topic an unsuitable one for judicial development, it is submitted that the House of Lords should, if the opportunity arises, take the opportunity to bring the case law into line so far as possible with present-day thinking on agency authority, which no longer needs a special and rather rigid notion of agency by operation of law, a notion which antedates the development of the doctrine of apparent authority, and even the full development of that of implied authority and depends on the existence of facts which may not be known or even knowable to the third party. 4–009

Development of the second category: restitutionary doctrine. If any wider principle of restitution in respect of necessitous intervention is to emerge from the cases in the second category, however, creative development of a different order would be required. In 1924 McCardie J., in a case of the first category, spoke strongly in favour of enlarging the whole doctrine of agency of necessity, and was prepared in principle to apply it to an agent for purchase who was unable because of wartime conditions to forward goods purchased to his principal in Romania and resold them in England.[61] The dicta were, however, doubted by Scrutton L.J. three years later in a case of the second category,[62] and other dicta against extension of the reasoning can be cited.[63] Proper analysis has been hampered by the running together of the two 4–010

---

[59] *The Choko Star* [1990] 1 Lloyd's Rep. 516, Illustration 2.
[60] n. 59 above. The judgment of Sheen J. at first instance repays study.
[61] *Prager v. Blatspiel, Stamp & Heacock Ltd* [1924] 1 K.B. 566. In this category, extension in cases where the principal has forbidden the act might be easier: *cf. Tetley & Co. v. British Trade Corp.* (1922) 10 Ll. Rep. 678; above, para. 4–006.
[62] *Jebara v. Ottoman Bank* [1927] 2 K.B. 254, 270–271 (decision revsd. [1928] A.C. 269) (selling goods overseas after outbreak of war).
[63] *Gwilliam v. Twist* [1895] 2 Q.B. 84, 87 *per* Lord Esher M.R. (substitute driver where official driver drunk); *Sachs v. Miklos* [1948] 2 K.B. 23, 35–36 *per* Lord Goddard C.J.

categories. Any attempt at development within the second category has to contend initially with the dictum of Bowen L.J. in 1886 that "work or labour done or money expended by one man to preserve or benefit the property of another do not according to English law create any lien upon the property saved, nor even, if standing alone, create any obligation to repay the expenditure."[64] Nevertheless, though they were said by Bowen L.J. to be a special exception, the rules of maritime salvage,[65] including the decision in *The Winson*, can be used to justify movement towards generalisation; as can certain cases concerning the payment of funeral expenses of a deceased person.[66] On the other hand it has been held that no lien arises in favour of a person who succours a stray animal,[67] or conveys timber on the bank of a river to a place of safety.[68] Though writers strongly advocate the development of generalised principle, the picture remains unclear and the case law very limited indeed. But other doctrines may sometimes secure a similar result by different means. Thus where there is an established cause of action, the damages awarded may cover expenses incurred in emergencies[69]; and a person who seeks to recover property may sometimes be able to do so only if he pays for work done on it.[70] The appropriate reasoning must be found outside the law of agency, and further discussion is beyond the scope of this work.[71]

4–011   **Agency of deserted wives.** Until comparatively recently a line of cases whereby a deserted wife was regarded as having, even if forbidden to do so, authority to pledge her husband's credit for necessaries was said to be a further instance of agency of necessity and agency by operation of law. These cases made any general principle behind the notion even more difficult to extract, for the necessity in such cases was that of the agent and not of the principal. This seems another example of agency

---

[64] *Falcke v. Scottish Imperial Insurance Co.* (1886) 34 Ch.D. 234. See Birks, *Introduction to the Law of Restitution* (1989), pp. 194 *et seq.*

[65] See Goff and Jones, *Law of Restitution* (4th ed.), Chap. 16.

[66] *Jenkins v. Tucker* (1788) 1 H.Bl. 90; *Tugwell v. Heyman* (1812) 3 Camp. 298; *Rogers v. Price* (1829) 3 Y. & J. 28; *Ambrose v. Kerrison* (1851) 10 C.B. 776; *Shallcross v. Wright* (1850) 12 Beav. 558; *Bradshaw v. Beard* (1862) 12 C.B.(N.S.) 344; *Rees v. Hughes* [1946] K.B. 517; *Croskery v. Gee* [1957] N.Z.L.R. 586. See also *Matheson v. Smiley* [1932] 2 D.L.R. 787 (medical expenses).

[67] *Binstead v. Buck* (1776) 2 Wm. Bl. 1117. But there may in appropriate cases be distress damage feasant. See *Sorrell v. Paget* [1950] 1 K.B. 252, where both matters are discussed. See also Protection of Animals Act 1911, s. 7.

[68] *Nicholson v. Chapman* (1793) 2 H.Bl. 254.

[69] *Schneider v. Eisovitch* [1960] 2 Q.B. 430 (tort); *Kolfor Plant Ltd v. Tilbury Plant Ltd* (1977) 121 S.J. 390 (sale of rejected goods).

[70] *Munro v. Wilmott* [1949] 1 K.B. 295; *Greenwood v. Bennett* [1973] 1 Q.B. 195.

[71] See Goff and Jones, *op.cit.* n. 65 above, Chap. 15 (which, since it approaches the law from a different angle, should be taken into account by any reader of this chapter); Birks, *op.cit.* n. 64 above, pp. 193 *et seq.*

law being deployed to achieve a desired result which did not at the time seem attainable by other means. This method of protecting deserted wives has, however, been superseded by other institutions for that purpose, and the doctrine inherent in the cases has in consequence been abolished in England by statute.[72] Discussion of these cases is therefore omitted: a full account appeared in the 13th edition of this work.

Illustrations

(1) A salvor, after the completion of the salvage operation, warehouses salved goods at a nearby port, principally to preserve them but partly with a view to preserving his lien. He asks the cargo owner to make arrangements to accept the goods at that port. The cargo owner does not respond. The salvor was bailee of the cargo owner from the time the goods were put into the vessels which he provided, and even if the salvage service was finished when the vessels arrived at the port, he remained bailee of the cargo owner thereafter. As such he had a duty to the cargo owner to take reasonable measures to preserve the cargo, and a correlative right to charge its owner with the warehousing expenses, which had been reasonably incurred in fulfilling that duty.[73]

4–012

(2) A ship strands in the River Parana in Argentina. The master signs a salvage agreement on Lloyd's Open Form with Greek salvors, though local salvors are available. There is only one cargo owner, who could have been consulted but was not. The master has no authority to sign for cargo (as opposed to the ship itself) except under the agency of necessity rules, which are not satisfied because of the lack of consultation, quite apart from the question whether the act of the master was reasonable or the third party was aware of the lack of consultation.[74]

(3) A ship strands. The master contacts his owners, who notify him that a tug will be sent. By chance the captain of another tug with different owners is completing a salvage service nearby. He notices the stranded ship, goes to it and offers his services. The master takes this to be the tug sent by his owners and signs a salvage agreement. As his owners are already sending another tug, he is not authorised to do so, and the agency of necessity rules do not apply: but his owners are nevertheless liable under the doctrine of apparent authority.[75]

---

[72] See above, para. 3–069.
[73] *China Pacific S.A. v. Food Corp. of India (The Winson)* [1982] A.C. 939. *Quaere*, however, whether the salvage service was really terminated: if it had not been, the case would have been more easily solved.
[74] *Industrie Chimiche Italia v. Alexander G. Tsavliris & Sons Maritime Co. (The Choko Star)* [1990] 1 Lloyd's Rep. 516.
[75] *The Unique Mariner* [1978] 1 Lloyd's Rep. 438.

CHAPTER 5

SUB–AGENCY

Article 36

WHEN AGENT MAY DELEGATE HIS AUTHORITY

5–001
(1) An agent may not delegate his authority in whole or in part except with the express or implied authority of the principal.[1]

(2) The authority of the principal is implied in the following cases:

(a) Where the principal knows and accepts, at the time of the agent's appointment, that the agent intends to delegate his authority.[2]

(b) Where the authority conferred is of such a nature as to necessitate its execution wholly or in part by means of a sub-agent.[3]

(c) Where the employment of a sub-agent is justified by the usage of the particular trade or business in which the agent is employed, provided that such usage is not unreasonable, and not inconsistent with the express terms of the agent's authority.[4]

(d) Where in the course of the agent's employment unforeseen circumstances arise which render it necessary for the agent to employ a sub-agent.[5]

(e) Where, from the conduct of the principal or of the principal and the agent, it may reasonably be presumed to have been intended that the agent should have power to employ a sub-agent.[6]

(3) The above principles are inapplicable where the act done or to be done is purely ministerial and does not involve confidence or discretion.[7]

---

[1] *De Bussche v. Alt.* (1878) 8 Ch.D. 286, 310–311 (Illustration 7). It seems that the converse position is taken by French CC, art. 1994; *cf.* BGB, para. 664. As to apparent authority see Comment.

[2] *Quebec & Richmond Railway Co. v. Quinn* (1858) 12 Moo.P.C. 232, 265 (English contractor employed to construct railroad in Canada).

[3] *Quebec & Richmond Railroad Co. v. Quinn*, n. 2 above.

[4] *De Bussche v. Alt*, n. 1 above. See also Article 31.

[5] *De Bussche v. Alt*, n. 1 above; *cf. Gwilliam v. Twist* [1895] 2 Q.B. 84; *Harris v. Fiat Motors Ltd* (1906) 22 T.L.R. 556 (revsd on other grounds, (1907) 23 T.L.R. 504). See also Chap. 4.

[6] *De Bussche v. Alt*, n. 1 above. See also *Re Deutsch* (1976) 82 D.L.R. (3d) 567 (consul as administrator of estate had power to delegate).

[7] See Illustration 5; *Rossiter v. Trafalgar Life Ass. Assn.* (1859) 27 Beav. 377 (insurance proposal); *Hemming v. Hale* (1859) 7 C.B. (N.S.) 487 (attorney's clerk); *Allam & Co. Ltd*

Comment

The general rule is that an agent may not delegate the discretions to   5–002
act for another which are reposed in him: *delegatus non potest delegare*.
This maxim is founded on the confidential nature of the contract of
agency: whenever authority is coupled with a discretion or confidence it
must, as a rule, be exercised by the agent in person.[8] "The reason is
fairly obvious: the risks of agency are substantial, and a person has a
right not to be represented, save at his own election and by an agent of
his   own   choice."[9]   Thus   auctioneers,[10]   factors,[11]   liquidators,[12]
brokers,[13] estate agents,[14] solicitors,[15] etc., have normally no implied
authority to employ deputies or sub-agents to exercise their powers.

Ministerial acts. On the other hand an agent may delegate the   5–003
performance of purely ministerial or ancillary acts, unless there is
evidence of usage not permitting this[16]: and in general other, non-
fiduciary functions of persons who have agency powers may be
performed vicariously in accordance with normal contractual principles.
This is not delegation.

Effect of unauthorised delegation. Where the agent is not authorised   5–004
to delegate and does so, acts performed by a purported sub-agent will
not be valid, where validity is in question, nor bind or entitle the
principal[17]; payment to such sub-agent will not rank as payment to the
principal[18]; the principal is not, of course, liable to the sub-agent for

---

v. Europa Poster Services Ltd [1968] 1 W.L.R. 638 (solicitor acting for agent gave notice
to terminate licence agreement); *The Berkshire* [1974] 1 Lloyd's Rep. 185, 188; *Lep
International Pty Ltd v. Atlanttrafic Express Service Inc.* (1987) 10 N.S.W.L.R. 614
(signature of bill of lading); *Parkin v. Williams* [1986] 1 N.Z.L.R. 294, Illustration 4
(Statute of Frauds).

[8] *De Bussche v. Alt*, n. 1 above. See also *Restatement*, §§ 18, 78–81.

[9] Mechem, *Outlines of Agency* (4th ed.), p. 50.

[10] *Coles v. Trecothick* (1804) 9 Ves.Jun. 234.

[11] *Solly v. Rathbone* (1814) 2 M. & S. 298.

[12] Illustration 5.

[13] *Cockran v. Irlam* (1813) 2 M. & S. 301; *Henderson v. Barnewall* (1827) 1 Y. & J.
387.

[14] *John McCann & Co. v. Pow* [1974] 1 W.L.R. 1643. See also *Benjamin v. Clothier*
(1969) 210 EG 29; *Maloney v. Hardy and Moorsehead* (1970) 216 EG 1582.

[15] *Re Becket, Purnell v. Paine* [1918] 2 Ch. 72. But see Illustration 6 as to London
agents.

[16] See Illustrations 4, 5, and other authorities cited above, n. 7.

[17] Illustrations 3 and 5.

[18] *Dunlop & Sons v. De Murrieta & Co.* (1886) 3 T.L.R. 166 (shipping agent acting for
shipbrokers); *Maloney v. Hardy and Moorsehead*, n. 14 above; *John McCann & Co. v.
Pow*, n. 14 above.

commission[19]; the sub-agent has no lien against the principal[20]; and the agent may be liable in respect of money received by such a person[21] and in general for wrongful execution of his authority.[22] But an agent may be expressly authorised to delegate; he may have implied authority to do so in the situations specified in this Article; or his act in doing so may be ratified.[23]

5–005   **Apparent authority.** The principle here stated is one of actual authority, but the rules of apparent authority may also apply where third parties are involved, and to these the Article is also relevant. For in the absence of specific representation or conduct, the third party will be entitled to assume that the agent had the authority to delegate where such authority to do so would normally be implied. In such a case he will be entitled to make that assumption even though the authority to delegate had actually been negatived between principal and agent, provided that he did not know of this.[24]

5–006   **Administrative law.** The same maxim *delegatus non potest delegare* is often invoked in administrative law to declare invalid the exercise of powers by persons other than those to whom they have been entrusted. Some cases purport to distinguish between delegation and appointment of an agent, on the basis that the second is permitted but the first is not: other cases treat the two notions as the same. The cases arise in diverse contexts and "abound in terminological inconsistencies"[25]: it is doubtful whether agency terminology assists in clarifying or solving the problems. An account of them is beyond the scope of this work and should be sought in specialised books.[26] One point may however be noted: that a government Minister may normally act through departmental officials without infringing the maxim.[27]

---

[19] *Schmaling v. Tomlinson* (1815) 6 Taunt. 147; *Mason v. Clifton* (1863) 3 F. & F. 899.

[20] *Solly v. Rathbone* (1814) 2 M. & S. 298; see Article 70.

[21] *Mackersy v. Ramsay, Bonars & Co.* (1843) 9 C. & F. 818; *Re Mutual Aid Permanent Benefit B.S.* (1883) 49 L.T. 530; *National Employers Mutual General Insurance Assn. Ltd v. Elphinstone* [1929] W.N. 135; *Balsamo v. Medici* [1984] 1 W.L.R. 951; *Trading and General Investment Corp. v. Gault, Armstrong & Kemble Ltd (The Okeanis)* [1986] 1 Lloyd's Rep. 195.

[22] *e.g.* Illustration 1.

[23] *e.g. Keay v. Fenwick* (1876) 1 C.P.D. 745. See Articles 13–20.

[24] See Article 74.

[25] de Smith, *Judicial Review of Administrative Action* (4th ed.), p. 301.

[26] *e.g.* de Smith, *op. cit*, n. 25 above, pp. 298 *et seq.*; Craig, *Administrative Law* (3rd ed.), pp. 309–310; see also *O'Reilly v. State Bank of Victoria Commissioners* (1983) 153 C.L.R. 1; Dixon, (1987) 11 Sydney L.Rev. 326.

[27] *Carltona Ltd v. Commissioner of Works* [1943] 2 All E.R. 560, 563.

Illustrations

(1) A shipmaster was authorised to sell certain goods. He was held **5–007** to have no implied authority to send them on to another person for sale when he could not himself find a purchaser, and was liable in respect of them. [28]

(2) A notice to quit given by the agent of an agent is not sufficient without further evidence of authority or ratification. [29]

(3) An agent buys property at a sale by auction, and the auctioneer enters his name as buyer without objection by the principal, who is present at the sale. The entry is sufficient memorandum of the contract as against the principal. [30] But entry by the auctioneer's clerk would not suffice unless there was other evidence of authority. [31] And where a tenant for life had power to lease, and a memorandum of the contract for a lease was signed by his agent's clerk with the approval of the agent and in the ordinary course of business it was held that the memorandum was not sufficient to satisfy the Statute of Frauds, not having been proved to have been signed by a duly authorised agent within the meaning of that statute. [32]

(4) Attorneys under a power of attorney may delegate the signature of an agreement for sale to the auctioneer. [33]

(5) An agent has authority to draw bills of exchange in the principal's name. Signature by the agent's clerk is sufficient if it is in accordance with the usual practice. [34] So, an authority given to an agent to indorse a particular bill in the principal's name may be delegated, because such acts are purely ministerial and involve no discretion. Where four liquidators had no power to authorise one of their number to accept bills of exchange on behalf of them all, it was held that they might authorise him to accept a particular bill on their behalf, because the execution of the former authority would involve discretion, whereas the latter was an authority to do a purely ministerial act. [35]

(6) A country solicitor has implied authority to act through his London agent when necessary or usual in the ordinary course of

---

[28] *Catlin v. Bell* (1815) 4 Camp. 183.

[29] *Doe d. Rhodes v. Robinson* (1837) 3 Bing.N.C. 677. But *cf. Allam & Co. v. Europa Poster Services Ltd* [1968] 1 W.L.R. 638 (notice given by solicitor of company).

[30] *White v. Proctor* (1811) 4 Taunt. 209; *Emmerson v. Heelis* (1809) 2 Taunt. 38.

[31] *Bell v. Balls* [1897] 1 Ch. 663; *Bird v. Boulter* (1833) 4 B. & Ad. 443.

[32] *Blore v. Sutton* (1817) 3 Mer. 237. These questions would not now arise in the same form because of the different requirements of the Law of Property (Miscellaneous Provisions) Act 1989, s. 2.

[33] *Parkin v. Williams* [1986] 1 N.Z.L.R. 294.

[34] *Re Marshall, ex p. Sutton* (1788) 2 Cox 84. See also *Lord v. Hall* (1848) 2 C. & K. 698; *Brown v. Tombs* [1891] 1 Q.B. 253.

[35] *Re London and Mediterranean Bank, ex p. Birmingham Banking Co.* (1868) L.R. 3 Ch.App. 651, 653–654.

business: thus the issue of proceedings by his London agent acting as such is valid.[36] Where a London agent has the general conduct of an action, he has the same general authority in conducting it, including authority to compromise, as the country solicitor employing him, in the absence of any express limits on such general authority.[37] But a solicitor cannot delegate his entire employment to his London agent so as to make the agent his client's solicitor: a retainer to a country solicitor does not justify an action in which the London agents are the solicitors on the record.[38]

(7)   A shipowner employed merchants carrying on business at Hong Kong, Shanghai and Yokohama to sell a ship at any port where the ship might from time to time in the course of employment under charter happen to be. The merchants had authority to appoint a sub-agent with branches at Nagasaki and other Japanese ports.[39]

(8)   A trustee may employ a broker when investing trust funds and may pay the purchase-money to him; the trustee will not be liable for any loss thereby occasioned if he follows the usual and regular course of business adopted by ordinary prudent persons.[40] This principle applies even if the trustee is paid for his services,[41] and where a co-trustee is employed as a broker under a clause in the trust instrument.[42] Apart from these general principles, the ability of a trustee to delegate his powers is governed by the Trustee Act 1925, ss.23 and 25 (the latter as amended by section 9 of the Powers of Attorney Act 1971).[43]

Article 37

RELATION BETWEEN PRINCIPAL AND SUB-AGENT

5–008

(1)   The acts done on the principal's behalf by a sub-agent whose appointment was authorised or ratified by the principal bind the principal as if they had been performed by the agent himself.[44]

(2)   The relation of principal and agent may be established by an agent between his principal and a sub-agent if the agent is expressly or impliedly authorised to constitute such relation, or

---

[36] *Solley v. Wood* (1852) 16 Beav. 370. See Article 37, Illustrations 5, 6.
[37] *Re Newen, Carruthers v. Newen* [1903] 1 Ch. 812.
[38] *Wray v. Kemp* (1884) 26 Ch.D. 169; *Re Scholes & Sons* (1886) 32 Ch.D. 245; see also *Re Beckett, Purnell v. Paine* [1918] 2 Ch. 72.
[39] *De Bussche v. Alt* (1878) 8 Ch.D. 286.
[40] *Speight v. Gaunt* (1883) 9 App.Cas. 1.
[41] *Jobson v. Palmer* [1893] 1 Ch. 71.
[42] *Shepherd v. Harris* [1905] 2 Ch. 310.
[43] See Snell, *Equity* (29th ed.), pp. 265–270; and recommendations in Law Com. No. 220 (1994).
[44] See Comment. As to apparent authority, see below, para. 5–012.

if his act is ratified, and it is the intention of the agent and of such sub-agent that such relation should be constituted.[45]

(3)   But there is no privity of contract between a principal and a sub-agent as such merely because the delegation was effected with the authority of the principal; and in the absence of such privity the rights and duties arising out of any contracts between the principal and the agent, and between the agent and the sub-agent, respectively, are only enforceable by and against the immediate parties to those contracts.[46] However, the sub-agent may be liable to the principal as a fiduciary, in tort, and possibly in other respects.[47]

Comment

Rule (1). The acts of an authorised sub-agent bind the principal. This is not because the sub-agent is the principal's agent: "it is rather that he is bound by the act of his own agent, who, in this instance, is (properly) doing the act through the sub-agent."[48] Thus he may receive notification or be held to have acquired knowledge through a sub-agent[49]; signature by a sub-agent may bind him[50]; issue of process by a sub-agent may be valid[51]; he may be bound by a contract made by a sub-agent[52]; and payment to a sub-agent may rank as payment to the principal.[53] These propositions are obvious where the sub-agent is in privity of contract with the principal, but the cases cited show that the same results obtain where he is not.

The consequences of authorised sub-delegation between principal and sub-agent depend on the way in which this was effected. There are two possibilities.

Rule (2). Privity of contract. The agent may appoint another agent for the principal, whether in substitution for,[54] or in addition to,[55]

5–009

5–010

---

[45] *De Bussche v. Alt* (1878) 8 Ch.D. 286, Illustration 7.

[46] *New Zealand & Australian Land Co. v. Watson* (1881) 7 Q.B.D. 374, Illustration 1; *Calico Printers Assn. Ltd v. Barclays Bank Ltd* (1931) 145 L.T. 51; *Schwensen v. Ellinger, Heath, Western & Co.* (1949) 83 Ll.Rep. 79, 81; *Kahler v. Midland Bank Ltd* [1950] A.C. 24; *Balsamo v. Medici* [1984] 1 W.L.R. 951, Illustration 2. This statement was approved in *Henderson v. Merrett Syndicates Ltd* [1994] 3 W.L.R. 761, 796.

[47] *Powell & Thomas v. Evan Jones & Co.* [1905] 1 K.B. 11; *Henderson v. Merrett Syndicates Ltd*, n. 46 above. See Comment.

[48] Mechem, *Outlines of Agency*, (4th ed.), p. 51.

[49] See Article 97, Illustration 16; *cf. ibid.*, Illustration 19.

[50] See Article 36, Illustrations 3, 5.

[51] See Article 36, Illustration 6.

[52] Illustration 7.

[53] *Hemming v. Hale* (1859) 7 C.B.(N.S.) 487; *Maloney v. Hardy and Moorsehead* (1970) 216 EG 1582, 1586; but *cf.* p. 1583.

[54] *e.g. Schwensen v. Ellinger, Heath, Western & Co.*, n. 46 above (wartime conditions): but in this case it seems that the principal himself appointed the new agent.

[55] See Illustration 7; *Ecossaise S.S. Co. Ltd v. Lloyd, Low & Co.* (1890) 7 T.L.R. 76.

himself, as in Rule (3) above. Complete handing-over of functions is obviously unlikely to be authorised, except as regards particular geographical locations,[56] a specific time or in abnormal circumstances.[57] This may create privity of contract between the principal and the new agent, and the full consequences of agency ensue. Since this all may occur where the new agent is to perform different functions from those performed by the appointing agent (*e.g.* where a manager hires staff), and where the appointing agent has no agency relationship with the person appointed, there will be many cases where the terms "sub-agency" and "delegate" will be inappropriate, and it has been suggested that such a person should not be called a sub-agent at all.[58] He is in fact a co-agent. But usage in the cases is indiscriminate.

There may be express authority to delegate by this means, or there may be ratification.[59] But it seems that such authority will not readily be implied.[60] However, where it does exist, the duty of the appointing agent is normally no more than to exercise due care in making the appointment,[61] and he does not, without further circumstances (*e.g.* if he is a *del credere* agent or undertakes a duty of supervision), undertake that the appointed agent will perform the work adequately.[62]

5–011   **Rule (3). No privity of contract.** The agent may equally appoint his own agent to do the requisite work, as in Rule (1) above; again, authority may be express or implied or there may be ratification. The prima facie rule seems to be that a delegation has been effected by this means[63]: this is not surprising as it retains the responsibility of the

---

[56] *e.g. De Bussche v. Alt* (1878) 8 Ch.D. 286, Illustration 7.

[57] *e.g. Schwensen v. Ellinger, Heath, Western & Co.*, n. 46 above.

[58] *Restatement*, Appendix, reporter's note to § 5.

[59] *e.g. Keay v. Fenwick* (1876) 1 C.P.D. 745.

[60] See *Calico Printers Assn. Ltd v. Barclays Bank Ltd* (1931) 145 L.T. 51. But *cf. De Bussche v. Alt* (1878) 8 Ch.D. 286, Illustration 7; *Keay v. Fenwick*, n. 59 above; *Ecossaise S.S. Co. Ltd v. Lloyd, Low & Co.*, n. 55 above. Country solicitors do not normally have the power to create such privity between their clients and their London agents: see Article 36, Illustration 6. But compare the position of solicitors or strockbrokers employing stockbrokers; *Blackburn v. Mason* (1893) 68 L.T. 510. See Article 28, Illustration 3.

[61] *Restatement*, §§ 405, 406; *cf. Thomas Cheshire & Co. v. Vaughan Bros. & Co.* [1920] 3 K.B. 240, 259; *Ecossaise S.S. Co. Ltd v. Lloyd, Low & Co.*, n. 55 above; *Fry v. Tapson* (1884) 28 Ch.D. 268; *Re Weall* (1889) 42 Ch.D. 674.

[62] *Sampson v. Wilson* [1995] 3 W.L.R. 455; *Aiken v. Stewart Wrightson Members Agency Ltd* [1995] 1 W.L.R. 1281. There are also cases on the Liability of directors for acts of Co-directors. And see Article 118.

[63] *Calico Printers Assn. Ltd v. Barclays Bank Ltd*, n. 60 above; *Royal Products Ltd v. Midland Bank Ltd* [1981] 2 Lloyd's Rep. 194. See also *Trengrouse & Co. v. Official Assignee of Steeds* (1896) 14 N.Z.L.R. 636.

person in whom trust is reposed. Thus, for the default of such a person the agent is normally responsible [64]; and if such person receives money for the principal, that is sufficient to charge the agent with its receipt. [65]

The full position of such a person, who may genuinely be called a sub-agent, is not, however, fully worked out in English law. The tacit assumption in the cases seems to be that if the sub-agent is not appointed to be in privity with the principal, he is only in privity with the agent and owes common law and fiduciary duties only to the agent. This, however, is another manifestation of the assumption, which is queried elsewhere in this book, that *either* the agent drops out altogether, *or* the so-called agent is not an agent at all and deals as principal with the outside world. There can be no objection in principal to the notion of an agent who has power to subdelegate, and to appoint a sub-agent, on the basis that he and sub-agent are both liable to the principal.

It is therefore arguable that the very fact that such a sub-agent binds the principal when acting in connection with the principal's affairs shows that he is to be regarded as an agent of the principal, and that he should be also directly liable to the principal. In a sense, this is a contract for the benefit of a third party, and if ways can be devised to give the principal rights against the sub-agent, they are to be welcomed. [66] In the United States, reasoning along these lines made it possible to say that a "sub-agent is liable to the principal for negligence in performing or failing to perform duties undertaken for the principal. He is also under a duty to account for anything received for the principal, and is liable as a fiduciary for any breach of a fiduciary duty." [67] It seems that the principal may also be liable to indemnify the sub-agent. [68] These propositions do not rest on contract: indeed the sub-agent is not liable to the principal for breach of contract, for he normally has no contract with him, nor is the principal liable to the sub-agent for remuneration. [69]

---

[64] *Re Mitchell* (1884) L.J.Ch. 342; *Meyerstein v. Eastern Agency Co. Ltd* (1885) 1 T.L.R. 595; *Ecossaise S.S. Co. Ltd v. Lloyd, Low & Co.* (1890) 7 T.L.R. 76; *Stewart v. Reavell's Garage* [1952] 2 Q.B. 545; *Swire v. Francis* (1877) 3 App.Cas. 106. But *cf. Thomas Cheshire & Co. v. Vaughan Bros. & Co.*, n. 61 above. This would apply even where the delegation was unauthorised.

[65] *Matthews v. Haydon* (1786) 2 Esp. 509; *Mackersy v. Ramsays, Bonars & Co.* (1843) 9 C. & F. 818; *Skinner & Co. v. Weguelin, Eddowes & Co.* (1882) C. & E. 12; *National Employers' Mutual General Insurance Assn. Ltd v. Elphinstone* [1929] W.N. 135; *Trading and General Investment Corp. v. Gault, Armstrong & Kemble Ltd (The Okeanis)* [1986] 1 Lloyd's Rep. 195. This would apply even where the delegation was unauthorised: see above, para. 5–004.

[66] Seavey (1955) 68 Harv.L.Rev. 658, 666–667; also printed as *Restatement*, Appendix, reporter's note to § 5 (a valuable article).

[67] *Restatement*, n. 66 above, at pp. 33–34.

[68] *ibid.*

[69] *ibid.*

In England, however, there is a long-standing authority that the lack of privity between principal and sub-agent means that not only is the principal not liable to the sub-agent for remuneration,[70] but also that the sub-agent has in general no duty to account to the principal,[71] and can be sued by the principal neither in contract nor in restitution.[72] It has also been held that the sub-agent is not liable to the principal for negligently performing the work[73]; and the rules as to indemnity are normally taken as contractual, so that there would be no liability to indemnify.[74] On the other hand such a sub-agent has been held to be a fiduciary for the purpose of disgorging a bribe[75]; he has in some cases a lien against the principal[76]; and if he is a solicitor the court may, in the exercise of its jurisdiction over solicitors, order him to pay to the principal money received for the principal in the course of the sub-agency.[77]

The present position as to the rules of law affecting the sub-agent in England is not, however, as firmly fixed as might appear. In *Junior Books Ltd v. Veitchi Co. Ltd*[78] the House of Lords held a subcontractor liable in negligence to the owner of premises on which he did work, where the negligence caused purely financial loss. The standing of this case is doubtful,[79] but it has more recently been held that Lloyd's managing agents were liable in tort to "indirect names", *i.e.* persons

---

[70] *Schmaling v. Tomlinson* (1815) 6 Taunt. 147; *Mason v. Clifton* (1863) 3 F. & F. 899.
[71] Illustration 4. The cases mainly relate to solicitors acting for trusts.
[72] *Robbins v. Fennell* (1847) 11 Q.B. 248, Illustration 5; *Cobb v. Becke* (1845) 6 Q.B. 930, Illustration 6; *Stephens v. Badcock* (1832) 3 B. & Ad. 354; *Sims v. Brittain* (1832) 4 B. & Ad. 375; but *cf. Robbins v. Heath* (1848) 11 Q.B. 257n; *Collins v. Brook* (1860) 5 H. & N. 700. It has been held that money received for the principal is not impressed with a trust: *New Zealand & Australian Land Co. v. Watson* (1881) 7 Q.B.D. 374, Illustration 1; but this may be true of an ordinary agent: *Henry v. Hammond* [1913] 2 K.B. 515, followed in *Neste Oy v. Lloyd's Bank Plc* [1983] 2 Lloyd's Rep. 658. See above, para. 6–043.
[73] *Calico Printers Assn. v. Barclays Bank Ltd* (1931) 145 L.T. 151 (a case prior to *Donoghue v. Stevenson*: see below).
[74] See Comment to Article 64; *Cairns, Noble & Co. Ltd v. Ashwin & Co.* (1920) 5 Ll.L.Rep. 120 (ship's agent).
[75] *Powell & Thomas v. Evan Jones & Co.* [1905] 1 K.B. 11, Illustration 8 (where it was also held that there was privity); but *cf. New Zealand & Australian Land Co. v. Watson*, n. 72 above; *Royal Products Ltd v. Midland Bank Ltd* [1981] 2 Lloyd's Rep. 194. In any case, the claim to the bribe would now be regarded as proprietary: *Att.-Gen. for Hong Kong v. Reid* [1994] 1 A.C. 324: see Article 50. See further Finn, *Fiduciary Obligations* (1977) pp. 177–178, 202–203.
[76] Article 70.
[77] *Ex p. Edwards* (1881) 8 Q.B.D. 262; see Illustration 5.
[78] [1983] 1 A.C. 520.
[79] *D & F Estates Ltd v. Church Commissioners for England* [1989] A.C. 177, 202, 215; *Murphy v. Brentwood D.C.* [1991] 1 A.C. 397, 466, 481. For a more vigorous view see Dillon L.J. in *Simaan Contracting Co. v. Pilkington Glass Ltd (No. 2)* [1988] Q.B. 758, 784. In the *Henderson* case, n. 80 below, opinion was reserved: see p. 791.

with whom they had no privity of contract, and as regards whom they were in effect subcontractors.[80] The liability was based on the notion of assumption of responsibility, which was treated as the basis of the leading case of *Hedley Byrne & Co. Ltd v. Heller & Partners Ltd.*[81] It was, however, stressed that the persons concerned "hold themselves out as possessing a special expertise ... the Names ... placed implicit reliance on that expertise"[82]; and it seems clear that the relationship between the parties was extremely close, much more so than in the *Junior Books* case. In other cases it was said that an action in tort would be "short circuiting the contractual structure ... put in place by the parties. It cannot therefore be inferred from the present case that other sub-agents will be directly liable to the agent's principal in tort."[83] Nevertheless, the position is that in appropriate cases of assumption of responsibility towards a principal who relies on the agent's profession of skill, an action in tort may lie.

The decision as to restitution (money had and received) rests on the view that such actions are basically contractual and affected by privity of contract[84]: it is now more possible to maintain that restitution is subject to its own rules.[85] Likewise the assumption as to liability to indemnify rests on the notion that such liability is contractual: there is some authority that the duty may arise independently of contract.[86] The action of account has always been separate,[87] and the decision that such a sub-agent may be a fiduciary[88] indicates that in appropriate cases he may be ordered to account; the general proposition to be derived from the cases is only that solicitors acting for trustees are not held to account together with the trustees without further indication that this would be appropriate.[89] It may well be that the situation of such a sub-agent is not susceptible to any general rule, but the freeing of this part of the

---

[80] *Henderson v. Merrett Syndicates Ltd* [1994] 3 W.L.R. 761, Illustration 3; citing *Punjab National Bank v. de Boinville* [1992] 1 Lloyd's Rep. 7.

[81] [1964] A.C. 465.

[82] At p. 776.

[83] At p. 790; citing as an example *Simaan Contracting Co. v. Pilkington Safety Glass Ltd (No. 2)*, n. 79 above (a case on construction sub contracts). A case where a sub-agent had earlier been held not liable in tort is *Balsamo v. Medici* [1984] 1 W.L.R. 951, Illustration 2. It is submitted that the decision in that case was correct but much of the reasoning extremely doubtful even at the time, and certainly in the light of subsequent developments. See Whittaker (1985) 48 M.L.R. 86.

[84] See *Robbins v. Fennell* (1847) 11 Q.B. 248; *Cobb v. Becke* (1845) 6 Q.B. 930; *Stephens v. Badcock*, n. 72 above; cf. *Cowern v. Nield* [1912] 2 K.B. 419; *Sinclair v. Brougham* [1914] A.C. 398; *R. Leslie Ltd v. Sheill* [1914] 3 K.B. 607.

[85] See, e.g. *Lipkin Gorman v. Kopnale Ltd* [1991] 2 A.C. 548.

[86] See Comment to Article 64.

[87] See Comment to Article 52: despite dicta that there is a "fundamental principle" that "the action in account is one in contract" in *Balsamo v. Medici* [1984] 1 W.L.R. 951, 961.

[88] Above, n. 75.

[89] See Illustration 4.

law from the shackles of privity of contract would be a satisfactory step. For otherwise the courts may yield to the temptation of holding that there is complete privity in order to secure an appropriate result. This is arguably what happened in the leading case of *De Bussche v. Alt*.[90]

5-012   **Apparent authority.** This Article again deals with actual authority. But it should be remembered that the principles of apparent authority still apply where third parties are involved. Thus a person appointed as agent to the principal by another agent may be able to rely on the apparent authority of the appointing agent if there was some specific representation by the principal, or if the case is one where authority to delegate would normally be implied despite instructions not to delegate given by the principal to his agent but unknown to the appointed agent. And a person dealing with an agent so appointed may be able to rely on the principal's holding out such person as his agent, or on the apparent authority of the appointing agent to make the appointment. So also a person may be able to rely on apparent authority to appoint him a sub-agent, *e.g.* where he wishes to exercise the lien of a sub-agent.[91]

Where, however, the appointment of the sub-agent is without actual authority, and there is no apparent authority, the principal will not in general be bound by the acts of such sub-agent.[92]

Illustrations

5-013   (1) A factor was employed to sell goods on a *del credere* commission. The factor, with the principal's authority, employed a broker on an ordinary commission to sell the goods. The broker sold the goods and received the proceeds, and made payments on account to the factor from time to time. While the balance of the proceeds was still in the hands of the broker, the factor, being then indebted to the broker in respect of other independent transactions, became bankrupt. Held, (i) that there was no privity of contract between the principal and the broker; (ii) that the broker was not liable to account to the principal for the proceeds of the goods sold; (iii) that the principal was not entitled to recover the balance of the proceeds from the broker in the factor's name without allowing the amount due from the factor to the broker in respect of other transactions to be set off, though the broker had reason to believe that the factor was acting as an agent.[93]

---

[90] (1878) 8 Ch.D. 286, Illustration 7. See also *Powell & Thomas v. Evan Jones & Co.* [1905] 1 K.B. 11, Illustration 8; *Maloney v. Hardy and Moorsehead* (1970) 216 EG 1582.
[91] And see *Restatement*, § 5; Illustration 5.
[92] See *Schmaling v. Tomlinson* (1815) 6 Taunt. 147; *Mason v. Clifton* (1863) 3 F. & F. 899.
[93] *New Zealand & Australian Land Co. v. Watson* (1881) 7 Q.B.D. 374.

(2)   The Italian owner of a vintage car asks a friend to sell it for him in England and remit the proceeds to the owner's mother-in-law in England. The friend sells the car but has to return to Italy before the proceeds have been received. Without the owner's knowledge he asks an English associate to receive and transmit the money. By his own negligence the associate is tricked out of the money. The associate is not liable in tort to the owner. [94]

(3)   "Names" investing in the Lloyd's market entrust their business to "members' agents". These agents further entrust the business to "managing agents". The managing agents handle the investors' funds negligently. They have no privity of contract with the names, only with the managing agents. They are liable in tort directly to the names. [95]

(4)   An agent, being expressly authorised to do so, appointed a solicitor as sub-agent to manage the principal's affairs. The sub-agent took over their entire management, and communicated with the principal direct. Held, that the sub-agent was not liable to render an account of his agency to the principal. [96]

(5)   The London agent of a country solicitor, in the ordinary course of business, receives, as such, the proceeds of a cause in which he is engaged. There is no privity of contract between the client and the London agent, and the client cannot recover the proceeds from him as money received to the client's use. [97] So, a London agent, in the ordinary course of business, gives credit to the country solicitor and not to the client, and has no remedy, except his lien, against the client for costs, and such lien, as against the client, is limited to the amount due from the client to the country solicitor. [98] The court may, however, in exercise of its summary jurisdiction over its own officers, order a London agent to pay over to the client money received, the agent claiming to retain the amount in satisfaction of a debt due to him from the country solicitor, [99] or having received it without the authority of either the country solicitor or the client. [1]

---

[94] *Balsamo v. Medici* [1984] 1 W.L.R. 951. But see above, n. 83. A similar decision was reached in a more substantial banking case, *Calico Printers Assn. v. Barclays Bank Ltd* (1931) 145 L.T. 51, but this was prior even to *Donoghue v. Stevenson*.
[95] *Henderson v. Merrett Syndicates Ltd* [1994] 3 W.L.R. 761. See also *Aiken v. Stewart Wrightson Agency* [1995] 1 W.L.R. 1281
[96] *Lockwood v. Abdy* (1845) 14 Sim. 437. And see *Att.-Gen. v. Earl of Chesterfield* (1854) 18 Beav. 596; *Re Spencer* (1881) 51 L.J.Ch. 271.
[97] *Robbins v. Fennell* (1847) 11 Q.B. 248. And see *Hannaford v. Syms* (1898) 79 L.T. 30; *cf. Collins v. Brook* (1860) 5 H. & N. 700. See in general Cordery, *Solicitors* (8th ed.), pp. 279–281 *et seq.*
[98] *Ex p. Edwards* (1881) 8 Q.B.D. 262; affirming 7 Q.B.D. 155. See further Article 70, Illustration 3.
[99] *Ex p. Edwards*, n. 98 above; *Hanley v. Cassam* (1847) 11 Jur. 1088.
[1] *Robbins v. Fennell*, n. 97 above; but *cf. Robbins v. Heath* (1848) 11 Q.B. 257n.

(6)   A client gives money to his solicitor to pay a debt and costs. The solicitor remits the amount, by means of his own cheque, to his London agent for the purpose of paying such debt and costs. The agent retains the amount in satisfaction of a debt due to him from the solicitor. The agent is not liable to the client in an action for money had and received to the client's use.[2] So, if a London agent receives money improperly, the remedy of the client is against his own solicitor, not against the agent.[3]

(7)   A ship was consigned to A, an agent in China, for sale, a minimum price being fixed. A employed B to sell the ship in circumstances in which he had authority to do so.[4] B, being unable to find a purchaser, bought the ship himself at the minimum price, and subsequently resold it at a large profit. It was held that privity of contract existed between the principal and B, and that B was liable to account to the principal for the profit made on the resale.[5]

(8)   Shipowners employ agents to obtain for them a loan secured by means of debentures on their ships. The agents, with the shipowners' consent, employ a sub-agent, who negotiates such a loan but accepts a commission from the lender. The shipowners can recover this sum from the sub-agent, whether or not they are in privity of contract with him.[6] The sub-agent cannot, however, be compelled to enforce the contract for the commission for the benefit of the principal.

---

[2] *Cobb v. Becke* (1845) 6 Q.B. 930. See, however, *Ex p. Edwards*, n. 98 above.

[3] *Gray v. Kirby* (1834) 2 Dowl. 601. See, however, *Robbins v. Fennell*, n. 97 above; *Robbins v. Heath*, n. 1 above.

[4] See Article 36, Illustration 7.

[5] *De Bussche v. Alt.* (1878) 8 Ch.D. 286; *Tarn v. Scanlan* [1928] A.C. 34.

[6] *Powell & Thomas v. Evan Jones & Co.* [1905] 1 K.B. 11. Some of what is said in this case requires reconsideration in the light of *Att.-Gen. for Hong Kong v. Reid* [1994] 1 A.C. 324; see Article 50.

CHAPTER 6

DUTIES OF AGENTS TOWARDS THEIR PRINCIPALS

Introductory Note

In legal systems where agency is fragmented into certain typical sorts **6–001** of activity, it may be possible to lay down fairly detailed rules as to the duties of agents towards their principals. The immense breadth of the agency concept at common law means that it is not easy to do so in a general work on agency. Many agents work under written contracts which contain detailed provisions as to the agent's duties, and perhaps specify the circumstances in which the principal can terminate the contract for breach by the agent. They may contain provisions which require to be measured against the rules relating to contracts in restraint of trade, and also considered in the light of E.C. law. The same is true of distributorship contracts.[1] Other persons exercising agency powers may be parties to contracts of employment and entitled to the protections of employment law. Beyond this, the question is one of interpretation. Where the contract is silent, the court may be willing to find implied terms: although the English courts are traditionally reluctant to do this, there are circumstances where they will do so.[2] But often the question is one of interpretation of an oral transaction. And some agents, *e.g.* canvassing agents, undertake no duties. They are simply entitled to certain contractual rights if they do certain things, though they may be liable for various forms of misconduct.[3] Again, some persons to whom the term "agent" may be applied act gratuitously: there may be difficulties in ascribing a liability to them for acting in a way which is unsatisfactory to the principal, and even more in holding them liable when they have undertaken to act but have not done so. All this means that the common law duties of an agent can only be referred to in very general terms, which indicate the sorts of way in which an agent may be held in breach of duty.[4] In one area,

---

[1] *e.g. Decro-Wall International S.A. v. Practitioners in Marketing Ltd* [1971] 1 W.L.R. 361; *Wickman Machine Tool Sales Ltd v. L. Schuler A.G.* [1974] A.C. 235.
[2] See *Liverpool City Council v. Irwin* [1977] A.C. 239; Chitty, *Contracts* (27th ed.), Vol. 1, Chap. 13, below, para. 7–001.
[3] Above, paras. 1–017 *et seq.*; below, para. 7–016.
[4] For a list of the agent's duties at common law see *Restatement*, §§ 377 *et seq.*

however, a specialised body of law has developed, and is still developing. This is the law relating to the fiduciary obligations of agents, which is a development of the rules of equity originally applicable to express trustees. The principles of fiduciary obligation are not confined to agents, but apply to agents among others, because of the special trust which is reposed in them. It is only in this area that it can be said that special rules on the duties of agents towards their principals can be identified. Sometimes the fiduciary obligations give rise to implied terms in the contract. But more often they are best regarded as operating independently of contract.

1.—Duties of Performance

Article 38

Contractual Agent's Duty to Perform His Undertaking

6–002   An agent who is appointed by contract is bound to act in accordance with the terms of that contract and not exceed his authority.

Comment

6–003   This rule is fundamental to every contractual agency. The agent must comply strictly with the terms of what he has agreed to do, and is in breach of contract if he exceeds his authority on the one hand, or fails to carry it out on the other.[5] Thus, a solicitor who is retained to conduct an action and instructed not to compromise it will be in breach of contract if he does compromise it without his client's instructions, although both he and counsel may consider that a settlement is in the client's best interests and strongly advise in favour of such a course.[6] Likewise, counsel may not compromise an action contrary to his instructions, however prudent he may consider a settlement to be.[7] On

---

[5] See Illustrations; *Smith v. Lascelles* (1788) 2 T.R. 187; *Comber v. Anderson* (1808) 1 Camp. 523; *Barber v. Taylor* (1839) 5 M. & W. 527; *L.S. Harris Trustees Ltd v. Power Packing Services (Hermit Road) Ltd* [1970] 2 Lloyd's Rep. 65; *Restatement*, § 377.

[6] *Fray v. Voules* (1859) 1 E. & E. 839; *Butler v. Knight* (1867) L.R. 2 Ex. 109; *The Hermione* [1922] P. 162; *Apatu v. Peach Prescott & Jamieson* [1985] 1 N.Z.L.R. 50, 64. But if he has no instructions to the contrary, a solicitor may compromise an action, provided that he acts bona fide with reasonable skill and the compromise is in the interests of his client: see Article 30, Illustration 5; para. 6–018 below.

[7] *Swinfen v. Lord Chelmsford* (1860) 5 H. & N. 890; *Neale v. Gordon Lennox* [1902] A.C. 465; *cf. Harvey v. Phillips* (1956) 95 C.L.R. 235. It is doubtful whether the barrister's immunity from action in respect of alleged negligence in litigation will often be relevant in this context: *Donnellan v. Watson* (1990) 21 N.S.W.L.R. 335.

the other hand, even if the principal's instructions are foolhardy, the agent must carry out what he has agreed to do.[8] He may sometimes be under a duty to warn and advise, but if such advice is ignored, he is bound to carry out the terms of the agency contract and may be liable to his principal for breach of contract if he does not do so.[9] Likewise, he must not exceed his authority and may be liable to his principal if he does so.

Exceeding authority: apparent authority and ratification. Sometimes an unauthorised act of the agent may bind the principal. This occurs where the agent has apparent, though no actual, authority, *viz.* he appears to a reasonable third party to have authority[10]; and when the principal chose to ratify an act done on his behalf without authority.[11] In such cases the question may arise as to whether the agent is liable to the principal for exceeding his authority. In the case of apparent authority the matter seems fairly clear; on principle, the agent has caused loss by exceeding his authority and must answer for it.[12] The second case, that of ratification, is perhaps more arguable, inasmuch as the principal has chosen to ratify when he need not have done so, and there is authority by way of general dicta that ratification validates an unauthorised act for all purposes.[13] There can however obviously be circumstances where a principal ratifies, not because he wishes to do so but because he finds it commercially expedient or even essential. In such a case it must be asked whether, while ratifying the contract, the principal has waived the agent's breach of duty. "Often the facts will lead to both ratification and exoneration, but not always."[14]

6–004

---

[8] See *R.H. Deacon & Co. Ltd v. Varga* (1972) 30 D.L.R. (3d) 653; affd. 41 D.L.R. (3d) 767n (stockbroker); Illustration 4; *Volkers v. Midland Doherty* (1985) 17 D.L.R. (4th) 343, Illustration 4 to Article 41.

[9] See *Boyce v. Rendells* [1983] E.G.D. 26, 37.

[10] See Article 74.

[11] See Articles 13–20.

[12] *cf. Papé v. Westacott* [1894] 1 Q.B. 272; *Thompson v. Howley* [1977] 1 N.Z.L.R. 16; *Restatement*, §§ 383, 386, 401. He may also sometimes commit a crime by so doing: see *R. v. Charles* [1977] A.C. 177. See, however, views to the contrary expressed in *Great Atlantic Insurance Co. v. Home Insurance Co.* [1981] 2 Lloyd's Rep. 219, 222; noted, [1982] J.B.L. 39.

[13] *e.g. Wilson v. Tunman and Fretson* (1843) 6 M. & G. 236, 242.

[14] *Suncorp Insurance and Finance v. Milano Assacurazioni S.p.A.* [1993] 2 Lloyd's Rep. 225, 235 *per* Waller J. See also *Restatement*, § 416; Mechem, *Treatise on the Law of Agency* (2nd ed.) §§ 492–493; *Mineworkers' Union v. Brodrick*, 1948 (2) S.A.L.R. 959, 979. See also Comment to Article 20. Sometimes the agent in may be protected by an exclusion clause. In *Darlington Futures Ltd v. Delco Australia Pty. Ltd* (1986) 161 C.L.R. 500 an agent who by unauthorised commodity transactions caused loss to the client was not protected by one form of words in the contract but under another could limit his liability to $100. The general statements in the case merit approval, but the final result seems surprising.

6–005   **Estate and other canvassing agents.** On the traditional analysis, the normal contract of an estate agent is unilateral, *i.e.* the agent only earns commission by performing the act entitling him to it. Until then he is under no duty to act. He is only under such a duty if a bilateral contract can be inferred, which will normally be so if he is a "sole" or "exclusive" agent.[15] The same reasoning may be applied to other canvassing agents acting on commission. If this analysis is correct, the estate agent acting, or failing to act, in respect of such a contract cannot be liable under the reasoning given in this and the Article immediately following. An assertion of this sort was described in one case as "startling",[16] but no other reasoning was offered and the proposition is consistent with the assumptions behind this sort of contract. But the agent may be liable if a collateral contract can be inferred and the omission or conduct in question is a breach of it; or in tort, as where he gives negligent advice or a negligent valuation,[17] or if he can be regarded as having assumed responsibility and not carried through what he assumed[18] (as is also true in the case of gratuitous agents[19]); or sometimes for breach of fiduciary duty.[20]

6–006   **Commercial Agents.** The Commercial Agents (Council Directive) Regulations 1993 lay down duties for commercial agents as there defined. In particular, a commercial agent must in performing his duties "look after the interests of his principal and act dutifully and in good faith".[21] The regulations are dealt with in Chapter 11.

Illustrations

6–007   (1) A was instructed by P to sell certain shares when the funds reached 85 or more. It was held that he was bound to sell when the funds reached 85, and had no discretion to wait until they went higher.[22]
(2) A, an auctioneer, was instructed by P to sell some furniture for ready money only. A sold the furniture to X, taking a bill of exchange from him. A was liable to P for the proceeds of sale on X's default.[23]

---

[15] See Comment to Article 58.
[16] *Prebble & Co. v. West* (1969) 211 EG 831, 832 *per* Edmund Davies L.J.
[17] *Kenny v. Hall, Pain & Foster* [1976] E.G.D. 629, Illustration 6 to Article 42.
[18] See *Henderson v. Merrett Syndicates Ltd* [1988] 3 W.L.R. 761 *per* Lord Goff. But this reasoning is unlikely to extend to pure non-feasance: below, para. 6–027.
[19] Article 44.
[20] See Articles 45, 46.
[21] Reg. 3(1); see also reg. 3(2) (duties regarding the transactions entrusted to him, supplying information to the principal and compliance with instructions).
[22] *Bertram, Armstrong & Co. v. Godfray* (1830) 1 Knapp 381. See also *Dufresne v. Hutchinson* (1810) 3 Taunt. 117.
[23] *Ferrers v. Robins* (1835) 2 C.M. & R. 152. See also *Williams v. Evans* (1866) L.R. 1 Q.B. 352.

(3) A foreign merchant (P) sent a bill of lading to his English correspondent (A) with instructions to insure the goods and sell them for P's account. A did not wish to accept P's instructions, but, with the intention of safeguarding P's interests by getting the goods insured, indorsed the bill of lading over to X, who insured the goods. A was held liable to P, because, having accepted the bill of lading by indorsing it, he was bound to carry out P's instructions in full. [24]

(4) A company was formed for the purpose of purchasing the goodwill and assets of a partnership. At the time the partnership was deeply in debt, and shortly after the purchase the whole business failed. The company brought proceedings against one of its directors for negligence in purchasing the partnership when he knew it was in difficulties. Held, an agent who was expressly authorised to do an act which was itself imprudent, and one which the principal ought not, as a matter of prudence, to have authorised, was not liable for the consequences of doing it. The director, as an agent of the company, had been expressly authorised to buy the partnership, and was not liable for having done so. [25]

Article 39

CONTRACTUAL AGENT'S DUTY TO OBEY FURTHER INSTRUCTIONS GIVEN BY PRINCIPAL

(1) Subject to any special circumstances indicating the contrary,   **6–008**
    the agent is bound to obey all lawful and reasonable instructions of his principal in relation to the manner in which the agent carries out his duties.

(2) In determining what is reasonable the court will have regard to all the circumstances of the case, including the nature of the agency and the customs, practices and ethics of the business to be undertaken by the agent.

Comment

There is little direct authority for the proposition contained in this   **6–009**
Article, [26] for it is almost self-evident. The instructions must not extend the ambit of the original contract; they must not compel the agent to do

---

[24] *Corlett v. Gordon* (1813) 3 Camp. 472. See also *Smith v. Lascelles* (1788) 2 T.R. 187.
[25] *Overend, Gurney & Co. v. Gibb* (1872) L.R. 5 H.L. 480; and see *Commerce Realty Ltd v. Olenyk* (1957) 8 D.L.R. (2d) 60.
[26] See *Julien Praet & Cie S.A. v. H.G. Poland Ltd* [1960] 1 Lloyd's Rep. 416, 441–442; *L.S. Harris Trustees Ltd v. Power Packing Services (Hermit Road) Ltd* [1970] 2 Lloyd's Rep. 64. See also *Restatement*, § 385, for a general discussion of this problem.

anything not originally contemplated as coming within the scope of what he promised to do. On the other hand, in most contracts, there will be an area within which instructions may properly be given and must be obeyed. Instructions which involve the performance of an illegal act normally need not be obeyed.[27] In the case of a professional person he or she will be bound to a considerable extent by the rules and ethical standards of the profession and could not be required to perform an act which was contrary to those rules or standards.[28]

Article 40

AMBIGUOUS INSTRUCTIONS

6–010   Where the principal's instructions are ambiguous (*viz.* capable of bearing two or more interpretations), if the agent fairly and honestly assumes them to bear one of those interpretations and acts accordingly, he will not be in breach of contract by so acting.[29]

Comment

6–011   This is certainly a general principle of the law of agency, and can be applied elsewhere.[30] But it must necessarily have limits. If the agent realised or ought to have realised that the instructions were ambiguous,

---

[27] See *e.g. Cohen v. Kittell* (1889) 22 Q.B.D. 680; *Donovan v. Invicta Airways Ltd* [1970] 1 Lloyd's Rep. 486. If the instructions involve performing an illegal act, the agent may not be liable if he carries them out negligently: *T. Cheshire v. Vaughan Bros. & Co.* [1920] 3 K.B. 240, where an agent instructed to effect a p.p.i. policy failed to disclose a material fact. But see *Fraser v. B.N. Furman (Productions) Ltd* [1967] 1 W.L.R. 898; *Everett v. Hogg, Robinson & Gardner Mountain (Insurance) Ltd* [1973] 2 Lloyd's Rep. 217; *L.B. Martin Construction Ltd v. Gagliardi* (1978) 91 D.L.R. (3d) 393.

[28] Thus a stockbroker is only required to carry out a sale of shares in accordance with the rules of the Stock Exchange and cannot be required to act other than in accordance with those rules: *Hawkins v. Pearse* (1903) 9 Com.Cas. 87; *Cunliffe-Owen v. Teather & Greenwood* [1967] 1 W.L.R. 1421.

[29] *Ireland v. Livingston* (1872) L.R. 5 H.L. 395, Illustration 1 to Article 26; *Comber v. Anderson* (1808) 1 Camp. 523; *Bertram, Armstrong & Co. v. Godfray* (1830) 1 Knapp. 381, Illustration 1 to Article 38; *Boden v. French* (1851) 10 C.B. 886; *Cobridge S.S. Co. Ltd v. Bucknall S.S. Lines Ltd* (1910) 15 Com.Cas. 138; *Weigall & Co. v. Runciman & Co.* (1916) 85 L.J.K.B. 1187, Illustration 3 to Article 26; *Pariente v. Lubbock* (1856) 8 De G.M. & G. 5; *Lindsay, Gracie & Co. v. Barter & Co.* (1885) 2 T.L.R. 4; *Loring v. Davis* (1886) 32 Ch.D. 625; *Miles v. Haslehurst & Co.* (1906) 12 Com.Cas. 83; *International Paper Co. v. Spicer* (1906) 4 C.L.R. 739, 751; *Larsen v. Anglo-American Oil Co. Ltd* (1924) 20 Ll.Rep. 40, 67; *Brown & Gracie Ltd v. F.W. Green & Co. Pty. Ltd* [1960] 1 Lloyd's Rep. 289. And see in general Article 26.

[30] See *Woodhouse A.C. Israel Cocoa Ltd S.A. v. Nigerian Produce Marketing Co.* [1972] A.C. 741; *Miles v. Haslehurst & Co.*, n. 29 above; *Veljkovic v. Vrybergen* [1985] V.R. 419, 424.

he ought, if the circumstances so permit, to seek clarification from his
principal before starting to act.[31]

Article 41

Contractual Agent's Duty to Carry Out Contract with Dispatch

(1) Subject to circumstances indicating the contrary, a term will   **6–012**
    normally be implied into a contract of agency that the agent
    should carry out his obligations with reasonable dispatch. What
    is reasonable will depend on all the circumstances of the
    case.[32]

(2) If an agent appointed by a contract cannot, or will not, carry
    out his orders when instructed or within a reasonable time he
    must inform his principal.[33]

Comment

The principle expressed in this Article is part of the agent's duty to   **6–013**
exercise the required degree of care in and about the performance of his
duties. It is also a general rule of contract that where no time for
performance is stated, the contract must be performed within a
reasonable time having regard to all the circumstances of the case.[34] It
has been said that a stipulation as to the time of performance will prima
facie not be held to be of the essence of a contract.[35] These and similar

---

[31] See the *Woodhouse A.C. Israel Cocoa* case, n. 30 above, at p. 772; *European Asian
Bank A.G. v. Punjab and Sind Bank* [1983] 1 W.L.R. 652, 656; *Veljkovic v. Vrybergen*,
n. 30, above (request to "get insurance").

[32] *Varden v. Parker* (1798) 2 Esp. 710; *Barber v. Taylor* (1839) 5 M. & W. 527,
Illustration 1; *Turpin v. Bilton* (1843) 5 M. & G. 455; *Potter v. Equitable Bank* (1921) 8
Ll.Rep. 291, 332; *World Transport Agency Ltd v. Royte (England) Ltd* [1957] 1 Lloyd's
Rep. 381.

[33] *Smith v. Lascelles* (1788) 2 T.R. 187; *Prince v. Clark* (1823) 1 B. & C. 186; *Callander
v. Oelrichs* (1838) 5 Bing.N.C. 58, Illustration 2; *Smith v. Price* (1862) 2 F. & F. 748;
Cassaboglou v. Gibb (1883) 11 Q.B.D. 797; *Tallerman v. Rose* (1886) 15 L.T. 450;
Salvesen & Co. v. Rederi A/B Nordstjernan [1905] A.C. 302; *Mark Lever & Co. Ltd. v.
W. Wingate & Johnson Ltd* (1950) 84 Ll.Rep. 156; *John Koch Ltd v. C. & H. Products
Ltd* [1956] 1 Lloyd's Rep. 59; *Havas v. Carter*, 515 P. 2d 397 (1975); *Fine's Flowers Ltd v.
General Accident Ass. Co. of Canada* (1977) 81 D.L.R. (3d) 139, 149 (Illustration 3);
Volkers v. Midland Doherty (1985) 17 D.L.R. (4th) 393, Illustration 4; *Youell v. Bland
Welch & Co. Ltd* (the *Superhulls Cover* case) (*No. 2*) [1990] 2 Lloyd's Rep. 431, 446–447.

[34] See, *e.g. Pantland Hick v. Raymond & Reid* [1893] A.C. 22; *Sims & Co. v. Midland
Ry. Co.* [1913] 1 K.B. 103; *Hartwells of Oxford Ltd v. B.M.T.A.* [1951] Ch. 50; *Monkland
v. Jack Barclay Ltd* [1951] 2 K.B. 252.

[35] *United Scientific Holdings Ltd v. Burnley B.C.* [1978] A.C. 904, 940; *Law of Property
Act* 1925, s. 41. See *Chitty, Contracts* (27th ed.), Vol. 1, §§ 21–010 *et seq.*; Treitel, *Law of
Contract* (9th ed.), pp. 739 *et seq.*

expressions do not mean that a time stipulation is merely a target date: if it is appropriately expressed, failure to comply would give rise to an action in damages.[36] The expression simply means that the contract cannot be treated as discharged for breach of that term as such. And the contract may expressly state[37] or be interpreted on the basis[38] that time is of the essence. Finally, in the case of the obligation to complete in transactions regarding land, and perhaps other obligations, and possibly outside land transactions also, one party can give notice requiring performance within a reasonable time, and failure to comply with this may entitle him to treat the contract as discharged.[39]

Illustrations

6–014   (1) P instructed A to purchase 150 bales of cotton for P's account and to send him the bill of lading. A failed to release the bill of lading to P for some days after the arrival of the goods in the United Kingdom. He was held to have been in breach of contract in failing to send the bill to P within a reasonable time, which was within 24 hours of the arrival of the goods.[40]

(2) P, a merchant in England, instructed A, his correspondent in America, to effect an insurance on certain special terms upon a cargo of wheat to be shipped by P from London to Baltimore. A tried in vain to effect an insurance on the special terms requested and eventually, without informing P, insured on the usual terms. Held that A was in breach of duty in failing to tell P that he could not carry out P's instructions relating to special insurance.[41]

---

[36] *Raineri v. Miles* [1981] A.C. 1050.

[37] *Steedman v. Drinkle* [1916] 1 A.C. 275; *Brickles v. Snell* [1916] 2 A.C. 599; *Harold Wood Brick Co. v. Ferris* [1935] 2 K.B. 198; *Mussen v. Van Diemen's Land Co.* [1938] Ch. 253.

[38] See, *e.g. Tilley v. Thomas* (1867) L.R. 3 Ch.App. 61; *Tadcaster Tower Brewery v. Wilson* [1897] 1 Ch. 705, 710; *Lock v. Bell* [1931] 1 Ch. 35; *Hare v. Nicoll* [1966] 2 Q.B. 130. Stipulations as to time in mercantile contracts may well be of the essence: *Bunge Corp. v. Tradax Export S.A.* [1981] 1 W.L.R. 711, 725; but stipulations as to the time of payment are not of the essence in a contract for the sale of goods unless a contrary intention appears from the contract: Sale of Goods Act 1979, s. 10.

[39] See, *e.g. Stickney v. Keeble* [1915] A.C. 386; *Finkielkraut v. Monohan* [1949] 2 All E.R. 234; *Behzadi v. Shaftesbury Hotels Ltd* [1992] Ch. 1; but *cf. Re Olympia & York Canary Wharf Ltd* (No. 2) [1993] B.C.C. 159. As to other contracts see *Charles Rickards Ltd v. Oppenhaim* [1950] 1 K.B. 616; Beale, *Remedies for Breach of Contract* (1980), pp. 87 *et seq.*; and see Treitel, *Law of Contract* (9th ed.), pp. 743–744.

[40] *Barber v. Taylor* (1839) 5 M. & W. 527.

[41] *Callander v. Oelrichs* (1838) 5 Bing.N.C. 58 (but see the criticism of the case on the question of damages in Duer, *Law and Practice of Marine Insurance* (1845), Vol. 2, pp. 222–225). See also *Hood v. West End Motor Car Packing Co.* [1917] 2 K.B. 38, 47: "When a person is instructed to procure an insurance he is bound to use reasonable care and skill to effect the policy. If he is unable to procure the policy, he must at once inform his principal of his inability to do so."

(3) An insurance broker is instructed to obtain "full coverage". He obtains cover for a number of risks but not for those which in fact occurred. He is liable for failure to obtain the cover promised; or alternatively, for failure to warn that he had not obtained it. [42]

(4) A representative of a firm of stockbrokers is instructed at 4.30 p.m. to buy a quantity of designated stock "at the market price first thing in the morning". He accepts the instructions but does not carry them out when he arrives at 7 a.m. because he thinks it more prudent to wait for the arrival of the representative who usually deals with that customer. That representative arrives between 8.30 and 9 a.m., at which time the order is referred to him. But at 8.45 a.m. dealings in the shares are suspended, and when they are resumed the shares have doubled in price. The firm is liable to the client for loss of profits. [43]

Article 42

CONTRACTUAL AGENT'S DUTY TO USE DUE SKILL AND CARE

Every agent acting for reward is bound to exercise such skill, care   **6–015** and diligence in the performance of his undertaking as is usual or necessary in or for the ordinary or proper conduct of the profession or business in which he is employed, or is reasonably necessary for the proper performance of the duties undertaken by him.

Comment

Contract, tort or both? A gratuitous agent's liability, if any, cannot lie   **6–016** in contract and must clearly lie in tort. [44] Where the agency is contractual, however, it is obvious that the primary action is one for breach of contract. Where what is alleged is negligence, as it often is, the question then arises whether it is possible to sue in tort instead of contract. There may be advantages in doing so, particularly in connection with the running of limitation periods. For in contract time runs from the moment of the breach; in tort, since the gist of the action is damage, it runs from when damage is suffered. [45] The matter has been one of dispute for a considerable time in common law jurisdictions. For

---

[42] *Fine's Flowers v. General Accident Co. of Canada* (1977) 81 D.L.R. (3d) 139; see also *Youell v. Bland Welch & Co. Ltd* (the *Superhulls Cover* case) (*No. 2*) [1990] 2 Lloyd's Rep. 431 (failure to inform assured that reinsurance subject to 48-month cut-off).
[43] *Volkers v. Midland Doherty* (1985) 17 D.L.R. (4th) 343. See also *R.H. Deacon & Co. v. Varqa* (1972) 30 D.L.R. (3d) 653; affd. (1973) 41 D.L.R. (4th) 767n.
[44] See Article 44.
[45] Some relief is provided by Limitation Act 1980, s. 2.

England, the House of Lords has now decided that an action in tort may concurrently lie,[46] with the incidental advantages that this may bring.[47]

6–017   **Degree of skill and care.** The degree of skill and care which may be expected of an agent acting for reward has been stated many times[48] and is similar in principle to the normal duty of care in negligence. An agent employed for the purpose of effecting a contract between the principal and a third party must use due skill and care in making that contract. Thus, a broker is under a duty not to sell goods at less than the best obtainable price[49] and an estate agent must use reasonable care to ascertain the general solvency of tenants.[50] Agents must use proper care to ensure that contracts they make are binding in law.[51] An agent does not, however, guarantee the contract; his duty is to exercise reasonable care in making it.

Many agents for reward will be professional agents. They must show the skill and care to be expected of those engaged in such a profession.[52] Not only must they be adequately qualified; they must take reasonable care to keep themselves up to date with current

---

[46] *Henderson v. Merrett Syndicates Ltd* [1994] 3 W.L.R. 761. See also *Midland Bank Trust Co. Ltd v. Hett, Stubbs & Kemp* [1979] Ch. 384, holding a solicitor liable in contract and tort, the reasoning of which was approved in the *Henderson* case; *Central Trust Co. v. Rafuse* [1986] 2 S.C.R. 147; (1986) 31 D.L.R. (4th) 481 (same result in Canada). The matter seems uncertain in Australia and New Zealand: see the *Henderson* case at pp. 786–787.

[47] As to the pleading of contributory negligence in contract cases see Treitel, *Law of Contract* (9th ed.), pp. 886 *et seq.*; Chitty, *Contracts* (27th ed.), Vol. 1, §§ 26–019 *et seq.*; *Forsikringsaktieselskapet Vesta v. Butcher* [1986] 2 All E.R. 488; affd. on other grounds [1989] A.C. 352; *Youell v. Bland Welch & Co. Ltd* (the *Superhulls Cover* case) (*No. 2*) [1990] 2 Lloyd's Rep 431.

[48] See, *e.g. Beal v. South Devon Ry. Co.* (1864) 3 H. & C. 337, 341 for the classical statement which forms the basic of this Article. See also *Boorman v. Brown* (1842) 3 Q.B. 511; *Price v. Metropolitan House Investment and Agency Co. Ltd* (1907) 23 T.L.R. 630; *Commonwealth Portland Cement Co. Ltd v. Weber, Lohmann & Co. Ltd* [1905] A.C. 66, Illustration 8; *Weld-Blundell v. Stevens* [1920] A.C. 956; *Whitehouse v. Jordan* [1981] 1 W.L.R. 246; *Maynard v. West Midlands R.H.A.* [1984] 1 W.L.R. 632; *Restatement*, § 379(1).

[49] *Solomon v. Barker* (1862) 2 F. & F. 726. For other cases see Stoljar, p. 274, n. 31.

[50] *Heys v. Tindall* (1861) 1 B. & S. 296, Illustration 5. See also *Carlile Steamship Co. v. Simpson, Spence & Young* (1926) 25 Ll.Rep. 278; *Dampskibsselskab Halla v. Catsell & Co.* (1928) 30 Ll.Rep. 284.

[51] *Grant v. Fletcher* (1826) 5 B. & C. 436; *Neilson v. James* (1882) 9 Q.B.D. 546; *Scott and Horton v. Godfrey* [1901] 2 K.B. 726; *Rainbow v. Howkins & Sons* [1904] 2 K.B. 322; *McManus v. Fortescue* [1907] 2 K.B. 1.

[52] *Lanphier v. Phipos* (1838) 8 C. & P. 475; *Hart and Hodge v. Frame, Son & Co.* (1839) 6 C. & F. 193; *Lee v. Walker* (1872) L.R. 7 C.P. 121; *New Zealand Farmers, &c., Ltd v. National Mortgage and Agency Co. of New Zealand Ltd* [1961] N.Z.L.R. 969; *Duchess of Argyll v. Beuselinck* [1972] 2 Lloyd's Rep. 172; *Wimpey Construction UK Ltd v. Poole* [1984] 2 Lloyd's Rep. 499. See also *Restatement*, § 380 (duty to act with propriety). See further Article 30.

developments in their profession.[53] Their duty is not, however, not to make any mistakes; it is only to use the required degree of care.

Discretion. If the agent has a discretion to exercise he must use   **6–018** proper care and skill in doing so. Thus a solicitor may compromise a case in the absence of instructions to the contrary from his principal, but he must exercise proper care and skill in arranging the compromise.[54] A similar situation may arise where an agent cannot obtain instructions from his principal but some action has to be taken by him. If he acts in a way which he reasonably considers to be in the principal's best interests and exercises the proper degree of care he will not be liable.[55]

Information.[56] An agent is, in general, under a duty to keep his   **6–019** principal informed about matters which are of his concern. Thus, a solicitor must inform his client of any overtures of settlement[57] and a broker must inform his principal of any contracts made on his behalf.[58] An estate agent must notify his principal of offers received up to the time of exchange of contracts.[59] A ship's agent must likewise inform his principal of any facts which the principal ought to know in order to make full disclosure to underwriters.[60] Moreover, an insurance broker owes a special duty of disclosure, not only to his principal but to the underwriters. This duty, for breach of which he may be liable to his principal, arises from the nature of the insurance contract, which is *uberrimae fidei.*[61]

---

[53] See *Park v. Hammond* (1816) 6 Taunt. 495, Illustration 2; *a fortiori* a solicitor must take reasonable care to keep himself abreast with changes in the law.

[54] *Chown v. Parrott* (1863) 14 C.B.(N.S.) 74. See above, para. 6–003; Article 30, Illustration 5.

[55] *Moore v. Mourgue* (1776) 2 Cowp. 479; *Smith v. Cologan* (1786) 2 T.R. 188n.; *East India Co. v. Henchman* (1791) 1 Ves.Jun. 287; *Gwatkin v. Campbell* (1854) 1 Jur.(N.S.) 131; *Lagunas Nitrate v. Lagunas Syndicate* [1899] 2 Ch. 392; *Morten v. Hilton, Gibbes & Smith* (1908), reported in [1937] 2 K.B. 176n. (H.L.), Illustration 9; *Re Cobridge and Bucknall S.S. Lines Ltd* (1910) 15 Com.Cas. 138; *Gokal Chand-Jagan Nath v. Nand Ram Das-Atma Ram* [1939] A.C. 106.

[56] *cf. Restatement*, § 381.

[57] *Sill v. Thomas* (1839) 8 C. & P. 762. For recent examples see *McKaskell v. Benseman* [1989] 1 N.Z.L.R. 75 (offensive letter from solicitors acting for other side); *Waimond Pty Ltd v. Byrne* (1989) 18 N.S.W.L.R. 642 (failure to guard interests of client when they were prejudiced by another client).

[58] *Johnson v. Kearley* [1908] 2 K.B. 514. See also *Dampskibsselskab Halla v. Catsell & Co.* (1928) 30 Ll.Rep. 284; *Dunton Properties Ltd v. Coles, Knapp & Kennedy* (1959) 174 EG 723.

[59] *Keppel v. Wheeler* [1927] 1 K.B. 577, Illustration 6 to Article 62; see also Estate Agents (Undesirable Practices) (No. 2) Order 1991 (S.I. 1991 No. 1032), Sched. 3 para. 2.

[60] *Proudfoot v. Montefiore* (1867) L.R. 2 Q.B. 511.

[61] See Marine Insurance Act 1906, s. 19, and *Blackburn Low & Co. v. Vigors* (1887) 12 App. Cas. 531, 537, 541.

6–020   **Special skill.** Some agents may be regarded as holding themselves out as possessed of special skills. In such cases it would seem that the standard of care which they owe should be higher. Thus in one case where a provincial auctioneer was held not liable for failure to recognise pictures possibly by Stubbs, the decision was affected by the fact that they were described "general practitioners"[62]: it would seem that a person offering more specialised skills should be liable if they are not exercised.[63]

6–021   **Dealing for competitors.** A question which arises frequently in connection with distributorship contracts concerns the extent to which the distributor is entitled to deal on behalf of the principal's competitors. The principles are obviously relevant to the resolution of similar disputes where an agent is involved. Usually the matter turns on an express contractual provision, or the inference to be drawn from other contractual provisions. Thus a promise to "push the sale" of a brand of whisky was not complied with by inaction and merely not preferring other brands, and was also broken in the circumstances by soliciting orders for other brands.[64] Where there were no clear terms, the Court of Session held that there is no principle that the agent will not "even in an outside matter" act in such a way as to bring his interests in conflict with those of his principal: thus an agent (perhaps a distributor) was entitled to deal also in competing products.[65] But an exclusive licensing and distributorship agreement requiring the agent to "make every endeavour" has been held terminable on the grounds that the agent sold similar products of competitors.[66] In a leading Australian case it was held that there was no term to be implied that a distributor would not do anything "inimical" to the market for the manufacturer's products, since a "best efforts" obligation made this unnecessary. But it was also held that it was a breach of contract to defer fulfilling orders for the manufacturer's products in anticipation of filling them himself.[67] Such acts by the distributor could perhaps in some circumstances amount to a breach of fiduciary duties.[68]

---

[62] *Luxmoore-May v. Messenger May Baverstock* [1990] 1 W.L.R. 1009, 1020.

[63] See *Restatement*, § 379; *Duchess of Argyll v. Beuselinck* [1972] 2 Lloyd's Rep. 172, 183–184; but *cf. Wimpey Construction U.K. Ltd. v. Poole* [1984] 2 Lloyd's Rep. 499, 506.

[64] *B. Davis Ltd v. Tooth & Co. Ltd* [1937] 4 All E.R. 118. And see *James Shaffer Ltd v. Findlay Durham & Brodie* [1953] 1 W.L.R. 106.

[65] *Lothian v. Jenolite Ltd* 1969 S.C. 111.

[66] *Re Arbitration between Deb Chemical Proprietaries Ltd and Dreumex Chemie B.V.,* Q.B.D., November 2, 1979; European Law Letter, Feb. 1980, p. 4.

[67] *Hospital Products Ltd v. United States Surgical Corp.* (1984) 156 C.L.R. 41; but *cf. Artifakts Design Group Ltd v. N.P. Rigg Ltd* [1993] 1 N.Z.L.R. 196.

[68] See the *Hospital Products* case, n. 67, *supra, per* Mason J.; Articles 45 *et seq.*

Illustrations

(1) "[A solicitor's liability] is the same as anybody else's liability; **6–022**
having regard to the degree of skill held out to the public by solicitors,
does the conduct of the solicitor fall short of the standard which the
public had been led to expect of the solicitor?"[69] A solicitor "is bound
to bring a fair and reasonable amount of skill to the performance of his
professional duty."[70]

(2)   An insurance broker is bound to exercise reasonable and proper
care, skill and judgment in obtaining a policy to cover his principal's
interests and protecting his principal generally in relation to the underwriters.[71] The expert evidence of other brokers may be called to prove
what is the requisite standard of care. A broker is bound to keep himself
up to date on the current developments of the law relating at least to that
part of the business of insurance with which he is concerned.[72] If he does
give advice on points of insurance law generally he must take reasonable
care to ensure that such advice is correct.[73] He must act with due speed
in obtaining insurance cover[74] and if he cannot obtain such cover he must
at once inform his principal.[75] He may be liable if he erroneously and
negligently informs his principal that cover is unobtainable, with the
result that the principal does not make further attempts to obtain it.[76] He
may also be liable in tort to others than his client.[77]

---

[69] *Simmons v. Pennington* [1955] 1 W.L.R. 183, 188 *per* Hodson L.J., citing with approval
this dictum from a judgment of Harman J. (unreported).
[70] *Parker v. Rolls* (1854) 14 C.B. 691, 695 *per* Talfourd J. See in general Cordery,
Solicitors (8th ed.), Chap.6. A solicitor may be liable to others than his client: *White v.
Jones* [1995] 2 W.L.R. 187 (prospective beneficiary); and if he acts for those on both sides
of a transaction (*e.g.* a conveyance) he may owe duties to both: *Mortgage Express Ltd v.
Bowerman & Partners, The Times,* August 1, 1995.
[71] *Chapman v. Walton* (1833) 10 Bing. 57; *Osman v. J. Ralph Moss Ltd* [1970] 1 Lloyd's
Rep. 313; *Claude R. Ogden & Co. Pty. Ltd v. Reliance Fire Sprinkler Co. Pty. Ltd* [1975] 1
Lloyd's Rep. 52; *Fine's Flowers v. General Accident Assurance Co. of Canada* (1977) 81
D.L.R. (3d) 139; *Warren v. Henry Sutton & Co.* [1976] 2 Lloyd's Rep. 276; *Cherry v. Allied
Insurance Brokers Ltd.* [1978] 1 Lloyd's Rep. 274; *McNealy v. Pennine Insurance Co. Ltd*
[1978] 2 Lloyd's Rep 18; *cf. O'Connor v. B.D. Kirby & Co.* [1972] 1 Q.B. 90; *Provincial
Insurance Australia Pty. Ltd v. Wood Products Pty. Ltd* (1991) 25 N.S.W.L.R. 541, 556
("go through with the insured the list of exceptions in the policy secured").
[72] *Park v. Hammond* (1816) 6 Taunt. 495; *The Ultra Processor* (1983) Lloyd's Maritime
Law Newsletter, September 15, 1983 (S.C., B.C.); *Provincial Insurance Australia Pty. Ltd
v. Consolidated Wood Products Pty. Ltd* n. 72 above at p. 556 ("pointing out legal
pitfalls").
[73] *Sarginson Bros. v. Keith Moulton & Co.* (1942) 73 Ll.Rep. 104.
[74] *Turpin v. Bilton* (1843) 5 M. & G. 455.
[75] See Article 41. See also *Youell v. Bland Welch & Co. Ltd* (the *Superhulls Cover* case)
(*No. 2*) [1990] 2 Lloyd's Rep. 431, 445. As to insurance brokers generally see McGillivray
and Parkington, *Insurance Law* (8th ed.), §§ 378 *et seq.*; Clarke, *Law of Insurance Contracts*
(1989), Chap. 9; Hodgin, *Insurance Intermediaries: Law and Regulation* (1992).
[76] *Sarginson Bros. v. Keith Moulton & Co.,* n. 73 above; *Markal Investments Ltd v.
Morley Shafron Agencies Ltd* (1987) 44 D.L.R. (4th) 745.
[77] *Punjab National Bank v. de Boinville* [1992] 1 W.L.R. 1138 (to assignee of policy).

(3)   A patent agent is "bound to bring reasonable and ordinary care and knowledge to the performance of his duty as such skilled agent."[78] He is bound to know and keep abreast of the most recent decisions of the courts relating to the business of obtaining patents.[79]

(4)   Brokers who are employed to sell goods are bound to employ due care and diligence in obtaining the best available price.[80]

(5)   An estate agent was employed to let houses and was paid a commission of 5 per cent for doing so. It was held that he was bound to use reasonable care to ascertain the solvency of the tenants.[81] "The house agent must use reasonable care and diligence in ascertaining the condition of a person before he introduces him to the landlord as a tenant. It cannot be supposed that the commission of 5 per cent is to be paid for only putting the name of the owner and the particulars of the premises upon the house agent's books for the information of those who may come to make inquiries at his office."[82]

(6)   An estate agent suggests a "reasonable asking price" of £100,000 to a prospective seller of land. He is then asked to act for the seller and does not suggest any change to the asking price. The advice was negligent. He is liable for negligent valuation when the seller buys another property at a price which proves ruinous when the original land can only be sold for £36,000.[83]

(7)   In the case of an ordinary commercial transaction a freight forwarder will not be negligent if he fails to insure the goods.[84] But in the case of a transaction involving a private individual where the goods are known to be valuable the agent may be negligent if he neither insures the goods nor refers immediately to his principal for

---

[78] *Lee v. Walker* (1872) L.R. 7 C.P. 121, 125 *per* Brett J.

[79] *Lee v. Walker*, n. 78 above.

[80] *Solomon v. Barker* (1862) 2 F. & F. 726. See also *Grant v. Fletcher* (1826) 5 B. & C. 436; *Sivewright v. Richardson* (1852) 19 L.T.(o.s.) 10; *Alexander & Co. v. Wilson Holgate & Co.* (1923) 14 Ll.Rep. 538.

[81] *Heys v. Tindall* (1861) 1 B. & S. 296; and see *P.G. Prebble & Co. v. West* (1969) 211 EG 831; *Brutton v. Alfred Savill, Curtis & Henson* [1971] E.G.D. 497; *Faruk v. Wyse* [1988] 2 EGLR 26. But neither the facts of the engagement nor the cause of action are clear in these cases.

[82] *Heys v. Tindall*, n. 81 above, at p. 298, *per* Cockburn C.J. *arguendo*. As to the liability of an exclusive agent for not trying hard enough, see *Styles v. Rogers Realty Ltd* (1987) 43 D.L.R. (4th) 629. See further as to estate agents Murdoch, *Law of Estate Agency and Auctions* (3rd ed.), pp. 106 *et seq.*

[83] *Kenney v. Hall, Pain & Foster* [1976] E.G.D. 629; see Brazier (1977) 41 Conv. 233.

[84] *W.L.R. Traders (London) Ltd v. British & Northern Shipping Agency and Leftley Ltd* [1955] 1 Lloyd's Rep. 554; *Club Speciality (Overseas) Inc. v. United Marine (1939) Ltd* [1971] 1 Lloyd's Rep. 482. See also Hill, *Freight Forwarders* (1974); *British Shipping Laws*, Vol. 13, §§ 635–656; Scrutton, *Charterparties* (19th ed.), pp. 42–46; *Contracts for Carriage of Goods*, ed. Yates (1993), Chap. 7, "Freight Forwarders."

instructions.[85] In the former instance he may expect his principals to have made their own arrangements for insurance. In the latter case the principal may well not have made any such arrangements. The agent may well also be liable if he fails to make appropriate claims against the carrier.[86]

(8) A contracted to lighter and load certain machinery, and pass it through the custom-house. It was common knowledge that import duties were about to be imposed on machinery, and A might have cleared it in time to escape the taxation, but did not do so, though he cleared it within the time prescribed by the customs regulations. In an action against A for the amount of the duty paid, it was held that there was no evidence to go to the jury of any negligence or breach of duty for which he would be liable.[87]

(9) Stockbrokers who were speculating on P's instructions had to know from P before the end of the accounting period which of P's accounts to close and which to leave open. They were unable to obtain instructions from P and so they closed some and left others open, exercising their discretion in what they considered to be in P's interests. In fact it would have been better to have closed all the accounts, and P sued them for negligence. Held, that they had acted reasonably and in P's best interests.[88] "I think brokers so situated were not only entitled but bound to carry through the transaction in the reasonable way they honestly thought most to the advantage of their principal and themselves, and that they did so. These considerations dispose of the case."[89]

(10) An auctioneer who sells goods has no duty to get in the price, even though he has the right to sue for it.[90] An auctioneer asked to express a view on the sale of pictures is liable for the negligence of a valuer whose advice he seeks and transmits to the client; but the formation of a wrong view may not be negligent.[91]

---

[85] *Von Traubenberg v. Davies, Turner & Co. Ltd* [1951] 2 Lloyd's Rep. 462.

[86] *Marbrook Freight Ltd v. K.M.I. (London) Ltd* [1979] 2 Lloyd's Rep. 341.

[87] *Commonwealth Portland Cement Co. v. Weber, Lohmann & Co. Ltd* [1905] A.C. 66. See also *World Transport Agency Ltd v. Royte (England) Ltd* [1957] 1 Lloyd's Rep. 381.

[88] *Morten v. Hilton, Gibbes & Smith* (1908) [1937] 2 K.B. 176n. (H.L.). See also *Samson v. Frazier Jelke & Co.* [1937] 2 K.B. 170; *Stafford v. Conti Commodity Services Ltd* [1981] 1 All E.R. 691; *Merrill Lynch Futures Inc. v. York House Trading Ltd, The Times,* May 24, 1984 (losses on commodity market are not of themselves evidence of negligence by broker); *Drexel Burnham Lambert Ltd N.V. v. El Nasr* [1986] 1 Lloyds Rep. 356, 366–367 (commodity broker).

[89] *Morten v. Hilson, Gibbes & Smith,* n. 88 above, at p. 178, *per* Lord Loreburn L.C.

[90] *Fordham v. Christie, Manson & Woods* [1977] E.G.D. 94. *cf. Brown v. Staton* (1816) 2 Chit. 353.

[91] *Luxmoor-May v. Messenger May Baverstock* [1990] 1 W.L.R. 1009. As to the duties of auctioneers see further *Alchemy (International) Ltd v. Tattersalls Ltd* [1985] 2 EGLR 17; Murdoch, *Law of Estate Agency and Auctions* (3rd ed.), pp. 290 *et seq.*

Article 43

NOT LIABLE TO PRINCIPAL IN RESPECT OF CONTRACTS ENTERED INTO ON HIS BEHALF

6–023   An agent is in general not liable to his principal on contracts made by him between his principal and third parties.[92]

Comment

6–024   This is the general rule: the essence of the notion of agency is that the agent drops out of the transaction. But just as the agent may in some case be liable to, and entitled to sue, the third party,[93] so also he may be liable to his principal, by express or implied agreement or by usage. This may occur, for example, when he is a *del credere* agent,[94] or where he in some other way agrees to answer to his principal in respect of transactions which he negotiates; where he in some respects deals as principal with a person for whom he is in other respects an agent (*e.g.* an insurance broker[95]); or where he acts also as agent for the third party and undertakes liability to his first principal as such agent.[96] And of course the entering into of the transaction may be a breach of duty under the principles stated in the previous Articles.

Article 44

LIABILITY OF GRATUITOUS AGENTS

6–025   A gratuitous agent will be liable to his principal if in carrying out the work he fails to exercise the degree of care which may reasonably be expected of him in all the circumstances.[97]

Comment

6–026   **Liability in tort.** There is no general requirement in the law of agency that an agent has a contract with his principal, and the external position between principal and third party can certainly be changed by a

---

[92] *Varden v. Parker* (1798) 2 Esp. 710; *Alsop v. Sylvester* (1823) 1 C. & P. 107; *Risbourg v. Bruckner* (1858) 3 C.B.(N.S.) 812.

[93] See Articles 100–105, 109–110.

[94] See above, para. 1–036.

[95] *Universo Insurance Co. of Milan v. Merchants Marine Insurance Co.* [1897] 2 Q.B. 93; MacGillivray and Parkington, *Insurance Law* (8th ed.), §§ 1378–1381; and see *Wilson v. Avec Audio-Visual Equipment Ltd* [1974] 1 Lloyd's Rep. 81.

[96] *e.g. Queensland Investment Co. v. O'Connell* (1896) 12 T.L.R. 502 (stockbroker).

[97] See Comment.

gratuitous agent.[98] The internal position between principal and agent however, is, in such a case only imperfectly enforceable. Where there is no contract between principal and agent, it would seem that the alleged agent cannot be liable for pure failure to do what he undertook to do without consideration. However, he can certainly be liable in tort for negligently failing to complete, or to complete with due care, work which he has undertaken and upon which he has embarked. Thus a person who gratuitously agrees to procure insurance for another may owe a duty of care in respect of the manner in which he does so.[99] Not all the cases which can be cited as instances of such a duty are necessarily to be regarded as true cases of gratuitous agency—some involve at the very least a strongly commercial background, in that the agent is a professional person who has either already earned commission (as where he obtains insurance and subsequently undertakes gratuitously to change it) or may hope to do so in the future.[1] In some he is already agent for the other side to the transaction.[2] However, the proposition itself seems clearly established.[3]

Non-feasance. The dividing line between not carrying out the work at all and carrying it out negligently, or negligently failing to carry out part of it, whether as a gratuitous agent or not, must obviously be exceedingly fine in some instances. Some time ago it was suggested that where a gratuitous agent has undertaken to do a particular task, he owes a duty of care to his principal if he knows that, because he has accepted the undertaking, the principal has refrained from instructing anyone else to do the work or otherwise acted in reliance. At least, it was suggested, the agent must inform his principal if he is not going to

6–027

---

[98] See Article 3.

[99] *Wilkinson v. Coverdale* (1793) 1 Esp. 74; *Norwest Refrigeration Services Pty Ltd v. Bain Dawes (W.A.) Pty Ltd* (1984) 157 C.L.R. 149, 168–170 (Illustration 6); *Veljkovic v. Vrybergen* [1985] V.R. 419; *Youell v. Bland Welch & Co. Ltd* (the *Superhulls Cover* case) (*No. 2*) [1990] 2 Lloyd's Rep. 431. But when his principal is a company, he does not necessarily owe a duty to its directors personally: *Verderame v. Commercial Union Ass.Co., The Times*, April 2, 1992.

[1] See *General Accident Fire & Life Assurance Corp. Ltd v. Tanter (The Zephyr)* [1985] 2 Lloyd's Rep. 529, 537 *per* Mustill L.J. This could be true of *Gomer v. Pitt & Scott* (1922) 12 Ll.Rep.115, Illustration 5, and many insurance broker cases.

[2] As in *Donaldson v. Haldane* (1840) 7 C. & F. 762, Illustration 4; *Al-Kandari v. J.R. Brown & Co.* [1987] Q.B. 514, Illustration 13 to Article 115; and in various other's cases where the agent of one party is held to owe a duty to the other, as to which see *Avery v. Salie* (1972) 25 D.L.R. (3d) 495 and Article 115.

[3] It is clearly accepted in *Chaudhry v. Prabakhar* [1989] 1 W.L.R. 29, though see discussion of this case below. See also *Wallace v. Tellfair* (1786) 2 T.R.188n.; *Smith v. Lascelles* (1788) 2 T.R. 187; *Seller v. Work* (1801) Marsh. Ins. 305; *Thorne v. Deas* (1809) 4 Johns N.Y.R. 84; *Massey v. Banner* (1820) 1 Jac. & W. 241; *Balfe v. West* (1853) 13 C.B. 466; *Turnbull v. Garden* (1869) 38 L.J. Ch. 331.

perform the task undertaken, and he must do so in time to enable the principal not to suffer damage by having insufficient time to instruct anyone else.[4] However, authority justifying liability in tort for pure failure to act is difficult to find. Thus in one case an insurance broker acting who, having placed all risks insurance with underwriters, gratuitously undertook to a reinsurance underwriter in respect of the same risks to obtain further signatures on a slip and failed to do so, causing loss to the reinsurer, was held at first instance liable in tort[5]; but the Court of Appeal was able to detect an implied contractual promise to justify the liability, and doubt was expressed as to the appropriateness of a tort action.[6] Although the House of Lords formerly cast doubt on the significance of the notion of assumption of responsibility as a basis of negligence liability,[7] there has more recently been in two cases[8] a movement back towards such reasoning, which indeed stems directly from *Hedley Byrne Ltd v. Heller & Partners Ltd*[9] itself. But both cases involve misfeasance, and it is not easy to justify a tort liability on facts indicating no more than a failure to do an act promised.[10] However, the line between this and failure to go through with a responsibility undertaken is a fine one.

6–028   **Estoppel.** In jurisdictions willing to recognise an estoppel liability based on reliance only, it might be possible to hold the gratuitous agent who completely fails to act liable on this basis to a person who acted or refrained from acting on the basis of the agent's undertaking.[11]

6–029   **Exclusions of liability.** A person may in principle limit what he undertakes by some form of disclaimer or exclusion clause.[12] Although

---

[4] See *Restatement*, § 378; Powell, p. 303; Seavey, *Studies in Agency* (1949) pp. 395–400; (1951) 64 Harv.L.R.913; Prosser, *Selected Topics on the Law of Torts* (1953), p. 380; *Wallace v. Tellfair*, n. 3 above.
[5] *General Accident Fire and Life Ass.Corp.Ltd v. Tanter (The Zephyr)* [1984] 1 Lloyd's Rep. 58.
[6] [1985] 2 Lloyd's Rep. 529: see p. 538, where Mustill L.J. refers to negligence liability as applicable to an "obligation to avoid doing something, or to avoid doing something badly." He also says that "doing something badly may often involve a neglect to carry out an act which would turn bad performance into adequate performance."
[7] *Smith v. Eric S. Bush* [1990] 1 A.C. 831; *Caparo Industries Plc. v. Dickman* [1990] 2 A.C. 605.
[8] *Spring v. Guardian Assurance Plc.* [1994] 3 W.L.R. 354 (negligent letter of reference); *Henderson v. Merrett Syndicates Ltd* [1994] 3 W.L.R. 761 (negligent management by sub-agent).
[9] [1964] A.C. 435.
[10] See *Restatement*, § 378, caveat: "When the gratuitous agent has not entered upon performance, it is not clear that liability will be imposed."
[11] See *Waltons Stores (Interstate) Ltd v. Maher* (1988) 164 C.L.R. 387; *Amalgamated Investment and Property Co. Ltd v. Texas Commerce International Bank Ltd* [1982] Q.B. 84.
[12] As in the leading case of *Hedley Byrne & Co. Ltd v. Heller & Partners Ltd* [1964] A.C. 465 itself.

it was arguable that such reservations were not exclusions of liability at all, but rather determined the scope and degree of the tortious duty undertaken, it has been held by the House of Lords that they may be treated as exclusions, and hence subject to section 2(2) of the Unfair Contract Terms Act 1977, which imposes a requirement of reasonableness on exclusions of liability for loss caused by negligence.[13]

Standard of care. It was formerly customary to state, and earlier **6–030** editions of this work did state, that the duty of care owed by a gratuitous agent was one of such skill and care as persons ordinarily exercise in their own affairs. This idea, which is similar to the *diligentia quam suis rebus* of Roman law (where different contracts had different prescribed levels of care), was derived in English law from old cases on bailment, which suggested (in like manner) that whereas a contractual bailee was liable for negligence, a gratuitous bailee was only liable for gross negligence.[14] But as Rolfe B. remarked in 1843,[15] gross negligence can be said to be no more than negligence with a vituperative epithet; and the determination of fixed standards for different types of case is not a technique now used by English law. Ormerod L.J. said in 1962[16]:

> "It seems to me that to try and put a bailment, for instance, into a watertight compartment—such a gratuitous bailment on the one hand, and bailment for reward on the other—is to overlook the fact that there might well be an infinite variety of cases, which might come into one or the other category. The question that we have to consider in a case of this kind, if it is necessary to consider negligence, is whether in the circumstances of this particular case a sufficient standard of care has been observed by the defendants or their servants."

This view has now been specifically accepted for gratuitous agency. In *Chaudhry v. Prabakhar*[17] a person undertook to find a suitable second-hand car for a friend to buy, and negligently recommended a car which had been in an accident. He was held liable in tort. The case was argued as turning on the duty owed by a gratuitous agent, though it is not clear that the defendant was in inspecting the car appropriately described as an agent[18]; indeed it is not clear that he should have been regarded as undertaking any duty at all, though this was expressly conceded and the

---

[13] *Smith v. Eric S. Bush*, n. 7 above.
[14] See *Coggs v. Bernard* (1703) 2 Ld.Raym.909; see also *Wilson v. Brett* (1843) 11 M.&W. 113; *Giblin v. McMullen* (1869) L.R. 2 P.C. 317; *Moffat v. Bateman* (1869) L.R.3 P.C. 115. But *cf. Port Swettenham Authority v. T.W.Wu & Co.* [1979] A.C. 580.
[15] *Wilson v. Brett*, n. 14 above, at p. 115.
[16] *Houghland v. R.R. Low (Luxury Coaches) Ltd* [1962] 1 Q.B. 694, 698; see also *Grill v. General Iron Screw Collier Co.* (1866) L.R. 1 C.P. 694, 698.
[17] [1989] 1 W.L.R. 29.
[18] He subsequently took a cheque for part of the purchase price and passed it to the seller, so could perhaps be regarded as having negotiated, or at least introduced, the sale.

case decided on the basis of the concession.[19] In substance accepting the view put forward[20] in the Comment (but not the Article itself) in the previous edition of this work, the Court of Appeal can be said to have taken the overall view that the agent's duty is "that which may be reasonably expected of him in all the circumstances."[21] Factors relevant to the determination of the standard owed are whether the agent is paid, and if so whether he exercises any trade, profession or calling; and where he is unpaid, the skill and experience which he has or represents himself as having.[22]

Illustrations

6–031   (1) A gratuitously undertakes to arrange an insurance policy on P's cargo. He then changes his mind and decides not to do so. P's cargo is lost, but it has been said that P has no claim against A.[23] *Sed quaere*. If A started to make the necessary arrangements but negligently failed to answer letters from the underwriters so that no policy was effected, or if A obtained a policy but negligently failed to obtain cover against the usual risks, *semble*, P would have a claim against A for the loss he suffered.

(2) E purchased a motor car from X. It was agreed that X's insurance would be transferred to E. E then arranged with X's insurance brokers for them to arrange the transfer. The insurers were not satisfied with the information given them by the brokers relating to E and in default of any answer to their questions cancelled the temporary insurance which they had granted. The brokers failed to inform E, who later had an accident. Held, the brokers were liable to indemnify E against the sums he had to pay in consequence of the accident. They were liable for their negligence notwithstanding that they were acting gratuitously.[24]

(3) A general merchant undertakes, without reward, to enter a parcel of P's goods at the custom-house together with a parcel of his own. By mistake he enters both parcels under the wrong denomination of goods, and both parcels are, in consequence, seized. He has not held himself out as having any special skill in this respect (*i.e.* he is not a

---

[19] A concession doubted by May L.J. at pp. 38–39.
[20] In a passage originally written by Mr Brian Davenport Q.C.
[21] See Stuart-Smith L.J. at p. 34; see also Stocker L.J. at p. 37.
[22] See p. 34.
[23] See Duer, *Law and Practice of Marine Insurance* (1845), Vol. 2, pp. 128–130, who comments unfavourably on the hardship inflicted on P, who has trusted A to carry out his promise.
[24] *London Borough of Bromley v. Ellis* [1971] 1 Lloyd's Rep. 97.

broker or customs clerk) and is therefore not liable to P, because he has taken as much care with P's goods as with his own.[25]

(4)   A writer to the signet was employed to invest money for a client and did so without obtaining adequate security. He charged no fee for his services but was held liable to the lenders for his negligence.[26]

(5)   P asked A, a shipping agent, to check with P's bank to ensure that the marine insurance policy on certain of P's goods covered a voyage to Lisbon. A acted gratuitously in accepting this request. He obtained an oral assurance from the bank but did not look at the terms of the policy itself (although he had been requested by P to "see the policy"). A was liable, since he had not shown that care which a reasonably careful man of business would have exercised in his own affairs.[27]

(6)   The owner of a fishing vessel is required by his banker to get it insured. He contacts the manager of a fisherman's co-operative which he has recently joined, and which has said that it can obtain insurance for members at a reduced rate. The vessel is added to the co-operative's fleet policy, but the manager fails to tell the owner that the insurance is inoperative if the vessel does not have a certificate of survey. A loss occurs and the insurers repudiate liability because of the absence of such a certificate. The co-operative is liable.[28]

(7)   Solicitors make a will for a testatrix and retain it. On her death they make no effort to locate the executor and notify him of the will for six years, during which time the main asset, a house, lies vacant and falls into decay. The solicitors are liable to the executor.[29]

2.—FIDUCIARY DUTIES

Article 45

AGENT'S FIDUCIARY DUTIES

An agent owes to his principal fiduciary duties (duties of loyalty).[30]   **6–032**

---

[25] *Shiells v. Blackburne* (1789) 1 Hy.Bl. 158.

[26] *Donaldson v. Haldane* (1840) 7 C. & F. 762. See also *Dartnall v. Howard & Gibbs* (1825) 4 B. & C. 345; *Whitehead v. Greetham* (1825) 2 Bing. 464.

[27] *Gomer v. Pitt & Scott* (1922) 12 Ll.Rep. 115.

[28] *Norwest Refrigeration Services Pty Ltd v. Bain Dawes (W.A.) Pty Ltd* (1984) 157 C.L.R. 149.

[29] *Hawkins v. Clayton* (1988) 164 C.L.R. 539.

[30] The literature is enormous: only some can be cited here. See Goff and Jones, *Law of Restitution* (4th ed.), Chaps. 32, 33; Meagher, Gummow and Lehane, *Equity Doctrines and Remedies* (3rd ed.), Chap. 5; Finn, *Fiduciary Obligations* (1977), Part II (to which the writer is much indebted and much of which is still completely valid); *Equity and Commercial Relationships* (Finn ed., 1987), Chaps. 6, 7; Shepherd, *Law of Fiduciaries*
—cont. on next page

6–033   **Fiduciary duties.** The essence of fiduciary duties has been well expressed in the following statement: "A person will be a fiduciary in his relationships with another when and in so far as that other is entitled to expect that he will act in that other's interests or (as in a partership) in their joint interests, to the exclusion of their several interests."[31] Such duties arise in equity, and stem from the extension, which is not confined to agency situations, of the duties and responsibilities imposed by courts of equity upon express trustees. The attribution of such duties to persons who are not trustees forms a significant area where the common law techniques of strict interpretation of contract, and reluctance to imply terms which the parties did not choose to make express, are modified by different techniques.[32] There is much authority that agents can owe such duties. These fiduciary duties apply whether or not the agency is gratuitous: they do not depend on the fact that the principal is paying for the agent's services.

6–034   **Agent as fiduciary.** An agent in the strict sense of the word holds a power to affect the legal relations of his principal.[33] This power is conferred by the law in the implementation of the supposed intentions of the parties; but it is not surprising that the law also imposes controls on the way in which the holder of such a strong power may behave towards the person who conferred it. This is not a situation like the more usual one regulated by the law in which the parties are in an adverse commercial relationship, for example a simple hire of services. Agency services are services of a special kind. Even when no such power to affect legal relations was conferred, as in the "incomplete agency" case of canvassing agent,[34] the relationship of the parties still imparts an undertaking by one to act in the interests of the other rather than his own, and this likewise, though to a lesser extent, justifies the law's intervention.

It has recently been said by Lord Browne-Wilkinson, however, in the context of an agent's fiduciary obligations, that "Agency is a contract made between principal and agent . . . like every other contract, the

---

—cont. from previous page
(1981); Powell, pp. 312 *et seq.*; Fridman, pp. 156 *et seq.*; Stoljar, Chap. 13; *Restatement*, §§ 387–409; Dowrick (1954) 17 M.L.R. 24; Sealy [1962] C.L.J. 69; [1963] C.L.J. 119; Jones (1968) 84 L.Q.R. 472; (1970) 86 L.Q.R. 463; Weinrib (1975) 25 U.Toronto L.J.1; Shepherd (1981) 97 L.Q.R. 51; Flannigan (1987) 9 O.J.L.S. 285; (1990) 54 Sask. L. Rev. 45; and further material cited in the following pages.
[31] Finn, *Commercial Aspects of Trusts and Fiduciary Obligations* (McKendrick ed., 1992), p. 9. See also *Restatement*, § 387: "Unless otherwise agreed, an agent is subject to a duty to his principal to act solely for the benefit of the principal in all matters connected with his agency."
[32] See Goodhart and Jones, (1980) 43 M.L.R. 489.
[33] Article 1.
[34] Above, para. 1–017.

rights and duties of the principal and agent are dependent upon the terms of the contract between them, whether express or implied."[35] Although other dicta of a similar nature can be cited,[36] not everyone may agree with the emphasis inherent in this statement. Agency need not be contractual; and the notion of fiduciary obligation stems from equity and is independent of contract. It is submitted that the law's control over the agent's exercise of his powers of intervention is not to be derived from contract terms alone. As Lord Mustill said in a subsequent case: "The essence of a fiduciary obligation is that it creates obligations of a different character from those deriving from the contract itself."[37]

Even where the relationship is contractual (as it normally will be), the matter is too important to be left entirely to the agreement of the parties and the interpretation of that agreement. This is an area where the unequal standing of contracting parties has for more than a century been recognised as requiring relief. The relief is principally given by the application of fiduciary duties, though other equitable (or partly equitable) doctrines such as duress or undue influence may on occasion be relevant. The agreement of the parties or the background of the case may certainly, however, establish that the relationship is not one of agency or otherwise justify modification of the normal standards[38]—even to increase them.[39]

Development of doctrine. The duties of fiduciaries such as agents have been developed over the last century and a half to accommodate the difference between express trustees and others who hold special powers similar in varying degrees to those of the trustee. In particular, the position of the company director was at one time a focal point of such development; hence cases on promoters and directors figure   **6–035**

---

[35] *Kelly v. Cooper* [1993] A.C. 205, 213–214 (Illustration 8). See also *Clark Boyce v. Mouat* [1994] 1 A.C. 428, 437; *Henderson v. Merrett Syndicates Ltd* [1994] 3 W.L.R. 761, 798–800; Heydon, (1995) 110 L.Q.R.1.

[36] *e.g. Lamb v. Evans* [1893] 1 Ch.218 *per* Bowen L.J.

[37] *Re Goldcorp Exchange Ltd* [1995] 1 A.C. 74, 98. See also *Yasuda Fire and Marine Ins. Co. of Europe Ltd v. Orion Marine Ins. Underwriting Agency Ltd*, [1995] Q.B. 174, 186, *per* Colman J.: "The rights and obligations arising as a matter of law from the existence of duty-creating relationships, such as bailment, are not in principle displaced by contractual rights and obligations unless the contract provides that such rights and obligations are to be excluded or includes remedies which are inconsistent with the duties attributable as a matter of law to the relationship."

[38] See *Hospital Products Ltd v. U.S. Surgical Corp.* (1984) 156 C.L.R. 41, 96–97 *per* Mason J.; below, para. 6–051.

[39] *e.g. Cia. Fianciera "Soleada" S.A. v. Hamoor Tanker Corp. Inc. (The Borag)* [1980] 1 Lloyd's Rep. 111 (revsd. on a different point [1981] 1 W.L.R. 274) (where unusual terms were held to impose a higher duty of loyalty than the general duty to which agents are held).

prominently in the illustrations and footnotes to this part of the book. There is, however, still some tendency to go too far and refer to fiduciaries as actual trustees and to talk in terms of "trust property". Though often not incorrect, this can be misleading, for it may lead to the application of rules which have been formulated in a strict fashion for those undertaking express trusteeship. Such rules may well be inappropriately harsh when applied to one who is not a trustee but merely a fiduciary. Likewise the approach may lead to the assumption that money or property held or received by the fiduciary acting as such, and its proceeds, are necessarily trust property which belongs in equity to the person to whom the duty is owed. But in some cases the use of such property reasoning may be unacceptable—for example as conferring the right to profits, or an unjustified priority in bankruptcy—whereas the conferring of a right *in personam* on the beneficiary of the duty would be acceptable even though no contractual, tortious or restitutionary action is available at common law. Conversely, the use of such phraseology may lead to the conclusion that if the agent is not subject to a trustee's duties, or there is nothing that can be called trust property, or a proprietary remedy against him is not appropriate, he owes no fiduciary duties at all; this may be equally misleading.

6–036   **Duties of loyalty.** The duties are therefore best separately designated as fiduciary duties, and if this word is thought to become too easily confused with the notion of genuine trusteeship, the *Restatement* phraseology, "duties of loyalty",[40] may be used in this context as carrying less specific overtones. Controversy exists as to when these duties exist; as to their extent in particular situations; and as to the remedies by which they may be given effect to. Such reasoning has been more developed in common law jurisdictions outside England, especially Canada[41]; but it seems to be on the increase everywhere. It should not, however, be taken too far; and it may be that the dictum of Lord Browne-Wilkinson quoted above should be interpreted as a warning against excessive use of such reasoning. It is sometimes imprecisely and mistakenly invoked to justify results which would indeed be more appropriately attributed to express or implied contract terms; but other possibilities are duress, undue influence, unconscionability, tort, or

---

[40] See § 367.
[41] *e.g. Bromley L.B.C. v. G.L.C.* [1983] 1 A.C. 768, 815; *Guerin v. R.* [1984] 2 S.C.R. 335; (1984) 13 D.L.R. (4th) 321 (public law: *cf. Tito v. Waddell (No. 2)* [1977] Ch. 106); *Canson Enterprises Ltd v. Boughton & Co.* [1991] 3 S.C.R. 534; (1991) 85 D.L.R. (4th) 129 (solicitors). See also *Frame v. Smith* [1987] 2 S.C.R. 99; (1987) 42 D.L.R. (4th) 81 *per* Wilson J. (refusal of access to children); *Norberg v. Wynrib* [1992] 2 S.C.R. 226; (1992) 92 D.L.R. (4th) 449 (doctor and patient); and see *DHL International (NZ) Ltd v. Richmond Ltd* [1993] 3 N.Z.L.R. 10 (international courier service: no fiduciary responsibility).

even, if such could be developed, a requirement of good faith in commercial transactions.[42]

Attribution of duties: are all agents always fiduciaries? Turning first to the question of how the incidence of the duties should be explained, it will be noted that the formulations in Article 1 and in the present Article treat the relationship of principal and agent as by definition a fiduciary one, and therefore in effect say that every agent is a fiduciary and hence owes fiduciary duties. This can be criticised on the basis that not every person who can be described by the word "agent" is subject to fiduciary duties; and that a person who certainly is so to be described may owe such duties in some respects and not in others. Hence it is said that there may be a "non-fiduciary agent", and that in some functions an acknowledged agent may not act as fiduciary. This is true, but largely a matter of words. The fact that neither "agent" nor "fiduciary" have agreed meanings make it to some extent a matter of choice how best to formulate the application of the rules. Rather than talk of a "non-fiduciary agent" it seems better to say that where an agent does not act in a fiduciary capacity (*e.g.* because he has specific instructions), this is a reflection of the scope of his duties and the boundaries of the equitable rules.

Another view is that the approach should rather be to identify the general circumstances in which a fiduciary duty may arise and note these as situations in which agents may sometimes, but do not always, find themselves. Thus in *Phipps v. Boardman*[43] Lord Upjohn said: "The facts and circumstances must be carefully examined to see whether in fact a purported agent and even a confidential agent is in a fiduciary relationship to his principal. It does not necessarily follow that he is in such a position (see *In re Coomber*)." And in the case referred to, *Re Coomber*,[44] Fletcher Moulton L.J. said, in a much-quoted passage[45]:

> "It is said that the son was the manager of the stores and therefore was in a fiduciary relationship to his mother. This illustrates in a most striking form the danger of trusting to verbal formulae. Fiduciary relations are of many different types; they extend from the relation of myself to an errand boy who is bound to bring me back my change up to the most intimate and confidential relations which can possibly exist between one party and another where the one is wholly in the hands of the other because of his infinite trust in him. All these are cases of fiduciary relations, and the courts have again and again, in cases where there has been a fiduciary relation, interfered and set aside acts

---

[42] See Finn, "The Fiduciary Principle" in *Equity, Fiduciaries and Trusts* (Youdan ed. 1989), Chap. 1.
[43] [1967] 2 A.C. 46, 127; followed in *Hendy Lennox (Industrial Engines) Ltd v. Grahame Puttick Ltd* [1984] 1 W.L.R. 485.
[44] [1911] 1 Ch. 723.
[45] At pp. 728–729.

which, between persons in a wholly independent position, would have been perfectly valid. Thereupon in some minds there arises the idea that if there is any fiduciary relation whatever any of these types of interference is warranted by it. They conclude that every kind of fiduciary relation justifies every kind of interference. Of course that is absurd. The nature of the fiduciary relation must be such that it justifies the interference. There is no class of case in which one ought more carefully to bear in mind the facts of the case, when one reads the judgment of the Court on those facts, than cases which relate to fiduciary and confidential relations and the action of the Court with regard to them. In my opinion there was absolutely nothing in the fiduciary relations of the mother and the son with regard to this house which in any way affected this transaction."

It is certainly true that fiduciary relationships arise in situations other than those of agency. Nevertheless, it is submitted that the fact that an agent in the strictest sense of the word has a power to alter his principal's legal position makes it appropriate and salutary to regard the fiduciary duty as a typical feature of the paradigm agency relationship. To do so will not mislead so long as two things are borne in mind.

The first is that the word "agent" can be used in varying senses, and not all persons to whom the word is applied are agents in the full (or sometimes, any) legal sense. A canvassing, or introducing agent,[46] for instance, may do no more than bring two parties together and thus may in many situations do nothing involving the incidence of fiduciary responsibilities at all; though equally he can, as has been stated above, in some circumstances become liable for breach of such duties, as when he conceals from his principal the existence of further offers.[47] A distributor or franchisee, though sometimes called an agent, is in most respects in a position commercially adverse, rather than fiduciary, to the person whose goods he distributes: he buys and resells.[48] But again it is conceivable that circumstances might give him knowledge of and power over his principal's affairs which could justify the imposition of some fiduciary duties[49]; and this is quite apart from the possibility that he may also in some circumstances exercise true agency functions, for

---

[46] Above, para. 1–017.

[47] *Keppel v. Wheeler* [1927] 1 K.B. 577, Illustration 6 to Article 62; *Jackson v. Packham Real Estate Ltd* (1980) 109 D.L.R. (3d) 277; and see *Regier v. Campbell-Stuart* [1939] Ch. 766, Illustration 17 to Article 47. Or gives information to third parties about those he has introduced. But *cf. Knoch Estate v. John Picken Ltd* (1991) 83 D.L.R. (4th) 447.

[48] See *Jirna Ltd v. Mister Donut of Canada Ltd* (1971) 22 D.L.R. (3d) 639; affd. (1973) 40 D.L.R. (3d) 303; see also *Keith Henry & Co. Pty. Ltd v. Stuart Walker & Co. Pty. Ltd* (1958) 100 C.L.R. 342; *Lothian v. Jenolite Ltd*, 1969 S.C. 11; *Hospital Products Ltd v. U.S. Surgical Corp.* (1984) 156 C.L.R. 41 (a leading case on this point, where the court was divided); *Watson v. Dolmark Industries Ltd* [1992] 3 N.Z.L.R. 311; above, paras. 1–029, 6–021.

[49] This might even be so of the franchisor's position *vis-à-vis* the franchisee: *cf.* the *Mister Donut* case, n. 48 above.

example as regards complaints concerning the goods, and be subject to fiduciary duties in that respect.

The second matter which should be borne in mind is that the *extent* of the fiduciary duty may vary from case to case. For example, a person who is certainly an agent in general, but who is authorised on a particular occasion to carry out an exactly specified act, may on the occasion act in no more than a ministerial capacity, even though he affects his principal's legal position.[50] In other situations the duty may be, by virtue of the circumstances, limited; or restricted or even excluded by contract.

Extent of duties: profits made. The duties may in general be expressed as requiring the agent to prefer the interests of his principal to his own. Hence he must not "promote his personal interest by making or pursuing a gain in circumstances in which there is a conflict or a real or substantial possibility of a conflict between his personal interests and those of the persons whom he is bound to protect."[51] The paradigm application of these principles is to benefits received by the agent in breach of these duties, as where he makes a secret profit not disclosed to his principal, accepts a bribe, or makes a profit from his principal's property or confidential information, or by exploiting his position as agent; all of these are considered in the following Articles. It can be said that such profits are received at the principal's expense, and are to be regarded as belonging to the principal. Such reasoning is not available under normal contract principles. In this context there are many dicta suggesting that the operation of these fiduciary duties, once it has been determined that they apply, is of the utmost strictness. Rules have been said to be "rigid"[52]: the fact that there is a mere possibility of action by the agent in the future which may be contrary to the interests of his principal is said to render him in breach of duty in respect of money or property acquired, even though the possibility is slender or is actually known not to have occurred by the time of the litigation, or even if the principal has benefited from the agent's activities.[53] Plainly some of the rules are justified by their supposed deterrent effect.[54] An often-cited dictum of this sort is that of Lord Cranworth L.C.:

6–038

---

[50] *e.g. Volkers v. Midland Doherty* (1985) 17 D.L.R. (4th) 343 (Illustration 4 to Article 41); see also *R.H. Deacon & Co. v. Varga* (1972) 30 D.L.R. (3d) 653; affd. (1973) 41 D.L.R. (4th) 767n.
[51] *Hospital Products Ltd v. U.S. Surgical Corp.* (1984) 156 C.L.R. 41, 103 *per* Mason J.
[52] *e.g. Phipps v. Boardman* [1965] Ch. 992, 1030; *Parker v. McKenna* (1874) L.R. 10 Ch.App. 96, 124–125. See also *Meinhard v. Salmon*, 164 N.E. 545, 546 *per* Cardozo C.J. ("unbending and inveterate").
[53] *e.g. Phipps v. Boardman* [1967] 2 A.C. 46, Illustration 4 to Article 49.
[54] See Shepherd, *Law of Fiduciaries* (1981), pp. 142 *et seq.*

"It is a rule of universal application, that no one, having such duties to discharge, shall be allowed to enter into engagements in which he has, or can have, a personal interest conflicting, or which possibly may conflict, with the interest of those whom he is bound to protect. So strictly is this principle adhered to that no question is allowed to be raised as to the fairness or unfairness of a contract so entered into."[55]

Many of these formulations are, however, in origin related to situations involving express trustees; they should therefore be viewed with some caution and not applied indiscriminately outside that context. Apparently harsh decisions can, also, often be explained in modern terms as based on presumptions applied to prevent too easy evasion of the rules; or on other grounds which do not require the use of such strict formulations.[56] The overriding consideration is that "the precise scope of [the obligation] must be moulded according to the nature of the relationship."[57]

6–039   **Losses caused.** A fiduciary may, as may a trustee, also cause loss to the person for whom he is fiduciary (in this context, his principal). Often, as when he gives inappropriate advice or fails to advise or to act generally as a reasonable person in his position would act, he can be regarded as liable in contract, and perhaps also in tort; for professionals such as solicitors are liable in both.[58] But a trustee is liable in equity, for example for dissipating, or failing to invest, the trust property; and such reasoning may extend by analogy to fiduciaries. It may then be asked what difference it makes to regard the duty of a fiduciary in this respect as equitable rather than the result of breach of an implied contract term at common law. There is authority that where there is a contract liability, a different scope of duty will not be secured by suing in tort in those cases where a tort action is concurrently available[59]: it may be asked why the result should be different where the alternative action derives from equity. The first answer to this question is that the rules for implication of terms at common law are strict and, at least at present, not easily invoked[60]; but the principles of equity applicable to fiduciary obligations are, at least for agents, long established, and

---

[55] *Aberdeen Ry. Co. v. Blaikie Bros.* (1854) 1 Macq. 461, 471.

[56] Shepherd, *op. cit.* n. 54 above at pp. 126–127.

[57] *New Zealand Netherlands Society "Oranje" Inc. v. Kuys* [1973] 1 W.L.R. 1126, 1130, *per* Lord Wilberforce. See also *Birtchnell v. Equity Trustee, Executor and Agency Co. Ltd* (1929) 42 C.L.R. 384, 408; *Tufton v. Sperni* [1952] 2 T.L.R. 516.

[58] See *Henderson v. Merrett Syndicates Ltd* [1994] 3 W.L.R. 761; Article 42.

[59] *Tai Hing Cotton Mill Ltd v. Liew Chong Hing Bank Ltd* [1986] A.C. 80, 107: see also *Henderson v. Merrett Syndicates Ltd*, above, at p. 781.

[60] *Liverpool C.C. v. Irwin* [1977] A.C. 239; *B.P. Refinery (Westernport) Pty. Ltd v. Hastings Shire Council* (P.C.) (1977) 52 A.L.J.R. 20; *Codelfa Construction Pty Ltd v. State Rail Authority of New South Wales* (1982) 149 C.L.R. 337; above, para. 7–001.

therefore easier to deploy.[61] Secondly, although where there is a contract its terms may exclude the fiduciary obligations which would otherwise exist, nevertheless, if this is not clearly done, so as to modify or change the nature of the relationship contemplated, the fiduciary duties may be regarded as surviving where the common law techniques of interpretation might suggest that they are not operative.[62] Finally, although there would be no profit to hold on trust, the equitable remedies may still be different from those available at common law.[63]

If therefore the equitable analysis is pursued, it must take account of the fact that a trustee is chargeable not only with profits made at the expense of the trust but also with losses caused to the trust estate by his breach of trust, including profits which would have accrued if there had been no breach.[64] On this analogy, the fiduciary also may be made liable on an equitable basis where he causes loss by the breach of a fiduciary obligation, as where he acts wrongly in respect of money or property held on trust or fails to make disclosure when he ought and thereby causes loss.[65] Here the analogy of the trustee must be even more cautiously applied. Even though there may be a need for one, it has been regarded as difficult to ground a true action *in personam* in equity,[66] which has traditionally used proprietary reasoning, and where the phrase *in personam* often has a procedural rather than a substantive connotation related to the original powers of courts of equity: "equity acts *in personam*". Even the action of account, to which reference is often made by speaking of a "duty to account" and the like, can be said to be in essence one for the taking of accounts from a trustee.[67] Such reasoning leads naturally to the idea of holding the agent liable to account for profit on a proprietary basis; and some might regard it as stopping there. It would not, however, be right to do so. Indeed, the proprietary aspect of the duty to account for profits can be regarded as based on independent reasoning, whereas an important result of the fiduciary duties between principal and agent is a duty to account for losses where common law might not give a remedy.

---

[61] *e.g. Moody v. Cox and Hatt* [1917] 2 Ch. 71 (solicitor).

[62] Below, para. 6–051.

[63] Below, para. 6–045.

[64] See, *e.g.* Snell, *Equity* (29th ed.), pp. 284 *et seq.* As to liability for interest, see Article 54.

[65] See *Re West of England & South Wales District Bank, ex p. Dale & Co.* (1879) 11 Ch.D. 772, 778.

[66] The only clearly accepted equitable action *in personam* in England is the rule of administration of estates recognised in *Re Diplock* [1948] Ch. 465; affd. *sub nom. Ministry of Health v. Simpson* [1951] A.C. 251. And see *Daly v. Sydney Stock Exchange Ltd* (1986) 160 C.L.R. 371.

[67] See Article 52; but note para. 6–094. See also below, paras. 6–076, 6–079.

6–040 **Conflict of duty and duty.** A different, but related situation in which an agent can cause loss to his principal is where he acts for two principals and does not disclose to one his involvement with the other. In this situation the agent does not prefer his own interest, but equally does not act entirely in the interests of either single principal. There may be breach of the duty of loyalty in the sense that the loyalty must be undivided. In such cases he may cause loss to one by failure to disclose information acquired in connection with the other—information, indeed, the disclosure of which would be a breach of duty to the other.[68] In some such cases it may be held that there is no breach of duty at all, as where an estate agent acts for the vendors of adjacent or nearby properties and is regarded as entitled to do so.[69] Where there is a duty, its breach may be remediable in tort by way of fraud or negligence; or by way of an action for breach of contract. But it may also derive from equity. "Fully informed consent apart, an agent cannot lawfully place himself in a position in which he owes a duty of care to another which is inconsistent with his duty to his principal."[70] The result of such a breach of the duty is again likely to be a loss to the principal concerned, rather than a profit by the agent.

6–041 **Remedies.** In respect of the remedies by which the principal can enforce the fiduciary duties of the agent, there is considerable flexibility. It is indeed this flexibility which is sometimes the object of alleging breach of fiduciary duties rather than a mere breach of contract. For example, the court may if it finds it appropriate set aside a transaction generated through the agent. It may grant an injunction. It may award damages for breach of contract, in tort or in lieu of injunction; it may make an award on a restitutionary basis; it may order an account in equity, whether of profits or with a view to ordering compensation; it may grant specific restitution of property. The nature of the remedy will depend on the particular situation in question.[71] In some jurisdictions the mingling of law and equity has been used to justify a very wide flexibility of remedy, one far greater than would be likely to commend itself to an English court, at any rate at present.[72] A full analysis of this ongoing controversy is beyond the scope of this book: but some reference must be made to the topics discussed in the following pages.

---

[68] Below, para. 6–047.
[69] *Kelly v. Cooper* [1993] A.C. 205, Illustration 8.
[70] *North & South Trust Co. v. Berkeley* [1971] 1 W.L.R. 470, 484–485 *per* Donaldson J.
[71] In *Yasuda Fire and Marine Ins. Co. of Europe Ltd v. Orion Marine Ins. Underwriting Agency Ltd* [1995] Q.B. 174, declarations and an order of specific performance were granted to permit the principal to inspect the agent's computer-held records.
[72] This is especially so in New Zealand. See, *e.g. Day v. Mead* [1987] 2 N.Z.L.R. 443 (contributory negligence); *McKaskell v. Benseman* [1989] 3 N.Z.L.R. 75 (damages); *Aquaculture Corp. v. New Zealand Green Mussel Co. Ltd* [1990] 3 N.Z.L.R. 299.

Proprietary or personal remedies? A question the answer to which   **6–042** can be very significant is whether the principal's remedies against the agent are proprietary or personal. A proprietary remedy for breach of fiduciary duty is an application of equity's main technique, of requiring the legal owner of money or other property to hold it as trustee; it involves the notion that the agent holds such money or property on constructive trust. The money or property belongs in equity to the principal. A personal remedy on the other hand holds him liable to pay money to the principal as upon an obligation. As has been stated above, such obligations can often in agency situations be derived from common law independently of the fiduciary duties, being formulated by way of breach of implied terms of a contract, restitution or even in tort.

Some of the advantages of a proprietary remedy from the point of view of the principal are that (i) the principal is generally entitled to any profits made with his money or property[73]; (ii) if the agent mixes the money with his own, the principal will be entitled to the contents of the mixture, or anything acquired by expenditure from the mixture, up to the value of his input[74]; (iii) the property will not in general be available to the agent's creditors in his bankruptcy[75]; (iv) the principal may be able to trace the money, not only against the agent but also into the hands of third parties[76]; (v) the doctrine of laches will apply rather than the provisions of the Limitation Acts[77]; (vi) the principal may be able to obtain an order for the return of specific property and an interim order for its preservation pending trial.[78]

When agent holds property as trustee. The first question which arises   **6–043** in this context is whether money or other property transferred to an agent in connection with his agency function is his absolutely, subject to

---

[73] *Docker v. Somes* (1834) 2 My. & K. 655. See Finn, *Fiduciary Obligations* (1977), Chap. 18. This may include interest (see Article 54); an account attributing the profits in a mixed fund to the constituent elements of it: see *Scott v. Scott* (1963) 109 C.L.R. 649; *Re Tilley's Will Trusts* [1967] Ch. 1179; Article 52; and sometimes an award in respect of savings effected for the trustee by the use of the property: see Finn, *op cit.*, pp. 127–129.
[74] *Lupton v. White* (1808) 15 Ves. 432; *Cook v. Addison* (1868) L.R. 7 Eq. 466; *Re Oatway* [1903] 2 Ch. 356; *James Roscoe (Bolton) Ltd v. Winder* [1915] 1 Ch. 62; *Bishopsgate Investment Management Ltd v. Homan* [1995] Ch. 211: see also *Re Tilley's Will Trusts* [1967] Ch. 1179. But the matter is sometimes put on the basis that the defendant can prove that something is his: see *Van Rassel v. Kroon* (1953) 87 C.L.R. 298 (lottery ticket); *Warman International Ltd v. Dwyer* (1995) 69 A.L.J.R. 362, 369–370.
[75] *Quistclose Investments v. Rolls Razor Ltd* [1970] A.C. 567.
[76] See Article 93.
[77] Limitation Act 1980, s. 21(1)(*b*); older cases, of course, related to earlier legislation. See, *e.g.* Illustrations 1, 3. But nor does the Act apply to "equitable relief"; s. 36.
[78] R.S.C., Ord. 29, r. 2. But this procedure may have lost some of its importance since the widening from international to domestic situations of the so-called *Mareva* injunction: see *e.g.* Colman, *Practice and Procedure of the Commercial Court* (3rd ed.), Chap. 6.

a duty to pay it to his principal, or is held on (express) trust—as for example where he becomes insolvent while holding funds derived from his relationship with his principal, whether emanating from his principal or emanating from a third party but destined for his principal. Sometimes the answer turns on the contract between principal and agent: it is clear in this context and in general that the existence of a contractual relationship of debtor and creditor between the parties does not prevent the existence of a simultaneous trust relationship, or a fiduciary relationship of a less onerous nature involving nevertheless that certain money or property is held on trust.[79] Thus it may be provided expressly between principal and agent that money received is so held. At other times the intention to create a trust may be inferred; the matter turns on the interpretation, according to general principles, of the intentions of the parties.[80] It is sometimes said that there is a prima facie duty on an agent to keep the principal's money and property separate[81]; but it may be that even this is overstated.[82] Earlier editions of this book suggested that the situations where a trust has been held to exist largely fall into two broad categories: (i) where money or property has been specifically entrusted to the agent by the principal to hold for his benefit or to use for a specific purpose[83]; and (ii) where money or property has been handed to the agent by a third party to hold or convert into a specific property for the benefit of the principal.[84] These are useful indications, though the cases are not all easily reduced to such form.[85] But the present trend seems to be to approach the matter more functionally and to ask whether the trust relationship is appropriate to

---

[79] See *Quistclose Investments Ltd v. Rolls Razor Ltd* A.C. 567; *Re Kayford* [1975] 1 W.L.R. 279; *Carreras Rothmans Ltd v. Freeman Matthews Treasure Ltd* [1985] Ch. 207; *General Communications Ltd v. Development Finance Corp. of New Zealand* [1990] 3 N.Z.L.R. 406.

[80] See *Scott on Trusts* (4th ed.), § 12.2.

[81] See *Palette Shoes Pty Ltd v. Krohn* (1937) 58 C.L.R. 1, 30; *Westpac Banking Corp. v. Savin* [1985] 2 N.Z.L.R. 41, 49. See also *Cohen v. Cohen* (1929) 42 C.L.R. 91, 101–102.

[82] See the valuable discussions by the Court of Appeal of New South Wales in *Walker v. Corboy* (1990) 19 N.S.W.L.R. 382; Article 51.

[83] *e.g. Burdick v. Garrick* (1870) L.R. 5 Ch.App. 233, Illustration 1; *Flitcroft's case* (1882) 21 Ch.D. 519; *Dooby v. Watson* (1888) 39 Ch.D. 178; *North American Land and Timber Co. Ltd v. Watkins* [1904] 2 Ch. 233, Illustration 3; *Royal Norwegian Government v. Calcutta Marine Engineering Co. Ltd* [1960] 2 Lloyd's Rep. 431 (but compare this case with *Potters (A Firm) v. Loppert* [1973] Ch. 399; and see Article 54).

[84] *e.g. Littlewood v. Williams* (1815) 6 Taunt. 277; *Mathew v. Brise* (1851) 14 Beav. 341; *Seagram v. Tuck* (1881) 18 Ch.D. 296; *Brown v. I.R.C.* [1965] A.C. 244, Illustration 1 to Article 54. *cf. ex p. Dale & Co.* (1879) 11 Ch.D. 772.

[85] *e.g.* as to stockbrokers: *Hancock v. Smith* (1889) 41 Ch.D. 456: *Re Wreford* (1897) 13 T.L.R. 153 (trustee of client account); see also *Re Ararimu Holdings Ltd* [1989] 3 N.Z.L.R. 487; *cf. King v. Hutton* (1860) 83 L.T. 68 (not a trustee); and auctioneers: *Re Cotton, ex p. Cooke* (1913) 103 L.T. 310 (trustee); *cf. Murphy v. Howlett* [1960] E.G.D. 231 (not a trustee).

the commercial relationship in which the parties find themselves[86]; whether it was appropriate that money or property should be, and whether it was, held separately, or whether it was contemplated that the agent should use the money, property or proceeds of the property as part of his normal cash flow in such a way that the relationship of debtor and creditor is more appropriate.[87] The latter would not, for example, be appropriate for an agent of a type who is not normally expected to handle money for his principal at all.[88] A relevant consideration also is whether money or property was received in pursuance of a single transaction for which the agent was appointed,[89] or as part of a group of transactions in respect of which a general account was to be rendered later or periodically.[90] Although the issue does not arise in many of the cases, a central question, really one of policy, perhaps too often overlooked (because not directly in issue), is whether the rights of the principal are sufficiently strong, and differentiatable from other claims, for him to be given priority in respect of them on the agent's bankruptcy;[91] though this can also be achieved by an equitable lien.[92] Sometimes with this in mind the position is secured by statute or regulation providing that particular types of functionary (*e.g.* estate agents and solicitors) hold clients' money on trust, pay into client accounts and keep trust accounts.[93]

Proprietary remedies in respect of profits made in breach of duty. The   **6–044** question of the availability of such proprietary remedies in connection

---

[86] See *New Zealand and Australian Land Co. v. Watson* (1881) 7 Q.B.D. 374, 382.

[87] See *King v. Hutton*, n. 85 above; *Henry v. Hammond* [1913] 2 K.B. 515, Illustration 4; *Neste Oy v. Lloyd's Bank Plc.* [1983] 2 Lloyd's Rep. 658, Illustration 5; *Stephens Travel Service Inc. Pty Ltd v. Qantas Airways Ltd* (1988) 13 N.S.W.L.R. 331 (dist. in *Canadian Pacific Airlines Ltd v. Canadian Imperial Bank of Commerce* (1987) 42 D.L.R. (4th) 375; affd. (1990) 71 O.R. (2d) 63); *Walker v. Corboy*, n. 82 above; *Kingscroft Insurance Co. Ltd v. H.S. Weavers (Underwriting Agencies) Ltd* [1993] 1 Lloyd's Rep. 187.

[88] *e.g.* an employee: the Rt.Hon. Lord Justice Millett, [1993] Restitution L.Rev.7, 25; and see above, Article 28.

[89] *e.g. Westpac Banking Corp. v. Savin* [1985] 2 N.Z.L.R. 41 (agent for sale).

[90] See *Kirkham v. Peel* (1880) 43 L.T. 171, 172; affd. (1881) 44 L.T. 195, Illustration 2; *Re Arthur Wheeler & Co.* (1933) 102 L.J.Ch. 341; *Walker v. Corboy* (1990) 9 N.S.W.L.R. 382.

[91] Parts of the preceding passage, as it appeared in the 15th ed. of this book, were approved and applied by Lord Goff of Chieveley in the context of equitable lien in *Lord Napier and Ettrick v. Hunter* [1993] A.C. 713, 744.

[92] As in *Lord Napier and Ettrick v. Hunter*, n. 91 above. As to such liens see Phillips, *Interests in Goods* (Palmer and McKendrick eds., 1993), Chap. 25.

[93] Estate Agents Act 1979, ss. 13–16 (in fact, persons engaged in "estate agency work") (see Murdoch, *Law of Estate Agency and Auctions* (3rd ed.), pp. 220 *et seq.*; Murdoch, *The Estate Agents and Property Misdescriptions Acts* (3rd ed.), Chap. 3D); Financial Services Act 1986, s. 55 (below, para. 6–053); see also Solicitors Act 1974, s. 32; Insurance Brokers Registration Act 1977, s. 11. See further *Walker v. Corboy*, n. 90 above. As to interest, see Article 54.

with profits made by the agent from breaches of duty has been much discussed.[94] Where the agent has made profits from his breach of duty the two key advantages to the proprietary claim are the entitlement of the principal to those profits and the priority in bankruptcy; and both being derived from property reasoning, the two tend to go together. But a strong case can be made for the rightness of this association; equity proceeds on the basis that what ought to have been done has been done, and the agent may be assumed therefore, whatever his real intentions, to have made all profits on the principal's behalf, and to hold them for the principal on constructive trust. Since the profits were never meant to be the agent's property at all, the creditors in the agent's bankruptcy have no legitimate claim to them.[95] There is much to be said for this view, though it should be borne in mind that the protection of the principal in the agent's bankruptcy can also be achieved by the more flexible (because less governed by authority), more remedial and less drastic technique of imposing an equitable lien.[96]

Such a result is difficult to attain under an ordinary action for breach of contract or in tort, where the general measure of damages compensates for loss only[97]; though suggestions have been made that such damages could sometimes include the contract-breaker's or tortfeasor's profit. In any case such an action does not always seem appropriate on the facts. Another possibility is, however, to use a more obligation-based approach in equity and say that while the agent should give up profits to his principal, there is no reason why the principal should have priority in the agent's bankruptcy in respect of them, rather than rank as an ordinary creditor with the rest. Hence what is needed is often no more than an *in personam* remedy for an account of profits, which, having no bankruptcy implications, could be more readily awarded.[98]

A more extreme approach is to draw a sharp distinction between right and remedy, and to use whatever remedy is required to achieve a fair result. On this basis the constructive trust can be treated as purely remedial and imposed to justify an appropriate monetary award covering profits, on the basis of the facts operative at the time of the

---

[94] See, *e.g.* the Hon.Mr.Justice Gummow, "Unjust Enrichment, Restitution and Proprietary Remedies", in *Essays on Restitution*, (Finn ed., 1990), Chap. 2; Youdan, "The Fiduciary Principle: the Applicability of Proprietary Remedies", in *Equity, Fiduciaries and Trusts*, (Youdan ed., 1989), Chap. 3; Goode, "Property and Unjust Enrichment" in *Essays on the Law of Restitution* (Burrows ed., 1991), Chap. 9.

[95] The Rt Hon. Lord Justice Millett, [1993] Restitution L.Rev.7.

[96] See *Lord Napier and Ettrick v. Hunter* [1993] A.C. 713.

[97] *Surrey C.C. v. Bredero Homes Ltd* [1993] 1 W.L.R. 1361.

[98] See *Warman International Pty Ltd v. Dwyer* (1995) 69 A.L.J.R. 362; *cf.* Birks, [1987] L.M.C.L.Q. 421.

judgment.[99] It is not clear whether those who advocate such reasoning intend the insolvency implications: it is quite possible not.[1] Some of the cases in which this approach has been taken are against the background of family law, where the need for flexibility is well accepted. In commercial situations the matter may be more arguable.

The view supported by most authority is, however, that profits made by the agent in breach of his fiduciary obligations are held for the principal on a full (*i.e.* non-remedial) constructive trust with proprietary implications. The former leading decision in *Lister & Co. v. Stubbs*[2] held nevertheless that in the case of an agent taking *bribes*, there is no proprietary remedy in favour of the principal; and a subsequent decision explained that the remedies for bribery are, apart from rescission of the contract entered into by the principal, actions *in personam* (on what would now be called a restitutionary basis) at common law.[3] *Lister & Co. v. Stubbs* was usually criticised; though it was also defended on the basis that there is no reason to give the principal a priority in bankruptcy or an entitlement to profits in respect of bribes, and that a remedy *in personam* was perfectly adequate in this as in many other situations.[4] As against this it could be argued that the bribe is simply an additional consideration which the third party was willing to pay, which the agent is to be regarded as holding for his principal, and to which the agent was never entitled. There is no reason why it should go to his other creditors, nor why there should be a special rule for bribes alone of the ways in which an agent may profit unfairly.[5] This latter view has recently been adopted by the Privy Council in *Att.-Gen. for Hong Kong v. Reid,*[6] in which it was held, not following (though not, technically, overruling) *Lister v. Stubbs*, that bribes are like other improper profits to be regarded as held on trust for the principal. If, however, the agent had passed on the profit without recognisable proceeds, it would seem that he should also be liable *in personam*.

Remedies in respect of losses. The above reasoning concerns profits   6–045
made by the agent at the principal's expense. But it has already been

---

[99] *e.g. Lac Minerals Ltd v. International Corona Resources Ltd* [1989] 2 S.C.R. 574; (1989) 61 D.L.R. (4th) 14; and see *Elders Pastoral Ltd v. Bank of New Zealand* [1989] 2 N.Z.L.R. 180; affd. on other grounds [1991] 1 N.Z.L.R. 385 (P.C.); *Powell v. Thompson* [1991] 1 N.Z.L.R. 597. See Symposium, "The Remedial Constructive Trust" in *The Frontiers of Liability* (Birks ed., 1994), vol. 2, pp. 165 *et seq.*
[1] See Youdan, n. 94 above.
[2] (1890) 45 Ch.D.1.
[3] *Mahesan v. Malaysian Government Officers' Co-operative Housing Society* [1979] A.C. 374; see Article 50.
[4] See, *e.g.* Watts, (1994) 110 L.Q.R. 278.
[5] Millett, *op. cit.* n. 95 above; approved in *Att.-Gen. for Hong Kong v. Reid*, n. 6 below. There is some problem as to where this reasoning stops
[6] [1994] 1 A.C. 324.

pointed out that fiduciaries may cause losses. There is also authority,[7] reinforced by the speech of Lord Haldane L.C. in *Nocton v. Ashburton*,[8] for a further equitable jurisdiction to award compensation against a fiduciary in respect of loss caused. The objective of such an award is not the same as the objective of awards of damages at common law, which are directed towards pure proven loss: it is "to effect a restitution to the estate".[9] It is therefore not necessarily governed by the established common law principles of damages regarding time of assessment, causation, remoteness, contributory negligence and so forth,[10] though it is not usually suggested that it creates proprietary rights.[11] In respect of causation, however, it has recently been held that where a solicitor wrongfully paid away money held on trust he was only liable for loss which would not have otherwise ocurred.[12] This casts doubt, at least in England, on strong earlier dicta regarding non-disclosure.

"When a party, holding a fiduciary relationship, commits a breach of his duty by non-disclosure of material facts, which his constituent is entitled to know in connection with the transaction, he cannot be heard to maintain that disclosure would not have altered the decision to proceed with the transaction ... . Once the court has determined that the non-disclosed facts were material, speculation as to what course the constituent, on disclosure, would have taken is not relevant."[13]

---

[7] See Gummow, *op. cit. supra*, n. 38; *Canson Enterprises Ltd v. Boughton & Co.* [1991] 3 S.C.R. 534; (1991) 85 D.L.R. (4th) 129 (solicitor); *Hodgkinson v. Simms* [1994] 3 S.C.R. 377, (1994) 117 D.L.R. (4th) 161 (accountant).

[8] [1914] A.C. 398, Illustration 6. But *cf. Henderson v. Merrett Syndicates Ltd* [1994] 3 W.L.R. 761, 798–799 *per* Lord Browne-Wilkinson.

[9] *Re Dawson* [1966] 2 N.S.W.R. 211, 214–216 *per* Street J.: approved by the Supreme Court of Canada in *Guerin v. R.* [1984] 2 S.C.R. 335, 360; (1984) 13 D.L.R. (4th) 321, 365; and by Brightman J. in *Bartlett v. Barclays Bank Trust Co. Ltd (No. 2)* [1980] Ch. 515, 543; and followed in *Target Holdings Ltd v. Redferns* [1994] 2 All E.R. 337. See also *Robinson v. Abbott* (1894) 20 V.L.R. 346; *McKenzie v. McDonald* [1927] V.L.R. 134; *Catt v. Marac Australia Ltd* (1986) 9 N.S.W.L.R. 639; *Hill v. Rose* [1990] V.R. 129; *Commonwealth Bank of Australia v. Smith* (1991) 102 A.L.R. 453; *Wan v. McDonald* (1992) 105 A.L.R. 473; Heydon, (1994) 110 L.Q.R. 328.

[10] See the Hon. Mr Justice Gummow, "Compensation for Breach of Fiduciary Duty" in *Equity, Fiduciaries and Trusts* (Youdan ed. 1989), Chap. 2; Meagher, Gummow and Lehane, *Equity Doctrines and Remedies* (3rd ed.), Chap. 23; Davidson, (1982) 13 Melb.U.L. Rev.349; Davies, "Equitable Compensation: Causation and Foreseeability" in *Equity, Fiduciaries and Trusts* (Waters ed. 1993), Chap. 14; McDermott, *Equitable Damages* (1994); *The Borag* [1980] 1 Lloyd's Rep. 111, 125. But *cf. Ohm Pacific Sdn. Bhd. v. Ng Hwee Chen Doreen* [1994] 2 Singapore L.R. 576.

[11] See *Daly v. Sydney Stock Exchange Ltd* (1986) 160 C.L.R. 371. But *cf. Space Investments Ltd v. Canadian Imperial Bank of Commerce Trust Co. (Bahamas) Ltd* [1986] 1 W.L.R. 1072. Contrast *Re Goldcorp Exchange Ltd* [1995] 1 A.C. 74.

[12] *Target Holdings Ltd v. Redferns* [1995] 3 W.L.R. 352, Illustration 9.

[13] *Brickenden v. London Loan and Savings Co.* [1934] 3 D.L.R. 465, 469 (P.C.) *per* Lord Thankerton; see also *Raso v. Dionigi* (1993) 100 D.L.R. (4th) 459. On the general problem see Heydon, (1994) 110 L.Q.R. 328.

It must, however, be acknowledged that in England the authority for using fiduciary reasoning in connection with the mere causing of loss is (outside the context of express trust) at present not plentiful; and that an (inevitably more limited) liability in this respect can frequently be justified by reference to breach of implied contract terms, though with different remedial results.[14] Equally, non-liability in respect of loss suffered by the principal can sometimes be justified on the basis of the lack of any implied terms.[15]

Application of fiduciary duties other than between individual persons.   **6–046** The principles stated above, especially those as to profits made by the fiduciary, were developed largely in the context of single agents and single principals, though there were some cases involving partnerships. Their application to companies, and even to large partnerships, has yet to be worked out. Thus an agent is not permitted to act on both sides of the same transaction without disclosure; but different parts of a company, or of solicitors' or accountants' firms, may do so at the same time in absolute good faith, without the company or firm necessarily being aware that this is happening. This has been called by Professor Finn a "same matter" conflict.[16] A company or firm may act for a client in respect of a particular matter, and subsequently act for another client who is on the other side of the dispute: this may be called a "former client" conflict. A company or firm may acquire knowledge from a client in respect of one matter, and an employee or partner may then move employment and subsequently act for another client in another matter to which information gained in connection with the first matter may be relevant: this may be called a "separate matter" conflict. Finally, part of a company or firm may appear to act in an agency or at least advisory capacity for a client while another part is acting in a different capacity in respect of the same client, for example as a seller or market-maker. This may be called a "fair dealing" conflict; such

---

[14] *e.g. Keppel v. Wheeler* [1927] 1 K.B. 577 (non-disclosure by estate agent of later offer); *The Borag* [1980] 1 Lloyd's Rep. 111, 125 (ship managers caused vessel to be detained).

[15] *Kelly v. Cooper* [1993] A.C. 205, Illustration 8; *Henderson v. Merrett Syndicates Ltd* [1994] 3 W.L.R. 761, 799–800 *per* Lord Browne-Wilkinson.

[16] In what follows I have drawn heavily on, and adopted the terminology of the essay by Professor Paul Finn (now the Hon. Justice Finn), "Fiduciary Law and the Modern Commercial World", in *Commercial Aspects of Trusts and Fiduciary Obligations*, (McKendrick ed. 1992), Chap. 1, pp. 19–36. I am much indebted to this exposition, to which the reader is referred for greater detail and more persuasive reasoning. I have also made much use of the valuable Law Com.C.P.No. 124, *Fiduciary Duties and Regulatory Rules* (1992).

conflicts are not confined to conglomerates, though in modern conditions are more likely to arise in that context.

Of these conflicts the first three raise general questions of agency law, and stem from the agent's duty of loyalty. There is likely to be a conflict between the right of one client (principal) that information regarding his business is not disclosed to anyone else, and the right of another that the agent, as fiduciary, make available to him all knowledge that he has and does not conceal relevant information. It may be sought to remedy these by the creation of so-called "Chinese Walls", that is, by arrangements which seek to isolate the business activities of different parts of firms from each other.

6–047   **Situation 1: "same matter" conflicts.** This situation concerns companies and firms which, for example through different departments or partners, are simultaneously involved as agents on the two sides of a transaction. Against the background of the situation of the single agent, it is clear that this would, if not disclosed, involve a breach of duty.[17] The agent must therefore in such a situation disclose to each party the extent of his double employment,[18] so that that party can decide for himself whether to continue using the services of the agent. Furthermore, he must make further disclosure if an actual conflict of interests between clients arises[19]; and if at that point he has information acquired on behalf of one party which would be relevant to the other, his position is extremely difficult, for an unauthorised disclosure would be a breach of duty to the first party, and a concealment of the information a breach towards the second. In the corporate context it seems unlikely that non-statutory law will accept either ignorance of the conflict or Chinese Walls as a defence to proceedings for breach of duty in such cases.[20] The agent should avoid the conflict arising in the first place.

6–048   **Situation 2: "former client" conflicts.** The problems here have usually arisen in connection with solicitors. A person in one firm who has knowledge or access to it about a client's affairs moves to another firm which is acting against that client. The first question is the extent to which he is deemed to have knowledge from his previous employment. Should knowledge of relevant information be presumed? and should it

---

[17] See *North & South Trust Co. v. Berkeley* [1971] 1 W.L.R. 470, Illustration 3 to Article 5. See also above para. 2–013; below, para. 6–060.

[18] *Moody v. Cox and Hatt* [1917] 2 Ch. 71 (solicitor).

[19] See *Farrington v. Rowe McBride & Partners* [1985] 1 N.Z.L.R. 83; *Day v. Mead* [1987] 2 N.Z.L.R. 443.

[20] See *Harrods Ltd v. Lemon* [1931] 2 K.B. 157, Illustration 8 to Article 62; *Standard Investments Ltd v. Canadian Imperial; Bank of Commerce* (1985) 22 D.L.R. (4th) 410.

be imputed to all persons involved in the first organisation?[21] The second is the extent to which he or his new firm are to be restrained from acting in the matter: for if strict controls are imposed, the choice of the second client of legal representation may become much restricted, especially in communities where there are not many lawyers, or law firms with suitable resources, available. The case law so far suggests that the interest of the first client in confidence will normally prevail over those of the second in being able to choose a lawyer; and that the second company or firm will be restrained from acting if any danger of disadvantage to the first client by imparting of confidential information to the second is reasonably apprehended.[22] The value of a Chinese Wall within the first or second firm, or both, *i.e.* an administrative arrangement which should exclude the person concerned from either receiving or imparting the relevant information, has been viewed with some scepticism by the courts, albeit in the context of solicitors, to whom certain special considerations concerned with the administration of justice apply.[23]

Situation 3: "separate matter" conflicts. These raise straight conflicts between the duty not to disclose in respect of the first matter, and the duty to place all information at the disposal of the client in the second. As Megarry V.-C. said in connection with a solicitor: "A solicitor must put at his client's disposal not only his skill but also his knowledge, so far as it is relevant; and if he is unwilling to reveal his knowledge to his client, he should not act for him. What he cannot do is to act for the client and at the same time withold from him any relevant knowledge that he has."[24] Similar reasoning can be applied to other professionals.   **6–049**

There can be no doubt that the disclosure of the first client's information will (unless specifically authorised) be a breach of contract towards that client; no development of rules to cover such situations is likely to change this. It can be argued that the information which the

---

[21] See *Mallesons Stephen Jaques v. K.P.M.G. Peat Marwick* (1990) 4 W.A.R. 357 (imputed).

[22] "Rightly anticipated": *Re a Firm of Solicitors* [1992] Q.B. 959, following *Rakusen v. Ellis, Munday & Clarke* [1912] 1 Ch. 831. See also *Re a Solicitor* (1987) 131 S.J. 1063. In *In re a Firm of Solicitors*, [1995] 3 All E.R. 482, Lightman J. held that the burden of proof was on the solicitor. In *McDonald Estate v. Martin* [1990] 3 S.C.R. 1235, *sub nom. Martin v. Gray* (1990) 77 D.L.R. (4th) 249, the Supreme Court of Canada by a majority preferred a rebuttable presumption that information would be imparted. This approach was regarded as too strict in Singapore: *Alrich Development Pte Ltd v. Rafiq Jumabhoy* [1994] 3 Singapore L.R. 1. See also *National Mutual Holdings Pty v. Sentry Corp.* (1987) 87 A.L.R. 539.

[23] *David Lee (Lincoln) Ltd v. Coward Chance* [1991] Ch. 259; *Re a Firm of Solicitors*, n. 22 above. See Law Com. C.P. No. 124, n. 16 above, pp. 144–149.

[24] *Spector v. Ageda* [1973] Ch. 30, 48.

second client "buys" is limited to that held by the fiduciary independently of that acquired through his client or clients, with the result that there need be no breach of duty at all. It has been so held, in effect, in the case of an estate agent who did not disclose information coming to her when acting for an adjacent proprietor.[25] But failure to disclose known facts to the second client may sometimes be fraud; or it may falsify advice given and so cause avoidable and foreseeable loss to the second client.[26] In this situation it may be that a Chinese Wall defence would be more acceptable, if it indicated that the precautions taken were such as effectively to prevent the knowledge from the first transaction being available to those handling the second. However, there may be problems when a person with oversight of two departments is aware of the conflict or its possibility; or if one department is aware that information may be available elsewhere in the firm. If the problem has been foreseen and provided for, the terms on which the agent accepts engagement from the second client may afford protection here, subject to the difficulties discussed below.

6–050   **Situation 4: "fair dealing" conflicts.** The fourth situation raises the problems created by the abolition of "single capacity" rules in some stock and other markets, including the securities markets of the United Kingdom. The functions previously performed by persons and organisations which were certainly agents (*e.g.* stockbrokers) may now be performed by parts of multi-function companies which advise clients, undertake execution of orders and may then sell securities which they themselves hold, or have purchased for the purpose, or in which they have an interest. Chinese Walls have no relevance here; indeed the problem could arise with a sole trader. In view of the stringency of the duties which can be imposed by fiduciary law, organisations which act in such markets in a potentially fiduciary capacity must seek to define the scope of their duties by way of contract terms, quite regardless of the requirements of specific forms of regulation. The most obvious example is that of providers of financial services, who may well appear to act as (what would previously have been called) agents, or at least advisers, but also may now act, sometimes by way of a different part of the organisation, in ways which are potentially adverse to any fiduciary responsibilities which they may have: examples have already been given.

Such changes in the patterns of dealing are accompanied by the making, by delegated legislation, of principles, rules and codes for the

---

[25] *Kelly v. Cooper* [1993] A.C. 205, Illustration 8.
[26] "We have been given no sufficient reason for permitting a person to avoid one fiduciary obligation by accepting another which conflicts with it": *Black v. Shearson, Hammill & Co.* 72 Cal.Rptr. 157, 161 (1968); and see *Moody v. Cox and Hatt* [1917] 2 Ch. 71.

proper conduct of business, of which the most relevant in the United Kingdom are those made under the Financial Services Act 1986. It is important here for the law to maintain the strength of fiduciary duties and to recognise that a person engaged to act on another's behalf is undertaking thereby to prefer that other's interests to his own and must be held to his undertaking. At the same time it must be recognised that commercial patterns change, and that as in other areas of activity some of those who were formerly intermediaries may adopt a new role as independent traders. Further, it is important not to set requirements such that financial services become impossible to carry out to the standards set by the law, for this would be subverting the mechanisms established under the aegis of statute by those authorised to establish them. These mechanisms may sometimes indeed be stronger and more effective than the rules of the general law, because they cover situations to which fiduciary duties might not apply, and also because they may be more specific and addressed to identified forms of dealing. For example, the so-called "riskless principal" who buys on specific instructions and immediately sells to his client is not unlike an agent in doing so and may be required to disclose his mark-up.

Common law: contract clauses. Some persons exercising pure agency functions in the old sense may remain in this sphere of activity; and others who normally act as principals may undertake agency functions, or something like them, as by promising "best execution". But in many cases an appropriate professional description or contract clause can be used to seek to make clear that a securities firm is not an agent, but rather a financial adviser and/or dealer. Although certain fiduciary duties may perhaps attach to them as advisers, these will be more limited than those attaching to pure agents[27]; and of course a dealer would not prima facie be under fiduciary duties at all.   6–051

Such contract terms will therefore in some way purport to exclude or restrict the fiduciary duties which might otherwise arise. It is plain that a fiduciary could not exclude his liability for fraud or deliberate breach of contract.[28] Beyond that, the background against which such clauses must be viewed is as follows. Recent dicta of high authority, already quoted, suggest that all agency is contractual and that the rights and duties of the parties to such a contract stem entirely from the contract between them.[29] These dicta can be regarded as highly relevant in this

---

[27] See *Burns v. Kelly Peters & Associates Ltd* (1987) 41 D.L.R. (4th) 577; Finn, "Fiduciary Law and the Modern Commercial World" in *Commercial Aspects of Trusts and Fiduciary Obligations* (McKendrick ed., 1992), 7, 10–11.

[28] *S. Pearson & Son Ltd v. Dublin Corp.* [1907] A.C. 351, 355, 362; Treitel, *Law of Contract* (9th ed.), p. 223.

[29] *Kelly v. Cooper* [1993] A.C. 205, 213–214 (Illustration 8).

context, and may be taken to suggest that the background against which intermediaries act, and the general understandings in the type of business, may establish that there are no fiduciary duties, or very limited duties, in certain situations, and that no specific contractual exclusions are therefore required: the principles of interpretation and implied terms will be adequate. It has earlier been submitted, however, that this purely contractual approach is open to question.[30] Although the common law is actually weak on the implied terms to be attributed to different types of contract, the relationship of agency is established as one with its own special features, which indeed the Comment to this Article sets out to describe; and certain types of term can be actually inconsistent with it, and so unacceptable, at least if the relationship is to remain one of agency. Thus it was long ago held in *Robinson v. Mollett*[31] that a usage of the market which allowed an agent to buy to become a seller to his principal was inconsistent with the relationship of agency and so invalid against a principal unless he was aware of it. On this basis, an apparent agent who seeks by a contract term to reserve the power to act in a way inconsistent with agency can therefore only achieve this in one of two ways. The first, and less drastic, is to acknowledge the agency but disclose the potential conflict of interest in such a way as to obtain the consent of the principal to it: for the fiduciary duty is only one of disclosure. The second, and more drastic, is to make clear that the obligation undertaken is not one of agency (in the sense to which the fiduciary duties attach) at all.

There can be no reason of principle why either of these should not be done,[32] but each would require a clearly drafted clause: the first, to make full disclosure, the second, to make clear that the substance of the relationship is in fact different from what it might otherwise be. As to the first, there is authority in another context that a general disclosure is not sufficient: the principal must receive sufficient disclosure to enable him to decide whether or not to utilise the services of the person in question,[33] and this seems correct in principle. As to the second, a person who accepts engagement on the basis that he is an agent, or appears to be such, or more generally describes himself or behaves in such a way as to suggest that he offers to act in the interests of the party who employs him, may find it difficult to establish the validity of a

---

[30] Above, para. 6–034.

[31] (1874) L.R. 7 H.L. 802, Illustration 8 to Article 31.

[32] *cf. Hayim v. Citibank N.A.* [1987] A.C. 730 (clause reducing duties of executor of will towards beneficiaries); *Movitex Ltd v. Bulfield* [1988] B.C.L.C. 104 (modification of self-dealing rules in company's articles). As to trustees excluding themselves from liability see Matthews, [1989] Conv. 42.

[33] *Farrington v. Rowe McBride & Partners* [1985] 1 N.Z.L.R. 83, 92–93. See in general Law Com.C.P. No.124, n. 16 above, pp. 106 *et seq.*

clause which purports to indicate that he may not be an agent after all, in that, while perhaps charging a commission (even if it is described as a "handling charge"), he may without warning sell his own shares to his principal and so forth. Such a purported disclosure may simply be held inconsistent with the basic obligation undertaken. To achieve or confirm a change of status from what would otherwise appear to be the case, he must indicate the capacity in which he acts, or that capacity must be open and notorious: it seems doubtful whether a clause indicating that he *may* on occasions change his role would be sufficient. The circumstances in which such problems can arise are too varied, and often too specialised, for more than general indications of approach to be suggested. But it would not be right for the claims of technical progress to be allowed to erode the duties rightly imposed on those who hold themselves as acting in the interests of others.

Unfair Contract Terms Act 1977. A contract clause seeking to make clear that a person who might be an agent is not, or might in some circumstances not be acting as such, may also be caught by the Unfair Contract Terms Act 1977, which could require it to assessed against the "requirement of reasonableness".[34] Here, however, conceptual problems may arise.[35] The relevant provision will normally be section 3, which operates where one party deals "as consumer or on the other's written standard terms of business." One of these two requirements may often be satisfied; but then the wording of the section is entirely geared to exclusions or restrictions of "breach of contract", "contractual performance" and "contractual obligation".[36] The section therefore seems to apply only to such duties as can be regarded as contractual and normal to the type of transaction; and we are therefore remitted to the problem, discussed above,[37] as to the extent to which the agent owes duties of loyalty and the extent to which, in so far as he does, these are contractual. It has been submitted there that there are some duties of an agent which are purely fiduciary and not contractual: if this is so, the Act may not affect such duties at all, though the normal principles of interpretation of contract terms would of course still apply. Conversely, it could be argued that a clause establishing the nature of the function of

6–052

---

[34] See in general Chitty, *Contracts* (27th ed.), Vol. 1, §§ 14–045 *et seq.* Problems may also arise, but in a different way, where the Unfair Terms in Consumer Contracts Regulations (S.I. 1994 No. 3159) apply.

[35] Cl.1(e) of Sched.1 to the Act excludes from its scope "any contract so far as it relates to the creation or transfer of securities or of any right or interest in securities." This appears on its face to relate to provisions concerning the transfer of the securities themselves and not to the function performed by the person effecting the transfer.

[36] See Treitel, *Law of Contract* (9th ed.), pp. 232–233.

[37] Above, para. 6–034.

a person in question is not an exclusion clause within the Act at all, and so is immune from the requirement of reasonableness. Reasoning of this type has, however, been rejected, albeit in a slightly different context, by the House of Lords.[38]

In response to either argument, the strongest part of section 3 is section 3(2)(b)(i), which does not rely on the idea of existing contractual obligations at all: under it a person cannot "claim to be entitled to render a contractual performance substantially different from that which was reasonably expected of him", except in so far as the clause is reasonable under the Act. It is this provision which gets nearest to approaching the problems outlined above and it may accordingly prove to be of most value where the exclusions used by a person who might be taken to be offering agency or similar functions are such that a reasonable person using that person's services would not have anticipated their effect.

The financial market in the United Kingdom is, as has already been stated, regulated by techniques laid down by statute, the Financial Services Act 1986.[39] In so far as the 1977 Act, and its "requirement of reasonableness", is applicable, it seems likely that compliance with such provisions would be strong evidence of the reasonableness of a particular contract term.

6–053   **Public law: the Financial Services Act 1986.**[40] We come finally to the legislation itself. Various provisions of the Financial Services Act authorise the making of principles, rules and codes which may potentially affect fiduciary duties. The principal rule-making authority is the Secretary of State for Trade and Industry, but the powers are largely delegated to the Securities and Investments Board (SIB). Thus section 55 empowers the making of rules concerning clients' money; section 81 as to the rights and obligations of participants in authorised unit trust schemes; and section 48(2)(g) as to disclosure. Most conspicuous is section 48(2)(h), which (like section 48(2)(g) filling out general powers conferred by section 48(1)) allows the making by statutory instrument of rules "enabling or requiring information obtained by an authorised person in the course of carrying out one part of his business to be witheld by him from persons with whom he deals in the course of

---

[38] *Smith v. Eric S. Bush* [1990] 1 A.C. 831.

[39] See below.

[40] The Act is a specialised topic which has generated its own literature. See, for example, Blair, *Financial Services: the New Core Rules* (1991); White, *Regulation of Securities and Futures Dealing* (1992); McVea, *Financial Conglomerates and the Chinese Wall* (1993); Cranston, (1990) 16 Brooklyn J.Int.Law 125; Lomnicka and Powell, *Encyclopedia of Financial Services Law* (1987); *Financial Services: Law and Practice* (1993).

carrying out another part and for that purpose enabling or requiring persons employed in one part of that business to withold information from those employed in another part." This is taken to refer to the setting up of Chinese Walls; and a rule made under the Act makes provision to give effect to such arrangements.[41] The view can be taken that rules so made can alter the rights and duties of the parties as they would otherwise be determined by the rules of private law[42] in the particular context of financial services, for example in the first three conflict situations referred to above. Equally, rules made under section 48(2)(g) might affect situations of the fourth type. It seems very doubtful, however, whether the power to alter basic protective rules of law could be conferred on a rule-making body in this way and by such general wording. Compliance with such standards might, however, as indicated above, be evidence of statutory reasonableness; or be a guide to the extent of the fiduciary obligation; to trade usage; or more simply as to the understandings of the parties to a contract. The provisions as to clients' money, on the other hand, raise no such problems, for the way in which a fiduciary holds money is in any case variable in accordance with the context.[43]

Illustrations

(1)   An agent in London had a power of attorney from his principal **6–054** in America to sell his English property and invest the proceeds at he thought fit. The agent, who was a solicitor, paid the interest received from the investments into the account of his firm. Held, he was a trustee of the profits and must account for them. Accordingly the Statute of Limitations did not run against the principal.[44]

(2)   A selling agent agrees to sell goods in India against an advance. He pays 85 per cent of the price to the principal and then sells the goods. He uses the balance of the price to buy goods in India and sell them in England, which is very profitable to him. Held, the agent does not have to account to the principal for the profit but only for the balance of the price, since he is not in a fiduciary position in relation to the money.[45]

(3)   An agent was employed to buy timber lands for a company. All these had already been bought up and he recommended the company to buy prairie land instead. The company agreed and sent the agent money

---

[41] SIB Core Conduct of Business Rules, rule 36 "Chinese Walls".
[42] Law Com. C.P. No. 124, n. 16 above, pp. 176 *et seq.*
[43] See above, para. 6–042.
[44] *Burdick v. Garrick* (1870) L.R. 5 Ch. App. 233.
[45] *Kirkham v. Peel* (1880) 43 L.T. 171; affd. (1880) 44 L.T. 195.

for that specific purpose. It was later discovered that the agent had charged the company more than he had himself paid for the land. Held, as the money had been sent to the agent for investment in a specified manner, he was a trustee of the improper profit and so could not plead the Statute of Limitations.[46]

(4) An agent is employed to sell cargo from a wrecked ship for average adjusters. After deducting claims for salvage and other expenses, £96 remains in his hands. He is not bound to keep the proceeds of sale of the cargo in a separate fund, and he is not a trustee of the £96 but only a debtor to his principal.[47]

(5) Shipping agents are placed in funds by shipowners from time to time to enable them to discharge jetty and river dues, pilotage and towage, berth fees and similar expenses on ships which visit the local port, and for their agency fee. They do not hold the money in trust, but in their insolvency and in respect of claims by their bank to set off other debts they are simply debtors to the shipowners in respect of money received and not disbursed.[48]

(6) A solicitor is associated with a client in transactions relating to the development of land. He persuades the client to release part of a mortgage over land on which he (the solicitor) has a second mortgage; this advances the solicitor's security and leaves the client with insufficient security. The solicitor does not explain to the client the advantage which the solicitor gains from this, nor fully explains other matters relating to the release. The solicitor is liable for the loss caused to the client.[49]

(7) A solicitor acts for the purchaser of land. He does not disclose that between the apparent vendor of the land and the purchaser there is an intermediate vendor, for whom he has acted, who bought from the original vendor and resold at a profit; and he conveys the property direct from the original vendor to the ultimate purchaser and bills the entire cost of the transaction to the purchaser. Subsequently a warehouse is built on the acquired land, but because of the negligence of the engineer and the pile-driving contractor the purchaser suffers loss, not all of which he recovers from the contractors concerned. The solicitor is liable for the profit made by the intermediate purchaser, but not for the subsequent losses.[50]

---

[46] *North American Land and Timber Co. v. Watkins* [1904] 1 Ch. 242; [1904] 2 Ch. 233.
[47] *Henry v. Hammond* [1913] 2 K.B. 515. See also *Wilsons and Furness-Leyland Line v. British and Continental Shipping Co.* (1907) 23 T.L.R. 397.
[48] *Neste Oy v. Lloyd's Bank Plc.* [1983] 2 Lloyd's Rep. 658, following *Henry v. Hammond*, n. 47 above; one particular payment was held on trust.
[49] *Nocton v. Ashburton* [1914] A.C. 398.
[50] *Canson Enterprises Ltd v. Boughton & Co.* [1991] 3 S.C.R. 534; (1991) 85 D.L.R. (4th) 129 cf. *Hodgkinson v. Simms* [1994] 3 S.C.R. 377, (1994) 117 D.L.R. (4th) 161 (accountant).

(8) An estate agent acts for the vendor of land and negotiates a sale of it "subject to contract". She is subsequently asked by the prospective purchaser if she can assist in obtaining a sale to him of the adjacent land, for the owner of which she has previously acted unsuccessfully. She approaches that second owner and gives minimal advice in respect of the price; she does not disclose that the offeror has just entered into a "subject to contract" arrangement in relation to the adjacent land. The information would have been of consequence to the second vendor, as the purchaser desired to secure a "family compound" of the two properties. The second vendor sells the property. The estate agent is not liable for loss (in so far as provable) suffered by the second vendor, and is not disentitled to commission, for there is "an implied term of the contract with such an agent that he is entitled to act for other principals selling competing properties and to keep confidential the information obtained from each of his principals." [51]

(9) Solicitors acting for purchasers of land receive money lent by mortgagees, for whom they are also acting, and release it to the purchaser without authority before the mortgage security is executed. The security is later executed. The borrower defaults and the property is repossessed and sold for less than the mortgage debt. The solicitors are liable, not to replace the trust estate, but to compensate the mortgagee for loss which he would not have suffered but for the breach of duty. [52]

Article 46

DUTY TO MAKE FULL DISCLOSURE

An agent may not enter into a transaction in which his personal interest, or his duty to another principal, may conflict with his duty to his principal, unless his principal, with full knowledge of all the material circumstances and of the nature and extent of the agent's interest, consents. [53]	6–055

---

[51] *Kelly v. Cooper* [1993] A.C. 205 (P.C.): as to the implied term see p. 214 *per* Lord Browne-Wilkinson. *Sed quaere* in view of the fact that advice was given and because the reasoning relies on the proposition that all agency is contractual. The decision may be correct for estate agents, who are only imperfectly agents (above, para. 1–017) and are known to act for many principals. It is doubtful whether its reasoning should be generalised. Both parties would have benefited from disclosure by the agent. The fiduciary duties were treated as regulated, not by the express terms of any contract, but by an *implied* term that they did not apply. See [1994] J.B.L. 147; and further as to estate agents in this context Murdoch, *Law of Estate Agency and Auctions* (3rd ed.), pp. 110–116.
[52] *Target Holdings Ltd v. Redferns* [1995] 3 W.L.R. 352.
[53] See Comment.

Comment

6–056   **General principle: profits.** The general principle covering liability of fiduciaries in respect of profits is well stated as follows:

"There is a wide variety of formulations of the general principle of equity requiring a person in a fiduciary relationship to account for personal benefit or gain. The doctrine is often expressed in the form that a person 'is not allowed to put himself in a position where his interest and duty conflict'[54] or 'may conflict'[55] or that a person 'is not to allow a conflict to arise between duty and interest'[56] As Sir Frederick Jordan pointed out however[57] this, read literally, 'represents rather a counsel of prudence that a rule of equity' ... Notwithstanding authoritative dicta to the effect that the 'use of fiduciary position' doctrine is but an illustration or part of a wider 'conflict of interest and duty' doctrine ... the two themes, while overlapping, are distinct ... Stated comprehensively in terms of the liability to account, the principle of equity is that a person who is under a fiduciary obligation must account to the person to whom the obligation is owed for any benefit or gain (i) which has been obtained or received in circumstances where a conflict or significant possibility of conflict existed between his fiduciary duty and his personal interest in the pursuit or possible receipt of such a benefit or gain or (ii) which was obtained or received by use or by reason of his fiduciary position or of opportunity or knowledge resulting from it. Any such benefit or gain is held by the fiduciary as constructive trustee."[58][59]

In a sense this Article does no more than draw attention to the guiding principles contained within the broader duty of loyalty, of which principles more specific applications appear in subsequent Articles. Problems of the causing of loss, and of non-proprietary remedies, have been alluded to under the previous Article.[59a]

Thus an agent may not without full disclosure buy his principal's property nor sell his own property to his principal.[60] He may not make

---

[54] *Bray v. Ford* [1896] A.C. 44, 51.
[55] *Phipps v. Boardman* [1967] 2 A.C. 46, 123.
[56] *New Zealand Netherlands Society "Oranje" Inc. v. Kuys* [1973] 1 W.L.R. 1126, 1129.
[57] Jordan, *Select Legal Papers* (1983), p. 115.
[58] See *Keith Henry & Co. Pty Ltd v. Stuart Walker & Co. Pty Ltd* (1958) 100 C.L.R. 342, 350.
[59] *Chan v. Zacharia* (1984) 154 C.L.R. 178, 198–199 *per* Deane J. See also *Burton v. Wookey* (1822) 6 Madd. 367; *Rothschild v. Brookman* (1831) 2 Dow. & Cl. 188; *Parker v. McKenna* (1874) L.R. 10 Ch.App.96, 118; *Re Birt* (1883) 22 Ch.D. 604; *Bray v. Ford* [1896] A.C. 44, 51–52; *Lindgren v. L.&P. Estates Ltd* [1968] Ch. 572; *North and South Trust Co. v. Berkeley* [1971] 1 W.L.R. 470; the Rt.Hon. Lord Justice Millett, [1993] Restitution L.Rev. 7, 16: "A fiduciary will not be allowed to retain any advantage acquired in violation of the rule."
[59a] See above, paras. 6–039, 6–044, 6–045.
[60] Article 47.

secret profits by exploiting the property, confidential information or special knowledge of his principal[61]; nor may he do so by means depending on the exercise of his position as agent.[62] He may not take a bribe or a secret commission from the other side to a transaction.[63] In each of these cases his own interest is likely to be at variance with that of his principal. The rules sometimes are said to apply even though there has in fact been no conflict, but merely because there was a possibility of one: but whether this approach will always be strictly implemented may be open to question.[64]

The general principle may however also take in certain other cases which cannot readily be reduced into the specific categories indicated above. Thus an agent who sells not to himself but to a company in which he has an interest does not buy his principal's property, but his fiduciary duties may be breached.[65] The same would be the case where a company in which he has a interest sells to his principal.[66] Again, an agent who competes with his principal to the subversion of his principal's business may be restrained, or held liable to disgorge his profits as an alternative to or over and above any liability for breach of contract. The argument may be that the profits are or ought to be regarded as being those of the principal's business.[67] Reasoning of this type is particularly found in connection with employment contracts.[68] Sometimes such an agent may be held to have made a profit from his principal's property, or because of his position as agent: but this explanation may not always fit the facts, and more general reasoning may be required.

Disclosure. The duty does not actually prohibit the adoption of a   **6–057** position or the entering into of transactions in which such a conflict might occur; it rather prohibits doing so without disclosure of all material facts to the principal so as to obtain his consent.[69] In this sense

---

[61] Article 48.

[62] Article 49.

[63] Article 50.

[64] See below, para. 6–079.

[65] Illustration 1.

[66] Illustration 2.

[67] See Finn, *Fiduciary Obligations* (1977), Chap. 24; Goff and Jones, *Law of Restitution* (4th ed.), pp. 660–661; *Re Thomson* [1930] 1 Ch. 203; Illustration 4; *cf.* Partnership Act 1890, s. 30.

[68] Thus the duty of loyalty is sometimes expressed in master and servant terminology: "the servant undertakes to serve his master with good faith and fidelity": *Robb v. Green* [1895] 2 Q.B. 315, 320. This expression is also to be found in *Wessex Dairies Ltd v. Smith* [1935] 2 K.B. 80; *Hivac Ltd v. Park Royal Scientific Instruments Ltd* [1946] Ch. 169; *Sanders v. Parry* [1967] 1 W.L.R. 753, Illustration 4; *Headway Construction Co. Ltd v. Downham* (1974) 233 E.G. 675, Illustration 17 to Article 47.

[69] *New Zealand Netherlands Society "Oranje" Inc. v. Kuys* [1973] 1 W.L.R. 1126.

the rule may, as suggested in the Comment to the previous Article, differ in application from the less flexible rules relevant to express trustees. Consent of the principal is not uncommon. But it must be positively shown. The burden of proving full disclosure lies on the agent[70] and it is not sufficient for him merely to disclose that he has an interest[71] or to make such statements as would put the principal on inquiry.[72]

6–058   **Custom or usage.** A custom or usage which converts an agent into a principal or otherwise gives him an interest at variance with his duty is prima facie unreasonable,[73] and will therefore be ineffective unless known of and consented to by the principal.[74]

6–059   **Disclosure by agent of his own breaches of duty.** Until recently the leading case of *Bell v. Lever Bros. Ltd*[75] was taken to establish that an employee, and hence an agent, was under no duty to disclose his own breaches of contract. This may be true as a broad proposition relating to employees in general. But the Court of Appeal has held that in appropriate circumstances an employee may be under a duty to disclose breaches of duty by other employees, whether inferior or superior.[76] And it has been said at first instance that the appellant in *Bell v. Lever Bros Ltd* was not a director of the company to which he did not disclose his breaches (but rather an employee of that company appointed as director of another company) and that had he been a director he would have owed the company fiduciary duties.[77] If this result is correct, the agent's fiduciary responsibilities may sometimes impose on him a duty to disclose his own breaches to his principal.

---

[70] *Dunne v. English* (1874) L.R. 18 Eq. 524. On the analogy of concurrence with breach of trust, it should not be necessary to show that the principal knew that what he was consenting to was a breach of duty, so long as he knew clearly what it was: *Re Pauling's Settlement Trusts* [1962] 1 W.L.R. 86, 108.

[71] *Imperial Mercantile Credit Association Co. v. Coleman* (1873) L.R. 6 H.L. 189; *Alexander v. Automatic Telephone Co.* [1900] 2 Ch. 56; *Gluckstein v. Barnes* [1900] A.C. 240; *Gray v. New Augarita Porcupine Mines* [1952] 3 D.L.R. 1 (P.C.).

[72] *Dunne v. English,* n. 70 above, *cf. Swale v. Ipswich Tannery Co. Ltd* (1906) 11 Com.Cas. 88, 86–97.

[73] *Robinson v. Mollett* (1875) L.R. 7 H.L. 802, Illustration 8 to Article 31; *Hamilton v. Young* (1881) 7 L.R.Ir. 289, Illustration 5; *Tetley v. Shand* (1871) 25 L.T. 658; *Anglo-African Merchants Ltd v. Bayley* [1970] 1 Q.B. 311; *North and South Trust Co. v. Berkeley* [1971] 1 W.L.R. 470: *Cec. McManus Realty Ltd v. Bray* (1970) 14 D.L.R. (3d) 564, 568: *cf. Jones v. Canavan* [1971] 2 N.S.W.L.R. 243.

[74] See Article 31.

[75] [1932] A.C. 161.

[76] *Sybron Corp. v. Rochem Ltd* [1984] Ch. 112, Illustration 6.

[77] *Horcal Ltd v. Gatland* [1983] I.R.L.R. 459: affd. without reference to this point [1984] I.R.L.R. 288.

Duty to another principal: agent acting for both parties.[78] Another   **6–060**
manifestation of the agent's fiduciary duty is that he must not serve two
principals whose interests may conflict. So he may not act for both
parties to a transaction unless he ensures that he fully discloses all the
material facts to each party and obtains their informed consent to his so
acting.[79] Thus a solicitor who is a trustee of trust property which is for
sale should not act as solicitor for the purchaser and may be liable in
respect of non-disclosure of information known to him as trustee if he
does[80]; an agent who is employed to negotiate a loan may not receive a
commission from the lender;[81] a hotel broker who is acting for the
vendor of an hotel may not also claim commisson from the purchaser[82];
and an insurance broker (who is the assured's agent) may not act as
agent for underwriters in obtaining an assessor's report, because such
report may be adverse to the assured's claim against underwriters.[83]
Any custom to the contrary will not be upheld.[84] It is not material that
the agent is acting gratuitously for one or both parties; the mere fact of
being agent for two or more parties who may have adverse interests is
improper unless all principals have given their informed consent. If,
however, it is notorious that agents do act for both sides to a transaction
or the agent explains all the circumstances fully to the principal and the
principal consents to the agent receiving two commissions, he cannot
subsequently call the agent to account for the commission paid by the
other party,[85] nor can he himself refuse to pay his own commission.[86]
Even if the agent is improperly acting for two opposing principals, the

---

[78] For further discussion see above, paras. 2–013, 6–047 et seq.

[79] This passage was cited with approval by Megaw J. in *Anglo-African Merchants Ltd v. Bayley* [1970] 1 Q.B. 311, 323 and by Douglas J. in *Dargusch v. Sherley Investments Pty. Ltd* [1970] Qd.R. 338, 347; see also *Eagle Star Insurance Co. Ltd v. Spratt* [1971] 2 Lloyd's Rep. 116, 133; *McDonnell v. Barton Realty Ltd* [1993] 3 N.Z.L.R. 418. cf. *Swain v. Law Society* [1983] 1 A.C. 598 (statutory scheme for solicitors' insurance).

[80] *Moody v. Cox and Hatt* [1917] 2 Ch. 71; *cf. Clark Boyce v. Mouat* [1994] 1 A.C. 428.

[81] *Re a Debtor* [1927] 2 Ch. 367; *Advanced Realty Funding Corp. v. Bannink* (1979) 106 D.L.R. (3d) 137. *Cf. Turner v. Laurentide Financial Realty Corp. (Western) Ltd* (1979) 97 D.L.R. (3d) 429.

[82] *Fullwood v. Hurley* [1928] 1 K.B. 498; *cf. Foster v. Reaume* [1924] 2 D.L.R. 951.

[83] *Anglo-African Merchants Ltd v. Bayley*, n. 79 above; *North and South Trust Co v. Berkeley* [1971] 1 W.L.R. 470, Illustration 3 to Article 5.

[84] *Bartram & Sons v. Lloyd* (1903) 88 L.T. 286; revsd. on other grounds (1904) 90 L.T. 357; *Fullwood v. Hurley* [1928] 1 K.B. 498; *Cec. McManus Realty Ltd v. Bray* (1970) 14 D.L.R. (3d) 564, 568; cases cited at n. 83 above; and compare *Jones v. Canavan* [1971] 2 N.S.W.L.R. 243. See also *Knoch Estate v. Jon Picken Ltd* (1991) 83 DLR (4th) 447.

[85] *Re Haslam and Hier-Evans* [1902] 1 Ch. 765, Illustration 7 to Article 50. This reasoning would presumably cover the "buyer's premium" charged by some auctioneers. As to auctioneers bidding for third parties, see Murdoch, *Law of Estate Agency and Auctions* (3rd ed.), pp. 297–298.

[86] *Harrods Ltd v. Lemon* [1931] 2 K.B. 157, Illustration 8 to Article 62; *cf. Owen v. Trickett* (1908) 27 N.Z.L.R. 950.

court will not normally make an order on the application of one of the principals which will result in the agent breaking his confidence towards his other principal, at least where that other principal has acted in good faith.[87]

6–061 **Statutory requirements.** Sometimes disclosure is required by statute or statutory instrument. Thus persons engaged in estate agency work are in some circumstances required to disclose to their clients services which they or persons connected with them offer to purchasers[88]; or that they or persons connected with them are seeking to acquire an interest in the land concerned.[89]

Illustrations

6–062 (1) An agent for sale sells to a company of which he is a director and large shareholder. The sale is not binding on the principal.[90]

(2) A director of a company may not sell to his company articles which he, or a firm in which he has an interest, manufactures. Any such contract is voidable by the company, quite apart from the question of its fairness, since a director is not permitted to enter into transactions in which his own interest is in conflict with his duty to promote the interests of the company.[91]

(3) Factory-owners employed a surveyor to prepare a specification of repairs for submission to the War Damage Commission and to supervise the repair work as it was done by a building company. After the preparation of a specification, but before any repair work was done, the surveyor became the managing director of the building company and told the factory-owners of his new position. The surveyor placed himself in a position where his duty and interest conflicted and this was a breach

---

[87] *North and South Trust Co. v. Berkeley* [1971] 1 W.L.R. 470, Illustration 3 to Article 5; but see (1972) 35 M.L.R. 78; Rider (1978) 42 Conv. 114. See also *Vehicle and General Insurance Co. Ltd v. Elmbridge Insurances* [1973] 1 Lloyd's Rep. 325, where effect was (surprisingly) given to a clause by which an insurance broker agreed to hold money received from clients in trust for the insurance company.

[88] Estate Agents (Undesirable Practices) Order 1991 (S.I. 1991 No. 1032) (made under Estate Agents Act 1979, s. 18), reg. 2; see Murdoch, *The Estate Agents and Property Misdescriptions Acts* (3rd ed.), Chap. 3A; *Law of Estate Agency and Auctions* (3rd ed.), pp. 206–211. The civil remedy is that the contract may be unenforceable: Estate Agents Act 1979, s. 18(5). Regulations to similar effect are made under s. 48(2) of the Financial Services Act 1986, but here breach may give rise to a civil action in damages if the plaintiff is a private investor: ss. 62, 62A. See Lomnicka and Powell, *Encyclopedia of Financial Services Law* (1987); *Financial Services: Law and Practice* (1994).

[89] Estate Agents (Undesirable Practices) (No 2) Order 1991, *supra*, Sched. 1 para. 2; see Murdoch, *op.cit.* n. 88 above, pp. 212–213.

[90] *Salomons v. Pender* (1865) 3 H. & C. 639.

[91] *Aberdeen Ry. Co. v. Blaikie Bros.* (1854) 1 Macq. 461.

of his contract. But he was entitled to recover his fees since the factory-owners had acquiesced in his continuance as their agent.[92]

(4) A solicitor engaged an assistant to undertake, among other business, the work of an important client. During his employment, the assistant agreed with the client to leave the employment of the solicitor in order to set up in practice on his own. The client agreed that, if he did so, the client would transfer his work to the assistant. Held, in so acting, the assistant was in breach of the implied term of his agreement to serve the plaintiff with good faith and fidelity. He was, accordingly, liable in damages to his principal.[93]

(5) A broker was authorised to sell certain shares, and pay himself certain advances out of the proceeds. A custom whereby he might himself take over the shares at the price of the day, in the event of him being unable to find a purchaser at an adequate price, was unreasonable, and such a transaction was not binding on the principal unless he had notice of the custom at the time when he gave the broker the authority, even if a forced sale of the shares would inevitably have realised less than the price given by the broker.[94] So a custom whereby an agent for sale of a ship may himself purchase at the minimum price if he cannot find a purchaser was held to be unreasonable.[95]

(6) The European zone controller of an international chemical company engages with other employees in setting up and operating rival businesses in competition with the company. He is in breach of duty in not disclosing the misconduct of the other employees, and on the terms of the company's pension scheme the company need not make certain payments to him and can recover sums paid.[96]

Article 47

DUTY TO MAKE FULL DISCLOSURE WHERE HE DEALS WITH HIS PRINCIPAL

(1) Where an agent enters into any contract or transaction with his   **6–063**
     principal, or with his principal's representative in interest, he
     must act with perfect good faith, and make full disclosure of
     all the material circumstances, and of everything known to him

---

[92] *Thornton Hall v. Wembley Electrical Appliances Ltd* [1947] 2 All E.R. 630.
[93] *Sanders v. Parry* [1967] 1 W.L.R. 753. See also *Aubanel and Alabaster Ltd v. Aubanel* (1949) 66 R.P.C. 343; *State Vacuum Stores v. Phillips* [1954] 3 D.L.R. 621.
[94] *Hamilton v. Young* (1881) 7 L.R.Ir. 289; *Rothschild v. Brookman* (1831) 2 Dow. & Cl. 188. But *cf.* Article 47, Illustration 9.
[95] *De Bussche v. Alt* (1878) 8 Ch.D. 286.
[96] *Sybron Corp. v. Rochem Ltd* [1984] Ch. 112. See Comment above.

223

respecting the subject-matter of the contract or transaction which would be likely to influence the conduct of the principal or his representative.[97]

(2) Where any question arises as to the validity of any such contract or transaction, or of any gift made by a principal to his agent, the burden of proving that no advantage was taken by the agent of his position, or of the confidence reposed in him, and that the transaction was entered into in perfect good faith and after full disclosure, lies upon the agent.[98]

Comment

6–064   **Purchase from principal.** A long-established line of cases indicates that a person who stands in a position of a confidential character in respect of the property of another, which would include many types of agent, cannot purchase it for himself without full and fair disclosure of all the facts to the principal.[99] The onus in such a case is on the agent to show that the price was adequate, that the sale was as advantageous to his principal as any other sale he could have obtained from a third party, and that he disclosed all the relevant facts to his principal before the purchase and that the principal gave his informed consent.[1] The rule

---

[97] *Collins v. Hare* (1928) 2 Bli.(N.S.) 106; *Jones v. Thomas* (1837) 2 Y. & C.Ex. 498; *Molony v. Kernan* (1842) 2 Dr. & War. (Ir.) 31; *Charter v. Trevelyan* (1844) 11 C. & F. 714; *Savery v. King* (1856) 5 H.L.Cas. 627; *Waters v. Shaftesbury* (1866) 14 L.T. 184; *Parker v. McKenna* (1874) L.R. 10 Ch.App. 96; *Ward v. Sharp* (1884) 53 L.J.Ch. 313; *Demerara Bauxite Co. v. Hubbard* [1923] A.C. 673; but *cf. Hanson v. Lorenz & Jones* [1987] 1 F.T.L.R. 23 (agent enters joint venture with principal). And see Illustrations; *Restatement*, §§ 389–393; Finn, *Fiduciary Obligations* (1977) Chap. 20 and pp. 223–228; Meagher, Gummow and Lehane *Equity Doctrines and Remedies* (3rd ed.), pp. 147 *et seq.* The problem of "self-contracting" raises in civil law jurisdictions theoretical problems to which the common law, largely concerned with protection of the principal, has paid little attention. See Badr (1982) 30 Am.J.Comp.L. 255.

[98] See material cited above, n. 97.

[99] *Gibson v. Jeyes* (1801) 6 Ves. 266; *Lowther v. Lowther* (1806) 13 Ves. 95; *Austin v. Chambers* (1838) 6 C. & F. 1, 37; *Rothschild v. Brookman* (1831) 2 Dow. & Cl. 188; *Dally v. Wonham* (1863) 33 Beav. 154; *Dunne v. English* (1874) L.R. 18 Eq. 524, Illustration 4; *McPherson v. Watt* (1877) 3 App.Cas. 254, Illustration 3; *Imeson v. Lister* (1920) 149 L.T.Jo. 446; *McKenzie v. McDonald* [1927] V.L.R. 143; *Christie v. McCann* (1972) 27 D.L.R. (3d) 544; *Lunghi v. Sinclair* [1966] W.A.R. 172; *Headway Construction Co. Ltd v. Downham* (1974) 233 E.G. 675, Illustration 17.

[1] *Gibson v. Jeyes*, n. 99 above; *Holman v. Loynes* (1854) 4 De G.M. & G. 270; *Savery v. King* (1856) 5 H.L.Cas. 627, 655–656; *Spencer v. Topham* (1856) 22 Beav. 573; *Gresley v. Mousley* (1862) 31 L.J.Ch. 537; *Pisani v. Att.Gen. for Gibraltar* (1874) L.R. 5 P.C. 516; *Ward v. Sharp* (1883) 53 L.J.Ch. 313; *Wright v. Carter* [1903] 1 Ch. 27; *Moody v. Cox & Hatt* [1917] 2 Ch. 71; *Demerara Bauxite Co. Ltd v. Hubbard* [1923] A.C. 673; *Christie v. McCann*, n. 99 above. Such is the authority. But a modern approach would be to look to the disclosure: if a fully-informed principal wishes to deal on terms adverse to himself, he should be allowed to do so.

extends to sub-agents, who may themselves be fiduciaries.[2] It also applies to agents who take leases from their principals.[3] In this respect a fiduciary differs in some degree from a trustee, because a purchase of the trust property by a trustee is voidable at the instance of any beneficiary unless it can be proved that all the beneficiaries consented.[4] Where a solicitor purchases from a client, it is important (if not essential) that the client should have had independent advice; otherwise, the solicitor will have difficulty in showing that the transaction was a fair one.[5] Such advice may be appropriate in other relationships also.

Sale to principal. Similarly, an agent may not sell his own property to his principal without full and fair disclosure and the obtaining of his principal's informed consent[6]; nor may he lease his own property to his principal without full disclosure. However fair the transaction may be, it can still be set aside by the principal if there has not been full disclosure.[7] Cases suggesting a more lenient rule have not been followed.[8]   6–065

Agent with specific instructions. Where, however, the agent has specific instructions to buy or sell at a particular price and no element of   6–066

---

[2] *Ex p. James* (1803) 8 Ves. 337; *Hobday v. Peters* (1860) 28 Beav. 349; *De Bussche v. Alt* (1878) 8 Ch.D. 286; *Powell & Thomas v. Evan Jones & Co.* [1905] 1 K.B. 11; *Blair v. Martin* [1929] N.Z.L.R. 225; *Christie v. McCann* (1972) 27 D.L.R. (3d) 544; *Palinko v. Bower* [1976] 4 W.W.R. 118; Finn, *Fiduciary Obligations* (1977), pp. 177–178, 202–203; and see Article 37.

[3] *Selsey v. Rhoades* (1824) 2 S. & St. 41; affd. (1827) 2 Bli. (N.S.) 1, Illustration 19. See also *Aaran Acceptance Corp. v. Adam* (1987) 37 D.L.R. (4th) 133 (loan).

[4] *Ex p. Lacey* (1802) 6 Ves. 625; *Ex p. James*, n. 2 above; *Campbell v. Walker* (1800) 5 Ves. 678; (1807) 13 Ves. 601. But *cf. Holder v. Holder* [1968] Ch. 353, an unusual case as to which see Goff and Jones, *Law of Restitution* (4th ed.), pp. 649–651. See Snell, *Equity* (29th ed.), pp. 249 *et seq.*; Goff and Jones, *op. cit.*, pp. 648–652; Finn, *Fiduciary Obligations* (1977), pp. 182–185, suggesting that there is little difference.

[5] *Allison v. Clayhills* (1907) 97 L.T. 709; *McMaster v. Byrne* [1952] 1 All E.R. 1362, Illustration 8; *Wintle v. Nye* [1959] 1 W.L.R. 284. See also *Cutts v. Salmon* (1852) 21 L.J.Ch. 750; *King v. Anderson* (1874) 8 I.R.Eq. 625; *Spector v. Ageda* [1973] Ch. 30, where Megarry J. said that a solicitor should in ordinary circumstances refuse to act for a client in relation to a transaction when he is himself a party with an adverse interest in that transaction.

[6] *Massey v. Davies* (1794) 2 Ves. 317; *Gibson v. Jeyes* (1801) 6 Ves. 266; *Rothschild v. Brookman* (1831) 2 Dow. & Cl. 188; *Bentley v. Craven* (1853) 18 Beav. 75; *Lucifero v. Castel* (1887) 3 T.L.R. 371; *Tetley v. Shand* (1871) 25 L.T. 658; *Skelton v. Wood* (1894) 71 L.T. 616; *Kuhlirz v. Lambert Brothers* (1913) 18 Com.Cas. 217; *Tito v. Waddell (No. 2)* [1977] Ch. 106, 240–244; Goff and Jones, *Law of Restitution* (4th ed.), pp. 653–654.

[7] *Aberdeen Ry. Co. v. Blaikie Bros.* (1854) 1 Macq. 461, Illustration 2 to Article 46; *Transvaal Lands Co. v. New Belgium (Transvaal) Land and Development Co.* [1914] 2 Ch. 488; *Gray v. New Augarita Porcupine Mines* [1952] 3 D.L.R. 1 (P.C.).

[8] *e.g. Charter v. Trevelyan* (1844) 11 C. & F. 714, 732. Distinguish the doctrine of undue influence, as to which see Snell, *Equity* (29th ed.), pp. 551 *et seq.* But see also *CIBC Mortgages Plc. v. Pitt* [1994] 1 A.C. 200, 209 *per* Lord Browne-Wilkinson; and n. 1 above.

advice or discretion is involved, there may be cases where he is free to sell his own property to the principal or buy the principal's property himself, there being no possibility of conflicting interest.[9]

6–067   **Person who has ceased to be agent.** Difficult questions arise if the agent deals with his principal after he has ceased to be an agent. It appears that the duty to disclose can continue, but whether it does so in any particular case in fact will depend on all the circumstances of the case. For example, if the confidence created by the agency relationship still exists at the time of the transaction,[10] or if the agent has a personal ascendancy over his principal, or if he has acquired special knowledge during his employment relating to the subject-matter of the transaction, a court will be inclined to hold that the duty of disclosure is still binding on the agent.[11] Thus a solicitor's duty to disclose may last longer that the duty of a less confidential agent, *e.g.* a stockbroker.[12] An agent cannot, of course, claim that his own breach of duty terminates his agency and that therefore he is no longer bound to make full disclosure in any transaction that afterwards takes place between himself and his principal.[13] Conversely, it appears that an agent is under no duty to disclose to his principal anything relating to a contract which is to come into effect only after the agency relationship is at an end. Thus an agent may negotiate the terms of a new employment before he has left his old one, provided that he does not let his interest conflict with his duty. If he is in breach of contract, the principal is adequately safeguarded by his right to damages.[14]

6–068   **Remedies of principal.** If the agent fails to make full disclosure, his principal may take one of the following courses appropriate to the particular circumstances of the case. He may rescind the contract, or

---

[9] See *Kelly v. Enderton* [1913] A.C. 191; *Dalgety & Co. v. Gray* (1919) 26 C.L.R. 249, 265 (P.C.) (loan to principal); *Jones v. Canavan* [1972] 2 N.S.W.L.R. 236 (stockbroker); *R.H. Deacon & Co. v. Varga* (1972) 30 D.L.R. (3d) 653; affd. (1973) 41 D.L.R. (3d) 767 (stockbroker); *cf. Thompson v. Meade* (1891) 7 T.L.R. 698 (stockbroker); *cf. Beer v. Lea* (1913) 29 O.L.R. 255; *Bentley v. Nasmith* (1912) 46 S.C.R. 477; *McMaster v. Byrne* [1952] 1 All E.R. 1362, Illustration 8. And see Finn, *Commercial Aspects of Fiduciary Obligations* (McKendrick ed., 1992), Chap. 1, pp. 37–39.

[10] *Carter v. Palmer* (1842) 8 C. & F. 657.

[11] *Allison v. Clayhills* (1907) 97 L.T. 709; *Demerara Bauxite Co. v. Hubbard* [1923] A.C. 673. See also *Edwards v. Meyrick* (1842) 2 Hare 60; *Montesquieu v. Sandys* (1811) 18 Ves. 302; *Learmonth v. Bailey* (1875) 1 V.L.R. 122.

[12] Compare Illustrations 8 and 9.

[13] *Regier v. Campbell-Stuart* [1939] Ch. 766, Illustration 16; *McLeod & More v. Sweezey* [1944] 2 D.L.R. 145. *Quaere* whether, if the principal is in breach of duty, the agent's obligation can continue. If the principal becomes an alien enemy, it may well be that the agent's duties of loyalty come to an end: *Nordisk Insulinlaboratorium v. Gorgate Products Ltd* [1953] Ch. 430, 442 (Illustration 11).

[14] *Julien Praet et Cie S.A. v. H.G. Poland Ltd* [1962] 1 Lloyd's Rep. 566, 578–581; *Sanders v. Parry* [1967] 1 W.L.R. 573.

affirm the contract and claim any profit which the agent has made.[15] If he chooses to rescind, it does not matter that the contract has been executed or that the property has meanwhile decreased in value,[16] but he must take proceedings within a reasonable time after discovering the truth about the transaction or he will be taken to have acquiesced.[17] The principal may choose, however, to affirm the contract and, if rescission is no longer possible,[18] he must affirm.[19] He will usually be able to claim the profit any agent has made, for it is deemed to have been made on his behalf. Alternatively, if the complaint is of loss he may claim damages for breach of contract, or conceivably under the principle of *Nocton v. Ashburton*.[20] Thus, where an agent has bought his principal's property, the principal can claim any profit on a resale[21] or the difference between the value of the property and the price the agent gave.[22]

However, where the agent sells his property to the principal, it seems that a distinction is to be drawn between the situation in which the agent is instructed to find a seller but secretly buys property which he then sells to the principal, making a profit for himself, and the situation in which the agent sells property which was his own before the agency was created. In the first situation the agent will be liable to account for any profit he has made from the transaction, since he will be presumed to have bought on his principal's behalf and to have been holding on trust for him.[23] But in the second situation he was not acting on the

---

[15] *Bentley v. Craven* (1853) 18 Beav. 75; *Rea v. Bell* (1852) 18 L.T.(o.s.) 312; *Gray v. New Augarita Porcupine Mines* [1952] 3 D.L.R. 1 (P.C.); *Hely-Hutchinson v. Brayhead Ltd.* [1968] 1 Q.B. 549; *Robinson v. Randfontein* [1921] App.D. 168, 178.

[16] *Armstrong v. Jackson* [1917] 2 K.B. 822.

[17] *De Montmorency v. Devereux* (1840) 7 C. & F. 188; *Champion v. Rigby* (1830) 1 Russ. & M. 539; affd. (1840) 9 L.J.(o.s.) Ch. 211; *Flint v. Woodin* (1852) 9 Hare 618; *Lyddon v. Moss* (1859) 4 De G. & J. 104; *Clanricarde v. Henning* (1861) 30 Beav. 175; *Wentworth v. Lloyd* (1863) 32 Beav. 467.

[18] *e.g.* because the property has already been conveyed to a sub-purchaser. For sub-purchases *pendente lite*, see *Trevelyan v. White* (1839) 1 Beav. 588.

[19] The onus is on the agent to show that the principal has affirmed: *Cavendish-Bentinck v. Fenn* (1887) 12 App.Cas. 652, 666 (Illustration 15). Before affirmation can take place, the principal must know the full facts, including the fact that he could rescind the transaction if he so wished: *Crowe v. Ballard* (1790) 2 Cox Eq.Cas. 253; *Osry v. Hirsch* [1922] Cape P.D. 531; *Holder v. Holder* [1968] Ch. 353; *Peyman v. Lanjani* [1985] Ch. 457.

[20] [1914] A.C. 932; above para. 6–045.

[21] *Barker v. Harrison* (1846) 2 Coll. 546; *De Bussche v. Alt* (1878) 8 Ch.D. 286; *Blackham v. Haythorpe* (1917) 23 C.L.R. 156; *Headway Construction Co. Ltd v. Downham* (1974) 233 E.G. 675, Illustration 17.

[22] *Hall v. Hallett* (1784) 1 Cox Eq.Cas. 134.

[23] *Massey v. Davies* (1794) 2 Ves. 317; *Benson v. Heathorn* (1842) 1 Y. & C.Ch.Cas. 326; *Tyrrell v. Bank of London* (1862) 10 H.L.Cas. 26; *Kimber v. Barber* (1872) L.R. 8 Ch.App. 56; *Regier v. Campbell-Stuart* [1939] Ch. 766, Illustration 16.

principal's behalf and will not be accountable for profits made: the usual remedy will be rescission, for no profit has been made within the scope of the agency.[24] However, this distinction may not survive the modern flexibility of remedies.[25] If this remedy is lost for any reason, *e.g.* because *resitutio in integrum* is impossible, it seems that the only right is to damages as above.[26] This right, too, will be lost if the contract is affirmed in such a manner as to show that the principal does not intend to pursue his rights against the agent.[27] In any case the agent's right to commission on the transaction is lost.[28]

6–069 **Gifts.** The nature of the relationship between principal and agent may lead to the application of a different, but related, rule, the presumption of undue influence, to a gift received by an agent from his principal,[29] and indeed to other transactions between them. On this basis the gift may be set aside unless it can be proved that undue influence was not exercised. The rule has often been applied between solicitor and client or counsel and lay client.[30] Any gift made by a client to his solicitor is presumed to have been made under undue influence and his presumption is not rebutted merely because the client has employed a completely separate and independent solicitor to advise about the gift.[31] This presumption will be applied although the solicitor-client relationship has come to an end, provided that there is still a relationship of confidence and trust between the parties. But a gift can be supported

---

[24] *Re Cape Breton Co.* (1885) 29 Ch.D. 795; affirmed *sub nom. Cavendish-Bentinck v. Fenn* (1887) 12 App.Cas. 652, Illustration 15; *Robinson v. Randfontein* [1921] App.D. 168, 179.

[25] See Goff and Jones, *Law of Restitution* (4th ed.), p. 655.

[26] *Jacobus Marler Estates Ltd. v. Marler* (1913) 85 L.J.P.C. 167n; *P. & O. S.N. Co. v. Johnson* (1938) 60 C.L.R. 189, 213. This topic is discussed in *Walden Properties Ltd v. Beaver Properties Pty. Ltd* [1973] 2 N.S.W.L.R. 815, 835–837.

[27] This would appear to be the effect of *Re Cape Breton Co.*, n. 24 above as approved by the P.C. in *Burland v. Earle* [1902] A.C. 83. See also *Cook v. Deeks* [1916] 1 A.C. 554; *Tracy v. Mandalay Pty Co.* (1953) 88 C.L.R. 215; Sealy [1963] C.L.J. 119, 132–135. But see Finn, *Fiduciary Obligations* (1977), p. 225.

[28] *Keppel v. Wheeler* [1927] 1 K.B. 577, 592; *Lunghi v. Sinclair* [1966] W.A.R. 172; Article 62.

[29] *Hunter v. Atkins* (1834) 3 Myl. & K. 113; *Union Fidelity Trustee Co. of Australia Ltd v. Gibson* [1971] V.R. 573. See in general *National Westminster Bank Plc v. Morgan* [1985] A.C. 686; Snell, *Equity* (29th ed.), pp. 551–558, Finn, *op. cit.* n. 27 above, Chap. 16.

[30] *Broun v. Kennedy* (1864) 4 De G.J. & S. 217.

[31] *Morgan v. Minnett* (1877) 6 Ch.D. 638; *Saunderson v. Glass* (1742) 2 Atk. 296; *Middleton v. Welles* (1785) 4 Bro.P.C. 245; *Wright v. Proud* (1806) 13 Ves. 136; *Tomson v. Judge* (1885) 3 Drew. 306; *O'Brien v. Lewis* (1863) 32 L.J.Ch. 569; *Liles v. Terry* [1895] 2 Q.B. 679; *Wright v. Carter* [1903] 1 Ch. 27. For a solicitor to accept a gift without ensuring that his client has received independent legal advice can amount to professional misconduct: *Re a Solicitor* [1975] Q.B. 475.

if the court is satisfied that it is perfectly fair and proper in all the circumstances.

"The court, in dealing with such a transaction, starts with the presumption that undue influence exists on the part of the donee, and throws upon him the burden of satisfying the court that the gift was uninfluenced by the position of the solicitor. Secondly, this presumption is not a presumption which is entirely irrebuttable, though it is one which is extremely difficult to be rebutted."[32]

The rule will apply to gifts to near relatives of the solicitor,[33] but it does not apply to trifling gifts.[34] The rule may be applied somewhat less strictly to gifts by will but the solicitor must ensure that the client receives independent legal advice and is fully capable of understanding what he is doing.[35] The desirability of independent advice applies to other relationships also.[36]

The illustrations which follow represent a large spread of mainly nineteenth-century case law on this topic. It seems appropriate to retain these at present rather than seek to concentrate on the most recent cases. For the direction which the law is taking is not yet clear, and furthermore varies from jurisdiction to jurisdiction.   **6–070**

Illustrations

Purchase from principal

(1) A solicitor purchases property from his client's trustee in bankruptcy. He must make a full disclosure of all the knowledge acquired by him respecting such property during the time when he was acting as solicitor for the bankrupt.[37]   **6–071**

(2) A solicitor purchased property from a former client, and concealed a material fact. Another solicitor acted for the client in this transaction, but he did not possess all the necessary information and somewhat neglected his duty. The transaction was set aside.[38]

---

[32] *Wright v. Carter* [1903] 1 Ch. 27, 57, *per* Stirling L.J.
[33] See, *e.g. Willis v. Barron* [1902] A.C. 271.
[34] *Rhodes v. Bate* (1866) L.R. 1 Ch.App. 252; *Wright v. Carter*, n. 32 above.
[35] See for a discussion of this topic Cordery, *Solicitors* (8th ed.), pp. 17–18; *cf. Re Tyler* [1967] 1 W.L.R. 1269, 1276, where it is said that the court will require evidence which will satisfy it beyond doubt. Because the burden of proof in a civil case is never more than the balance of probabilities, this must mean that the presumption to be displaced is a heavy one.
[36] *e.g. O'Sullivan v. Management Agency and Music Ltd* [1985] Q.B. 428 (musician and manager).
[37] *Luddy's Trustees v. Peard* (1886) 33 Ch.D. 500. See also *Boswell v. Coaks* (1884) 27 Ch.D. 424 (revsd. on the evidence, *sub nom. Coaks v. Boswell* (1886) 11 App.Cas. 232).
[38] *Gibbs v. Daniel* (1862) 4 Giff. 1 *cf. Guest v. Smythe* (1870) L.R. 5 Ch.App. 551 (solicitor's name appeared on particulars of sale only).

(3)　A Scottish attorney purchased four houses from his clients, doing so in the name of his brother. He did not disclose that he was the real purchaser of two of the houses. The House of Lords refused to order specific performance of the contract. [39]

(4)　Two persons become partners to sell a mine. One represents to the other that he has found a purchaser. Actually he has arranged to share with the purchaser in the profits made by floating a company to buy and work the mine. He must share the profit he makes with the other. [40]

(5)　An auctioneer, who was employed to sell an estate, purchased it himself. The transaction was set aside, after an interval of thirteen years. [41] So, an agent of a trustee for sale or of a mortgagee selling under his power of sale, who is employed as agent in the matter of the sale, [42] cannot purchase the property sold [43]; and a solicitor who conducts a sale of property must not purchase it without a full explanation to the vendor. [44]

(6)　A broker is employed to sell goods. He sells them ostensibly to A, really to A and himself jointly. While the goods are still in possession of the broker, he becomes bankrupt, A also being insolvent. The principal may repudiate the contract and recover the goods specifically from the trustee in bankruptcy of the broker. [45]

(7)　An agent for the management of trust property purchased part of such property from the *cestui que trust*. Held, that the circumstances being highly disadvantageous to the seller, the burden lay on the agent to prove that the transaction was right and honest, and that in the circumstances the lack of disinterested advice was fatal. [46]

(8)　M owned shares in a Canadian company. He granted X an option to purchase them for $30,000. X assigned the option to B, who was the solicitor to the company and had until recently been solicitor to M. B exercised the option. At that time active negotiations for the take-over of the company were taking place and that fact was known to B

---

[39] *McPherson v. Watt* (1877) 3 App.Cas. 254. See also *Lewis v. Hillman* (1852) 3 H.L.Cas. 607; *Cane v. Allen* (1814) 2 Dow. 289; *Uppington v. Bullen* (1842) 2 Dr. & War. 184; *Murphy v. O'Shea* (1845) 8 I.Eq.R. 329; *Crowe v. Ballard* (1790) 2 Cox.Eq.Cas. 253.
[40] *Dunne v. English* (1874) L.R. 18 Eq. 524.
[41] *Oliver v. Court* (1820) 8 Price 127. See also *Haywood v. Roadknight* [1927] V.L.R. 512. But laches may afford a defence: see *Wentworth v. Lloyd* (1863) 32 Beav. 467.
[42] See *Nutt v. Easton* [1899] 1 Ch. 873; affd. on other grounds [1900] 1 Ch. 29.
[43] *Whitcomb v. Minchin* (1820) 5 Madd. 91; *Martinson v. Clowes* (1882) 21 Ch.D. 857; *Lawrance v. Galsworthy* (1857) 3 Jur.(N.S.) 1049. *Cf. Bath v. Standard Land Co.* [1911] 1 Ch. 618 and *Orme v. Wright* (1839) 3 Jur. 19; *ibid.*, 972.
[44] *Re Bloye's Trust* (1849) 1 Mac. & G. 488; *Ex p. James* (1803) 8 Ves. 337.
[45] *Ex p. Huth, re Pemberton* (1840) Mont. & C. 667.
[46] *King v. Anderson* (1874) 8 I.R.Eq. 625. See also *Dally v. Wonham* (1863) 33 Beav. 154.

when he exercised the option. As a result of the take-over B later sold the shares for $127,000. Held, although B was no longer M's solicitor, the confidential relationship between them still subsisted and B was under a duty to make full disclosure to M before he purchased the shares from him.[47]

(9)   A stockbroker is commissioned to buy for a client. The client is unable to meet the amount due on settlement. In accordance with normal procedures the broker sells the shares. This is a valid closing of the account and he is entitled to indemnity.[48] He also repurchases them himself. This is legitimate[49] unless the repurchase is sufficiently a part of the same transaction that he secures a preferential price because the market-maker does not have to carry the shares. In the latter case the broker may be liable for a secret profit.[50]

(10)   Dealers employ agents to grant future options in cocoa. The agents do so and then take the options themselves. They fail to notify the dealers that the options have been declared. This is not merely a breach of their duties as agents, but rather, since their own taking of the options was valid, the options in respect of which no declarations were made by them lapse.[51]

(11)   A Danish corporation deposited insulin in an English bank shortly before the outbreak of war. When the Germans invaded Denmark the corporation became an alien enemy and the property vested in the Custodian of Enemy Property, who sold it to the defendants. The defendants had been the English selling agents of the corporation before the war; they now resold the insulin at a profit. Held, as the defendants had not acquired any special or secret knowledge about the insulin while they were the corporation's agents, they were under no fiduciary duty regarding it and were not accountable for the profit they made on resale.[52]

Sale to principal

(12)   A firm of brokers were authorised to purchase goods. They delivered bought notes to the principal which purported to be notes of a contract of which the brokers guaranteed performance, but which did   6–072

---

[47] *McMaster v. Byrne* [1952] 1 All E.R. 1362.

[48] *Macoun v. Erskine, Oxenford & Co.* [1901] 2 K.B. 493; *Walter and Gould v. King* (1897) 13 T.L.R. 270; *Christoforides v. Terry* [1924] A.C. 566. But a direct purchase by the broker himself would be voidable: *Re Finlay* [1913] 1 Ch. 565. See also *Jones v. Canavan* [1972] 2 N.S.W.L.R. 236 (custom of "marrying" buying and selling transactions held reasonable).

[49] See cases cited above.

[50] *Erskine, Oxenford & Co. v. Sachs* [1901] 2 K.B. 504.

[51] *Limako B.V. v. Hentz & Co. Inc.* [1979] 2 Lloyd's Rep. 23.

[52] *Nordisk Insulinlaboratorium v. Gorgate Products Ltd* [1953] Ch. 430.

not disclose the sellers. The principal paid the brokers their commission and a deposit, and subsequently discovered that one of the brokers intended to perform the contract himself. The principal was held to be entitled to repudiate the contract, and the brokers were ordered to repay the deposit and commission, with interest, since no agent can become a principal and deal on that footing without full and fair disclosure. [53]

(13) A stockbroker was employed to purchase certain shares. He purchased the shares from his own trustee without informing the principal of the fact. The transaction was set aside, after an interval of many years, without inquiry whether a fair price was charged or not. [54]

(14) A director proposes to contract with his company, it being provided by the articles of association that directors may contract with the company on disclosing their interest. It is his duty to declare the full extent and exact nature of his interest. [55]

(15) A company was formed to purchase certain coal areas in Newfoundland. It purchased these areas from A, who was a trustee for B and had been so for some time before the formation of the company. B was one of the directors of the company but did not disclose that he was beneficially interested in the coal areas. When the company was wound up, the shareholders, with full knowledge of the circumstances, decided to sell the coal areas. They realised a smaller sum than expected, but rescission of the original contract of purchase was now impossible. Held, any claim to damages had been forfeited by the affirmation of the contract, and any claim to B's profit was unsustainable as B had not acquired the property with a view to selling it to the company but owned it already. [56]

(16) A, an estate agent, agreed with B that A would furnish B with particulars of houses which A might think suitable for purchase by B. A, having found a suitable house, procured C to purchase it for £2,000, the purchase-money being provided by A; and thereupon purported to

---

[53] *Wilson v. Short* (1848) 6 Hare 366. See also *Robinson v. Mollett* (1874) L.R. 7 H.L. 802, Illustration 8 to Article 31; *Skelton v. Wood* (1894) 71 L.T. 616; *Stange & Co. v. Lowitz* (1898) 14 T.L.R. 468; *Nicholson v. J. Mansfield & Co.* (1901) 17 T.L.R. 259. *Cf. Ellis & Co.'s Trustee v. Watsham* (1923) 155 L.T.Jo. 363 ("bought of ourselves as principals"—held sufficient disclosure).
[54] *Gillett v. Peppercorne* (1840) 3 Beav. 78. See also *Rothschild v. Brookman* (1831) 2 Dow. & Cl. 188; *King, Viall & Benson v. Howell* (1910) 27 T.L.R. 114; *Oelkers v. Ellis* [1914] 2 K.B. 139; *Armstrong v. Jackson* [1917] 2 K.B. 822.
[55] *Imperial Mercantile Credit Co. v. Coleman* (1873) L.R. 6 H.L. 189; *Gluckstein v. Barnes* [1900] A.C. 240. *cf. Chesterfield & Boythorpe Colliery Co. v. Black* (1877) 37 L.T. 740.
[56] *Re Cape Breton Co.* (1885) 29 Ch.D. 795; affd. *sub nom. Cavendish-Bentinck v. Fenn* (1887) 12 App.Cas. 652. See also *Jacobus Marler Estates Ltd v. Marler* (1913) 85 L.J.P.C. 167n.; *Walden Properties Ltd v. Beaver Properties Pty Ltd* [1973] 2 N.S.W.L.R. 815, 836.

buy it from C for £4,500. A then informed B that he had purchased the house for £4,500, and offered it to B for £5,000, representing that this price would allow a profit to A of £500. B purchased the house from A for £5,000. Held, that A was the agent of B for the purpose of furnishing particulars of suitable houses; that though an agent might terminate the relationship of principal and agent by selling to his principal property which belonged to himself, it was his duty to act honestly and faithfully, and, if he concealed material facts, the relationship was not terminated by such a transaction; and that A, having concealed the true nature of the transaction, was liable to account to B for all profits obtained by A without B's knowledge and consent.[57]

(17) P engaged A to ascertain the owners of properties adjacent to a site he was developing. A did so but dishonestly told P that he had failed. A then made an agreement with P whereby he agreed for a commission to acquire the properties for P. He then formed a company and acquired the properties for £42,000. This company then sold the properties to P for £57,000. Held, A was liable to P for the profit of £15,000 and damages of £3,000 for loss of the chance to acquire the properties for less than £42,000. P was entitled to avoid the contract with A and was not liable to A for commission in respect of other transactions.[58]

Other dealings by agent with principal

(18) If a solicitor takes a mortgage from his client, the court will not   6–073
enforce any unusual stipulations in the mortgage disadvantageous to the client,[59] and will restrain the solicitor from exercising his rights as mortgagee in an unfair or inequitable manner.[60] Where a power of sale exercisable at any time was inserted in such a mortgage without the usual proviso requiring interest to be in arrear or notice to be given, and the solicitor sold the property under the power, he was held liable to the client in damages as for an improper sale, it not being shown that he had explained to the client the unusual nature of the power.[61]

(19) A steward contracts with his employer for a lease. He must show that he is giving as high a rent as it would have been his duty to

---

[57] *Regier v. Campbell-Stuart* [1939] Ch. 766. See Murdoch, *Law of Estate Agency and Auctions* (3rd ed.), pp. 110–116.
[58] *Headway Construction Co. Ltd v. Downham* (1974) 233 E.G. 675.
[59] *Cowdry v. Day* (1859) 1 Giff. 316; *Eyre v. Hughes* (1876) 2 Ch.D. 148. See also *Gray v. Dalgety & Co. Ltd* (1916) 21 C.L.R. 509.
[60] *Macleod v. Jones* (1883) 24 Ch.D. 289; *Pearson v. Benson* (1860) 28 Beav. 598.
[61] *Readdy v. Pendergast* (1887) 56 L.T. 790; *Cockburn v. Edwards* (1881) 18 Ch.D. 449; *Craddock v. Rogers* (1884) 53 L.J.Ch. 968. *cf. Pooley's Trustee v. Whetham* (1886) 2 T.L.R., 808. See in general Cordery *Solicitors* (8th ed.), pp. 13 *et seq.*

obtain from a third party and that his employer was fully informed of every circumstance affecting the value of the property which was, or ought to have been, within the steward's knowledge.[62]

(20) A woman lends money on mortgage to persons who have for many years acted as her property and mortgage security advisers. Later she discharges the mortgage, no payment having been made under it. The presumption of undue influence not being rebutted, the discharge is set aside.[63]

Article 48

AGENT USING PRINCIPAL'S PROPERTY TO ACQUIRE BENEFIT FOR HIMSELF

6–074 An agent may not, without the informed consent of his principal, use his principal's property, or confidential information acquired during the course of the agency, to acquire a benefit (*i.e.* a secret profit) for himself.[64]

Comment

6–075 **Property.** It has long been established that if the agent makes any secret profit from the use of his principal's property, he is accountable to his principal for that profit, unless the principal with full knowledge of the circumstances consents to the retention of it by the agent.

> "It is quite clear that if an agent uses property, with which he has been entrusted by his principal, so as to make a profit for himself out of it, without his principal's consent, then he is accountable for it to his principal ... Likewise with information or knowledge which he has been employed by his principal to collect or discover, or which he has otherwise acquired, for use of his principal, then again if he turns it to his own use, so as to make a profit by means of it for himself, he is accountable ... "[65]

The fact that the agent's liability can be based on his holding identifiable property of the principal makes this an obvious example where the duties of a trustee can be said to be extended to the agent. But it can also be regarded as a simple example of the general principle stated in Article 47, that the agent must not without disclosure enter into a transaction in which his interest and his duty may conflict. It is

---

[62] *Selsey v. Rhoades* (1824) 2 S. & St. 41; affd. (1827) 1 Bli.(N.S.) 1. See also *Watt v. Grove* (1805) 2 Sch. & Lef. 492; *Waters v. Shaftesbury* (1866) 14 L.T. 184; *Molony v. Kernan* (1842) 2 Dr. & War. 31; *Ker v. Lord Dungannon* (1841) 1 Dr. & War. (Ir.) 509.
[63] *Union Fidelity Trustee Co. of Australia Ltd v. Gibson* [1971] V.R. 573.
[64] See Comment; Stoljar pp. 293–299; Fridman (1968) 3 Manitoba L.J. 17.
[65] *Phipps v. Boardman* [1965] Ch. 992, 1030, *per* Pearson L.J.

not, of course, *any* use by the agent of his principal's property which attracts this liability: in many circumstances some form of use is contemplated. It is use leading to an undisclosed profit to which the rule applies.

Under this principle can also be brought the case where an agent is treated as holding in trust money he has received from his principal, with the result that he is liable for interest on it or may be required to account for profits.[66] Such profits would not of course be secret. All these liabilities appear to attract a proprietary remedy; but the remedy can also be expressed as involving an account of profits, which has been said to be personal.[66a]

Confidential information.[67] There is also no doubt that if an agent   **6–076**
uses confidential information acquired as a result of his agency he may be liable to his principal in respect of it.[68] On one view, this is explicable on the basis that such information is property.[69] But "perhaps the most sterile of the debates which have arisen around the subject of information received in confidence is whether or not such information should be classified as property."[70] For it is only in certain circumstances, difficult of definition, that information is protected, and the criteria for ascertaining this are not the same as those used to

---

[66] Above, para. 6–043.

[66a] See *Warman International Ltd v. Dwyer* (1995) 69 A.L.J.R. 362, 367 *et seq.*; above, para. 6–044; below, paras. 6–079, 6–094.

[67] See Goff and Jones, *Law of Restitution* (4th ed.), pp. 661–665; Chap. 35; Finn, *Fiduciary Obligations* (1977), Chap. 19; Curry, *Breach of Confidence* (1984); Jones (1970) 86 L.Q.R. 463; *Att.-Gen. v. Jonathan Cape Ltd* [1976] Q.B. 752. The Law Commission (No. 110, Cmnd. 8388 (1981)) recommended the creation of statutory tort liability. This would have left much of the liability arising from fiduciary relationships as a separate area of law. See for a general summary of the report, Jones [1982] C.L.J. 40.

[68] *Phipps v. Boardman* [1967] 2 A.C. 46, Illustration 4 to Article 49; *Peter Pan Manufacturing Corporation v. Corsets Silhouette Ltd* [1964] 1 W.L.R. 96, Illustration 6; *Att.-Gen. v. Guardian Newspapers Ltd (No. 2)* [1990] 1 A.C. 109, 288; Jones, [1989] C.L.P. 49.

[69] See *Phipps v. Boardman,* n. 68 above. Lord Hodson (at p. 107) and Lord Guest (at p. 115) were clearly of the opinion that information and knowledge can be property; Lord Cohen said (at p. 102) that information was not "property in the strict sense of that word" and Lord Upjohn, in his dissenting speech (at pp. 127–128), was clear that information as such is not property at all but that where it is confidential, equity will intervene to prevent its transmission. Viscount Dilhorne, in his dissenting speech, said (at pp. 89–90) that information and knowledge can be treated as property. The Court of Appeal ([1965] Ch. 992) had no doubt that information was property and that an agent is thus accountable for any profit derived from it. The House of Lords seems to have based its decision that the appellants should account on their position as fiduciaries rather than on the information which they used.

[70] Finn, *op. cit.* n. 67 above, p. 131. See also Millett, [1993] Restitution L.Rev. 7, 11: "owes more to metaphor than to legal reality."

determine whether property reasoning is inherently appropriate. "If only some information is described as property, *i.e.* information protected by the courts, to call that information property is merely to add yet another consequence to a decision taken for reasons quite unrelated to property considerations."[71]

The principle is not, however, peculiar to the law of agency; if any fiduciary exploits confidential information which he acquires in the course of his relationship with his beneficiary, he is in breach of his fiduciary duty and if, as is usually the case with an agent, he has a contract with his principal, he will probably be in breach of contract also.[72] But the duty may be independent of contract or even of a standing relationship. It seems that if any person receives information which he knows or ought to know[73] is confidential and uses that information for his own profit, he is so liable whether there is any previous relationship between him and the plaintiff or not.[74] "The law on this subject does not depend on any implied contract. It depends on the broad principle of equity that he who has received information in confidence shall not take unfair advantage of it. He must not make use of it to the prejudice of him who gave it without obtaining his consent."[75] It may therefore be said that the rule is not a special one applicable to fiduciaries, but rather that the receipt of confidential information may impose an obligation not to misuse it.[76]

---

[71] *ibid.* p. 132.
[72] *Lamb v. Evans* [1893] 1 Ch. 218, Illustration 5; *Robb v. Green* [1895] 2 Q.B. 315; *Duchess of Argyll v. Duke of Argyll* [1967] Ch. 302; *Westminster Chemical N.Z. Ltd v. McKinley* [1973] 1 N.Z.L.R. 659; *New Zealand Needle Manufacturers Ltd v. Taylor* [1975] 2 N.Z.L.R. 33; *Investors Syndicate Ltd v. Versatile Investments Ltd* (1983) 149 D.L.R. (3d) 46.
[73] *Coco v. A.N. Clark (Engineers) Ltd* [1969] R.P.C. 41, 48; and see *Printers and Finishers Ltd v. Holloway* [1965] R.P.C. 239, 252; *Att.-Gen. v. Jonathan Cape Ltd* [1976] Q.B. 752. *cf. United Sterling Corp. Ltd v. Felton* [1974] R.P.C. 162. See also *Union Carbide Corp. v. Naturin Ltd* [1987] F.S.R. 538; *Att.-Gen. v. Guardian Newspapers Ltd (No. 2)* [1990] 1 A.C. 109, 281.
[74] *Saltman Engineering Co. Ltd v. Campbell Engineering Co.* (1948) [1963] 3 All E.R. 413n.; *Talbot v. General Television Corp. Pty. Ltd* [1981] R.P.C. 1; *Fraser v. Thames Television Ltd* [1984] Q.B. 44.
[75] *Seager v. Copydex Ltd* [1967] 1 W.L.R. 923, 931, *per* Lord Denning M.R. The liability extends to persons to whom information is further transmitted. See Finn, *Fiduciary Obligations* (1977), pp. 152–156; *Schering Chemicals Ltd v. Falkman Ltd* [1982] Q.B. 1, Illustration 7; *Wheatley v. Bell* [1982] 2 N.S.W.L.R. 544. But different considerations may arise where information is received in confidence which ought in the public interest to be disclosed to one who has a proper interest to receive it: *Initial Services Ltd v. Putterill* [1968] 1 Q.B. 396; *Fraser v. Evans* [1969] 1 Q.B. 349; *Hubbard v. Vosper* [1972] 2 Q.B. 84; *Church of Scientology v. Kaufman* [1973] R.P.C. 635. *cf. Schering Chemicals Ltd v. Falkman Ltd*, above; *Lion Laboratories Ltd v. Evans* [1985] Q.B. 526.
[76] *cf.* above, para. 6–037.

Once the information is readily available to the public it has ceased to be confidential. It will then no longer be a breach of confidence for the agent to make use of it.[77]

A principal whose confidential information has been used by his agent has various remedies open to him.[78] He may seek an injunction to restrain the agent from making any further use of the information[79]; he may sue for damages for breach of contract in an appropriate case. Where a contractual action is not available, there is authority that damages may be awarded in equity to cover the price which the owner would have charged for the information,[80] and it seems that this award may be independent of damages in lieu of injunction under Lord Cairns' Act.[81] The principal may also sue for an account of the profits made by the agent from his use of the confidential information.[82] It seems however that the court will in such situations determine the appropriate remedy rather than permit the plaintiff to elect.[83] Finally, whether or not the information can properly be described as the property of the

---

[77] *O'Mustad & Son v. Dosen* (1928) [1964] 1 W.L.R. 109n.; *Cranleigh Precision Engineering Ltd v. Bryant* [1965] 1 W.L.R. 1293, 1314–1319; *Speed Seal Products Ltd v. Paddington* [1985] 1 W.L.R. 1327; *Att.-Gen. v. Guardian Newspapers (No. 2)* [1990] 1 A.C. 109, esp. at p. 285.

[78] For a detailed consideration of remedies see Goff and Jones, *Law of Restitution* (4th ed.) pp. 661–665; Finn, *Fiduciary Obligations* (1977), pp. 163 *et seq*; Gurry, *Breach of Confidence* (1984).

[79] *Merryweather v. Moore* [1892] 2 Ch. 518; *Lamb v. Evans* [1893] 1 Ch. 218, Illustration 5; *Robb v. Green* [1895] 2 Q.B. 315; *Peter Pan Manufacturing Co. Ltd v. Corsets Silhouette Ltd* [1964] 1 W.L.R. 96, Illustration 6; *Coco v. A.N. Clark (Engineers) Ltd* [1969] R.P.C. 41;*Dunford & Elliott Ltd v. Johnson & Firth Brown Ltd* [1977] 1 Lloyd's Rep. 505. cf. *Amber Size and Chemical Co. Ltd v. Menzel* [1913] 2 Ch. 239; *Baker v. Gibbons* [1972] 1 W.L.R. 693. The grant of an injunction is of course discretionary: see *Att.-Gen. v. Guardian Newspapers Ltd (No. 2)* [1990] 1 A.C. 109.

[80] *Saltman Engineering Co. Ltd v. Campbell Engineering Co.* (1948) [1963] 3 All E.R. 413n. *Seager v. Copydex Ltd* [1967] 1 W.L.R. 923, where Lord Denning M.R. says at p. 932 that there is to be an inquiry as to damages as "it may not be a case for an injunction"; for the principle upon which the damages were to be assessed see *Seager v. Copydex Ltd (No. 2)* [1969] 1 W.L.R. 809; *Interfirm Comparison (Australia) Pty. Ltd v. Law Society of N.S.W.* [1975] 2 N.S.W.L.R. 104; *Dowson & Mason Ltd v. Potter* [1986] 1 W.L.R. 1419. And see Illustration 4.

[81] See *Nicro-Therm Electrical Co. Ltd v. Percy* [1956] R.P.C. 272; [1957] R.P.C. 207; *Seager v. Copydex Ltd*, n. 80 above. But see *English v. Dedham Vale Properties Ltd* [1978] 1 W.L.R. 93 111–112.

[82] *Peter Pan Manufacturing Corp. Ltd v. Corsets Silhouette Ltd* [1964] 1 W.L.R. 96, Illustration 6; cf. *Lever v. Goodwin* (1887) 36 Ch.D. 1; *Att.-Gen. v. Guardian Newspapers Ltd (No. 2)* [1990] 1 A.C. 109, 288; *Dart Industries Inc. v. Decor Corp. Pty. Ltd* (1993) 179 C.L.R. 101.

[83] *English v. Dedham Vale Properties Ltd.*, n. 81 above. For more advanced reasoning in the context of remedies see *Aquaculture Corp. v. New Zealand Green Mussel Co. Ltd* [1990] 3 N.Z.L.R. 289 (exemplary damages); *Watson v. Dolmark Industries Ltd* [1992] 3 N.Z.L.R. 311; *Lac Minerals Ltd v. International Corona Resources Ltd* [1989] 2 S.C.R. 574; (1989) 61 D.L.R. (4th) 14 (constructive trust).

principal, it seems that an agent who has made profits for himself by making use of it is a trustee of those profits for the principal; though where no fiduciary is involved and the recourse is simply to general principle the matter is more arguable, for the action for an account of profits can be said to be personal. [84]

Illustrations

6–077   (1)   The master of a ship was authorised to employ the vessel to the best advantage; he could not procure remunerative freight and so loaded her with cargo of his own. Held, he must account to the owners for the profit to be made on the sale of the cargo and not merely for a reasonable freight. [85]

(2)   A telegraph company erected and maintained a "special wire" alongside a railway line in Newfoundland. The railway company were by contract entitled to use the wire in and about their railway business but were not entitled to transmit any commercial messages except for the account of the telegraph company. In fact they used it in part for their shipping business and other commercial undertakings. Held, they were accountable to the telegraph company for all the profits made and that they held these profits in trust for the company. [86]

(3)   A client instructs a stockbroker to buy a certain quantity of stock in a company and "carry at 8%". The stockbroker deals with the shares so bought on his own account. He must account for his profits. [87]

(4)   B is managing director of a company publishing a trade journal for the timber industry. With the company's consent, he is also manager and principal shareholder of another company which publishes a "Lumberman's Atlas". He inserts in the journal free advertisements for the Atlas. He must refund to his employer company a reasonable charge for doing so. [88]

(5)   The proprietor of a trade directory employed canvassers to obtain advertisements from traders for insertion in the directory. He discovered that the canvassers were proposing to assist a rival

---

[84] See *Lees v. Nuttall* (1829) 1 Russ. & M. 53; affd. (1834) 2 My. & K. 819; *Triplex Safety Glass Co. Ltd v. Scorah* [1938] Ch. 211; *Boardman v. Phipps* [1965] Ch. 992; [1967] 2 A.C. 46; the *Lac Minerals* case, above; *Warman International Ltd v. Dwyer* (1995) 69 A.L.J.R. 362, 367; above, para. 6–044; below, para. 6–094.

[85] *Shallcross v. Oldham* (1862) 2 Johns. & H. 609. See also *Gardner v. M'Cutcheon* (1842) 4 Beav. 534; *Diplock v. Blackburn* (1811) 3 Camp. 43.

[86] *Reid-Newfoundland Co. v. Anglo-American Telegraph Co. Ltd* [1912] A.C. 555. See as to this unusual case Finn, *Fiduciary Obligations* (1977), p. 99. The wire remained the property of the company.

[87] *Thornley v. Tilley* (1925) 36 C.L.R. 1; see also *Langton v. Waite* (1868) L.R. 6 Eq. 165 (revsd. on other grounds (1869) L.R. 4 Ch.App. 402); *McLaughlin v. Solloway* [1936] S.C.R. 127; [1938] A.C. 247; *cf. King v. Hutton* [1900] 2 Q.B. 504.

[88] *B.C. Timber Industries Journal v. Black* [1934] 3 D.L.R. 31.

publication with similar advertisements after their agreement with his had come to an end. Held, the canvassers were not entitled to use material or information obtained while in the plaintiff's employment for the purpose of this publication.[89]

(6) English licensees of the patents for brassières were shown in confidence new designs not yet on the market. They made use of this information to design their own brassières and then terminated their licence from the plaintiffs. Held, the plaintiffs were entitled (a) to an injunction restraining the defendants from making and selling brassières made from the new designs; (b) to an account of the profits from the brassières already sold; and (c) to an order for delivery up or destruction of the offending goods.[90]

(7) A drug company, to combat unfavourable publicity as to the side-effects of one of its drugs, engages a specialist in television training to train its executives to put the company's point of view effectively when interviewed on television. The person engaged himself engages an experienced broadcaster to assist. During the courses the latter acquires information which he subsequently uses in making a documentary film in conjunction with a television company. The showing of the film is a breach of confidence and may be restrained by injunction.[91]

Article 49

AGENT USING POSITION TO ACQUIRE BENEFITS FOR HIMSELF

An agent may not use his position to acquire for himself a benefit (*i.e.* a secret profit) from a third party. He must account to his principal for any benefit so obtained.[92]   **6–078**

Comment

Secret profit. On the account here given of the fiduciary duties of an agent, this is a residual principle, insofar as it does not rely on the notion of using the principal's property, though it does seek to suggest that acquisitions *become* the principal's property. As such it is difficult to formulate, for the various aspects of the fiduciary's duties overlap to   **6–079**

---

[89] *Lamb v. Evans* [1893] 1 Ch. 218. For the extent to which names and addresses not in a written list may be confidential information which a defendant may be restrained from using, see *Baker v. Gibbons* [1972] 1 W.L.R. 693; *Investors Syndicate Ltd v. Versatile Investments Inc.* (1983) 149 D.L.R. (3d) 46. See also *Faccenda Chicken Ltd v. Fowler* [1987] Ch. 117.

[90] *Peter Pan Manufacturing Corp. Ltd v. Corsets Shilhouette Ltd* [1964] 1 W.L.R. 96.

[91] *Schering Chemicals Ltd v. Falkman Ltd* [1982] Q.B. 1.

[92] See Comment and Illustrations; *Meinhard v. Salmon* 164 N.E. 545 (1928), *per* Cardozo C.J.

a very considerable extent. It is often traced back to the law of express trusts. In *Keech v. Sandford*[93] property was leased to a trust, and when the lease determined the trustee renewed it for his own personal benefit. It was held that the trustee held the benefit of the lease on trust for his beneficiaries. The rule undoubtedly to some extent performs a cautionary role. "I very well see" said Lord King L.C. "if a trustee on refusal to renew might have a lease to himself, few trust estates would be renewed to *cestui que use*."[94]

The application of the principle to fiduciaries is of course limited in the sense that, as elsewhere, full disclosure of all the material facts will displace it.[95]

It seems that the rule as to renewals is absolute; and it has been held that it extends also to purchases of the reversion.[96] Beyond this, however, clearly not everything acquired in the course of the agency relationship can be made the subject of account to the principal. The question where the line should be drawn is a difficult one. Attempts have been made to link the liability to notions such as use or misuse of position or of opportunities acquired in that position, and in the case of companies, of "corporate opportunity"; but these are probably unduly restrictive.[97] It can be said that the test is to ask whether acquisitions on the agent's own account would be inconsistent with his undertaking to act for his principal. It will be inconsistent where the benefit is acquired within the scope of the activities which the agent has undertaken to pursue on his principal's behalf; or where the agent uses his position or connection with the principal to obtain a benefit[98]; or obtains one while holding himself out to another party as representing the principal.[99] The mere possibility that he might at some time in the future be called on to act for the principal in the relevant matter is, on some authority, sufficient to impose liability on him even though when he makes the

---

[93] (1726) Sel.Cas.t. King 61.

[94] See also *Bray v. Ford* [1896] A.C. 44, 51–52; *Chan v. Zacharia* (1984) 154 C.L.R. 178.

[95] *New Zealands Netherlands Society "Oranje" Inc. v. Kuys* [1973] 1 W.L.R. 1126.

[96] *Protheroe v. Protheroe* [1968] 1 W.L.R. 519; see also *Re Biss* [1903] 2 Ch. 40; Snell, *Equity* (29th ed.), pp. 245 *et seq.*; Finn, *Fiduciary Obligations* (1977), Chap. 23; Meagher, Gummow and Lehanes, *Equity Doctrines and Remedies* (3rd ed.), pp. 134–136.

[97] See the significant judgment of Laskin J. in *Canadian Aero Service Ltd v. O'Malley* [1974] S.C.R. 592; (1973) 40 D.L.R. (3d) 371, Illustration 8.

[98] See Illustrations 2, 3, 5, 8. See also *Keogh v. Dalgety & Co. Ltd* (1916) 22 C.L.R. 402. The reasoning is also applied somewhat inappropriately in public law: see Illustration 11.

[99] As was perhaps the case in *Phipps v. Boardman*, Illustration 4, where it was arguably by purporting to act as agents for the trust that the defendants acquired the necessary information to enable them to obtain control of the company. But see the dissenting judgment of Lord Upjohn. See also *Fine Industrial Commodities v. Pauling* (1954) 71 R.P.C. 253.

profit he has not so been called on.[1] This however is open to doubt, unless he is under a pre-existing duty to act in that way.[2] The agent may be liable even though at the time he makes the profit he has ceased to act as agent for the principal: indeed, the person concerned may often have resigned as agent precisely in order to pursue the profit.[3] A person who acts as agent without authority may also be liable under this principle.[4] If, however, the profit is made on a transaction which can be regarded as completely outside any agency relationship, then the agent will not be accountable for it.[5]

The rule when applicable is a strict one, and all profits must be accounted for even if, in acquiring them, the agent has incurred a risk of loss,[6] and the principal could not himself have made the profit, has suffered no injury or even has made a profit himself.[7] However, the court may make an allowance to the fiduciary for his skill and expenditure in making the profit;[8] and sometimes this appears to approach a share in the profit.[9]

A claim made under the principle set out in this Article is often, of course, advanced in conjunction with a claim that the agent has used property or information belonging to his principal to acquire a benefit

---

[1] See *Phipps v. Boardman*, n. 99 above, where it was said that the solicitor might at some time be called on to advise whether to apply to the court for permission for the trust to increase its holding in the company.

[2] See *Re Thomson* [1930] 1 Ch. 203; *British Syphon Co. v. Homewood* [1956] 1 W.L.R. 1190; Finn, *Fiduciary Obligations* (1977), pp. 244–246.

[3] See Illustrations 7, 8.

[4] See Illustration 10.

[5] See Illustrations 1, 6, 9 and *Aas v. Benham* [1891] 2 Ch. 244, esp. at p. 256. This case was distinguished in *Phipps v. Boardman*, n. 99 above, on the ground that it was a partnership case, and that in such cases a partner works in a defined area of business so that it is possible to determine whether a transaction is within the scope of the partnership; it will be more difficult for a general agent in a fiduciary position to show that a profit was acquired outside the scope of his agency. See *per* Hodson L.J. at p. 108 and *per* Guest L.J. at p. 117. See also *London School Board v. Northcroft* (1892), *Hudson's Building and Engineering Contracts* (10th ed.), p. 192; *Re Charles Selz Ltd's Patent Application* (1953) 71 R.P.C. 158.

[6] See *e.g. Burrell v. Mossop* (1888) 4 T.L.R. 270; *Williams v. Stevens* (1866) L.R. 1 P.C. 352.

[7] *Parker v. McKenna* (1874) L.R. 10 Ch.App. 96; *Phipps v. Boardman* [1967] 2 A.C. 46, a case where the principal acquired great benefit as a result of the fiduciaries' action: *Industrial Development Consultants Ltd v. Cooley* [1972] 1 W.L.R. 443, Illustration 7; *Warman International Ltd v. Dwyer* (1995) 69 A.L.J.R. 362.

[8] *Phipps v. Boardman*, n. 99 above; but *cf. Guinness Plc. v. Saunders* [1990] 2 A.C. 663. See also *Yates v. Finn* (1880) 13 Ch.D. 839; *Re Jarvis* [1958] 1 W.L.R. 815; *Paul A. Davies (Australia) Pty. Ltd v. Davies* [1983] 1 N.S.W.L.R. 440.

[9] See *O'Sullivan v. Management Agency and Music Ltd* [1985] Q.B. 428; *Re Duke of Norfolk's Settlement Trusts* [1962] Ch. 61; *Re Berkeley Applegate (Investment Consultants) Ltd* [1989] Ch. 32; *Estate Realties Ltd v. Wignall* [1992] 2 N.Z.L.R. 615; *Warman International Ltd v. Dwyer*, n. 7 above.

for himself[10]: but the present principle is wider, since, as stated above, it is not confined to situations where trust property can be readily identified. Since there is, until it is generated, no property to which the right can attach, it can be said that the only remedy is a duty to account, which is personal[10a]; but it can be argued to the contrary that the agent is deemed to act properly and generate or acquire the property for the principal, which would lead to a proprietary claim. [10b]

6–080

Companies. [11] Promotors and directors are not allowed to retain profits made which should belong to their companies. In the case of promoters, the duty is not to make a secret profit in the promotion, and difficulties occur in determining to whom disclosure should be made; there are also problems as to profits made after the promotion. [12] In the case of directors, the rule arises out of their fiduciary relationship to their companies[13] and no director may retain any benefit acquired in the conduct of his company's business unless the particulars of such benefits are fully explained to and are approved by the shareholders. [14] "Directors, no doubt, are not trustees, but they occupy a fiduciary position towards the company whose board they form. Their liability in this respect does not depend upon breach of duty but upon the proposition that a director must not make a profit out of property acquired by reason of his relationship to the company of which he is a

---

[10] e.g. *Phipps v. Boardman*, see Article 48.
[10a] cf. *Warman International Ltd v. Dwyer*, n. 7 above. See paras. 6–044, 6–075, 6–094.
[10b] cf. *Att.-Gen. for Hong Kong v. Reid* [1994] 1 A.C. 324; the Rt. Hon. Lord Justice Millett, [1993] Restitution L.Rev. 7.
[11] See Gower, *Modern Company Law* (5th ed.), Chaps 12, 21; Pennington, *Company Law* (4th ed.), pp. 525 *et seq.*, 586 *et seq*; Sealy [1967] C.L.J. 83.
[12] See *Erlanger v. New Sombrero Phosphate Co.* (1878) 3 App.Cas. 1218; *Gluckstein v. Barnes* [1900] A.C. 240. See also *Bagnall v. Carlton* (1877) 6 Ch.D. 371; *Emma Silver Mining Co. v. Lewis & Sons* (1879) 4 C.P.D. 396; *Emma Silver Mining Co. v. Grant* (1879) 11 Ch.D. 918; *Whaley Bridge Calico Printing Co. v. Green* (1879) 5 Q.B.D. 109; *Lydney and Wigpool Ore Co. v. Bird* (1886) 33 Ch.D. 85; *Re Cape Breton Co.* (1885) 29 Ch.D. 795; affd. *sub nom. Cavendish-Bentinck v. Fenn* (1887) 12 App.Cas. 652; *Lagunas Nitrate Co. v. Lagunas Syndicate* [1899] 2 Ch. 392; *Re Lady Forrest (Murchison) Gold Mine* [1901] 1 Ch. 582; *Re Leeds & Hanley Theatres of Varieties* [1902] 2 Ch. 809; *Ommium Electric Palaces Ltd v. Baines* [1914] 1 Ch. 332; *Jacobus Marler Estates Ltd v. Marler* (1916) 85 L.J.P.C. 167n.; *Jubilee Cotton Mills v. Lewis* [1924] A.C. 958; *Tracy v. Mandelay Pty. Ltd* (1953) 88 C.L.R. 215.
[13] *Percival v. Wright* [1902] 2 Ch. 421; but cf. *Briess v. Woolley* [1954] A.C. 333; *Coleman v. Myers* [1977] 2 N.Z.L.R. 225.
[14] *Aberdeen Ry. Co. v. Blaikie* (1854) 1 Macq. 461, Illustration 2 to Article 46; *Imperial Mercantile Credit Assn. v. Coleman* (1873) L.R. 6 H.L. 189; *Selangor United Rubber Estates Ltd v. Cradock (No. 3)* [1968] 1 W.L.R. 1555; *Wallersteiner v. Moir* [1974] 1 W.L.R. 991; *Furs Ltd v. Tomkies* (1936) 54 C.L.R. 583; *G.E. Smith Ltd v. Smith* [1952] N.Z.L.R. 470; *Guinness Plc. v. Saunders* [1990] 2 A.C. 663; and see Illustrations; Wedderburn [1958] C.L.J. 93, 99 *et seq.*

director."[15] This applies even though the directors act without fraud and in good faith[16]; moreover, if the director has obtained a benefit which in equity belongs to the company, a resolution passed by reason of the director's majority shareholding cannot confirm the situation and state that the company has no interest in the benefit so obtained.[17] Many of the secret profit cases actually concern directors.[18]

Illustrations

(1) Commission agents who were also merchants were employed to ship and sell goods abroad. They did so and purchased other goods with the proceeds. They were not bound to account for the profit on the sale of the goods bought with the proceeds, because such profit was not made in the course of or by means of the agency. They were only bound to account for the proceeds of the goods sold on the principal's behalf.[19]

(2) Three directors of a company which carried on the business of railway construction contractors obtained for themselves a contract to build a railway line to the exclusion of the company. They concealed this from the fourth director until the contract was obtained. Held, they held the benefit of the contract on behalf of the company.[20]

(3) A company wished to purchase the leases of two cinemas from X which, with a cinema it already owned, were to be transferred to a subsidiary company and then sold to a third party. The intention was that the company should own all the shares in the subsidiary. X required personal guarantees of the rent so long as the subscribed capital of the subsidiary was below a certain amount. It being difficult to secure such guarantees, and the company not having the money to subscribe further, the directors of the company and their solicitor personally subscribed for the remainder of the capital. When the directors sold their shares they made a profit which they could not keep for themselves but held for the benefit of their company, even after the company had been sold. The solicitor was however unaffected.[21]

(4) A will created a trust which included a shareholding in a private company. X, the solicitor who had been acting for the trust, and Y, a beneficiary, decided that the best way to protect the interests of the trust was to gain control of the company and this they did by purchasing sufficient extra shares in the company with their own money. By holding

6–081

---

[15] *Regal (Hastings) Ltd v. Gulliver* [1967] 2 A.C. 134n., 159, *per* Lord Porter.

[16] *Regal (Hastings) Ltd v. Gulliver*, above, at p. 144.

[17] *Cook v. Deeks* [1916] 1 A.C. 554, Illustration 2.

[18] See Illustrations.

[19] *Kirkham v. Peel* (1881) 44 L.T. 195; *cf. Union Government v. Chappell* [1918] Cape P.D. 462.

[20] *Cook v. Deeks* [1916] 1 A.C. 554; see Wedderburn [1958] C.L.J. 93, 99 *et seq.*

[21] *Regal (Hastings) Ltd v. Gulliver* [1967] 2 A.C. 134n. See Wedderburn [1958] C.L.J. 93, 99 *et seq.*

themselves out as acting on behalf of the trust, they acquired both the opportunity to bid for the further shares and also confidential information which satisfied them that the purchase of the shares would be a good investment. As a result of the changes in control of the company X and Y and the trust made considerable profits. They had made formal disclosure to two trustees but not to the third; and later, when the estate had been administered, disclosure to the beneficiaries had not been complete. Held, X and Y were accountable to the trust for the profit made on the shares which they had purchased with their own money, as they had used their position to make a profit for themselves as well as the trust. X and Y could, however, claim remuneration for their expenses and labour in taking over the company.[22]

(5) Two mine prospectors employed X to stake asbestos mineral claims for them in Manitoba. X received information about the area from them, explored the area and reported that there was no asbestos there. However, in the course of his prospecting he discovered that there were other valuable minerals in the area. Shortly afterwards he staked claims to these minerals for himself and made a considerable profit. Held, he was under a duty to disclose all he had learnt about the area to his principals and he must account for the profits made within the area he agreed to explore.[23]

(6) The board of directors of a mining company consider a proposition put up by an outsider for mining in an area near to the company's holdings, and reject it. Individual directors contact the outsider and put up the money for the venture, taking advice from the company's consulting geologist. They are not liable to account for profits.[24]

(7) C was managing director of the plaintiffs, a company which carried on business as construction consultants. As such, he was

---

[22] *Phipps v. Boardman* [1967] 2 A.C. 46. This is a stern and perhaps somewhat exceptional decision: there is much force in the dissenting judgment of Lord Upjohn. A crucial reason seems to have been that X and Y purported, at any rate initially, to be acting for the trust: there was certainly no pre-existing agency relationship. The company was also a private one and information could not be obtained from its public documents. The trust could not have purchased shares in the company without leave of the court and in some speeches reliance is placed, perhaps questionably, on the fact that it was possible that at some time in the future the solicitor would be asked to advise in this respect; on the question of remuneration: *cf. Guinness Plc. v. Saunders* [1990] 2 A.C. 663 (also a strict decision). See Finn, *Fiduciary Obligations* (1977), pp. 242 *et seq.*; Fridman (1968) 84 L.Q.R. 224; Rider (1978) 42 Conv. 114; Bishop and Prentice (1983) 46 M.L.R. 289; *Chan v. Zacharia* (1984) 154 C.L.R. 178, 204–205 *per* Deane J.

[23] *McLeod and More v. Sweezey* [1944] 2 D.L.R. 145.

[24] *Peso Silver Mines Ltd v. Cropper* [1966] S.C.R. 673; (1966) 58 D.L.R. (2d) 1, a controversial case: see (1967) 30 M.L.R. 450; Beck (1971) 49 Can.B.R. 80; Prentice (1972) 50 Can.B.R. 623. See also *Mid-Western News Agency Ltd v. Vanpinxteren* (1975) 62 D.L.R. (3d) 555; *Evans v. Anderson* (1977) 76 D.L.R. (3d) 482.

negotiating with E for a contract. E made it clear to him that he had no intention of contracting with the plaintiffs but indicated that he might be prepared to contract with C personally. At a subsequent interview with the chairman of the plaintiffs, C did not tell him of E's offer but falsely told him that he was seriously ill. For this reason he was given permission by the plaintiffs to resign at once instead of working out his contractual period of notice. Having resigned from the plaintiff's employment C at once made a contract with E. Held, C had allowed his personal interest to conflict with his duty as a director of the plaintiffs. Notwithstanding that the plaintiffs had sustained no loss (because E was not willing to contract with them) C was ordered to account to the plaintiffs for all his profits from his contract with E. [25]

(8)   The executive president and vice-president of a company engage in preliminary prospecting towards an extensive aerial mapping project to be paid for by a government. They subsequently form a separate company and obtain the contract in competition with their previous company. They must account for profits. [26]

(9)   The managing director of a company formed to exploit mining licences is poised to exploit successful negotiations. The collapse of one of the company's shareholders leaves it without working capital. The managing director takes the licences in his own name, resigns as managing director (but not as a director) and forms his own company to exploit the concession. He explains the full position and the inherent risks to the Board, which decides to pursue the concession no further and permit him to do what he wants with the licence. He is not liable to account. [27]

(10)   The prospective purchaser of property applies for planning permission in respect of it in the vendor's name without telling the vendor. He must account for profits made as the result of the application. [28]

(11)   A sergeant in the Army stationed at Cairo, while in uniform, accompanied civilian lorries containing illicit goods through Cairo,

---

[25] *Industrial Development Consultants Ltd v. Cooley* [1972] 1 W.L.R. 443; see [1972A] C.L.J. 222; (1972) 35 M.L.R. 655. See also *Green & Clara Pty. Ltd v. Bestobell Industries Pty. Ltd* [1982] W.A.L.R. 1.
[26] *Canadian Aero Service Ltd v. O'Malley* [1974] S.C.R. 592; (1973) 40 D.L.R. (3d) 371: see Beck (1975) 53 Can. B.R. 771. See also *Abbey Glen Property Corp. v. Stumborg* (1978) 85 D.L.R. (3d) 35; (1979) 42 M.L.R. 215; and in general as to those cases Gower, *Modern Company Law* (5th ed.), pp. 567 *et seq.*
[27] *Queensland Mines Ltd v. Hudson* (1978) 52 A.L.J.R. 399 (P.C.): see (1979) 42 M.L.R. 711. See also *Island Export Finance Ltd v. Umunna* [1986] B.C.L.C. 460.
[28] *English v. Dedham Vale Properties Ltd* [1978] 1 W.L.R. 93. This is an unusual case as the person concerned was in effect treated as a "self-appointed" agent: see Beatson, *Use and Abuse of Unjust Enrichment* (1991), pp. 241–243; (1978) 94 L.Q.R. 347; (1978) 41 M.L.R. 474.

enabling them to pass the civilian police without inspection. He was paid large sums of money for his services. The military authorities took possession of the money, and the sergeant petitioned the Crown for its return. Held, he could not recover the money. He had obtained the money by reason of his employment, but in dereliction of his duty—by using his position as a sergeant and the uniform to which his rank entitled him; the Crown could retain the money—at least against the sergeant—even though it was earned by a criminal act.[29]

Article 50

LIABILITY OF AGENTS IN RESPECT OF BRIBES AND SECRET COMMISSIONS

6–082   When an agent receives or arranges to receive any money or property by way of bribe or secret commission in the course of his agency from a person who deals or seeks to deal with his principal, he is liable to his principal jointly and severally with that person—

(1)   in restitution for the amount of the bribe or secret commission;

(2)   in tort, for any loss suffered by the principal from entering into the transaction in respect of which the bribe or secret commission was given or promised[30];

and the bribe, if it was paid, is held on constructive trust for the principal.[31]

Comment

6–083   **Bribes.** "If a gift be made to a confidential agent with the view of inducing the agent to act in favour of the donor in relation to transactions between the donor and the agent's principal and that gift is secret as between the donor and the agent—that is to say, without the knowledge and consent of the principal—then the gift is a bribe in the view of the law."[32] However, where the payment is not for a corrupt

---

[29] *Reading v. Att.-Gen.* [1951] A.C. 507; but it is doubtful whether the principles of fiduciary obligation are appropriate in such public law situations: see Finn, *Fiduciary Obligations* (1977), pp. 214–215; Goff and Jones, *Law of Restitution* (4th ed.), pp. 666–667. See also *Att.-Gen v. Goddard* (1929) 98 L.J.K.B. 743; *Hawrelak v. City of Edmonton* (1975) 54 D.L.R. (3d) 45.

[30] *Mahesan v. Malaysia Government Officers Co-operative Housing Society Ltd* [1979] A.C. 374, Illustration 8. See in general Goff and Jones, *Law of Restitution* (4th ed.), pp. 666 *et seq.*; Finn, *Fiduciary Obligations* (1977), pp. 211 *et seq.* See further Article 98 as to the position between principal and third party.

[31] *Att.-Gen. for Hong Kong v. Reid* [1994] 1 A.C. 324. See in general the Rt. Hon. Lord Justice Millett, [1993] Restitution L.Rev. 7.

[32] *Hovenden & Sons v. Millhoff* (1900) 83 L.T. 41, 43, *per* Romer L.J.

purpose it is more appropriate to refer to the arrangement as a secret commission. The reasoning applies also to commissions given by way of discount on payment[33] and to promised commissions and discounts as well as to paid ones.[34] Older cases did not necessarily regard such commissions as bribes but might simply treat the agent as bound to account to his principal on the ground that the money or property had been received for him.[35] It is now clear however that the agents are liable in respect of bribes and secret commissions in restitution or in tort;[36] and that the bribe if paid is held on trust for the principal.[37] But the principle does not apply to small gifts made after the conclusion of a transaction related to services performed by the agent himself,[38] unless it appears that such gifts were expected when the transaction was entered into, or are intended to affect future transactions.[39] A large gift however might be regarded as received for the principal. Nor does it apply to payments and the like from independent third parties, though these may create a liability for a secret profit[40]; nor to discounts obtained on transactions independent of the agency relationship.[41]

Disclosure. Active concealment is not necessary: it is sufficient that   **6-084** the principal did not know of the bribe.[42] Furthermore, to free the agent from liability, the disclosure must be such as to enable the principal to understand the implications of the arrangement: thus a partial disclosure may be insufficient.[43] If the relevant elements are proved, it is irrelevant to show that the agent has not in fact been

---

[33] *e.g. Turnbull v. Garden* (1869) 38 L.J.Ch. 331, Illustration 2. Sometimes such transactions can be treated as a sale by the agent to his principal: see *Kimber v. Barber* (1872) L.R. 8 Ch.App. 56; Article 47.

[34] *Grant v. Gold Exploration & Development Syndicate Ltd* [1900] 1 Ch. 233; though the agent can only be liable in restitution where he has received the money.

[35] *e.g. Fawcett v. Whitehouse* (1829) 1 Russ. & M. 132; *Turnbull v. Garden,* n. 33 above.

[36] *Mahesan's case,* n. 30 above, at p. 383.

[37] *Att.-Gen. for Hong Kong v. Reid,* n. 31 above.

[38] *The Parkdale* [1897] P. 53, Illustration 1. See also *Meadow Schama & Co. v. C. Mitchell & Co. Ltd* (1973) 228 EG 1511 (sum promised after commission earned: not a bribe).

[39] See Article 98, Illustration 1.

[40] *Armagas Ltd v. Mundogas S.A., (The Ocean Frost)* [1985] 1 Lloyd's Rep. 1, 19–20, but *cf.* 83. But the third party may be affected by the bribe if it was given or promised by his agent acting in the course of his employment: see the same case on appeal [1986] A.C. 717, 743–744 *per* Robert Goff L.J.

[41] See *London School Board v. Northcroft* (1892) Hudson's Building and Engineering Contracts (10th ed.), p. 192.

[42] *Temperley v. Blackrod Mfg. Co. Ltd* (1907) 71 J.P. 341. *Cf. Rowland v. Chapman* (1901) 17 T.L.R. 669 (knowledge of solicitor).

[43] *Bartram & Sons v. Lloyd* (1904) 90 L.T. 357. See also *Christie v. McCann* (1972) 27 D.L.R. (3d) 544. The onus is on the agent: *Jordy v. Vanderpump* (1920) 64 S.J. 324.

influenced or departed from his duty to his principal,[44] for the acceptance of or agreement to receive a bribe is of itself a breach of his general fiduciary duty, as giving him an interest contrary to his duty to his principal.[45]

If however the principal knows that the agent has been paid such a commission and consents, he cannot afterwards claim against the agent[46]: similarly, where he leaves the agent to look to the other party for his remuneration or knows that he will receive something from the other party, he cannot object on the ground that he did not know the precise particulars of the amount paid. Such situations often occur in connection with usage and custom of trades and markets.[47] Where no usage is involved, however, the principal's knowledge may require to be more specific.

6–085   **Remedies.** The principal has various remedies open to him when he discovers that his agent has been bribed. If the bribe has been paid and is in money, he can sue the agent for its amount[48] in an action which was in earlier cases regarded as lying in equity[49] but was subsequently treated as an action in restitution.[50] A sub-agent is similarly liable despite the absence of privity of contract.[51] In this action the person who gave the bribe is also liable jointly and severally.[52] If the bribe is

---

[44] *Harrington v. Victoria Graving Dock Co.* (1978) 3 Q.B.D. 549; *Shipway v. Broadwood* [1899] 1 Q.B. 369; *Re a Debtor* [1927] 2 Ch. 367.

[45] *Shipway v. Broadwood*, n. 44 above, at p. 373. Statements that the recipient is conclusively presumed to have been influenced (*e.g. Hovenden v. Millhoff* (1900) 83 L.J. 41; *Industries and General Mortgage Co. v. Lewis* [1949] 2 All E.R. 573, 578), are therefore beside the point: the Rt. Hon. Lord Justice Millett, [1993] Restitution L.Rev. 7, 13, n. 42.

[46] *Great Western Insurance Co. of New York v. Cunliffe* (1874) L.R. 9 Ch.App. 525; *Re Haslam and Hier-Evans* [1902] 1 Ch. 765; *P.&O. S.N. Co. v. Johnson* (1938) 60 C.L.R. 189; *cf. Federal Supply and Cold Storage of South Africa v. Angehrn & Piel* (1910) 80 L.J.P.C. 1 (in which an acceptance of an agent's denial that he had received a bribe was held not to be condonation or consent, where he had in fact done so).

[47] See Illustration 9.

[48] *Morison v. Thompson* (1874) L.R. 9 Q.B. 480; *Hay's Case* (1875) L.R. 10 Ch.App. 593; *Boston Deep Sea Fishing and Ice Co. v. Ansell* (1888) 39 Ch.D. 339; *Lister & Co. v. Stubbs* (1890) 45 Ch.D. 1; *Att.-Gen. v. Goddard* (1929) 98 L.J.K.B. 743 (but see Article 49, Illustration 11); *Ardlethan Options Ltd v. Easdown* (1916) 20 C.L.R. 285, 292. See Public Bodies Corrupt Practices Act 1889, s. 2(b) for power of the court to order a recipient of a bribe, who has been convicted under that Act, to pay the amount or value of the bribe to the public body concerned.

[49] *Fawcett v. Whitehouse* (1829) 1 Russ. & M. 132.

[50] *Mahesan v. Malaysia Government Officers' Co-operative Housing Society Ltd* [1979] A.C. 374, Illustration 8.

[51] *Att.-Gen. v. Goddard*, n. 29 above; *Powell & Thomas v. Evan Jones & Co. Ltd* [1905] 1 K.B. 11, Illustration 8 to Article 37.

[52] *Mahesan's case*, n. 50 above; see Article 98.

given in property, older cases say that the agent is liable for the value of the property at the highest value which it had while in his possession.[53] Interest is payable from the date when the bribe was received.[54] It is now clear also, although the contrary view held sway for many years,[55] that the bribe is to be regarded as the property of the principal and held on trust as such.[56] This will be an advantageous claim if the agent is insolvent, or if the property increases in value:[57] there is no indication that it affects the remedy *in personam*.

In addition, the agent and the person giving the bribe are jointly and severally liable in deceit for any loss suffered.[58] This action will be preferable to the restitutionary and proprietary claims where the loss suffered exceeds the amount of the bribe, or the bribe has decreased in value; and as regards the action against the agent, where the bribe has not yet been paid. The principal cannot however recover under all heads and must elect before judgment.[59]

An agent who takes a bribe may also forfeit his right to commission or remuneration that he would have otherwise received[60]; he may also lose his right to indemnity.[61] The principal is justified in dismissing without notice any agent who accepts a bribe in the course of his agency[62] and such a dismissal will still be justifiable, even if the bribery is not discovered until after the agent has been dismissed.[63] The

---

[53] *McKay's Case* (1878) 2 Ch.D. 1; *Pearson's Case* (1877) 5 Ch. D. 336; *Nant-y-glo and Blaina Iron Co. v. Grave* (1878) 12 Ch.D. 738; *Eden v. Ridsdales Railway Lamp & Lighting Co. Ltd* (1889) 23 Q.B.D. 368; see Illustration 4. It is not clear on what basis a bribe in services would be quantified.

[54] *Nant-y-glo and Blaina Iron Co. v. Grave*, n. 53 above; *Boston Deep Sea Fishing and Ice Co. v. Ansell* (1888) 39 Ch.D. 339, 353, 372 (Illustration 3).

[55] *Lister & Co. v. Stubbs* (1890) 45 Ch.D. 1; *Powell & Thomas v. Evan Jones & Co.* [1905] 1 K.B. 11. See Meagher, Gummow and Lehane, *Equity Doctrines and Remedies* (3rd ed.), pp. 153 *et seq.*

[56] *Att.-Gen. for Hong Kong v. Reid* [1994] 1 A.C. 324; and see above, para. 6–044.

[57] *ibid.* at p. 331.

[58] *Mahesan's case*, n. 50 above; see Article 98; (1978) 41 M.L.R. 603; (1978) 94 L.Q.R. 344; Needham, (1979) 95 L.Q.R. 536. *Quaere* whether there can be situations where the requirements of deceit cannot be established.

[59] *Mahesan's case*, n. 50 above, not following dicta in *Salford Corp. v. Lever* [1891] 1 Q.B. 168 and *Hovenden & Sons v. Millhoff* (1900) 83 L.T. 41. See Tettenborn (1979) 95 L.Q.R. 68.

[60] See Article 57 and *Cec. McManus Realty Ltd v. Bray* (1970) 14 D.L.R. (3d) 564; *Meadow Schama & Co. v. C. Mitchell & Co. Ltd* (1973) 228 EG 1511. But not necessarily in respect of other transactions: *cf. Hippisley v. Knee Bros.* [1905] 1 K.B. 1; *P. & O. S.N. Co. v. Johnson* (1938) 60 C.L.R. 189; 216–217. And see Article 62.

[61] *Stange & Co. v. Lowitz* (1898) 14 T.L.R. 468; *Nicholson v. J. Mansfield & Co.* (1901) 17 T.L.R. 259. See Article 65.

[62] *Bulfield v. Fournier* (1895) 11 T.L.R. 282; *Swale v. Ipswich Tannery Ltd* (1906) 11 Com. Cas. 88; *Temperley v. Blackrod Manufacturing Co. Ltd* (1907) 71 J.P. 341; *Federal Supply and Cold Storage Co. of South Africa v. Angehrn & Piel* (1910) 80 L.J.P.C. 1.

[63] *Boston Deep Sea Fishing & Ice Co. v. Ansell* (1888) 39 Ch.D. 339, Illustration 3.

principal may also rescind the transaction between himself and the third party.[64] But the liability of the agent persists whichever the principal does, and if the principal has received the bribe he is entitled to keep it and need not give credit for it in the rescission.[65]

6–086   **Criminal law.** Lastly, corrput dealings with agents are a criminal offence. Thus, an agent who accepts or agrees to accept a bribe is at common law guilty of conspiracy.[66] By the Prevention of Corruption Act 1906, s.1,[67] if any agent[68] corruptly[69] accepts, or obtains, or agrees to accept, or attempts to obtain for himself or for any other person, any gift or consideration,[70] as an inducement or reward for doing, or forbearing to do, or for having done, or forborne to do, any act in relation to his principal's[71] affairs[72] or business, or for showing or forbearing to show favour or disfavour to any person, in relation thereto, he is guilty of an offence. Any person who corruptly gives, or agrees to give, or offers any such gift or consideration is similarly guilty.[73]

---

[64] See *Taylor v. Walker* [1958] 1 Lloyd's Rep. 490; Article 98.

[65] *Logicrose v. Southend United Football Club* [1988] 1 W.L.R. 1256.

[66] *R. v. Barber* (1887) 3 T.L.R. 491. See also *R. v. Whitaker* [1914] 3 K.B. 1283; *R. v. De Kromme* (1892) 66 L.T. 301 (incitement to conspire).

[67] See also Public Bodies Corrupt Practices Act 1889; Prevention of Corruption Act 1916; *R. v. Andrews-Weatherfoil Ltd* [1972] 1 W.L.R. 118; and see generally Archbold, *Criminal Pleading, Evidence and Practice* (1994), Vol. 2, §§ 31–161 *et seq.*

[68] Includes any person employed by or acting for another: s. 1(2); and also any person serving under the Crown or under any corporation or any municipal borough, county or district council: s. 1(3). See *Templeton v. H.M. Advocate* 1988 S.L.T. 171.

[69] See *R. v. Wellburn* (1979) 69 Cr.App.R. 254. Where the consideration has been received by an employee of Her Majesty or of a government or public body (including any local or public authority) from a person, or the agent of a person, holding, or seeking, a contract from Her Majesty or from a government department or public body, corruption is presumed until the contrary is proved: 1916 Act, ss. 2, 4; *R. v. Jenkins* (1923) 87 J.P. 115. It is sufficient to establish the contrary by reasonable probability: *R. v. Carr-Briant* [1943] K.B. 607. The prosecution need prove only that a bribe was taken as an inducement to show favour. It need not prove that favour was in fact shown: *R. v. Carr* [1957] 1 W.L.R. 165; *R. v. Mills* (1978) 68 Cr.App.R. 154. See also *R. v. Barrett* [1976] 1 W.L.R. 946; *R. v. Manners* [1978] A.C. 43.

[70] Includes valuable consideration of any kind: 1906 Act, s. 1(2). See *R. v. Braithwaite* [1983] 1 W.L.R. 385.

[71] Includes an employer: 1906 Act, s. 1(2); and see *Morgan v. D.P.P.* [1970] 3 All E.R. 1053.

[72] Pecuniary interest need not be involved: *Att.-Gen. v. Goddard* (1929) 98 L.J.K.B. 743.

[73] 1906 Act, s. 1(1). The subsection also provides against the use of documents containing false statements, with intent to deceive the principal. See *R. v. Tweedie* [1984] Q.B. 729.

Illustrations

(1) The master of a ship receives three payments totalling £45 by   **6–087**
way of gratuity for efficient discharge of cargo. This is not a bribe and
he may retain the money.[74]

(2) A requested B to provide an outfit for A's son. B did so, and
obtained certain discounts, but charged A the full prices. The discounts
were disallowed, although B did not charge any commission as an
agent.[75]

(3) A director of a company who was a shareholder in two other
companies accepted bonuses from such other companies, in consideration of his giving them orders on behalf of the first company. He also
took a commission, which was unknown to his company, on a contract
for the building of a number of boats. The articles of association
provided that the directors might contract with the company. Held, that
he was accountable to the company for the bonuses and the secret
commission with interest; and that the bribery justified the dismissal of
the director, although it was not discovered until after the dismissal.[76]

(4) The secretary of a company, when making a contract on behalf
of the company with the vendor, stipulated that he should receive, and
subsequently did receive, from the vendor 600 fully paid-up shares.
Held, that he must account to the company for the highest value borne
by the shares during the time they were held by him, which in this case
was assumed to be the nominal value.[77]

(5) A director of a company, before the transactions between the
promoter and the company had been finally completed, accepted his
qualification shares from the promoter. The director had to account to
the company for the highest value attributable to the shares during the
time they were held by him, with interest on such value from the date
the shares were transferred to him to the date of the action.[78] So, if a
director receives the money to pay for his qualification shares, he must
account for the amount received, with interest from the date of its
receipt.[79] Where a promoter sold shares to a director, the director was
compelled to account for the difference between the nominal value of
the shares and the price he paid for them.[80]

---

[74] *The Parkdale* [1897] P. 53.
[75] *Turnbull v. Garden* (1869) 38 L.J.Ch. 331. See also *Hippisley v. Knee Bros.* [1905] 1
K.B. 1, Illustration 5 to Article 62; *North American Land and Timber Co. Ltd v. Watkins*
[1904] 1 Ch. 242; [1904] 2 Ch. 233, Illustration 3 to Article 45.
[76] *Boston Deep Sea Fishing & Ice Co. v. Ansell* (1888) 39 Ch.D. 339; see also *Temperley
v. Blackrod Manufacturing Co. Ltd* (1907) 71 J.P. 341.
[77] *McKay's Case* (1875) 2 Ch.D. 1.
[78] *Nant-y-glo & Blaina Iron Co. v. Grave* (1878) 12 Ch.D. 738; *Pearson's Case* (1877) 5
Ch.D. 336; *Eden v. Ridsdale's Railway Lamp & Lighting Co. Ltd* (1889) 58 L.J.Q.B. 579;
Mitcalfe's Case (1879) 13 Ch.D. 169.
[79] *Hay's Case* (1875) L.R. 10 Ch.App. 593; *McLean's Case* (1885) 55 L.J.Ch. 36; *cf.*
Archer's Case [1892] 1 Ch. 322.
[80] *Weston's Case* (1879) 10 Ch.D. 579.

(6) A assisted B in the negotiations for the building of a ship by C for B, B agreeing to pay A a sum for his services. The negotiations with C were conducted through D, a shipbroker, who was to receive commission from C. Unknown to B, A and D arranged that A should take half of D's commission. Held, B could recover from A the latter's share of the commission.[81]

(7) A solicitor, who was retained by A to act for him in negotiation for the purchase of a patent, had previously received a commission note from the owner of the patent agreeing to pay him commission in the event of a purchaser being found. A purchased the patent and the solicitor, with A's knowledge, received the commission from the seller. Held, that he was not accountable to A for the commission, having made full disclosure.[82]

(8) The agent of a housing society, for a bribe of $122,000 arranges that a third party should buy land at a low price and sell it to the society at a profit. The third party buys the land for $456,000 and sells it to the society for $944,000. The society recovers the $122,000 from the agent and also sues him for $443,000, being the third party's net profit. The society must elect between one claim and the other before judgment is entered.[83]

(9) It was usual for underwriters to allow all intermediaries, for punctual payment of premiums, a percentage as discount, or 12 per cent calculated on the yearly profits, in addition to the ordinary commission of 5 per cent on each reinsurance. A company, having made no inquiry as to the remuneration paid by the underwriters, and not being aware of the 12 per cent allowance, employed Baring Bros. as agent to negotiate business. After the agent (who received no remuneration from the company) had been paid the usual allowance of 12 per cent for more than eight years, the company discovered it and claimed to have it paid over to them as secret profit. It was held that they were not entitled to recover.[84] This decision was followed by the Court of Appeal in a later case, on the ground that every person who employs another as his agent with the knowledge that the agent receives remuneration from third persons, and who does not choose to inquire what the charges of the agent will be, must allow all the usual and customary charges of such an

[81] *W.A. Phillips, Anderson & Co. v. Euxine Shipping Co.* [1955] 2 Lloyd's Rep. 512.
[82] *Re Haslam and Hier-Evans* [1902] 1 Ch. 765.
[83] *Mahesan v. Malaysia Government Officers' Co-operative Housing Society Ltd* [1979] A.C. 374. For periodical literature on this case see n. 58 above.
[84] *Great Western Insurance Co. of New York v. Cunliffe* (1874) L.R. 9 Ch.App. 525; see also *Leete v. Wallace* (1888) 58 L.T. 577; *Norreys v. Hodgson* (1897) 13 T.L.R. 421, where an agent who was instructed to procure a loan from an insurance company which required a policy on the life of the principal was held entitled to retain the commission on the policy.

agent, and is not entitled to dispute them because he was not aware of the extent of the remuneration usually received by such agents.[85]

(10)   An agent accepts a bribe in connection with the grant of a concession. The facts are discovered and the agent accounts for most of the bribe to his principal. The principal rescinds the concession. He may keep the bribe: if he has not received it he can still recover it from the agent. He is under no obligation to give credit for it to the third party in the rescission.[86]

Article 51

DUTY TO KEEP PROPERTY OF PRINCIPAL SEPARATE AND PRESERVE CORRECT ACCOUNTS

It is the duty of an agent—   6–088

(1)   where he holds money or property belonging to his principal, to keep it separate from his own and from that of other persons[87];

(2)   to preserve and be constantly ready with correct accounts of all his dealings and transactions in the course of his agency[88];

(3)   to produce to the principal, or to a proper person appointed by the principal, all books and documents in his hands relating to the principal's affairs.[89]

Comment

(1)   **Separation of property.** If an agent is entrusted with the money   6–089
or property of his principal, he must keep it separate from his own. If he is sued for an account and has failed to keep his principal's property separate, he will be liable for the contents of the mixture or anything acquired by expenditure from it, up to the value of the input.[90] This

---

[85] *Baring v. Stanton* (1876) 3 Ch.D. 502; *cf. Queen of Spain v. Parr* (1869) 39 L.J.Ch. 73; *E. Green & Son Ltd v. G. Tughan & Co.* (1913) 30 T.L.R. 64. *cf. Copp v. Lynch* (1882) 26 S.J. 348.

[86] *Logicrose v. Southend United Football Club* [1988] 1 W.L.R. 1256.

[87] *Gray v. Haig* (1855) 20 Beav. 219; *Clarke v. Tipping* (1846) 9 Beav. 284; *Palette Shoes Pty Ltd v. Krohn* (1937) 58 C.L.R. 1, 30. *cf.* above, para. 6–043.

[88] *Gray v. Haig*, n. 87 above; *Clarke v. Tipping*, n. 87 above; *Pearse v. Green* (1819) 1 J. & W. 135; *Turner v. Burkinshaw* (1867) L.R. 2 Ch.App. 488; *Collyer v. Dudley* (1823) T. & R. 421; *Utz v. Carver* [1972] 1 N.S.W.L.R. 407. *cf. Re Lee, ex p. Neville* (1868) L.R. 4 Ch.App. 43. See *Restatement*, § 346.

[89] *Dadswell v. Jacobs* (1887) 34 Ch.D. 278; *Re Burnand, ex p. Baker, Sutton & Co.* [1904] 2 K.B. 68 (bankruptcy of agent); *Re Ellis & Ellis* [1908] W.N. 215; 25 T.L.R. 38 (bankruptcy of principal).

[90] See material cited above, para. 6–042, n. 74.

obligation only arises, however, in connection with money or property which is beneficially owned by the principal; in such a case the agent will be in the position of a trustee.[91] In other cases however the court will infer that the parties intended the relationship of debtor and creditor on the ground that a duty to keep money separate would be an unintended restriction on the agent's commercial activity.[92]

6–090   (2) **Accounts.** An agent is under an obligation to keep an accurate account of all transactions entered into on his principal's behalf[93] and he must be ready at all time to produce it to his principal.[94] If he fails to keep and preserve correct accounts, everything is presumed against him.

> "In such a case ... I am compelled to ... presume everything most unfavourable to him, which is consistent with the rest of the facts which are admitted or proved."[95]

The agent need not, however, produce records of transactions which do not concern the principal,[96] nor need he produce detailed items which his principal has agreed expressly or impliedly not to require of him.[97]

6–091   (3) **Documents.** The principal is entitled to have delivered up to him at the termination of the agency all documents concerning his affairs which have been prepared by the agent for him. In each case it is necessary (unless, as may be the case, the ownership of the documents

---

[91] See, *e.g. Burdick v. Garrick* (1870) L.R. 5 Ch.App. 233, Illustration 1 to Article 45. The Estate Agents Act 1979, s. 13, requires clients' money to be held on trust (but see Article 54 as to interest). The same is the case with solicitors: Solicitors Act 1974, ss. 32–33. See above, paras. 6–042–6–044; also Murdoch. *The Estate Agents and Property Misdescriptions Acts* (3rd ed.); Cordery, *Solicitors* (8th ed.), pp. 305–306.

[92] See *Henry v. Hammond* [1913] 2 K.B. 515; *Neste Oy v. Lloyd's Bank Plc* [1983] 2 Lloyd's Rep. 658; *Walker v. Corboy* (1990) 19 N.S.W.L.R. 398; and generally above, para. 6–043; Article 45, Illustrations 1–5. See also Financial Services Act 1986, s. 55.

[93] *Chedworth v. Edwards* (1802) 8 Ves. 46; *White v. Lincoln* (1803) 8 Ves. 363; *Tindall v. Powell* (1858) 32 L.T.(o.s.) 8; and cases cited at n. 88, above. Some agents are under a statutory obligation to keep special forms of accounts, *e.g.* solicitors under the Solicitors' Accounts Rules 1975, the Solicitors' Trust Accounts Rules 1975 and the Solicitors' Accounts (Deposit Interest) Rules 1975. Agents to sell horticultural produce must also keep special accounts under the Horticultural Produce (Sales on Commission) Act 1926. It will be a breach of duty wrongfully to disclose the account to third parties: see *Fogg v. Gaulter and Blane* (1960) 110 L.J. 718; *Yasuda Fire and Marine Ins. Co. of Europe Ltd v. Orion Marine Ins. Underwriting Agency Ltd* [1995] Q.B. 174 (right still existed though contract terminated by repudiatory breach).

[94] *Pearse v. Green* (1819) 1 J. & W. 135; *Turner v. Burkinshaw* (1867) L.R. 2 Ch.App. 488.

[95] *Gray v. Haig* (1855) 20 Beav. 219, 226, *per* Romilly M.R.; see also *Jenkins v. Gould* (1827) 3 Russ. 385.

[96] *Gerard v. Penswick* (1818) 1 Swan. 533; *Heugh v. Garrett* (1875) 44 L.J.Ch. 305.

[97] *Hunter v. Belcher* (1864) 2 De G.J. & S. 194.

is settled by the contract between the parties) to decide whether the document in question came into existence for the purpose of the agency relationship or for some other purpose, *e.g.* in pursuance of a duty to give professional advice. Thus land agents have been ordered to hand over memorandum books, a private rental and cash book and a field book[98]; an architect was ordered to deliver up the plans of a house after the work had been completed and paid for.[99] Both the land agents and the architect were considered to be agents. But memoranda prepared by quantity surveyors for their own use in measuring up buildings were held to be their own property[1]; and documents, books, maps and plans prepared by rating valuers employed to give advice and assistance to a county council remained the property of the valuers.[2] In *Chantrey Martin v. Martin*[3] the Court of Appeal held that working papers, draft and final accounts, notes and calculations and draft tax computations, brought into being by chartered accountants in the course of auditing a company's accounts, were the property of the accountants, the relationship being that of professional person and client; while correspondence between the accountants and the Inland Revenue relating to the company's tax liability was conducted by the accountants as the company's agents, so that original and copy letters comprising such correspondence belonged to the company. Where a document was prepared by the agent for the third party, the agent, though in breach of his duty to his principal in preparing it, was held not bound or entitled to give his principal inspection or possession of it.[4]

The agent may sometimes however exercise a lien over such documents.[5]

Article 52

DUTY TO ACCOUNT

An agent may be required to account in equity to his principal.   6–092

Comment

History. The action of account was an ancient common law action 6–093
first used against bailiffs and receivers.[6] It fell gradually into disuse

---

[98] *Beresford v. Driver* (1851) 14 Beav. 387.
[99] *Gibbon v. Pease* [1905] 1 K.B. 810, in which the Court of Appeal held that a custom to the contrary would be unreasonable.
[1] *London School Board v. Northcroft* (1889), Hudson, *Law of Building and Engineering Contracts* (10th ed.) p. 192.
[2] *Leicestershire C.C. v. Michael Faraday & Partners* [1941] 2 K.B. 205.
[3] [1953] 2 Q.B. 286; and see *Floydd v. Cheney* [1970] Ch. 602.
[4] *North and South Trust Co. v. Berkeley* [1971] 1 W.L.R. 470, Illustration 3 to Article 5.
[5] Article 67.
[6] See Fifoot, *History and Sources of the Common Law* (1952), pp. 268–277; Jackson, *History of Quasi-Contract* (1936) pp. 9–17; Stoljar, pp. 299–300; (1964) 80 L.Q.R. 203.

when the Court of Chancery began to exercise jurisdiction in matters of account: the Chancery procedure could be used to compel a defendant to make discovery on oath and so was superior. It became settled that the action was available not only against trustees but also against other fiduciaries such as agents[7] (but not in favour of agents against their principals[8]).

Before the fusion of law and equity there were various rules to determine when an action of account lay in equity. Thus if there was a fiduciary situation between the principal and his agent, or if there was a suspicion of fraud, or if the accounts were complicated, the agent could be compelled to account in equity: otherwise, the principal could only bring his action in the courts of Common Law.[9] Since the Judicature Acts, however, any division of the High Court has the jurisdiction originally vested in the previous courts of Common Law and Chancery. By virtue of section 61 and Schedule 1 of the Supreme Court Act 1981, actions for an account are usually to be assigned to the Chancery Division, but actions for simple accounts can be heard in the Queen's Bench Division[10]; if an action is started in the Queen's Bench Division it can be transferred to an Official Referee or the Chancery Division and usually will be transferred if the accounts are complicated.[11]

6–094   **Substantive significance.** The duty to account is in this sense simply a liability to the exercise of certain sorts of procedures used in courts of equity for the ascertainment of the true position between trustee or other fiduciary and beneficiary. As such it can be regarded as no more than a procedure ancillary to the ascertainment of other rights[12]: though the remedy does of course provide a sanction for, and hence the basis of, the duty to keep accounts and make them available to the principal.[13] However, the liability to account in equity has also a certain substantive significance in that it may lead to a judgment of the court for the payment of the money shown to be due on the account, whether arising from liabilities for breach of trust, constructive trust, contract etc., or on other grounds such as tracing. Further, when the agent cannot explain exactly what has happened to money or property, presumptions may be made against him which will impose substantive

---

[7] See in general Snell, *Equity* (29th ed.), pp. 687 *et seq.*
[8] *Beaumont v. Boultbee* (1802) 7 Ves. 599; *Mackenzie v. Johnston* (1819) 4 Madd. 373.
[9] See esp. *Foley v. Hill* (1848) 2 H.L.Cas. 28; *Navulshaw v. Brownrigg* (1852) 2 De G.M. & G. 441.
[10] *York v. Stowers* [1883] W.N. 174.
[11] *Leslie v. Clifford* (1884) 50 L.T. 590; and see R.S.C., Ord. 43.
[12] This is borne out by the wording of s. 23 of the Limitation Act 1980, which refers to the "claim which is the basis of the duty to account".
[13] Article 51.

liabilities on him. It is also frequently said that the agent has a general fiduciary obligation to account. Although on orthodox doctrine most claims in pursuance of such an obligation are regarded as proprietary, and amount to claims to profits attributable to what has been designated as the principal's property,[14] a more general and less precise notion of accounting (which is particularly relied on in some cases relating to confidential information[15]) may assist also in the development of an equitable action *in personam* against the agent, which would not carry the sometimes inappropriate consequences on bankruptcy of the agent which would follow from a true proprietary claim.[16]

The account. The actual taking of accounts can be a long and complex   **6–095** matter, and it has been said in the context of dissolution of partnership that such a judgment may be "often oppressive."[17]

An agent will usually be held to be bound by his own accounts; thus if they show that he has credited his principal with money received, the agent will be presumed to have received that money and will be liable for it to his principal.[18] But the agent will not be liable if the account shows that the money has not, in fact, been received,[19] or if the principal's accounts show that the agent has not received the money.[20] Similarly, if the agent, after submitting an account which shows money in his hands, later corrects the accounts and the principal does not disagree with such correction,[21] or if the agent shows he has made a mistake, he will not be accountable to his principal.[22]

In an action of account the agent will be allowed to deduct all reasonable expenses incurred on his principal's behalf,[23] unless such deduction is contrary to the terms of the agency agreement.[24]

---

[14] See above, para. 6–044.
[15] See above, paras. 6–076, 6–079.
[16] See *ibid.*; *Warman International Pty Ltd v. Dwyer* (1995) 69 A.L.J.R. 362, 366 *et seq.*
[17] *Lindley and Banks on Partnership* (16th ed.), p. 635. See also *Docker v. Somes* (1834) 2 My. & K. 655, 673; *Wedderburn v. Wedderburn* (1838) 4 My. & Cr. 41.
[18] *Shaw v. Picton* (1825) 4 B. & C. 715. See also *Shaw v. Woodcock* (1827) 7 B. & C. 73 (where the submission of accounts showing amounts received and allowing the principal to draw on the agent for the amounts was held sufficient evidence to go to the jury to establish a personal obligation on the agent to pay); *Skyring v. Greenwood* (1825) 4 B. & C. 281; *Owens v. Kirby* (1861) 30 Beav. 31; *Cave v. Mills* (1862) 7 H. & N. 913. *Quaere* whether personal representatives of the agent are similarly bound: see *Kaland Singh v. Gir Prasad Das* (1913) 17 *Calcutta Weekly Notes* 1060.
[19] *Shaw v. Dartnall* (1826) 6 B. & C. 56, 65.
[20] *Shaw v. Dartnall,* above, at pp. 65–66.
[21] *ibid.*
[22] *Shaw v. Picton* (1825) 4 B. & C. 715; *Dails v. Lloyd* (1848) 12 Q.B. 531; *cf. Worrall v. Peters* (1902) 32 S.C.R. 52.
[23] *Dale v. Sollet* (1767) 4 Burr. 2133 (expenses of fighting an action for principal); *East India Co. v. Blake* (1673) C.temp.F. 117 (entertainment expenses); *cf. Baring v. Stanton* (1876) 3 Ch.D. 502.
[24] See *Bath v. Standard Land Co. Ltd* [1911] 1 Ch. 618.

6–096   **Account stated.** If an account is agreed, the principal can sue on an account stated.[25] This may be a mere acknowledgment of a debt, and in that case the agent may show that no such debt in fact existed; or it may be an account containing debts on both sides in which the parties have agreed that the debts of one should be set against the debts of the other and only the balance paid. In the latter case the agent may only dispute the account where there are items which, if paid, would be recoverable by him on the basis of a total failure of consideration.[26] This second form of account stated is also called a settled account. It is not always clear when an account will be held a settled account. There must be mutual debts, since if all the accounting has to be done by one party, there cannot be a settling of accounts.[27] Once the principal has approved the accounts, they are settled,[28] and if the principal enters the account as agreed in his books and either pays the balance or recognises in some other way that the account is correct, there is also a settled account.[29] It has been held that a principal, who received an account and kept it for two years without objection could not later maintain it was not a settled account.[30] But there will not be a settled account where a principal allows part of his agent's claim but is silent as to the rest.[31]

The general rule is that settled accounts will not be reopened,[32] but the principal may be given leave to surcharge and falsify them, if they are drawn up under a mistake.[33] Thus, where a partnership account recorded £1,950 as lent to the plaintiff, whereas only £1,000 was in fact advanced, it was held that the amount could be corrected without the whole account being reopened.[34]

But where the agent has been guilty of fraud (whether legal or equitable)[35] or the accounts have been settled under undue influence,[36]

---

[25] See also Chitty, *Contracts* (27th ed.), Vol. 1, §§ 29–134 *et seq.*

[26] *Siqueira v. Noronha* [1934] A.C. 332; *Laycock v. Pickles* (1863) 4 B. & S. 497.

[27] *Anglo-American Asphalt Co. Ltd v. Crowley Russell & Co. Ltd* [1945] 2 All E.R. 324.

[28] *East India Co. v. Mainston* (1676) 2 Cas. in Cha. 218.

[29] *Ovington v. Bell* (1812) 3 Camp. 237; *Hunter v. Belcher* (1864) 2 De G.J. & S. 194; *McKellar v. Wallace* (1853) 8 Moo.P.C. 378.

[30] *Tickel v. Short* (1751) 2 Ves.Sen. 239; but see the Canadian case of *Smith v. Redford* (1872) 19 Grant 274.

[31] *Farquhar v. East India Co.* (1845) 8 Beav. 260.

[32] *Parkinson v. Hanbury* (1867) L.R. 2 H.L. 1; Goff and Jones, *Law of Restitution* (4th ed.), pp. 228–229. See also *Re Webb* [1894] 1 Ch. 73.

[33] *Mozeley v. Cowie* (1877) 47 L.J.Ch. 271; *Hardwicke v. Vernon* (1798–99) 4 Ves. 411; *Gething v. Keighley* (1878) 9 Ch.D. 547; *Cheese v. Keen* [1908] 1 Ch. 245. See also R.S.C., Ord. 43, r. 5.

[34] *Gething v. Keighley* (1878) 9 Ch.D. 547; *cf. Daniell v. Sinclair* (1881) 6 App.Cas. 181.

[35] *Beaumont v. Boultbee* (1802) 5 Ves. 485; *Clarke v. Tipping* (1846) 9 Beav. 284, as mentioned by Jessel M.R. in *Williamson v. Barbour* (1877) 9 Ch.D. 529; *Hardwicke v. Vernon* (1808) 14 Ves. 504; *Walsham v. Stainton* (1863) 1 De G.J. & S. 678.

[36] *Watson v. Rodwell* (1879) 11 Ch.D. 150; *Coleman v. Mellersh* (1850) 2 Mac. & G. 309; *Lewes v. Morgan* (1817) 5 Price 42; *Jones v. Moffett* (1846) 3 J. & L. 636; *Ward v. Sharp* (1883) 53 L.J.Ch. 313.

the accounts may be reopened from the commencement of the agency. In such cases lapse of time is no defence and proof of one fraudulent overcharge has been held sufficient to entitle the principal to have the agent's accounts reopened for a period of 20 years.[37] When accounts have been drawn up between fiduciaries and their beneficiaries, the courts have been astute to reopen them if there is any suspicion of underhand dealing.[38] So, where there were incorrect entries, and amounts unexplained and unaccounted for in the accounts of a deceased agent of a company, who was also a large shareholder in the company, his accounts were reopened after his death for a period of 25 years.[39]

The illegality of a transaction entered into by an agent is not a bar to an action by the principal for an account,[40] unless the contract of agency is itself illegal, in which case money paid to the agent may be irrecoverable.[41]

<h3 style="text-align:center">Article 53</h3>

C<small>OMMON</small> L<small>AW</small> D<small>UTY TO</small> P<small>AY</small> O<small>VER</small> M<small>ONEY</small> H<small>ELD TO</small> U<small>SE</small>
OF P<small>RINCIPAL</small>

Subject to the provisions of Article 72, an agent who holds or **6–097** receives money to the use of his principal is bound to pay over or account for that money at the request of his principal, notwithstanding claims made by third persons, even if the money has been received in respect of a void or illegal transaction.[42]

<h3 style="text-align:center">Comment</h3>

The principle expressed in this Article is a principle of common law **6–098** which applies wherever an agent holds money to the use of his principal. Thus if the agent has received money on his principal's behalf, or if the agent in breach of his duty to the principal has received a bribe, the

---

[37] *Williamson v. Barbour* (1877) 9 Ch.D. 529; *Coleman v. Mellersh* (1850) 2 Mac. & G. 309.

[38] *Williamson v. Barbour,* above; *Re Webb* [1894] 1 Ch. 73; *Cheese v. Keen* [1908] 1 Ch. 245; *cf. Newman v. Payne* (1793) 2 Ves. 199.

[39] *Stainton v. Carron Co.* (1857) 24 Beav. 346.

[40] *Williams v. Trye* (1854) 18 Beav. 366.

[41] *Knowles v. Haughton* (1805) 11 Ves. 168; *Battersby v. Smyth* (1818) 3 Madd. 110; *Sykes v. Beadon* (1879) 11 Ch.D. 170; and see Article 53.

[42] See, *e.g. Edgell v. Day* (1865) L.R. 1 C.P. 80; *Blaustein v. Maltz, Mitchell & Co.* [1937] 2 K.B. 142, Illustration 7 to Article 56; *Eames v. Hacon* (1881) 18 Ch.D. 347, Illustration 6 to Article 56; *Nickolson v. Knowles* (1820) 5 Madd. 47; *Harsant v. Blaine, Macdonald & Co.* (1887) 56 L.J.Q.B. 511; *Martin v. Pont* [1993] 3 N.Z.L.R. 25, Illustration 6; Goff and Jones, *Law of Restitution* (4th ed.), pp. 515–516; see also Illustrations 1, 2.

principal can sue the agent in restitution.[43] Further, if the principal has entrusted money to his agent for a particular purpose which the agent has not carried out, the principal can recover that money on the same basis.[44] When available, such common law actions in restitution have long been alternatives to an account.[45] Where the money can be regarded as held in trust, however, a proprietary remedy will be available, and may be preferable.[46]

The principal cannot make his claim in restitution until the agent has either received the money[47] or has been credited with it in his own account with a third party.[48] This does not mean that the principal must wait until the agent admits he has received the money; if, for example, the principal employs an agent to sell goods for him and the agent does not account to the principal within a reasonable time, it may be presumed in the absence of evidence to the contrary that the agent has received money for the goods.[49] It is not settled whether demand has to be made by the principal for his money before he can start his action against the agent, but on general principles it seems that the right to money held to the principal's use accrues as soon as it comes into the agent's hands and that no demand should be necessary.[50] It may be, however, that a claim for interest on such a claim will only run from the date of a demand for payment and its refusal.[51]

An agent usually discharges his liability by handing over the money or property he has received to his principal, but he may also pay a third party in accordance with the principal's instructions[52]; he will also be discharged if he pays a third party in obedience to the instructions of the

---

[43] Powell, pp. 324–326: *Eisentrager v. Lyneham* [1952] St.R.Qd. 232. See Article 50.

[44] *Parry v. Roberts* (1835) 3 A. & E. 118; *Hill v. Smith* (1844) 12 M. & W. 618; *Martin v. Pont*, n. 42 above; *cf. Thomas v. Da Costa* (1818) 8 Taunt. 345, *Livingstone v. Elmslie* (1902) 21 N.Z.L.R. 640 (money paid by husband to be paid to wife on her obtaining a divorce could not be recovered). Probably an action for money had and received will not lie against an agent entrusted with money for a particular purpose until the agent violates his duty by applying it for some other purpose, or otherwise shows an intention not to be bound by his obligation: *Hardman v. Bellhouse* (1842) 9 M. & W. 596; *Ehrensperger v. Anderson* (1848) 3 Exch. 148; *Whitehead v. Howard* (1820) 2 B. & B. 372.

[45] Stoljar, pp. 301–302.

[46] See above, paras. 6-042—6-043.

[47] *Varden v. Parker* (1798) 2 Esp. 710.

[48] *Andrew v. Robinson* (1812) 3 Camp. 199; but if the principal and the third party have a common agent, an entry in the books of such agent will not be conclusive: see *McLarty v. Middleton* (1858) 6 W.R. 379; 9 W.R. 861.

[49] *Hunter v. Welsh* (1816) 1 Stark. 224.

[50] There are confusing dicta in actions for money paid under a mistake of fact: see *Freeman v. Jeffries* (1869) L.R. 4 Ex. 189; *Baker v. Courage & Co.* [1910] 1 K.B. 56; see further Goff and Jones, *Law of Restitution* (4th ed.), pp. 124–125.

[51] See, *e.g.* *Edgell v. Day* (1865) L.R. 1 C.P. 80; *Harsant v. Blaine, Macdonald & Co.* (1887) 56 L.J.Q.B. 511. See also Article 54.

[52] *McCarthy v. Colvin* (1839) 9 A. & E. 607; *Blyth v. Whiffin* (1872) 27 L.T. 330, 333.

court.[53] Furthermore, an agent, in accounting for money received to the use of his principal, is entitled to set off all just allowances and any sums expended by him with the authority of the principal,[54] even if they were spent for an unlawful purpose[55]; but if the authority to deal with the money in an unlawful manner is revoked before the agent has used the money, the principal can recover.[56]

Even though the agent receives money for his principal in respect of a transaction which is void or illegal, the principal can sue his agent in restitution. Thus if an agent is employed to make bets and he wins money, he must pay it over to the principal, although the betting transactions are themselves void[57]; similarly, if an agent is employed to sell shares, he cannot retain the money he receives by saying that the sale is illegal by Act of Parliament.[58] But if the contract between the principal and agent is itself illegal, then the principal cannot recover any money received by the agent. The reason is that since both parties are equally to blame, the court will not assist the plaintiff: *ex turpi causa non oritur actio.*[59]

---

[53] *Brown v. Farebrother* (1888) 58 L.J.Ch. 3.

[54] *Dale v. Sollett* (1767) 4 Burr. 2133; *Curtis v. Barclay* (1826) 5 B. & C. 141; *Wemys v. Greenwood, Cox and Hammersley* (1827) 5 L.J.(o.s.) K.B. 257; *Potter v. Fowler* (1837) 6 L.J.Ch. 273; *Cropper v. Cook* (1868) L.R. 3 C.P. 194; *Roxburghe v. Cox* (1881) 17 Ch.D. 520; cf. *Monkwearmouth Flour Mill Co. Ltd v. Lightfoot* (1897) 13 T.L.R. 327; *Dorf v. Neumann, Luebeck & Co.* (1924) 40 T.L.R. 405; *Bath v. Standard Land Co. Ltd* [1911] 1 Ch. 618. The agent cannot retain money where his right to do so has not yet accrued: *Wilkinson v. North Surburban Properties Ltd* [1959] E.G.D. 218. In contracts for work and labour the defendant may have the right to make deductions in respect of defective performance of contractual services: see, *e.g. Hanak v. Green* [1958] 2 Q.B. 9. Such deductions cannot be made in respect of a claim for marine freight: *Aries Tanker Corp. v. Total Transport Ltd (The Aries)* [1977] 1 W.L.R. 185; and this exception has been held to apply also to a claim against an agent for freight: *James & Co. v. Chinecrest Ltd* [1979] 1 Lloyd's Rep. 126.

[55] *Bayntun v. Cattle* (1833) 1 Moo. & R. 265.

[56] *Bone v. Ekless* (1860) 5 H. & N. 925; *Taylor v. Bowers* (1876) 1 Q.B.D. 291.

[57] *De Mattos v. Benjamin* (1894) 63 L.J.Q.B. 248, Illustration 3; *Bridger v. Savage* (1885) 15 Q.B.D. 363; overruling *Beyer v. Adams* (1857) 26 L.J.Ch. 841. But cf. *A.R. Dennis & Co. v. Campbell* [1978] Q.B. 365. See also Treitel, *Law of Contract* (9th ed.), pp. 478–479.

[58] *Bousfield v. Wilson* (1846) 16 M. & W. 185; *Tenant v. Elliot* (1797) 1 B. & P. 3; *Farmer v. Russell* (1798) 1 B. & P. 296; *Sharp v. Taylor* (1849) 2 Ph. 801; see also *Sykes v. Beadon* (1879) 11 Ch.D. 170; *Thomson v. Thomson* (1802) 7 Ves. 470.

[59] *Booth v. Hodgson* (1795) 6 T.R. 405; *Catlin v. Bell* (1815) 4 Camp. 183; *Knowles v. Haughton* (1805) 11 Ves. 168; *Battersby v. Smyth* (1818) 3 Madd. 110, with which cf. *Davenport v. Whitmore* (1836) 2 My. & Cr. 177; *Harry Parker Ltd v. Mason* [1940] 2 K.B. 590, Illustration 2. The question whether a principal should be able to recover money illegally paid to his agent is difficult. The *Restatement*, § 412, adopts the general rule that the agent should be liable to pay over the proceeds of an illegal act to his principal unless to do so would be to commit a crime, or they were obtained by committing a crime or for the purpose of committing a crime or for the purpose of committing a very serious crime. See also, generally, Goff and Jones, *Law of Restitution* (4th ed.), pp. 515–516; Merkin (1981) 97 L.Q.R. 420, 437–439.

Where money is wrongfully obtained by an agent or is paid to him under a mistake of fact or for a consideration which wholly fails he can resist an action by his principal on the grounds that he has repaid it to the person who paid it to him[60]; and where money is paid to an agent in respect of a voidable contract, he can show that the contract has been rescinded and the money repaid, even where the contract was rescinded solely on the ground of his own fraud.[61]

Where an agent is appointed by two or more persons jointly, he is not discharged unless he accounts to them all, except where the principals are partners.[62] But an agent who has been severally appointed by one person cannot refuse to account separately to him on the ground that others are jointly interested in the money in the agent's hands.[63]

Illustrations

6–099   (1)   B granted an annuity to C and D guaranteed the payment of the instalments. B was in arrears with his instalments and at the same time owed money for another reason to C's agent, E. E made an application to B and D for the payment of the instalments and as a result of this application and D's insistence B paid a sum of money to E. Held, E could not keep the money as payment for his own debt but had received it on C's behalf and must account for it.[64]

(2)   P employed A to place £12,000 in bets on a horse in a race at Nottingham, and relied on A's false representations that they could make the bets without affecting the starting price by placing £6,000 with street bookmakers and the rest with bookmakers all over the country. This was contrary to the Street Betting Act 1906, which prohibited bets with street bookmakers, and there was also a conspiracy to make a sham bet on another horse in order to deceive the public. The horse lost and P paid A £11,875, which represented the full sum due to A less a small amount which A owed P. When P discovered that A had never placed the money at all in the belief that the horse would lose, he claimed the return of the money as had and received to his use. Held, as the money had been handed to A for an illegal purpose, P could not recover any of the money he had paid.[65]

---

[60] See Article 113.

[61] *Murray v. Mann* (1848) 2 Exch. 538, Illustration 4; *cf. Stevens v. Legh* (1853) 2 C.L.R. 251 and *Field v. Allen* (1842) 9 M. & W. 694.

[62] *Lee v. Sankey* (1872) L.R. 15 Eq. 204; *Innes v. Stephenson* (1831) 1 M. & R. 145; for authority to the contrary see *Husband v. Davis* (1851) 10 C.B. 645. See Article 11.

[63] *Roberts v. Ogilby* (1821) 9 Price 269; and see *Suart v. Welch* (1839) 4 Myl. & Cr. 305; Article 56.

[64] *Shaw v. Picton* (1825) 4 B. & C. 715.

[65] *Harry Parker Ltd v. Mason* [1940] 2 K.B. 590.

(3)   A turf commission agent is employed to make bets. He must pay over to the principal the amount of any winnings actually received by him in respect of such bets, though the bets themselves are void by the Gaming Act 1845, and though in consequence of the Gaming Act 1892 he would not be able to recover from the principal the amount of any losses paid in respect of the bets.[66]

(4)   An agent sells a horse and receives the purchase-money. The sale is subsequently rescinded on the ground of the agent's fraud, and the purchase-money is repaid. The agent is not liable to the principal for the amount of the purchase-money.[67]

(5)   A factor raises money by wrongfully pledging the goods of his principal. The principal may adopt the transaction, and treat the money raised as money had and received to his use.[68]

(6)   P gives money to an accountant to invest. The accountant's daughter misappropriates it. The accountant is liable for its return.[69]

Article 54

LIABILITY FOR INTEREST

(1)   Where an agent holds money which belongs in law or equity to his principal, any interest earned in respect of that money belongs to the principal, and the agent must account to him for it.   **6–100**

(2)   Subject to the discretion of the court under section 35A of the Supreme Court Act 1981,[70] an agent who receives money in breach of his fiduciary duties, or who fails to pay his principal on demand, must pay interest on it from the date of his default.

Comment

Rule (1). If the agent holds money as trustee for his principal, he may not keep for himself anything earned with that money.[71] The claim for interest is alternative to a proprietary claim for profits[72] and sometimes merely interest is claimed because of the difficulty of establishing what   **6–101**

---

[66] *De Mattos v. Benjamin* (1894) 63 L.J.Q.B. 248; *Bridger v. Savage* (1885) 15 Q.B.D. 363.

[67] *Murray v. Mann* (1848) 2 Exch. 538.

[68] *Bonzi v. Stewart* (1842) 5 Scott N.R. 1, 26; 4 M. & G. 295.

[69] *Martin v. Pont* [1993] 3 N.Z.L.R. 25.

[70] Added by Administration of Justice Act 1982, s. 15.

[71] See *Att.-Gen. v. Alford* (1855) 4 De G.M. & G. 843; *Brown v. I.R.C.* [1965] A.C. 244; above, paras. 6–042 *et seq.*

[72] *Re Davis* [1902] 2 Ch. 314.

the profits are, or because the result has been not to make a profit but to effect a saving. When the agent is under a duty to invest and does not do so, he may under this head be liable for the interest which should have been received.[73] It is not, however, clear exactly when such a duty arises; there are dicta suggesting that a holder of trust money is always liable for interest if he knows that the money has this character,[74] but there are cases holding that there is no liability where it is proved that no profit was made.[75]

6–102   **Estate agents.** In *Potters (A Firm) v. Loppert*[76] Pennycuick V.-C. held that an estate agent was under no obligation to account for the interest earned by him on a sum deposited with him to hold as stakeholder. The decision related to a pre-contract deposit, but the reasoning applies equally to contract deposits. The basis of the decision was that the agent was not a trustee and was liable only in contract or restitution. A better reason for the rule might be that although the agent holds as trustee, there is a usage that he is entitled to the income in return for his services in holding the deposit.[77] The rule is of ancient origin[78] and it is open to question whether such a rule is appropriate to modern times, particularly in view of the size of some deposits on commercial and other property. It is now however provided by the Estate Agents Act 1979 that money received in the course of estate agency work by way of pre-contract or contract deposit is held on trust[79] and must be paid into a client account[80]; there is provision for

---

[73] *Burdick v. Garrick* (1870) L.R. 5 Ch.App. 233, Illustration 2. As to the amount of interest see Snell, *Equity* (29th ed.), pp. 288–289; *Supreme Court Practice*, 1995, 6/2/9 *et seq.*

[74] *Moons v. De Barnales* (1826) 1 Russ. 301; *Att.-Gen. v. Alford*, n. 71 above, at p. 851; and see Finn, *Fiduciary Obligations* (1977), pp. 114–115.

[75] *e.g. Turner v. Burkinshaw* (1867) L.R. 2 Ch.App. 488.

[76] [1973] Ch. 399.

[77] See Goode (1976) 92 L.Q.R. at p. 371, n. 44.

[78] Pennycuick V.-C. followed *Harrington v. Hoggart* (1830) 1 B. & Ad. 577, a case concerning an auctioneer decided in the Court of King's Bench which was a claim in assumpsit not based upon principles of equity. However the court cited an unreported dictum of Lord Eldon and upon this basis said that their decision was not at variance with any rule of equity. (Yet the case had been argued partly on the basis that the agent was a trustee and therefore not obliged to obey the instructions of the vendor to put the money out to earn interest). The defendant auctioneer was treated as if he were a banker and his position was contrasted with that of an agent. See also below, Illustrations 1–3 to Article 113; *Royal Norwegian Government v. Calcutta Marine Engineering Co. Ltd* [1960] 2 Lloyd's Rep. 431.

[79] ss. 12, 13. "Estate agency work" is defined in s. 1 and applies only to some of the work performed by estate agents. See in general Murdoch, *The Estate Agents and Property Misdescriptions Acts* (3rd ed.), Chap. 13D; *Law of Estate Agency and Auctions* (3rd ed.), pp. 220 *et seq.*

[80] s. 14.

the making of accounts regulations requiring payment of interest.[81] These detailed requirements supersede the normal consequences of a trusteeship in such cases[82]; but the regulations made do not in fact require payment of interest on money received as stakeholder.[83]

Solicitors. A solicitor may hold property on trust, depending on the   **6–103** circumstances.[84] In many cases however money held for clients is paid into general client account. In *Brown v. I.R.C.*[85] it was held that the solicitor had no right to the interest earned on such money, whatever the difficulty of accounting as between the clients concerned. The matter was subsequently regulated by statute[86] under which rules may be made providing for payment of interest on client accounts[87]: beyond this no interest is due.[88] It is apparently assumed that these rules are not applicable to money received as stakeholder.

Financial services. For details on this topic the reader is referred to   **6–104** specialised works.[89]

Rate of interest. The rate of interest may vary in accordance with   **6–105** whether the agent has, or may be presumed to have, made more money by his breach, or whether the misconduct is serious.[90] Old cases used 4 per cent on the basic simple interest rate, with 5 per cent and compound interest for the special cases. However, more recently, and not surprisingly, higher rates have been ordered.[91]

Rule (2). In general there was no right to interest on money received   **6–106** for a principal and not held in trust unless the agent was guilty of a breach of fiduciary obligation or refused to pay his principal on demand.

---

[81] s. 15.

[82] s. 13(3).

[83] See Estate Agents (Accounts) Regulations 1981 (S.I. 1981 No. 1520), reg. 7.

[84] *e.g. Burdick v. Garrick* (1870) L.R. 5 Ch.App. 233, Illustration 2.

[85] [1965] A.C. 244, Illustration 1.

[86] See Solicitors Act 1974, ss. 32, 33.

[87] Solicitors Accounts Rules, 1986; Solicitors' Trust Accounts Rules 1986; Solicitors Accounts (Deposit Interest) Rules 1988.

[88] Solicitors Act 1974, s. 33(3).

[89] See Financial Services Act 1986, ss. 48, 55, 63A; Lomnicka and Powell, *Encyclopedia of Financial Services Law* (1987); *Financial Services: Law and Practice* (1994).

[90] See *Burdick v. Garrick* (1870) L.R. 5 Ch.App. 233, 241–242; *Wallersteiner v. Moir (No. 2)* [1975] Q.B. 373, 397; Snell, *Equity* (29th ed.), pp. 288–289; Finn, *Fiduciary Obligations* (1977), pp. 115–117; *Supreme Court Practice*, 1995, 6/2/9 *et seq.*

[91] *Wallersteiner v. Moir (No. 2)*, n. 90 above. And see *O'Sullivan v. Management Agency and Music Ltd* [1985] Q.B. 428.

In these latter cases there was such a right in equity though not at common law,[92] and the same considerations as those mentioned above were applicable in calculating the rate of interest. The decisions on this point were largely rendered obsolete by section 3 of the Law Reform (Miscellaneous Provisions) Act 1934, which gave the court a wide discretion to award interest on all or any part of any debt or damages for which judgment is given at such rate as it thinks fit for the whole or any part of the period between the date when the cause of action arose and judgment. These powers are now contained in the Supreme Court Act 1981 as amended.[93] The 1934 provision used the words "proceedings tried" and thus did not apply to a default judgment, nor perhaps to certain other situations. In such cases it was sometimes still necessary to rely on the equitable rather than on the statutory jurisdiction.[94] The wording of the (amended) Supreme Court Act, referring simply to "proceedings ... before the High Court," is wider.[95] There is still, however, no power to award interest where money is paid after delay but before proceedings for recovery have begun.

Illustrations

6–107 (1) A solicitor held sums of money on deposit in his clients' account. This account earned interest which, in accordance with common practice, the solicitor kept for himself as part of the profits of his firm. Held, the solicitor was in a fiduciary position in relation to his clients and that the interest accordingly belonged to them. The practice of the solicitor retaining the interest for himself could not be permitted.[96]

(2) A solicitor was authorised by power of attorney to sell certain property and invest the proceeds. He paid the proceeds into the account of his firm, who made use of the money. Held, that he must pay interest at the rate of 5 per cent.[97]

---

[92] See *e.g. Pearse v. Green* (1819) 1 J. & W. 135; *Wolfe v. Findlay* (1847) 6 Hare 66; *Edgell v. Day* (1865) L.R. 1 C.P. 80; *Harsant v. Blaine, Macdonald & Co.* (1887) 56 L.J.Q.B. 511; *Boston Deep Sea Fishing and Ice Co. v. Ansell* (1888) 39 Ch.D. 339; *Barclay v. Harris* (1915) 85 L.J.K.B. 115; *Webster v. British Empire Mutual Life Assurance Co.* (1880) 15 Ch.D. 169.

[93] S. 35A, inserted by Administration of Justice Act 1982, s. 15. See *Supreme Court Practice*, 1991, 6/2/9/ *et seq.*

[94] See *Wallersteiner v. Moir (No. 2)* [1975] Q.B. 373; *Gardner Steel Ltd v. Sheffield Bros. (Profiles) Ltd* [1978] 1 W.L.R. 916.

[95] *President of India v. La Pintada Compania Navigacion S.A. (The La Pintada)* [1985] A.C. 104; *cf. Hungerfords v. Walker* (1989) 171 C.L.R. 125.

[96] *Brown v. I.R.C.* [1965] A.C. 244. The problems presented to solicitors by this case have been met in part by the Solicitors Accounts (Deposit Interest) Rules 1988, made under the Solicitors Act 1974, ss. 32 and 33.

[97] *Burdick v. Garrick* (1870) L.R. 5 Ch.App. 233. *Cf. Chedworth v. Edwards* (1802) 8 Ves. Jun. 48.

(3)   An agent, who undertook to invest his principal's money in the funds, kept large balances in his hands. Held, that he must pay interest on such balances.[98]

Article 55

AGENT ACQUIRING LAND IN OWN NAME

If an agent who agrees to acquire land on behalf of his principal **6–108** acquires it in his own name or on his own behalf he becomes a trustee of it for his principal.[99]

Comment

An agent must not retain any property or money which ought to **6–109** belong to his principal. This Article is concerned with the situation where an agent is employed for a specific purpose, *e.g.* to purchase land for his principal. The rule, however, is not limited to purchases; it applies, for example, to leases. Thus, where an agent took a lease in his own name which he had been instructed to take jointly for himself and his principal, it was decided that he held it on trust for the benefit of both himself and his principal.[1]

The assumption behind this rule is that at least in the case of land, neither a disclosed nor an undisclosed principal can claim that conveyance to the agent vests property in the principal. This rule is at least to some extent based on the special methods required for the conveyance of land and the strict rules as to deeds. It is conceivable that in the case of chattels an undisclosed principal at least may sometimes claim that property is by transfer to his agent vested in him, rather than held on trust.[2]

If the agent purports to sell to the principal the property which he has acquired in his own name (and which he therefore holds on trust), the

---

[98] *Browne v. Southouse* (1790) 3 Bro.C.C. 107; *Barwell v. Parker* (1751) 2 Ves. 364.

[99] *Lees v. Nuttall* (1829) 1 Russ. & M. 53; (1834) 2 Myl. & K. 819; *Austin v. Chambers* (1837) 6 C. & F. 1, 36–40. In *Bartlett v. Pickersgill* (1760) 1 Cox 15 and *James v. Smith* [1891] 1 Ch. 384; affd. (1892) 65 L.T. 544, there was held to be a trust in favour of the principal, but one which he could not enforce as it did not comply with s. 7 of the Statute of Frauds. In *Rochefoucauld v. Boustead* [1897] 1 Ch. 196 this limitation was overruled but the cases are still authority for the principle expressed in the Article. See also *Taylor v. Salmon* (1838) 4 Myl. & Cr. 134, 139; *Trench v. Harrison* (1849) 17 Sim. 111; *Cave v. Mackenzie* (1877) 46 L.J.Ch. 564. See further Comment to Article 9; Youdan [1984] C.L.J. 306.

[1] *Atkins v. Rowe* (1728) Mos. 39; *Taylor v. Salmon*, n. 99 above; *Raleigh v. McGrath* (1877) 3 V.L.R. 250.

[2] See Article 91.

sale is of no effect, since the agent is already holding it on trust for his principal. Accordingly, the principal can recover from the agent anything he has paid in excess of the price paid by the agent for the property. It also follows that the agent holds this excess on trust for the principal until it is claimed from him.[3]

Illustration

6–110   A agrees with B to bid at an auction for property which they both want and promises that if he acquires it he will cede part to B. A holds that part on trust for B and cannot claim to own the whole.[4]

3.—ESTOPPEL

Article 56

AGENT'S ESTOPPEL AS TO PRINCIPAL'S TITLE

6–111   (1) Where an agent is in possession of property in his capacity as agent, he is estopped from asserting that he has a better title to it than his principal, for his possession is deemed to be that of his principal.[5]

(2) An agent is estopped from asserting that a third party has a better right than his principal to receive money held by him as agent for or on account of his principal or owed by him as agent to his principal.[6]

(3) But an agent who is a bailee of chattels from his principal as bailor may in any action for wrongful interference with them show that a third party has a better right than his principal as respects all or any part of the interest claimed by the principal or in right of which he sues.[7]

Comment

6–112   Although the word "estoppel" is not much used in the cases relating to these propositions, the first and second constitute situations where an agent is not allowed to make such allegations against his principal, and they can conveniently be regarded as based on a form of estoppel. The

---

[3] cf. *Regier v. Campbell-Stuart* [1939] Ch. 766, Illustration 16 to Article 47, and *Bentley v. Craven* (1853) 18 Beav. 75.

[4] *Chattock v. Muller* (1878) 8 Ch.D. 177; applied in *Pallant v. Morgan* [1953] Ch. 43.

[5] *Cooper v. De Tastet* (1829) Tamlyn 177, 179; *Williams v. Pott* (1871) L.R. 12 Eq. 149, 151.

[6] *Blaustein v. Maltz, Mitchell & Co.* [1937] 2 K.B. 142, Illustration 7.

[7] Torts (Interference with Goods) Act 1977, s. 8(1).

third was formerly a case where estoppel reasoning was articulately applied: but this has been reversed by statute.

An agent who is in possession of property in his capacity as agent cannot acquire title against his principal under the Limitation Act, for he is estopped from denying that his possession is that of the principal. [8]

"An agent cannot well get an adverse title, unless he can very distinctly shew that what he has done is in respect of title, and not in respect of his agency". [9]

Moreover, an agent may not set up his own title as true owner against a prescriptive title acquired by his principal through him. Thus, where an agent received rents for 25 years and paid them to his principal, it was the principal who acquired the statutory title by limitation, since the agent was not permitted to deny that the principal acquired it through him. [10]

Again, if the agent has received money for his principal as a result of his agency he cannot assert that a third party has a better right to receive it than his principal. [11]

"The law is perfectly clear that an agent receiving money rightfully for his principal is not liable in respect of that money to the owner of the money even where the principal, upon receiving it, would be bound to pay it over to the owner." [12]

This rule applies where the relationship between principal and agent is merely that of creditor and debtor. A *fortiori* the agent cannot assert a third party's rights to money which he holds as trustee for his principal.

Until recently there was a third rule whereby an agent was prevented from making a claim adverse to his principal, and here the term estoppel was more frequently used. [13] Where the agent was also a bailee

---

[8] *Ward v. Carttar* (1865) L.R. 1 Eq. 29, Illustration 2; *Smith v. Bennett* (1874) 30 L.T. 100; *Lyell v. Kennedy* (1889) 14 App.Cas. 437, Illustration 1. He must possess as agent and not in any other capacity, but it is for the agent to prove that he was not acting as agent, and the burden of proof is heavy: *White v. Bayley* (1861) 10 C.B.(N.S.) 227; *Markwick v. Hardingham* (1880) 15 Ch.D. 339; *Re Hobbs* (1887) 36 Ch.D. 553; *Bell v. Marsh* [1903] 1 Ch. 528.

[9] *Att.-Gen. v. Corporation of London* (1850) 2 Mac. & G. 247, 259, *per* Lord Cottenham L.C.

[10] *Williams v. Pott* (1871) L.R. 12 Eq. 149, Illustration 3.

[11] *Dixon v. Hamond* (1819) 2 B. & A. 310, Illustration 5; *Roberts v. Ogilby* (1821) 9 Price 269, Illustration 5; *Suart v. Welch* (1839) 4 Myl. & Cr. 305; *Eames v. Hacon* (1881) 18 Ch.D. 347, Illustration 6; *Davie v. Sachs* [1911] Cape P.D. 992; *Mangena v. Moyatusi* [1918] App.D. 650; *Blaustein v. Maltz, Mitchell & Co.* [1937] 2 K.B. 142, Illustration 7. However, it seems that the agent may deny his principal's title to money (or chattels) received by the agent as a result of the principal's fraud on a third party: *Field v. Allen* (1842) 9 M. & W. 694; *Murray v. Mann* (1848) 2 Exch. 538; *Cheesman v. Exall* (1851) 6 Exch. 341.

[12] *Blaustein v. Maltz, Mitchell & Co.,* n. 11 above, at p. 156, *per* Scott L.J.

[13] e.g. *Kahler v. Midland Bank Ltd* [1950] A.C. 24, 38.

of his principal, he was bound by a rule that a bailee may not assert that a third party has a better right to the property than has the bailor. [14] There were exceptions to this: a bailee might rely on a third party's title if he had handed the goods over to him or if he defended the bailor's claim by authority of and on behalf of the third party. [15] The exceptions did not apply if the bailee had accepted the bailment or attorned to the bailor with knowledge of the third party's claim. [16]

But now by virtue of section 8(1) of the Torts (Interference with Goods) Act 1977, "in any action for wrongful interference with goods the defendant is entitled to show, in accordance with rules of court, that a third party has a better right than the plaintiff as respects all or part of the interest claimed by the plaintiff or in right of which he sues, and any rule of law (sometimes called *jus tertii*) to the contrary is abolished." The purpose of this legislation was in general to end multiplicity of actions[17]; and to that end the defendant's proper course is to apply for joinder of the named *tertius*. [18]

Illustrations

6–113   (1)   A receives the rents of certain properties as an agent, and pays them into a separate account at his own bank. The principal dies intestate. A continues to receive the rents for more than 12 years after the death of the principal, stating to several of the tenants that he is acting for the heir, whoever he may be. Thirteen years afterwards, a purchaser from the heir brings an action against A, claiming possession of the property and an account of the rents and profits. A claims the property as his own, and pleads the Statute of Limitations. The plaintiff is entitled to possession of the property, and an account of all the rents and profits received by A, which were held in trust. [19]

(2)   A solicitor paid off a mortgage debt due from a client, and entered into possession of the mortgaged property. Held, that he must

---

[14] Clerk and Lindsell, *Torts* (16th ed.) § 21–77; Palmer, *Bailment* (2nd ed.), pp. 265 *et seq.*; Spencer Bower, *Estoppel by Representation* (3rd ed.), pp. 211 *et seq.*
[15] *Biddle v. Bond* (1865) 6 B. & S. 225; *Rogers, Sons & Co. v. Lambert & Co.* [1891] 1 Q.B. 318; *Ross v. Edwards & Co.* (1895) 73 L.T. 100; *Kahler v. Midland Bank Ltd* [1950] A.C. 24.
[16] *Re Sadler, ex p. Davies* (1881) 19 Ch.D. 86; *Eastern Construction Co. Ltd v. National Trust Co. and Schmidt* [1914] A.C. 197, 210; *Wilson v. Lombank* [1963] 1 W.L.R. 1294, 1297.
[17] See Law Reform Committee, 18th Report, Cmnd. 4774 (1971), §§ 51–78; Clerk and Lindsell, *Torts* (16th ed.), §§ 21–79, 21–80; Palmer; *Bailment* (2nd ed.), pp. 283 *et seq.* See also *De Franco v. Commissioner of Police for the Metropolis, The Times*, May 8, 1987.
[18] See s. 8(2) of the Act; R.S.C., Ord. 15, r. 10A.
[19] *Lyell v. Kennedy* (1889) 14 App.Cas. 437. And see *Smith v. Bennett* (1874) 30 L.T. 100.

be taken to have acted as the agent of the client, and therefore (a) was not a mortgagee in possession, and (b) was not entitled to set up the Statute of Limitations in an action by the client for redemption.[20]

(3) A receives the rents of certain property as B's agent for more than 12 years, and duly pays them over to B. B thereby acquires a good prescriptive title to the property, in the absence of fraud, even if A was the true owner.[21]

(4) A makes advances for the purpose of a mine, in order to obtain ore, which he consigns to B for sale, B undertaking to account to him for the proceeds. B cannot set up any paramount title to the ore, or dispute A's right to the proceeds, on the ground that there are rights of third persons existing independently of the contract between A and B.[22]

(5) A ship which is the property of A is transferred to B as security for a debt. B insures the ship for and on behalf of A & Co., and charges them with the premiums. The ship is lost, and B receives the insurance money. B must pay over the money, after deducting the amount of his debt, to A & Co., and cannot set up A's title, having insured for and on behalf of A & Co.[23] So an insurance broker who receives money under a policy cannot dispute the claim of his principal on the ground that other persons are interested in the subject-matter of the insurance.[24]

(6) E died intestate in Ireland and letters of administration were granted to P. Part of E's assets were in India and P sent a power of attorney to F & Co., who obtained letters of administration for the benefit of P. They collected his Indian assets, paid his debts and sent the assets to A, their English agents. A refused to hand the assets over to P without the concurrence of E's next-of-kin. Held (the next-of-kin making no claim), A could not set up any third party's title against P.[25]

(7) B was engaged to Miss J. Her father, J, gave him a cheque for £172.10s., the amount of the deposit on the intended matrimonial home, as a gift conditional on the marriage taking place. B paid the cheque into his bank account and sent his own cheque for the same sum to the estate agent, B then instructed M (who was J's son-in-law) to act for him as solicitor in the purchase of the house. The engagement between B and Miss J was broken off and B instructed M to reclaim the deposit, which he did. M refused to pay B the amount of the deposit

---

[20] *Ward v. Carttar* (1865) L.R. 1 Eq. 29.
[21] *Williams v. Pott* (1871) L.R. 12 Eq. 149.
[22] *Zulueta v. Vinent* (1852) 1 De G.M. & G. 315. But see Illustration 8.
[23] *Dixon v. Hamond* (1819) 2 B. & A. 310.
[24] *Roberts v. Ogilby* (1821) 9 Price 269. But if money is paid by B to A to hold for P, it cannot be claimed by P until A has acknowledged the agency: *Wediake v. Hurley* (1830) 1 C. & J. 83; *Stephens v. Badcock* (1832) 3 B. & Ad. 354; Article 114.
[25] *Eames v. Hacon* (1881) 18 Ch.D. 347.

since J had ordered him not to do so and had told M to account to J for it. Held, (i) the relationship between B and M was that of principal (creditor) and agent (debtor); (ii) the principle of *jus tertii* as applied to bailments had no application to a sum of money; and (iii) M could not plead J's orders and must account to B for the money.[26]

(8) A wrongfully distrains B's goods and delivers them to C, an auctioneer, for sale, C having at the time no knowledge of B's adverse claim. B subsequently gives notice of his title to C, and claims the proceeds.[27] C may now, if sued by A, apply for B to be joined as a party.[28]

---

[26] *Blaustein v. Maltz, Mitchell & Co.* [1937] 2 K.B. 142.

[27] cf. *Biddle v. Bond* (1865) 6 B. & S. 225; *Rogers & Co. v. Lambert & Co.* [1891] 1 Q.B. 318; *Ross v. Edwards & Co.* (1895) 73 L.T. 100.

[28] Torts (Interference with Goods) Act 1977, s. 8; see Comment; and in the context of auctioneers Murdoch, *Law of Estate Agency and Auctions* (3rd ed.), pp. 301–304.

CHAPTER 7

RIGHTS OF AGENTS AGAINST THEIR PRINCIPALS

Introductory Note

Duties of co-operation. Legal systems which categorise types of agent **7–001** and seek to lay down the incidents of the various legal relationships may well prescribe duties of principals towards their agents just as they prescribe duties of agents towards their principals. English law however has traditionally viewed the principal as the person requiring protection, against wrongful use of the agent's powers, and have paid little attention to the position of the agent. Thus it was long ago held that the principal was under no duty to account on a fiduciary basis to the agent[1]; and in general the view that the principal has fiduciary duties towards the agent is not one that is often put forward. Equally, the limited body of law relating to the common law duties owed by agents towards their principals has no obvious counterpart concerning duties owed towards agents by their principals.

The fiduciary duties of an agent are however acknowledged to be manifestations of a wider principle which is not confined to agents, and there can be no general reason why a principal should not find himself under a fiduciary responsibility towards his agent, even if the situation would be rarer than those imposing fiduciary responsibilities on the agent.[2] So also there can be no objection to a principal being liable to his agent in tort: the existence of a contractual action between them may regulate or modify the duties owed, but does not exclude tort liability based on general principles.[3] As to contract, however, parties drafting agency contracts (or related contracts such as distributorship

---

[1] *Padwick v. Stanley* (1852) 9 Hare 627; *cf. Padwick v. Hurst* (1854) 18 Beav. 575.

[2] Fiduciary duties in a franchisor were denied in *Jirna v. Mister Donut of Canada Ltd* (1973) 40 D.L.R. (3d) 303; criticised by Shepherd (1981) 97 L.Q.R. 51, 59; and see Brown (1971) 49 Tex.L.Rev. 650, suggesting that franchising should be regarded as creating a fiduciary relationship. But see *Hospital Products Ltd v. U.S. Surgical Corp.* (1984) 156 C.L.R. 41 *per* Mason and Deane JJ. (on *duties* of a distributor). *cf.* para. 6–039, n. 8.

[3] *Henderson v. Merrett Syndicates Ltd* [1994] 3 W.L.R. 761, explaining *Tai Hing Cotton Mill Ltd v. Liu Chong Hing Bank Ltd* [1986] A.C. 80.

contracts) are well advised to deal specifically with the duties of the principal. The rules as to implication of terms at common law are strict: such terms can only be implied to implement the general nature of a recognised type of relationship or transaction (such as landlord and tenant), or to give business efficacy to a particular transaction.[4]

Although the relevant cases do not cite the principal/agent relationship as coming within the first category of implication, and perhaps indeed could not because of the varied ways in which agency relationships arise, connected relationships, e.g. master and servant, are discussed,[5] and there are in fact many cases discussing the basic nature of particular types of agency transactions.[6] It may well be therefore that the courts will not be unwilling under the first category to find certain elemental duties of co-operation by a principal with his agent,[7] at least in those situations which involve a fiduciary relationship between the parties.[8] In cases of a more obviously commercial nature, such as distributorship, they may be more cautious.[9] A number of cases, not easy to reconcile, discuss the implication of terms in connection with the termination of the agent's authority.[10] Other cases consider more generally when a term will be implied that the principal will not prevent the agent from earning commission.[11] Except where the analogy of employment contracts is available[12] both groups use the second of the techniques above mentioned, viz. they deny the possibility of a general implication and only find terms when this is necessary to give business efficacy to a transaction. There is therefore nothing in the law sufficiently specific to make the formulation of a general Article on the principal's inherent duties towards the agent appropriate. The Restatement[13] lists certain general duties in this connection; these include a

---

[4] See Liverpool City Council v. Irwin [1977] A.C. 239; Shell U.K. Ltd. v. Lostock Garage Ltd [1976] 1 W.L.R. 1187, 1195–1197; Chitty, Contracts (27th ed.), Vol. 1, Chap. 13; Treitel, Law of Contract (9th ed.) pp. 185 et seq.

[5] e.g. Lister v. Romford Ice and Cold Storage Co. Ltd [1957] A.C. 555, esp. at pp. 576 and 594; Spring v. Guardian Assurance Plc [1994] 3 W.L.R. 354.

[6] e.g. the normal estate agent's contract, discussed in Luxor (Eastbourne) Ltd v. Cooper [1941] A.C. 108, esp. at pp. 137 et seq. and L.J. Hooker Ltd. v. W.J. Adams Estates Pty. Ltd (1977) 138 C.L.R. 52, esp. at pp. 73 et seq. See also W.T. Lamb & Sons v. Goring Brick Co. Ltd [1932] 1 K.B. 710 ("sole selling agents": distributorship).

[7] See in general Burrows (1968) 31 M.L.R. 390; Lücke (1973) 5 Adelaide L.Rev. 32; Kerr (1980) 97 S.A.L. Rev. 550.

[8] cf. Lamb v. Evans [1893] 1 Ch. 218, per Bowen L.J.

[9] See Hospital Products Ltd v. United States Surgical Corp. (1984) 156 C.L.R. 41 (as to the duties of distributors); cf. Mona Oil Equipment Supply Co. Ltd v. Rhodesia Railways Ltd [1949] 2 All E.R. 1014.

[10] See Comment to Article 125.

[11] Article 60.

[12] See Martin-Baker Aircraft Co. Ltd v. Canadian Flight Equipment Ltd [1955] 2 Q.B. 556; below, para. 10–037.

[13] §§ 432–437.

duty not to interfere unreasonably with agent's work, to give relevant information, to keep and render accounts, and "to conduct himself so as not to harm the agent's reputation, nor to make it impossible for the agent, consistently with his reasonable self-respect or personal safety, to continue in the employment."[14] While these may be useful reminders of appropriate standards, it is submitted that they are no more than that. It remains appropriate therefore to list as the basic rights of an agent only those which follow.

Commercial agents. The Commercial Agents (Council Directive)   **7–002**
Regulations 1993, however, lay down duties for the principals of commercial agents as there defined. In particular, a principal must act "dutifully and in good faith".[15] The regulations are dealt with in Chapter 11.

1.—REMUNERATION

Article 57

WHETHER AGENT ENTITLED TO ANY REMUNERATION

(1)   An agent is only entitled to remuneration for his services as   **7–003**
agent if either the express or implied terms of the agency contract, if any, so provide or he has a right in restitution to claim on a *quantum meruit*.

(2)   Where the contract contains express terms providing for remuneration to be paid, the agent cannot normally claim remuneration other than in accordance with those terms. In the absence of such express terms the right to claim any remuneration, and the amount and terms of payment of such remuneration, are determined by such terms as may be implied into the contract.

(3)   In deciding what terms are to be implied the court will have regard to all the circumstances of the case, including the nature and length of the services, the express terms of the contract and the customs, usages and practices of the particular area of activity. In the absence of any factors to the contrary, a term will be implied that the agent is entitled to reasonable remuneration.[16]

---

[14] § 437.
[15] Reg. 4(1).
[16] See Comment.

Comment

7–004   **Contractual claim.** Apart from claims in restitution, the rendering of services to another, however long continued, creates no right to remuneration unless the agency contract expressly or impliedly makes provision for such payments. If there are no express terms relating to remuneration, terms providing for remuneration will only be implied where the circumstances are such as to indicate that the parties intended that there should be remuneration.[17] In general, however, the mere employment of a professional person raises a presumption that it was intended that he should be remunerated unless there are circumstances indicating the contrary.[18]

In respect of some contracts, particularly the contract of sale, failure to agree on the price would be a very strong indication that no contract had been concluded. In the case of the contract of agency, however, the question of the agent's remuneration is less central, and if it is found that remuneration was intended, its amount can be determined by reference to scales or even by what is reasonable.[19]

What terms may be implied into the contract will depend upon the normal rules for the implication of terms into contracts.[20] In particular, no terms may be implied which would be inconsistent with the express terms.[21] Thus, if the express terms provide for remuneration which seems unduly low, no term may be implied which will give a more reasonable remuneration.[22] But if the agent performs services at the

---

[17] *Reeve v. Reeve* (1858) 1 F. & F. 280; *Foord v. Morley* (1859) 1 F. & F. 496. See also *Hulse v. Hulse* (1856) 17 C.B. 711. The *Restatement* suggests that a promise to pay for services is to be implied unless those services are trivial or there are other indications to the contrary (§ 411), but no English authority has yet gone so far as to suggest that this principle is applicable here.

[18] *Miller v. Beale* (1879) 27 W.R. 403, Illustration 6; *Manson v. Baillie* (1855) 2 Macq. 80; *Gibbon v. Budd* (1863) 2 H. & C. 92; *Landless v. Wilson* (1880) 8 R. 289; *Turner v. Reeve* (1901) 17 T.L.R. 592; *Corbin v. Stewart* (1911) 28 T.L.R. 99 (the practice of one doctor charging no fee for attendance on the children of another doctor was a circumstance displacing the general rule); *Way v. Latilla* [1937] 3 All E.R. 759, Illustration 3; Supply of Goods and Services Act 1982, s. 15.

[19] *cf.* Supply of Goods and Services Act 1982, s. 15.

[20] See above, para. 7–001.

[21] *Broad v. Thomas* (1830) 7 Bing. 99; *Read v. Rann* (1830) 10 B. & C. 438; *Phillipps v. Briard* (1856) 25 L.J.Ex. 233; *Alder v. Boyle* (1847) 4 C.B. 635; *Green v. Mules* (1861) 30 L.J.C.P. 343, Illustration 8; *Barnett v. Isaacson* (1888) 4 T.L.R. 645; *Lott v. Outhwaite* (1893) 10 T.L.R. 76; *Harley & Co. v. Nagata* (1917) 34 T.L.R. 124; *Moor Line Ltd v. Louis Dreyfus & Co.* [1918] 1 K.B. 89; *Howard Houlder & Partners Ltd v. Manx Islands S.S. Co.* [1923] 1 K.B. 110; *Burrough's Adding Machine Ltd. v. Aspinall* (1925) 41 T.L.R. 276; *Jones v. Lowe* [1945] K.B. 73; *Fairvale Ltd v. Sabharwal* [1992] 2 EGLR 27. But a trade custom or usage may be used to interpret a contract, provided that it is not inconsistent with the express terms: *Caine v. Horsefall* (1847) 1 Exch. 519; *Allan v. Sundius* (1862) 1 H. & C. 123; *Parker v. Ibbetson* (1858) 4 C.B.(N.S.) 346.

[22] *Kofi Sunkersette Obu v. Strauss & Co.* [1951] A.C. 243, Illustration 1.

request of the principal which are outside the duties for which the contract expressly provides for remuneration, a term may exceptionally be implied that a reasonable sum shall be paid for such services.[23] If the contract provides that the amount of remuneration shall be in the discretion of the principal, the court may not decide what sum should be paid; to do so would be to re-write the contract and usurp the principal from the function which the parties agreed should be his.[24] But if the contract expressly or impliedly provides that a reasonable sum shall be payable, the court will determine what is a reasonable sum and the terms on which it should be paid.[25] In the absence of a contrary indication as to the amount payable, the term which will be implied is for a reasonable sum on reasonable terms. What is reasonable will depend upon all the circumstances of the case.[26]

Scales: implied terms and custom. The fact that a professional person normally charges on a fixed scale, such as a scale of charges laid down by his professional body which provides for a varying percentage of the total sum involved, does not *ipso facto* entitle him to remuneration according to that scale. He must show that the scale was incorporated into the contract either by express term or otherwise. If it is not incorporated expressly he may show that the scale is to be implied by custom; but the custom must, of course, be reasonable if it is to bind the other party.[27] In the absence of express or implied incorporation of a scale, the implied term will be that the professional person is only entitled to a reasonable sum, although the scale may provide the measure of or an indication of what a reasonable sum might be.[28] The

7–005

---

[23] *Marshall v. Parsons* (1841) 9 C. & P. 656; *Williamson v. Hine Bros.* [1891] 1 Ch. 390.
[24] *Kofi Sunkersette Obu v. Strauss & Co.*, n. 22 above; *Re Richmond Gate Property Co. Ltd* [1948] 1 W.L.R. 335, where the articles of a company provided (from Table A in the Companies Act 1948) for "such remuneration as the directors may determine". This was held to exclude any implied term because the contract provided expressly for the directors to determine the sum payable and any implied term would have been contrary to the express terms.
[25] *Way v. Latilla* [1937] 3 All E.R. 759, Illustration 3; *Powell v. Braun* [1954] 1 W.L.R. 401; *Gross Fine & Krieger Chalfen v. Clifton* (1974) 223 EG 837.
[26] As to the amount, see *Cohen v. Paget* (1814) 4 Camp. 96; *Rucker v. Lunt* (1863) 3 F. & F. 959; *Great Western Insurance Co. v. Cunliffe* (1874) L.R. 9 Ch.App. 525; *Baring v. Stanton* (1876) 3 Ch.D. 502; *Stubbs v. Slater* [1910] 1 Ch. 632; *Campbell v. National Trust Co. Ltd* [1931] 1 D.L.R. 705 (P.C.); *Hugh V. Allen & Co. v. A. Holmes Ltd* [1969] 1 Lloyd's Rep. 348. As to the conditions, see *Broad v. Thomas* (1830) 7 Bing. 99; *Hall v. Benson* (1836) 7 C. & P. 711; *Burnett v. Bouch* (1840) 9 C. & P. 620.
[27] See Article 31.
[28] *Upsdell v. Stewart* (1793) Peake 255 (in which a surveyor attempted to prove a trade custom that he was entitled to 5 per cent of the cost of the works. Of this custom, Lord Kenyon said: "as to the custom offered to be proved, the course of robbery on Bagshot Heath might as well be proved in a court of justice"); *Footner v. Joseph* (1859) 3 L.C.J. 233; affd. 5 L.C.J. 225 (Canada); *Debenham v. King's College, Cambridge* (1884) 1

—cont. on next page

court may have regard to the negotiations of the parties in order to ascertain the value which each of them put upon the services.[29] It has been suggested that where the agent performs services which are not geared to producing particular results, the sum should be ascertained on the basis of time and trouble, unless a custom incorporating a scale can be established; but that where an agent employed to achieve results achieves those results, assessment of a reasonable sum by reference to a scale may be more appropriate.[30]

7–006 **Fiduciaries.** The fiduciary nature of the agent's functions may mean that he cannot charge for his services without the informed consent of the person or persons to whom the fiduciary duty is owed.[31] There are equitable[32] and statutory[33] exceptions to this rule, often concerning solicitors.

7–007 **Estate agents.** Under section 18 of the Estate Agents Act 1979 a person who enters into a contract with another under which the agent will engage in estate agency work must give the client certain information regarding the remuneration payable and other sums (such as advertising and other expenses) which may become payable.[34] If he does not do so, the contract is unenforceable except pursuant to an

---

—*cont. from previous page*
T.L.R. 170; *Brocklebank v. Lancashire & Yorkshire Ry. Co.* (1887) 3 T.L.R. 575; *Drew v. Josolyne* (1888) 4 T.L.R. 717 (in which Lord Coleridge said that he would never sanction surveyors being paid not with reference to the work done but on a percentage of the amount involved. A similar view was expressed by Younger J. in *Faraday v. Tamworth Union* (1917) 86 L.J.Ch. 436, Illustration 5); *Farthing v. Tomkins* (1893) 9 T.L.R. 566; *Wilkie v. Scottish Aviation Ltd* 1956 S.C. 198, Illustration 4. See also *Gibbon v. Pease* [1905] 1 K.B. 810 (custom that architect can retain plans after payment unreasonable); *Att.–Gen. v. Drapers' Company* (1869) L.R. 9 Eq. 69; *Buckland and Garrard v. Pawson & Co.* (1890) 6 T.L.R. 421; *Turner v. Reeve* (1901) 17 T.L.R. 592; *Re Wolfe* [1952] 2 All E.R. 595; *Frank Swain v. Whitfield Corp. Ltd* (1962) 183 E.G. 479; *Graham & Baldwin v. Taylor, Son & Davis* (1965) 109 S.J. 793.
[29] *Way v. Latilla* [1937] 3 All E.R. 759, Illustration 3, following *Scarisbrick v. Parkinson* (1869) 20 L.T. 175.
[30] Murdoch [1981] Conv. 424. doubting the cases cited at Illustration 10.
[31] *e.g. Sheriff v. Axe* (1827) 4 Russ 33 (commission agent became executor); *Williams v. Barton* [1927] 2 Ch. 9 (stockbroker's clerk was trustee); *cf. Douglas v. Archbutt* (1858) 2 De G. & J. 148 (trustee acted as auctioneer); and see *Re Northcote's Will Trusts* [1949] 1 All E.R. 442 (charge for getting in foreign assets allowable by foreign law). See in general Articles 45–50; Finn, *Fiduciary Obligations* (1977), pp. 206–208.
[32] The rule in *Cradock v. Piper* relating to solicitor trustees: see Snell, *Equity* (29th ed.), pp. 255–257; Cordery, *Solicitors* (8th ed.), pp. 177–178.
[33] Rules made under the Insolvency Act 1986.
[34] See in general Murdoch, *The Estate Agents and Property Misdescriptions Acts 1979* (3rd ed.); *Law of Estate Agency and Auctions* (3rd ed.); below, paras. 7–020, 7–037. "Estate agency work" is defined in s. 1; it only covers some of the functions normally performed by estate agents. The notice must be in writing: Estate Agents (Provision of Information) Regulations 1991 (S.I. 1991 No. 859) reg. 4 (made under s. 30 of the Act).

order of the court. It is arguable however that this provision does not apply to the normal estate agent's agreement, which involves a unilateral offer by the client, and under which the agent enters into no contract until he earns his commission by introducing a purchaser or something similar.[35] When this analysis is applicable, it may be difficult to justify any implication that these should be any form of payment where commission is not earned, at least in contract. But regardless of this reasoning, the time at which the information must be given is specified by regulation.[36]

Barristers. A barrister has no legal right to receive any fee or remuneration for services rendered by him in his capacity as a barrister, nor is any promise to pay him for such services binding.[37]   **7–008**

Quantum meruit where no contractual right. If services are rendered   **7–009** by the agent not pursuant to a contract, but they were freely accepted by the principal with full knowledge, or (perhaps) from which he incontrovertibly benefits, the courts may, on principles of restitution, award a reasonable sum to the agent as remuneration on a *quantum meruit*.[38] Thus, the original contract under which the services were rendered may have been a nullity, because for example, subsequently rescinded[39] or made without authority (ratification being impossible),[40] or it may have contained terms so vague or uncertain as to make it unenforceable,[41] or the parties may have provided that remuneration

---

[35] See below, para. 7–015.

[36] Estate Agents (Provision of Information) Regulations 1991, above, reg. 3(1): "when communication commences between the estate agent and the client or as soon as is reasonably practicable thereafter provided it is at a time before the client is committed to any liability towards the estate agent."

[37] *Kennedy v. Broun* (1863) 13 C.B.(N.S.) 677; *Broun v. Kennedy* (1864) 4 De G.J. & S. 217, affirming 33 Beav. 133; *Re May* (1858) 4 Jur.(N.S.) 1169; *Wells v. Wells* [1914] P. 157; *Re Sandiford (No. 2)* [1935] Ch. 681; and see generally *Rondel v. Worsley* [1969] 1 A.C. 191.

[38] See Goff and Jones, *Law of Restitution* (4th ed.), pp. 3–4, 18–26, 477–487. But *cf.* Birks in *Essays on the Law of Restitution* (Burrows ed. 1991), Chap. 5 and material there cited. In some of the authorities *quantum meruit* is used to describe a claim in contract for a reasonable sum due under an implied term of that contract. It is, perhaps, preferable to avoid this terminology, which may lead to confusion between a claim under a contract and a claim in restitution where no contract exists and may, further, cause the normal principles for the implication of terms into a contract to be overlooked. *cf.* below, para. 7–024.

[39] *Faraday v. Tamworth Union* (1917) 86 L.J.Ch. 436, Illustration 5. This case may be difficult to reconcile with the earlier Scottish case of *Boyd & Forrest v. Glasgow & S.W. Ry. Co.*, 1915 S.C. 20 (H.L.) (reported also as a note in [1915] A.C. 526).

[40] *Craven-Ellis v. Canons Ltd* [1936] 2 K.B. 403. See also *William Lacey (Hounslow) Ltd. v. Davis* [1957] 1 W.L.R. 932.

[41] See *Turner v. Webster*, 24 Kan. 38 (1880) for a clear illustration of this principle which was considered in a wider context in *Scammell v. Ouston* [1941] A.C. 251. See also
—cont. on next page

shall be such as they shall subsequently agree but they thereafter fail to reach agreement.[42] In these cases no contract may exist and there can therefore be no express or implied terms relating to remuneration.

7–010   Contractual right. This situation must, of course, be distinguished from that in which P asks A to perform a service and A does so. Request and performance will normally create a contract and, subject to the considerations discussed above, reasonable remuneration will be payable pursuant to an implied term of that contract rather than give rise to a claim upon a *quantum meruit* in restitution. Equally, the contract may itself provide for reasonable remuneration where for some reason commission is not earned.[43]

7–011   Commercial agents. The Commercial Agents (Council Directive) Regulations 1993 provide for remuneration in the absence of agreement.[44] The Regulations are discussed in Chapter 11.

Illustrations

7–012   (1)   A company engaged A to act as its agent for the purchase and shipment of rubber to the company. The contract of engagement provided that "the company has agreed to remunerate my services with a monthly sum of fifty pounds. . . . A commission is also to be paid to me . . . which I have agreed to leave to the discretion of the company." A claimed a commission on all rubber purchased by him for the company. The Privy Council held that it could not determine the basis and rate of commission and that to do so would be to vary the existing contract by transferring to the court the exercise of a discretion vested in the company.[45]

—*cont. from previous page*
Jaques v. Lloyd D. George & Partners Ltd [1968] 1 W.L.R. 625, where the contract was void for uncertainty and no remuneration was payable, and *John Meacock & Co. v. Abrahams* [1956] 1 W.L.R. 1463, Illustration 9.

[42] *Loftus v. Roberts* (1902) 18 T.L.R. 532. The courts will be keen to find a contract if they can by implying reasonable terms, especially when the parties have proceeded a long way under the supposed contract: *F. & G. Sykes (Wessex) Ltd v. Fine Fare Ltd* [1967] 1 Lloyd's Rep. 53. But cf. *Courtney & Fairbairn Ltd v. Tolaini Bros. (Hotels) Ltd* [1975] 1 W.L.R. 297; *Mallozzi v. Carapelli S.p.A.* [1975] 1 Lloyd's Rep. 229. See also *Hillas & Co. Ltd v. Arcos Ltd* (1932) 38 Com.Cas. 23; *May & Butcher v. R.* (1929) reported [1934] 2 K.B. 17n.; *Foley v. Classique Coaches Ltd* [1934] 2 K.B. 1; *British Bank of Foreign Trade Ltd v. Novinex* [1949] 1 K.B. 623; *National Coal Board v. Galley* [1958] 1 W.L.R. 16; *Luanda Exportadora v. Wahbe Tamari* [1967] 2 Lloyd's Rep. 353, 361.

[43] See Illustration 10.

[44] Reg. 6(1).

[45] *Kofi Sunkersette Obu v. Strauss & Co.* [1951] A.C. 243. See also *Taylor v. Brewer* (1813) 1 M. & S. 290; *Roberts v. Smith* (1859) 4 H. & N. 315; *Mann v. Shell Petroleum Ltd* [1961] C.L.Y. 1440; *Re Richmond Gate Property Co. Ltd* [1965] 1 W.L.R. 335. But cf. *Sudbrook Trading Estate Ltd v. Eggleton* [1983] 1 A.C. 444.

(2)   A entered into an agreement which provided: "I hereby agree to enter your service as a weekly manager, and the amount of payment I am to receive I leave entirely for you to determine." He served in that capacity for six weeks. It was held that he was entitled, in an action on a *quantum meruit*, to recover such an amount as the employer, acting in good faith, ought to have awarded. [46]

(3)   A alleged that he had agreed with P that he should send P information relating to gold mines and concessions in Africa and that P should give him a reasonable share in the same and pay a reasonable sum for the information. Held, there was no concluded contract between the parties as to the amount of the share and the court could not complete the contract for the parties, but that there was an employment contract between the parties which clearly indicated that A was not to work gratuitously; a term would be implied under which A was entitled to reasonable remuneration. In fixing the amount, the court could have regard to the negotiations between the parties in order to ascertain what value they had themselves placed upon the service. [47]

(4)   W was employed by S to act as valuer, adviser and witness in arbitration proceedings. No provision was made for his fees. After the work was completed W prepared a bill of charges, made up in accordance with the Scale of Professional Charges of the Royal Institution of Chartered Surveyors, amounting to £3,009. S paid him £1,000 and he sued for the balance. Held, fees would be payable according to the Scale if it was customary to pay according to the Scale and if the resulting fee was reasonable. If W could not prove the incorporation of the Scale by custom the court would fix a reasonable fee. [48]

(5)   F was employed by the defendants to act as surveyor for them in connection with an arbitration. The contract provided that he should be paid a percentage fee on Ryde's Scale of Professional Charges, but as a result of an innocent misrepresentation by the defendants, F thought that his percentage would be based on the entire amount in issue whereas the contract provided that it should be based only on the defendants' share. Held, (i) the contract could be rescinded by F for the defendants' innocent mispresentation, (ii) F was entitled to reasonable remuneration on a *quantum meruit*, (iii) such remuneration was to be fixed in accordance with the work actually done and not on a percentage of values. Ryde's Scale was therefore ignored. [49]

---

[46] *Bryant v. Flight* (1839) 5 M. & W. 114. The basis of the decision is obscure. See also *Peacock v. Peacock* (1809) 2 Camp. 45; *Jewry v. Busk* (1814) 5 Taunt. 302; *Bird v. M'Gahey* (1849) 2 C. & K. 707; *Powell v. Braun* [1954] 1 W.L.R. 401 where it was clear that the parties intended a reasonable sum to be paid.

[47] *Way v. Latilla* [1937] 3 All E.R. 759.

[48] *Wilkie v. Scottish Aviation Ltd* 1956 S.C. 198.

[49] *Faraday v. Tamworth Union* (1917) 86 L.J.Ch. 436.

(6)   A engages an auctioneer to sell property on his behalf. It is implied that A is to pay the auctioneer the usual and reasonable commission. [50]

(7)   A contract provided that an agent should receive commission on all sales effected or orders executed by him. By a custom of the trade, no commission was payable in respect of bad debts. It was held that the agent was entitled to commission on all sales effected by him, including those resulting in bad debts, the trade custom being inconsistent with the express terms of the contract. [51]

(8)   P employed A to find a purchaser or mortgagee for property. A introduced N to P and negotiations started between them. These negotiations flagged and P agreed with A that A should write N a letter and that if N made an advance or purchased *in consequence* of the letter P would pay A £100. N purchased but gave evidence that he was not influenced by the letter. It was held that A was entitled to no remuneration since (i) the subsequent agreement had replaced the original agreement, (ii) the terms of the subsequent agreement left no room for a claim on a *quantum meruit*, and (iii) the event specified in the subsequent agreement had not taken place. [52]

(9)   P, a second mortgagee, gave A instructions to sell the property by auction. The contract between P and A provided that if a sale was effected between the date of receipt of instructions and the date of the auction, commission was payable on the same scale as for a sale by auction. On the day before the auction the mortgagor redeemed the mortgages and sold the property himself. Held, (i) A was not entitled to commission since the event on which commission was due had not taken place, (ii) no claim on a contractual *quantum meruit* lay because P had received no advantage and the contract provided for the events on which payment became due. [53]

(10)   An agent introduces suitable purchasers to a prospective vendor, but takes no part in negotiations. The relevant scale provides commission for "seeking and negotiating" but not for seeking and finding without negotiating. It also provides for *quantum meruit* on

---

[50] *Miller v. Beale* (1879) 27 W.R. 403. As to the remuneration of auctioneers on a sale by the court, and the relevant practice, see *Re Wolfe, Heller v. Wolfe* [1952] 2 All E.R. 545 and *Supreme Court Practice, 1995*, notes to R.S.C., Ord. 31, r. 2. And see in general Murdoch, *Law of Estate Agency and Auctions* (3rd ed.), pp. 340–342.

[51] *Bower v. Jones* (1831) 8 Bing. 65. *cf. Caine v. Horsefall* (1847) 1 Exch. 519; and see *Read v. Rann* (1830) 10 B. & C. 438; *Broad v. Thomas* (1830) 7 Bing. 99; *Harley v. Nagata* (1917) 34 T.L.R. 124. And see Article 58.

[52] *Green v. Mules* (1861) 30 L.J.C.P. 343. This decision may today be regarded as somewhat harsh.

[53] *John Meacock & Co. v. Abrahams* [1956] 1 W.L.R. 1463. See also *Fairvale Ltd. v. Sabharwal* [1992] 2 EGLR 27; *cf. Bernard Marcus & Co. v. Ashraf* [1988] 1 EGLR 7; Murdoch, *Law of Estate Agency and Auctions* (3rd ed.), pp. 337–340.

"abortive work." Remuneration may be assessed on the basis of trouble taken, at considerably less than the scale fee.[54]

Article 58

AGENTS' REMUNERATION DUE UPON THE HAPPENING OF AN EVENT

(1) Where an agent is entitled to his remuneration upon the happening of a future event, his entitlement does not arise until that event has occurred.

7–013

(2) The event upon which the agent's entitlement to remuneration arises is to be ascertained from the terms of the agency contract.

(3) Where the event upon which the agent's entitlement to remuneration arises does not occur, the agent will not be entitled to receive remuneration on a *quantum meruit* unless provision for this is expressly made in the agency contract, or unless a term to such effect can be implied into the agency contract in order to give it business efficacy or otherwise to give effect to the intentions of the parties.[55]

Comment

General rule. This Article should be read in conjunction with Articles 59 and 60. The rule stated above is fundamental to the remuneration of the large number of agents who are paid by way of a commission on transactions which they bring about for their principals. The commission may be payable on many separate transactions, as in the case of a selling agent,[56] or it may be payable on a single transaction, as in the case of an estate agent acting for a private vendor. The principle stated is, however, of general application.[57] The agent must prove that the

7–014

---

[54] *Sinclair Goldsmith v. Minero Peru Comercial* [1978] E.G.D. 194, following *Reif Diner & Co. v. Catalytic International Inc.* (1978) 246 EG 743. See also *Hoddell v. Smith* [1976] E.G.D. 217; *Hampton & Sons v. Trade and General Securities Ltd* (1978) 250 EG 451; *Lewis & Graves v. Harper*, *ibid.* 1287. But see Murdoch [1981] Conv. 424 and *Law of Estate Agency and Auctions* (3rd ed.), pp. 159–161, 170–172, questioning these decisions; above, para. 7–005. See further *Debenham Tewson & Chinnocks v. Rimington* [1990] 2 EGLR 21; *Michael Elliott & Partners Ltd v. U.K. Land Plc* [1991] 1 EGLR 39.

[55] See Comment.

[56] See, *e.g. Lockwood v. Levick* (1860) 8 C.B.(N.S.) 603. *Del credere* commission is due and payable, in the absence of any special terms to the contrary, as soon as the contract is made in respect of which it is claimed: *Solly v. Weiss* (1818) 8 Taunt. 371; *Caruthers v. Graham* (1811) 14 East 578.

[57] *Lara v. Hill* (1863) 15 C.B.(N.S.) 45; *Alder v. Boyle* (1847) 4 C.B. 635; *Horford v. Wilson* (1807) 1 Taunt. 12; *Platt v. Depree* (1893) 9 T.L.R. 194; *Passingham v. King* (1898) 14 T.L.R. 392; *Re Sovereign Life Assce. Co., Salter's Claim* (1891) 7 T.L.R. 602; *Skinner v. Andrews & Hall* (1910) 26 T.L.R. 340; but *cf. Peacock v. Freeman* (1888) 4

—cont. on next page

event has occurred upon which remuneration becomes due is one of law to be determined from the construction of the terms of agency contract.

> "It is a settled rule for the construction of commission notes and the like documents which refer to the remuneration of an agent that a plaintiff cannot recover unless he shows that the conditions of the written bargain have been fulfilled. If he proves fulfilment he recovers. If not, he fails. There appears to be no halfway house, and it matters not that the plaintiff proves expenditure of time, money and skill."[58]

In most instances the question whether the event has occurred presents no great difficulties. For example, if the agent is engaged to bring about a contract for his principal his entitlement to commission will arise if and when the contract is made. He had then done what he was engaged to do. However, owing largely to the number of stages involved in a contract for the purchase of real property, the commission of an estate agent has been the subject of many decisions in the courts; the estate agent frequently wishes to earn his commission at a stage earlier than at which his principal enters into the contract the agent was engaged to bring about.

7–015   **Estate agents.**[59] Although there are a great many cases concerning the entitlement of the estate agent to receive commission from his principal, "commission contracts are subject to no peculiar rules or principles of their own; the law which governs them is the law which governs all contracts and all questions of agency."[60] There are, therefore, no special rules of law relating to estate agents' contracts although the application to these of some of the basic principles of the law of contract presents considerable difficulty.

7–016   **Nature of estate agent's contract.** The nature of the estate agent's contract was analysed by Lord Russell of Killowen in *Luxor (Eastbourne) Ltd v. Cooper.*[61] He said that "contracts by which owners

---

—cont. from previous page

T.L.R. 541. Many of the early cases must be regarded with caution in view of the leading decision in *Luxor (Eastbourne) Ltd v. Cooper* [1941] A.C. 108, *e.g. Fisher v. Drewett* (1878) 48 L.J.Ex. 32; *Fuller v. Eames* (1892) 8 T.L.R. 278; *Green v. Lucas* (1876) 33 L.T. 584; *Vulcan Car Agency Ltd v. Fiat Motors Ltd* (1915) 32 T.L.R. 73; and the dicta on substantial performance in *Rimmer v. Knowles* (1874) 30 L.T. 496.

[58] *Howard Houlder & Partners Ltd v. Manx Isles S.S. Co.* [1923] 1 K.B. 110, 113–114, *per* McCardie J.

[59] See Murdoch, *Law of Estate Agency and Auctions* (3rd ed.), Chap. 5 (also discussing, at pp. 332 *et seq.*, commission and remuneration of auctioneers); Murdoch (1975) 91 L.Q.R. 357; Samuels (1969) 113 S.J. 885; Seepersad (1969) 119 N.L.J. 407; Kerr [1973] N.I.L.Q. 1; Hall (1985) 14 U. Qd.L.J. 26. The nature of the estate agent's contract was considered in detail, and the relevant cases reviewed, in Ash, *Willing to Purchase* (1963).

[60] *Luxor (Eastbourne) Ltd. v. Cooper* [1941] A.C. 108, 124 *per* Lord Russell of Killowen (Illustration 1 to Article 60).

[61] n. 60 above.

of property, desiring to dispose of it, put it in the hands of agents on commission terms, are not (in default of specific provisions) contracts of employment in the ordinary meaning of those words. No obligation is imposed on the agent to do anything. The contracts are merely promises binding on the principal to pay a sum of money upon the happening of a specified event, which involves the rendering of some service by the agent. There is no real analogy between such contracts, and contracts of employment by which one party binds himself to do certain work, and the other binds himself to pay remuneration for the doing of it."[62] The normal estate agent's contract is therefore said to be a unilateral contract, the agent not being bound to do anything if he does not wish to do so. A "sole" or "exclusive" agency agreement is however said to raise a bilateral contract. There are difficulties of analysis which are discussed below.[63]

Entitlement to commission. Whenever an estate agent claims his   **7–017** remuneration the court must determine, as a matter of construction of the particular agency contract concerned, whether the event has occurred upon which the agent's entitlement to remuneration accrues. "No general rule can be laid down by which the rights of the agent or the liability of the principal under commission contracts are to be determined. In each case these must depend upon the exact terms of the contract in question, and upon the true construction of those terms."[64] A useful statement of the relevant principles is that of Jenkins L.J. in *Midgley Estates Ltd v. Hand*[65]:

"So far as any general principle is deducible from the authorities, their effect may, I think, be thus summarised: The question depends on the construction of each particular contract, but prima facie the intention of the parties to a contract of this type is likely to be that the commission stipulated for should only be payable in the event of an actual sale resulting.... That is, broadly, speaking, the intention which, as a matter of probability, the court should be disposed to impute to the parties. It follows that general or ambiguous expressions, purporting, for instance, to make the commission payable in the event of the agent 'finding a purchaser' or ... 'selling the property,' have been construed as meaning that the commission is only to be payable in the event of an actual and completed sale resulting, or, at least, in the event of the agent succeeding in introducing a purchaser who is able and willing to purchase the property. That is the broad general principle in the light of which the question of construction should be approached; but this does not

---

[62] At p. 124.
[63] See Comment to Article 60.
[64] *Luxor (Eastbourne) Ltd v. Cooper* [1941] A.C. 108, 124 *per* Lord Russell of Killowen.
[65] [1952] 2 Q.B. 432, 435–436.

mean that the contract, if its terms are clear, should not have effect in accordance with those terms, even if they do involve the result that the agent's commission is earned and becomes payable although the sale in respect of which it is claimed, for some reason or another, turns out to be abortive."

Clear and unambiguous words must, therefore, be used if the commission is to be payable without an actual sale taking place,[66] since it is "the common understanding of men . . . that the agent's commission is payable out of the purchase price."[67] But as fast as the courts have held that one particular formula will not entitle the agent to commission before the contract of sale is made, so have estate agents devised new formulae in an endeavour to achieve this result. The reported cases are therefore no more than illustration of the strict criteria which the courts have applied, and many of the contractual formulae used in them must be regarded as obsolete in so far as they clearly will not achieve what the agent generally desires to do, viz., to secure his right to commission as soon as he produces someone who shows a serious interest in buying the property. It must also be remembered that in the purchase of real property in England and Wales the contractual arrangements will, unlike a normal commercial contract, generally fall into three distinct stages.

(1) *Agreement "subject to contract"*. The third party makes an offer "subject to contract" or "subject to survey" and, if this is accepted, pays a deposit to the estate agent. This transaction is not normally, in law, a contract to purchase the property and either party is free to withdraw from further negotiations for any, or even no, reason.[68]

---

[66] See also *Luxor (Eastbourne) Ltd v. Cooper* [1941] A.C. 108, 129. The *contra proferentem* rule was applied in *Price, Davies & Co. v. Smith* (1929) 141 L.T. 490, 494; *Jacques v. Lloyd D. George & Partners Ltd* [1968] 1 Q.L.R. 625, 632; *Block Bros. Realty Ltd v. Viktoria* (1974) 42 D.L.R. (3d) 474. See also *Mustafa v. K. G. Palos* [1972] E.G.D. 797.

[67] *Dennis Reed Ltd v. Goody* [1950] 2 K.B. 277, 284, *per* Denning L.J.; *H.W. Liebig & Co. v. Leading Investments Ltd* [1986] 1 S.C.R. 70, 79–82; (1985) 25 D.L.R. (4th) 161, 176–179. (But an argument, based on this statement, that a contract contained an implied term that the estate agent was entitled to commission from the purchase money held by the vendor's solicitor was rejected in *W.A.Ellis Services Ltd v. Stuart Wood* [1993] 2 EGLR 43.) See also *Jaques v. Lloyd D. George*, n. 66 above, where Lord Denning M.R. said that if the agency contract provided for payment of commission other than on the conclusion of business, it was the agent's duty to inform his principal; if not, the agent might be unable to recover. This statement goes further than other cases and may be difficult to reconcile with the general principle that a person is presumed to have read his contract. The contract provided that commission was payable if the agent should be "instrumental in introducing a person willing to sign a document capable of becoming a contract to purchase at a price which at any stage of the negotiations has been agreed " by the prospective vendor. The court held that these words were too vague to be enforceable.

[68] *Chillingworth v. Esche* [1924] 1 Ch. 97; *Eccles v. Bryant* [1948] Ch. 93. But as to "subject to survey" and "subject to satisfactory survey" see *Astra Trust v. Adams* [1969] 1

(2) *Contract.* The parties sign and, normally through their solicitors, exchange contracts. From the moment of exchange of contracts, but not until then, they are contractually bound[69] (subject to the ordinary rules, such as those relating to void and voidable contracts).

(3) *Completion.* This is normally effected through solicitors. The vendor's solicitor hands the title deeds to the purchaser's solicitor in exchange for a banker's draft for the balance of the purchase price with an adjustment for outgoings from the date of contract. The estate agent generally wants to be entitled to his commission at stage (1); the courts have rarely held that he is entitled to it before stage (2) and sometimes even not until stage (3).

In a work of this nature it is not appropriate to consider every reported case in which an estate agent has claimed commission and, indeed, there is a very large number of such cases.[70] All that is possible is to consider some of the leading cases in which forms of wording then common were used, in order thereby to illustrate the general principle. It should be noted also that differences in conveyancing practice, and in the functions of an estate agent, may lead to differences in decision between jurisdictions. For example, in some countries an estate agent may be expected to procure a purchaser's signature to the contract and take a deposit.[71]

Introduction of a "purchaser". The simplest practical form of estate agent's contract provides that commission shall be payable on the "introduction of a purchaser".[72] Sometimes the agent is merely asked to "find a purchaser"[73] or to "find someone to buy".[74] In these cases   7–018

Lloyd's Rep. 81, doubted in *The Merak* [1976] 2 Lloyd's Rep. 250, 254; *Ee v. Kakar* (1979) 40 P. & C.R. 223; and in general Treitel, *Law of Contract* (9th ed.), pp. 58–62.

[69] *Eccles v. Bryant,* n. 68 above.

[70] See Murdoch (1982) 264 EG 419, 513. Almost all the older cases of importance were examined in Ash, *Willing to Purchase* (1963).

[71] See, *e.g. Pemberton v. Action Realty Ltd* [1986] 1 N.Z.L.R. 286.

[72] *Jones v. Lowe* [1945] K.B. 73. As to the meaning of "introduce", see *D.C. Wylde & Co. v. Sparg* 1977 (2) S.A.L.R. 75: in the context the word meant "to direct the attention of a person who has not applied his mind in that direction to the fact that a property is for sale, or to a material element of the sale not previously appreciated by him." See also *John D. Wood & Co. v. Dantata* [1987] 2 EGLR 23, 25 *per* Nourse L.J. ("the leading or bringing in of the purchaser to that transaction"); *Peter Yates & Co. v. Bullock* [1990] 2 EGLR 24. A clause entitling to commission on introduction will not in the absence of other indications entitle to commission on introductions effected before the making of the contract providing for commission: *Samuel & Co. v. Sanders Bros.* (1886) 3 T.L.R. 145.

[73] *Fowler v. Bratt* [1950] 2 K.B. 96.

[74] *McCallum v. Hicks* [1950] 2 K.B. 271. See also *Alder v. Boyle* (1847) 4 C.B. 635; *Lott v. Outhwaite* (1893) 10 T.L.R. 76; *Chapman v. Winson* (1904) 91 L.T. 17; *Henry v. Gregory* (1905) 22 T.L.R. 53; *Timms v. Carofaro* (1989) 53 S.A.S.R. 572 ("effect a sale ... substantially the transaction contemplated by the contract").

there must, it seems, be a binding contract to purchase before there can be any question of entitlement to commission.[75] Moreover, if after contract and before completion the purchaser withdraws for any reason, the agent's entitlement will (unless specific performance is obtained[76]) be lost because the person introduced was not a "purchaser".[77] On the other hand, if the *vendor* defaults after contract but before completion, the agent's entitlement is normally not lost; the vendor may not rely upon the fact that it was his own wrong *vis-à-vis* the person introduced which prevented the contract from proceeding to completion.[78]

7–019   **Introduction of a person "ready, willing and able to purchase".** Use of the above expressions was unsatisfactory to those agents who wanted to be entitled to their commission at an earlier stage than exchange of contracts. Accordingly, some agents provided that their commission was to be earned on the introduction of a person who was "ready, willing and able to purchase."[79] Sometimes one or more of the adjectives was dropped (*e.g.* a person "willing and able to purchase"[80]). It does not matter what adjectives are used; the principle which the courts have applied in the construction of such contracts is the same. The agent must prove that the person he introduced fulfilled the qualifications provided in the contract.

---

[75] See *McCallum v. Hicks*, n. 74 above; *James v. Smith* (1921) [1931] 2 K.B. 317n; *Blake & Co. v. Sohn* [1969] 1 W.L.R. 1412. But the right to commission is not lost because the parties later vary the contract: *Lord v. Trippe* (1977) 51 A.L.J.R. 574.

[76] See *Boots v. E. Christopher & Co.* [1952] 1 K.B. 89, 98 where Denning L.J. also suggests that if the vendor sues, and obtains full damages including commission payable to the agent, commission would be due. In *H.W. Liebig & Co. v. Leading Investments Ltd* [1986] 1 S.C.R. 70, 86; (1985) 25 D.L.R. (4th) 161, 181–182 LaForest J. suggests that the agent may in such a case be entitled to some form of restitutionary award. But the vendor is not bound to sue and may settle the case: *ibid.*

[77] *James v. Smith*, n. 75 above; *Martin v. Perry and Daw* [1931] 2 K.B. 310; *Poole v. Clarke & Co.* [1945] 2 All E.R. 445. If the contract expressly or impliedly provides that commission is to be paid out of the purchase price, no commission will be due if the purchase price is not paid: *Bull v. Price* (1831) 5 M. & P. 2; *Martin v. Tucker* (1885) 1 T.L.R. 655; *Beningfield v. Kynaston* (1887) 3 T.L.R. 279; *Knight, Frank & Rutley v. Gordon* (1923) 39 T.L.R. 399; *Price, Davies & Co. v. Smith* (1929) 141 L.T. 490; *Boots v. E. Christopher & Co.* [1952] 1 K.B. 89. See also *Fidcott v. Friesner* (1895) 11 T.L.R. 187; *Foster's Agency Ltd v. Romaine* (1916) 32 T.L.R. 545.

[78] *Luxor (Eastbourne) Ltd v. Cooper* [1941] A.C. 108, 126, 142; *Dennis Reed Ltd v. Goody* [1950] 2 K.B. 277, 285. See also *Alpha Trading Ltd v. Dunnshaw-Patten Ltd* [1981] Q.B. 290, Illustration 3 to Article 60.

[79] *e.g. Keningtons v. Regional Properties Ltd* [1946] E.G.D. 86; *Dennis Reed Ltd v. Nicholls* [1948] 2 All E.R. 914; *Lewis & Tucker v. Lee* (1949) 153 EG 342; *Bennett & Partners v. Millett* [1949] 1 K.B. 362; *Berry Estates v. Burgess* (1949) 153 EG 343; *Brown & Co. v. Michaels* (1949) 153 EG 511; *E.P. Nelson & Co. v. Rolfe* [1950] 1 K.B. 139; *E.P. Nelson v. Lyons* (1949) 154 EG 376; *Murdoch Lownie v. Newman* [1949] 2 All E.R. 783; *Dennis Reed Ltd v. Goody* [1950] 2 K.B. 277.

[80] *Graham & Scott (Southgate) Ltd v. Oxlade* [1950] 2 K.B. 257.

At first, commission was fairly readily awarded to the agent on such wording,[81] but in 1950 it became clear that the courts would apply a strict test to decide whether the agent's entitlement had arisen. In *Graham and Scott (Southgate) Ltd v. Oxlade*[82] the Court of Appeal held that if a prospective purchaser made an offer which was subject to any conditions, such as "subject to contract" or "subject to survey", this showed that he was not "willing to purchase" because he had reserved for himself a *locus poenitentiae*. Only an unqualified offer, capable of acceptance by the vendor, would show that the prospective purchaser was "willing". The court overruled a number of cases at first instance[83] and explained its own earlier and apparently inconsistent decision in *E.P. Nelson & Co. v. Rolfe*[84] as having turned on the fact that the prospective purchaser's willingness and ability were there admitted. Shortly afterwards, in *Dennis Reed Ltd v. Goody*,[85] the Court of Appeal repeated its decision in *Oxlade*'s case, holding that a person who made a conditional offer to purchase was not shown to be "willing" to purchase. This strict approach has generally been followed by the courts. In *Dellafiora v. Lester*[86] where, after contract, the vendor's landlord refused to consent to the assignment of the lease to the person introduced and the parties did not proceed further, the Court of Appeal held that this showed that the person introduced was not "able" to purchase and the agent was therefore not entitled to commission. In *Christie, Owen & Davies v. Stockton*[87] the contract provided that commission should be payable if, *inter alia*, the vendor withdrew "after having accepted an offer to purchase by a person able and willing to enter into a formal contract." The agents introduced a person and a price was agreed "subject to contract." During negotiations the vendor withdrew. Slade J. held that the agent was not entitled to commission. The language was not clear and unequivocal and there were no agreed

---

[81] *e.g. Dennis Reed Ltd v. Nicholls* [1948] 2 All E.R. 914; *Bennett & Partners v. Millett* [1949] 1 K.B. 362; *Knight, Frank and Rutley v. Fraser*, 1974 S.L.T. 50.

[82] [1950] 2 K.B. 257.

[83] *Giddys v. Horsfall* [1947] 1 All E.R. 460; *Bennett & Partners v. Millett* [1949] 1 K.B. 362; and probably by implication disapproved of some of the reasoning in *Dennis Reed Ltd v. Nicholls* [1948] 2 All E.R. 914. This latter case was regarded as overruled by Denning L.J. in *Dennis Reed Ltd. v. Goody* [1950] 2 K.B. 277, 289.

[84] [1950] 1 K.B. 139.

[85] [1950] 2 K.B. 277. A month later the Court of Appeal held in *Bennett, Walden & Co. v. Wood* [1950] 2 All E.R. 134 that an offer "subject to contract" did not entitle the agent to commission when the agency contract provided that commission was due when the agent "secured an offer."

[86] [1962] 1 W.L.R. 1208. The form of wording in the case was unusual, but the case was decided on whether the potential purchaser was "able". The Court of Appeal expanded the definition given in earlier cases in which it had suggested that the ability to purchase related to financial ability; the potential purchaser must be "able" in every way.

[87] [1953] 1 W.L.R. 1353.

terms since the whole matter was "subject to contract." Under these circumstances the principle of *Oxlade*'s case applied. A rather similar attempt to claim commission failed in *A.L. Wilkinson Ltd v. Brown*.[88] Commission was due on the introduction of a person "prepared to enter into a contract to purchase" at an agreed price. A person was introduced and a price "agreed" but the offer to purchase was conditional on the potential purchaser selling his own house. Before contract the vendor sold elsewhere. The Court of Appeal held that there was only an expectancy that a contract would be signed and that there was therefore no introduction of a suitably qualified person.

In the above cases the agent failed because the event upon which the commission became due had not occurred. That event was defined by the contract as being the introduction of a person having certain qualifications ("ready, willing and able to purchase"). The person introduced did not have those qualifications and the commission thus had not become due. Whether the person introduced did have those qualifications is a question of fact and if the agent does introduce such a person, he is entitled to his commission even if no sale contract is thereafter concluded because the potential vendor declines to enter into a contract with that person. Thus in *Christie Owen & Davies Ltd v. Rapacioli*[89] the defendant instructed the plaintiff agents to help him find a purchaser of his business and to quote a price of £20,000. The agency contract provided that commission was payable in the event of the plaintiffs "effecting an introduction either directly or indirectly of a person ... ready able and willing to purchase [for £20,000] or any other price." The plaintiffs introduced a person who was prepared to purchase for £17,700 and this offer was accepted "subject to contract." The parties' solicitors thereafter negotiated and a draft contract was prepared, engrossed and signed by the potential purchaser. The defendant then decided to proceed no further with the sale. The Court of Appeal held that the plaintiffs were entitled to succeed in their claim to commission. The person whom they had introduced was willing to contract with the defendant in terms acceptable to him until the moment of his withdrawal. The court expressly approved a passage from the judgment of Bucknill L.J. in *Dennis Reed Ltd. v. Goody*,[90] who said,

---

[88] [1966] 1 W.L.R. 194. See also *Gerlach v. Pearson* [1950] V.L.R. 321 ("secure a purchaser": offer "subject to finance": no commission due).

[89] [1974] Q.B. 781. The court followed *A.L. Wilkinson Ltd v. O'Neil* (1961) 181 EG 137. See also *John E. Trinder & Partners v. Haggis* (1951) 158 EG 4 (not cited in the *Christie* case but decided on similar principles). The court declined to follow *Martin, Gale & Wright v. Buswell* [1961] E.G.D. 418 in view of the different grounds of decision given by the court. See also *Walters v. John Crisp Pty Ltd* (1982) 64 F.L.R. 299 (Aus.) ("if you or anyone else obtains a person who is ready, willing and able to purchase the property ... a full fee is payable to the listing agent").

[90] [1950] 2 K.B. 277.

"... the plaintiffs' claim to commission is not established merely by showing that the person whom they introduced was able and willing to purchase the property at any one particular moment of time: they must prove that he was ready, able and willing to purchase up to the time when either an enforceable contract for the purchase of the house is made between the parties or, alternatively, up to the time when the vendor refuses to enter into such a contract on terms on which the purchaser is willing to purchase and the vendor was at one time willing to sell."[91] It should be noted that the wording is the contract in *Rapacioli*'s case was particularly precise. Although there are suggestions in the judgments that some of Lord Denning's earlier dicta may have gone too far, it is not clear that this is so.[92]

The problem raised by this case is that the prospective purchaser's willingness must be measured against some terms on which he is to be "willing to purchase". In theory it might be possible to specify in the agency contract all the terms which the prospective purchaser must be willing to accept; only if he agreed to those terms would he be a "willing" purchaser for the purposes of the agency contract. But in practice this would be unacceptable in view of the fact that negotiations between prospective purchaser and prospective vendor are inevitable. Furthermore, neither party would be willing to accept such provisions before the market has been tested. The prospective purchaser's willingness has therefore been tested by the courts against the terms on which the prospective vendor is prepared to sell. The difficulty is that the "subject to contract" situation is not a simple offer and acceptance situation; at any time until exchange of contracts the prospective vendor can change the terms on which he is prepared to sell and his willingness is thus only a temporary willingness until that time. The most that can be said is that until exchange of contracts the prospective vendor has expressed the view that in due course he will be willing to sell on certain terms provided that he does not change his mind thereafter. In holding that the prospective purchaser's willingness may be tested against terms which at one time the prospective vendor was prepared to accept, the court was referring only to this temporary manifestation of preparedness to accept which could at any time be altered *vis-à-vis* the prospective purchaser. A conclusive willingness can only be tested at the moment of exchange of contracts because it is only at this moment that it is known what the prospective vendor's terms are, and thus whether the prospective purchaser is "willing to purchase" on those terms. The Court of Appeal was therefore prepared to look for a willingness on the part of the prospective vendor for the purposes of the agency contract

---

[91] *ibid.* at p. 283.
[92] See *H.W. Liebig & Co. v. Leading Investments Ltd* [1987] 1 S.C.R. 70, 82; (1986) 25 D.L.R. (4th) 161, 179 *per* LaForest J.

which was not yet a willingness to sell for the purposes of the sale contract.

These difficulties had been foreseen by Denning L.J. (as he then was) in *McCallum v. Hicks*.[93] He said, "A person may not properly be said to be 'willing' to purchase, so as to entitle the agent to commission, unless he is irrevocably willing, that is, unless he has given irrevocable proof of his willingness by entering into a binding contract to purchase."[94] Only then could the prospective purchaser be said to be "willing to purchase" on terms acceptable to the prospective vendor. This remark of Denning L.J. was expressly disapproved by the Court of Appeal in *Christie Owen & Davies Ltd v. Rapacioli*,[95] as was a similar statement by the same judge in *Dennis Reed Ltd v. Goody*.[96] A problem of a similar nature arose indirectly in *Ackroyd & Sons v. Hasan*.[97] The agents' contract there provided that their commission was due in the event of their introducing "a party prepared to enter into a contract to purchase [on certain terms set out in the agency contract] or on such other terms to which [the vendor might] assent." The terms of sale were agreed "subject to contract" between the potential purchaser's and the potential vendor's solicitors, but the vendor had not yet agreed to what her solicitors had negotiated. She withheld this agreement and no contract was ever made. The Court of Appeal held that, on the facts, the agents had failed to prove that the vendor had assented to the terms. At first instance, Winn J. had said[98] that in his view "assent" meant legally binding assent. In the Court of Appeal Upjohn and Ormerod L.JJ. expressed their strong disagreement with this view.[99] Upjohn L.J. said that whether the vendor had assented[1] was "purely a

---

[93] [1950] 2 K.B. 271.
[94] *ibid.* at p. 276.
[95] [1974] Q.B. 781, 787, 790, 791. But see *H.W. Liebig & Co. v. Leading Investments Ltd*, n. 92 above.
[96] [1950] 2 K.B. 277, 287–288.
[97] [1960] 2 Q.B. 144.
[98] [1959] 1 W.L.R. 706, 712 "... in that context the word 'assent' means: finally assent at the last moment of time at which you, the property owner, will be entitled, when the negotiations have proceeded to that final stage, to say: 'These are the terms precisely to which I give my concluded and considered assent.' I do not think it permissible to construe in favour of the estate agent and against the property owner in such a contract as this the word 'assent' as meaning: 'give a half-considered assent on the basis that it seems at the moment to be all right, but possibly with a mental reservation, due to advice received from the solicitor, that there is no final commitment on this matter until the time comes for exchanging the formal contracts.'"
[99] [1960] 2 Q.B. 144, 156 (Upjohn L.J.), 162 (Ormerod L.J.).
[1] In *Martin Gale & Wright v. Buswell* [1961] E.G.D. 418 Upjohn L.J. made it clear that what the vendor's solicitor had "agreed" with the potential purchaser's solicitor was not the "assent" which had to be proved since the solicitor, in the absence of express authority could not bind his client. What had to be proved was that the vendor assented to the draft contract prepared by the solicitor.

question of fact" and that, for example, it could be strongly argued that a vendor could be shown to assent by having signed his part of the contract notwithstanding that he withdrew before exchange. Sellers L.J.,[2] however, was not satisfied that Winn J.'s view was wrong or that commission could be due where the assent of the vendor fell short of communicated assent so as to conclude a contract. He reserved consideration of this question until it might arise on another set of facts. The view of the majority of the court was that which was accepted in *Christie Owen & Davies v. Rapacioli*.[3] The court in that case recognised that a situation might well arise where the potential vendor might well have to pay two commissions, one to the agent who introduced a person who was willing to purchase on terms on which the principal had at one time been willing to sell but from which he had withdrawn, and another to the agent through whom he finally sold. Such a conclusion in this context seems however at variance with the statement of Lord Wright in *Luxor (Eastbourne) Ltd. v. Cooper*[4] that "the commission agreement is, however, subordinate to the hoped for principal agreement of sale. It would be strange if what was preliminary or accessory should control the freedom of action of the principal in regard to the main transaction which everyone contemplates might never materialise."

Where however the agent does introduce a person who signs an offer to purchase, but at the time he does so the principal has already accepted an offer from another buyer introduced by another agent, it has been held that no commission is due, on the basis that the right to commission is subject to an implied restriction that the property has not already been sold. This implication is a natural one for most transactions.[5]

Estate Agents (Provision of Information) Regulations 1991.[6] By these   7–020
regulations, an estate agent using in the course of estate agency work[7] the phrase "ready, willing and able purchaser" must explain the intention and effect of these words in writing in a way described in the regulations.[8] Failure to comply with this obligation makes the contract

---

[2] [1960] 2 Q.B. 144, 166–167.
[3] n. 95 above.
[4] [1941] A.C. 108, 138–139.
[5] *A.A. Dickson & Co. v. O'Leary* (1979) 254 EG 731, following *E.P. Nelson & Co. v. Rolfe* [1950] 1 K.B. 139 on this point. But it is certainly possible for a vendor to be liable for two commissions: para. 7–029 below.
[6] S.I. 1991 No. 859, made under s. 30(1) of the Estate Agents Act 1979.
[7] As to which see Estate Agents Act 1979, s. 1; Murdoch, *Law of Estate Agency and Auctions* (3rd ed.), pp. 185 *et seq.*; and in general Murdoch, *The Estate Agents and Property Misdescriptions Acts* (3rd ed.).
[8] Reg. 5.

unenforceable except by order of the court. [9] The explanation required is as follows:

> "A purchaser is a 'ready, willing and able' purchaser if he is prepared and is able to exchange unconditional contracts for the purchase of your property.
>
>   You will be liable to pay remuneration to us, in addition to any other costs or charges agreed, if such a purchaser is introduced by us in accordance with your instructions and this must be paid even if you subsequently withdraw and unconditional contracts for sale are not exchanged, irrespective of your reasons." [10]

Where the contract wording varies, the explanation must be given with appropriate modifications. [11] It may be that this requirement, in calling for clearer drafting, will avoid in the future some of the difficulties of the past. The older cases must, however, be noted as examples of the problems to be avoided. It should be noted that the explanation given by the regulations, while inappropriate to estate agents seeking *tenants*, is more favourable to the estate agent than some of the judicial decisions on it and similar wording. [12]

7–021   **Other types of estate agent contracts.** Some of the difficulties discussed above have been avoided where the agent has stipulated for his commission upon the introduction by him of a person who signs or enters into a legally binding contract to purchase. The event here is clearly defined, even if it may not be sufficiently advanced in time to please all estate agents. Thus, in *Midgley Estates Ltd v. Hand* [13] and *Scheggia v. Gradwell* [14] the agents were held entitled to their commission although, in the former case, the purchaser withdrew after contract and, in the latter, the contract that was signed would not have been enforced by specific performance. In each case the event, the signature of a legally binding contract, had occurred. On the other hand, in *Peter Long & Partners v. Burns* [15] the agents' claim to commission failed because the contract was voidable due to an innocent misrepresentation. They had therefore not introduced a person who had entered into a

---

[9] Estate Agents Act 1979, s. 18(5).

[10] Regulations, Sched.

[11] Reg. 5(1)(2). As to the time at which notice must be given, see regs. 3, 5(3).

[12] It does not require that the transaction proceeds as far as the exchange of contracts. See Murdoch, *Law of Estate Agency and Auctions* (3rd ed.), pp. 205–206.

[13] [1952] 2 Q.B. 432.

[14] [1963] 1 W.L.R. 1049. In *A.L. Wilkinson Ltd. v. Brown* [1966] 1 W.L.E. 194, 202–203 Salmon L.J. described the *Scheggia* type of contract as "a ridiculous bargain" and said that the scope of that decision ought not to be extended. See also *Jaques v. Lloyd D. George & Partners Ltd* [1968] 1 W.L.R. 625, 632.

[15] [1956] 1 W.L.R. 1083. *cf. Chris Hart (Business Sales) Ltd v. Currie* 1992 S.L.T. 544 (concluded contract conditional on transfer of licence of public house by licensing board; licence not transferred; commission due).

legally binding contract. Another format entitles the agent to commission if he introduces a person "with whom we have not been in prior communication, and who subsequently completes" a contract. This avoids problems of effective cause[16] and appears effective.[17] Where commission contracts with different terms are used, this may result in two commissions being payable.[18]

Where the person or group introduced subsequently completes the transaction by means of a newly formed company, subsidiary or syndicate, it may be held that the person introduced has completed the purchase, though by means of others,[19] subject to considerations of effective cause.[20]

The most satisfactory way for the agent to ensure that he becomes entitled to his commission upon an introduction seems to be to avoid all references to the ultimate contract or to purchasers. Thus in *Drewery and Drewery v. Ware-Lane*[21] the agents' contract provided that commission was to be due when a "prospective purchaser" signed the agents' "purchaser's agreement" and the vendor signed the agents' "vendor's agreement". Both these documents were "subject to contract" but both were signed. The Court of Appeal held that the agents were entitled to their commission notwithstanding that the prospective purchaser was unable to obtain a mortgage and so never entered into a contract to purchase. The court held that the expression "prospective purchaser" did not require that the person introduced must be ready, willing or able but simply that he must bona fide contemplate purchasing.[22] This condition had been fulfilled. But in *Mustafa v. K.G. Palos*[23] the contract provided that commission was payable to a mortgage broker in the event of "an offer of mortgage" on terms set out in the agency contract. The agent found a building society which offered

---

[16] See Article 59.

[17] *Brian Cooper & Co. v. Fairview Estates (Investments) Ltd* [1987] 1 EGLR 18.

[18] e.g. *Lordsgate Properties Ltd v. Balcombe* [1985] 1 EGLR 20; *Bernard Marcus & Co. v. Ashraf* [1988] 1 EGLR 7 (auctioneer); *Peter Yates & Co. v. Bullock* [1990] 2 EGLR 24. It is also possible that there may be two effective causes: *Lordsgate Properties Ltd v. Balcombe*, above: see para. 7–029 below.

[19] *Di Dio Nominees Pty Ltd v. Brian Mark Real Estate Pty Ltd* [1992] 2 V.R. 732.

[20] *Gunn v. Showell's Brewery Co. Ltd* (1902) 50 W.R. 659, Illustration 12 to Article 59.

[21] [1960] 1 W.L.R. 1204.

[22] Even this difficulty could, it seems, have been overcome by substituting "person" in the agency contract for "prospective purchaser".

[23] [1972] E.G.D. 797. The principles expressed in this case seem entirely at variance with those expressed in *Christie Owen & Davies Ltd v. Rapacioli* [1974] Q.B. 781 although the two cases can, perhaps, be reconciled on their particular facts and contractual terms. On "obtain an offer" see *Cash v. George Dundas Realty Ltd* [1976] 2 S.C.R. 796; (1975) 59 D.L.R. (3d) 605; on "arrange a mortgage" see *Capital Management Corp. v. Hackett Development* (1971) 18 F.L.R. 362 (Aus.); and on "subject to our offer being accepted" see *Richard Ellis v. Pipe-Chem (Holdings) Ltd* [1981] E.G.D. 222.

to grant a mortgage but the prospective vendor then withdrew from the sale negotiations. The Court of Appeal held that commission was not due because an "offer of mortgage" meant an offer which actually led to a mortgage.

7–022   **Custom.**[24] Just as custom cannot entitle an agent to commission where it is unreasonable or contrary to the express terms of the contract,[25] it also cannot debar an agent from commission where it is unreasonable, or where the terms of the contract entitle the agent to commission.[26]

7–023   **Conclusion.** The cases discussed in this Article are no more than illustrations of the strict criteria applied. It cannot be too strongly emphasised that each case falls to be decided with reference to the general principles: "first, when an agent claims that he has earned the right to commission, the test is whether upon the proper interpretation of the contract between the principal and agent the event has happened upon which commission is to be paid. Secondly, there are no special principles of construction applicable to commission contracts with estate agents. Thirdly, contracts under which a principal is bound to pay commission for an introduction which does not result in a sale must be expressed in clear language."[27]

7–024   **Claims on a quantum meruit.**[28] In the nineteenth century it was commonly thought that if an agent was prevented from earning his commission he was nevertheless entitled to receive a reasonable sum on

---

[24] See Article 31.
[25] Above, para. 3–034.
[26] *Les Affréteurs Reunis Société Anonynyme v. Leopold Walford (London) Ltd* [1919] A.C. 801.
[27] *Ackroyd & Sons v. Hasan* [1960] 2 Q.B. 144, 154, *per* Upjohn L.J.
[28] The expression *quantum meruit* is used in at least two different senses in the cases: (i) to describe a claim in restitution; (ii) to describe a claim in contract for a reasonable sum. Such a claim must be based on an express or implied term in the agency contract. *Cf.* para. 7–009 above. In many of the authorities no distinction is made between the two different uses of the expression and it is often not clear to which the court intended to refer. The matter is further complicated because the courts have sometimes been referring to the principle expressed in *Planché v. Colburn* (1831) 8 Bing. 14 that in certain circumstances, where an innocent party has rendered services under a contract which has been terminated by him because of the other party's breach, he may waive the claim for breach of contract and sue in restitution on a *quantum meruit* to recover a reasonable sum for his services. The extent of this principle is doubtful in the light of modern developments of the law of contract, but see Goff and Jones, *Law of Restitution* (4th ed.), pp. 424 *et seq.* Because the principle depends essentially on breach of contract and termination, it is doubtful after *Luxor (Eastbourne) Ltd v. Cooper* [1941] A.C. 108 whether it can have any application to an estate agent's contract.

a *quantum meruit*. But, as was frequently also pointed out,[29] such suggestions were contrary to principle. A claim for a contractual *quantum meruit* must be based on an implied contractual term that a reasonable sum is payable in the circumstances. Where the contract expressly provides for remuneration on the happening of an event, any such implication would be contrary to this express term and so could not be made. "It was said that there was an implied contract to pay the agent a *quantum meruit* for his services. The answer was that there could be no implied contract when there was an express contract."[30] The principle is, perhaps, most clearly to be found in *Howard Houlder & Partners Ltd v. Manx Isles S.S. Co.*[31] and *Bentall, Horsley & Baldry v. Vicary.*[32] In the latter case an estate agent claimed on a *quantum meruit* when the vendor sold the property himself, although the agent had been appointed the sole agent. McCardie J. held that the principal was not in breach of contract. Of the agent's claim on a *quantum meruit* he said[33]:

> "Undoubtedly ... [the agent] did work and incurred expense. But this is quite a usual feature of an estate agent's vocation when he works under a commission note which only gives him a right to recover commission when he fulfils the terms of the note. He runs the risk of losing his labour and expense unless he can comply with the conditions of the bargain. There is no scope in the present case for the operation of the doctrine of *quantum meruit*."

It may, however, be that the intention of the parties was that the principal should pay the agent a reasonable sum if the event upon the happening of which remuneration was due did not occur. The contract may make express provision to this effect.[34] Alternatively, the implication of a term to this effect might be necessary to give business efficacy to the contract or otherwise to effect the clear intention of the parties. But it is clear that such an implication would only be made in the most exceptional cases.[35]

---

[29] *e.g. Martin v. Tucker* (1885) 1 T.L.R. 655; *Peacock v. Freeman* (1888) 4 T.L.R. 541; *Barnett v. Isaacson* (1888) 4 T.L.R. 645; *Re Sovereign Life Assce. Co., Salter's Claim* (1891) 7 T.L.R. 602; *Lott v. Outhwaite* (1893) 10 T.L.R. 76.
[30] *Lott v. Outhwaite*, above, at p. 77, *per* Lindley L.J.
[31] [1923] 1 K.B. 110.
[32] [1931] 1 K.B. 253.
[33] [1931] 1 K.B. at p. 262. See also for a more modern example *Fairvale Ltd v. Sabharwal* [1992] 2 EGLR 27.
[34] *e.g. Sinclair Goldsmith v. Minero Peru Comercial* [1978] E.G.D. 194; *Reif Diner & Co. v. Catalytic International Co.* (1978) 246 EG 743, Illustration 10 to Article 57. For the amount payable see para. 7–005 above.
[35] *e.g. Firth v. Hylane Ltd* [1959] E.G.D. 212. The agency contract there provided that if the agent could find a purchaser willing to purchase the property for £35,000 he would receive £1,000 commission. This figure for commission was admitted to be high and in the nature of a bonus. The property was eventually sold for £31,000 to a person introduced by

—*cont. on next page*

7–025   **Overpaid commission.** Sometimes advance payments of commission exceed the amounts actually due when the contract is terminated. In such a case it is a matter of interpretation of each contract whether there is or is not an implication that such overpayments must be repaid.[36]

7–026   **Commercial agents.** The Commercial Agents (Council Directive) Regulations 1993 contain provisions as to entitlement to commission.[37] These are discussed in Chapter 11.

Article 59

WHETHER AGENT IS EFFECTIVE CAUSE OF TRANSACTION

7–027   Subject to any special terms or other indications in the contract of agency, where the remuneration of an agent is a commission on a transaction to be brought about, he is not entitled to such commission unless his services were the effective cause of the transaction being brought about.[38]

Comment

7–028   The principle stated in this Article is no more than a particular example of the wider principle stated in the preceding Article. But there exists a body of cases on the notion of "effective cause" which is sufficiently discrete to require segregation. Where the agent is to be remunerated upon the happening of an event, the question whether that event has occurred depends upon the facts of the case and the express or implied terms of the agency contract. Many agents are employed upon terms that if a certain transaction is brought about, they will be entitled to a commission calculated by reference to the amount of the consideration passing in that transaction or to a stated fee. Sometimes the transaction is carried out but has not been brought about as a result of the agent's efforts. Sometimes the agent has played a part in bringing about the transaction but only a small part, or he has only achieved a

---

—*cont. from previous page*
the agent. The Court of Appeal said it did not make sense for the agent to be paid nothing if the property fetched less than £35,000 and held that the parties had merely defined how the commission was to be quantified. They had, therefore, not excluded payment of a reasonable sum for work done by the agent at the principal's request. The court awarded £450 plus £100 expenses. See also *Boots v. E. Christopher & Co.* [1952] 1 K.B. 89, 98–99; Article 60.
[36] See *Rivoli Hats Ltd v. Gooch* [1953] 1 W.L.R. 1190; *Clayton Newbury Ltd v. Findlay, ibid.* 1194n; *Bronester Ltd v. Priddle* [1961] 1 W.L.R. 1294; *Prudential Assurance Co. Ltd v. Rodriguez* [1982] 2 N.Z.L.R. 54.
[37] Regs. 7–12.
[38] See Comment; Murdoch, (1985) 276 EG 742 and 877.

partial success. Sometimes the principal has carried out a different transaction from the one the agent was employed to bring about but the substitute transaction was nevertheless the result of the agent's efforts. For example, an agent may have been employed to find a purchaser for a house. He introduces a person who is only willing to take a long lease of the house and the principal thereafter decides to grant such a lease rather than sell. Has the agent earned his commission? The matter may take a more complicated form. For example, an agent is employed to find a purchaser for part of the business being carried on by the principal. He introduces a potential purchaser, but after direct negotiations between the principal and the potential purchaser, the two of them agree to establish a new company with the principal as minority shareholder and transfer the business to that company in exchange for shares. The final transaction is different in substance from the sale the agent was employed to achieve but was carried out in substitution for that sale without the agent having caused or even been aware of the change. Has the agent earned his commission?

The answers to these questions depend upon the express or implied terms of the relevant agency contract. But a large number of them interpret the agent's contract in connection with a sale on the basis that to be entitled to commission the agent must be the, or at least an, effective cause of the sale. This seems to result "from the use in the agency agreements of expressions such as 'find a purchaser' or 'introduce a purchaser'.... It would have been quite artificial to suppose that the parties intended that the agent should earn his commission simply by finding an individual who, independently of any further action by the agent, later agreed to buy the subject property."[39] Where the contract is in such terms as "You are employed to find a purchaser of the property," the above result flows as a result of a constructional implication. Where there is no such term, the implication will only be made to give business efficacy to the contract. Where the ultimate transaction is different from and carried out in substitution for the contract which the agent was employed to bring about, the same implication will be made and the court will ask whether the agent was the effective cause of the particular transaction which the principal entered into.[40] The fact of a substitute transaction may be evidence of a

---

[39] *Doyle v. Mt. Kidston Mining and Exploration Pty Ltd* [1984] 2 Qd.R. 386, 392 *per* McPherson J.

[40] *Gunn v. Showell's Brewery Co. Ltd* (1902) 18 T.L.R. 659, Illustration 12; *Burchell v. Gowrie and Blockhouse Collieries Ltd* [1910] A.C. 614; *Price Davies & Co. v. Smith* (1929) 141 L.T. 490; *Stewarts & Lloyds Ltd v. Zoess, The Times*, July 5, 1955 (H.L.); *Jack Windle Ltd v. Brierley* [1952] 1 All E.R. 398 (doubted [1981] E.G.D. at p. 245); *Chamberlain and Willows v. H.B.S. (Trust) Ltd* [1952] E.G.D. 443; *Poulter v. Doggett* (1964) 115 L.J. 76; *Allen v. Anderson* [1969] N.Z.L.R. 951; *Levers v. Dunsdon* [1968] E.G.D. 280.

299

break in the chain of causation. But it should be noted that in some cases the terms of the contract or the nature of the transaction mean that there is no room for this implication.[41]

The general principle is well stated in *Millar, Son & Co. v. Radford*[42] where the defendant employed the plaintiff to find a purchaser of property or, failing that, a tenant. A tenant was found and commission was paid. Fifteen months later the tenant purchased the property and the plaintiff claimed commission on the sale although he had not been concerned with the property since the letting. In holding that the plaintiff was not entitled to commission Collins M.R. said[43]: "It is important to point out that the right to commission does not arise out of the mere fact that agents had introduced a tenant or purchaser. It is not sufficient to show that the introduction was a *causa sine qua non*. It is necessary to show that the introduction was an efficient[44] cause in bringing about the letting or the sale. Here the plaintiffs fail to establish what is a condition precedent to their right to commission—*viz.*, that they have brought about the sale. It is open to the defendant[45] in an action like this to say either that, though the plaintiffs effected a sale, they were not his agents, or that, though they were his agents, they had not effected the sale. If the defendant proves either the one or the other, the plaintiffs fail to make out their case."[46]

7–029   **"The" or "a"?** There is doubt as to whether the rule is more helpfully formulated by requiring that the agent's act be "the effective cause" or merely "an effective cause". The word "the" is used in this Article: but it should be noted that in various places, including the passage quoted in the paragraph above, the indefinite article "a" is used.[47] It is certainly true that the agent can be entitled to his commission though there are other events which could be called causes of the transaction. Thus if the agent introduces a person who becomes the purchaser "it is nothing to the point . . . that that person would have become the purchaser without

---

[41] See *David Leahy (Aust.) Pty. Ltd v. McPhersons Ltd* [1991] 2 V.R. 367, Illustration 18; *Brian Cooper Ltd. v. Fairview Estates (Investments) Ltd* [1987] 1 EGLR 18.

[42] (1903) 19 T.L.R. 575. For cases on almost identical facts, see *Toulmin v. Millar* (1887) 58 L.T. 96, Illustration 4; *Nightingale v. Parsons* [1914] 2 K.B. 621.

[43] (1903) 19 T.L.R. 575, 576.

[44] The word "efficient" has changed its meaning since 1903. The modern equivalent is "effective" (see, *e.g. Allan v. Leo Lines Ltd* [1957] 1 Lloyd's Rep. 127, 133).

[45] The burden of proving entitlement to commission rests on the agent throughout. By using the expression "it is open to the defendant" Collins M.R. can mean no more than that the defendant may assert; the plaintiff agent must, of course, disprove the assertions.

[46] The passage has, for the sake of clarity, been altered from the indirect speech of the original report to direct speech.

[47] See also *Burchell v. Gowrie and Blockhouse Colleries Ltd* [1910] A.C. 614, 624, where both phrases are used.

the intervention of the agent, or that the principal's own efforts were also an effective cause of the sale."[48] But it is submitted that it is the word "effective" which is the most significant "'Effective cause' means more than simply 'cause'. The inquiry is whether the actions of the agent really brought about the relation of buyer and seller, and it is seldom conclusive that there were other events which could each be described as a cause of the ensuing sale. The factual inquiry is whether a sale is really brought about by the act of the agent."[49] In a recent case where a submission was made that the better usage was "*an* effective cause", Woolf L.J. said that this could create problems where there are "two or more effective causes, each of which could be the object of a claim for commission."[50] A situation of two genuinely effective causes of equal potency is unlikely, though possible,[51] and it seems better to retain the word "the". But a vendor may more easily sometimes become liable for two (or more) commissions on the same sale by virtue of the specific terms of two (or more) agency contracts.[52]

Apart from the general principle that in the absence of other indications the agent must be the effective cause of the transaction taking place, no clear principles can be easily derived from the many cases on this topic. No precise definition of "effective cause" in this context has yet been given by an English court.[53] Accordingly, any conclusions to be drawn from these cases must be advanced with hesitation.

The agent will normally be entitled to his commission if he causes a person to negotiate with his principal and contract, no substantial break in the negotiations having taken place. It appears that the agent does not have to complete or even take part in the negotiations,[54] nor

---

[48] *L.J. Hooker Ltd. v. W.J. Adams Estates Pty Ltd* (1977) 138 C.L.R. 52, 58 *per* Barwick C.J. For an example see *Doyle v. Mt. Kidston Mining & Exploration Pty Ltd* [1984] 2 Qd.R. 386.

[49] *ibid.*, at p. 86 *per* Jacobs J. See also *Tufton Associates v. Dilmun Shipping* [1992] 1 Lloyd's Rep. 71, 78 ("cause which had the greatest efficacy" not the last).

[50] *Brian Cooper & Co. v. Fairview Estates (Investments) Ltd* [1987] 1 EGLR 18, 20.

[51] It occurred in *Lordsgate Properties Ltd v. Balcombe* [1985] 1 EGLR 20, Illustration 19.

[52] See *Bernard Marcus & Co. v. Ashraf* [1988] 1 EGLR 7 (auctioneer); *Peter Yates & Co. v. Bullock* [1990] 2 EGLR 24; para. 7–021 above.

[53] The *Restatement*, § 448, states that "an agent is an 'effective cause' ... when his efforts have been sufficiently important in achieving a result for the accomplishment of which the principal has promised to pay him, so that it is just that the principal should pay the promised compensation to him." This definition is open to the objection that it begs the question.

[54] *Re Beale, ex p. Durrant* (1888) 5 Morr. 37, Illustration 8; *Green v. Bartlett* (1863) 14 C.B.(N.S.) 681, Illustration 9; *Mansell v. Clements* (1874) L.R. 9 C.P. 139; *Barnett v. Brown & Co.* (1890) 6 T.L.R. 463; *Steere v. Smith* (1885) 2 T.L.R. 131; *Burton v. Hughes* (1885) 1 T.L.R. 207; *Thompson, Rippon & Co. v. Thomas* (1896) 11 T.L.R. 304; *Brandon*

—cont. on next page

arrange any meeting[55] nor persuade either party to enter into the contract. Further, he is still entitled to his commission if the principal contracts at a lower price or on other terms than the agent was authorised to offer, provided that the agent was the effective cause and the express or implied terms of the agency contract are such as to show that the remuneration was payable upon the happening of the transaction which actually resulted.[56]

The agent will not normally be entitled to his commission if the third party who ultimately contracts has his attention drawn to the possibility of contracting by means other than those intended by the agent to bring about the contract.[57] Moreover, the fact that one agent introduces a person who ultimately purchases after a later introduction by another agent will not necessarily entitle the first agent to commission.[58] In such a case the court must determine which of the two agents was the effective cause of the transaction taking place.[59] On the whole, it may be said that the first introducer has more often succeeded. But it is possible that a sale might have two effective causes.[60]

7–030   **Commercial agents.** The Commercial Agents (Council Directive) Regulations 1993 contain provisions on entitlement to commission which parallel the "effective cause" rule.[61] The Regulations are discussed in Chapter 11.

—cont. from previous page
v. *Hanna* [1907] 2 I.R. 212; *Walker, Fraser and Steele v. Fraser's Trustees*, 1910 S.C. 222; *Burchell v. Gowrie and Blockhouse Collieries Ltd* [1910] A.C. 614; *Howard Houlder & Partners Ltd v. Manx Isles S.S. Co. Ltd* [1923] 1 K.B. 110; *Bow's Emporium Ltd v. A.R. Brett & Co. Ltd* (1928) 44 T.L.R. 194; *Bartlett v. Cole* [1963] E.G.D. 452, Illustration 15; *Burns v. Coomber* [1966] E.G.D. 110; *F.P. Rolfe & Co. v. George* [1969] E.G.D. 331; *McKeag Harris Realty & Development Co. Ltd v. Builders' Mutual Assets Ltd* (1968) 66 W.W.R. 512; *Knight, Frank & Rutley v. Fraser*, 1974 S.L.T. 50. But if he simply advises his principal, he may not be the effective cause: *Hoddell v. Smith* [1976] E.G.D. 217.
    [55] See, e.g. *Green v. Bartlett* (1863) 14 C.B.(N.S.) 681, Illustration 9.
    [56] *Allan v. Leo Lines Ltd* [1957] 1 Lloyd's Rep. 127, Illustration 2; *Poulter v. Dogget* (1964) 115 L.J. 76; *Allen v. Anderson* [1969] N.Z.L.R. 951. See also *Spiess v. Taylor* (1984) 271 EG 196 (no effective cause where property offered at wrong price: *sed quaere*); *Connell Estates v. Begej* [1993] 2 EGLR 35 (commission on sale by part exchange).
    [57] Illustrations 9, 13 and 16. See also *D.C. Wylde & Co. v. Sparg*, 1977 (2) S.A.L.R. 75 (eventual purchaser knew about property already). But cf. *Cobbs Property Services Ltd v. Liddell-Taylor* [1990] 1 EGLR 49.
    [58] *Murray v. Currie* (1836) 7 C. & P. 584; *Barnett v. Brown* (1890) 6 T.L.R. 463; *Curtis v. Nixon* (1871) 24 L.T. 706, Illustration 3; *Davis v. Trollope & Sons* [1943] 1 All E.R. 501; *Bartlett v. Cole* [1963] E.G.D. 452, Illustration 15; *Chesterfield & Co. Ltd. v. Zahid* [1989] 2 EGLR 24. Sometimes the matter may turn on who "introduced": e.g. *Terry Martel Real Estate Ltd v. Lovette Investments Ltd* (1981) 123 D.L.R. (3d) 387.
    [59] *John D. Wood & Co. v. Dantata* [1987] 2 EGLR 23. See also *Chasen Ryder & Co. v. Hedges* [1993] 1 EGLR 47. If two different agents are claiming commission from the principal he cannot normally interplead: *Greatorex & Co. v. Shackle* [1895] 2 Q.B. 249. See also Article 72.
    [60] *Lordsgate Properties Ltd v. Balcombe* [1985] 1 EGLR 20, Illustration 19.
    [61] Reg. 7(1).

Illustrations

(1) A employs B, a broker, to procure a charter for a ship. B   **7–031**
introduces C, who is also a broker, C introduces D, who negotiates for
but does not enter into a charterparty. D informs E that the ship is
available and E charters her from A. B is not entitled to commission,
the transaction being too remote a consequence of his introduction.[62]

(2) A employs B to find a purchaser for a ship. B, acting on behalf
of A, contracts with C that C will receive a commission if he finds a
purchaser. X, acting through D, asks C to find a ship for purchase and
C gives X the name of A's ship. Various offers and counter-offers are
passed through C, the last being rejected by A. Shortly afterwards A
sells the ship to X privately. C is entitled to his commission, the
introduction of X being the effective cause of the sale. The fact that the
final sale was at a different figure from any that passed through C did
not mean that C was not the real cause of the sale taking place at all.[63]

(3) An estate agent lets a house for a term of years, the tenant
having the option of taking it for a further term. The tenant declines to
exercise this option but agrees to take the house for a further term at a
lower rent. The first agent is not entitled to commission on the further
term since he was not the proximate cause of the reletting.[64]

(4) An agent is employed to let an estate and procures a tenant. The
tenant subsequently buys the estate without any further communication
with the agent. The agent is not entitled to any commission on the
sale.[65]

(5) An agent employed to sell property on commission is not
entitled to commission if he and the principal agree together that he
shall be the purchaser himself, unless they expressly agree that
commission shall be payable on such a sale.[66]

(6) An agent, employed to find a purchaser of property at a
specified price, brings it to the notice of a government department

---

[62] *Wilkinson v. Martin* (1837) 8 C. & P. 1. And see *Ellis v. May & Co.* (1960) 110 L.J.
140 (introduction of mortgage broker: no commission for "arranging mortgage").
[63] *Allan v. Leo Lines Ltd* [1957] 1 Lloyd's Rep. 127. The facts have been slightly
simplified for the sake of clarity.
[64] *Curtis v. Nixon* (1871) 24 L.T. 706. See also *Ex p. Chatteris* (1874) 22 W.R. 289;
Lofts v. Bourke (1884) 1 T.L.R. 58.
[65] *Toulmin v. Millar* (1887) 58 L.T. 96 (reported on another point (1887) 12 App.Cas.
746). The test there laid down by Lord Watson that "in order to found a legal claim for
commission there must not only be a causal, there must also be a contractual relation
between the introduction and the ultimate transaction of sale" is difficult to understand
and does not seem in practice to have been applied. See also *Millar, Son & Co. v.
Radford* (1903) 19 T.L.R. 575 and *Nightingale v. Parsons* [1914] 2 K.B. 621 for cases on
almost identical facts.
[66] *Hocker v. Waller* (1929) 29 Com.Cas. 296. See also *Barnett v. Isaacson* (1888) 4
T.L.R. 645, Illustration 14.

which, after negotiations to purchase fail, compulsorily acquires it at a lower price and against the wishes of the principal. The agent is not entitled to commission. He was employed only to find a ready and willing purchaser at a price which the principal voluntarily accepts. [67]

(7) A entered into an agreement with B in the following terms: "In case of your introducing a purchaser [of a certain business] of whom I approve, or capital which I should accept, I could pay you 5 per cent commission, provided no one else is entitled to commission in respect of the same introduction." B introduced C, who advanced £10,000 by way of loan, and B was duly paid his commission in respect of that advance. Some months afterwards, A and C entered into an agreement for a partnership, C advancing a further £4,000 by way of capital. Held, that B was not entitled to commission on the £4,000, that amount having been advanced in consequence of the negotiations between A and C for a partnership, with which B had nothing to do. [68]

(8) A, who was employed by B to find a purchaser for certain property, introduced C to B, but C could not accept B's terms. Shortly afterwards B became bankrupt. Further negotiations took place between C and B's trustee in bankruptcy, resulting in a sale of the property three weeks after the original introduction. Held, A's introduction brought about the sale and he was entitled to prove in the bankruptcy for his commission. [69]

(9) A, an auctioneer and estate agent, was employed by P to sell the island of Herm by auction or otherwise. He put it up for auction and the reserve price was not reached. Afterwards T, who had attended the auction, asked A for and was given P's name. T then approached P direct and eventually purchased the island from him. Shortly before the sale P wrote to A withdrawing A's authority to sell. Held, A was the *causa causans* of the sale and was entitled to commission. [70]

(10) A employed B to sell an estate in lots. C bought certain lots and B received commission on them. At this stage C refused to buy further lots. A then withdrew B's authority, and 27 months later C bought the remaining lots by private contract. Held, that the jury were entitled to find that the ultimate sale was not due to B's intervention. [71]

---

[67] *Hodges & Sons v. Hackbridge Park Residential Hotel Ltd* [1940] 1 K.B. 404. See also *Battams v. Tompkins* (1892) 8 T.L.R. 707; *Beable v. Dickerson* (1885) 1 T.L.R. 654; *Thompson v. British Berna Motor Lorries Ltd* (1917) 33 T.L.R. 187. *Cf. Price, Davies & Co. v. Smith* (1929) 141 L.T. 490 and *O'Connor Real Estate Ltd v. Flynn* (1969) 3 D.L.R. (3d) 345.
[68] *Tribe v. Taylor* (1876) 1 C.P.D. 505. See also *Boyd v. Tovil Paper Co. Ltd* (1884) 4 T.L.R. 332.
[69] *Re Beale, ex p. Durrant* (1888) 5 Morr. 37.
[70] *Green v. Bartlett* (1863) 14 C.B.(N.S.) 681. See also *Bayley v. Chadwick* (1878) 39 L.T. 429; *Wilkinson v. Alston* (1879) 48 L.J.Q.B. 733; *Ong Kee Ming v. Quek Yong Kang* [1991] 3 M.L.J. 294.
[71] *Lumley v. Nicholson* (1886) 34 W.R. 716. Compare *Jack Windle Ltd v. Brierley* [1952] 1 All E.R. 398.

(11)   An estate agent, A, was instructed by P to offer a house for sale. It was agreed that he should receive 2½ per cent commission if he found a purchaser or a guinea for his services if the house was sold without his intervention. T called on A and received a card to view the house. T viewed it and after negotiations though a friend of P, he ultimately bought it. Held, there was evidence for the jury that the house was sold through the intervention of A so as to entitle him to commission. [72]

(12)   Two brewery companies agreed to pay A a commission on all licensed properties or businesses they might purchase through his introduction. A submitted a brewery for their consideration. The companies decided that the most advantageous course was for them to promote a new company to buy the brewery. Held, the position was the same as if the companies had bought the brewery themselves and sold it to the new company. A was accordingly entitled to his commission. [73]

(13)   A introduced T to P, his principal, as a possible purchaser of certain property belonging to P, but no agreement between them was reached. P subsequently sold the property by auction, T being the purchaser. Held, A was not entitled to his commission. [74]

(14)   A agreed to pay B a commission of £5,000 in the event of B introducing a purchaser of A's business. B failed to find a purchaser, but introduced C, an accountant, as a person who might be able to introduce a purchaser. C eventually himself bought the property at the proposed price after deducting the commission which he was to have been paid in the event of his finding a purchaser. Held, that there was no evidence that B had introduced a purchaser of the business, he having introduced C, not as a purchaser, but as an agent to find a purchaser, and that B could not recover either the agreed commission or

---

[72] *Mansell v. Clements* (1874) L.R. 9 C.P. 139. See also *Barnett v. Brown* (1890) 6 T.L.R. 463; *Steere v. Smith* (1885) 2 T.L.R. 131; *Burton v. Hughes* (1885) 1 T.L.R. 207; *Thompson, Ripon & Co. v. Thomas* (1896) 11 T.L.R. 304; *Brandon v. Hanna* [1907] 2 I.R. 212; *Howard Houlder & Partners Ltd v. Manx Isles S.S. Co.* [1923] 1 K.B. 110; *Burns v. Coomber* [1966] E.G.D. 110; *McKeag Harris Realty & Development Co. Ltd v. Builders Mutual Assets Ltd* (1968) 64 W.W.R. 208, affd. (1968) 66 W.W.R. 512.

[73] *Gunn v. Showell's Brewery Co. Ltd & Crosswell's Ltd* (1902) 50 W.R. 659 (see also at first instance (1901) 17 T.L.R. 563); *Di Dio Nominees Pty Ltd v. Brian Mark Real Estate Pty Ltd* [1992] 2 V.R. 732. See also *Glendinning v. Cavanagh* (1908) 40 S.C.R. 414; *Stratton v. Vachan and Wilson* (1911) 44 S.C.R. 395; *McBrayne v. Imperial Loan Co* (1913) 13 D.L.R. 448; *Levers v. Dunsdon* [1968] E.G.D. 280; *L.J. Hooker Ltd v. W.J. Adams Estates Pty Ltd*, Illustration 17; *Lord v. Trippe* (1977) 51 A.L.J.R. 574; and n. 40 above.

[74] *Taplin v. Barrett* (1889) 6 T.L.R. 30. See also *Green v. Mules* (1861) 30 L.J.C.P. 343, Illustration 8 to Article 57; *Lofts v. Bourke* (1884) 1 T.L.R. 58; *Coles v. Enoch* [1939] 3 All E.R. 327, Illustration 16. cf. *Walker, Fraser and Steele v. Fraser's Trustees* 1910 S.C. 222.

a *quantum meruit*, the claim for a *quantum meruit* being excluded by the express terms of the contract.[75]

(15)   A employed B to sell his café. B introduced C, who wanted to buy but could not without a loan, and who eventually went to new agents for a lower-priced business. The new agents also had A's business on their books, and assured C of finance, advising him to employ a solicitor for the purchase. The new agents' finance fell through but C's solicitor found finance and C bought. Held, the removal of the financial problem made B's introduction which had otherwise been successful the effective cause of the purchase. *Semble*, if the new agents had been able to supply finance they would have been the effective cause.[76]

(16)   P, who was the owner of a shop suitable for a pin-table arcade, arranged with A to pay him a commission if A could find a tenant. A telephoned C, a manufacturer of pin-tables, and told him of the shop. C said he wanted to consult his partner. T overheard the telephone conversation and asked C for the address. C merely said it was "in Victoria". T went to Victoria, found the shop, and arranged a lease direct with P. Held, A was not entitled to commission. The deliberate withholding of the address by C broke the chain of causation and A was not the direct or efficient cause of T becoming the tenant.[77]

(17)   An agent is engaged to locate a satisfactory purchaser for land at a satisfactory price. The agent introduces two persons, L and H, who conduct real property development operations though a number of companies including A Co. L makes several unsuccessful offers. The vendor had independently been in touch with another development company of which B Co. was a subsidiary. A Co. and B Co. enter into a joint venture agreement; B Co. buys the land and makes an allotment of shares to A Co. The agent had played no part in introducing either company and did not know of the joint venture. He is not entitled to commission.[78]

(18)   A "business broker" states terms to company X upon which it will act in the acquisition of other businesses. A fee is payable if a company or business submitted by the broker is acquired by the

[75] *Barnett v. Isaacson* (1888) 4 T.L.R. 645.
[76] *Bartlett v. Cole* [1963] E.G.D. 452; *cf. Robert Drummond v. Mangles* [1981] E.G.D. 265; *Hartnell v. Taylor, Cook v. Bromwich* [1982] E.G.D. 436. See also *Rungay v. Forrester* (1967) 63 D.L.R. (2d) 338; *Tufnell v. Richard Costain Ltd* (1968) 209 EG 705; *Christie & Co. v. Jones* [1966] E.G.D. 439; *Glentree Estates Ltd v. Gee* [1981] E.G.D. 235; *cf. Jack Windle Ltd v. Brierley* [1952] 1 All E.R. 398 as a case where the finance was provided by the *seller*; doubted in *Glentree Estates Ltd v. Gee*, above; *Peter Yates & Co. v. Bullock* [1990] 2 EGLR 24.
[77] *Coles v. Enoch* [1939] 3 All E.R. 327. See also *Antrobus v. Wickens* (1865) 4 F. & F. 291.
[78] *L.J. Hooker Ltd v. W.J. Adams Estates Pty. Ltd* (1977) 138 C.L.R. 52. (The judgments in this case repay study.)

company. In 1982 the broker introduces a business. Negotiations ensue but are abandoned. In 1985 the business is transferred to a public listed company. In 1987 company X effects a takeover of the listed company. The broker's fee is due.[79]

(19) X engages the services of two agents, each of which introduces the same prospective purchaser. X's son tells the second agents that he has an offer through the first agents, and the second agents tell this to the prospective purchaser, who raises his offer, neither he nor the second agent realising that he is bidding against himself. The two agents are both effective causes of the eventual sale.[80]

Article 60

Agent Prevented by Principal from Earning Remuneration

The principal will only be liable for preventing the agent from earning his remuneration when the implication of a promise that he will not do so is necessary to give business efficiacy to the contract, or otherwise to effect the intention of the parties.[81]   7–032

Comment

If the agent claims that he is entitled to damages because his principal has wrongfully deprived him of the opportunity to earn his remuneration, he must be able to show some contractual promise of which the principal is in breach. Where there is an express promise on which the agent can rely, no difficulty will arise. But where there is no express promise the question will arise whether any, and if so what, promise can be implied.   7–033

Earlier case law. For many years it was thought that the principal was under a duty not to deprive the agent of the opportunity of earning his commission. This view was first expressed in *Prickett v. Badger*.[82] A series of confused cases followed,[83] the basis of the supposed principle   7–034

---

[79] *David Leahy (Aust.) Pty Ltd. v. McPherson's Ltd* [1991] 2 V.R. 362. See also *Brian Cooper Ltd. v. Fairview Estates (Investments) Ltd* [1987] 1 EGLR 18 ("introduce a tenant ... with whom we have not been in previous communication and who subsequently completes a lease").

[80] *Lordsgate Properties Ltd v. Balcombe* [1985] 1 EGLR 20.

[81] See Comment.

[82] (1856) 1 C.B.(N.S.) 296.

[83] These are considered in detail in Ash, *Willing to Purchase* (1963). They include *Green v. Lucas* (1875) 33 L.T. 584; *Fisher v. Drewett* (1878) 48 L.J.Q.B. 32; *Roberts v. Barnard* (1884) 1 Cab. & El. 336; *Grogan v. Smith* (1890) 7 T.L.R. 132; *Fuller v. Eames* (1892) 8 T.L.R. 278; *Nosotti v. Auerbach* (1899) 15 T.L.R. 140; *Brinson v. Davies* (1911) 105 L.T. 134; *Hankinson v. Vickers* [1931] E.G.D. 16.

never being fully worked out. Most of the cases concerned agents, *e.g.* estate agents, who were entitled to receive a commission if they brought about a certain transaction for their principals. It was realised, however, that the principal could not be held liable in the context of sale of land when he did *any* act which had the effect of preventing the agent from earning commission; for the vendor may be taken normally to wish to retain some element of discretion. The supposed rule became therefore more and more tenuous. In *G. Trollope & Sons v. Martyn Bros.*[84] the Court of Appeal held that the principal of an estate agent would be liable in damages to the agent if (but only if) he unreasonably withdrew from negotiations with the potential purchaser with the result that the agent could not earn his commission. However, the dissenting judgment of Scrutton L.J. revealed the fallacies in the reasoning of the majority of the court, and in *Luxor (Eastbourne) Ltd v. Cooper*[85] the House of Lords expressly overruled *G. Trollope & Sons v. Martyn Bros.*

7–035   **Estate agent's contract.** In *Luxor's* case the House made a detailed examination of the estate agent's contract. The peculiarity of the usual version of this arrangement is that the agent is not under an obligation to do anything.[86] Hence in the typical situation the principal makes a continuing or single offer of a unilateral contract only, which the agent accepts by introducing a purchaser or whatever else is required by the terms of the particular offer.[87] Sometimes a letter following the engagement may contain wording purporting to create a bilateral contract, inasmuch as it contains undertakings that the agent will use his best endeavours and so forth.[88] Although there can be no objection in

---

[84] [1934] 2 K.B. 436. This case was followed in *G. Trollope & Sons v. Caplan* [1936] 2 K.B. 382; *Kahn v. Aircraft Industries Corp. Ltd* [1937] 3 All E.R. 476; *Harrods Ltd v. Geneen* [1938] 4 All E.R. 493; *Way & Waller Ltd v. Verrall* [1939] 3 All E.R. 533.

[85] [1941] A.C. 108, Illustration 1. Most of the cases cited in nn. 83 and 84 above must now be taken to have been wrongly decided, or at least decided on the wrong principles. In general, any case on this topic before *Luxor's* case should be regarded with caution. It is suggested that the statement in *J.H. Milner & Son v. Percy Bilton* [1966] 1 W.L.R. 1582, 1588 that "the estate agent who has been employed to sell a particular house can sue for damages if his authority is withdrawn" was made *per incuriam*, especially since the judge relied upon *G. Trollope & Sons v. Martyn Bros.*

[86] See Comment to Article 58.

[87] *L.J. Hooker Ltd v. W.J. Adams Estates Pty. Ltd* (1977) 138 C.L.R. 52, 73. A different type of analysis, which tends to discount the conceptual difference between unilateral and bilateral contracts, is however suggested by Lord Wilberforce in *A.M. Satterhwaite & Co. v. New Zealand Shipping Co. Ltd (The Eurymedon)* [1975] A.C. 154, 167–168; followed by Barwick C.J. in *Port Jackson Stevedoring Pty. Ltd v. Salmond & Spraggon (Australia) Pty Ltd (The New York Star)* [1979] 1 Lloyd's Rep. 298, 305–306, whose judgment was endorsed by the Privy Council [1981] 1 W.L.R. 138, 148.

[88] See Murdoch (1977) 242 EG 609; *cf.* McConnell (1983) 265 EG 547. In two cases the confirming letter appears to have been treated as effective: *Way & Waller Ltd v. Ryde* [1944] 1 All E.R. 9 and *John E. Trinder & Partners v. Haggis* (1951) 158 EG 4. Murdoch,

principle to a new contract being subsequently formed in this way, or indeed to the initial contract being a bilateral one, the authoritative way in which the normal agency contract is analysed in *Luxor*'s case means that such an interpretation of the facts would be difficult to establish.

On the unilateral analysis, the next question is whether the principal is to be regarded as promising not to deprive the agent of commission. Although the speeches in the case speak of implied *terms*, it is submitted that if the contract is truly unilateral, the requirement would be for the implication of an implied collateral *contract*.[89] However this be, the House, having interpreted the nature of the transaction, treated the question of implication as a question of business efficacy and held that such implication was not appropriate. It was improbable that the principal would wish to fetter his freedom of choice by binding himself *vis-à-vis* his agent not to withdraw unreasonably from negotiations when he was free *vis-à-vis* the potential purchaser to withdraw at any time for any reason. Furthermore, the agent earns a considerable commission if successful: he likewise takes the business risk that if his efforts are unsuccessful he earns nothing.[90]

"Sole" and "exclusive" agency. Where the agent is appointed "sole" agent, however, it is established that if the principal then employs a second agent who earns the commission on the transaction which the first agent should have earned, the first agent is entitled to damages.[91] The normal view of such a transaction is that it is a bilateral contract, the consideration for the principal's promise not to sell through another agent being the agent's undertaking to use his best endeavours to sell the property.[92] Alternatively, it could be said that the contract is still

7–036

---

op. cit. above, suggests that they are inconsistent with *Toulmin v. Millar* (1887) 58 L.T. 96, Illustration 4 to Article 59.

[89] *Contra*, Treitel, *Law of Contract* (9th ed.), pp. 38–39. And see n. 87 above.

[90] See also *Burns Fry Ltd v. Khurana* (1985) 20 D.L.R. (4th) 245.

[91] *Milsom v. Bechstein* (1898) 14 T.L.R. 159; *Hampton & Sons Ltd v. George* [1939] 3 All E.R. 627; *Newton v. Erickson* (1951) 157 EG 414. Where the agent was employed to effect a single transaction the damages will be calculated by reference to the sum at which it is proved that the plaintiff agent could have found a purchaser: *Hampton & Sons Ltd v. George*, above; *De Coning v. Monror Estate and Investment Co. (Pty) Ltd* 1974 (3) S.A. 72. Where the agent was employed generally, the damages will, on the principles expressed in *Roberts v. Elwells Engineers Ltd* [1972] 2 Q.B. 586, be what he has lost in consequence of the breach, *i.e.* what he would have been expected to earn, less any saved expenses. An account is not the appropriate relief. Nor, under this reasoning, is commision due: but see below, para. 7–037.

[92] *C. Christopher & Co. v. Essig* [1948] W.N. 461; *Mendoza & Co. v. Bell* (1952) 159 EG 372; *Hampton & Sons v. Chapman* [1952] C.P.L. 24; *Galan v. Alekno* [1950] 3 D.L.R. 9; *Fidelity Trust Co. v. Rudy* (1957) 23 W.W.R. 668; *Bradley-Wilson (1954) Ltd v. Canyon Gardens Ltd* (1965) 53 W.W.R. 413; *cf. Midland Business Agency v. Apted* (1971) 218 EG 1727, where the supposed consideration was illusory.

unilateral, but that this is a case where a collateral contract not to revoke will readily be implied, which would not be the case in the first and more general situation.[93] This seems however a more artificial interpretation and where an ordinary bilateral contract can be found it is probably better to use this analysis rather than have recourse to collateral contracts. Normally however the principal will still not be in breach of contract by negotiating the sale of the property himself, for the mere appointment of a sole agent does not imply any prohibition on the principal from so acting.[94] Some agency contracts may, however, expressly prohibit the principal from selling other than through the agent during the period of the sole agency[95]: these are sometimes called "exclusive" or "sole selling" agency contracts.[96] Again, provision may be made that commission must nevertheless be paid to the agent though the principal sells the property himself.[97] It would seem, however, that the principal can still *withdraw* the property.[98] Similar problems arise with distributorship contracts, though here a prohibition on the principal selling himself may more easily be inferred.[99] But in all cases the interpretation of the contract is crucial: decisions cannot be based entirely on the phrase used.[1]

7–037   Estate Agents (Provision of Information) Regulations 1991.[2] Where the terms "sole selling rights" or "sole agency" are used in the course of estate agency work[3] the estate agent must give an explanation of their meaning in the way described in the regulations.[4] Failure to do so

---

[93] Murdoch (1975) 91 L.Q.R. 357.

[94] *Bentall, Horsley & Baldry v. Vicary* [1931] 1 K.B. 253; *Sadler v. Whittaker* (1953) 162 EG 404.

[95] *e.g. Snelgrove v. Ellringham Colliery Co.* (1881) 45 J.P. 408; *Chamberlain & Willows v. Rose* [1924] E.G.D. 356; *Property Choice Ltd v. Fronda* [1991] 2 EGLR 249. They are common in auctioneers' contracts: see *Bernard Marcus & Co. v. Ashraf* [1988] 1 EGLR 7. See also *Chinnock v. Sainsbury* (1860) 30 L.J.Ch. 409; *Lamb & Sons v. Goring Brick Co. Ltd* [1932] 1 K.B. 710.

[96] *Brodie Marshall & Co. (Hotel Division) v. Sharer* [1988] 1 EGLR 21, 22.

[97] *e.g. Tredinnick v. Browne* (1921), cited in *Bentall, Horsley & Baldry v. Vicary* [1931] 1 K.B. 253, 260.

[98] See Murdoch, *Law of Estate Agency and Auctions* (3rd ed.), p. 162.

[99] *W.T. Lamb & Sons v. Goring Brick Co. Ltd* [1932] 1 K.B. 710: see above, para. 1–029.

[1] *Murphy Buckley & Keogh Ltd. v. Pye (Ireland) Ltd* [1971] I.R. 57; *G.F. Galvin (Estates) Ltd v. Hedigan* [1985] I.L.R.M. 295, 300, where it was apparently argued that "sole selling agency" allowed the vendor to sell personally, but "exclusive selling rights" did not.

[2] S.I. 1991 No. 859, made under s. 30 of the Estate Agents Act 1979.

[3] As to which, see Estate Agents Act 1979, s. 1; Murdoch, *Law of Estate Agency and Auctions* (3rd ed.), pp. 185 *et seq.*; and in general Murdoch, *The Estate Agents and Property Misdescriptions Acts* (3rd ed.).

[4] Reg. 5.

makes the estate agency contract unenforceable, except pursuant to an order of the court.[5] It should be noted that the forms prescribed in the regulations[6] entitle the estate agent to actual commission rather than, as under the common law, to damages for breach of the special contract term. They also appear to entitle him to commission on a mere "introduction", without requirement of effective cause,[7] though not where the principal withdraws the property. Where the contract wording varies, the explanation must be given with appropriate modifications.[8]

Principles of general application. It would seem that the principles **7–038** referred to above are of general application in connection with agents acting on commission. Where the transaction is interpreted as a unilateral contract, and the agent has no duty to do anything, the agent could only be protected by an implied collateral contract not to revoke, and although there are dicta in another context that a promise not to revoke the offer of such a contract will in general be implied,[9] it is submitted that these are too wide. Where the contract is bilateral, the question is one of implication of terms. Since the contract for an agent working on commission is not one of which general incidents are worked out,[10] in both cases there will only be implications on the basis of "business efficacy",[11] and such implications will therefore be rare. It may however be that the implication of a *term* is easier than the implication of a *contract*, since the latter is to some extent inconsistent

---

[5] Estate Agents Act 1979, s. 18(5).
[6] In the Schedule. They are as follows.
"Sole selling rights.
  You will be liable to pay remuneration to us, in addition to any other costs or charges agreed, in each of the following circumstances—
  if unconditional contracts for the sale of the property are exchanged, in the period during which we have sole selling rights, even if the purchaser was not found by us but by another agent or by any other person, including yourself;
  if unconditional contracts for the sale of the property are exchanged after the expiry of the period during which we have sole selling rights but to a purchaser who was introduced to you during that period or with whom we had negotiations about the property during that period."
"Sole agency.
  You will be liable to pay remuneration to us, in addition to any other costs or charges agreed, if at any time unconditional contracts for the sale of the property are exchanged—
  with a purchaser introduced by us during the period of our sole agency or with whom we had negotiations about the property during that period; or
  with a purchaser introduced by another agent during that period."
[7] See Murdoch, *Law of Estate Agency and Auctions* (3rd ed.), pp. 203–205.
[8] Regs. 5(1)(2). As to the time at which notice must be given, see Regs. 3, 5(3).
[9] *Daulia Ltd v. Four Millbank Nominees Ltd* [1978] Ch. 231, 239 *per* Goff L.J.
[10] See *Liverpool City Council v. Irwin* [1977] A.C. 239.
[11] See above, para. 7–001; below, para. 7–040.

with, or at least modifies the nature of the transaction as already determined.

7–039   **Dismissal.** The most obvious way of preventing the agent from earning his commission is by terminating his authority or dismissing him. Whether or not this constitutes a breach of contract at all turns on the interpretation of the contract (if any) and in particular on its provisions (if any) relating to appointment for a specified period and to termination by either party: or on the interpretation of an offer of a unilateral contract, and any additional promises that may be implied with such an offer. The matter is dealt with under "Termination of authority" in Article 125.

7–040   **Prevention by other means.** Terms may by the same techniques be implied against prevention by other means. The nature of the promise will vary from case to case. The term sometimes[12] might be that the principal will not do *anything* to prevent the agent from earning the commission as contemplated. Or it might be that there are certain things which the principal must not do. It has been held that a term was to be implied to prevent a vendor from "playing a dirty trick on the agent ... a term which prevents the vendor from acting unreasonably to the possible gain of the vendor and the loss of the agent"; as by breaking the contract on performance of which the agent is entitled to commission.[13] A further implication might be that if the principal does prevent the agent from earning commission on the happening of an event but, as contemplated by the contract, the agent has had to spend money and undertake work, the principal will pay him on a *quantum meruit* for what he has already done.[14] It is clear from *Luxor*'s case that such a contractual promise will not normally be implied into an estate agent's engagement in general, and it is probable that such an implication will be made only in an exceptional case. Where the agent cannot perform his duties under the agency contract without the active cooperation of his principal, a promise can sometimes be implied that such cooperation will be forthcoming.[15] This implication is an example

---

[12] But not in an estate agent situation: above, para. 7–036.

[13] *Alpha Trading Ltd v. Dunnshaw-Patten Ltd* [1981] Q.B. 290, 306, *per* Templeman L.J. (Illustration 3). See further cases cited at Illustration 3.

[14] This is, perhaps, the most satisfactory explanation of *Inchbald v. Western Neilgherry Coffee, Tea and Cinchona Plantation Co. Ltd* (1864) 17 C.B.(N.S.) 733. In *Luxor (Eastbourne) Ltd. v. Cooper* [1941] A.C. 108, 147, Lord Wright said that he could not understand *Inchbald's* case unless it was treated as analogous to a case of wrongful dismissal. Its authority must be regarded as doubtful.

[15] *Mona Oil Equipment & Supply Co. Ltd v. Rhodesia Railways Ltd* [1949] 2 All E.R. 1014. See also *Luxor (Eastbourne) Ltd v. Cooper* [1941] A.C. 108, 118, 148; *Mackay v. Dick* (1881) 6 App.Cas. 251; *Colley v. Overseas Exporters* [1921] 3 K.B. 302. See also Burrows (1968) 31 M.L.R. 390; Lücke (1973) 5 Adelaide L.Rev. 32.

of the general rule and can again only be made in so far as it is necessary "to make the contract workable."[16]

Remuneration after termination.[17] In some types of agency contract   **7–041** the question will arise whether the agent is entitled to remuneration after the contract has been terminated. This remuneration will usually take the form of commission on business introduced before the contract was terminated.

In all cases the test is whether, as a matter of construction of the agency contract, the parties intended that the agent should be entitled to be paid commission after termination. The older authorities held there must be clear and unequivocal words to entitle the agent to such commission,[18] but this has been doubted[19]; it seems that the normal rules for the implication of terms into a contract must be applied.[20] The necessary term will not readily be implied to give business efficacy to the contract, but the many cases on this topic turn on the particular form of words under consideration.

In *Sellers v. London Counties Newspapers*[21] it was suggested that the intention to pay commission after termination can more readily be found in the case of an agent who is an independent contractor than when he is a servant.[22] A further indication is, perhaps, that the right to be paid (so that a debt is actually due from the principal to the agent) may accrue a considerable period after the right to receive payment has been earned.[23] In such a case it may be said that it is quite likely that the contract may have been terminated, for whatever reason, during the

---

[16] *Mona Oil Equipment & Supply Co. Ltd. v. Rhodesia Railways Ltd*, n. 15 above, at p. 1018, *per* Devlin J.; and see *Secretary of State for Employment v. Associated Society of Locomotive Engineers and Firemen (No. 2)* [1972] 2 Q.B. 455.

[17] Sometimes called "continuing commission". This subject is considered in detail in Powell, pp. 364–369.

[18] *Nayler v. Yearsley* (1860) 2 F. & F. 41; *Boyd v. Mathers and "South Africa" Ltd* (1893) 9 T.L.R. 443; *Gerahty v. Baines & Co. Ltd* (1903) 19 T.L.R. 554; *Marshall v. Glanvill* [1917] 2 K.B. 87, 92; *Ward v. Spivack* [1957] I.R. 40.

[19] *Sellers v. London Counties Newspapers* [1951] 1 K.B. 784. See also *Westralian Farmers Ltd v. Commonwealth Agricultural Service Engineers Ltd* (1936) 54 C.L.R. 361.

[20] See *Roberts v. Elwells Engineers Ltd* [1972] 2 Q.B. 586.

[21] n. 19 above.

[22] See also *Salomon v. Brownfield and Brownfield Guild Pottery Society Ltd* (1896) 12 T.L.R. 239; *Cramb v. Goodwin* (1919) 35 T.L.R. 477 and *Faulkner v. Cooper & Co. Ltd* (1899) 4 Com.Cas. 213; *Marshall v. Glanvill* [1917] 2 K.B. 87. Two leading cases in which commission was held to be recoverable after termination of the agency contract were both cases where the contract was not analogous to a master and servant contract: *Bilbee v. Hasse & Co.* (1889) 5 T.L.R. 677; affd. *The Times*, January 16, 1890; *Levy v. Goldhill* [1917] 2 Ch. 297.

[23] *Sellers v. London Counties Newspapers* [1951] 1 K.B. 784 at pp. 784, 798–799; *Gold v. Life Assurance Company of Pennsylvania* [1971] 2 Lloyd's Rep. 164.

interval between these two events. A similar situation may arise where the commission is received over a long period, such as under a contract of hire.

Even if the contract provides for commission on "repeat orders" by customers introduced by the agent there may still be no right to commission after termination. The parties may only have intended to refer to repeat orders taken while the agency subsisted.[24] However, if the court finds that the parties did intend that commission should be paid on certain transactions regardless of whether the agency still subsisted, the court will award damages or order an assessment of damages. An account and order of payment of the sums due from time to time is not appropriate.[25]

7–042   Commercial agents. The Commercial Agent (Council Directive) Regulations 1993 contain provisions regarding remuneration after termination.[26] They are discussed in Chapter 11.

Illustrations

7–043   (1)   An agent indicates willingness to introduce a purchaser for two cinemas if paid commission. He introduces a prospective purchaser but the vendor decides not to proceed with the sale. The agent is not entitled to commission.[27]

(2)   Shipbrokers procured a charter of a vessel for 18 months which provided for a commission of 2½ per cent on hire paid under it and any continuation of it. After four months the owners sold the vessel. The brokers were unable to recover commission for the remainder of the charter period.[28]

(3)   Agents introduced buyers to sellers, who entered into a contract of sale. A contract between agents and sellers provided, in consideration for the introduction, for commission calculated per metric ton sold on

---

[24] *Crocker Horlock Ltd v. B. Lang & Co. Ltd* [1949] 1 All E.R. 526. See also in general *Hilton v. Helliwell* [1894] 2 I.R. 94; *Morris v. Hunt & Co.* (1896) 12 T.L.R. 187; *Barrett v. Gilmour & Co.* (1901) 17 T.L.R. 292; *Weare v. Brimsdown Lead Co.* (1910) 103 L.T. 429; *Bickley v. Browning, Todd & Co.* (1913) 30 T.L.R. 134; *Sales v. Crispi* (1913) 29 T.L.R. 491; *Leak v. Charles & Sons Ltd* (1948) 92 S.J. 154.
[25] *Roberts v. Elwells Engineers Ltd* [1972] 2 Q.B. 586, overruling *Wilson v. Harper, Son & Co.* [1908] 2 Ch. 370 and *British Bank for Foreign Trade v. Novinex* [1949] 1 K.B. 623 on this point.
[26] Reg. 8.
[27] *Luxor (Eastbourne) Ltd v. Cooper* [1941] A.C. 108.
[28] *L. French & Co. Ltd. v. Leeston Shipping Co. Ltd* [1922] 1 A.C. 451. See this case explained by Bingham L.J. in *Marcan Shipping (London) Ltd v. Polish S.S. Co.* [1989] 2 Lloyd's Rep. 138. See also Article 125 and Illustrations.

performance of the sale contract, and for certain other payments in connection with the demurrage payable at the port of discharge. The sellers failed to perform the contract, forfeited a performance bond and settled additionally with the buyers. Held, a term was to be implied that "the vendors will not deprive the agents of their commission by committing a breach of the contract between the vendors and the purchaser which releases the purchaser from its obligation to pay the purchase price."[29]

Article 61

SPECIFIC ENFORCEMENT OF AGENCY CONTRACT

The performance of a contract of agency will not normally be enforced by an order for specific performance or other similar order.[30]   **7–044**

Comment

Specific performance exceptional. A contract of agency is by its nature a personal contract; the relationship between the parties is of a fiduciary character and depends upon mutual confidence. It has long been established that the courts will not normally enforce the continuation of such a contract, whether directly by an order for specific performance or indirectly by injunction.[31] The normal remedy for breach of contract by the principal is therefore an action for damages. But because these specific remedies are equitable they are discretionary and it is therefore not possible to state that the principle has no exceptions. In this context the contract of agency has many similarities   **7–045**

---

[29] *Alpha Trading Ltd v. Dunnshaw-Patten Ltd* [1981] Q.B. 290; see (1982) 45 M.L.R. 220; *George Moundreas & Co. S.A. v. Navimpex Centrala Navala* [1985] 2 Lloyd's Rep. 515; *Orient Overseas Management and Finance Ltd v. File Shipping Co. Ltd (The Energy Progress)* [1993] 1 Lloyd's Rep. 355; *cf. Marcan Shipping (London) Ltd v. Polish S.S. Co.*, n. 28 above; *Sun Alliance Pensions Life and Investments Services Ltd v. Webster* [1991] 2 Lloyd's Rep. 410; *Micklefield v. S.A.C. Technology Ltd* [1990] 1 W.L.R. 1002. Sometimes such events are specifically provided for: see *Christie & Vesey Ltd v. Maatschappij, etc. Helvetia N.V. (The Helvetia–S)* [1960] 1 Lloyd's Rep. 540. *cf. White v. Turnbull Martin & Co.* (1898) 3 Com.Cas. 183.

[30] See in general Chitty, *Contracts* (27th ed.), Vol. 1, Chap. 27; Treitel, *Law of Contract* (9th ed.), pp. 918 *et seq.*; Meagher, Gummow and Lehane, *Equity Doctrines and Remedies* (3rd ed.), Chap. 20; Spry, *Equitable Remedies* (4th ed.); Sharpe, *Injunctions and Specific Performance* (2nd ed.).

[31] See Fry, *Specific Performance* (6th ed.), p. 50; *Chinnock v. Sainsbury* (1860) 30 L.J.Ch. 409 (auctioneer); *Mortimer v. Beckett* [1920] 1 Ch. 571; *Page One Records Ltd v. Britton* [1968] 1 W.L.R. 157; *Denmark Productions Ltd v. Boscobel Productions Ltd* [1969] 1 Q.B. 699.

with the contract of employment: indeed some agents may be employees. In *Hill v. C.A. Parsons & Co. Ltd*[32] the Court of Appeal gave an interim injunction to an employee to restrain his employers from dismissing him.[33] The court made clear the wholly exceptional nature of the case[34]: the employers had full confidence in the employee and were being forced to dismiss him in breach of contract under pressure from a trade union. However, subsequent cases have also indicated a greater readiness to enforce performance,[35] and it seems that specific performance or remedies creating a similar effect may now be more readily obtained. The continuation of confidence is clearly a factor of importance, especially in the field of agency where the agent represents the principal *vis-à-vis* third parties and can bring him into contractual relationship with them.[36] Where the agent is a sole agent, it is particularly hard to envisage the contract being specifically enforced; in that event the principal would be obliged to cease carrying on the business in question or to continue it through the agency of someone in whom he may have lost confidence and against whom he is currently engaged in litigation. In other cases the principal may have a right to terminate the contract,[37] or the agent himself may have only limited rights, *e.g.* because his contract is unilateral.[38] But a distributorship or franchising contract may perhaps more readily be specifically enforced, or at least supported by an injunction against dealing with others.[39]

---

[32] [1972] 1 Ch. 305. See also *Tito v. Waddell (No. 2)* [1977] Ch. 106, 321, 322; *Posner v. Scott-Lewis* [1987] Ch. 25; *Irani v. Southampton, etc. Health Authority* [1985] I.C.R. 80.

[33] s. 236 of the Trade Union and Labour Relations (Consolidation) Act 1992 prohibits a court, whether by an order for specific performance or an injunction, from compelling an employee to do any work or attend at any place for the doing of any work.

[34] The exceptional nature of the relief granted in *Hill v. C.A. Parsons & Co. Ltd* was emphasised in *Sanders v. Ernest A. Neale Ltd* [1974] I.C.R. 565 and *Chappell v. Times Newspapers Ltd* [1975] 1 W.L.R. 482.

[35] See *C.H. Giles & Co. Ltd. v. Morris* [1972] 1 W.L.R. 307, esp. at p. 318; *Sky Petroleum Ltd v. V.I.P. Petroleum Ltd* [1974] 1 W.L.R. 576; *Sudbrook Trading Estate Ltd v. Eggleton* [1983] 1 A.C. 444.

[36] The importance of continued confidence was stressed in *Page One Records Ltd v. Britton* [1968] 1 W.L.R. 157 where the manager of a very successful group of young musicians was refused an injunction which would have had the effect of enforcing his agency contract.

[37] See Article 125.

[38] As in the case of an estate agent: see above, para. 7–035. See also *Chinnock v. Sainsbury* (1860) 30 L.J.Ch. 409 (auctioneer); *Metropolitan Electric Supply Co. Ltd v. Ginder* [1901] 2 Ch. 799.

[39] *e.g. Decro-Wall International S.A. v. Practitioners in Marketing Ltd* [1971] 1 W.L.R. 361; *Evans Marshall & Co. v. Bertola S.A.* [1973] 1 W.L.R. 349, esp. at p. 379 (injunction cases). See also *Donnell v. Bennett* (1883) 22 Ch.D. 835; *Atlas Steels (Australia) Pty Ltd v. Atlas Steels Ltd* (1948) 49 S.R. (N.S.W.) 157; *Pasen v. Dominion Herb Distributors Inc* (1968) 67 D.L.R. (2d) 405; affd. 69 D.L.R. (2d) 651. *Cf. Paxton v. Spira* (1965) 54 D.L.R. (2d) 627.

Subsistence of contract. It was formerly considered that a contract of   **7–046**
employment could be unilaterally terminated by either party[40] and that
a court would therefore not grant a declaration that such a contract still
subsisted. But in *Francis v. Kuala Lumpur Councillors*[41] the Privy
Council said that in exceptional circumstances such a declaration might
be made, and in *Decro-Wall International S.A. v. Practitioners in
Marketing Ltd*[42] a majority of the Court of Appeal expressed the view
that an employment contract could not be unilaterally terminated by one
party and that such a contract was not an exception to the general
principles of the law of contract in this respect. The latter case
concerned not a contract of employment but a distributorship contract;
and it has been held that the reasoning applies to pure agency.[43] Many
difficulties however remain unresolved.[44] A declaration that a contract
still subsists is, however, a discretionary remedy and it is clear that the
circumstances must be exceptional before it will be granted.

Article 62

No Remuneration for Unauthorised Transactions or in Cases
of Misconduct or Breach of Duty

An agent is not entitled to remuneration—   **7–047**

    (1) in respect of any unauthorised transaction[45] which is not
          ratified by the principal[46];
    (2) in respect of transactions in relation to which he is in breach of
          his duties as agent, such breach going to the root of the
          contract or otherwise justifying the principal's repudiation of
          the liability to pay.[47]

---

[40] *e.g. Vine v. National Dock Labour Board* [1957] A.C. 488; *Cranleigh Precision
Engineering Ltd v. Bryant* [1965] 1 W.L.R. 1293; *Denmark Productions Ltd v. Boscobel
Productions Ltd* [1969] 1 Q.B. 699; *Roberts v. Elwells Engineers Ltd* [1972] Q.B. 586;
Sanders v. Ernest A. Neale Ltd [1974] I.C.R. 565.

[41] [1962] 1 W.L.R. 1411, 1417–1418.

[42] [1971] 1 W.L.R. 361. See also *Gunton v. Richmond-upon-Thames L.B.C.* [1981] Ch.
448; *London Transport Executive v. Clarke* [1981] I.C.R. 355. *Cf. Sport International
Bussum B.V. v. Inter-Footwear Ltd* [1984] 1 W.L.R. 776 (no relief against forfeiture).

[43] *Atlantic Underwriting Agencies Ltd v. Cia. di Assicurazione di Milano S.p.A.* [1979] 2
Lloyd's Rep. 240.

[44] See Kerr (1984) 47 M.L.R. 30; Treitel, *Law of Contract*, (9th ed.), pp. 927 *et seq*;
Chitty, *Contracts* (27th ed.), §§ 27–013 *et seq.*

[45] Illustrations 1, 2, 3.

[46] As in *Keay v. Fenwick* (1876) 1 C.P.D. 745. See Articles 13–20.

[47] See Comment.

Comment

7–048   **Unauthorised transactions.** Commission is by its nature only payable in respect of transactions expressly or impliedly authorised or ratified. Where authority is wrongfully withdrawn, however, there may be an action for breach of contract.

7–049   **Breach of duty by agent.** Where the agent is in serious breach of his duty to his principal, the principal can refuse to pay commission in respect of the transaction as to which the agent is in breach[48]: if the agent is appointed by the principal for a fixed time in circumstances entitling him to notice[49] the principal may terminate his employment or agency contract summarily and decline to pay the agent's current salary or wages.[50] But commission earned, and salary or wages already due, at the time of the breach must normally be paid.[51] This is simply an application of the law as to discharge of contract by breach.[52]

A breach of duty such as to justify refusal of remuneration may be described in various ways. In some cases it may be sufficient to say that commission has not been earned, without reference to discharge of the contract of agency, if any: this reasoning has been used where the agent has wrongfully delegated his duties[53] or stated a wrong asking price for the property leading to its sale at less than the vendor intended.[54] But in other cases it may be appropriate to say more generally that the agent's breach goes to the root of the contract,[55] or that his dereliction of duty is itself a repudiation of his obligations which may be accepted by the principal.[56] Even a slight breach by the agent of the strict obligations arising from his fiduciary character, *e.g.* where the agent accepts a bribe, or himself purchases (without disclosure) his principal's

---

[48] *Salomons v. Pender* (1865) 3 H. & C. 639, Illustration 4; *Andrews v. Ramsay & Co.* [1903] 2 K.B. 635, Illustration 4; *Rhodes v. Macalister* (1923) 29 Com.Cas. 19.

[49] See Comment to Article 125.

[50] *Boston Deep Sea Fishing & Ice Co. v. Ansell* (1888) 39 Ch.D. 339; *Rhodes v. Macalister*, n. 48 above, at p. 29; *Shepherd v. Felt and Textiles of Australia Ltd* (1931) 45 C.L.R. 359. See further Article 50.

[51] *ibid.*

[52] See Chitty, *Contracts* (27th ed.), Vol. 1, §§ 24–001 *et seq.*; Treitel, *Law of Contract* (9th ed.),Chap. 19; Treitel (1967) 30 M.L.R. 139; Lord Devlin [1966] C.L.J. 192.

[53] *Beable v. Dickerson* (1885) 1 T.L.R. 654; *John McCann & Co. v. Pow* [1974] 1 W.L.R. 1643.

[54] *Spiers v. Taylor* (1984) 271 EG 196.

[55] *Thornton Hall & Partners v. Wembley Electrical Appliances Ltd* [1947] 2 All E.R. 630, 634; *cf. Keppel v. Wheeler* [1927] 1 K.B. 577, 592.

[56] *Boston Deep Sea Fishing & Ice Co. v. Ansell* (1888) 39 Ch.D. 339, 365. And see *Hurst v. Holding* (1810) 3 Taunt. 32 (agent himself prevented performance); *Styles v. Rogers Realty Ltd* (1987) 43 D.L.R. (4th) 629 (exclusive agent did not use reasonable efforts to sell land).

property, is normally regarded as fatal[57] and may be described as a breach going to the root of the contract[58]; though in such cases it may sometimes also be said that an agent so acting is not acting as agent at all but as buyer, or generally not within the scope of his authority.[59] In other cases, especially of professional agents, it may be said that he has been guilty of gross neglect or misconduct,[60] or lack of due diligence,[61] or dishonesty[62]; or again that his acts have by his own default been entirely valueless and useless to his principal and do not therefore qualify him for commission.[63] Again even a slight breach of duty or omission may bar him from remuneration if the obligation is treated as entire, for such an obligation cannot be sued upon by an agent until he has completely performed it.[64]

There can obviously however be cases where the agent effects severable transactions, and in these cases the rule depriving him of commission will only apply to those in respect of which he is in breach of duty[65]; or where the breach does not go to the whole contract.[66] There has also been some tendency to hold commission recoverable when the agent makes an honest mistake, even if that mistake renders him liable in damages.[67] And there may be a waiver of the agent's breach[68]: but this is not implied from the fact that the principal takes

---

[57] *Boston Deep Sea Fishing & Ice Co. v. Ansell*, n. 56 above; *Salomons v. Pender* (1865) 3 H. & C. 639, Illustration 4; *Andrews v. Ramsay & Co.* [1903] 2 K.B. 635, Illustration 4; *Rhodes v. Macalister* (1923) 29 Com.Cas. 19; *Price v. Metropolitan House Investment Agency Co. Ltd* (1907) 23 T.L.R. 630; *L.S. Harris Trustees Ltd v. Power Packing Services (Hermit Road) Ltd* [1970] 2 Lloyd's Rep. 65 (breach of confidence); *Greenwood v. Harvey* [1965] N.S.W.R. 1489 (discussed by Baxt (1967) 7 Aus. Lawyer 55); *Cec. McManus Realty Ltd v. Bray* (1970) 14 D.L.R. (3d) 564; *Ian Scott & Co. v. Medical Installations Co. Ltd* [1981] E.G.D. 228 (attempt to extract extra commission); *Ocean City Realty Ltd v. A. & M. Holdings Ltd* (1987) 36 D.L.R. (4th) 94. But this is not always so: *cf. Hippisley v. Knee Bros.* [1905] 1 K.B. 1, Illustration 5; *Keppel v. Wheeler*, n. 55 above, at p. 592.
[58] *Thornton Hall & Partners v. Wembley Electrical Applicances Ltd* [1947] 2 All E.R. 630, 634.
[59] *Salomons v. Pender*, n.57 above; *Andrew v. Ramsay*, n.48 above.
[60] *White v. Lady Lincoln* (1803) 8 Ves. 363 (failure by solicitor to keep accounts; but the principle of this case does not apply when the solicitor is not the general agent of the client: *Re Lee, ex p. Neville* (1868) L.R. 4 Ch.App. 43); *Huntley v. Bulwer* (1839) 6 Bing.N.C. 111.
[61] *Moneypenny v. Hartland* (1824) 1 C. & P. 352.
[62] *Rhodes v. Macalister* (1923) 29 Com.Cas. 19; *Andrews v. Ramsay & Co.* [1903] 2 K.B. 635, Illustration 4.
[63] *Huntley v. Bulwer* (1839) 6 Bing.N.C. 111; *Denew v. Daverell* (1813) 3 Camp. 451, Illustration 10; *Hamond v. Holiday* (1824) 1 C. & P. 384 (shipbroker); *Hill v. Featherstonhaugh* (1831) 7 Bing. 569 (attorney).
[64] Such may be the case with solicitors' retainers to conduct actions: *Underwood, Son & Piper v. Lewis* [1894] 2 Q.B. 306; *Cachia v. Isaacs* (1985) 3 N.S.W.L.R. 366. But *cf. Warmingtons v. McMurray* (1937) 52 T.L.R. 381; *Caldwell v. Treloar* (1982) 30 S.A.S.R. 202.
[65] Illustration 5.
[66] See Illustrations 5, 6.
[67] See Illustrations 6, 7.
[68] Illustration 8; *Thornton Hall & Partners v. Wembley Electrical Appliances Ltd* [1947] 2 All E.R. 630.

the benefit of the transaction negotiated by the agent,[69] for that is not relevant to the contract between agent and principal; nor from the fact that he recovers a bribe from the agent.[70] Some of these latter rules seem penal in operation, and it is on this basis that they are justified in the cases.[71]

Illustrations

7–050   (1)   A is employed on commission to procure a loan upon certain terms. Before anything is done the principal varies the terms. A is unable to procure the loan on the terms as varied, but obtains an offer on the original terms, which the principal refuses to accept. A is not entitled to any commission, though he may be entitled to damages for breach of contract.[72]

(2)   An agent is employed on commission to sell certain property. His authority is revoked by the death of the principal, but he subsequently sells the property, and the principal's executors confirm the sale. The agent is not entitled to recover the agreed commission from the executors unless they recognise the terms of his employment, but he may be entitled upon a *quantum meruit*.[73]

(3)   An auctioneer, who is employed to sell property by auction, sells it by private contract. He is not entitled to commission.[74]

(4)   An agent, who is employed to sell certain land, sells it to a company in which he is a director and large shareholder. He is not entitled to commission upon the sale, even if it is adopted and confirmed by the principal.[75] So, if an agent for sale fraudulently takes a secret commission from the purchaser, he is not only accountable to the principal for the secret commission, but is not entitled to remuneration from the seller; and if the seller pays him commission in ignorance of the facts, he is entitled to recover it.[76]

(5)   An auctioneer, employed to sell property on the terms that he should be paid a certain commission and out-of-pocket expenses, received discounts from printers and advertisers, and charged the principal in full without deducting the discounts, in the honest belief

---

[69] *Salomons v. Pender* (1865) 3 H. & C. 639; *Rhodes v. Macalister* (1923) 29 Com.Cas. 19.
[70] *Andrews v. Ramsay & Co.* [1903] 2 K.B. 635.
[71] See esp. *Rhodes v. Macalister*, n. 69 above; Articles 50, 98.
[72] *Toppin v. Healey* (1863) 11 W.R. 466.
[73] *Campanari v. Woodburn* (1854) 15 C.B. 400. As to *quantum meruit* see above, paras. 7–009, 7–024.
[74] *Marsh v. Jelf* (1862) 3 F. & F. 234; *Gillow & Co. v. Lord Aberdare* (1892) 9 T.L.R. 12.
[75] *Salomons v. Pender* (1865) 3 H. & C. 639.
[76] *Andrews v. Ramsay & Co.* [1903] 2 K.B. 635. See also *Harrington v. Victoria Graving Dock Co.* (1878) 3 Q.B.D. 549; *cf. Turner v. Laurentide Financial Realty Corp. (Western) Ltd* (1979) 97 D.L.R. (3d) 429. See also Articles 50, 98.

that he was entitled to retain them. It was held that, though he must account for the discounts, he was entitled to commission, as he had not acted fraudulently, and as the receipt of the discount was incidental to his main duty of selling the goods.[77] So, where a commission agent fraudulently overcharged his principal in respect of some transactions, but acted honestly in other separate and distinct transactions, it was held that he was entitled to commission on the transactions in which he had acted honestly.[78]

(6) An agent, employed to find a purchaser, procured an offer, which the vendor accepted, subject to contract. Subsequently, a higher offer was made by another party to the agent, which, in the bona fide belief that he had fulfilled his duty, he failed to communicate to the vendor, and the vendor concluded a contract with the person whose offer had been accepted. The vendor recovered as damages from the agent the difference between the price fixed by the concluded contract and the higher offer. Held, that, in the circumstances, the agent was entitled to commission on the price so fixed.[79]

(7) An agent firm introduces purchasers whose offer is accepted subject to contract. The agents' branch manager hears of difficulties which the vendors are having concerning the house to which they hope to move. He thinks it his duty to tell the prospective purchasers and does so. The sale nearly falls through, but the vendors terminate the agents' instructions and sell the property to the same purchasers directly: they move into rented accommodation. The agents are entitled to commission, though they would have been liable in damages had loss resulted to the vendor.[80]

(8) The estate department of a company acting for the vendor of a house introduced a purchaser, and, in ignorance of the agency, the building department of the company acted for the purchaser and made a report on the house which had the effect of reducing the price. Subsequently the company discovered that they had been acting in this way and made an offer to the vendor to invite the purchaser to obtain

---

[77] *Hippisley v. Knee Bros.* [1905] 1 K.B. 1. See (1905) 21 L.Q.R. 102.

[78] *Nitedals Taendstikfabrik v. Bruster* [1906] 2 Ch. 671. But *cf. Headway Construction Co. Ltd v. Downham* (1974) 233 E.G. 675 (whole commission agreement voidable for fraud).

[79] *Keppel v. Wheeler* [1927] 1 K.B. 577. It is easy to see that the commission which would have been paid should be deducted from the damages, but *quaere* whether the court was right in saying that it was *recoverable* by the agent. But see Murdoch (1974) 232 E.G. 1021, supporting the case and criticising *John McCann & Co. v. Pow* [1974] 1 W.L.R. 1643. See also Estate Agents (Undesirable Practices) (No. 2) Order 1991 (S.I. 1991 No. 1032), Sched. 3, para. 2.

[80] *Robinson Scammell & Co. v. Ansell* [1985] 2 EGLR 41; see also *Eric V. Stansfield v. South East Nursing Home Services Ltd* [1986] 1 EGLR 29.

an independent report on the house. The vendor refused and completed the sale at a reduction of the agreed price, the reduction being due to the work required to be done as a result of the report. Held, that although the company had committed a breach of their duty as agents, since the principal with full knowledge of this breach had completed the sale at the reduced price, he had affirmed the transaction and the agent was entitled to commission.[80a]

(9) An agent was employed by a lessee to find a purchaser of leasehold premises which were subject to a covenant prohibiting the carrying on of any business other than that of a music seller without the consent of the lessor. Several tailors made offers to the lessee to buy the premises for £2,500, but the lessee, believing that the lessor would not consent, did not approach him upon the matter. The agent, having an offer from a tailor of £2,250, and having obtained an assurance from the lessor that he would consent to a tailor's business being carried on upon the premises, concealed from the lessee the fact that the lessor had so assured his consent and the nature of the business of the person making the offer, and induced the lessee to accept £2,250. Held, that the agent was not entitled to any commission.[81]

(10) An auctioneer employed to sell an estate negligently omitted to insert in the conditions of sale a proviso usually inserted in them, and in consequence of the omission the sale was rendered nugatory. Held, that he was not entitled to any compensation or remuneration for his services, although the particulars of the sale had been submitted to the principal and were not objected to by him.[82]

Article 63

No Remuneration in Respect of Unlawful or Wagering Transactions

7-051   (1)   An agent may be debarred from recovering remuneration for his services if at the time when the services were rendered he was not legally qualified to act in the capacity in which he claims the remuneration, or if the enforcement of his contract of agency is affected in some other way by statute or statutory instrument.[83]

[80a] *Harrods Ltd v. Lemon* [1931] 2 K.B. 157. See also *Dargusch v. Sherley Investments Pty Ltd* [1970] Qd.R. 338. Cf. *Jones v. Canavan* [1972] 2 N.S.W.L.R. 236.
[81] *Heath v. Parkinson* (1926) 136 L.T. 128.
[82] *Denew v. Daverell* (1813) 3 Camp. 451.
[83] Illustrations 1, 2, 3; and see Comment.

(2) An agent cannot recover any remuneration in respect of any transaction which is obviously, or to his knowledge, unlawful,[84] or unlawful by virtue of legislation which is to be interpreted as affecting contracts which involve the doing of acts prohibited by it, or in respect of any contract or agreement rendered null and void by the Gaming Act 1845, or of any services in relation to or connection with such a transaction.[85]

Comment

Rule (1). Incapacity to act. There are frequently statutory or other   **7–052** requirements regarding capacity to act in certain professional and similar activities. An obvious example is the Solicitors Act 1974, referred to in Illustration 1. So also in Australia, New Zealand and elsewhere real estate agents require licences.[86] Unqualified persons cannot normally recover remuneration. But the exact result must in each case turn on the terms of the legal provisions imposing the requirement of qualification. Sometimes the very acting as agent for the particular person in certain ways is unlawful.[87] Some statutes prevent persons exercising agency functions from suing on the agency contract in certain circumstances.[88] Other statutes simply prescribe penalties.[89]

Rule (2). Illegal transactions. Except where it emanates from the   **7–053** Gaming Act 1892, this rule is an application of the common law principles as to illegal contracts, which should be considered, as developed by cases most of which are not relevant to agency, in each

---

[84] Illustrations 4, 5, 6; and see Comment. See also *Allkins v. Jupe* (1877) 2 C.P.D. 375 (illegal insurance); *Harrington v. Victoria Graving Dock Co.* (1878) 3 Q.B.D. 549 (corrupt contract).

[85] Gaming Act 1892; see Comment.

[86] See, *e.g.* Real Estate Agents Act 1963, s. 79 (New Zealand); Auctioneers and Agents Act 1941, s. 42 (N.S.W.) (these statutes also require appointment in writing); Auctioneers and House Agents Acts 1947 and 1967 (Ireland) as to which see *Somers v. Nicholls* [1955] I.R. 83.

[87] *e.g.* Accommodation Agencies Act 1953; see *Saunders v. Soper* [1975] A.C. 239; Partington (1975) 125 New L.J. 148; Cartwright (1979) 123 S.J. 577; Szekely (1984) 12 Aus. Bus. Law Rev. 408. See also *Phoenix General Ins. Co. of Greece S.A. v. Halvanon Ins. Co.* [1988] Q.B. 216 (Insurance Companies Act 1982, s. 2: effect reversed by Financial Services Act 1986, s. 132).

[88] See Illustrations 2, 3.

[89] *e.g.* Insurance Brokers (Registration) Act 1977, s. 22(1) (false self-description) (but in respect of investment business, insurance intermediaries are affected by the Financial Services Act 1986: see in general Hodgin, *Insurance Intermediaries: Law and Practice* (1992)). See also *SCF Finance Co. Ltd v. Masri (No. 2)* [1987] Q.B. 1002 (accepting deposits: Banking Act 1979, s. 1).

situation individually.[90] The formulation in the Article gives no more than the most general of guidelines.

7–054   **Wagering transactions.** It seems that before 1892 commission was recoverable by agents employed to make wagers[91] just as indemnity was recoverable.[92] But this was reversed by the Gaming Act 1892, which provides that any promise, express or implied, to pay any sum of money by way of commission, fee, reward or otherwise, in respect of any contract or agreement rendered null and void by the Gaming Act 1845, or of any services in relation-thereto or connection therewith, shall be null and void, and no action shall be brought or maintained to recover any such sum of money. The main difficulties have occurred in connection with speculation on the Stock Exchange.[93]

Illustrations

7–055   (1)   No costs are recoverable in respect of anything done by any unqualified person acting as a solicitor.[94]

(2)   An estate agent who enters into a contract with another under which he will engage in estate agency work and who fails to supply to his client information as required by the Estate Agents Act 1979 or statutory instrument made under it cannot enforce the contract, whether by legal action or the exercise of a lien over the client's money, except pursuant to an order of the court.[95]

(3)   Any contract entered into in the course of carrying on an investment business by a person who is not an authorised or exempted person cannot be enforced without the leave of the court.[96]

(4)   An action was brought for work done and money expended in buying shares in a company which affected to act as a body corporate without authority by charter or statute and was therefore illegal. Held,

---

[90] See Treitel, *Law of Contract* (9th ed.), Chap. 11.
[91] *Knight v. Fitch* (1855) 15 C.B. 566.
[92] See Comment to Article 65.
[93] See Article 65, Illustration 11.
[94] Solicitors Act 1974, s. 25(1). (See also Employment Agencies Act 1973, s. 6.) "Costs" includes fees, charges, disbursements, expenses and remuneration: *ibid.* s. 87(1). For "unqualified person" see *ibid.* s. 87(1) as amended and s. 1. See also *ibid.* s. 25(2); *Kent v. Ward* (1894) 70 L.T. 612; *Re Sweeting* [1898] 1 Ch. 268; *Browne v. Barber* [1913] 2 K.B. 553; *Hudgell Yeates & Co. v. Watson* [1978] Q.B. 451; Cordery, *Solicitors* (8th ed.), p. 35.
[95] Estate Agents Act 1979, s. 18(5); above, paras. 7–007, 7–037; *Solicitors' Estate Agency (Glasgow) Ltd v. MacIver* 1993 S.L.T. 23; *Connell Estate Agents v. Begej* [1993] 2 EGLR 35; Murdoch, *Law of Estate Agency and Auctions* (3rd ed.), pp. 200 *et seq.*; Murdoch, *The Estate Agents and Property Misdescriptions Acts* (3rd ed.). As to lien, see Articles 66–70.
[96] Financial Services Act 1986, s. 5. See Lomnicka and Powell, *Encyclopedia of Financial Services Law* (1987).

that the action was not maintainable because it arose out of an unlawful transaction.[97]

(5) Commission was claimed by a broker for procuring freight. Held, that the fact that the charterparty in respect of which commission was claimed would be illegal unless the charterer obtained certain licences was no answer to the action, it not being part of the broker's duty to see that the licences were obtained.[98]

(6) Claims for remuneration for attending auctions for the purpose of "puffing" prices,[99] and claims for remuneration for procuring the sale of public offices,[1] are unenforceable.

2.—REIMBURSEMENT AND INDEMNITY

Article 64

REIMBURSEMENT OF EXPENSES AND INDEMNITY FROM LIABILITIES INCURRED IN COURSE OF AGENCY

Subject to the provisions of Article 65, every agent has a right against his principal to be reimbursed all expenses and to be indemnified against all losses and liabilities incurred by him in the execution of his authority[2]: and where the agent is sued for money due to his principal, he has a right to set off the amount of any such expenses, losses or liabilities,[3] unless the money due to the principal is held on trust.[4]   **7–056**

Comment

The rule here given is normally stated in such general terms,[5] but its juristic basis may require attention. In the nineteenth century actions at   **7–057**

---

[97] *Josephs v. Pebrer* (1825) 3 B. & C. 639.

[98] *Haines v. Busk* (1814) 5 Taunt. 521.

[99] *Walker v. Nightingale* (1726) 4 Bro.P.C. 193.

[1] *Stackpole v. Earle* (1761) 2 Wil.K.B. 133; *Parsons v. Thompson* (1790) 1 Hy.Bl. 322; *Waldo v. Martin* (1825) 4 B. & C. 319.

[2] See Comment and Illustrations; *Restatement*, §§ 438, 439 and reporter's notes thereto; Chapter 3 as to authority.

[3] Illustrations 4, 5. And see Goff and Jones, *Law of Restitution* (4th ed.), pp. 361–362.

[4] See *Stumore v. Campbell & Co.* [1892] 1 Q.B. 314; *Re Mid-Kent Fruit Factory* [1896] 1 Ch. 567; above, paras. 6–042 *et seq.*

[5] e.g. *Thacker v. Hardy* (1878) 4 Q.B.D. 685, 687. The principle is also stated in even wider terms that do not confine it to agency: see *Dugdale v. Lovering* (1875) L.R. 10 C.P. 196; *Sheffield Corp. v. Barclay* [1905] A.C. 392; *Secretary of State for India v. Bank of India Ltd* [1938] 2 All E.R. 797; *Guaranty Trust Co. v. James Richardson & Son* (1963) 39 D.L.R. (2d) 517. But *cf. Cory & Son Ltd v. Lambton & Hetton Collieries Ltd* (1916) 86 L.J.K.B. 401.

law were based on the common count for money paid, and it was not often necessary to distinguish between contractual and what would now be called restitutionary claims.[6] The procedural reforms of the nineteenth century led to greater attention being paid to substantive issues, and it is possible that at the present day it might matter how the claim was classified in a particular case.

7–058   **Contract.** Where the agency agreement is contractual, the agreement to reimburse and indemnify, if not express,[7] can be regarded as an implied term of the contract that operates unless clearly excluded. There is thus no difficulty in such cases in holding that the principal is liable to reimburse and indemnify the agent for all payments made and liabilities incurred within the agent's express or implied authority.[8] This would include not only payments that the principal is legally bound to make, but also payments which the agent is legally bound to make though the principal would not be liable for them,[9] cases where the agent is bound by the usage of a market,[10] cases where the agent makes an authorised but gratuitous payment on the principal's behalf,[11] cases where the agent makes a payment which could not have been enforced but which there is a strong and legitimate pressure to make,[12] cases where the agent, though under a liability, has as yet suffered no loss,[13] and cases where a payment is reasonably but mistakenly made by the agent.[14] Cases where the agent acts beyond his instructions[15], or interferes without request would not however be included.

---

[6] See Stoljar, *Law of Quasi-Contract* (1964), pp. 127 *et seq.*; *Bowlby v. Bell* (1846) 3 C.B. 284; *Pawle v. Gunn* (1838) 4 Bing.N.C. 445.

[7] As in *Toplis v. Grane* (1839) 5 Bing.N.C. 636; *Moore v. Moore* (1611) 1 Bulst. 169.

[8] As to whether the right of indemnity can arise before the agent has suffered loss by meeting the liability, see *Firma C-Trade S.A. v. Newcastle P. & I. Assn. (The Fanti and The Padre Island)* [1991] 2 A.C. 1; *McIntosh v. Dalwood (No. 4)* (1930) 4 S.R. (N.S.W.) 415.

[9] *Adams v. Morgan & Co.* [1924] 1 K.B. 751, Illustration 6; *Brittain v. Lloyd* (1845) 14 M. & W. 762.

[10] See Illustration 11; there were many old cases on the usage of the London Stock Exchange, but most are now obsolete. As to customs and usages of markets, see Article 31.

[11] *Brittain v. Lloyd*, n. 9 above, at p. 773; *Pawle v. Gunn* (1838) 4 Bing.N.C. 445, 448–449.

[12] *Rhodes v. Fielder, Jones and Harrison* (1919) 89 L.J.K.B. 15, Illustration 10; *Schneider v. Eisovitch* [1960] 2 Q.B. 430. The position as to the payment of lost bets was altered by the Gaming Act 1892; see Article 65.

[13] *Lacey v. Hill, Crowley's Claim* (1874) L.R. 18 Eq. 182, Illustration 7. Where the agent has incurred a liability, his right to indemnity has arisen, and a purported revocation of his authority to discharge it is ineffective. See below, para. 10–010.

[14] See Illustration 8.

[15] *Islamic Republic of Iran Shipping Lines v. Zannis Cia. Naviera S.A. (The Tzelepi)* [1991] 2 Lloyd's Rep. 265.

Restitution. But where the agency is not contractual and the law of   **7–059**
contract cannot be relied on, the agent's claim is only restitutionary[16]
and confined to the reimbursement of payments made by the agent
under compulsion, in respect of which the ultimate liability is on the
principal, and the benefit of which the principal obtains.[17] It does not,
therefore, extend to the full indemnity which the contractual right might
give. Normally speaking, agency is contractual: but circumstances can
arise where it is not, *e.g.* because one of the parties is a minor, or
because the agent has not been properly appointed.[18] In some cases
there may still be room for the implication of an independent contract
to indemnify, created by the request of one party to another to do
something, accompanied by a promise to indemnify against loss incurred
by so doing.[19] But in others it may be necessary to rely on the
restitutionary remedy, which will normally (though not always, because
not limited by the scope of the agent's authority) be narrower in scope.
However, the right of indemnity exists also in equity, and where the
agent can invoke the assistance of equity,[20] *e.g.* as trustee[21] or surety,
the limitations imposed by the common law rules of restitution will not
apply: the right to indemnity may therefore be wider.[22]

Right of reimbursement superseded by remuneration. It should be   **7–060**
borne in mind that in many cases the right of reimbursement of *expenses*
will not apply, because any expense incurred is taken to be covered by
the remuneration. Thus in some areas estate agents do not seek to
recover the cost of advertising, for this is taken to be included in their

---

[16] See Goff and Jones, *Law of Restitution* (4th ed.), Chap. 14, taking (at pp. 359–360) a
distinction between reimbursement and indemnity, and attributing a special restitutionary
meaning to the former.
[17] See *Brook's Wharf & Bull Wharf Ltd v. Goodman Bros.* [1937] 1 K.B. 534; *Owen v.
Tate* [1976] Q.B. 402; *Liberian Insurance Agency Inc. v. Mosse* [1977] 2 Lloyd's Rep. 560;
The Pindaros [1983] 2 Lloyd's Rep. 635; Goff and Jones, *op. cit.* n. 16 above.
[18] *cf. Craven-Ellis v. Canons Ltd* [1936] 2 K.B. 403.
[19] See *Dugdale v. Lovering* (1875) L.R. 10 C.P. 196; *Sheffield Corp. v. Barclay* [1905]
A.C. 392; *Yeung Kai Yung v. Hong Kong and Shanghai Banking Corp.* [1981] A.C. 787;
Naviera Mogar S.A. v. Soc. Metallurgique de Normandie (The Nogar Marin) [1988] 1
Lloyd's Rep. 412 (implication turns on form of individual case). *Cf. Guaranty Trust Co. of
New York v. Hannay & Co.* [1918] 2 K.B. 623. There are even dicta in these cases
suggesting that the obligation is wider than a contractual obligation. But in *Yeung Kai
Yeung's* case it was suggested (at pp. 799–800) that the rule in the *Sheffield* case might
require reconsideration in view of the Civil Liability (Contribution) Act 1978: below, para.
7–067.
[20] See *Lacey v. Hill, Crowley's Claim* (1874) L.R. 18 Eq. 182, Illustration 7;
Wallersteiner v. Moir (No. 2) [1975] Q.B. 373 (minority shareholder suing on behalf of
company).
[21] *Cf. Adams v. Morgan & Co.* [1924] 1 K.B. 751, Illustration 6; *Campbell v.
Larkworthy* (1894) 9 T.L.R. 528.
[22] See Snell, *Equity* (29th ed.), pp. 257–259.

commission, if earned, and if no commission is earned the expenditure is a business loss in respect of which no reimbursement can be claimed.[23] Many office and professional expenses are likewise taken to be covered by the remuneration payable.

Illustrations

7–061   (1) A employs B to find a purchaser for certain bark. C agrees with B to purchase the bark, subject to its being equal to sample. B, being offered a *del credere* commission by A, accepts A's draft for the price of the bark, and in due course pays the amount of the draft. C then refuses the bark, which is not equal to sample. B is entitled to recover from A the amount of the draft paid by him.[24]

(2) An auctioneer is instructed to sell certain property, and after he has incurred liabilities in reference to his employment, his authority is revoked by the principal. The principal must indemnify him against the liabilities.[25]

(3) An accommodation bill is drawn and accepted for the purpose of raising money for the benefit of the drawer and acceptor. The drawer instructs a bill broker to get the bill discounted. It is the common practice for bill brokers to give a general guarantee to the bankers who discount their bills, and not to indorse each bill discounted on behalf of their customers. The bill is dishonoured, and the broker becomes liable to the bankers upon such a guarantee. The broker is entitled to recover from the acceptor the amount that he is compelled to pay in pursuance of such guarantee, with interest, it being a liability incurred in the execution of his authority in the ordinary course of his business as a bill broker.[26]

(4) A broker, in accordance with a reasonable custom of the particular market in which he was employed, rendered himself personally responsible for the price of goods bought on behalf of his principal, and duly paid for the goods. Held, that he was entitled to set off the amount so paid, in an action by the principal's trustee in bankruptcy for money due to the principal.[27]

---

[23] But see *Bernard Thorpe & Partners v. Flannery* (1977) 244 EG 129, where such expenses were recoverable on the terms of the contract. It is usually said that neither auctioneers nor estate agents are normally entitled to expenses: see Murdoch, *Law of Estate Agency and Auctions* (3rd ed.), pp. 177–178, 342–343.

[24] *Hooper v. Treffry* (1847) 1 Exch. 17; but distinguish *Simpson v. Swan* (1812) 3 Camp. 291.

[25] *Warlow v. Harrison* (1859) 1 E. & E. 309, 317; *Brittain v. Lloyd* (1845) 14 M. & W. 762.

[26] *Re Fox, Walker & Co., ex p. Bishop* (1880) 15 Ch.D. 400.

[27] *Cropper v. Cook* (1868) L.R. 3 C.P. 194. And see *Anglo-Overseas Transport Co. Ltd v. Titan Industrial Corp. (United Kingdom)* [1959] 2 Lloyd's Rep. 152; *Perishables Transport Co. Ltd v. N. Spyropoulos (London) Ltd* [1964] 2 Lloyd's Rep. 379.

(5)   An agent, who had general authority to receive and sell goods on behalf of the principal, in good faith brought an action against a third person who wrongfully withheld possession of the goods. In an action by the principal for the proceeds of the goods it was held that the agent was entitled to set off the amount of the costs incurred by him in the proceedings to recover the goods. [28]

(6)   The seller of a business carries it on between the date of contract and the date of completion on the buyer's account, a clause in the contract expressly providing for indemnity. He may obtain indemnity for supertax which he is obliged to pay, even though the buyer, being a corporation, would not be liable for supertax. [29]

(7)   A stockbroker incurred liabilities on the Stock Exchange on behalf of his principal. The stockbroker subsequently paid a composition on the amount of his debts (including such liabilities), and by a rule of the Stock Exchange he could not be sued for the balance of such debts without the permission of the committee. The principal was bound to indemnify him to the full extent of the liabilities incurred on his behalf. [30]

(8)   An agent incurs damages and expenses in defending an action on behalf of his principal. He is entitled to reimbursement of such damages and expenses if he was acting within the scope of his authority in defending the action, and the loss was not caused by his own default. [31] Where an agent, exercising his best judgment, compromised an action brought against him in respect of a contract made on behalf of the principal, who had notice of the action, and had not given any instructions as to the course to be pursued, it was held that the agent was entitled to indemnity, although the plaintiff could not, in the circumstances, have succeeded in the action. [32]

(9)   A acted as B's agent for the purchase of goods from C. The terms included immediate payment, made by A, of £1,000, which would be forfeited if the contract were cancelled. Subsequently, believing that B would not be able to perform the contract, A without authority cancelled the contract, and the £1,000 was forfeited. A claimed to be

---

[28] *Curtis v. Barclay* (1826) 5 B. & C. 141; *Williams, Torrey & Co. v. Knight* [1894] P. 342, 349.

[29] *Adams v. Morgan & Co.* [1923] 2 K.B. 234; [1924] 1 K.B. 751. *Cf. Re Hollebone's Agreement* [1959] 1 W.L.R. 536.

[30] *Lacey v. Hill, Crowley's Claim* (1874) L.R. 18 Eq. 182; *Fraser v. Equitorial Shipping Co. Ltd (The Ijaola)* [1979] 1 Lloyd's Rep. 103.

[31] *Frixione v. Tagliaferro & Sons* (1856) 10 Moo.P.C. 175; *The James Seddon* (1866) L.R. 1 A. & E. 62; *Re Wells & Croft, ex p. Official Receiver* (1895) 72 L.T. 359; *Williams v. Lister & Co.* (1913) 109 L.T. 699; *Re Famatina Development Corp. Ltd* [1914] 2 Ch. 271; *Simpson and Miller v. British Industries Trust Ltd* (1923) 39 T.L.R. 286.

[32] *Pettman v. Keble* (1850) 9 C.B. 701. See also *Broom v. Hall* (1859) 7 C.B.(N.S.) 503; *The Millwall* [1905] P. 155, 174; *Wallersteiner v. Moir (No. 2)* [1975] Q.B. 373.

reimbursed by B in respect of the £1,000 paid out. Held, that although the cancellation by A was a breach of the contract of agency for which B might obtain damages (though none could be shown here, for, on the facts, the £1,000 would have been lost in any case), yet the £1,000 had been paid by A, and his right to reimbursement accrued when it was paid, before the breach; and the £1,000 was therefore recoverable. [33]

(10) A country solicitor requests his London agent to instruct counsel. The litigation is successful, but some of the costs are disallowed. The country solicitor purports to revoke the authority of the London solicitor to pay fees to counsel. The London solicitor nevertheless pays. Counsel could not have sued for the fees, but the London agent might have been guilty of professional misconduct had he not paid them. He is entitled to an indemnity in respect of the fees paid out, and may retain money in his hands for this purpose. [34]

(11) A freight forwarder is by custom of the market obliged to undertake personal liability for dead freight when his customer provides insufficient cargo. He may recover the sum paid from his customer. [35]

Article 65

CASES WHERE REIMBURSEMENT OR INDEMNITY NOT AVAILABLE

7–062   (1) An agent may be debarred from recovering reimbursement or indemnity if at the time when the services were rendered he was not legally qualified to act in the capacity in which he claims the reimbursement or indemnity, or if the enforcement of his contract of agency is in some other way affected by statute or statutory instrument.

    (2) An agent is not entitled to reimbursement of expenses incurred by him, nor to indemnity against losses or liabilities—

        (a) in respect of any unauthorised act or transaction which is not ratified by the principal, except where the agent has a right of action in restitution [36];

---

[33] *John Koch Ltd v. C. & H. Products Ltd* [1956] 2 Lloyd's Rep. 59; *cf. World Transport Agency v. Royte (England) Ltd* [1957] 1 Lloyd's Rep. 381.

[34] *Rhodes v. Fielder, Jones and Harrison* (1919) 89 L.J.K.B. 15.

[35] *Anglo Overseas Transport Co. Ltd v. Titan Industrial Corp. (United Kingdom) Ltd* [1959] 2 Lloyd's Rep. 152; *Perishables Transport Co. Ltd v. N. Spyropoulos (London) Ltd* [1964] 2 Lloyd's Rep. 379. *Cf. Wilson v. Avec Audio-Visual Equipment Ltd* [1974] 1 Lloyd's Rep. 81 (insurance broker not personally liable to insurance company so not entitled to indemnity).

[36] See Comment; Illustrations 1, 2; *Frixione v. Tagliaferro & Sons* (1856) 10 Moo.P.C. 175, 196.

(b) in consequence of his own negligence, default, insolvency or breach of duty[37];

(c) in respect of any act or transaction which is obviously, or to his knowledge, unlawful,[38] or unlawful by virtue of legislation which is to be interpreted as affecting contracts which involve the doing of acts prohibited by it; except where he is entitled to contribution towards damages for which he is liable in tort[39];

(d) in respect of any contract or agreement rendered null and void by the Gaming Act 1845.[40]

Comment

Rule (1). The statutory provisions which prevent certain agents and others acting in certain capacities from recovering commission normally apply also to reimbursement and indemnity, at least in so far as claims for these arise in contract.[41]   7–063

Rule (2): unauthorised acts. It is obvious that the contractual duty to reimburse and indemnify cannot operate where the act is unauthorised and not ratified[42]; there may however be cases where, though it is not possible to rely on the contractual right, an action in restitution is available.[43]   7–064

Where agent at fault. Where the expenses and liabilities only arise because of the agent's fault, it is obvious that there is no liability to indemnify[44]: and it should be noted that the reasoning covers liability arising from the agent's bankruptcy, where the bankruptcy was not occasioned by the agent's activities on behalf of the principal.[45] Where the expenses and liabilities do not so arise, but the agent is in repudiatory breach of his duties as agent, contractual indemnity may be   7–065

---

[37] *Thacker v. Hardy* (1878) 4 Q.B.D. 685, 687; *Frixione v. Tagliaferro & Sons*, n. 36 above; Illustrations 3, 4; *Restatement*, § 440. and see *Gregory v. Ford* [1951] 1 All E.R. 121: there may be circumstances in which an agent can recover his losses by a different cause of action.
[38] See Comment; Illustrations 5–9; below, para. 7–066; *Restatement*, § 440.
[39] Under the Civil Liability (Contribution) Act 1978: see Comment.
[40] Gaming Act 1892; Illustrations 10, 11.
[41] See Article 63, Illustrations 2, 3.
[42] See Comment to Article 64.
[43] See above, para. 7–059; *Restatement*, § 439(e).
[44] See Illustration 3.
[45] *Duncan v. Hill* (1873) L.R. 8 Ex. 242, Illustration 4.

refused on grounds similar to those relating to refusal of remuneration discussed under Article 62.[46] The principal may sometimes, however, incur a liability in restitution as indicated under Article 64.

7–066   **Unlawful transactions.** Here again, as in Article 63, the wording gives only the most general indication of the applicable rules: too much turns on the nature of the illegality for a more precise formulation to be possible.[47] But it should be noted that provisions forbidding unqualified persons from recovering remuneration may not apply to mere reimbursement and indemnity.[48]

7–067   **Joint tortfeasors.** The old rule was that a tortfeasor could recover neither contribution nor indemnity from the person at whose request or on whose behalf the tort was committed,[49] and this was based on the maxim *ex turpi causa non oritur actio.* But "where one person requests another to commit or where they jointly commit an indifferent act, of which the illegality does not appear, but which may subsequently be proved to be tortious, the contractual relation may arise; and where one party induces another party by fraud to commit a tortious act, and that other party does not in fact know and need not be presumed to know that he was doing an unlawful act, he may have redress or contribution."[50] And even where the act is obviously unlawful, contribution may now be recoverable by statute. By the Civil Liability (Contribution) Act 1978, s. 1(1),[51] any person liable in respect of damage suffered by another person may recover contribution from any other person liable in respect of the same damage, whether jointly with him or otherwise. Nothing in the Act however affects express or implied

---

[46] See, *e.g. Hurst v. Holding* (1810) 3 Taunt. 32 (agent prevented goods reaching principal); *Ellis v. Pond* [1898] 1 Q.B. 426 (wrongful sale by stockbroker); *Solloway v. McLaughlin* [1938] A.C. 247 (fraud of agent). It can also be said that a person cannot claim an indemnity in respect of the consequences of his own wrong; or that the allowing of an indemnity would promote circuity of action. See *Goulandris Bros. Ltd v. Goldman & Sons* [1958] 1 Q.B. 74, esp. at pp. 94–98; Comment to Article 62. *Cf. J.O. Lund Ltd v. Anglo Overseas Transport Co. Ltd* [1955] 1 Lloyd's Rep. 142.

[47] See, *e.g.* Illustration 6.

[48] See Solicitors Act 1974, s. 25(2); Cordery, *Solicitors* (8th ed.), pp. 91–92; Real Estate Agents Act 1963 (New Zealand), s. 79. But *cf.* Estate Agents Act 1979, s. 18(5).

[49] *Merryweather v. Nixan* (1799) 8 T.R. 186; *Shackell v. Rosier* (1836) 2 Bing.N.C. 634; *W.H. Smith & Son v. Clinton & Harris* (1908) 99 L.T. 840.

[50] *W.H. Smith & Son v. Clinton & Harris,* n. 49 above at p. 841 (and see Defamation Act 1952, s. 11). See *Adamson v. Jarvis* (1827) 4 Bing. 66, Illustration 9; *Betts & Drewe v. Gibbins* (1834) 2 A. & E. 57; *Toplis v. Grane* (1839) 5 Bing.N.C. 636 (*cf. Cory & Son Ltd v. Lambton & Hetton Collieries Ltd* (1916) 86 L.J.K.B. 401); *Dugdale v. Lovering* (1875) L.R. 10 C.P. 196; *Thacker v. Hardy* (1878) 4 Q.B.D. 685, 687.

[51] Replacing Law Reform (Married Women and Tortfeasors) Act 1935, s. 6.

contractual or other right to indemnity.[52] The amount of contribution is such as the court may find just and equitable having regard to that person's extent of responsibility for the damage; and the court has power to exempt from liability or direct a complete indemnity.[53] But the Act does not render enforceable any agreement for indemnity which would not have been enforceable apart from it.[54] The ready implication of a promise to indemnify by one who requests another to act[55] may sometimes exclude these provisions, and it has been suggested that the cases on such implication may require reconsideration.[56]

Wagering transactions. The contractual obligation to reimburse extends to situations where the agent pays money that neither he nor the principal could be legally compelled to pay, but non-payment of which would involve serious consequences and the payment of which can therefore be treated as authorised.[57] Pursuant to this it was held that where an agent paid lost bets he could recover indemnity from his principal.[58] But the Gaming Act 1892, s. 1, provides that any promise, express or implied, to pay any person any sum of money paid[59] by him under or in respect of any contract or agreement rendered null and void by the Gaming Act 1845 shall be null and void, and no action shall be brought or maintained to recover any such sum of money. The main difficulties have occurred in connection with speculation on the Stock Exchange.[60]   **7–068**

Illustrations

(1) A authorises B, a broker, to effect a marine insurance policy. After the underwriters have signed the slip, but before a binding contract is made, A revokes B's authority. B, nevertheless, effects the policy, and pays the premiums. B cannot recover the premiums from A, having acted without authority.[61]   **7–069**

---

[52] s. 7(3).
[53] s. 2(1).
[54] s. 7(3).
[55] Above, para. 7–059.
[56] *Yeung Kai Yung v. Hong Kong and Shanghai Banking Corp.* [1981] A.C. 787, 799–800.
[57] See Comment to Article 64.
[58] *Read v. Anderson* (1884) 13 Q.B.D. 779. So also a plea of gaming and wagering was before the Act of 1892 no answer to an action by a stockbroker for differences paid on his clients behalf: *Rosewarne v. Billing* (1863) 15 C.B.(N.S.) 316; *Hannan v. Beeton* (1889) 5 T.L.R. 703.
[59] Includes any sum to be paid: *Levy v. Warburton* (1901) 70 L.J.K.B. 708.
[60] See Illustration 11.
[61] *Warwick v. Slade* (1811) 3 Camp. 127.

(2) A authorises B and C to insure his life in their names. They insure in the names of B, C and D, and pay the premiums. They are not entitled to recover the amount of the premiums from A, not having strictly pursued their authority. [62]

(3) A solicitor undertook a prosecution for perjury, and agreed that he would only charge out-of-pocket expenses. The prosecution failed in consequence of the negligent way in which the indictment was drawn. Held, that the solicitor was not entitled to recover the disbursements. [63] So, an auctioneer is not entitled to be indemnified against a loss incurred by him in consequence of his own mistake on a point of law as to which he ought to have been competent. [64] And where the manager of the stud stock department of a company conducting activities connected with agriculture is asked to buy "top rams" and because of lack of knowledge of terms used by sheep breeders buys rams which are not "tops" no reimbursement is due. [65]

(4) A stockbroker is instructed by his principal to carry over stock to the next settlement. Before the next settling day the broker becomes insolvent and is declared a defaulter, in consequence of which the stock is sold at a loss. The principal is not bound to indemnify the broker, the loss having been caused by the broker's insolvency. [66]

(5) A purchased shares as a broker, not being duly licensed as the law then required. Held, that he was entitled to recover from the principal the price of the shares, which he was compelled to pay, such payment not being an essential part of the duty of a broker, although, in consequence of not being licensed, he could not recover any commission or remuneration. [67]

(6) A broker effects an illegal insurance on behalf of his principal, and pays the premium. He is not entitled to recover from the principal the amount of the premium, or any other payments made by him in respect of such insurance. [68]

(7) An election agent made payments which were illegal under the Corrupt Practices Acts. He could not recover the amount of any such payments from the candidate employing him. [69]

---

[62] *Barron v. Fitzgerald* (1840) 6 Bing.N.C. 201. As to instructions given to stockbrokers, see *Johnson v. Kearley* [1908] 2 K.B. 514; *Aston v. Kelsey* [1913] 3 K.B. 314; *Blaker v. Hawes and Brown* (1913) 109 L.T. 320.

[63] *Lewis v. Samuel* (1846) 8 Q.B. 685.

[64] *Capp v. Topham* (1805) 6 East 392.

[65] *New Zealand Farmers Co-operative Distributing Co. Ltd v. National Mortgage and Agency Co. of New Zealand Ltd* [1961] N.Z.L.R. 969.

[66] *Duncan v. Hill* (1873) L.R. 8 Ex. 242. This case is retained here on account of the general significance of the reasoning.

[67] *Smith v. Lindo* (1858) 5 C.B.(N.S.) 587.

[68] *Ex p. Mather* (1797) 3 Ves. 373.

[69] *Re Parker* (1882) 21 Ch.D. 408.

(8) A employs B to purchase smuggled goods. B purchases the goods and pays for them. B cannot recover the price from A, even if A obtains possession of the goods.[70]

(9) A instructs B, an auctioneer, to sell goods of which A has no right to dispose, B having no knowledge of any defect in A's title. B sells the goods, and duly pays over the proceeds to A. B is afterwards compelled to pay to the true owner the value of the goods. A must indemnify B, the transaction not being obviously, or to B's knowledge, unlawful.[71]

(10) A makes a bet with B, and loses. C, at A's request and on his behalf, pays B the amount of the bet. C cannot recover the amount from A.[72]

(11) A, intending to speculate, employs a broker to buy and sell stock on the Stock Exchange, the broker being aware that A does not intend to accept the stock bought, or deliver the stock sold, on his behalf, but expects the broker to arrange that only differences shall be paid or received. The broker makes the contracts on A's behalf, and becomes personally liable on them. The broker is entitled to indemnity, because the transactions entered into by him on the Stock Exchange are real contracts for the purchase and sale of stock, and not gaming or wagering contracts.[73] But if the broker agrees with the persons with whom he contracts on behalf of his principal, or if it is the intention of both parties to the contract that no stock or shares shall be bought or sold, but only differences paid or received, it is nonetheless a wagering contract though there is a superadded provision that either party may at his option require completion.[74] On the other hand, if either party intends that stock or shares shall be delivered and paid for, the contract is not a wagering contract, even if it provides for the payment of an enhanced price in the event of the stock or shares being taken up.[75]

---

[70] *Ex p. Mather, supra.*

[71] *Adamson v. Jarvis* (1827) 4 Bing. 66.

[72] *Tatam v. Reeve* [1893] 1 Q.B. 44; *Gasson v. Cole* (1910) 26 T.L.R. 468.

[73] *Thacker v. Hardy* (1878) 4 Q.B.D. 685; *Forget v. Ostigny* [1895] A.C. 318; *Barnett v. Sanker* (1925) 41 T.L.R. 660; *Ironmonger & Co. v. Dyne* (1928) 44 T.L.R. 497; *Weddle, Beck & Co. v. Hackett* [1929] 1 K.B. 321; *Woodward v. Wolfe* [1936] 3 All E.R. 529; *E. Bailey & Co. Ltd v. Balholm Securities Ltd* [1973] 2 Lloyd's Rep. 404; *Jackson Securities Ltd v. Cheesman* (1986) 4 N.S.W.L.R. 484. See also *Woodward & Co. v. Koefoed* (1921) 62 D.L.R. 431; *Topper Grain Co. Ltd v. Mantz* [1926] 2 D.L.R. 712. As to the validity of options, see *Buitenlandsche Bankvereeniging v. Hildesheim* (1903) 19 T.L.R. 641; *Sadd v. Foster* (1897) 13 T.L.R. 207; *Cunliffe-Owen v. Teather and Greenwood* [1967] 1 W.L.R. 1421.

[74] *Universal Stock Exchange v. Strachan* [1896] A.C. 166; *Re Gieve* [1899] 1 Q.B. 794; *H.W. Franklin & Co. Ltd v. Dawson* (1913) 29 T.L.R. 479. But the position is altered by the Financial Services Act 1986: see *City Index Ltd v. Leslie* [1992] Q.B. 98.

[75] *Philp v. Bennett & Co.* (1901) 18 T.L.R. 129. These cases are retained here on account of their general significance: present-day procedures are, however, different. See Financial Services Act 1986, s. 63(1).

3.—LIEN

Article 66

DEFINITIONS OF GENERAL AND PARTICULAR POSSESSORY LIENS

7–070 (1) A possessory lien is the right of a person who has possession of goods or chattels belonging to another to retain possession of them until the satisfaction of some debt or obligation by the owner of the goods or chattels. [76]

(2) Where the right is to retain possession in respect of a general balance of account, or until the satisfaction of debts or obligations incurred independently of the goods or chattels subject to the right, it is called a general lien. Where the right is confined to debts and obligations incurred in respect of the goods and chattels subject to the right, it is called a particular lien.

Comment

7–071 **Introduction.** The cases collected in this section go beyond agency law as such; and many of them are old and reflect practices that may no longer obtain. It seems, however, worth preserving the collection and updating it, for they remain the only authority on many of the matters which they decide, and excellent illustrations from which the principles may be understood.

7–072 **Liens.** A possessory lien involves the right to retain only[77]: it does not involve the right to sell the goods except in special circumstances,[78] *e.g.* where trade usage or statute permit. Indeed, a person who sells thereby destroys his lien and becomes liable in conversion.[79] But such a lien confers not only a defence against the principal (who cannot sue in conversion since he has not the immediate right to possess), but also the right to sue in conversion, where the goods are wrongfully removed, against the principal or third parties, for it involves possession and may confer an immediate right to possession.[80]

---

[76] See *Hammonds v. Barclay* (1802) 2 East 227, 235.

[77] This may carry with it the right to direct movement. Thus a shipping agent who had a lien over a bill of lading was held justified in having the goods brought back home: *Edwards v. Southgate* (1862) 10 W.R. 528.

[78] *Smart v. Sandars* (1848) 5 C.B. 895. Nor, of itself, does it confer the right of stoppage in transit: see Article 71.

[79] *Sibel v. Springfield* (1863) 8 New Rep. 36.

[80] *Rogers v. Kennay* (1846) 9 Q.B. 592; *Dicas v. Stockley* (1836) 7 C. & P. 587; *Bryans v. Nix* (1839) 4 M. & W. 775.

Strictly speaking, liens are given by law only; but an analogous right can be regarded as arising by contract,[81] and it is a right of this latter type that an agent has. Particular liens are favoured by the law, but general liens are "founded in custom only, and are therefore to be taken strictly."[82]

Article 67

POSSESSORY LIEN OF AGENTS

(1) An agent has a general or particular possessory lien on the   **7–073**
goods and chattels of his principal in respect of all lawful claims he may have as such agent against the principal, for remuneration earned, or advances made, or losses or liabilities incurred, in the course of the agency, or otherwise arising in the course of the agency,[83] provided—

    (a) that the possession of the goods or chattels was lawfully obtained by him in the course of the agency, and in the same capacity as that in which he claims the lien[84];

    (b) that there is no agreement inconsistent with the right of lien; and

    (c) that the goods or chattels were not delivered to him with express directions, or for a special purpose, inconsistent with the right of lien.[85]

(2) The possessory lien of an agent is a particular lien only, except where he has a general lien by agreement, express or implied, with his principal. Such an agreement may be implied from a course of dealing between the principal and agent, or from an established custom or usage.[86]

Comment

Clear authority for the general proposition as to the lien of an agent is   **7–074**
difficult to find. This is not surprising, for the word agent can be applied

---

[81] *Gladstone v. Birley* (1817) 2 Mer. 401, 404.

[82] *Houghton v. Matthews* (1803) 3 B. & P. 485, 494; *Rushforth v. Hadfield* (1805) 6 East 519; (1806) 7 East 224; *Bock v. Gorrissen* (1860) 2 De G.F. & J. 434, 443.

[83] Illustrations 1–4; *Restatement*, § 464; and see Comment. For a discussion of choice of law problems, see Chesterman (1973) 22 I.C.L.Q. 213.

[84] Illustrations 5, 6; and see Comment.

[85] Illustrations 7–11.

[86] *Bock v. Gorrissen*, n. 82 above; *Rushforth v. Hadfield*, n. 82 above; *Holderness v. Collinson* (1827) 7 B. & C. 212; *Langley, Beldon & Gaunt Ltd v. Morley* [1965] 1 Lloyd's Rep. 297. Custom is not easy to establish: see Article 31.

in many situations, and no doubt some persons to whom the word could be applied would have no lien. For example, an estate agent will not normally hold property of his principal upon which he could exercise a lien.[87] Equally, there will be many cases where a person who has agency powers holds his principal's property in circumstances quite inconsistent with his having a lien over it.[88] But in general it is is established by the cases that an agent is entitled to a lien over the property of his principal in respect of payments, liabilities etc. relating to matters connected with that property. This seems in many cases to be a development of the older lien of a craftsman who makes repairs to a chattel;[89] but it was developed by cases on factors, brokers, auctioneers and other undoubted agents.

7–075   **When exercisable.** There is little authority on when the lien is exercisable, and in particular on whether it can only be exercised when the principal's breach is repudiatory in nature. It does not seem that the contract must be brought to an end before the remedy can be exercised. But it has been said that "common sense suggests that where the agency is of a continuing nature, it will not usually survive the exercise by the agent of rights inconsistent with those of the principal over goods which are the very subject-matter of the agency; and this would appear to indicate that the principal's conduct must at least be of a repudiatory nature, even if not formally treated by the agent as such."[90] In general it would seem that the fiduciary relationship between principal and agent will require the agent to exercise the right with consideration for his principal, and that the relationship will not survive its exercise.[91]

7–076   **Goods and chattels.** In principle, a lien operates over goods and chattels only, including those choses in action which are represented by documents, often called securities, which can themselves be treated as goods and chattels—for example, insurance policies, share certificates, bills of exchange. It is sometimes said that the lien extends to funds or money held: thus in connection with bankers it has been said that "All

---

[87] But he may hold a deposit: see para. 7–076 below. For an attempt by an estate agent to claim rights over proceeds of sale held by his principal's solicitor, see *W.A. Ellis Services Ltd v. Stuart Wood* [1993] 2 EGLR 43.

[88] See *Ariston Products Pty Ltd v. Egan* (1977) 3 A.C.L.R. 418 (accountant).

[89] See *Woodworth v. Conroy* [1976] Q.B. 884, 890 (accountant); but *cf. Ariston Products Pty Ltd v. Egan*, n. 88 above. See also *R. v. South Devon Ry. Co.* (1850) 15 Q.B. 1043 (arbitrator); *Ridgway v. Ley* (1856) 25 L.J.Ch. 584 (Parliamentary agent); *Fraser v. Equitorial Shipping Co. Ltd (The Ijaola)* [1979] 1 Lloyd's Rep. 103 (consulting marine engineer).

[90] *Compania Financiera "Soleada" S.A. v. Hamoor Tanker Corp. Inc. (The Borag)* [1980] 1 Lloyd's Rep. 111, 122, *per* Mustill J. (revsd. on a different point [1981] 1 W.L.R. 274).

[91] See *Restatement*, comment *b* to § 464.

moneys paid into a bank are subect to a lien,"[92] and the auctioneer's
lien has been said to be over goods and their proceeds. It is however
difficult to see how a lien can be exercised over money, which will
normally be the actual property of the holder subject to an obligation to
account for it. It seems that reference to a lien over money should in
many cases be explained as references to the agent's right to set-off and
counterclaim when sued by the principal for the money.[93] In the case of
an auctioneer it may also refer to the auctioneer's right to sue for the
price upon a separate contract, and then retain it; or to the rule that the
third party may not, to the extent of the auctioneer's lien, set off against
the auctioneer claims which he has against the vendor.[94] In other
circumstances it may refer to an equitable assignment by way of
charge[95]; or to an equitable lien arising out of the position of the parties
towards each other, as in the case of solicitor and client.[96] In so far as
an estate agent has a lien, it is likely to be over a deposit which belongs
to his client.[97]

Possession. The agent must possess the goods: "there can be no lien   **7–077**
upon any property unless it is in the possession of the party who claims
the lien."[98] But the possession may be held for the agent by another:
thus in *Bryans v. Nix*[99] an agent's lien was held to arise where the
principal delivered a cargo to a barge-master employed by him together
with documents indicating that the barge-master was to hold the cargo
for the agent. And it has been held that an agreement, made for

[92] *Misa v. Currie* (1876) 1 App.Cas. 554, 569.
[93] See Paget, *Law of Banking* (10th ed.), pp. 496, 501 *et seq.*; *Benjamin's Sale of Goods*
(4th ed.), § 22–136; *Halesowen Presswork and Assemblies Ltd v. Westminster Bank Ltd*
[1971] 1 Q.B. 1, 33–34, 46; the decision was reversed by the House of Lords on another
point ([1972] A.C. 785), but see the judgments of Viscount Dilhorne at p. 802 and of Lord
Cross at p. 810. See also *Richmond Shipping Ltd v. D/S and A/S Vestland (The Vestland)*
[1980] 2 Lloyd's Rep. 171, 181.
[94] See Illustration 1; below, para. 9–027.
[95] See *Re Welsh Irish Ferries Ltd* [1986] Ch. 471; *The Annangel Glory* [1988] 1 Lloyd's
Rep. 45; *Itex Italgrani Export S.A. v. Care Shipping Corp. (The Cebu (No. 2))* [1990] 2
Lloyd's Rep. 316; *Kingscroft Insurance Co. v. H.S. Weavers (Underwriting) Agencies Ltd*
[1993] 1 Lloyd's Rep. 187, 194–195.
[96] See Snell, *Equity* (29th ed.), Part IV, Chap. 10; *Hewett v. Court* (1983) 149 C.L.R.
639 esp. at p. 663.
[97] See Murdoch, *Law of Estate Agency and Auction* (3rd ed.), p. 178. This would
usually only be so on completion. His right to exercise the "lien" could be affected by
failure to comply with the information requirements of the Estate Agents Act 1979 and
statutory instruments made thereunder: see para. 7–007 above.
[98] *Shaw v. Neale* (1858) 6 H.L.Cas. 581, 601.
[99] (1839) 4 M. & W. 775, distinguishing *Kinloch v. Craig* (1789) 3 T.R. 119; (1790) 3
T.R. 783. See also *Evans & Evans v. Nichol & Nichol* (1841) 3 M. & G. 614; *Hammonds
v. Barclay* (1802) 2 East 227. cf. *Kruger v. Wilcox* (1755) Amb. 252; *Taylor v. Robinson*
(1818) 2 Moo. 730, Illustration 5; *Nicholas v. Clent* (1817) 3 Price 547.

valuable consideration, to hand over a bill of lading to an agent for the purpose of giving him security over the goods represented by it gives the agent the right in equity to the bill of lading and possession of the goods, as against the principal and his creditors.[1] Further, the lien is not lost by giving the goods to be held by another specifically on behalf of the person entitled to the lien.[2] On the other hand, even though the goods are in the agent's custody and control, they may not be in his possession, unless he performs some overt act taking them into his possession.[3]

7–078   **Lawfully obtained.** A lien cannot be acquired by a wrongful act. Thus if an agent obtains goods from his principal by misrepresentation, he has no lien over them, though the circumstances in other respects are such that he would have been a lien if the goods had been obtained lawfully.[4] And where the agent takes goods without authority, or is given goods by the principal after the latter's bankruptcy,[5] he acquires no lien.

7–079   **In the same capacity.** Even a general lien will not extend to the retaining of goods by an agent in satisfaction of debts incurred previous to or outside the agency.[6] Thus a factor's general lien did not entitle him to retain goods in respect of rent that was owing to him but which was unconnected with his operations as factor,[7] or in respect of transactions performed by him in some other capacity.[8] This requirement to some extent overlaps with those next referred to.

7–080   **No inconsistent agreement and goods not delivered in circumstances inconsistent with lien.** The scope of these two requirements, which overlap, will be apparent from the Illustrations.[9] It should be noted that the lien will not easily be displaced.[10]

---

[1] *Re Evans, ex p. Barber* (1843) 3 M.D. & De G. 174; *Lutscher v. Comptoir d'Escompte de Paris* (1876) 1 Q.B.D. 709. This is an equitable charge: see *Benjamin's Sale of Goods* (4th ed.), § 18–089.

[2] *McCombie v. Davis* (1805) 7 East 5; see Article 69. A more modern example is the trust receipt. *Aliter* if the delivery is a conversion.

[3] See *Hatton v. Car Maintenance Co. Ltd* [1915] 1 Ch. 621 (owner could remove car from company's premises at will: company had no lien).

[4] cf. *Madden v. Kempster* (1807) 1 Camp. 12.

[5] *Nichols v. Clent* (1817) 3 Price 547; *Copland v. Stein* (1799) 8 T.R. 199.

[6] *Houghton v. Matthews* (1803) 3 B. & P. 485, Illustration 6. See also *Tellrite Ltd v. London Confirmers Ltd* [1962] 1 Lloyd's Rep. 236.

[7] *Houghton v. Matthews*, n. 6 above, at pp. 494–495.

[8] *Dixon v. Stansfeld* (1850) 10 C.B. 398, Illustration 7.

[9] 8–11.

[10] See, *e.g. Brandao v. Barnett* (1846) 12 C. & F. 787, Illustration 10; *London Chartered Bank of Australia v. White* (1879) 4 App.Cas. 413; *Re London & Globe Finance Corp.* [1902] 2 Ch. 416.

General liens. Factors,[11] marine insurance brokers,[12] stockbrokers,[13]   **7–081**
solicitors,[14] bankers,[15] wharfingers[16] and packers[17] are among those
who have been held to have a general lien by implication from custom.
On the other hand it has been held that a confirming house was not a
modern version of the factor, and had no such lien[18]; and the old cases
on the packer's lien were based on the packer being to some extent a
factor and again may not avail those who conduct for different sorts of
business in a modern context, *e.g.* a freight forwarder[19] or a
consolidator[20] in the absence of proof of custom. Further details should
be sought in specialised works. The manager of a business may likewise
have such a lien[21]: but in view of the extensive subject-matter of the
lien it could equally be regarded as particular.

Solicitors' charging lien. A solicitor has a lien on the property of the   **7–082**
client in his possession and an equitable lien on property recovered or
preserved through his instrumentality.[22] But under section 73 of the
Solicitors' Act 1974 a court may also declare a solicitor entitled to a
charge upon property recovered or preserved through his instrumentality, and conveyances done or operating to defeat that charge are valid
except against a bona fide purchaser for value. This latter is often
referred to as a "charging lien", but it depends upon the order of the
court.[23]

Maritime liens. A shipmaster has a maritime lien over the ship and   **7–083**
freight for their wages and for disbursements and liabilities properly

---

[11] *Kruger v. Wilcox* (1755) Amb. 252; *Godin v. London Assurance Co.* (1758) 1 W.Bl.
103; *Baring v. Corrie* (1818) 2 B. & A. 137; Illustrations 5, 6, 7.
[12] *Mann v. Forrester* (1814) 4 Camp. 60; *Westwood v. Bell* (1815) 4 Camp. 349; *Fisher v.
Smith* (1878) 4 App.Cas. 1.
[13] *Jones v. Peppercorne* (1858) John. 430; *Re London & Globe Finance Corp.* [1902] 2
Ch. 416; *John D. Hope & Co. v. Glendinning* [1911] A.C. 419.
[14] *Barratt v. Gough-Thomas* [1951] Ch. 242.
[15] *Brandao v. Barnett* (1846) 12 C. & F. 787; *London Chartered Bank of Australia v.
White* (1879) 4 App.Cas. 413; *Misa v. Currie* (1876) 1 Ap..Cas. 554.
[16] *Naylor v. Mangles* (1794) 1 Esp. 109; *Spears v. Hartly* (1800) 3 Esp. 81; *cf.
Holderness v. Collinson* (1827) 7 B. & C. 212; *Jowitt & Sons v. Union Cold Storage Co.*
[1913] 3 K.B. 1 (lien by contract only).
[17] *Re Witt, ex p. Shubrook* (1876) 2 Ch.D. 489.
[18] *Tellrite Ltd v. London Confirmers Ltd* [1962] 1 Lloyd's Rep. 236. See also *Ahlers v.
Broome & Greene Ltd* (1938) 62 Ll.Rep. 163; *Rolls Razor Ltd v. Cox* [1967] 1 Q.B. 552.
[19] See *Langley, Beldon & Gaunt Ltd v. Morley* [1965] 1 Lloyd's Rep. 297, 305.
[20] *Chellaram & Sons (London) Ltd v. Butlers Warehousing and Distribution Ltd* [1978] 2
Lloyd's Rep. 412. As to warehousemen, see *Majeau Carrying Co. Pty. Ltd v. Coastal
Rutile Ltd* (1973) 129 C.L.R. 48.
[21] See Illustrations 2, 3.
[22] See Snell, *Equity* (29th ed.), Part IV, Chap. 10; Cordery, *Solicitors* (8th ed.), Chap.
8. As to priority between a Mareva injunction and solicitors' liens, see *Prekookeanska
Plovidba v. L.N.T. Lines S.R.L.* [1989] 1 W.L.R. 753.
[23] See further Cordery, *Solicitors* (8th ed.), pp. 254 *et seq.*

made or incurred by him on account of the ship.[24] Maritime liens, which are enforced by Admiralty action *in rem*, do not depend on possession, and attach to the ship from the moment when the claim arsies: they can have effect even against a bona fide purchaser for value.[25]

7–084   **"Statutory liens".** Certain Admiralty claims can be enforced by proceeding *in rem* against the ship: by virtue of section 20(2)(*p*) of the Supreme Court Act 1981 this includes "any claim by a master, shipper, charterer or agent in respect of disbursements made on account of the ship." This procedure in certain respects creates claims enforceable against the ship, and the result is sometimes referred to as a "statutory lien": but the procedure is a special one and connected neither with the general law of liens nor with that of agency.[26]

Illustrations

7–085   (1)   An auctioneer who is employed to sell goods has a lien on the goods for his charges and commission.[27]

(2)   A carries on a business in his own name as agent for B. B becomes bankrupt. A, being liable to the creditors of the business by reason of his having carried it on in his own name, has a lien upon the goods and chattels in his possession belonging to B to the extent of such liability.[28]

(3)   A carries on a business in his own name as agent for B, and deals with the possession of the goods of the business as if he were the owner of them. He accepts certain bills of exchange drawn by B. Both become bankrupt. A's trustee in bankruptcy has a lien upon the goods

---

[24] Merchant Shipping Act 1970, s.18.
[25] See further Thomas, *Maritime Liens* (1980). An insurance broker's claim for the cost of hull insurance was heid not covered in *Bain Clarkson Ltd v. Owners of the Ship "Sea Friends"* [1991] 2 Lloyd's Rep. 322. A managing agent may perhaps be an agent for the purposes of this section: see *The Corona Energy* (unrep.), 1977 folio no. 174. See also *The Westport (No. 3)* [1966] 1 Lloyd's Rep. 342.
[26] See in general Thomas, *op. cit.* n. 25 above; Meeson, *Admiralty Jurisdiction and Practice* (1993). For an example in the agency context see *The Ohm Mariana* [1993] 2 Singapore L.R. 698.
[27] *Williams v. Millington* (1788) 1 H.Bl. 81; *Robinson v. Rutter* (1855) 4 E. & B. 954; *Webb v. Smith* (1885) 30 Ch.D. 192. As to his lien over any deposit paid, see *Skinner v. Trustee of the Property of Reed* [1967] Ch. 1194; and above, para. 7–076. In *Skinner's* case the amount outstanding on the mortgage exceeded the purchase price, so the auctioneer had no lien. See in general Murdoch, *Law of Estate Agency and Auctions* (3rd ed.), pp. 347–350.
[28] *Foxcraft v. Wood* (1828) 4 Russ. 487.

in A's possession to the extent of A's liability upon current bils as well as for other amounts due to him from B.[29]

(4) An agent was appointed by a company to sell goods on their behalf in a shop taken for that purpose, and it was agreed that he should from time to time accept bills representing the value of the goods in his hands for sale. Goods were consigned to the agent, and he accepted a bill for their value. Before the bill became due, the company was wound up, and the liquidators took possession of and sold the goods. Held, that the agent, having paid the bill, had a lien upon the goods for the amount, and was entitled to be repaid out of the proceeds thereof in preference to the other creditors of the company.[30]

(5) A bought goods as a factor for and on behalf of B, and it was agreed that the goods should remain upon the premises of the seller at a rent to be paid by B. After a time A was requested by the seller to remove the goods, but did not do so. Subsequently, without B's authority or instructions, A removed the goods to his own premises, and about the same time a petition in bankruptcy was presented against B. Held, that the possession of the goods continued in B, and that A had therefore no lien upon them.[31]

(6) A, a factor, sold goods in his own name on B's behalf to C. C subsequently sent goods to A for sale, never having employed him as a factor before. C became bankrupt. A had no lien upon C's goods for the price of the goods sold by him on B's behalf.[32]

(7) A factor insures a ship on his principal's behalf as insurance broker, the transaction being quite distinct and separate from his duties as factor. His general lien does not extend to the policy of insurance, because he did not acquire it in the capacity of factor.[33] So, if a policy is left merely for safe custody in an agent's hands, he has no general lien over it for advances.[34] Where a partner deposited a lease with a banker to secure a particular advance to himself personally, it was held that the banker had no lien over it for the general balance due from the firm.[35]

(8) A life policy was deposited at a bank, with a memorandum charging it with overdrafts not exceeding a specified amount. Held, that the banker's general lien was excluded by the special contract, such contract being inconsistent with the existence of a general lien on the policy.[36] If a factor expressly agrees to deal in a particular way with the

---

[29] *Re Fawcus, ex p. Buck* (1876) 3 Ch.D. 795.
[30] *Re Pavy's Patent Felted Fabric Co.* (1876) 1 Ch.D. 631.
[31] *Taylor v. Robinson* (1818) 2 Moo.C.P. 730.
[32] *Houghton v. Matthews* (1803) 3 B. & P. 485.
[33] *Dixon v. Stansfeld* (1850) 10 C.B. 398.
[34] *Muir v. Fleming* (1822) D. & R.N.P. 29.
[35] *Wolstenholm v. Sheffield Union Banking Co. Ltd* (1886) 54 L.T. 746.
[36] *Re Bowes, Strathmore v. Vane* (1886) 33 Ch.D. 586. See also *Re Laurence, ex p. M'Kenna, City Bank Case* (1861) 3 De G.F. & J. 629.

proceeds of goods deposited with him for sale, his general lien is excluded.[37] But the lien is not excluded unless the contract is clearly inconsistent with its existence.[38] Thus, where certain securities were deposited with stockbrokers for a specific loan, and they were given a power of sale, it was held that their general lien extended to such securities.[39] So, an agreement that there shall be monthly settlements does not affect the lien of an insurance broker for premiums upon policies in his hands.[40] And the general lien of a factor is not excluded merely because he acts under special instructions to sell in his principal's name and at a particular price.[41]

(9) A consigns goods to B, who transfers the bill of lading to his factor C, to secure £1,000. B becomes bankrupt. C has no lien on the bill of lading for a general balance due from B, and A may stop the goods in transit, subject to C's claim for £1,000.[42]

(10) Certain exchequer bills were deposited at a bank, to be kept in a box under lock and key, the key being kept by the customer. The bills were subsequently entrusted to the bank, with instructions to obtain the interest on them, and get them exchanged for new bills, and to deposit the new bills in the box as before. Held, that the banker's lien did not attach to the original bills or to those for which they were exchanged, the special purpose for which they were placed in his hands being inconsistent with a right of general lien.[43]

(11) A factor, who acted as such for the owners of a ship, asked the master to let him have the certificate of registry for the purpose of paying certain duties at the custom house. Held, that his general lien as a factor did not attach to the certificate.[44]

Article 68

CONFINED TO RIGHTS OF PRINCIPAL, EXCEPT IN THE CASE OF MONEY OR NEGOTIABLE SECURITIES

7–086   (1) The possessory lien of an agent attaches only upon goods or chattels in respect of which the principal has, as against third

---

[37] *Walker v. Birch* (1795) 6 T.R. 258; See also *Buchanan v. Findlay* (1829) 9 B. & C. 738; *Bock v. Gorrissen* (1860) 2 De G.F. & J. 434; *Frith v. Forbes* (1862) 4 De G.F. & J. 409; *Rolls Razor Ltd v. Cox* [1967] 1 Q.B. 552.

[38] *Brandao v. Barnett* (1846) 12 C. & F. 787; *Re European Bank, Agra Bank Claim* (1872) L.R. 8 Ch.App. 41; *Davis v. Bowsher* (1794) 5 T.R. 488.

[39] *Jones v. Peppercorne* (1858) John. 430. See also *Re London & Globe Finance Corp.* [1902] 2 Ch. 416.

[40] *Fisher v. Smith* (1878) 4 App.Cas. 1.

[41] *Stevens v. Biller* (1883) 25 Ch.D. 31; *König v. Brandt* (1901) 84 L.T. 748.

[42] *Spalding v. Ruding* (1843) 6 Beav. 376.

[43] *Brandao v. Barnett* (1846) 12 C. & F. 787.

[44] *Burn v. Brown* (1817) 2 Stark. 272.

parties, the power to create the lien, and except in the case of money or negotiable securities, and subject to any statutory provision to the contrary,[45] is confined to the rights of the principal in the goods or chattels at the time when the lien attaches, and is subject to all rights and equities of third parties available against the principal at that time.[46]

(2)   The lien of an agent over negotiable securities deposited with him by or in the name of the principal is not affected by the rights or equities of third parties, and is as effectual as if the principal were the absolute owner of such money or securities, provided that at the time when the lien of the agent attaches he has no notice of any defect in the title of the principal to them.[47]

Comment

No one can create a lien beyond his own interest. This means that not only does a lien take effect subject to the interests existing in the property concerned at the time that any money first becomes due in respect of which it may be exercised, but also that a subsequent disposition of the goods by the owner, in principle and subject to the circumstances of the disposition, freezes the lien at the sum due at that time: notice of such interests or dispositions to the person having the lien is (in the case of legal interests in ordinary chattels) irrelevant.[48] On the other hand, to the extent to which dispositions are subject to the lien, it is equally irrelevant whether or not the person taking under such disposition had notice of the lien: nor can he acquire priority to it by giving notice.[49]

7–087

The position as regards negotiable instruments depends not on special rules as to liens, but on the normal rules of negotiability. Notice of previous interests in or subsequent dealings as to the goods is therefore relevant, in so far as it may prevent the person claiming the lien from being a holder in due course.[50]

---

[45] *e.g.* Factors Act 1889; Sale of Goods Act 1979, ss. 24–26. (See Article 89.)

[46] See Illustrations; *Att.-Gen. v. Trueman* (1843) 11 M. & W. 694; *Cuthbert v. Robarts, Lubbock & Co.* [1909] 2 Ch. 226, 233.

[47] See Illustration 9.

[48] *Blunden v. Desart* (1842) (Ir.) 59 R.R. 753, Illustration 8 (authorities reviewed); see also *Watson v. Lyon* (1855) 7 De G.M. & G. 288; *Young v. English* (1843) 7 Beav. 10; *Jeffryes v. Agra & Masterman's Bank* (1866) L.R. 2 Eq. 674; cases cited at Illustration 4. As to equitable interests see, *e.g. Re Gross, ex p. Kingston* (1871) L.R. 6 Ch.App. 632.

[49] *West of England Bank v. Batchelor* (1882) 51 L.J.Ch. 199.

[50] See Bills of Exchange Act 1882, ss. 27(3), 29.

Illustrations

(1)   A solicitor or other agent can have no lien on the share register or minute book of a company, because the directors have no power to create any lien that could interfere with the use of such register or book for the purposes of the company. So, no lien can attach upon such books of a company as, under the articles of association or the Companies Acts, ought to be kept at the registered office of the company.[51] And where documents come into the hands of a solicitor pending the winding up of a company, he cannot claim any lien on them that would interfere with the winding up.[52] But the fact that a company has issued debentures as a floating security does not prevent an agent from acquiring a lien on the title deeds of the company, and such a lien has priority to the claims of the debenture holders.[53]

(2)   The directors of a building society, which has no borrowing powers, overdraw the banking account of the society, and agree that certain deeds deposited at the bank shall be held as security for the general balance. The transaction is *ultra vires*, and the banker has no lien on the deeds for the overdraft. He is, however, in equity, entitled to hold them as security for so much of the money advanced as he can show to have been actually applied in payment of the debts and liabilities of the society.[54]

(3)   A solicitor or other agent is employed by trustees. He normally has no lien on the trust funds for his expenses.[55]

(4)   Deeds are deposited with a solicitor by a tenant for life. The solicitor has no lien on the deeds as against the remainderman.[56] The lien of a solicitor upon deeds and papers deposited with him by a client is confined to the rights of the client in them, and is subject to all rights and equities of third persons available against the client.[57] So, a solicitor or other agent has no lien, as such, on the separate property of a partner for the obligations of the firm.[58]

(5)   A mortgage is paid off, and the property is reconveyed to the mortgagor. The mortgagee's solicitor has no lien as against the

---

[51] *Re Capital Fire Ins. Assn.* (1883) 24 Ch.D. 408; *Re Rapid Road Transit Co.* [1909] 1 Ch. 96; Companies Act 1985, ss. 352, 353.
[52] *Re Anglo-Maltese Hydraulic Dock Co. Ltd* (1885) 54 L.J.Ch. 730.
[53] *Brunton v. Electrical Engineering Corp.* [1892] 1 Ch. 434. See also *Re Dee Estates Ltd, Wright v. Dee Estates Ltd* [1911] 2 Ch. 85.
[54] *Cunliffe v. Blackburn Benefit Building Society* (1884) 9 App.Cas. 857; see Article 95.
[55] *Staniar v. Evans* (1886) 3 T.L.R. 215; *Worrall v. Harford* (1802) 8 Ves. 4; *Lightfoot v. Keane* (1836) 1 M. & W. 745; *Hall v. Laver* (1842) 1 Hare 571; *Francis v. Francis* (1854) 5 De G.M. & G. 108; Cordery, *Solicitors* (8th ed.), pp. 60–61.
[56] *Turner v. Letts* (1855) 20 Beav. 185; 7 De G.M. & G. 243; *Ex p. Nesbitt* (1805) 2 Sch. & Lef. 279.
[57] *Hollis v. Claridge* (1813) 4 Taunt. 807; *Furlong v. Howard* (1804) 2 Sch. & Lef. 115; *Pelly v. Wathen* (1851) 1 De G.M. & G. 16; Cordery, *Solicitors* (8th ed.), p. 236–238.
[58] *Turner v. Deane* (1849) 3 Exch. 836; *Watts v. Christie* (1849) 11 Beav. 546.

mortgagor on the title deeds for costs due from the mortgagee, except the cost of the reconveyance, even if such costs were incurred in respect of the mortgaged property, *e.g.* the costs of an attempted sale by the mortgagee.[59] So, where a mortgagor borrowed the title deeds from the mortgagee and sold the property, it was held that the solicitor of the mortgagor, to whom the deeds were handed for the purpose of completing the sale, had no lien over them for costs due from the mortgagor in respect of other transactions.[60]

(6) A sells goods to B, and ships them to B's order. Before the goods arrive, A and B agree to rescind the contract for sale. The wharfinger cannot, on the arrival of the goods at his wharf, claim a lien on them as against A, for a general balance due from B.[61] So, a wharfinger has no lien on goods, as against a buyer, for charges becoming due from the seller after the sale.[62]

(7) A, an owner of land, deposits the title deeds at a bank as security for his general balance, and subsequently contracts to sell the land to B, who has notice of the terms of the deposit. The banker has notice of the sale, but continues to account, and makes fresh advances to A, who pays in sums from time to time. B pays the purchase-money to A, by instalments, without notice of such advances. A having paid into the bank sums exceeding in the aggregate the amount owing to the bank at the time of the contract of sale, the banker has no lien on the title deeds or charge on the land as against B, though on the general balance there was always a debt due to the bank.[63]

(8) A client deposits deeds with a solicitor. Judgment is subsequently obtained against the client. The solicitor's lien does not extend to costs becoming due after the date of the judgment.[64]

(9) A banker borrowed a specific sum of money from a stockbroker, with whom he deposited, as security, negotiable instruments belonging to third persons. The banker dealt as a principal with the broker, having had many previous transactions with him, and there was nothing to lead the broker to believe that the securities were not the property of the banker. Held, that the broker's general lien for the balance due to him from the banker attached upon the securities, although the banker had been guilty of gross fraud.[65] So, the general lien of a banker upon

---

[59] *Re Llewellin* [1891] 3 Ch. 145; *Wakefield v. Newbon* (1844) 6 Q.B. 276.
[60] *Young v. English* (1843) 7 Beav. 10.
[61] *Richardson v. Goss* (1802) 3 B. & P. 119.
[62] *Barry v. Longmore* (1840) 12 A. & E. 639.
[63] *London and County Banking Co. Ltd. v. Ratcliffe* (1881) 6 App.Cas. 722 (a case on mortgage: see now Law of Property Act 1925, s. 94. But Lord Blackburn refers also to lien). See Paget, *Law of Banking* (10th ed.), pp. 499–501.
[64] *Blunden v. Desart* (1842) (Ir.) 59 R.R. 753.
[65] *Jones v. Peppercorne* (1858) John. 430.

negotiable instruments deposited with him is not affected by the circumstance that the customer who deposits them is acting as agent for a third person,[66] nor by equities between the customer and third persons.[67] But an agent has no lien upon a negotiable instrument, as against the true owner, for advances made after notice of a defect in the title of the principal.[68]

Article 69

How Lien Extinguished or Lost

7–089

(1) The lien of an agent is extinguished or lost—

   (a) by tender to him of the sume due[69];

   (b) by his entering into any agreement,[70] or acting in any capacity,[71] which is inconsistent with the continuance of the lien;

   (c) by waiver.[72]

(2) The lien of an agent is extinguished by his voluntarily[73] parting with the possession of the goods or chattels subject to it,[74] except where the circumstances in which he parts with possession are consistent with the continuance of the lien and are such as to show that he intends to retain the lien.[75]

(3) The lien of an agent is not affected by the fact that the claim secured by it becomes barred by limitation,[76] or that the principal becomes insolvent, or sells or otherwise deals with the goods or chattels subject to the lien, after the lien has attached.[76a]

---

[66] *Brandao v. Barnett* (1846) 12 C. & F. 787; *Baker v. Nottingham & Nottinghamshire Banking Co. Ltd* (1891) 60 L.J.Q.B. 542.

[67] *Misa v. Currie* (1876) 1 App.Cas. 554; *Johnson v. Robarts* (1875) L.R. 10 Ch.App. 505.

[68] *Solomons v. Bank of England* (1791) 13 East 135 (but this is hardly clear authority); Bills of Exchange Act 1882, ss.27(3), 29.

[69] See Comment.

[70] Illustration 1; *How v. Kirchner* (1857) 11 Moo.P.C. 21.

[71] Illustrations 2, 3.

[72] See Comment; Illustrations 4, 5, 6, 7; Sale of Goods Act 1979, s. 43(1)(c).

[73] See *Tibmor Pty Ltd v. Nashlyn Pty Ltd* [1989] 1 Qd.R. 610 (obligatory payment into court did not extinguish lien).

[74] Illustration 8; *Kruger v. Wilcox* (1755) Amb. 252; *Bligh v. Davies* (1860) 28 Beav. 211.

[75] Illustrations 9, 10, 11.

[76] *Spears v. Hartly* (1800) 3 Esp. 81; *Re Broomhead* (1847) 5 D. & L. 52; *Curwen v. Milburn* (1889) 42 Ch.D. 424; *Re Carter, Carter v. Carter* (1885) 55 L.J.Ch. 230. The statute can be said to bar the remedy, not the right.

[76a] The last two propositions follow from the nature of the lien as a right *in rem*.

Comment

Tender. Acceptance or refusal of a valid tender extinguishes the lien. 7–090
But a lien is not necessarily lost by a claim for more than the sum due,
unless the claimant gives no details from which the correct sum can be
calculated, or makes it clear that he insists on an incorrect sum.[77]

Waiver. A waiver is implied whenever the conduct of the agent is 7–091
such as to indicate an intention to abandon the lien, or is inconsistent
with the continuance of it.[78] The situations referred to in Rule (1)(b)
are in fact no more than examples of implied waiver. Questions of
tender are also sometimes expressed in terms of waiver.[79]

Parting with possession. The lien of an agent is not affected where he 7–092
was induced to part with possession of the goods by fraud,[80] or
possession was obtained from him unlawfully or without his consent.[81]
In such cases, the lien continues, and the person entitled to it can sue in
conversion, whether or not he has recovered possession, and if he has
recovered possession, even where he did so by a trick.[82] Nor is the lien
affected by the fact that the goods are given by the agent to another to
hold on his behalf,[83] even where that other is himself the principal, if
the agreement to retain the lien is clear: an example where this occurs is
the commercial situation covered by the trust receipt.[84] Where the agent
simply delivers the goods with a purported unilateral reservation of the
lien to which the receiver has not agreed, it is arguable that the lien is
lost, on the grounds that such terms of receipt cannot be unilaterally
imposed. It has however been decided that the lien is maintained, and
that if the receiver does not agree to the terms under which the goods
are delivered he must give notice to the lienor to remove them.[85] It
appears that in some cases, where the subject-matter of the lien comes
lawfully back into the claimant's hands after he has voluntarily parted
with it, the lien revives, even for sums due before possession was lost.[86]

---

[77] *Albemarle Supply Co. Ltd. v. Hind & Co.* [1928] 1 K.B. 307.
[78] *e.g.* Illustrations 4, 5.
[79] *e.g. Scarfe v. Morgan* (1838) 4 M. & W. 270. The principle seems to be similar to
that of election: a person may waive a contract term which is to his benefit. Obviously
there can also be estoppels as to whether there has been or will be a waiver.
[80] *Wallace v. Woodgate* (1824) R. & M. 193.
[81] *Dicas v. Stockley* (1836) 7 C. & P. 587; *Re Carter, Carter v. Carter* (1885) 55 L.J.Ch.
230.
[82] *Bristol (Earl) v. Wilsmore* (1823) 1 B. & C. 514.
[83] *Wilson v. Kymer* (1813) 1 M. & S. 157; *McCombie v. Davis* (1805) 7 East 5.
[84] See Illustration 10; *Benjamin's Sale of Goods* (4th ed.), §§ 18–090 *et seq.*
[85] *Caldwell v. Sumpters* [1972] Ch. 478, Illustration 11, at first instance and on appeal.
[86] *Levy v. Barnard* (1818) 8 Taunt. 149 (marine insurance policy); *Caldwell v. Sumpters*
[1972] Ch. 478, 488. But a general lien, at any rate, does not do so where he has
—*cont. on next page*

Illustrations

7-093 (1) The holder of a lien allows the owner of the goods free access to the goods for the purpose of using and returning them: he may be held to have lost his lien. [87]

(2) A solicitor acts for both mortgagor and mortgagee in carrying out a mortgage. The solicitor thereby loses his lien on the title deeds of the mortgaged property for costs due from the mortgagor, even if the costs were incurred prior to the mortgage, and even if the deeds are not permitted to be taken out of the solicitor's possession. [88]

(3) A solicitor prepares a marriage settlement, on the instructions of the intended husband, and retains it in his possession after the marriage. He has no lien on the settlement as against the trustees, the cost of preparing it being payable by the husband. [89]

(4) An agent causes goods upon which he has a lien to be taken in execution at his own suit. He thereby waives the lien, though the goods are sold to him under the execution, and are never removed from his premises. [90]

(5) Upon a demand being made against an agent by his principal for a chattel upon which the agent has a lien, the agent claims to retain the chattel on some other ground, without mentioning the lien. He thereby waives the lien. [91]

(6) A solicitor, having a lien for costs, takes a security for them, and does not tell the client that he intends to reserve the lien. He is deemed to waive the lien, it being the duty of a solicitor, if he intends to reserve his lien in such a case, to explain to the client that such is his intention. [92]

—*cont. from previous page*

meanwhile discovered that the person with whom he is dealing is only an agent, or where dispositions of the goods have meanwhile been made: see *Near East Relief v. King, Chasseur & Co. Ltd* [1930] 2 K.B. 40, 44–45; Article 70.

[87] *Forth v. Simpson* (1849) 13 Q.B. 680; *cf. Albermarle Supply Co. Ltd v. Hind & Co.* [1928] 1 K.B. 307. See also *Hatton v. Car Maintenance Co. Ltd* [1915] 1 Ch. 621.

[88] *Re Nicholson, ex p. Quinn* (1883) 53 L.J.Ch. 302; *Re Snell* (1877) 6 Ch.D. 105; *Re Mason and Taylor* (1878) 10 Ch.D. 729.

[89] *Re Lawrance, Bowker v. Austin* [1894] 1 Ch. 556.

[90] *Jacobs v. Latour* (1828) 5 Bing. 130.

[91] *Weeks v. Goode* (1859) 6 C.B.(N.S.) 367; *Boardman v. Sill* (1808) 1 Camp. 410n. The rule is different from that applicable to discharge of contract by breach, where a person who gives an invalid reason for treating the contract as discharged may subsequently justify his conduct by a valid reason.

[92] *Re Morris* [1908] 1 K.B. 473; *Re Taylor, Stileman & Underwood* [1891] 1 Ch. 590; *Bissill v. Bradford & District Tramway Co. Ltd* (1893) 9 T.L.R. 337; *Re Douglas Norman & Co.* [1898] 1 Ch. 199. It seems, therefore, that the solicitor's position is somewhat unfavourable. See Cordery, *Solicitors* (8th ed.), p. 249.

(7)   An agent entitled to a lien takes other security for the claim. He may be deemed to waive the lien,[93] but only if the nature of the security,[94] or the circumstances in which it is taken,[95] are inconsistent with the continuance of the lien, or indicate an intention to abandon it. The taking of a bill of exchange will usually be no more than conditional acceptance of a particular mode of payment.[96]

(8)   An agent delivers goods, on which he has a lien, on board a ship, to be conveyed on account and at the risk of the principal. The agent thereby surrenders his lien on the goods, and he has no power to revive it by stopping the goods in transit.[97]

(9)   A, as a solicitor, on the instructions of a mortgagor, prepares and engrosses a reconveyance, which he sends to the solicitor of the mortgagee with a request that he will hold it on A's account, he having a lien thereon. The mortgagee executes the reconveyance. A's lien is not, in the circumstances, prejudiced by his parting with the possession of the engrossment, nor by its being executed by the mortgagee as a deed, and he can restrain the mortgagee's solicitor from transferring the deed to a subsequent purchaser of the land.[98]

(10)   An agent gives up a chattel in order that the principal may sell it and account for the proceeds to the agent; he does not thereby lose his lien on the chattel.[99]

(11)   The intending vendor of property changes her solicitor during negotiations. The former solicitor claims a lien on the deeds. The new solicitor requires the deeds in connection with the sale. At the request of the new solicitor, the former solicitor gives them up, accompanying them by a letter saying that they are sent "on the understanding that you will hold them to our order." The new solicitor immediately writes refusing to agree to these terms, but does not offer the deeds back. The former solicitor's lien continues: if the new solicitors were not willing to hold the deeds on these terms they should have told the former solicitors to come and take them back.[1]

---

[93] *Cowell v. Simpson* (1809) 16 Ves. 275 (note payable three years later); *Hewison v. Guthrie* (1836) 2 Bing.N.C. 755 (bill at 12 months); *Mason v. Morley (No. 1)* (1865) 34 Beav. 471.

[94] *Angus v. McLachlan* (1883) 23 Ch.D. 330.

[95] See *The Albion* (1872) 27 L.T. 723.

[96] *Gunn v. Bolckow, Vaughan & Co.* (1875) L.R. 10 Ch.App. 491; *cf. Tamvaco v. Simpson* (1866) L.R. 1 C.P. 363; *W.J. Alan & Co. Ltd v. El Nasr Export & Import Co.* [1972] 1 Q.B. 189.

[97] *Sweet v. Pym* (1800) 1 East 4; *Hathesing v. Laing* (1873) 17 Eq. 92. See, however, Article 71.

[98] *Watson v. Lyon* (1855) 7 De G.M. & G. 288.

[99] *North Western Bank Ltd v. Poynter, Son & Macdonalds* [1895] A.C. 56; see also *Albemarle Supply Co. Ltd v. Hind & Co.* [1928] 1 K.B. 307; *Benjamin's Sale of Goods* (4th ed.), §§ 18–090 *et seq.* as to trust receipts.

[1] *Caldwell v. Sumpters* [1972] Ch. 478. See Comment.

[2] See Article 89 as to the Factors Act.

Article 70

Lien of Sub-Agents

7-094

(1) Except where otherwise expressly provided by statute,[2] a sub-agent who is employed by an agent in circumstances where the agent has no actual or apparent authority to delegate his functions has no lien over the goods or chattels of the principal as against the principal.[3]

(2) Where a sub-agent is employed by an agent in circumstances where the agent has actual or apparent authority to delegate without creating privity of contract between principal and agent, the sub-agent—

(a) has the same right of lien, general or particular, against the principal, over the goods and chattels of the principal, in respect of claims arising in the course of the sub-agency, as he would have had against the agent if the agent had been the owner of the goods and chattels; and such right of lien is not liable to be defeated by any settlement between the principal and the agent to which the sub-agent is not a party[4];

(b) has the same right of general lien over the goods and chattels of the principal in respect of all claims, whether arising in the course of the sub-agency or not, as he would have had against the agent if the agent had been the owner of the goods and chattels; provided that, as against the principal, such right of lien is available only to the extent of the lien, if any, to which the agent would have been entitled if the goods and chattels had been in his possession[5]; and

(c) has the same right of lien, general or particular, over the goods and chattels of the principal, as he would have had against the agent if the agent had been the owner of the goods and chattels, where that at the time when the lien attaches he believes on reasonable grounds that the agent is the owner of the goods and chattels and is acting in the matter on his own behalf.[6]

---

[3] Illustration 1. As to when the agent has the power to affect the legal position of his principal, see Chap. 3. And see in general *Restatement*, § 465. As to cases where bailees have authority to place goods in the hands of persons who may subsequently claim a lien against the owner, see *Cassils & Co. v. Holden Wood Bleaching Co.* (1914) 84 L.J.K.B. 834; *Tappenden v. Artus* [1964] 2 Q.B. 185; *Chellaram & Sons (London) Ltd v. Butlers Warehousing and Distribution Ltd* [1978] 2 Lloyd's Rep. 412; Article 27, Illustration 10.
[4] Illustration 2.
[5] Illustration 3.
[6] Illustrations 4–6.

Comment

Unauthorised delegation. Where the agent for a disclosed principal   **7–095**
delegates his duties but has no authority, actual or apparent, to do so, it
is obvious that the principal's position cannot be affected.[7] The
remainder of the Article applies to cases where delegated performance
is authorised, but the creation of privity between principal and sub-agent
is not.[8] In cases where such privity does exist, the so-called sub-agent is
actually an agent of the principal and entitled to an agent's normal
remedies against him.[9]

General rule. But where delegation to a sub-agent is authorised by   **7–096**
virtue of actual or apparent authority, the principal can be regarded as
having contemplated that the sub-agent would acquire a lien: the
general rule, therefore, set out in Rule (2)(a), is that the sub-agent's
lien against the principal is confined to claims arising in the course of
performance of the duties properly delegated to him. However, where
the agent himself has an interest in the principal's property by way of
lien,[10] the sub-agent is entitled to exercise a lien to that extent against
the principal, as stated in Rule (2)(b). Both these rules can be regarded
as applications of the principle that no one can create a lien beyond his
own interest.[11]
Against the agent, of course, the sub-agent has the normal rights of
an agent against his principal.

Undisclosed principal. It has long been established that, as stated in   **7–097**
Rule 2(c), when the agent does not disclose the existence of his
principal, the sub-agent may exercise against such principal the full lien
that would have been available against the agent had that agent in fact
been principal, to the extent that such lien had accrued up to the time
of discovery of the principal[12]—provided, of course, that the delegation
was within the authority of the agent. The basis of this rule seems to be
the notion that an undisclosed principal intervenes on the contract of his
agent subject to equities already accrued,[13] and there is no tendency in
the cases regarding lien to require some fault in the principal that could
be treated as raising an estoppel.[14] However, since the agent is

---

[7] Illustration 1.
[8] See Article 37.
[9] *ibid.*
[10] Illustration 3.
[11] See Comment to Article 68.
[12] *Westwood v. Bell* (1815) 4 Camp. 349; Marine Insurance Act 1906, s.53(2).
[13] *Montagu v. Forwood* [1893] 2 Q.B. 350, 355–356.
[14] Compare the position as regards set-off: see Comment to Article 83.

authorised, it would seem that on discovery of the principal the sub-agent is remitted to his position under Rule 2(a).

Although a lien revives, at any rate in some cases, where possession of the goods is recovered,[15] it has been held that the general lien of a marine insurance broker on a policy does not revive when at the time that he recovers possession he has notice that the person with whom he had dealt was only an agent,[16] and this seems to be a rule applicable to all general liens, based on the fact that the regained possession is a new possession.[17] It would not, however, apply where the first possession is lost not voluntarily, but by fraud or a trick.[18]

Illustrations

7–098   (1) A factor delegated his authority to a sub-agent, without the assent of the principal. The sub-agent, who knew that the goods did not belong to the factor, had no lien on the principal's goods, even for duties paid in respect of those goods.[19]

(2) An agent, with the authority of his principal, employs an insurance broker to effect a policy for his principal, the broker being aware that the agent is acting for a principal. The principal pays the agent the amount of the premiums due in respect of the policy. Nothwithstanding such payment, the broker has a lien upon the policy for premiums paid by him in respect of it, or for which he is liable.[20] But he has no lien, as against the principal, for a general balance due from the agent in respect of other transactions.[21]

(3) As against the solicitor employing him, a London agent has a general lien upon all moneys received and documents deposited with him in the course of his employment,[22] but as against the client, his general lien is limited to the amount due from the client to the country solicitor.[23] As against both the country solicitor and the client, he has a

---

[15] *Levy v. Barnard* (1818) 2 Moo.C.P. 34 (marine insurance policy).

[16] *Near East Relief v. King, Chasseur & Co. Ltd* [1930] 2 K.B. 40; see Marine Insurance Act 1906, s. 53.

[17] Powell, pp. 375–376.

[18] See Comment to Article 69.

[19] *Solly v. Rathbone* (1814) 2 M. & S. 298; *Snook v. Davidson* (1809) 2 Camp. 218. And see *Chellaram & Sons (London) Ltd v. Butlers Warehousing and Distribution Ltd* [1978] 2 Lloyd's Rep. 412 (uncontemplated sub-bailment).

[20] *Fisher v. Smith* (1878) 4 App.Cas. 1; Marine Insurance Act 1906, s. 53(2).

[21] *Mildred v. Maspons* (1883) 8 App.Cas. 874; *Maanss v. Henderson* (1801) 1 East 335; *Man v. Shiffner* (1802) 2 East 523; Marine Insurance Act 1906, s. 53(2); *Fairfield Shipbuilding & Engineering Co. Ltd v. Gardner Mountain & Co. Ltd* (1911) 104 L.T. 288.

[22] *Lawrence v. Fletcher* (1879) 12 Ch.D. 858; *Bray v. Hine & Fox* (1818) 6 Price 203; *Re Jones and Roberts* [1905] 2 Ch. 219.

[23] *Ex p. Edwards* (1881) 8 Q.B.D. 262; *Moody v. Spencer* (1822) 2 D. & R. 6; *Waller v. Holmes* (1860) 1 John. & H. 239; *Peatfield v. Barlow* (1869) L.R. 8 Eq. 61.

lien upon money recovered and documents deposited with him in a particular suit, for the amount of his agency charges and disbursements in connection with that suit. [24]

(4)   An agent, on behalf, and with the authority, of his principal, employs an insurance broker to effect a policy, the broker having no notice, and being unaware, that he is dealing with an agent. The broker has a lien on the policy for the general balance due to him from the agent, and is entitled to apply the proceeds of the policy in payment of such balance, notwithstanding that he has, in the meantime, received notice of the principal's rights. [25]

(5)   A, a commission agent, employed B, a broker, to buy certain goods, B having no knowledge that A was acting as an agent. B bought and paid for the goods and retained the warrants relating to them. A was in fact acting for C, and C paid A for the goods. B, on A's instructions, resold the goods, and applied the proceeds in reduction of a running account between himself and A. In an action by C against B for converting the goods, it was held that B was not liable, because at the time of the sale he had a lien on goods for the balance due to him from A. [26]

(6)   A employed B to collect general average contributions under an insurance policy. B, in the ordinary course of business, employed C, an insurance broker, to collect the contributions, C being unaware that B was acting as an agent. C collected the contributions, and B became bankrupt. Held, in an action by A against C for the contributions, as money had and received to his use, that C was entitled to set off the amount of a debt due to him from B. [27]

4.—OTHER MISCELLANEOUS RIGHTS

Article 71

RIGHTS IN RESPECT OF GOODS BOUGHT IN OWN NAME

Where an agent, by contracting personally, [28] renders himself solely liable for the price of goods bought on behalf of his principal, the property in the goods, as between the principal and the agent, vests   **7–099**

---

[24] *Dicas v. Stockley* (1836) 7 C. & P. 587; *Lawrence v. Fletcher*, n. 22 above. See Cordery, *Solicitors* (8th ed.), p. 242.

[25] *Mann v. Forrester* (1814) 4 Camp. 60; *Westwood v. Bell* (1815) 4 Camp. 349; Marine Insurance Act 1906, s.53(2).

[26] *Taylor v. Kymer* (1832) 3 B. & Ad. 320.

[27] *Montagu v. Forwood* [1893] 2 Q.B. 350. And see *New Zealand, etc., Land Co. v. Watson* (1881) 7 Q.B.D. 374; Article 83.

[28] See Comment and Article 100.

in the agent, and does not pass to the principal until he pays for the goods, or the agent intends that it shall pass[29]; and the agent has the same rights with regard to the disposal of the goods, and with regard to stopping them in transit, as he would have had if the relation between him and his principal had been that of seller and buyer.[30]

Comment

7–100   An agent who obtains goods for his principal may genuinely buy them from the third party and resell them to the principal.[31] In such a case he has all the normal remedies of a seller, and is under the liabilities of a seller, except in so far as circumstances indicate otherwise.

But another interpretation of his functions is possible: he may deal with the third party as principal, while remaining in the status of agent towards his own principal—*i.e.* his remuneration will (normally[32]) be by commission rather than by profit on resale, and his duty would not be the absolute one of a seller, but rather that of an agent to exercise due diligence in carrying out the principal's instructions.[33] This is one of the interpretations put on the function of a commission merchant in the leading case of *Ireland v. Livingston*.[34] It is referred to elsewhere in this book as "indirect representation".[35] The specialised group of cases on which this Article is based concern nineteenth-century examples of (what appears to be) this situation: they are indeed the only cases which can be said to concern it. The assumptions behind them are not easy to get into.

In such a case the agent may nevertheless have, as against his principal, some of the remedies regarding the goods which are available to unpaid vendors. It has long been established that the right of stoppage in transit could apply, not being confined to genuine

---

[29] *Cassaboglou v. Gibb* (1883) 11 Q.B.D. 797, 803–804, 806–807, Illustration 4.

[30] Sale of Goods Act 1979, s. 38(2); and see Comment; *Restatement*, § 466.

[31] See above, paras. 1–030 *et seq.* Provided that he is not in breach of his fiduciary duties in doing so: see Article 31, Illustration 9; Articles 47, 49.

[32] See above, para. 1–030.

[33] See *Casaboglou v. Gibb*, n. 29 above; *Bolus & Co. Ltd v. Inglis Bros. Ltd* [1924] N.Z.L.R. 164, 174; *Witt & Scott Ltd v. Blumenreich* [1949] N.Z.L.R. 806; *Anglo-African Shipping Co. of New York Inc. v. J. Mortimer Ltd* [1962] 1 Lloyd's Rep. 610 (but note the dissenting opinion of Diplock L.J.). See above, para. 1–015.

[34] (1872) L.R. 5 H.L. 395, 404–405, 412, 416. The position of such a merchant seems similar to that of the *commissionaire* or indirect agent of some continental systems. But compare expressions used elsewhere; and see *ex p. Miles* (1885) 15 Q.B.D. 39, 42; *Brown & Gracie v. F.W. Green Pty. Ltd* [1960] 1 Lloyd's Rep. 289 *per* Lord Denning. See further Hill (1972) 3 J. Maritime Law and Commerce, 307, esp. at pp. 318–324 (a valuable article); (1968) 31 M.L.R. 623; above, para. 1–018.

[35] Above, para. 1–018.

vendors[36]: the unpaid vendor's lien has also been extended to such a case.[37] In any case the agent has a lien as such, but the unpaid vendor's rights may be exercised by a person who has never acquired property or possession.[38] The effect of these cases was put into statutory form in section 38(2) of the Sale of Goods Act 1979 which extends the rights of the unpaid seller against the goods to "any person who is in the position of a seller, as, for instance ... a consignor or agent who has himself paid, or is directly responsible for, the price." This indicates that such a person has not only the rights of lien and stoppage in transit but also that of resale.

Whether an agent in such a position can reserve property so as to be able to exercise the right of withholding delivery, as opposed to a lien, is open to argument. It used to be said that the normal rule for agents is that the goods become the property of the principal as soon as they are consigned to him.[39] On one view, an agent who does something that would normally reserve property, e.g. takes a bill of lading to his own order, reserves a lien only: if he is to reserve property he must be acting not as agent but as seller, as it is difficult to see under what transaction the goods would otherwise eventually become the property of the principal.[40] On another view, he may in appropriate cases still be an agent, but may reserve and subsequently transmit property nevertheless.[41] There may be little difference in practice, for even where an agent would be for the above purposes treated as a seller, it is clear that he cannot act as a seller to the exclusion of his instructions and sue his principal for non-acceptance of goods bought[42]; he cannot sue for the price of goods as on a sale[43]; the measure of damages for breach of contract is not that of a contract of sale[44]; and the agent will often not answer for breach of warranty of quality.[45] Property will presumably

---

[36] *Feise v. Wray* (1802) 3 East 93, Illustration 1; *cf. Siffken v. Wray* (1805) 6 East 371. See also *The Tigress* (1863) 32 L.J.Ad. 97; *Hawkes v. Dunn* (1831) 1 C. & J. 519.

[37] See *Imperial Bank v. London & St. Katharine Docks Co.* (1877) 5 Ch.D. 195, Illustration 2.

[38] *Jenkyns v. Usborne* (1844) 7 M. & G. 678.

[39] *Hathesing v. Laing* (1873) L.R. 17 Eq. 92, 101; *Re Tappenbeck, ex p. Banner* (1876) 2 Ch.D. 278, 287 (Illustration 3). And see Article 91.

[40] See *Benjamin's Sale of Goods* (4th ed.), §§ 18–084 et seq.; Blackburn, *Contract of Sale* (3rd ed.), p. 352.

[41] See *Cassaboglou v. Gibb* (1883) 11 Q.B.D. 797, 804, 806; see also *Jenkyns v. Brown* (1849) 14 Q.B. 496; *Schuster v. McKellar* (1857) 7 E. & B. 704; *Falk v. Fletcher* (1865) 18 C.B.(N.S.) 403; *Re Tappenbeck, ex p. Banner*, n. 39 above; *The Prinz Adelbert* [1917] A.C. 586, 590; Sale of Goods Act 1979, s. 38(2).

[42] *Tetley v. Shand* (1871) 25 L.T. 658, Illustration 5; *White v. Benekendorff* (1873) 29 L.T. 475; *cf. Robinson v. Mollett* (1875) L.R. 7 H.L. 802, Illustration 8 to Article 31.

[43] *Seymour v. Pychlau* (1817) 1 B. & A. 14.

[44] *Cassaboglou v. Gibb*, n. 41 above.

[45] See *J.S. Robertson (Australia) Pty Ltd v. Martin* (1950) 94 C.L.R. 30.

357

pass by intention,[46] but not in accordance with the rules for sales laid down in the Sale of Goods Act 1979 as such. In view of these points, it is doubtful whether there is much utility in calling the agent a seller, and it is submitted that the second view is preferable.

A third way in which an agent who contracts personally may act is by making a contract between his principal and the third party and adding his own liability to it: the possibilities in this respect are discussed elsewhere.[47] The cases cited for the propositions above do not apply to such a situation. If appropriate, he can here presumably reserve property, and may certainly exercise his agent's lien. If he discharges his principal's liability, it seems that he also has the unpaid vendor's rights.[48] It is not clear whether or not he has these rights when he is simply liable but has not been called upon to pay, *e.g.* where his principal is insolvent.[49]

Illustrations

7–101   (1)   P instructs A, a factor in Hamburg, to procure and ship wax for him. A buys wax in his own name, ships to P's order, and draws on P for the price. P becomes insolvent. A can stop in transit.[50]

(2)   D, a broker, buys goods lying in a warehouse from C for unnamed principals. D obtains a delivery order, and delivers it to Z, his principals. Z pledge their interest in the goods to X and indorse the order to X. X requests the warehouse to attorn to him. Before the warehouse has done so Z becomes insolvent, and D, knowing nothing of X, pays C and obtains another delivery order. D can exercise the unpaid vendor's lien against X and Z.[51]

(3)   P employs A in South America to buy goods. A buys goods in his own name using money raised by bills drawn on P. A ships the goods, taking a bill of lading to P's order. The bills of exchange are not all paid. A has the right to stop in transit, but no further rights against the goods once the transit is ended.[52]

(4)   P requests A in Hong Kong to buy and ship a certain kind of opium. A ships the wrong kind of opium. P sues A. The measure of

---

[46] See *Cassaboglou v. Gibb*, n. 41 above, at pp. 803–804.

[47] See Comment to Article 100.

[48] See Sale of Goods Act 1979, s. 38(2); *Imperial Bank v. London & St. Katharine Docks Co.* (1877) 5 Ch.D. 195. See further as to this case, and especially as to the reference to the Mercantile Law Amendment Act, Benjamin, *Sale of Personal Property* (8th ed.), pp. 882–883.

[49] See Blackburn, *Contract of Sale* (3rd ed.), p. 352; *Cassaboglou v. Gibb*, n. 41 above, at p. 804; Sale of Goods Act 1979, s. 38(2).

[50] *Feise v. Wray* (1802) 3 East 93.

[51] *Imperial Bank v. London & St. Katharine Docks Co.*, n. 48 above.

[52] *Re Tappenbeck, ex p. Banner* (1876) 2 Ch.D. 278.

damages is not the difference between the value of the opium ordered and that shipped, as on a sale, but the loss actually sustained by P in consequence of the opium not being as ordered, the contract being one of agency.[53]

(5) P requests A, a cotton broker, to buy cotton gradually at 8¼d if A cannot do better. A purchases in his own name at $8^1/_{16}$d and $7^{13}/_{15}$d and sends P a bought note for the cotton at 8¼d. P discovers what has happened and repudiates the transaction. The contract is not one of sale and A cannot sue for non-acceptance: also, he is in breach of his duties as agent.[54]

Article 72

RIGHT TO INTERPLEAD

(1) Where adverse claims whether legal or equitable, are made **7–102** upon an agent in respect of any money, goods, or chattels in his possession, and he claims no interest in the subject-matter of the dispute other than for costs or charges, he may claim relief by way of interpleader,[55] even as against his own principal whose title he has acknowledged,[56] provided that he had no notice of the adverse claim at the time of the acknowledgment.[57]

(2) Where the agent claims a lien on property as against the owner, whoever he may be, the lien is not such an interest as deprives him of the right to interplead in respect of the ownership of the property[58]; but where he claims a lien or any other interest in the property, or part of it, other than for costs or charges, as against a particular claimant, he is not permitted to interplead.[59]

---

[53] *Cassaboglou v. Gibb* (1883) 11 Q.B.D. 797.

[54] *Tetley v. Shand* (1871) 25 L.T. 658.

[55] R.S.C. Ord. 17. See in general *Supreme Court Practice, 1995.*

[56] *Tanner v. European Bank Ltd* (1866) L.R. 1 Ex. 261; *Attenborough v. St. Katharine's Dock Co.* (1878) 3 C.P.D. 450; *Ex p. Mersey Docks and Harbour Board* [1899] 1 Q.B. 546; Illustrations 1 to 6. As to interpleader on claims by agent and undisclosed principal, see *Meynell v. Angell* (1863) 32 L.J.Q.B. 14.

[57] *Re Sadler, ex p. Davies* (1881) 19 Ch.D. 86. If he had such notice he would formerly have been estopped from denying his principal's title. But by virtue of s. 8(1) of the Torts (Inference with Goods) Act 1977 he may now apply for joinder of the third party in such a situation. See Article 56 and Comment.

[58] *Attenborough v. St. Katharine's Dock Co.*, n. 56 above; *Cotter v. Bank of England* (1833) 3 Moo. & S. 180.

[59] *Mitchell v. Hayne* (1824) 2 Sim. & S. 63; *Moore v. Usher* (1835) 7 Sim. 383. But *cf. Best v. Hayes* (1863) 1 H. & C. 718, Illustration 6.

Illustrations

7–103   (1) An agent has funds in his hands, upon which a third person claims to have been given a lien by the principal. The agent may interplead as against his principal and the third person. [60]

(2) A instructs a stockbroker to sell shares, and sends him the share certificate and blank transfers. The shares are claimed by B, who alleges that they were obtained from him by fraud. A sues the broker, claiming the return of the certificate and transfers. The broker may interplead. [61]

(3) A, a part-owner of a vessel, instructs B, a broker, to insure the vessel. B receives an amount due under the policy in respect of a loss, and the whole of the amount is claimed by A. A sues B for the whole amount, and certain other part-owners sue him for part thereof. B may interplead. [62]

(4) A deposits goods with B, a wharfinger, and afterwards requests him to transfer them to the name of C, reserving to himself a right to draw samples. B enters the goods in C's name. D then claims them as paramount owner, and A acquiesces in his claim. C also claims them. B may interplead as against C and D. [63]

(5) A entrusted a policy to B for a specified purpose. C, who had pledged the policy with A, and A each brought an action against B for the policy. Held, that B was entitled to interplead. [64]

(6) A, an auctioneer, sells goods on behalf of B, and whilst a portion of the proceeds is still in his hands, receives notice of a claim by C. B sues A for the balance of the proceeds. A may deduct his expenses and charges and interplead as to the residue. [65]

(7) Two estate agents claim commission in respect of the sale of the same property. There is a possibility that the vendor may be under an obligation to pay commission to both. He may not interplead. [66]

---

[60] *Smith v. Hammond* (1833) 6 Sim. 10.

[61] *Robinson v. Jenkins* (1890) 24 Q.B.D. 275.

[62] *Suart v. Welch* (1839) 4 My. & C. 305.

[63] *Mason v. Hamilton* (1831) 5 Sim. 19; *Pearson v. Cardon* (1831) 2 Russ. & M. 606; *Ex p. Mersey Docks and Harbour Board* [1899] 1 Q.B. 546.

[64] *Tanner v. European Bank* (1866) L.R. 1 Ex. 261.

[65] *Best v. Hayes*, n. 59 above; *cf. Mitchell v. Hayne*, n. 59 above; *Wright v. Freeman* (1879) 48 L.J.Q.B. 276; *Ingham v. Walker* (1887) 3 T.L.R. 448 (claims against auctioneer not co-extensive; seller claims price paid, buyer claims damages).

[66] *Greatorex & Co. v. Shackle* [1895] 2 Q.B. 249; *Dominion Factors Pty Ltd v. L.J. Hooker Ltd* [1963] N.S.W.R. 573.

CHAPTER 8

RELATIONS BETWEEN PRINCIPALS AND THIRD PARTIES

1—CONTRACT

Article 73

DISCLOSED PRINCIPAL: GENERAL RULE

(1) A disclosed principal, whether named or unnamed, may sue or **8–001** be sued on any contract made on his behalf, and in respect of any money paid or received on his behalf, by his agent acting within the scope of his actual authority or whose acts are validly ratified.[1]

(2) So far as concerns deeds, bills of exchange, promissory notes and cheques, this Article must be read subject to Articles 79 and 80.

Comment

Rule (1). This Article states the basic principle of contractual agency, **8–002** that an agent acting within the scope of his actual authority, express or implied, binds and entitles his principal. As such it does no more than link up this section with Chapter 3, where many relevant authorities will be found. Ratification will also, subject to the rules peculiar to that branch of the law, achieve the same result.[2] The usual explanation of the rights and liabilities of the principal is that he has in fact made the contract, and this explanation is, if the action used be regarded as contractual, indeed made necessary by the doctrine of consideration and the related rules of privity of contract.[3] But it is by no means clear that it disposes of all the difficulties. The plain fact is that business

---

[1] *cf. Restatement*, §§ 144, 292.

[2] See Chap. 2, Section 3.

[3] See *Freeman & Lockyer v. Buckhurst Park Properties (Mangal) Ltd* [1964] 2 Q.B. 480, 502.

convenience requires that one person be in some cases liable and entitled on the contract of another; and the historical evolution of the above rule has been complex.[4]

8-003   **Written evidence: Statute of Frauds. The old law.** Under section 40 of the Law of Property Act 1925, contracts for the sale of land and certain similar contracts were unenforceable without a note or memorandum, signed by the party to be charged. Such a document might instead be signed by an agent "thereunto by him lawfully authorised".[5] The cases on this provision and its predecessor, section 4 of the Statute of Frauds 1677, "decide that to satisfy the statute the agreement or memorandum must name or identify two parties who are contractually bound to each other."[6] Therefore, if an agent made an agreement in such terms that he was himself liable as a contracting party, the memorandum would satisfy the statute,[7] and would not cease to do so because the other party knew that the agent was acting as an agent.[8] In such a case, and also in the case where the principal was undisclosed, the contract was enforceable by or against either principal or agent, for the effect of the introduction of the principal was to add the liability of a new party to the agent's already existing liability.[9] But where the agreement was made by the agent in such terms that he was not himself liable as a contracting party, the principal could sue or be sued only if his name appeared in the memorandum, or if, from the description of him therein, his identity as a party was clear.[10] Thus where an agent signed as agent for an unnamed principal, there might be no memorandum satisfying the statute, unless a custom existed making him personally liable in a manner not inconsistent with the form of signature, so that his signature alone could suffice.[11]

The same rules presumably applied and still apply to contracts of guarantee, which were also governed by the Statute of Frauds, and remain so governed, the wording of which regarding authorisation is the same as that later reproduced in section 40.[12]

---

[4] See Chap. 1; Powell, pp. 148–150; Stoljar, pp. 32–41.

[5] As to authorisation of such an agent, see above, para. 2–018.

[6] *Basma v. Weekes* [1950] A.C. 441, 454 *per* Lord Reid.

[7] *Filby v. Hounsell* [1896] 2 Ch. 737, as interpreted by Younger L.J. in *Lovesey v. Palmer* [1916] 2 Ch. 233.

[8] *Basma v. Weekes*, n. 6 above; disapproving dicta of Luxmoore L.J. in *Smith-Bird v. Blower* [1939] 2 All E.R. 406; *Davies v. Sweet* [1962] 2 Q.B. 300.

[9] *Higgins v. Senior* (1841) 8 M. & W. 834; *Calder v. Dobell* (1871) L.R. 6 C.P. 486; *Basma v. Weekes*, n. 6 above. See also *Morris v. Wilson* (1859) 5 Jur.(N.S.) 168.

[10] *Lovesey v. Palmer* [1916] 2 Ch. 233.

[11] See *Dale v. Humfrey* (1857) 7 E. & B. 266; affd. (1858) E.B. & E. 1004; Article 102.

[12] See *Bateman v. Phillips* (1812) 15 East 272; *Garrett v. Handley* (1825) 4 B. & C. 664. See also *Marginson v. Ian Potter & Co.* (1976) 136 C.L.R. 161 (where principal already liable, his promise to pay was not a guarantee).

The new law. Section 40 of the 1925 Act, however, was repealed and   **8–004**
replaced by section 2 of the Law of Property (Miscellaneous Provisions)
Act 1989, which requires that such contracts actually be in writing,
signed by each party. This provision also allows signature by agents, but
in different words: it requires that the signature be "by or on behalf of
each party to the contract." Although the Law Commission Working
Paper which eventually led to the Act avowed an intention to "let the
ordinary principles of agency operate"[13] it is not clear how they were
intended to do so. If the agent signs for a principal whom he names, the
matter is straightforward. At the other extreme, if he signs "as agent
only" and no principal is named in or identifiable from the document,
the contract is presumably not in writing, the name of one of the parties
being missing. But if the agent signs in such a way as to make himself
personally liable, but is also stated to be acting on behalf of an unnamed
principal, or is in fact acting on behalf of a completely undisclosed
principal, the situation is more difficult of analysis. It can be said that
the change from a mere requirement of authorisation to the wording
"by or on behalf of" means that the signature must now be *avowedly*
"on behalf of" the party concerned, and hence that in neither of the
above cases can the principal now sue or be sued. This seems correct,
and consonant with the policy of the Act of requiring that the full terms
of the contract be in writing, rather than merely evidenced by a note or
memorandum.[14] But it can be argued alternatively that an agent signs
"on behalf of" the principal whenever he signs with authority to do so
and intending to act for his principal. On this basis the previous law
remains valid, and the unnamed or undisclosed principal may enforce
the contract or have it enforced against him. If that is so, it is then,
however, necessary to inquire whether or not the unnamed or
undisclosed principal is a party to the contract entered into by the agent,
or to some other contract: for if it was to some other contract, writing
and his signature would be required for that. It seems clear that the
undisclosed principal is a party to the same contract as the agent[15]; and
although doubt may now be cast on whether the unnamed principal of
an agent who undertakes personal liability is a person alternatively as
opposed to cumulatively liable, as older cases suggest, it is clear that his
liability, whether joint or joint and several, is normally on the same
contract as that of the agent.[16] But, as stated above, the view that the
law has been changed (albeit without this being stated in the relevant
Law Commission reports[17]) seems preferable.

---

[13] Law Com.W.P.No.92 (1985), s. 5.16.
[14] *Spiro v. Glencrown Properties Ltd* [1991] Ch. 537, 541. The requirements for
satisfying s. 2 are laid down in *Commission for the New Towns v. Cooper (G.B.) Ltd*
[1995] 2 W.L.R. 677.
[15] Article 78.
[16] See Comment to Article 100.
[17] See Law Com.W.P.No.92 (1985); Law Com.No. 164 (1987).

8–005   **Auctions.** The provisions of section 2 do not apply to sales by public auction[18] and hence it appears that no writing is needed for such sales.[19]

8–006   **Cases where agent also liable and entitled.** The fact that the principal instructs an agent who operates in a market by the rules or customs of which the agent is personally liable and entitled on contracts which he makes within it does not in general exclude the principal's right to sue and be sued, for the agent's rights and duties are simply additional to those of the principal and not inconsistent with them.[20] If the rules or customs require that the agent be solely liable and entitled, and the principal knows of them, he may be regarded as instructing the agent on that basis.[21] If, however, he does not know of them, he only assents to such rules or customs as are reasonable,[22] and such a rule may not be.[23]

8–007   **Foreign principal.** Certain nineteenth-century cases held that a *foreign* principal could neither sue nor be sued on his agent's contracts. The rule was based on the notions that such a principal did not authorise his English agent to establish privity of contract between him and English suppliers; and that the English contracting party did not authorise its agent to establish privity of contract with foreign dealers. Therefore the agent was himself the contracting party and there was not in form any exception to normal agency principles. The rule, if such it was, is now obsolete, though the fact that the principal is foreign may be relevant to the question whether the agent is liable in addition to his principal. Since the case law was, and what remains still is, principally relevant to the liability of the agent rather than that of the principal, it is dealt with under Article 100.

8–008   **Knowledge of third party that agent not authorised.** If the principal does something indicating that he withdraws the authority, but does not communicate this to the agent, the agent still has actual authority. But if

---

[18] s. 2(5)(*b*).

[19] It is arguable that s. 40 of the 1925 Act is not repealed in the case of public auctions, since the repealing provision (s. 2(8)) appears in s. 2, which by its own wording does not apply to sales by public auction. But s. 2(8) also states in brackets that it supersedes s. 40 and this is probably enough to prevent what would be a surprising result.

[20] See, *e.g. Levitt v. Hamblet* [1901] 2 K.B. 53 as an example of many cases concerning the former rules of the London Stock Exchange. And see in general below, para. 9–014.

[21] As in *Morrison, Kekewich & Co. v. Mendel* (1888) 5 T.L.R. 153.

[22] Article 31.

[23] See *Morrison, Kekewich & Co. v. Mendel*, n. 21 above. But *cf. Cunliffe-Owen v. Teather & Greenwood* [1967] 1 W.L.R. 1421 (usage that only members can declare options reasonable).

in such circumstances that withdrawal of authority comes to the notice of the third party, the third party probably cannot hold the principal liable, not only as regards apparent authority[24] but also on principles of actual authority.[25]

Restitution: right of principal to recover money paid by agent. A disclosed principal is entitled to sue for the recovery of money paid by an agent on the principal's behalf where the payment is made under a mistake of fact or any other circumstances ordinarily entitling a person paying money to recover it from the payee.[26]   **8–009**

The question has arisen of the effect on the principal's right to recover money paid by an agent under a mistake of fact in the circumstance that, when the payment is made, some other agent has knowledge of the true facts. It has been said that "where ... a limited liability company is concerned and payments are made under a bona fide mistake of fact by an authorised agent of the company, the fact that some other agent of the company may have had full knowledge of all the facts does not disentitle the company to recover the money so paid, provided that the agent with the full knowledge does not know that the payments are being made on an erroneous basis."[27] Presumably this principle applies also where the payment is made on behalf of any other kind of corporation or of a natural person.

Restitution: liability of principal. A disclosed principal may also be liable for money paid to his agent as such in connection with transactions effected within the agent's authority, even though he has not received it.[28]   **8–010**

The Illustrations which follow only concern restitution: the general proposition of the Article is too obvious to require examples.

Rule (2). The general rule is displaced in the case of deeds and negotiable instruments, where special significance is attached to the wording of the documents used. These are therefore dealt with separately.   **8–011**

---

[24] Article 74.

[25] See Wright (1937) 15 Can.B.R. 196, criticising *Robert Simpson Co. v. Godson* [1937] 1 D.L.R. 454 (to the contrary effect); *Restatement*, § 7, comment *d*, § 144, comment *e. cf.* above, para. 2–032.

[26] See Illustration 1. For the right of the agent to recover money, see Article 112.

[27] *Turvey v. Dentons (1923) Ltd* [1953] 1 Q.B. 218, 224 *per* Pilcher J.; applying the stronger case of *Anglo-Scottish Beet Sugar Corp. Ltd v. Spalding U.D.C.* [1937] 2 K.B. 607, where "the carelessness of the various officials of the company was more pronounced than any carelessness" existing in the later case. See also below, para. 8–183.

[28] Illustration 2; for further discussion see Articles 94, 95. As to the *agent's* liability, see Article 113.

Illustrations

8–012　　(1)　A custom-house officer took exorbitant fees from a shipmaster. Held, that the owner of the vessel had a right to sue to recover the amount paid in excess of the proper fees.[29]

(2)　An agent appointed by the managing owner of a ship demanded too much freight from the consignees of certain goods, and refused to deliver the goods until payment. The consignees paid the amount demanded, under protest, and sued one of the part-owners of the ship for the excess. Held, that he was liable, though no portion of the money had come to his hands.[30]

Article 74

APPARENT (OR OSTENSIBLE) AUTHORITY

8–013　　Where a person, by words or conduct, represents or permits it to be represented that another person has authority to act on his behalf, he is bound by the acts of that other person with respect to anyone dealing with him as an agent on the faith of any such representation, to the same extent as if such other person had the authority that he was represented to have, even though he had no such actual authority.[31]

Comment

8–014　　**Doctrine of apparent authority.** This Article seeks to formulate the general doctrine of apparent (sometimes called, alternatively ostensible) authority. It should be read together with the three Articles following. Under this doctrine a principal may be bound by the acts of an agent which he has not authorised, and has even forbidden. Most western systems of law have found the necessity for some type of reasoning which at least imposes liability, if it does not confer the right to sue, in

---

[29] *Stevenson v. Mortimer* (1778) Cowp. 805; see also *Holt v. Ely* (1853) 1 E. & B. 795; *Taylor v. Smith* (1926) 38 C.L.R. 48.
[30] *Coulthurst v. Sweet* (1866) L.R. 1 C.P. 649.
[31] See *Pickering v. Busk* (1812) 15 East. 38; *Pickard v. Sears* (1837) 6 A. & E. 469; *Reynell v. Lewis* (1846) 15 M. & W. 517; *Freeman v. Cooke* (1848) 2 Exch. 654; *Smith v. M'Guire* (1858) 3 H. & N. 554; *Robinson v. Tyson* (1888) 9 L.R. (N.S.W.) 297; *International Paper Co. v. Spicer* (1906) 4 C.L.R. 739; *Freeman & Lockyer v. Buckhurst Park Properties (Mangal) Ltd* [1964] 2 Q.B. 480; *Hely-Hutchinson v. Brayhead Ltd* [1968] 1 Q.B. 549; *R. v. Charles* [1977] A.C. 177, 183; *Armagas Ltd v. Mundogas S.A. (The Ocean Frost)* [1986] A.C. 717, 777. For an extended consideration of policy issues, see Hetherington (1966) 19 Stanford L.Rev. 76; see also Rubenstein (1958) 44 A.B.A.J. 849.

situations such as those covered by this doctrine. The English version is plainly based on the notion of a representation by the principal. The leading case which is constantly cited, is *Freeman & Lockyer v. Buckhurst Park Properties (Mangel) Ltd*,[32] in which Diplock L.J. said:

> "An 'apparent' or 'ostensible' authority ... is a legal relationship between the principal and the contractor created by a representation, made by the principal to the contractor, intended to be and in fact acted upon by the contractor, that the agent has authority to enter on behalf of the principal into a contract of a kind within the scope of the 'apparent' authority, so as to render the principal liable to perform any obligations imposed upon him by such contract. To the relationship so created the agent is a stranger. He need not be (although he generally is) aware of the existence of the representation but he must not purport to make the agreement as principal himself. The representation, when acted upon by the contractor by entering into a contract with the agent, operates as an estoppel, preventing the principal from asserting that he is not bound by the contract. It is irrelevant whether the agent had actual authority to enter into the contract."[33]

Applicable outside contract. The dictum concerns contract, where the main application of the doctrine is to be found. The doctrine also applies, however, in respect of transfer of property[34]; and sometimes also in other contexts such as tort[35] and questions of notice.[36]   **8–015**

Liability only. Normally, of course, the actual and apparent authorities will coincide, and it will be unnecessary for the doctrine of apparent authority to be invoked. But when it is, the full consequences of the agency relationship do not flow, for the doctrine is primarily concerned with the question whether the principal is bound. Apparent authority is not therefore the same as implied authority, though older cases did not always make the distinction now recognised, or at least in the form in which it is now recognised: in the judgments, recourse was more often had to the notion of the wide implied authority of a general agent.[37] Even some more recent cases have tended to confuse the two.[38] Therefore, although apparent authority has twice been mentioned, and juxtaposed with actual authority, in the discussion of the   **8–016**

---

[32] [1964] 2 Q.B. 480, Illustration 31.
[33] At p. 503.
[34] Article 85.
[35] Article 92.
[36] Article 97.
[37] Above, para. 1–039.
[38] See *e.g. Ryan v. Pilkington* [1959] 1 W.L.R. 403, and explanations of that case in *Burt v. Claude Cousins & Co. Ltd* [1971] 2 Q.B. 426, 438, 448–449, 454, *Barrington v. Lee* [1972] 1 Q.B. 326, 336, 341, and *Sorrell v. Finch* [1977] A.C. 728.

agent's authority,[39] its main treatment is given here. It is further developed in the specialised context of disposition of property by the agent in Article 85. Reference should also be made to Article 21, which deals with the rare case where a person not hitherto an agent may bind his supposed principal under this doctrine as if he was; and to Article 123, where the application of the doctrine in cases of termination of authority is discussed.

It will be seen that the formulation is basically in terms of estoppel, and that this explanation of the doctrine receives articulate support from the dictum quoted. There are however certain difficulties in this explanation, as will appear: the matter is reverted to after the formulation has been analysed.

8–017   **Represents by words or conduct.** There must be a representation made. This seems to occur in three main ways. It may be express (whether orally or in writing)[40]; or implied from a course of dealing[41]; or it may be made "by permitting the agent to act in some way in the conduct of the principal's business with other persons."[42] A further way in which such a representation may be made, by entrusting the agent with the indicia of ownership of property, is dealt with in connection with dispositions of property.[43]

8–018   **Two types of case.** It may be suggested that the idea of apparent authority can be divided into two types of case. First, cases where there is something that can be said to be a genuine representation (orally, in writing, by course of dealing or by allowing the agent to act in certain ways, *e.g.* entrusting him with the conduct of particular negotiations[44] or allowing him to run a business that appears to be the principal's business[45]) by the principal of the agent's authority, on which the third party relies: such cases could be called cases of "genuine apparent authority" and more easily (but not always perfectly) based on estoppel.

---

[39] Comments to Articles 1, 22.

[40] Illustrations 13, 22.

[41] Illustrations 7, 21; Article 77, Illustration 1.

[42] *Freeman & Lockyer v. Buckhurst Park Properties (Mangal) Ltd* [1964] 2 Q.B. 480, 503 (managing director). See, *e.g. Collen v. Gardner* (1856) 21 Beav. 540 (steward); *Howard v. Sheward* (1886) L.R. 2 C.P. 148; *Baldry v. Bates* (1885) 52 L.T. 620 (horse dealers).

[43] See Articles 85–87.

[44] *Crabb v. Arun D.C.* [1976] Ch. 179, 183; *I.R.C. v. Ufitec Group Ltd* [1977] 3 All E.R. 924, Illustration 33; *Egyptian International Foreign Trade Co. v. P.S. Refson & Co. Ltd (The Raffaella)* [1985] 1 Lloyd's Rep. 36, 41 (Illustration 11); *Magripilis v. Baird* [1926] St.R.Qd. 89, 96 (H.C. of A.: "accredited as his legal agents and medium of communication").

[45] *Gurtner v. Beaton* [1993] 2 Lloyd's Rep. 369, Illustration 5.

Secondly, cases where the representation is only of a very general nature, and arises only from the principal's putting the agent in a specific position carrying with it a usual authority,[46] *e.g.* making him a partner[47] or appointing him managing director,[48] or using the services of a professional agent, *viz.*, someone whose occupation normally gives him a usual authority to do things of a certain type, *e.g.* a solicitor.[49] It is said that "by so doing the principal represents to anyone who becomes aware that the agent is so acting that the agent has authority to enter on behalf of the principal into contracts with other persons of the kind which an agent so acting in the course of his principal's business has usually 'actual' authority to enter into."[50] Here the notion of representation to the third party seems more artificial and the connection of the principal's liability with estoppel is thus more difficult to maintain.[51] It seems further that in this category the authority which the third party is entitled to infer is that which would normally be implied between principal and agent, and it is of this that the court receives evidence. But the third party may be quite ignorant of what authority would be so implied, *e.g.* of what authority a "branch manager" of an insurance company normally has.[52] In this respect the protection of the "reasonable third party" is limited.

Categories not mutually exclusive. It is, however, important to note   **8–019** that these two categories are not mutually exclusive. There may be additional representations by the principal, peculiar to the case in question, over and above the putting into a position carrying authority. Where it is not clear what authority a person in the particular position would normally have, such factors may be crucial.[53] The representation will normally be of an authority of some generality: although there is no reason why there should not be a representation of authority to enter into a specific transaction only, such a case would be rare, especially where the third party knows of the lack of general authority.[54]

---

[46] See Articles 29, 30.

[47] Partnership Act 1890, ss. 5, 14.

[48] *Hely-Hutchinson v. Brayhead Ltd* [1968] 1 Q.B. 549, 583.

[49] *Waugh v. H.B. Clifford & Sons Ltd* [1982] Ch. 374, Illustration 16.

[50] *Freeman & Lockyer v. Buckhurst Park Properties (Mangal) Ltd*, n. 42 above, at p. 503 *per* Diplock L.J.

[51] See below.

[52] See *British Bank of the Middle East v. Sun Life Insurance Co. of Canada (U.K.) Ltd* [1983] 2 Lloyd's Rep. 9 (H.L.), Illustration 10 to Article 77, a harsh decision for this reason. See also *Cleveland Manufacturing Co. v. Muslim Commercial Bank Ltd* [1981] 2 Lloyd's Rep. 646 (shipping agent); *Ricci Burns Ltd v. Toole* [1989] 1 W.L.R. 993, 1007.

[53] As in *Egyptian International Foreign Trade Co. v. Soplex Wholesale Supplies Ltd (The Raffaella)* [1985] 2 Lloyd's Rep. 36, Illustration 11.

[54] See *Armagas Ltd v. Mundogas S.A. (The Ocean Frost)* [1986] A.C. 717, 777.

8–020   **Representation need not be deliberate.** This general analysis suggests that the words of Diplock L.J., which appear to require that the representation be deliberate, and certainly say that it must be actually *intended* to be acted on, are perhaps too narrow. This wording does not appear elsewhere in his judgment.

8–021   **Permits it to be represented: authority to make representations as to authority of others.** The representation as to authority need not be made by the principal himself: it may obviously be made by an intermediate agent with actual authority to do so. More difficulties arise as to apparent authority. It seems correct in principle to say that an agent can have apparent authority to make representations as to the authority of other agents, provided that his own authority can finally be traced back to a representation by the principal or to a person with actual authority from the principal to make it.[55] However, such apparent authority would in general only be attributed to a person who would normally have actual authority to act within that particular sphere of activity.[56] An agent would, therefore, not usually be regarded as having apparent authority, simply because he is or appears to be permitted to answer inquiries, to attribute authority to another agent, unless he was or appeared to be authorised to conduct that business or that part of the business to which the transaction related.[57]

8–022   **Permits it to be represented: representation by agent himself.** As already stated, the essence of apparent authority is an appearance emanating from the principal. Therefore the representation must be made by the principal, or by another agent authorised to act for the principal. It is usually said that a representation by the agent himself that he has authority cannot create apparent authority, unless the principal can be regarded as having in some way instigated or permitted it, or put the agent in a position where he appears to be authorised to

---

[55] There are, however, dicta appearing to require actual authority in the agent whose representation is relied on as creating apparent authority, in cases connected with companies. It is submitted that *Crabtree-Vickers Pty Ltd. v. Australian Direct Mail Advertising Co. Ltd* (1975) 133 C.L.R. 72 may go too far in following these and requiring such actual authority, which need not exist except at the ultimate level: see [1983] J.B.L. 409; *Cromwell Corp. Ltd v. Sofrana Immobilier (N.Z.) Ltd* (1992) N.Z.C.L.C. 67, 997; below, paras. 8–022, 8–041.

[56] This seems clear from *British Bank of the Middle East v. Sun Life Assurance Co. of Canada Ltd* [1983] 2 Lloyd's Rep. 9 (H.L.), Illustration 10 to Article 77; see esp. p. 17. See, however, *Canadian Laboratory Supplies Ltd. v. Engelhard Industries of Canada Ltd* [1979] 2 S.C.R. 787, (1979) 97 D.L.R. (3d) 1, where the Supreme Court of Canda differed as to the effect of an inquiry as to an employee's authority to sell, made to a company's purchasing agent, while agreeing on the effect of that made to a Vice-President (Operations).

[57] See also below, paras. 8–022, 8–023.

make it.[58] "All 'ostensible' authority involves a representation by the principal as to the extent of the agent's authority. No representation by the agent as to the extent of his authority can amount to a 'holding out' by the principal."[59] Thus in *Armagas Ltd v. Mundogas S.A. (The Ocean Frost)*[60] where a person was known to have no authority and did not claim to have it, but wrongly stated that he had obtained authority from his managing director, it was held that there was no apparent authority.

Exceptions. However, pragmatic exceptions eat into this principle. **8–023** There may be cases where an agent would normally have authority if certain facts were true, and the agent gives the impression that they are. Thus the master of a ship has authority to sign bills of lading, but only if the goods are on board: a third party holder of the bill is entitled to rely on his signature, which attests that they were.[61] And a solicitor may be authorised to enter into a guarantee on behalf of his partners or employers if the firm holds the client's money or has good reason to expect that it will do so: the third party cannot know whether the underlying facts are true, yet may be able to rely on the solicitor's apparent authority. In one case on such facts[62] it was said that "the banks, knowing that Mr E was a practising solicitor with an established firm, were entitled to assume the truth of what he said unless alerted to the fact that the contrary might be the case." Further, an agent who has no authority to contract may sometimes have authority to say whether particular contract terms will be enforced,[63] or even to say whether the principal is performing the contract, or whether a proposal is accepted or not.[64]

---

[58] *Colonial Bank v. Cady and Williams* (1890) 15 App.Cas. 267, 273; *De Tchihatchef v. Salerni Coupling Ltd* [1932] 1 Ch. 330, 342; *Fay v. Miller, Wilkins & Co.* [1941] Ch. 360, 365; *Freeman & Lockyer v. Buckhurst Park Properties (Mangal) Ltd* [1964] 2 Q.B. 480, 505; *Restatement*, § 162. Cf. Partnership Act 1890, s. 14(1). But see *Hely-Hutchinson v. Brayhead Ltd* [1968] 1 Q.B. 549, 563–564 (affd. on another ground at p. 573); *Canadian Laboratory Supplies Ltd v. Engelhard Industries of Canada Ltd* [1979] 2 S.C.R. 787, 800; (1979) 97 D.L.R. (3d) 1, 10. The latter dictum is discussed by Fridman, (1983) 13 Manitoba L.J. 1.

[59] *Att.-Gen. for Ceylon v. Silva* [1953] A.C. 461, 479 *per* Mr. L.M.D. de Silva. See also *Lanyon v. Blanchard* (1811) 2 Camp. 597; *New Zealand Tenancy Bonds Ltd v. Mooney* [1986] 1 N.Z.L.R. 280; *Essfood v. Crown Shipping (Ireland) Ltd* [1991] I.L.R.M. 97.

[60] [1986] A.C. 717, Illustration 11 to Article 77.

[61] Carriage of Goods by Sea Act 1992, s. 4. But it was not always so: see below, para. 8–068, n. 82.

[62] *United Bank of Kuwait Ltd v. Hammoud* [1988] 1 W.L.R. 1051 *per* Staughton L.J. (Illustration 10).

[63] *State Rail Authority of New South Wales v. Heath Outdoor Pty Ltd* (1987) 7 N.S.W.L.R. 170, 184 *per* McHugh J.A. (albeit in a dissenting judgment). See also *Legione v. Hateley* (1983) 152 C.L.R. 406; compare different reasoning in *Waltons Stores (Interstate) Ltd v. Maher* (1988) 164 C.L.R. 387.

[64] See *International Paper Co. v. Spicer* (1906) 4 C.L.R. 739.

From this it is only a small step to say that the agent has authority to say whether he has been authorised. It is this final step which is not approved in *The Ocean Frost*.[65] But the step appears recently to have been taken (despite difficulties of reconciling what is said in *The Ocean Frost*) in *First Energy (U.K.) Ltd v. Hungarian International Bank Ltd*.[66] The decision is supported in the leading judgment of Steyn L.J. on the basis of the importance of protecting third parties. But it is submitted that even if the decision can be supported on its facts, any easy admission of the agent's statement of his own authority as creating apparent authority involves a departure from the basic principles of apparent authority, for which no general justifying principle seems ready to hand. As was said in an American case, "Apparent authority loses all of its apparency when the third party knows that actual authority is lacking."[67] Although cases where an agent is authorised to say whether facts which confer authority on him can occur and have occurred, situations where this reasoning is legitimate should be specialised and unusual.[68]

8–024   **Representation of law.** The representation must be one of fact: on general principles a pure representation of law is not sufficient.[69]

8–025   **With respect to anyone dealing with him as an agent.** It is obvious that if the third party does not know of the existence of any principal, this doctrine cannot apply, as when the agent purports to deal as principal.[70] A representation that does not come to the notice of the third party is no representation. The mere fact that the principal enables the agent to commit fraud by putting him in a position where he can do so is not, without more, decisive.[71] Thus the doctrine does not apply if the principal represents that the agent is the *owner* of goods or of a

---

[65] See especially *per* Robert Goff L.J. in the Court of Appeal, [1986] A.C. at pp. 730–735, quoted by Lord Keith of Kinkel in the House of Lords, *ibid.* at p. 777.

[66] [1993] 2 Lloyd's Rep. 194, Illustration 12: see Reynolds, (1993) 110 L.Q.R. 21.

[67] *Home Owners Loan Corp. v. Thornburgh* 106 P 2d 511, 512 (S.C. Okl., 1940).

[68] See *Armagas Ltd v. Mundogas S.A.*, n. 60 above, at p. 777; *Restatement*, §§ 168–172. See also *Berryere v. Firemans Fund Insurance Co.* (1965) 51 D.L.R.(2d) 603 (doubted in *The Ocean Frost*); *Jensen v. South Trail Mobile Ltd* (1972) 28 D.L.R.(3d) 233; *Cypress Disposal Ltd v. Inland Kenworth Sales (Nanaimo) Ltd* (1975) 54 D.L.R.(3d) 598; *Savill v. Chase Holdings (Wellington) Ltd* [1989] 1 N.Z.L.R. 257, 304–306, 313–314.

[69] But see *De Tchihatchef v. Salerni Coupling Ltd* [1932] 1 Ch. 330; below, para. 9–063.

[70] *A.L. Underwood Ltd v. Bank of Liverpool* [1924] 1 K.B. 775; *Farquharson Brothers & Co. v. King & Co.* [1902] A.C. 325, Illustration 7 to Article 86; *Freeman & Lockyer v. Buckhurst Park Properties (Mangal) Ltd* [1964] 2 Q.B. 480, 503. But it is possible that the doctrine of undisclosed principal may apply: see Article 78.

[71] *Farquharson Brothers & Co. v. King & Co.*, n. 70 above; *Morris v. C.W. Martin & Sons Ltd* [1966] 1 Q.B. 716; Article 76.

business, though here the related doctrine of apparent ownership,[72] or that of undisclosed principal,[73] may be relevant.

On the faith of any such representation. This involves two elements.   **8–026**

(1) The representation must be made to a third party or to a number of third parties. Old cases speak of holding out to the world,[74] but this is a loose expression[75]: "the 'holding out' must be to the particular individual who says he relied on it, or under such circumstances of publicity as to justify the inference that he knew of it and acted upon it."[76]

Nevertheless, the holding out may be quite general. If the analogy of estoppel were followed strictly, it is arguable that there could be no apparent authority where the principal at the time of making the representation by his words or his conduct had no third party or parties in contemplation, for it would be difficult to say that he had made a representation with the intent that it should be acted on[77]: it is clear however, that in many cases a third party can simply rely on the agent's having the authority usual to a person in his position (usual authority[78]), unless that third party knew that the agent had no such authority.

Where negligent conduct is relied on, a similar requirement operates, in that it is frequently said that there must be a duty of care towards the person who deals with the agent.[79] But the circumstances in which such a duty arises are not clear, and it seems that a duty may be owed to quite a wide class of persons[80]: some cases speak of it being owed to the world.[81] The case-law on this topic is far from clear, but is better developed in the area of dispositions by agents entrusted with property[82]: the contract cases are usually explicable on the basis of representation only.

---

[72] Article 86.

[73] Article 78.

[74] *e.g. Whitehead v. Tuckett* (1812) 15 East 400, 411.

[75] *Dickinson v. Valpy* (1829) 10 B. & C. 128, 140.

[76] *Farquharson Brothers & Co. v. King & Co.* [1902] A.C. 325, 341 *per* Lord Lindley; *cf. Restatement*, § 8, comment *b*, § 27, comment *b*.

[77] See Comment to Article 21.

[78] See above, para. 8–018; Powell, p. 37; Articles 22, 29, 30.

[79] *Swan v. North British Australasian Co. Ltd* (1863) 2 H. & C. 175, 182; *R.E. Jones Ltd. v. Waring & Gillow Ltd* [1926] A.C. 670, 693; *Mercantile Bank of India Ltd v. Central Bank of India Ltd* [1938] A.C. 287, 298–299; *Wilson & Meeson v. Pickering* [1946] K.B. 422, 425; *Mercantile Credit Co. Ltd v. Hamblin* [1965] 2 Q.B. 242, 271; *Moorgate Mercantile Co. Ltd v. Twitchings* [1977] A.C. 890.

[80] See *Swan v. North British Australasian Co. Ltd*, n. 79 above, at p. 182; *Mercantile Credit Co. Ltd v. Hamblin*, n. 79 above.

[81] *Saunders v. Anglia Building Society* [1971] A.C. 1026, 1038.

[82] See Articles 85–87, where some of the cases here cited appear as Illustrations.

(2)　The third party must have relied on the representation. This is of course another aspect of the same point. The third party cannot hold the principal liable if there is no causal connection between the representation and his dealing with the agent. This requirement of directness is obvious, but is particularly clear in cases of estoppel by conduct, where not only must there be a duty of care owed to the third party, but the breach of that duty must be the proximate cause of the damage to that third party.[83]

Thus he cannot hold the principal liable if he did not believe that the agent had authority, despite the appearance of authority,[84] or if he was not aware of the circumstances giving rise to apparent authority. He may also be unable to do so if he has notice of the terms of the agent's authority: this is discussed under Article 75.[85]

Further, he must in some way have relied on the representation. If the analogy of common law estoppel by representation is strictly followed, the acting must have been to his detriment, and this requirement is stated in several cases.[86] Others, however, speak simply of alteration of position, or acting on the faith of the representation,[87] and it seems that there need be no more than an entering into a contract in reliance on the representation.[88] This tends to make this aspect of the doctrine merge with the previous one.

---

[83] *Swan v. North British Australasian Co. Ltd*, n. 79 above, at p. 182; *Farquharson Brothers & Co. v. King & Co.* [1902] A.C. 325; *Mercantile Credit Co. Ltd v. Hamblin*, n. 79 above; *Welch v. Bank of England* [1955] Ch. 508; *Arnold v. Cheque Bank* (1876) 1 C.P.D. 578; *Coventry v. Great Eastern Ry. Co.* (1883) 11 Q.B.D. 776; *Bell v. Marsh* [1903] 1 Ch. 528; *MacFisheries Ltd v. Harrison* (1924) 93 L.J.K.B. 811; *General & Finance Facilities Ltd v. Hughes* (1966) 110 S.J. 847; *Moorgate Mercantile Co. Ltd v. Twitchings* [1977] A.C. 890.

[84] See *Bloomenthal v. Ford* [1897] A.C. 156.

[85] Where the third party has written notice from the principal as to the extent of the agent's authority, it requires a strong case to establish an apparent authority beyond this: *Australian Bank of Commerce v. Perel* [1926] A.C. 737.

[86] *Howard v. Hudson* (1853) 2 E. & B. 1; *George Whitechurch Ltd v. Cavanagh* [1902] A.C. 117; *Farquharson Brothers & Co. v. King & Co.* [1902] A.C. 325; *Mac Fisheries Ltd v. Harrison* (1924) 93 L.J.K.B. 811; *Wilson & Meeson v. Pickering* [1946] K.B. 422; *Norfolk County Council v. Secretary of State for the Environment* [1973] 1 W.L.R. 1400.

[87] *Pickard v. Sears* (1837) 6 A. & E. 469; *Freeman v. Cooke* (1848) 2 Exch. 654; *Cornish v. Abington* (1859) 4 H. & N. 549; *Rama Corp. v. Proved Tin and General Investments* [1952] 2 Q.B. 147; *Freeman & Lockyer v. Buckhurst Park Properties (Mangal) Ltd* [1964] 2 Q.B. 480, 503.

[88] *Freeman & Lockyer v. Buckhurst Park Properties (Mangal) Ltd*, n. 87 above; *Cleveland Mfg. Co. Ltd v. Muslim Commercial Bank Ltd* [1981] 2 Lloyd's Rep. 646, 650; *Polish S.S. Co. v. A.J. Williams Fuels (Overseas Sales) Ltd (The Suwalki)* [1989] 1 Lloyd's Rep. 511, 514; *Arctic Shipping Co. Ltd v. Mobilia A.B. (The Tatra)* [1990] 2 Lloyd's Rep. 51, 59; *Restatement*, § 8, comment *d*. In *Silver v. Ocean Steamship Co. Ltd* [1930] 1 K.B. 416 it was held that the taking up of a bill of lading was sufficient evidence of reliance on it to raise an estoppel: see at pp. 428, 434, 441.

Scope of the doctrine. The general doctrine here stated applies to   8–027
cases where the person concerned is not, apart from the estoppel, an
agent at all (an unusual situation) [89]; to cases where he has some
authority, but not authority to do what he has in fact done; to cases
where he would have such authority but for the existence of reservations
unknown to the third party; and to cases where he previously had
authority, but this has, unknown to the third party, been terminated. [90]

Doctrine does not validate act for all purposes. The doctrine of   8–028
apparent authority validates the agent's act as regards the third party;
but it does not necessarily make it valid as regards the agent himself,
who may be liable to his principal for breach of duty if the breach is not
waived. [91]

Relationship of apparent authority with estoppel. There is much   8–029
argument as to whether apparent authority should be regarded as based
on estoppel or not. [92] It is obvious from what has already been said that
the prevailing view in England is that it should. "Ostensible or apparent
authority ... is merely a form of estoppel, indeed, it has been termed
agency by estoppel, and you cannot call in aid an estoppel unless you
have three ingredients: (i) a representation, (ii) a reliance on the
representation, and (iii) an alteration of your position resulting from
such reliance. [93]
   The main difficulties with this approach have already been referred
to. They are, first, the fact that the representation giving rise to the
estoppel is in this area permitted to be very general indeed, [94] and
second, that the detriment incurred by the representee may be small. [95]
Of these, the first is clearly the important. The idea that by allowing his
agent to act in certain ways the principal is making representations to

---

[89] See Illustrations 1–6; Article 21.
[90] As to hidden reservations, see Illustrations 13–23, 26; as to termination of authority,
see Illustrations 24, 25 and Article 123.
[91] See Comments to Articles 20 and 38.
[92] Powell, pp. 68–72; Fridman, Chap. 6; Stoljar, pp. 25–36; *Restatement*, § 8, comment
d and Appendix, reporter's note to § 8; Seavey (1920) 29 Yale L.J. 859; Montrose (1938)
16 Can.B.R. 757.
[93] *Rama Corp. v. Proved Tin and General Investments* [1952] 2 Q.B. 147, 149–150 *per*
Slade J.; *Freeman & Lockyer v. Buckhurst Park Properties (Mangal) Ltd* [1964] 2 Q.B.
480, 503; *R. v. Charles* [1977] A.C. 177, 183; *Egyptian International Foreign Trade Co. v.
Soplex Wholesale Supplies Ltd (The Raffaella)* [1985] 2 Lloyd's Rep. 36, 41; *Armagas Ltd
v. Mundogas S.A. (The Ocean Frost)* [1986] A.C. 717, 777. See also other cases cited
above, n. 31; Ewart, *Estoppel* (1900), Chap. XXVI; Spencer Bower, *Estoppel by
Representation* (3rd ed.), pp. 181 *et seq.*; Mechem, *Outlines of Agency* (4th ed.), §§ 86 *et
seq.*
[94] See above, para. 8–017.
[95] See above, para. 8–026.

third parties is an artificial one, especially where the "representation" simply amounts to putting someone in a position which carries usual authority, or using the services of a professional person whose activities carry a usual authority.[96] The *Restatement* distinguishes clearly between cases where the principal is bound under the principles of estoppel and cases where his liability is to be attributed to some wider principle.[97] If a genuine estoppel is looked for, the category might indeed be even narrower than that marked off above as "genuine apparent authority."[98] In the editions of this work edited by Bowstead himself it can be said that such a distinction was in fact made, though later writings have enabled it to be more clearly stated. The Article above, which now stands for all apparent authority, by its reference to "representations" may be regarded as having been intended to refer to "genuine" estoppel cases. The broader notion was dealt with in Article 80 of the 8th edition (the last edited by Bowstead himself) as follows: "Every act done by an agent in the course of his employment on behalf of his principal, and within the apparent scope of his authority, binds the principal, unless the agent is in fact unauthorised to do the particular act, and the person dealing with him has notice that in doing such act he is exceeding his authority."[99] It will be noted that this last formulation approaches the terminology now reserved for the liability of an employer for the torts of his employee. It is not in accord with current thinking in contract law.

Those common lawyers who reject the idea of estoppel have indeed mostly argued for some sort of extension of the tort principles of this type[1]; or based themselves on the objective analysis applicable to the formation of contract and argued that it applies equally to the formation of contracts through agents.[2] There is much to be said for the latter view, for recent developments in estoppel have tended to stress that the consequences of the estoppel should only be sufficient to satisfy the equity raised,[3] which would not be appropriate in many agency

---

[96] See Articles 29, 30; *e.g. Waugh v. H.B. Clifford & Sons Ltd* [1982] Ch. 374, Illustration 16, where the dicta go some way towards attributing an independent position to the agent.

[97] See §§ 140, 141; 8 and comment *d*; 8B and comment *b*.

[98] Above, para. 8–018.

[99] *cf.* Partnership Act 1890, s. 5. This Article, in the form in which it appeared in the 4th ed., was relied on by counsel in *Lloyd v. Grace, Smith & Co.* [1912] A.C. 716. It was also cited with approval by the Court of Appeal in *Navarro v. Moregrand Ltd* [1951] 2 T.L.R. 674 and *Ryan v. Pilkington* [1959] 1 W.L.R. 403. But it was severely criticised by Falconbridge in (1939) 17 Can. B.R. 248, 255–256; and see *Armagas Ltd v. Mundogas S.A. (The Ocean Frost)* [1986] A.C. 717, 779 *et seq.*

[1] Wright (1935) 1 U. Toronto L.J. 40–41; Mearns (1962) 42 Va.L.Rev. 50; Bester (1972) 89 S.A.L.J. 49; Comment to Article 22.

[2] Cook (1905) 5 Col.L.R. 36; (1906) 6 Col.L.R. 34; Conant (1968) 47 Neb.L.Rev. 678.

[3] *e.g.* Brennan J. in *Commonwealth of Australia v. Verwayen* (1990) 170 C.L.R. 394.

situations. History however tends to support the estoppel view. It is certainly true that cases on master and servant and cases on principal and agent have not always been clearly separated, that some of the old cases on what is now called apparent authority reached their results without reference to estoppel, on broader notions such as that of the implied authority of a general agent, [4] and that it can be said to be to some extent accidental that the idea that a person is not normally bound without at least his apparent consent has remained better entrenched in the law of contract than in tort. [5] But cases on agency and the related notion of apparent ownership which use what would now be called estoppel reasoning can be traced back many years, and indeed some of them seem to figure among the origins of the general doctrine of estoppel. [6]

There is in any case no doubt that the prevailing approach in England is and has been in terms of representation and estoppel, at any rate as regards the agent's contracts. [7] Although it is arguable that little difference results from the approach adopted, [8] the separation of some of the cases where the representation is of too general a nature to give rise to the doctrine of estoppel strictly interpreted can be used to develop a special category of "usual authority," based on some far wider notion of the responsibility of a person for the acts of his agents. Into this certain other intractable cases can be assimilated which could have the effect of considerably widening the principles of agency as at present understood. It is submitted elsewhere that as a general doctrine such an approach, the purpose of which is to protect bona fide third parties, [9] is too vague. [10]

Even on the law as it stands, however, the notion of usual authority assists in illuminating certain difficult matters related to apparent authority, *e.g.* the liability of companies for the acts of their agents, discussed below.

---

[4] See *Smith v. M'Guire* (1858) 3 H. & N. 554; Stoljar, Chap. 3. See also Partnership Act 1890, s. 5; Thomas (1971) 6 Victoria U. of Wellington L.Rev. 1. Development on the continent of Europe was certainly not based on any principle like that of estoppel; Müller-Freienfels (1964) 13 Am.J.Comp.L. 193, 341. See also Articles 2, 29.

[5] Wright, *op. cit.* n. 1 above.

[6] See, *e.g. Pickering v. Busk* (1812) 15 East 38; *Pickard v. Sears* (1837) 6 A. & E. 469; *Freeman v. Cooke* (1848) 2 Exch. 654.

[7] See above, n. 93. As to the agent's disposition of property, which raises slightly different considerations, see *Eastern Distributors Ltd v. Goldring* [1957] 2 Q.B. 600, 611; Comment to Article 85.

[8] Mechem, *Outlines of Agency* (4th ed.), § 90.

[9] See Müller-Freienfels in *Civil Law in the Modern World* (Yiannopoulos ed. 1965), pp. 87–88: appearance "corresponds to causal explanations but has nothing to do with considerations of value."

[10] See Comment to Article 22.

8–030   **Other estoppels.** Even though the principal is not bound under the doctrine of apparent authority, he may be liable by virtue of some other estoppel: though the requirements for his liability may vary slightly in accordance with the type of estoppel involved. Thus if he can be regarded as having represented, after the time of the supposed transaction, that the supposed agent had had at the time of the transaction authority to enter into it, he may be regarded as estopped by representation.[11] Sometimes mere inaction, or a failure to disavow a transaction, might give rise to an estoppel, as where a principal through his agent allows it to appear that he is a party to a contract[12] or that an action in relation to a contract has been taken on his behalf[13]: but there would need to be a duty to take action of some kind.[14] It is usually said that this form of estoppel, like others, requires that the representee has acted to his detriment on the faith of the representation.[15] But under the doctrine of estoppel by convention, if *both* parties act on the basis of a certain assumption as to a state of fact, they may be estopped from going back on this merely because of the unconscionability of departing from the agreed assumption, without any clear representation having been made or proof of detriment[16]; and this could extend to an assumption as to the existence of a contract.[17] But the view is often

---

[11] A possible interpretation of *Spiro v. Lintern* [1973] 1 W.L.R. 1002, Illustration 34.

[12] *Pacol Ltd v. Trade Lines Ltd (The Henrik Sif)* [1982] 1 Lloyd's Rep. 456.

[13] *The Stolt Loyalty* [1993] 2 Lloyd's Rep. 281 (affd. without reference to this point [1995] 1 Lloyd's Rep. 598), doubting dicta in *Shearson Lehman Hutton Inc. v. Maclaine Watson & Co. Ltd* [1989] 2 Lloyd's Rep. 570, 596.

[14] *Spiro v. Lintern*, n. 11 above; *The August Leonhardt* [1985] 2 Lloyd's Rep. 28; *The Henrik Sif*, n. 12 above; *The Stolt Loyalty*, above; *The Indian Grace (No. 2)* [1994] 2 Lloyd's Rep. 331, 344.

[15] *Spiro v. Lintern*, n. 11 above, at pp. 1012–1013; *cf.* Treitel, *Law of Contract* (9th ed.), p. 105. It is doubtful whether, as in promissory estoppel, more than reliance should be required: as Dixon J. said in *Grundt v. Great Boulder Pty Gold Mines Ltd* (1937) 59 C.L.R. 641, 674: "The real detriment or harm from which the law seeks to give protection is that which would flow from the change of position if the assumption were deserted that led to it." (As to promissory estoppel, see *Société Italo-Belge, &c. v. Palm and Vegetable Oils Sdn. Bhd. (The Post Chaser)* [1982] 1 All E.R. 19, 27.)

[16] *Amalgamated Investment and Property Co. Ltd v. Texas Commerce Intl. Bank Ltd* [1982] Q.B. 84, following Spencer Bower and Turner, *Estoppel by Representation* (3rd ed.) p. 157. See, however, *Norwegian American Cruises A/S v. Paul Munday Ltd (The Vistafjord)* [1988] 2 Lloyd's Rep. 343, 352; *The Captain Gregos (No. 2)* [1990] 2 Lloyd's Rep. 395, 405; *The Indian Grace (No. 2)*, n. 14 above, at pp. 345–346. In so far as this can be regarded as involving a mistaken statement of law, the doctrine has been said nevertheless to apply: see *The Vistafjord*, above, at p. 351; but such statements can often be described as being of fact. See in general Treitel, *Law of Contract* (9th ed.), pp. 111–115; Chitty, *Contracts* (27th ed.), Vol. 1, §§ 3–080 *et seq.*

[17] This is a possible interpretation of *Spiro v. Lintern*, n. 11 above; and may well be the correct interpretation of *Worboys v. Carter* [1987] 2 EGLR 1, where *Spiro v. Lintern* was followed. See also the view of the minority of the High Court of Australia in the leading Australian case of *Waltons Stores (Interstate) Ltd v. Maher* (1988) 164 C.L.R. 387.

expressed that this form of estoppel cannot be used to create of itself a right of action.[18] Since estoppel can in appropriate cases do so,[19] including an estoppel as to whether a contract exists,[20] it is not clear why great efforts should be made to avoid explaining cases as having this effect.

Can the principal sue in contract? No doubt where the principal is   8–031
sued on a contract within the apparent authority of an agent, he can make counterclaims as well as adduce defences. But if it is correct that, as suggested above, the doctrine is connected with estoppel, it seems clear that he cannot of his own motion sue on such a contract without ratifying it.[21] Ratification would not normally be a difficult matter, and could presumably be inferred from the bringing of a counterclaim. The question will only be of practical significance where ratification is for some reason impossible, *e.g.* because of difficulties about ratification in part[22] or as to the time of ratification.[23] The present law is that ratification is possible though the third party has meanwhile purported to withdraw from the contract.[24] Were it otherwise, the question whether the principal can sue on a contract binding him under the doctrine of apparent authority would assume more practical significance. In general it seems appropriate to apply the safeguards on ratification[25] to such actions by principals; and if this is correct, it provides also a practical reason for adhering to the results imposed by the estoppel theory.

Some special cases are now discussed.

Agents of companies.[26] In general, companies can *only* act through   8–032
agents, except in the comparatively rare situations where a person acting for the company is in a sufficiently significant position within it for his acts to rank, for the purpose of a particular legal rule, not as acts on the company's behalf, but rather as acts of the company itself.[27] Yet it may

---

[18] Treitel, *op. cit.* n. 16 above, pp. 113–114.
[19] *e.g.* in connection with land: *ibid.*, pp. 125 *et seq.*
[20] See *The Henrik Sif*, n. 12 above.
[21] *Contra*, Powell, p. 70. Different views were expressed on the point by the Ontario Court of Appeal in *Canadian Laboratory Supplies Ltd v. Engelhard Industries of Canada Ltd* (1977) 78 D.L.R. (3d) 232. On appeal the case was decided on different grounds: [1979] 2 S.C.R. 787, (1979) 97 D.L.R. (3d) 1.
[22] As in the *Canadian Laboratory Supplies* case, n. 21 above.
[23] Above, 2–077; Article 19.
[24] *Bolton Partners v. Lambert* (1889) 41 Ch.D. 295: see Article 18.
[25] See Article 19.
[26] See in general Gower, *Modern Company Law* (5th ed.), Chap. 8. See also the leading cases of *Freeman & Lockyer v. Buckhurst Park Properties (Mangal) Ltd* [1964] 2 Q.B. 480 and *Hely-Hutchinson v. Brayhead Ltd* [1968] 1 Q.B. 549.
[27] Above, para. 1–022.

be extremely difficult for a person dealing with another who purports to be the agent of a company to know whether that person can be or is in fact authorised to do what he purports to do. The question of the apparent authority of agents of companies is therefore extremely important. But it is, not surprisingly, complicated by special factors peculiar to company law. The complications which previously existed have now been somewhat changed, but not eliminated, by recent statutory provisions.[28] Full guidance should be sought in works on company law: what follows seeks only to give general indications as to the impact on agency law of these special factors.[29]

8–033   **Ultra vires doctrine.** The first complication is the doctrine of *ultra vires*. Under this doctrine a company was not bound by a contract or (in some cases) other act into which by virtue of the objects clause in its memorandum it had no capacity to enter, or which it similarly had no capacity to perform.[30] This doctrine was sometimes interpreted rather widely so as to cover situations where the activity was authorised but the motive for the doing of it was improper, or where the exercise of a power was in the circumstances illegal, or where delegation to particular officers was not authorised by the memorandum or articles. More recent case law, however, confined the *ultra vires* doctrine to strict questions of capacity—that is to say, to matters outside the actual objects clause in the company's memorandum; the other matters go rather to questions of authority of an agent and notice to the third party.[31] Nevertheless, even in a limited form it remained a trap in respect of the apparent authority of a company's agent: the activity in which he was engaged might be *ultra vires* in the narrower sense and hence his act simply void as against the company, whatever the appearance of authority to the third party. The E.C. First Directive on Company Law[32] required member states to abolish this doctrine in order to ensure security of transactions between companies and those with whom they deal.

8–034   **Constructive notice of company's public documents.** There was also a doctrine, of rather uncertain scope, under which a person dealing with a company was deemed to have constructive notice of what appeared in

---

[28] For guidance on the law applicable before these provisions came into effect, the reader should consult earlier editions of this work and of works on company law. Attention needs to be paid to the different dates on which the reforms were brought into effect.

[29] There are special rules with respect to charitable companies: see s. 111 of the Companies Act 1989, amending the Charities Act 1960.

[30] *Ashbury Railway Carriage and Iron Co. v. Riche* (1875) L.R. 7 H.L. 653 (unanimous vote of ratification by the shareholders could not validate an *ultra vires* transaction).

[31] *Rolled Steel Products (Holdings) Ltd v. British Steel Corp.* [1986] Ch. 246.

[32] 68/151/EEC, Article 7.

its public documents. It was not clear exactly what these documents were, but they certainly included its memorandum and articles. Thus he might in particular be deemed to know not only of limitations on the company's authorised activities but also of restrictions on delegation contained in its articles. As stated above, sometimes such matters of delegation had been taken into the *ultra vires* rule; but if it was wrong to do so, the significance of the constructive notice rule for such situations became greater. The third party might not be able to rely on what would otherwise be apparent authority under agency law because he was deemed to have constructive notice of the company's objects and of restrictions on the power to delegate to agents. Even complete abolition of the *ultra vires* rule could still leave the third party with constructive notice that the act performed was outside the objects clause, or one that could not be done by the agent in question, and hence in either case unauthorised, with the result that he could not rely on what might otherwise be the apparent authority of that agent. The rule only applied against the third party: it did not apply in his favour.[33]

Common law: the rule in Turquand's case. The public documents of a   **8–035**
company may provide that a power *can* be delegated: but they may require some special procedure, for example a resolution of a general meeting; or special procedures may be laid down by the directors for the exercise of ordinary powers, for example a requirement that a cheque on the company's account needs signatures of persons authorised in particular ways.[34] The third party may have no way of finding out whether or not these procedures may have been followed. This problem was dealt with, after the introduction of the system of incorporation by registration, by judicial decision. Under the rule in *Royal British Bank v. Turquand*[35] a third party acting in good faith is entitled to assume that the relevant procedures of "indoor management", the details of which were not available to him, have been complied with. He is not, however, entitled to assume from the mere fact that authority was possible that it had actually been conferred. This could only be assumed where under the general principles of agency there would normally be apparent authority. This requires that the company, by a representation traceable back to an authorised officer, has held out the agent as having authority: either by appointing him to a position which would normally

---

[33] *Rama Corp. Ltd v. Proved Tin & General Investments Ltd* [1952] 2 Q.B. 147, 149; *Freeman & Lockyer v. Buckhurst Park Properties (Mangal) Ltd* [1964] 2 Q.B. 480, 504, 508.
[34] e.g. *Mahony v. East Holyford Mining Co.* (1875) L.R. 7 H.L. 869.
[35] (1856) 6 E. & B. 327, Illustration 27; *Mahony v. East Holyford Mining Co.*, n. 34 above. A director might in some circumstances rank as a third party for the purposes of this rule: *Hely-Hutchinson v. Brayhead Ltd* [1968] 1 Q.B. 549; affd. on other grounds *ibid.*, 573.

carry such authority, or by representing that he has been appointed to it, or by some more specific holding out.[36] If this was so, compliance with internal procedures might be assumed.

8–036   **Statutory reforms: ultra vires.** Limited provisions protecting third parties dealing with companies in section 9(1) of the European Communities Act 1972, later re-enacted as section 35 of the Companies Act 1985, proved inadequate to abolish the *ultra vires* doctrine completely,[37] particularly in that they failed to distinguish between issues of corporate capacity and directors' authority. Section 108 of the Companies Act 1989 therefore replaced the then existing section 35 with a new and specific provision. The new section 35(1), substituted by the 1989 Act, provides that "the validity of an act done by a company shall not be called in question on the ground of lack of capacity by reason of anything in the company's memorandum."[38] This provision effectively removes *ultra vires* as a relevant factor in the company's external relations in this context, and hence from questions of apparent authority; though internally, as between the company and its directors *ultra vires* acts are not permissible and may give rise to the directors being liable for breach of duty.[39] To preclude the *ultra vires* doctrine being reintroduced by the back door, the rights of shareholders are curtailed: no proceedings lie by a shareholder against a company to make it comply with the provisions of the memorandum where the act to be restrained is in fulfilment of a legal obligation of the company, including one binding only by virtue of section 35(1).[40]

8–037   **Constructive notice.** As indicated above, mere abolition of the *ultra vires* rule would not protect third parties adequately unless the constructive notice rule was also abolished, for that could lead to the conclusion that the third party was deemed to know that the act was

---

[36] *cf.* above, para. 8–018.

[37] For discussion of s. 9(1), see Prentice (1973) 89 L.Q.R. 518; Sealy [1973] C.L.J. 1; Farrar and Powles (1973) 36 M.L.R. 270; Hirstenstein (1973) 123 N.L.J. 312.

[38] This could be interpreted as directed only towards a specific limitation in the memorandum. Such an interpretation would not be justified. The leading cases made it clear that the objects of a company not only positively conferred capacity but also negatively restricted the company from acting outside its powers. Further, such an interpretation would be contrary to the obligation to implement the First Directive. On the obligation to interpret national law in a way which harmonises with the wording and purpose of relevant directives, see *Litster v. Forth Dry Dock and Engineering Co. Ltd* [1990] 1 A.C. 546; and in the context of company law, *Marleasing S.A. v. La Comercial Internacional de Alimentacion S.A.* [1992] 1 C.M.L.R. 305.

[39] See s. 35(2)(3). (Subs. (3) permits ratification by special resolution: this does not exonerate the directors unless there is a separate resolution to this effect.)

[40] See s. 35(2). The company must, however, be under a legal obligation: thus the exercise of a mere option imposing no obligation could be restrained.

outside the objects and could not be authorised. Protection was also needed against the constructive notice rule for cases where the articles gave no power to delegate, or actually prohibited delegation, either at all or to particular persons. Provisions protecting third parties were first enacted in section 9(1) of the European Communities Act 1972, but these proved not only inadequate to abolish the *ultra vires* rule, as stated above, but also unsatisfactory in general. Improved provisions now appear in sections 35A and 35B of the 1985 Act, which were inserted by section 108 of the Companies Act 1989, and section 711A of the 1985 Act, inserted by section 142 of the 1989 Act, though this provision has not yet been brought into effect.

Companies Act 1985, section 35A. Section 35A(1) overrides any   **8–038** question of constructive notice by providing that the power of the directors to bind the company, or to authorise others to do so, shall be deemed, in the case of a person "dealing" with a company in "good faith" to be "free of any limitation under the company's constitution". The company's constitution includes not only its memorandum and articles, but also any resolution of the shareholders or the effect of the unanimous consent of the shareholders. [41]

Central to the operation of the section are the concepts of dealing and good faith. Both these concepts are defined. As regards dealing, the definition is self-explanatory and is framed broadly so as to cover any transaction or other act to which the company is a party. [42] The definition of good faith is not so straightforward. First, a person will be presumed to be acting in good faith. [43] Secondly, a person will not be regarded as acting in *bad* faith by reason *only* that he knows that the act is beyond the powers of the directors. [44] The adverb "only" is critical. It is intended to distinguish situations where the directors are exceeding their authority from those where they are actually abusing it. In the first situation mere knowledge of this fact will not result in a person dealing with the company being unable to enforce his transaction; and this goes further than the normal rules of apparent authority. But where he knows or is to be taken to know that the directors are abusing their authority, there will be no such protection. [45] There are also provisions curtailing a shareholder's internal right to enforce the memorandum and

---

[41] s. 35A(3). See, *e.g. Cane v. Jones* [1980] 1 W.L.R. 1451.

[42] s. 35A(2)(*a*).

[43] Subs. 2(*c*). But on the authority of *International Sales and Agencies Ltd v. Marcus* [1982] 3 All E.R. 551, on the 1972 wording, the burden is on the third party to establish that he dealt with the company within the wording.

[44] Subs. 2(*b*). A person acts in good faith if he acts genuinely and honestly in the circumstances, *i.e.*, the test is subjective: *Barclays Bank Ltd v. T.O.S.G. Trust Fund Ltd* [1984] B.C.L.C. 1, 18 (on the predecessor provision to the current s. 35).

[45] This distinction is required by Article 9(2) of the First Directive.

articles against the directors, which parallel those previously referred to in connection with section 35. [46] However, if one of the third parties is a director of the company or its holding company, or is associated with such a director, or is a company with which such a director is associated, the transaction is in certain circumstances voidable against him. [47] In this respect, it can be said that the *ultra vires* doctrine survives. This provision gives effect to a policy that the protection against *ultra vires* given to third parties in general should normally not be extended to third parties who are also directors or otherwise involved with the company.

8–039   **Sections 35B and 711A.** These provisions are intended to deal with the doctrine of constructive notice in this context. At present this is sought to be achieved by section 35B, which provides that "A party to a transaction with a company is not bound to enquire as to whether it is permitted by the company's memorandum or as to any limitation on the power of the directors to bind the company or authorise others to do so." This adds little to sections 35 and 35A. More significant, but not at the time of writing in force, is section 711A(1), under which "A person shall not be deemed to have notice of any matter merely because of its being disclosed in any document kept by the registrar of companies (and thus available for inspection) or made available by the company for inspection." A limit on this is, however, provided by subsection (2), which provides that "This does not affect the question whether a person is affected by notice of any matter by reason of a failure to make such inquires as ought reasonably to be made." This has little effect where it is the powers of the board of directors that are in issue, for section 35A, with its reference to the power to authorise others, protects the third party. Where the authority in issue is that of an officer of the company, however, the subsection seems simply to preserve the relevant part of the existing law of apparent authority.

8–040   **The overall position: dealing with directors.** Where the third party deals with the board of directors, or with a person actually authorised by it, his position is well protected by section 35. This is further reinforced by section 285 of the 1985 Act, under which "The acts of a director or manager are valid notwithstanding any defect that may afterwards be discovered in his appointment or qualification." [48]

---

[46] Subss. (4), (5).

[47] Companies Act 1985, s. 322A (inserted by s. 109 of the Companies Act 1989).

[48] This provision is not excluded by s. 292(2) (void resolution to appoint): *ibid.* However, it only applies where there is a defect in an appointment actually made and not where there is no appointment: *Morris v. Kanssen* [1946] A.C. 459 (obviously a difficult distinction).

Dealings with other agents of the company. In respect of other   8–041
agents, including individual directors, however, the third party is in a
less protected position. He cannot be affected by anything in the
company's memorandum. He is also entitled, if acting in good faith, to
assume by virtue of section 35A that the board of directors has power to
authorise others to bind the company. But he can only assume that it
has exercised this power by virtue of the common law rules, in
particular the "indoor management" rule: and for these there must, as
before, be a holding out by the company. This may be by appointing a
person to an office carrying a usual authority,[49] *e.g.* managing director,
or representing that it has done so.[50] In such a case all acts within that
authority will bind the company,[51] but not acts outside it. The holding
out may also, as in apparent authority generally, be by more specific
conduct, as by granting powers of attorney without restriction,[52] or
regularly accepting the acts of the agent in question.[53] But pursuant to
the general doctrine, there is no protection, even in such a case, for a
third party who has notice of the lack of authority[54] or is put on inquiry
by the facts of the transaction.[55]

In the leading case on apparent authority, which also relates to the
agents of companies, Diplock L.J. said that in such cases "the
representation must be made by a person or persons who had 'actual'
authority to manage the business of the company either generally or in
respect of those matters to which the contract relates."[56] This must now
be read subject to section 35A of the Companies Act 1985, above. But
on the general principle, the High Court of Australia has followed this

---

[49] See Articles 22, 29.

[50] *Freeman & Lockyer v. Buckhurst Park Properties (Mangal) Ltd* [1964] 2 Q.B. 480,
Illustration 31.

[51] *Mahony v. East Holyford Mining Co.* (1875) L.R. 7 H.L. 869; *Biggerstaff v. Rowlatt's
Wharf* [1896] 2 Ch. 93, Illustration 28; *British Thomson-Houston Co. Ltd v. Federated
European Bank Ltd* [1932] 2 K.B. 176, as explained in *Freeman & Lockyer v. Buckhurst
Park Properties (Mangal) Ltd*, n. 50 above; *Clay Hill Brick & Tile Co. Ltd v. Rawlings*
[1938] 4 All E.R. 100; *Freeman & Lockyer v. Buckhurst Park Properties (Mangal) Ltd*,
above (Illustration 31); *Panorama Developments (Guildford) Ltd v. Fidelis Furnishing
Fabrics Ltd* [1971] 2 Q.B. 711, Illustration 32. *cf. Kreditbank Cassel GmbH v. Schenkers*
[1927] 2 Q.B. 147; *Rama Corp. Ltd v. Proved Tin and General Investments Ltd* [1952] 2
Q.B. 147.

[52] *Mercantile Bank of India Ltd v. Central Bank of India Ltd* [1938] 1 All E.R. 52.

[53] See *First Energy (U.K.) Ltd v. Hungarian International Bank Ltd* [1993] 2 Lloyd's
Rep. 194, Illustration 12.

[54] *Morris v. Kanssen* [1946] A.C. 459; *Howard v. Patent Ivory Co.* (1888) 38 Ch.D. 156.
Cf. Hely-Hutchinson v. Brayhead Ltd [1968] 1 Q.B. 549; affd. on other grounds at p. 573.

[55] *A.L. Underwood Ltd v. Bank of Liverpool* [1924] 1 K.B. 775; *Liggett v. Barclays
Bank* [1928] 1 K.B. 48; *Houghton & Co. v. Nothard, Lowe & Wills* [1927] 1 K.B. 246,
Illustration 15; and see Article 75.

[56] *Freeman & Lockyer v. Buckhurst Park Properties (Mangal) Ltd*, n. 50 above, at
p. 506.

wording and refused to find apparent authority in a person whose authority was represented by a person who only had apparent authority to do so.[57] It is submitted, however, that whether or not the decision is correct on the facts, this goes too far: so long as the authority *ultimately* traces back to a person with actual authority (subject to section 35A), that should be sufficient.[58]

Case law as to what usual authority should be attributed to the various company officials other than directors is limited and mostly out of date. As in the case of solicitors, accountants and the like, modern evidence should be required as to what can be regarded as normal.[59] Old cases tended to attribute limited authority to persons designated as "managers", and to company secretaries. But some more recent decisions recognise greater authority in such persons[60]; and the role of the chairman of the directors has developed since the nineteenth century, though it varies from company to company.[61]

8–042   **Execution of documents.** Section 36A of the Companies Act 1985 (also inserted by the 1989 Act), which abolishes the necessity for a corporate seal, further provides that in favour of a purchaser a document shall be deemed to be duly executed if it purports to be signed by a director and the secretary or by two directors.[62]

8–043   **Forgery.** As under apparent authority generally,[63] the company can be bound, though the agent effects a forgery in the sense of executing an unauthorised signature. But an actual counterfeit signature would simply be a nullity.[64] There may, however, be an estoppel against setting up a forgery in either sense.[65] A view is possible that unauthorised use of the company seal is a special matter of indoor

---

[57] *Crabtree-Vickers Pty Ltd v. Australian Direct Mail Advertising and Addressing Co. Pty Ltd* (1975) 133 C.L.R. 72.

[58] See *British Bank of the Middle East v. Sun Life Assurance Co. of Canada (U.K.) Ltd* [1983] 2 Lloyd's Rep. 9, Illustration 10 to Article 77, where the apparent authority of an intermediate agent was discussed. See also above, para. 8–021.

[59] See above, para. 3–028.

[60] *e.g. Panorama Developments (Guildford) Ltd v. Fidelis Furnishing Fabrics Ltd* [1971] 2 Q.B. 711, Illustration 32 (company secretary).

[61] See *Hely-Hutchinson v. Brayhead Ltd* [1968] 1 Q.B. 549.

[62] See also Foreign Companies (Execution of Documents) Regulations 1994 (S.I. 1994 No. 150).

[63] See Article 76.

[64] *Northside Developments Pty Ltd v. Registrar-General* (1990) 170 C.L.R. 146.

[65] *Greenwood v. Martin's Bank Ltd* [1933] A.C. 51; *M'Kenzie v. British Linen Co.* (1881) 6 App.Cas. 82; *Fung Kai Sun v. Chan Fui Hing* [1951] A.C. 489; *Rowe v. B. & R. Nominees Pty. Ltd* [1964] V.R. 477; *Welch v. Bank of England* [1955] Ch. 508; *Spiro v. Lintern* [1973] 1 W.L.R. 1002.

management of the company and governed by special rules: but the view that ordinary principles of agency are involved seems preferable.[66]

The Crown. Employees of the Crown are all servants of the Crown   **8–044** and do not employ each other.[67] And apparent authority may be extremely difficult to prove in a Crown or other public agent, for in *Att.-Gen. for Ceylon v. Silva*[68] it was said that "no public officer, unless he possesses some special power, can hold out on behalf of the Crown that he or some other public officer has the right to enter into a contract in respect of the property of the Crown when in fact no such right exists."[69] However, this was a clear case, inasmuch as the agent's powers were limited by delegated legislation, and to hold otherwise would have been to give a Crown official a dispensing power to validate *ultra vires* acts. Another clear case occurs where to bind the Crown would be to permit an officer of the Crown to fetter the Crown's freedom of action to do its public duty.[70] Subject to these important reservations, however, it may be possible to establish apparent authority in the normal way[71]; though where it is argued that one officer held out another as having authority, it will be necessary to establish the actual (or sometimes apparent) authority of that officer to do so.[72] It may also be difficult to distinguish this form of estoppel from other estoppels, *e.g.* as to whether the relevant authority has taken a decision.[73] Further, if

---

[66] See *Northside Developments Ltd v. Registrar-General*, n. 64 above, at pp. 164.

[67] *Raleigh v. Goschen* [1898] 1 Ch. 73; *Bainbridge v. Postmaster-General* [1906] 1 K.B. 178; *Moukataff v. B.O.A.C.* [1967] 1 Lloyd's Rep. 396, 423–424.

[68] [1953] A.C. 461. See also *Comeau v. Province of New Brunswick* (1973) 36 D.L.R. (3d) 763 (welfare official); *Director of Posts and Telegraphs v. Abbott* (1974) 22 F.L.R. 157 (clerk in telephone office).

[69] At p. 479 *per* Mr L.M.D. de Silva. *Cf. Robertson v. Minister of Pensions* [1949] 1 K.B. 227: see as to this case *Howell v. Falmouth Boat Construction Co.* [1951] A.C. 837, 845, 849 and *Commissioners of Crown Lands v. Page* [1960] 2 Q.B. 274.

[70] See *Southend-on-Sea Corp. v. Hodgson (Wickford) Ltd* [1962] 1 Q.B. 416; *Union S.S. Co. of New Zealand Ltd v. C.I.R.* [1962] N.Z.L.R. 656; *Director of Posts and Telegraphs v. Abbott*, n. 68 above.

[71] *cf. J.E. Verreault et Fills Ltée v. Att.-Gen. for Quebec* [1977] 1 S.C.R. 41; (1975) 57 D.L.R. (3d) 403; Hilliard (1976) 54 Can.B.R. 401; *Commonwealth v. Crothall Hospital Services (Aust.) Ltd* (1981) 54 F.L.R. 439; *cf. Director of Posts and Telegraphs v. Abbott*, n. 68 above. As to the apparent authority of a Consul-General see *Tasita Pty Ltd v. Sovereign State of Papua New Guinea* (1991) 34 N.S.W.L.R. 691.

[72] See above, para. 8-021.

[73] See *Miles v. McIlwraith* (1883) 8 App.Cas. 120; *Att.-Gen. for Ceylon v. Silva* [1953] A.C. 461, 480; *P. v. P.* [1957] N.Z.L.R. 854; *P. v. P. (No. 2)* [1958] N.Z.L.R. 349; *Wells v. Minister of Housing and Local Government* [1967] 1 W.L.R. 1000; *Lever Finance Ltd. v. Westminster (City) London B.C.* [1971] 1 Q.B. 222; *Norfolk C.C. v. Secretary of State for the Environment* [1973] 1 W.L.R. 1400; *Co-operative Retail Services Ltd v. Taff-Ely B.C.* (1979) 39 P. & C.R. 223; *Rootkin v. Kent C.C.* [1981] 1 W.L.R. 1186; *Western Fish Products Ltd v. Penwith D.C.* [1981] 2 All E.R. 204; Craig, *Administrative Law* (3rd ed.), Chaps. 18, 19.1.

the supposed doctrine of usual authority is accepted as a separate notion from that of apparent authority (which it has been suggested is not so), [74] the Crown could perhaps be held liable under it, [75] since no specific holding out is required—unless it be suggested that policy reasons still make the doctrine inapplicable to the Crown. The interaction of public and private law principles makes the area a difficult one.

Illustrations [76]

8–045 Creation of an agent

(1) A was in B's counting-house, apparently entrusted with the conduct of B's business. Held, that a payment to A on B's account operated as a payment to B, although A was not, in fact, employed by B. [77]

(2) A professional organiser of fairs and exhibitions ordered supplies for a fair using note paper on which the defendant's names appeared as an "executive committee." They were held liable for the supplies notwithstanding that the fair was a proprietary concern belonging to the organiser, since the suppliers were led to believe that the committee was responsible for the management of the fair. [78]

(3) Goods are ordered for an unincorporated charitable institution on behalf of the person who first managed the institution. A committee of governors is later formed which tacitly acquiesces in the continued supply of goods. A member of the committee is liable. [79]

(4) A, the tenant and licensee of a public-house, agreed with B and the owners of the public-house that B should become tenant in place of

---

[74] See Article 22.

[75] See Treitel [1957] P.L. 335, suggesting that *Robertson v. Minister of Pensions*, n. 69 above, may be an example of this. The possibility of usual authority was ignored in *Miles v. McIlwraith*, n. 73 above, but that was a criminal case.

[76] See further, Illustrations to Article 77 for examples of situations where principals are *not* bound.

[77] *Barrett v. Deere* (1828) Moo. & M. 200. The situation is obviously an unusual one. See also *Galbraith & Grant v. Block* [1922] 2 K.B. 155; *Bocking Garage v. Mazurk, The Times*, Feb. 4, 1954; *Guest v. J. Davy (Liverpool) Ltd* (unreported), Liverpool Autumn Assizes, Nov. 18, 1966.

[78] *F. Mildner & Sons v. Noble* [1956] C.L.Y. § 32; *The Times*, March 8, 1956; see also *Pilot v. Craze* (1888) 52 J.P. 311; *Royal Albert Hall Corp. v. Winchilsea* (1891) 7 T.L.R. 362; *Povey v. Taylor* (1966) 116 New L.J. 1656. See also *Derham v. Amev Life Insurance Co. Ltd* (1981) 56 F.L.R. 34, where the supply of business cards, letterheads, etc. to an insurance representative was held evidence of holding out. The agent was a sub-contractor and had no contractual relationship with the principal.

[79] *Glenester v. Hunter* (1831) 5 C. & P. 62; *Luckombe v. Ashton* (1862) 2 F. & F. 705; *Harper v. Granville-Smith* (1891) 7 T.L.R. 284. *Cf. Royal Albert Hall Corp. v. Winchilsea*, n. 78 above; *Draper v. Earl Manvers* (1892) 9 T.L.R. 73. See further Article 109; Keeler (1971) 34 M.L.R. 615; Fletcher (1979) 11 U.Qd.L.J. 53 and material there cited.

A, but the licence was not transferred to B, and A's name remained painted over the doorway. C, not knowing that A was the licensee, supplied goods at the public-house to B; and afterwards discovered that A was the licensee and sued him for the price of the goods. Held, that the agreement that B should occupy a position as tenant which could only be lawfully occupied by A did not make B the agent of A in relation to C; and that there was no estoppel in the matter between A and C, because whatever misrepresentations had been made, they had not reached C nor caused him to act to his detriment.[80]

(5)   A person is employed by a company to service their aircraft and teach some of its employees to fly. The company permits him to run an air taxi business under a name which gives the impression that the business is part of theirs. Neither the company nor the person concerned is licensed to do such work. An aircraft crashes while on such work. The company has held out the person concerned as its agent and is the carrier.[81]

(6)   The holder of a stolen cheque card and cheque book may, by virtue of the statements on the card, have apparent authority to communicate to a third party the offer of the card issuer to honour a cheque supported by it.[82]

Extension of existing authority   8–046
(7)   A occasionally employed B to purchase goods from C and duly recognised such purchases. Subsequently, B purchased goods from C for his own use, C believing him to be buying them on behalf of A, and giving credit to A. Held, that it was a question of fact whether A had, by his conduct, held out B as his agent to purchase the goods.[82a]

(8)   The assignee of a life policy which was voidable if the assured went beyond Europe, in paying the premiums to the local agent of the assurance company, told him that the assured was in Canada. The agent said that that would not avoid the policy, and continued to receive the

---

[80] *Mac Fisheries Ltd v. Harrison* (1924) 93 L.J.K.B. 811; *cf. Smith v. M'Guire* (1858) 3 H. & N. 554; *Dunn v. Shanks* [1932] N.I. 66. See also *Charrington Fuel Oil v. Parvant Co., The Times,* December 28, 1988 (C.A.) (property changes hands; new owners request previous suppliers, who have no notice of change, to continue; no apparent authority to bind former owners).

[81] *Gurtner v. Beaton* [1993] 2 Lloyd's Rep. 369. See also *Lease Management Services Ltd v. Purnell Secretarial Services Ltd* [1993] Tr.L. Rep. 337 (finance company estopped from saying employee of supplying company not its agent).

[82] *First Sport Ltd v. Barclays Bank Plc.* [1993] 1 W.L.R. 1229.

[82a] *Todd v. Robinson* (1825) 1 Ry. & M. 217; *Gilman v. Robinson* (1825) 1 Ry. & M. 226. See also *International Paper Co. v. Spicer* (1906) 4 C.L.R. 739; *Swiss Air Transport Co. Ltd v. Palmer* [1976] 2 Lloyd's Rep. 604. *cf. Bailey & Whites Ltd v. House* (1915) 31 T.L.R. 583 (carelessness over paying for unordered goods did not constitute a course of dealing); *Slingsby v. District Bank Ltd* [1932] 1 K.B. 544, 566. As to course of dealing see also Illustration 21; Article 77, Illustration 1.

premiums until the death of the assured. Held, that the company was estopped by the representation of its agent from saying that the policy was avoided by the absence of the assured. [82b] So, where a shipmaster signed a bill of lading containing a statement that the freight had been paid, it was held that the owners were estopped from claiming the freight from an indorsee for value of the bill of lading. [83]

(9) A was in debt to a company for goods supplied by its branch at X, and also for goods supplied by its branch at Y. He entered into a deed of assignment for the benefit of his creditors. The company's agent at X branch assented to the deed, but its agent at Y branch refused to assent. The company sued A for the debt incurred at Y branch. Held, that the company was bound by the first assent given by its agent at X branch as to all debts due from A, and was precluded from maintaining the action. [84]

(10) E, in one case as a salaried partner of a firm of solicitors, and in the other as an employed solicitor of a different firm, makes representations that funds becoming available to his firm will be transferred to a bank or to a customer of the bank: on the security of these undertakings the bank makes loans. The firms are bound. [85]

(11) The documentary credits manager of a trading bank signs a guarantee without, as he should have done, obtaining a director's assent and a counter-signature. Evidence indicates that practice regarding the authority of such officials is varied, but there are other indications from which it appears that the bank has entrusted the handling of this particular matter to the manager. The bank is bound. [86]

(12) The senior manager in charge of the Manchester office of a foreign bank operating in London is known to have no authority to agree loan facilities of the type requested, and a previous letter offering such a facility was signed by a director and an assistant director. He writes a letter offering a facility. He has apparent authority to notify to the prospective borrower that his superiors in London have approved the transaction and is interpreted as having done so: the bank is bound. [87]

[82b] *Wing v. Harvey* (1854) 5 De G.M. & G. 265. See Clarke, *Law of Insurance Contracts*, §§ 8–2A1, 20–7C. *cf.* Article 77, Illustration 8.

[83] *Howard v. Tucker* (1831) 1 B. & Ad. 712. See also *Compania Naviera Vasconzada v. Churchill & Sim* [1906] 1 K.B. 237; *Silver v. Ocean Steamship Co. Ltd* [1930] 1 K.B. 416 (statements as to apparent order and condition of goods shipped); *The Nea Tyhi* [1982] 1 Lloyd's Rep. 606 (shipment under deck); Article 77, Illustration 2.

[84] *Dunlop Rubber Co. Ltd v. Haigh & Sons* [1937] 1 K.B. 347.

[85] *United Bank of Kuwait Ltd v. Hammoud* [1988] 1 W.L.R. 1051; see [1989] J.B.L. 63.

[86] *Egyptian International Foreign Trade Co. v. Soplex Wholesale Supplies Ltd (The Raffaella)* [1985] 2 Lloyd's Rep. 36.

[87] *First Energy (U.K.) Ltd v. Hungarian International Bank Ltd* [1993] 2 Lloyd's Rep. 194.

Reservations in authority not known to third party   8–047

(13) An agent was entrusted by his principal with a document containing a written consent signed by the principal to do a particular act, but the agent was told not to give the consent, except on certain conditions which were not specified in the document. The agent consented unconditionally. Held, that the principal was bound, though he had signed the document without having read it.[88] So, where A gave B a power of attorney to charge and transfer in any form whatever any estate, etc., "following A's letters of instructions and private advices which, if necessary," should "considered part of these presents," it was held that A was bound by a mortgage on his property executed by B, although as between A and B the mortgage was not authorised.[89] So, where a principal wrote: "I have authorised A to see you, and, if possible, to come to some amicable arrangement" and gave A private instructions not to settle for less than a certain amount, it was held that he was bound by A's settlement for less than that amount, the instructions not having been communicated to the other party.[90]

(14) A gives B a signed form of promissory note or acceptance in blank, with authority on certain conditions to fill it up and convert it into a bill of exchange or promissory note for a certain amount. B fills it up in breach of the conditions and for a larger amount than was authorised, and negotiates it to C, who takes it in good faith and for value, without notice of the circumstances. A is liable to C on the bill or note as filled up, for he is estopped from denying its validity as between himself and C.[91] It would be otherwise if C had had notice of the circumstances in which the document was issued.[92] or if B had not been authorised to fill up or negotiate the instrument except on the receipt of instructions from A in that behalf.[93]

(15) An agent was given authority, in cases of emergency, to borrow money on exceptional terms outside the ordinary course of business. A third person, in good faith and without notice that the agent was exceeding his authority, lent money to him on such exceptional terms. Held, that the principal was bound, although in the particular case the emergency had not arisen.[94]

---

[88] *Duke of Beaufort v. Neeld* (1845) 12 C. & F. 248.

[89] *Davy v. Waller* (1899) 81 L.T. 107.

[90] *Trickett v. Tomlinson* (1863) 13 C.B.(N.S.) 663.

[91] *Lloyd's Bank Ltd v. Cooke* [1907] 1 K.B. 794. But *quaere* whether this and related cases should be regarded as agency cases: they are more properly to be attributed to general estoppel principles. See also Bills of Exchange Act 1882, s. 20. See further, Byles, *Bills of Exchange* (26th ed.), Chap. 4; below, para. 8–133, n. 16; *General & Finance Facilities Ltd v. Hughes* (1966) 110 S.J. 847.

[92] *Hatch v. Searles* (1854) 24 L.J.Ch. 22.

[93] *Smith v. Prosser* [1907] 2 K.B. 735; see also *Baxendale v. Bennett* (1878) 3 Q.B.D. 525.

[94] *Montaignac v. Shitta* (1890) 15 App.Cas. 357.

(16)   A solicitor is entrusted with the conduct of litigation for clients who are defendants. A compromise is contemplated involving the purchase of property by the defendants at a valuation. The clients tell him not to agree to the appointment of a valuer, but these instructions do not reach the person handling the matter, who agrees the terms of the compromise and the appointment of a valuer. The client is bound.[95]

(17)   An auctioneer is instructed to sell goods by auction, a reserve price being fixed. By mistake he sells without reserve. The principal is bound by the sale,[96] unless the conditions of sale expressly provide that the lot is offered subject to a reserve price.[97]

(18)   A solicitor is authorised to sue for a debt. A tender of the debt to his managing clerk operates as a tender to the client, although the clerk was instructed not to receive payment of the particular debt, unless at the time of the tender he disclaims any authority to receive the money.[98]

(19)   At a meeting of the provisional directors of a proposed company it was resolved that the company should be advertised, and the secretary was directed to take the necessary steps for that purpose. The secretary employed an advertising agent and upon being asked on what authority he was acting, showed the agent the prospectus and resolution. Held, that the jury were justified in finding the directors who were parties to the resolution liable for the expenses of the advertising agent, though they had allowed their names to appear as provisional directors on the faith of a promise by the secretary to find all the preliminary expenses.[99]

(20)   A charterparty provides that the master, who is appointed by the owners, shall sign bills of lading as the agent of the charterers only. The owners are liable on a bill of lading signed by the master, to a person who ships goods with notice of the charterparty but without notice of its terms.[1]

---

[95] *Waugh v. H.B. Clifford & Sons Ltd* [1982] Ch. 374. See also *Thompson v. Howley* [1977] 1 N.Z.L.R. 16; Kenny (1982) 126 S.J. 663; Foskett (1982) 79 L.S.Gaz. 57.

[96] *Rainbow v. Howkins* [1904] 2 K.B. 322.

[97] *McManus v. Fortescue* [1907] 2 K.B. 1. See also *Fay v. Miller, Wilkins & Co.* [1941] Ch. 360.

[98] *Moffat v. Parsons* (1814) 1 Marsh. 55; *Kirton v. Braithwaite* (1836) 1 M. & W. 310; *Finch v. Boning* (1879) 4 C.P.D. 143. *cf. Bingham v. Allport* (1833) 1 N. & M. 398. And see *Re Buckley and Bienefelt* (1976) 13 A.L.R. 291; Cordery, *Solicitors* (8th ed.), p. 82.

[99] *Maddick v. Marshall* (1864) 17 C.B.(N.S.) 829; *Riley v. Packington* (1867) L.R. 2 C.P. 536; *cf. Burbidge v. Morris* (1865) 3 H. & C. 664. As to company promoters, see further Gower, *Modern Company Law* (5th ed.), pp. 306 *et seq.*

[1] *Manchester Trust v. Furness* [1895] 2 Q.B. 539; *cf. Baumwoll Manufactur von Carl Scheibler v. Furness* [1893] A.C. 8, where the master was appointed by the demise charterer.

(21) A man who has regularly paid bills in respect of contracts made by his wife.[2] or otherwise shown his acquiescence in such contracts, as by directing alterations to goods supplied,[3] revokes his wife's authority to pledge his credit. His wife nevertheless orders further goods from a tradesman who does not know of the prohibition. The man is liable. The same would be true if the debt was incurred in similar circumstances by a person who lived with him but was not his wife.[4] But apparent authority does not necessarily arise merely because he has met one bill,[5] or accompanied the person concerned shopping,[6] nor did it arise where the goods were supplied to a different address from that originally used.[7]

(22) A signs an underwriting agreement purporting to give B authority to apply for shares in a company in A's name and on his behalf, and hands it to an agent of the promoters, with a letter stating that the agreement was signed, and is only to hold good, on certain conditions. The agreement is delivered to B, who applies for the shares, and they are duly allotted to A, neither B nor the company having any notice of the letter or conditions. A is bound as a shareholder, though the conditions were not complied with.[8]

(23) A ship requires salvage services. Its owners arrange for a salvage tug. Coincidentally, another tug appears and offers assistance. The master takes it to be the tug ordered by the owners and signs a salvage agreement. He would normally be authorised to do so, but on this occasion is not because other arrangements have been made. The owners are bound.[9]

Termination of authority not known to third party   **8–048**

(24) A had for some years managed a shop belonging to B and ordered goods in B's name from C, and B had duly paid for them. A absconded, called on C and bought goods in B's name, and took them away. Held, that B was liable for the price of the goods.[10]

(25) A gave his wife authority to deal with a tradesman and held her out to the tradesman as his agent. Later he became mentally incapable, but the tradesman had no knowledge of this. A was held liable on

[2] *Debenham v. Mellon* (1880) 16 App.Cas. 24, 36; *Drew v. Nunn* (1879) 4 Q.B.D. 661; *Hawthorne Bros. v. Reilly* [1949] V.L.R. 137. See also above, Article 33.

[3] *Jetley v. Hill* (1884) C. & E. 239.

[4] *Ryan v. Sams* (1848) 12 Q.B. 460.

[5] *Durrant v. Holdsworth* (1886) 2 T.L.R. 763.

[6] *Seymour v. Kingscote* (1922) 38 T.L.R. 586.

[7] *Swan & Edgar Ltd v. Mathieson* (1910) 103 L.T. 832; *cf. Filmer v. Lynn* (1835) 4 N. & M. 559. See also Illustration 7; Article 77, Illustration 1.

[8] *Ex p. Harrison, re Bentley & Co. & Yorkshire Breweries Ltd* (1893) 69 L.T. 204.

[9] *The Unique Mariner* [1978] 1 Lloyd's Rep. 438. See above, para. 4–008.

[10] *Summers v. Solomon* (1857) 7 E. & B. 879; *Trueman v. Loder* (1840) 11 A. & E. 589.

contracts made by his wife with the tradesman after he became incapable. [11]

(26) A manager has authority to conclude sales. He enters into negotiations for a sale. During the negotiations and unknown to the third party his authority to contract is restricted in the case of sales above a certain value, approval of a higher authority being required. After the imposition of the restriction he nevertheless makes a sale. The company is bound. [12]

8–049 **Agents of companies**

(27) By the articles of association of a company, the directors are authorised to borrow on bond as may from time to time be authorised by general resolution of the company. The directors borrow £1,000 on a bond, no such resolution having been passed. Held, that the company is liable on the bond, the lender having no notice of the irregularity. For a person who, when dealing with a company, relies upon a power contained in the articles of association to appoint agents or to delegate powers to them is entitled, within limits, to assume that necessary formalities and conditions that are matters of the internal management of the company have been observed and complied with. [13]

(28) The directors of a company had power, by the articles of association, to delegate such of their powers as they thought fit to a managing director. Held, that the company was bound by the acts, with the scope of such powers, of a person who acted to their knowledge as managing director, though there was no evidence that he had been duly appointed or that the powers of the directors had been delegated to him, the person dealing with him having acted in good faith and without notice of any want of authority. [14]

(29) By the articles of a fruit importing company the directors were authorised to delegate their powers. One of the directors, acting without authority, purported to make an agreement on behalf of the company whereby a loan was made (by a fruit broker) to another fruit importing company of which he was also a director, and the lender was granted the right to sell on commission the fruit imported by both companies, retaining the commission against the loan to the second company. The lender required confirmation from the secretary of the first company, who, also acting without authority, gave it. The first company was not bound by the agreement, as the acts concerned were not within the

---

[11] *Drew v. Nunn* (1879) 4 Q.B.D. 661. See further Article 123 for discussion of this case.

[12] *Rockland Industries Inc. v. Amerada Minerals Corp. of Canada Ltd* [1980] 2 S.C.R. 2; (1980) 108 D.L.R. (3d) 513.

[13] *Royal British Bank v. Turquand* (1856) 6 E. & B. 327.

[14] *Biggerstaff v. Rowlatt's Wharf Ltd.* [1896] 2 Ch. 93.

usual authority of a director and a secretary, and the articles not having been read by the lender, no apparent authority arose.[15]

(30) A trading company, having power by its memorandum of association to borrow money and give security and to act through agents, gave a power of attorney to an agent empowering him to borrow and give security. Held, that the company was bound by the acts of the agent acting within the apparent scope of the authority so constituted, notwithstanding that the agent may have exceeded the authority actually given to him as between himself and the company, provided that (as the law then stood) nothing in the articles of association prohibited the company from borrowing through such an agent.[16]

(31) A and B formed a company to purchase and resell a large estate. A and B, together with a nominee of each of them were the directors of the company. A agreed to pay the running expenses of the company and to reimburse himself out of profits. A instructed architects to apply for planning permission and to do other work in connection with the estate. The company was held liable for the architects' fees, though A had never been appointed managing director.[17]

(32) A company secretary hires cars, saying that they are needed to meet customers of the company at London Airport and drive them to the company's factory at Leeds. He uses the cars for purposes of his own. The company is bound by the contracts of hire, since the secretary has apparent authority to act in such matters of administration.[18]

(33) The directors of a company permit the chairman and majority shareholder to conduct negotiations, together with the company's solicitor, to enter into a contract to sell shares. The contract binds the company.[19]

Other estoppels   **8–050**

(34) A husband who owns a house asks his wife to put into the hands of estate agents, and this she does. An offer is made to the estate

---

[15] *Houghton & Co. v. Nothard, Lowe & Wills* [1927] 1 K.B. 246; affd. on other grounds [1928] A.C. 1.

[16] *Mercantile Bank of India Ltd v. Chartered Bank of India, Australia and China* [1937] 1 All E.R. 231. The headnote is misleading in suggesting that the estoppel arose from the articles rather than the power of attorney: see Gower, *Modern Company Law* (5th ed.), p. 192, note 28. For the present position see above, para. 8–034.

[17] *Freeman & Lockyer v. Buckhurst Park Properties (Mangal) Ltd* [1964] 2 Q.B. 480.

[18] *Panorama Developments (Guildford) Ltd v. Fidelis Furnishing Fabrics Ltd* [1971] 2 Q.B. 711. Earlier decisions giving a very limited actual, and so apparent, authority to a company secretary were said to be obsolete in view of changed practice: see *Barnett, Hoares & Co. v. South London Tramways Co.* (1887) 18 Q.B.D. 815; *Ruben v. Great Fingall Consolidated* [1905] A.C. 439; *George Whitechurch Ltd v. Cavanagh* [1902] A.C. 117; *Kleinwort, Sons & Co. v. Associated Automatic Machine Corp.* (1934) 50 T.L.R. 244. See [1972A] C.L.J. 44; *cf.* Article 77, Illustration 3.

[19] *I.R.C. v. Ufitec Group Ltd* [1977] 3 All E.R. 924.

agents, who telephone the wife. She instructs them to accept it and authorises them over the telephone to sign a contract, which they do. She has no authority on her husband's behalf to contract to sell the property. Later the purchasers become aware that the house belongs to the husband. However, the husband subsequently behaves as if the purchase had been authorised, as by receiving visits from the purchasers and allowing repairs. He gives his wife a power of attorney to transfer the house, and goes abroad. She subsequently conveys the house to another purchaser. The husband is estopped from saying that she had had no authority, and the first contract is binding on him.[20]

(35)   The solicitors of a plaintiff pursuing a bill of lading claim seek from the agents of the P. & I. insurers an extension of time in respect of the time bar of Article III.6 of the Hague Rules. They ask for this extension from the "owners". The ship is under demise charter and the appropriate defendants, from whom extension should have been sought via the same agents, are the demise charterers. The agents grant an extension on behalf of the "owners", who would not be liable. The demise charterers, who are the appropriate defendants, later allege that this was not granted on their behalf and that the claim against them is therefore time-barred. They are estopped from doing so, as if the extension was really to be interpreted as not granted on their behalf their agents must have been aware of the mistake and it was unconscionable to take advantage of it.[21]

Article 75

NO UNAUTHORISED ACT BINDING WITH RESPECT TO PERSONS WITH NOTICE

8–051   No act done by an agent in excess of his actual authority is binding on the principal with respect to persons having notice that in doing the act the agent is exceeding his authority.[22]

Comment

8–052   This proposition is mainly relevant to apparent authority: but it seems also true of the rare, almost hypothetical case where the third party

---

[20] *Spiro v. Lintern* [1973] 1 W.L.R. 1002; *Worboys v. Carter* [1987] 2 EGLR 1.

[21] *The Stolt Loyalty* [1993] 2 Lloyd's Rep. 281 (affd. without reference to this point [1995] 1 Lloyd's Rep. 598). But some difficulty is caused by the fact that the same agents acted for both parties: should they have alerted the plaintiffs to the fact that the proper defendant was not the one of their clients who was being sued, but another client who was not?

[22] *cf.* Partnership Act 1890, s. 5. See *Lysaght Bros & Co. Ltd v. Falk* (1905) 2 C.L.R. 421; *Combulk Pty. Ltd v. TNT Management Pty. Ltd* (1993) 113 A.L.R. 214.

knows that the agent's authority has been withdrawn but the agent does not.[23] It arises naturally from the estoppel basis of the doctrine of apparent authority, which requires that the third party deal with the agent on the faith of the principal's representation.[24] Situations of express notice cause no difficulty.[25] The problem is to know what constitutes notice, and when there is a duty to inquire. It is often said that neither constructive[26] nor presumed[27] notice apply in commercial transactions. This certainly excludes the full doctrine of constructive notice of equitable interests in land, whereby a person may be deemed to have notice of property interests which would have come to his knowledge if such inquiries and inspections had been made as ought reasonably to have been made.[28] But there can be no doubt that in many situations where it is relevant to know whether one person has knowledge of facts, including those raising the doctrine of apparent authority, the court may infer from the circumstances that the person concerned must have known of the facts in question or at least must have been suspicious to the extent that further inquiries would have been appropriate in the context.[29]

It seems that the proper approach in commercial cases is to apply the objective interpretation which one person is entitled to put on another's words and conduct. The matter was well elucidated in a judgment of Neill J. relating to the imposition of a constructive trust on a person who buys goods which are being sold in breach of duty at undervalue—admittedly a different context.[30] He said:

> "In deciding whether a person in the position of the defendants had actual notice, (a) the court will apply an objective test and look at all the circumstances; (b) if by an objective test clear notice was given liability cannot be avoided by proof merely of the absence of actual knowledge; (c) a person will be deemed to have had notice of any fact to which it can be shown that

---

[23] See above, para. 8–008.

[24] Article 79. Continental systems, from a different starting-point, may tend towards a different result and may even conclude that a third party can hold the principal liable though he knows of the lack of authority, simply because of the position of the agent. The principal's remedy is to remove the agent. But efforts may also be made to avoid such results by the use of other doctrines such as that of good faith. See Schmitthoff, 1970 I Hague *Recueil des Cours* at pp. 120–121; Müller-Freienfels (1964) 13 Am.J. Comp.L. 192, 211 *et seq.*, 341 *et seq.*

[25] See Illustration 1.

[26] *Manchester Trust v. Furness* [1897] 2 Q.B. 539.

[27] *Eagle Star Insurance Co. Ltd v. Spratt* [1971] 2 Lloyd's Rep. 116, 128.

[28] See Law of Property Act 1925, s. 199(1).

[29] The passage was approved and applied in *Combulk Pty. Ltd v. TNT Management Pty Ltd* (1993) 113 A.L.R. 214. See also *Alliance & Leicester B.S. v. Edgestop Ltd* [1993] 1 W.L.R. 1462.

[30] *Feuer Leather Corp. v. Frank Johnston & Sons Ltd* [1981] Com.L.Rep. 251, Illustration 7; and see *Standard Bank v. Bank of Tokyo* [1995] 2 Lloyd's Rep. 167, 175.

he deliberately turned a blind eye ...; (d) on the other hand, the court will not expect the recipient of goods to scrutinise commercial documents such as delivery notes with great care; (3) there is no general duty on the buyer of goods in an ordinary commercial transaction to make inquiries as to the right of the seller to dispose of the goods; (f) the question becomes, looking objectively at the circumstances which are alleged to constitute notice, do those circumstances constitute notice? This must be a matter of fact and degree to be determined in the particular circumstances of the case .... The burden of proving a bona fide purchase for value without notice rests on the person who assets it."

This particular dictum is cited here because, although uttered in the context of constructive trust, it appears specially appropriate to the sort of commercial situations in which the doctrines of apparent authority and apparent ownership are relied on. Although the topic has been further developed in the area of constructive trusts, the dictum retains, it is submitted, validity for this context. Indeed, the case seems more readily analysed as a bona fide purchaser case at common law than as a constructive trust case.[31] In more specialised contexts, especially banking, higher duties have sometimes been imposed and more elaborate analysis undertaken.[32]

But the distinction between commercial and other transactions cannot in any event be precise. For pragmatic, if not for analytical purposes, the difference seems to lie mainly in the divergence between the settled practices of conveyancers dealing with land, which it is well known may be subject to trust and other interests, and in respect of which certain types of inquiry and investigation are normal and the varied practices which may be thought appropriate to other areas of activity. The rules regarding notice and knowledge in the context of constructive trust may be developing on the basis that a court will impute knowledge to a person who is guilty of commercially unacceptable conduct.[33] "The good sense of the general rule in relation to ordinary commercial transactions where there is no time or opportunity to make inquiries is obvious. But it would be very surprising if the law today was that the mere fact that a transaction was a commercial transaction was sufficient to prevent any duty of inquiry ever arising whatever the circumstances, particularly so many years after the confluence of the separate streams of equity and common law."[34]

---

[31] See Articles 85, 86, 89 esp. para. 8–152, below.
[32] See the careful distinctions taken by Peter Gibson J. in *Baden Delvaux v. Société Générale, & Co., S.A.* [1983] B.C.L.C. 325; affd. [1985] B.C.L.C. 258; below para. 9–129.
[33] *Cowan de Groot Properties Ltd v. Eagle Trust Plc* [1992] 4 All E.R. 700, 760–761 *per* Knox J., quoted below, para. 9–129.
[34] *Baden Delvaux v. Société Générale, & Co., S.A.*, n. 32 above, at p. 414 *per* Peter Gibson J. See also *Shearson Lehman Bros. Inc. v. Maclaine Watson & Co. Ltd (No. 2)* [1988] 1 W.L.R. 16, 28 *per* Lord Bridge of Harwich.

Knowledge of agent of third party. The knowledge of an agent of the   8–053
third party will often be attributed to the third party himself: this is
dealt with in Article 97.[35]

Some special instances may be taken as examples.

Powers of attorney. In the case of a disposition of land by an agent   8–054
purporting to act under a power of attorney, there will doubtless be a
duty to examine the power. But even in other situations the power itself
will often constitute the only holding out by the principal: therefore the
third party can only rely on it if he has examined it,[36] unless there are
other circumstances creating apparent authority, such as the position or
profession of the agent, or other acts by the principal indicating
authority, *e.g.* acceptance of similar acts by the agent in the past.[37]
However, where such an inspection would not reveal the want of
authority, failure to make it is not relevant: and if the act appears to be
authorised, the third party cannot be expected to inquire further into
the agent's motives for doing it unless there are special reasons (*e.g.*
some irregular practice) for doubt.[38]

Acts within usual authority. Where the agent is acting within the usual   8–055
authority of a person holding the position which he holds, *e.g.* that of
managing director,[39] or of a professional agent exercising such functions
as the agent is exercising, *e.g.* in former days, a factor,[40] or exercises
functions combining the two, *e.g.* a solicitor conducting litigation[41] there
will not normally be any duty to inquire[42] unless the transaction is
abnormal or there are further circumstances giving grounds for

---

[35] See esp. *Dresser v. Norwood* (1864) 17 C.B.(N.S.) 466, Illustration 12 to Article 97.
[36] See *Jacobs v. Morris* [1902] 1 Ch. 816, Illustration 3; *National Bolivian Navigation Co. v. Wilson* (1880) 5 App.Cas. 176, 209. There used to be statutory requirements for the filing of powers of attorney: see Law of Property Act 1925, s. 125(1); Trustee Act 1925, s. 25. By virtue of s. 2 of the Power of Attorney Act 1971 filing is no longer possible, though powers filed prior to the commencement of the Act may still be inspected. As to less formal written authority, see *Suncorp Insurance & Finance v. Milano Assecurazioni S.p.A.* [1993] 2 Lloyd's Rep. 225, 233 ("onus on the third party to ask to see that authority where the agent is acting close to the border of what is usual": *per* Waller J.)
[37] See *e.g.* Article 74, Illustration 7.
[38] *Hambro v. Burnand* [1904] 2 K.B. 10, Illustration 1 to Article 76.
[39] See Articles 29, 74.
[40] See Articles 2, 30.
[41] *Waugh v. H.B. Clifford & Sons Ltd* [1982] Ch. 374, Illustration 16 to Article 74 (compromise: "officious" of other side to demand to be satisfied as to authority).
[42] *Borries v. Imperial Ottoman Bank* (1873) L.R. 9 C.P. 38; see also *Smith v. M'Guire* (1855) 3 H. & N. 554; *Knight v. Matson & Co.* (1902) 22 N.Z.L.R. 293 (horse dealer). Some of the cases used the concept of general agent in this connection: see Comments to Articles 2, 29.

suspicion—for instance, in the area of banking practice, where the agent pays the principal's money into his own bank account,[43] or uses a signed blank transfer for what might well, to an outsider, be his own purposes.[44]

8-056   **Acts outside usual authority.** An agent acting outside such authority as that indicated above is acting abnormally, and in the absence of other indications of authority there may well be a duty to inquire. Thus a contract of sale of goods by a commodity broker in his own name would not, at any rate according to former usage, normally be authorised, and apparent authority might not be easy to establish.[45] So also where it is notorious that usual authority is specially limited by trade usage, *e.g.* in particular markets, there may be no apparent authority, though some of the cases applying such reasoning are open to criticism.[46]

8-057   **Representation of limited authority only.** If the representation is of limited authority only, there will obviously be no liability where that authority is exceeded.[47]

8-058   **Bills of exchange.** In the case of bills of exchange, promissory notes and cheques, it has been long established that a signature *per procurationem* operates as notice that the agent has but a limited authority to sign, and the principal is only bound if the agent in so signing was acting within the limits of his actual authority.[48] But the fact that the agent is acting for his own benefit is of itself immaterial if he is acting within such limits.[49]

8-059   **Public documents: companies.** It was formerly possible to say that registration of the public documents of a company was notice of limitations of authority contained in them. The matter is a specialist part of company law now regulated by statute.[50]

---

[43] *Midland Bank Ltd v. Reckitt* [1933] A.C. 1, Illustration 3 to Article 76.
[44] *Sheffield v. London Joint Stock Bank Ltd* (1888) 13 App.Cas. 333; *Levy v. Richardson* (1890) 5 T.L.R. 236; *Colonial Bank v. Cady and Williams* (1890) 15 App.Cas. 267.
[45] *Cooke & Sons v. Eshelby* (1887) 12 App.Cas. 271, Illustration 7 to Article 83; *Baring v. Corrie* (1818) 2 B. & A. 137.
[46] See Article 77, Illustration 2.
[47] *Forman & Co. Pty. Ltd v. The Liddesdale* [1900] A.C. 190; *Russo-Chinese Bank v. Li Yau Sam* [1910] A.C. 174; *Doey v. L. & N.W. Ry. Co.* [1919] 1 K.B. 623.
[48] Bills of Exchange Act 1882, s. 25. See Chalmers and Guest, *Bills of Exchange* (14th ed.), pp. 208 *et seq.*
[49] *Bryant, Powis & Bryant v. Quebec Bank* [1893] A.C. 170; Article 76, Illustration 1.
[50] See above, paras. 8–032 *et seq.*

Agents of the Crown. A person dealing with an agent whose powers   **8–060**
are fixed by statute or statutory instrument or other delegated legislation
ought to inquire into them, for such an agent can by law have no
authority to contract beyond such limits; unless there is some holding
out, which can only be effected by an official with power to do so, and
would be difficult to establish. [51]

Statutes. The inquiries made by a third party may also be relevant to   **8–061**
the application of statutes, under which the third party may need to
establish that he acted in good faith. [52]

Response to inquiries. Sometimes the response to an inquiry may be   **8–062**
indecisive. For example, the person of whom the inquiry is made may, if
he is not himself the principal (as in the case of a company), say that he
will investigate and make further contact but may not do so. [53] In such a
case there may be apparent authority if his conduct is such as to give the
impression that the authority questioned exists. Any response, whether
indirect in this way or direct, will however only bind the principal if
given by the principal himself or by an agent with authority to make it.
Such authority will normally only be attributed to a person authorised to
deal with the particular business in question [54]: it is difficult to believe
that authority to give answers to inquiries which bind the employer will
easily be inferred. [55]

Illustrations

(1) General conditions of sale state that auctioneers have no   **8–062**
authority to make representations in relation to the property sold.
Contrary to this, the auctioneers state that no schemes for compulsory
purchase or the like affect the property. Such representations are not
within their apparent authority. [56]

(2) A authorised his son to take delivery of a mare, provided that a
certain warranty was given, and told the owner so. The son took away

---

[51] See *Att.–Gen. for Ceylon v. Silva* [1953] A.C. 461; above, para. 8–044.

[52] *e.g.* Sale of Goods Act 1979, ss. 25, 26; Factors Act 1889, s. 2 (Article 89); Bills of Exchange Act 1882, s. 29.

[53] See *Canadian Laboratory Supplies Ltd v. Engelhard Industries of Canada Ltd* [1979] 2 S.C.R. 787, (1979) 97 D.L.R. (3d) 1.

[54] See *British Bank of the Middle East v. Sun Life Assurance Co. of Canada (U.K.) Ltd* [1983] 2 Lloyd's Rep. 9, Illustration 10 to Article 77; above, para. 8–022.

[55] But see Grönfors [1962] *Scandinavian Studies in Law* 97, 104, discussing the position of a person "to whom telephone customers are referred".

[56] *Overbrooke Estates v. Glemcombe Properties Ltd* [1974] 1 W.L.R. 1335, holding also that such a clause is not within Misrepresentation Act 1967, s. 3. *Mendelssohn v. Normand Ltd* [1970] 1 Q.B. 177 is somewhat difficult to reconcile with this decision: see Coote [1975] C.L.J. 17. It was followed in *Collins v. Howell-Jones* [1981] E.G.D. 207.

the mare without the warranty in question. Held, that the son's act did not amount to an acceptance of the mare, so as to bind the father.[57]

(3) An agent, purporting to act under a power of attorney, which he represented gave him full power to borrow, borrowed money from A, and misapplied it. The agent produced the power, which did not in fact authorise the loan, but A acted on his representation, and did not read the power. Held, that A must be taken to have had notice of the terms of the power, and that the principal was not bound by the loan.[58]

(4) Cattle are brought to an auctioneer for sale by a dealer who normally buys and resells on his own account, but has on one previous occasion, to the auctioneer's knowledge, sold on account of another. The auctioneer is not fixed with notice that on this occasion the dealer is again acting for that other.[59]

(5) A accepts a bill of exchange drawn by B, and delivers it to B to be held by him for A's use. B indorses the bill to C for a loan, having told C that it belongs to A, and that he (B) has no authority to deal with it. A is entitled to recover the bill or its value from C.[60]

(6) A indorses a bill of exchange "pay B or order for my use." B's bankers discount the bill and pay the proceeds to B's account. The bankers are liable to A for the amount, because the restrictive indorsement operated as notice that the bill did not belong to B.[61]

(7) A dealer in an established market buys goods which are sold at undervalue in circumstances suggesting that the seller is in difficulties. The dealer is not thereby fixed with notice that the seller is selling goods which are not his own in breach of his obligations to the owner.[62]

Article 76

FRAUD OF AGENT

8–063   An act of an agent within the scope of his actual or apparent authority does not cease to bind his principal merely because the agent was acting fraudulently and in furtherance of his own interests.

---

[57] *Jordan v. Norton* (1838) 4 M. & W. 155.
[58] *Jacobs v. Morris* [1902] 1 Ch. 816.
[59] *Knight v. Matson & Co.* (1902) 22 N.Z.L.R. 293; see also *Curlewis v. Birkbeck* (1863) 3 F. & F. 894.
[60] *Evans v. Kymer* (1830) 1 B. & Ad. 528.
[61] *Lloyd v. Sigourney* (1829) 5 Bing. 525; Bills of Exchange Act 1882, s. 35. See Byles, *Bills of Exchange* (26th ed.), pp. 239–240; Chalmers and Guest, *Bills of Exchange* (14th ed.), pp. 313 *et seq.*
[62] *Feuer Leather Corp. v. Frank Johnston & Sons Ltd* [1981] Com.L.Rep. 251 (a case on constructive trust: see above, para. 8–052 and Comment to Article 117). See also *Re Funduk and Horncastle* (1973) 39 D.L.R. (3d) 94 (car).

Comment

This principle is general, applicable to cases of actual[63] and **8–064** apparent[64] authority; in tort[65]; in the disposition of property[66]; a similar result even appears in criminal cases.[67] But for the principal to be responsible under agency principles the agent must normally have been acting within the scope of his actual or apparent authority.[68] It is a well-known proposition that the mere fact that the principal by appointing an agent gives that agent the opportunity to steal or otherwise to behave fraudulently does not without more make him liable.[69] Conversely, the fact that an agent is acting in furtherance of his own interests may negative actual authority[70] and put the third party on notice as regards apparent authority.[71] As regards forgery, a forger may profess not to act *for* but *as* the person whose document he forges[72]; and a counterfeit document may of itself be ineffective.[73]

It can be argued that the general rule does not apply to undisclosed principals, in that their liability is anomalous and based on the fact that they benefit from the contract: in such a case an undisclosed principal would not benefit and so should not be liable.[74] But this is only one

---

[63] Illustration 1.

[64] Illustration 2; *Bryant, Powis & Bryant v. Quebec Bank* [1893] A.C. 170, 180; *A.L. Underwood Ltd v. Bank of Liverpool* [1924] 1 K.B. 775, 791–792; *Lloyds Bank v. Chartered Bank of India, Australia & China* [1929] 1 K.B. 40; *Uxbridge Permanent Benefit Building Society v. Pickard* [1939] 2 K.B. 248; *Alliance and Leicester B.S. v. Edgestop Ltd* [1993] 1 W.L.R. 1462.

[65] *Lloyd v. Grace, Smith & Co.* [1912] A.C. 716; *Uxbridge Permanent Benefit Building Society v. Pickard*, n. 64 above; *Morris v. C.W. Martin & Sons Ltd* [1966] 1 Q.B. 716.

[66] Many of the cases involve fraud on the part of the agent: see, *e.g.* *Oppenheimer v. Attenborough & Son* [1908] 1 K.B. 221; *Canadian Laboratory Supplies Ltd v. Engelhard Industries of Canada Ltd* [1979] 2 S.C.R. 787, (1979) 97 D.L.R. (3d) 1; *cf. De Gorter v. Attenborough & Son* (1904) 21 T.L.R. 19.

[67] See *Moore v. Brester Ltd* [1944] 2 All E.R. 515.

[68] See *Ruben v. Great Fingall Consolidated*, n. 69 below; *Morris v. C.W. Martin & Sons Ltd*, n. 69 below; *Polkinghorne v. Holland* (1934) 51 C.L.R. 143 (partner). But see also Articles 74 and 85–87; and as to vicarious liability in tort Article 92.

[69] *Farquharson Bros. & Co. v. King & Co.* [1902] A.C. 325. Illustration 7 to Article 86; *Ruben v. Great Fingall Consolidated* [1906] A.C. 439; *Morris v. C.W. Martin & Sons Ltd* [1966] 1 Q.B. 716, 726, 737, 740–741; *Leesh River Tea Co. v. British India Steam Navigation Co.* [1967] 2 Q.B. 250; *Koorangang Investments Pty. Ltd v. Richardson & Wrench Ltd* [1982] A.C. 462, Illustration 4.

[70] See Article 97, Illustration 11. Especially when the agent is practising a fraud on the principal himself: *Kwei Tek Chao v. British Traders and Shippers Ltd* [1954] 2 Q.B. 459.

[71] Illustration 3; and see Article 75.

[72] A possible explanation of *Ruben v. Great Fingall Consolidated* [1906] A.C. 439.

[73] For the ways in which forgery may be committed, see Forgery and Counterfeiting Act 1981, ss. 1, 2–5; also para. 2–055 above. As to estoppel against setting up a forgery, see cases cited above, para. 8–043, n. 65.

[74] See Comment to Article 78.

view as to the rationale of an undisclosed principal's liability and the proposition is doubtful.[75] It is however true that it may be more difficult to establish that the agent was acting on behalf of the undisclosed principal in such a case; for whether or not the principal is bound turns on the undisclosed intentions of the agent, and where an agent was acting in his own interests it may be difficult to establish that he was nevertheless intending to act for the principal.

Illustrations

8–065   (1)   A is authorised in writing to act as the agent of B for the purpose of underwriting policies of insurance, and carrying on the ordinary business of underwriting, at Lloyd's, in the name and on behalf of B, in accordance with the usual custom of Lloyd's. A, in his own interests, and in abuse of his authority, underwrites a guarantee policy in B's name, the assured acting in good faith, but having no knowledge of the existence of the written authority or of its terms. It is in the ordinary course of business at Lloyd's to underwrite such policies, and A was therefore acting within the scope of his actual authority, though in fraud of B. B is bound by the policy.[76]

(2)   A was entrusted by B with the letting of B's flat. A, as a condition of granting C a tenancy of the flat, demanded an illegal premium which C paid to A. The premium was recoverable by C by virtue of the Landlord and Tenant (Rent Control) Act 1949, s.2(5). Held, that C could recover the premium from B.[77]

(3)   A gave B a power of attorney authorising him to draw cheques on A's banking account and apply the money for A's purposes. B fraudulently drew cheques on A's account, signing the cheques "A by B his attorney," and paid the cheques into his own banking account to meet an overdraft. B's bankers applied the cheques in reduction of the overdraft without making inquiries as to B's authority. Held, that B's bankers were bound by the terms of B's actual authority, which did not extend to paying B's debts with A's money; that they had converted the cheques; and as, from the form of the cheques, they had notice that the money was not B's money, they were negligent in not making inquiry as to B's authority and therefore could not avail themselves of the

---

[75] cf. *Restatement*, § 199.

[76] *Hambro v. Burnand* [1904] 2 K.B. 10: see (1903) 17 Harv.L.Rev. 56; (1934) 50 L.Q.R. 228–230; (1935) 1 U Toronto L.J. 42–43; (1972) 89 S.A.L.J. 60–63. See also *Refuge Ass. Co. Ltd v. Kettlewell* [1909] A.C. 243.

[77] *Navarro v. Moregrand Ltd* [1951] 2 T.L.R. 674. Cf. *Barker v. Levinson* [1951] 1 K.B. 342. See also *Credit Services Investments Ltd v. Evans* [1974] 2 N.Z.L.R. 683; *Gordon v. Selico Co. Ltd* [1986] 1 EGLR 71.

protection of the Bills of Exchange Act 1882, s. 82, and were liable to A for the amount of the cheques.[78]

(4) An employee of valuers is told not to issue valuations for a particular group of companies. He nevertheless does so, on his employer's headed notepaper, and signs it with his employer's name, it not appearing on the valuation who prepared it. The valuation is negligent. His employers are not liable.[79]

Article 77

Disclosed Principal Not Bound by Acts Outside Actual or Apparent Authority

A disclosed principal is not bound by an act of his agent which is **8–066** outside the scope of the agent's implied or apparent authority unless the principal in fact authorised the agent to do the particular act or ratified it. This Article is subject to the provisions of Articles 86 to 89.[80]

Comment

This Article simply completes the account of actual and apparent **8–067** authority by further examples of principals who are not bound. It should be read in conjunction with the Article following, Article 78, concerning the doctrine of the undisclosed principal.

Illustrations

(1) A, a stockbroker, employed B, a clerk, to whom he allowed a **8–068** commission on orders obtained by him and accepted by A. B was not authorised to accept orders on A's behalf. On three occasions C gave orders to B, which were passed on to A, and executed by him, A sending contract notes to C. C made payment in respect of the first two orders by cheques payable to A's order, and in respect of the third order by a cheque payable to B's order. The cheques were delivered to B, and passed on to A, who duly credited C. Subsequently, C gave orders to B, who did not transmit them to A, but made out bought

---

[78] *Midland Bank Ltd v. Reckitt* [1933] A.C. 1; *John v. Dodwell and Co. Ltd* [1918] A.C. 563; *Nelson v. Larholt* [1948] 1 K.B. 339. See Article 75; Cheques Act 1957, s. 4.

[79] *Kooragong Investments Pty Ltd v. Richardson & Wrench Ltd* [1982] A.C. 462; criticised, [1982] C.L.J. 36.

[80] Partnership Act 1890, s. 7. As to ratification see Chap. 2, Section 3. Difficulty may occur in determining whether the act of an agent, especially one in breach of a fiduciary duty, is simply a nullity under this rule or is voidable under equitable rules. See Baxter [1970] C.L.J. at pp. 295 *et seq.*

notes on which he forged A's signature, and handed them to C. C gave cheques in payment to B, who misapplied them. It was held that there was no evidence that A had held out B as authorised to accept orders on his behalf, and that A was under no liability in respect of the orders subsequent to the first three. [81]

(2)   The master of a ship signs a bill of lading on behalf of the owner stating that goods of a particular mercantile quality have been received on board. The goods are of a different quality. The owner is not bound by the statement; for to ascertain such matters is quite outside the scope of the functions and capacities of a ship's master. [82]

(3)   The secretary of a company fraudulently, and without the knowledge of the directors, represented to A that if he took certain shares he would be appointed solicitor to the company, and subsequently that he had been so appointed. A, on the faith of the representations, applied for the shares, which were allotted to him. Held, that A was bound by the contract to take the shares, the representations being outside the scope of the secretary's authority. [83] So, where the secretary of a tramway company made a representation as to the financial relations of the company, and it was not shown that he was authorised to make the representation, it was held that the company was not bound, it not being part of the ordinary duties of such an official to make such representations on behalf of the company. [84]

(4)   Where an estate agent who is employed to procure a purchaser at a certain price enters into a contract of sale, the principal is not

---

[81] *Spooner v, Browning* [1898] 1 Q.B. 528. As to course of dealing see also Article 74, Illustrations 7, 21.

[82] *Cox, Patterson & Co. v. Bruce & Co.* (1886) 18 Q.B.D. 147. The case on which this decision was based, *Grant v. Norway* (1851) 10 C.B.(N.S.) 665, which held that a master did not bind his owner if he signed for goods not on board, was reversed in England by section 4 of the Carriage of Goods by Sea Act 1992. The reasoning of that case had appeared obsolete for a long time; yet there was substantial authority which made no difficult for any tribunal but the House of Lords to establish this. See the judgment of Sheen J. in *The Nea Tyhi* [1982] 1 Lloyd's Rep. 606. But the present application of the reasoning is acceptable.

[83] *Newlands v. National Employers' Accident Association Ltd* (1885) 54 L.J.Q.B. 428.

[84] *Barnett, Hoares & Co. v. South London Tramways Co.* (1887) 18 Q.B.D. 815; *Ruben v. Great Fingall Consolidated* [1906] A.C. 439. The authority of a company secretary in administrative matters was, however, considerably enlarged by *Panorama Developments (Guildford) Ltd v. Fidelis Furnishing Fabrics Ltd* [1971] 2 Q.B. 711, Illustration 32 to Article 74; and though these examples do not concern administration they may require reconsideration in view of what was said in that case as to changing practice. There is authority that a company secretary has no apparent authority to certify transfers: *George Whitechurch Ltd v. Cananagh* [1902] A.C. 117, and *Kleinwort, Sons & Co. v. Associated Automatic Machine Corp.* (1934) 50 T.L.R. 244; but in so far as these cases depend on authority, doubt is cast on them by the *Panorama* case, and they are also open to the same criticism as *Grant v. Norway*, n. 82 above. See Gower, *Modern Company Law* (5th ed.), pp. 161–163.

bound unless he in fact authorised the agent to make the contract on his behalf, because it is not within the ordinary scope of such an agent's authority to enter into binding contracts on his principal's behalf.[85]

(5)   An estate agent, not being authorised to do so, takes a deposit from a prospective purchaser of land in a transaction "subject to contract." The prospective vendor is not liable.[86]

(6)   The manager of a tied public-house, who had authority to deal with particular persons only, bought spirits from a person with whom he had no authority to deal. Held, that the principal was not bound, it being usual for such managers to be restricted to particular persons from whom to purchase spirits.[87]

(7)   A bank manager guaranteed the payment of a certain draft. It was not within the ordinary scope of a bank manager's authority to give such a guarantee, and the bank therefore was not liable on it unless he was expressly authorised to give it.[88]

(8)   The local agent of an insurance company contracted on behalf of the company to grant a policy. Held, that it was not within the ordinary scope of the authority of such an agent to make such a contract (as opposed to issuing a cover note[89]), and that the company was not bound unless it could be shown that the agent had actual authority.[90] So an insurance company has been held not bound by the acceptance of a premium by its agent after the time for payment of the premium had expired.[91]

(9)   An insurance broker, being authorised to effect an insurance, agreed with a company for a policy on certain terms. The policy was duly executed by the company and the broker was debited with the amount of the premium. The broker, having been paid the premium by his principal, told the company that the insurance was a mistake, and fraudulently cancelled without the principal's authority. The principal was entitled to enforce the contract against the company, it being no part of a broker's usual authority to cancel contracts made by him.[92]

(10)   The "unit manager" of an insurance company, whose only authority is to transmit proposals for life assurance or loans on mortgage to higher officers of the company, purports to bind the company to

---

[85] See Article 30, Illustration 6.
[86] *Sorrell v. Finch* [1977] A.C. 728. See Articles 94, 113; below, para. 9–024.
[87] *Daun v. Simmins* (1879) 41 L.T. 783.
[88] *Re Southport & West Lancashire Banking Co.* (1885) 1 T.L.R. 204.
[89] See, *e.g. Wilkinson v. General Accident Fire and Life Assurance Corp. Ltd* [1967] 2 Lloyd's Rep. 182; and see *Stockton v. Mason* [1978] 2 Lloyd's Rep. 430 (broker) (a puzzling case: see [1979] J.B.L. 169).
[90] *Linford v. Provincial, etc., Ins. Co.* (1864) 34 Beav. 291.
[91] *Acey v. Fernie* (1840) 7 M. & W. 151. See Clarke, *Law of Insurance Contracts* (2nd ed.), §§ 8–2A1 *et seq.*
[92] *Xenos v. Wickham* (1866) L.R. 2 H.L. 296.

guarantee a loan. The lender writes to the "general manager" of the company asking whether the "unit manager" is authorised to do this. There is no "general manager": the letter is answered by a "branch manager," who describes himself as such, and whose authority is similar to that of a unit manager. He purports to confirm the authority. He has neither actual nor apparent authority to do so and the company is not bound. [93]

(11) The Chartering Manager and Vice-President (Transportation) of a company, authorised to negotiate the sale of a ship belonging to the company, purports to enter into a simultaneous agreement to take it back on charter, the charter containing unusual terms. The third party knows that the Vice-President has no authority to enter into such a charter without approval from higher in the company. The Vice-President falsely states that he has obtained such approval. The company is not bound. [94]

(12) A shipping agent is authorised to arrange for the shipment of goods and prepare the necessary documents, including those to be presented under a letter of credit. An employee prepares a draft, signs and indorses it in blank on behalf of the customer, and the money is paid to the agency firm. The authority to prepare the documents does not represent that the firm has authority to receive payment under the credit, and payment to the firm is invalid: the bank must pay again. [95]

Article 78

UNDISCLOSED PRINCIPAL: RIGHTS AND LIABILITIES

8–069   (1) An undisclosed principal may sue or be sued on any contract made or his behalf, or in respect of money paid or received on his behalf, by his agent acting within the scope of his actual authority. [96]

---

[93] *British Bank of the Middle East v. Sun Life Assurance Co. of Canada (U.K.) Ltd* [1983] 2 Lloyd's Rep. 9 (H.L.). See above, para. 8–018.
[94] *Armagas Ltd v. Mundogas S.A. (The Ocean Frost)* [1986] A.C. 717. But *cf. Egyptian International Foreign Trade Co. v. Soplex Wholesale Supplies Ltd* [1985] 2 Lloyd's Rep. 36, Illustration 11 to Article 74. But *cf. First Energy (U.K.) Ltd v. Hungarian International Bank Ltd* [1993] 2 Lloyd's Rep. 194, Illustration 12 to Article 74.
[95] *Cleveland Mfg. Co. Ltd v. Muslim Commercial Bank Ltd* [1981] 2 Lloyd's Rep. 646.
[96] See Comment; Illustrations 1, 2, 3; *Thomson v. Davenport* (1829) 9 B. & C. 78, 90; *Sims v. Bond* (1833) 5 B. & Ad. 389; *Browning v. Provincial Insurance Co. of Canada* (1873) L.R. 5 P.C. 263, 272; *Moto Vespa S.A. v. Mat (Britannia Express) Ltd* [1979] 1 Lloyd's Rep. 175; *Siu Yin Kwan v. Eastern Insurance Co. Ltd* [1994] 2 A.C. 199, 207 (Illustration 12). *cf. Restatement*, §§ 186, 302. As to what is an undisclosed principal in this context see below, paras. 8–072, 8–074. As to money paid see *Duke of Norfolk v. Worthy* (1808) 1 Camp. 337, Illustration 3 (action by principal); *Transvaal & Delagoa Bay Investment Co. v. Atkinson* [1944] 1 All E.R. 579 (liability of principal); Articles 94, 95, 113. The doctrine was recently applied in *Boyter v. Thomson* [1995] 3 W.L.R. 36.

(2) (Perhaps), an undisclosed principal may also be sued on any contract made on his behalf, or in respect of money received on his behalf, by his agent acting within the authority usually confided to an agent of that character, not withstanding limiations put upon that authority as between principal and agent.[97]

(3) Where an agent enters into a contract, oral or written, in his own name evidence is admissible to show who is the real principal, in order to charge him or entitle him to sue on the contract.[98]

(4) But the rights of the undisclosed principal to sue and his liability to be sued on a contract made by his agent may be excluded by the terms of the contract, express or implied.[99]

(5) So far as concerns deeds, bills of exchange, promissory notes and cheques, this Article must be read subject to Articles 79 and 80.

Comment

Rule (1). Undisclosed principal doctrine. This is a statement of the common law doctrine of undisclosed principal. The proposition that such a principal can in appropriate circumstances sue and be sued on a contract made by his agent may be surprising, but is well established. Its origin is said to lie in the right of the principal of a factor to intervene in the factor's bankruptcy, to claim his goods or the unpaid price of them; and later to sue in respect of the whole contract.[1] This somehow led to more generalised reasoning whereby such a principal was entitled to sue on his agent's contracts in general; and it became established that he was liable also. Such a conclusion is certainly difficult to accommodate within standard theories of contract, which emphasise, even though under objective criteria, the consent of the parties. It should be remembered however that the doctrine was formed before such theories had acquired prominence.[2] There are judicial dicta to the effect that the contract is that of the undisclosed principal, just as in cases of disclosed principal,[3] and some decisions can only be justified on this reasoning.[4]

8–070

---

[97] *Watteau v. Fenwick* [1893] 1 Q.B. 346, 348. See Comment; Illustrations 4, 5, 6; *cf. Restatement*, §§ 194, 195.

[98] See Comment; Illustrations 7, 8.

[99] *Siu Yin Kwan v. Eastern Insurance Co. Ltd* [1994] 2 A.C. 199, 207 (Illustration 12).

[1] Stoljar, pp. 203–211; Goodhart and Hamson (1932) 4 C.L.J. 320.

[2] Müller-Freienfels (1953) 16 M.L.R. 299.

[3] *Keighley, Maxsted & Co. v. Durant* [1901] A.C. 240, 261; *Said v. Butt* [1920] 3 K.B. 497, 500 (Illustration 11).

[4] *e.g. Cooke & Sons v. Eshelby* (1887) 12 App.Cas. 271, Illustration 7 to Article 83; below, para. 8–111.

But, subject to the intervention of the principal, the agent can sue on such a contract and even recover the principal's loss by way of damages; and can be sued on it.[5] There are also special rules whereby a third party cannot be prevented by the intervention of the principal from exercising his rights against the agent[6] nor (normally) from using against the principal defences which he had against the agent.[7] These cast doubt on such dicta and decisions[8] and highlight an uneasy tension between two organising theories, that the contract is that of the agent and that the contract is that of the principal. It is difficult to deny that the undisclosed principal is really a third party intervening on a contract which he did not make, and this view has recently been accepted in the Court of Appeal.[9]

Even as an exception to the rules of privity of contract, however, the doctrine is unusual, since the *tertius* is not mentioned, nor indeed contemplated by one of the parties, and furthermore takes liabilities as well as rights. Another suggestion therefore is that the basis of the doctrine is similar to that of assignment[10]: but there is no evidenced transfer, formal or informal, nor are the rights of the agent extinguished; and the principal receives liabilities as well as rights. It can be said further that the undisclosed principal takes burdens because he receives benefits: but this does not explain why he receives benefits. Sometimes it is argued that the agent is trustee for the undisclosed principal, but it has been held in the context of the *res judicata* doctrine that, as regards the third party, the agent is not to be so regarded,[11] and in any case the principal who intervenes has control over litigation in a way that a trust beneficiary would not.[12] Nevertheless, some aspects of the relation between principal and agent are undoubtedly to be accounted for, here as elsewhere, on the basis of trust, or at least of analogous fiduciary duties.[13] The doctrine is probably best explained simply as one of commercial convenience, and its justice is disputable.[14]

---

[5] Below, paras. 9–011, 9–012.

[6] *O'Herlihy v. Hedges* (1803) 1 Sch. & Lef. 123 (specific performance in favour of a principal may be refused unless the agent will enter into or continue personal covenants with third party); *Montgomerie v. United Kingdom Mutual Steamship Assn.* [1891] 1 Q.B. 370, 372. See below, paras 8–098, 9–012.

[7] *Siu Yin Kwan v. Eastern Insurance Co. Ltd* [1994] 2 A.C. 199, 207 (Illustration 12); Article 81.

[8] See Comments to Articles 82, 83.

[9] *Welsh Development Agency v. Export Finance Co. Ltd* [1992] B.C.L.C. 148; see pp. 173, 182.

[10] Goodhart and Hamson (1932) 4 C.L.J. 320.

[11] *Pople v. Evans* [1969] 2 Ch. 255; and see *Allen v. F. O'Hearn & Co.* [1937] A.C. 213.

[12] Below, para. 9–012.

[13] Higgins (1965) 28 M.L.R. 167; and see Comment to Article 45.

[14] See Pollock (1887) 3 L.Q.R. 358; (1896) 12 L.Q.R. 204; (1898) 14 L.Q.R. 2; Ames (1909) 18 Yale L.J. 443; Lewis (1909) 9 Col.L.Rev. 116; Mechem (1910) 23 Harv.L.Rev.

"It has often been doubted" said Blackburn J. "whether it was originally right so to hold: but doubts of this kind come now too late."[15] The Privy Council has recently rejected the analogy of assignment.[16] This throws the law back on the tensions between the two approaches described above. Reasoning based on the notion, at first glance straightforward, that the contract is that of the principal should therefore be regarded with caution.

It has been suggested in a leading judgment on a different topic that the rule "can be rationalised as avoiding circuity of action."[17] It is true that in continental systems similar results can sometimes be achieved by circuitous routes: the principal may sue as assignee of the agent's rights, and the third party may exercise the agent's right of indemnity against the principal.[18] It is said indeed that the simplicity of the common law doctrine is admired by some continental jurists.[19] But the principal's right to sue is perhaps more easily justified on this basis than his liability to be sued.[20] Indeed, the generalisation of what was apparently in origin a limited right of intervention into an arm of general agency principle causes serious problems, many of which are still unsolved.[21]

Authority and ratification. The agent must have actual authority, 8–071 though this may of course be express or implied. It has been held, and is often said, that the doctrine of ratification does not apply to undisclosed principals.[22] The reason usually given is that if it did, one person could too easily intervene on the contracts of another. This is certainly true where the person whose acts another seeks to ratify initially had no authority at all. Indeed, in such a case there would be no one who could be called an undisclosed principal, and the proposition would simply mean that a person cannot become an

---

513; Seavey (1920) 29 Yale L.J. 859; Montrose (1938) 16 Can.B.R. 770–771; Weinrib (1975) 21 McGill L.J. 298; Geva (1979) 25 McGill L.J. 32; Stoljar, pp. 228–233; Rochvarg (1989) 34 McGill L.J. 286; Barnett (1987) 75 Calif. L.Rev. 1969.

[15] *Armstrong v. Stokes* (1872) L.R. 7 Q.B. 598, 604.

[16] *Siu Yin Kwan v. Eastern Insurance Co. Ltd* [1994] 2 A.C. 199, Illustration 12.

[17] *Freeman & Lockyer v. Buckhurst Park Properties (Mangal) Ltd* [1964] 2 Q.B. 480, 503 *per* Diplock L.J. *Cf.* Ames, *op. cit.* n. 14 above; Higgins, *op. cit.* n. 13 above.

[18] Müller-Freienfels (1955) 18 M.L.R. 33: Schmitthoff, 1970 I Hague *Recueil des Cours* 115, 114–145.

[19] Müller-Freienfels (1953) 16 M.L.R. 299.

[20] See below, para. 12-002; Zweigert and Kötz, *Introduction to Comparative Law* (tr. Weir) (2nd ed.), Vol. 2, pp. 98 *et seq.*; *cf.* Ames (1909) 18 Yale L.J. 443, 449; Geva (1975) 25 McGill L.J. 32.

[21] *e.g.* as to capacity: below, para. 8–075; and in connection with dispositions of property: see Article 91.

[22] *Keighley, Maxsted & Co. v. Durant* [1901] A.C. 240, Illustration 3 to Article 15. Schmitthoff calls this a "remarkable restriction": 1970 I Hague *Recueil des Cours* at p. 148. See also Seavey (1954) 21 U.Chi.L.Rev. 248; Rochvarg (1989) 34 McGill L.J. 286. As to ratification in general, see Chap. 2, section 3.

undisclosed principal by ratifying the act of another, which is doubtless correct. It is not clear that such reasoning is so appropriate where the agent already has some authority, but exceeds it. It is arguable that in such a situation a principal who chooses to ratify should be liable; and that he should also be able to sue, the third party being protected by the various safeguards against unfair operation of the doctrine of ratification.[23] Of these, the case for the liability of the principal, which can hurt no one but the principal, is obviously the stronger. The leading case,[24] however, which is a decision of the House of Lords, concerns just this situation and holds the principal not liable.

8–072   **What is an undisclosed principal?** A more difficult question is that of the nature of the authority which must be conferred. Here two views can be justified from the cases. One view is that for the doctrine to operate the principal must have authorised the agent to bring him into contractual privity with the third party. If this view, which in some respects seems obvious,[25] is correct, the application of the doctrine is confined to two types of case. The first occurs where the principal wishes to be a party to a contract, but wishes also to conceal the fact that he is doing so, perhaps because he does not wish it to be known that he has entered the market. The second is that where the agent does not disclose the existence of his principal, perhaps because he does not wish the third party on the next transaciton to bypass him and go direct to the principal; and the principal either acquiesces in this or makes no inquiry as to the agent's practice.[26]

The other view is that whatever the principal's intentions, he is affected by this doctrine whenever he uses the services of an intermediary who works on agency basis, *viz.* undertakes only to use his best endeavours, does not act as an independent merchant or supplier of services but takes a commission on the transaction arranged, and so forth,[27] even though the principal does not intend to be a party to any

---

[23] Article 19.

[24] *Keighley, Maxsted & Co. v. Durant*, n. 22 above: see above, para. 2–059.

[25] *e.g.* the agent may do something quite outside the contemplated sphere of action, as by delegating his function. It is clear that in such a case the principal would not be liable or entitled. See *New Zealand and Australian Land Co. v. Watson* (1881) 7 Q.B.D. 374; *Kaltenbach v. Lewis* (1885) 10 App.Cas. 617, Illustration 9 to Article 83; Goodhart and Hamson (1932) 4 C.L.J. 320, 330–335. See also *The Astyanax* [1985] 2 Lloyd's Rep. 109.

[26] There may even be cases where the agent acts contrary to instructions in not disclosing his principal's name: *Ex p. Dixon, re Henley* (1876) 4 Ch. D. 133. Swedish law differentiates between cases where the principal is undisclosed in his own interest and cases where he is undisclosed in the interests of the agent. In the former case it seems that he will be liable and entitled; in the latter, entitled but not liable: Grönfors [1962] *Scandinavian Studies in Law* 97, 100, 122–123.

[27] See above, paras. 1–013—1–015 *et seq.*

contracts made. This would bring within the scope of the doctrine situations where the principal uses the services of an intermediary who deals with the outside world as principal, but as regards his own principal acts as agent—the indirect agency of the civil law.[28] In such a case the entitlement and liability of the principal would be superimposed by the law irrespective of the intentions of the parties, and contrary of course to the normal result in civil law countries recognising this notion.[29]

Although the question does not appear to have been squarely faced, the majority of dicta directly or by implication favour the first view.[30] Many of these are based on the assumption, discussed earlier in this book,[31] that the category of indirect representation cannot exist at all: that either there is true agency or a contract (usually of sale) between principals.[32] But they also include the formidable authority of Lord Blackburn,[33] who was in favour of the recognition of indirect representation,[34] but apparently without applying this particular common law consequence to it. On the other hand there is authority for the second view[35]: also, the situation of the nineteenth century factor must often have been within the second category, and the origin of the doctrine is normally attributed to his position.[36] Indeed, if the doctrine is confined to cases in the first category, it applies comparatively rarely, and many of the situations in which it applies would be ones where the existence of the principal was concealed in a way making the fairness of his intervention doubtful. Further, the accepted rationale of the rule, which is normally regarded as connected with priority in the agent's bankruptcy, would suggest the second view. The question creates a significant uncertainty within the doctrine. For example, the answer to

---

[28] Above, para. 1–018; see also Article 71.

[29] Foreign commentators sometimes recognise the undisclosed principal situation as being a parallel to indirect agency: see *e.g.* Hamel, *Le Contrat de Commission* (Paris, 1949) pp. 310–327. But the foreign principal rule, a direct exception to the undisclosed principal doctrine, would in fact have prevented intervention or liability of foreign principals: see *e.g. Hutton v. Bulloch* (1874) L.R. 9 Q.B. 572.

[30] *e.g.* (and especially) *Hutton v. Bulloch*, n. 29 above; and the foreign principal cases, below, para. 9–018.

[31] Above, para. 1–019.

[32] *e.g. Anglo-African Shipping Co. of New York Ltd v. J. Mortner Ltd* [1962] 1 Lloyd's Rep. 610 *per* Diplock L.J.

[33] See the decision in *Armstrong v. Stokes* (1872) L.R. 7 Q.B. 598, Illustration 7 to Article 82; also *Elbinger Actiengesellschaft v. Claye* (1873) L.R. 8 C.B. 313.

[34] See *Robinson v. Mollett* (1875) L.R. 7 H.L. 802, 809–810 (but the majority regarded the arrangement as inconsistent with the nature of agency: see Article 31, Illustration 8); *Ireland v. Livingston* (1872) L.R. 5 H.L. 395.

[35] *Maspons y Hermano v. Mildred, Goyeneche & Co.* (1882) 9 Q.B.D. 530; affd. on other grounds (1883) 8 App.Cas. 874. See Reynolds [1983] C.L.P. 119, 128–133.

[36] Above, para. 8–070; and see above, para. 1–040.

the following problem is obscure. If the principal authorises and instructs the agent to deal in the principal's name, *i.e.* saying that he acts for a principal and naming him as the person for whom he acts, but the agent does not and deals in his own name, is the principal affected by the undisclosed principal doctrine? On the second view he probably is. On the first, it would seem that the agent is not authorised to act for the principal in the way in which he did, and the principal is outside the transaction.

8–073   **Intention of the agent.** Although the intention of one party uncommunicated to the other is not usually relevant to the legal effect of a transaction, it is plain that this must be a case where intention is relevant: if the agent intended to act for his own profit and not on the principal's behalf, the principal cannot intervene or be sued.[37]

8–074   **Degree of knowledge of the third party.** The obvious situation for the operation of the doctrine is that where the third party does not know of the involvement of any principal. Many cases suggest or imply that a third party dealing with an apparent principal has no duty of inquiry as to whether that person has anyone behind him[38]; that he need not establish that he had no knowledge of a principal's existence[39]; and that constructive notice of it is not to be attributed to him.[40] But there are several decisions which go further and apply the undisclosed principal doctrine to situations where the third party is actually aware that the agent sometimes deals for himself and sometimes on behalf of others but does not know which is true on this occasion[41]; to situations where the third party is aware of the existence (possibly even the name) and involvement of the principal, but is not clear as to his exact relationship with the agent[42]; and even to situations where he is aware that the

---

[37] *Siu Yin Kwan v. Eastern Insurance Co. Ltd* [1994] 2 A.C. 199, 207 (Illustration 12). *cf. Restatement,* § 199. See the question discussed in the context of unnamed principals in *National Oilwell (U.K.) Ltd v. Davy Offshore Ltd* [1993] 2 Lloyd's Rep. 582, 597; above, para. 2–063. See also *A. Tomlinson (Hauliers) Ltd v. Hepburn* [1966] A.C. 451.

[38] *Fish v. Kempton* (1849) 7 C.B. 687; *Ex p. Dixon, re Henley* (1876) 4 Ch.D. 133.

[39] *Borries v. Imperial Ottoman Bank* (1873) L.R. 9 C.P. 38. See also *Semenza v. Brinsley* (1865) 18 C.B.(N.S.) 467; *Knight v. Matson & Co.* (1902) 22 N.Z.L.R. 293.

[40] *Greer v. Downs Supply Co.* [1927] 2 K.B. 28.

[41] *Baring v. Corrie* (1818) 2 B. & A. 137; *Cooke & Sons v. Eshelby* (1887) 12 App.Cas. 271, Illustration 7 to Article 83; and perhaps *Armstrong v. Stokes* (1872) L.R. 7 Q.B. 598, Illustration 7 to Article 82.

[42] *Addison v. Gandassequi* (1812) 4 Taunt. 574; *Paterson v. Gandasequi* (1812) 15 East 62; *Teheran-Europe Co. Ltd v. S.T. Belton (Tractors) Ltd* [1986] 2 Q.B. 545 (where the Court of Appeal was undecided whether the case was one of unnamed or of undisclosed principal); and perhaps *Pyxis Special Shipping Co. Ltd v. Dritsis & Kaglis Bros. Ltd (The Scaplake)* [1978] 2 Lloyd's Rep. 380.

principal is using the intermediary's services on an agency basis but that the principal does not wish to become a party to the agent's contract.[43] In all these cases the first requisite would of course be that the agent was liable as a contracting party: otherwise the transaction would lack certainty.[44] It is possible that the first two situations would really be better analysed as involving disclosed but unnamed principals, if a rule that the agent of such a principal was prima facie personally liable could be adopted, for they seem to be brought within the undisclosed principal doctrine by the desire to hold the agent liable and entitled as well as the principal, or otherwise to use reasoning applicable to undisclosed rather than fully disclosed principals.[45] Whether the third situation invokes the undisclosed principal rules has already been discussed.[46] Here again there are significant uncertainties as to the application of the doctrine.

Capacity of agent. Although the doctrine is here explained on the general basis that the principal intervenes on the agent's contract, this need not mean that the agent who acts for an undisclosed principal must, contrary to the normal rule for agents,[47] have capacity. There are sufficient inelegancies in the doctrine for it to be appropriate to examine each situation on its merits rather than by reference to formulae. If the agent's contract is unenforceable for lack of capacity, it is possible that the principal may nevertheless be able to intervene, and is liable, although the agent could not sue or be sued.[48]   **8–075**

Contract in writing. The question whether an undisclosed principal can intervene on a contract signed only by his agent and the third party is undetermined. He certainly was able to do so under section 40 of the Law of Property Act 1925, which re-enacting the Statute of Frauds 1677 required a note or memorandum of the contract. But section 2 of the Law of Property (Miscellaneous Provisions) Act 1989 requires that the   **8–076**

---

[43] *Maspons y Hermano v. Mildred, Goyeneche & Co.* (1882) 9 Q.B.D. 530; affd. on other grounds (1883) 8 App.Cas. 874. *Browning v. Provincial Insurance Co. of Canada* (1873) L.R. 5 P.C. 263 also seems to concern such a person.

[44] See *Public Trustee v. Taylor* [1978] V.R. 289 ("for himself or as agent for an undisclosed principal"—agent personally liable so transaction valid).

[45] See below, para. 9–014.

[46] Above, para. 8–072.

[47] Article 5.

[48] See Weinrib (1975) 21 McGill L.J. 298, criticising *Commonwealth Trust Co. v. De Witt* (1973) 40 D.L.R. (3d) 113, in which the fact that it acted for an undisclosed principal was held actually to *confer* capacity on a corporate agent. But, the reverse would be more logical: the incapacity should prevent the principal's involvement. The case is also criticised in (1976) 40 Sask.L.Rev. 291. In *Danziger v. Thompson* [1944] K.B. 654, Illustration 8, specific performance was decreed against an undisclosed principal whose agent was a minor: but the facts and decision are not clear, and the contract was probably one of those binding minors.

contract actually be in writing and signed by or an behalf of the parties. The matter is discussed elsewhere.[49]

8–077   **Merger and election.** It seems to have been at least in part unease about the justifiability of the doctrine which led to the application of rules as to merger and election, whereby the third party may be able to sue principal or agent, but not both.[50] These are separately discussed under Article 84. They operate in one direction only: the third party cannot elect as to by whom he is sued; though he may be able to insist on exercising rights against the agent despite the principal's intervention,[51] and, as explained below, there are cases where the principal may not be permitted to intervene at all.[52]

8–078   **Rule (2).** This Rule represents the proposition to be derived from a Divisional Court case of 1893 which has achieved a surprising prominence. Its correctness is however most doubtful.

In *Watteau v. Fenwick*[53] the owner of an hotel sold his business to a firm of brewers, who retained him as their manager. The licence was taken out in his name and his name was painted over the door. It was agreed that he should buy all supplies other than bottled ales and mineral waters from the brewers. In breach of this stipulation he bought cigars on credit from the plaintiffs, and the brewers were held liable on this contract. The case cannot be explained on the basis of apparent authority, since the principal was undisclosed,[54] and there was no actual authority. It was in fact based on a wider principle. Wills J. said[55]:

> "Once it is established that the defendant was the real principal, the ordinary doctrine as to principal and agent applies—that the principal is liable for all the acts of the agent which are within the authority usually confided to an agent of that character, notwithstanding limitations, as between the principal and the agent, put upon that authority. It is said that it is only so where there has been a holding out of authority—which cannot be said where the person supplying the goods knew nothing of the existence of a principal. But I do not think so. Otherwise in every case of undisclosed principal, or at least in every case where the fact of there being a principal was undisclosed, the secret limitation of authority would prevail and defeat the action of the person

---

[49] See Comment to Article 73.

[50] *e.g. Kendall v. Hamilton* (1879) 4 App.Cas. 504, 544.

[51] See *O'Herlihy v. Hedges*, above, para. 8–070, n. 6.

[52] Below, para. 8–080.

[53] [1893] 1 Q.B. 346 Illustration 5; criticised (1893) 9 L.Q.R. 111; (1893) 7 Harv.L.Rev. 49; (1893) 37 S.J. 280; Ewart, *Estoppel* (1900), pp. 246 *et seq.*

[54] Though Goodhart and Hamson seek so to explain it: see (1932) 4 C.L.J. 320, 336, but *cf.* Wright (1935) 13 Can.B.R. 116, 120; Montrose (1939) 17 Can.B.R. 693, 696; Powell, pp. 75–76.

[55] At pp. 348–349.

dealing with the agent and then discovering that he was an agent and had a principal."

This proposition, which can be regarded as suggesting a special form of usual authority,[56] is however extremely dubious. It was supported by two arguments: an analogy with the law of partnership, and an earlier case in the Queen's Bench, *Edmunds v. Bushell and Jones.*[57] The analogy with the law of partnership has long since been shown to be wrong.[58] *Edmunds v. Bushell and Jones* is a case where the facts are not clear[59] and there may have been apparent authority: in any case the dicta in the short judgments cast doubt on the reasoning employed. Thus Shee J. said[60]: "The natural inference when a person allows an agent to carry on a particular business as an ostensible principal, is that he clothes him with every authority incidental to a principal in the business." But this involves confusion: a principal has no authority and deals on his own account.[61]

The case has been followed, and indeed preferred to other authority which might appear contrary,[62] by the Divisional Court in a case subsequently reversed on other grounds,[63] and it has been distinguished.[64] The supposed doctrine of *Watteau v. Fenwick*[65] is therefore tentatively reproduced here. But the Supreme Court of Ontario[66] and the Court of Appeal of British Columbia[67] have refused to follow it; and doubt has been cast on it in the High Court of Australia[68] and in England.[69] It is submitted that it is in fact inconsistent with the basic principles of agency law as subsequently established, which make it clear

---

[56] See Comment to Article 22.

[57] (1865) L.R. 1 Q.B. 97, Illustration 4.

[58] See Lindley and Banks, *Partnership* (16th ed.), p. 251; Pollock (1893) 9 L.Q.R. 111; Montrose (1939) 17 Can.B.R. 693, 699 *et seq.* (but as to some of the points made, see Thomas (1971) Vic.U. of Wellington L.R. 1); Powell, pp. 76–77, *Construction Engineering (Aust.) Pty. Ltd v. Hexyl Pty. Ltd* (1985) 155 C.L.R. 541.

[59] See Montrose, *op. cit.*, n. 58 above, pp. 697–699; (1893) 37 S.J. 280.

[60] At p. 100.

[61] *cf.* Ewart, *Estoppel* (1900), Chap. XVII.

[62] *Daun v. Simmins* (1879) 41 L.T. 783.

[63] *Kinahan & Co. v. Parry* [1910] 2 K.B. 389, revsd. [1911] 1 K.B. 459, Illustration 6.

[64] See *Johnston v. Reading* (1893) 9 T.L.R. 200; *Lloyd's Bank Ltd v. Swiss Bankverein* (1912) 107 L.T. 309 (affd. 108 L.T. 143); *Jerome v. Bentley* [1952] 2 All E.R. 114.

[65] n. 53 above.

[66] *McLaughlin v. Gentles* (1919) 51 D.L.R. 383; see also *Becherer v. Asher* (1896) 23 Ont.App. 202.

[67] *Sign-o-Lite Plastics Ltd v. Metropolitan Life Insurance Co.* (1990) 73 D.L.R. (4th) 541.

[68] *International Paper Co. v. Spicer* (1906) 4 C.L.R. 739, 763. The Privy Council made no attempt to use such reasoning in the earlier case of *Miles v. McIlwraith* (1883) 8 App.Cas. 120.

[69] See *The Rhodian River*, n. 75 below. See also *Re Att.-Gen.'s Reference (No. 1 of 1985)* [1986] Q.B. 491, 506.

that liability can only be based on actual or apparent authority.[70] If the doctrine is adopted, therefore, this should only be done on the basis of a conscious advance on the previous accepted theories of agency, made for the purpose of extending liability.[71] Thus the *Restatement* would regard this as an example of "inherent agency power."[72]

Although such an extension might on the face of it appear progressive, it is not easy to justify a general rule of liability on such a loose basis. Recent decisions of the House of Lords[73] and Privy Council,[74] while not adverting expressly to the point, are not consistent with any trend to extend liability beyond situations where authority exists or appears to exist. In another recent case Bingham J. said that the argument advanced for the unsuccessful defendant in *Watteau v. Fenwick* seemed to him in principle correct.[75] It is submitted that the supposed doctrine is too vague to be satisfactorily employed.[76] It is sometimes suggested that the actual decision in *Watteau v. Fenwick* can be explained on the basis of apparent ownership[77]: but this would be an extension of that doctrine, which only applies to dispositions of property and perhaps to contracts to dispose of property, and which requires not only that the owner of property must have given another possession of the property, but also done something more, so as to raise an estoppel against him.[78] Had execution been sought against the property, that doctrine might conceivably have applied: but it would not (again unless the case indicates an extension of the doctrine) make the brewer liable for the money.[79] Other explanations of the decision, *e.g.* that the brewer had received and used the goods and was liable on that basis only,[80] are possible, should they be thought necessary.

---

[70] See Comment to Article 22; Hornby [1961] C.L.J. 239. In *A.L. Underwood Ltd v. Bank of Liverpool* [1924] 1 K.B. 775, 792, Scrutton L.J. said "Just as you cannot ratify the act of an agent who did not profess to act for you ... so in my view you cannot rely on the apparent authority of an agent who did not profess in dealing with you to act as agent." See also above, para. 1–024.

[71] Montrose (1939) 17 Can.B.R. 693; Bester (1972) 89 S.A.L.J. 49.

[72] See §§ 8A, 140, 194, 195 and Appendix, reporter's note to § 161; the notion is discussed in the Comment to Article 22. See also Seavey (1955) 1 Howard L.J. 79.

[73] *Moorgate Mercantile Co. Ltd v. Twitchings* [1977] A.C. 890, Illustration 8 to Article 86; *British Bank of the Middle East v. Sun Life Assurance Co. of Canada (U.K.) Ltd* [1983] 2 Lloyd's Rep. 9, Illustration 10 to Article 77.

[74] *Kooragang Investments Pty. Ltd v. Richardson & Wrench Ltd* [1982] A.C. 462, Illustration 4 to Article 76.

[75] *Rhodian River Shipping Co. S.A. v. Holla Maritime Corp. (The Rhodian River)* [1984] 1 Lloyd's Rep. 373, 379.

[76] See also Comment to Article 22.

[77] Hornby, *op. cit.*, n. 70 above; Conant (1968) 47 Neb.L.Rev. 678; Mechem, *Outlines of Agency* (4th ed.), §§ 173–176. This receives some support from the cases dealing with set-off against the agent: see Article 83.

[78] Article 86.

[79] Ewart, *Estoppel* (1900), p. 247.

[80] Ferson (1951) 4 Vand.L.Rev. 260, 280.

It does not appear that the supposed doctrine of this case enables the principal to sue, any more than does that of apparent authority: and the principal being undisclosed, there can be no ratification.[81]

Rule (3). Contract in writing: evidence to show who is the real   **8–079** **principal.** In *Humble v. Hunter*[82] the argument was accepted that where the contract was in writing, the intervention of the undisclosed principal might be prevented under the parol evidence rule, as being inconsistent with the written contract.[83] This was contrary to the rationale of the cases on the Statute of Frauds, referred to above, which is that the effect of the principal's intervention is to add a contracting party, not to exclude one.[84] Though the case has been followed,[85] it has more often been distinguished,[86] and it has also been judicially questioned.[87] It is obvious that if such a view was readily taken, the intervention of an undisclosed principal would be almost impossible. It is therefore submitted that the undisclosed principal can only be excluded from intervening under the proposition stated in Rule (4) of this Article, and that evidence of such a principal will be admitted unless the exclusion of such a principal is expressed or implied by the terms of the contract, written or unwritten, as explained below.[88] Indeed the dicta of Lord

---

[81] Above, para. 8–071.

[82] (1848) 12 Q.B. 310, Illustration 7.

[83] But compare the arguments of counsel with the judgment given. However, such was the interpretation put on the case in *Formby Brothers v. Formby*, n. 85 below. The argument had been rejected in *Wilson v. Hart* (1817) 1 Moo.C.P. 45.

[84] See above, para. 8–076; Comment to Article 73.

[85] *Formby Brothers v. Formby* (1910) 102 L.T. 116 ("proprietor"), where the court would have followed *Humble v. Hunter* but was prevented by the fact that the matter had not been raised in the lower court (and see on this case Stoljar, p. 223, n. 25); *Rederiaktiebolaget Argonaut v. Hani* [1918] 2 K.B. 247 ("as charterer") (but see Lord Shaw in *Drughorn v. Rederiaktiebolaget Transatlantic* [1919] A.C. 203); *Fawcett v. Star Car Sales Ltd* [1960] N.Z.L.R. 406, 420–425.

[86] *Killick & Co. v. Price & Co. & Lingfield S.S. Co. Ltd* (1896) 12 T.L.R. 263; *Drughorn Ltd v. Rederiaktiebolaget Transatlantic* [1919] A.C. 203 ("charterer"); *Danziger v. Thompson* [1944] K.B. 654, Illustration 8 ("tenant"); *Epps v. Rothnie* [1945] K.B. 562 ("landlord"); *O/Y Wasa S.S. Co. & N.V. Stoomschip Hannah v. Newspaper Pulp & Wood Export* (1949) 82 Ll.L.Rep. 936 ("disponent owner") (where there is a full review of the authorities); *Murphy v. Rae* [1967] N.Z.L.R. 103 ("vendor"); *The Astyanax* [1985] 2 Lloyd's Rep. 109 ("disponent owner": held to act personally).

[87] *Killick & Co. v. Price & Lingfield S.S. Co. Ltd*, n. 86 above, at p. 264 (but see *Formby Brothers v. Formby*, n. 85 above); *Drughorn Ltd v. Rederiaktiebolaget Transatlantic*, n. 86 above at p. 209; *Epps v. Rothnie*, n. 86 above, at p. 565.

[88] *Finzel, Berry & Co. v. Eastcheap Dried Fruit Co.* [1962] 1 Lloyd's Rep. 370, 375; *Murphy v. Rae*, n. 86 above; *Teheran-Europe Co. Ltd v. S.T. Belton (Tractors) Ltd* [1968] 2 Q.B. 545, 552; Davies (1968) 8 U. of W.A.L.Rev. 534; Fridman (1968) 84 L.Q.R. 224, 239–244; McLauchlan, *The Parol Evidence Rule* (Wellington, N.Z., 1976), Chap. 13.

Denman C.J. in *Humble v. Hunter* itself afford some support for this view,[89] and *Humble v. Hunter* may be explained as an example, if a curious one, of such exclusion. This would be a true application of the parol evidence rule to this situation. The relation between the two rules—the rule of law dealing with exclusion of the principal by the express or implied terms of the contract, and the rule of evidence against variation of written contracts by extrinsic evidence—has often been misunderstood.[90]

8–080   **Rule (4). Express or implied exclusion of undisclosed principals.**[91] It is obvious that where the agent contracts for a named principal, no other principal may intervene.[92] Equally, where there is an express term of the contract that the agent is the only party to it, there can be no intervention by an undisclosed principal.[93] It may indeed be prudent to insert such clauses into contracts where it is desired to exclude the possibility of intervention.[94] There can, however, be cases where the agent impliedly contracts that he is principal, or that no other party is involved.[95] Sometimes this implication is derived from the interpretation of words descriptive of the agent himself, and of the contract as a whole, that he alone answers the description in question: this is probably the best interpretation of the cases cited in the preceding paragraph, and it seems that (if the cases are all to be treated as correct) whereas the words "owner" or "proprietor" may perhaps raise such an implication,[96] descriptions of the agent as "landlord", "tenant",

---

[89] See the case explained by a court containing two of the same judges in *Schmaltz v. Avery* (1851) 12 Q.B. 655, 660. See also *Drughorn Ltd v. Rederiaktiebolaget Transatlantic* [1919] A.C. 203, 207 ("a term of the contract that he should contract as owner of that property"); *O/Y Wasa S.S. Co. v. Newspaper Pulp & Wood Export* (1949) 82 Ll.L.Rep. 936.

[90] See Landon (1945) 61 L.Q.R. 130; (1946) 62 L.Q.R. 20; McLauchlan, *op. cit.* n. 88 above.

[91] Ivamy (1951) 18 *Solicitor* 245; Goodhart and Hamson (1932) 4 C.L.J. 320; Powell, pp. 154–166; Glanville Williams, (1945) 23 Can.B.R. 397–416; *Restatement*, §§ 186, 189, 302, 303, 309, 310 and Appendix, reporter's note to § 304.

[92] *Phillips v. Duke of Bucks* (1683) 1 Vern. 227. *Cf. M'Auliffe v. Bicknell* (1835) 2 Cr.M. & R. 263. But see Article 110.

[93] *United Kingdom, etc., Assn. v. Neville* (1887) 19 Q.B.D. 110, Illustration 9; *J.A. Rayner (Mincing Lane) Ltd v. Department of Trade and Industry* [1990] 2 A.C. 418, 516 ("The contract is made between ourselves and yourselves as principals, we alone being liable to you for its performance"). This exception was criticised as illogical by Williston, *Contracts*, rev. ed., § 286. See also *Bart v. British West Indian Airways* [1967] 1 Lloyd's Rep. 239, 243–249, 284–287 (contract regulated by Warsaw Convention).

[94] A non-assignment clause would not necessarily be effective: below, n. 3.

[95] See *Finzel, Berry & Co. v. Eastcheap Dried Fruit Co.* [1962] 1 Lloyd's Rep. 370, 375. It is possible that *Greer v. Downs Supply Co.* [1927] 2 K.B. 28 and *Collins v. Associated Greyhound Racecourses* [1930] 1 Ch. 1 could be so explained, but see below, nn. 6 and 10.

[96] *e.g. Davis v. Capel* [1959] N.Z.L.R. 825.

"disponent owner", "charterer" or "vendor" are less likely to do so.[97] In these cases intervention by an undisclosed principal would be inconsistent with the contract on which he seeks to intervene. "The terms of the contract may, expressly or by implication, exclude the principal's right to sue, and his liability to be sued."[98] But such cases must be exceptional, for if the doctrine were interpreted widely it would make the intervention of an undisclosed principal extremely difficult, whereas in fact it is clear that this is not so. The question is, therefore, when will such an implication be made?

It was formerly arguable that some guidance could be obtained by applying the analogy of the assignment rules, and that it could be said that where the benefit of a contract is not assignable, or its burden could not be vicariously performed,[99] the undisclosed principal cannot intervene.[1] This view has, however, been rejected by the Privy Council in the (perhaps unusual) case of an insurance policy which was unassignable, but where it was found that the identity of the assured was a matter of indifference to the insurer.[2] The main limiting rule is simply therefore that as to express or implied exclusion of the principal.[3] It is clear that this will not often apply. It has been said that "in an ordinary commercial context" it may be assumed that a person is "willing to treat as a party to the contract anyone on whose behalf the agent may have been authorised to contract, unless either the other party manifests his unwillingness or there are other circumstances which would lead the agent to realise that the other party was not so willing."[4]

But there may be other cases where the third party would not have dealt with the principal and objects to his intervention. Are there any

---

[97] See nn. 85, 86, 88 above. Goodhard and Hamson describe such implied exclusion as arising only in "highly peculiar circumstances": (1932) 4 C.L.J. 320, 356. But the decision as to "tenant" can be criticised: *infra*, below, n. 23.

[98] *Siu Yin Kwan v. Eastern Insurance Co. Ltd* [1994] 2 A.C. 199, 207 (Illustration 12) *per* Lord Lloyd of Berwick.

[99] See Chitty, *Contracts* (27th ed.) Vol. 1, §§ 19–024 *et seq.*, 19–046 *et seq.* Intervention on a sale would under this rule rarely be disallowed, for both in the case of assignment and in the case of undisclosed principal, the liability of the original contracting party to the third party remains. But intervention on a loan would rarely be permitted.

[1] This was the view of Goodhart and Hamson (1932) 4 C.L.J. 320.

[2] *Siu Yin Kwan v. Eastern Insurance Co. Ltd* [1994] 2 A.C. 199, Illustration 12. Had it not been for findings of fact, the case would be a straightforward one of unnamed principal: the insurers knew the occupation of the agents and that they did not own the ship. The case seems in fact to be another where facts appropriate to unnamed principals distort the rules for undisclosed principals: see above, para. 8–074.

[3] See *Restatement*, §§ 189, 303, where it is suggested that a specific *non-assignment* clause would not directly exclude the intervention of an undisclosed principal but would provide evidence that the parties intended to exclude such a principal.

[4] *Teheran-Europe Co. Ltd v. S.T. Belton (Tractors) Ltd* [1968] 2 Q.B. 545, 555 *per* Diplock L.J., described by Lord Lloyd of Berwick in the *Siu Yin Kwan* case, n. 2 above, as a "beneficial assumption".

other grounds on which the third party may do so? In *Said v. Butt*[5] a theatre critic bought, as undisclosed principal through an agent, a ticket for a first night performance. He was refused admission. He was held not entitled to sue for breach of contract, apparently on the ground that the formation of the contract was affected by mistake. But this reasoning involves the assumption that the contract is between third party and undisclosed principal, and as we have seen the validity of this reasoning is limited.[6] Further, it does not provide useful guidance: if the contract is made (as this was) with a named person, on such reasoning no other person can ever be a party to it. Since the first night was largely by invitation, this may have been a case where an implied exclusion of the, or any, principal was appropriate: and this may be the best explanation of the decision.

It has been suggested that there should be a simple rule that the undisclosed principal cannot intervene when he knew or should have known at the time of the contract that the principal would not have dealt with him[7]: this rule may be a fair one, but it can only be justified on grounds of being an exception to an admitted anomaly, designed to prevent that anomaly from going too far and interfering with the commercial convenience for which it arose. It would be easier to refuse an order of specific performance in such a case than to refuse an action in damages. But it is probable that such a case would have to be a strong one, for in *Dyster v. Randall & Sons*[8] despite dicta that the result might be otherwise in a case "in which some personal consideration

---

[5] [1920] 3 K.B. 497, Illustration 11. The action was actually against the manager of the theatre for inducing breach of contract. See also *Smith v. Wheatcroft* (1878) 9 Ch.D. 223, 230; *Nelthorpe v. Holgate* (1844) 1 Col.C.C. 203.

[6] See para. 8–070 above; Glanville Williams, (1945) 23 Can.B.R. 397–414; Goodhart and Hamson (1932) 4 C.L.J. 320. *Said v. Butt* is to some extent supported by *Greer v. Downs Supply Co.* [1927] 2 K.B. 28, where a third party made a contract with an agent because the agent owed him money which could be set off, and the undisclosed principal was not permitted to intervene. But the judgments in the case are unsatisfactory (see (1945) 23 Can.B.Rev. 411–412) since it is clear that the set-off could have been used against the principal in any case: see Article 83. See also *Collins v. Associated Greyhound Racecourses Ltd* [1930] 1 Ch. 1 (but on this case see n. 10 below); *Campbellville Gravel Supply Ltd v. Cook Paving Co. Ltd* (1968) 70 D.L.R. (2d) 354.

[7] Treitel, *Law of Contract* (9th ed.), p. 647; see also *Smith v. Wheatcroft*, n. 5 above at p. 230; *Humble v. Hunter* (1848) 12 Q.B. 310, 313 (the undisclosed principal "shall not come forward so as unfairly to prejudice the party sued"). It derives some support from the judgment of Diplock L.J. in *Teheran-Europe Co. Ltd v. S.T. Belton (Tractors) Ltd*, quoted above.

[8] [1926] Ch. 932, Illustration 10, criticised, *Restatement*, Appendix, at p. 524. *Cf. Nash v. Dix* (1898) 78 L.T. 445, where it was held that there was no agency but a purchase for resale. See Smith, [1972B] C.L.J. 197, 219 *et seq.*, considering the relation between these cases and *Berg v. Sadler and Moore* [1937] 2 K.B. 158. See also *Garnac Grain Co. Inc. v. H.M.F. Faure & Fairclough Ltd* [1968] A.C. 1130n.

formed a material ingredient,"[9] a person who through an agent bought land which he knew that the owner would not sell to him was held entitled to specific performance on the grounds that the contract was assignable.[10] There seems to be no satisfactory case where intervention has been prevented on the basis of such a rule and no more, and it would seem that such knowledge by the third party is to be treated as relevant to the implied terms of the contract and no more.

The question whether a principal could, if sued, himself plead that the contract was one excluding his intervention does not appear to have been considered, but there seems no reason why he should not.

Where the contract is procured by misrepresentation, fraudulent or innocent, by agent or principal, the third party may have a defence to an action upon it,[11] and may be able to take proceedings to rescind it.[12] This is not, however, a situation where the principal's intervention is excluded: the contract is simply unenforceable by anyone against the third party. And the rights to rescind and repudiate can be lost. Non-disclosure may sometimes constitute misrepresentation in the rare cases where there is a duty to disclose,[13] but normally failure to mention the principal's existence does not without more constitute misrepresentation.[14]

Discovery against principal. It has been held that where the principal is the real plaintiff and the agent has no interest in the proceedings other than the right to bring them, proceedings by the agent may be stayed unless the principal discloses documents which he would be required to do if he had been a party to the contract.[15] It was said in the case that if there was an undisclosed principal, this would necessarily follow; but in view of the interest of the agent of an undisclosed principal in the contract made, as explained above, this seems doubtful.   8–081

---

[9] At p. 939.

[10] See also *Collins v. Associated Greyhound Racecourses Ltd* [1930] 1 Ch. 1 discussed by Goodhart and Hamson (1932) 4 C.L.J. 320, 352 *et seq.* where an undisclosed principal was not allowed to intervene on a contract to underwrite shares. But the main reason was that he sought to rescind the contract for misrepresentation, which would have prejudiced the third party's rights against the tenant.

[11] *Archer v. Stone* (1898) 78 L.T. 34.

[12] See *Garnac Grain Co. Inc. v. H.M.F. Faure & Fairclough Ltd* [1966] 1 Q.B. 650 at first instance; in C.A., *ibid.* at pp. 685–686; affd. by H.L. [1968] A.C. 1130n. See also Article 81; *Restatement*, § 304.

[13] Chitty, *Contracts* (27th ed.), Vol. 1, §§ 6–009 *et seq.* In general, it may be easier to resist an action for specific performance than to obtain rescission; but see the cases cited in the next note, where specific performance was granted.

[14] *Dyster v. Randall & Sons* [1926] Ch. 932, Illustration 10; criticised, *Restatement*, Appendix at p. 524; *Nash v. Dix* (1898) 78 L.T. 445.

[15] *Abu Dhabi National Tanker Co. v. Product Star Shipping Co. (The Product Star)* [1992] 2 All E.R. 20. And see below, para. 9–010.

8–082   Deeds, bills, notes and cheques. As explained in the following Articles, the doctrine does not apply to deeds, bills, notes or cheques. Deeds depend strictly on their wording. Negotiable instruments pass from hand to hand in circumstances which make it important that the rights and liabilities shall relate only to those persons appearing on the face of the document.

Illustrations

8–083   (1)   S, a solicitor, practised in the name of S and C. C was also a solicitor, but acted as clerk to S. Held, that S, being the real principal, was entitled to sue alone upon a contract made in the name of the firm. [16]

(2)   Gunpowder is bought by a person who appears to be acting on his own account. At a later stage the seller discovers that the buyer was agent for certain mine-owners. He may sue the mine-owners. [17]

(3)   An agent entered into a contract in his own name for the purchase of property, and paid a deposit. Held, that on the default of the vendor, the principal was entitled to sue for the return of the deposit. [18]

(4)   A owned a business, which was carried on in the name of B with B as manager. B appeared to be the principal. The drawing and accepting of bills of exchange were incidental to the ordinary conduct of such a business. A forbade B to draw or accept bills. B accepted a bill in the name in which the business was carried on. Held, A was liable on the bill. [19] *Sed quaere.*

(5)   The manager and licensee of an hotel carried on business in his own name, the principal being undisclosed. The manager was forbidden by the principal to buy cigars on credit, but he bought cigars on credit. Held, the principal was liable for the price of the cigars, it being within the authority usually confided to the manager of an hotel to buy such goods on credit. [20] *Sed quaere.*

(6)   A appointed B as the manager of an hotel owned by A, and the licence was taken out in the name of B, who appeared to be the principal. A told B to order spirits from a certain brewery only, but B disregarded this instruction and ordered whisky from C. Held, A was liable to C for the price of the whisky. [21] *Sed quaere.*

---

[16] *Spurr v. Cass, Cass v. Spurr* (1870) L.R. 5 Q.B. 656. See also *Cothay v. Fennell* (1830) 10 B. & C. 671.

[17] See *Curtis v. Williamson* (1874) L.R. 10 Q.B. 57.

[18] *Duke of Norfolk v. Worthy* (1808) 1 Camp. 337.

[19] *Edmunds v. Bushell and Jones* (1865) L.R. 1 Q.B. 97. See Comment.

[20] *Watteau v. Fenwick* [1893] 1 Q.B. 346. See Comment.

[21] *Kinahan & Co. v. Parry* [1910] 2 K.B. 389. See Comment. But the decision was reversed [1911] 1 K.B. 459, on the ground that there was no evidence that the manager had not bought the goods for his own use.

(7) An agent executed a charterparty in his own name, and was described in the contract as the owner of the vessel. It was held that the principal was not entitled to give evidence to show that the agent contracted on his behalf, so as to enable him to maintain an action on the contract, because such evidence was inconsistent with the statement that the agent was the owner of the vessel. [22]

(8) The expression "tenant" does not negative agency, and oral evidence has been held admissible to show that a person described in a tenancy agreement as the tenant in fact entered into the agreement as agent for another. [23]

(9) A is the managing part-owner of a ship. He becomes a member of a mutual insurance association, and insures the ship under the rules and regulations of that association. By the terms of the policy and rules of the association, the right to recover in respect of losses, and the liability for contributions in the nature of premiums, are confined to members of the association. The other part-owners, not being members of the association, cannot, as undisclosed principals of A, sue for any losses, nor can they be sued for contributions due in respect of the policy, even if A fails to pay them, because the right and liability of the principals to sue and be sued are excluded by the terms of the contract. [24] It would be otherwise, if the liability for contributions is thrown by the policy on the persons assured, without reference to whether they are members of the association or not; or if it is provided that the persons assured shall be liable therefor as if they were members. [25]

(10) P, a developer, knew that T would not sell land to him, and therefore bought it through A, who did not disclose that he was acting as agent. A later requested T to cancel the contract, but P sued for specific performance. Held, he was entitled to succeed. [26] So also when in a similar case the persons wishing to buy the land (a committee of Roman Catholics) knew that the sellers (trustees of a Congregational chapel) would not sell to them, and offered an intermediary a

---

[22] *Humble v. Hunter* (1848) 12 Q.B. 310.

[23] *Danziger v. Thompson* [1944] K.B. 654; *Hanstown Properties Ltd v. Green* (1977) 246 EG 917, C.A. The reasoning is criticised by McLauchlan, *The Parol Evidence Rule* (Wellington, N.Z. 1976) p. 137 on the grounds that the identity of a tenant is likely to be of importance. *Cf. Carberry v. Gardiner* (1936) 36 S.R. (N.S.W.) 559 (assignment of lease).

[24] *United Kingdom Mutual Steamship Assurance Assn. v. Nevill* (1887) 19 Q.B.D. 110; *Montgomerie v. United Kingdom Mutual Steamship Assn.* [1891] 1 Q.B. 370.

[25] *Ocean Iron Steamship Insurance Assn. Ltd v. Leslie* (1889) 22 Q.B.D. 722n; *Great Britain 100 A1 Steamship Insurance Assn. v. Wyllie* (1889) 22 Q.B.D. 710; *British Marine Mutual Insurance Co. v. Jenkins* [1900] 1 Q.B. 299.

[26] *Dyster v. Randall & Sons* [1926] Ch. 932: criticised, *Restatement, Appendix*, at p. 524; *Williams v. Bulat* [1992] 2 Qd.R. 566.

commission to buy the land and resell it to them: but here there was no agency.[27]

(11) P wished to see the first night of a play at a theatre of which T was managing director, but knew that T would not allow a ticket to be sold to him on account of allegations he had previously made about T. He bought a ticket through an intermediary, but when he appeared at the theatre he was refused admission on T's instructions. Held, he could not sue T for inducing a breach of contract by the company that owned the theatre, for there was no breach of contract in refusing him admission: the contract was one on which he had no right to intervene as undisclosed principal.[28]

(12) Shipping agents took out workmen's compensation insurance on the crew of a vessel owned by others. The policy is not assignable, but it is not established that the insurers knew that the agents were not the employers of the crew, and it is found as a fact that the identity of the employers of the crew is a matter of indifference to them. The owners of the vessel can claim under the policy.[29]

Article 79

DEEDS

8–084

(1) Subject to the following exceptions, a principal may not sue or be sued on any deed *inter partes*, even if it is expressed to be executed on his behalf, unless he is described as a party to it and it is executed in his name.[30]

(2) Where an agent who has entered into a deed in his own name is a trustee for his principal of the rights under the deed, the principal may enforce such rights in proceedings to which the agent is a party as plaintiff or defendant.[31]

(3) By virtue of the Law Property Act 1925, s. 56(1), a person may take an immediate interest in land or other property, or the benefit of any condition, right of entry, covenant or agreement over or respecting land or other property, although he is not named as a party to the conveyance or other instrument.

---

[27] *Nash v. Dix* (1898) 78 L.T. 445.
[28] *Said v. Butt* [1920] 3 K.B. 497. See Comment. As to the tort liability, see below, para. 9–115.
[29] *Siu Yin Kwan v. Eastern Insurance Co. Ltd* [1994] 2 A.C. 199, a case on Third Parties (Rights against Insurers) legislation. See above, n. 2.
[30] Illustrations 1–4. See also *Restatement*, §§ 151, 191, 296, 303. The formalities required for deeds are now laid down by the Law of Property (Miscellaneous Provisions) Act 1989, s. 1.
[31] *Harmer v. Armstrong* [1934] Ch. 65, Illustration 5.

(4) By virtue of the Powers of Attorney Act 1971, s. 7(1), the donee of a power of attorney may, if he thinks fit, execute any instrument with his own signature, and, where sealing is required, with his own seal, by the authority of the donor of the power; and every document executed in that manner shall be as effective as if executed or done by the donee with the signature and seal of the donor of the power.

Comment

Rule (1) is an exception to the general principles stated in Articles 73   **8–085** and 74, and to the rules as to undisclosed principal stated in Article 78, and results from the strict rules concerning deeds. It requires signature in a form such as "A, by B his attorney."[32] But the exact form might not matter, for example "B for A" is acceptable.[33] The rules are to some extent modified by statute: and where the deed is not *inter partes* the principal may, if a covenantee, sue in any case.[34] And in general a right of action may be assigned by the normal procedures.

Rule (2) is straightforward from the point of view of principle: if the   **8–086** trustee will not sue, the beneficiary may, joining the trustee as co-defendant. The question when a trust arises, of course, causes more difficulty.[35]

Rule (3) embodies section 56 of the Law of Property Act 1925, the   **8–087** exact application of which is open to dispute and is beyond the scope of this book.[36] It may clearly entitle the principal to sue on the agent's deed in some cases.

Rule (4). Powers of attorney. The effect of section 7(1) of the Powers   **8–088** of Attorney Act 1971 (which supersedes section 123(1) of the Law of Property Act 1925)[37] is not clear. The previous rule was that the holder of a power of attorney should exercise it in the principal's name, *i.e.* sign the principal's name and use his seal.[38] Otherwise the principal, at

---

[32] *Combe's Case* (1613) 9 Co.Rep. 75a; *Frontin v. Small* (1726) 2 Ld.Raym. 1418; *White v. Cuyler* (1795) 6 T.R. 176; *Wilks v. Back* (1802) 2 East 142. *cf.* above, para. 2–023.

[33] *Wilks v. Back*, n. 32 above; and see *Lawrie v. Lees* (1880) 14 Ch. D. 249.

[34] *Cooker v. Child* (1673) 2 Lev. 74; *Sunderland Marine Insurance Co. v. Kearney* (1851) 16 Q.B. 925.

[35] See Snell, *Equity* (29th ed.), p. 96.

[36] See *Beswick v. Beswick* [1968] A.C. 58; Chitty *Contracts* (27th ed.), Vol. 1, §§ 18–056, 18–057.

[37] Re-enacting Conveyancing Act 1881, s. 46.

[38] The requirement of sealing is as abolished by the Law of Property (Miscellaneous Provisions) Act 1989, s. 1, which also provides that in certain circumstances solicitors and licensed conveyancers are conclusively presumed to be authorised to deliver the instrument.

any rate, would not at common law be bound or entitled, though in some cases the agent himself might be bound.[39] It is clear that the agent may now in certain circumstances use his own name and seal and nevertheless render the principal liable and entitled. The first problem is as to whether the section by its words requires that he should have specific authority to act in his own name. Earlier editions of this book took the view (on the former legislation) that it does, but the wording of the section is not clear and it seems unlikely that such authority is required.[40] The second problem is as to whether the principal must in such a case be named in the deed. It seems likely that he must, as otherwise the rule that an undisclosed principal cannot intervene on a deed would have been abolished, yet in *Harmer v. Armstrong*[41] it was clearly assumed to exist, apart from the exception as to trust beneficiaries recognised in that case. The effect of the section is therefore to allow execution by an attorney in his own name: but the principal should be mentioned in the body of the deed, and though it may not be strictly necessary,[42] it is highly desirable that the attorney should express that he executes as attorney or on behalf of the principal, though he need not be so careful in the formula used as under the old law. It is not clear whether the agent is himself discharged from liability in cases where he would hitherto have been bound. The former provision said that the deed "shall be as effectual to all intents" as if the agent had executed it in the principal's name. This made it arguable that the agent was discharged. The removal of these words may be thought to make such a construction less likely. If the provision does have this effect, it would assimilate the law as to deeds with that as to other written contracts.

The provision operates without prejudice to any statutory direction that an instrument is to be executed in the name of an estate owner, and is an alternative to the procedure prescribed by section 74(3) and (4) of the Law of Property Act 1925, (as amended), which deal with execution of conveyances by or on behalf of corporations.[43]

---

[39] See *Appleton v. Binks* (1804) 5 East 148, Illustration 1 to Article 104. It would be more difficult for him to show that he was entitled to sue: see *Frontin v. Small* (1726) 2 Ld.Raym. 1418.

[40] Powell, p. 178; Davidson's *Concise Precedents in Conveyancing* (21st ed.), Vol. 2, p. 447.

[41] [1934] Ch. 65, Illustration 5. (Though in that case the authority had in any case not been given by deed.)

[42] See *Re Whitley Partners Ltd* (1886) 32 Ch.D. 337, 338; but *cf.* Wolstenholme and Turner, *The Conveyancing Acts* (3rd ed.) (1883), p. 99.

[43] s.7(2), (3).

Illustrations

(1) An agent entered into a contract by deed in his own name, the **8–089** principal not being named in it. It was held that the principal was not liable to be sued on the contract. [44]

(2) A shipmaster executed a charterparty by deed in his own name "as agent for the owners." Held, that the owners were not entitled to sue for the freight, because they were not parties to the deed. [45]

(3) An attorney, who was authorised in writing to execute a lease, signed and sealed the lease in and with his own name and seal. It was held that the principal was not entitled to sue on the covenants in the lease, though they were expressed to be made by the tenant with the landlord, because the deed was not executed in his name. [46]

(4) A by deed transferred shares to B. In consequence of the winding up of the company, the transfer could not be registered, and A was compelled to pay a call. A had no right of action for indemnity against B's principal, for whom B acted in taking the transfer. [47]

(5) By a contract under seal made between A and B, A agreed to purchase the copyright in certain periodicals from B. A in fact entered into the contract as agent and trustee for himself and C. Held, in an action brought by C against A and B for a declaration that A was agent and trustee as stated above and for specific performance, that as the agency and trusteeship of A had been established and all necessary parties were before the court, there was jurisdiction to decree specific performance. [48]

Article 80

Bills, Notes and Cheques

(1) A principal is not liable on a bill of exchange, promissory note **8–090** or cheque unless his signature appears on it [49]: but it is not necessary that he should sign with his own hand, it is sufficient if his signature is written by some person by or under his authority. [50]

(2) No person can be liable as acceptor of a bill except the person on whom it is drawn, except where it is accepted for honour. [51]

---

[44] *Re International Contract Co., Pickering's Claim* (1871) L.R. 6 Ch.App. 525.
[45] *Schack v. Anthony* (1813) 1 M. & S. 573.
[46] *Berkeley v. Hardy* (1826) 5 B. & C. 355; *Lord Southampton v. Brown* (1827) 6 B. & C. 718. But the result might now be different by virtue of s.56 of the Law of Property Act 1925.
[49] *Viscount Torrington v. Lowe* (1868) L.R. 4 C.P. 26.
[48] *Harmer v. Armstrong* [1934] Ch. 65.
[49] Bills of Exchange Act 1882, ss. 23, 89.
[50] *ibid.* s.91(1).
[51] *ibid.* s.17(1); *Polhill v. Walter* (1832) 3 B. & Ad. 114; *Steele v. M'Kinlay* (1880) 5 App.Cas. 754. As to acceptance for honour, see Bills of Exchange Act 1882, ss.65–68.

Comment

8–091   These rules can be justified on the ground that negotiable instruments are likely to come into the hands of persons who have no knowledge of the circumstances in which they were issued. Such persons must be able to rely on what appears on the face of the instrument. Undisclosed principals are not liable.

8–092   **Rule (1)** provides another exception to the general rules as to the liability of a principal on his agent's transactions stated in Articles 73, 74 and 78: he cannot be liable on a bill when his name does not appear on it, although his signature may be effected by an agent. If the agent simply writes the principal's name, there is no difficulty. In other cases, the form of representative signature is regulated by section 26 of the Bills of Exchange Act 1882, which reads:

> "(1)   Where a person signs a bill as drawer indorser or acceptor, and adds words to his signature, indicating that he signs for or on behalf of a principal, or in a representative character, he is not personally liable thereon; but the mere addition to his signature of words describing him as an agent, or as filling a representative character, does not exempt him from personal liability.
>
> (2)   In determining whether a signature on a bill is that of the principal or that of the agent by whose hand it is written, the construction most favourable to the validity of the instrument shall be adopted."

Subsection (1) lays down the standard rule for representative signatures. In cases of drawing or indorsing the question is usually as to whether the principal or the agent is the drawer or indorser; to this subsection (2) is not normally relevant, and the matter is decided by application of the main rule, which is discussed elsewhere.[52]
    It should be noted that forged and unauthorised signatures do not bind principals,[53] though a principal may be precluded from setting up the forgery,[54] and may ratify an unauthorised signature.[55] A signature by procuration operates as notice that the agent has but a limited

---

[52] See Article 105. For full citation of the many cases relevant to this section, see Byles, *Bills of Exchange* (26th ed.), pp. 65 *et seq.*; Chalmers and Guest, *Bills of Exchange* (14th ed.), pp. 215 *et seq.*

[53] Bills of Exchange Act 1882, s.24. But as to the meaning of this provision, see Chalmers and Guest, *op. cit.*, n. 52 above, pp. 165 *et seq.*

[54] *Greenwood v. Martins Bank Ltd* [1933] A.C. 51. See further above, para. 8–043.

[55] Chap. 2, Section 3.

authority to sign, and the principal is only bound by such signature if the agent in so signing was acting within the limits of his authority.[56]

Rule (2). Since only the drawee can be liable as acceptor, it may be   **8–093** important to know whether or not a signature is valid as an acceptance; and here section 26(2) may be more often relevant. It seems that where the bill is drawn on an agent, the principal cannot be liable on the agent's acceptance, even though the agent accepts in the principal's name or in a representative character, and with his authority.[57] Where the bill is drawn on the principal, if the agent accepts in the principal's name or using representative words the principal will be liable: but if he accepts in his own name or using descriptive words, the principal will not be liable (and nor will the agent). In either case section 26(2), with its presumption of validity, assists in doubtful cases only: it does not reverse the rule as to representative signatures, nor does it prevent clearly inappropriate signatures from being inoperative.[58]

As regards partnerships, the signature of the firm is equivalent to those of the partners[59]: otherwise, the names of all partners sought to be held liable would have to appear in accordance with section 23 of the Bills of Exchange Act 1882.

The above rules relate to the suing of the principal: whether or not he can sue depends on whether he is the payee, or a holder of the bill, in accordance with the general law.

Illustrations

(1) A bill of exchange is drawn on "Artitalia," a partnership. One   **8–094** partner accepts it with the authority of the other but signs her own name. The other partner is not liable on the bill.[60]

(2) A duly authorised agent draws or indorses a bill, or indorses a note or cheque, in his own name. The principal is not liable on it.[61]

(3) A promissory note is signed "The JS Laundry Ltd, JS, Managing Director." JS is not liable; the company would be.[62]

(4) A promissory note in the form "We promise to pay ... etc." is signed "C D, Director, E F, Secretary, The FE Ltd." The signatories are personally liable and the company is not.[63]

---

[56] Bills of Exchange Act 1882, s.25.
[57] *ibid.* s.17; *Polhill v. Walter* (1832) 3 B. & Ad. 114; *Steele v. M'Kinlay* (1880) 5 App.Cas. 754. For the liability of the agent in this case, see Article 105.
[58] *Britannia Electric Lamp Works v. D. Mandler & Co. Ltd* [1939] 2 K.B. 129.
[59] Partnership Act 1890, s.6. As regards companies, see Companies Act 1985, s.37.
[60] *Geo. Thompson (Aust.) Pty. Ltd v. Vitadello* [1978] V.R. 199.
[61] *Ducarrey v. Gill* (1830) M. & M. 450. And see *Leadbitter v. Farrow* (1816) 5 M. & S. 345, 350.
[62] *Chapman v. Smethurst* [1909] 1 K.B. 927. See also *Britannia Electric Lamp Works Ltd v. D. Mandler & Co. Ltd* [1939] 2 K.B. 129.
[63] *Brebner v. Henderson* 1925 S.C. 643.

(5)   A bill of exchange is addressed to A B, and is accepted "A B for and on behalf of C D." C D is not liable as acceptor, even if A B was expressly authorised to accept the bill on his behalf.[64]

Article 81

Defences to Action by or Against Principal

8–095   (1)   Where a principal sues the other party to a contract made through an agent, the other party has all the defences which he would have had against the principal if the principal had himself made the contract in the same circumstances.[65]

(2)   Where an undisclosed principal sues the other party to a contract, the other party may, in addition to the defences mentioned above, plead all defences which accrued against the agent before he had reasonable notice that the agent was not acting for himself.[66]

(3)   Where the other contracting party sues the principal, the principal, whether disclosed or undisclosed, can plead against him all defences arising out of the transaction with the agent, and defences personal to himself, but not defences personal to the agent.[67]

Comment

8–096   There is little direct English authority for these rules, which closely follow the wording of the *Restatement*, but it is submitted that they are logically correct, though many points of detail remain unsettled. The propositions in Article 83 should be taken as an elaboration of these rules in a specific context.

8–097   **Rule (1). General rule.** The contract being with the principal, the third party should be able to use all defences arising out of the contract itself, and all defences available against the principal himself (*e.g.* set-off, the fact that he is an alien enemy) but not defences and set-offs[68] which he may have against the agent but which are not connected with the instant transaction. It is clear that he can allege fraud,[69]

---

[64] *Polhill v. Walter* (1832) 3 B. & Ad. 114.
[65] See Comment. *cf. Restatement*, §§ 298, 299.
[66] See Comment. *cf. Restatement*, § 308.
[67] See Comment. *cf. Restatement*, §§ 180, 203.
[68] As to payment to or set-off with agent on the same transaction see Article 83.
[69] *Archer v. Stone* (1898) 78 L.T. 34 (action by agent); *Raphael v. Goodman* (1838) 8 A. & E. 565; *Foster v. Green* (1862) 7 H. & N. 881; *Ludgater v. Love* (1881) 44 L.T. 694.

misrepresentation,[70] non-performance, illegality and mistake, where these are attributable to the agent, just as he could against the agent. And where he has such a defence, he can also take proceedings for rescission and restitution.[71] The relevant act of the agent must, however, have been within the authority of that agent, actual or apparent, or else the principal is obviously not affected by it.[72] Where there is fraud or misrepresentation by the principal himself, *a fortiori* this will be a defence to the third party.[73] It was held at first instance in *Garnac Grain Co. Inc. v. H.M.F. Faure and Fairclough Ltd*[74] that where an agent sued on a contract made on behalf of an undisclosed principal, it would be a defence to prove that the contract was induced by the fraud of the undisclosed principal. The decision was reversed on other grounds, but this view was accepted in the Court of Appeal.[75] *A fortiori* such fraud could be pleaded if the undisclosed principal was himself plaintiff.

Rule (2). Undisclosed principal. Here, as a starting-point, the same   **8–098**
rule should apply, *mutatis mutandis*. But as the contract is initially made between third party and agent, the third party should not be prejudiced by the intervention of the undisclosed principal. Therefore the third party should in addition be able to plead against the principal all defences against the agent, including personal defences such as set-offs which accrued before he had reasonable notice of the principal's existence.[76] In the case of settlement with the agent and set-off against the agent, however, some English cases indicate that these can only be pleaded against the principal where he was in some way at fault in misleading the third party: the matter is dealt with in Article 83.

Rule (3). Defences available to principal. The principal should be able   **8–099**
to plead defences arising out of the transaction, and defences personal to himself (*e.g.* that he is a minor, set-off in his favour)[77] but not defences personal to the agent (*e.g.* that the agent is a minor, set-off in favour of the agent), which only the agent could plead.

---

[70] *Mullens v. Miller* (1882) 22 Ch.D. 194; *Winch v. Winchester* (1812) 1 V. & B. 375; *Myers v. Watson* (1851) 1 Sim.(N.S.) 523. As to liability in tort, see para. 8–183 below.
[71] *Wilde v. Gibson* (1848) 1 H.L. Cas. 605; *Stevens v. Legh* (1853) 2 C.L.R. 251; *Wauton v. Coppard* [1899] 1 Ch. 92; *Whurr v. Devenish* (1904) 20 T.L.R. 385.
[72] But see above, para. 8–078.
[73] See *Mullens v. Miller*, n. 70 above.
[74] [1966] 1 Q.B. 650.
[75] See pp. 685–686. See also [1968] A.C. 1130n. (H.L.).
[76] *Sims v. Bond* (1833) 5 B. & Ad. 389, 393; *Browning v. Provincial Insurance Co. of Canada* (1873) L.R. 5 P.C. 263, 272–273; *Rabone v. Williams* (1785) 7 T.R. 360. And see above, para. 8–070; below, para. 9–012.
[77] See *Restatement*, § 203.

In *Collins v. Associated Greyhound Racecourses Ltd*[78] it was held that an undisclosed principal could not rescind, for misrepresentation in the prospectus, a contract to underwrite part of an issue of shares when he alone, and not the agent, was proved to have relied on the misrepresentation. This seems correct, and probably follows from the proposition that the third party cannot by the principal's intervention be deprived of his rights against the agent should be desire to exercise them[79]: the principal cannot therefore deprive him of them by rescinding the whole contract unless it is clear that the agent could do so, or at least that the agent would have a valid defence to proceedings against him.[80]

Article 82

SETTLEMENT BETWEEN PRINCIPAL AND AGENT AFFECTING RECOURSE TO PRINCIPAL

8–100

(1) Except as provided in this Article, a principal is not discharged by the circumstances that he has paid or settled or otherwise dealt to his prejudice with the agent.

(2) Where a debt or obligation has been contracted through an agent, and the principal is induced by the conduct of the creditor reasonably to believe that the agent has paid the debt or discharged the obligation or that the creditor has elected to look to the agent alone for its payment or discharge, and in consequence of such belief pays, or settles or otherwise deals to his prejudice with the agent, the creditor is not permitted to deny, as between himself and the principal, that the debt has been paid or the obligation discharged or that he has elected to give exclusive credit to the agent so as to discharge the principal.[81]

(3) (Semble,) where an undisclosed principal settles with his agent at a time when the third party still does not know that the agent acted for a principal, the principal is discharged.[82]

---

[78] [1930] 1 Ch. 1.

[79] Above, para. 8–098; *O'Herlihy v. Hedges* (1803) 1 Sch. & Lef. 123; see also *Montgomerie v. United Kingdom etc., Ass.* [1891] 1 Q.B. 370, 372.

[80] See Goodhart and Hamson (1932) 4 C.L.J. 320, 353 *et seq.* Despite dicta in the case to the contrary, it is doubtful whether this was a situation where the undisclosed principal could not intervene at all, for shares are transferable, and the agent would be liable for any loss.

[81] See Comment; *Restatement*, § 183; as to election, Article 84.

[82] See Comment.

Comment

General rule. In general, the right of a third party is not affected by   **8–101**
the fact that the principal has paid or otherwise adjusted his accounts
with the agent[83]: this is a transaction with which the third party has no
concern, and the mere fact that he delays in enforcing his claim, or in
making application to the principal for payment of the debt or discharge
of the obligation, is irrelevant, unless there are special circumstances
rendering the delay misleading.[84]

Exceptions. But there may be cases where such third party is   **8–102**
precluded from suing the principal, other than under the rules relating
to merger and election (though the two overlap).[85] Two different lines
of reasoning are to be found in the cases: (i) the principal may be
discharged in such a case where the third party has led him to suppose
that he should settle with the agent; (ii) the principal is discharged
where hardship would be caused to him if he were forced to pay the
third party.

First view: estoppel. The first view, a form of estoppel, is more   **8–103**
generally accepted. Thus the principal is discharged from liability by
paying the agent where the third party requests payment by the agent,[86]
or leads the principal to believe that the agent has paid,[87] or that he
looks to the agent alone for payment.[88] If this view is correct, since the
discharge of the principal is based on the action of the third party in
misleading him,[89] there can, at least normally, be no such discharge
while the principal is undisclosed, for the third party could not make

---

[83] *Kymer v. Suwercropp* (1807) 1 Camp. 109; *Waring v. Favenck* (1807) 1 Camp. 85;
Heald v. Kenworthy (1855) 10 Exch. 739; *Macfarlane v. Giannacopulo* (1858) 3 H. & N.
860; *Irvine & Co. v. Watson & Sons* (1880) 5 Q.B.D. 414.
[84] See *Davison v. Donaldson* (1882) 9 Q.B.D. 623, Illustration 6.
[85] See Article 84, esp. at para. 8–119.
[86] *Smyth v. Anderson* (1849) 7 C.B. 21. When the agent paid by the principal is also the
agent of the third party, normal principles of agency law must be invoked to ascertain
whether the agent has authority to receive payment for the third party. See *Miller v.
Douglas* (1886) 56 L.J.Ch. 91.
[87] *Horsfall v. Fauntleroy* (1830) 10 B. & C. 755; *Wyatt v. Hertford* (1802) 3 East 147,
Illustration 1; *MacClure v. Schemeil* (1871) 20 W.R. 168, Illustration 3; but *cf. Irvine &
Co. v. Watson & Sons* (1880) 5 Q.B.D. 414, Illustration 5.
[88] *Smith v. Ferrand* (1827) 7 B. & C. 19, Illustration 2; *Smethurst v. Mitchell* (1859) 1 E.
& E. 623, as explained in *Davison v. Donaldson,* n. 84 above; *cf. Hopkins v. Ware* (1869)
L.R. 4 Ex. 268, Illustration 4. A further line of reasoning appears here which is not clearly
distinguished: that of taking the agent's bill in satisfaction of the principal's debt. See
below, para. 8–121, n. 47.
[89] *Kymer v. Suwercropp* (1807) 1 Camp. 109; *Heald v. Kenworthy* (1855) 10 Exch. 739;
Irvine & Co. v. Watson & Sons (1880) 5 Q.B.D. 102; *ibid.,* 414; *Davison v. Donaldson*
(1882) 9 Q.B.D. 623.

any representation to someone of whose existence he was at the time of making the supposed representation ignorant.[90]

8–104   **Second view: prejudice of principal.** The second view is that the third party cannot sue the principal where the principal would be unfairly prejudiced were he to do so.[91] This is a looser formulation which stresses the position the principal rather than that of the third party and has its origin in old cases,[92] some of which can now be, and have been, re-explained in terms of the first view.[93] But this second view, if correct, could of course apply to undisclosed principals, and it was so applied in *Armstrong v. Stokes*,[94] where it was held that a third party could not sue an undisclosed principal who had in good faith paid the agent at a time when the third party still knew of no principal. In that case a reconciliation of the two views previously attempted by Parke B.,[95] that it would only be an unfair prejudice to the principal for the third party to sue him where that third party had by his conduct induced the principal to believe that a settlement had been made with the agent, was specifically rejected by Blackburn J.

But in the leading cases of *Irvine & Co. v. Watson & Sons*[96] and *Davison v. Donaldson*[97] the views of Parke B. were preferred, and *Armstrong v. Stokes* was explained as a special case where the third party, by virtue of local usage,[98] dealt with the agent as sole principal and it was reasonable for the principal to believe that he had so dealt.

8–105   **Different rule for undisclosed principals.** It is submitted that any difficulty there may be is caused by an assumption that the same rule should be applied to disclosed and to undisclosed principal cases, and in particular by a failure to distinguish between disclosed but unnamed principals and true undisclosed principals. As has already been pointed out, the true undisclosed principal's position is a very special one.[99]

---

[90] See *Campbell v. Hicks* (1858) 28 L.J.Ex. 70. This argument is, however, not found to be conclusive in other situations: see Articles 78(2), 86, 87.

[91] Some cases even refer to an alteration of the accounts between principal and agent as avoiding the principal's liability: *Thomson v. Davenport*, n. 92 below; *Curtis v. Williamson* (1874) L.R. 10 Q.B. 57. But this must be too wide: see, *e.g. Waring v. Favenck* (1807) 1 Camp. 85 (principal cannot set off against third party money owed to him by agent).

[92] Principally the judgment of Bayley J. in *Thomson v. Davenport* (1829) 9 B. & C. 78.

[93] See *Smyth v. Anderson* (1849) 7 C.B. 21 and *Wyatt v. Hertford* (1802) 3 East 147, Illustration 1, explained in *Heald v. Kenworthy*, n. 89 above; *Smethurst v. Mitchell* (1859) 1 E. & E. 623 explained in *Davison v. Donaldson*, n. 89 above.

[94] (1872) L.R. 7 Q.B. 598, Illustration 7.

[95] In *Heald v. Kenworthy* (1855) 10 Exch. 739.

[96] (1880) 5 Q.B.D. 414, Illustration 5.

[97] (1882) 9 Q.B.D. 623, Illustration 6.

[98] Among Manchester commission merchants: see above, para. 1–018; also Article 71.

[99] Above, paras. 8–072 *et seq.*

Where the principal is disclosed, the first, or estoppel view is clearly appropriate: and this is so whether he is named or unnamed. It seems to be the latter situation which *Irvine & Co. v. Watson & Sons*[1] and *Davison v. Donaldson*[2] concern. In a true undisclosed principal situation, however, the third party deals on the credit of the agent alone and reasoning based on the notion that the contract is that of the principal (the estoppel view) is inappropriate. Rather it may be said that the principal "has done his duty to customers of the agent if he has seen to it that the agent is properly kept in funds to meet his obligations."[3] Thus where at the time of payment the third party still gave credit to the agent and knew of no principal, it may be right to hold the principal discharged. This was in fact the situation to which Blackburn J. confined his decision in *Armstrong v. Stokes*[4]; he specifically excluded "the case of the broker, who avowedly acts for a principal (though not necessarily named)." Of the three judges in *Irvine & Co. v. Watson & Sons*[5] only one, Bramwell L.J., doubted whether the undisclosed principal case was rightly distinguished from the general rule.[6] A special rule for undisclosed principal situations is therefore tentatively formulated above.

Illustrations

(1)   A creditor takes a security from the agent of his debtor, and gives the agent a receipt for the debt. The principal deals to his detriment with the agent on the faith of the receipt. The principal is discharged from liability to the creditor.[7]   **8–106**

(2)   An agent of a debtor offers to pay the debt either in cash or by a bill of exchange. The creditor takes a bill in payment, and it is dishonoured. If the agent had funds of the principal's with which to pay the debt, or if the principal deals to his prejudice with the agent on the faith of his having paid it, the principal is discharged from liability to the creditor.[8]

---

[1] n. 96 above.

[2] n. 97 above. Also *Thomson v. Davenport* (1829) 9 B. & C. 78. See further *Sopwith Aviation & Engineering Co. Ltd v. Magnus Motors Ltd* [1928] N.Z.L.R. 433 (principal disclosed).

[3] Mechem, *Principles of Agency* (4th ed.), § 186. See Reynolds, [1983] C.L.P. 119, 133–135. See also (1947) 18 Mississippi L.J. 436.

[4] n. 98 above. But *cf.* Higgins (1965) 28 M.L.R. 167, 175–178.

[5] n. 96 above.

[6] See pp. 417–418; *cf.* Baggallay L.J. at p. 419 and Brett L.J. at p. 421. See also the judgment of Jessel M.R. in *Davison v. Donaldson* (1892) 9 Q.B.D. 623, 628.

[7] *Wyatt v. Hertford* (1802) 3 East 147; *Smyth v. Anderson* (1849) 7 C.B. 21: see n. 93 above.

[8] *Smith v. Ferrand* (1827) 7 B. & C. 19. But see n. 88 above.

(3)   Goods were sold, on the terms that they should be paid for cash on delivery, to an agent who appeared to be buying on his own account. The seller omitted to enforce cash payment, and the principal, not knowing that the seller had not been paid, paid the agent for the goods. Held, that the principal was discharged.[9]

(4)   The agent of a debtor paid the debt by means of his own cheque, and the creditor neglected to present the cheque for four weeks, when it was dishonoured and the agent absconded. There was a reasonable chance that the cheque would have been honoured if it had been presented within three weeks, and the principal had dealt to his detriment with the agent on the faith of the payment. Held, that the principal was discharged.[10]

(5)   A employed a broker to buy oil. The broker bought from B, telling him that he was acting for a principal, the terms being that the oil should be paid for by "cash on or before delivery." B delivered the oil without payment, and A, not knowing that B had not been paid, in good faith paid the broker. The broker soon afterwards became insolvent, and B sued A for the price of the oil. It was proved that it was not the invariable custom in the oil trade to insist on prepayment in the case of a sale for "cash on or before delivery." Held, that, in the absence of such an invariable custom, the mere omission to insist on prepayment was not such conduct as would reasonably induce A to believe that the broker had paid for the oil, and that, therefore, A was liable to B for the price.[11]

(6)   Stores are sold to the managing owner of a ship. The supplier applies for payment but does not obtain it. The managing owner's principal settles accounts with his agent three months after the goods were supplied, and again two years later. More than three years after the supply of the goods, the agent becomes bankrupt. There has been no such conduct on the part of the supplier as to prevent his suing the principal.[12]

(7)   Commission merchants, who act sometimes for themselves and sometimes as agents, regularly buy shirting from X on credit. X never inquires whether the commission merchants are acting for themselves or not. They subsequently stop payment. It is discovered that the shirting was bought for Y on a commission basis and sent to him after being bleached. Y had paid for the shirtings the day after receipt and before the commission merchant stopped payment. Y is not liable to pay again.[13]

---

[9] *MacClure v. Schemeil* (1871) 20 W.R. 168 (but the judgments proceed principally on the basis of election). *cf. Kymer v. Suwercropp* (1807) 1 Camp. 109.
[10] *Hopkins v. Ware* (1869) L.R. 4 Ex. 268; *cf. Everett v. Collins* (1810) 2 Camp. 515.
[11] *Irvine & Co. v. Watson & Sons* (1880) 5 Q.B.D. 102; *ibid.*, 414.
[12] See *Davison v. Donaldson* (1882) 9 Q.B.D. 623.
[13] *Armstrong v. Stokes* (1872) L.R. 7 Q.B. 598.

Article 83

SETTLEMENT WITH OR SET-OFF AGAINST AGENT AFFECTING RIGHTS OF PRINCIPAL

(1) Except as provided in this Article, the defendant, in an action **8–107** by the principal, has no right to set off any claim he may have against the agent personally[14]; and the principal is not bound by a payment to or settlement with the agent unless that payment or settlement was made in the ordinary course of business and in a manner actually or apparently authorised by him.[15]

(2) A person who, in dealing with an agent, reasonably believes that the agent is the principal in the transaction is discharged from liability by payment to or settlement with the agent in any manner which would have operated as a discharge if the agent had been the principal, and is entitled, as against the principal, to the same right of set-off in respect of any debt due from the agent personally as he would have been entitled to if the agent had been the principal; provided that he had not, at the time when the payment to or settlement took place, or the set-off accrued, received notice that the agent was not in fact the principal.[16]

Comment

Rule (1). General rule. A set-off against an agent is a defence against **8–108** him personally: therefore the third party cannot use it against a disclosed principal by virtue of the rules stated in Article 81, unless this is authorised by the principal.[17] And the third party is only discharged by settlement with the agent if the latter had authority, actual or apparent, to receive it, in accordance with the principles explained in Chapter 3.[18] However, if the money is paid over to the principal the third party is, obviously, discharged. And there are cases where an agent, for example an auctioneer, may be regarded as contracting independently with the third party.[19] In such a case, the right of the principal to sue on the contract is subservient to that of the agent: and a

---

[14] *i.e.* unconnected with the instant transaction. See Illustrations 6–10; *Restatement*, § 299.
[15] See Comment and Illustrations 1–3. See also *Mooney v. Williams* (1905) 3 C.L.R. 1.
[16] See Comment.
[17] As in *Barker v. Greenwood* (1837) 2 Y. & C.Ex. 414, Illustration 2 to Article 28; *Stewart v. Aberdein* (1838) 4 M. & W. 211. *Cf. Young v. White* (1844) 7 Beav. 506.
[18] See esp. Article 28.
[19] See below, paras. 9–009, 9–021.

payment to or settlement with the agent may operate as a discharge, notwithstanding that the person making the payment or settlement has had notice from the principal or trustee in bankruptcy not to pay the agent; and such payment or settlement may be by way of set-off or settlement of accounts between the agent and the person making the settlement.[20]

8–109   **Rule (2). Undisclosed principal.**[21] Where the principal is undisclosed, and the third party therefore believes that the agent is dealing on his own account, the third party may use all the defences, including set-offs and other matters personal to the agent,[22] which had already accrued (whether on the original account or not, and whether previously or subsequently to the original transaction[23]) against the agent prior to the discovery of the principal,[24] and is discharged by payment to the agent prior to such time.[25] So also the third party, before he has notice of the principal's existence, may vary the contract by agreement with the agent.[26]

All this is obviously reasonable, but the principle justifying it is not certain, and there may be differences of application, depending upon what that principle is. One approach, which, it is submitted, is the better, would favour the third party, and holds him entitled to take advantage of such defences provided he believed the agent to be principal, on the ground that the principal intervenes on the agent's contract and must do so, like an assignee, subject to equities.[27]

The other approach concentrates on the position of the principal[28] and only holds him bound by such defences if he has done something towards misleading the third party, as by giving the agent possession of

---

[20] Illustrations 4, 5. See also below, para. 10–010.

[21] See Derham, *Set-Off* (1987), pp. 175 *et seq.*; Wood, *English and International Set-Off* (1989), Chap. 19.

[22] See Article 81, Illustrations 1, 3; *Rabone v. Williams* (1785) 7 T.R. 360n.; *George v. Clagett* (1979) 7 T.R. 359; *Ex p. Dixon, re Henley* (1876) 4 Ch.D. 133. Where there are mutual credits between the agent and the other contracting party, in order to constitute a right of set-off as against the principal, each of the debts must be liquidated: *Turner v. Thomas* (1871) L.R. 6 C.P. 610.

[23] It is submitted that this is the best view, though there seems to be no clear authority. For an exhaustive, though now dated, summary of English and American cases on this and related topics, see 53 A.L.R. Annotated 414 (1928).

[24] Illustrations 9, 10; *Mann v. Forrester* (1814) 4 Camp. 60.

[25] *Coates v. Lewes* (1808) 1 Camp. 444; *Curlewis v. Birkbeck* (1863) 3 F. & F. 894.

[26] *Blackburn v. Scholes* (1810) 2 Camp. 341.

[27] *cf. Rabone v. Williams* (1785) 7 T.R. 360n.; *George v. Clagett* (1797) 7 T.R. 359; *Ramazotti v. Bowring* (1859) 7 C.B.(N.S.) 851, 856; *Turner v. Thomas* (1871) L.R. 6 C.P. 610, 613; *Montgomerie v. U.K. Mutual Steamship Assn.* [1891] 1 Q.B. 370, 372. And see Article 81(2).

[28] See *Baring v. Corrie* (1818) 2 B. & A. 137.

goods. The fact that he is bound is said to depend on estoppel.[29] This reasoning seems to arise to some extent from a confusion with the rules as to apparent ownership,[30] where the validity of a disposition of property is in issue and an estoppel is required to displace the operation of the property-protecting maxim *nemo dat quod non habet*. In the present case, however, the validity of the contract is not disputed and no special reasoning is therefore required: a person contracting with another is surely entitled to assume that the other contracts for himself and that he can therefore safely pay the other or plead set-off against him unless he has reason to believe the contrary, and to this the fault, or lack of it, of a person unknown to him is not conclusive. Further, it is difficult to see how a person can ever rely on the representation of someone of whom he has not heard: the same criticism applies to the doctrine of apparent ownership, and this has therefore to receive a special and somewhat involved justification in terms of estoppel by conduct,[31] which can here be avoided. Finally, the conditions giving rise to estoppel in this case appear to fall short of those required to give rise to apparent ownership: it is now settled that apparent ownership is not created by merely giving the possession of goods to another,[32] whereas it seems that the estoppel in this situation is raised by such conduct without more.[33]

Notice as to principal's existence. Under each approach it is clear   8–110
that, while it is said that the doctrine of constructive notice is not applicable in commercial transactions,[34] the third party may be taken to have notice that the agent has or may have a principal, *e.g.* by the

---

[29] *Cooke & Sons v. Eshelby* (1887) 12 App.Cas. 271, 278 (Illustration 7); *cf.* p. 283. See also *Fish v. Kempton* (1849) 7 C.B. 687; *Ramazotti v. Bowring* (1859) 7 C.B.(N.S.) 851; *Drakeford v. Piercy* (1866) 7 B. & S. 515.

[30] Article 86. See the same confusion in *Lloyds & Scottish Finance Ltd v. Williamson* [1965] 1 W.L.R. 404. But *cf.* Mechem, *Outlines of Agency* (4th ed.), §§ 177–183.

[31] See Article 86 and Comment.

[32] See Article 86.

[33] *Borries v. Imperial Ottoman Bank* (1873) L.R. 9 C.P. 38; *Rabone v. Williams*, n. 27 above; *George v. Clagett*, n. 27 above; *Ex p. Dixon, re Henley* (1876) 4 Ch.D. 133; *Knight v. Matson & Co.* (1903) 22 N.Z.L.R. 293. The old cases usually required that possession be given to a *factor*, who had authority to and often did sell in his own name, as opposed to a broker who should not—indeed the distinction between them was largely worked out in this connection: see *Baring v. Corrie*, n. 28 above; *Semenza v. Brinsley* (1865) 18 C.B.(N.S.) 467; *Drakeford v. Piercy* (1866) 7 B. & S. 515. *Cooke & Sons v. Eshelby*, n. 29 above; para. 1–040, above. If these were the only cases, this could rank as an extra feature over and above delivery of possession (see Comment to Article 86). But the doctrine was also applied to brokers: see *Coates v. Lewis* (1808) 1 Camp. 444; *Blackburn v. Scholes* (1810) 2 Camp. 341; and in any case, decisions could not turn on that distinction today. This difference seems to have been ignored in *Lloyds & Scottish Finance v. Williamson*, n. 30 above, where these cases were cited, but passing of property was in issue.

[34] *Manchester Trust v. Furness* [1895] 2 Q.B. 539; *Greer v. Downs Supply Co.* [1927] 2 K.B. 28; *Borries v. Imperial Ottoman Bank* (1873) L.R. 9 C.P. 38; but see Article 75 and above, para. 8–074.

nature of the agent's occupation[35] or because the fact or possibility is known to his own agent.[36] Under the first approach there would not be an equity in favour of the third party: under the second, this prejudice would not have been caused by the principal's conduct.

8–111   **Preferable approach.** Although the second approach was adopted by the House of Lords in *Cooke & Sons v. Eshelby*[37] it is submitted that, as in the case of settlement by the principal with the agent, previously discussed,[38] the difficulty arises from the failure to distinguish between disclosed principal cases and undisclosed principal cases. The latter type of case is a very special one and may not be rightly subsumed under normal agency principles.[39] The estoppel approach is based on the notion that the contract is that of the principal, and hence is again only appropriate to the case of the disclosed principal, whether named or unnamed.

Where the third party knows of no principal and this is reasonable in the circumstances it seems inappropriate and indeed unfair to him to require fault in the principal before set-off against the agent may be valid or settlement with the agent effective. The third party may have dealt with the agent precisely because the agent was indebted to him. Where the principal cannot be said to have been at fault, his intervention could on the estoppel approach only be prevented under the rules preventing intervention which is inconsistent with the express or implied terms of the contract,[40] rules which are of rare application.[41] It is therefore submitted that in the case of undisclosed principals, the analogy of the assignee intervening subject to equities should be followed, and Rule (2) has been modified to permit this.[42] *Cooke & Sons v. Eshelby*[43] is a marginal case where the agent (a broker)

---

[35] Notably if he is a broker: *Baring v. Corrie* (1818) 2 B. & A. 137, which was a leading case on the position of brokers as opposed to factors (see above, n. 33); *Cooke & Sons v. Eshelby* (1887) 12 App.Cas. 271. It is not, of course, necessary that the actual principal is known: *Maanss v. Henderson* (1801) 1 East 335; *Semenza v. Brinsley*, n. 33 above: *Mildred v. Maspons* (1883) 8 App. Cas. 874.

[36] *Dresser v. Norwood* (1864) 17 C.B.(N.S.) 446, Illustration 6.

[37] (1887) 12 App. Cas. 271, Illustration 7: treated as correct in *Cooper v. Strauss & Co.* (1898) 14 T.L.R. 233 and *Wester Moffat Colliery v. Jeffrey* 1911 S.C. 346. See also *Owens v. Harris Bros.* (1932) 34 W.A.L.R. 110. In *Montagu v. Forwood* [1893] 2 Q.B. 350, Illustration 10, the emphasis on fault is not so strong, and indeed on the facts stated in the official report it is not easy to see how the principal was at fault. But further facts appear in the report at 69 L.T. 371. See also Powell, pp. 174–178.

[38] Article 82.

[39] See Comment to Article 78.

[40] As in *Greer v. Downs Supply Co.* [1927] 2 K.B. 28.

[41] See above, para. 8–080.

[42] The wording in earlier editions was "A person who, in dealing with an agent, is led by the conduct of the principal to believe, and does in fact believe ... etc."

[43] (1887) 12 App.Cas. 271, Illustration 7.

sometimes dealt on his own account and sometimes as an agent: the third party said that he had no belief one way or the other as to which was the case on this occasion. It is thus not clear whether the principal should have been treated as undisclosed or merely as unnamed. The decision against the third party may or may not have been a fair one on the facts.[44]

The two approaches will normally yield the same result: for a principal who uses the services of an agent whom he directs not to disclose his name, or who he knows does not disclose the existence of his principals, can be regarded as leading the third party to suppose that the agent acts for himself.[45] The same is true where, as often, he gives the agent possession of goods. But there can be a difference. Where he does not transfer such possession, and does not do anything that facilitates the deception of the third party, but simply tells the agent to contract in his (the principal's) name, and the agent disobeys and contracts in his own name, the principal would on the estoppel view not be bound by set-offs against, and payments to, the agent.[46]

Illustrations

(1) A traveller offers a sample of goods to a tradesman with whom he has had previous dealings: the tradesman knows that the traveller is probably acting for someone else. The tradesman orders coats as per sample, and they are sent to him by the supplier. The traveller was working for the supplier on this occasion only, having represented to the supplier that he could obtain an order from the tradesman. Payment to the traveller, there being an invoice bearing the supplier's name, is no discharge to the tradesman.[47]   **8–112**

(2) A firm employed A, a traveller, to carry with him for sale parcels of sponges. It was A's duty, on concluding a bargain, to forward particulars of the transaction to the firm. The firm would then send to the customer an invoice and (monthly) a statement of account. The statement of account contained three notices: (1) "Cheques to be crossed." (2) "All cheques to be made payable to the firm." (3) "No receipt valid unless on firm's printed form to be attached hereto." B dealt thus with the firm for some years. Between 1905 and 1908 A sold three parcels of sponges to B. In respect of two of these sales A induced B to pay by cheque payable to him. For the third parcel B paid A in cash. A had no authority to receive in payment anything except crossed

---

[44] It was criticised by Pollock (1887) 3 L.Q.R. 358. See also Reynolds [1983] C.L.P. 119, 122–125.

[45] See *Semenza v. Brinsley* (1865) 18 C.B.(N.S.) 467; *Ex p. Dixon, re Henley* (1876) 4 Ch.D. 133 (where the agent acted contrary to instructions).

[46] *Restatement*, § 306, comment *a*. But *cf. Ex p. Dixon, re Henley*, n. 45 above.

[47] *Butwick v. Grant* [1924] 2 K.B. 483. See also Article 28.

cheques in favour of the firm. A fraudulently appropriated the three sums to himself. Held, that the payments to A were valid against the firm, for the notices in the statements of accounts did not contain sufficient intimation to their customer that A was not authorised to receive payment for goods delivered in cash or by a cheque in his favour cashable at once.[48]

(3) A broker sells goods in the name of his principal to A, who pays the broker for them. The broker absconds without paying over the money to the principal. A is liable to the principal for the price of the goods, unless the broker had authority, or was held out by the principal as having authority, to receive payment, and the mere fact that the principal had on previous occasions authorised him to receive payment for goods sold on his behalf is not sufficient evidence of such authority or holding out.[49]

(4) A factor who has a lien on goods for advances sells the goods in his own name. The buyer, though he knew that the factor was acting as an agent, is, to the extent of the factor's lien, discharged by a payment to him, even if the payment be by way of set-off,[50] or be made after the bankruptcy of the principal, and after notice from the trustee in bankruptcy not to pay the factor.[51]

(5) A factor who had a lien on goods in excess of the value sold the goods to A, to whom he was indebted. The factor became bankrupt. A gave credit for the price of the goods, and proved in the bankruptcy for the residue of his debts against the factor. Held, that this settlement was a good answer to an action by the principal against A for the price.[52]

(6) A broker bought goods on behalf of A from a factor who sold them on behalf of B. The broker knew that the factor sold the goods on behalf of a principal, but A thought that he was selling his own goods. B sued A for the price. Held, that A was bound by the knowledge of his broker, and therefore had no right to set off a debt to him from the factor.[53]

(7) A broker who was entrusted by his principal with the possession of goods sold them in his own name without disclosing the principal. The buyer knew that the broker sometimes sold goods in his own name, though acting as a broker, and sometimes sold goods of his own, and in this case had no particular belief one way or the other. Held, that the

---

[48] *International Sponge Importers Ltd v. Andrew Watt & Sons* [1911] A.C. 279. See also Article 28.

[49] *Linck, Moeller & Co. v. Jameson & Co.* (1885) 2 T.L.R. 206.

[50] *Warner v. M'Kay* (1836) 1 M. & W. 591.

[51] *Drinkwater v. Goodwin* (1775) Cowp. 251.

[52] *Hudson v. Granger* (1821) 5 B. & A. 27. These cases, like that of the auctioneer, are nowadays best explained as involving collateral contracts. See below, paras. 9–009, 9–021.

[53] *Dresser v. Norwood* (1864) 17 C.B.(N.S.) 466. See the same case, Article 97, Illustration 12.

buyer was not entitled, in an action by the principal for the price, to set off a debt due from the broker personally.[54]

(8)   A, who acted as shipping agent for B, a merchant in Havana, consigned in his own name to C a cargo of tobacco. C, according to his instructions, insured the cargo for the benefit of all concerned, having had notice that there was a principal. The cargo was lost, and the insurance money was paid to C after he had received notice that B claimed it. Held, that C was not entitled to set off, as against B, debts due to him from A personally.[55]

(9)   Goods were consigned to an agent for sale. The agent pledged the goods to brokers as security for a specific advance, and authorised them to sell. The broker sold the goods, but before receiving the proceeds had notice that the principal was the owner, and that he claimed the proceeds. Held, that the principal was entitled to the balance of the proceeds after deducting the amount of the advance, and that the brokers were not entitled to set off such balance against a general account due to them from the agent.[56] It would be otherwise, if they had received the proceeds in the bona fide belief that they belonged to the agent, and had credited the amount in the account with the agent before receiving notice of the principal's claim.[57]

(10)   A employed B to collect general average contributions under an insurance policy. B instructed a broker to collect the contributions, the broker believing him to be the principal. B became bankrupt. In an action by A against the broker for the contributions, as money received to his use, it was held that the broker was entitled to set off a debt due from B.[58]

Article 84

MERGER AND ELECTION: RELEASE OF PRINCIPAL

(1)   Where an agent enters into a contract on which he is **8–113** personally liable, and judgment is obtained against him on it, the judgment, though unsatisfied is, so long as it subsists, a bar to any proceedings against the principal, undisclosed or (perhaps) disclosed, on the contract.

(2)   (Perhaps), where an agent enters into a contract on behalf of an undisclosed principal or on such terms that he is personally

---

[54] *Cooke & Sons v. Eshelby* (1887) 12 App.Cas. 271.

[55] *Mildred, Goyeneche & Co. v. Maspons y Hermano* (1883) 8 App.Cas. 874.

[56] *Kaltenbach v. Lewis* (1885) 10 App.Cas. 617. See on this case (1932) 4 C.L.J. 320, 333–334.

[57] *ibid.*; *New Zealand and Australian Land Co. v. Watson* (1881) 7 Q.B.D. 374.

[58] *Montagu v. Forwood* [1893] 2 Q.B. 350. See also *Knight v. Matson & Co.* (1903) 22 N.Z.L.R. 293; *Curlewis v. Birkbeck* (1863) 3 F. & F. 894.

liable on it together with his principal, and the other contracting party, discovering or knowing or discovering who is the real principal, elects to pursue his rights against the agent, he is bound by his election and cannot afterwards sue the principal on the contract. The question whether or not he has so elected is a question of fact.

(3) Except as provided in this Article, the liability of the principal, whether disclosed or undisclosed, upon a contract made on his behalf is not affected by fact that the agent is personally liable on the contract.[59]

Comment

8–114   **Questions of principle.** The propositions stated above represent a conservative attempt to state the law emerging from the many and rather confused decisions on this topic. They are, however, difficult propositions to justify in principle.[60] It is difficult to see in principle why, where principal and agent are both liable on a contract, any doctrine of merger or election should bar a person who has proceeded against one from proceeding against the other. Only satisfaction of the claim should normally be a bar.

The real basis of such notions of merger and election seems to be an assumption, common in older cases, that the contract was *either* with the principal *or* with the agent. In cases of disclosed principal these were in effect alternative interpretations of the facts: but it seems to have been applied also to undisclosed principals and their agents on the basis that there was alternative liability as a matter of substantive law. But it is now clear that there can be cases where the agent is liable together with the disclosed principal[61]: and there seems no real reason why this should not be so in the case of the undisclosed principal also. To such analysis, the idea of merger or election in respect of alternative liabilities seems inappropriate.

Only three lines of reasoning appear available to justify the results stated in the Article as formulated. The first is that the principal and the

---

[59] See Comment. For an extended treatment of the problems in this area see Reynolds (1970) 86 L.Q.R. 318 (on which, however, it is hoped that the present text represents some advance). See also Clayton (1925) 3 Texas L. Rev. 384; Merrill (1933) 12 Nebr.L.Bull. 100; (1953) 34 Nebr.L.Rev. 613; Hill [1967] J.B.L. 125–128; Sargent and Rochvarg (1982) 36 U. Miami.L.Rev. 411; Seavey, *Studies in Agency* (1949), pp. 215–219, 330–331; Stoljar, pp. 216–219. *Cf.* Indian Contract Act, s.223, the interpretation of which has caused difficulties: Pollock & Mulla, *Indian Contract and Specific Relief Acts* (10th ed.), pp. 922–924. As to the position in Scotland see Phillips 1993 J.R. 133.

[60] See a valuable discussion of this topic by Thomas J. in *L.C. Fowler & Sons Ltd v. St Stephen's College Board of Governors* [1991] 3 N.Z.L.R. 304.

[61] See below, para. 9–006.

agent are liable jointly. If there is only one obligation, it can be said that judgment against one can release the other. This would be solely a doctrine of merger: any notion of election would be irrelevant. This is certainly a possible interpretation of some cases where *disclosed* principal and agent are both liable on a contract. But it is by no means the only one: indeed, it is an unlikely one.[62] Further, there seems no reason at all to apply it to *undisclosed* principals and their agents, and indeed it has not been applied to them. In any case, the rule that judgment against one person jointly liable releases the other was abolished in England by statute in 1978, so that the reasoning now fails, at any rate in England.[63]

The second possible justification is that the liability of principal and agent is, where they are both liable to the third party, as a matter of substance an *alternative* liability. The leading case of *United Australia Ltd v. Barclays Bank Ltd*,[64] concerning waiver of tort, accepts a distinction as to choice between inconsistent rights and choice between alternative remedies. In the first, election is required; but in the second the right to proceed is (probably[65]) only lost by satisfaction of the claim. The standard example of the first is the right to treat a contract as discharged for breach, or to forfeit a lease: once this is done, the party concerned cannot proceed on the basis that the contract or lease subsists. An example in the context of agency is the right or power to ratify.[66] It is possible, and indeed is assumed in the *United Australia* case itself,[67] that the liabilities of agent and *undisclosed* principal are inconsistent in such a way as to require election between rights. This can only really be justified as a special analysis applicable in this context to situations of *undisclosed* principals. But as to disclosed principals, although a third party *could* enter into a contract with a disclosed principal and agent on the basis that their liability was alternative, it is difficult to see that in normal situations there would be any reason for doing so,[68] and hence for a court to put such an interpretation on the facts. The problem in the disclosed principal situation seems rather to be one of alternative remedies against persons who are both liable. Modern analysis of the situation where the agent is liable together with the principal has made this clearer than it was before.[69] As stated above, older cases tended to assume that *either* the principal *or* the agent was

---

[62] See *ibid.*
[63] Civil Liability (Contribution) Act 1978, s.3.
[64] [1941] A.C. 1.
[65] *cf.* [1941] A.C. at pp. 3, 21, 30.
[66] See Article 17; *Verschures Creameries Ltd v. Hull and Netherlands S.S. Co. Ltd* [1921] 2 K.B. 608.
[67] See [1941] A.C. at p. 30.
[68] But see below, para. 9–021 as to certain types of brokerage arrangements.
[69] See Comment to Article 100.

liable. Such reasoning more easily raises the possibility of an argument that the third party must choose. There has also sometimes been, as in other areas, a lack of clarity in distinguishing a true undisclosed principal from a mere unnamed though disclosed principal,[70] which may have added to the confusion.

It does, however, seem that the liability of agent and *undisclosed* principal is on present authority to be regarded as an alternative one: and since the whole doctrine of the undisclosed principal can be said to be anomalous anyway,[71] it cannot be said that such a view is demonstrably wrong, even if there is not much to commend it.[72] If this is so, the governing principle could be regarded either as one of merger or as one of election. If it is one of merger, manifestation of choice to sue one or the other would have no relevance; but a judgment against one would discharge the other, and where it is against the agent, even where it was taken without knowledge of the principal. If the principle is the broader one of election, the third party has an election or choice as to with whom he wishes to regard the contract as having been. When he has manifested this choice he cannot thereafter change course. Until he realises the existence of the undisclosed principal, of course, he is not able to make a valid election, for on general principles a choice cannot be exercised by one who does not know that he has it.[73] Though the narrower, merger principle predominates, the election approach has been taken in some cases, including the *United Australia* case itself.[74] A compromise position is that judgment is the only true election.[75]

The third justification is this. There are many situations where a person does not allege that both agent and principal were liable to him, but cannot decide on the correct interpretation of the facts whether his contract was with one or the other; and therefore sues both in the alternative and leaves the court to decide the question. Or again, he may allege one interpretation and the other party may in defence allege another. Here the court is asked to decide between two mutually inconsistent legal interpretations of the facts. Once a final judgment has been obtained on this issue of fact, the matter is *res judicata*. This is obviously not a matter of merger; but neither is it one of election between inconsistent rights. In this situation, at least in theory, one interpretation is right and the other simply wrong. The matter is rather one of finality of decision as to the proper legal analysis of facts; or

---

[70] See above, para. 8–074.
[71] See Comment to Article 78.
[72] See *L.C. Fowler & Sons Ltd v. St Stephen's College Board of Governors* [1991] 3 N.Z.L.R. 304.
[73] Below, para. 8–121.
[74] See [1941] A.C. at p. 30.
[75] See cases cited above para. 8–119, n. 20.

sometimes as to restrictions on the advancing of mutually inconsistent allegations. Difficulties arise in particular when it is sought to reopen the issue in connection with judgments subject to appeal, and as to default and summary judgments, and some of the leading cases concern procedural problems arising in such situations.[76] In such situations there is an element of choice in a rather special sense. The third party may choose which interpretation to allege, and sue on that basis. If the action is undefended, or summary judgment is given, that interpretation is in theory adopted by the court. But this happened merely at the choice of the plaintiff. Had the case proceeded to trial the court might have decided on a different interpretation of the facts. So the third party has certainly made a choice of a sort; but it is not an election between inconsistent rights, to each of which he is entitled, it is, rather, a pragmatic choice as to against whom to start proceedings in an uncertain situation. However, the dicta in these cases are sometimes uncompromisingly general. Both for default and summary judgments, the procedural decisions are given on the apparent basis that the liability in issue is alternative. This, it is submitted, is not correct. It is these cases which are productive of the most confusion.

It may be added that there are other situations where the third party may do an act which is relevant to the establishment of liability at a much earlier stage, e.g. enter principal or agent in his books as debtor. This is even less an election in respect of legal rights: it is simply an act which may assist in interpreting the initial intentions of all possible parties with respect to any contractual position between them.[77]

The last technique which may be applied is that of estoppel. By the principle of equitable estoppel, a person who represents that he intends to take a particular course of action may be debarred from going back

---

[76] e.g. Morel Bros. & Co. Ltd v. Earl of Westmorland [1904] A.C. 11; Moore v. Flanagan [1920] 1 K.B. 919. See also the cases on default judgments cited below, para. 8–116. The leading Australian case of Petersen v. Moloney (1958) 84 C.L.R. 91 may be of this type. Here the purchaser of land paid the vendor's estate agent and the question was whether the agent had authority to receive payment: the eventual answer was "no". The vendor sued the purchaser and his agent in the alternative: and it was held that a judgment against the agent which was subject to appeal did not prevent judgment against the purchaser. Here the inconsistent interpretations were that the purchaser had paid and the agent was liable to the vendor; or that the purchaser had not paid and was still liable to pay, and hence the agent not liable to the vendor. However, it can be said that the action against the agent was a ratification of the agent's act in receiving the money, which would have involved a need to elect between inconsistent rights. But ratification was not argued: see p. 93. In any case, the decision concerns an action by a principal against *his own agent*—not by the third party (despite some argument to the contrary: see pp. 93, 97–98). It accepts the view that judgment alone constitutes election. It was followed in *Bain Securities Ltd v. Curmi* (1990) 1 A.C.S.R. 794, which was a true case of a third party suing agent and undisclosed principal. See also *Con-Stan Industries of Australia Pty Ltd v. Norwich Winterthur Insurance (Australia) Ltd* (1986) 160 C.L.R. 226.

[77] See below, para. 8–120.

449

on that representation if there is some element of reliance making it inequitable to do so. [78] By other forms of estoppel, for example estoppel by convention, a person who acts on the basis of a particular assumption of facts or interpretation may be debarred from going back on it. [79] These and similar lines of reasoning may sometimes debar a person who has taken one course of action in such a dispute from going back on it. They are not, however, the same as election.

8–115   **The *Restatement*.** It will be seen that the clearest case for the application of some doctrine of merger or election is the specialised one of the undisclosed principal, where the view that the liability is substantively alternative certainly can, though it need not, be taken. The alternative liability can, as has been stated, be attributed either to a merger rule, or to a wider rule of election. The *Restatement* accordingly provides, in deference to the case law of the time, but contrary to the inclinations of the Reporter, Professor Seavey, [80] for release of the agent of an undisclosed principal by judgment against the principal. [81] This is taken as a rule of merger only: no role is left for election. [82] But it only provides for release of the undisclosed *principal* by judgment against the *agent* provided that it was taken with knowledge of the principal's connection with the transaction [83]—an exception which, as the Reporter recognised [84] could be justified under a principle of election, but is contrary to the principle of merger on an alternative liability. It is nevertheless a gloss which can readily be understood. The *Restatement* also preserves the application of estoppel. [85] In the area of disclosed principal it allows for loss of the right of action only if the parties contracted jointly, in which case there is a merger once judgment is given [86]: this is not now relevant in English law. It also again allows for estoppel. [87] It is difficult to see that any other analysis can really be appropriate. However, the English cases are such and so numerous as to require special treatment: it is (unfortunately) difficult to say that they at present justify the formulation in this Article of rules such as those of the *Restatement*.

---

[78] See *Société Italo-Belge, &c. v. Palm and Vegetable Oils (M) Sdn Bhd (The Post Chaser)* [1982] 1 All E.R. 19: note the reference to election reasoning (though in a different context) at the end of the judgment.

[79] See above, para. 8–030.

[80] See Comment to s.210; 7 Proc. Am. Law Inst. 257 (1929): "We do not think that it is a sound theory, sound common sense or good justice."

[81] § 337.

[82] §§ 209, 237.

[83] s.210.

[84] See Comment to § 210.

[85] § 337.

[86] § 184(1).

[87] § 336.

These general points being made, discussion follows of the case law on which the actual wording of the Article is based.

Rule (1). Judgment. Undisclosed principal. It is well established in **8–116** England that if the third party obtains judgment against the agent of an undisclosed principal, he can no longer sue the principal, even though he obtained judgment in ignorance of the fact that the agent had been acting for another, and so of his full rights, and even though the judgment is unsatisfied.[88] The rule seems to be based on two arguments. The first is that there is only one obligation, which is merged in the judgment.[89] The analogy is with the case of joint debtors:[90] but the reasoning seems rather that the obligation is an alternative one. This is reinforced by a rather rough and ready argument, that the liability of the undisclosed principal involves an interpretation of the facts inconsistent with that involving the agent's liability, and the third party cannot have it both ways: the principal's liability is in a sense a windfall, and the third party cannot complain if the windfall turns out to be of limited value.[91] But, as stated above this rule relating to joint debtors has been changed by statute.[92] And what may be called the "windfall" argument can be regarded as reneging on the doctrine of undisclosed principal itself. It seems that in the late nineteenth century the doctrine came to be thought of as inconsistent with basic contract theory, and limitations were consequently placed on it. Such inconsistency was not of itself a valid reason for the limitations imposed. It seems clear, however, that the present rule for undisclosed principals, that the obligation is alternative, can only be changed by the House of Lords.

Disclosed principal. The cases indicate that the same doctrine of **8–117** merger applies to situations where both agent and principal are liable on the contract, but where the existence of the principal is disclosed: it has been applied to cases of named principals[93] and *a fortiori* would apply

---

[88] *Priestly v. Fernie* (1863) 3 H. & C. 977, Illustration 1 (not a convincing case: see n. 53 below, nor a case on a true undisclosed principal, since ships are known to have owners); *Kendall v. Hamilton* (1879) 4 App.Cas. 504, 513–515.

[89] *Kendall v. Hamilton*, n. 88 above, at p. 515; *M. Brennen & Sons Mfg. Co. Ltd v. Thompson* (1915) 33 Ont.L.T. 465, 471–472; *Marginson v. Ian Potter & Co.* (1976) 136 C.L.R. 161.

[90] *Kendall v. Hamilton*, n. 88 above, was in fact the leading case on joint debtors, though paradoxically it takes the position of the undisclosed principal as a paradigm.

[91] *Kendall v. Hamilton*, n. 88 above, at p. 544.

[92] Civil Liability Contribution Act 1978, s.3.

[93] *Morel Bros & Co. Ltd v. Earl of Westmorland* [1904] A.C. 11; *Sullivan v. Sullivan* [1912] 2 I.R. 116, 127–128; *Moore v. Flanagan* [1920] 1 K.B. 919; *R.M.K.R.M. (A Firm) v. M.R.M.V.L. (A Firm)* [1926] A.C. 761, Illustration 2; *Debenhams Ltd v. Perkins* (1925) 133 L.T. 252, 254; *Barrington v. Lee* [1972] 1 Q.B. 326. See also the leading Australian case of *Petersen v. Moloney* (1958) 84 C.L.R. 91; as to which see above, n. 76.

to cases of unnamed principals, who are in any case nearer to undisclosed principals. It has also been applied to recovery of judgment for part only of an undivided debt.[94] In the disclosed principal situation, however, the doctrine is even more difficult to justify. The "windfall" argument is completely inapplicable. The "one obligation" argument, though relied on,[95] is as regards joint obligations again now rendered obsolete by statute,[96] and there seems in the case of a disclosed principal little reason to regard the obligation as alternative.[97] In those circumstances where the third party may be regarded as having stipulated for the liability of both agent and principal, it may be thought that he does so in order to make sure of satisfaction: the dual liability would be of much reduced utility if lost by a mere unsatisfied judgment against one party. It has been suggested above that the extension of the merger doctrine to disclosed principal situations is due to two things: a failure, as in other contexts,[98] to distinguish an unnamed principal situation from a true undisclosed principal situation[99]; and a failure to analyse adequately the nature of the agent's liability in cases where he is liable together with his principal.

Older cases tended to assume that *either* the principal *or* the agent was liable. But modern analysis[1] indicates that an agent liable together with his principal may in principle be liable jointly, jointly and severally, as surety, on a separate contract, or in the alternative. Joint liability, with its technical rules, is rarely appropriate: it applies to partners,[2] but not normally to husband and wife.[3] The possibilities of suretyship[4] and separate contracts[5] are also recognised. But in this context of the taking

---

[94] *French v. Howie* [1906] 2 K.B. 674.
[95] *Moore v. Flanagan*, n. 93 above, at pp. 925–926.
[96] Above, n. 92.
[97] See *L.C. Fowler & Sons Ltd v. St Stephen's College Board of Governors* [1991] 3 N.Z.L.R. 304, 311–312 (Illustration 7); and above, para. 8–114.
[98] *cf.* above, paras. 8–074, 8–105, 8–111.
[99] *cf.* above, para. 8–114. See also *Priestly v. Fernie* (1865) 3 H. & C. 977, n. 88 above.
[1] See Comment to Article 100.
[2] Partnership Act 1890, s.9.
[3] *Morel Bros. & Co. Ltd v. Earl of Westmorland*, n. 93 above. *Cf. Swanton Seed Service Ltd v. Kulba* (1968) 68 D.L.R. (2d) 38.
[4] *Imperial Bank v. London & St Katharine Docks Co.* (1877) 5 Ch.D. 195, 200; *Fleet v. Murton* (1871) L.R. 7 Q.B. 126, 132. See also *Young v. Schuler* (1883) 11 Q.B.D. 651; *Rutherford v. Ounan* [1913] 2 I.R. 265, 268.
[5] *Barclays Bank Ltd v. Williams* (1971) 115 S.J. 674 (breach of warranty of authority); *M. Brennen & Son Mfg. Co. Ltd v. Thompson* (1915) 33 Ont.L.R. 465, 469–470. But *cf. Benton v. Campbell, Parker & Co.* [1925] 2 K.B. 410, 414, where it is contemplated that election may apply between the separate causes of action against the auctioneer and his vendor. Sometimes the agent's liability comes to an end by its terms on the acceptance of a contract by the third party with the principal. This could formerly occur on the Stock Exchange: see *Grissell v. Bristowe* (1868) L.R. 4 C.P. 36; *Maxted v. Paine* (1869) L.R. 4 Ex. 203, affd. (1871) L.R. 6 Ex. 132; (1929) 39 Yale L.J. 265; below, para. 9–021.

of proceedings against one or the other, there are a surprising number of assertions against joint and several liability and in favour of alternative liability.[6] Indeed the doctrine of merger has in some cases been applied where it might appear that the agent against whom judgment was obtained was in fact not liable at all,[7] so that the judgment should have been regarded as abortive and as being no bar to subsequent proceedings against a person who was liable[8]: it has also been extended to actions in restitution in respect of deposits paid to estate agents in "subject to contract" situations.[9] But many cases[10] where the doctrine of merger has been held to operate should probably be explained by the proposition that where claims are made against principal and agent in the alternative, on the basis that the facts justify the liability of one or the other, but not both, judgment against one, unless set aside, involves *res judicata* in favour of the other. Whatever the arguments, the true interpretation of the facts is now settled.[11] This is based on the idea, not that both are substantively liable in the alternative, but that one is and the other is not. But it is submitted that the law urgently requires clarification. There should be no scope for merger in most disclosed principal case. But it may be that in England, because of the weight of authority, again only the House of Lords can say so.[12]

There can, of course, be cases where on any criterion the agent's liability is separate. Thus a wife may order goods for herself, and other, identifiably different, goods as agent for her husband.[12a] In another case an agent negotiated a sale of patents by his principal, and received the

---

[6] See cases cited above, n. 93; *Murray v. Delta Copper Co. Ltd* [1925] 4 D.L.R. 1061, 1067.

[7] See the R.S.C. Ord. 14 cases cited on the liability of husband wife: *Morel Bros. & Co. Ltd v. Earl of Westmorland*, n. 93 above (discussed (1970) 86 L.Q.R. at p. 338–340); *French v. Howie* [1906] 2 K.B. 674; *Sullivan v. Sullivan* [1912] 2 I.R. 116; *Moore v. Flanagan* [1920] 1 K.B. 919. See also *Cross & Co. v. Matthews and Wallace* (1904) 91 L.T. 500 (default judgment: discussed (1970) 86 L.Q.R. at pp. 341–342); *Cyril Lord (Carpet Sales) v. Browne* (1966) 111 S.J. 51 (default summons: discussed (1970) 86 L.Q.R. at pp. 342–343). But *cf. Longman v. Hill* (1891) 7 T.L.R. 639; *Petersen v. Moloney* (1951) 84 C.L.R. 91; *Goodey v. Garriock* [1972] 2 Lloyd's Rep. 369 (Order 14).

[8] On the basis of *Isaacs & Sons v. Salbstein* [1916] 2 K.B. 139, discussed below; *Longman v. Hill*, n. 7 above.

[9] *Barrington v. Lee* [1972] 1 Q.B. 326, Illustration 6. But on this fact situation see *Sorrell v. Finch* [1977] A.C. 728, Illustration 4 to Article 94.

[10] Perhaps the Order 14 cases on husband and wife, cited above n. 7.

[11] See above, para. 8–114; *Reardon Smith Line Ltd v. Cayzer, Irvine & Co. Ltd* (1929) 35 Com.Cas. 270; see also *Beadon v. Capital Syndicate* (1912) 28 T.L.R. 427; *Clark v. Urquhart* [1930] A.C. 28. As to setting aside of judgments, see below.

[12] But see *L.C. Fowler & Sons Ltd v. St Stephen's College Board of Governors* [1991] 3 N.Z.L.R. 304, where a bold line was taken.

[12a] *Debenham's Ltd v. Perkins* (1925) 133 L.T. 252.

price, which he retained. The principal later agreed to repurchase the patents and gave the third party a cheque, which was dishonoured. It was held that the third party had separate causes of action against the agent as stakeholder, and against the principal on the cheque and the agreement to repurchase.[13] It has also been held that where judgment had been obtained against a firm (Salbstein Bros.) which was never proved to exist or to be liable, this was no bar to a subsequent action on the same facts against a person (H. Salbstein) who was liable.[14] And where the actions are in tort the position is different: principal and agent are joint tortfeasors.[15]

8–118   **Setting aside of judgments.** It seems in principle correct to say that where a judgment against the agent is set aside on the merits, *i.e.* as being wrong, it is no bar to another action against the principal[16]: but that a judgment may not simply be set aside by consent for this purpose.[17] But the cases are not clear.[18]

8–119   **Rule (2). Election. Undisclosed principal.** Some cases state the doctrine under which the third party may not sue both agent and undisclosed principal as applying to situations short of judgment.[19] If this is correct, the bar must be caused by the notion of election, or manifestation of choice, rather than merger. The basis of such a doctrine must again be that the obligations of agent and principal are as a matter of substantive law alternative at the election of the third party. There are, however, cases which speak of judgment as the only proof of

---

[13] *B. O. Morris Ltd v. Perrott & Bolton* [1945] 1 All E.R. 567. See also *Bucknell v. O'Donnell* (1922) 31 C.L.R. 40; *Goldrei Foucard & Son v. Russian Chamber of Commerce* [1918] 1 K.B. 180.

[14] *Isaacs & Sons v. Salbstein* [1916] 2 K.B. 139; followed in *Maxform S.p.A. v. Mariani and Goodville* [1979] 2 Lloyd's Rep. 385; affd. [1981] 2 Lloyd's Rep. 54.

[15] See below, para. 8–187; *Derham v. Amev Life Assurance Co. Ltd* (1981) 56 F.L.R. 34.

[16] See *Partington v. Hawthorne* (1888) 52 J.P. 807 (explained in *M. Brennen & Sons Mfg. Co. Ltd v. Thompson* (1915) 33 Ont. L.R. 465, 470–471); *Buckingham v. Trotter* (1901) 1 S.R.(N.S.W.) 253; *Petersen v. Moloney* (1951) 84 C.L.R. 91; *Goodey v. Garriock* [1972] 2 Lloyd's Rep. 369 (Ord. 14).

[17] *Hammond v. Schofield* [1891] 1 Q.B. 453 (Ord. 14).

[18] Difficulty is caused by *Cross & Co. Ltd v. Matthews & Wallace* (1904) 91 L.T. 500 (default summons: discussed (1970) 86 L.Q.R. at pp. 341–342); *Cyril Lord (Carpet Sales) v. Browne* (1966) 111 S.J. 51 (default summons: discussed (1970) 86 L.Q.R. at pp. 342–343); and the cases on husband and wife cited above. A default judgment was set aside in *Kohn v. Devon Mortgage Ltd* (1983) 3 D.L.R. (4th) 466 (revsd. on other grounds (1985) 20 D.L.R. (4th) 480).

[19] *Curtis v. Williamson* (1874) L.R. 10 Q.B. 57, Illustration 4; *United Australia Ltd v. Barclays Bank Ltd* [1941] A.C. 1, 30; *Clarkson Booker Ltd v. Andjel* [1964] 2 Q.B. 775, 794, Illustration to Article 106; *Chestertons v. Barone* [1987] 1 EGLR 15, 17.

election.[20] Here also the famous case of *Scarf v. Jardine*,[21] which requires election between inconsistent liabilities in partnership law, is sometimes invoked. But, as in the case of judgment against joint debtors, the situation here is not quite the same and need not be treated in the same way.[22] "Elective liability" between two parties is a strange concept for the law. The problem is made easier, however, by the fact that though many cases speak of election, virtually every case in the field of undisclosed principal holds that the acts in question are insufficient to constitute election.[23] Only two have been traced which purport to hold that there has been a binding election short of judgment, and both can also be explained on the basis that the third party, after learning of the principal's existence, did an act which induced the principal to settle with, or alter his position as to the agent, and thereby debarred himself from looking to the principal.[24] Such cases are part of a well-established group which is not normally associated with the idea of election at all,[25] but rather with estoppel, the hallmark of which is some form of reliance. It is submitted therefore that though there is in a Court of Appeal case concerning an undisclosed principal[26] extensive discussion on the basis that the rights against principal and agent are inconsistent and subject to election (though the decision was that there had been no election), a third party should only be debarred from suing an undisclosed principal, short of an actual judgment against the agent, by an act which raises an estoppel against him, *e.g.* where after discovery of the principal he does an act leading the principal to suppose that he relied on the agent, or has been paid by the agent, or in some other way waives the liability of the principal in a manner relied on.[27] There are, however, recent dicta in the Court of Appeal maintaining the notion of election.[28]

---

[20] *Priestly v. Fernie* (1865) 3 H. & C. 977, 983–984; *Buckingham v. Trotter*, n. 16 above, at pp. 259, 261; *Petersen v. Moloney*, n. 16 above; *Morgan v. Lifetime Building Supplies Ltd* (1967) 61 D.L.R. (2d) 178; *Bain Securities Ltd v. Curmi* (1990) 1 A.C.S.R. 794.

[21] (1882) 7 App.Cas. 345; see also *Fell v. Parkin* (1882) 52 L.J.Q.B. 99.

[22] See (1970) 86 L.Q.R. at pp. 321–322, 327; Spencer Bower, *Estoppel by Representation* (1st ed.), p. 224; (2nd ed.), pp. 324–325; (3rd ed.), pp. 359–361.

[23] *Nelson v. Powell* (1784) 3 Doug. 410; *Taylor v. Sheppard* (1835) 1 Y. & C.Ex. 271; *Curtis v. Williamson* (1874) L.R. 10 Q.B. 57, Illustration 4; *Clarkson Booker Ltd v. Andjel* [1964] 2 Q.B. 775, Illustration to Article 106.

[24] *MacClure v. Schemeil* (1871) 20 W.R. 168, Illustration 3 to Article 82; *Smethurst v. Mitchell* (1859) 1 E. & E. 622 (explained in *Davison v. Donaldson* (1882) 9 Q.B.D. 623).

[25] See Article 82.

[26] *Clarkson Booker Ltd v. Andjel*, n. 23 above.

[27] See cases cited above, n. 24. But the taking of a bill or cheque from the agent will not normally produce such an estoppel: see cases cited below, n. 147. *Cf. Restatement*, §§ 209, 337; see also Corbin (1909) 19 Yale L.J. 221, 239.

[28] *Chestertons v. Barone* [1987] 1 EGLR 15, 17 *per* May L.J.

8–120   **Disclosed principal.** Again, in the case of disclosed principal there are clear dicta that where both principal and agent are liable, the third party must elect.[29] The criticisms made above of the merger doctrine for such cases apply *a fortiori* to any requirement of election. Only if the liabilities are in the alternative does the idea of election make sense[30]; and of the many possible interpretations which can be given to the situation where agent and principal are liable, alternative liability is an unlikely one.[31] In this area however most of the cases appear fairly obviously not to be based on election between two liabilities on an alternative contract at all, but on problems of formation of contract. The typical situation is that discussed in several nineteenth-century cases, where a third party deals with an agent in circumstances where either agent or principal might reasonably be regarded as the other contracting party. In principle the law of agency assumes that he is dealing with the principal, unless there are clear indications to the contrary[32]; but these there may be.[33] It is also clear that the third party may contract on the basis that both are liable to him.[34] Thus invoicing and debiting the agent or the like, which are sometimes spoken in terms of election, should perhaps really be classified in terms of offer or coutner-offer.[35] There are many cases dealing with this point where the idea of election is not employed at all.[36] Such situations may of course

---

[29] *Calder v. Dobell* (1871) L.R. 6 C.P. 486, 499 (Illustration 5); *Benton v. Campbell Parker & Co.* [1925] 2 K.B. 410, 414; *Murray v. Delta Copper Co.* [1925] 4 D.L.R. 1061, 1067; *Tedrick v. Big T Restaurants of Canada Ltd* [1983] 2 W.W.R. 135.

[30] *L.C. Fowler & Sons Ltd v. St Stephen's College Board of Governors* [1991] 3 N.Z.L.R. 304, 309 (Illustration 7).

[31] See above, para. 8–114.

[32] *Thomson v. Davenport* (1829) 9 B. & C. 78, 90. As to husband and wife, see Chap. 3, Section 4.

[33] *e.g. Addison v. Gandassequi* (1812) 4 Taunt. 574; *cf. Paterson v. Gandasequi* (1812) 15 East 62.

[34] *Calder v. Dobell*, n. 29 above, at p. 494; Comment to Article 100.

[35] *e.g. Thomson v. Davenport*, n. 32 above. See also cases on building subcontracts: *Young & Co. v. White* (1911) 28 T.L.R. 87; *Beigtheil & Young v. Stewart* (1900) 16 T.L.R. 177; cases on husband and wife: *Jewsbury v. Newbold* (1857) 26 L.J.Ex. 247; *Bentley v. Griffin* (1814) 5 Taunt. 356; *Metcalfe v. Shaw* (1811) 3 Camp. 22; *Callot v. Nash* (1923) 39 T.L.R. 292; shipping cases of various sorts: *Eastman v. Harry* (1875) 33 L.T. 800; *Whitwell v. Perrin* (1858) 4 C.B.(N.S.) 412; *Lamont v. Hamilton* 1907 S.C. 628; *Beliard, Crighton (Belgium) & Co. Ltd v. Charles Lowe & Partners Ltd* (1922) 13 Ll.Rep. 567; *The Huntsman* [1894] P. 214; and other cases regularly cited in this connection: *Bottomley v. Nuttall* (1858) 5 C.B.(N.S.) 122; *Dramburg v. Pollitzer* (1873) 28 L.T. 470; *Re Bowerman, ex p. Vining* (1836) 1 Deac. 555.

[36] *e.g.* as to husband and wife: *Lea Bridge District Gas Co. v. Malvern* [1917] 1 K.B. 803; as to ship stores: *Dawson (Ship Stores) v. Atlantica Co. Ltd* (1931) 40 Ll.Rep. 63; *Evans & Reid Coal Co. v. McNabb, Rougier & Co. Ltd* (1924) 18 Ll.Rep. 471; *Fraser-Johnston Engineering, etc., Co. v. Sam Isaacs (Aberdeen) Ltd* (1922) 12 Ll.Rep. 233; *Freimuller (Ships Stores) Ltd v. Ocean Carriers (London) Ltd* [1961] 2 Lloyd's Rep. 309; *Pearson v. Nell* (1860) 12 L.T. 607; *Thompson v. Finden* (1829) 4 C. & P. 158. See also

give rise to estoppels as in the case of undisclosed principals. It is therefore submitted that in this area also a supposed election (short of judgment) to have recourse to the agent does not bind the third party unless it again gives rise to some form of estoppel.[37] This does not, of course, remove any authority from the cases referred to above dealing with the question with whom the contract was made.

What constitutes election? If, however, contrary to what is suggested above, any doctrine of election (as opposed to one of estoppel) is applicable, on general grounds the person electing must know the facts,[38] and the election must be clear and unequivocal[39] and voluntary.[40] It may also be that it must occur within a reasonable time,[41] though cases on this point seem better attributed to estoppel.[42] The question is certainly one of fact.[43] The following have been held *not* to constitute election: debiting the agent in the third party's books[44]; demanding payment of the agent[45]; receipt of part payment from the agent[46]; taking a bill of exchange or cheque from the agent[47]; proving in the agent's bankruptcy[48]; pursuing a claim in arbitration

8–121

Williamson v. Barton (1862) 7 H. & N. 899; *Gardiner v. Heading* [1928] 2 K.B. 284; *Pennell v. Alexander* (1854) 3 E. & B. 283; *Thomas v. Edwards* (1836) 2 M. & W. 215; *Mortimer v. M'Callan* (1840) 6 M. & W. 58 (*cf. Stoneham v. Wyman* (1901) 6 Com.Cas. 174); *Format International Security Printers Ltd v. Mosden* [1975] 1 Lloyd's Rep. 37. As to ship repairs and stores see Article 101, Illustration 7; Article 103, Illustration 2.

[37] *cf. Restatement*, §§ 336 and comment.

[38] *Dunn v. Newton* (1884) C. & E. 278; *Clarkson Booker Ltd v. Andjel* [1964] 2 Q.B. 775, 792; *Pyxis Special Shipping Co. Ltd v. Dritsas & Kaglis Bros. Ltd (The Scaplake)* [1978] 2 Lloyd's Rep. 380; *Kammins Ballrooms Co. Ltd v. Zenith Investments (Torquay) Ltd* [1971] A.C. 850, 882–883; *Peyman v. Lanjani* [1985] Ch. 457; *L.C. Fowler & Sons v. St Stephen's College Board of Governors* [1991] 3 N.Z.L.R. 304.

[39] *Clarkson Booker Ltd v. Andjel*, n. 38 above, at p. 792.

[40] *L.C. Fowler & Sons Ltd v. St Stephen's College Board of Governors*, n. 38 above.

[41] *Powell*, p. 272.

[42] *e.g. Smethurst v. Mitchell* (1859) 1 E. & E. 622.

[43] *Clarkson Booker Ltd v. Andjel*, n. 38 above, at p. 792.

[44] *Thomson v. Davenport* (1829) 9 B. & C. 78; *Calder v. Dobell* (1871) L.R. 6 C.P. 486, Illustration 5; *Eastman v. Harry* (1875) 33 L.T. 800; *Young & Co. v. White* (1911) 28 T.L.R. 87. This is really a matter of formation of contract: see above.

[45] *Calder v. Dobell*, n. 44 above; *Beigtheil & Young v. Stewart* (1900) 16 T.L.R. 177; *Eastman v. Harry*, n. 35 above; *cf. MacClure v. Schemeil* (1871) 20 W.R. 168, Illustration 3 to Article 82.

[46] *Ex p. Pitt* (1923) 40 T.L.R. 5.

[47] *Robinson v. Read* (1829) 9 B. & C. 449. Unless it is received in full satisfaction, which would be difficult to establish. See *Everett v. Collins* (1810) 2 Camp. 515; *Marsh v. Pedder* (1815) 4 Camp. 257; *Strong v. Hart* (1827) 6 B. & C. 160; *Smith v. Ferrand* (1827) 7 B. & C. 191; *The Huntsman* [1894] P. 214.

[48] *Curtis v. Williamson* (1874) L.R. 10 Q.B. 57, Illustration 5; *cf. MacClure v. Schemeil* n. 45 above; *Scarf v. Jardine* (1882) 7 App.Cas. 345; *Fell v. Parkin* (1882) 52 L.J.Q.B. 99; *Con-Stan Industries of Australia Pty Ltd v. Norwich Winterthur Insurance (Australia) Ltd* (1986) 160 C.L.R. 226.

457

against the agent[49]; serving a writ on the agent[50]; or obtaining leave to sign judgment against him under R.S.C. Order 14.[51] It has, however, recently been said that "the clearest evidence of election is at least the commencement of proceedings against one or other of the two relevant parties.[52]

8–122   **Rule (3).** The strength of this residual rule obviously varies in accordance with the validity of the doctrine of election above discussed. But the cases deciding that there has been no election far outnumber those holding that there has been.

8–123   **Substance or procedure?** A difficult question is whether the above rules are to be classified as rules of substance or procedure for the purposes of the conflict of laws. In general, the rules for undisclosed principal do appear to represent rules of substance whereby the principal is liable alternatively with the agent. Much of the law as to disclosed principals, on the other hand, seems to derive from procedural considerations concerning summary and default judgments; though questions of guarantee and joint and several liability would be substantive. The question which of two persons is a party to a contract is of course one of substance. The confused bases of the rules make generalisation extremely difficult.

Illustrations

8–124   (1) The master of a ship signs a bill of lading in his own name. The consignee obtains judgment against him on it, but the judgment is not satisfied. The consignee cannot thereafter sue the shipowner.[53]

(2) The Earl and Countess of Westmorland are sued jointly by a tradesman for wines and provisions ordered by the Countess. The Countess submits to summary judgment but the Earl obtains leave to defend. It is held that there is no evidence of joint liability; and that

---

[49] *Pyxis Special Shipping Co. Ltd v. Dritsas & Kaglis Bros. Ltd (The Scaplake)* [1978] 2 Lloyd's Rep. 380.
[50] *Clarkson Booker Ltd v. Andjel* [1964] 2 Q.B. 775 (actually here served on principal).
[51] *C. Christopher (Hove) Ltd v. Williams* [1936] 3 All E.R. 68.
[52] *Chestertons v. Barone* [1987] 1 EGLR 15, 17 *per* May L.J. Contrast *Bain Securities Ltd v. Curmi* (1990) 1 A.C.S.R. 794.
[53] *Priestly v. Fernie* (1865) 3 H. & C. 977. This leading case reads strangely to modern eyes. In present times the master (who appears to have been imprisoned for the debt in Melbourne) would not be liable at all. The assumption seems to have been that he was the sole contracting party; the argument put was that in the case of shipmasters the owners were, by maritime law and contrary to principle, liable also. The court applied what it said was a general rule that principal and agent were liable in the alternative.

having signed judgment against the wife the plaintiff cannot sue the husband as her principal. [54]

(3) The agent of a moneylender sues the agent of another moneylender on a debt and obtains judgment. Later the first moneylender sues the second moneylender on the same debt. The action is barred. [55]

(4) A bought goods in his own name on behalf of B. The seller discovered that B was the principal, and subsequently, A having filed a liquidation petition, a clerk of the seller, for the purpose of proving in the liquidation, made an affidavit treating A as the debtor, and the affidavit was duly filed. The seller could still sue B for the price of the goods. [56]

(5) A broker is authorised to buy cotton, but not to disclose his principal's name. Being unable to obtain a contract on his own credit, he reveals the principal's name and bought and sold notes are exchanged between him and the seller naming the principal as the buyer. The goods are invoiced to the broker, but, the market falling, he refuses to accept the goods. The seller threatens both with legal proceedings, but subsequently sues the principal. He is not precluded from doing so. [57]

(6) The seller of a house instructs two estate agents. B makes an offer subject to contract and pays a deposit to each agent. The sale does not proceed. One estate agent returns the deposit, the other does not. B obtains judgment against the second agent, but it is unsatisfied. Even if the principal is liable in respect of the deposit, an action against him is barred by the judgment against the agent. [58]

(7) An agent acting for a school contracts on the school's behalf, with a firm which arranges such tours, for a sporting tour for the school. The school pays its agent, who passes on some of the money to the firm and disappears. The firm obtains a default judgment against the agent for the remainder, but it is not satisfied. Later the firm sues the school. The school is liable and the firm's action is not barred by election or

---

[54] *Morel Bros. & Co. Ltd v. Earl of Westmorland* [1904] A.C. 11 (where the husband's liability was affected by the rules as to presumptions of authority: see Article 33). See also *Sullivan v. Sullivan* [1912] 2 I.R. 116, where the court regretted the conclusion to which it regarded itself as bound to come; *Moore v. Flanagan* [1920] 1 K.B. 919, a claim by a milliner and dressmaker, where Scrutton L.J. said that the rule was "extremely technical" but Atkin L.J. robustly said that "Any ill result to the plaintiff arises from her abuse of the procedure under Order XIV."
[55] *R.M.K.R.M. (A Firm) v. M.R.M.V.L. (A Firm)* [1926] A.C. 761 (discussed (1970) 86 L.Q.R. at pp. 337–338).
[56] *Curtis v. Williamson* (1874) L.R. 10 Q.B. 57.
[57] *Calder v. Dobell* (1871) L.R. 6 C.P. 486.
[58] *Barrington v. Lee* [1972] 1 Q.B. 326 (noted (1972) 88 L.Q.R. 184). But as to the principal's liability see now *Sorrell v. Finch* [1977] A.C. 728, Illustration 4 to Article 94.

judgment, the judgment against the agent being against one who was not liable to the firm at all.[59]

2—DISPOSITIONS OF PROPERTY

Article 85

DISPOSITIONS OF PRINCIPAL'S PROPERTY BY AGENT ACTING WITHIN ACTUAL OR APPARENT AUTHORITY

8–125   A principal is bound by dispositions of property made by his agent acting within the scope of such agent's actual or apparent authority or which are ratified.[60]

Comment

8–126   It is obvious that a disposition within an agent's actual authority, express or implied, transfers property, whether the principal is disclosed or not[61]; and an unauthorised disposition can be ratified.[62] Equally, the doctrine of apparent authority must in principle, apply here, as in other parts of the law of agency. However, in two respects considerable difficulties affect its application.

First, the doctrine of apparent authority is often said to be based on estoppel.[63] An estoppel in general operates only between two parties and their privies. Yet the result of a disposition which is effective under the doctrine of apparent authority is to confer "a real title and not merely a metaphorical title by estoppel,"[64] *viz.* a title which can be transmitted to persons unable to rely on the estoppel, and which will bind not only a volunteer but also a bona fide purchaser from the person estopped.[65] This is recognised in section 21(1) of the Sale of

---

[59] *L.C. Fowler & Sons Ltd v. St Stephen's College Board of Governors* [1991] 3 N.Z.L.R. 304.

[60] See Comment. As to actual authority, see Chap. 2; as to apparent authority, see Article 74; as to ratification, see Articles 13–20. For extended discussion of this difficult topic, see Powell, pp. 80–97; Stoljar, Chap. 5; Fridman, Chap. 12.

[61] An example would be a distributor of goods which he holds under a "Romalpa" clause: he is generally authorised to resell them. Such a person is not usually however a true agent. See above; below, para. 8–162.

[62] For examples, see Illustrations to Article 17.

[63] See Comment to Article 74.

[64] *Eastern Distributors Ltd v. Goldring* [1957] 2 Q.B. 600, 611, *per* Devlin J. (Illustration 5 to Article 86).

[65] *Eastern Distributors Ltd v. Goldring*, n. 64 above, at p. 611. But where the interests of the person concerned are adverse to those of the person estopped, *e.g.* as a creditor, he may not be bound by the estoppel: see *Heane v. Rogers* (1820) 9 B. & C. 577; *Richards v. Johnston* (1859) 4 H. & N. 660; *Richards v. Jenkins* (1887) 18 Q.B.D. 451; *Geddes v. M'Donnell* (1896) 22 V.L.R. 330; *Curtis v. Perth & Fremantle Bottle Exchange Co. Ltd* (1914) 18 C.L.R. 17, 23, 28; Ewart, *Estoppel* (1900), pp. 196–221; Spencer Bower,

Goods Act 1979, which gives as an exception to the maxim *nemo dat quod non habet* the case where "the owner of the goods is by his conduct precluded from denying the seller's authority to sell."[66] Hence cases in this area can be used in support of the proposition that the doctrine of apparent authority does not depend on estoppel[67]; or in support of the idea that an agent may have powers transcending his actual and apparent authority.[68] Yet the terminology of estoppel is much used in the English cases.

Second, a basic tenet of this part of the law is that the mere entrusting of goods or documents of title to an agent does not confer apparent authority to dispose of them, for otherwise "no one would be safe in parting with the possession of anything."[69] A person in possession of goods may be a bailee; a person in possession of documents of title may be a mortgagee or a mere depositary. The cases therefore constantly indicate the necessity for some further act on the part of the owner beyond the mere parting with possession.

It is suggested in the main discussion of the doctrine of apparent authority[70] that two types of case seem to be involved: those involving a more specific representation, on which the third party relies, where the principal's liability can fairly easily be based on estoppel, and those involving only a general representation made by putting the agent in a position carrying with it a usual authority, where the liability of the principal is more difficult to explain in terms of estoppel; though these categories overlap and are not mutually exclusive. So in the first category, an agent may in this context have apparent authority by virtue of having been entrusted with goods or documents of title together with a further indication that he has authority to dispose of them. It is

---

Estoppel by Representation (3rd ed.), § 126. The solution to this difficulty turns on the extent to which apparent ownership and apparent authority are separate from the general rules of estoppel.

[66] This provision only applies to a sale as opposed to an agreement to sell: *Shaw v. Commissioner of Police of the Metropolis* [1987] 1 W.L.R. 1332.

[67] See *Eastern Distributors Ltd v. Goldring*, n. 64 above; *cf.* W. H. Goodhart (1957) 73 L.Q.R. 455.

[68] See Comment to Article 22.

[69] *Weiner v. Gill* [1905] 2 K.B. 172, 182; *Cole v. North Western Bank* (1872) L.R. 10 C.P. 354, 362; *Farquharson Brothers & Co. v. King & Co.* [1902] A.C. 325, Illustration 7 to Article 86; *Johnson v. Crédit Lyonnais* (1877) 3 C.P.D. 32; *Fry v. Smellie* [1912] 3 K.B. 282, Illustration 3 to Article 87; *Jerome v. Bentley & Co.* [1952] 2 All E.R. 114; *Central Newbury Car Auctions Ltd v. Unity Finance Ltd* [1957] 1 Q.B. 371, Illustration 4 to Article 86; *Moorgate Mercantile Co. Ltd v. Twitchings* [1977] A.C. 890, 902–904 (Illustration 8 to Article 86.). A further reason given is that otherwise there would be no need of the Factors Act: the existence of those Acts may have militated against subsequent extension of the common law rules, at any rate as regards goods.

[70] See Comment to Article 74.

difficult to find a clear case of this where the disposition is not binding by virtue of a contract,[71] but if an agent is given goods and a written authority to pledge them, his disposition will be valid notwithstanding that there are secret limits on his authority which he does not disclose. Again, in the second category the entrusting of goods to an agent, *e.g.* in former times a factor, who in the way of business normally had authority to sell, will create apparent authority,[72] and a disposition in the ordinary course of business of such an agent will be effective: but here a clear modern case is difficult to find because such an agent would normally come under the wider principles of the Factors Act.[73]

There are two other ways in which the courts have sought to validate unauthorised dispositions by agents in possession of goods or documents of title.

(1) *Apparent ownership.* Where the owner has allowed his agent to have possession of goods or documents of title and also in some way let him appear to be *owner* of the goods or the property represented by the document of title, the agent's unauthorised disposition may be valid. This is not really a rule of agency, inasmuch as the person concerned is not thought to be an agent and need not in fact be such: but the reasoning in the cases is virtually identical to that relating to apparent authority and indeed the majority of the cases on property dispositions by agents lie in this area rather than in that of true apparent authority. The interconnection between the two is shown by the fact that Chalmers, in his first commentary on the Sale of Goods Act,[74] cited cases on apparent ownership as cases where the owner is precluded from denying the seller's authority to sell.[75] One difference however should

---

[71] A possible example is *Davy v. Waller* (1899) 81 L.T. 107. See also *Robinson v. Montgomeryshire Brewery Co. Ltd* [1896] 2 Ch. 841; *cf. Jameson v. Union Bank of Scotland* (1913) 109 L.T. 850. The third party must of course rely on the appearance of authority: see *Raffoul v. Esanda Ltd* [1970] 3 N.S.W.R. 8.

[72] *Pickering v. Busk* (1812) 15 East 38, Illustration 1 to Article 86. As to the distinction between brokers and factors see above, para. 1–040.

[73] Article 89. A possible modern example is *Fuller v. Glyn, Mills, Currie & Co.* [1914] 2 K.B. 168, as explained in *Mercantile Bank of India Ltd v. Central Bank of India Ltd* [1938] A.C. 287 and in *Tobin v. Broadbent* (1947) 75 C.L.R. 378. In *Shearson Lehman Brothers Inc. v. Maclaine, Watson & Co. Ltd* [1988] 1 W.L.R. 16, 28 it was said that authority to pass property may be more easily inferred than authority to enter into an obligation: "business would come to a standstill if persons who receive documents from clerks and secretaries, acting in the course of their employment, were not entitled to assume that these documents were sent with the authority of the employer": *per* Lord Bridge of Harwich.

[74] *Sale of Goods* (2nd ed.) (1894).

[75] A common root for both doctrines is *Pickering v. Busk*, n. 72 above. The relevant section of the Sale of Goods Act, s.21, is sometimes cited in apparent ownership cases: see *J. Sargent (Garages) Ltd v. Motor Auctions (West Bromwich) Ltd* [1977] R.T.R. 121.

be noted. The fact that a sale is not in the ordinary course of business may be evidence that it is not within the apparent authority: but this point would not be relevant where the agent actually appeared to own the goods.[76] The doctrine of apparent ownership is dealt with in the following Article.

(2) *Delivery plus authority to make a disposition.* A number of cases, mostly dealing with land, tend to suggest a proposition that where the principal delivers possession of documents of title, and authorises the agent to make certain property dispositions, he may be bound when the agent makes other, unauthorised dispositions. Though this may be a reasonable idea, it does not accord with agency doctrines, inasmuch as there is in these cases no actual or apparent authority (or apparent ownership), and the position between principal and agent is not relevant to the position of the third party (though references to that position tend to creep into cases in all categories). It seems to be based on reasoning applicable to problems of priority in land law, and any more general validity is therefore doubtful. It is dealt with in Article 87.

Other estoppels. It should be noted finally that even though a disposition is not valid under any of the above rules, the principal may by his conduct subsequent to it be estopped from alleging its invalidity; or from alleging in general that the property is his. This conduct may take the form of a positive representation; in other cases there must be a duty to speak or disclose.[77]   **8–127**

Article 86

Doctrine of Apparent Ownership

Where a principal, by words or conduct, represents or permits it to be represented that his agent is the owner of any property, any sale, pledge, mortgage or other disposition for value of the property by the agent is as valid against the principal as if the agent were its owner, with respect to anyone dealing with him on the faith of such representation.[78]   **8–128**

---

[76] *Motor Credits (Hire Finance) Ltd v. Pacific Motor Auctions Pty. Ltd* (1963) 109 C.L.R. 87, reversed on other grounds [1965] A.C. 867; but *cf. General Distributors Ltd v. Paramotors Ltd* [1962] S.A.S.R. 1.

[77] *West v. Dillicar* [1920] N.Z.L.R. 139; [1921] N.Z.L.R. 617; *Fung Kai Sun v. Chan Fui Hing* [1951] A.C. 489; *Spiro v. Lintern* [1973] 1 W.L.R. 1002. See also *M'Kenzie v. British Linen Co.* (1881) 6 App.Cas. 82; *Greenwood v. Martin's Bank Ltd* [1933] A.C. 51. See in general above, para. 8–030.

[78] See Comment.

Comment

8–129   Where, in such a case the agent's disposition is authorised, it is valid under ordinary doctrine; if necessary, the principal can be referred to as undisclosed. But the above proposition embraces also more complex cases which do not strictly depend on agency principles, for there is no actual authority, and the third party does not think that the agent is an agent, but the owner. The proposition in the Article is in fact a specific formulation of a more general proposition which is not confined to disposition by persons who are already agents. But the cases are usually confused with cases on agency, and agency terminology used.[79]

The rule is regarded, perhaps more clearly than that of apparent authority, as based on estoppel,[80] though it is an even vaguer application of this notion than is the idea of apparent authority, for, apart from the fact that the estoppel confers title,[81] it is difficult to see that a third party can rely on the representation or conduct of someone of whose existence he may not be aware. The estoppel is said to be based on representation or conduct. Although the two are often difficult to distinguish, *e.g* in the case of signature of a document, the latter is usually more appropriate, since the word "representation" implies a communication from the principal to the third party, and, as stated above, in many cases the third party does not know of the principal at all. The rules seem to be effectively the same whichever is relied on.[82] Where the notion of representation is employed, it is said that it must be made to a person or group of persons,[83] though as the group can apparently be quite a wide one this is necessarily vague in its application. Where negligent conduct is relied on, it is often said that

---

[79] See *Rimmer v. Webster* [1902] 2 Ch. 163, Illustration 6; *Central Newbury Car Auction Ltd v. Unity Finance Ltd* [1957] 1 Q.B. 371, Illustration 4; *Eastern Distributors Ltd v. Goldring* [1957] 2 Q.B. 600, Illustration 5; *Jerome v. Bentley & Co.* [1952] 2 All E.R. 114; *Stoneleigh Finance Ltd v. Phillips* [1965] 2 Q.B. 537; above, para. 8–126, Sale of Goods Act 1979, s.21 (referred to in such a situation in *J. Sargent (Garages) Ltd v. Motor Auctions (West Bromwich) Ltd* [1977] R.T.R. 121).

[80] See cases cited below, nn. 84, 90; indeed some of these cases are seminal for the doctrine of estoppel in general. But *cf. Eastern Distributors Ltd v. Goldring*, n. 79 above, at p. 611.

[81] But see Comment to Article 85, esp. para. 8–126, n. 65.

[82] *Mercantile Bank of India Ltd v. Central Bank of India Ltd* [1938] A.C. 287, 298–299. See also *Bell v. Marsh* [1903] 1 Ch. 528, 541.

[83] "The 'holding out' must be to the particular individual who says he relied on it, or under such circumstances of publicity as to justify the inference that he knew of it and acted upon it": *Dickinson v. Valpy* (1829) 10 B. & C. 128, 140, approved in *Farquharson Bros. & Co. v. King & Co.* [1902] A.C. 325, 341 (Illustration 7). As to representation through an agent see *Moorgate Mercantile Co. Ltd v. Twitchings* [1977] A.C. 890, Illustration 8.

there must be a duty of care,[84] breach of which is the proximate cause of the deception of the third party.[85] But it seems that the duty can be owed to a wide class of persons, and indeed some cases speak of it being owed to all the world.[86] Although this reasoning does not invoke the rules applicable to the establishment of a cause of action in tort,[87] and may indeed be criticized as adding a gloss to the statute,[88] it does go beyond the mere requirement that loss to a third party is foreseeable. Not only must such loss be foreseeable, it must also be a loss which the principal is culpable in failing to guard against: there cannot be negligence in the air. On this latter question there are therefore guidelines to be extracted from the case-law.

Here again, as in the case of apparent authority, the principal is not bound merely because he has let the agent have goods and/or documents of title[89]: he must have done something more, e.g. allowed property to stand in the agent's name,[90] given the agent an acknowledgment that the agent has bought and paid for the goods,[91] signed a document offering to buy the goods from the agent or a third

---

[84] *Swan v. North British Australasian Co. Ltd* (1863) 2 H. & C. 175, 182; *R. E. Jones Ltd v. Waring & Gillow Ltd* [1926] A.C. 670, 693; *Mercantile Bank of India Ltd v. Central Bank of India Ltd*, n. 82 above, disapproving dicta in *Commonwealth Trust v. Akotey* [1926] A.C. 72; *Wilson & Meeson v. Pickering* [1946] K.B. 422, 425; *Mercantile Credit Co. Ltd v. Hamblin* [1965] 2 Q.B. 242, 271; *Moorgate Mercantile Co. Ltd v. Twitchings*, n. 83 above; *Beverley Acceptances Ltd v. Oakley* [1982] R.T.R. 434, 439, Illustration 9.

[85] *Swan v. North British, etc. Co. Ltd.*, n. 84 above, where this was not so because the agent stole share certificates from the principal.

[86] *Swan v. North British, etc. Co.*, n. 84 above; *Gallie v. Lee* [1969] 2 Ch. 17, 36, 48 (affd. *sub nom. Saunders v. Anglia Building Society* [1971] A.C. 1004).

[87] See *Saunders v. Anglia Building Society*, n. 86 above, at pp. 1026, 1038.

[88] See *Thomas Australia Wholesale Vehicle Trading Co. Pty Ltd v. Marac Finance Australia Ltd* (1985) 3 N.S.W.L.R. 452 esp. at pp. 458–459; *Leonard v. Ielasi* (1987) 46 S.A.S.R. 495.

[89] cf. Illustrations 7–9; *Motor Credits (Hire Finance) Ltd v. Pacific Motor Auctions Pty Ltd* (1963) 109 C.L.R. 87, 99 (revsd. on other grounds [1965] A.C. 867). A car registration document is not such a document of title: *J. Sargent (Garages) Ltd v. Motor Auctions (West Bromwich) Ltd* [1977] R.T.R. 121; *Beverley Acceptances Ltd v. Oakley* [1982] R.T.R. 417, Illustration 9. Lord Denning M.R. consistently took a different view: *ibid.*

[90] Illustrations 1, 2; *Dyer v. Pearson* (1824) 3 B. & C. 38; *Pickard v. Sears* (1837) 6 A. & E. 469; *Freeman v. Cooke* (1848) 2 Exch. 654; *Henderson & Co. v. Williams* [1895] 1 Q.B. 521; *Leonard v. Ielasi*, n. 88 above. See also *Lloyds & Scottish Finance v. Williamson* [1965] 1 W.L.R. 404, *sed quaere* what was the extra feature in that case. The court seems to have applied the rules as to settlement with an agent discussed in Article 82: but these do not require more than possession of goods, and the principal seeks to affirm the transfer and require a second payment. Unless the case can be justified on the basis of *Brocklesby v. Temperance Building Society*, discussed under Article 87, it is probably best treated, as it seems to have been at first instance, as a case of actual authority.

[91] Illustration 6.

party[92]: or (perhaps) entrusted the goods to a person who in the normal course of business sells goods that are his own.[93] Further, in all these cases the representation must be relied on: a person who did not believe that the agent was owner cannot found on this doctrine.[94] But it is not at all clear how far this goes: in particular, the question of the duty of care owed by those who sign documents in blank, which is not of course confined to agency situations, is a vexed one.[95] It seems that no estoppel will normally arise against a person who gives his agent share certificates accompanied by signed blank transfers,[96] for this could be used as a method of effecting a mortgage. It has been suggested that, apart from cases of specific representation and (possibly) entrusting to a person who normally sells goods that are his own, any estoppel is confined to the case of negotiable instruments,[97] viz. (presumably), instruments intended to become negotiable instruments[98]: where incomplete documents are deposited merely for custody there is apparently no negligence.[99] More recent authority however indicates doubt as to whether it should be so limited, even if cases in other areas would be rare.[1] The formulation of principles is so difficult that the

---

[92] Illustrations 4, 5.

[93] *Motor Credits (Hire Finance) Ltd v. Pacific Motor Auctions Pty Ltd*, n. 89 above.

[94] *Motor Credits (Hire Finance) Ltd v. Pacific Motor Auctions Pty Ltd*, n. 89 above; *Pickering v. Busk* (1812) 15 East 38; *Motor Finance and Trading Co. Ltd v. Brown* [1928] S.A.S.R. 153, *Sed quaere.*

[95] See Pickering (1939) 55 L.Q.R. 400; Ewart, *Estoppel* (1900), pp. 438 *et seq.*

[96] *France v. Clark* (1884) 26 Ch.D. 257; *Hutchison v. Colorado Mining Co.* (1886) 3 T.L.R. 265; *Fox v. Martin* (1895) 64 L.J.Ch. 473, Illustration 2 to Article 87; *cf.* cases on the negligent custody of company seals: *Bank of Ireland v. Evans' Trustees* (1855) 5 H.L. Cas. 389; *Merchants of Staple v. Bank of England* (1888) 21 Q.B.D. 160; *Lewes Sanitary Steam Laundry v. Barclay & Co. Ltd* (1906) 22 T.L.R. 737. But a duty of care was held to exist in *Fuller v. Glyn, Mills, Currie & Co.* [1914] 2 K.B. 168. This case is difficult to reconcile with *Fox v. Martin*, above, and the matter turns on the correct propositions to be derived from *Colonial Bank v. Cady and Williams* (1890) 15 App.Cas. 267. It was explained in *Mercantile Bank of India Ltd v. Central Bank of India Ltd* [1938] A.C. 287, 302–303 as a case where the agent, a stockbroker, had a usual authority to pledge: this explanation was accepted by Starke and Dixon JJ. in *Tobin v. Broadbent* (1947) 75 C.L.R. 378, but Latham C.J. thought the case "not satisfactorily supported by authority." See further *Chomley v. Union Bank of Australia Ltd* [1951] S.A.S.R. 152; *Pan-Electric Industries Ltd v. Sim Lim Finance Ltd* [1993] 3 Singapore L.R. 242 (authorities reviewed).

[97] *Wilson & Meeson v. Pickering* [1946] K.B. 422, 427; *Swan v. North British, &c., Co.*, n. 84 above. This, if correct, would explain *Lloyds Bank v. Cooke* [1907] 1 K.B. 794; but *cf.* (1945) 9 M.L.R. 298. That case can also be based on the doctrine of *Brocklesby v. Temperance Building Society*, but this doctrine is itself doubtful: see Article 87. See also Bills of Exchange Act 1882, s.20; Article 74, Illustration 14.

[98] Powell, p. 90.

[99] *Smith v. Prosser* [1907] 2 K.B. 735.

[1] *Mercantile Credit Co. Ltd v. Hamblin* [1965] 2 Q.B. 242, 279; *Gallie v. Lee* [1967] 2 Ch. 17, 48 (affd. *sub nom. Saunders v. Anglia Building Society* [1971] A.C. 1004); *Union Credit Bank Ltd v. Mersey Docks and Harbour Board* [1899] 2 Q.B. 205, 210; *United Dominions Trust Ltd v. Western* [1976] Q.B. 513; *Gator Shipping Corp. v. Trans-Asiatic Oil Ltd S.A. (The Odenfeld)* [1978] 2 Lloyd's Rep 357, 375–378.

courts have frequently been forced back on the famous dictum of Ashurst J., "Whenever one of two innocent persons must suffer by the acts of a third, he who has enabled such third person to occasion the loss must sustain it."[2] But this hardly furnishes a precise guide: whether a person has "enabled" seems to turn on the criteria indicated above.[3]

Agent as trustee. The doctrine is inapplicable where the principal 8–130 vests property in the agent as trustee,[4] for "a person is entitled to leave his property, whatever it may be, in the name of a trustee."[5] But in such a case the principal's interest could of course be defeated by a bona fide purchaser for value of the legal estate without notice.[6]

Notice. The question of notice is discussed under Article 75.   8–131

Illustrations

(1)   The purchaser of hemp lying at wharves in London has, at the 8–132 time of the purchase, the hemp transferred in the wharfinger's books into the name of the broker who effected the purchase for him and whose ordinary business it was to buy and sell hemp. An unauthorised sale by the broker passes property.[7]

(2)   A, though the agency of B, a broker, obtained a loan on a mortgage of stock, and afterwards permitted the security to be transferred to B's banker, who had no notice of A's title and believed that B was the owner of the stock. B sold the stock, which was transferred by the banker to the purchaser, and, having paid off the loan, converted the balance to his own use. Held, that A had no remedy against the banker.[8]

(3)   A broker, having effected an insurance policy in his own name, was permitted to retain possession of it for the purpose of receiving the proceeds. The broker pledged the policy. Held, that the pledgee was

---

[2] *Lickbarrow v. Mason* (1787) 2 T.R. 63, 70.

[3] *Farquharson Bros & Co. v. King & Co.* [1902] A.C. 325, 342, Illustration 7; *R. E. Jones Ltd v. Waring & Gillow Ltd* [1926] A.C. 670, 693; *Jerome v. Bentley & Co.* [1952] 2 All E.R. 114, 118; *Central Newbury Car Auctions Ltd v. Unity Finance Ltd* [1957] 1 Q.B. 371, 389 (Illustration 4).

[4] *Shropshire Union Railways and Canal Co. v. R.* (1875) L.R. 7 H.L. 496; *Burgis v. Constantine* [1908] 2 K.B. 484.

[5] *Burgis v. Constantine,* n. 4 above, at p. 498.

[6] The above cases involved subsequent equitable mortgagees, who were postponed to the equitable owners.

[7] *Pickering v. Busk* (1812) 15 East 38.

[8] *Marshall v. National Provincial Bank* (1892) 61 L.J.Ch. 465; *Bentinck v. London Joint Stock Bank* [1893] 2 Ch. 120.

entitled, as against the principal, to retain the advance out of the proceeds of the policy.[9]

(4)   B agrees to buy A's car on hire-purchase and signs documents proposing to buy it from a finance company. A lets B have car and registration document and drive away. Later B sells the car, with the registration document, to a third party who is ignorant of B's lack of title. The third party does not acquire title, since possession of the car is not apparent ownership of it and the registration document contains a warning that the person holding it may or may not be the owner.[10]

(5)   A wishes to borrow money on the security of his car. He agrees to a dealer representing to a finance company that he (the dealer) owns the car, and signs in blank documents agreeing to buy the car on hire-purchase from the finance company. The dealer fills in the documents and purports to sell the car to the company, who duly hire it to A. A is estopped from denying the dealer's authority to sell the car to the finance company.[11]

(6)   R gives a broker a mortgage bond and instructs him to sell it. The broker induces R to execute transfers of the bond to him, acknowledging receipt of purchase money (though R has received nothing). The broker submortgages the bond to W. The submortgage binds R.[12]

(7)   F, timber merchants, warehouse timber with a dock company and instruct the company to accept all orders signed by their clerk. The clerk gives orders transferring timber to himself under an assumed name and under that name fraudulently sells it to K. F can recover the timber from K.[13]

(8)   A finance company transferring a car on hire purchase negligently fails to register the transaction with H.P. Information Ltd, an independent organisation to which 95 per cent of such finance

---

[9] *Callow v. Kelson* (1862) 10 W.R. 193. See also *Williams v. Allsup* (1861) 10 C.B.(N.S.) 417.
[10] *Central Newbury Car Auctions Ltd v. Unity Finance Ltd* [1957] 1 Q.B. 371 (see (1957) 73 L.Q.R. 309); *Astley Industrial Trust Ltd v. Miller* [1968] 2 All E.R. 36; *J. Sargent (Garages) Ltd v. Motor Auctions (West Bromwich) Ltd* [1977] R.T.R. 121.
[11] *Eastern Distributors Ltd v. Goldring* [1957] 2 Q.B. 600; *Stoneleigh Finance Ltd v. Phillips* [1965] 2 Q.B. 537; *Snook v. London & West Riding Investments Ltd* [1967] 2 Q.B. 786; *cf. Mercantile Credit Co. Ltd v. Hamblin* [1965] 2 Q.B. 242.
[12] *Rimmer v. Webster* [1902] 2 Ch. 163; *Abigail v. Lapin* [1934] A.C. 491. See also *Shaw v. Commissioner of Police of the Metropolis* [1987] 1 W.L.R. 1332. Contrast *Debs v. Sibec Developments Ltd* [1990] R.T.R. 91 (document signed under duress does not found estoppel by representation).
[13] *Farquharson Bros. & Co. v. King & Co.* [1902] A.C. 325; see (1902) 18 L.Q.R. 18; ibid., 159. See also *Mercantile Bank of India Ltd v. Central Bank of India Ltd* [1938] A.C. 287; *cf. Canadian Laboratory Supplies Ltd v. Engelhard Industries of Canada Ltd* [1979] 2 S.C.R. 787, (1979) 97 D.L.R. (3d) 1.

companies belong and which maintains a central register of hire-purchase agreements. Another member, a motor dealer, inquires as to the existence of any agreement on the car, and on being told none is recorded, buys it. The first company can assert its interest because (a) the answer does not allege that there *is* no such agreement; (b) H.P.I. are independent suppliers of information and not agents for their members (in this case the finance company); (c) the members owe no duty to each other to register agreements.[14]

(9)   The pledgee of two valuable motor-cars who keeps them in a shed in the yard of his premises lends the owner the keys, and the registration document of one, supposedly to enable the owner to show the cars to insurers. The owner executes bills of sale on the cars. The first pledgee is not estopped from setting up his prior interest.[15]

Article 87

Dispositions by Agents Entrusted with Title Deeds of Property

(Perhaps), where a principal entrusts his agent with the possession   **8–133** of the indicia of title to property, and authorises him to raise money on their security, any security given by the agent on the property for money advanced, though for a higher amount than he was authorised to raise, is valid against the principal, provided that the person taking the security acts in good faith, and without notice that the agent is exceeding his authority.[16]

Comment

A person who holds the indicia of title to another's property has no   **8–134** apparent authority to sell or mortgage it from his holding alone, for he may well, for example, be a mortgagee; nor has he apparent ownership.[17] The cases on which this Article is based seek to find in the

---

[14] *Moorgate Mercantile Co. Ltd v. Twitchings* [1977] A.C. 890. See also *Cadogan Finance Ltd v. Lavery* [1982] Com.L.Rep. 248 (aircraft); *Debs v. Sibec Developments Ltd* [1990] R.T.R. 91 (failure to report robbery to police).

[15] *Beverley Acceptances Ltd v. Oakley* [1982] R.T.R. 417 (Lord Denning M.R. dissenting). See also *McManus v. Eastern Ford Sales Ltd* (1981) 128 D.L.R. (3d) 246.

[16] *Brocklesby v. Temperance Building Society* [1895] A.C. 173, Illustration 1; *Perry-Herrick v. Attwood* (1857) 2 De G. & J. 21; *Rimmer v. Webster* [1902] 2 Ch. 163; *Fry v. Smellie* [1912] 3 K.B. 282, Illustration 3. *Brocklesby's* case was followed in *Lloyd's Bank v. Cooke* [1907] 1 K.B. 794, but this difficult case should probably be explained on the grounds of estoppel by conduct. (See *Wilson & Meeson v. Pickering* [1946] K.B. 422; above, para. 8–129, n. 97.) It was also referred to with approval by the Court of Appeal in *Abbey National B.S. v. Cann* [1989] 2 F.L.R. 265; affd. on other grounds [1991] 1 A.C. 56.

[17] Articles 85, 86.

fact that the principal has, unknown to the third party, given the agent authority to effect some sort of disposition of the goods, an additional element validating his unauthorised disposition. It is however difficult to justify such a proposition on principle. The underlying notion seems to be that where a person is given documents of title with authority to use them for the purpose of raising money, the owner of the documents cannot take advantage of any limitation in point of amount placed on the agent's authority as against a lender who had no notice of such limitation. [18] This may be a reasonable idea, but it is not in accord with well-established rules of agency to the effect that where an agent acts outside his actual authority, his principal is only bound where there is apparent authority, or where the contract is ratified. [19] The fact that the agent, unknown to the third party, has some limited authority in the relevant direction should, it is submitted, make no difference in the absence of ratification, apparent authority, or apparent ownership.

One of the leading cases, *Brocklesby v. Temperance Building Society*, [20] could be explained on the ground that the agent had, in addition to the deeds, a document conferring on him an apparent authority to pledge them, [21] but the relevance of this was discounted in the judgments and emphasis placed on the existence of some initial authority, and the possible injustice to third parties if the unauthorised pledge was not valid. In another leading case, *Fry v. Smellie*, [22] an agent who was given share certificates and a signed blank transfer, and instructed to borrow not less than a certain sum, borrowed less than the stipulated sum, and the owner of the shares was held bound. It could be argued that the deposit of share certificates together with such a transfer gives apparent ownership, or gives an apparent authority to borrow on their security, [23] but there was authority against this, [24] based on a practice of effecting mortgages by the use of such documents. Again the initial authority was held to make the difference. It is indeed difficult to escape the significance of the initial authority if this line of cases is to be accepted.

---

[18] *Brocklesby v. Temperance Building Society* [1895] A.C. 173, 180–181.

[19] *cf. Keighley Maxsted & Co. v. Durant* [1901] A.C. 240. And the distinction between exceeding authority and doing an act right outside the authority would be difficult to operate. It is, however, defended by Atiyah [1965] J.B.L. 130, 136; *Sale of Goods* (8th ed.), p. 358. *Cf.* Ewart, *Estoppel* (1900), pp. 244–246.

[20] [1895] A.C. 173, Illustration 1.

[21] Powell, p. 84.

[22] [1912] 3 K.B. 282, Illustration 3; criticised by Powell, pp. 82–83.

[23] See *per* Farwell L.J. at p. 296. See also *Tobin v. Broadbent* (1947) 75 C.L.R. 378, 405–406.

[24] *Fox v. Martin* (1895) 64 L.J.Ch. 473, Illustration 2.

The rule seems to originate from cases of priority of mortgages of land,[25] where it takes the form that if a mortgagee of property permits the mortgagor to have possession of the title deeds for the purpose of giving a security on the property, any security given for value by the mortgagor thereon has priority to the claim of the mortgagee, provided that the person taking the security acts in good faith and without notice to the mortgage.[26] But in this rather different area, priority is largely regulated by conduct rendering the equities unequal as between the parties, or displacing the superiority of the legal estate, and it is obvious that conduct of one party, even where unknown to the other, could be taken into account in this sort of inquiry.[27] Thus gross negligence with regard to the deeds displaces the claim of a prior or legal mortgagee.[28] Although it is said that the cases are not based on this rule as to gross negligence,[29] their rationale is most imprecisely stated,[30] and their relation to agency cases not fully worked out.[31] Further, many mortgage

---

[25] See the doctrine discussed by Millett J. in *Macmillan Inc. v. Bishopgate Investment Trust Plc (No. 2)* [1995] 1 W.L.R. 978 (where counsel had described it as "the arming principle"). Millett J. said that it was "indeed part of the law of priorities and not of agency" (at p. 1012).

[26] *Perry-Herrick v. Attwood* (1857) 2 De G. & J. 21; *Briggs v. Jones* (1870) L.R. 10 Eq. 92; *Clarke v. Palmer* (1882) 21 Ch.D. 124. *Cf. Colyer v. Finch* (1856) 5 H.L.Cas. 905; *Northern Counties Insurance Co. v. Whipp* (1884) 26 Ch.D. 482; *Hunt v. Elmes* (1861) 30 L.J.Ch. 255; *Cottey v. National Provincial Bank Ltd* (1904) 20 T.L.R. 607. The connection between the rule and these mortgage cases is supported by the fact that in *Northern Counties Insurance Co. v. Whipp*, above, at pp. 492–493 it is suggested that it is *only* where the delivery was for the purpose of raising money that a prior mortgagee who fails to retain the deeds (as opposed to one who fails to obtain them) is postponed.

[27] "To hold that a person who advances money on an estate, the title deeds of which are under such circumstances left in the hands of the mortgagor, is not to have preference would be to shut our eyes to the plainest equity": *Perry-Herrick v. Attwood*, n. 26 above, at p. 39, *per* Lord Cranworth L.C. "A person who puts it in the power of another to deceive and to raise money must take the consequences; he cannot afterwards rely on a particular or a different equity": *Briggs v. Jones*, n. 26 above, at p. 98, *per* Lord Romilly M.R.

[28] See in general Waldock, *Law of Mortgages* (2nd ed.), pp. 392, *et seq.*, 420 *et seq.* (though the interpretation given of the cases here discussed at p. 393 is, it is submitted, erroneous). *Quaere* to what extent this differs from estoppel by conduct: see, *e.g. Rimmer v. Webster* [1902] 2 Ch. 163, 172; Ashburner, *Principles of Equity* (2nd ed.), pp. 453 et seq.

[29] *Perry-Herrick v. Attwood*, n. 26 above, at pp. 37, 39.

[30] See *Perry-Herrick v. Attwood*, n. 26 above, discussed in *Briggs v. Jones*, n. 26 above, at p. 98; *Hunter v. Walters* (1870) L.R. 11 Eq. 292, 318; *Clarke v. Palmer*, n. 26 above, at p. 129; *Manners v. Mew* (1885) 29 Ch.D. 725, 732; *Northern Counties Insurance Co. v. Whipp*, n. 26 above, at pp. 492–493; *Fox v. Hawks* (1879) 13 Ch.D. 822, 834; *National Provincial Bank v. Jackson* (1886) 33 Ch.D. 1, 12; *Jones v. Rhind* (1869) 17 W.R. 1091; *Lloyds Bank v. Bullock* [1896] 2 Ch. 193, 198.

[31] In land cases the tendency is to think in terms of priority of estates and to consider what conduct will displace the holder of an earlier title. In chattel cases, the reasoning used is more likely to follow the maxim *nemo dat quod non habet* unless there is apparent authority or apparent ownership. Cases involving shares may employ either type of reasoning.

cases can also be explained on the ground of apparent ownership, in that the mortgagee, by returning the mortgagor's own deeds to him (or allowing him to hold them), whether *simpliciter* or with some false acknowledgment of receipt of the mortgage debt,[32] has enabled the mortgagor to appear as the owner of unencumbered property. Similar reasoning can be applied to other mortgage cases.[33]

The leading cases contain dicta which are very difficult to reconcile with the normal principles of agency law,[34] and it is submitted that, if the reasoning contained in them cannot be regarded as wrong, they should at any rate not be regarded as supporting a proposition any wider than that set out in the Article. One case, *Rimmer v. Webster*,[35] suggests that where the agent has authority to sell, an unauthorised pledge may be effective. This is however even more difficult to reconcile with other authority,[36] and the case is probably best explained on its other ground of decision, that of apparent ownership.[37]

8–135   **Forgery.** Forged instruments do not confer rights, and if the agent counterfeits a signature, seal or document in a situation such as those above, no rights are transferred by the forged document.[38] But if the forgery consists only in signing or sealing without authority it may be ratified.[39]

8–136   **Notice.** The question of notice is discussed under Article 75.

---

[32] *e.g. Rice v. Rice* (1854) 2 Drew. 73. *Cf. Martinez v. Cooper* (1826) 2 Russ. 198.

[33] *e.g. Robinson v. Montgomeryshire Brewery Co.* [1896] 2 Ch. 841; *cf. Jameson v. Union Bank of Scotland* (1913) 109 L.T. 850.

[34] Including references to "equitable estoppel": *Fry v. Smellie* [1912] 3 K.B. 282, 299. *Cf. Eastern Distributors Ltd v. Goldring* [1957] 2 Q.B. 600, 611. The doctrine seems to have been nurtured by Farwell L.J., who sat in most of the cases.

[35] [1902] 2 Ch. 163, Illustration 6 to Article 86.

[36] See *Fox v. Martin* (1895) 64 L.J.Ch. 473, Illustration 2; *Hutchison v. Colorado Mining Co.* (1886) 3 T.L.R. 265. This situation will often be covered by section 2 of the Factors Act 1889: see *Lloyd's Bank Ltd v. Bank of America, etc.* [1938] 2 K.B. 147, Illustration 6 to Article 89, and this seems to be the proper approach to it.

[37] See *Tsang Chuen v. Li Po Kwai* [1932] A.C. 715, 728–729; *Abigail v. Lapin* [1934] A.C. 491, 508; Article 86. The case was distinguished in *Jerome v. Bentley & Co.* [1952] 2 All E.R. 114; and there are signs of a similar approach in *Lloyds & Scottish Finance v. Williamson* [1965] 1 W.L.R. 404. This case was, however, treated also as a case of apparent authority, and is probably even better explained as a case of actual authority. There are similar suggestions in *Mercantile Credit Co. Ltd v. Hamblin* [1965] 2 Q.B. 242, 276, 277. See also *Union Credit Bank Ltd v. Mersey Docks & Harbour Board* [1899] 2 Q.B. 205.

[38] Illustration 4.

[39] See above, para. 2–055. And a person may be estopped from setting up forgery: see *ibid.*

Illustrations

(1)   The owner of deeds entrusts them to an agent, with authority to pledge them for a certain sum. The agent pledges them for a larger sum to a person who takes them in good faith and without notice of the limit on the agent's authority. The owner is not entitled to recover the deeds except on repayment of the full amount advanced on them. [40]

(2)   A authorises B, stockbroker, to sell certain shares and entrusts him with the certificates and a blank transfer of the shares for that purpose. B deposits the blank transfer and certificates with his banker as security for an advance to himself. The banker has no title to the shares as against A. [41]

(3)   A gives B share certificates and a signed blank transfer, authorising him to borrow not less than £250. B borrows £100. The mortgage is valid, because B was authorised to borrow. [42]

(4)   A solicitor is employed to obtain a loan of £100 on a mortgage of certain property, and is entrusted with the title deeds for that purpose. He forges a mortgage deed for £400, and misappropriates the whole sum. The mortgage is void, and the client is not liable to the mortgagee, even to the extent of £100. [43]

Article 88

DEALINGS WITH MONEY AND NEGOTIABLE SECURITIES

(1)   Where an agent, in consideration of an antecedent debt or   **8–137**
liability, or for any other valuable consideration, pays or negotiates money or negotiable securities in his possession to a person who receives the same in good faith and without notice that the agent has not authority so to pay, title in the money or negotiable securities passes that person.

(2)   A thing is deemed to be done in good faith within the meaning of this Article when it is in fact done honestly, whether it is done negligently or not.

Comment

Bills of exchange. The position is here regulated by statute: the holder   **8–138**
in due course of a negotiable instrument, *i.e.* a person who receives it in the circumstances specified in Rule (1) of this Article, acquires title to it

---

[40] *Brocklesby v. Temperance Building Society* [1895] A.C. 173.

[41] *Fox v. Martin* (1895) 64 L.J.Ch. 473; *Hutchison v. Colorado Mining Co.* (1886) 3 T.L.R. 265. But *cf. Rimmer v. Webster* [1902] 2 Ch. 163, Illustration 6 to Article 86; *Fuller v. Glyn, Mills, Currie & Co.* [1914] 2 K.B. 168 (see above, para. 8–126, n. 73).

[42] *Fry v. Smellie* [1912] 3 K.B. 282.

[43] *Painter v. Abel* (1863) 2 H. & C. 113; see also *Fox v. Hawks* (1879) 13 Ch.D. 822.

free from defects in title of prior parties,[44] and subsequent transferees deriving title through a holder in due course have the same rights unless parties to fraud or illegality affecting the bill.[45] The doctrine of constructive notice does not apply in this branch of the law.[46]

8-139   **Money.** Money has been called a "negotiable chattel",[47] and partakes both of the nature of chattels and of the nature of negotiable instruments. When the principal's money is transferred by the agent to a third party but has not yet passed into currency (*e.g.* coins of a set kept in a case), and the agent has no actual or apparent authority to transfer the property, and none of the exceptions to the maxim *nemo dat quod non habet* apply, it can be recovered at common law, no property having passed.[48] But where it is paid as money for valuable consideration to a person having no notice of the lack of authority (both of these requirements applying in the modified form laid down for bills of exchange[49]), it cannot be recovered, because it has passed into currency.[50] Such money could not normally be identified in any case: but even if it could, the rule would apply.[51]

Illustrations

8-140   (1)   A, having bought on the Stock Exchange scrip which was issued in England by the agent of a foreign government, and which purported to entitle the bearer, on payment of £100, to receive a bond for that amount, entrusted the scrip to a broker. The broker pledged the scrip as security for a debt owing by himself, the pledgee taking it in good faith

---

[44] Bills of Exchange Act 1882, ss.38, 29(2); but see s.81 ("not negotiable" crossing). For definition of "holder in due course" see s.29(1) (2); for definition of "valuable consideration", see s.27(1). For special rules as to bankers see ss.60, 80, 82; Cheques Act 1957, s.4.

[45] *ibid.* s.29(3).

[46] *ibid.* s.90; see Rule (2) above; *Goodman v. Harvey* (1836) 4 A. & E. 870; *Raphael v. Bank of England* (1855) 17 C.B. 161; *Jones v. Gordon* (1877) 2 App.Cas. 616; Illustration 2. But this simply means that there is no duty to inquire: it may be found as a fact that a person must have been suspicious: *cf.* Article 75.

[47] *Banque Belge pour l'Etranger v. Hambrouck* [1921] 1 K.B. 321, 329. See Mann, *Legal Aspect of Money* (5th ed.), pp. 9–13.

[48] See Article 90.

[49] As to consideration, see Rule (1) above. As to notice, see Rule (2); *Raphael v. Bank of England* (1855) 17 C.B. 161; *Lloyds Bank Ltd v. Swiss Bankverein* (1913) 108 L.T. 143; *Nelson v. Larholt* [1948] 1 K.B. 339, 343–344.

[50] *Miller v. Race* (1758) 1 Burr. 452, 457; *Clarke v. Shee & Johnson* (1774) 1 Cowp. 197, 200; *Wookey v. Pole* (1820) 4 B. & A. 1, 7; *Lipkin Gorman v. Karpnale* [1991] 2 A.C. 548. But its proceeds may be recovered from the agent if they are identifiable: see Article 90.

[51] *Miller v. Race* (1758) 1 Burr. 452, 457.

and without notice that the broker was not authorised so to pledge it. Held, that the scrip being negotiable in the same manner as the bond which it represented would be, the pledgee acquired a good title, as against A, to the extent of the pledge.[52]

(2) A broker fraudulently pledged with a banker negotiable securities belonging to various principals, as security for an advance. The banker acted in good faith, but had no knowledge whether the securities were the property of the broker, or whether he had authority to pledge them, or not, and made no inquiries. Held, that the banker had a good title to the securities, as against the principals, to the extent of the advance.[53]

(3) An agent fraudulently applies moneys of his principal in the purchase of overdue bills, which he sells to a company. The company has no title to the bills as against the principal, overdue bills not being negotiable instruments.[54]

Article 89

DISPOSITIONS PROTECTED BY THE FACTORS ACT 1889

Where a mercantile agent is, with the consent of the owner, in possession of goods, or of the documents of title to goods, any sale, pledge or other disposition of the goods made by him when acting in the ordinary course of business of a mercantile agent is as valid as if he were expressly authorised by the owner of the goods to make the same: provided that the person taking under the disposition acts in good faith and has not, at the time of the disposition, notice that the agent has not authority to make the same.[55]   **8–141**

Comment

Historical. The Factors Act 1889 is a consolidation, with changes and improvements, of a series of Acts dating from 1823, the general purpose of which was to protect bona fide purchasers in mercantile   **8–142**

---

[52] *Goodwin v. Robarts* (1876) 1 App.Cas. 476; *Rumball v. Metropolitan Bank* (1877) 2 Q.B.D. 194; *Edelstein v. Schuler* [1902] 2 K.B. 144; *Bechuanaland Exploration Co. v. London Trading Bank Ltd* [1898] 2 Q.B. 658.

[53] *London Joint Stock Bank v. Simmons* [1892] A.C. 201; *Bentinck v. London Joint Stock Bank* [1893] 2 Ch. 120; *Mutton v. Peat* [1900] 2 Ch. 79; *Lloyds Bank Ltd v. Swiss Bankverein* (1913) 108 L.T. 143. *Cf. Sheffield v. London Joint Stock Bank* (1888) 13 App.Cas. 333.

[54] *Re European Bank, ex p. Oriental Commercial Bank* (1870) L.R. 5 Ch.App. 358. And see Article 90.

[55] Factors Act 1889, s.2(1). *cf.* Uniform Commercial Code, s.2–403(2), a much simpler and wider provision. For Australian and New Zealand cases, see Sutton, *Sales and Consumer Law in Australia and New Zealand* (1983), Chap. XV.

transactions.[56] It should be noted that it involves making a distinction between such transactions and non-mercantile transactions, a distinction familiar in civil law countries but not prominent in the common law. In general it may be said that the Act both confirmed and altered the law, the latter principally by validating not only unauthorised sales by agents. which would often have been effective at common law if the agent was a person in the business of selling,[57] but also unauthorised pledges, which would not normally be effective under the common law rules.[58] The Acts take their name from the factor, a well-known type of commercial agent of the nineteenth century who regularly dealt with goods in his own name,[59] though that operation was not confined to factors. But the operations of business intermediaries are now conducted in different ways from those in use in the nineteenth century, and the main application of the Act seems nowadays to be in respect of situations of much more casual agency, such as that of a motor car dealer obtaining offers for a customer, or a commercial traveller carrying samples. The term "Factors Act" is therefore in some ways misleading[60]: "Mercantile Agents Act" would give a better indication of the ambit of the legislation, and in some common law jurisdictions titles of this sort are adopted.

8–143   **Mercantile agent.** The term was introduced by the 1889 Act.[61] A mercantile agent is an agent having, in the customary course of his business as such agent, authority either to sell goods, or to consign goods for the purpose of sale, or to buy goods, or to raise money on the security of goods.[62] This excludes, *e.g.* shop assistants, carriers and warehousemen.[63] But it does not appear that such a person need follow a recognised occupation as commercial agent of a known sort,[64]

---

[56] See Munday (1977) 6 Anglo-Am.L.Rev. 221, 243 *et seq.*
[57] Under the doctrines of apparent authority and apparent ownership: see Articles 85, 86.
[58] See Stoljar, Çhap. 5; *Cole v. North Western Bank* (1875) L.R. 10 C.P. 354.
[59] See above, para. 1–040; *Heyman v. Flewker* (1863) 13 C.B.(N.S.) 519, 527–528.
[60] See *Rolls Razor Ltd. v. Cox* [1967] 1 Q.B. 552, 578.
[61] Previous statutes used the words "agent entrusted." Therefore cases on such statutes should be viewed with caution, though it has been said that the wording of the 1889 Act represents the results of decisions on the earlier wording: *Oppenheimer v. Attenborough & Son* [1907] 1 K.B. 510, 514. Statutes in other jurisdictions also may use the older wording: Sutton, *op. cit.* n. 55 above.
[62] s.1(1).
[63] *Lowther v. Harris* [1927] 1 K.B. 393, Illustration 3; *Cole v. North Western Bank*, n. 58 above; *Lamb v. Attenborough* (1862) 1 B. & S. 831, Illustration 1; *Heyman v. Flewker* (1863) 13 C.B.(N.S.) 519.
[64] There are dicta to the contrary in *Heyman v. Flewker*, n. 63 above, and *Hastings Ltd v. Pearson* [1893] 1 Q.B. 62, but the latter case was disapproved in *Weiner v. Harris* [1910] 1 K.B. 285. See also *Davey v. Paine Bros. (Motors) Ltd* [1954] N.Z.L.R. 1122.

and a person may be a mercantile agent though he acts for one princpal only, or for an isolated transaction. [65] However, a person who agrees to find a purchaser for goods for another as a friend is not a mercantile agent on these facts alone, [66] nor is a person who only buys and sells on his own behalf. [67] If a person receives goods when not a mercantile agent and subsequently becomes one, the section will not apply unless there is further consent to his possession of the goods subsequent to his acquisition of the character of mercantile agent. [68]

With the consent of the owner. Such consent is presumed in the absence of evidence to the contrary. [69] Where the agent has, with such consent, been in possession of the goods or documents, a disposition which would have been valid if the consent had continued is valid notwithstanding determination of the consent, provided that the person taking under the disposition had not, at the time thereof, notice that the consent had been determined. [70] Where the agent has obtained possession of documents of title through being or having been, with such consent, in possession of the goods or of other documents of title to them, his possession of the former documents is deemed to be with such consent. [71] Where the owner consents to possession by the agent, the operation of the Act is not defeated by the fact that the consent was obtained by deception or fraud, [72] unless the owner did not intend the agent to have possession at all. [73]

8–144

The word "owner" may cover a person who would not strictly be so called, but without whose concurrence the goods cannot be sold even by the true owner, *e.g.* a pledgee whose right of sale has not arisen who returns documents of title to the pledgor under a trust receipt. [74]

---

[65] *Lowther v. Harris*, n. 63 above; *Weiner v. Harris*, n. 64 above; *Heyman v. Flewker*, n. 63 above; *Mortgage Loan & Finance Co. of Australia Ltd v. Richards* (1932) 32 S.R.(N.S.W.) 50; *Thoresen v. Capital Credit Corp. Ltd* (1962) 37 D.L.R. (2d) 317, 327 (decision revsd. (1964) 43 D.L.R. (2d) 94).

[66] *Budberg v. Jerwood & Ward* (1934) 51 T.L.R. 99.

[67] *Belvoir Finance Co. Ltd v. Harold G. Cole & Co. Ltd* [1969] 1 W.L.R. 1877.

[68] *Heap v. Motorists Advisory Agency Ltd* [1923] 1 K.B. 577, 588.

[69] s.2(4).

[70] See s.2(2). *cf.* Article 123.

[71] s.2(3).

[72] *Whitehorn Bros. v. Davison* [1911] 1 K.B. 463; *Pearson v. Rose & Young Ltd* [1951] 1 K.B. 275; *Folkes v. King* [1923] 1 K.B. 282; *Du Jardin v. Beadman Bros.* [1952] 2 Q.B. 712; *Ingram v. Little* [1961] 1 Q.B. 31, 70.

[73] *Pearson v. Rose & Young Ltd*, n. 72 above; *Stadium Finance Ltd v. Robbins* [1962] 2 Q.B. 664. This might be the case where the agent obtains the goods as the result of a mistake on the part of the owner as to the agent's identity, where such identity is material: see *Lake v. Simmons* [1927] A.C. 487. See also Illustration 4.

[74] *Lloyds Bank Ltd v. Bank of America National Trust and Savings Association* [1938] 2 K.B. 147, Illustration 6; see also *Beverley Acceptances Ltd v. Oakley* [1982] R.T.R. 417, Illustration 10.

8–145   **In possession.** It is provided that a person is deemed to be in possession of goods or documents when they are in his actual custody, or are held by any other person subject to his control, or for him, or on his behalf.[75] It has been held that a person who pledges goods for less than their value retains sufficient control to make a further pledge for the balance valid against the principal.[76] But if he simply pledges the goods twice and the first pledgee has possession, this provision cannot be used to validate the second pledge against the first pledgee.[77] The possession must be held by the agent in his capacity as a mercantile agent: the fact that the person in possession is a mercantile agent makes no difference if he is not in possession of the goods for a purpose in some way connected with his business as a mercantile agent, *e.g.* where goods are deposited for repair with a person who is also a dealer, or let to a dealer on hire-purchase.[78] If it were not so, when a furnished house was let to an auctioneer he might acquire power to dispose of the furniture.[79] But it does not seem that it is necessary for the owner to have contemplated that the agent would dispose of all the goods: thus where pictures were sent to the owner of a gallery, some for sale but some for display only, the Act was held to apply to all.[80]

8–146   **Goods.** The term includes wares and merchandise,[81] but not certificates of stock.[82] It was suggested in *Pearson v. Rose & Young Ltd*[83] that where a person obtained possession of a car with the consent of the owner but of the registration document without such consent, he had not obtained "goods" with the owner's consent because "goods" in

---

[75] s.1(2). See *Brown & Co. v. Bedford Pantechnicon Co.* (1889) 5 T.L.R. 449.
[76] *Portalis v. Tetley* (1867) L.R. 5 Eq. 140.
[77] *Beverley Acceptances Ltd v. Oakley*, n. 74 above.
[78] *Staffs Motor Guarantee Ltd v. British Motor Wagon Co. Ltd* [1934] 2 K.B. 305; *Lowther v. Harris* [1927] 1 K.B. 393; *Pearson v. Rose & Young Ltd* [1951] 1 K.B. 275; *Stadium Finance Ltd v. Robbins*, n. 73 above; *Astley Industrial Trust Ltd v. Miller* [1968] 2 All E.R. 36; *Belvoir Finance Co. Ltd v. Harold G. Cole & Co. Ltd* [1969] 1 W.L.R. 1877; *Henderson v. Prosser* [1982] C.L.Y. § 21 (car left for valeting); *Schafhauser v. Shaffer and National Finance Co.* [1943] 3 D.L.R. 656; *Universal Guarantee Pty. Ltd v. Metters Ltd* [1966] W.A.R. 74 ("display or return"); *McManus v. Eastern Ford Sales Ltd* (1981) 128 D.L.R. (3d) 246. The criticism of the *Staffs Motor Guarantee* case in *Pacific Motor Auctions Pty. Ltd v. Motor Credits (Hire Finance) Ltd* [1965] A.C. 867 applies only to the point in relation to s.25(1) of the Sale of Goods Act 1893 (now s.24 of 1979 Act).
[79] See *Cole v. North Western Bank* (1875) L.R. 10 C.D. 354, 369 *per* Blackburn J.
[80] *Moody v. Pall Mall Deposit & Fowarding Co. Ltd* (1917) 33 T.L.R. 306; *sed quaere* (an inadequately reported case). See also *Fuentes v. Montis* (1868) L.R. 3 C.P. 268, 284; *Turner v. Sampson* (1911) 27 T.L.R. 200, Illustration 5; *Pearson v. Rose & Young Ltd*, n. 78 above, at p. 288. But *cf. Stadium Finance Ltd v. Robbins* [1962] 2 Q.B. 664, 674, on which see Hornby (1962) 25 M.L.R. 719.
[81] s.1(3).
[82] *Freeman v. Appleyard* (1862) 32 L.J.Ex. 175.
[83] [1951] 1 K.B. 275.

the Act means in this connection the car together with the registration document.[84] But this reasoning was not accepted in *Stadium Finance Ltd v. Robbins*,[85] and *Pearson v. Rose & Young Ltd* can be otherwise explained (though the alternative explanation is equally unsatisfactory).[86]

Documents of title to goods. This expression includes any bill of **8–147** lading, dock warrant, warehouse keeper's certificate, and warrant or order for the delivery of goods, and any other document used in the ordinary course of business as proof of the possession or control of goods, or authorising, or purporting to authorise, either by indorsement or by delivery, the possessor of the document to transfer to receive the goods thereby represented.[87] This is wider than the notion of "document of title" at common law, which is effectively confined to bills of lading.[88] A motor-vehicle registration document is in England not a document of title.[89]

Sale, pledge or other disposition. The meaning of "sale" is clear from **8–148** the Sale of Goods Act 1979.[90] It should be noted that there is not, as there is in other provisions,[91] any requirement of delivery. "Pledge" includes any contract pledging or giving a lien or security on goods, whether in consideration of an original advance, or of any further or continuing advance, or of any pecuniary liability.[92] A pledge of the documents of title to goods is deemed to be a pledge of the goods.[93] The Act thus applies to pledges for antecedent debts: but where the goods are pledged, without authority, for an antecedent debt or liability of the pledgor, the pledgee acquires no further right to the goods than

---

[84] See esp. at p. 290.
[85] [1962] 2 Q.B. 664. See also (1951) 67 L.Q.R. 3; Powell, pp. 228–229; *Paris v. Goodwin* [1954] N.Z.L.R. 823.
[86] See below, para. 8–151.
[87] s.1(4).
[88] See *Benjamin's Sale of Goods* (4th ed.) § 18–005.
[89] *Joblin v. Watkins & Roseveare Motors Ltd* [1949] 1 All E.R. 47; see also *Pearson v. Rose & Young Ltd*, n. 78 above; *Central Newbury Car Auctions Ltd v. Unity Finance Ltd* [1957] 1 Q.B. 371, Illustration 4 to Article 86; *Moorgate Mercantile Co. Ltd v. Twitchings* [1977] A.C. 890, Illustration 8 to Article 86; *J. Sargent (Garages) Ltd v. Motor Auctions (West Bromwich) Ltd* [1977] R.T.R. 121; *Beverley Acceptances Ltd v. Oakley* [1982] R.T.R. 417. Lord Denning M.R. consistently took a different view: *ibid.*
[90] s.2.
[91] *e.g.* Sale of Goods Act 1979, ss.24, 25.
[92] s.1(5).
[93] s.3; Illustration 8. The transfer of a document may be by indorsement, or where the document is by custom or by its express terms transferable by delivery, or makes the goods deliverable to the bearer, then by delivery: s.11.

could have been enforced by the pledgor at the time of the pledge.[94] Where the goods are pledged without authority in consideration of the delivery or transfer of other goods or documents of title to goods, or of a negotiable security, the pledgee acquires no right or interest in the goods so pledged in excess of the value of the goods, documents or security when so delivered or transferred in exchange.[95] It has been held in Canada that the Act applies where the goods are pledged along with other goods to secure a loan based on the total value of all the goods so pledged.[96]

8–149   Other disposition. Sales and pledges have consideration: but it seems that "other dispositions" must equally not be gratuitous, for it is provided that the consideration necessary for the validity of a sale, pledge or other disposition may be any valuable consideration.[97] But it would in any case be rare for a gratuitous transfer to be in the normal course of business of a mercantile agent. Entrusting goods to an auctioneer for sale is not a pledge or other disposition within the meaning of the Act, though the auctioneer makes advances on the goods.[98]

8–150   Time of disposition. It seems that the sale, pledge or other disposition must occur at the same time as the possession is held.[99]

8–151   Acting in the ordinary course of business of a mercantile agent.[1] This requirement must be distinguished from the requirement that the agent have authority to deal with goods in the customary course of his business as a mercantile agent. If he has no such authority, he is not a mercantile agent within the Act: but even if he is, the section may not apply, because he acts outside the ordinary course of business, *e.g.* by selling outside business premises, or out of business hours.[2] But it is irrelevant whether or not he sells in his own name, and it seems that

---

[94] s.4; Illustration 8.
[95] s.5.
[96] *Thoresen v. Capital Credit Corp.* (1964) 43 D.L.R. (2d) 94; and see *Kaltenbach v. Lewis* (1885) 10 App.Cas. 617; but *cf. City Bank of Sydney v. Barden* (1908) 9 S.R. (N.S.W.) 41.
[97] See s.5. "Consideration" includes exchange: *ibid.* As to "disposition" see *Worcester Works Finance Ltd v. Cooden Engineering Co. Ltd* [1972] 1 Q.B. 210.
[98] *Waddington & Sons v. Neale & Sons* (1907) 96 L.T. 786; *Roache v. Australian Mercantile Land & Finance Co. Ltd (No. 2)* [1966] 1 N.S.W.L.R. 384.
[99] *Beverley Acceptances Ltd v. Oakley* [1982] R.T.R. 417, Illustration 10.
[1] Ivamy (1951) 18 *Solicitor* 28, 31.
[2] *Oppenheimer v. Attenborough & Son* [1908] 1 K.B. 221, 230–231 (Illustration 7). But see *Newtons of Wembley Ltd v. Williams* [1965] 1 Q.B. 560, where the sale of a second-hand car in Warren Street in London was held to be within the ordinary course of business.

provided the general requirements relating to sales by mercantile agents are fulfilled, it is not relevant whether the agent is acting within the ordinary course of business of his particular type of mercantile agent, nor whether the circumstances of the transaction in question are normal. [3] Thus a diamond broker may be acting in the ordinary course of business of a mercantile agent within the meaning of the Act in pledging diamonds entrusted to him for sale, although by the custom of the trade such a broker has no authority to pledge diamonds so entrusted to him. [4] But it is not in the ordinary course of business for a mercantile agent to ask a friend to pawn goods entrusted to him: in order that the pledgee may be protected, the agent must pledge the goods himself, or by a servant or agent employed in the ordinary course of business. [5] A sale by a dealer on terms that the price is to be paid direct to one of the dealer's creditors would probably not be in the ordinary course of business, [6] nor a forced sale to provide security for a debt owed by the agent, [7] nor a sale the profits of which went to the agent, [8] nor a sale of an entire stock-in-trade, [9] nor, perhaps, in some cases, the sale of a car in England without the registration document. [10]

In each case the special facts of the transaction may, however, be evidence that the receiver did not act in good faith, *e.g.* if there is an unduly high rate of interest, [11] the price was unduly low, [12] or it is well known that such an agent has not authority to make the type of

---

[3] *Janesich v. Attenborough & Son* (1910) 102 L.T. 605; *Ceres Orchard Partnership v. Fiatagri Australia Pty Ltd* [1995] 1 N.Z.L.R. 112 (citing further authority).

[4] *Oppenheimer v. Attenborough & Son*, n. 2 above.

[5] s.6; *De Gorter v. Attenborough & Son* (1904) 21 T.L.R. 19.

[6] See *Lloyds & Scottish Finance Ltd v. Williamson* [1965] 1 W.L.R. 404; *Biggs v. Evans* [1894] 1 Q.B. 88 (the other point on which the Act was excluded was doubted in *Turner v. Sampson* (1911) 27 T.L.R. 200). But a sale on credit could be: *Tingey v. Chambers* [1967] N.Z.L.R. 785.

[7] *Motor Credits (Hire Finance) Ltd v. Pacific Motor Auctions Pty. Ltd* (1963) 109 C.L.R. 87 (revsd. on other grounds [1965] A.C. 867); *Nash v. Barnes* [1922] N.Z.L.R. 303.

[8] *Raffoul v. Esanda Ltd* [1970] 3 N.S.W.R. 8.

[9] *Mortimer-Rae v. Barthel* (1979) 105 D.L.R. (3d) 289.

[10] *Pearson v. Rose & Young Ltd* [1951] 1 K.B. 275; *Stadium Finance Ltd v. Robbins* [1962] 2 Q.B. 664; *Lambert v. G. & C. Finance Corp.* (1963) 107 S.J. 666. *Sed quaere*: should this be a matter relevant to the buyer's good faith? *cf. Folkes v. King* [1923] 1 K.B. 282; *Oppenheimer v. Attenborough & Son*, n. 2 above; *Janesich v. Attenborough & Son*, n. 3 above; *Durham v. Asser* (1968) 67 D.L.R. (2d) 574; *Astley Industrial Trust v. Miller* [1968] 2 All E.R. 36 (document left with licensing authority for taxing purposes). As to different practice in Australia see *Magnussen v. Flanagan* [1981] 2 N.S.W.L.R. 926. As to sale on part-exchange basis see *Davey v. Paine Bros. (Motors) Ltd* [1954] N.Z.L.R. 1122.

[11] *Janesich v. Attenborough & Son* (1910) 102 L.T. 605.

[12] *Heap v. Motorists Advisory Agency Ltd* [1923] 1 K.B. 577, 591; *Davey v. Paine Bros. (Motors) Ltd* [1954] N.Z.L.R. 1122, 1130.

disposition involved.[13] Indeed, the demarcation between matters of ordinary course of business and good faith is not clear, and they do not always operate as separate requirements.

In *Pearson v. Rose & Young Ltd*[14] it was suggested that where a car dealer obtains possession of a car with the consent of the owner, but obtains the registration document without such consent, a sale by him of car and registration document is not in the ordinary course of business. This is dubious: provided the book was supplied to the buyer, its provenance should be irrelevant, for the sale is perfectly regular on its face.[15] The case can be explained on other grounds, but these are equally unsatisfactory.[16] It was followed in *Stadium Finance Ltd v. Robbins*,[17] but in this case it appears that the buyer was given neither the registration document nor the ignition key (which the owner had retained) when he bought the car, which might perhaps indicate that the sale was not in the ordinary course of business.[18]

8–152   **Good faith and absence of notice.** This must be proved by the third party.[19] "Good faith" is not defined, but on the analogy of the Sale of Goods Act[20] it may be assumed that the standard is one of honesty: a thing is done in good faith if it is done honestly, whether negligently or not. It is often said that constructive notice is not relevant in commercial transactions.[21] The court may, however, infer that the third party must have known of the lack of authority, *e.g.* in the circumstances discussed above; and in general the courts have in other contexts, especially that of constructive trust, imposed something akin to a duty to inquire.[22] In the case of a disposition by two or more persons who are acting in the transaction as partners, want of good faith on the part of any one of them may deprive all of the protection of the statute.[23]

---

[13] *Oppenheimer v. Attenborough & Son* [1908] 1 K.B. 221, Illustration 7.
[14] [1951] 1 K.B. 275.
[15] See (1951) 67 L.Q.R. 3.
[16] See above, para. 8–146.
[17] [1962] 2 Q.B. 664. See Hornby (1962) 25 M.L.R. 719; Thornley [1962] C.L.Y. § 139; (1972) 78 L.Q.R. 468.
[18] See above, n. 10 and text.
[19] *Heap v. Motorists Advisory Agency Ltd*, n. 12 above; *Stadium Finance Ltd v. Robbins* [1962] 2 Q.B. 664, 673. Yet under s.23 of the Sale of Goods Act 1979, the burden is on the original owner: *Whitehorn Bros. v. Davison* [1911] 1 K.B. 463.
[20] s.61(3). See also *Barclays Bank Ltd v. T.O.S.G. Trust Fund Ltd* [1984] B.C.L.C. 1, 18 ("genuinely and honestly in the circumstances of the case"); *Ceres Orchard Partnership v. Fiatagri Australia Pty Ltd* [1995] 1 N.Z.L.R. 112, 117 ("must have known or must have suspected and wilfully shut his eyes to the means of knowledge available").
[21] See Article 75; *Re Funduk and Horncastle* (1973) 39 D.L.R. (3d) 94.
[22] See n. 20 above; Comments to Articles 75, 117. As to knowledge of adverse claims as preventing bona fides see *Carl Zeiss Stiftung v. Herbert Smith & Co. (No. 2)* [1969] 2 Ch. 276.
[23] *Oppenheimer v. Frazer & Wyatt* [1907] 2 K.B. 50.

Undisclosed principal. It should be noted that the act applies **8–153** notwithstanding that the third party believes the agent to be the owner of the goods: what is relevant is that the agent is a mercantile agent in possession, etc., not that the third party thinks he is.[24] Thus the Act applies to agents of undisclosed as well as disclosed principals.

Miscellaneous. An agreement made with a mercantile agent through a **8–154** clerk or other person authorised in the ordinary course of business to make contracts of sale or pledge on his behalf is deemed to be an agreement with the agent.[25] The Act is in amplification and not in derogation of other powers of an agent.[26] But nothing in it authorises an agent to exceed or depart from his authority as between him and his principal, or exempts him from any liability, civil or criminal, for so doing[27]; or prevents the owner from recovering goods from an agent or his trustee in bankruptcy before a sale or pledge; or from redeeming pledged goods, before sale, on satisfying the claim for which they were pledged and paying to the agent, if required, money in respect of which he would have a lien; or from recovering from a pledgee any balance in his hands as the proceeds of sale, after deducting the amount of his lien.[28]

The protection given by sections 24 and 25 of the Sale of Goods Act 1979 to dispositions by sellers and buyers in possession after sale extends to dispositions by them through mercantile agents; and the peculiar wording of section 25(1) leads to the apparent conclusion that where a buyer is in possession after sale, advantage can only be taken of its provisions if he sells, though a private person, in the ordinary course of business of a mercantile agent.[29] Therefore cases on the application of this section may be relevant to the interpretation of section 2 of the Factors Act 1889.[30]

Where an owner of goods has given possession of the goods to an agent for the purpose of consignment or sale, or has shipped goods in the name of the agent, and the consignee of the goods has not had knowledge that the agent is not the owner of the goods, the consignee,

---

[24] *Oppenheimer v. Attenborough & Son* [1908] 1 K.B. 221, 229 (Illustration 7).
[25] s.6.
[26] s.13.
[27] s.12(1).
[28] s.12(2).
[29] See *Newtons of Wembley Ltd v. Williams* [1965] 1 Q.B. 560, a case on s.9 of the Factors Act 1889, which is largely reproduced in s.25(1) of the Sale of Goods Act 1979. But *cf. Langmead v. Thyer Rubber Co. Ltd* [1947] S.A.S.R. 29; *Jeffcott v. Andrew Motors Ltd* [1960] N.Z.L.R. 721.
[30] *e.g. Newtons of Wembley Ltd v. Williams*, n. 29 above (sale of second-hand car in street market); *Pacific Motor Auctions Pty. Ltd v. Motor Credits (Hire Finance) Ltd* [1965] A.C. 867.

in respect of advances made to or for the use of the agent, has the same lien on the goods as if the agent were the owner of the goods, and may transfer any such lien to another person; but this does not limit or affect the validity of any sale, pledge or other disposition by a mercantile agent.[31]

8–155   **Exclusion of the Act.** It is not possible to contract out of the provisions of the Factors Act; but if a mercantile agent is in possession as buyer of the goods and not as mercantile agent they will not apply.[32]

8–156   **Market overt.** There was formerly a principle under which a bona fide purchaser in certain markets could acquire title to goods even though they were stolen: this was called the rule of market overt. It has now been abolished by statute.[33]

Illustrations

8–156A   (1) A wine merchant's clerk, permitted to have the possession for the purpose of his master's business of dock warrants for wine belonging to his master, fraudulently pledges the warrants for an advance to himself. The transaction is not protected by the Factors Act, because the clerk is not a mercantile agent within the meaning of the Act.[33a]

(2) A, a manufacturing jeweller, supplies jewellery to B, a retail jeweller, on sale or return, on the terms that it is to remain the property of A until it is sold or paid for—B, after selling it, to retain half the difference between the cost price and selling price, by way of remuneration, and to remit the balance of the proceeds to A. B is merely A's agent for sale, and therefore a mercantile agent within the meaning of the Act.[34]

(3) L wishes to sell furniture and a tapestry. He stores it in a house and engages P, an art dealer who has a shop nearby, to sell it on commission: he permits P to occupy a flat in the house and to show the items to customers. P is a mercantile agent but is not in possession of the goods. P pretends that he has sold the tapestry to W, and L permits

---

[31] Factors Act 1889, s.7. See *Mildred, Goyeneche & Co. v. Maspons y Hermano* (1883) 8 App.Cas. 874, 883.

[32] See *Weiner v. Gill* [1906] 2 K.B. 574; *Kempler v. Bravingtons* (1925) 41 T.L.R. 519. *cf. Weiner v. Harris* [1910] 1 K.B. 285, Illustration 2. This distinction can be criticised: see Stoljar, p. 124.

[33] Sale of Goods (Amendment) Act 1994, effective January 3, 1995. For the old law see *Benjamin's Sale of Goods* (4th ed.), §§ 7–016 *et seq.*

[33a] *Lamb v. Attenborough* (1862) 1 B. & S. 831. See also *Farquharson Bros. & Co. v. King & Co.* [1902] A.C. 325, Illustration 7 to Article 86.

[34] *Weiner v. Harris* [1910] 1 K.B. 285; *cf. Weiner v. Gill* [1906] 2 K.B. 574; *Universal Guarantee Pty. Ltd v. Metters Ltd* [1966] W.A.R. 74 (electrical goods "on consignment").

him to remove it. P sells it to H. He was at the time of sale in possession of the tapestry with L's consent and the sale is valid.[35]

(4) An agent employed by a foreign principal to negotiate sales in London obtains an offer from A, which the principal accepts. The principal specially indorses to A the bill of lading for the goods, and sends it to the agent to be exchanged for A's acceptance. The agent, without the principal's authority, agrees with A to cancel the contract, and subsequently induces him to indorse the bill of lading by representing that it was specially indorsed by mistake, and then, having obtained possession of the goods by means of the bill of lading, pledges them for an advance. The pledge is not protected by the Factors Act, because the agent did not obtain possession of the goods with the consent of the principal. The principal, therefore, is entitled to recover the goods from the pledgee.[36]

(5) The owner of a picture asks a dealer to hang it in his gallery and report any offers he may receive for it. The dealer sells it and disappears. The sale is valid.[37]

(6) A company pledged bills of lading with A, a bank, as security for bills of exchange or advances. A handed the bills of lading back to the company upon terms contained in trust receipts, whereby the company was authorised to sell the goods and undertook to hold the proceeds in trust for A. The company pledged the bills of lading with B, a bank, to secure advances. B acted in good faith and without notice that the company was not entitled so to pledge the bills of lading. A claimed the bills of lading from B. Held, that A was owner of the goods represented by the bills of lading within the meaning of the Factors Act; but that the company was a mercantile agent in possession of the bills of lading within the meaning of the Act and that the pledge to B was valid.[38]

(7) A diamond broker asks a diamond dealer to let him have some diamonds to show to two firms of diamond merchants to whom he says he thinks he can sell them. The dealer lets him have diamonds for this purpose, but the broker, instead of showing them to any merchant, pledges them. The pledge is valid.[39]

(8) A broker is authorised to sell goods, and is entrusted with the bill of lading for them by their owner. By means of the bill of lading he obtains dock warrants for the goods, and without the authority of the principal, pledges the warrants with his banker as security for an overdraft, the banker taking them in good faith, and without notice that in so pledging them he is exceeding his authority. Before receiving

---

[35] *Lowther v. Harris* [1927] 1 K.B. 393.
[36] *Vaughan v. Moffatt* (1868) 38 L.J.Ch. 144.
[37] *Turner v. Sampson* (1911) 27 T.L.R. 200.
[38] *Lloyds Bank Ltd v. Bank of America National Trust and Savings Association* [1938] 2 K.B. 147. See *Benjamin's Sale of Goods* (4th ed.), § 18–092.
[39] *Oppenheimer v. Attenborough & Son* [1908] 1 K.B. 221.

notice of the want of authority, the banker, on the faith of the pledge, permits the overdraft to be increased. So far as concerns the overdraft existing at the time of the pledge, the principal is only bound by the pledge to the extent of any lien the broker had on the goods at that time, and may redeem the goods upon payment to that extent, and payment of the amount overdrawn since the date of the pledge. If the broker has a lien in excess of the full amount of the overdraft, the principal must, if required, also pay to the broker the amount of the excess before he is entitled to redeem the goods.[40]

(9)   A factor is entrusted with the possession of goods for sale. The principal revokes his authority, and demands the return of the goods. The factor refuses to return the goods, and then fraudulently sells and delivers them to a person who purchases them in good faith, and without notice that the factor has no authority to sell them, or that he is in possession of the goods without the consent of the owner. The principal is bound by the sale, but may sue in his own name for the price, subject to any right of set-off the purchaser may have against the factor.[41]

(10)   A person pledges two cars and possession is transferred to the pledgee. He subsequently asks to borrow the keys and one registration document (the other not being available), ostensibly to show them to insurance representatives. He actually shows the car to representatives of a finance house; and by virtue of having done so he is later able to execute a bill of sale in favour of the finance house. The disposition is not protected by the Factors Act as (a) he never regained possession of the goods; (b) the registration document is not a document of title; (c) the disposition did not occur at the same time as any possession that he might have had.[42]

Article 90

PRINCIPAL'S RIGHT TO FOLLOW PROPERTY INTO HANDS OF THIRD PARTIES

8–157   Subject to the provisions of Articles 85 to 89, where an agent disposes of the property or money of his principal in a manner not authorised, ratified or otherwise valid, the principal is entitled, as against the agent and third parties, to recover that property or money, or the proceeds of that property or money, wherever they may be found, provided that they can be traced in accordance with the rules of common law and equity.[43]

---

[40] s.12(2).
[41] s.12(3).
[42] *Beverley Acceptances Ltd v. Oakley* [1982] R.T.R. 417.
[43] See Comment.

Comment

Tracing at common law. Where an agent holds the property or money **8–158** of his principal and disposes of it in a manner authorised, title passes. So also it passes by virtue of the special rules of the law of agency in cases of apparent authority,[44] and where one of the exceptions to the rule *nemo dat quod non habet* applies.[45] Otherwise the property or money remains the property of the principal, who may have the right to trace and claim it at common law.[46] This he can do so long as it is identifiable,[47] whether tangible[48] or intangible,[49] and even if it is converted into a different form of property,[50] provided that there is no admixture of other property or money. The primary action for enforcing the principal's property right is that of conversion,[51] but in some cases an action in restitution will be appropriate, though this really affirms property in the defendant, because the claim is for money, which is not identifiable.[52] Either of these lies against a recipient who has parted with what he has received; but in the case of the restitutionary action a defence of change of position is potentially applicable to a recipient who has changed his position in good faith in such a way that it would be inequitable to require him to make restitution in whole or in part.[53] Both these actions are strictly to be classified as actions *in personam*,[54] though the right on which they are based is sometimes thought of as

---

[44] Articles 74, 85.

[45] Articles 85–89.

[46] *Lang v. Smyth* (1831) 7 Bing. 284, 292; *Farquharson Bros. & Co. v. King & Co.* [1902] A.C. 325. The principal may have sufficient title to trace where the agent draws money from the principal's bank account, for the bank's indebtedness is a chose in action belonging to the principal: see *Lipkin Gorman v. Karpnale Ltd* [1991] 2 A.C. 548. Where the transfer is authorised or ratified, the principal may of course sometimes be able to trace against the *agent*; but that is not relevant in this context. See Article 45.

[47] *Taylor v. Plumer* (1815) 3 M. & S. 562, 575 (Illustration 1). (It is by no means clear that this is really a common law case, though it is normally treated as such.)

[48] *e.g.* coins in a bag: *Taylor v. Plumer*, n. 47 above, at p. 565.

[49] *Banque Belge pour l'Etranger v. Hambrouck* [1921] 1 K.B. 321 (unmixed bank balance); *Agip (Africa) Ltd v. Jackson* [1990] Ch. 265; [1991] Ch. 547 (effect of bank clearing mechanisms).

[50] *e.g. Taylor v. Plumer*, n. 47 above (draft converted into stock and bullion). An unpaid debt in respect of the sale of the property would presumably be recoverable: *cf. Re Wood, ex p. Boden* (1873) 28 L.T. 174; and see Illustration 8.

[51] *e.g. Farquharson Bros. & Co. v. King & Co.* [1902] A.C. 325; *Gompertz v. Cook* (1903) 20 T.L.R. 106.

[52] See *Calland v. Lloyd* (1840) 6 M. & W. 26; *Marsh v. Keating* (1834) 1 Bing.N.C. 198; *Scott v. Surman* (1742) Willes 400; *Banque Belge pour l'Etranger v. Hambrouck* [1921] 1 K.B. 321, *per* Atkin L.J.

[53] *Lipkin Gorman v. Karpnale Ltd* [1991] 2 A.C. 548. See McKendrick, (1992) 55 M.L.R. 377; Goff and Jones, *Law of Restitution* (4th ed.), Chap. 40; Burrows, *Law of Restitution* (1993), Chap. 15.

[54] *Lipkin Gorman v. Karpnale Ltd.*, n. 53 above, at p. 572.

proprietary and hence may be spoken of as if *in rem*. It is, however, not easy to see that on the common law as at present understood claims in restitution (as opposed to conversion for chattels) can lie against a recipient subsequent to the first[55]; if they do, they should not lie against a person who gave value in good faith[56] or against a recipient who has parted with the money.[57] Claims more readily classifiable as *in rem* may also be asserted in other ways, such as bankruptcy proceedings,[58] in an action for a declaration,[59] by way of defence to an action in conversion,[60] and in proceedings regarding the registration of shares.[61] There is, however, no general common law action *in rem*, viz. no general action of a proprietary nature.

8–159   **Tracing in equity.** In equity there is also a right to trace,[62] and this is greater because its mechanism, which involves the imposition of a notional lien, can be applied to a mixed fund.[63] But it requires that there be an initial breach of trust or fiduciary relationship; for the equitable right is not triggered unless there has been an initial equitable proprietary relationship.[64] This requirement is sometimes said to be paradoxical, since it attributes greater force to the principal's equitable title than to his legal ownership, though equity always recognised legal ownership.[65] There is, however, a decision, standing by itself, which detected a fiduciary relationship between banks arising merely from payment by one to the other and so almost *ad hoc*.[66] This may seem

---

[55] See the Rt Hon. Lord Justice Millett, (1991) 107 L.Q.R. 71, 77–79. The only relevant authority is the *Banque Belge* case, n. 52 above; see discussion of it in *Agip (Africa) Ltd v. Jackson*, n. 49 above, but *cf.* McKendrick [1991] L.M.C.L.Q. 378, 384–386. But consider also *Lipkin Gorman v. Karpnale Ltd*, n. 53 above.

[56] Unless this is to be regarded as a manifestation of the change of position defence, as to which see Birks, [1989] L.M.C.L.Q. 296, 301–302; [1991] L.M.C.L.Q. 473, 490–492; the Rt Hon. Lord Justice Millett, (1991) 107 L.Q.R. 71, 82.

[57] *Agip (Africa) Ltd v. Jackson* [1990] 1 Ch. 265, 287.

[58] See below, para. 8–161.

[59] *e.g. Banque Belge pour l'Etranger v. Hambrouck*, n. 52 above.

[60] *e.g. Taylor v. Plumer* (1815) 3 M. & S. 562, Illustration 1.

[61] *e.g. France v. Clark* (1884) 26 Ch.D. 257; *Hutchison v. Colorado United Mining Co. & Hamill, Hamill v. Lilley* (1887) 3 T.L.R. 265; *Colonial Bank v. Cady and Williams* (1890) 15 App.Cas. 267; *Fox v. Martin* (1895) 64 L.J.Ch. 473, Illustration 2 to Article 87.

[62] See Snell, *Equity* (29th ed.), pp. 297 *et seq.*; Goff and Jones, *Law of Restitution* (4th ed.), Chap. 2; Burrows, *Law of Restitution* (1993) pp. 57 *et seq.*

[63] But see *Banque Belge, &c. v. Hambrouck*, n. 52 above, at pp. 335–336, suggesting that the common law may not have been so circumscribed.

[64] *Re Diplock* [1948] Ch. 465, 530 (affd. [1951] A.C. 251).

[65] Goff and Jones, *op. cit.* n. 62 above at pp. 83 *et seq.* The Court of Appeal of New Zealand did not accept this restriction in *Elders Pastoral Ltd v. Bank of New Zealand Ltd* [1989] 2 N.Z.L.R. 180 (affd. [1991] 1 N.Z.L.R. 385).

[66] *Chase Manhattan Bank N.A. v. Israel British Bank Ltd* [1981] Ch. 105; see Tettenborn [1980] C.L.J. 272; Jones, *ibid.*, 275.

difficult to justify, but if correct may take some of the sting out of the equitable requirement.[67] It is also true that where an agent holds property entrusted to him by his principal, he often does so as fiduciary[68]; and in other cases he may have control over his principal's money as a fiduciary in a way that gives equal access to the right to trace.[69]

The right in equity consists of a notional lien (sometimes referred to as a charge) on the fund or property, whether mixed or not, held by the agent or by a subsequent holder.[70] The right operates against one who takes with notice[71] or a volunteer,[72] but not against a bona fide purchaser for value without notice,[73] nor where the property or (more usually) money sought to be traced has ceased to be identifiable, e.g. because, being money, it has been spent without identifiable proceeds,[74] or has passed into an overdrawn bank account.[75]

Constructive trust. Whether or not there is a right to trace, a person **8–160** receiving trust property or property affected by some other fiduciary interest with notice, actual or constructive, of the trust or fiduciary interest may nevertheless be liable to account as constructive trustee. It is usually assumed that this is a separate head of liability, effectively *in personam*, based on different principles, and that it is only on this ground that a recipient who has parted with the property would still be liable, and could be required to account for profits, but the question is

---

[67] Not completely, because the issue was not whether the money could be traced into the defendant's hands, but whether he had any of the money left: see *Agip (Africa) Ltd v. Jackson* [1990] Ch. 265, 290 (affd. [1991] Ch. 547). The decision was plainly affected by the fact that the bank was insolvent. See also *Sinclair v. Brougham* [1914] A.C. 398; *Neste Oy v. Lloyd's Bank Plc* [1983] 2 Lloyd's Rep. 658, 666; *Westdeutsche Landesbank Girozentrale v. Islington L.B.C.* [1994] 1 W.L.R. 938; *Re Goldcorp* [1995] 1 A.C. 74.

[68] See Comment to Article 45.

[69] *Agip (Africa) Ltd v. Jackson* [1990] 1 Ch. 265.

[70] *Re Hallett's Estate* (1880) 13 Ch.D. 696, 709; *Hopper v. Conyers* (1866) L.R. 2 Eq. 549. Where the property or proceeds are clearly identifiable, the beneficiary may elect to take them without recourse to a lien. For problems connected with mixed bank accounts, see Illustration 3. For a more complex modern example of tracing see *El Ajou v. Dollar Land Holdings Plc.* [1993] 3 All E.R. 717; decision revsd. [1994] 2 All E.R. 685; *El Ajou v. Dollar Land Holdings Plc (No. 2)* [1995] 2 All E.R. 213.

[71] *Re Diplock, Diplock v. Wintle* [1948] Ch. 465, 539 (affd. [1951] A.C. 251).

[72] *ibid.* But an innocent volunteer may sometimes have an equal equity to share with the principal, where his own money has been mixed with the fund; *Sinclair v. Brougham* [1914] A.C. 398; Maudsley (1959) 75 L.Q.R. 234, 249–252.

[73] *ibid.*; *Thorndike v. Hunt* (1859) 3 De G. & J. 563. As to the meaning of "notice" in this context see *Polly Peck International Plc v. Nadir (No. 2)* [1992] 4 All E.R. 769, 781–782 (but see Bryan (1993) 109 L.Q.R. 368).

[74] *Re Diplock*, n. 71 above, at pp. 546–550; *Re Hallett & Co.* [1894] 2 Q.B. 237; *Ex p. Hardcastle, re Mawson* (1881) 44 L.T. 523.

[75] *Bishopgate Investment Management Ltd v. Homan* [1995] Ch. 211.

controversial.[76] The matter is discussed in connection with the liability of the agent to his principal[77] and again in connection with the liability of the agent to third parties[78]; but of course the principles apply equally to third parties who receive money *from* agents.[79]

8–161   **Bankruptcy.** Bankruptcy of the agent involves the clearest case of a claim *in rem*, inasmuch as the principal seeks to assert that money or goods are his, and to extricate them from the agent's bankruptcy. The basic rule is that property held by the bankrupt the legal title to which is in his principal, and property held by him in trust, or as a fiduciary, is not liable to be seized: this extends to property that can be traced at law or in equity.[80] But once the property can no longer be traced, the principal becomes an ordinary creditor with the rest. Debts owed to the principal are not owed to the agent and so can be recovered by the principal. Some debts owed to the agent could be regarded as held in trust for the principal and so rank as property held on trust.

8–162   **"Romalpa" clauses.** Considerable difficulties can be caused by the use of so-called "Romalpa" clauses, whereby a supplier of goods may seek to protect himself against the bankruptcy of the person to whom he supplies them by reserving title not only in the goods themselves, but also sometimes in the proceeds of their resale, and even into the product of mixing and manufacturing processes to which they may be subjected. Sometimes such provisions contain a "current account" clause, which reserves title not only pending payment in respect of the goods concerned, but also so long as any debt is outstanding between the parties. Apart from problems of identification of goods and appropriation of payments to particular consignments, the main danger from the point of view of the supplier is that they may be held to create some sort of charge and hence be void for non-registration. Therefore, though such arrangments are not normally related to agency re-lationships at all but rather to that of seller and buyer, attempts may be made to draft or interpret them as creating agency features, even though the transaction concerned is inappropriate to such interpretation. Thus it may be suggested that a buyer of goods under such a clause resells as

---

[76] See *Re Montagu's Settlement Trusts* [1987] Ch. 264, 285; but *cf.* the Rt. Hon. Lord Justice Millett, (1991) 107 L.Q.R. 71, 80–81.

[77] Article 45.

[78] Article 117.

[79] See below, para. 9–132 as to the duties and liabilities of banks.

[80] See Insolvency Act 1986 s.283(3); Williams and Muir Hunter, *Bankruptcy* (19th ed.), pp. 260–280 (not reproduced in the subsequent *Muir Hunter on Personal Insolvency* (1988)). A number of old illustrations concerning bankruptcy of agents were collected in the 15th edition of the present work (1985).

agent and holds the proceeds as trustee. As stated, agency reasoning is usually not at all appropriate to such situations, and may indeed create unexpected and unsatisfactory side-effects, for example that the supplier is liable as undisclosed principal on a resale by his purchaser.[81]

Distress.[82] The law of distress anomalously[83] permits distress to be levied on the goods of third parties on the premises of the tenant. There are exceptions to this rule.[84] One is where goods or chattels are entrusted to a person who carries on a trade or business in which the public are invited to entrust their goods or chattels to him for the purpose of being carried, wrought, worked up or managed in the way of such trade or business. The goods or chattels, while on the premises of that person, or on other premises hired by him for any such purpose, are exempt from distress.[85] This may affect certain sorts of agent, particularly auctioneers. The controlling dicta in *Simpson v. Hartopp*[86] refer to persons exercising a "public trade", but it is submitted that the formulation above is more instructive.[87] The reason behind the exception is "public policy for the benefit of trade."[88]   **8–163**

Illustrations

(1) A broker misapplied his principal's money by purchasing stock and bullion, and absconded. He was adjudicated bankrupt on the day upon which he received and misapplied the money. On being arrested he surrendered the securities for the stock and bullion to the principal. Held, that the principal was entitled to retain the securities as against the trustee in bankruptcy.[89]   **8–164**

---

[81] See in general Chitty, *Contracts* (27th ed.), Vol. 2, §§ 41–135 *et seq.*; *Benjamin's Sale of Goods* (4th ed.), §§ 5–113 *et seq.*
[82] See in general Eddy, *Law of Distress* (3rd ed.).
[83] *Clarke v. Millwall Dock Co.* (1886) 17 Q.B.D. 494, 499.
[84] See *Simpson v. Hartopp*, n. 85 below.
[85] *Gisbourn v. Hurst* (1710) 1 Salk. 249; *Simpson v. Hartopp* (1744) Willes 512; *Wood v. Clarke* (1831) 1 Cr. & J. 484; *Swire v. Leach* (1868) 18 C.B.(N.S.) 479; *Miles v. Furber* (1873) L.R. 8 Q.B. 77; *Challoner v. Robinson* [1908] 1 Ch. 49. The Law of Distress Amendment Act 1908 permits certain persons, including a person who has no interest in premises on which goods are taken, to serve a notice on the landlord stating the circumstances; after which any distress on the property of that person may be illegal. If this procedure is followed by the owner of the goods, the immunity from distress may be enlarged.
[86] n. 85 above.
[87] See *Challoner v. Robinson* [1908] 1 Ch. 49; Illustration 12.
[88] *Lyons v. Elliott* (1876) 1 Q.B.D. 210, 214. See also *Miles v. Furber*, n. 85 above, at p. 83; *Muspratt v. Gregory* (1838) 3 M. & W. 677.
[89] *Taylor v. Plumer* (1815) 3 M. & S. 562; *Re Hulton, ex p. Manchester and County Bank* (1891) 39 W.R. 303; *Re Dodds, ex p. Brown* (1891) 60 L.J.Q.B. 599. See also *Marsh v. Keating* (1834) 1 Bing. (N.C.) 198.

(2) An agent who was entrusted with bills to get discounted mixed them with his own property, absconded, and became bankrupt. He was arrested with money in his possession which was the produce of portions of the mixed property. Held, that the principal was entitled, in preference to the other creditors, to a first charge on such money for the amount of the bills.[90]

(3) Money is paid to a broker by his principal for application in a particular way. The broker pays the money into his own account at a bank, and becomes bankrupt before applying it as directed. The principal is entitled to the money as against the broker's trustee in bankruptcy.[91] If, in such a case, the agent has drawn on the account, the principal has a charge on the balance in the banker's hands, the amounts so drawn being deemed to be drawn out of the agent's own moneys, whenever they were paid in,[92] so long as the balance exceeds the trust moneys.[93] Where the moneys of several principals have been paid into the account, their charges have priority in the inverse order of the payments, the balance being deemed to consist of the trust moneys most recently paid in.[94]

(4) An agent who was employed to sell certain goods mixed them with goods of his own, and consigned the whole of the goods together to a factor for sale, representing to his principal that he had sold his goods, and debiting himself with the amount of the supposed prices. The agent having become bankrupt, the principal was held entitled to have the proceeds of the mixed property marshalled, so as to throw advances made by the factor, as far as possible, on to the agent's own goods.[95]

(5) A factor becomes bankrupt. Goods in his hands for sale, fresh goods directly bought with the proceeds of sale of such goods, and unmatured bills and notes received by him as the price of goods sold, must, subject to his lien, be returned to the principal, and may be

---

[90] *Frith v. Cartland* (1865) 34 L.J.Ch. 301.

[91] *Re Strachan, ex p. Cooke* (1876) 4 Ch.D. 123; *Hancock v. Smith* (1889) 41 Ch.D. 456; *Re Arthur Wheeler* (1933) 102 L.J.Ch. 341. See also *Re Cotton, ex p. Cooke* (1913) 108 L.T. 310 (auctioneer). *Cf. Re Hallett & Co., ex p. Blane* [1894] 2 Q.B. 237; *Re Mawson, ex p. Hardcastle* (1881) 44 L.T. 523; *King v. Hutton* [1900] 2 Q.B. 504; *Wilsons & Furness-Leyland Line Ltd v. British & Continental Shipping Co. Ltd* (1907) 23 T.L.R. 397.

[92] *Re Hallett's Estate* (1880) 13 Ch.D. 696; *Re Wreford* (1897) 13 T.L.R. 153; *Banque Belge pour l'Etranger v. Hambrouck* [1921] 1 K.B. 321. See also *Re Oatway* [1903] 2 Ch. 356.

[93] *James Roscoe (Bolton) Ltd v. Winder* [1915] 1 Ch. 62.

[94] *Re Stenning* [1895] 2 Ch. 433. See also *Re Diplock* [1948] Ch. 465 (affd. [1951] A.C. 251). This is subject to contrary intention: see *Barlow Clowes International Ltd v. Vaughan* [1992] 4 All E.R. 22.

[95] *Broadbent v. Barlow* (1861) 3 De G.F. & J. 570; *Re Holland, ex p. Alston* (1868) L.R. 4 Ch.App. 168; *Re Burge, Woodall & Co., ex p. Skyrme* [1912] 1 K.B. 393.

recovered by him from the trustee in bankruptcy.[95] The price of goods already sold may, subject to the agent's lien, be recovered by the principal from the purchaser,[96] and, if paid to the trustee in bankruptcy, may be recovered from him by the principal.[97]

(6) The chief accountant of a company fraudulently alters a cheque duly signed on the company's behalf, with the effect that it is credited to another company with which the paying company has no connection, and from there paid out on instructions. It is assumed that the directors of the latter company have no knowledge of the reason behind the transaction. They are liable for money still in their possession.[98]

(7) A partner in a firm of solicitors fraudulently draws money from the company's account and spends it gambling at a casino. The firm may recover the money from the casino subject to a defence of change of position.[99]

Distress   8–165

(8) Goods are entrusted to a factor or auctioneer for sale. They are not liable to distress for the rent of the premises of the factor or auctioneer.[1]

(9) An auctioneer hires a room for the purpose of a sale by auction. Goods or chattels sent to the room for sale are privileged from distress, though the room was hired only for the particular occasion.[2]

(10) A employs an auctioneer to sell goods by auction on A's premises. B sends goods to A's premises, to be sold with A's goods. The goods of both A and B are liable to distress for rent due from A in respect of the premises.[3]

(11) Corn is entrusted to a factor for sale. Not having a warehouse of his own, he deposits the corn in the warehouse of a granary keeper. The corn is privileged from distress for the rent of that warehouse.[4]

(12) A was an agent for the sale of carpets manufactured by B, and the name of B, as well as that of A, was painted outside the premises upon which A carried on business. A also acted as agent for the sale,

---

[95] *Scott v. Surman* (1742) Willes 400; *Whitecomb v. Jacob* (1710) 1 Salk. 160; *Godfrey v. Furzo* (1733) 3 P.Wms. 186. See also *Ex p. Sayers* (1800) 5 Ves. 169.
[96] *Scott v. Surman*, n. 95 above; *Re Wood, ex p Boden* (1873) 28 L.T. 174.
[97] See cases cited above, n. 95.
[98] *Agip (Africa) Ltd. v. Jackson* [1990] Ch. 265; [1991] Ch. 247.
[99] *Lipkin Gorman v. Karpnale Ltd* [1991] 2 A.C. 548.
[1] *Williams v. Holmes* (1853) 8 Exch. 861; *Adams v. Grane* (1833) 1 C. & M. 380; *Gilman v. Elton* (1821) 6 Moo.C.P. 243; *Findon v. M'Laren* (1845) 6 Q.B. 891.
[2] *Brown v. Arundell* (1850) 10 C.B. 54.
[3] *Lyons v. Elliott* (1876) 1 Q.B.D. 210.
[4] *Matthias v. Mesnard* (1826) 2 C. & P. 353.

upon the same premises, of carpets manufactured by C, and was entitled to carry on other agency business, though he did not do so. Held, that the goods of B and C were not exempt from distress for the rent of the premises, because A did not carry on a trade or business in which the public were invited to entrust their goods to him.[5]

(13) Motor car manufacturers send a chassis to dealers for exhibition purposes. It is not privileged from distress.[6]

Article 91

DISPOSITIONS TO AGENT

8–166   (1) Where a purported transfer of property in goods is made to the agent of a disclosed principal, and the agent receives it as such acting within his actual or apparent authority, the property in the goods is transferred to the principal if such is the intention of the parties to the transfer.

(2) (Perhaps), where a purported transfer of property in goods is made to the agent of an undisclosed principal and the agent is authorised to receive it and does so intending to act as agent, the property in the goods is transferred to the undisclosed principal if such is the intention of the agent and the principal, unless the principal knows that the transferor would not have transferred the property in the goods to him.

(3) (Perhaps), where there is an attornment by the holder of goods to the agent of an undisclosed principal and the agent is authorised to receive it and does so intending to act as agent, the principal has the right to treat the attornment as being to him unless the principal knows that the holder of the goods would not have attorned to him.[7]

Comment

8–167   The question of the effect of dispositions *by* an agent of his principal's property raises problems of transfer of property by a non-owner. That of the effect of dispositions *in favour of* the agent, on the other hand, raises quite different problems regarding the relevance of the intention of the parties to the transfer of property and possession.

---

[5] *Tapling & Co. v. Weston* (1883) C. & E. 99.
[6] *Simms Manufacturing Co. v. Whitehead* [1909] W.N. 95. See also *Challoner v. Robinson* [1908] 1 Ch. 49 ("managed" includes, if it is not equivalent to, "disposed of").
[7] See Comment; Goode, *Proprietary Rights and Insolvency in Sales Transactions* (2nd ed.), Chap. III.

Disclosed principal. Property in goods is transferred by delivery, and   **8–168**
in some cases (particularly contracts of sale of goods)[8] by intention.
There is no objection to the acquisition of property through an agent.
Hence a transfer of goods, whether by delivery or mere intention, to an
agent who in receiving possession or assenting to receive property
without possession acts for a disclosed principal, named or unnamed,
will pass property to the principal, provided that all the other conditions
normally required for the passing of property[9] are satisfied. It would of
course be necessary that the agent was acting within his actual or
apparent authority: since the acquisition of property is usually an
advantage, cases where there was no authority of either sort would be
the exception rather than the rule. Where *possession* is also transferred
to the agent, however, this rests with him, though by a pre-existing
intention he may immediately constitute himself bailee for his principal.
As bailee he possesses: his principal does not.[10]

Undisclosed principal. When however there is a transfer to a person   **8–169**
who is acting as agent for an undisclosed principal and intends to receive
for his principal, the position becomes very difficult to analyse. The
operation of the undisclosed principal doctrine outside the realm of pure
contract raises many problems, the solutions to which have hardly been
considered. On one view, transfer of property is not the same as
contract, and the passage of property does not necessarily occur in
pursuance of a contract. Hence the intentions of the parties must be
looked at in isolation from any contractual implications. On this basis
the intention of the transferor is only to transfer to the agent, and a
concealed intention of the agent to acquire for another should not be
able to produce a different effect. If the agent wishes to make a further
transfer to his principal this can be instantly effected, as regards
property, by intention alone: but the property will have passed through
the agent for a *scintilla temporis*, which may have legal significance, *e.g.*
for bankruptcy or tax purposes. Again, *possession* will pass to the agent,
though he may immediately, by virtue of his intention, become bailee to
the principal.

It may furthermore be argued that in a contract situation the
undisclosed principal doctrine involves an element of intervention. The
undisclosed principal intervenes on a transaction entered into by the

---

[8] Sale of Goods Act 1979, s.17.

[9] *e.g.* that the goods are ascertained: see Sale of Goods Act 1979, s.16 (as modified by
Sale of Goods (Amendment) Act 1995).

[10] See Paton, *Bailment in the Common Law* (1952), pp. 6–9; Pollock and Wright,
Possession in the Common Law (1888), pp. 57–60. As to possession of documents by an
agent for the purpose of *subpoena duces tecum* see *Rochfort v. Trade Practices
Commission* (1982) 153 C.L.R. 134 and cases there cited.

agent which is valid in itself; and the third party may elect to sue the principal on such a transaction, but need not do so. Such an element of choice can be said to be inappropriate in property transactions: there cannot be a right to possess in both principal and agent. It is also true that agents taking conveyances of land are held to act as trustees for their principals and not to vest property in their principals directly[11]: but these cases seem to depend on the fact that written instruments are used which by their words purport to vest the land in the agent.

As against these arguments it may be said that the formation of obligation is, at least prima facie, of an even more personal nature than the transfer of property. The latter rids the transferor of obligations rather than creates them, and does not produce a continuing relationship: it is often, perhaps usually, a matter of indifference to a transferor who receives the goods with which he intends to part. If an undisclosed principal can intervene on an obligation, *a fortiori* he should be able to intervene on a transfer of property, which usually occurs in pursuance of an obligation. It may even be argued that in the case of sale of goods the requirement of intention of the parties[12] is supplied by the transferor's intention to transfer and the undisclosed principal's intention to receive, though these have no reference to each other. These propositions are strengthened by the usual view that the origin of the undisclosed principal doctrine lay in the desire to protect the principal in the agent's bankruptcy.[13] For that purpose it is obviously important that the principal's title should be protected from the moment of acquisition of goods for the principal by the agent.

If the principal has the right to intervene and claim property, that right is presumably subject to the exception to which intervention on a contract is subject: that it must not be excluded by the express or implied terms of the transaction.[14] It is arguable also that the exception goes further than this and that he cannot claim that property vested in him automatically (rather than by a further transfer from the agent) where he knows that the transferor would not have transferred to him.[15]

8–170   **Attornment.** An attornment in respect of goods occurs where the possessor of goods, whether himself the transferor or the bailee of the transferor, acknowledges that he holds, and possesses, for another. There is authority that such an attornment creates a fresh bailment by

---

[11] Article 55.

[12] Sale of Goods Act 1979, s.17.

[13] See above, para. 8–070.

[14] See above, para. 8–080: *Maynegrain* case, n. 17 below, at p. 153: "unless the terms of the attornment or of the arrangements for the making of that attornment require A.N.Z. to be treated as the only attornee."

[15] See above, para. 8–080.

means of a constructive delivery and redelivery.[16] It may be used to pass property to a buyer: but it may instead create a pledge in favour of the attornee. Attornment to the agent of a disclosed principal acting as such may plainly rank as attornment to the principal. If intention is the key to the effect of attornment, the intention where the agent's principal is undisclosed is, however, only to attorn to the agent. Indeed, any other conclusion could be said to lead to there being a constructive delivery to two persons, each of whom effects a redelivery. But again it can be argued that, since attornment will usually occur in pursuance of a contract, the undisclosed principal's intervention should not be disallowed in such a case when it is allowed in the case of contract; and that not only should attornment be capable of passing property to an undisclosed principal, it should also (subject to the same provisos regarding cases where the attornor did not or would not have attorned to the principal) be capable of constituting him a pledgee. Such a conclusion has been reached by the Court of Appeal of New South Wales in *Maynegrain Pty. Ltd v. Compafina Bank,*[17] the facts of which are summarised below.

Estoppel. In the above case there was an additional complication: the   **8–171** goods in respect of which an attornment (for the purposes of creating a security) was made were part of an undivided bulk, and the court assumed (it is submitted, correctly[18]) that there can be no possession, and hence no bailment, of such unascertained goods. Therefore as a pure attornment, *viz.* a constructive delivery and redelivery, the act concerned (the issue of a warehouse receipt) was ineffective. In such cases however there is authority that an attornment also operates by way of estoppel, in that it prevents the person attorning from denying that he in fact holds goods as described for the attornee.[19] A further doctrinal point therefore arises: can a warehouseman be estopped against someone whose existence he has not contemplated? This turns on the scope of his representation, not on any notion of intervention. Again there is a choice. On one view, it may be immaterial to a holder of goods to whom they are transferred, for whom he holds or to whom the receipt which he has signed is shown. On another, estoppel raises

---

[16] *Dublin City Distillery Ltd v. Doherty* [1914] A.C. 823, 852; *Official Assignee of Madras v. Mercantile Bank of India Ltd* [1935] A.C. 53, 58.

[17] [1982] 2 N.S.W.L.R. 141, Illustration below; reversed on the facts (1984) 58 A.L.J.R. 389 (P.C.). See Goode, *op. cit.* n. 7 above, at pp. 11–12.

[18] But see *Hayman & Son v. M'Lintock* 1907 S.C. 936; *Benjamin's Sale of Goods* (4th ed.), §§ 18–055, 18–133.

[19] *Knights v. Wiffen* (1870) L.R. 5 Q.B. 660; *Coventry, Sheppard & Co. v. G.E. Ry. Co.* (1883) 11 Q.B.D. 776. See also *Alicia Hosiery Ltd v. Brown, Shipley & Co. Ltd* [1970] 1 Q.B. 195, 206.

the question of who is contemplated as likely to rely on the representation, and a statement specifically addressed to one person may well not be intended to be relied on by another, at any rate where a document of title is not involved.[20] The analogy of share certificates,[21] which are not documents of title, suggests the adoption of the first view, and indeed to differentiate in result between cases where the goods are specific and cases where they are part of a bulk seems wrong. The court not surprisingly held that the estoppel applied likewise: granted the first decision, it would have been unsatisfactory to decide differently on this issue.

Illustration

8–172   A warehouseman, holding imported goods for a customer at the customer's request, for purposes of creating a security, issues a warehouse receipt for a quantity of goods, part of an undivided mass, for the account of a local bank. He subsequently delivers some of the goods at the customer's direction. The local bank to whom he issued the receipt was in fact agent for another bank which has actually advanced money to the owner of the goods. The lending bank can intervene and, as bailor, sue the warehouseman in conversion.[22]

3—WRONGS

Introductory Note

8–173   **Torts.** The primary application of the principles of agency so far expounded is in the field of contract and the related field of dispositions of property, though there are of course other fields where such or similar principles operate. The law of tort, however, uses different techniques. Anyone considering the application of agency principles in the law of tort is initially faced with the fact that when that branch of the law deals with liability of one person for the acts of another, the question normally turns not on the authority of the person who committed the tort, but on whether he was the servant (or employee) of the person sought to be held liable, or an independent contractor. An

---

[20] cf. *V/O Rasnoimport v. Guthrie & Co.* [1966] 1 Lloyd's Rep 1, where a signature as agent was held to constitute a contractual offer of authority to persons taking up the document.

[21] *Re Bahia and San Francisco Ry. Co. Ltd* (1868) L.R. 3 Q.B. 584; see Gower, *Modern Company Law* (5th ed.), p. 394; Spencer Bower, *Estoppel by Representation* (3rd ed.), pp. 116 *et seq.*

[22] *Maynegrain Pty. Ltd v. Compafina Bank* [1982] 2 N.S.W.L.R. 141. But the decision was reversed on the facts on the basis that the local bank had assented to the delivery: (1984) 58 A.L.J.R. 389 (P.C.).

agent may be either (or indeed, in the case of a gratuitous agent, neither). A very rough summary of the usual view would be to say that a person is liable for torts committed by another which he specifically instigates or authorises, or which are committed by his servant acting within the course of employment, or which involve a breach of a personal duty owed by him, though the acts leading to such breach were actually performed by another (usually an independent contractor).

Vicarious liability in the law of tort seems also to have a different basis from agency in contract. In contract the agent is not normally liable, and the effect of agency rules is in the majority of cases to establish the primary liability of the person with whom the third party intended to deal. But in tort the actual tortfeasor is in principle liable, and the effect of vicarious liability is to add a defendant, often unknown to and uncontemplated by the victim; on one view its purpose is simply to find a defendant who can pay.[23]

It might then seem that agency is excluded in tort altogether. There are however various ways in which considerable interrelation with the law of agency exists and these prevent a total separation between agency in contract and vicarious liability in tort. They may be enumerated as follows, with the reservation that, as is obvious, the categories are not mutually exclusive.

(a) Parallels from one part of the law have long been cited in the other[24] and the terminologies of master and servant and principal and agent have been and still are readily interchanged: the same applies to the phrases "course of employment" and "scope of authority."[25]

(b) The clear dichotomy between contract and tort which was made from the late nineteenth century was not made in earlier times,[26] and is now again subject to considerable doubts and reservations.

---

[23] Atiyah, *Vicarious Liability in the Law of Torts* (1967), Chaps. 1, 2; and see *Rose v. Plenty* [1976] 1 W.L.R. 141, 147.

[24] "There has never been a time when cases on master and servant were not cited as authority in the law of principal and agent, and vice versa": Street, *Foundations of Legal Liability* (1906), Vol. 2, p. 454.

[25] Had there been separate commercial courts, the result might have been otherwise; the terminology of agency is a commercial one, but that of master and servant has long been rooted in the common law. See Holdsworth, *H.E.L.* VIII, p. 227. See also *e.g.* Pollock, *Contracts* (15th ed.), pp. 58 *et seq.*; *Barwick v. English Joint Stock Bank* (1867) L.R. 2 Ex. 259, 266; *Swire v. Francis* (1877) 3 App.Cas. 106; *Holdsworth v. City of Glasgow Bank* (1880) 5 App.Cas. 317, 326–327; *Lloyd v. Grace, Smith & Co.* [1912] A.C. 716, 734–735; *Uxbridge Permanent Benefit B.S. v. Pickard* [1939] 2 K.B. 248, 254; *Navarro v. Moregrand Ltd* [1951] 2 T.L.R. 674; *Morris v. C.W. Martin & Sons Ltd* [1966] 1 Q.B. 716, 726; *Heaton's Transport (St Helen's) Ltd v. T. & G.W.U.* [1973] A.C. 15, 99; *Rose v. Plenty*, n. 23 above. Statutes relating to tort may use the term "agent": see Crown Proceedings Act 1947, s.2(1)(*a*) (below, para. 8–186): National Health Service Act 1946, s.13(1).

[26] Especially as regards representations: Stoljar, pp. 64–67.

(c)   Ancillary notions primarily related, according to modern ideas, to contractual agency, e.g. ratification, have on occasion been useful in the field of tort.[27]

(d)   Certain persons whom the law of tort, as expounded above, might for the sake of consistency describe as servants seem in common speech more appropriately described as agents, especially where their duties involve commercial matters such as the making of contracts, dispositions of property, etc. Thus a shipmaster who sells the cargo wrongfully,[28] a solicitor's managing clerk dealing with a mortgage who defrauds the person with whom he is dealing,[29] or a bailiff levying distress wrongfully[30] may well be servants (or independent contractors), but the term "agent" may nevertheless be used when the principal is made liable for their torts committed in the course of their professional activities. On the other hand though a bus driver could be an agent for buying petrol, he is certainly more likely to be called a servant if he is involved in a collision on the way to get it.[31] In some cases the term used may depend simply on whether a tort leading to personal injuries is involved, or an economic tort, e.g. deceit.

(e)   Torts of misrepresentation have a primary association with contract, are often committed by a person who has authority to make contracts, and are frequently litigated in connection with a contract.[32] Here it may seem natural to talk of representations by an agent, whether he is a servant or an independent contractor, and to speak in terms of authority rather than course of employment.[33] It is arguable whether or not such reasoning limits the results which pure tort reasoning would reach.

(f)   There is a further group of tort cases where agency principles seem especially relevant, because it is sought to hold a principal liable for the torts of his agent where the normal rules as to master and

---

[27] Indeed ratification may be older than the idea of agency. But it is probably now confined to cases of conversion and trespass: see Comment to Article 14. Agency terminology may also be used where a servant does acts upon which the tortiousness of further acts may depend, e.g. invites persons on to land where they would otherwise be trespassers: Hillen & Pettigrew v. I.C.I. Alkall Ltd [1936] A.C. 65; Young v. Box & Co. [1951] 1 T.L.R. 789.

[28] Ewbank v. Nutting (1849) 7 C.B. 797.

[29] Lloyd v. Grace, Smith & Co. [1912] A.C. 716, Illustration 11 to Article 92; Uxbridge Permanent Benefit Building Society v. Pickard [1939] 2 K.B. 248, Illustration 12 to Article 92.

[30] Article 92, Illustration 17.

[31] Limpus v. London General Omnibus Co. Ltd (1862) 1 H. & C. 526.

[32] See, e.g. Mercantile Credit Co. v. Garrod [1962] 3 All E.R. 1103 (a case on partnership); Armagas Ltd v. Mundagas S.A. (The Ocean Frost) [1986] A.C. 717. Liability may arise in deceit; in negligence under Hedley Byrne & Co. Ltd. v. Heller & Partners Ltd [1964] A.C. 465; or under the Mispresentation Act 1967, s.2(1).

[33] Ferson (1948) 2 Vand.L.Rev. 1.

servant, and as to independent contractors, might not easily permit of such a result being achieved. In this area, agency reasoning may arguably extend the tort liability. Such cases have principally arisen in England in connection with deceit only, but the idea can perhaps be extended to torts of representation generally and perhaps also to other torts involving statements.

(g) In one unique line of cases one person is held liable for the tort of another who is certainly neither his servant nor his independent contractor, but who can be said in some sense to be acting for him—in most cases by driving a car. These cases, often referred to as involving the notion of "casual delegation", are sometimes explained as based on agency.

Attempts can be and have been made to unify all agency in contract and tort into one set of principles,[34] and even, abandoning the terminology of master and servant, to seek to establish the types of authority as the guiding criteria in tort as well as contract.[35] If there is a separate notion of usual authority,[36] it is plainly of much assistance for this: some of the rules relating to independent contractors would be incorporated here and some related to the personal duty of the principal. Though there is plenty of useful material in the cases,[37] such an exercise is a creative and theoretical one involving a development of the law beyond the form in which it is at present stated and understood in England. It has already been suggested that such attempts are of doubtful validity in pure contract situations,[38] and they do not seem to illuminate tort situations either.

For the elucidation of the law as at present applied it is more appropriate to set out briefly an indication of the basic rules as to liability in tort, based on the distinction between servants and independent contractors, and to suggest the ways in which agency reasoning may arguably be regarded as modifying the results which the pure tort reasoning might reach. This requires consideration of the last three categories, (e), (f) and (g) above mentioned. Of these, the first two may be regarded as involving genuine applications of agency principles in the law of tort, the tort being committed by an agent in the course of representing someone else.[39] The third does not, it is

---

[34] *cf. Restatement*, § 2. And see above, para. 1–024 *et seq.*

[35] See Powell, pp. 184–194; Fridman, Chap. 13. *cf.* Ferson (1951) 4 Vand.L.Rev. 260; Conant (1968) 48 Neb.L.Rev. 42; Tedeschi (1969) 4 Israel L.Rev. 1; Atiyah, *Vicarious Liability in the Law of Torts* (1967), Chap. 9.

[36] See Comment to Article 22; above, para. 8–078.

[37] See material cited at n. 25 above; cases relating to false imprisonment cited at Article 92, Illustration 5; cases on solicitors and bailiffs cited at Article 92, Illustration 17. *cf.* Partnership Act 1890, s.10.

[38] See Comment to Article 22.

[39] See paras. 8–177 and 8–180 below.

submitted, in fact stem from those principles. But the cases are frequently explained on the basis of agency, and treatment of them is required for the sake of completeness.[40]

The tort of deceit raises special problems regarding the states of mind of principal and agent, or master and servant, and since this tort is pre-eminently connected with contract these difficulties also require discussion.[41]

Article 92

Liability of Principal for Torts Committed by Agent

8–174

(1) If an agent is the servant of his principal, the principal is liable for loss or injury caused by the wrongful act of the agent when acting in the course of his employment.[42]

(2) A principal is liable for loss or injury caused by the tort of his agent, whether or not his servant, in the following cases:

   (a) if the wrongful act was specifically instigated, authorised[43] or ratified[44] by the principal;

   (b) if the wrongful act amounts to a breach by the principal of a duty personal to himself, liability for non-performance or non-observance of which cannot be avoided by delegation to another[45];

   (c) (perhaps) in the case of a statement made in the course of representing the principal made within the actual or apparent authority of the agent: and for such a statement the principal may be liable notwithstanding that it was made for the benefit of the agent alone and not for that of the principal.[46]

(3) Where principal and agent are both liable for a wrongful act committed by the agent they are joint tortfeasors.[47]

---

[40] See para. 8–182 below.

[41] See para. 8–183 below.

[42] See Comment: Salmond and Heuston, *Torts* (20th ed.), Chap. 21; Clerk and Lindsell, *Torts* (16th ed.), Chap. 3; Atiyah, *Vicarious Liability in the Law of Torts* (1967), Parts II, IV, V. But as to torts of representation see below, para. 8–177.

[43] Illustrations 14, 15; Atiyah, *op cit.* n. 42 above, Chap. 27; *C. Evans & Sons Ltd v. Spritebrand Ltd* [1985] 1 W.L.R. 317.

[44] See Article 14.

[45] *Cassidy v. Minister of Health* [1951] 2 K.B. 343, 363; *Riverstone Meat Co. Pty Ltd v. Lancashire Shipping Co. Ltd (The Muncaster Castle)* [1961] A.C. 807; *Salsbury v. Woodland* [1970] 1 Q.B. 324. See Salmond and Heuston, *op. cit.* n. 42 above, part. VIII.

[46] See Comment; Article 76. *cf.* Partnership Act 1890, s.10. As to apparent authority, see Article 74.

[47] *Jones v. Manchester Corp.* [1952] 2 Q.B. 852, 869. See para. 8–187 below.

(4) In this Article, save where the context requires otherwise, "act" includes "omission," and phrases which include the word "act" are capable of any necessary consequential modification.

Comment

Rule (1). Servants. This gives a brief indication of the liability of a   **8–175** principal for the acts of his servant. A definition of "servant" is given in Article 2. A servant acts in the course of his employment if he commits any wrongful act authorised by the employer or does an act within the scope of his duties as a servant in a wrongful and unauthorised manner.[48] He may act in the course of his employment notwithstanding that the employer has expressly prohibited the act done[49]: whether the prohibited act is or is not in the course of the servant's employment depends upon whether the prohibition is such as merely regulates the conduct of the servant within the scope of his employment or is such as limits the sphere of that employment itself.[50] A servant may act in the course of his employment notwithstanding that the act is done for the benefit of the servant alone and not for that of the employer.[51]

Transferred employment.[52] A servant may be in the general   **8–176** employment of A, but, as the result of arrangements made between A and B, he may be acting as the servant of B, so as to make B, and not A, responsible for his tort at the relevant time.[53] The test is whether the servant is transferred, or only the use and benefit of his work,[54] and this depends upon the extent to which A places the servant under the control and at the disposition of B.[55] The question of control will be

---

[48] See *Poland v. John Parr & Sons Ltd* [1927] 1 K.B. 236, 240; *Bugge v. Brown* (1919) 26 C.L.R. 110; Salmond and Heuston, *op cit.*, n. 42 above, p. 457.

[49] Illustrations 7–10.

[50] See *Plumb v. Cobden Flour Mills Co. Ltd* [1914] A.C. 62, 66–67; *Canadian Pacific Ry. Co. v. Lockhart* [1942] A.C. 591, 599; *Rose v. Plenty* [1976] 1 W.L.R. 141; *Harrison v. Michelin Tyre Co. Ltd* [1985] 1 All E.R. 918; *Kooragang Investments Pty Ltd v. Richardson & Wrench Ltd* [1982] A.C. 462, Illustration 9.

[51] Illustrations 11–13. *Cf.* Article 76.

[52] See Clark and Lindsell, *Torts* (16th ed.), § 3–15.

[53] *Century Insurance Co. Ltd v. Northern Ireland Road Transport Board* [1942] A.C. 509, 513.

[54] *ibid.* at pp. 509, 513, 516.

[55] *Cameron v. Nystrom* [1893] A.C. 308, 312; *Century Insurance Co. Ltd v. Northern Ireland Road Transport Board*, n. 53 above at p. 517. See also *Chua Chye Leong Alan v. Grand Palace De-luxe Nite Club Pte Ltd* [1993] 3 Singapore L.R. 449 ("parking jockey" supplied by independent contractor to night club for valet parking "servant or agent" of night club).

determined by deciding where the authority lies to direct, or to delegate to, the servant the manner in which the work is to be done.[56] Where a servant is lent with a machine, such as a crane, "it is easier to infer that the general employer continues to control the method of performance," since the driver remains responsible to him for the safe keeping of the machine.[57] The agreement between the principals does not determine the question, although it may help to determine such relevant matters as, *e.g.* who pays the servant or can dismiss him, how long the alternative service is to last, and what machinery is to be employed.[58] Each case must depend on its own circumstances.[59] Prima facie, responsibility for the negligence of the servant rests upon the master who engaged him and generally employs him, and the burden upon the general employer to shift that responsibility to the hirer is a heavy one.[60]

8–177   **Torts of misrepresentation.** Torts of misrepresentation involve reliance by the plaintiff. This suggests that the principal should not be liable for the mispresentations of his agent who is also a servant unless the third party was justified in relying on them, *viz.* unless they were made within the agent's actual or apparent authority, which of course they may be.[61] This viewpoint has recently been adopted by the House of Lords, at least as regards the tort of deceit.[62] It is arguable that it puts limits on "the course of employment" test which would otherwise be applied in a tort case, for an agent authorised to make a contract who makes false representations outside his actual or apparent authority in connection

---

[56] *Mersey Docks and Harbour Board v. Coggins & Griffith* [1947] A.C. 1, 12.
[57] *Mersey Docks and Harbour Board v. Coggins & Griffith*, above at p. 17; *Ready Mixed Concrete (East Midlands) Ltd v. Yorkshire Traffic Area Licensing Authority* [1970] 2 Q.B. 397, 404. See also *Garrard v. A.E. Southey & Co.* [1952] 2 Q.B. 174; *Denham v. Midland Employers Mutual Ass. Ltd* [1955] 2 Q.B. 437; *Bhoomidas v. Port of Singapore Authority* [1978] 1 All E.R. 956 (P.C.).
[58] *Mersey Docks and Harbour Board v. Coggins & Griffith*, n. 56 above.
[59] *Ready Mixed Concrete (East Midlands) Ltd v. Yorkshire Traffic Area Licensing Authority*, n.57 above, at p. 406.
[60] *Mersey Docks and Harbour Board v. Coggins & Griffith* [1947] A.C. 1, 10; *Ready Mixed Concrete (East Midlands) Ltd v. Yorkshire Traffic Area Licensing Authority*, n.57 above, at p. 404.
[61] *e.g.* Illustration 19. *cf. Bank of Montreal v. Young* (1966) 60 D.L.R. (2d) 220 (bank manager not authorised to advise on investments).
[62] *Armagas Ltd v. Mundogas S.A. (The Ocean Frost)* [1986] A.C. 717 (Illustration 25). See also *Hamlyn v. John Houston & Co.* [1901] 1 K.B. 81 (partner liable for bribery by other partner in course of obtaining information which he had been authorised to obtain by legitimate means); *George Whitechurch Ltd v. Cavanagh* [1902] A.C. 117; *Slingsby v. District Bank Ltd* [1933] 2 K.B. 588; *Kleinwort, Sons & Co. v. Associated Automatic Machine Corp. Ltd* (1934) 151 L.T. 1. But *cf.* (on the last case and in general) Wright (1935) 13 Can.B.R. 116.

with it can be said to be doing an act within the scope of his duties in a wrongful manner. The preferable view is however that the suggested rule sets true limits on the scope of employment in respect of torts of misrepresentation: the dealings which the servant is employed to enter into are in this respect to be identified with reference to his authority. The third party should not have relied on statements neither actually nor apparently authorised at all. Liability for other wrongs committed in connection with authorised activities (*e.g.* assault, negligent driving) remains; in this respect the course of employment test is wider than "authority" reasoning. [63]

Rule 2(a). The principal's liability where the tort is specifically authorised or ratified is obvious: he has effectively committed the tort himself, and the liability is not truly vicarious. **8–178**

Rule 2(b). This is no more than a general formulation, on which not too specific reliance should be placed, intended to give some indication of the law on the controversial subject of liability for independent contractors. If the rule as set out is correct, such liability as there is may be said to be not truly vicarious, though the whole question remains very open. [64] **8–179**

Rule 2(c). Liability based only on agency reasoning. The third category causes the most difficulty. The formula suggested here is put forward tentatively. It is suggested above that where an agent commits a tort of misrepresentation, the terminology of authority is appropriate: he renders his principal liable when he makes the misrepresentation within the scope of his authority and the misrepresentation is acted on. In the case of a servant it is clear that at least in the tort of deceit this authority terminology controls the normal tort "course of employment" test, which cannot be used to invoke a wider vicarious liability. [65] But it is submitted further that "authority" reasoning may also be used to *create* liability in one person for another who is not his servant, and for whom there is no liability under the principles relating to independent contractors set out in Rule 2(b). The reasoning is somewhat limited. It should apply to an agent "when the function entrusted is that of representing the person who requests his performance in a transaction **8–180**

---

[63] See *Navarro v. Moregrand Ltd* [1951] 2 T.L.R. 674, 680, Illustration 21 *per* Denning L.J. But *cf. Heaton's Transport Ltd (St Helen's) v. T. & G.W.U.* [1973] A.C. 15, 99. See also Illustrations 3, 4, 11, 12. As to defamation, see *Riddick v. Thames Board Mills Ltd* [1977] Q.B. 881.

[64] See McKendrick (1990) 53 M.L.R. 770; *Cashfield House v. Sinclair* [1995] 1 N.Z.L.R. 4520.

[65] *Armagas Ltd v. Mundogas S.A. (The Ocean Frost)* [1986] A.C. 717; see above, para. 8–177.

with others, so that the very service to be performed consists in standing in his place and assuming to act in his right and not in an independent capacity."[66] Thus it has been held that an estate agent, who is not a servant, may have authority to make representations about property for which he is seeking a buyer or tenant, so that his principal is liable for their falsity.[67] So also the vendor of land may be liable for false statements wilfully or negligently made by his solicitor in answer to inquiries.[68] Both of these involve torts of misrepresentation. But such reasoning may perhaps be extendable further. In *Colonial Mutual Life Assurance Society Ltd v. Producers' and Citizens' Cooperative Co. of Australia Ltd*,[69] from which the above quotation is taken, the High Court of Australia held an insurance company liable for defamation of another company committed by its agent (not a servant) in the course of soliciting business. An English case in which similar suggestions appear is *Uxbridge Permanent Benefit Building Society v. Pickard*,[70] where a solicitor was held liable for the fraud of his managing clerk, though this could be explained on the basis of the established rules as to master and servant. There are also cases where the agent was not a servant, and the possibility of his nevertheless having acted within his authority so as to render his principal liable was discussed, but negatived on the facts.[71]

It has therefore been suggested that a person should be liable in respect of all tortious statements, whether in deceit, negligence, defamation or injurious falsehood, made by his agent in the course of representing him, provided that the statement made was within a category which the agent had actual or apparent authority to make.[72] and it is this proposition which is tentatively formulated here. It would in fact be an extension of the reasoning in Rule 2(a) above. It would, however, exclude loss caused by acts to which such "authority" reasoning cannot be related. Thus it has been held in South Africa that

---

[66] *Colonial Mutual Life Assurance Society Ltd v. Producers and Citizens Cooperative Co. of Australia Ltd* (1931) 46 C.L.R. 41, *per* Dixon J. See also *The Litsion Pride* [1985] 1 Lloyd's Rep 437, 513–514; *N.Z. Guardian Trust v. Brooks* [1995] 1 W.L.R. 4.

[67] See Illustrations 19–22.

[68] *Cemp Properties (U.K.) Ltd v. Dentsply Research and Development Corp.* [1989] 2 EGLR 196 (Misrepresentation Act 1967, s.2(1)); *Gran Gelato Ltd v. Richcliff Group Ltd* [1992] Ch. 560 (Misrepresentation Act 1967, s.2(1)) (criticised by Cane, (1992) 108 L.Q.R. 539); and see *Derham v. Amev Life Insurance Co. Ltd* (1981) 56 F.L.R. 34 (fraud of insurance agent).

[69] (1931) 46 C.L.R. 41, Illustration 23. See also cases there cited.

[70] [1939] 2 K.B. 248, Illustration 12.

[71] *Bradford Third Equitable B.S. v. Borders* [1941] 2 All E.R. 205; *Kwei Tek Chao v. British Traders and Shippers Ltd* [1954] 2 Q.B. 459; *Strover v. Harrington* [1988] Ch. 390, Illustration 8 to Article 97 (Misrepresentation Act 1967, s.2(1)).

[72] See Atiyah, *Vicarious Liability in the Law of Torts* (1967), Chaps. 9, 10.

an insurance company was not liable for the negligent driving of its agent who was taking a doctor to examine a prospective client.[73]

Relevance of agent's personal liability. The general reasoning 8–181 proposed has one more difficulty to overcome. In tort law, liability for the torts of another presupposes in general that the other has committed a tort. But in torts of misrepresentation there is also authority that an agent owes a duty of care to his principal only and hence not to the third party with whom his principal is dealing unless he can be regarded as undertaking some special responsibility towards that third party. Thus it has been held that a solicitor acting for the vendor in conveyancing who answers inquiries made on behalf of the purchaser owes no duty of care to the purchaser.[74] It is, however, assumed in the judgment that the vendor himself would be liable.[75] It is difficult to see how this can be so unless the solicitor is regarded as no more than a manifestation of the vendor, which as unsupported reasoning can hardly be correct. The problem is one of misrepresentation causing pure economic loss.[76] If the agent had by negligence caused destruction of or damage to the person or property of the third party he would certainly in principle be liable.[77] But in the case of misrepresentation, and perhaps sometimes other tortious liability, what is required is an assumption of responsibility,[78] and it is certainly arguable that a person acting for one person who is dealing with another may be regarded as prima facie undertaking duties only towards the person for whom he acts and not to third parties.

There seem to be only two possible answers to this problem. The first is that in some cases of torts of mispresentation the principal may be taken to be liable directly, despite the fact that the agent is not liable. This is not impossible: all that is required is an extension to tort cases of the normal agency reasoning whereby the agent drops out of the transaction unless there are other indications that he undertakes a duty.[79] This of course he may, and arguably did in the case referred to,

---

[73] *Colonial Mutual Life Assurance Society Ltd v. Macdonald* 1931 A.D. 412, Illustration 24. See also *Eggington v. Reader* [1936] 1 All E.R. 7, Illustration 6. But *cf. Dobson v. Holderness* [1975] 2 N.Z.L.R. 749; *Nelson v. Raphael* [1979] R.T.R. 437, cases, however, which move into the area of "casual delegation": see para. 8–182 below.

[74] *Gran Gelato Ltd v. Richcliff Group Ltd* [1992] Ch. 560, Illustration 22. See Cane (1992) 108 L.Q.R. 539; and *cf. Punjab National Bank v. de Boinville* [1992] 1 W.L.R. 1138, where employees of insurance brokers were held to owe a duty of care to an assignee of the policy broked.

[75] See also *Cemp Properties (U.K.) Ltd v. Dentsply Research and Development Corp.* [1989] 2 EGLR 196.

[76] It occurs also in cases where it is argued that directors of companies have undertaken personal liability: see below para. 9–114.

[77] *Colonial Mutual Life Assurance Society Ltd v. Macdonald*, n. 73 above.

[78] *Henderson v. Merrett Syndicates Ltd* [1994] 3 W.L.R. 761, 773 *et seq.*; and see the cases on company directors cited below, para. 9–114.

[79] See Article 73; Fleming, *Law of Torts* (8th ed.), pp. 369–370; below, paras. 8–183, 8–184 and cases cited, in which the term "agent" is frequently used.

where there was a direct and erroneous answer, which the solicitor giving it knew would be relied on, on behalf of another.

The second is that the decision above referred to is wrong and that the agent should more easily in such circumstances be regarded as undertaking responsibility towards the third party; but that only when he does can the principal be liable for him, and then only if he is an employee or he is an independent contractor and the duty is non-delegable. The latter approach is more in accord with normal tort reasoning[80]; but the former, while less tidy, may be more sensitive to the application of agency principles to tort situations, an application which is probably inevitable once liability for pure economic loss caused by misrepresentation is accepted as giving rise to an action. It also provides support for the idea that the act is that of the principal.

8–182   Casual delegation.[81] This is a distinct line of cases holding that the owner[82] of a motor-car or other conveyance[83] or chattel[84] may be liable for the negligence of one whom he permits to use it on his behalf. The vast majority of the cases concern the use of cars. The liability appears to extend to any case in which A drives B's car in pursuance of B's order, instruction or request for a purpose in which B has an interest[85]: as where A is driving the car on a trial run in order to advise a prospective purchaser[86]; or where A is driving the car to a place where he will meet B for the purpose of taking a holiday together[87]; or where A is driving during the course of a pleasure outing with B.[88] Liability is excluded if B has by contract or bailment abandoned control of the car to A[89]; and there is no question of liability where A is merely driving with B's permission for the purpose of his own in which B has no

---

[80] See Cane, n. 74 above.

[81] Atiyah, *Vicarious Liability in the Law of Torts* (1967), Chap. 13; Clerk and Lindsell, *Torts* (16th ed.) §§ 3–49 *et seq.*

[82] A person other than the owner may be liable on the same principle: *Wheatley v. Patrick* (1837) 2 M. & W. 650; *Scarsbrook v. Mason* [1961] 3 All E.R. 767 (but this case extends the principle very far); *Rogers v. Night Riders* [1983] R.T.R. 324 (minicab booking agency: also an extended liability). An obvious example would be a person buying a car on hire-purchase. But *cf. Nottingham v. Aldridge* [1971] 2 Q.B. 739 (employer not liable for negligent driving of employee proceeding to training course in own car).

[83] *Booth v. Mister* (1835) 7 C. & P. 66 (cart); *Wheatley v. Patrick*, n. 82 above (horse and chaise); *"Thelma" (owners) v. University College School* [1953] 2 Lloyd's Rep 613 (rowing eight).

[84] *Launchbury v. Morgans* [1973] A.C. 127, 135, 138, 144, 145.

[85] *Launchbury v. Morgans*, above; *Vandyke v. Fender* [1970] 2 Q.B. 292; *cf. Nottingham v. Aldridge*, n. 82 above; *Ansin v. R & D Evans Ltd* [1982] 1 N.Z.L.R. 184. See further Howard (1971) 34 M.L.R. 568; Jolowicz [1971] C.L.J. 195; [1972A] C.L.J. 209.

[86] *Samson v. Aitchison* [1912] A.C. 844; see also *Nelson v. Raphael* [1979] R.T.R. 437.

[87] *Ormrod v. Crosville Motor Services Ltd* [1953] 1 W.L.R. 1120; *cf. Klein v. Caluori* [1971] 1 W.L.R. 619 (return of car borrowed without permission).

[88] *Pratt v. Patrick* [1924] 1 K.B. 488; see also *Carberry v. Davies* [1968] 1 W.L.R. 1103.

[89] *Samson v. Aitchison*, n. 86 above; *Hewitt v. Bonvin* [1940] 1 K.B. 188; *Chowdhary v. Gillot* [1947] 2 All E.R. 541.

interest, as where B lends A the car in order that A may drive to the theatre[90] or take his (A's) friends home.[91] Where it is not clear why the car was being used, the fact of ownership is *some* evidence of delegation, but does not raise a presumption.[92] Such liability can be and has been explained by saying that the driver is the agent of the owner to drive and manage the car,[93] though "'agency' in contexts such as these is merely a concept, the meaning and purpose of which is to say 'is vicariously liable.'"[94] But liability has also been said to be based on the retention of control by the person concerned.[95] Such control is probably not to be regarded as establishing the relationship of master and servant,[96] but rather as showing that the act is that of the owner and so the negligence his. Since, however, the control may be rather a theoretical one, for the owner may be absent,[97] the best explanation of these cases may in fact be simply that there is a breach of a duty personal to the owner of taking care in managing the car when it is being used for his own purposes, which duty he cannot avoid by delegating the task of driving to another.[98] At all events the cases form a reasonably discrete group, and though the terminology of agency is used, as in other areas, for convenience, it is submitted that they do not form the basis of any special rules relating or peculiar to agency. "It is easier to see the direction in which the branch grows than to understand

---

[90] *Britt v. Galmoye* (1928) 44 T.L.R. 294; see also *Norwood v. Navan* [1981] R.T.R. 457 (shopping expedition by unlicensed driver).

[91] *Hewitt v. Bonvin*, n. 89 above; *Launchbury v. Morgans* [1973] A.C. 127.

[92] *Rambarran v. Gurrucharran* [1970] 1 W.L.R. 556; *Hewitt v. Bonvin*, n. 91 above; *Manawatu County v. Rowe* [1956] N.Z.L.R. 78.

[93] See *Hewitt v. Bonvin*, n. 89 above at pp. 194–196; *Smith v. Moss* [1940] 1 K.B. 424; *Ormrod v. Crosville Motor Services Ltd* [1953] 1 W.L.R. 1120; *Norton v. Canadian Pacific Steamships Ltd* [1961] 1 W.L.R. 1057, 1061; *Launchbury v. Morgans*, n. 91 above at pp. 138, 140, 144, 149.

[94] *Launchbury v. Morgans*, n. 91 above, at p. 135 *per* Lord Wilberforce.

[95] *Samson v. Aitchison* [1912] A.C. 844; *Trust Co. v. T.H.I. de Silva* [1956] 1 W.L.R. 376 (where the person in control was acting in the course of his employment, and so rendered his employer liable); *Launchbury v. Morgans*, n. 91 above, at p. 135; *Ansin v. R. & D. Evans Ltd* [1982] 1 N.Z.L.R. 184 (no control).

[96] *Norton v. Canadian Pacific Steamships Ltd*, n. 93 above.

[97] *Parker v. Miller* (1926) 43 T.L.R. 408; *Richards v. Shard* (1914) 31 T.L.R. 24; *Launchbury v. Morgans*, n. 91 above.

[98] *Norton v. Canadian Pacific Steamships Ltd* [1961] 1 W.L.R. 1057, 1063; *Nottingham v. Aldridge* [1971] 2 Q.B. 739; *Launchbury v. Morgans*, n. 91 above; and see *Rogers v. Night Riders* [1983] R.T.R. 324, where the defendant was a minicab booking agency, and the car, which was owned and operated independently, appeared to the injured party to be in use for the defendant's purposes. *Cf.* the rules as to liability for independent contractors. In *Moynihan v. Moynihan* [1975] I.R. 192, such reasoning is applied to impose liability on a mother for the negligence of her daughter towards a small child. See also *Dobson v. Holderness* [1975] 2 N.Z.L.R. 749 (liability for farm fire) and the "parking jockey" case cited above, n. 55.

the support it obtains from the main trunk of traditional doctrine governing vicarious responsibility."[99]

8-183   **Deceit: division of ingredients.**[1] The tort of deceit, where agency terminology is frequently used, raises special problems where agents are involved, in so far as it requires a false statement made, with the intention that it should be acted on, "knowingly, or without belief in its truth, or recklessly, careless whether it be true or false."[2] Is the principal to be liable to a third party where (for instance) the agent made a representation innocently, believing it to be true, and the principal knew of the untruth of the statement but did not know that it was being made? In such case no individual is guilty of personal fraud: there is an "innocent division of ingredients."[3] But are the acts and minds of principal and agent to be regarded as so far one that, by taking the agent's statement and the principal's knowledge together, the principal can be held liable to the third party in deceit? There was some authority that they were[4]: but the law later clarified by the decision of the Court of Appeal in *Armstrong v. Strain*[5] and is best stated in a series of propositions.

(a)   The principal is liable if he authorised the agent to make the false representation which he (the principal) knew to be untrue (or did not believe to be true), whether the agent knew the truth or not.[6]

(b)   The principal is liable if, while not expressly authorising the agent to make the false representation, he knew it to be untrue and was guilty of some positive wrongful conduct, as by consciously permitting the agent to remain ignorant of the true facts, so as to prevent the disclosure of the truth to the third party, if the third party should ask the agent for information, or in the hope that the agent would make some false representation.[7]

---

[99] *Soblusky v. Egan* (1960) 103 C.L.R. 215, 229 *per* Dixon J.

[1] Powell, pp. 200–207; Salmond and Heuston, *Torts* (20th ed.), pp. 389–390; Devlin (1937) 53 L.Q.R. 344; Wright (1937) 15 Can.B.R. 716; Gower (1952) 15 M.L.R. 232; Unger (1952) 15 M.L.R. 508; Müller-Freienfels in *Civil Law in the Mordern World* (Yiannapoulos ed., 1965), 77, 120–124.

[2] *Derry v. Peek* (1889) 14 App.Cas. 337, 374 *per* Lord Herschell.

[3] The language of Devlin J. in (1937) 53 L.Q.R. 344 and in *Armstrong v. Strain* [1951] 1 T.L.R. 856 (at first instance).

[4] See the confusing discussion in *Woyka & Co. v. London & Northern Trading Co.* (1922) 10 Ll.Rep. 110.

[5] [1952] 1 K.B. 232; affirming [1951] 1 T.L.R. 856, Illustration 20.

[6] If the agent knew the truth, they are jointly and severally liable; if not, the principal is alone liable for his own tort committed through the agent as an innocent instrument. *cf.* above, para. 8–181.

[7] *Ludgater v. Love* (1881) 44 L.T. 694; *Cornfoot v. Fowke* (1840) 6 M. & W. 358, 370, 372, 373–374; *Gordon Hill Trust Ltd v. Segall* [1941] 2 All E.R. 379, 390; *Awaroa*

(c) The principal is liable if the agent made the false representation fraudulently, it being within the scope of his actual or apparent authority and within the course of his employment, to make such a representation,[8] sometimes even where the representation reached the third party by way of another innocent agent,[9] or by way of the innocent principal himself,[10] because in such a case the innocent second agent or principal may be no more than a conduit pipe for the fraud of the guilty agent.[11]

(d) The principal is not liable if the agent made the false representation innocently, the principal knowing the true facts but not having authorised the agent to make the representation, nor knowing that it would be made, nor being guilty of fraudulent conduct as in (b) above.[12]

(e) Conversely, the principal is not liable if he himself made the false representation innocently, notwithstanding that the agent knew the true facts.[13]

Similar situations now actionable in negligence. The problems centred around *Armstrong v. Strain* arose from attempts to invoke the tort of deceit in respect of actions that were in substance in respect of negligent misrepresentation—largely in respect of misrepresentations made by the agents of companies. Since *Hedley Byrne & Co. Ltd v. Heller & Partners Ltd*[14] it has been established that an action in negligence may   8–184

Holdings Ltd v. Commercial Securities & Finance Ltd [1976] 1 N.Z.L.R. 19. Presumably this would be equally so if the wrongful conduct was of another agent of the principal acting in the course of his employment, the principal being innocent.

[8] *Barwick v. English Joint Stock Bank* (1867) L.R. 2 Ex. 259; *Briess v. Woolley* [1954] A.C. 333, Illustration 19; *Egger v. Viscount Chelmsford* [1965] 1 Q.B. 248, 261; *Mackay v. Commercial Bank of New Brunswick* (1874) L.R. 5 P.C. 394. See also *Hern v. Nichols* (1701) 1 Salk. 289; *Udell v. Atherton* (1861) 7 H. & N. 172, *per* Pollock C.B. and Wilde B. Unless the fraud of the agent is primarily practised on the principal himself: *Kwei Tek Chao v. British Traders & Shippers Ltd* [1954] 2 Q.B. 459.

[9] *London County Freehold & Leasehold Properties Ltd v. Berkeley Property & Investment Co. Ltd* [1936] 2 All E.R. 1039, as explained in *Anglo-Scottish Beet Sugar Corp Ltd v. Spalding U.D.C.* [1937] 2 K.B. 607; approved by the Court of Appeal in *Armstrong v. Strain* [1952] 1 K.B. 232.

[10] *S. Pearson & Son Ltd v. Dublin Corp.* [1907] A.C. 351, as explained in *Anglo-Scottish Beet Sugar Corp. Ltd v. Spalding U.D.C.*, n. 9 above.

[11] *S. Pearson & Son Ltd v. Dublin Corp.*, n. 10 above, at p. 367.

[12] *Armstrong v. Strain*, n. 9 above; *Cornfoot v. Fowke* (1840) 6 M. & W. 358; *Gordon Hill Trust v. Segall* [1941] 2 All E.R. 379.

[13] See *Anglo-Scottish Beet Sugar Corp. Ltd v. Spalding U.D.C.*, n. 9 above. "You cannot add an innocent state of mind to an innocent state of mind and get as a result a dishonest state of mind": *per* Devlin J. in *Armstrong v. Strain* [1951] 1 T.L.R. 856, 872. The same reasoning would apply where the relevant knowledge was possessed by another agent.

[14] [1964] A.C. 465.

in principle lie in such cases, and the rules stated above are therefore of less importance. It is now possible in appropriate cases to sue the principal as if for his own statement where the statement was negligently made by an agent[15]; or where, though no one person can be said to have been negligent, the totality of the operations of the principal in the particular respect can be regarded as negligent.[16] The same is true of actions under section 2 of the Mispresentation Act 1967.[17]

8–185   **Corporations.** Corporations can be held liable like individuals. Thus corporations can be sued for conversion,[18] wrongful distress,[19] false imprisonment,[20] trespass to land or goods,[21] and, as regards cases where a specific mental element may be involved, defamation,[22] malicious prosecution[23] and fraud.[24]

Where it is necessary to show authority or ratification specifically, a corporation acts through its primary representatives:

"In such a case, the court must fashion a special rule of attribution for the particular substantive rule. This is always a matter of interpretation: given that it was intended to apply to a company, how was it intended to apply? Whose act (or knowledge, or state of mind) was *for this purpose* intended to count as the act, etc., of the company? One finds the answer to this question by applying the usual canons of interpretation, taking into account the language of the rule (if it is a statute) and its content and policy."[25]

---

[15] Thus in *Mutual Life and Citizen's Assurance Co. v. Evatt* [1971] A.C. 793 it was alleged that the defendant company gave advice "by itself, its servants and agents." See also *Ministry of Housing and Local Government v. Sharp* [1970] 2 Q.B. 223; *Esso Petroleum Co. Ltd v. Mardon* [1976] Q.B. 801; *Box v. Midland Bank Ltd* [1979] 2 Lloyd's Rep 391; Stephens [1974] C.L.P. 59, 70–75.

[16] See *W.B. Anderson & Sons v. Rhodes (Liverpool) Ltd* [1967] 2 All E.R. 850; *McInerny v. Lloyd's Bank Ltd* [1974] 1 Lloyd's Rep 246.

[17] *Howard Marine and Dredging Co. Ltd v. A. Ogden & Sons (Excavations) Ltd* [1978] Q.B. 574. See also *Gosling v. Anderson* (1972) 223 E.G. 1743, 1745 *per* Lord Denning M.R. Although this section uses the analogy of fraud in imposing liability, it seems that the fraud rules as to division of ingredients will not be applied. *cf.* Atiyah and Treitel (1967) 30 M.L.R. 369, 374.

[18] *Yarborough v. Bank of England* (1812) 16 East 6; *Giles v. Taff Vale Ry.* (1853) 2 E. & B. 822; *Barnett v. Crystal Palace Co.* (1861) 4 L.T. 403.

[19] *Eastern Counties Ry. Co. v. Broom* (1851) 6 Exch. 314; *Smith v. Birmingham Gas Co.* (1834) 3 L.J.K.B. 165.

[20] Illustration 5.

[21] *Maund v. Monmouthshire Canal Co.* (1842) 4 Man. & G. 452.

[22] Illustration 23.

[23] *Cornford v. Carlton Bank* [1899] 1 Q.B. 392.

[24] *Ranger v. Great Western Ry. Co.* (1854) 5 H.L.Cas. 72; *Barwick v. English Joint Stock Bank* (1867) L.R. 2 Ex. 259; *Mackay v. Commercial Bank of New Brunswick* (1874) L.R. 5 P.C. 394.

[25] *Meridian Global Funds Management Asia Ltd v. Security Commission* [1995] 3 W.L.R. 413, 419 *per* Lord Hoffmann. For further discussion of this notion see above, para. 1–022.

The Crown.[26] The Crown Proceedings Act 1947 provides that the   **8-186**
Crown is subject to all those liabilities in tort to which, if it were a
private person of full age and capacity, it would be subject in respect
of torts committed by its servants or agents: provided that no
proceedings lie against the Crown by virtue of this provision in
respect of any act or omission of a servant or agent of the Crown
unless the act or omission would apart from the provisions of the Act
give rise to a cause of action in tort against that servant or agent or
his estate.[27] The words "servant or agent" cause some difficulty. It is
arguable that there is nowadays no such person as a servant of the
Crown in the strict sense, but it has been said that there is a large
category of persons, including civil servants, whom "the Crown
(through or with the advice of a Minister) controls ... and directs
their activities in a way which ... makes the term 'servant' quite
appropriate."[28] As regards agents, it is provided that "agent ...
includes an independent contractor,"[29] but the inference from this is
that the word covers also persons other than independent contractors.
It is submitted that the effect of the use of the word is to leave it in
no doubt that the Crown is to be liable in those cases in which an
ordinary person would be liable for the torts of his agent.[30] It seems
that the word covers also those public bodies that act on behalf of
the Crown, though there is little authority on which bodies are to be
regarded as agents of the Crown for this purpose.[31]

By section 2(6) of the Act the Crown is not liable by virtue of section
2 for any act, neglect or default of any *officer* of the Crown, unless that
officer was (i) directly or indirectly appointed by the Crown, and (ii)
paid wholly out of the Consolidated Fund, moneys provided by
Parliament, or any other fund certified by the Treasury for the purposes
of the subsection, or was holding an office in respect of which the
Treasury certifies that the holder would normally be so paid. The term
"officer" has a different connotation from "servant" or "agent," but the
Act provides that "officer" includes "servant."[32] Where the officer is a

---

[26] See Clerk and Lindsell, *Torts* (16th ed.), §§ 2–02 *et seq.*
[27] Crown Proceedings Act 1947, s.2(1)(*b*) and proviso. See Atiyah, *Vicarious Liability in the Law of Torts* (1967), pp. 391 *et seq.*
[28] *Bank voor Handel en Scheepvaart N.V.* v. *Administrator of Hungarian Property* [1954] A.C. 584, 616, *per* Lord Reid, rejecting dicta of Devlin J. at first instance, [1952] 1 All E.R. 314, 319.
[29] s.38(2).
[30] *cf.* Diamond [1978] L.M.C.L.Q. 225, 250, 251 (on "servant or agent" under the Hague-Visby Rules); as to when this is so, see above.
[31] Treitel [1957] P.L. 320, 327 *et seq.* See also Griffith (1952) 9 U. Toronto L.J. 169; *Moukataff v. B.O.A.C.* [1967] 1 Lloyd's Rep 396.
[32] s.38(2). See, as to the term "officer", *Moukataff v. B.O.A.C.*, above, at p. 413.

servant, liability for his acts arises by virtue of section 2(1)(*a*) above; where he is not, and is also not an agent of the Crown, *e.g.* because he exercises an independent public function, the Crown's liability seems to arise under section 2(3), which provides that where an officer of the Crown commits a tort while performing or purporting to perform functions conferred or imposed on him by law, the liability of the Crown shall be such as it would have been had the functions been conferred or imposed solely by virtue of instructions lawfully given by the Crown.[33] In either case, the main effect of section 2(6) was to exclude liability for the police: a police officer is a servant neither of the Crown[34] nor of the local authority that pays him,[35] and was exempted from the operation of section 2(3) by this subsection. But now, by virtue of section 48 of the Police Act 1964, the chief officer of police of any area is liable in respect of torts committed by constables under his control in the performance of their functions in like manner as a master is liable in respect of torts committed by his servants in the course of their employment, the police fund being charged with the payment of damages and costs awarded.

The purpose of the proviso initially referred to seems to be to preserve any defences open to the tortfeasor, but these would be available by virtue of the general rules of vicarious liability in any case.[36]

8–187   **Effect of judgment against principal or agent: contribution.**[37] Where the principal is liable for the torts of his agent, or the master for those of his servant, they are in principle to be regarded as joint tortfeasors.[38] At common law judgment against one such tortfeasor released the others[39] and there was no general right of contribution between them.[40] The Law Reform (Married Women and Tortfeasors) Act 1935[41]

---

[33] But see Atiyah, *op. cit.* n. 27 above, p. 392; it is arguable that the liability still arises under s.2(1) and therefore that the Crown is not liable at all for a public officer who is not a servant or agent.

[34] *Att.-Gen. for New South Wales v. Perpetual Trustee Co.* [1955] A.C. 457.

[35] *Fisher v. Oldham Corp.* [1930] 2 K.B. 364.

[36] Though before the Law Reform (Husband and Wife) Act 1962, the Crown would not have been liable in a case like *Broom v. Morgan* [1953] 1 Q.B. 597. For further suggestions see Street, *Governmental Liability* (1953), pp. 37–38; Glanville Williams, *Crown Proceedings* (1948), p. 45; Clerk and Lindsell, *op. cit.* n. 26 above, § 2–04.

[37] See in general Glanville Williams, *Joint Torts and Contributory Negligence* (1951); Salmond and Heuston, *Torts* (20th ed.), pp. 437 *et seq.*; Clerk and Lindsell, *Torts* (16th ed.), §§ 2–53 *et seq.*; *N.Z. Guardian Trust Ltd v. Brooks* [1995] 1 W.L.R. 96.

[38] *Jones v. Manchester Corp.* [1952] 2 Q.B. 852, 869.

[39] *Merryweather v. Nixan* (1788) S.T.R. 186.

[40] *Brinsmead v. Harrison* (1872) L.R. 7 C.P. 547.

[41] s.6.

abolished the first rule; and also made provision for contribution between such tortfeasors. The Civil Liability (Contribution) Act 1978[42] repealed the relevant part of the 1935 Act, extending the right to contribution to situations where one wrongdoer was not liable in tort (but rather for breach of contract or trust)[43] and also making improved provision for the right to contribution,[44] dealing with two cases which previously had been controversial. These were whether a tortfeasor who had settled a claim against him was entitled to contribution: and whether contribution could be recovered from a person who had been sued to judgment and held not liable in circumstances in which he would have been liable had he been sued at some other time or in some other way. The Act binds the Crown.[45]

The master can often, however, recover an indemnity at common law apart from statute,[46] for a servant is under a duty to take reasonable care in the execution of his duties, and if he breaks this duty the measure of damages may be the loss he has caused his master, who has had to answer for his tort.[47] Where an agent can be brought under this reasoning, he may similarly be liable.[48] But if his master or principal is himself at fault, the agent or servant may not be liable under this head.[49]

However, even if the master or principal was at fault, he may be able to recover such sum as the court considers just and equitable by way of contribution under the Act: and where he is not at fault he can equally sue under the statute, instead of at common law, and may recover 100 per cent contribution.[50] But he has no right to recover contribution where the agent is completely innocent, for here he is himself under a duty to indemnify the agent.[51]

---

[42] See Law Com. No. 79 (1977).

[43] ss.2, 4, 6. But *release* of one joint tortfeasor still releases the others.

[44] ss.1, 2, 7(3).

[45] s.5

[46] The right to do so is preserved by Civil Liability (Contribution) Act 1978, s.7(3).

[47] *Lister v. Romford Ice & Cold Storage Co.* [1957] A.C. 555. But the effect of this case has been circumvented in practice: see Gardiner (1959) 22 M.L.R. 652; Clerk and Lindsell, *Torts* (16th ed.), § 2–65.

[48] See Articles 42 and 44 as to the duties owed by contractual and non-contractual agents.

[49] See *Jones v. Manchester Corp.* [1952] 2 Q.B. 852, 865. But *cf.* Atiyah, *Vicarious Liability in the Law of Torts* (1967), pp. 428–430. See also *Adamson v. Jarvis* (1827) 4 Bing. 66, Illustration 9 to Article 65 for the converse case where an agent recovers indemnity because innocent.

[50] *Ryan v. Fildes* [1938] 3 All E.R. 517; *Semtex v. Gladstone* [1954] 1 W.L.R. 945; *Harvey v. R.G. O'Dell* [1958] 2 Q.B. 78. This may be useful where for some reason the common law action is not available, as in *Harvey v. R.G. O'Dell.*

[51] See *Adamson v. Jarvis* (1827) 4 Bing. 66, n. 49 above; and Article 65 generally.

515

Illustrations

8–188   The course of the servant's employment
(1)   The driver of a tanker, whose duty included the delivery of petrol into storage tanks, while transporting petrol from the tanker to a storage tank at a garage, struck a match to light a cigarette and threw the lighted match on the floor, thereby causing a fire. Held, that his employer was liable for the damage so caused by the negligent act of the driver, which was done in the course of his employment.[52]
(2)   An assistant storekeeper at a warehouse is inconvenienced by a lorry belonging to a customer, which is blocking the entrance. Without making any inquiries of anyone he attempts to move the lorry and causes personal injuries to another. His employers are liable.[53]
(3)   The manager of a branch of a furniture business, while repossessing goods under a hire-purchase contract, assaults the hirer. His employer is liable.[54]
(4)   An employee of a garage, after serving a customer with petrol, incorrectly thinking that the customer was about to depart without paying or giving up the necessary coupons, pursued him and abused him. The customer paid and delivered the coupons and then said that he would report the employee to his employers. The employee struck the customer. Held, the assault had no connection with the discharge of the employee's duty to his employers, who were therefore not liable.[55]
(5)   The manager of a shop detains a person suspected of shoplifting. The person detained is innocent. The manager's employer may be liable for false imprisonment.[56]

---

[52] *Century Insurance Co. Ltd v. Northern Ireland Road Transport Board* [1942] A.C. 509; *Jefferson v. Derbyshire Farmers Ltd* [1921] 2 K.B. 281; *Staton v. National Coal Board* [1957] 1 W.L.R. 893.
[53] *Kay v. I.T.W. Ltd* [1968] 1 Q.B. 140; cf. *Beard v. London General Omnibus Co.* [1900] 2 Q.B. 530; and see *Ilkiw v. Samuels* [1963] 1 W.L.R. 991; *Nelson v. Raphael* [1979] R.T.R. 437 (person demonstrating controls of car to buyer).
[54] *Dyer v. Munday* [1895] 1 Q.B. 742. cf. Illustration 17. And see *Hamlyn v. John Houston & Co.* [1903] 1 K.B. 81 (bribery).
[55] *Warren v. Henlys* [1948] 2 All E.R. 935: cf. *Pettersson v. Royal Oak Hotel Ltd* [1948] N.Z.L.R. 136; *Deatons Pty Ltd v. Flew* (1949) 79 C.L.R. 370: *Keppel Bus Co. Ltd v. Salad bin Ahmed* [1974] 1 W.L.R. 1082; *Auckland Workingmen's Club v. Rennie* [1976] 1 N.Z.L.R. 278. See further as to assaults by servants and agents Rose (1977) 40 M.L.R. 420; Clerk and Lindsell, *Torts* (16th ed.), § 3–25; Atiyah, *Vicarious Liability in the Law of Torts* (1967), pp. 276–280.
[56] See *Neville v. C. & A. Modes Ltd* 1945 S.C. 175. An account of such a case heard in York is reported in *The Times* of September 30, 1983. The older cases often concerned the giving of a person into custody, and drew a distinction between preservation of the employer's property and a mere desire to punish. See *e.g. Bank of New South Wales v. Owston* (1879) 4 App.Cas. 270; *Abrahams v. Deakin* [1891] 1 Q.B. 516. Police officers are more likely nowadays to arrest on their own responsibility: see *Meering v. Graham-White Aviation Co. Ltd* (1919) 122 L.T. 44; but cf. *Martin v. Watson* [1995] 3 W.L.R. 318 (malicious prosecution). See further Atiyah, *op. cit.* n. 55 above, pp. 266–267.

liable for damage caused by the agent's negligent driving. The agent was not the servant of the principal.[57]

Prohibited acts   8–189

(7)   A bus driver, in order to prevent a rival bus from overtaking him, drove his bus across the road and caused the rival bus to overturn. The driver had instructions from his employers not to race with or obstruct other buses. Held, that the employers were liable, the wrongful act being done in the course of the driver's employment.[58]

(8)   The driver of a vehicle had authority to carry his employer's servants, but had been expressly forbidden to carry other persons, and a notice to this effect was displayed in the vehicle. The driver gave a lift to a person who was not a fellow-employee and who, in dismounting, suffered injury. Held, the driver acted outside the course of his employment, so that the employer was not liable.[59]

(9)   The employee of a firm of valuers is instructed not to make valuations for certain companies. He nevertheless does so on the vendor's headed notepaper, it not appearing who made the valuation. The valuation is negligent. The valuers are not liable for it.[60]

(10)   An employee of A, in disregard of a written notice issued to A's employees prohibiting the use of privately owned cars for the purpose of A's business unless adequately protected by insurance, used his own uninsured car for the purpose of ordinary work, and by negligent driving injured the plaintiff. Held, that the means of transport was incidental to the execution of what the servant was employed to do; that the prohibition merely limited the way in which, or means by which, the servant was to execute the work; and that A was liable to the plaintiff.[61]

Wrong of servant or agent committed for his own benefit   8–190

(11)   A solicitor's managing clerk who had a general authority to conduct conveyancing business induced a widow to give him instructions to realise properties with a view to reinvestment of the proceeds. For that purpose she handed him her title deeds, for which he gave her a receipt in his principal's name; and, at his request, she signed two documents, which were not read over or explained to her, and which

---

[57] *Eggington v. Reader* [1936] 1 All E.R. 7; *cf.* Illustration 24.
[58] *Limpus v. London General Omnibus Co.* (1862) 1 H. & C. 526.
[59] *Conway v. George Wimpey & Co. (No. 2)* [1951] 2 K.B. 266; *Twine v. Bean's Express Ltd* [1946] 1 All E.R. 202. *Cf. Young v. Edward Box & Co. Ltd* [1951] 1 T.L.R. 789.
[60] *Kooragang Investments Pty. Ltd v. Richardson & Wrench Ltd* [1982] A.C. 462 (criticised, [1982] C.L.J. 36).
[61] *Canadian Pacific Ry. Co. v. Lockhart* [1942] A.C. 591; *L.C.C. v. Cattermoles (Garages) Ltd* [1953] 1 W.L.R. 997.

were in fact conveyances of the properties to the clerk. He afterwards disposed of the properties for his own benefit. The principal was liable for the fraud. [62]

(12) A solicitor's managing clerk was authorised to carry out conveyancing business and to borrow money from building societies, on behalf of clients, upon security of mortgage. He obtained an advance from a building society by producing a deed which he knew to be forged. Held, he was acting within the scope of his apparent authority and his principal was liable for the fraud, despite that the fact that it involved a forgery. [63]

(13) A, at the request of B, a transport contractor, committed goods to B's servants for carriage by road. In the course of their employment B's servants stole the goods so received. Held, B was liable to A for the value of the goods. [64]

8–191   Authority to commit the wrongful act

(14) A, the chairman at a meeting, at the request of B, who took part in the meeting, made a defamatory statement concerning C, and both A and B expressed a desire that the reporters present would take notice of the case. Correct reports having been published, it was held, in an action by C for libel, that there was evidence for the jury of publication by A and B through the reports, whom they had made their agents. [65]

(15) A, being hired to sing at a music-hall, and being permitted to choose his own song, sang a song infringing B's copyright. No control was exercised by the proprietor of the music-hall to prevent infringement of copyright. Held, that there was sufficient evidence of authority to sing the song complained of to justify a verdict for B in an action against the proprietor for the infringement. [66]

8–192   Liability for acts of agent

(16) An unnecessary sale by a shipmaster of any part of the cargo, where the sale, though unauthorised, is within the general scope of the

---

[62] *Lloyd v. Grace, Smith & Co.* [1912] A.C. 716.

[63] *Uxbridge Permanent Benefit Building Soc. v. Pickard* [1939] 2 K.B. 248. As to the liability of a solicitor to the disciplinary action of the court for the misdeeds of his clerk, see *Myers v. Elman* [1940] A.C. 282.

[64] *United Africa Co. Ltd v. Saka Owoade* [1955] A.C. 130; *Morris v. C.W. Martin & Sons* [1966] 1 Q.B. 716, overruling *Cheshire v. Bailey* [1905] 1 K.B. 237; *Mendelssohn v. Normand Ltd* [1970] 1 Q.B. 177.

[65] *Parkes v. Prescott* (1869) L.R. 4 Ex. 169. *cf. Lucas v. Mason* (1875) L.R. 10 Ex. 251. See Gatley, *Libel and Slander* (8th ed.), §§ 237 *et seq.*

[66] *Monaghan v. Taylor* (1886) 2 T.L.R. 685; *Marsh v. Conquest* (1864) 17 C.B. 418; *cf. Performing Rights Society Ltd v. Ciryl Theatrical Syndicate Ltd* [1924] 1 K.B. 1; *C. Evans & Sons Ltd v. Spritebrand Ltd* [1985] 1 W.L.R. 317. See Copinger and Skone James, *Copyright* (13th ed.), §§ 8–139, 9–30, 11–10, 11–11, 11–15.

authority conferred upon the master by the owners of the ship, is a conversion for which the owners are liable.[67]

(17) A landlord is liable for wrongful distress committed by a bailiff acting on the landlord's behalf and within the scope of the bailiff's authority.[68] But he is not liable for an unauthorised assault committed by the bailiff in levying a distress, at any rate if the person assaulted was not interfering with the distress.[69]

(18) A principal is liable for infringement by his employee or agent, acting in the course of his employment or within the scope of his authority, of a patent,[70] trade mark[71] or copyright.[72]

(19) A director starts negotiations for a contract without authority, and makes fraudulent misrepresentations. He is later authorised to negotiate, and takes no steps to correct the misrepresentations. The company is liable.[73]

(20) An estate agent tells a prospective purchaser of a bungalow that any building society will lend £1,200 on a mortgage of it. The bungalow is in fact structurally unsound, but the estate agent was not fraudulent in making such statements. The owners of the bungalow, for whom the estate agent was acting, knew of the unsoundness, but not that the estate agent had made such a representation. The owner is not liable in deceit for the agent's false statement, it not having been proved that he deliberately kept the agent in ignorance of the facts.[74]

---

[67] *Ewbank v. Nutting* (1849) 7 C.B. 797. And see Illustration 18.

[68] See, *e.g. Hurry v. Richman and Sutcliffe* (1831) 1 M. & Rob. 126; *Freeman v. Rosher* (1849) 13 Q.B. 780; *Hasseler v. Lemoyne* (1858) 5 C.B.(N.S.) 530. But the basis of liability is not clear: some cases put it on the basis of express authorisation or ratification only. also sheriffs are liable for the acts of their officers: *Hooper v. Lane* (1857) 6 H.L.Cas 443. But the sheriff himself is the agent of the court and the execution creditor is not liable for his acts unless he specifically authorised them: *Barclays Bank v. Roberts* [1954] 1 W.L.R. 1212. However, a solicitor is the agent of the execution creditor, so that if he by indorsement of the writ directs the sheriff to seize the goods of the wrong party, the client is liable for the acts of the sheriff as so directed: *Jarmain v. Hooper* (1843) 6 Man. & G. 827; *Morris v. Salberg* (1889) 22 Q.B.D. 614; *Lee v. Rumilly* (1891) 55 J.P. 519; *cf. Condy v. Blaiberg* (1891) 55 J.P. 580. The same applies if the solicitor issues execution after the debt has been paid: *Bates v. Pilling* (1826) 6 B. & C. 38; *Clissold v. Cratchley* [1910] 2 K.B. 244. But he has no authority to direct the seizure of particular chattels, and the client will not be liable if he does this: *Smith v. Keal* (1882) 9 Q.B.D. 340; *Hewitt v. Spiers & Pond* (1896) 13 T.L.R. 64; and see *Williams v. Williams & Nathan* [1937] 2 All E.R. 559; *Barclays Bank v. Roberts*, above. These lines of cases are well established, but their basis and their reconciliation with more recent authorities on vicarious liability are a difficult matter. See Atiyah, *Vicarious Liability in the Law of Torts* (1967), pp. 136–142.

[69] *Richards v. West Middlesex Waterworks Co.* (1885) 15 Q.B.D. 660. See Illustrations 3, 4 above.

[70] *Betts v. Neilson* (1868) L.R. 3 Ch.App. 429.

[71] *Tonge v. Ward* (1869) 21 L.T. 480.

[72] Illustration 15 above.

[73] *Briess v. Woolley* [1954] A.C. 333.

[74] *Armstrong v. Strain* [1952] 1 K.B. 232. As to liability under s.2(1) of the Misrepresentation Act 1967, see *Gosling v. Anderson* (1972) 223 E.G. 1743. As to liability

—cont. on next page

(21)   An estate agent demands a premium from a person who wishes to acquire the tenancy of a flat. The premium is illegal. It is recoverable from the landlord though the agent kept the money himself and the taking of the premium was not within his actual authority.[75]

(22)   A solicitor acting for the vendor in a conveyancing transaction negligently makes false statements in answer to inquiries. The vendor is liable in respect of the statements but the solicitor is not.[76]

(23)   A canvasser and agent was engaged by an insurance company under an agreement one of the terms of which prohibited him from defaming any other person or institution. While attempting to obtain business, he made defamatory statements concerning another assurance company. It was held that in doing so he was acting not independently but as a representative of the first assurance company conducting negotiations for that company, and that the company was liable for his statements.[77]

(24)   An agent employed by an assurance company drives a doctor to make the necessary examination of a person who wishes to propose for life insurance. He drives negligently and the doctor is injured. The company is not liable.[78]

(25)   The Chartering Manager and Vice-President (Transportation) of a company, authorised to negotiate the sale of a ship belonging to the

---

—cont. from previous page
in negligence, see *Presser v. Caldwell Estates Pty. Ltd* [1971] 2 N.S.W.L.R. 471; *cf. Thompson v. Aiken* (1977) 2 B.C.L.R. 23. As to the authority of an estate agent, see Article 30, Illustration 6.

[75] *Navarro v. Moregrand Ltd* [1951] 2 T.L.R. 674. See also *Credit Services Investments Ltd v. Evans* [1974] 2 N.Z.L.R. 653. *Cf. Kabel v. Ronald Lyon Espanola S.A.* (1968) 208 E.G. 265.

[76] *Cemp Properties (U.K.) Ltd v. Dentsply Research and Development Corp.* [1989] 2 EGLR 196 (Misrepresentation Act 1967, s.2(1)); see also *Strover v. Harrington* [1988] Ch. 390 (Misrepresentation Act 1967, s.2(1), Illustration 8 to Article 97: no liability on facts); *Gran Gelato Ltd v. Richliff Group Ltd* [1992] Ch. 560 (Misrepresentation Act and common law negligence: criticised by Cane (1992) 108 L.Q.R. 539); and as to surveyors *Thompson v. Henderson & Partners Pty. Ltd* (1989) 51 S.A.S.R. 43 (negligence); and as to insurance agents *Derham v. Amev Life Insurance Co. Ltd* (1981) 56 F.L.R. 34 (fraud).

[77] *Colonial Mutual Life Assurance Society Ltd v. Producers' and Citizens Co-operative Assurance Co. Ltd. of Australia* (1931) 46 C.L.R. 41. The case was referred to with approval in *Derham v. Amev Life Assurance Co. Ltd* (1981) 56 F.L.R. 34, where an insurance company was held liable for the fraud of an agent with whom it had no contractual relation. See further as to defamation *Whitfield v. S.E. Ry. Co.* (1858) E.B. & E. 115; *Nevill v. Fine Arts Assurance Co.* [1895] 2 Q.B. 156; [1900] A.C. 68; *Citizens' Life Assurance Co. Ltd. v. Brown* [1904] A.C. 423; *Ellis v. National Free Labour Assn.* (1905) 7 F. 629; *Finburgh v. Moss Empires Ltd* 1908 S.C. 928; *Fitzsimons v. Duncan and Kemp & Co.* [1908] 2 I.R. 483; *Glasgow Corp. v. Lorimer* [1911] A.C. 209; *Aiken v. Caledonian Ry. Co.* 1913 S.C. 66; *Egger v. Viscount Chelmsford* [1965] 1 Q.B. 248; Atiyah, *Vicarious Liability in the Law of Torts* (1967) pp. 274–276. As to partners see *Meekins v. Henson* [1964] 1 Q.B. 472.

[78] *Colonial Mutual Life Assurance Society Ltd v. Macdonald* 1931 A.D. 412.

company, purports to enter into a simultaneous agreement to take it back on charter. The third party knows that the Vice-President has no authority to enter into such a charter without approval from higher in the company, but believes the Vice-President when he falsely says that he has obtained such approval. There is no apparent authority; nor therefore is the company vicariously liable for the deceit of its agent. [78a]

<h3 style="text-align:center">Article 93</h3>

MISREPRESENTATIONS BY AGENT AS TO CREDIT OF THIRD PARTIES

No action can be maintained against a principal in deceit or under   **8–193**
section 2(1) of the Misrepresentation Act 1967 in respect of any representation as to the character, conduct, credit, ability, trade or dealings of another person, to the intent that such other person may obtain credit, unless such representation is in writing signed by the principal [78b]; the signature of an agent is not sufficient, even if expressly authorised by the principal, except in the case of a limited company. [78c]

Comment

This Article reproduces the effect of the Statute of Frauds   **8–194**
Amendment 1828 (Lord Tenterden's Act), the purpose of which was to prevent a person against whom the Statute of Frauds was pleaded in respect of a guarantee evading the protection of the Statute by suing in tort. [79] It was subsequently established that it applied only to actions in deceit, the form of action which would have been used at the time, and not to those in negligence, where the gist of the tort is said to lie not in the representation but in the breach of a duty of care. [80] It is also confined to representations as to creditworthiness. [81] However, the wording of section 2(1) of the Misrepresentation Act 1967, which uses

---

[78a] *Armagas Ltd v. Mundogas S.A. (The Ocean Frost)* [1986] A.C. 717.

[78b] Statute of Frauds Amendment Act 1828 (Lord Tenterdens' Act) s.6. The actual wording reads: "May obtain credit, money or goods upon, unless etc,": see *Lyde v. Barnard* (1836) 1 M. & W. 101, 104. For a case on similar Scottish legislation see *Clydesdale Bank Ltd v. Paton* [1896] A.C. 381.

[78c] See Comment. There is a useful discussion of this provision (which led to its repeal in New South Wales) in Report LRC 57 of the New South Wales Law Reform Commission (1988).

[79] See *Williams v. Mason* (1873) 28 L.T. 232.

[80] *Banbury v. Bank of Montreal* [1918] A.C. 626; *W.R. Anderson & Sons v. Rhodes (Liverpool) Ltd* [1967] 2 All E.R. 850; *Diamond v. Bank of London and Montreal Ltd* [1979] Q.B. 333.

[81] *Diamond v. Bank of London and Montreal Ltd,* above.

the referent of fraud liability, appears to produce the result that section 6 applies also to claims under that provision.[82]

It was held in *Swift v. Jewsbury and Goddard*[83] that signature of an agent was not sufficient under the Act. "If you mean to charge a person with a fraudulent act ... you shall not charge that person unless you can produce his own handwriting for the statement of fraud by which you say you have been misled."[84] However, this caused difficulties with the emerging doctrine of corporate personality. A corporation can only sign by agents, and hence it might appear that a fraudulent misrepresentation signed by the agent of a corporation would never render the corporation liable. In *Hirst v. West Riding Union Banking Co. Ltd*[85] it was therefore argued that the Act only applied to natural persons and not to corporations at all. The proposition was rejected and the Act held effective to protect the Bank against liability for a fraudulent representation as to credit signed by a local manager. On this basis companies would not be liable except perhaps where reasoning that the signature is that of the company itself can be deployed. This was done in *UBAF Ltd v. European American Banking Corp. Ltd*,[86] where a company was held liable for a fraudulent misrepresentation as to credit signed by its Assistant Secretary.

Article 94

MONEY, ETC., MISAPPROPRIATED BY AGENT

8–195   Where the money of a third party is received by an agent while acting within the scope of his authority or in respect of a transaction ratified by the principal, and misapplied by him, or is received by the principal and misapplied by the agent, the principal is liable to repay the third party.[87]

Comment

8–196   The authority of the agent may of course be actual or apparent.[88] This rule, which is based on section 11 of the Partnership Act 1890, is

---

[82] *UBAF v. European American Banking Corp.*, n.86 below.
[83] (1874) L.R. 9 Q.B. 301.
[84] *per* Lord Coleridge C.J. at p. 312.
[85] [1901] 2 K.B. 560.
[86] [1984] Q.B. 713. See now *Meridian Global Funds Management Asia Ltd v. Securities Commission* [1995] 3 W.L.R. 413; above, paras. 1–022, 8–185.
[87] See Illustrations. *cf.* Partnership Act 1890, s.11, which refers to "money *or property*", as to which see Atiyah, *Vicarious Liability in the Law of Torts* (1967), pp. 119–121. As to the agent's liability see Article 113.
[88] *Trott v. National Discount Co.* (1900) 17 T.L.R. 37.

placed here for convenience, since it relates to the liability of a principal for the wrongs of his agent, but it does not follow that the liability is always in tort. Sometimes situations arise where the liability of the principal is indeed in tort for the fraud or conversion of his agent[89]: but sometimes the action may be in restitution,[90] and sometimes it is sufficient to say that a payment made in respect of a contract is binding whatever may have happened to it,[91] or that there is a breach of contract, whether or not the facts also constitute a tort.[92]

Illustrations

(1)   A local manager, acting as agent for a bank, induced a lady to invest money in paying off a certain mortgage. The money was paid to him for that purpose, and he misappropriated it. Held, that he was acting within the scope of his apparent authority in receiving the money, which must therefore be deemed to have been received by the bank, and that the bank was liable to repay it.[93]   **8–197**

(2)   An agent, acting apparently in the ordinary course of business, sent an account to A, representing that certain advances had been made on his account, and drew on him for the amount. It was within the scope of the agent's authority to make advances of that kind, but he had in fact misappropriated the money, and had not made the advances. A accepted and paid the bill. Held, that the principal was liable to A for the amount.[94]

(3)   An auctioneer receives a deposit in connection with a concluded contract, and does not pay it over to the vendor. The vendor is liable whether the auctioneer received it as agent for the vendor or as stakeholder.[95]

(4)   An estate agent receives a deposit on a transaction "subject to contract," whether expressly "as stakeholder" or without any indication of the capacity in which he was to hold it, and does not pay it over to the prospective vendor. The vendor is not liable unless the agent received it as agent for him, having authority to do so.[96]

---

[89] *Swire v. Francis* (1877) 3 App.Cas. 106, Illustration 2.

[90] *Thompson v. Bell* (1854) 10 Exch. 10, Illustration 1; *cf. Russo-Chinese Bank v. Li Yau Sam* [1910] A.C. 174. Again, the principal may be a trustee: see *Hackney v. Knight* (1891) 7 T.L.R. 254.

[91] *Thompson v. Bell*, n. 90 above, at p. 14 ("the money is still in the hands of the bank").

[92] *National Bank of Lahore v. Sohan Lal*, A.I.R. 1965 S.C. 1663.

[93] *Thompson v. Bell* (1854) 10 Exch. 10. *Cf. Bishop v. Jersey (Countess)* (1854) 2 Drew. 143; *Russo-Chinese Bank v. Li Yau Sam* [1910] A.C. 174. See also *Royal Globe Life Assurance Co. Ltd v. Kovacevic* (1979) 22 S.A.S.R. 78.

[94] *Swire v. Francis* (1877) 3 App.Cas. 106.

[95] See Article 113, Illustrations 2 and 3 and cases cited.

[96] *Sorrell v. Finch* [1977] A.C. 728. *Cf. Branwhite v. Worcester Works Finance Ltd* [1969] 1 A.C. 552. See *ibid.*, Illustration 3 and cases cited.

Article 95

MONEY APPLIED BY AGENT FOR BENEFIT OF PRINCIPAL

8–198   Where, by any wrongful act of an agent, or by an unauthorised act which is not ratified, the money of the third party is obtained and applied for the benefit of the principal, the principal is liable in equity to restore such money to the extent that it has been so applied.[97]

Comment

8–199   This applies notwithstanding that the third party knew that the agent was not authorised to obtain or receive money,[98] for its basis is not liability for the acts of the agent, but a wider principle akin to a doctrine of subrogation, whereby the third party is entitled to stand in the same position as the principal's creditor when the money has been paid over. There is no true subrogation, however, because the third party is not entitled to the benefit of the securities of the creditor,[99] and it has been suggested that the true basis of the principle is that an unauthorised loan is adopted or validated *pro tanto*.[1] The main application of the wider principle lay in cases of *ultra vires* borrowing by companies, where the view could have been taken that the transaction, though *ultra vires*, had not added to the liabilities of the company, which remain unchanged[2]: but there is a similar rule in the case of loans for necessaries purchased by minors[3] and in some cases the doctrine, or a similar doctrine, has been applied to situations of money obtained by fraud.[4] The money must be used by the defendant himself or his authorised agent: the principle does not apply where a third party discharges the defendant's debt without authority.[5] It is uncertain how far the words "for his benefit" in this Article should be stretched: the cases concern discharge

---

[97] See Comment.
[98] *Reversion Fund & Insurance Co. v. Maison Cosway Ltd* [1913] 1 K.B. 364, Illustration 1, interpreting *Bannatyne v. D. & C. McIver* [1906] 1 K.B. 103; accepted in *Rolled Steel Products (Holdings) Ltd v. British Steel Corp.* [1986] Ch. 246, 300, 307.
[99] *ibid.* at p. 377.
[1] Goff and Jones, *Law of Restitution* (4th ed.), p. 625; see pp. 622 *et seq.* where there is a full discussion of these and related cases. See also *Hazlewood v. West Coast Securities Ltd* (1974) 49 D.L.R. (3d) 46, affd. (1976) 68 D.L.R. (3d) 172; and *cf. Orakpo v. Manson Investments Ltd* [1978] A.C. 95.
[2] *Blackburn Building Society v. Cunliffe, Brookes & Co.* (1882) 22 Ch.D. 61, 71 (see also (1884) 9 App.Cas. 857). The scope of this doctrine is now much reduced: see above, paras. 8–036 *et seq.*
[3] *Marlow v. Pitfield* (1719) 1 P.Wms. 558. See also *City Bank of Sydney v. McLaughlin* (1909) 9 C.L.R. 615 (person of unsound mind).
[4] Illustration 2. See also *Barrow v. Bank of New South Wales* [1931] V.R. 323, deriving a wider doctrine from *Refuge Assurance Co. Ltd v. Kettlewell* [1909] A.C. 243.
[5] *Re Cleadon Trust Ltd* [1939] Ch. 286.

of his legal liabilities, but it has been suggested that the principle can apply wherever the money is used on any purpose authorised by the defendant,[6] *e.g.* in making authorised but gratuitous payments.

It should be noted that a similar result may sometimes be obtained without the aid of equity, by invoking the doctrine of tracing at common law. If the money has been paid into the principal's bank account, he may be liable to an action in restitution.[7]

Illustrations

(1) The managing director of a company borrows money on the company's behalf without authority. The lender knows that he has no authority, but expects that the company will adopt the loan. The company does not do so, but the money is spent by the managing director in discharging existing legal debts of the company. The company must repay the money.[8]

8–200

(2) The secretary of a company forges and discounts certain bills of exchange, and pays the proceeds to his own account, upon which he draws cheques in favour of the company. The company is liable to the discounter to the extent that the proceeds of the bills have been applied for its benefit.[9]

(3) A manager who had no authority to borrow money or overdraw his principal's account, having overdrawn the account and misapplied the money, borrowed £20 for the alleged purpose of paying the principal's workmen (but really to make up the defalcations), paid it into the principal's account, and drew on the account to pay the workmen. Held, that the £20 having been applied for the benefit of the principal, he was liable to repay the amount to the lender.[10]

4.—ADMISSIONS BY AND NOTICE TO AGENTS

Article 96

WHEN AGENT'S ADMISSIONS ARE EVIDENCE AGAINST THE PRINCIPAL

(1) An admission or representation made by an agent[11] may be received in evidence as an admission binding the principal only in the following cases:

8–201

---

[6] See Lindley and Banks, *Partnership* (16th ed.), §§ 12–196, 12–197; Goff and Jones, *op cit.* n. 1 above, p. 625.
[7] Illustration 3; see Article 90.
[8] *Reversion Fund & Insurance Co.* v. *Maison Cosway Ltd* [1913] 1 K.B. 364. See also *Bannatyne* v. *D. & C. McIver* [1906] 1 K.B. 103.
[9] *Ex p. Shoolbred* (1880) 28 W.R. 339. See also *Hazlewood* v. *West Coast Securities Ltd* (1974) 49 D.L.R. (3d) 46, affd. (1976) 68 D.L.R. (3d) 172.
[10] *Reid* v. *Rigby & Co.* [1894] 2 Q.B. 40.
[11] As regards admissions by partners, see Partnership Act 1890, s.15; Lindley and Banks, *Partnership* (16th ed.), §§ 12–17 *et seq.*

(a) Where it was made as part of a communication expressly authorised by the principal;

(b) Where it has reference to some matter or transaction upon which the agent was engaged on the principal's behalf at the time when the admission or representation was made, and the making thereof was within the ordinary course of that activity; [12]

(c) Where it has reference to some matter or transaction respecting which the person to whom the admission or representation was made had been expressly referred by the principal to the agent for information. [13]

(2) A report made by an agent to his principal cannot be put in evidence against the principal by a third person as an admission made on behalf of the principal. [14]

Comment

8–202   Where it is sought to prove an agent's admissions against his principal, the existence of the agency must be proved. Thus it has been held that an admission by a mother did not bind her son in affiliation proceedings. [15] But in commercial situations slight evidence of agency has been accepted. [16]

Where there is agency, "it is important to distinguish between authority to do an act and authority to talk about it." [17] The scope of the agent's authority as regards the making of admissions may be much

---

[12] Illustrations 1–6. And see Cross, *Evidence* (7th ed.), pp. 585–587; Phipson, *Evidence* (14th ed.), §§ 24–42 *et seq.*; *Restatement*, §§ 284–291 and Appendix, reporter's notes to § 284. *cf.* Partnership Act 1890, s.15. The rule here given is one of the law of evidence. But similar reasoning appears in other contexts, where the matter should properly be classified as one of substantive law, though the terminology in nineteenth-century cases is frequently confused. Thus questions may arise concerning statements in bills of lading signed by the master of a ship: see Article 77, Illustration 2; Scrutton, *Charterparties* (19th ed.), Articles 59–61. And there are many cases on acknowledgment and part payment by agents under the Limitation Acts: see Limitation Act 1980, ss.29–31; *Burt v. Palmer* (1804) 5 Esp. 145; *Anderson v. Sanderson* (1817) 2 Stark, 204; *Linsell v. Bonsor* (1835) 2 Bing.N.C. 241; *Whitehouse v. Abberley* (1845) 1 C. & K. 642; *Re Hale, Lilley v. Foad* [1899] 2 Ch. 107; *Re Coliseum (Barrow) Ltd* [1930] 2 Ch. 44; *Re Edwards' Will Trusts* [1937] Ch. 553; *Ledingham v. Bermejo Estancia Co.* [1947] 1 All E.R. 749; *Re Transplanters (Holding Company) Ltd* [1958] 1 W.L.R. 822. See also above, para. 2026
[13] Illustration 7.
[14] Illustrations 8, 9.
[15] *G. (A.) v. G. (T.)* [1970] 2 Q.B. 643; see Article 4. *Quaere* as to whether the evidence here might have been admitted under the Evidence Act 1938.
[16] See *Edwards v. Brookes (Milk) Ltd* [1963] 1 W.L.R. 795.
[17] Morgan (1929) 42 Harv.L.Rev. 461, 464.

narrower than that of his authority to make contracts or dispose of property, for in the latter cases the interests and possible losses of third parties must more directly be borne in mind. Thus in the absence of express authority to make the communication during which an admission is made, not only must the transaction about which the admission was made have been one upon which the agent was concerned on the principal's behalf at the time of the admission,[18] but also it must have been within his authority to make admissions, or at least to effect the relevant communication,[19] and this may be difficult to establish.[20] Beyond this the principal will not be bound. Authority to make admissions is a type of implied authority, but the implication should be made with caution. Apparent authority, strictly so-called, is not here relevant, since the idea of acting on a representation is not material to the law of evidence, which deals with proof of facts[21]: the more general notion of usual authority,[22] at any rate as a form of implied authority, will, however, apply.[23]

Authority to make admissions regarding past transactions will rarely be inferred,[24] and the admission of a servant will seldom be admissible in an action in which it is sought to make his master vicariously liable for his acts, since the courts have taken the view that authority to do the act resulting in the tort does not involve authority to make admissions about the tort.[25] This view can be criticised.[26]

The rules given above are rules of the law of evidence, under which admissions of the parties to a suit and their agents are receivable in

---

[18] *The Prinses Juliana* [1936] P. 139 (report by pilot made subsequent to time when he was acting as pilot not admissible): *Betham v. Benson* (1818) Gow 45 (letter written prior to contract in connection with another transaction).
[19] *Sed quaere* whether these are more than aspects of the same rule that there must be authority to make an admission, not lightly to be inferred. *Cf. Restatement*, § 286, esp. comment *c*, referring to statements concerning matters "upon which the agent is authorised to speak."
[20] See, *e.g. Wagstaff v. Wilson* (1832) 4 B. & Ad. 339; *R. v. Downer* (1880) 43 L.T. 445 (solicitors); *Maxwell v. I.R.C.* [1959] N.Z.L.R. 708 (accountant); *Garth v. Howard and Fleming* (1832) 1 M. & Scott 628 (pawnbroker's assistant); *R. v. Evans* [1981] Crim.L.R. 699 (solicitor's managing clerk).
[21] *Restatement*, § 286, comment *b*, and Appendix, pp. 497–498. But *cf. Edwards v. Brookes (Milk) Ltd* [1963] 1 W.L.R. 795; *H. Clark (Doncaster) Ltd v. Wilkinson* [1965] Ch. 694.
[22] See Comment to Article 22.
[23] *e.g. Kirkstall Brewery Co. v. Furness Ry. Co.* (1874) L.R. 9 Q.B. 468, Illustration 1.
[24] *Peto v. Hague* (1804) 5 Esp. 134; *Snowball v. Goodricke* (1833) 4 B. & Ad. 541; *Tunley v. Evans* (1845) 14 L.J.Q.B. 116; *The Prinses Juliana* [1936] P. 139.
[25] *Burr v. Ware R.D.C.* [1939] 2 All E.R. 688; *Johnson v. Lindsay* (1889) 53 J.P. 599; *Price Yards Ltd v. Tiverton Transport Ltd* (1958) 11 D.L.R. (2d) 669. This rule is connected with the previous one. *Cf. Restatement*, § 288.
[26] Logan (1939) 55 L.Q.R. 490; Cross, *Evidence* (7th ed.), p. 588; *Botes v. van Deventer*, 1966 (3) S.A.L.R. 182.

evidence as one of the exceptions to the rule against hearsay. But evidence which may not be received as an admission may nevertheless be received by virtue of other rules of the law of evidence, *e.g.* under the Evidence Act 1938, and under sections 2(1), 4(1) and 5(1) of the Civil Evidence Act 1968. These latter provisions could, for example, permit the reception of the evidence in Illustrations 2, 4, 8 and 9. The Act however preserves the common law rules. [27]

Illustrations

8–203   (1)   A parcel sent by railway was lost in transit. The station-master, in the ordinary course of his duty, made a statement to the police as to the absconding of a porter. Held, that the statement was admissible in evidence as an admission by the railway company. [28]

(2)   In an action against a railway company for not delivering certain cattle within a reasonable time, it appeared that a night inspector of the company, a week after the alleged cause of action arose, in answer to the question why he had not sent on the cattle, said that he had forgotten them. Held, that this admission did not bind the company, because it was not within the scope of the inspector's authority to make admissions as to past transactions. [29]

(3)   A shipmaster contracted by charterparty to carry certain goods. In an action against the shipowners for not carrying and delivering certain of the goods, letters written by the master to the plaintiff were admitted in evidence to show that the goods had been duly received. [30]

(4)   A solicitor or counsel is retained to conduct an action. Statements made by him in the conduct and for the purposes of the action are evidence against the client. [31] But statements made by him in casual conversation, and not in the course and for the purposes of the action, are not. [32] So statements made by a solicitor for the purposes of one action cannot be used as evidence in another action which the solicitor is conducting on behalf of the same client[33]; and admissions

---

[27] See ss.1(1), 9(1), (2)(*a*).

[28] *Kirkstall Brewery Co. v. Furness Ry. Co.* (1874) L.R. 9 Q.B. 468. See also *Ruddy v. Midland Great Western Ry. Co.* (1880) 8 L.R.Ir. 224; *Edwards v. Brookes (Milk) Ltd*, [1963] 1 W.L.R. 795; *Fraser Henleins Pty. Ltd v. Cody* (1945) 70 C.L.R. 100.

[29] *Great Western Ry. Co. v. Willis* (1865) 18 C.B.(N.S.) 748, but see the explanation of this case in Cross, *Evidence* (7th ed.), p. 586; *Johnson v. Lindsay* (1889) 53 J.P. 599; *Burr v. Ware R.D.C.* [1939] 2 All E.R. 688; *Scott v. Fernhill Stud Poultry Farm Pty Ltd* [1963] V.R. 12.

[30] *British Columbia Sawmill Co. v. Nettleship* (1868) 37 L.J.C.P. 235.

[31] *Marshall v. Cliff* (1815) 4 Camp. 133; *Haller v. Worman* (1861) 3 L.T. 741; *R. v. Turner* (1975) 61 Cr.App.R. 67; *Smart v. Pepper and Casswell* (1987) 26 A.C.R. 40.

[32] *Petch v. Lyon* (1846) 9 Q.B. 147; *Wilson v. Turner* (1808) 1 Taunt. 398; *Young v. Wright* (1807) 1 Camp. 139; *Richardson v. Peto* (1840) 1 Man. & G. 896; *R. v. Evans* [1981] Crim.L.R. 699.

[33] *Blackstone v. Wilson* (1857) 26 L.J.Ex. 229.

made by counsel at a trial have been held not to be binding at a new trial which had been ordered by the Court of Appeal.[34]

(5) An officer or member of a corporation or company answers interrogatories on its behalf. The answers may be read as an admission by the corporation or company.[35]

(6) The secretary of a tramway company represented that certain money was due from the company. Held, that the company was not estopped by such representation from saying that the money was not due, because it was not within the scope of the secretary's authority to make any such representation.[36]

(7) A refers B to C for information concerning a particular matter. Statements made by C to B respecting such matter are evidence against A.[37]

(8) The chairman of a company makes a statement at a meeting of shareholders. The statement is not an admission made on behalf of the company and cannot be put in evidence as such against the company by any third party, because it is not made to a third party.[38]

(9) An agent writes letters to his principal containing an account of transactions performed on his behalf. The letters cannot be put in evidence against the principal by third parties as admissions made on behalf of the principal because not made to third parties.[39]

Article 97

WHEN NOTICE TO AGENT EQUIVALENT TO NOTICE TO PRINCIPAL

(1) A notification given to an agent is effective as such if the agent **8–204** receives it within the scope of his actual or apparent

---

[34] *Dawson* v. *Great Central Ry. Co.* (1919) 88 L.J.K.B. 1177. See also *H. Clark (Doncaster) Ltd* v. *Wilkinson* [1965] Ch. 694 (admission made in interlocutory proceedings may be withdrawn unless estoppel raised).

[35] *Weisbach, etc., Co.* v. *New Sunlight Gas Lighting Co.* [1900] 2 Ch. 1. See also *Industrial Distributions (Central Scotland) Ltd* v. *Quinn* 1984 S.C.C.R. 5; *Ahern* v. *R.* (1988) 165 C.L.R. 87; *Claiborne Industries Ltd* v. *National Bank of Canada* (1989) 59 D.L.R. (4th) 533; *Beach Petroleum NL* v. *Johnson* (1993) 115 A.L.R. 411.

[36] *Barnett* v. *South London Tramways Co.* (1887) 18 Q.B.D. 815 (but this is probably not a case on the law of evidence); *Bruff* v. *Great Northern Ry. Co.* (1858) 1 F. & F. 344. But see as to company secretaries *Panorama Developments (Guildford) Ltd* v. *Fidelis Furnishing Fabrics Ltd* [1971] 2 Q.B. 711, Illustration 32 to Article 74.

[37] *Williams* v. *Innes* (1808) 1 Camp. 364; *Hood* v. *Reeve* (1828) 3 C. & P. 532.

[38] *Re Devala Provident Gold Mining Co., ex p. Abbott* (1883) 22 Ch.D. 593. *Contra, The Solway* (1885) 10 P.D. 137, doubted in *Admiralty Commissioners* v. *Aberdeen Steam Trawling and Fishing Co.* 1909 S.C. 335; *Swan* v. *Miller, Son and Torrence* [1919] 1 I.R. 151. And see *Re Djambi (Sumatra) Rubber Estates Ltd* (1912) 107 L.T. 631.

[39] *Langhorn* v. *Allnutt* (1812) 4 Taunt. 511. But *cf. Warner* v. *Women's Hospital* [1954] V.L.R. 410.

authority,[40] whether or not it is subsequently transmitted to the principal, unless the person seeking to charge the principal with notice knew that the agent intended to conceal hi.: knowledge from the principal.[41]

(2)   The law imputes to the principal and charges him with all notice or knowledge relating to the subject-matter of the agency which his agent acquires or obtains while acting as such agent.[42]

(3)   Where an agent is authorised to enter into a transaction in which is own knowledge is material, or where the principal has a duty to investigate or make disclosure, the knowledge of the agent may be attributed to the principal whether it was acquired in connection with the agency or not.[43]

Comment

8–205   This Article gives an indication of the applicable rules, but the notion that the knowledge of an agent is that of the principal is (as is apparent from the Illustrations) frequently invoked in cases of varying types and its full applications are not clearly determined. "When a question of notice, or knowledge, arises, we find ourselves overwhelmed in a sea of authorities, not altogether reconcilable with each other."[44] The *Restatement* seeks to lay down exhaustive rules[45] but there is not enough material in the English cases for such an exercise. This Article is formulated to make a division between cases of notification and mere notice or knowledge. This distinction has been forcefully argued by academic writers,[46] is adopted in the *Restatement*,[47] and has received judicial support in New Zealand.[48] It is based on the fact that in some cases of a more specific type of giving of information, use of the notion of an authority to receive it, not only actual but also apparent, seems natural and appropriate.

---

[40] *Tanham v. Nicholson* (1872) L.R. 5 H.L. 561, Illustration 3; and see Comment.
[41] *Blackley v. National Mutual Life Assn. of Australasia Ltd* [1972] N.Z.L.R. 1038, Illustration 7. See also *Norwegian American Cruises A/S v. Paul Mundy Ltd (The Vistafjord)* [1988] 2 Lloyd's Rep 343, 354.
[42] This formulation is taken from Mechem, *Law of Agency* (2nd ed.), s.183.
[43] See *El Ajou v. Dollar Land Holdings Plc* [1994] 2 All E.R. 685, 702 *per* Hoffmann L.J.
[44] *Taylor v. Yorkshire Insurance Co. Ltd* [1913] 2 Ir.R. 1, 21 *per* Palles C.B.
[45] See §§ 9–11, 268–282.
[46] Powell, pp. 236–244; Wright (1935) 1 U. Toronto L.J. 17, 52 n. 5; Falconbridge (1939) 17 Can.B.R. 248, 259; Seavey (1916) 65 U.Pa.L.Rev. 1 (a very valuable article): but *cf.* Fridman, pp. 318–319.
[47] §§ 9, 268–282.
[48] *Blackley v. National Mutual Life Assn. of Australasia Ltd* [1972] N.Z.L.R. 1038 *per* Turner P (Illustration 7).

The *Restatement* defines notification as "a formal act intended by the notifier to affect his rights arising from transactions with or by another with respect to the interests of the one notified"[49]; an obvious example is a notice to quit.[50] The reasoning has, however, been extended to certain situations where information is received by an insurance agent,[51] and in a recent formulation it has been extended to communications in general, "whether informative (such as the state of health of an insured) ... or performative (such as a notice to quit)."[52] This may be a useful extension, though there are dangers in applying such reasoning to negotiations concerning insurance, where not all knowledge held by the agent can easily be designated as a "communication", and the other criteria set down below as to mere notice and knowledge will often seem more relevant. For this reason the *Restatement* term "notification" is retained in the Article for the present, and not superseded by "communication".

Basis of rules. In notification cases, as stated above, the terminology   **8–206** of agency can readily be resorted to: the agent has authority to receive a notice to quit, or a formal disclosure of information, and so forth. But where the third party *knows* that the agent does not intend to pass on the notification, he cannot rely on authority reasoning any more than he could in the central applications of the notions of actual and apparent authority.[52a]

In notice or knowledge cases on the other hand, this terminology does not seem so natural[53]; but the idea that the principal must in certain circumstances be infected by the agent's knowledge does seem natural, whatever the justification for it. Two lines of reasoning can justify such a conclusion. The first is that of the identity of principal and agent: "every act of the agent, within the scope of his authority, is the act of the principal. Consequently all knowledge acquired by the agent when acting in the scope of his authority is the knowledge of the principal."[54] This reasoning would limit the imputation of knowledge to cases where it is acquired when the agent is acting for the principal, and as such does not accord with all the decisions.

---

[49] § 268, comment *a*.

[50] See *Tanham v. Nicholson* (1872) L.R. 5 H.L. 561, 569–570 (Illustration 3) *per* Lord Hatherley L.C. (but Lord Westbury and Lord Colonsay relied on the presumption that notice had been passed on); *Marsden v. City & County Ass. Co.* (1865) L.R. 1 C.P. 232; *Financings Ltd v. Stimson* [1962] 1 W.L.R. 1184, Illustration 6; *Blackley v. National Mutual Life Assn. of Australasia Ltd*, n. 48 above, Illustration 7; Consumer Credit Act 1974, ss.57, 69, 102; *Restatement*, § 268.

[51] *Blackley v. National Mutual Life Assn. of Australasia Ltd*, n. 48 above.

[52] *El Ajou v. Dollar Land Holdings Plc* [1994] 2 All E.R. 685, 703 *per* Hoffmann L.J.

[52a] See Article 75.

[53] *Restatement*, §§ 273; 272 comment *q*.

[54] *Taylor v. Yorkshire Insurance Co. Ltd* [1913] 2 Ir.R. 1, 21 *per* Palles C.B.

The second is that there is a presumption that where the agent has notice or knowledge of a matter relevant to the principal, it is presumed to have been passed on to the principal, at least where the situation is one in which there is a duty to do so.[55] The presumption is said to be rebuttable[56]; but it seems that it will not easily be rebutted except in cases where the agent is actually practising, or is a party to practising, a fraud on the principal, so that there is a moral certainty that the information will not be communicated.[57] This explanation would obviously take in some cases of knowledge acquired by the agent outside the scope of the agency, and as such it is somewhat more satisfactory, though it is obviously "rather a justification for the rule than a reason for it".[58] The question of knowledge acquired outside the agency is returned to below.[59]

It has, however, been held in a notification cases that where there is no evidence of authority to receive notification there may nevertheless be reliance on the presumption that notice was passed on[60]; presumably this would not be so where a special form of notification is required, but it does show some overlap between the notification and notice/knowledge rules.

8–207 **Fraud of agent.** It is clear, on the one hand, that the mere fact that the agent does not communicate his knowledge or information which he has, from fraudulent or other motives, is not sufficient to negative notice to the principal[61]: at the other extreme it is clear also that where the third party had actual knowledge that the agent would not pass information on (*e.g.* because he is a party to the fraud together with the agent), the principal will not be treated as having notice.[62] It may be that the second is the only case where the agent's fraud will prevent a *notification* being effective, the reasoning being that there is no actual authority and that the third party is not in such a case relying on apparent authority.[63] "He cannot take advantage of a known breach of

---

[55] *Wyllie v. Pollen* (1863) 32 L.J.Ch. 782, 783; *Waldy v. Gray* (1875) L.R. 20 Eq. 238, 252; *Bradley v. Riches* (1878) 9 Ch.D. 189, 196.

[56] *A/S Rendal v. Arcos Ltd* [1937] 3 All E.R. 577 (H.L.).

[57] See below, para. 8–207.

[58] Mechem, *Agency* (2nd ed.), s.1806.

[59] Below, para. 8–209.

[60] *A/S Rendal v. Arcos Ltd,* n. 56 above. See also *Brewin v. Briscoe* (1859) 2 E. & E. 116, Illustration 16; *Saffron Walden Second Benefit Building Society v. Rayner* (1877) 14 Ch.D. 406, Illustration 5.

[61] *Atterbury v. Wallis* (1856) 25 L.J.Ch. 792; and see Illustrations: *Bunbury v. Hibernian Bank* [1908] 1 I.R. 261.

[62] *Sharpe v. Foy* (1868) L.R. 4 Ch.App. 35; *Re Fitzroy Bessemer Steel Co. Ltd* (1884) 50 L.T. 144.

[63] *Blackley v. National Mutual Life Assn. of Australasia Ltd* [1972] N.Z.L.R. 1038, 1049.

faith."[64] In other cases the notification will be validly effected whatever subsequently became of it.[65]

In knowledge cases, however, the presumption that information will be passed on may also be nullified by proof that the agent was defrauding the principal in that transaction, whether or not the third party knew this: it can, in such a case, be said that there was a moral certainty that the information would not be communicated,[66] or that communication would require disclosure of the very fraud being practised upon the agent by the principal,[67] or that the agent was not acting for the principal when he received the information.[68] The mere suppression of a document is not sufficient fraud.[69] "It must be made out that distinct fraud was intended in the very transaction, so as to make it necessary for the [agent] to conceal the fact from his [principal] in order to defraud him."[70] But it is not clear that this old doctrine is entirely desirable; it seems out of accord with the approach of tort cases where employers are held responsible for the fraud of their employees.[71]

Time when effective. A notification should take effect on receipt[72]: knowledge however should often only be regarded as effective from the time when it was or ought to have been received by the principal.[73]   **8–208**

When information acquired. A notification will, in accordance with the rationale stated above, only affect the principal if it is given as such[74] to the agent while he is acting within his actual or apparent authority. Thus a notification given outside business hours might not be effective.   **8–209**

---

[64] Seavey (1916) 65 U.Pa.L.Rev. 1, 8.
[65] *Tanham v. Nicholson* (1872) L.R. 5 H.L. 561, Illustration 3; *Graves v. Legg* (1857) 2 H. & N. 210. See also Illustration 7.
[66] *Thompson v. Cartwright* (1863) 33 Beav. 178, 185 (affd. (1863) 2 De G.J. & S. 10).
[67] *Waldy v. Gray* (1875) L.R. 20 Eq. 238, 251–252; *Kennedy v. Green* (1834) 3 My. & K. 699. *Re European Bank* (1870) L.R. 5 Ch.App. 358; *Re Hampshire Land Co.* [1891] 2 Ch. 743; *Houghton & Co. v. Nothard, Lowe & Wills* [1928] A.C. 1; *Kwei Tek Chao v. British Traders & Shippers Ltd* [1954] 2 Q.B. 459; *Stoneleigh Finance Ltd v. Phillips* [1965] 2 Q.B. 537; *United Dominions Trust (Ireland) Ltd v. Shannon Caravans Ltd* [1976] I.R. 225; *Belmont Finance Corp v. Williams Furniture Ltd* [1979] Ch. 250; *Wall v. New Ireland Assurance Co. Ltd* [1965] I.R. 385; *Cricklewood Holdings Ltd v. C.V. Quigley & Sons Nominees Ltd* [1992] 1 N.Z.L.R. 463.
[68] *Espin v. Pemberton* (1859) 3 De G. & J. 547, 555; *Cave v. Cave* (1880) 15 Ch.D. 639, 644; *Restatement,* § 282. This supports the wording of this Article.
[69] *Atterbury v. Wallis* (1856) 25 L.J.Ch. 792.
[70] *Rolland v. Hart* (1871) L.R. 6 Ch.App. 678, 682–683, *per* Lord Hatherley L.C.
[71] *e.g. Lloyd v. Grace, Smith & Co.* [1912] A.C. 716. See Watts [1992] N.Z. Recent Law Review 223; and the balancing of the two principles by Phillips J. in *Deutsche Ruckversicherung Aktiengesellschaft v. Walbrook Ins. Co. Ltd* [1995] 1 Lloyd's Rep. 153.
[72] *Restatement,* § 270.
[73] *Restatement,* § 278.
[74] See, *e.g. Re Sketchley, ex p. Boulton* (1857) 1 De G. & J. 163; *ex p. Carbis* (1834) 4 D. & Ch. 354.

As to notice or knowledge, however, the position is more difficult. There are certainly cases holding that when knowledge was acquired by an agent prior to his acquiring that capacity, or at a time when he was not acting for the principal, that knowledge is not to be attributed to the principal[75]; and in the case of purchasers of land, knowledge acquired in other transactions is now excluded by statute.[76] There are also cases to the contrary. Some of these cases were explained on the basis that there was a "duty to know", or that the agent's knowledge had been bought.[77] A more general line of reasoning, often invoked, is that the agent has a duty to pass the information on to his principal[78]: it will be seen that this links with the second of the two organising explanations given above.[79] It will also be noted that there are cases where an agent's fiduciary duties may require him *not* to pass on information.[80] The matter has recently been considered in the Court of Appeal, where Hoffmann L.J. rejected the incidence of the *agent's* duty to make disclosure to his *principal* as irrelevant, and the court held that knowledge of the fraudulent provenance of money was not to be attributed to the principal, even though the agent probably did have a duty to disclose it to that principal.[81] He suggested that in this area there are two categories of case where the agent's knowledge will be attributed to the principal. The first is "cases in which the agent is authorised to enter into a transaction in which his own knowledge is material." These cases are not to be regarded as cases of imputation of knowledge: "rather, the agent's knowledge affects the terms of performance of a contract which he concludes on behalf of his principal."[82] There is here some danger of overlap with certain "notification" cases.[83] The second is "cases in which the *principal* has a

---

[75] *e.g.* Illustrations 20, 21. *cf. Welsbach Incandescent Gas Lighting Co. v. New Sunshine Incandescent Co.* [1900] 2 Ch. 1. See also *Wilde v. Gibson* (1848) 1 H.L.Cas. 605.

[76] Below, para. 8–211.

[77] *Taylor v. Yorkshire Insurance Co.* [1913] 2 I.R. 1, 20–21; *Jessett Properties Ltd v. U.D.C. Finance Ltd* [1992] 1 N.Z.L.R. 138. It is forcefully argued by Seavey (1916) 65 U.Pa.L.Rev. 1, 23 *et seq.*, and set out in the *Restatement*, § 276, that in principle, time and manner of acquisition are irrelevant in knowledge cases, though there may be no duty to remember and hence cases where knowledge is not inferred. See further Mechem, *Principles of Agency* (4th ed.), p. 90, n. 22. But an approach from this angle does not square with what is said in the English cases.

[78] *e.g. Restatement*, § 272: "concerning a matter as to which he acts within his power to bind the principal or upon which it is his duty to give the principal information".

[79] Above, para. 8–206.

[80] See above, paras. 6–040 *et seq.*; a recent example is *Halifax Mortgage Services Ltd v. Stepsky*, Ch.D., June 16, 1995 (solicitor).

[81] *El Ajou v. Dollar Land Holdings Plc* [1994] 2 All E.R. 685.

[82] At p. 702. *e.g* Illustration 12; *Turton v. L. & N.W. Ry.* (1850) 15 L.T. (o.s.) 92 (knowledge of contract terms from earlier occasion); *The Vistafjord* [1988] 2 Lloyd's Rep 343 (estoppel by convention). But see the *Deutsche Ruckversicherung* case, n. 71 above, at pp. 164–165.

[83] (Emphasis supplied). Above, para. 8–205.

duty to investigate or to make disclosure" where "he may have to disclose not only facts which he knows but also material facts of which he could expect to be told by his agents."[84] The judgment suggests, however, that other categories could be detected.[85]

Agents of companies. These lines of reasoning may obviously cause   **8–210** difficulty in the case of agents of companies, for there may be situations where the information required by one agent is available elsewhere in the company; it may perhaps also have been acquired at an earlier time. In some such cases it may, because of a time gap or a gap between departments (for example, as to renewals of insurance and new proposals), not be appropriate to attribute the information to the person handling the particular matter on behalf of the company.[86] There may also be cases where one part of the company may have a duty not to disclose to the other.[87]

It may, however, also be necessary to consider whether the company *itself* has information. For this purpose the "directing mind" reasoning[88] may be used and it may be held that since a person of sufficient significance in the company's operations is aware of something, the company itself is. It has been held that the "directing mind" need not be a person with general management and control: it may be necessary only to identify the person who had management and control in relation to the act or omission in point.[89] This reasoning may be more appropriate in situations where attempts to attribute notice via particular individuals by way of agency principles fail.[90]

Law of Property Act 1925, s. 199(1)(ii).[91] This section provides that a   **8–211** purchaser of property[92] for valuable consideration shall not be

---

[84] At p. 702. *e.g.* Illustrations 11, 13, and many cases on insurance, as to which see in general Clarke, *Law of Insurance Contracts* (2nd ed.), Chap. 8, *Simner v. New India Ass. Co. Ltd*, Q.B.D., June 22, 1994 (Judge Diamond Q.C.).

[85] *ibid.* See also *Det Danske Hedeselskabet v. K.D.M. International Plc* [1994] 2 Lloyd's Rep 535 (relevance of knowledge of agents in the aware of interrogatories: reference to a person "for whose knowledge" the interrogated party "is responsible": *per* Colman J. at p. 538).

[86] *Malhi v. Abbey Life Assurance Co. Ltd*, C.A., May 26, 1994, distinguishing *Evans v. Employers Mutual Life Assn. Ltd* [1936] 1 K.B. 505 and other authority; see also *F.A.M.E. Ins. Co. Ltd v. Spence* [1958] N.Z.L.R. 735. See in general Clarke, *op. cit.* n. 84 above, s.20–7Cl.

[87] Above, paras. 6–047 *et seq.*

[88] Above, paras. 1–022, 8–185.

[89] *Meridian Global Funds Management Asia Ltd* [1995] 3 W.L.R. 413, 419; *El Ajou v. Dollar Land Holdings Plc.* [1994] 2 All E.R. 685, 706.

[90] *El Ajou v. Dollar Land Holdings Plc.*, above (Illustration 25).

[91] Re-enacting Conveyancing Act 1882, s.3.

[92] Unless the context otherwise requires, "property" includes any thing in action and any interest in real or personal property: s.205(1)(xx).

prejudicially affected by notice of any instrument, fact or thing unless it is within his own knowledge, or would have come to his knowledge if such inquiries or inspections had been made as ought reasonably to have been made by him; or *in the same transaction* with respect to which a question of notice to the purchaser arises, it has come to the knowledge of his counsel, as such,[93] or of his solicitor, or other agent, as such, or would have come to the knowledge of his solicitor or other agent, as such, if such inquiries and inspections had been made as ought reasonably to have been made by the solicitor or other agent.[94]

Illustrations

8–212 Notification

(1) An underwriter sought to avoid a policy on the ground of the non-disclosure of a material fact. The fact had been disclosed to his solicitor, but had not been communicated to him. Held, that he was not bound by the disclosure to his solicitor, it not being in the ordinary course of a solicitor's employment to receive notice as to mercantile business.[95]

(2) Notice of withdrawal of an application for shares was given during business hours to a clerk at the registered office of the company, the clerk stating that the secretary was out. Held, that it operated as notice to the company.[96]

(3) A notice to quit is served at the house of a tenant upon a servant whose duty it is to deliver it to the tenant. That is good service on the tenant though the servant does not deliver the notice to him.[97]

(4) Notice of a bankruptcy petition against an execution debtor is given to the man left in possession by the sheriff. That does not operate as notice to the sheriff, because the man in possession is only his agent for the purpose of levying, selling the goods, and handing over the proceeds.[98]

(5) Notice of an incumbrance was given to a solicitor who had been employed by trustees in all matters relating to the trust in which professional assistance was required, but who had not been authorised to receive notices on their behalf, and the solicitor wrote accepting the notice on behalf of the trustees. Held, that the notice to the solicitor did

---

[93] *i.e.* as *his* agent; see *Re Cousins* (1886) 31 Ch.D. 671; *Taylor v. London & County Banking Co.* [1901] 2 Ch. 231; *cf. Meyer v. Charters* (1918) 34 T.L.R. 589.
[94] See *Maxfield v. Burton* (1873) L.R. 17 Eq. 15.
[95] *Tate v. Hyslop* (1885) 15 Q.B.D. 368.
[96] *Re Brewery Assets Corp., Truman's Case* [1894] 3 Ch. 272.
[97] *Tanham v. Nicholson* (1872) L.R. 5 H.L. 561. See also *Townsend Carriers Ltd v. Pfizer Ltd* (1977) 33 P. & C.R. 361.
[98] *Re Holland, ex p. Warren* (1885) 1 T.L.R. 430.

not operate as notice to the trustees, solicitors not being, as such, standing agents of their clients to receive notices on their behalf.[99]

(6) A car dealer may be the agent of the finance company for whom he acts, to receive notification of revocation of offer from a prospective hirer.[1]

(7) B proposes for life insurance. After a medical examination the company accepts the proposal, acceptance not to be completed till the first premium is paid and a banker's order signed. The agent who communicates this acceptance knows at the time of doing so that B has just been admitted to hospital and has undergone an operation, but does not tell the company. The premium is paid and a bankers' order signed (by B's wife). The company cannot repudiate the policy for non-disclosure, there having been notification of the facts to the agent, who had apparent authority to receive it. Suspicion, short of actual knowledge or positive belief, by B's wife that the information would not be passed on does not vitiate the notification.[2]

(8) In negotiations for the sale of a house, a misrepresentation is made in the particulars that it is on main drainage. This is subsequently corrected by the vendor's agent in a letter to the purchaser's solicitor. The solicitor does not pass on the information. The purchaser is deemed to have notice for the purposes of an action by him under s. 2(1) of the Misrepresentation Act 1967: his loss was caused not by reliance on the continuing representation but by his solicitor's failure to communicate the correction to him.[3]

(9) An agent with a power of attorney for several principals to purchase racehorses borrows money for the purpose from a bank. The bank makes disclosures requisite under credit contract legislation to the attorney. It has made the disclosure to his principals thereby.[4]

Notice   8–213

(10) An an agent of an insurance company negotiated a contract of insurance with a man who had lost the sight of an eye. Held, that company must be deemed to have had notice that the assured had lost the sight of an eye, and that it could not avoid the contract on the ground of non-disclosure by him of that fact.[5]

---

[99] *Saffron Walden Second Benefit Building Society v. Rayner* (1880) 14 Ch.D. 406.

[1] *Financings Ltd v. Stimson* [1962] 1 W.L.R. 1184. See Consumer Credit Act 1974, ss.57, 69, 102.

[2] *Blackley v. National Mutual Life Association of Australasia Ltd* [1972] N.Z.L.R. 1038.

[3] *Strover v. Harrington* [1988] Ch. 390.

[4] *National Australia Finance Ltd v. Fahey* [1990] 2 N.Z.L.R. 482.

[5] *Bawden v. London, Edinburgh & Glasgow Ass. Co.* [1892] 2 Q.B. 534. And see *Hough v. Guardian Fire & Life Ass. Co.* (1902) 18 T.L.R. 273; *Holdsworth v. Lancashire & Yorkshire Insurance Company* (1907) 23 T.L.R. 521; *Thornton-Smith v. Motor Union Insurance Co. Ltd.* (1913) 30 T.L.R. 139; *Golding v. Royal London Auxiliary Insurance*

—cont. on next page

(11) An insurance proposal form signed by the proposer contained untrue answers which were warranted to be true and which formed the basis of the contract. The answers were filled in by the insurance company's agent, whom the proposer had required or permitted to fill in the form after informing him of the true facts. Held, that the company were entitled to repudiate liability on the ground of the untrue answers. The agent, in filling in the form, was the agent of the proposer. If the agent knew that the answers were untrue, he was committing a fraud which prevented his knowledge being the knowledge of the company; if he did not know, he had no knowledge to be imputed to the company.[6]

(12) A broker bought goods from a factor, knowing from other experience that he was selling on behalf of a principal. Held, that the principal for whom the broker acted must be deemed to have had notice that the factor was not selling his own goods.[7]

—cont. from previous page

Co. Ltd. (1914) 30 T.L.R. 350; Keeling v. Pearl Life Ass. Co. Ltd. (1923) 129 L.T. 573. But these cases became doubtful in view of Newsholme Bros. v. Road Transport & General Ins. Co. Ltd. [1929] 2 K.B. 356, Illustration 11, and represent a view of the facts which was subsequently less easily taken. Thus in Newsholme's case Scrutton L.J. said: "The decision in Bawden's case is not applicable to a case where the agent himself, at the request of the proposer, fills up the answers in purported conformity with information supplied by the proposer." See Clarke, Law of Insurance Contracts (2nd ed.), §§ 10–2 et seq. But cf. Illustration 7; and see n. 6 below.

[6] Newsholme Bros. v. Road Transport & General Ins. Co. Ltd [1929] 2 K.B. 356 (where there is a full review of the authorities); Biggar v. Rock Life Ass. Co. [1902] 1 K.B. 516; Jumna Khan v. Bankers and Traders Insurance Co. Ltd. (1925) 37 C.L.R. 451; Dunn v. Ocean Accident & Guarantee Ltd. (1933) 50 T.L.R. 32; Facer v. Vehicle & General Insurance Co. [1965] 1 Lloyd's Rep 113; O'Connor v. B.D.B. Kirby & Co. [1972] 1 Q.B. 90. This is now the prevailing view. But it does not always yield just results, and in some contexts and countries, e.g. where illiteracy is prevalent, it must yield most unfair results. Attempts are sometimes therefore made to evade it, on grounds which are not very clear: see Stone v. Reliance Mutual Insurance Society Ltd [1972] 1 Lloyd's Rep. 469 (noted (1972) 88 L.Q.R. 462; Tan Lee Meng (1975) 17 Malaya L.Rev. 104); Blanchette v. C.I.S. Ltd (1973) 36 D.L.R. (3d) 561, following Stone's case; Woolcott v. Excess Insurance Co. Ltd [1979] 1 Lloyd's Rep. 231; Deaves v. C.M.L. Fire & General Insurance Co. Ltd (1978) 143 C.L.R. 24; Moxness v. Co-operative Fire and Casualty Co., (1979) 95 D.L.R. (3d) 365; Jeyeretnam, [1991] 2 M.L.J. lxvii, suggesting a distinction between situations where the information disclosed to the agent is contradicted by the signed proposal form and situations where the information supplements or clarifies the contents of the form; Clarke, op. cit. n. 5 above. See also Illustration 7, where the idea of notification is employed. Sometimes the matter is regulated by statute, e.g. New Zealand Insurance Law Reform Act 1977, s. 10. See also Australian Insurance (Agents and Brokers) Act 1985 (Cth.). Clauses providing that the person filling in the form is the agent of the proposer are probably not caught by s.3 of the Misrepresentation Act 1967, which gives the court discretion to disallow reliance on certain exemption clauses: cf. Overbrooke Estates Ltd v. Glencombe Properties Ltd [1974] 1 W.L.R. 1335; Collins v. Howell-Jones [1981] E.G.D. 207.

[7] Dresser v. Norwood (1864) 17 C.B.(N.S.) 466. See this case explained in El Ajou v. Dollar Land Holdings Plc [1994] 2 All E.R. 685, 702. See also Apthorp v. Neville & Co. (1909) 23 T.L.R. 575 (printing contract: agent knew manuscript defamatory).

(13) A ship was driven on a rock and damaged. The master afterwards wrote a letter to the owner, but did not communicate the fact of the ship having been damaged, and, subsequent to the receipt of the letter, the owner insured the ship. Held, that the master ought to have communicated the fact, and that therefore the owner must be deemed to have had knowledge of it at the time of the insurance.[8] So, where an agent shipped goods, and, having heard of a loss, purposely refrained from telegraphing to the principal because he thought it might prevent him from insuring, it was held that it was his duty to have telegraphed, and that an insurance effected by the principal after the time when he would have received the telegram was void on the ground of non-disclosure of material facts.[9]

(14) A broker was employed to effect an insurance, but did not effect it. Subsequently, another broker effected a policy in respect of the same risk on behalf of the same principal. It was sought to avoid the policy on the ground of the non-disclosure of material fact which had come to the knowledge of the first-mentioned broker in the course of his employment, but which he had not communicated to the principal, and which was not known either to the principal or to the broker who effected the policy. Held, that the policy was valid, there being no duty on the first broker to communicate the knowledge he had acquired.[10]

(15) A had a dog, which was kept at his stables under the care and control of his coachman. The coachman's knowledge of the ferocity of the dog was equivalent to A's knowledge.[11] So, where the wife of A occasionally attended to his business, which was carried on upon premises where a dog was kept, and B made a complaint to her, for the purpose of its being communicated to A, that the dog had bitten B's nephew, it was held that that was evidence of scienter on the part of A.[12] So also, where complaints were made of a publican's dog to his barman.[13] But the mere fact that a servant knows a dog to be

---

[8] *Gladstone v. King* (1813) 1 M. & S. 35.

[9] *Proudfoot v. Montefiore* (1867) L.R. 2 Q.B. 511. And see Marine Insurance Act 1906, s.19.

[10] *Blackburn Low & Co. v. Vigors* (1887) 12 App.Cas. 531: see a comment on this case in *Deutsche Ruckversicherung v. Wallbrook Ins. Co. Ltd* [1995] 1 Lloyd's Rep. 153, 164. *cf. Blackburn v. Haslam* (1888) 21 Q.B.D. 144; *The Litsion Pride* [1985] 1 Lloyd's Rep. 437, 513–514. See also *Wilson v. Salamandra Ass. Co. of St Petersburg* (1903) 88 L.T. 96 (knowledge of Lloyd's agents not imputed to underwriters).

[11] *Baldwin v. Casella* (1872) L.R. 7 Ex. 325; Animals Act 1971, s.2(2). See North, *The Modern Law of Animals* (1972), pp. 58 *et seq.*

[12] *Gladman v. Johnson* (1967) 36 L.J.C.P. 153. It seems that this and the following case are still relevant despite the wording of s.2(2) of the Animals Act 1971: North, *op. cit.* n. 11 above, pp. 66 *et seq.*

[13] *Applebee v. Percy* (1874) L.R. 9 C.P. 647.

dangerous is no evidence of scienter on the part of the master, where the servant has nothing to do with the care or control of the dog, and has not the control of the premises or place where it is kept.[14]

(16) The solicitor of a judgment creditor, having issued execution against the debtor, instructed A, a solicitor at the place where the execution was levied, to take an assignment of the goods seized from the sheriff. A did so, after having received notice of an act of bankruptcy by the debtor. Held, that the creditor must be deemed to have taken the assignment with notice of the act of bankruptcy.[15] So, if a solicitor, with the consent of his client, puts his managing clerk in his place to conduct and manage the matter, notice of an act of bankruptcy to the clerk operates as notice to the solicitor and to the client.[16]

(17) A solicitor induced a client to advance money on a mortgage of land which he held as trustee and afterwards induced another client to advance money on the same land. Held, that the last-mentioned client must be deemed to have had notice of the prior mortgage.[17]

(18) A solicitor, in the course of a transaction on his client's behalf, became a party to a fraud on the client. Held, that that did not operate as notice to the client of the fraudulent act, because no person would be likely to disclose his own fraud to the person defrauded.[18] So, where the directors of a company took part in a misfeasance against the company, it was held that their knowledge did not operate as notice to the company of the misfeasance.[19]

(19) A solicitor sells or mortgages property, and himself draws the purchase or mortgage deed and carries the transaction through on behalf, and with the consent, of the purchaser or mortgagee. The purchaser or mortgagee is deemed to have notice of all incumbrances

---

[14] *Stiles v. Cardiff Steam Navigation Co.* (1864) 33 L.J.Q.B. 310; *Cleverton v. Uffernel* (1887) 3 T.L.R. 509; *Colget v. Norrish* (1886) 2 T.L.R. 471; North, *op. cit.*, n. 11 above, pp. 62 *et seq.* See also *The Cawood III* [1951] P. 270 (knowledge of lightermen as to warning notice on jetty not attributed to employers); *Diment v. N.H. Foot Ltd* [1974] 1 W.L.R. 1927 (knowledge of agents regarding user of right of way not attributed to absent owner of land). cf. *The Gudermes* [1991] 1 Lloyd's Rep. 456 (knowledge of appointed inspectors that ship had no cargo heating arrangements attributed to principals: decision revsed. [1993] 1 Lloyd's Rep. 311).

[15] *Brewin v. Briscoe* (1859) 2 E. & E. 116; *Rothwell v. Timbrell* (1842) 1 Dowl.(N.S.) 778.

[16] *Re Ashton, ex p. McGowan* (1891) 64 L.T. 28; *Pike v. Stephens* (1848) 12 Q.B. 465; *Pennell v. Stephens* (1849) 7 C.B. 987.

[17] *Rolland v. Hart* (1871) L.R. 6 Ch.App. 678. And see *Le Neve v. Le Neve* (1747) 1 Ves. Sen. 64.

[18] *Cave v. Cave* (1880) 15 Ch.D. 639; *Kennedy v. Green* (1834) 3 M. & K. 699; *Thompson v. Cartwright* (1863) 33 Beav. 178 (affd. (1863) 2 De G.J. & S. 10); *Waldy v. Gray* (1875) L.R. 20 Eq. 238.

[19] *Re Fitzroy Bessemer Steel Co. Ltd* (1884) 50 L.T. 144.

known to the solicitor, even if the solicitor fraudulently conceals them.[20] But the mere fact that the purchaser or mortgagee employs no solicitor does not mean that, when the vendor or mortgagor is a solicitor and prepares the documents, he constitutes such vendor or mortgagor his solicitor.[21]

(20)   The secretary or a director of a company, while attending a funeral as a relative of the deceased, acquires knowledge of certain facts concerning the company's business. That does not operate as notice to the company of such facts.[22]

(21)   A solicitor who was employed to transfer a mortgage knew that there were incumbrances on the property subsequent to such mortgage. Held, that his knowledge did not operate as notice of the incumbrances to the transferee, because the incumbrances were not material to the transfer, for which alone the solicitor was employed.[23]

(22)   If a person is secretary of two companies, knowledge acquired by him as secretary of one of the companies need not be imputed to the other company.[24]

(23)   Directors of a banking company who had no voice in the management of the accounts acquired knowledge of certain circumstances relating to the accounts. Held, that this did not operate as notice of such circumstances to the company.[25]

(24)   On the sale of land, one firm of solicitors acts for the vendor, another for the purchaser. The two firms are in fact constituted by the same two partners. Knowledge acquired by one firm in acting for the vendor is not to be attributed via the other firm to the purchaser.[26]

(25)   Money which in fact consists of misappropriated trust funds is lent to a company. It is sought to charge the company with knowing

---

[20] *Atterbury v. Wallis* (1856) 25 L.J.Ch. 792 (see explanation in *Waldy v. Gray* (1875) L.R. 20 Eq. 238); *Re Weir, Hollingworth v. Willing* (1888) 58 L.T. 792; *Boursot v. Savage* (1866) L.R. 2 Eq. 134 (see (1916) 65 U. Pa.L.Rev. 34); *Dryden v. Frost* (1837) 3 M. & C. 670; *Sheldon v. Cox* (1764) 2 Eden 224; *Dixon v. Winch* [1900] 1 Ch. 736. Some of the distinctions taken are not convincing. See also *Burnard v. Lysnar* [1927] N.Z.L.R. 757 (knowledge by solicitor of true nature of transaction).

[21] *Espin v. Pemberton* (1859) 3 De G. & J. 547; *Hewitt v. Loosemore* (1851) 9 Hare 449. But he may be affected by such notice as he would have had had he employed a solicitor: *Kennedy v. Green*, n. 18 above; *Boursot v. Savage*, n. 20 above.

[22] *Société Générale de Paris v. Tramways Union Co.* (1884) 14 Q.B.D. 424.

[23] *Wyllie v. Pollen* (1863) 32 L.J.Ch. 782; *Brittain v. Brown & Millar* (1871) 24 L.T. 504 (*cf. Restatement*, § 279). See also *Wythes v. Labouchere* (1859) 3 De G. & J. 593; *Wells v. Smith* [1914] 3 K.B. 722; *Wilkinson v. General Accident, etc., Corp.* [1967] 2 Lloyd's Rep. 182.

[24] *Re Fenwick, Stobart & Co., Deep Sea Fishery Co.'s Claim* [1902] 1 Ch. 507; *Re Hampshire Land Co.* [1896] 2 Ch. 743; *Re David Payne & Co. Ltd* [1904] 2 Ch. 608; *Belmont Finance Corp. v. Williams (No. 2)* [1980] 1 All E.R. 393. See also *The Hayle* [1929] P. 275.

[25] *Powles v. Page* (1846) 3 C.B. 16; *Re Carew's Estate Act* (1862) 31 Beav. 39, *Cf. Ex. p. Agra Bank, Re Worcester* (1868) L.R. 3 Ch.App. 555. But *cf.* Illustration 25.

[26] *Campbell v. M'Creath* 1975 S.C. (Ct. of Sess.) 81.

receipt of trust property.[27] The fact that the funds were misappropriated is known to a Swiss "fiduciary agent" who acts as broker in the transaction. He is also a director and chairman of the company, is claimed to be the ultimate beneficial owner of the company and signed the relevant agreement regarding the loan. Although as broker he has a duty to disclose the facts to the company and does not do so, the company itself has no duty to inquire into their provenance and hence has no notice through him as their broker in the matter. But his position as a director and chairman of the company acting in connection with this transaction means that he is for this purpose the "directing mind and will" of the company, and the company itself has direct knowledge, not through an agent, that trust funds are involved, sufficient to make it liable for knowing receipt.[28]

5—BRIBERY OF AGENT

Article 98

RIGHTS OF PRINCIPAL WHERE AGENT BRIBED

8–214

(1) Every contract made or act done by an agent under the influence of bribery, or, to the knowledge of the other contracting party, in violation of his duty to his principal, is voidable against the other party by the principal.[29]

(2) Where an agent is induced by bribery to depart from his duty to his principal, the third party who bribed or promised the bribe to the agent is liable jointly and severally with the agent to the principal—

(a) in restitution, for the bribe; or
(b) in tort, for any loss sustained by the principal from entering into the transaction in respect of which the bribe was given.[30]

Comment

8–215

"For the purposes of the civil law a bribe means the payment of a secret commission, which only means (i) that the person making the payment makes

---

[27] See Article 117.
[28] *El Ajou v. Dollar Land Holdings Plc* {1994] 2 All E.R. 685; following on the first point *Re David Payne & Co. Ltd* [1904] 2 Ch. 608. See para. 8–210 above.
[29] *Panama & South Pacific Telegraph Co. v. India Rubber, etc., Co.* (1875) L.R. 10 Ch.App. 515. See Comment and Illustrations 1–3. See also *Gaunt v. Gold Star Insurance Co. Ltd* [1991] 2 N.Z.L.R. 341, a decision turning on the wording of New Zealand legislation regarding insurance intermediaries.
[30] *Mahesan v. Malaysian Government Officers' Co-operative Housing Society Ltd* [1979] A.C. 374; see below.

it to the agent of the other person with whom he is dealing; (ii) that he makes it to that person knowing that that person is acting as the agent of the other person with whom he is dealing; and (iii) that he fails to disclose to the other person with whom he is dealing that he has made that payment to the person whom he knows to be the other person's agent."[31]

The meaning of the notion of bribe has already been discussed in connection with the relationship between agent and principal.[32] The offer or acceptance of a bribe has, however, Draconian results not only in this respect but also as regards the third party. For, as the above quotation suggests, the third party is regarded as a party to the agent's breach of duty[33] even where he thought that the agent would tell or had told the principal of the bribe, since it is prima facie wrongful.[34] But the basis of the rules is wider notion that the payment gives rise to a conflict of interest.[35] The same consequences therefore ensue where there is other surreptitious dealing by the agent whereby he puts himself in a position where his interest and duty may conflict: for the principal is entitled to the disinterested advice of the agent. In these cases the third party is implicated where he knows of or is wilfully blind to an interest of the agent in the transaction between them; or where he is unaware of the agent's interest but aware that the agent does not intend to disclose the dealing to the principal.[36] He is also liable where he originally arranged for the bribe not knowing of the agency, but continued and entered into the contract after he had learned of it.[37]

Therefore the main contract can be rescinded against him either *ab initio* or, if it is too late for this, terminated for the future.[38] The

---

[31] *Industries & General Mortgage Co. Ltd v. Lewis* [1949] 2 All E.R. 573, 575 *per* Slade J.; followed, *Taylor v. Walker* [1958] 1 Lloyd's Rep. 490, Illustration 3. See also *Anangel Atlas Cia. Naviera S.A. v. Ishikawajima-Harima Heavy Industries Co. Ltd* [1990] 1 Lloyd's Rep. 167, 171 *per* Leggott J.: "More succinctly it may be said that a bribe consists in a commission or other inducement which is given by the third party to an agent as such, and which is secret from the principal."

[32] See Article 50.

[33] *Panama & South Pacific Telegraph Co. v. India Rubber, etc., Co.* (1875) L.R. 10 Ch.App. 515, 526. See Article 45.

[34] *Shipway v. Broadwood* [1899] 1 Q.B. 369, 373 (Illustration 2); *Grant v. Gold Exploration and Development Syndicate Ltd* [1900] 1 Q.B. 233, 248–250; *Taylor v. Walker*, n. 31 above at pp. 509–513.

[35] *Anangel Atlas Cia. Naviera S.A. v. Ishikawajima-Harima Heavy Industries Co. Ltd* [1990] 1 Lloyd's Rep. 167, 171.

[36] *Logicrose Ltd v. Southend United F.C.* [1988] 1 W.L.R. 1256, 1260–1262, holding that the test is the same as in the "knowing assistance" cases. But as regards these the law has now been restated: see below, para. 9–130; but *cf.* this para., text to n. 54.

[37] *Grant v. Gold Exploration and Development Syndicate Ltd*, n. 34 above.

[38] *Panama & South Pacific Telegraph Co v. India Rubber, etc., Co.*, n. 33 above; *Chadler v. Bradley* [1897] 1 Ch. 315; *Re a Debtor* [1927] 2 Ch. 367; *Taylor v. Walker*, n. 31 above; *Armagas Ltd v. Mundogas S.A. (The Ocean Frost)* [1986] A.C. 717, 742–743. The contract may sometimes be treated as outside the agent's authority: see *Matthews v.*

—*cont. on next page*

principal may refuse to proceed,[39] and recover money paid[40]; and he may do this even if he had previously, in ignorance of the bribery, terminated the contract on insufficient grounds;[41] and if the principal has recovered the bribe, this does not constitute affirmation of the transaction.[42] Where the bribe is paid or agreed upon, or, when originally unauthorised, adopted after the making of the contract, the matter probably turns on the general principles of breach of contract, *viz.* the significance of the arrangement to the performance of the contract.[43]

The English cases concern bribes paid or promised by third parties themselves, or readily imputable to such third parties. Where a bribe is paid or promised by an agent of the third party without that third party's knowledge, it has been held that the third party is affected by it when the agent has acted within the tort notion of course of employment, this being appropriate because of the tortious nature of the claim in damages as now established.[44] It has been suggested that rescission, as opposed to damages, might be appropriate even where the agent was not so acting.[45]

The principal may sue the agent and the third party, who are jointly and severally liable for the bribe and for any additional loss which may have been caused to the principal. Older case law suggested that the third party's liability was without taking into account any sum recovered from the agent.[46] Such a rule was almost penal in operation and highly

---

—*cont. from previous page*
Gibbs (1860) 30 L.J.Q.B. 55. The principal can also enforce the contract should he so wish: see *Odessa Tramways Co. v. Mendel* (1878) 8 Ch.D. 235; *Moody v. Cox and Hatt* [1917] 2 Ch. 71. And see Article 50.

[39] Illustrations 1, 2; *Maxwell v. Port Tennant Patent Steam Fuel & Coal Co.* (1857) 24 Beav. 495; *Bartram & Sons v. Lloyd* (1904) 90 L.T. 357.

[40] *Panama & South Pacific Telegraph Co. v. India Rubber, etc., Co.* (1875) L.R. 10 Ch.App. 515.

[41] *Alexander v. Webber* [1922] 1 K.B. 642; *cf. Boston Deep Sea Fishing & Ice Co. v. Anstell* (1888) 39 Ch.D. 339.

[42] *Grant v. Gold Exploration and Development Syndicate* [1900] 1 Q.B. 233, 251; *Logicrose v. Southend United F.C.*, n. 36 above, at pp. 1262–1263.

[43] *Armagas Ltd v. Mundogas S.A. (The Ocean Frost)* [1985] 1 Lloyd's Rep. 1, 18–22, following the view of Mellish L.J. in *Panama & South Pacific Telegraph Co. v. India Rubber, etc., Co.*, n. 33 above, at pp. 531–532 and applying *Hong Kong Fir Shipping Co. Ltd v. Kawasaki Kisen Kaisha Ltd* [1962] 2 Q.B. 26. The decision was reversed on other grounds, [1986] A.C. 717 (C.A. and H.L.).

[44] *Armagas Ltd v. Mundogas S.A.*, n. 43 above in C.A., [1986] A.C. at pp. 744–745, following *Barry v. Stoney Point Canning Co.* (1917) 55 S.C.R. 51. See also *Hamlyn v. John Houston & Co.* [1903] 1 K.B. 81.

[45] *Ibid.* per Robert Goff L.J., [1986] A.C. at p. 745.

[46] *Salford Corp. v. Lever* [1891] 1 Q.B. 168, Illustration 4; *Morgan v. Elford* (1876) 4 Ch.D. 352; *Phosphate Sewage Co. v. Hartmont* (1877) 5 Ch.D. 394; *cf. Lands Allotment Co. v. Broad* (1895) 13 R. 699; *Grant v. Gold Exploration & Development Syndicate Ltd* [1900] 1 Q.B. 233; *Cohen v. Kuschke & Co. and Koenig* (1900) 83 L.T. 102.

surprising, inasmuch as it seemed to allow double recovery[47] and its origin may have been influenced by the rule, applicable at the time of the leading case, that judgment against one tortfeasor released the others[48]: it was important to establish the briber's liability as separate from the restitutionary liability of the agent for the bribe. The law however was clarified in *Mahesan v. Malaysian Government Officers' Co-operative Housing Society Ltd*[49] in which it was held that the notion that there could be cumulation was unjustified and inconsistent with the principle as to election laid down in *United Australia Ltd v. Barclays Bank Ltd.*[50]

It was also difficult to see how the action against the briber should be classified. One view was that it should be regarded as lying in deceit, intention of the briber and proof of reliance being irrelevant. Where no loss could be proved either, such liability was to be explained on the basis that the damages would be presumed to be at least the amount of the bribe.[51] This would however involve tort liability without actual loss or damage and is contrary to principle in this and other respects. It is now clear that the plaintiff has alternative remedies against the briber.

"(1) to recover from him the amount of the bribe as money had and received, or (2) to recover, as damages for tort, the actual loss which he has sustained as a result of entering into the transaction in respect of which the bribe was given; but ... he need not elect between these alternatives before the time has come for judgment to be entered in his favour in one or other of them."[52]

The former cause of action is based on the proposition that "he is entitled to treat the benefit obtained by or promised to the agent as part of the consideration which should have been received by the principal (if he is a vendor) or as excess consideration provided by the principal (if he is a purchaser)."[53] It does not, however, involve any receipt by the briber; rather, he expends money. Hence it does not fit easily with

---

[47] Pollock, (1891) 7 L.Q.R. 99. But there does not seem to have been actual double recovery in any of the cases. *cf.* however Tettenborn (1979) 95 L.Q.R. 68, who defends this possibility.

[48] *Brinsmead v. Harrison* (1872) L.R. 7 C.P. 547 (abolished by the Law Reform (Married Women and Tortfeasors) Act 1935). See the argument in *Salford Corp. v. Lever* [1891] 1 Q.B. 168.

[49] [1979] A.C. 374, Illustration 8 to Article 50; see Needham, (1979) 95 L.Q.R. 536; (1978) 94 L.Q.R. 344; (1978) 41 M.L.R. 603. *cf.*, however, Tettenborn, *op. cit.* n. 47 above.

[50] [1941] A.C. 1. The agent is also liable on a proprietary basis: see above, para. 6–085. But there is no indication that this extinguishes the personal liability of agent or third party.

[51] See *Hovenden & Sons v. Millhoff* (1900) 83 L.T. 41; *Industries & General Mortgage Co. v. Lewis* [1949] 2 All E.R. 573; *Grant v. Gold Exploration and Development Syndicate Ltd* [1900] 1 Q.B. 233.

[52] *Mahesan's* case, n. 30 above, at p. 383 *per* Lord Diplock; but see above, n. 50.

[53] *Logicrose Ltd v. Southend United F.C.* [1988] 1 W.L.R. 1256, 1263 *per* Millett J.

normal principles of restitutionary liability, though the explanation given above certainly suggests enrichment. Now that the basis of accessory liability in respect of breach of fiduciary duty has been clarified, it may be that the briber's liability would be best explained under this head.[54] The cause of action in tort will be advantageous where the loss exceeds the amount of the bribe. It might also more easily be available when the bribe has not been paid but merely promised: though it appears that the action in restitution may also lie in such a case.[55] But it is still not clear whether the third party can ever disprove his tort liability in such situations.

Where the bribe is already in the hands of the principal, he need not, if he rescinds, account for it to the third party: although it may be treated as part of the consideration, he is not bound so to treat it, and may treat it as in effect a gift not paid under the contract at all.[56] He must, however, account for other sums received.

Illustrations

8–216   (1)   A person who dealt with an agent gave him a gratuity in order to influence him generally in favour of the giver. The agent was in fact so influenced in making a contract with the giver on the principal's behalf. Held, that the contract was voidable by the principal, although the gratuity was not given in direct relation to the particular contract.[57]

(2)   A agreed to buy a pair of horses from B, provided A's agent certified that they were sound. B secretly offered the agent a certain sum if the horses were sold, and the agent accepted the offer. The agent certified that the horses were sound. Held, that A was not bound by the contract whether the agent was in fact biased by the offer made to and accepted by him or not.[58]

(3)   A person injured in a road accident employs a "claims service" to negotiate a tort claim. The service uses an assessor, who tells the insurer that he will recommend acceptance of the insurer's offer if the

---

[54] See below, para. 9–130; see also Birks, *Introduction to the Law of Restitution* (1985), pp. 337–339; *Eaves v. Hickson* (1861) 30 Beav. 136. There are hints of this in *Logicrose Ltd v. Southend United F.C.*, n. 53 above: see p. 126; above, n. 36.

[55] *Grant v. Gold Exploration and Development Syndicate*, n. 42 above (but see on this case *Mahesan's* case, n. 30 above, at pp. 382–383); and the dictum of Millett J. quoted above ("or promised to"). See also *Whaley Bridge Calico Printing Co. v. Green* (1879) 5 Q.B.D. 109.

[56] *Logicrose v. Southend United F.C.* [1988] 1 W.L.R. 1256, 1263–1264 (Illustration 6); *Grant v. Gold Exploration and Development Syndicate*, n. 42 above, at p. 251.

[57] *Smith v. Sorby* (1875) 3 Q.B.D. 552n; *Hough v. Bolton* (1885) 1 T.L.R. 606. See also *Galloway v. Pedersen* (1915) 34 N.Z.L.R. 513 (specific performance refused).

[58] *Shipway v. Broadwood* [1899] 1 Q.B. 369.

insurer pays his fee. The plaintiff settles. The sum is a bribe and he can rescind the settlement and pursue his claim for damages. [59]

(4) An agent contracted, on behalf of a corporation, for a supply of coals, the persons with whom he contracted making him an allowance of 1s. per ton, and charging 1s. per ton more than the market price, to enable them to make the allowance. The corporation, on discovering the bribery, sued the person who supplied the coals for the amount so overcharged. Held, that the defendants were liable, and that the fact that the agent had deposited with the corporation the amount of the bribe, and the corporation had agreed to allow him what was recovered from the defendants, constituted no defence. [60]

(5) By paying a bribe of $18,000, third parties sell land to a Government and make a profit of $67,940. They are liable for the latter sum, but the $18,000 is subsumed into it. The fact that the Government resold the land at prices whereby it recovered its costs is irrelevant. [61]

(6) An agent accepts a bribe in connection with the grant of a licence to operate a market on his principal's land. On learning of this the principal rescinds the contract. He need not give credit for the amount of the bribe, which he is entitled to recover from the agent whether as not he adopts the transaction, and which he can treat as a gift to him. [62]

---

[59] *Taylor v. Walker* [1958] 1 Lloyd's Rep. 490.
[60] *Salford Corp. v. Lever* [1891] 1 Q.B. 168. See Comment, text to nn. 47, 48.
[61] *Att.-Gen. for Nova Scotia v. Christian* (1974) 49 D.L.R. (3d) 742.
[62] *Logicrose v. Southend United F.C.* [1988] 1 W.L.R. 1256.

RELATIONS BETWEEN AGENTS AND THIRD PARTIES

1.—CONTRACT

Article 99

GENERAL RULE

9–001   In the absence of other indications, when an agent makes a contract, purporting to act solely on behalf of a disclosed principal, whether named or unnamed, he is not liable to the third party on it. Nor can he sue the third party on it.[1]

Comment

9–002   "There is no doubt whatever as to the general rule as regards an agent, that where a person contracts as agent for a principal, the contract is the contract of the principal and not that of the agent; and, prima facie, at common law the only person who may sue is the principal and the only person who can be sued is the principal."[2] This is so even where the principal himself is not in fact bound because the agent was not authorised; and even where the agent is a *del credere* agent and as such liable to the principal for the third party's debt.[3] This basic prima facie result is often expressed in the maxim that the agent "drops out" of the transaction, an expression which, though convenient, may be misleading if pushed too far.[4]

However, the mere fact that a person acts as agent and is known to do so does not necessarily negate his involvement in the transaction. It has been said that "it is not the case that, if a principal is liable, his

---

[1] See Comment.

[2] *Montgomerie v. U.K. Mutual S.S. Assn. Ltd* [1891] 1 Q.B. 370, 371 *per* Wright J. See also *Paquin v. Beauclerk* [1906] A.C. 148; *Restatement*, §§ 320, 328.

[3] *Bramwell v. Spiller* (1870) 21 L.T. 672. See above, para. 1–036.

[4] See Müller-Freienfels (1963) 12 Am.J.Comp.L. 272, 278.

agent cannot be. The true principle of law is that a person is liable for his engagements (as for his torts) even though he acts for another, unless he can show that by the law of agency he is to be held to have expressly or impliedly negatived his personal liability."[5]

Thus it is possible for an agent to be a contracting party instead of or in addition to his principal, as explained in the next Article. Agents are also normally held to warrant their authority to act even when they are not liable on the contract itself[6]; and they may be liable on other collateral contracts.[7] Agents may also of course be liable in tort.[8]

Illustrations

(1) A solicitor is prima facie not personally liable for the expenses of **9–003** skilled or other witnesses retained or subpoenaed by him.[9] Nor is he personally liable for sheriff's fees merely because in the course of his duty he lodges a writ at the sheriff's office for execution.[10] In such matters he is deemed to act merely as the agent of his client, unless he expressly pledges his personal credit. But a solicitor who employs a particular bailiff to levy execution may be prima facie personally liable to such bailiff for the fees, if it is the usual course of business for the solicitor to pledge his personal credit in such a case.[11] The same is true where he employs another solicitor.[12]

(2) A broker sent a contract note in the following form: "I have this day sold you, on account of B, etc." (signed) "A B, broker." Held, that the broker had no right of action in his own name against the buyer for refusing to accept the goods.[13] So, where a broker sent a contract note

---

[5] *Yeung Kai Yung v. Hong Kong and Shanghai Banking Corp.* [1981] A.C. 787, 795, *per* Lord Scarman. See also *ex p. Hartop* (1806) 12 Ves. Jun. 349, 352: "for the application of that rule, the agent must name his principal as the person to be responsible," *per* Lord Erskine L.C. This quotation makes the same point; but it should not be taken to require that the agent actually give the name of the principal, merely that he indicate that he acts as agent for a principal.

[6] Articles 112, 113.

[7] See *Yeung Kai Yung v. Hong Kong and Shanghai Banking Corp.*, n. 5 above (Illustration 5 to Article 100).

[8] Article 115.

[9] *Robins v. Bridge* (1837) 3 M. & W. 114; *Lee v. Everest* (1857) 2 H. & N. 285; *Wakefield v. Duckworth* [1915] 1 K.B. 218 (order for photographs to be used in connection with a trial). *Cf. Cocks v. Bruce, Searl and Good* (1904) 21 T.L.R. 62 (shorthand writer: solicitor liable).

[10] *Royle v. Busby* (1880) 6 Q.B.D. 171, following *Mayberry v. Mansfield* (1846) 9 Q.B. 754.

[11] *Newton v. Chambers* (1844) 13 L.J.Q.B. 141; *Maile v. Mann* (1848) 2 Exch. 608 as explained in *Royle v. Busby*, n. 10 above. See further Cordery, *Solicitors* (8th ed.), pp. 98–99.

[12] *Scrace v. Whittington* (1823) 2 B. & C. 11; and see *Porter v. Kirtlan* [1917] 2 I.R. 138.

[13] *Fairlie v. Fenton* (1870) L.R. 5 Ex. 169.

as follows: "Mr. L, I have this day bought in my own name for your account, of AKT, etc." (signed) "A B, broker," it was held that he was acting as agent of AKT; that the words "bought in my own name" were inserted to inform the purchaser that the broker was liable to the vendor; and that the broker had no right to sue L for the price.[14]

(3) A shipmaster signs bills of lading as agent for the owners. He can sue for freight neither under the bills nor on an implied contract.[15] Nor can he sue on an implied contract to pay demurrage.[16]

(4) The manager of a mutual insurance association subscribes a policy on behalf of the members of the association. He cannot sue in his own name for contributions due from the member effecting the policy, though the rules of the association purport to give him such a power.[17]

Article 100

WHEN AGENT HAS RIGHTS AND LIABILITIES

9–004   An agent who makes a contract on his principal's behalf is liable to or entitled to sue the third party in accordance with the terms of any contractual engagement, whether upon the same contract or upon some independent contract, into which he has entered.[18]

Comment

9–005   **Agent may be liable or entitled.** As has been stated in the Comment to the previous Article, there is no reason why an agent should not be entitled and/or liable on the contract which he has made for his principal, or upon a separate but related contract. "In all cases the parties can by the express contract provide that the agent shall be the person liable either concurrently with or to the exclusion of the principal."[19] The question whether an agent who has made a contract on behalf of his principal is to be deemed to have contracted personally, and, if so the extent of his liability, depends on the intention of the

---

[14] *Fawkes v. Lamb* (1862) 31 L.J.Q.B. 98.

[15] *Repetto v. Millar's Karri and Jarrah Forests Ltd* [1901] 2 K.B. 306. A signature without qualification anywhere else in the document (see Article 101) could perhaps still make the master a contracting party: see p. 310 and *Atkinson v. Cotesworth* (1825) 3 B. & C. 647. But such a signature would be rare in a commercial context today. See also *Smith v. Plummer* (1818) 1 B. & A. 575; *cf. Cawthron v. Trickett* (1864) 15 C.B.(N.S.) 754.

[16] *Brouncker v. Scott* (1811) 4 Taunt. 1; *Evans v. Forster* (1830) 1 B. & Ad. 118. *Cf. Jesson v. Solly* (1811) 4 Taunt. 52.

[17] *Evans v. Hooper* (1875) 1 Q.B.D. 45; *Gray v. Pearson* (1870) L.R. 5 C.P. 568.

[18] See Comment.

[19] *Montgomerie v. U.K. Mutual S.S. Assn.* [1891] 1 Q.B. 370, 372, *per* Wright J. See also *Fawkes v. Lamb* (1862) 31 L.J.Q.B. 98, 100.

parties to be deduced from the nature and terms of the particular contract and the surrounding circumstances, including any binding custom.[20] As in all matters of formation of contract, the test is objective.[21] The rules can be most easily articulated in related to written contracts, where the use of a particular form of words may constitute an agent a contracting party though it is on the underlying facts doubtful whether he intended to become such.[22]

It is sometimes said that an agent can be liable to the third party without being entitled to sue, but cannot be entitled to sue without being liable, for then there would be no consideration to support his right to sue.[23] This is true in the sense that a collateral contract can more easily be constructed on the basis that the agent, in return for the third party's dealing with his principal, undertakes also personal liability on the main contract. But the converse position can also exist, though it may be less likely: a third party may, in return for being introduced to the principal or for some other benefit, be held to make the same promise to the agent as he does to the principal. Thus a person buying goods at auction is liable to the auctioneer for the price: but the auctioneer's reciprocal promise to him may be extremely limited and certainly does not involve liability on the contract of sale itself.[24]

Agent's liability. Where an agent is potentially liable, the terms of his liability may require careful analysis. Except as regards the undisclosed principal, discussed below, no general rules have been laid down by the courts. The possibilities seem to be as follows. **9–006**

(1) *Sole liability of agent.* The agent may be solely liable, *i.e.* although perhaps authorised to do so, he has not created any contract binding his principal at all but has made the contract in his own name. The majority of the cases seem to assume this as the main interpreation of a situation involving the agent's personal liability[25]: other interpretations have often been justified by reference to special circumstances

---

[20] This sentence was quoted with approval in *Maritime Stores Ltd v. H.P. Marshall & Co. Ltd* [1963] 1 Lloyd's Rep. 602, 608.

[21] *The Swan* [1968] 1 Lloyd's Rep. 5, 12.

[22] See *Fisher v. Marsh* (1865) 6 B. & S. 411; *Sika Contracts Ltd v. B.S. Gill* (1978) 9 Build. L.R. 11, Illustration 9 to Article 101; Articles 101–102, 104–105.

[23] *Fawkes v. Lamb* (1862) 31 L.J.K.B. 98, 101; *Fairlie v. Fenton* (1870) L.R. 5 Ex. 169, 172. See criticism of the dicta in these cases by Stoljar, pp. 245–247.

[24] In some cases the consideration would seem to be the release by the auctioneer of his lien when he delivers the goods; see *Chelmsford Auctions v. Poole* [1973] Q.B. 542, Illustration 17; below, para. 9–021.

[25] See in general *Parker v. Winslow* (1857) 7 E. & B. 942, 947 ("An agent is liable personally if he is the contracting party: and he may be so though he names his principal"); *Gadd v. Houghton* (1876) 1 Ex.D. 357, 360 ("It seems extraordinary that there should be any doubt whether this binds the principal or the agent"); *H.O. Brandt &*

—cont. on next page

such as trade custom,[26] or (as in the case of the auctioneer) lien or special property.[27] In such a case the agent's position *vis-à-vis* his principal may still be regulated by the law of agency, *viz.* he is remunerated on a commission basis, undertakes only to use his best endeavours, must not accept discounts or bribes, etc.; or it may be regulated by some other set of rules, *e.g.* those governing the relationship of buyer and seller or consignor and carrier.[28] This is not the concern of the third party.

This is not however the only possibility. "There is nothing to prevent an agent entering into a contract on the basis that he is himself to be liable to perform it as well as his principal."[29] Other possibilities may have been too easily overlooked in the past,[30] though there are signs that they may be more readily recognised in the future.[31] It is suggested below that they may be particularly relevant in considering unnamed principal situations. The remainder of this list enumerates them.

(2) *Joint or joint and several obligation.* The agent may be held jointly or jointly and severally liable together with his principal. Joint liability applies to partners,[32] but not normally to husband and wife.[33]

—*cont. from previous page*
Co. v. *H.N. Morris & Co. Ltd* [1917] 2 K.B. 784, 793 ("Prima facie when a person signs a document in his own name ... he is the person liable on the contract"). For specific examples may be cited cases on solicitors: *Hall v. Ashurst* (1883) 1 C. & M. 714, 718; *Iveson v. Conington* (1823) 1 B. & C. 160, 162; *Tanner v. Christian* (1855) 4 E. & B. 591, 597–598, all of which should be considered with *Lavan v. Walsh* [1964] I.R. 87; and cases on ship repairs and stores, where the contract is often with the local agent placing the order. See Article 103, Illustration 2. See also *Salsi v. Jetspeed Air Services Ltd* [1977] 2 Lloyd's Rep. 57 (air freightage broker); *Pitzel v. Saskatchewan Motor Club Travel Agency Ltd* (1983) 149 D.L.R. (3d) 122 (travel agent).

[26] See below, para. 9–014.
[27] As to which see below, para. 9–009.
[28] See above, paras. 1–030 *et seq.*
[29] *International Ry. v. Niagara Parks Commission* [1941] A.C. 328, 342, *per* Luxmoore L.J. See also *Young v. Schuler* (1887) 11 Q.B.D. 651; *Elbinger Actiengesellschaft v. Claye* (1873) L.R. 8 Q.B. 313, 317; *Calder v. Dobell* (1871) L.R. 6 C.P. 486, 494; *Montgomerie v. U.K. Mutual S.S. Assn.* [1891] 1 Q.B. 370, 372; *The Swan* [1968] 1 Lloyd's Rep. 5.
[30] Stoljar, pp. 234–238. And see Blackburn, *Contract of Sale* (3rd ed.), p. 352.
[31] See *The Swan*, n. 29 above (Illustration 6); *Gardiner v. Heading* [1928] 2 K.B. 284; *Teheran-Europe Co. Ltd v. S.T. Belton (Tractors) Ltd* [1968] 2 Q.B. 53, 59–60; [1968] 2 Q.B. 545, 558; *Wolfe Stevedores (1968) Ltd v. Joseph Salter's Sons Ltd* (1971) 16 D.L.R. (3d) 334; *Burt v. Claude Cousins & Co. Ltd* [1971] 2 Q.B. 426, 455; *Format International Security Printers Ltd v. Mosden* [1975] 1 Lloyd's Rep. 37; *Et Biret Cie S.A. v. Yukiteru Kaiun KK (The Sun Happiness)* [1984] 1 Lloyd's Rep. 381; *Stag Line Ltd v. Tyne Shiprepair Group Ltd (The Zinnia)* [1984] 2 Lloyd's Rep. 211. But *cf. Wilson v. Avec Audio-Visual Equipment Ltd* [1974] 1 Lloyd's Rep. 81, 83, where such liability is said to require "clear and precise evidence of a very special relationship"; *N. & J. Vlassopulos Ltd v. Ney Shipping Ltd (The Santa Carina)* [1977] 1 Lloyd's Rep. 478, Illustration 3 to Article 103; *Foalquest Ltd v. Roberts* [1990] 1 EGLR 50. See also below, paras. 9–011—9–014.
[32] Partnership Act 1890, s. 9.
[33] *Morel Bros. & Co. Ltd v. Earl of Westmorland* [1904] A.C. 11; *cf. Hoare v. Niblett* [1891] 1 Q.B. 781; *Swanton Seed Service Ltd v. Kulba* (1968) 68 D.L.R. (2d) 38.

Joint liability is subject to certain technical rules which may make it inappropriate to an agency relationship[34]: so, though to a lesser degree, is joint and several liability.[35]

(3) *Suretyship.* He may be a surety for his principal, that is to say he may guarantee the principal's obligation; or contract to indemnify the third party in respect of its non-performance. This is to be distinguished from *del credere* agency, where the agent's liability is to his principal, not to the third party. Here again suretyship in general, and guarantee in particular, are subject to special rules which may not be appropriate to the particular situation.[36] The possibility is however occasionally referred to.[37]

(4) *Collateral contract.* He may undertake a separate liability on a separate or collateral contract which is not one of suretyship. A contract of indemnity is of course a specialised form of such a contract. Consideration can often be found by the entry into the main contract with the principal. Examples of such contract are found in cases of warranty of authority[38] and auctioneers.[39] It has been held that a stockbroker may warrant the genuineness of a share transfer which he presents for registration.[40]

(5) *Alternative liability.* He may undertake a liability alternative to that of the principal, the choice to lie with the third party. Though this interpretation seems to be assumed by some of the cases on election, it is submitted that there is little to commend it.[41]

Such cases as do recognise the liability of the agent do not, however, usually consider further the nature of that liability, because the question is not relevant. Many old cases raise questions of the Statute of Frauds or of parol evidence, and concern the question whether the fact that a written contract mentions only principal or agent necessarily excludes

---

[34] See Glanville Williams, *Joint Obligations* (1949); but see Civil Liability (Contribution) Act 1978, s. 3.

[35] *e.g.* release of one debtor releases all: see Glanville Williams, *op. cit.* above, p. 135.

[36] *e.g.* giving time to the principal debtor releases the surety: Chitty, *Contracts* (27th ed.), Vol. 2, §§ 42–052 *et seq.* See also Rowlatt, *Principal and Surety* (5th ed.); Glanville Williams, *op. cit.* n. 34 above, pp. 121 *et seq.* Guarantees may require written evidence under the Statute of Frauds.

[37] *Imperial Bank v. London and St Katharine Docks Co.* (1877) 5 Ch.D. 195, 200; *Fleet v. Murton* (1871) L.R. 7 Q.B. 126, 132; see also *Young v. Schuler* (1883) 11 Q.B.D. 651; *Rutherford v. Ounan* [1913] 2 I.R. 265, 268.

[38] Article 107.

[39] Below, paras. 9–009, 9–021; Illustrations 11–14, 17–19. It may be that the position of the nineteenth-century factor would today be explicable in such terms, but it is no longer relevant to seek to explain it. See below, para. 9–009.

[40] *Yeung Kai Yung v. Hong Kong & Shanghai Banking Corp.* [1981] A.C. 787, Illustration 5.

[41] See Comment to Article 84.

the other.[42] Others are simply concerned with the question whether the agent can be sued, regardless of whether the principal can, or whether the agent who has paid on a contract is entitled to indemnity as having discharged a legal liability resting on him: they go no further than is necessary for the particular decision. The area is therefore not yet properly mapped.

9–007   **Election.** When principal and agent are both liable, the doctrines of merger and election may apply, and the third party may be debarred from suing one by obtaining judgment against, or even perhaps simply electing to look to, the other.[43] But this only operates where the two remedies available to the third party are inconsistent, and this may not be so in all cases. The nature of the liability assumed by the agent may therefore be crucial, but it has received insufficient attention in the cases.

9–008   **Agent's right to sue.** The question of the agent's right to sue certainly arises less frequently than that of his liability,[44] and it seems that the incorporation of the agent into the contract has more normally the purpose of securing his liability. In any case, the right to sue can often be specifically assigned to the agent when this is thought desirable. On the analysis given above of the possible interpretations of the agent's liability, headings (1) (2) and (4) could also involve the right to sue. Plainly, the agent who makes the contract as sole contracting party can sue on it as well as be held liable.[45] An agent who is a party to a joint or joint and several obligation can sue on it, subject to the technical rules applicable.[46] And a collateral contract made by agent with the third party may give the agent the right to sue on it: a conspicuous example is that of the auctioneer, who can sue for the price of the goods or land sold.[47] On the other hand, a contract of suretyship does not, and a contract of indemnity would not normally, confer a right to sue; and the cases suggesting alternative liability do so in connection with the *third party's* right to choose between principal and agent. In so far as any question arises between these two as to who should sue, it would

---

[42] See Article 102; *Higgins v. Senior* (1841) 8 M. & W. 834; *Calder v. Dobell* (1871) L.R. 6 C.P. 486; *Basma v. Weekes* [1950] A.C. 441; *Davies v. Sweet* [1962] 2 Q.B. 300.

[43] See Articles 84, 106.

[44] Though it has arisen where the principal is fictitious or non-existent, or where the agent is his own principal: see Articles 109, 110.

[45] *e.g. Short v. Spackman* (1851) 2 B. & Ad. 962. For a modern example where this was probably the case see *Anglo-African Shipping Co. of New York Inc. v. J. Mortner Ltd* [1962] 1 Lloyd's Rep. 610.

[46] *e.g.* a partner: *cf.* Co. Litt. 182A. See also *Jung v. Phosphate of Lime Co. Ltd* (1868) L.R. 3 C.P. 139.

[47] Below, para. 9–021; Illustrations 11–14, 17–19.

probably be solved by reference to the subordinate position of the agent *vis-à-vis* the principal.[48]

Lien and special property. A number of cases, mostly on nineteenth-   **9–009**
century factors and auctioneers, suggest that certain types of agent can
sue because they have a special property in or lien upon the subject-
matter of the contract or a beneficial interest in the completion
thereof.[49] It is however clear that the mere fact that an agent has an
interest in the completion of the contract, *e.g.* because he hopes to earn
commission on it, does not entitle him to sue upon it.[50] The cases are in
the modern context best explained as particular collateral contracts,
upon which there is long-standing authority conferring specific rights and
imposing specific duties upon these types of agent. The case law on the
factor may be obsolete, but the auctioneer's contract is still of
importance.[51] The possibility of detecting such contracts in new
circumstances is not of course closed.

Agent suing on behalf of principal. Another group of old cases   **9–010**
suggests that the agent can in general sue on behalf of his disclosed
principal and recover his principal's loss.[52] They should be viewed with
extreme caution. Many date from a time when there was no method of
assigning legal choses in action, communications did not make it easy
for foreign contracting parties to sue in England, contract rights under
bills of lading were not transferable,[53] and the central contractual
doctrines now accepted had not been fully worked out. The distinction
between a right of suit and a right to recover substantial damages was
not taken in some of these early cases. However the matter would have
been viewed at the time, it is submitted that most of them would not

---

[48] Below, para. 9–012.
[49] The wording of Article 119 of the 1st edition of this book.
[50] *e.g. Bramwell v. Spiller* (1870) 21 L.T. 672 (*del credere* agent); *Fairlie v. Fenton* (1870) L.R. 5 Ex. 169; *Turnbull & Jones Ltd v. Amner & Sons* [1923] N.Z.L.R. 673.
[51] See below, para. 9–021; also above, para. 1–040.
[52] *Davis v. James* (1770) 5 Burr. 2680; *Moore v. Wilson* (1787) 1 T.R. 659; *Joseph v. Knox* (1813) 3 Camp. 320; *Atkinson v. Cotesworth* (1825) 3 B. & C. 647; *Dunlop v. Lambert* (1839) 6 Cl. & F. 600; *Mead v. S.E. Ry.* (1870) 18 W.R. 735. Also cases indicating that admissions by principal or agent are admissible against the other: *Bauerman v. Radenius* (1792) 7 T.R. 663; *Smith v. Lyon* (1813) 3 Camp. 465; *Welstead v. Levy* (1831) 1 M. & Rob. 138; and on discovery; *Willis & Co. v. Baddeley* [1892] 2 Q.B. 324 (but *cf. James Nelson & Sons Ltd v. Nelson Line (Liverpool) Ltd* [1906] 2 K.B. 217); *Abu Dhabi National Tanker Co. v. Product Star Shipping Ltd* [1992] 2 All E.R. 20. The *Restatement*, §§ 364 *et esq.*, appears to try to follow the older doctrines (as to which see Mechem, *Treatise on the Law of Agency* (2nd ed.), Vol. 2, Chap. 6) and some of its propositions seems very doubtful for modern English law. See esp. § 371 and examples.
[53] A problem dealt with by the Bills of Lading Act 1855 (now replaced by the Carriage of Goods by Sea Act 1992).

now be followed or would be otherwise explained. An action brought for another by an agent authorised to do so should nowadays be brought in the name of the principal.[54]

To modern eyes the correct analysis must be that where the agent is a party to the, or a, contract with the third party he has the right to sue on it. The question then arises as to what he can recover. It was affirmed in the leading case of *The Albazero*[55] that the measure of damages for breach of contract is "generally the financial loss which the plaintiff has sustained by reason of the defendant's failure to perform the contract according to its terms."[56] But there are exceptions to this rule that the plaintiff can only recover his own loss. First, trustees can recover the loss suffered by their beneficiaries.[57] This is a matter of equity.[58] There are also, however, exceptions at common law. They were cited by Lord Diplock in *The Albazero*, as follows.[59] First, bailees can recover the value of the goods bailed to them even though the loss would ultimately fall on the bailor[60]; *a fortiori* an owner of goods who has possession or the immediate right to possess can recover their value as a matter of course whatever his actual loss may be.[61] Secondly, there are cases where an insurer is subrogated to the rights of the insured and recovers a loss in respect of which the insured has been reimbursed.[62] Thirdly, those who insure goods in appropriate terms may be able to recover the value of the goods insured even though the actual loss is suffered by another person interested.[63] And lastly, those who consign goods to others may be able to do the same.

"In a commercial contract concerning goods where it is in the contemplation of the parties that the proprietary interests in the goods may be transferred from one owner to another after the contract has been entered into and before the breach which causes loss or damage to the goods, an original party to the contract, if such be the intention of them both, is to be treated in law as having entered into the contract for the benefit of all persons who have or

---

[54] *Jones v. Gurney* [1913] W.N. 72; and see *Moores v. Hopper* (1807) 2 B. & P.N.R. 411.

[55] [1977] A.C. 774. The judgments of all three courts and the arguments before the House of Lords repay study.

[56] *ibid.* at p. 841, *per* Lord Diplock.

[57] See *Les Affréteurs Réunis S.A. v. Leopold Walford (London) Ltd* [1919] A.C. 801.

[58] It may sometimes be relevant that the agent is a *constructive* trustee: see *per* Dillon L.J. in *Darlington B.C. v. Wiltshier Northern Ltd* [1995] 1 W.L.R. 68, 75.

[59] See pp. 846–847.

[60] *The Winkfield* [1902] P. 42.

[61] *Obestain Inc. v. National Mineral Development Corp. Ltd (The Sanix Ace)* [1987] 1 Lloyd's Rep. 265.

[62] *The Charlotte* [1908] P. 206; and see *The Albazero*, n. 55 above, at p. 846.

[63] See *A. Tomlinson (Hauliers) Ltd v. Hepburn* [1966] A.C. 451; *Petrofina (U.K.) Ltd v. Magnaload Ltd* [1984] Q.B. 127.

may acquire an interest in the goods before they are lost or damaged, and is entitled to recover by way of damages for breach of contract the actual loss sustained by those for whose benefit the contract is entered into."[64]

This is not, however, applicable where the contract is transferred to the consignee, or, if the initial contract is a charterparty, where the consignee acquires rights under a bill of lading.[65] In all these four cases the proceeds of the action would be held in trust for those suffering actual loss.[66]

Of these the third, relating to insurance for others, is most commonly explained as an agency rule[67]; and if it is such, it allows an agent to sue for his principal's loss, albeit in a limited context. However, it is not clear that this is the correct analysis. The judgments in the leading case of *A. Tomlinson (Hauliers) Ltd v. Hepburn*[68] stress the notion that goods may be insured by a person with an interest in them so as to cover the interests of others, whether present or future. In such a case the plaintiff would recover on *his own* contract. Reliance is often placed on wide dicta regarding actions on insurance policies by agents in *Provincial Insurance Co. of Canada v. Leduc*[69]; but the case itself still concerned insurance by a part-owner for the other part-owner. Other decisions can be explained on the basis that the agent is in the circumstances a *trustee* for others;[70] but this is by no means true of every agency situation.[71] Though it has been held at first instance that the principle as to actions by agents on insurance policies is a general one[72] it is not in fact clear that there is such a principle.

However, recent authority in connection with building contracts makes further exceptions to the general rule. The exact basis of the reasoning is not clear, though the preference seems to be for an extension of Lord Diplock's fourth exception; but it seems that where it is contemplated that the loss may be suffered by a third party and it cannot otherwise be recovered, the contracting party may recover it.[73]

---

[64] *The Albazero*, n. 55 above, at p. 847, *per* Lord Diplock.

[65] *ibid.* at pp. 847–848.

[66] *ibid.* at p. 846.

[67] See *Waters v. Monarch Fire and Life Ins. Co.* (1856) 5 E. & B. 870. As to actions by principals, see *National Oilwell (U.K.) Ltd v. Davy Offshore Ltd* [1993] 2 Lloyd's Rep. 582.

[68] [1965] A.C. 451.

[69] (1874) L.R. 6 P.C. 224, 244.

[70] See *Woodar Investment Development Ltd v. Wimpey Construction U.K. Ltd* [1980] 1 W.L.R. 277, 294 (H.L.), referring to *Lloyd's v. Harper* (1880) 16 Ch.D. 290.

[71] See *Allen v. F. O'Hearn & Co.* [1937] A.C. 213, 218.

[72] *Transcontinental Underwriting Agency S.R.L. v. Grand Union Ins. Co. Ltd* [1987] 2 Lloyd's Rep. 409, 415.

[73] See *Linden Gardens Trust Ltd v. Lenesta Sludge Disposals Ltd* [1994] 1 A.C. 45 (assignment); *Darlington B.C. v. Wiltshier Northern Ltd* [1995] 1 W.L.R. 68. See Treitel, *Law of Contract* (9th ed.), pp. 545–547.

Whatever the principle turns out to be, it may sometimes enable an agent to recover, on his own contract, elements of his principal's loss.

9–011   The case of the contract made by the agent of an *undisclosed* principal acting for his principal, however, requires special treatment in this context, for here the contract is that of the agent and it is clear that the agent must be able to sue on it just as he is liable upon it,[74] even though he may be eventually liable to transfer the proceeds of the action to his principal. Unless he is a trustee, he cannot recover his principal's loss as such, only his own.[75] The loss in respect of which damages are awarded may be suffered by his principal and not by him, and because of the limited nature of the agent's duties towards his principal may not be loss for which he is required to answer to his principal,[76] though to be recoverable it must be within the loss contemplatable by the other party to the transaction.[77] Equally, the agent may be reimbursed by the principal for his loss. There is Scottish authority that the agent may nevertheless recover in such cases, and this seems correct.[78] The situation may be likened to that of an injured plaintiff to whose rights the insurer who has paid him is subrogated. Equally, it is submitted that a buyer of goods which prove to be shoddy may recover the difference in value even though he resold them under a contract which effectively excluded his liability, or gave them away as a gift.[79] This is again not a case where the agent recovers the principal's loss; rather, it is one where the agent seeks to recover the contemplatable loss arising out of the breach of contract, and it is held no defence to the party in breach to prove that by virtue of the plaintiff's dealings with someone else the incidence of the actual loss may be different. However, the reasoning that the third party contemplates loss suffered by another[80] cannot here be used. It does not follow that the proceeds of the action are necessarily held on trust: the agent may be under an obligation to adjust the position on an *in personam* basis.[81] If this reasoning is correct for cases where the undisclosed principal can intervene, *a fortiori* it must be correct in the rare cases where his intervention is excluded.[82]

---

[74] See Comment to Article 78 and below, para. 9–012.

[75] *Allen v. F. O'Hearn & Co.* [1937] A.C. 213, 218: "The supposed agent's rights would be to recover the damage suffered by him on the footing that he had been principal."

[76] See *Anglo-African Shipping Co. of New York Inc. v. J. Mortner Ltd* [1962] 1 Lloyd's Rep. 610.

[77] *cf. Cory v. Thames Ironworks Co.* (1868) L.R. 3 Q.B. 181.

[78] *Craig & Co. v. Blackater* 1923 S.C. 472, though the decision is in part based on *Joseph v. Knox* (1813) 3 Camp. 320, as to which see comments in *The Albazero*. It was followed (perhaps dubiously) in *James Laidlaw & Son v. Griffin* 1968 S.L.T. 278.

[79] *cf. Slater v. Hoyle & Smith Ltd* [1920] 2 K.B. 11; *Joyner v. Weeks* [1891] 2 Q.B. 31.

[80] See above.

[81] *cf. Henry v. Hammond* [1913] 2 K.B. 515; above, para. 6–043.

[82] Above, para. 8–080.

Some special situations are now discussed.

Undisclosed principal. Where the principal is undisclosed at the time   **9–012**
of contracting, the contract is made with the agent, and he is personally
liable and entitled on it. The principal also may intervene to sue, and
may be sued, but the latter only subject to the general rule that nothing
must prejudice the right of the third party to sue the agent if he so
wishes. [83] This is therefore a case where both agent and principal are
liable and entitled. The problems of damages are discussed above. The
doctrine of election, referred to above, may raise problems when the
agent is sued.

In this context it is often said that the right of the principal is superior
to that of the agent, and it is a defence for the third party to prove that
the principal has intervened and claimed payment or damages, or that
the agent's authority to sue is otherwise terminated. On principle this
seems correct[84]; though some of the cases usually cited for the
proposition would now be otherwise explained. [85] This subordination
may also apply where the agent of a *disclosed* principal is a joint and
several creditor of the third party; his right is presumably secondary to
that of the principal. [86] The question of damages has been dealt with
above.

Interrogatories as to existence of undisclosed principal. It has been   **9–013**
held that in an action by the vendor for specific performance of a
contract of sale of land, the plaintiff is not entitled to interrogate the
defendant for the purpose of ascertaining whether he was acting as
agent for an undisclosed principal. [87] And in general it would seem that,
the contract being that of the agent, he is under no duty when suing or
sued to disclose the existence of his principal.

Unnamed principal. Difficult problems must frequently occur in the   **9–014**
case of unnamed principals. Where the agent gives the third party to
understand that he acts for another, as by reference to "our principals",
"our clients", etc., there may indeed be cases where the third party can

---

[83] See Comment to Article 78; *O'Herlihy v. Hedges* (1803) 1 Sch. & Lef. 123;
Montgomerie v. U.K. Mutual SS Assn. [1891] 1 Q.B. 370, 372. See also *Sargent v. Morris*
(1820) 3 B. & Ald. 277, 281. As to principal's liability where agent lacks capacity, see
above, para. 8–075.
[84] *cf. Restatement*, § 302, comment *c*; § 368, comments *d, e, f*; 370. Some support may
perhaps be derived from *Sadler v. Leigh* (1815) 4 Camp. 195 and *Gardiner v. Davis* (1825)
2 C. & P. 49.
[85] *e.g. Rogers v. Hadley* (1821) 2 H. & C. 227.
[86] *cf. Restatement*, § 370.
[87] *Sebright v. Hanbury* [1916] 2 Ch. 245. But as to discovery against the principal, see
above, para. 8–081.

be regarded as being willing to deal with the principal, whoever he is. Indeed it has been said that in an ordinary commercial transaction such willingness may be assumed by the agent in the absence of other indications.[88] But this may sometimes be an improbable construction to put on the situation; at the other end of the scale, therefore, such facts may give rise, or assist in giving rise, to the inference that the third party deals only with the agent (the problem of the agent's position vis-à-vis his principal being irrelevant to the third party). But there is a middle course. The *Restatement*[89] suggests a rule that when the agent acts for a principal whose existence is known but who is not identified at the time of contracting, the agent is unless otherwise agreed a party to the contract, and the inference is that he is liable in addition to and not in substitution for the principal (though sometimes his liability may cease on disclosure of the principal's identity). Though the fact that the agent does not name his principal is obviously relevant in determining whether he contracts personally, such a general proposition has actually been rejected in England in respect of unwritten contracts,[90] and in the Supreme Court of Canada in respect of a written contract.[91] But the wording of written contracts may certainly give rise to the agent being a party to the contract in such a case.[92] And there are many cases showing that in such situations the court will recognise a trade usage that a commercial agent, *e.g.* a broker, is personally liable, particularly if his principal is unnamed.[93] Here again the exact terms of the agent's engagement with the third party require careful analysis. The trade

---

[88] *Teheran-Europe Co. Ltd v. S.T. Belton (Tractors) Ltd* [1968] 2 Q.B. 545, 555 *per* Diplock L.J. See also *Thomson v. Davenport* (1829) 9 B. & C. 78.

[89] § 321.

[90] *N. & J. Vlassopulos Ltd v. Ney Shipping Co. (The Santa Carina)* [1977] 1 Lloyd's Rep. 478, Illustration 3 to Article 103. But equally it may make clear that he acts as agent: see the *Chartwell Shipping* case, n. 91 below; *Southwell v. Bowditch* (1876) 1 C.P.D. 374.

[91] *Chartwell Shipping Ltd v. Q.N.S. Paper Co. Ltd* [1989] 2 S.C.R. 683; (1989) 62 D.L.R. (4th) 36, Illustration 8 to Article 101, on the basis that "to add a burden of proof on the mandatary would blur the focus of analysis: the goal is to identify the intentions of the parties" (*per* L'Heureux Dubé J. at pp. 745, 78).

[92] *e.g. Tudor Marine Ltd v. Tradax Export S.A. (The Virgo)* [1976] 2 Lloyd's Rep. 135, Illustration 6 to Article 101.

[93] *Dale v. Humfrey* (1858) E.B. & E. 1004 (oil); *Cropper v. Cook* (1868) L.R. 3 C.P. 194 (wool); *Fleet v. Murton* (1871) L.R. 7 Q.B. 126 (fruit); *Hutchinson v. Tatham* (1873) L.R. 8 C.P. 482 (charterparty); *Imperial Bank v. London & St. Katharine Docks Co.* (1877) 5 Ch.D. 195 (fruit); *Bacmeister v. Fenton, Levy & Co.* (1883) C. & E. 121 (rice); *Pike v. Ongley* (1887) 18 Q.B.D. 708 (hops); *Thornton v. Fehr & Co.* (1935) 51 Ll.Rep. 330 (tallow); *Anglo Overseas Transport Ltd v. Titan Industrial Corp. (United Kingdom) Ltd* [1959] 2 Lloyd's Rep. 152; *Perishables Transport Co. v. N. Spyropoulos (London) Ltd* [1964] 2 Lloyd's Rep. 379 (forwarding agents). *Cf. Wilson v. Avec Audio-Visual Equipment Ltd* [1974] 1 Lloyd's Rep. 81 (no such custom as to insurance brokers). See further Article 102.

custom cases, which arise mostly in the context of the rules of evidence, on the whole do seem to assume that the agent's liability is additional to that of his principal[94]: a collateral contract[95] and suretyship[96] are also sometimes suggested. The doctrine of election, referred to above, may again cause problems.

The most difficult cases may perhaps be those where the third party deals with an agent who is known normally to act for principals or in a situation where persons dealing frequently act for principals, but there is no indication as to whether or not that is so on this occasion. This was of course a common situation with the nineteenth-century factor, who was distinguished from a broker on the basis that a broker could be *assumed* to be dealing on behalf of a principal[97]; and cases of this type are associated with the growth of the undisclosed principal doctrine.[98] Problems may also arise in connection with bidders at auction sales.[99] Such cases may indeed fall to be considered under the undisclosed principal doctrine, in which case the contract is with the agent, subject to the principal's right to intervene and liability to be sued. But more rigorous analysis may require them to be considered in connection with the possible rules for unnamed principal cases.[1]

If there is in unnamed principal cases not even a prima facie rule that the agent is liable together with the principal, the agent may sometimes appear to be free from liability in cases where he should arguably be regarded as undertaking it. In such cases the courts may classify the principal as undisclosed rather than unnamed in order to secure the liability of the agent. The undisclosed principal rules may then themselves be confused by considerations which are really relevant to the unnamed principal situation. For example, it has been held that a third party cannot set off against the principal a debt accruing before he had notice of the principal's existence unless the principal was in some way at fault in misleading him[2]—a rule appropriate to unnamed principal situations where the existence of a principal is from the start envisaged, but not to true undisclosed principals. It is therefore

---

[94] See *e.g. Pike v. Ongley*, n. 93 above.
[95] *Hutchinson v. Tatham*, n. 93 above (collateral contract coming into effect if name of principal not given; *cf.* the suggestion in the *Restatement*, n. 89 above); *Reid v. Dreaper* (1861) 6 H. & N. 813.
[96] *Imperial Bank v. London and St. Katharine Docks Co.*, n. 93 above.
[97] *Baring v. Corrie* (1818) 2 B. & A. 137. The factor's contract could perhaps also be treated as collateral: above, para. 9–009.
[98] *e.g. Armstrong v. Stokes* (1872) L.R. 7 Q.B. 598; see Articles 78, 82.
[99] See Illustration 4.
[1] See the differing views taken by Lord Denning M.R. and Diplock L.J. in *Teheran-Europe Co. Ltd v. S.T. Belton (Tractors) Ltd* [1968] 2 Q.B. 545; *Marsh & McLennan Pty Ltd v. Stanyers Transport Pty Ltd* [1994] 2 V.R. 232; Comment to Article 78.
[2] *Cooke & Sons v. Eshelby* (1887) 12 App.Cas. 271: see Comment to Article 82.

submitted that the courts should be willing to adopt a rule of at least prima facie liability together with an unnamed principal unless it is absolutely clear that the person concerned acted as agent only.[3]

9–015   **Interrogatories as to name of principal.** It is not clear whether an agent acting for an unnamed principal can be compelled to disclose his principal's name by interrogatory.[4]

9–016   **Fictitious or non-existent principal.** Such situations have given rise to specialised case law in the context of companies in the course of formation and unincorporated associations. This is discussed separately.[5]

9–017   **Agent his own principal.** Some cases suggest that where the agent has no principal, *viz.* is his own principal, he is personally liable and entitled. This seems contrary to general principle; but since such a proposition is not infrequently put forward, this topic also is separately discussed.[6]

9–018   **Foreign principal.**[7] There long existed a strong presumption of fact[8] (so strong that a court was "justified in treating it as a matter of law"[9]) that where an agent in England contracted on behalf of a foreign principal, disclosed or undisclosed, the agent assumed personal liability and had no authority to pledge the principal's credit by establishing privity of contract between the principal and the third party.[10] The presumption could be displaced by clear evidence of authority. Further, the effect of the presumption was to render the agent alone liable and entitled on the contract; so that when it was clear that the agent contracted only as agent, and that it was not intended that he should be

---

[3] See Reynolds [1983] C.L.P. 119.

[4] See *Hersom v. Bernett* [1955] 1 Q.B. 98; *Thöl v. Leask* (1855) 10 Exch. 704; *Hancocks v. Leblache* (1878) 3 C.P.D. 197; *Sebright v. Hanbury* [1916] 2 Ch. 245.

[5] See Article 109.

[6] See Article 110.

[7] Hudson (1957) 35 Can.B.Rev. 336; (1960) 23 M.L.R. 695; (1966) 29 M.L.R. 353; (1969) 32 M.L.R. 207. The term "foreign principal" does not seem to be a very precise one, but it is normally taken to mean a principal who does not reside or carry on business in England or Wales. However, the purpose of the rule indicates what sort of person might be regarded as a foreign principal, and it is very doubtful whether principals in Scotland, Northern Ireland or even the Irish Republic should be treated as foreign.

[8] *Paterson v. Gandasequi* (1812) 15 East 62; *Smyth v. Anderson* (1849) 7 C.B. 21; *Dramburg v. Pollitzer* (1872) 28 L.T. 470; *Glover v. Langford* (1892) 8 T.L.R. 628; *Malcolm Flinn & Co. v. Hoyle* (1893) 63 L.J.Q.B. 1; *Harper & Sons v. Keller, Bryant and Co. Ltd* (1915) 84 L.J.K.B. 1696.

[9] *Armstrong v. Stokes* (1872) L.R. 7 Q.B. 598, 605.

[10] *Armstrong v. Stokes*, above; *Elbinger, etc. v. Claye* (1873) L.R. 8 Q.B. 313; *Hutton v. Bulloch* (1874) L.R. 9 Q.B. 572; and see cases cited in n. 8 above.

personally liable, there was no room for the presumption, which could not operate inconsistently with the clear purport of the contract.[11] The presumption was not affected by the fact that the contract was in writing: most, if not all, of the cases concern such contracts.

The status of this presumption was discussed in many cases, and though it could be questioned,[12] it is sometimes said to have reflected both a preference by foreign merchants to use an intermediary who did not bring them into privity of contract with a merchant in another country, especially where the contract involved bulk supplies from several English sources; and also the reluctance of English businessmen to enter into transactions which might involve them in problems of the conflict of laws or the possibility of having to sue in a foreign jurisdiction, or both,[13] especially where the contract concerned bulk supplies from overseas sources. The latter reasoning seems more significant to modern eyes, since the foreign merchant's contract with his English intermediary may not be governed by English law. The banker's commercial credit system performs a similar function in to some extent localising the transaction. More recent cases tended to treat the fact that the principal was foreign as one to be taken into account but no more.[14] In *Teheran-Europe Co. Ltd v. S.T. Belton (Tractors) Ltd*,[15] where air compressors were ordered for use in Iran, the Court of Appeal held that the presumption itself no longer exists, for "the usages of the law merchant are not immutable." But the fact that the principal is foreign is not irrelevant. Diplock L.J. said[16]:

"The fact that the principal is a foreigner is one of the circumstances to be taken into account in determining whether or not the other party to the contract was willing, or led the agent to believe that he was willing, to treat as a party to the contract the agent's principal, and, if he was so willing, whether the mutual intention of the other party and the agent was that the agent should be personally entitled to sue and liable to be sued on the contract as well as his principal. But it is only one of many circumstances, and as respects the creation of privity of contract between the other party and the principal its weight may be minimal, particularly in a case such as the present where the terms of payment are cash before delivery and no credit is extended by the

---

[11] *Miller, Gibb & Co. v. Smith & Tyrer Ltd* [1917] 2 K.B. 141.

[12] See *Miller, Gibb & Co. v. Smith & Tyrer Ltd*, above, at p. 162; *Holt & Moseley v. Cunningham & Partners* (1949) 83 Ll.Rep. 141.

[13] See *Armstrong v. Stokes* (1872) L.R. 7 Q.B. 598, 605; Hill (1968) 31 M.L.R. 623, 637–639; Munday (1977) 6 Anglo-Am.L.Rev. 221, 235 *et seq.*

[14] *H.O. Brandt & Co. v. Morris & Co.* [1917] 2 K.B. 784; *Rusholme and Bolton and Roberts Hadfield v. S.G. Read & Co.* [1955] 1 W.L.R. 146; *Cox v. Sorrell* [1960] 1 Lloyd's Rep. 471; *Anglo-African Shipping Co. of New York Inc. v. J. Mortner Ltd* [1962] 1 Lloyd's Rep. 610, 617, 621; *Maritime Stores v. H.P. Marshall & Co. Ltd* [1963] 1 Lloyd's Rep. 602.

[15] [1968] 2 Q.B. 545.

[16] At p. 558.

other party to the principal. It may have considerably more weight in determining whether the mutual intention of the other party and the agent was that the agent should be personally liable to be sued as well as the principal, particularly if credit has been extended by the other party.[17]

9-019   **Confirming houses in international sales.**[18] A confirming house provides specialised agency functions for an overseas buyer who wishes to import goods. The normal purpose of the intervention of a confirming house is so that the seller, in a transaction between himself and an overseas buyer, shall have someone in his own country to look to in respect of performance of the contract: like the banker's commercial credit, it performs the function of reducing the possibility of becoming involved in questions of the conflict of laws or of suing in foreign jurisdictions. A confirming house may, on instructions, act for the buyer as agent only, and if so is not liable to the seller.[19] Alternatively, it may act as merchant, *viz.* by buying from the seller and reselling to its principal, the buyer.[20] Neither of these arrangements realy involves confirmation. A transaction involving confirmation will normally be intended to result in privity of contract being established between seller and confirming house.[21] In some cases the confirming house may be liable on a collateral contract whereby it answers in some way for the performance of the buyer's contract.[22] In other cases the confirming house may be solely liable to the seller, creating no privity between buyer and seller, but still remaining as an agent in relation to the buyer rather than a seller to its own principal: this possibility, which involves the notion of what is sometimes called the "commission agent," has not yet been fully explored.[23] It is clear that the fact that a confirming house acts as principal in one respect does not mean that it cannot act as agent in another, *e.g.* as a forwarding agent, and vice

---

[17] As to which see *Fraser v. Equitorial Shipping Co. Ltd (The Ijaola)* [1979] 1 Lloyd's Rep. 103.

[18] Hill (1972) 3 J. Maritime Law and Commerce 307; Schmitthoff (1970) 1 *Hague Recueil des Cours* at pp. 154–157; *The Export Trade* (9th ed.), pp. 296–302; [1957] J.B.L. 17.

[19] cf. *Bolus & Co. Ltd v. Inglis Bros. Ltd* [1924] N.Z.L.R. 164; *Stunzi Sons Ltd v. House of Youth Pty Ltd* [1960] S.R.(N.S.W.) 220.

[20] See the dissenting judgment of Diplock L.J. in *Anglo-African Shipping Co. of New York Inc. v. J. Mortner Ltd* [1962] 1 Lloyd's Rep. 610.

[21] *Sobell Industries Ltd v. Cory Bros. & Co.* [1955] 2 Lloyd's Rep. 82, 89.

[22] *Sobell Industries Ltd v. Cory Bros. & Co.*, above (Illustration 7).

[23] *Rusholme and Bolton and Roberts Hadfield v. S.G. Read & Co.* [1955] 1 W.L.R. 146 and *Anglo-African Shipping Co. of New York Inc. v. J. Mortner Ltd*, n. 20 above, may be examples of this. See paras. 1–018—1–019 above; Hill, *op. cit.* n. 18 above, at pp. 318–324; (1968) 31 M.L.R. 623; *Bolus & Co. Ltd v. Inglis Bros. Ltd*, n. 19 above, at pp. 174–175; *Downie Bros. v. Henry Oakley & Sons* [1923] N.Z.L.R. 734; *Scott v. Geoghegan & Sons Pty. Ltd* (1969) 43 A.L.J.R. 243; *Isaac Gundle v. Mohanlal Sunderji* (1939) 18 Kenya L.Rep. 137; Comment to Article 71.

versa.[24] A confirming house that does undertake liability to the seller may answer for more than the mere solvency of the buyer: subject to the terms of the particular contract and to the commercial understanding of the transaction, it is subject to litigation on the contract in general.[25] So also it may sue the seller, or assign its rights of action to the buyer.

Del credere agents. The position of a *del credere* agent is to be **9–020** contrasted with that of a confirming house. A *del credere* agent is normally the agent of the seller, not of the buyer. Thus, though he answers to the seller, he is not undertaking to the third party that his principal will perform a contract, but is undertaking to his principal that the third party will.[26] Equally, he cannot sue the third party.[27] A confirming house on the other hand is normally agent of the buyer, and thus answers to the seller not as agent but as a party to the contract of sale.[28] Its duty to the buyer is therefore usually greater than that of a *del credere* agent, whose obligation is confined to answering for the failure by the other contracting parties, owing to insolvency or the like, to pay ascertained sums which may become due from them as debts.[29] However, situations may occur where it is difficult to distinguish between the two.[30]

Auctioneers. Auctioneers provide examples of liability on what must **9–021** be explained in modern terms (however the matter is put in old cases) as collateral contracts. Where an auctioneer sells a specific chattel by auction for a disclosed principal, he is not liable upon the contract of sale,[31] nor does he impliedly warrant the title of his principal, although the name of the principal has not been disclosed to the buyer.[32] But he warrants that he has authority to sell, and that he knows of no defect in

---

[24] *Anglo-African Shipping Co. of New York Inc. v. J. Mortner Ltd*, n. 23 above, at pp. 616–617; *Sobell Industries Ltd v. Cory Bros & Co.*, n. 21 above, at p. 90.

[25] *Sobell Industries Ltd v. Cory Bros & Co.*, n. 21 above (Illustration 7); *Rusholme, etc. v. Read*, n. 23 above.

[26] *Churchill & Sim v. Goddard* [1937] 1 K.B. 92.

[27] *Bramwell v. Spiller* (1871) 21 L.T. 672; Article 2. But sometimes a *del credere* agent may by special arrangment or by the usage of trade answer to both parties to a sale: see Hill (1968) 31 M.L.R. 623, 639, note 64. And see Illustration 22.

[28] See above.

[29] *Thomas Gabriel & Sons v. Churchill & Sim* [1914] 3 K.B. 1272; *Rusholme, etc. v. Read*, n. 23 above.

[30] See Hill, *op. cit.* above, n. 18. See further as to *del credere* agents, Comment to Article 2.

[31] *Elder Smith Goldsbrough Mort Ltd v. McBride* [1976] 2 N.S.W.L.R. 631, Illustration 14; *cf. Fraser v. Dalgety & Co. Ltd* [1953] N.Z.L.R. 126.

[32] *Benton v. Campbell, Parker & Co.* [1925] 2 K.B. 410; *Chelmsford Auctions Ltd v. Poole* [1973] Q.B. 542. The special situation where a sale merely goes through an auctioneer's books was analysed as a sale to the auctioneer and a resale by him in *Murphy v. Howlett* [1960] E.G.D. 231.

the title of his principal.[33] His contract with the buyer entitles him to sue for the price,[34] and is independent of the contract of sale, which he makes on behalf of the seller and to which he is not a party.[35] It is traditionally said to be based on his lien over or special property in the goods, and for this reason seems inappropriate to the sale of land,[36] though no doubt in such cases he may still be subject to contractual duties.[37]

Another example was provided by the jobber on the Stock Exchange, who contracted, through the broker, with the seller of shares, to find a purchaser to whom no legitimate objection could be taken. When he had done so, he effected a contract between seller and buyer and his own collateral undertaking was performed.[38] This method of trading is no longer used in England.

9–022   **Freight forwarders.** A freight forwarder may make a contract of carriage as agent for his principal, the consignor. Alternatively he may act as principal towards the outside world but himself secure or even charter space as principal. But recent cases have held that he has done so as agent, even though he has issued a bill of lading,[39] so that it is the consignor who is party to the contract of carriage: the forwarder may not be able to sue on it. This can only be a matter of interpretation: there can be no objection to a forwarder also being able to sue on the contract of carriage or a collateral contract, or to his acting as carrier.[40]

9–023   **Deposits: receipt as agent for vendor.** An agent, particularly an estate agent, auctioneer or solicitor acting in connection with the sale of land, may receive money from a third party to hold by way of deposit.

---

[33] *Peto v. Blades* (1814) 5 Taunt. 657; *Pollway Ltd v. Abdullah* [1974] 1 W.L.R. 493 (warranty of authority to sign memorandum and accept deposit entitled auctioneer to sue upon cheque for deposit). See further below, para. 9–027; Illustrations 11–14, 17–19; Murdoch, *Law of Estate Agency and Auctions* (3rd ed.), pp. 304 *et seq.*, 350 *et seq.*

[34] See Illustration 17.

[35] *Benton v. Campbell, Parker & Co.*, n. 32 above, at p. 416.

[36] See *Cherry v. Anderson* (1876) I.R. 10 C.L. 204; *Fisher v. Marsh* (1865) 6 B. & S. 411; *Evans v. Evans* (1834) 3 A. & E. 132; *cf. Cleave v. Moore* (1857) 3 Jur.(N.S.) 48.

[37] See *Pollway Ltd v. Abdullah*, n. 33 above.

[38] *Grissell v. Bristowe* (1868) L.R. 4 C.P. 36; *Maxted v. Paine* (1869) L.R. 4 Ex. 203, affd. (1871) L.R. 6 Ex. 132. See on these cases (1929) 39 Yale L.J. 265–271.

[39] *Carrington Slipways Pty Ltd v. Patrick Operations Pty Ltd* (1991) 24 N.S.W.L.R. 745. See also *Marston Excelsior Ltd v. Arbuckle Smith & Co. Ltd* [1971] 2 Lloyd's Rep. 306; *Hair & Skin Trading Co. Ltd v. Norman Airfreight Carriers Ltd* [1974] 1 Lloyd's Rep. 443; *J. Evans & Sons (Portsmouth) Ltd v. Andrea Merzario Ltd* [1976] 1 W.L.R. 1078; *The Maheno* [1977] 1 Lloyd's Rep. 81.

[40] *Thomas National Transport (Melbourne) Pty Ltd v. May & Baker (Aust.) Ltd* (1966) 115 C.L.R. 353; *Chas. Davis (Metal Brokers) Ltd v. Gilyott & Scott Ltd* [1975] 2 Lloyd's Rep. 57; *Salsi v. Jetspeed Air Services Ltd* [1977] 2 Lloyd's Rep. 57. See in general *Contracts for the Carriage of Goods* (Yates ed., 1993), Chap. 7.

Sometimes he receives this as agent for the vendor: this is the assumption in the case of solicitors[41] and estate agents[42] unless there are indications to the contrary. Old cases suggest that auctioneers, on the other hand, prima facie receive money in such circumstances not as agents but as stakeholders[43] though it is not clear why the rule for them should be different, and hence whether this interpretation is still correct. The consequence of receipt as agent is that it is the vendor who is liable if the sale goes off and the money is not returned.[44]

Stakeholders. Whatever the prima facie rule, circumstances frequently   9–024 arise where persons in these categories receive money as stakeholders. A person receiving money as stakeholder must hold or at least account for it pending the occurrence of the relevant event, and when this has occurred, pay it across in accordance with his instructions. He must not accede to the unilateral instructions of one of the parties to do otherwise, though he must accept the instructions of both of them, for example, to transfer the deposit to another stakeholder.[45] He does not hold the deposit in trust[46] and must pay it to one of the parties, usually the vendor, when the relevant event occurs. If he takes the view that it has, but his view is wrong, he is liable, but *in personam*.[47] It is sometimes said that in such a case he is agent of both parties[48]; but it seems rather that he receives the money from the purchaser under a specific and separate obligation as principal.[49] It appears from the auctioneer cases that the vendor also is liable if the stakeholder defaults[50]; but the agent's obligation is clearly a separate one from that

---

[41] *Ellis v. Goulton* [1893] 1 Q.B. 350, 352–353 (Illustration 1 to Article 113); *Tudor v. Hamid* [1988] 1 EGLR 251, 255. This has the advantage for the purchaser that he has a lien on the property to the extent of the deposit: *Whitehead & Co. Ltd v. Watt* [1902] 1 Ch. 835; *cf. Combe v. Lord Swaythling* [1947] Ch. 625. See also *Skinner v. Trustee of the Property of Reed* [1967] Ch. 1194.

[42] *Ojelay v. Neosale Ltd* [1987] 2 EGLR 167, 168.

[43] *Harington v. Hogart* (1830) 1 B. & Ad. 577; *Furtado v. Lumley* (1890) 6 T.L.R. 168.

[44] Article 113.

[45] *Rockeagle Ltd v. Alsop Wilkinson* [1992] Ch. 47 (despite solicitors having an interest in retaining it against debts owed by vendor). His lien is confined to so much as becomes the property of the vendor: *Skinner v. Trustee of the Property of Reed*, n. 41 above. As to interest, see Article 54.

[46] *Hastingwood Property Ltd v. Saunders Bearman Anselm* [1991] Ch. 114; *Potters (A Firm) v. Loppert* [1973] Ch. 399.

[47] *Hastingwood Property Ltd v. Saunders Bearman Anselm*, above.

[48] *Collins v. Stimson* (1883) 11 Q.B.D. 142, 144.

[49] *Hastingwood Property* case, n. 46 above, at p. 123. See also *Berry v. Hodson* [1989] 1 Qd.R. 361 (knowledge of stakeholder not imputed to vendor).

[50] *Fenton v. Browne* (1807) 14 Ves. 144; *Annesley v. Muggridge* (1816) 1 Madd. 593, 596; *Rowe v. May* (1854) 18 Beav. 613; *Christie v. Robinson* (1907) 4 C.L.R. 1338; *Swindle v. Knibb* (1929) 29 S.R.(N.S.W.) 325; *Grant v. O'Leary* (1955) 93 C.L.R. 587; *Goding v. Frazer* [1967] 1 W.L.R. 286, 290–291; *Barrington v. Lee* [1972] 1 Q.B. 326, 335;

—cont. on next page

of his principal. The obligation is probably contractual, the consideration for his promise being that he has the use of the money without accounting for interest[51]; but alternatively it may lie in restitution, though this head of restitution is not yet well worked out in English law.[52]

Where the agent receives money under a pre-contract situation in the sale of land "subject to contract", as estate agents sometimes do, he is often also said to hold as stakeholder, and it has indeed been said that this is the appropriate interpretation where there are no other indications.[53] In this context the term "stakeholder" has at best a specialised meaning, however, and would be better avoided,[54] for the holder is under a duty to return the money to the prospective purchaser on demand at any time before he has paid it away on the completion of the contract in accordance with instructions.[55] Such a person is probably better described as agent of the purchaser, authorised to hold and pay away the money unless that authority is revoked. Here the fact that the agent must be ready to return the money on mere demand is more plausibly treated as consideration for his entitlement to interest.[56] In such cases the vendor is not liable if the estate agent defaults.[57]

9–025   **Express restriction of liability.** Where an agent contracts personally, his liability may be expressly restricted to certain events. The cesser clause in a charterparty may be cited as an example.[58] Older forms of the clause provide that the charterer signs as agent for others, and that his liability to the shipowner is to cease as soon as the cargo is shipped,

---

—cont. from previous page
Ojelay v. Neosale Ltd [1987] 2 EGLR 167, 168; *Thomson Hill Pte. Ltd v. Chang Erh* [1992] 2 Singapore L.R. 769; Murdoch, *Law of Estate Agency and Auctions* (3rd ed.), pp. 312–319. The rule seems to be based on the idea that the vendor appoints the stakeholder: *quaere* whether it should apply when he cannot easily be said to have done so, as where it is the purchaser's solicitor who holds the money. But in the *Thomson Hill* case, above, it was held that the same result ensued because the parties have in such a case by mutual consent made the purchaser's solicitor the stakeholder.

[51] *Potters (A Firm) v. Loppert* [1973] Ch. 399, following *Harington v. Hoggart* (1830) 1 B. & Ad. 577; and see *Smith v. Hamilton* [1951] Ch. 174, 184. See also Article 54.

[52] See *Chillingworth v. Esche* [1924] 1 Ch. 97. See also as to this point *Burt v. Claude Cousins & Co. Ltd* [1975] 1 Q.B. 426, 449; *Barrington v. Lee* [1972] 1 Q.B. 326, 337; *Potters (A Firm) v. Loppert* [1973] Ch. 399, 413–414; (1976) 92 L.Q.R. 484; Article 113, Illustration 2.

[53] *Burt v. Claude Cousins & Co. Ltd*, n. 52 above, *per* Lord Denning M.R. and Sachs L.J. But see *Desmond v. Brophy* [1985] I.R. 449, where it was held on the facts that a solicitor received such a deposit as agent for the prospective vendor.

[54] *Maloney v. Hardy and Moorsehead* [1971] 2 Q.B. 442n.

[55] *Sorrell v. Finch* [1977] A.C. 728, 749 (Illustration 4 to Article 94).

[56] See *Potters (A Firm) v. Loppert*, n. 52 above, at pp. 414–415.

[57] *Sorrell v. Finch*, n. 55 above. See also Article 113, Illustration 3.

[58] Below, para. 9–090.

the shipowner holding a lien for unpaid charges. Under it the charterer's liability may cease as specified and be superseded by the liability of the holders of the bills of lading.[59] Such clauses, which are the subject of extensive case law,[60] do not necessarily involve true agency by the charterer, for he may not at the time of contracting have a principal or principals as required. He may intend to procure that other shippers fill the ship with general cargo and pay the freight between them. Indeed he may in the end ship himself. Later forms of the clause do not refer to agency.

Agents of the Crown. Prior to 1947, no action for breach of contract lay against the Crown, except where permitted by statute. However, as the Crown was to all intents and purposes liable in contract by Petition of Right, no special rule was avowedly applied to agents of the Crown, who were therefore, like other agents, not liable unless they had contracted personally. But they would rarely be held to do so,[61] which is doubtless fair when the magnitude of commitment involved in some government contracts is considered. Cases of personal liability are however not impossible,[62] and indeed where the "agent" is a public body there is no particular difficulty about them: in such a case at any rate it is also possible for the Crown and the agent to be liable together.[63] The Crown can now be sued directly by virtue of the Crown Proceedings Act 1947, but the rules as to the liability and entitlement to sue of an agent of the Crown remain unchanged. **9–026**

Defences.[64] Where the agent is sued on the main contract, he can presumably plead defences arising out of the contract, and defences personal to himself, but not defences personal to the principal. Where the agent sues, the third party can likewise plead defences on the main transaction, but not defences against the agent personally unless the principal was undisclosed. **9–027**

---

[59] *Oglesby v. Yglesias* (1858) E.B. & E. 930; *Milvain v. Perez* (1861) 3 E. & E. 495.

[60] See in general Scrutton, *Charterparties* (19th ed.), pp. 178 *et seq.*

[61] See *Palmer v. Hutchinson* (1881) 6 App.Cas. 619; *Macbeath v. Haldimand* (1786) 7 T.R. 172; also *Kenny v. Cosgrave* [1926] I.R. 517. As to the liability of agents of the Crown for breach of warranty of authority, see Comment to Article 107.

[62] Illustrations 8–10. But these are special cases: a private individual contracting on behalf of the Crown (as opposed to a public body specially incorporated by statute, or a private person making arrangements on his own behalf) does not seem to be liable, and dicta that he is free from liability have been couched in strong terms: see, *e.g. Gidley v. Palmerston* (1822) 3 B. & B. 275, 286–287.

[63] *International Ry. Co. v. Niagara Parks Commission* [1941] A.C. 328 (again a case on a public body, incorporated by statute with the power to sue and be sued).

[64] See Derhem, [1985] C.L.J. 384; *Set-Off* (1987), pp. 192–204; Wood, *English and International Set-Off* (1989), Chap. 19.

But where the agent sues on a separate or collateral contract, defences available on the main contract may not be available against him, depending on the terms of his contract as interpreted by the court. The best example of this is the case of auctioneers.[65] Auctioneers, as stated above, make a separate and quite independent contract with the buyer which renders them subject to certain liabilities and also entitles them to sue. Payment to or set-off against the principal are therefore normally no defence to the auctioneer's claim.[66] But it may sometimes be a defence if the auctioneer knew of such a set-off, for then the contract with him may be otherwise interpreted, or if the auctioneer apparently waived his right by allowing goods to be taken away contrary to normal practice without asking for payment.[67] And if the auctioneer's principal did not own the goods, the auctioneer has no one from whom he can derive an interest in the goods, and payment to the true owner will discharge a purchaser.[68] Further, the auctioneer's right to sue may sometimes be extinguished if he has received his commission, for here an equity may be raised against him.[69] Similar reasoning was applied to nineteenth-century factors, who likewise had a lien, and sometimes (less obviously) to brokers.[70]

The contract on which the agent sues may be independent of the main contract to such an extent that defences against him may be pleaded though he effectively sues for his principal. Thus it has been held that an underwriter may set off, in an action by a broker for insurance money due to a client, debts owed by the broker to the underwriter.[71]

9–028   Estoppel as to whether a party to contract. There may be circumstances when, although he is not on true analysis a party to the contract, an agent conducts himself towards the third party as though he is. In such circumstances an estoppel may be raised against him. This has recently been held to occur in connection with the demise clause, a bill of lading clause which purports to create a contract with the shipowner where the ship is not owned by or chartered by demise to the party issuing the bill of lading.[72] Under such clauses the party issuing the bill of lading acts as agent only. But where such a party conducted

---

[65] See *Derham, Set-Off* (1987), pp. 192–194.
[66] Illustration 18.
[67] Illustration 19.
[68] *Dickenson v. Naul* (1833) 4 B. & Ad. 638; and see *Fraser v. Dalgety & Co. Ltd* [1953] N.Z.L.R. 126.
[69] Illustration 19; but *cf.* 18. See in general Murdoch, *Law of Estate Agency and Auctions* (3rd ed.).
[70] See Illustrations 20, 21; above, para. 9–009.
[71] *Gibson v. Winter* (1833) 5 B. & Ad. 96.
[72] See Scrutton, *Charterparties* (19th ed.), p. 71.

himself as if he was the contracting party, and the third party proceeded on this basis with the result that his action against the true principal became time-barred, it was held that the party issuing the bill was estopped from alleging that he was not a party to the contract.[73]

Warranty of authority. An agent who contracts on behalf of his principal is normally regarded as warranting his authority to do so. This special collateral contract is treated separately in Article 107.   9–029

Tort. An agent may of course be liable to the third party in deceit. There may also be circumstances in which the agent assumes a duty of care towards the third party. This would not involve liability on the promise, but in respect of negligent representation, or sometimes negligent conduct.[74]   9–030

Statute. Section 18 of the Estate Agents Act 1979, in combination with regulations made under the Act,[75] impose on estate agents certain duties of disclosure to third parties of any personal interest in a transaction.[76] These have, however, no civil sanction and are only enforceable in so far as they may trigger the enforcement powers of the Director General of Fair Trading.   9–031

Illustrations

Liability of agent

(1)   A acted as the London agent of C & Co., who were paper manufacturers in Vienna. B, by letter, ordered paper from A, who in his own name acknowledged the letter, and promised to supply the paper in certain quantities at certain times. A portion of the paper was delivered, and on B complaining to A respecting the non-delivery of the remainder, A stated that it was the default of C & Co. B then wrote to C & Co. telling them of the position of affairs, and the excuses made by A. Subsequently B sued A for breach of contract. Held, that A, having contracted personally, was liable, and that B's letter to C & Co. did not amount to an election by B to substitute C & Co. for A as the   9–032

---

[73] *Pacol Ltd v. Trades Lines Ltd (The Henrik Sif)* [1982] 1 Lloyd's Rep. 456, applying reasoning in *Amalgamated Investment & Property Co. Ltd v. Texas Commerce International Bank Ltd* [1982] Q.B. 84; *Taylors Fashions Ltd v. Liverpool Victoria Trustee Co. Ltd, ibid.* 133n. See further above, para. 8–030.

[74] See Article 115.

[75] Estate Agents (Undesirable Practices) Order 1991 (S.I. 1991 No. 1032).

[76] See Murdoch, *Law of Estate Agency and Auctions* (3rd ed.), pp. 213–218; *The Estate Agents and Property Misdescriptions Acts* (3rd ed.), Chap 3C.

contracting parties.[77] Some weight was attached to the circumstance that the principals were foreign.[78]

(2)   Where solicitors instructed stockbrokers to sell stock belonging to A, and enclosed a blank transfer signed by A, it was held that the instructions to sell were given by the solicitors as principals and that they were liable when A objected to the registration of the transfer.[79]

(3)   An agent signed in his own name, without mentioning his principal, an undertaking to accept shares in a company, and the shares were allotted to him. Subsequently, the principal took a larger number of shares, in satisfaction, as the agent said, of his undertaking. Held, that the agent having personally accepted the shares, was liable as a contributory.[80]

(4)   An agent buys goods at a sale by auction, and gives his own name, which is entered as that of the buyer. He is personally liable, unless it is clearly proved that he did not intend to bind himself, and that the auctioneer knew that.[81]

(5)   A stockbroker in Hong Kong presenting share transfers for registration has been held to promise that he will indemnify the person to whom he presents them against the consequences of registering them; and may also be held to warrant their genuineness.[82]

(6)   A fishing vessel is owned by R, who forms a company to hire it from him and operate it. Repairs are ordered by R on the company's notepaper, signed "R, Director". Although R undoubtedly contracts as agent for the company, he also, as owner of the vessel, undertakes personal liability.[83]

---

[77] *Dramburg v. Pollitzer* (1873) 28 L.T. 470. *cf. J.S. Robertson (Aust.) Pty. Ltd v. Martin* (1956) 94 C.L.R. 30. See Articles 84, 106. The "election" reasoning would not be so expressed today: see above, paras. 8–120, 9–028.

[78] See above, para. 9–018.

[79] *Hichens, Harrison Woolston & Co. v. Jackson & Sons* [1943] A.C. 266; and see *Lavan v. Walsh* [1964] I.R. 87; *Saxon v. Blake* (1861) 29 Beav. 438; *Hobhouse v. Hamilton* (1826) 1 Hog. 401 (Ir.); and see Article 99.

[80] *Re Southampton, Bird's Case* (1864) 4 De. G.J. & S. 200.

[81] *Williamson v. Barton* (1862) 7 H. & N. 899; *Chadwick v. Maden* (1851) 9 Hare 188. Presumably commercial usage in the type of auction sale in question would be relevant.

[82] *Yeung Kai Yung v. Hong Kong and Shanghai Banking Corp.* [1981] A.C. 787. *cf. Guaranty Trust Corp. of New York v. Hannay & Co.* [1918] 2 K.B. 623. And see below, para. 9–062.

[83] *The Swan* [1968] 1 Lloyd's Rep. 5; see also *R. & J. Bow Ltd v. Hill* (1930) 37 Ll.Rep. 46; *Format International Security Printers Ltd v. Mosden* [1975] 1 Lloyd's Rep. 37; *cf. Badgerhill Properties Ltd v. Cottrell* [1991] B.C.L.C. 805, Illustration 15 to Article 101. Compare comments by Legh-Jones (1969) 32 M.L.R. 325 and Reynolds (1969) 85 L.Q.R. 92. See also Prentice (1973) 89 L.Q.R. 518, 531, suggesting that the case is inconsistent with *Newborne v. Sensolid (Great Britain) Ltd* [1954] 1 Q.B. 45, Illustation 6 to Article 109 and *Henry Browne & Sons Ltd v. Smith* [1964] 2 Lloyd's Rep. 276. It could also be said that some of the dicta are inconsistent with what was subsequently said in *N. & J. Vlassopulos Ltd v. Ney Shipping Co. (The Santa Carina)* [1977] 1 Lloyd's Rep. 478.

(7)   A buyer in Turkey orders radio sets from an English manufacturer. The order is confirmed by an English confirming house and accepted by the seller. The buyer fails to accept full delivery. The confirming house is liable for the buyer's breach of contract.[84]

(8)   A naval commander, when employing a cook, undertook to pay him a certain sum per annum in addition to the government pay. Held, that the commander was personally liable to pay that sum, he having contracted personally, and not as an agent for the government.[85]

(9)   A clerk of a county court gave orders for the fitting up, etc., of the court-house. Held, that it was properly left to the jury to say whether he had contracted personally, and that, if he had, he was personally liable on the contract.[86]

(10)   The Commissioners of Public Works and Buildings entered into a contract with certain builders for the erection of public buildings. It was held that the Commissioners must be taken to have contracted for themselves, and not merely as agent for the Crown, and that they were liable to be sued by the builders for damages for breach of the contract.[87]

(11)   An auctioneer sold goods on behalf of a disclosed principal, the conditions of sale providing that the lots should be cleared within three days, and that if from any cause the auctioneer was unable to deliver, etc., the purchaser should accept compensation. Held, that the auctioneer, being in possession of the goods, and having contracted to deliver, was personally liable to the purchaser for non-delivery.[88]

(12)   In a case of a sale of standing corn with straw, to be removed at the purchaser's expense, it was held that the auctioneer contracted to give proper authority to enter and carry away the corn and straw, and undertook that he was in fact authorised to sell, but that he did not warrant the title.[89] Upon a sale of shares, which required transfer by

---

Illustration 3 to Article 103. As regards repairs to and stores for ships, see further cases cited above; Article 101, Illustration 7; Article 103, Illustration 2; *H.J. Lyons & Sando Ltd v. Houlson* [1963] S.A.S.R. 29; *Stag Line Ltd v. Tyne Shiprepair Group Ltd (The Zinnia)* [1984] 2 Lloyd's Rep. 211.

[84] *Sobell Industries Ltd v. Cory Bros. & Co. Ltd* [1955] 2 Lloyd's Rep. 82; see above, para. 9–019.

[85] *Clutterbuck v. Coffin* (1842) 3 M. & G. 842. See also *Cunningham v. Collier* (1785) 4 Doug. 233; *cf. Unwin v. Wolseley* (1787) 1 T.R. 674 (cases on deeds); *Rice v. Chute* (1801) 1 East 579.

[86] *Auty v. Hutchinson* (1848) 6 C.B. 266.

[87] *Graham v. Public Works Commrs.* [1901] 2 K.B. 781; *Roper v. Public Works Commrs.* [1915] 1 K.B. 45. The Commissioners were a public body incorporated by statute.

[88] *Woolfe v. Horne* (1877) 2 Q.B.D. 355.

[89] *Wood v. Baxter* (1883) 49 L.T. 45; *Benton v. Campbell Parker & Co.* [1925] 2 K.B. 410.

deed, the auctioneers, who were acting on behalf of an unnamed principal, were held liable in damages for failure to procure a transfer of the shares, upon the ground that they had agreed to do so.[90]

(13) Where a sale by auction is advertised as being "without reserve" it may be that the auctioneer impliedly contracts to accept the offer of the highest bona fide bidder, and is liable in damages for breach of such implied contract if he accept a bid from the vendor.[91] But an advertisement to the effect that certain goods will be sold on certain days does not amount to a contract to sell them, so as to entitle a person who acts on the advertisement to recover damages for loss of time or expense if the goods are not put up at all.[92]

(14) An auctioneer sells a bull at an auction of stud cattle. The bull proves infertile. The auctioneer is not liable for breach of the implied condition as to description and may sue for the price.[93]

Agent's right to sue

9–033   (15) A contract was made in the following form: "It is mutually agreed between J. & R. W., of the one part, and S J C, on behalf of G. & M. Rail Co., of the other part, etc." (signed) "J & R W, S J C." Held, that S J C was entitled to sue in his own name for breach of the contract, he having contracted personally.[94]

(16) A broker contracted in writing in his own name to buy goods, the seller being told that there was a principal. The broker then, under a general authority from the principal, contracted to resell. On hearing of the last-mentioned contract, the principal refused to have anything to do with the goods, and the broker acquiesced. The seller then refused to deliver. Held, that the broker, having contracted personally, had a right to recover damages for the non-delivery, and that the principal's renunciation of the contract did not affect that right.[95]

---

[90] *Franklyn v. Lamond* (1847) 4 C.B. 637; *Hanson v. Roberdeau* (1792) Peake 163.

[91] See *Warlow v. Harrison* (1858) 1 E. & E. 295, 309, which is some authority for the implication of such a contract. See Slade (1952) 68 L.Q.R. 238; (1953) 69 L.Q.R. 21; Gower (1952) 68 L.Q.R. 457; *Johnston v. Boyes* [1899] 2 Ch. 73. See as to this case *Wright v. Madden* [1992] 1 Qd. R. 343. *cf. Rainbow v. Howkins* [1904] 2 K.B. 322; *McManus v. Fortescue* [1907] 2 K.B. 1; *Richards v. Phillips* [1969] 1 Ch. 39. Compare the auctioneer's liability for breach of warranty of authority: Article 107.

[92] *Harris v. Nickerson* (1873) L.R. 8 Q.B. 286. On these auctioneer cases see in general Murdoch, *Law of Estate Agency and Auctions* (3rd ed.), pp. 305 *et seq.*

[93] *Elder Smith Goldsbrough Mort Ltd v. McBride* [1976] 2 N.S.W.L.R. 631; *cf. Fraser v. Dalgety & Co. Ltd* [1953] N.Z.L.R. 126.

[94] *Cooke v. Wilson* (1856) 1 C.B.(N.S.) 153; *Clay & Newman v. Southern* (1852) 7 Exch. 717; *H.O. Brandt & Co. v. H.N. Morris & Co.* [1917] 2 K.B. 784. *cf. Sharman v. Brandt* (1871) L.R. 6 Q.B. 720.

[95] *Short v. Spackman* (1831) 2 B. & Ad. 962.

(17) An auctioneer sells A's goods to a buyer who knows that they are A's property. The auctioneer may, nevertheless, sue in his own name for the price,[96] even where he has already been paid a sum sufficient to cover his commission and charges.[97] But if the contract can be treated by the buyer, who has not paid, as discharged for breach, it may be that the auctioneer cannot sue.[98]

(18) An auctioneer sued for the price of goods sold and delivered. The defendant pleaded that the plaintiff acted as an auctioneer, and that the defendant had paid the principal for the goods before action. Held, that the plea was bad, because the auctioneer would have had, as against the principal, a lien on the proceeds for charges, etc.[99] The defendant should have shown that, either by the conditions of sale or by facts accruing subsequently, payment to the principal was permitted in discharge of the plaintiff's claim.

(19) An auctioneer, on behalf of A, sold goods to B. A was indebted to B, and there was an agreement between them before the sale that the price of any goods bought by B should be set off against the debt, but the auctioneer had no notice of the agreement. The auctioneer permitted B to take away the goods, thinking that he was going to pay for them, B thinking that he was taking them in pursuance of his agreement with A. The auctioneer paid A on account and after receiving notice of the agreement between A and B, paid A the balance of the proceeds of the sale, such balance exceeding the amount of B's purchases. The auctioneer subsequently sued B for the price of the goods. Held, that the auctioneer's charges having been paid before action, and he having had notice of the agreement between A and B at the time of his payment to A (exceeding the amount for which he was suing B), the settlement between A and B constituted a good defence.[1] Here, the auctioneer was not really prejudiced by the settlement with the principal.

(20) A factor sold, in his own name, goods on which he had a lien for advances. While the advances were unpaid, the factor's right to sue the purchaser and compel payment had priority to that of the principal or his trustee in bankruptcy.[2]

---

[96] *Williams v. Millington* (1788) 1 H.Bl. 81.

[97] *Chelmsford Auctions Ltd v. Poole* [1973] Q.B. 542. See also *Fisher v. Marsh* (1865) 6 B. & S. 411. But this does not apply to the sale of land: above, para. 9–021.

[98] See *Dickenson v. Naul* (1833) 4 B. & Ad. 638; see also discussion in *Elder Smith Goldsbrough Mort Ltd v. McBride* [1976] 2 N.S.W.L.R. 631, 648; above, para. 9–021.

[99] *Robinson v. Rutter* (1855) 4 E. & B. 954.

[1] *Grice v. Kenrick* (1870) L.R. 5 Q.B. 340; *Holmes v. Tutton* (1855) 5 E. & B. 65; see explanation of these cases in *Chelmsford Auctions Ltd v. Poole*, n. 97 above, at p. 549. *cf. Manley & Sons Ltd v. Berkett* [1912] 2 K.B. 329. On these auctioneer cases, see in general Murdoch, *Law of Estate Agency and Auctions* (3rd ed.), pp. 350 *et seq.*

[2] *Drinkwater v. Goodwin* (1775) 1 Cowp. 251. See above, para. 1–040.

(21) A broker sold, in his own name, goods on which he had made advances. The buyer had no right, in an action by the broker for the price, to set off a debt due to him from the principal.[3]

(22) A, acting as *del credere* agent on behalf of B, a timber exporter, sold a cargo of timber to C. A, in accordance with the contract of agency, paid to B the price of the timber, less A's commission; and, in accordance with the contract of sale, C accepted bills of exchange drawn by A for the price of the timber. When the timber arrived, C rejected it on the ground that it was not as specified, and it was found that he was entitled so to do. C dishonoured his acceptances. Held, that A was not the trustee or agent of B in respect of A's rights as holder of the bills of exchange; that there was no failure of consideration for the bills, which were separate contracts between A and C, and were not affected by the failure of consideration under the contract for sale of the timber; and that C was liable to A for the amount of the bills.[4]

Article 101

WRITTEN CONTRACTS

9–034   The question whether the agent is to be deemed to have contracted personally, in the case of a contract in writing other than a deed, bill of exchange, promissory note or cheque, depends upon the intention of the parties, as appearing from the terms of the written agreement as a whole, the construction of which is a matter of law.[5]

Comment

9–035   In the context of a written contract, an agent may be held liable and entitled rather more easily than in unwritten contracts, because of the interpretation put by the court on words used. There is also a sizeable

---

[3] *Atkyns and Batten v. Amber* (1796) 2 Esp. 493. But this case was doubted in *Bramwell v. Spiller* (1870) 21 L.T. 672.

[4] *Churchill & Sim v. Goddard* [1937] 1 K.B. 92; *Hindle v. Brown* (1908) 98 L.T. 791; *Pollway Ltd v. Abdullah* [1974] 1 W.L.R. 493; *Pendergrast v. Chapman* [1988] 2 N.Z.L.R. 177. cf. *Barton, Thompson & Co v. Vigers Bros.* (1906) 19 Com.Cas. 175; *Jordeson & Co. v. London Hardwood Co.* (1913) 110 L.T. 666; *Flatau, Dick & Co. v. Keeping* (1931) 39 Ll.L.Rep. 42; *Turnbull & Jones Ltd v. Amner & Sons* [1923] N.Z.L.R. 673.

[5] See *Universal Steam Navigation Co. v. McKelvie* [1923] A.C. 492; *Bowes v. Shand* (1877) 2 App.Cas. 455; *The Swan* [1968] 1 Lloyd's Rep. 5, Illustration 6 to Article 100; Illustrations. See also criticism of the decisions in Stoljar, pp. 251–256.

body of case law in this area which can be cited as precedent in disputes.

The cases on this topic should only be treated as single instances exemplifying the application of a rather imprecise principle; much turns on the particular context of each contract. Some of the older cases have been overruled,[6] and some may not be able to stand—in particular those which turned on the assumption, at one time held, that the agent must be liable if the principal was not,[7] for it has been clear that in such cases his liability is based on a separate contract,[8] a warranty of authority.[9] Generalisations about particular formulae are dangerous.[10]

The following rules have, however, appeared in previous editions and still seem valid starting points.

(a) If the contract is signed by the agent in his own name without qualification, he is deemed to have contracted personally[11] unless a contrary intention plainly appears from other portions of the document.[12]

(b) The mere fact that the agent is described as an agent, director, secretary, manager, broker, etc., whether by words connected with or forming part of the signature,[13] or in the body of the contract,[14] and whether the principal is named or not, raises no presumption that the agent did not intend to contract personally; but here again an intention to contract as agent only may be gathered from the whole document and surrounding circumstances.[15]

---

[6] *e.g. Lennard v. Robinson* (1855) 5 E. & B. 125; overruled in *Universal Steam Navigation Co. v. McKelvie*, n. 5 above; *Paice v. Walker* (1870) L.R. 5 Ex. 173; disapproved in *Gadd v. Houghton* (1876) 1 Ex.D. 357.

[7] *Downman v. Williams* (1845) 7 Q.B. 103, Illustration 2; *Harper v. Williams* (1843) 4 Q.B. 219.

[8] *Lewis v. Nicholson* (1852) 18 Q.B. 503; *Jenkins v. Hutchinson* (1849) 13 Q.B. 744.

[9] Article 107.

[10] Two cases worth particular study are *Gadd v. Houghton* (n. 6 above), Illustration 10 and *Universal Steam Navigation Co. v. McKelvie* (n. 5 above), Illustration 12.

[11] Illustration 5. And see *Lavan v. Walsh* [1964] I.R. 87 and *Transcontinental Underwriting Agencies SRL v. Grand Union Insurance Co. Ltd* [1987] 2 Lloyd's Rep. 409, where this formulation is approved; *Farncombe v. Sperling* (1922) 66 S.J. 312; *Ernest Scragg & Son Ltd v. Perserverance Banking and Trust Co. Ltd* [1973] 2 Lloyd's Rep. 101; *Sika Contracts Ltd v. B.S. Gill* (1978) 9 Build. L.R. 11, Illustration 9.

[12] Illustrations 6, 10; *Concordia Chemische Fabrik Auf Actien v. Squire* (1876) 34 L.T. 824. But *cf.* Illustration 11, where the indications in the document were not sufficiently clear.

[13] *Hutcheson v. Eaton* (1884) 13 Q.B.D. 861 ("brokers"). As to the term "agent," see *Universal Steam Navigation Co. v. McKelvie*, n. 17 below, at p. 501: "When people add 'agent' to a signature to a contract, they are trying to escape personal liability, but are unaware that the attempt will fail." But see Comment to Article 102(1).

[14] Illustrations 1, 2 (first part), 4, 5.

[15] Illustrations 2 (second part), 3.

(c) But if the agent adds words to his signature, indicating that he signs an agent, or for or on behalf or on account of a principal, he is deemed not to have contracted personally,[16] unless it is plain from other portions of the document that, notwithstanding such qualified signature, he intended to bind himself.[17] This is so even though he does not name his principal.[18] But this proposition should be read subject to Article 102(2) regarding the liability of agents under trade custom.

As in other cases, care should be taken to ascertain exactly what liability an agent undertakes, if he does appear to contract personally.[19] Although most of the cases assume that the agent is the only party to the contract, this need not necessarily be so.[20] Extrinsic evidence is admissible to clarify a written contract,[21] provided that it is not inconsistent with the contract.[22] It is not impossible for a person to sign both for himself and also as agent of another.[23]

In the case of signatures for companies, a further distinction must be taken between cases where an agent signs as agent, which are governed by the above rules, and those where he signs *as* the company, *viz.* simply purports to authenticate the company's signature and so does not even sign as agent. In this latter case the agent's liability or right to sue will be difficult to establish.[24]

---

[16] Illustrations 11, 12.

[17] Illustration 13; *Paice v. Walker* (1870) L.R. 5 Ex. 173 (but this case was disapproved in *Gadd v. Houghton* (1876) 1 Ex.D. 357); *Weidner v. Hoggett* (1876) 1 C.P.D. 533. But such a contingency is unlikely: see *Universal Steam Navigation Co. v. McKelvie* [1923] A.C. 492, 499, *per* Lord Shaw, "But I desire to say that in my opinion the appending of the word 'agents' to the signature of a party to a mercantile contract is, in all cases, the dominating factor in the soloution of the problem of principal or agent. A highly improbable and conjectural case (in which this dominating factor might be overcome by other parts of the contract) may by an effort of the imagination be figured, but, apart from that, the appending of the word 'agent' to the signature is a conclusive assertion of agency, and a conclusive rejection of the responsibility of a principal, and is and must be accepted in that twofold sense by the other contracting party."

[18] *Southwell v. Bowditch* (1876) 1 C.P.D. 374, Illustration 3; *Chartwell Shipping Ltd v. Q.N.S. Paper Co. Ltd* [1989] 2 S.C.R. 683, (1989) 62 D.L.R. (4th) 36, Illustration 8.

[19] *Universal Steam Navigation Co. v. McKelvie*, n. 17 above, at p. 501. See Comment to Article 100.

[20] See *e.g. Stag Line Ltd v. Tyne Shiprepair Group Ltd (The Zinnia)* [1984] 2 Lloyd's Rep. 211, 216; above, para. 9–006.

[21] See *McCollin v. Gilpin* (1881) 6 Q.B.D. 516, Illustration 2; *Young v. Schuler* (1883) 11 Q.B.D. 651; *Automobiles Renault Canada Ltd v. Maritime Import Autos Ltd* (1961) 31 D.L.R. (2d) 592.

[22] See Article 102.

[23] See Illustration 13; Article 100.

[24] See *Newborne v. Sensolid (Great Britain) Ltd* [1954] 1 Q.B. 45, Illustration 6 to Article 109, *Black v. Smallwood* (1966) 117 C.L.R. 52, 61–62 (Illustration 7 to Article 109); above, para. 1–022; below, para. 9–080.

Illustrations

(1)   An agent entered into a written agreement to grant a lease of **9–036**
certain premises. He was described in the agreement as making it on
behalf of the principal, but in a subsequent portion of the document it
was provided that he (the agent) would execute the lease. Held, that the
agent was liable for a breach of the agreement, though the premises
belonged to the principal.[25]

(2)   The directors of a company signed a contract in the following
terms: "We, the undersigned, three of the directors, agree to repay £500
advanced by A to the company," and at the same time assigned to A, as
security, certain property belonging to the company. Held, that the
directors were personally liable.[26] But when an agent signed a contract
in the following form: "I undertake, on behalf of A (the principal), to
pay, etc." it was held that he was not personally liable.[27]

(3)   A broker sent a contract note in the following terms: "Messrs.
S.—I have this day sold by your order and for your account to my
principal, etc., one per cent. brokerage"; (signed) "W A B". Held, that
W A B was not personally liable in an action for goods sold.[28]

(4)   A solicitor wrote: "I hereby undertake to pay on behalf of these
creditors [his clients] two-thirds" of certain expenses. Held, that he was
personally liable.[29] So, the solicitor of the assignees of a bankrupt
tenant was held personally liable on an undertaking as follows: "I, as
solicitor to the assignees, undertake to pay the landlord his rent,
provided it do not exceed the value of the effects distrained."[30]

(5)   A charterparty was expressed to be made between A B and
C D, agent for E F & Son, and was signed by C D, without
qualification. Held, that C D was personally liable, though the principals
were named, there being nothing in the terms of the contract clearly
inconsistent with an intention to contract personally.[31]

---

[25] *Norton v. Herron* (1825) 1 C. & P. 648; *Tanner v. Christian* (1855) 4 E. & B. 591; *cf.*
Spittle v. Lavender (1821) 5 Moo.C.P. 270.
[26] *McCollin v. Gilpin* (1881) 6 Q.B.D. 516. See also *H.O. Brandt & Co. v. H.N. Morris
& Co.* [1917] 2 K.B. 784.
[27] *Downman v. Williams* (1845) 7 Q.B. 103; *Glover v. Langford* (1892) 8 T.L.R. 628;
W.T. Avery Ltd v. Charlesworth (1914) 31 T.L.R. 52.
[28] *Southwell v. Bowditch* (1876) 1 C.P.D. 374.
[29] *Hall v. Ashurst* (1833) 1 C. & M. 714; *Lavan v. Walsh* [1964] I.R. 87 ("sale to the
writer in trust for a client"). See also *Weidner v. Hoggett* (1876) 1 C.P.D. 533. *Cf.*
Allaway v. Duncan (1867) 16 L.T. 264.
[30] *Burrell v. Jones* (1819) 3 B. & A. 47; *Harper v. Williams* (1843) 4 Q.B. 219; *cf. Lewis
v. Nicholson* (1852) 18 Q.B. 503.
[31] *Parker v. Winlow* (1857) 7 E. & B. 942. See also *Cooke v. Wilson* (1856) 1 C.B.(N.S.)
153; *Hick v. Tweedy* (1890) 63 L.T. 765. *Cf.* Illustration 11.

(6) A charterparty states that it is entered into between "A, owners," and "B, charterers." A clause in it provides "This vessel was chartered on behalf of C." B is liable as charterer. [32]

(7) Repairs are arranged for a vessel by telex and a document is signed headed "Agreement between 'Cape Hatteras' and 'Astican' " (the repairers). The contract is with the owners of the *Cape Hatteras*, whoever they may be. [33]

(8) Ship's agents write to two firms "As Managing Operators for the charterers we are again pleased to appoint you as agents for the vessel's forthcoming call"; "On behalf of our principals we are again pleased to appoint you as agent for the above-mentioned vessel." The first letter is signed by them "C Shipping Ltd", the second "C Shipping Ltd as agents." They are not personally liable on either contract. [34]

(9) A tender is accepted in these words: "We have pleasure in informing you that your tender dated 19th July 1974 has been accepted ... Yours faithfully, BS, Chartered Civil Engineer." The signer is personally liable. [35]

(10) Fruit brokers in Liverpool signed in their own names without qualification a contract in the following form: "We have this day sold to you on account of J M & Co., Valencia, etc." Held, the brokers were not personally liable, the word "on account" clearly showing that there was no intention to contract personally. [36]

(11) A charterparty is signed "for A B, of L, C Bros., as agents." C Bros. are not liable, unless it clearly appears from the body of the contract that they intended to bind themselves. [37] So, where a contract

---

[32] *Tudor Marine Ltd v. Tradax Export S.A. (The Virgo)* [1976] 2 Lloyd's Rep. 135. See also *Pyxis Special Shipping Co. Ltd v. Dritas & Kaglis Bros. Ltd (The Scaplake)* [1978] 2 Lloyd's Rep. 380 (noted [1979] J.B.L. 150); *Jugoslavenska Linijska Plovidba v. Hulsman (The Primorje)* [1980] 2 Lloyd's Rep. 74; *Et. Biret et Cie S.A. v. Yukiteru Kaiun KK (The Sun Happiness)* [1984] 1 Lloyd's Rep. 381.

[33] *Astilleros Canarios S.A. v. Cape Hatteras Shipping Co. Inc. (The Cape Hatteras)* [1982] 1 Lloyd's Rep. 518; *Armour v. Duff & Co.* 1912 S.C. 120. Importance may be attached to the fact that if the contract is with the owner, it will often be possible to arrest a ship. *cf. Dawson (Ship Stores) v. Atlantica Co. Ltd* (1931) 40 Ll.Rep. 63 (contract with agent); *The Swan* [1968] 1 Lloyd's Rep. 5, Illustration 6 to Article 100 (contract with both: *ante* above, para. 9–006, n. 31). As to oral contracts see Article 103, Illustration 3.

[34] *Chartwell Shipping Ltd v. Q.N.S. Paper Co. Ltd* [1989] 2 S.C.R. 683, (1989) 62 D.L.R. (4th) 36.

[35] *Sika Contracts Ltd v. B.S. Gill* (1978) 9 Build. L.R. 11. See also *Fraser v. Equitorial Shipping Co. Ltd (The Ijaola)* [1979] 1 Lloyd's Rep. 103.

[36] *Gadd v. Houghton* (1876) 1 Ex.D. 357; disapproving *Paice v. Walker* (1870) L.R. 5 Ex. 173 (but see *Hough & Co. v. Manzanos & Co.* (1874) 4 Ex.D. 104); *Ogden v. Hall* (1879) 40 L.T. 751; *Mercer v. Wright, Graham & Co.* (1917) 33 T.L.R. 343, *Lester v. Balfour Williamson & Co.* [1953] 2 Q.B. 168; *cf. H.O. Brandt & Co. v. H.N. Morris & Co.* [1917] 2 K.B. 784.

[37] *Deslandes v. Gregory* (1860) 30 L.J.Q.B. 36; *Green v. Kopke* (1856) 18 C.B. 549; *Miller, Gibb & Co. v. Smith & Tyrer* [1917] 2 K.B. 141.

was signed "G W, J L, for C J M & Co.," it was held that G W and J L were not personally liable.[38]

(12) A charterparty was signed "For and on behalf of James McKelvie and Co. as agents, J.A. McKelvie," but James McKelvie & Co. were described in the body of the agreement as charterers. Held, that James McKelvie & Co. were not personally liable, the qualified signature indicating an intention to exclude personal liability.[39]

(13) An agent signed a contract—"p p A, J A & Co., A B." The contract contained a clause providing that A B should guarantee moneys due from his principal to the other contracting party. Parol evidence was admitted to show that A B intended to sign, not only as an agent, but also as a surety. Held, that such evidence was rightly admitted, and that he must be taken to have signed in both capacities.[40]

(14) An insurance policy is issued to "PN Bank, a/c E (Commodities) Ltd." The contract is with the bank.[41]

(15) A contract is signed "The Plumbing Centre, BT, Director." "The Plumbing Centre" is in fact the trade name of BP Ltd., whose name appears (inaccurately) at the foot of the page. The contract is with BP Ltd. under its trade name and BT is not liable on it.[42]

Article 102

ADMISSIBILITY OF EXTRINSIC EVIDENCE

(1) Where it is clear from the terms of a written contract made by an agent that he contracted personally, extrinsic evidence is not admissible to show that, notwithstanding the terms of the contract, it was the intention of the parties that he should not be personally liable on it, because such evidence would be contradictory to the written contract.[43]   **9–037**

---

[38] *Redpath v. Wigg* (1866) L.R. 1 Ex. 335; *Mahony v. Kekulé* (1854) 14 C.B. 390.

[39] *Universal S.N. Co. v. McKelvie* [1923] A.C. 492; overruling *Lennard v. Robinson* (1855) 5 E. & B. 125. See also *Kimber Coal Co. v. Stone & Rolfe Ltd* [1926] A.C. 414; *Dragages et Travaux Publics v. Gladhover Ltd* [1988] 1 H.K.L.R. 298 ("between G for and on behalf of N and the contractors").

[40] *Young v. Schuler* (1883) 11 Q.B.D. 651; *Ontario Marble Co. Ltd v. Creative Memorials Ltd* (1963) 39 D.L.R. (2d) 149; affd. (1964) 45 D.L.R. (2d) 244; *VSH Ltd v. BKS Air Transport Ltd* [1964] 1 Lloyd's Rep. 460; *Sun Alliance Pensions Life & Investments Services Ltd v. Webster* [1991] 2 Lloyd's Rep. 410; *Elpis Maritime Co. Ltd v. Marti Chartering Co. Inc. (The Maria D)* [1992] 1 A.C. 21.

[41] *Punjab National Bank v. de Boinville* [1992] 1 W.L.R. 1138.

[42] *Badgerhill Properties Ltd v. Cottrell* [1991] B.C.L.C. 805. See also *Vic Spence Associates v. Balchin* 1990 S.L.T. 10.

[43] *Higgins v. Senior* (1841) 8 M. & W. 834, Illustration 1; *Magee v. Atkinson* (1837) 2 M. & W. 440; *Sobell Industries v. Cory Bros.* [1955] 2 Lloyd's Rep. 82, Illustration 7 to Article 100; *Sika Contracts Ltd v. B.S. Gill* (1978) 9 Build. L.R. 11, Illustration 9 to Article 101; *Transcontinental Underwriting Agency S.R.L. v. General Union Insurance Co. Ltd* [1987] 2 Lloyd's Rep. 409; *Restatement*, § 323. But see Comment.

(2) But where it appears from the terms of a written contract made by an agent that he contracted as agent, extrinsic evidence is nevertheless admissible to show that, by custom or usage in the particular trade or business, an agent so contracting is liable either absolutely or conditionally in addition to the principal[44], provided that such custom or usage is not inconsistent with nor repugnant to the express terms of the written contract.[45]

Comment

9–038   **Rule (1).** It is sometimes said that parol or other extrinsic evidence may not be admitted to add to, vary or contradict a deed or written contract.[46] Such evidence may therefore not be adduced to delete an apparent contracting party (though it may be adduced to *add* a party, *e.g.* to establish the liability of the principal as well as the agent[47]). But this reasoning is only appropriate where the contract is exclusively contained in a document or documents: there may be documents (*e.g.* invoices) which do not purport to constitute the complete contract, and in such cases extrinsic evidence will certainly be admissible.[48]

Further, where a written document can be established not to represent the intention of the parties as clearly agreed, it can be rectified in equity: and there are a few cases holding that the fact that it would be rectified could be pleaded as a defence to a common law action.[49] This can apparently be pleaded even by a plaintiff,[50] and a party can plead that he is not liable, even though it is not established who, if anyone, is liable, provided it is clear that the true intention of

---

[44] Illustrations 2 to 4.

[45] Illustrations 5, 6. And see Article 31.

[46] *Jacobs v. Batavia & General Plantations Trust Ltd* [1924] 1 Ch. 287, 295 (an extreme formulation). See McLauchlan, *The Parol Evidence Rule* (Wellington, N.Z. 1976); Law Com. No. 154 (1986) for full discussion of this often misunderstood topic.

[47] *Higgins v. Senior*, n. 43 above, at p. 844. See further Comment to Article 73. As to cases where the principal is undisclosed, see Comment to Article 78.

[48] *Rogers v. Hadley* (1861) 2 H. & C. 227; *Holding v. Elliott* (1860) 5 H. & N. 117.

[49] *Wake v. Harrop* (1862) 1 H. & C. 202; affirming 6 H. & N. 768; *Cowie v. Witt* (1874) 23 W.R. 76. And see *Breslauer v. Barwick* (1876) 36 L.T. 52; *Mostyn v. West Mostyn Coal & Iron Co.* (1876) 1 C.P.D. 145; Supreme Court Act 1981, s. 49; *Restatement*, § 323. The possibility of a collateral contract to the same effect is discussed in a note on *Farncombe v. Sperling* (1922) 66 S.J. 312: it is possible that breach of a collateral contract might bar an action on the main contract (see *Benjamin's Sale of Goods* (4th ed.), para. 10–014). *Wake v. Harrop* was applied at first instance in Australia in *Alliance Acceptance Co. Ltd v. Oakley* (1987) 45 S.A.S.R. 148; but on appeal the decision was reversed on grounds which made *Wake v. Harrop* irrelevant: (1988) 48 S.A.S.R. 337.

[50] *Breslauer v. Barwick*, n. 49 above.

the parties was that the person concerned should not be. Thus where an agent made a charterparty and signed it "for X Co. A, agents" on the express undertaking that he was acting only as agent and that the use of this formula was the correct way of expressing this, he was held to have a good defence to an action on the charterparty.[51] Even if these cases are correct, situations where such clear evidence is available will be rare. It is not clear to what extent the defence is subject to the normal rules relating to the availability of rectification (*e.g.* that a third party must not be prejudiced), and, of course, the extent to which equity will relieve against mistakes of law as opposed to fact is in general by no means clear.[52] On general principles, any operative mistake would have to be common to the parties, or there would have to be some unconscionable conduct on the part of the person not mistaken.[53]

Rule (2). Where the agent signs a contract as agent only, he is prima facie not liable. However, the rules referred to above do not prevent evidence being adduced to establish who the principal is (though if the case is one regulated by the Statute of Frauds, the principal's identity must be clear from the memorandum[54]); or to establish that, notwithstanding the fact that the agent signed as agent, it was intended that he should in fact additionally be liable to some extent not inconsistent with the primary liability of the principal (in which case the agent's signature would satisfy the Statute of Frauds[55]). The cases in this area suggest that the agent may fairly readily be held liable together with, as opposed to instead of, his principal: usages that hold the agent liable have always been common[56] and may be increasing.[57]   **9–039**

Illustrations

(1) An iron commission agent receives an order to purchase iron from a named company but sends in return a sold note saying "We have this day sold ... to Messrs H & Sons ... " and signs it "JB & Co., WS" Although JB & Co. are "notoriously an agent" they are in this instance personally liable.[58]   **9–040**

---

[51] *Wake v. Harrop*, n. 49 above.

[52] See Kerr, *Fraud and Mistake* (7th ed.), pp. 133 *et seq.*

[53] As to ratification in general, see Snell, *Equity* (29th ed.), pp. 626 *et seq.*

[54] See *Lovesy v. Palmer* [1916] 2 Ch. 233; above, paras. 8–003, 8–004.

[55] See *Dale v. Humfrey* (1858) E.B. & E. 1004.

[56] See Illustrations; Marine Insurance Act 1906, ss. 53, 54. As to proof of custom or usage, see Article 31. Sometime the agent's liability ceases on naming a principal.

[57] See Comment to Article 100.

[58] *Higgins v. Senior* (1841) 8 M. & W. 834.

(2) An agent signed a charterparty expressly "as agent to merchants", the principals being unnamed. It was held that, although it plainly appeared that he did not intend to contract as principal, it might nevertheless be proved that, by a general custom, an agent so signing was, in the ordinary course of trade, personally liable on the contract in the event of his not identifying the principals within a reasonable time. Such a custom was not inconsistent with the terms of the contract as the primary liability was that of the unnamed principals.[59]

(3) A broker entered into a contract in the following terms: "Sold by A to Messrs. B, for and on account of owner, 100 bales of hops." An action was brought against A for not delivering the hops according to sample. Evidence of a custom in the hop trade, whereby a broker who does not identify his principal at the time of the contract is personally liable, was admitted, and the broker was held liable on the contract.[60]

(4) A and B, who were brokers, contracted in the following terms: "We have this day sold for your account to our principal, etc." (signed) "A and B, brokers." Some of the goods were accepted by the principal, whose name was declared by A and B before delivery, and an action was subsequently brought against A and B for not accepting the residue. Held, that they were personally liable, it being proved that by a custom in the particular trade, the broker was personally liable for his principal's default unless the name of the principal was inserted in the written contract.[61] So, by the usage of the London dry goods market, where a broker bought goods for an unnamed principal, he was personally liable for the price.[62]

(5) Brokers entered, as such, into a contract which contained a clause providing that they should act as arbitrators in the event of any dispute between the parties. Held, that evidence of a custom rendering them personally liable on the contract was inadmissible, because the custom was inconsistent with the clause appointing them arbitrators.[63]

(6) Agents sign a contract in a clearly representative capacity. It is argued that since their principals are foreign, they are personally liable.

---

[59] *Hutchinson v. Tatham* (1873) L.R. 8 C.P. 482 (collateral contract).
[60] *Pike v. Ongley* (1887) 18 Q.B.D. 708; *Dale v. Humfrey* (1858) E.B. & E. 1004 (similar custom in fruit trade); *Thornton v. Fehr* (1935) 51 Ll.Rep. 330 (tallow trade); *Anglo Overseas Transport Ltd v. Titan Industrial Corp.* [1959] 2 Lloyd's Rep. 152 (forwarding agents); *Perishables Transport Co. v. Spyropoulos* [1964] 2 Lloyd's Rep. 379 (air forwarding agents); *cf. Wilson v. Avec Audio-Visual Equipment Ltd* [1974] 1 Lloyd's Rep. 81 (no such usage for insurance broker).
[61] *Fleet v. Murton* (1871) L.R. 7 Q.B. 126 (fruit trade and colonial market). Similar custom in the rice trade: *Bacmeister v. Fenton Levy & Co.* (1883) Cab. & El. 121.
[62] *Imperial Bank v. London & St. Katharine Docks Co.* (1877) 5 Ch.D. 195 (agent held a surety).
[63] *Barrow & Bros. v. Dyster, Nalder & Co.* (1884) 13 Q.B.D. 635.

Even if such a custom exists, it would here be inconsistent with the contract.[64]

Article 103

ORAL CONTRACTS

Where an agent makes a contract which is not reduced to writing, the question whether he contracted personally, together with his principal or solely in his capacity as an agent is a question of fact.[65]   **9–041**

Comment

The proposition contained in this Article means nowadays little more   **9–042** than that general rules or presumptions cannot be laid down for such cases, whereas precedents can be cited on the interpretation of documents.[66] An appellate tribunal may also be more reluctant to interfere with findings of fact as to oral contracts[67]; and in many cases an appeal only lies on point of law.

Unnamed principals. One area in which the rule might be thought to exist is that of unnamed principals. The *Restatement*[68] suggests a rule that when the principal is unnamed the agent is prima facie liable together with him. In *The Santa Carina* (Illustration 2), however, the Court of Appeal refused to accept such a rule and said that the question was entirely one of fact; and that for the agent's liability there would have to be some indication, whether from trade custom[69] or special facts,[70] which did not exist in that case. This means that the presumption is that the agent is not liable unless there are indications to displace it.[71] It has already been suggested, however,[72] that the close connection of such cases with undisclosed principal cases, where the

---

[64] *Miller, Gibb & Co. v. Smith & Tyrer Ltd* [1917] 2 K.B. 141. As to the alleged custom, see para. 9–018 above.

[65] See Illustrations; *Castle v. Duke* (1832) 5 C. & P. 359; *Gurney v. Womersley* (1854) 4 E. & B. 133; *Lakeman v. Mountstephen* (1874) L.R. 7 H.L. 17; *Blake v. Melrose* [1950] N.Z.L.R. 781.

[66] *The Swan* [1968] 1 Lloyd's Rep. 5, 12.

[67] *e.g. Gardiner v. Heading* [1928] 2 K.B. 284.

[68] § 321; see above, para. 9–014.

[69] See Article 102.

[70] *e.g.* that the principal is foreign: see *Fraser v. Equitorial Shipping Co. Ltd (The Ijaola)* [1979] 1 Lloyd's Rep. 103; above, para. 9–018.

[71] See also *Wilson v. Avec Audio-Visual Equipment Ltd* [1974] 1 Lloyd's Rep. 81, 83.

[72] Above, para. 9–014.

agent *is* liable and entitled, mean that there is a good case for a prima facie rule as in the *Restatement*.

Illustrations

9–043   (1)   Brokers sell goods by auction and invoice them in their own names as sellers. It is a question of fact whether the invoice was intended to be the contract. If it was, the brokers are personally liable. If not, it is a question of fact whether they intended to contract personally. [73]
(2)   Stores are supplied to, or repairs effected on, a ship on the oral orders of the ship's agent. In appropriate cases the agent may be held to have assumed personal liability. [74]
(3)   Brokers on the Baltic Exchange order bunkers from other brokers, also members of the Baltic, for a ship at Penang. The order is given on the telephone without indication of the capacity in which either party is acting. The bunkers are not paid for. The first broker does not expect the second broker to effect the bunkering himself: the second broker knows that the first broker does not own ships. The first broker is not personally liable. [75]

Article 104

DEEDS

9–044   Where an agent is a party to a deed and executes it in his own name, he is personally liable and entitled on it, even when he is

---

[73] *Holding v. Elliott* (1860) 5 H. & N. 117.

[74] See *Fraser-Johnston Engineering, etc., Co. v. Sam Isaacs (Aberdeen) Ltd* (1922) 12 Ll.Rep. 233; *Beliard, Crighton (Belgium) Ltd v. Charles Lowe & Partners Ltd* (1922) 13 Ll.Rep. 567; *Evans & Reid Coal Co. Ltd v. McNabb, Rougier & Co. (Italy) Ltd* (1924) 18 Ll.Rep. 471; *J.D. McLaren & Co. v. Nomikos* [1961] 1 Lloyd's Rep. 318; *Freimuller (Ship Stores) v. Ocean Carriers (London) Ltd* [1961] 2 Lloyd's Rep. 309; *Victory Shipchandlers v. Leslie & Anderson Ltd* [1972] E. Africa L.Rep. 42. Sometimes the agent is made liable by statute: see New Zealand Sea Carriage of Goods Act 1940, s. 11(1) (ship's agents). See also *Lamont v. Hamilton* 1907 S.C. 628 (insurance); *H.J. Lyons & Sando Ltd v. Houlson* [1963] S.A.S.R. 29 (car repairs). *cf. Whitwell v. Perrin* (1858) 4 C.B.(N.S.) 412; *Eastman v. Harry* (1875) 33 L.T. 800. As to written contracts see Article 101, Illustration 7. The liability of a local agent may be an advantage: on the other hand where the contract is with the shipowner there may be a right to arrest a ship. *cf.* Article 100, Illustration 6; Article 101, Illustration 7.

[75] *N. & J. Vlassopulos Ltd v. Ney Shipping Ltd (The Santa Carina)* [1977] 1 Lloyd's Rep. 478. See also *Marina Shipping Ltd v. Laughton* [1982] Q.B. 1127; *A/S Hansen-Tangens Rederi III v. Total Transport Corp. (The Sagona)* [1984] 1 Lloyd's Rep. 194, 198–199. (shipping agent arranging port facilities acts for charterer); *Shipping Co. Uniform Inc. v. Intl. Transport Workers' Fedn. (The Uniform Star)* [1985] 1 Lloyd's Rep. 173.

described in the deed as acting for and on behalf of a named principal.[76]

Comment

This rule, which is an application of the strict rules relating to deeds,   **9-045** applies even though he executes it specifically on behalf of the principal: *a fortiori* if he executes it personally, merely adding descriptive words. To escape liability the agent must purport to execute the deed *as* the principal's deed.[77] However, by virtue of section 7(1) of the Powers of Attorney Act 1971[78] an agent with a power of attorney may execute a deed with his own signature and seal, and it may be that he is exempt from liability if he does so, at least so long as he indicates that he signs in a representative capacity. If so, the rules for deeds are now in these circumstances the same as for other written contracts. The matter is discussed elsewhere.[79]

Illustrations

(1) A, on behalf of B, contracted by deed to purchase certain   **9-046** houses, and covenanted that he (a) would pay £800 for them. The houses were destroyed. Held, that A was personally liable to pay the £800, although he had no effects in his hands belonging to B.[80] If A covenants under his own hand and seal for the act of B, A is personally liable, though he describes himself as covenanting for and on behalf of B.[81]

(2) A person signs a deed "signed as agent for and on behalf of CIC." CIC is a French company, but its corporate title is not given. The signer is personally liable.[82]

(3) A mortgagee by deed contracted for a tenancy of the mortgaged property, the contract being expressed to be made between the mortgagee "as agent, hereinafter called the landlord," and the tenant. Held, that it was a question of construction who was the lessor, and on the true construction the contract was that of the mortgagee, and that

---

[76] See Illustrations; *Plant Engineers (Sales) Ltd v. Davies* 113 S.J. 484 (liquidator); Article 79.

[77] See Article 79.

[78] Replacing Law of Property Act 1925, s. 123.

[79] Article 79.

[80] *Cass v. Rudele* (1692) 2 Vern. 280.

[81] *Appleton v. Binks* (1804) 5 East 148; *Bacon v. Dubarry* (1697) 1 Ld.Raym. 246.

[82] *Bailey v. de Kerangat*, C.A., December 7, 1993 (but the case was actually decided on general agency principles).

the mere use of the words "as agent" was not sufficient to prevent the demise operating on the legal estate of the mortgagee. [83]

Article 105

BILLS, NOTES AND CHEQUES

9–047
(1) An agent is not personally liable on a bill of exchange, promissory note or cheque unless his name appears on it. [84]

(2) Where a person signs a bill as drawer, indorser or acceptor, and adds words to his signature indicating that he signs for or on behalf of a principal, or in a representative character, he is not personally liable on it; but the mere addition to his signature of words describing him as an agent, or as filling a representative character, does not exempt him from personal liability. [85]

(3) But no person can be liable as acceptor of a bill except the person on whom it is drawn, except where it is accepted for honour. [86]

(4) In determining whether the signature on a bill is that of the principal or that of the agent by whose hand it is written, the construction most favourable to the validity of the instrument will be adopted. [87]

Comment

9–048
Rule (1). These rules are to be justified on the ground that negotiable instruments are likely to come into the hands of persons who have no knowledge of the circumstances in which they were issued; such persons must be able to rely on what appears on the fact of the instrument.

9–049
Rule (2). In this case the Bills of Exchange Act 1882 provides when the agent contracts personally and when for his principal. In cases of drawing or indorsement the question is usually merely whether principal or agent is liable, and the problem therefore is as to whether additional words are merely descriptive or indicate that the agent signs solely in a

---

[83] *Chapman v. Smith* [1907] 2 Ch. 97.
[84] Bills of Exchange Act 1882, ss. 23, 89. See *e.g. Maxform S.p.A. v. Mariani and Goodville* [1981] 2 Lloyd's Rep. 54. But see also Companies Act 1985, s. 349(4), below.
[85] *ibid.* s. 26(2). See *Rolfe Lubbell & Co. v. Keith* [1979] 1 All E.R. 80.
[86] See *ibid.*, s. 17(1). As to acceptance for honour, see ss. 65–68.
[87] *ibid.* s. 26(2).

representative capacity for another, *viz.* "says plainly 'I am the mere scribe.' "[88] If the agent signs solely in such a capacity and has authority, his principal is bound: if he has no authority, his principal is not bound, and the agent is liable for breach of warranty of authority.

Rule (3) raises difficulties. Where a bill is drawn on an agent but accepted by him in the principal's name and with his authority, the principal nevertheless cannot be bound[89]; but since the agent has not purported to act for himself, it seems that he cannot be bound either.[90] Where the bill is drawn on the principal and accepted by the agent in his own name without qualification, equally the agent cannot be liable.[91]

    9–050

Rule (4). Where however in acceptance cases such as those above it is not clear how the signature should be regarded, the presumption in favour of validity may assist in construing it as the signature of the drawee. The presumption only operates in cases of ambiguity,[92] and it is difficult to see that it can have much relevance in cases of drawing or indorsement, where the question is simply as to whether principal or agent is liable, for in both cases the signature will normally (*i.e.* in the absence or incapacity of one of the parties or the like) be operative.[93]

    9–051

Trade, firm and company names. Where an agent signs in a trade or assumed name, he is liable as if he had signed his own name[94]; and the signature of a firm is equivalent to the signature by the person so signing of the names of all the persons liable as partners in that firm.[95] Whether the director or other officer of a company who signs on behalf of the company is personally liable depends on ordinary principles of construction.[96] But by section 349(4) of the Companies Act 1985, if an officer of a company or a person on its behalf signs or authorises to be signed on behalf of the company any bill of exchange, promissory note, endorsement, cheque or order for money or goods in which the name of

    9–052

---

[88] *Leadbitter v. Farrow* (1816) 5 M. & S. 345, 349. For full citation of the main cases on signatures, see Byles, *Bills of Exchange* (26th ed.); Chalmers and Guest, *Bills of Exchange* (14th ed.).

[89] Bills of Exchange Act 1882, s. 17(1); *Polhill v. Walter* (1832) 3 B. & Ad. 114; *Steele v. M'Kinlay* (1880) 5 App.Cas. 754.

[90] Bills of Exchange Act 1882, s. 26(1).

[91] *ibid.* s. 17(1).

[92] See *Britannia Electric Lamp Works Ltd v. D. Mandler & Co. Ltd* [1939] 2 K.B. 129.

[93] But see *Elliott v. Bax-Ironside* [1925] 2 K.B. 301, Illustration 4, for an example where the presumption was invoked in such a case.

[94] Bills of Exchange Act 1882, s. 23(1).

[95] *ibid.* s. 23(2). See *Ringham v. Hackett* [1980] C.L.Y. § 158.

[96] See *Ferguson v. Wilson* (1866) L.R. 2 Ch.App. 77.

the company is not mentioned in legible characters, he is liable to a fine and is personally liable on it unless payment is made by the company.[97] This provision therefore constitutes an exception to the proposition contained in Rule (1).

Illustrations

9–053   (1)   An agent draws a bill in his own name. He is personally liable as drawer, even to a holder who knows that he is merely an agent, unless words are added to the signature, indicating that he signs merely as an agent.[98]

(2)   A shipmaster draws a bill on his owners in payment for necessaries, the bill concluding with the words "value received in 300 tons coal and disbursements ... supplied to my vessel to enable her to complete her voyage ... for which I hold my vessel, owners and freight responsible." The master is personally liable as drawer, there being nothing in the concluding words excluding such liability.[99]

(3)   An agent draws a bill in the name of his principal. The agent is not liable on the bill as drawer.[1]

(4)   A bill directed to a company was accepted in the following form: "Accepted ... —A B and C D, directors—F F E Ltd." This was the acceptance of the company. The drawer, however, required the bill to be indorsed by the company's directors. Accordingly, A B and C D signed on the back of the bill, "F F E Ltd, A B and C D, directors." Held, A B and C D were personally liable on the indorsement, because unless the indorsement was read as the personal indorsement of the directors, it added nothing to the validity of the bill.[2]

(5)   Directors have been held personally liable on promissory notes in the following forms:

---

[97] See *Dermatine Co. v. Ashworth* (1905) 21 T.L.R. 510; *Stacey v. Wallis* (1912) 106 L.T. 544; *Scottish and Newcastle Breweries Ltd v. Blair* 1967 S.L.T. 72; *Durham Fancy Goods Ltd v. Michael Jackson (Fancy Goods) Ltd* [1968] 2 Q.B. 839; *British Airways Board v. Parish* [1979] 2 Lloyd's Rep. 361; *Maxform S.p.A. v. Mariani and Goodville* [1981] 2 Lloyd's Rep. 54; *Lindholst & Co. A/S v. Fowler* [1988] B.C.L.C. 166; *Blum v. OCP Repartition S.A., ibid.,* 170; *Oshkosh B'Ghosh Inc. v. Dan Marbel Inc. Ltd* [1989] B.C.L.C. 507; *Rafsanjan Pistachio Producers Co-operative v. Reiss* [1990] B.C.L.C. 352. See also *Badgerhill Properties Ltd v. Cottrell* [1991] B.C.L.C. 805, Illustration 15 to Article 101.
[98] *Leadbitter v. Farrow* (1816) 5 M. & S. 345; *Sowerby v. Butcher* (1834) 4 Tyr. 320.
[99] *The Elmville* [1904] P. 319.
[1] *Wilson v. Barthrop* (1837) 2 M. & W. 863.
[2] *Elliott v. Bax-Ironside* [1925] 2 K.B. 301, applying Bills of Exchange Act 1882, s. 26(2). See also *Rolfe, Lubell & Co. v. Keith* [1979] 1 All E.R. 860, where parol evidence was admitted to displace the operation of s. 26(1) in case of ambiguity. *cf. Kettle v. Dunster and Wakefield* (1927) 43 T.L.R. 770.

   (a)   "We, directors of A B Company Limited, do promise to pay J D, etc."; sealed and signed by four directors without qualification.[3]

   (b)   "We, directors of A B Company, for ourselves and other shareholders of the company, jointly and severally promise to pay, etc., on account of the company"; signed without qualification.[4]

   (c)   "We promise to pay ... C D, Director, E F, Secretary, the F E Ltd."[5]

   (d)   "We, being members of the executive committee, on behalf of X Co-operative Society, do jointly promise to pay ... "[6]

(6) The secretary of a company signed a note in the following form: "I promise to pay, etc." (signed) "For M T and W Railway Company, J S, secretary." Held, that he was not personally liable.[7]

(7) A note was signed "The J S Laundry Ltd, J S, Managing Director." J S was not personally liable: the company would have been.[8]

Article 106

Merger and Election: Release of Agent

The liability of an agent on any contract made by him on behalf of   **9–054** his principal is discharged by the obtaining of judgment against the principal, and may perhaps be discharged where the third party elects to pursue his rights against the principal, in accordance with the principles stated in Article 84.

Comment

The relevant authorities mainly concern the release of the principal by   **9–055** the obtaining of judgment against, or electing to look to the agent, and are collected under Article 84. But the considerations applicable where the agent seeks to be discharged are obviously the same; thus, subject to the reservations there expressed, the obtaining of judgment against the

---

[3] *Dutton v. Marsh* (1871) L.R. 6 Q.B. 361; *Courtauld v. Saunders* (1867) 16 L.T. 562.

[4] *Penkivil v. Connell* (1850) 5 Exch. 381.

[5] *Brebner v. Henderson*, 1925 S.C. 643. See also *Landes v. Bradwell* (1909) 25 T.L.R. 478.

[6] *Gray v. Raper* (1861) L.R. 1 C.P. 694.

[7] *Alexander v. Sizer* (1869) L.R. 4 Ex. 102.

[8] *Chapman v. Smethurst* [1909] 1 K.B. 927; see also *Britannia Electric Lamp Works Ltd v. D. Mandler & Co. Ltd* [1939] 2 K.B. 129; *Bondina Ltd v. Rollaway Shower Blinds Ltd* [1986] 1 W.L.R. 517.

principal releases the agent,[9] and a clear manifestation of an intention to hold the principal liable would perhaps have the same effect.[10] But where there are separate causes of action, the rule would not apply,[11] for it is based on there being two inconsistent rights.[12] And, of course, where the principal is not liable at all, the agent cannot be released by any attempt to make the principal liable.

Illustration

9–056   Travel agents supply and credit A with tickets, which he buys in his own name. Subsequently they are informed by B Ltd that A was B Ltd's agent in the transaction. They write to both demanding payment, and threatening proceedings, and subsequently issue a writ against B Ltd. Hearing that B Ltd is going into liquidation, they discontinue these proceedings and sue A. A is liable, there having been no election on these facts.[13]

Article 107

WARRANTY OF AUTHORITY

9–057   (1)   Where a person, by words or conduct, represents that he has authority to act on behalf of another, and a third party is induced by such representation to act in a manner in which he would not have acted if that representation had not been made, the first-mentioned person is deemed to warrant that the representation is true, and is liable for any loss caused to such third party by a breach of that implied warranty, even if he acted in good faith, under a mistaken belief that he had such authority.[14]

(2)   Every person who purports to act as an agent is deemed by his conduct to represent that he is in fact duly authorised so to act,[15] except where the nature and extent of his authority, or the material facts from which its nature and extent may be

---

[9] *L.G.O.C. v. Pope* (1922) 38 T.L.R. 270.
[10] *Clarkson Booker Ltd v. Andjel* [1964] 2 Q.B. 775, Illustration.
[11] See for the nature of the possible causes of action, Comment to Article 100.
[12] See Comment to Article 84.
[13] *Clarkson Booker Ltd v. Andjel* [1964] 2 Q.B. 775; *cf. Beigtheil & Young v. Stewart* (1900) 16 T.L.R. 177. See also *Format International Security Printers Ltd v. Mosden* [1975] 1 Lloyd's Rep. 37.
[14] *Collen v. Wright* (1857) 7 E. & B. 301; affd. (1857) 8 E. & B. 647; *Yonge v. Toynbee* [1910] 1 K.B. 215; and see Comment; *Restatement*, § 329. But see below as to powers of attorney.
[15] *Collen v. Wright*, n. 14 above.

inferred, are fully known to the other contracting party,[16] or the purported agent expressly disclaims any present authority.[17]

Comment

Historical background. Early nineteenth-century cases found great **9–058** difficulty in identifying a basis of liability for the agent who acted without authority, and there was at one time a tendency to hold that the agent had contracted personally wherever it turned out that he had no authority.[18] This solution was not sustainable in principle,[19] except where the agent could genuinely be regarded as undertaking personal liability on the contract,[20] or conceivably where the agent was really acting for himself.[21] An agent who fraudulently professed authority would always be liable in deceit,[22] but the basis of an innocent agent's liability was not settled till *Collen v. Wright*.[23] where it was decided by a majority that he was liable on a separate, implied warranty of authority.

Where the agent is entirely innocent, this action is the only one available: where he is fraudulent, the plaintiff can sue for deceit or breach of warranty of authority at his option. Where he is negligent, it might be thought that a similar choice obtains in those cases where the negligence gives rise to liability in tort.[24] But the Court of Appeal of New Zealand has recently ruled against the existence of a duty of care in such circumstances,[25] on the ground that the contractual remedy is adequate and that to permit a tort remedy would create a vicarious liability in a principal who had not authorised the agent. However, the non-liability of the principal in such a case could be secured by the

---

[16] Illustrations 8, 9; see also *Beattie v. Ebury* (1872) L.R. 7 Ch.App. 777, 810 (affd. L.R. 7 H.L. 102).

[17] *Halbot v. Lens* [1901] 1 Ch. 344, Illustration 10; *Restatement*, § 331.

[18] *Downman v. Williams* (1845) 7 Q.B. 103; *Thomas v. Hewes* (1834) 2 C. & M. 519, 530n. See also the cases on contracts made on behalf of companies in the course of formation, below, para. 9–079; Radcliffe (1902) 18 L.Q.R. 364; *Randell v. Trimen* (1856) 18 C.B. 786; the judgment of Cockburn C.J. in *Collen v. Wright* (1857) 8 E. & B. 647; discussion in *Black v. Smallwood* (1966) 117 C.L.R. 52.

[19] *Lewis v. Nicholson* (1852) 18 Q.B. 503; *Jenkins v. Hutchinson* (1849) 13 Q.B. 744. For a modern example of what could be taken as similar reasoning see *Savills v. Scott* [1988] 1 EGLR 20, as to which see also [1989] J.B.L. 62.

[20] See Articles 100, 109.

[21] See Article 110.

[22] *Randell v. Trimen*, n. 18 above; *Polhill v. Walter* (1832) 3 B. & Ad. 114; *West London Commercial Bank v. Kitson* (1884) 13 Q.B.D. 360. And he may commit the offence of obtaining a pecuniary advantage by deception: *R. v. Charles* [1977] A.C. 177.

[23] (1857) 7 E. & B. 301; affd. (1857) 8 E. & B. 647.

[24] On the basis of *Hedley Byrne & Co. Ltd v. Heller & Partners Ltd* [1964] A.C. 465: see below, n. 33.

[25] *Kavanagh v. Continental Shelf (No. 46) Ltd* [1993] 2 N.Z.L.R. 648.

principle of *Armagas Ltd v. Mundogas S.A. (The Ocean Frost),*[26] under which vicarious liability in torts of misrepresentation modifies to meet the contractual position.[27] Granted therefore the general coexistence of actions in contract and tort, it seems doubtful whether the complete denial of a duty of care is necessary or appropriate, bearing in mind that there are other advantages of tort actions.

9–059   **Nature of liability.** The nature of the liability arising under this rule has been much discussed.[28] There are dicta in many of the cases which to modern eyes leave it doubtful whether the cause of action is to be classified as contractual or tortious. But in the absence of fraud an action in tort did not seem appropriate at the time: indeed, the possibility of an action for negligent misstatement has only recently become apparent. The assumption in the later nineteenth century that all actions must be classifiable into one group or the other eventually led to these actions being regarded as contractual, and contractual rules being applied.[29] The contract is normally unilateral, *viz.,* the agent offers to warrant his authority in exchange for the third party entering into a contract with the principal or otherwise acting as requested; the offer is accepted by the third party acting accordingly.[30] The result of the cause of action being classified as contractual is the strict liability customarily placed on parties who make contractual promises: the agent is in effect a guarantor of his authority. There are also repercussions as regards the damages obtainable.[31] An action in tort would require proof of fraud or negligence, and in the latter case, the existence of a duty of care. Where there is clear fraud, it might occasionally be preferable to sue in deceit, to obtain the possibly more liberal assessment of damages which may be employed in connection with that tort.[32] But the uncertainties of an action in negligence[33] have hitherto meant that the contractual action will normally be preferable.

---

[26] [1986] A.C. 717: see above, para. 8–177.
[27] It is, however, arguable (it is submitted, wrongly) that the principal of *Armagas v. Mundogas* is limited to fraud.
[28] Radcliffe (1902) 18 L.Q.R. 364; Holdsworth (1924) 40 L.Q.R. 1 (suggesting that the liability is quasi-contractual); Seavey (1920) 29 Yale L.J. 859, 886 *et seq.*; *Edwards v. Porter* [1923] 2 K.B. 538, 545–546 (but *cf.* on appeal, [1925] A.C. 1, 23, 45).
[29] See *Dickson v. Reuter's Telegram Co. Ltd* (1877) 3 C.P.D. 1, 5; *The Piraeus* [1974] 2 Lloyd's Rep. 266 (action contractual for the purposes of R.S.C., Ord. 11, r. 1(f) (g)).
[30] *V/O Rasnoimport v. Guthrie & Co. Ltd* [1966] 1 Lloyd's Rep. 1, 13.
[31] See Article 108.
[32] *Doyle v. Olby (Ironmongers) Ltd* [1969] 2 Q.B. 158; *Archer v. Brown* [1985] Q.B. 401; *Gould v. Vaggelas* (1984) 157 C.L.R. 215.
[33] Liability in tort in cases of lack of authority was specifically rejected in *Heskell v. Continental Express Ltd* [1950] 1 All E.R. 1033, Illustration 5 to Article 108. That case was said to require reconsideration in *Hedley Byrne & Co. Ltd v. Heller & Partners Ltd* [1964] A.C. 465, 532. But see above, para. 9–058.

Strict liability. There was at one time a tendency to confine the   9–060
remedy, as if on a tort, to cases where the agent was negligent[34]: but
this, as stated above, does not square with the supposed contractual
nature of the liability, and in *Yonge v. Toynbee*[35] the Court of Appeal
decided that an agent whose authority had, unknown to him, been
determined by the mental incapacity of his principal was liable for the
plaintiff's costs. The proceedings were in fact an appeal from an order
that the solicitors should pay these costs, and it is difficult to see how a
contractual action could arise in such a situation. But the reasoning of
the court is plainly directed towards the proposition that liability for
breach of warranty of authority is strict. The reasoning applies equally
to termination of authority by the principal's death, or, in the case of a
company, dissolution.[36] Cases to the contrary must therefore be
regarded as wrong.[37] The court quoted the words of Willes J. in *Collen
v. Wright*[38]:

> "I am of opinion that a person, who induces another to contract with him as
> the agent of a third party by an unqualified assertion of his being authorised
> to act as such agent, is answerable to the person who so contracts for any
> damages which he may sustain by reason of the assertion of authority being
> untrue ... The fact that the professed agent honestly thinks that he has
> authority affects the moral character of his act; but his moral innocence, so far
> as the person whom he has induced to contract is concerned, in no way aids
> such person or alleviates the inconvenience and damage which he sustains.
> The obligation which arises in such a case is well expressed by saying that a
> person, professing to contract as agent for another, impliedly, if not expressly,
> undertakes to or promises the person who enters into such contract, upon the
> faith of the professed agent being duly authorised, that the authority which he
> professes to have does in point of fact exist."

This can be regarded as a harsh rule, but it is to some extent mitigated
by a certain flexibility in the selection of cases appropriate for the
implication of a warranty.[39]

---

[34] *Salton v. New Beeston Cycle Co.* [1900] 1 Ch. 43; following *Smout v. Ilbery* (1842) 10
M. & W. 1.

[35] [1910] 1 K.B. 215, Illustration 12. See also *Starkey v. Bank of England* [1903] A.C.
114, 119.

[36] See pp. 227–228; para. 10–027 below. This was the situation dealt with in *Salton v.
New Beeston Cycle Co.* [1900] 1 Ch. 43, the actual decision in which has not been
questioned; see also *Babury Ltd v. London Industrial Plc* (1989) 139 N.L.J. 1596. But the
agent has statutory protection in the case of a power of attorney: see Article 124.

[37] Though *Smout v. Ilbery*, n. 34 above, may perhaps be supported on the grounds that
on the facts there was no warranty: "the continuance of the life of the principal was ... a
fact equally within the knowledge of both contracting parties": at p. 11. See *Yonge v.
Toynbee*, n. 35 above, at pp. 227–228; *Randall v. Trimen* (1856) 18 C.B. 786, 793.

[38] (1857) 8 E. & B. 647, 657–658.

[39] See below.

9–061   **Warranty not confined to misrepresentation resulting in contract.** The implication of a warranty is not confined to cases where the transaction with the person representing himself as having authority results in a contract with the principal.[40] "The rule to be deduced is, that where a person by asserting that he has the authority of the principal induces another person to enter into any transaction which he would not have entered into but for that assertion, and the assertion turns out to be untrue, to the injury of the person to whom it is made, it must be taken that the person making it undertook that it was true, and he is liable personally for the damage that has occurred."[41] Thus the doctrine has been applied where directors purported to pay a creditor by the use of debentures which the company had no power to issue, and to the presentation of a forged transfer.[42] Nor is the rule confined to cases where the person sought to be held liable is the person who was thought to have authority: there may be liability for a representation that another person has authority.[43] And there may be liability to a person unknown to the defendant who relies on the warranty, *e.g.* the indorsee of a bill of exchange or bill of lading containing a false representation of authority, though this (like many of the other points made) is difficult to accommodate within the framework of implied contract.[44] But there are limits: the mere fact that a person misrepresents a fact relevant to a third party does not mean that he asserts that he has authority to do so.[45]

9–062   **What is warranted?** The basic warranty is only that the agent has authority from his principal: this is something peculiarly within the agent's knowledge. If the principal proves unreliable, that is something in respect of which the third party could have made inquiries. Merely as agent, therefore, the agent does not warrant that his principal is

---

[40] See Illustrations 3, 6; *Brown v. Law* (1895) 72 L.T. 779; *British Russian Gazette Ltd v. Associated Newspapers Ltd* [1933] 2 K.B. 616; *Heskell v. Continental Express Ltd* [1950] 1 All E.R. 1033, 1042, where an attempt to put a limit on the rule was rejected; *Restatement*, § 329, comment *i*.

[41] *Firbank's Exors. v. Humphreys* (1886) 18 Q.B.D. 54, 60, *per* Lord Esher M.R.

[42] See Illustrations 3, 6.

[43] Illustrations 1, 4 and 9 can be so explained.

[44] *V/O Rasnoimport v. Guthrie & Co. Ltd* [1966] 1 Lloyd's Rep. 1, Illustration 11; following wide dicta in textbooks (mostly to be justified by reference to the words used in *Starkey v. Bank of England* [1903] A.C. 114) and dicta of A.L. Smith J. at first instance in *West London Commercial Bank v. Kitson* (1883) 12 Q.B.D. 157, 161 (treated by the Court of Appeal as a case of fraud: (1884) 13 Q.B.D. 360). However, the result is probably correct, and is accepted by *Restatement*, § 324, comment *a*. See also *New Georgia National Bank v. Lippman*, 249 N.Y. 307, 164 N.E. 108 (1928); Reynolds (1967) 80 L.Q.R. 189.

[45] *Salvesen v. Rederi A/B Nordstjernan* [1905] A.C. 302; *Jones v. Still* [1965] N.Z.L.R. 1071.

solvent,[46] or will perform the contract (if any). The difficulty arises however when the cause of lack of authority is that the principal has never existed, no longer exists, or lacks capacity. In England the leading case is *Yonge v. Toynbee*,[47] where the agent was held liable when his principal had without his knowledge become incapable. As stated above, the reasoning is expressly extended to cases where the principal has died.[48] If the agent warrants that his principal still exists, *a fortiori* he may be held to warrant that his principal has at some time existed.[49] Hence problems of the liability of promoters of companies not yet formed could sometimes perhaps be solved by the implication of this warranty.[50] In many situations where the principal, whether supposedly human or corporate, is non-existent, however, there is some degree of knowledge on both sides, so that the warranty may be excluded,[51] and in some cases, *e.g.* unformed companies and unincorporated associations, the agent has in fact been held liable on the contract itself.[52]

Cases holding the agent liable where the contract would be *ultra vires* the corporate principal, and certain other cases such as that of the non-existent principal, may require to be analysed as an extension of the warranty of authority. For in some of them the agent is held liable though the act would, even if authorised by the supposed principal, be a nullity, with the result that there would be no loss caused by the lack of authority.[53] Though *Collen v. Wright*[54] is frequently cited in these cases, it may sometimes be necessary to say that what is warranted is that, *e.g.* there is a power to issue debentures, that the document presented is genuine, and so forth.[55]

---

[46] See Article 108.

[47] [1910] 1 K.B. 215, Illustration 12. See also *Scott v. J.B. Livingston & Nicol* 1990 S.L.T. 305.

[48] See p. 227; *cf. Schlieske v. Overseas Construction Co. Pty. Ltd* [1960] V.R. 195; *Babury Ltd v. London Industrial Plc.* (1989) 139 N.L.J. 1596 (corporate principal had been dissolved).

[49] See *Simmons v. Liberal Opinion Ltd* [1911] 1 K.B. 966; *Russian & English Bank v. Baring Bros. & Co. Ltd* [1935] Ch. 120; *Salter v. Cormie* (1993) 108 D.L.R. (4th) 372.

[50] Such an action was successful in *Delta Construction Co. Ltd v. Lidstone* (1979) 96 D.L.R. (3d) 457; but failed on the issue of damages. See Article 108; Article 109; *Brownett v. Newton* (1941) 64 C.L.R. 439 (company not entitled to commence business); *Black v. Smallwood* (1966) 117 C.L.R. 52, 64; *Fernée v. Gorlitz* [1915] 1 Ch. 177 (principal a minor); *cf. Newborne v. Sensolid (Great Britain) Ltd* [1954] 1 Q.B. 45, 47; *Hawke's Bay Milk Corp. Ltd v. Watson* [1974] 1 N.Z.L.R. 236. The argument was successful in *Lomax v. Dankel* (1981) 29 S.A.S.R. 68.

[51] See below, para. 9–064.

[52] Article 109.

[53] Article 108; *Heskell v. Continental Express Ltd* [1950] 1 All E.R. 1033; Radcliffe (1902) 18 L.Q.R. 364; *cf. British Russian Gazette v. Associated Newspapers Ltd* [1933] 2 K.B. 616, 649.

[54] (1857) 8 E. & B. 647.

[55] See Illustrations 2–5; *Sheffield Corp. v. Barclay* [1905] A.C. 392. But as to the presentation of bills of exchange see *Guaranty Trust Co. of New York v. Hannay & Co.*

—*cont. on next page*

A situation could arise where an agent is authorised to sell goods by one whom he believes to be, but is not, their owner. If he warrants that he has the owner's authority, he is liable if he has not such authority. If, however, he warrants only that he has the authority of a principal (even unnamed), he is not liable, because he has such authority, even though his principal is not the owner. The second interpretation seems clearly preferable: the buyer has bought from a non-owner and should have recourse accordingly. The warranty of authority is only to protect him if there is no principal against whom he can have recourse.[56]

9–063   **Mistake of law.** The warranty will not be implied where the representation is one of law.[57] There may however be great difficulty in distinguishing representations of fact from representations of law.[58] Thus a representation that a company has power to borrow may be one of law if on the true construction of its memorandum it has no such power: but if the power could have been conferred by resolution, the representation may be of fact, that such a resolution has been passed.[59] Again, there may be a representation of the fact that the borrowing limit has not been exceeded.[60] Though there is no clear authority, it seems on principle that a wilfully false statement of law would give rise to liability in deceit, provided the other requirements (*e.g.* that the statement is likely to be acted on) were satisfied.[61]

9–064   **Rebuttal of the warranty.** The circumstances in which the warranty is implied create the possibility of considerable flexibility, and the strictness of the liability placed on the agent is in effect tempered by this technique. Thus where the agent disclaims authority, he avoids such liability,[62] unless the case is one where he contracts to obtain

---

—cont. from previous page
[1918] 2 K.B. 623; *Greenwood v. Martins Bank Ltd* [1933] A.C. 51, 59–60; *cf. Yeung Kai Yung v. Hong Kong and Shanghai Banking Corp.* [1981] A.C. 787, Illustration 5 to Article 100.
[56] See two notes, (1985) 102 S.A.L.J. 596, 603. See also *Scott v. J.B. Livingston & Nicol* 1990 S.L.T. 305, 307.
[57] Illustration 5; *Beattie v. Ebury* (1872) L.R. 7 Ch.App. 777; affd. L.R. 7 H.L. 102; *Saffron Walden Second Benefit Building Society v. Rayner* (1880) 14 Ch.D. 406.
[58] See *Eaglesfield v. Londonderry* (1876) 4 Ch.D. 693, 703 (affd. (1876) 38 L.T. 303), Illustration 5.
[59] See *Beattie v. Ebury* (1872) L.R. 7 Ch.App. 777, 800–803.
[60] *Weeks v. Propert* (1873) L.R. 8 C.P. 427.
[61] See *Beattie v. Ebury*, n. 59 above; *Eaglesfield v. Londonderry*, n. 58 above; *Hirschfeld v. London, Brighton & South Coast Ry. Co.* (1876) 2 Q.B.D. 1; *West London Commercial Bank v. Kitson* (1884) 13 Q.B.D. 360 (but none of these are clear authorities); Winfield and Jolowicz, *Tort* (13th ed.), pp. 264–265.
[62] *Halbot v. Lens* [1901] 1 Ch. 344, Illustration 10; *Restatement*, § 331. In *McManus v. Fortescue* [1907] 2 K.B. 1 it was held that if the purchaser had notice that there might be a reserve the auctioneer who knocked down an item short of the reserve was not liable for breach of warranty of authority when he refused to sign a memorandum of the sale. *Sed quaere*: see Murdoch, *Law of Estate Agency and Auctions* (3rd ed.), p. 312.

authority.[63] If the third party does not think that authority can be obtained, this may be a ground for negativing the implication of a warranty, though the fact that A does not think that B can perform his contract with A does not usually affect B's liability.[64] In some cases the third party may be taken to know of the limitation or lack of authority, so that there are no grounds for implying a warranty by the agent.[65] There will not, however, usually be any duty on a third party to inquire.[66]

Apparent authority. Where the agent has no actual authority, but contracts in circumstances in which the principal would be bound under the doctrine of apparent authority, it seems that the agent should be prima facie liable, for he has no authority: the fact that the principal could be held liable, however, would mean that the third party could prove no loss. Even if the principal were insolvent, the agent would not be liable, for he is only liable for loss arising out of the fact that he has no authority.[67] However, there are dicta that in a case of apparent authority there is no breach of warranty at all.[68]   9–065

Ratification. It may be assumed that the agent is not liable where the principal ratifies: here again there is no loss to the third party, and it may be argued that there was no breach of warranty at all.[69]   9–066

---

[63] *Halbot v. Lens*, n. 62 above, at p. 351.

[64] Powell, pp. 256–257.

[65] Illustrations 8, 9; and see *Beattie v. Ebury*, n. 61 above; *Dillon v. Macdonald* (1902) 21 N.Z.L.R. 45 (third party ought to have assumed authority expired); *Cook v. Williams* (1897) 14 T.L.R. 31 (third party ought to have known estate agent had no authority to sell); *cf. Austin v. Real Estate Listing Exchange* (1912) 2 D.L.R. 324 (list of properties for sale guaranteed by issuers).

[66] See *V/O Rasnoimport v. Guthrie & Co. Ltd* [1966] 1 Lloyd's Rep. 1, esp. at p. 11: though there are dicta to the contrary concerning the public documents of companies. And see *Schlieske v. Overseas Construction Co. Pty. Ltd* [1960] V.R. 195 where it was held that solicitors should have realised that the defendant company might have been dissolved. *cf.*, however, *Leggo v. Brown & Dureau Ltd* (1923) 32 C.L.R. 95 (plaintiff need not affirmatively establish reliance).

[67] See Article 108. It is difficult to see why this point was not considered in *Yonge v. Toynbee* [1910] 1 K.B. 215 in view of *Drew v. Nunn* (1879) 4 Q.B.D. 661, in which it had been held that there was apparent authority in an agent whose principal had become incapable: see Article 123. *cf.* Powers of Attorney Act 1971, s. 5(1) and (2); see Article 124.

[68] See *Rainbow v. Howkins* [1904] 2 K.B. 322, 326. Some doubt was cast on this case in *McManus v. Fortescue* [1907] 2 K.B. 1, but as regards the apparent authority of an auctioneer to sell without reserve, and in the later case there was notice that there might be a reserve (but see above, n. 62). See also *V/O Rasnoimport v. Guthrie*, n. 66 above at p. 10; *Mitsui & Co. Ltd v. Marpro Industrial Ltd* [1974] 1 Lloyd's Rep. 386.

[69] Unless perhaps the principal initially refused to ratify, thereby causing expense to the third party.

9–067   **Powers of attorney.** There is statutory protection for the agent where he acts in pursuance of a power of attorney which has been revoked: this is set out in Article 124.

9–068   **Agents of the Crown.** It was held in *Dunn v. Macdonald*[70] that an agent of the Crown was not liable for breach of warranty of authority where he purported to engage an employee on behalf of the Crown for a fixed period of three years and the plaintiff was dismissed, in accordance with the powers of the Crown to dismiss, within this period. This case is usually taken as authority for a general exemption from liability for breach of warranty of authority on the part of such agents on grounds of public policy: the implication of a warranty is "utterly inconsistent with the facts."[71] Though the majority of the judges involved in the case[72] took this view, the case can be explained as one involving a mistake of law.[73] Further, it could be argued that the defendant had in fact authority to engage the plaintiff, that the contract was impliedly subject to the Crown's right of dismissal, and that all that was held was that the agent did not warrant that the right of dismissal would not be exercised[74]—not a matter of authority at all. However, though an agent of the Crown can no doubt expressly warrant his authority, it is very doubtful whether he should be regarded as impliedly doing so in the same circumstances as other agents. His non-liability may be explained as based on the other party's being presumed to know of this; but such a presumption is somewhat artificial, and public policy may provide the best explanation.

9–069   **Procedure.** Where the authority of the agent is disputed by the person on whose behalf the contract is made, the person who made the contract may be joined with him as co-defendant and relief claimed against them alternatively.[75]

---

[70] [1897] 1 Q.B. 401; *ibid.*, 555; followed in *The Prometheus* (1949) 82 Ll.Rep. 859. See also *Kenny v. Cosgrave* [1926] I.R. 517. See Street, *Governmental Liability* (1953), p. 93; Nettheim [1975] C.L.J. 253.

[71] *ibid.* at p. 558.

[72] Charles J. at first instance; Lopes and Chitty L.JJ. in the Court of Appeal.

[73] See arguments before Charles J.

[74] See the judgment of Lord Esher M.R.

[75] See R.S.C., Ord. 15, r. 4; *Honduras Inter-Oceanic Ry. Co. v. Lefevre & Tucker* (1877) 2 Ex.D. 301; *Massey v. Heynes* (1888) 21 Q.B.D. 330; *Bennetts v. McIlwraith* [1896] 2 Q.B. 464; *Sanderson v. Blyth Theatre Co.* [1903] 2 K.B. 533. In such a case the court would, in the exercise of its discretion, normally order the unsuccessful defendant to pay the successful defendant's costs by making either a "Bullock Order" or a "Sanderson Order": see *Supreme Court Practice*, 1995, para. 62/A4/119; *Sanderson v. Blyth Theatre Co.*, above.

Illustrations

(1)   The directors of a company wrote a letter to the company's   **9–070**
bankers representing that A had been appointed manager and had
authority to draw cheques on the company's account, which, to the
knowledge of the directors, was already overdrawn. A further overdrew
the account, the directors having, in fact, no authority to overdraw.
Held, that the directors were liable to the bankers for breach of an
implied warranty that they had authority to overdraw.[76] But the mere
fact that directors of a company in that capacity sign cheques drawn on
the company's bankers after the account is overdrawn does not amount
to a representation that they have authority to overdraw the account, or
to borrow money on the company's behalf.[77]

(2)   A lent £70 to a building society, and received a certificate of the
deposit, signed by two directors. The society had no borrowing powers.
Held, that the directors were personally liable to A on an implied
warranty that they had authority to borrow on behalf of the society.[78]

(3)   The directors of a company issued a certificate for debenture
stock, which A agreed to accept in lieu of cash due to him from the
company, all the debenture stock that the company had power to issue
having already been issued. Held, that the directors were liable to A on
an implied warranty that they had authority to issue valid debenture
stock, although they had acted in good faith, not knowing that all the
stock had been issued.[79] So, where directors of a company which had
already fully exercised its borrowing powers issued a debenture bond, it
was held that the directors thereby impliedly warranted that they had
authority to issue a valid debenture.[80]

(4)   The directors of an unincorporated society held out the secretary
as having authority to borrow in excess of the amount prescribed by the
rules of the society. The secretary borrowed in excess of such amount,
and misappropriated the money. Held, that the directors were
personally liable to the lenders on an implied warranty of authority,
though they had not acted fraudulently.[81]

(5)   The directors of a company having no borrowing powers induce
A to advance money on the security of a Lloyd's bond, which they in

---

[76] *Cherry v. M'Dougall v. Colonial Bank of Australasia* (1869) 38 L.J.P.C. 49.
[77] *Beattie v. Ebury* (1872) L.R. 7 Ch.App. 777; affd. L.R. 7 H.L. 102.
[78] *Richardson v. Williamson* (1871) L.R. 6 Q.B. 276.
[79] *Firbank's Exors. v. Humphreys* (1886) 18 Q.B.D. 54; criticised (1902) 18 L.Q.R. 364.
cf. Elkington & Co. v. Hürter [1892] 2 Ch. 452 and Illustration 5.
[80] *Weeks v. Propert* (1873) L.R. 8 C.P. 427; *Whitehaven Joint Stock Banking Co. v.
Reed* (1886) 2 T.L.R. 353. *cf.* Illustration 5.
[81] *Chapleo v. Brunswick Building Society* (1881) 6 Q.B.D. 696. *cf. Smith v. Reed* (1886)
2 T.L.R. 442.

good faith represent to be a valid security, A being aware that the company has no borrowing powers. The directors are not liable on an implied warranty of authority, though the bond is invalid, because its validity is a question of law.[82] So, where directors issued certain stock and described it as No. 1 Preference Stock, in the erroneous belief that they had power to issue stock to rank with the No. 1 Preference Stock already issued, and A purchased some of the new stock, knowing that it was new stock, but believing that it would rank with the No. 1 Preference, it was held that the directors were not liable to make good the misrepresentation, because it was a misrepresentation as to a matter of law, and A had not been deceived by any misrepresentation of fact.[83]

(6) A stockbroker, acting in good faith, induces the Bank of England to transfer consols to a purchaser under a forged power of attorney. He is liable, in an action for breach of warranty of authority, to indemnify the Bank against the claim of the stockholder for restitution.[84]

(7) A acts as broker for both buyer and seller. He impliedly warrants to each that he is duly authorised to act on behalf of the other.[85]

(8) A ship-broker signs a charterparty—"by telegraphic authority; as agent." It is proved that such a form of signature is commonly adopted to negative the implication of any further warranty by the agent than that he has received a telegram which, if correct, authorises such a charterparty as he is signing. The ship-broker is not answerable for a mistake in the telegram.[86]

(9) H, a ship-broker, professes to make a charterparty on behalf of A, and signs it—"by telegraphic authority of B, G H as agent." B is A's agent, but A did not authorise the charterparty. H is liable for breach of an implied warranty that he has authority to make the charterparty on behalf of A, though he acted in good faith, believing that the telegram from B gave him such authority.[87]

(10) A signs a composition agreement with B on behalf of X, both A and B being aware that X has refused to enter into such an agreement, and taking the risk that X would again refuse to be bound. A does not warrant that X will accept the agreement.[88]

---

[82] *Rashdall v. Ford* (1866) L.R. 2 Eq. 750.
[83] *Eaglesfield v. Londonderry* (1876) 38 L.T. 303; affirming (1874) 4 Ch.D. 693.
[84] *Starkey v. Bank of England* [1903] A.C. 114; affirming decision of C.A. *sub nom. Oliver v. Bank of England* [1902] 1 Ch. 610.
[85] *Hughes v. Graeme* (1864) 33 L.J.Q.B. 335. See above, paras. 2–013, 6–047, 6–060.
[86] *Lilly, Wilson & Co. v. Smales, Eeles & Co.* [1892] 1 Q.B. 456.
[87] *Suart v. Haigh* (1893) 9 T.L.R. 488.
[88] *Halbot v. Lens* [1901] 1 Ch. 344.

(11)   A loading broker signed a bill of lading covering goods some of which were never shipped. As regards the goods not shipped his principal, the shipowner, was as the law then stood not bound. The loading broker was liable for breach of warranty of authority.[89]

(12)   Solicitors enter an appearance in an action for a client who has without their knowledge become incapable. The action is struck out. They are liable for the plaintiff's costs as having warranted their authority to act.[90]

(13)   Where a solicitor, without authority, prosecutes or defends an action, the action will in general be dismissed or the defences struck out on the motion of either the plaintiff or the defendant, and the solicitor so acting without authority will be ordered to pay all the costs occasioned thereby.[91]

Article 108

MEASURE OF DAMAGES FOR BREACH OF WARRANTY OF AUTHORITY

(1)   The measure of damages for breach of warranty of authority is   **9–071**
the loss which the parties should reasonably have contemplated as liable to result from the breach of warranty.[92]

(2)   Where a contract is repudiated by the person on whose behalf it was made on the ground that it was made without his authority, such loss is prima facie the amount of damages that could have been recovered from him in an action if he had duly authorised and subsequently refused to perform the contract, together with the costs and expenses (if any) incurred

---

[89] *V/O Rasnoimport v. Guthrie & Co. Ltd* [1966] 1 Lloyd's Rep. 1; noted (1967) 83 L.Q.R. 189. *cf.* Article 108, Illustration 5. The principal could now be bound by virtue of Carriage of Goods by Sea Act 1992, s. 4.

[90] *Yonge v. Toynbee* [1910] 1 K.B. 215—actually a case on the summary jurisdiction in respect of solicitors: see Illustration 13. See above, para. 9–062; below, para. 10–027.

[91] This is a different way of raising the same issue: no formal action is required and hence expense is saved, but the considerations taken into account appear to be the same. See *Supreme Court Practice,* 1995, § 3874; *Hubbart v. Phillips* (1845) 13 M. & W. 702; *Reynolds v. Howell* (1873) L.R. 8 Q.B. 398; *Nurse v. Durnford* (1879) 13 Ch.D. 764; *Newbiggin-by-the-Sea Gas Co. v. Armstrong* (1879) 13 Ch.D. 310; *Re Savage* (1880) 15 Ch.D. 557; *Schjott v. Schjott* (1881) 45 L.T. 333; *Fricker v. Van Grutten* [1896] 2 Ch. 649; *Gold Reefs of Western Australia v. Dawson* [1897] 1 Ch. 115; *Geilinger v. Gibbs* [1897] 1 Ch. 479; *Yonge v. Toynbee* [1910] 1 K.B. 215; *Simmons v. Liberal Opinion Ltd, re Dunn* [1911] 1 K.B. 966; *Porter v. Fraser* (1912) 29 T.L.R. 91; *Fernée v. Gorlitz* [1915] 1 Ch. 177; *Russian & English Bank v. Baring Bros. & Co. Ltd* [1935] Ch. 120; *Brendon v. Spiro* [1938] 1 K.B. 176; *Babury Ltd v. London Industrial Plc* (1989) 139 N.L.J. 1596. See Cordery, *Solicitors* (8th ed.), pp. 113 *et seq.*

[92] See *C. Czarnikow Ltd v. Koufos (The Heron II)* [1969] 1 A.C. 350; Illustrations; *Restatement,* § 329, comments *i, j*; McGregor, *Damages* (15th ed.), Chap. 29.

in respect of any legal proceedings reasonably taken against him on the contract. [93]

Comment

9–072   **Contractual principle.** The cause of action for breach of warranty of authority being classified as contractual, the damages are those required to put the plaintiff in the position in which he would have been had the warranty been made good, *viz.* had the representation of authority been true. "The damages, under the general rule, are arrived at by considering the difference in the position [the plaintiff] would have been in had the representation been true and the position he is actually in in consequence of it being untrue." [94]

9–073   **Insolvent principal.** Thus it has often been stated that when the principal is insolvent only nominal damages may be given, for a successful action against him would have produced no money. [95] However, the fact that the principal is insolvent does not necessarily mean that there will be no damages, if the result of the transaction would, if the agent had had authority, have been to make the third party a preferred creditor of the principal. In *Firbank's Executors v. Humphreys* [96] the plaintiffs were induced by the directors of a company to accept debenture stock in lieu of payment for services rendered, but such stock was null because the amount which the company had power to borrow had been exceeded. Had the company been solvent, the loss recoverable from the directors would probably have been nothing, as the plaintiffs could have sued the company on the original debt: but as it

---

[93] See Comment and Illustrations. But *cf. Chitholie v. Nash & Co.* (1973) 229 EG 786 (measure of damages available in lieu of specific performance in an action against principal under Lord Cairns' Act not applicable to claim against agent: but see McGregor, *Damages* (15th ed.), pp. 762–763 and below, n. 20).

[94] *Firbank's Executors v. Humphreys* (1886) 18 Q.B.D. 54, 60 *per* Lord Esher M.R. But *cf. Doyle v. Olby (Ironmongers) Ltd* [1969] 2 Q.B. 158, 168, where Winn L.J. used this passage to distinguish liability for breach of warranty of authority from liability for breach of contract and to liken it to liability in deceit. This does not seem to be correct, though of course in actions in respect of statements the question of loss actually incurred often has more prominence that the expectation interest, *viz.* the profit that might have been made: see, *e.g. Kwei Tek Chao v. British Traders and Shippers Ltd* [1954] 2 Q.B. 459; *McRae v. Commonwealth Disposals Commission* (1951) 84 C.L.R. 377. *Salvesen v. Rederi A/B Nordstjernan* [1905] A.C. 302 seems contrary to Winn L.J.'s suggestion.

[95] *Simons v. Patchett* (1857) 7 E. & B. 568, 574; *Spedding v. Nevell* (1869) L.R. 4 C.P. 212, 226; *Goodwin v. Francis* (1870) L.R. 5 C.P. 295, 308; *Richardson v. Williamson* (1871) L.R. 6 Q.B. 276, 279–280; *Weeks v. Propert* (1873) L.R. 8 C.P. 427, 439; *Re National Coffee Palace Co., ex p. Panmure* (1883) 24 Ch.D. 367, 372; *Restatement*, § 329, comment *j*.

[96] (1886) 18 Q.B.D. 54, Illustration 3 to Article 107.

was insolvent, this right was valueless, so that the loss was the par value of the debentures, since valid stock of this type retained its value.[97]

Transaction unenforceable against principal. Where no redress could   9–074
be obtained from the principal even if the agent had been authorised, there is again no loss. Thus in *Heskell v. Continental Express Ltd*[98] (Illustration 5) even authorisation of the signature by the principal would not have created a contract with the principal, since no goods had ever been shipped. The same results should follow where the contract is unenforceable against the principal because the principal is a company not yet formed,[99] or for lack of writing under the Statute of Frauds. The latter point arose in *Fay v. Miller, Wilkins & Co.*[1] and the agent was held liable specifically because it could be held that there was a sufficient memorandum, the argument that if there had been no such memorandum no damage could be shown being apparently accepted. However, the absence of a memorandum could between the contracting parties be outweighed by an act or acts of part performance. Can these be pleaded against the agent, to show that the contract with the principal would have been enforceable? It was held in 1876 that this could not be pleaded because the notion of part performance is one that affects the equities between two parties to a suit for specific performance.[2] This is a narrow view; but in England the Statute of Frauds now only applies to guarantees, so the matter is not of importance.

Costs of legal proceedings. The costs of legal proceedings may also be   9–075
recovered, provided that they were reasonable[3] and the fact that they might be brought was within the contemplation of the parties.[4] These will usually be proceedings against the principal, but the costs of defending proceedings brought by an unauthorised agent may also be

---

[97] *cf. Weeks v. Propert*, n. 95 above; *Whitehaven Joint Stock Banking Co. v. Reed* (1886) 2 T.L.R. 353. In neither case was there a pre-existing debt.
[98] [1950] 1 All E.R. 1033.
[99] *Delta Construction Co. Ltd v. Lidstone* (1979) 96 D.L.R. (3d) 457. See above, para. 9–062; Article 109.
[1] [1941] Ch. 360. See also *Pow v. Davies* (1861) 1 B. & S. 220 (seven year lease without deed: defence of ejectment action held unreasonable). But *cf. British Russian Gazette Ltd v. Associated Newspapers Ltd* [1933] 2 K.B. 616, 649.
[2] *Warr v. Jones* (1876) 24 W.R. 695; but in land contracts the doctrine of part performance is no longer relevant in England by virtue of the Law of Property (Miscellaneous Provisions) Act 1989.
[3] See *Hughes v. Graeme* (1864) 33 L.J.Q.B. 355, Illustration 7; *cf. Godwin v. Francis* (1870) L.R. 5 C.P. 295, Illustration 9. See also *Hammond & Co. v. Bussey* (1887) 20 Q.B.D. 79.
[4] See *Spedding v. Nevell* (1869) L.R. 4 C.P. 212, Illustration 8.

recovered,[5] as may the cost of defending proceedings brought by the supposed principal.[6] Persisting with proceedings after it has become clear that the agent was unauthorised may not however be reasonable.[7] It is not clear whether such expenses can be recovered in those cases where the transaction is unenforceable against the principal. In the case of an insolvent principal, it is submitted that they might be, on the basis that a plaintiff in an action for breach of contract may abandon his claim for the expectation interest and claim his expenses only.[8] In the other two cases discussed above, those of the purported transaction that is a nullity and of the contract unenforceable for lack of writing, it is submitted that expenses will not often be regarded as reasonably incurred. An attempt under the same principles to obtain the full loss caused to the plaintiff in such situations would be met by the defence that the loss was too remote,[9] for otherwise the rules as to the contractual measure of damages would be circumvented.

9–076   **Other warranties.** These propositions concern the warranty of authority. If the agent is held liable on some *other* warranty, as is suggested in the comment to the previous Article,[10] the damages would require to be calculated by reference to that warranty.

Illustrations

9–077   (1) Directors of a building society represent that they have authority to borrow money on behalf of the society, and A is induced to lend £70. The society being solvent, the measure of damages for breach of warranty of authority is £70, with interest at the rate agreed upon.[11]

(2) A contracted, on behalf of B, to buy a ship. A was not authorised so to do, and B repudiated the contract. The seller having resold the ship at a lower price (which was the best price that, acting reasonably, he could get), it was held that the measure of damages

---

[5] *Yonge v. Toynbee* [1910] 1 K.B. 215, Illustration 12 to Article 107; *Fernée v. Gorlitz* [1915] 1 Ch. 177.
[6] *Pow v. Davis* (1861) 1 B. & S. 220; *Oliver v. Bank of England* [1901] 1 Ch. 562, affd. on different grounds *sub nom. Starkey v. Bank of England* [1903] A.C. 114.
[7] Illustration 9.
[8] See *Anglia Television Ltd v. Reed* [1972] 1 Q.B. 60; *Collen v. Wright* (1857) 7 E. & B. 301, affd. (1857) 8 E. & B. 647; *Pow v. Davis*, n. 6 above (seven year lease not under seal: cost of repairs allowed); *Lloyd v. Stanbury* [1971] 1 W.L.R. 535; McGregor, *Damages* (15th ed.), §§ 50–51, Chap. 29; *CCC Films (London) Ltd v. Impact Quadrant Films Ltd* [1985] Q.B. 616.
[9] *cf. Heskell v. Continental Express Ltd, above* (Illustration 5).
[10] Above, para. 9–062.
[11] *Richardson v. Williamson* (1871) L.R. 6 Q.B. 276.

recoverable against A was the difference between the contract price and the price at which the vessel was resold.[12]

(3) A instructed B to apply for shares in a certain company. B by mistake applied for shares in another company, and they were duly allotted to A. The last-mentioned company was ordered to be wound up, and A's name was removed from the list of contributories on the ground that he had not authorised the application for shares. Held, that, A being solvent and the shares unsaleable, the liquidator of the company was entitled to recover from B the full amount payable on the shares.[13]

(4) A brought an action against a company in the United States, and recovered judgment for £1,000. An agent of the company in good faith represented that he had authority to settle for £300, and A agreed to accept that sum. The agent was, in fact, not authorised to settle. Held, that, the judgment against the company being, in the circumstances, unenforceable, A was entitled to recover £300 from the agent for the breach of warranty of authority.[14]

(5) Under a contract to sell goods to a foreign buyer, A, the seller, had to procure shipment of the goods. He registered cargo space for the goods, but did not enter into a contract of carriage. He arranged for the dispatch of the goods to the ship, but they were not dispatched. A did not know this, and applied for a bill of lading. A bill of lading was negligently issued by B, the shipowners' broker, the goods never having been received. A later had to pay damages to the buyer for non-delivery. A claimed damages against B for breach of warranty of authority to issue the bill of lading. Held, that A could not have recovered against the shipowners even if the bill of lading had been issued with their authority, for only receipt of the goods on behalf of the shipowner would here have concluded a contract; as they had never been received, there was no contract of carriage and the bill was a nullity. A's rights upon the bill was therefore not affected by B's lack of authority, and he could recover nothing against B.[15]

---

[12] *Simons v. Patchett* (1857) 7 E. & B. 568.
[13] *Re National Coffee Palace Co., ex p. Panmure* (1883) 24 Ch.D. 367.
[14] *Meek v. Wendt* (1888) 21 Q.B.D. 126. It is suggested in McGregor, *Damages* (15th ed.), p. 764, n. 38 that he should have received the costs of negotiating the settlement. As to an unauthorised settlement, see further *British Russian Gazette Ltd v. Associated Newspapers Ltd* [1933] 2 K.B. 616.
[15] *Heskell v. Continental Express Ltd* [1950] 1 All E.R. 1033 (on which see Grunfeld (1950) 13 M.L.R. 516); said to require reconsideration as regards the decision on negligence in *Hedley Byrne & Co. Ltd v. Heller & Partners Ltd* [1964] A.C. 465, 532. *cf.* *V/O Rasnoimport v. Guthrie & Co. Ltd* [1966] 1 Lloyd's Rep. 1, Illustration 11 to Article 107, where there was a contract of carriage and the plaintiff recovered the value of the goods not delivered plus interest.

(6)   A bought goods, professedly on behalf of B. The seller brought
an action for the price against B, which was dismissed with costs, on the
ground that A was not authorised by B. Held, that the seller was
entitled to recover from A the price of the goods, and also the costs
incurred in the action against B. [16]

(7)   A professed to sell property on behalf of B. Held, that A, not
being authorised to sell, was liable to the purchaser for the taxed costs
of a suit for specific performance against B, as well as for the value of
the contract. [17]

(8)   Where an agent without authority granted a lease, and the lessee
agreed to sell his interest, it was held that damages and costs recovered
against the lessee for breach of such agreement to sell could not be
recovered by him in an action against the agent for breach of warranty
of authority; but that the lessee was entitled to recover the value of the
lease, and the costs of a suit for specific performance against the
principal. [18]

(9)   A contracted to sell an estate to B, and sent him an abstract of
title, representing that he had the authority of the owners to sell. The
owners repudiated the contract and sold the estate at a higher price to
C. B sued the owners, continued the action after they had sworn
answers to interrogatories that A had no authority, and was nonsuited.
In an action by B against A, it was held that the measure of damages
for the breach of warranty of authority was (a) the costs of investigating
the title; (b) the costs of the action up to the time when the answers to
the interrogatories had been received and considered by the plaintiff's
legal advisers; and (c) the difference between the contract and market
prices of the estate, the price at which it was resold to C being prima
facie evidence of the market price; but that the loss on a resale of
horses, which were bought to stock the land before the investigation of
the title and without notice to A, was too remote, it not appearing that
the purchase of stock was contemplated by the parties when the contract
was made. [19]

(10)   A solicitor falsely warrants that he has authority to sell land,
and the vendor refuses to complete. The land rises in value between the

---

[16] *Randall v. Trimen* (1856) 18 C.B. 786. See also *Farley Health Products v. Babylon Trading Co.* [1987] C.L.Y. § 1126 (damages included cost of manufacturing, packing and shipping goods not paid for).
[17] *Hughes v. Graeme* (1864) 33 L.J.Q.B. 335; *Collen v. Wright* (1857) 8 E. & B. 647.
[18] *Spedding v. Nevell* (1869) L.R. 4 C.P. 212.
[19] *Godwin v. Francis* (1870) L.R. 5 C.P. 295. See also *Schlieske v. Overseas Construction Co. Pty. Ltd* [1960] V.R. 195 (action continued after indications received that principal, a company, dissolved); *McDonnell v. McGuinness* [1939] I.R. 223 (principal unable to make title: damages against agent limited by rule (no longer applicable in England) in *Bain v. Fothergill* (1874) L.R. 7 H.L. 158).

date of completion and the date of the action against the solicitor. He is liable for the difference in value between the purchase price and the value of the property at the date of judgment.[20]

Article 109

Principal Fictitious or Non-Existent

(1) At common law, where a person purports to contract on behalf of a principal, and the principal is a fictitious or non-existent person, the person so purporting to contract may sometimes be regarded as having contracted personally.[21]   **9–078**

(2) By statute, where a contract purports to be made by a company, or by a person as agent for a company, at a time when the company has not been formed, then subject to any agreement to the contrary, the contract has effect as a contract made with the person purporting to act for the company or as agent for it, and he is personally liable on the contract accordingly.[22]

Comment

Rule (1). The situation referred to in this Article normally arises where a person purports to act for a company not yet formed, or for an unincorporated association, which has no legal existence, neither of which can be bound. Where the third party was aware of the position at the time of contracting, it may sometimes be appropriate to conclude that the transaction was intended to have legal effect[23] and hence that the agent contracted personally, *viz.* is liable, and also entitled to sue. The only alternative interpretation would be that the third party knowingly entered into a transaction of the "subject to contract" or "subject to ratification" type.[24] Where the third party is not aware of the true position there may be more difficulty in applying either of these   **9–079**

---

[20] *Suleman v. Shahsavari* [1988] 1 W.L.R. 1181, distinguishing and in part not following *Chitholie v. Nash & Co.* (1973) 229 EG 786, above, n. 93.

[21] See Comment; *Kelner v. Baxter* (1866) L.R. 2 C.P. 174, Illustration 1; *Black v. Smallwood* (1966) 117 C.L.R. 52, Illustration 7; *Marblestone Industries Ltd v. Fairchild* [1975] 1 N.Z.L.R. 529; Gross (1971) 87 L.Q.R. 367; (1972) 18 McGill L.J. 512; Shapira (1975) 3 Otago L.Rev. 309.

[22] Companies Act 1985, s. 36C(1) (inserted by Companies Act 1989, s. 130(4)); see Comment; Prentice (1973) 89 L.Q.R. 518, 530–533; Farrar and Powles (1973) 36 M.L.R. 270; Collier and Sealy [1973] C.L.J. 1; Griffiths [1993] L.S. 241; Gower, *Modern Company Law* (5th ed.), pp. 306 *et seq.*

[23] See *Kelner v. Baxter*, n. 21 above, at p. 85.

[24] But there cannot be ratification in either case. See Article 15.

interpretations,[25] and in any case the agent cannot be treated as contracting personally where he clearly contracts as agent only.[26] The cases on companies to be formed[27] and perhaps more lenient towards the third party than those on unincorporated associations.[28] But even in the case of companies there is no actual rule of law that a person purporting to contract for an unformed company is necessarily (as opposed to by interpretation) personally liable on the contract[29]; it is all a matter of interpretation, perhaps aided by a presumption,[30] of law in the case of a written contract, and of fact in the case of an oral contract.[31] Further, such presumption as there is only applies to a person who purports to act *for* the company: if he purports to act *as* the unformed company, his act is simply a nullity and he cannot be held personally liable on it.[32]

Where the third party was at the time of contracting unaware of the true position it would seem that since an interpretation making the agent a party to the contract is so much more difficult to justify, analytically his contractual liability should be for breach of warranty of authority.[33] This has been suggested in the High Court of Australia.[34] There is however a difficulty. Such an action would probably yield no

---

[25] See *Wickberg v. Shatsky* (1969) 4 D.L.R. (3d) 540; *Jones v. Hope* (1880) 3 T.L.R. 247n., Illustration 4; *Restatement*, § 326.

[26] *Hollman v. Pullin* (1884) C. & E. 254, Illustration 5.

[27] Illustrations 1, 2. But *cf. Re Banque du Marchands de Moscou* [1952] 1 All E.R. 1269 as to a company that had been dissolved.

[28] Illustrations 3, 4, 5. See Powell, pp. 263–265; Lloyd, *Law of Unincorporated Associations* (1938); Keeler (1971) 34 M.L.R. 615; Fletcher (1979) 11 U. Qd. L.J. 53 and material there cited.

[29] *Newborne v. Sensolid (Great Britain) Ltd* [1954] 1 Q.B. 45, 50; *Black v. Smallwood* (1966) 117 C.L.R. 52; *Stott Land Development Corp. v. Dean* [1967] W.A.R. 86. For cases where there was no liability, see *e.g. Dairy Supplies Ltd v. Fuchs* (1959) 18 D.L.R. (2d) 408; *Hawke's Bay Milk Corp. Ltd v. Watson* [1974] 1 N.Z.L.R. 236; *Lomax v. Dankel* (1981) 29 S.A.S.R. 68.

[30] See *Marblestone Industries Ltd v. Fairchild* [1975] 1 N.Z.L.R. 529, 539–540; *Vickery v. Woods* (1952) 85 C.L.R. 336. But presumptions are perhaps out of fashion nowadays, and the tendency is to rely on interpretation only. See Oliver L.J. in *Phonogram Ltd v. Lane* [1982] Q.B. 938, 945–946.

[31] *Summergreene v. Parker* (1950) 80 C.L.R. 304, 323–324. See above.

[32] *Newborne v. Sensolid (Great Britain) Ltd* n. 29 above (Illustration 6); *Black v. Smallwood*, n. 29 above (Illustration 7); *Miller Associates (Australia) Pty Ltd v. Bennington Pty Ltd* (1975) 7 A.L.R. 144; *Western Radio Group Ltd v. McIsaac* (1989) 63 D.L.R. (4th) 433. See Fridman (1966) 116 New L.J. 1605; Baxt (1967) 30 M.L.R. 328. But a company can only act through agents, and *Newborne v. Sensolid* is open to criticism as turning on a technicality: see Gray (1953) 17 Conv. 217–219; Shapira (1975) 3 Otago L.Rev. 309; the judgment of Windeyer J. in *Black v. Smallwood*; and *cf. Elliott v. Bax-Ironside* [1925] 2 K.B. 301.

[33] *cf.* the situation where the agent is his own principal: see Article 110.

[34] *Black v. Smallwood* (1966) 117 C.L.R. 52, 64–65, *per* Windeyer J. See also *Scott v. J.B. Livingston & Nichol* 1990 S.L.T. 305, 307 (above, para. 9–062).

more than the cost of any abortive proceedings brought against the principal, because since the company has no existence and so no funds it would not be possible affirmatively to prove further loss arising from the lack of authority[35]: any effective liability would then require to be in deceit, or possibly in negligence.[36] In the case of a signature not on behalf of the company but *as* the company, to authenticate the company's signature, there is the further difficulty that the signer arguably does not profess agency. It may however be possible in either case to imply some sort of warranty that there is or is still an extent company as described, on the analogy of the cases in which directors were held liable in respect of transactions which even if authorised would have been *ultra vires* their companies.[37] This depends on the scope of the agent's warranty, which is discussed elsewhere.[38] But in the leading case of *Kelner v. Baxter*[39] Willes J. did not suggest using the reasoning he had employed nine years earlier in *Collen v. Wright*,[40] the leading case on warranty of authority.

Should it transpire that the agent is in fact his own principal, he might perhaps be held liable under the anomalous rule stated in the next Article. But it would be necessary to prove that he was his own principal: the conclusion would not follow from the mere fact that the supposed principal was not liable.[41]

Rule (2) reproduces section 36C(1) of the Companies Act 1985,[42] the intention of which is to give effect to the first EEC directive on company law. The purport of this directive is that any person who enters into a transaction on behalf of a company not yet formed[43] shall be personally liable on it unless the company on formation assumes the

9–080

---

[35] See Article 107. This argument was accepted in *Delta Construction Co. Ltd v. Lidstone* (1979) 96 D.L.R. (3d) 457; see also *Wickberg v. Shatsky* (1969) 4 D.L.R. (3d) 540; *General Motors Acceptance Corp. of Canada Ltd v. Weisman* (1979) 96 D.L.R. (3d) 159. It succeeded in *Lomax v. Dankel* (1981) 29 S.A.S.R. 68.

[36] See Article 115.

[37] See Article 107, Illustrations 2, 3, 4, 5; *Black v. Smallwood*, n. 34 above, at pp. 64–65; Palmer (1975) 9 U.Qd.L.J. 123. But *cf. Newborne v. Sensolid (Great Britain) Ltd.*, n. 29 above, at p. 47; *Hawke's Bay Milk Corp. Ltd v. Watson* [1974] 1 N.Z.L.R. 236.

[38] See para. 9–062 above.

[39] (1866) L.R. 2 C.P. 174, Illustration 1.

[40] (1857) 8 E. & B. 647; see Article 107.

[41] *Newborne v. Sensolid (Great Britain) Ltd* [1954] 1 Q.B. 45, Illustration 6.

[42] Inserted by Companies Act 1989, s. 130(4) and replacing s. 9(2) of the European Communities Act 1972. See Gower, *Modern Company Law* (5th ed.), pp. 306–310.

[43] The relevant EEC Directive refers to a company "en formation", *i.e.* already in the process of formation, which would by English law be liable and entitled in any case. In *Phonogram Ltd v. Lane* [1982] Q.B. 938, Illustration 8, the Court of Appeal noted the different wording of the then English statute and followed it.

obligation, or there is "a clear exclusion of personal liability."[44] It is now clear that the section imposes liability regardless of whether at common law the agent might have been held to sign as agent for the company or as authenticating the company's own signature.[45] Beyond this it has been restrictively interpreted. It does not apply when a contract is made on behalf of a company which exists but is in the process of changing its name[46]; nor when the company existed but has been dissolved[47]; and it applies only to companies formed and registered under the Companies Act 1985.[48] But although the statutory provision refers specifically only to liability of the agent, the remainder of the wording is consistent with the interpretation that the agent is also entitled to sue. Statutory provisions drafted to meet this problem in other common law jurisdictions are often more clearly formulated.[49]

Illustrations

9–081   (1)   A enters into a written contract on behalf of a company not yet incorporated. A is personally liable on the contract, even if he expresses himself as contracting on behalf of the future company; and parol evidence is not admissible to show that he did not intend to contract personally, because it is only by holding him personally liable that any effect at all can be given to the contract.[50]

(2)   The promoters of a future company borrowed money from a bank, to be repaid out of calls on shares. Held, that the promoters must be taken to have contracted that the money would be repaid out of calls, if the calls should prove sufficient, and if not, to pay personally.[51]

(3)   The managing committee of a club authorise the steward to order provisions for the use of the club. A supplies provisions on his orders, and invoices them to the club. If A looked to the funds of the

---

[44] *Phonogram Ltd v. Lane*, n. 43 above, at p. 944.

[45] *Phonogram Ltd v. Lane*, n. 43 above.

[46] *Oshkosh B'Gosh Inc. v. Dan Marbel Inc. Ltd* [1989] B.C.L.C. 507; *Vic Spence Associates v. Balchin* 1990 S.L.T. 10. See also *Badgerhill Properties Ltd v. Cottrell* [1991] B.C.L.C. 805 (company not properly named).

[47] *Cotronic (UK) Ltd v. Dezonie* [1991] B.C.L.C. 721.

[48] *Rover International Ltd v. Cannon Film Sales Ltd* [1987] B.C.L.C. 540; decision varied on other grounds [1989] 1 W.L.R. 912.

[49] *e.g.* Singapore Companies Act (cap. 185), s. 35.

[50] *Kelner v. Baxter* (1866) L.R. 2 C.P. 174 (further facts, 36 L.J.C.P. 94); *Wilson & Co. v. Baker Lees & Co.* (1901) 17 T.L.R. 473; *Rita Joan Dairies Ltd v. Thompson* [1974] 1 N.Z.L.R. 285; *Marblestone Industries Ltd v. Fairchild* [1975] 1 N.Z.L.R. 529. But *cf. Black v. Smallwood* (1966) 117 C.L.R. 52, Illustration 7. A company cannot ratify a contract made on its behalf before its incorporation: see Article 15.

[51] *Scott v. Ebury* (1867) L.R. 2 C.P. 255; *Coutts & Co. v. Irish Exhibition in London* (1891) 7 T.L.R. 313; *Drew, Wood & Son v. Heath* (1899) 8 T.L.R. 111. *cf. Royal Albert Hall Corp. v. Winchilsea* (1891) 7 T.L.R. 362.

club alone for payment, and contracted on the terms that if there were no such funds he should not be paid, the committee are not personally liable. But they are personally liable if he gave credit to them. Whether A gave credit to the committee or looked to the funds of the club alone is a question of fact.[52]

(4)   A, a colonel of a volunteer corps, contracts on behalf of the corps with B. A does not intend to pledge nor does B intend to accept, his personal credit, but both think that the corps as an entity may be bound. The corps cannot be bound. A is not personally liable on the contract.[53]

(5)   H makes a contract with P and signs it "on behalf of the Tunbridge Wells Medical Association, H." The association is unregistered at the time of the contract. H cannot sue on the contract since he contracted as agent only.[54] Nor can he be sued upon it.[55]

(6)   N enters into a contract for the sale of goods to S and signs the contract: "LN (London) Ltd, LN" LN (London) Ltd was not incorporated at the date of the contract. LN cannot sue on this contract, since he made it neither as agent nor as principal.[56] Nor can he be sued on it.[57]

(7)   S and C enter into a contract for the sale of land. They sign the contract: "Western Suburbs Holdings Pty. Ltd S, C, Directors." The company was not incorporated at the date of the contract. They cannot be sued personally on the contract.[58]

(8)   A written letter of contract is signed by the recipient "Signed by BL for and on behalf of Fragile Management Ltd." The company is never formed and the contract never performed. BL is personally liable by virtue of s. 9(2) of the European Communities Act 1972.[59]

---

[52] *Steele v. Gourley* (1887) 3 T.L.R. 772; *Collingridge v. Gladstone* (1890) 7 T.L.R. 60; *Harper v. Granville-Smith* (1891) 7 T.L.R. 284; *Bradley Egg Farm Ltd v. Clifford* [1943] 2 All E.R. 378. See also *Carlton Cricket and Football Social Club v. Joseph* [1970] V.R. 487; *cf. Peckham v. Moore* [1975] 1 N.S.W.L.R. 353. The members of the committee do not normally act as agents for the members: *Flemyng v. Hector* (1836) 2 M. & W. 172; *Todd v. Emly* (1841) 8 M. & W. 505; *Wise v. Perpetual Trustee Co. Ltd* [1903] A.C. 139; *cf. Cockerell v. Aucompte* (1857) 2 C.B.(N.S.) 440; *Ideal Films Ltd v. Richards* [1927] 1 K.B. 374; *Campbell v. Thompson* [1953] 1 Q.B. 445. See in general Keeler (1971) 34 M.L.R. 615; Fletcher (1979) 11 U.Qd.L.J. 53; above, para. 8–045.
[53] *Jones v. Hope* (1880) 3 T.L.R. 247n; and as to clubs see *Overton v. Hewett* (1887) 3 T.L.R. 246; *cf. Cross v. Williams* (1862) 31 L.J.Ex. 145; *Samuel Bros. Ltd v. Whetherly* [1908] 1 K.B. 184; *Lascelles v. Rathbun* (1919) 35 T.L.R. 347.
[54] *Hollman v. Pullin* (1884) C. & E. 254, 257.
[55] Semble; but see the judgment in *Hollman v. Pullin*, n. 54 above, at p. 257.
[56] *Newborne v. Sensolid (Great Britain) Ltd* [1954] 1 Q.B. 45.
[57] *ibid.* at p. 47; Illustration 7. But see *Hollman v. Pullin*, n. 54 above, at p. 257.
[58] *Black v. Smallwood* (1966) 117 C.L.R. 52, discussed by Fridman (1966) 116 N.L.J. 1605; *Hawke's Bay Milk Corp. Ltd v. Watson* [1974] 1 N.Z.L.R. 236.
[59] *Phonogram Ltd v. Lane* [1982] Q.B. 938. See above, para. 9–080.

Article 110

Agent Shown to be the Real Principal

9–082   (1)   Where a person professes to contract as agent, whether in writing or orally, and it is shown that he is, in fact, himself the principal, and was acting on his own behalf, he is (perhaps) personally liable on the contract.[60]

(2)   Where a person who enters into a contract professedly as an agent is in fact the real principal, he may (perhaps) sue on the contract:

(a)   where the identity of the contracting party is not a material element in the making of the contract, provided that he gives notice to the other contracting party, before action, that he is the real principal;

(b)   where it has been partly performed or otherwise affirmed by the other contracting party with knowledge that he is the real principal.[61]

Comment

9–083   These propositions have appeared in all editions of this book and are probably generally accepted[62]: but they have slender authority in their support and are difficult to justify on principle.

9–084   **Rule (1). Liability.** The cases usually cited in support of the agent's liability date from a time when the courts were searching for a way of holding the unauthorised agent personally liable.[63] At one time it was

---

[60] See Comment.

[61] See Comment.

[62] See *Leigh and Sillivan Ltd v. Aliakmon Shipping Ltd (The Aliakmon)* [1983] 1 Lloyd's Rep. 203, 207 (where counsel accepted the agent's right to sue in such a case) (for further proceedings see [1986] A.C. 785); *Fraser v. Thames Television Ltd* [1984] Q.B. 44, 54–55 (where Hirst J. appears to accept it).

[63] They are *Railton v. Hodgson* (1804) 4 Taunt. 576n.; *Jenkins v. Hutchinson* (1849) 13 Q.B. 744; *Carr v. Jackson* (1852) 7 Exch. 382; *Adams v. Hall* (1877) 37 L.T. 70; and *Gardiner v. Heading* [1928] 2 K.B. 284. In *Railton v. Hodgson* there seems to have been no clear indication of agency, and it appears that the liability of the agent might have been together with that of the supposed principal, the example of a factor being cited. The relevance of *Jenkins v. Hutchinson* is confined to the words "unless it be shown that he was the real principal." *Carr v. Jackson* contains similar dicta, but concerns a foreign principal (see above, para. 9–018) and a cesser clause (below, para. 9–090). These dicta are perhaps the strongest: but they seem contrary to later dicta of Brett J. in *Hutchinson v. Tatham* (1873) L.R. 8 C.P. 482 (which were only partly withdrawn by him in *Pike v. Ongley* (1887) 18 Q.B.D. 708). In any case the agent was held not liable. *Adams v. Hall* seems to be a straightforward case of the personal liability of an agent. *Gardiner v. Heading* is a case where it was not clear that the agent did contract as agent, though the third party thought that he was doing so: it contains dicta discussed below.

thought that if he had no authority he was always to be regarded as having contracted personally[64]: but this was not supportable,[65] and later decisions made it clear that his liability, where it could not be regarded as being a second, parallel liability on the contract itself,[66] was on a collateral warranty of authority.[67] However, when it could be established that the agent was the real principal, the case was naturally a simpler one, and views were sometimes expressed that in such a case he was personally liable.[68] But such reasoning is difficult to justify.

Named principal. If the agent in fact acts for himself, but outwardly for a named principal from whom he has no authority, and that principal is not liable on the basis of apparent authority,[69] it seems that (unless the principal ratifies[70]) the agent's liability ought to be for breach of warranty of authority or in tort. If he has not undertaken personal liability on the contract and so cannot be liable under it, it is contrary to the principal of objective interpretation in contract to establish intentions unknown to the third party. The main possible justification of the agent's liability on the contract is that an undisclosed principal can be sued when discovered.[71] But the anomalies of the undisclosed principal rules could be cited as authority for many breaches of principle, and this situation comes under no established rule relating to the undisclosed principal, whose liability is additional to the agent's: the analogy can go no further than providing another case where facts initially unknown to the third party can be invoked in his aid.

In *Gardiner v. Heading*[72] a builder did work on the orders of H, the director of a company for which the builder had previously done work on H's order. The builder addressed estimates to the company and after completing the work was paid some of his charges by the company. He was then told that the work was not for the company but for other principals. He sued H. H was held liable as the person who ordered the work, on the facts found by the judge of first instance. Scrutton L.J. asked[73]: "If a man who contracts with another thinking he is a principal may, on finding he is in truth an agent, sue the real principal, why

9–085

---

[64] *Thomas v. Hewes* (1834) 2 Cr. & M. 519, 530n.; *Downman v. Williams* (1845) 7 Q.B. 103. And see discussion in *Black v. Smallwood* (1966) 117 C.L.R. 52.
[65] See *Lewis v. Nicholson* (1852) 18 Q.B. 503; *Jenkins v. Hutchinson*, n. 63 above; *Black v. Smallwood*, n. 64 above.
[66] See Comment to Article 100.
[67] *Collen v. Wright* (1857) 8 E. & B. 647; see Article 107.
[68] See cases cited at n. 63 above.
[69] Article 74.
[70] *Re Tiedemann and Ledermann Freres* [1899] 2 Q.B. 66, Illustration 4 to Article 15.
[71] *Gardiner v. Heading* [1928] 2 K.B. 284, 290. See Article 78.
[72] Above.
[73] At p. 290.

should not the reverse hold good also? Why should not a man who contracts with another, thinking he is an agent, sue him when he finds out that he is the real principal?" But the passage goes on to exclude where "the supposed agent ... has expressly contracted as agent so as to exclude his liability as a principal party to that contract" and the dicta seem wider than was necessary for the decision of the case, which may be regarded as a straightforward decision on the objective interpretation of the facts surrounding the formation of the contract.

The only other justification for the agent's liability seems to be his right to sue in such a situation, but this is equally disputable, as appears below.

From the third party's point of view there are of course advantages in the agent's personal liability on the contract. Where the purported principal is bankrupt, an action for breach of warranty of authority would produce limited damages, for the loss caused to the third party by the agent's lack of authority is small.[74] If the agent is really himself the principal, it seems unfair that he should be able to take advantage of such a fortuitous circumstance.[75] But it can be argued that the third party's reliance was on the financial standing of the supposed principal, not on that of the agent.[76] If the fact that the agent was acting for himself can be genuinely established, however, liability would normally lie in deceit, which would be immune from the limits of the action for breach of warranty of authority.

9–086   **Unnamed principal.** If the agent does not name a principal, there is a possibility that he will be held to have contracted personally. This is another situation where, as previously suggested,[77] a rule of prima facie liability of the agent in such situations would yield fair results. However that be, where there is a trade usage to that effect this may override his appearing to contract as agent only.[78] But where he clearly does contract as agent only, and has no principal, analytically his liability should again be on a collateral contract that he has a principal fitting the description (if any) given,[79] and the danger of his producing an insolvent person is met by the fact that he would have to prove that he was in fact acting as agent for such person—otherwise he would be presumed to have acted for a solvent principal. Analogies from the law as to undisclosed principal are again unconvincing.

---

[74] See Article 108.
[75] See *Railton v. Hodgson* (1804) 4 Taunt. 576n., where this situation arose: but see n. 63 above.
[76] *cf.* Mechem, *Outlines of Agency* (4th ed.), p. 221.
[77] See Article 100, esp. at para. 9–014.
[78] Article 102(2).
[79] *Restatement*, § 329, comment *e*.

The notion that an agent would be liable on the contract in such a case was however apparently accepted in *Hersom v. Bernett*,[80] where a defendant gave evidence that his principal was X: this was rejected as false and he himself was held liable. Roxburgh J. said[81] that "a fundamental principle of justice requires that a defendant who has given false evidence that his principal was X should not be heard to say ... that his principal may have been somebody else, but must thereafter be treated as having no principal; or, in other words, as being himself the principal." The latter two propositions are not, with respect, equivalent, and it is submitted that the first proposition is the one properly applicable. The judge however seems to have applied the second: although he was not willing to find as a fact that the defendant was himself the principal,[82] he held that he should be treated as such because of his conduct. If the liability of the agent on the contract is to be accepted, this can only be on the somewhat tenuous basis that it provides a quick route to a desired result.[83] But the mere fact that the agent's act does not bind his purported principal does not mean that he is to be regarded as acting for himself[84]: there must be evidence that he actually is doing so, or (as in *Hersom v. Bernett*[85]) other circumstances preventing him from denying this.

Rule (2). Right to sue. Whereas the liability on the contract itself of the agent who is his own principal is an advantage to the third party, the agent's right to sue in such a case is not so and is even more difficult to justify.   **9–087**

Named principal. Although there is a strong dictum by Lord Ellenborough that "Where a man assigns to himself the character of agent to another whom he names, I am not aware that the law will permit him to shift his situation, and to declare himself the principal, and the other to be a mere creature of straw,"[86] it was held in *Rayner v. Grote*[87] that a person who had purported to sell goods as agent for   **9–088**

---

[80] [1955] 1 Q.B. 98, following a dictum in *Owen v. Gooch* (1797) 2 Esp. 567, 568.
[81] At p. 103.
[82] At p. 100.
[83] "I am sure it is justice. It is probably the law for that reason": *Gardiner v. Heading* [1928] 2 K.B. 284, 290; "It is not worth while to be learned on very plain matters": *Layng v. Stewart*, 1 Watts & S. (Pa.) 222 (1841), quoted by Mechem, *Outlines of Agency* (4th ed.), p. 221.
[84] cf. *Newborne v. Sensolid (Great Britain) Ltd* [1954] 1 Q.B. 45, Illustration 6 to Article 109; *Black v. Smallwood* (1966) 117 C.L.R. 52, Illustration 7 to Article 109.
[85] n. 80 above.
[86] *Bickerton v. Burrell* (1816) 5 M. & S. 383, 386.
[87] (1846) 15 M. & W. 359, Illustration 2. See also *Fellowes v. Lord Gwydyr* (1829) 1 Russ. & M. 83.

such a principal but who was really himself the seller could sue for non-acceptance where the third party had become aware of the true position and nevertheless continued with the contract. On this basis it might be argued that such a person can do so in any case, if he gives notice that he is the principal,[88] and provided that the third party is not clearly prejudiced.[89] But in such a case the contract is with the named principal, an identified person different from the agent, the agent being by the wording of the contract excluded from being a party, and it is extremely difficult to see how the agent can then intervene and claim the benefit of such a contract. For although mistake is not relevant in the formation of contract where it is not material, it should not be difficult for the third party to show that he intended to contract with the named principal only.[90] He should not be left to establish prejudice, which, in view of the fact that the benefit of contracts is usually assignable, might not be easy. It is submitted therefore that the case itself should be explained on the basis of novation. The agent having disclosed his own interest in the transaction, the third party accepted him as seller. In other circumstances it is highly doubtful whether the principal could intervene: this is supported by a dictum of Alderson B. in the case,[91] which has since been cited with approval.[92]

" . . . In many such cases, such as, for instance, the case of contracts in which the skill or solvency of the person who is named as the principal may reasonably be considered as a material ingredient in the contract, it is clear that the agent cannot then shew himself to be the real principal, and sue in his own name; and perhaps it may be fairly urged that this, in all executory contracts, if wholly unperformed, or if partly performed without the knowledge of who is the real principal, may be the general rule."

9–089   **Unnamed principal.** It was decided in *Schmaltz v. Avery*[93] that an agent who signed a charterparty containing a cesser clause purportedly as agent for an unnamed principal could show that he was himself the principal and sue on the contract, on the grounds that it was not of moment to the third party who contracted on such terms to whom he was liable, and that the agent could say that he was his own principal. Such a right is in danger of being inconsistent with the terms of the contract, especially where the contract can be said to be embodied in a document.[94] It is therefore submitted that, even on the most favourable

---

[88] *Bickerton v. Burrell*, n. 86 above; *Fellowes v. Lord Gwydyr*, n. 87 above. But *cf. Rogers v. Hadley* (1861) 2 H. & C. 227.

[89] *Rayner v. Grote*, n. 87 above.

[90] *cf. Hardman v. Booth* (1863) 1 H. & C. 803.

[91] (1846) 15 M. & W. 359, 365.

[92] In *Gewa Chartering B.V. v. Remco Shipping Lines Ltd. (The Remco)* [1984] 2 Lloyd's Rep. 205, Illustration 3.

[93] (1851) 16 Q.B. 655, Illustration 1.

[94] See Article 102.

view of the situation, the true analysis is that the contract in such cases is with the unnamed principal,[95] and that the agent can only intervene if he fits such description (if any) as has been given of the supposed principal.[96] Further, if the third party can establish that, with whomsoever he was willing to contract, he was not willing to contract with the agent, he should equally be able to say that he had no agreement with the agent.[97] In *Harper & Co. v. Vigers Bros.*[98] the plaintiff was allowed to sue on a charterparty which he had signed "as agent for owner," though the third party gave evidence that he would not have made the contract had he known that the agent was acting on his own behalf. Although the plaintiff was refused costs, it is submitted that the case goes further than necessary in following *Schmaltz v. Avery.* In both cases it is arguable that the agent was excluded by the terms of the contract, at least unless a trade usage was proved whereby persons so contracting could nevertheless declare themselves their own principals.[99]

Supposed rule doubtful. *Schmaltz v. Avery* is a case arising in the **9–090** context of a particular form of the cesser clause, a very specialised charterparty provision on which there is much case law. The purpose of such a clause is that the charterer can substitute for himself shippers or consignees of cargo whose positions are regulated by bills of lading and against whom the shipowner can recover outstanding charges by the exercise of his lien.[1] A charterer who uses such a clause may well have no principals: he may hope to procure others to ship or receive goods on bill of lading terms. Indeed, modern forms of the clause make no reference to agency. If the charterer cannot achieve his object, he may ship himself and/or consign to himself[2] in the absence of indications that he would not be an acceptable shipper or receiver of the cargo on bill of lading terms (which is unlikely if he is acceptable as charterer). Even if the clause contains a reference to agency, it implies initial involvement of the charterer. In *Schmaltz v. Avery* itself the dispute arose because the cargo was not taken on board, so that the question of the charterer's

---

[95] See Glanville Williams (1945) 23 Can.B.R. at pp. 397 *et seq.*; *cf. Hardman v. Booth* (1863) 1 H. & C. 803.
[96] *cf. Restatement*, § 369, comment *b.*
[97] *cf. Sowler v. Potter* [1940] 1 K.B. 271 (but this case is often criticised: see *e.g.* Cheshire and Fifoot, *Law of Contract* (12th ed.), pp. 251–252); *Hill S.S. Co. Ltd v. Hugo Stinnes Ltd* 1941 S.C. 324, 337.
[98] [1909] 2 K.B. 549.
[99] See *Hill S.S. Co. Ltd v. Hugo Stinnes Ltd*, n. 97 above, at p. 333; *cf.* Article 102.
[1] See Scrutton, *Charterparties* (19th ed.), Article 90. The modern form there given at n. 67 makes no reference to agency. See also above, para. 9–025.
[2] See *Gullischen v. Stewart Bros.* (1884) 13 Q.B.D. 317; *Hill SS. Co. v. Hugo Stinnes Ltd* 1941 S.C. 324.

initial liability did not arise: but it was held that he could sue. The general reasoning of the case has been criticised in Scotland[3] as being obsolete in view of the restatement of the rules as to interpretation of written contracts by the House of Lords in *Universal Steam Navigation Co. v. McKelvie*,[4] and is difficult to reconcile with the principles of law established since that time. The right to sue of an agent purporting to act for a *disclosed* principal is even more difficult to justify. It is equally difficult to support the agent's liability in such cases: indeed in the context of the cesser clause that liability can be regarded as contrary to other authority.[5] Analogies to the case of the undisclosed principal are misleading, as in that case the third party thinks that he is dealing with the agent, and the effect of the doctrine is to add a further right and liability of a further person.[6] The whole of this Article should therefore be viewed with caution and even suspicion, and the cases approached on the basis that in many if not all of them different reasoning would be used today.[7] In view of the existing case law, however, it does not seem appropriate to omit these propositions at present.

Even if the third party cannot plead that he made no contract with the agent, he can presumably plead misrepresentation in appropriate cases[8]; and all authorities agree that the agent cannot intervene when such intervention would prejudice the third party,[9] *e.g.* where the third party could show that he relied on liability of both agent and principal, or where the agent's liability as principal is by the terms of the contract less onerous than his liability as agent.[10] But this is similar to the rule preventing the intervention of the undisclosed principal in some situations,[11] and it might well be more difficult for the third party to establish such prejudice than merely to plead that the contract was made with the supposed principal and not with the agent. *Harper & Co. v. Vigers Bros.*,[12] indeed, shows clearly the difficulty of establishing prejudice.

---

[3] *Hill SS. Co. Ltd v. Hugo Stinnes Ltd* 1941 S.C. 324. And see *Sharman v. Brandt* (1871) L.R. 6 Q.B. 720. But it has been followed in Australia: see *MacCormac v. Bradford* [1927] S.A.S.R. 152; *Marzo v. Land and Homes (W.A.) Ltd* (1931) 34 W.A.L.R. 62.

[4] [1923] A.C. 492: see Article 101.

[5] *Oglesby v. Yglesias* (1858) E.B. & E. 930: see Scrutton, *op. cit.* n. 1 above, pp. 181–182.

[6] Article 78.

[7] But see *Restatement*, § 372 and comment.

[8] See *Newborne v. Sensolid (Great Britain) Ltd* [1954] 1 Q.B. 45, 48.

[9] *Rayner v. Grote* (1846) 15 M. & W. 359; *Hill SS. Co. Ltd v. Hugo Stinnes Ltd*, n. 3 above.

[10] *Hill SS. Co. Ltd v. Hugo Stinnes Ltd*, n. 3 above.

[11] See above, para. 8–080.

[12] [1909] 2 K.B. 549; above.

Whatever the correct view on this matter, the agent can only sue if he purported to contract as agent: if he purported to contract, *e.g.* as a company which was in fact not yet formed, he cannot sue as principal.[13]

Illustrations

(1) A signed a charterparty "as agent for the freighter," a cesser **9–091** clause being inserted therein limiting A's liability to certain events in view of his being an agent. A was himself the freighter. Held, that he might sue on the contract (the clause limiting his liability would be inoperative). It would be otherwise, if the other contracting party had relied on his character as agent, and would not have contracted with him had he known him to be the principal. The freighter, whoever he might have been, would have had a right to sue.[14]

(2) A, professedly as agent for a named principal, contracted in writing to sell certain goods. The buyer, with notice that A was the real principal, accepted and paid for part of the goods. Held, that A might sue for non-acceptance of the residue.[15]

(3) The chartering broker of a firm conducting various maritime commercial activities charters a vessel, the owners of which are given the impression that the charterers are a large trading group known to the owners' broker. The chartering broker actually intended to charter for his own firm and arrange by back-to-back charters a recharter to the trading group. The chartering broker's firm is not a party to the contract, which is between the owners and the trading group.[16]

Article 111

NO RIGHT OF ACTION FOR PROMISED BRIBES OR SECRET COMMISSIONS

No action can be maintained by an agent for recovery of any **9–092** property or money promised to be given to him by way of a bribe whether he was in fact induced by such promise to depart from his duty or not.[17]

---

[13] *Newborne v. Sensolid (Great Britain) Ltd*, n. 8 above (Illustration 6 to Article 109).

[14] *Schmaltz v. Avery* (1851) 15 Q.B. 655. But see Comment.

[15] *Rayner v. Grote* (1846) 15 M. & W. 359. But see Comment.

[16] *Gewa Chartering B.V. v. Remco Shipping Lines Ltd (The Remco)* [1984] 2 Lloyd's Rep. 205.

[17] *Harrington v. Victoria Graving Dock Co.* (1878) 3 Q.B.D. 549; *Laughland v. Millar* (1904) 6 F. 413; *Lemenda Trading Co. Ltd. v. African Middle East Petroleum Co. Ltd* [1988] Q.B. 448. But *cf. Meadow Schama & Co. v. C. Mitchell & Co. Ltd* (1973) 228 EG 1571 (sum promised after commission earned: not a bribe). And see Articles 50 and 98. Nor, of course, can the agent be sued for not performing the act which he was bribed to do: nor (normally) for return of the bribe to its donor. These are applications of the rules as to illegal contracts. See Chitty, *Contracts* (27th ed.), Vol. 1, Chap. 16.

2.—Restitution

Article 112

Right of Agent to Sue for Money Paid by Mistake, etc.

Where an agent pays money on his principal's behalf under a mistake of fact, or in respect of a consideration which fails, or in consequence of some fraud or wrongful act of the payee or otherwise under such circumstances that the payee is liable to repay the money, the agent may sue the payee for its recovery.[18]

Comment

9–094   In such cases the proper plaintiff is normally the principal: but the agent can sue also.[19] It may however be that where the agent is mistaken as to his authority to pay, but the money was owed by the principal, the agent would not be able to recover, as the mistake was not one as between plaintiff and defendant[20]: nor, of course, could the principal recover. But if the principal did not ratify the payment the debt would not be discharged and the principal would still be liable: in such a case it would be strange if the agent could not recover, and it is submitted that he can.[21]

Article 113

Duty of Agent to Repay Money Received for Use of Principal

9–095   (1) Except as provided in this Article, an agent is not personally liable to repay money received by him for the use of his principal.[22]

(2) Where money is paid to an agent for the use of his principal, and the circumstances are such that the person paying the money is entitled to recover it back, the agent is personally liable to repay such money in the following cases:

---

[18] *Stevenson v. Mortimer* (1778) 2 Cowp. 805; *Langstroth v. Toulmin* (1822) 3 Stark. 145; *Holt v. Ely* (1853) 1 E. & B. 795; *Colonial Bank v. Exchange Bank of Yarmouth Nova Scotia* (1885) 11 App.Cas. 84; *Royal Securities Corp. v. Montreal Trust Co.* (1966) 59 D.L.R. (2d) 666 (citing this Article) (affd. (1967) 63 D.L.R. (2d) 15); *Restatement*, § 23. As to the principal's right to sue, see Article 73.

[19] *Duke of Norfolk v. Worthy* (1808) 1 Camp. 337.

[20] *Barclay & Co. Ltd v. Malcolm & Co.* (1925) 133 L.T. 512.

[21] See Goff and Jones, *Law of Restitution* (4th ed.), pp. 124–125; *Walter v. James* (1871) L.R. 6 Ex. 124; *Colonial Bank v. Exchange Bank of Yarmouth, Nova Scotia*, n. 18 above.

[22] See Comment. As to the principal's liability see Articles 73, 94, 95.

(a) Where the agent contracts or acts personally, and the money is paid to him in respect of or pursuant to the contract or transaction.[23]

(b) Where the money is obtained by duress or by means of any fraud or wrongful act to which the agent is party or privy.[24]

(c) Where the money is paid under a mistake of fact, or under duress, or in consequence of some fraud or wrongful act, or generally under circumstances in which an immediate right of recovery arises, and repayment is demanded of the agent, or notice is given to him of the intention of the payer to demand repayment, before he has in good faith paid the money over to, or otherwise dealt to his detriment with, the principal in the belief that the payment was a good and valid payment.[25]

(d) Where the receipt of the money is outside the actual and apparent authority of the agent and is not ratified by the principal.[26]

Comment

Questions of principle. The cases of this subject indicate two different   **9–096** and possibly inconsistent lines of reasoning which could be taken in respect of recovery of money from an agent.[27] The first uses the notion that payment to an agent for the principal in respect of a matter on which the agent has actual or apparent authority to receive it is payment to the principal. Under this reasoning, unless there is a separate liability in the agent (as where the principal is undisclosed,[28] or where he is liable together with his principal, or where he himself commits a wrong), the proper defendant is the principal and the agent is not liable even where he has not passed the money on to the principal.[29] The money is in contemplation of law in the hands of the principal: for example, in the case of a deposit.

---

[23] See Comment; Article 100.
[24] See Comment.
[25] See Comment.
[26] e.g. *Sorrell v. Finch* [1977] A.C. 728, Illustration 4 to Article 94.
[27] Mechem, *Treatise on the Law of Agency* (2nd ed.), ss. 1432–1433. See in general Goff and Jones, *Law of Restitution* (4th ed.), pp. 750 *et seq.*; Burrows, *Law of Restitution* (1993), pp. 480 *et seq.*
[28] See *Agip (Africa) Ltd v. Jackson* [1990] 2 Ch. 265, 289 (decision affd. [1991] Ch. 547); the Rt. Hon. Lord Justice Millett, (1991) 107 L.Q.R. 71, 77. But the defence succeed in *Transvaal and Delagoa Bay Investment Co. v. Atkinson* [1944] 1 All E.R. 579.
[29] *Ellis v. Goulton* [1893] 1 Q.B. 350, Illustration 1.

The second line of reasoning uses the notion that where the agent holds money to which neither he nor his principal is entitled, it can be intercepted and recovered at this stage unless without knowledge of the claim he has paid it over to his principal. The case law on payment over is of considerable antiquity and has developed its own rules. It was formerly criticisable on the basis that if the agent was liable *in personam*, the fact that he no longer had the money should make no difference. It could now be justified as an example of the notion of change of position recently recognised in restitution cases[30]; but the cases certainly have their own, and anterior, existence and it can be argued that they should still be treated separately.[31]

The two lines of reasoning can, however, perhaps be assigned to their own spheres. First, some of the cases in which the agent is held liable do not really refer to agents but rather to persons only at best describable as intermediaries. In many cases they have been banks. Thus in *Kleinwort, Sons & Co. v. Dunlop Rubber Co.*[32] the price of goods sold was assigned to a bank and notice given to the debtor, who by mistake paid another bank which was itself assignee in respect of the price of other goods of the same seller. That bank was held liable to refund the money; but the finding of the jury that the second bank received the money as agent for the original seller does not really accord with the facts. Such cases have little relevance to agency law. These being eliminated, there is a difference between two types of case. The first comprises those where the liability to repay arises immediately on payment, as where money is paid by mistake. The second covers those where the money is rightly regarded as paid to the principal (even if the agent still has it) because he may be permanently entitled to it; but by virtue of subsequent events it becomes repayable, as where a deposit correctly paid is justifiably reclaimed.[33] In the first situation the right to intercept is more easily acceptable. This is especially so if the mistake is that of the third party alone, or if the money is paid because of the principal's fraud without involvement of the agent.[34] For in either case the principal has no right to the money at all. In the second case, where the money becomes reclaimable at a later stage then payment, it is right that the principal should alone be liable, for the agent may not be in a position to know whether the money is returnable, and the matter should be disputed between the principal and the third party.[35]

---

[30] *Lipkin Gorman v. Karpnale Ltd* [1991] 2 A.C. 548; see Goff and Jones, *Law of Restitution* (4th ed.), Chap. 40; Burrows, *Law of Restitution* (1993), Chap. 15.

[31] But see *Australia and New Zealand Banking Group Ltd v. Westpac Banking Corp.* (1988) 164 C.L.R. 662, 684; Burrows, *op. cit.* n. 27 above, pp. 484–486.

[32] (1907) 97 L.T. 263.

[33] As in *Ellis v. Goulton*, n. 29 above.

[34] As in *Owen & Co v. Cronk* [1895] 1 Q.B. 265.

[35] Mechem, *op. cit.* n. 27 above, s. 438.

Rule (1). In view of the above, however the matter should be   9–097
approached in a book on the law of restitution, it is most convenient in
a work on agency to start with the general agency-based rule that money
paid to an agent for his principal and received within the agent's actual
or apparent authority, or the receipt of which is ratified, is regarded as
having been paid to the principal and is recoverable from the principal
only. It will normally still be recoverable from the principal even when
it is also recoverable from the agent. Thus where a deposit is paid to an
agent and the transaction falls through, the money must be recovered
from the principal even though the agent has not paid it acrosss,[36]
unless the agent was a stakeholder, in which case he assumes personal
liability.[37]

Rule (2)(a). Where the agent acts personally, however, he is   9–098
obviously liable to repay,[38] and his liability is not confined to cases of
contract.[39] The question of when he contracts personally is discussed in
Article 100. In particular, an agent acting for an undisclosed principal
contracts personally and so is liable.[40] So also a stakeholder is
personally liable unless he has paid money away in accordance with his
instructions. But where both agent and principal are liable, the third
party may sometimes be prevented from suing the agent by reason of
merger or election.[41]

Rule (2)(b). "If any person gets money into his hands illegally, he   9–099
cannot discharge himself by paying it over to another."[42] Therefore,
where the agent is a party or privy to a wrong in respect of which
money is paid to him, the action lies against him and it is no defence to
allege that he has paid the money over to his principal.[43] This applies
whether he receives the money on his own account[44] or on behalf of the

---

[36] See *Ellis v. Goulton* [1893] 1 Q.B. 350, Illustration 1; *Sadler v. Evans* (1766) 4 Burr.
1984; *Duke of Norfolk v. Worthy* (1808) 1 Camp. 337.
[37] See Illustrations 2, 3; above, paras. 9–023, 9–024.
[38] Illustrations 4, 5; *Continental Caoutchouc & Gutta Percha Co. v. Kleinwort, Sons &
Co.* (1904) 90 L.T. 474.
[39] See *Baylis v. Bishop of London* [1913] 1 Ch. 127; *Wakefield v. Newbon* (1844) 6 Q.B.
276.
[40] Illustration 5 (though the principal here may have been unnamed rather than
undisclosed). But see *Transvaal and Delagoa Bay Investment Co. v. Atkinson* [1944] 1 All
E.R. 579, where the point was not argued. A trustee also acts personally: *King v. Stewart*
(1892) 66 L.T. 339.
[41] Article 106.
[42] *Townson v. Wilson* (1808) 1 Camp. 396, 397 *per* Lord Ellenborough.
[43] See Illustrations 6–9; *Steele v. Williams* (1853) 8 Exch. 625; *Wakefield v. Newbon*
(1844) 6 Q.B. 276; *Chappell v. Poles* (1837) 2 M. & W. 867; *Keegan v. Palmer* [1961] 2
Lloyd's Rep. 449.
[44] *Smith v. Sleap* (1844) 12 M. & W. 585, Illustration 9.

principal.[45] In *Snowdon v. Davis*,[46] Mansfield C.J. said that the reason that the agent was liable in that case (a case of duress of goods) was that the third party did not pay the money for the purpose of its being paid over to the principal, but "under the terror of process, to redeem his goods." But this would be so in a case where the agent was innocent, yet in such cases recovery is barred where the agent has paid the money over.[47] The true explanation is therefore that quoted at the beginning of this paragraph, that the agent as a party to the wrong is himself liable.[48] The principal will usually also be liable for the wrong, subject to the rules of merger and election.[49]

9–100   **Rule (2)(c).** "Where money has been paid under a mistake of fact to an agent, it may be recovered back from that agent, unless he has in the meantime paid it to his principal, or done something equivalent to payment to him, in which cases the recourse of the party who has paid the money is against the principal only."[50] This rule has been applied to a wide variety of agents.[51] Although the majority of the decisions and dicta concern money paid under mistake, the formulation of this Article has been extended to all cases where the very fact of payment creates an immediate liability to repay; in such cases, the agent is liable, and can only escape by proving payment over in the circumstances mentioned.[52]

---

[45] *Oates v. Hudson* (1851) 6 Exch. 346.

[46] (1808) 1 Taunt. 359, Illustration 6. See also *Steel v. Williams*, n. 43 above, at p. 632; *Oates v. Hudson*, n. 45 above, at p. 348.

[47] *e.g. Owen & Co. v. Cronk* [1895] 1 Q.B. 265.

[48] The statement by Baggallay L.J. in *Ex p. Edwards, re Chapman* (1884) 13 Q.B.D. 747, 751 (Illustration 7) is also probably too wide.

[49] Article 106.

[50] *Pollard v. Bank of England* (1871) L.R. 6 Q.B. 623, 630 *per* Blackburn J. See also *Buller v. Harrison* (1777) 2 Cowp. 565; *Continental Caoutchouc and Gutta Percha Co. v. Kleinwort, Sons & Co.* (1904) 90 L.T. 474; *Kleinwort, Sons & Co. v. Dunlop Rubber Co.* (1907) 97 L.T. 263; *Kerrison v. Glyn, Mills, Currie & Co.* (1911) 81 L.J.K.B. 465; *Transvaal and Delagoa Bay Investment Co. Ltd v. Atkinson* [1944] 1 All E.R. 579; *Australia and New Zealand Banking Group Ltd v. Westpac Banking Corp.* (1988) 164 C.L.R. 662; *Agip (Africa) Ltd v. Jackson* [1990] Ch. 265, 288–289.

[51] *e.g.* clerks: *Cary v. Webster* (1721) 1 Str. 480; solicitors: *Davys v. Richardson* (1888) 21 Q.B.D. 202; bankers: *Gowers v. Lloyds, etc., Foreign Bank* [1938] 1 All E.R. 766, Illustration 12; *Egyptian Intl. Foreign Trade Co. v. Soplex Wholesale Supplies Ltd. (The Raffaella)* [1984] 1 Lloyd's Rep. 102, affd. on other grounds [1985] 2 Lloyd's Rep. 36; auctioneers: *Galland v. Hall* (1888) 4 T.L.R. 761, Illustration 11 (but *cf.* Illustration 2); one railway company collecting money for another: *Taylor v. Metropolitan Ry.* [1906] 2 K.B. 55; cotton brokers: *Re Bourne, ex p. Bird* (1851) 4 De G. & S. 273; excise collectors: *Greenway v. Hurd* (1792) 4 T.R. 553; churchwardens: *Horsfall v. Handley* (1818) 8 Taunt. 136. See also Illustrations.

[52] *cf.* Goff and Jones, *Law of Restitution* (4th ed.), pp. 750 *et seq.* See *Cox v. Prentice* (1815) 3 M. & S. 344, 348; *Davys v. Richardson*, n. 51 above; *Galland v. Hall*, n. 51 above; *Owen & Co. v. Cronk* [1895] 1 Q.B. 265. But the agent may sometimes be liable in conversion in any case, *e.g.* in respect of a cheque: see Article 116.

The principal is however also liable, subject to the rules of merger and election.[53] Where the liability to repay arises subsequently, however, *e.g.* because of breach of contract, it seems that the more general rule (Rule (1)) applies and the agent is not liable even though he still has the money.[54]

Payment over. By modern thinking this may be an example of the **9–101** defence of change of position[55]; but the rules are long-established and quite fully worked out. For the agent to be immune from suit by reason of payment over, the mere fact that he has credited the principal with the amount is not sufficient to discharge him from liability: he must have "paid over the money which he received to the principal, or settled such an account with the principal as amounts to payment, or done something which so prejudiced his position that it would be inequitable to require him to refund."[56] Thus he may have given new credit,[57] or credited the sum to his principal in a settled account, or spent it on the instructions of his principal.[58] But where the agent has paid the money to the principal and received it back again, he again becomes liable.[59]

This rule does not enable an action to be maintained against the agent in a situation where the principal is, as a foreign sovereign, immune from suit.[60] And where the agent acts in a merely ministerial capacity, *e.g.* as a bank cashier, he is obviously not the proper defendant in an action.[61]

Rule 2(d). If the agent is not authorised to receive the money and the **9–102** principal is not bound under the doctrine of apparent authority and does not ratify the payment, even though it is said to be received for the

---

[53] Article 106.

[54] See cases cited at n. 36 above; *North Eastern Timber Importers v. Ch. Arendt & Sons* [1952] 2 Lloyd's Rep. 513; *Restatement*, §§ 339–340.

[55] See *Lipkin Gorman v. Karpnale Ltd* [1991] 2 A.C. 548; *Australia and New Zealand Banking Group Ltd v. Westpac Banking Corp.* (1988) 164 C.L.R. 662 *cf.* Burrows, *Law of Restitution* (1989), pp. 484–486.

[56] *Kleinwort, Sons & Co. v. Dunlop Rubber Co.* (1907) 97 L.T. 263, 265 *per* Lord Atkinson. See *Australia and New Zealand Banking Group Ltd v. Westpac Banking Corp.*, n. 55 above, at pp. 682–684; Watts (1991) 107 L.Q.R. 521, 525. And see *Buller v. Harrison* (1777) 2 Cowp. 565; *Cox v. Prentice* (1815) 3 M. & S. 344; *Scottish Met. Ass. Co. v. P. Samuel & Co.* [1923] 1 K.B. 348: *Bavis, Jnr. & Sims v. London & South Western Bank* [1900] 1 Q.B. 270. See also *M'Carthy v. Colvin* (1839) 9 A. & E. 607.

[57] See *Buller v. Harrison*, n. 56 above.

[58] See *Holland v. Russell* (1861) 1 B. & S. 424; affirmed (1863) 4 B. & S. 14, Illustration 10: see also Illustrations 11–12.

[59] *British American Continental Bank v. British Bank of Foreign Trade* [1926] 1 K.B. 328.

[60] *Rahimtoola v. Nizam of Hyderabad* [1958] A.C. 379.

[61] *cf. Restatement*, § 339, comment *g*.

principal, there is no way in which the principal can be liable, and it is the agent who must be sued.

Illustrations

9–103   (1)   The solicitor of the vendor at a sale by auction receives a deposit as agent for the vendor.[62] The sale goes off through the vendor's default. The purchaser cannot maintain an action against the solicitor for its return whether it has been paid over to the vendor or not. The purchaser's action is against the vendor.[63]

(2)   The auctioneer at a sale by auction receives a deposit as stakeholder[64] and pays it over to the vendor. He is personally liable to refund the amount on the default of the vendor, because it was his duty to hold it until the completion of the contract.[65] In such a case the principal is liable also.[66]

(3)   An estate agent arranges an agreement for the sale of land "subject to contract" and take a deposit. The sale never comes into effect and thus no contract is ever made. If he expressly took the deposit as stakeholder he is liable to the payer for its return,[67] and if he accepts it without indication as to the capacity in which he has taken it he is likewise liable,[68] though in both cases the term "stakeholder" is an unsatisfactory one.[69] It is irrelevant that he has paid the deposit over to his principal, for he would act wrongly if he did so. His liability is a personal one to the payor, whether in contract or in restitution. If he defaults, the principal is in such a case not liable.[70]

(4)   An agent discounts certain bills, and in good faith pays over the proceeds to his principal. The bills turn out to be forgeries. The

---

[62] The prima facie rule is that he does so: see the cases cited below, n. 63 and *Tudor v. Hamid* [1988] 1 EGLR 251, 255. This is also true of estate agents: *Ojelay v. Neosale Ltd* [1987] 2 EGLR 167, 168 as regards *contract* deposits. See also above, para. 9–023.

[63] *Ellis v. Goulton* [1893] 1 Q.B. 350; *Bamford v. Shuttleworth* (1840) 11 A. & E. 926; *Edgell v. Day* (1865) L.R. 1 C.P. 80; *Burt v. Claude Cousins & Co. Ltd* [1971] 2 Q.B. 426, 435 (estate agent); *Goodey v. Garriock* [1972] 2 Lloyd's Rep. 369: but *cf. Wilder v. Pilkington* [1956] J.P.L. 739, where *Ellis v. Goulton* was distinguished on grounds that are not clear.

[64] The prima facie rule stems to be that he does so, though *quaere* whether this is appropriate: see the cases cited below; and above, paras. 9–023, 9–024.

[65] *Burrough v. Skinner* (1770) 5 Burr. 2639; *Edwards v. Hodding* (1814) 5 Taunt. 815; *Gray v. Gutteridge* (1828) 3 C. & P. 40; *Furtado v. Lumley* (1890) 6 T.L.R. 168.

[66] *cf.* Illustration 3; see also above, para. 9–024.

[67] See *Burt v. Claud Cousins & Co. Ltd* [1971] 2 Q.B. 426, 435–436; *Rayner v. Paskell and Cann, ibid.,* 439n.; *Brodard v. Pilkington, ibid.,* 442n.; *Barrington v. Lee* [1972] 1 Q.B. 326.

[68] *Burt v. Claud Cousins & Co. Ltd.,* n. 67 above, *per* Lord Denning M.R. and Sachs L.J.

[69] See *Maloney v. Hardy and Moorsehead* [1971] 2 Q.B. 442n.; above, para. 9–024.

[70] *Sorrell v. Finch* [1977] A.C. 728, Illustration 4 to Article 94.

discounter has no remedy against the agent unless he indorsed or guaranteed the bills, or dealt as a principal with the discounter.[71] But the agent is personally liable to repay the amount, as upon a total failure of consideration, if he dealt as a principal with the discounter.[72]

(5) A bought goods from B, a broker acting for an undisclosed principal, and by mistake paid him too much. B gave his principal, who was largely indebted to him, credit for the amount received. Held, that B was liable to repay to A the amount paid in excess, on the grounds (a) that B dealt as principal with A, and (b) that the mistake accrued to B's personal benefit.[73]

(6) A sheriff issued a warrant of distress against A. The bailiff levied the debt on the goods of B, and, under pressure of the illegal distress, B paid the debt. Held, that the bailiff was personally liable to repay B, though he had paid the amount over to the sheriff.[74]

(7) Pending a bankruptcy petition, and with notice of the act of bankruptcy, a solicitor, as the agent of the petitioning creditor, received from the debtor various sums of money in consideration of the adjournment of the petition, and paid such sums over to his principal. Held, that the solicitor was personally liable to repay the amount to the trustee in bankruptcy, notwithstanding the payment over, because the money was obtained wrongfully.[75]

(8) An agent who acts for an executor *de son tort* is himself an executor *de son tort* and personally liable to account for assets collected by him, even after he has paid them over to his principal. Payment over is no defence in the case of wrongdoers.[76]

(9) An agent demands more money than is due, and wrongfully withholds documents from T, who pays him the amount demanded, under protest, in order to recover the documents. The agent is personally liable to T in respect of the amount overpaid, even after he has paid the money over to the principal.[77]

(10) An insurance broker received money from an underwriter in respect of a voidable policy, and settled with his principal for the amount, amongst other matters, without notice of the underwriter's intention to dispute the policy, and without fraud. Held, that the agent

---

[71] *Re Bourne, ex p. Bird* (1851) 4 De G. & S. 273.
[72] *Gurney v. Womersley* (1854) 4 E. & B. 133; *Royal Exchange Ass. v. Moore* (1863) 8 L.T. 242.
[73] *Newall v. Tomlinson* (1871) L.R. 6 C.P. 405.
[74] *Snowdon v. Davis* (1808) 1 Taunt. 359. *Cf. Goodall v. Lowndes* (1844) 6 Q.B. 464.
[75] *Ex p. Edwards, re Chapman* (1884) 13 Q.B.D. 747.
[76] *Sharland v. Mildon, Sharland v. Loosemore* (1846) 5 Hare 469; *Padget v. Priest* (1787) 2 T.R. 97. See Williams, Mortimer and Sunnucks, *Executors, Administrators and Probate* (1993), p. 97.
[77] *Smith v. Sleap* (1844) 12 M. & W. 585; *Oates v. Hudson* (1851) 6 Exch. 346.

was not liable to repay the amount to the underwriter, who had paid it to him under a mistake of fact.[78]

(11) An auctioneer sold certain shares by private contract, and received a deposit. The purchaser declined to complete, on the ground that the contract was void as not complying with the provisions of Leeman's Act,[79] and sued the auctioneer for the return of the deposit. Held, that, the auctioneer having paid over the amount of the deposit to the vendor before the repudiation of the contract, the purchaser was not entitled to recover, because the auctioneer was authorised to pay over the deposit to the vendor either on the completion of the contract or on the purchaser's refusal to complete, and such authority had not been revoked.[80]

(12) A, a pensioner, collected his pension from the Crown Agents for the Colonies through the defendant bank by means of receipt forms sent to him by the Crown Agents. Each receipt form contained a certificate that A was still alive. The forms when completed were sent by A to the bank, who obtained payment on A's behalf from the Crown Agents and credited A's account with the amount so obtained. A died. Thereafter, receipt forms containing a forged signature, purporting to be that of A, and a false certificate that A was still living, were sent to the bank by a person pretending to be A, and the bank, believing that the signatures and certificates were genuine and that A was still alive, collected the pension from the Crown Agents and credited the amount to A's account, from which it was withdrawn. The Crown Agents, having discovered that A was dead, sued the bank for the amount of the pension so collected after A's death. Held, that the money could not be recovered as money paid under a mistake of fact, as the bank had paid it over to a person who was their principal, and their belief that such person was A made no difference in this respect.[81]

Article 114

MONEY HELD TO USE OF THIRD PARTIES

9–104   (1) Except as is provided in this Article, an agent is not liable or accountable to any third party in respect of money in his hands which he has been directed or authorised by his principal to pay to any third party.[82]

---

[78] *Holland v. Russell* (1863) 4 B. & S. 14; *Shand v. Grant* (1863) 15 C.B.(N.S.) 324.
[79] Banking Companies (Shares) Act 1867; repealed by Statute Law Revision Act 1966.
[80] *Galland v. Hall* (1888) 4 T.L.R. 761.
[81] *Gowers v. Lloyds, etc., Foreign Bank* [1938] 1 All E.R. 766. See Goff and Jones, *Law of Restitution* (4th ed.), pp. 750–753.
[82] See Comment; Illustration 5; *Gibson v. Minet* (1824) 2 Bing. 7.

(2) Where a specific fund existing or accruing in the hands of an agent to the use of his principal is assigned or charged by the principal to or in favour of a third party, the agent is bound, upon receiving notice of the assignment or charge, to hold the fund, or so much thereof as is necessary to satisfy the charge, to the use of such third party.[83]

(3) Where an agent is directed or authorised by his principal to pay to a third party money out of a fund existing or accruing in his hands to the use of the principal, and he expressly or impliedly promises such third party to pay him, or to receive or hold such money on his behalf or for his use, he is personally liable to pay such third party, or to receive or hold such money on his behalf or for his use, as the case may be, even if he has had fresh instructions from the principal not to pay such third party.[84]

Comment

Rule (1) is the general rule: there is no privity of contract with such third party, and therefore no third party can sue. 9–105

Rule (2). This rule refers to cases where the chose in action has been assigned, whether *simpliciter* or by way of charge. The same rule would therefore apply to mere debts owed by the agent to the principal, though here of course the money could not be regarded as held to the use of the third person, whose action would be contractual. The reference to a "specific fund" in this rule is therefore dictated only by the subject of this section of the chapter: although the assignment must of course be of a specific chose in action,[85] it is not necessary that the chose in action be a fund as opposed to a debt (though the distinction is probably relevant for the purposes of Rule (3)). The complexities of the law of assignment of choses in action are beyond the scope of this work, but once an assignment has been duly made the assignee can sue for the money and the debtor must not pay the assignor, and is not discharged by doing so.[86] But an assignee takes subject to equities, and therefore the agent can plead against the third party set-offs he had against the principal before the assignment.[87] An assignment should be sharply distinguished from a mere authority to pay money out of a fund, which 9–106

---

[83] Illustration 1.

[84] See Comment and Illustrations 2–4.

[85] See *Citizens' Bank of Louisiana v. First National Bank* (1874) L.R. 6 H.L. 352.

[86] *Brandt's Sons & Co. v. Dunlop Rubber Co.* [1905] A.C. 454; *Brice v. Bannister* (1878) 3 Q.B.D. 569.

[87] *Roxburghe v. Cox* (1881) 17 Ch.D. 520, Illustration 1.

is revocable and gives no right to any third party[88] except as provided in Rule (3).

9–107   **Rule (3).** This refers to an "intractable mass of conflicting authority ... contradictory and unintelligible."[89] A large group of mainly nineteenth-century cases establishes that where an agent holds a fund for his principal and is directed by that principal to pay it to a third party, and notifies the third party that he is willing to do so, he becomes liable to the third party, and the principal's authority becomes irrevocable. It is now clear that the liability is in restitution, and it is submitted that the only way in which the cases can be justified in the light of modern notions is as a sort of attornment of money,[90] whereby the agent holds a fund for the principal and then attorns to the third party, this being evidenced by his promising to pay the third party. And it seems that such was the original doctrine: but the rule was extended in *Israel v. Douglas* (1789)[91] to cases where the agent was merely a debtor to the principal. This, of course, causes theoretical complications regarding what is now called privity of contract: but the modern notions of consideration, privity and assignment were not then fully worked out, and there followed a large number of cases purporting to explain the rule on the basis of novation,[92] assignment,[93] trust,[94] or declaration of agency in favour of the third party.[95] The rule was in the mid-nineteenth century again confined to the case of a fund, and recognised as involving an action not in contract but in restitution, in *Liversidge v. Broadbent*[96] and *Griffin v. Weatherby*.[97] More than a century later it was discussed in *Shamia v. Joory*,[98] where the full complexities were apparently not cited to Barry J., who decided that there was for this purpose no difference between a debt and a fund. But it is only this distinction, unsatisfactory though it may be, that prevents the rule from subverting many of the fundamental principles of the law of contract as

---

[88] *Brandt's Sons & Co. v. Dunlop Rubber Co.*, n. 86 above; *Ex p. Hall, re Whitting* (1879) 10 Ch.D. 615; *Rodick v. Gandell* (1852) 1 De G.M. & G. 763. And see Illustrations 1 and 5 and cases there cited.

[89] Jackson, *History of Quasi-Contract* (1936), pp. 99, 103. See *ibid.*, pp. 31 *et seq.*, 93 *et seq.*; Davies (1959) 75 L.Q.R. 220; Goff and Jones, *Law of Restitution* (4th ed.), Chap. 27; Winfield, *Province of the Law of Tort* (1931), pp. 135 *et seq.*; Yates (1977) 41 Conv. 49; Comment to Article 120.

[90] Goff and Jones, *op. cit.* n. 89 above.

[91] 1 H.Bl. 239.

[92] See cases cited at n. 1 below.

[93] See cases cited at n. 99 below.

[94] See *Re Douglass, ex p. Cotterill* (1837) 3 Mont. & Ayr. 376, 385.

[95] See *Lilly v. Hays* (1836) 5 A. & E. 548, 551.

[96] (1859) 4 H. & N. 603.

[97] (1869) L.R. 3 Q.B. 753.

[98] [1958] 1 Q.B. 448, Illustration 6; followed in a case involving a fund in *Dellas v. Kourtessis* [1962] V.R. 456.

now understood. It is submitted that the rule should therefore be confined to the case of a fund: but if it is to be extended to the case of a debt, it provides a rather curious type of quasi-assignment operating at common law. It does not follow logically that the arrangement should be irrevocable by the principal, especially where the third party is a mere donee, but this irrevocability seems too firmly rooted in the cases to be questioned.

The illustrations that follow have been left, apart from the addition of *Shamia v. Joory*, in the arrangement in which they appeared in the second edition of this work (1898), though a few which seem to have no modern relevance have been omitted. But it should be noted that the proper assessment of the cases cited is today a difficult matter. The doctrine of privity of contract and the rules of assignment and consideration are now established with reasonable clarity: therefore the issues should be looked at as being of principle, and the old cases viewed critically. In particular, cases that refuse to distinguish between a debt and a fund could be regarded as wrong in view of *Liversidge v. Broadbent* and *Griffin v. Weatherby* were it not for the authority of *Shamia v. Joory*. Many cases purporting to find an assignment[99] or a novation[1] can now be regarded as outdated: and cases refusing to allow a third party to sue unless there is consideration or assignment[2] should probably be regarded as wrong where a fund is involved, and possibly, if *Shamia v. Joory* is correct, where a debt is involved.

The formulation of the Article, however, which also dates from the second edition, is submitted as being correct.[3]

Illustrations

(1) A principal assigns to another money held by his agent to his   **9–108** use, and the assignee gives notice to the agent of the assignment. The agent is bound to account for the money to the assignee,[4] subject to any right of lien or set-off the agent may have against the principal at the time when he receives notice of the assignment.[5] So, if a debtor charges money in the hands of his agent with payment of the debt, the agent is liable to the creditor upon receiving notice of the charge.[6]

---

[99] *e.g. Crowfoot v. Gurney* (1832) 9 Bing. 372, Illustration 2; *Hutchinson v. Heyworth* (1838) 9 A. & E. 375; *Gardner v. Lachlan* (1838) 4 Myl. & C. 129; *Burn v. Carvalho* (1839) 4 Myl. & C. 690.
[1] *e.g. Walker v. Rostron* (1842) 9 M. & W. 411, Illustration 3; *Hodgson v. Anderson* (1825) 3 B. & C. 842; *Hamilton v. Spottiswoode* (1849) 4 Exch. 200.
[2] *e.g. Wharton v. Walker* (1825) 4 B & C. 163.
[3] The formulation in the first edition was in terms of the third party suing in contract.
[4] *Webb v. Smith* (1885) 30 Ch.D. 192; *Ex p. South* (1818) 3 Swan. 392; *Rodick v. Gandell* (1852) 1 De G.M. & G. 763; *Greenway v. Atkinson* (1881) 29 W.R. 560.
[5] *Roxburghe v. Cox* (1881) 17 Ch.D. 520; *Webb v. Smith*, n. 4 above.
[6] Cases cited at n. 4 above.

(2) A principal gives his agent authority to pay money to T, a third person. The agent promises T that he will pay him when the amount is ascertained. The agent is liable to T for the amount when it is ascertained, though in the meantime the principal has become bankrupt,[7] or has countermanded his authority.[8]

(3) A principal writes a letter authorising his agent to pay to A the amounts of certain acceptances, as they become due, out of the proceeds of certain assignments. A shows the letter to the agent, who assents to the terms of it. Before the acceptances fall due, the principal becomes bankrupt, and the agent pays the proceeds of the assignments to the trustee in bankruptcy. The agent is personally liable to A for the amounts of the acceptances as they become due.[9]

(4) A bill drawn on an agent is made payable out of a particular fund, and the agent promises to pay the holder when he receives money for the principal. The agent is liable to the holder, if he subsequently receives the money.[10]

(5) An acceptor of a bill pays money to a banker for the purpose of taking up the bill, and the banker promises to apply the money accordingly. The banker refuses to take up the bill, and claims to retain the money for a balance due to him from the acceptor. The drawer of the bill has no right of action, either at law or in equity, against the banker to compel him to apply the money to the payment of the bill, there being no privity of contract between them.[11] So, where an agent is authorised to pay a debt out of moneys in his hands, and there is no assignment of or charge on such moneys to or in favour of the creditor, the agent is not liable to the creditor, unless he expressly or impliedly contracts to pay him, or agrees to hold the money to his use.[12]

(6) A owes P money. P. who lives abroad, wishes to make a gift to T, and instructs A to pay some of the debt to T. A agrees, tells T that he will do so, and sends him a cheque, which is, however, incorrectly drawn. The cheque is returned by T to A for correction, but A makes no further effort to pay T. T can sue A in restitution.[13]

---

[7] *Crowfoot v. Gurney* (1832) 9 Bing. 372.

[8] *Robertson v. Fauntleroy* (1823) 8 Moo. C.P. 10.

[9] *Walker v. Rostron* (1842) 9 M. & W. 411; *Fruhling v. Schroder* (1835) 7 C. & P. 103; *Hamilton v. Spottiswoode* (1849) 4 Exch. 200; *Noble v. National Discount Co.* (1860) 5 H. & N. 225.

[10] *Stevens v. Hill* (1805) 5 Esp. 247; *Langston v. Corney* (1815) 4 Camp. 176.

[11] *Moore v. Bushell* (1857) 27 L.J.Ex. 3; *Hill v. Royds* (1869) L.R. 8 Eq. 290; *Johnson v. Robarts* (1875) L.R. 10 Ch.App. 505.

[12] *Williams v. Everett* (1811) 14 East 582; *Howell v. Batt* (1833) 5 B. & Ad. 504; *Malcolm v. Scott* (1850) 5 Exch. 601; *Brind v. Hampshire* (1836) 1 M. & W. 365; *Wedlake v. Hurley* (1830) 1 C. & J. 83; *Bell v. London & Northern Western Ry. Co.* (1852) 15 Beav. 548; *Morrell v. Wotten* (1852) 16 Beav. 197; *Scott v. Porcher* (1817) 3 Meriv. 652.

[13] *Shamia v. Joory* [1958] 1 Q.B. 448; *Dellas v. Kourtessis* [1962] V.R. 456. But see Comment above.

3.—Torts

Article 115

Agent Personally Liable for Torts and Other Wrongs

Where loss or injury is caused to any third party by any wrongful   **9–109**
act or omission of an agent while acting on behalf of his principal,
the agent is personally liable, whether he was acting with the
authority of the principal or not, to the same extent as if he was
acting on his own behalf,[14] unless the authority of the principal
justifies the wrong.[15]

Comment

General. It is in general no defence to an action against a tortfeasor   **9–110**
for the tortfeasor to prove that he acted under the authority,
instructions or orders of another.[16] In this respect tort liability differs
from contract liability. But, of course, where such authority, instructions
or orders make legal what might otherwise be tortious, there will be no
liability; and ratification also may make non-tortious what was tortious
when it was done.[17] Again, there are many cases where a person who
follows the instructions or orders of a person who has superior status or
skill may for that reason, not be negligent[18], and a person who acts
purely ministerially may likewise not be liable.[19]

Torts connected with contract. In contractual situations it is clear that   **9–111**
an agent may be liable to the third party in deceit, *e.g.* when he
deliberately misrepresents his authority.[20] It is also now clear that an
action in negligence may be brought upon a pre-contractual[21] and also a
contractual situation[22] against a contracting party himself. *A fortiori*
therefore the existence of a contractual situation does not bar an action

---

[14] See Illustrations; *Restatement*, §§ 343 *et seq.* He may be liable as joint tortfeasor with the principal: see below, para. 9–117.

[15] Illustrations 9, 10.

[16] *Bennett v. Bayes* (1860) 5 H. & N. 391, Illustration 1; *Heugh v. Earl of Abergavenny* (1874) 23 W.R. 40.

[17] Illustrations 9, 10. The reverse does not apply: an agent sued for defamation who pleads qualified privilege is not affected by the malice of his principal: *Egger v. Viscount Chelmsford* [1965] 1 Q.B. 248.

[18] See *Gold v. Essex C.C.* [1942] 2 K.B. 293.

[19] See Article 116.

[20] *Polhill v. Walter* (1832) 3 B. & Ad. 114; *Randell v. Trimen* (1856) 18 C.B. 786; *West London Commercial Bank v. Kitson* (1884) 13 Q.B.D. 360.

[21] *Esso Petroleum Co. Ltd v. Mardon* [1976] Q.B. 801.

[22] *Henderson v. Merrett Syndicates Ltd* [1994] 3 W.L.R. 761; *Midland Bank Trust Co. Ltd v. Hett, Stubbs & Kemp* [1979] Ch. 384.

against the agent of one of the contracting parties. It is also clear that the fact that the agent acts for one party does not prevent his owing, in appropriate cases, a duty of care to the other. Such liability is most likely to occur in connection with negligent misrepresentation.

9–112   **Negligence.** Although earlier authority on the leading case of *Hedley Byrne & Co. Ltd v. Heller & Partners Ltd*[23] suggested a narrow scope for the duty of care in respect of statements,[24] later authority expanded this[25] and was unaffected by subsequent decisions restricting the scope of liability for the negligent causing of financial loss in general.[26] However, "for there to be a duty of care there must be a foreseeability of damage and direct relationship which has come to bear the label of 'proximity' "[27]; in the present context it appears that what is required is an assumption of responsibility towards the third party.[28] There are several Commonwealth cases in which estate agents have been made liable for negligent misrepresentations not made within the scope of their authority on behalf of the vendor, to prospective purchasers of land.[29]

Outside this specialised context, authority is accumulating that where such assumption of responsibility and reliance has been shown, an agent may be held liable to a third party.[30] On the other hand it has recently been held that a solicitor for a vendor does not owe a duty of care to a purchaser in answering inquiries before lease: here it could not be said that there was an assumption of responsibility[31]; and it has been held in

---

[23] [1964] A.C. 465.
[24] *Mutual Life and Citizens' Assurance Co. Ltd v. Evatt* [1971] A.C. 793.
[25] *Esso Petroleum Co. Ltd v. Mardon* [1976] Q.B. 801.
[26] Especially *Murphy v. Brentwood D.C.* [1991] 1 A.C. 398.
[27] *Gran Gelato Ltd v. Richcliff (Group) Ltd* [1992] Ch. 560, 569 *per* Sir Donald Nicholls V.-C., summarising the effect of *Caparo Industries Plc. v. Dickman* [1990] 2 A.C. 605.
[28] See *Spring v. Guardian Assurance Plc* [1994] 3 W.L.R. 354 *per* Lord Goff of Chieveley; *Henderson v. Merrett Syndicates Ltd* [1994] 3 W.L.R. 761.
[29] *Dodds v. Dodds and Millman* (1964) 45 D.L.R. (2d) 472; *Bango v. Holt* (1971) 21 D.L.R. (3d) 66; *Avery v. Salie* (1972) 25 D.L.R. (3d) 495; *Olsen v. Poirier* (1978) 91 D.L.R. (3d) 123; *Chand v. Sabo Bros. Realty Ltd* (1979) 96 D.L.R. (3d) 445; *Komarniski v. Marien* (1979) 100 D.L.R. (3d) 81; *Roberts v. Montex Development Corp., ibid.*, 660; *Barrett v. J.R. West Ltd* [1970] N.Z.L.R. 789; *Richardson v. Norris Smith Real Estate Ltd* [1977] 1 N.Z.L.R. 152; *Roots v. Oentory Pty Ltd* [1983] 2 Qd.R. 745. But *cf. Alessio v. Jovica* (1973) 34 D.L.R. (3d) 107, revsd. in part (1973) 42 D.L.R. (3d) 242; *Jones v. Still* [1965] N.Z.L.R. 1071; *Presser v. Caldwell Estates Pty. Ltd* [1971] 2 N.S.W.L.R. 471; *Shing v. Ashcroft* [1987] 2 N.Z.L.R. 154.
[30] *Allied Finance and Investments Ltd v. Haddow & Co.* [1983] N.Z.L.R. 22 (solicitor) (see also *Tracy v. Atkins* (1980) 105 D.L.R. (3d) 632); *Computastaff Ltd v. Ingledew Brown Bennison & Garrett* (1983) 268 EG 906; *Garland v. Ralph Pay & Ransom* (1984) 271 EG 106 (selling agent employed by mortgagee liable to mortgagor); *Punjab National Bank Ltd v. de Boinville* [1992] 1 W.L.R. 1138 (insurance broker liable to assignee of policy); *McCullagh v. Lane Fox & Partners* [1994] 08 EG 118 (estate agent).
[31] *Gran Gelato v. Richcliff (Group) Ltd* [1992] Ch. 560, Illustration 15; see Cane (1992) 108 L.Q.R. 539.

New Zealand that an agent is not liable in negligence in respect of a false statement as to his authority.[32] There are also a few cases outside the scope of the *Hedley Byrne* principle, where an agent has been held liable to a third party for negligent action or even failure to act, or at any rate to continue acting, on the basis of assumption of responsibility.[33]

Misrepresentation Act 1967, s. 2(1). As regards actions under section   9–113
2(1) of the Misrepresentation Act 1967, its wording is confined to representations made by a party to a contract and does not cover misrepresentations by their agents, unless they also are parties to the contract.[34]

Companies. Where the agent acts for a company a further feature is   9–114
introduced, for to hold him personally liable may, especially in the case of one-man companies, be in effect to pierce, or at any rate to ignore, the corporate veil. In such cases clear evidence of a separate wrong, as by ordering the commission of a tort,[35] or a separate assumption of responsibility, will normally be looked for.[36]

An exception: inducement of breach of contract? In *Said v. Butt*[37]   9–115
McCardie J. held that an agent could not be liable for inducing a breach of contract by his principal. A major reason given was that the liability

---

[32] *Kavanagh v. Continental Shelf (No. 46) Ltd* [1993] 2 N.Z.L.R. 517; above, para. 9–058.
[33] e.g. *Fairline Shipping Corp. v. Adamson* [1975] Q.B. 180, Illustration 12; *Smith v. Eric S. Bush* [1990] 1 A.C. 831 (surveyor); *Al-Kandari v. J.R. Brown & Co.* [1988] Q.B. 665, Illustration 13; cf. *Trevor Ivory Ltd v. Anderson* [1992] 2 N.Z.L.R. 517. See also *Alder v. Dickson* [1955] 1 Q.B. 158 (shipmaster); *Morris v. C.W. Martin & Sons Ltd* [1966] 1 Q.B. 716 (sub-bailee); *Meates v. Att.-Gen.* [1983] N.Z.L.R. 308. But sometimes a contract between third party and agent can be detected: see *General Accident Fire & Life Insurance Corp. v. Tanter (The Zephyr)* [1984] 1 W.L.R. 100, where an insurance broker was in the Court of Appeal held liable in contract when the judge at first instance had held him liable in tort: [1984] 1 Lloyd's Rep. 58.
[34] *Resolute Maritime Inc. v. Nippon Kaiji Kyokai (The Skopas)* [1983] 1 W.L.R. 857, Illustration 16. Though an agent may be a party to the contract: see Article 100. For a case where a principal was held liable under the Act, see *Gosling v. Anderson* (1972) 223 EG 1743.
[35] See *Rainham Chemical Works v. Belvedere Fish Guano Co.* [1921] 2 A.C. 465, 476; *Performing Rights Society Ltd v. Ciryl Theatrical Syndicate Ltd* [1924] 1 K.B. 1, 14–15; *Mancetter Developments Ltd v. Garmanson Ltd* [1986] Q.B. 1212, 1217; *Chan Cheng Kum v. Wah Tat Bank Ltd* [1975] A.C. 507 (liability in conversion).
[36] See *Yuille v. B. & B. Fisheries (Leigh) Ltd* [1958] 2 Lloyd's Rep. 596 (personal injuries: liability); *Sealand of the Pacific Ltd v. Robert C. McHaffie Ltd* (1974) 51 D.L.R. (3d) 702 (misstatement: no liability); *Fairline Shipping Corp. v. Adamson* [1975] Q.B. 180, Illustration 12 (liability); *Morton v. Douglas Homes Ltd* [1984] 2 N.Z.L.R. 548 (building: liability); *C. Evans & Sons Ltd v. Spritebrand Ltd* [1985] 2 All E.R. 415 (infringement of copyright: refusal to strike out); cf. *Trevor Ivory Ltd v. Anderson* [1992] 2 N.Z.L.R. 517 (a valuable discussion: see also Watts, [1992] N.Z. Recent Law Review 219).
[37] [1920] 3 K.B. 597.

of the principal, for whom the agent acted, and who would be responsible, would not lie in tort but would rather be for breach of contract. This ground is not convincing.[38] Although the doctrine derives only from an alternative basis[39] for the decision of a judge of first instance, it has been assumed to be correct in other decisions[40] and the English Court of Appeal has said that it is now too late to upset it.[41] This seems unfortunate, for occasions for the matter to be considered by the House of Lords may not arise easily and it is not the sort of topic on which legislation could be expected.

9–116   **Vicarious immunity.**[42] It might be expected that where a principal has an immunity conferred upon him by contract, an agent working for him in respect of that contract would be entitled to the same immunity towards the third party.[43] The notion of privity of contract, however, prevents this result being easily achieved. It was held by the House of Lords in 1962 that there is no general doctrine of vicarious immunity in English law.[44] On the other hand the agent will be protected where a contract can be construed between agent and third party under which the agent is entitled to the immunities conferred by the main contract on the principal,[45] and the principal can sometimes be regarded as having, acting in the capacity of agent for his own agent, negotiated such a contract of immunity for the agent.[46] Although difficulties might be expected in finding the consideration supplied by the agent, the Privy Council brushed these aside and held that there was an implied contract between a consignor of goods and the stevedore at the port of discharge

---

[38] See *Welsh Development Agency v. Export Finance Co. Ltd* [1992] B.C.L.C. 148, 173, 191.
[39] The first basis for the decision concerned the doctrine of the undisclosed principal: see above, para. 8–080.
[40] *G. Scammell & Nephew Ltd v. Hurley* [1929] 1 K.B. 419, 443, 449; *D.C. Thomson & Co. Ltd v. Deakin* [1952] Ch. 646, 680, 681; *O'Brien v. Dawson* (1942) 66 C.L.R. 18, 32, 34; *Rutherford v. Poole* [1953] V.L.R. 130, 135–136; *Official Assignee v. Dowling* [1964] N.Z.L.R. 578, 580–581; *Telemetrix Plc v. Modern Engineers of Bristol (Holdings) Plc* [1985] B.C.L.C. 213, 217. See also *Cooke Strait Skyferry Ltd v. Dennis Thompson International Ltd* [1993] 2 N.Z.L.R. 72.
[41] *Welsh Development Agency v. Export Finance Co. Ltd*, n. 38 above at pp. 171–173, 179–182, 191. See Oditah, [1992] J.B.L. 541, 565–569.
[42] Treitel, *Law of Contract* (9th ed.), pp. 567 *et seq.*; Chitty, *Contracts* (27th ed.), Vol. 1, §§ 14–034 *et seq.*
[43] *Restatement*, § 347, esp. comment *b*.
[44] *Scruttons Ltd v. Midland Silicones Ltd* [1962] A.C. 446; *Dunlop Pneumatic Tyre Co. v. Selfridge* [1915] A.C. 847.
[45] This is a possible explanation of *Elder Dempster & Co. v. Paterson Zochonis & Co.* [1924] A.C. 522; discussed in *Scruttons v. Midland Silicones*, n. 44 above; but see *The Pioneer Container*, n. 51 below.
[46] *Hall v. North Eastern Ry. Co.* (1875) L.R. 10 Q.B. 437.

entitling the stevedore to the limitations and immunities of the bill of lading.[47] There may also be other ways of conferring immunity on the agent. In particular, the principal can contract to indemnify the agent against claims made on him, and insert into the main contract a clause whereby the third party promises not to sue the agent. If the third party is made aware of the indemnity provision, the liability under it will become the measure of loss caused to the principal if the third party does sue the agent. In such a case the principal may be able to have the third party's action against the agent stayed,[48] or even, if all the parties are before the court, dismissed.[49]

Similar considerations apply where the agent seeks to rely as against the third party on an immunity conferred by his contract with the principal. If a contract with the third party on such terms can be inferred, he will be protected.[50] And here there is recent authority that if the owner of goods expressly or impliedly authorises sub-bailment of them on the sub-bailee's terms (as where he authorises sub-bailment "on any terms") and the sub-bailee has sufficient notice that a person other than the bailee (his bailor) is interested in the goods, the sub-bailee's terms may be invoked against the owner.[51] The true merits of both situations are still obscured by a general suspicion of exemption clauses: it is submitted that, subject to appropriate safeguards, agents ought to be able to take advantage of exemption clauses intended to cover them.[52]

Effect of judgment against principal or agent: contribution. Where the principal is liable for the torts of his agent they are in principle joint tortfeasors. Questions relating to the effect of judgment and contribution have been considered in Chapter 8.[53]   **9–117**

The Crown. Agents of the Crown are liable for their torts[54]; indeed, until the Crown Proceedings Act 1947, they alone were liable, and the   **9–118**

---

[47] *New Zealand Shipping Co. Ltd v. A.M. Satterthwaite & Co. Ltd (The Eurymedon)* [1975] A.C. 154; *Port Jackson Stevedoring Pty. Ltd v. Salmond & Spraggon (Australia) Pty. Ltd (The New York Star)* [1981] 1 W.L.R. 138.
[48] *cf. Gore v. Van Der Lann* [1967] 2 Q.B. 31; and see *Nippon Yusen Kaisha v. Intl. Import and Export Co. Ltd (The Elbe Maru)* [1978] 1 Lloyd's Rep. 206.
[49] *Snelling v. John G. Snelling Ltd* [1973] Q.B. 87. *Quaere* whether the agent himself could plead the promise as a defence by virtue of the reasoning in *Hirachand Punamchand v. Temple* [1911] 2 K.B. 330; Birks (1975) 1 Poly.L.Rev. 39.
[50] *Pyrene Co. Ltd v. Scindia Navigation Co. Ltd* [1954] 2 Q.B. 402, as explained in *Scruttons Ltd v. Midland Silicones Ltd* [1962] A.C. 446, 471.
[51] *The Pioneer Container* [1994] 2 A.C. 324; following dicta in *Morris v. C.W. Martin & Sons* [1966] 1 Q.B. 716, 730.
[52] See English Law Com. C.P. No. 121 (1991).
[53] See Comment to Article 92.
[54] See Wade, (1991) 107 L.Q.R. 4. But there are exceptions as to the armed forces: Crown Proceedings Act 1947, s. 10; and as to carriage of mail: Post Office Act 1969, s. 29

—cont. on next page

Crown was not, and an action could only be brought against the tortfeasor in his private capacity. Orders from the Crown, without more, do not justify torts.[55] To this there is one exception, that of Act of State. Where an agent of the Crown, whose act is duly authorised or ratified by the Crown, commits what would otherwise be a tort to an alien not resident in British territory, and the act is committed outside British territory, Act of State will be a defence to any action against him.[56] It may also be a defence in respect of an act against an enemy alien within British territory.[57] Whether it can be pleaded as a defence in respect of acts against British subjects outside British territory is not clear.[58] In view of the many changes within the Commonwealth over recent years there is much connected with the doctrine that may require reconsideration.[59]

Illustrations

9–119   (1)   An agent signed a distress warrant, and after the warrant was issued, but before it was executed, refused a tender of the rent. Held, that the agent was personally liable for the illegal distress.[60]

(2)   The manager of a bank signed a letter, as such, falsely and fraudulently representing that the credit of a certain person was good. Held, that the manager was personally liable in an action for deceit.[61]

(3)   A solicitor who is employed to conduct the sale of an estate advises trustees to conceal an incumbrance from a mortgagee. He is personally liable with the trustees for the concealment.[62]

(4)   A solicitor, on his client's instructions, presents a bankruptcy petition against A, knowing that A has not committed any act of bankruptcy. An action is maintainable against the solicitor for maliciously, and without reasonable and probable cause, presenting such petition, and causing A to be adjudged bankrupt.[63]

(5)   A, a printer, is employed to print pictures which are an infringement of copyright. A, though not aware of the infringement of

---

—cont. from previous page
as amended by British Telecommunications Act 1981 and Telecommunications Act 1984. See *American Express Co. v. British Airways Board* [1983] 1 W.L.R. 701.

[55] *Entick v. Carrington* (1765) 19 St.Tr. 1029.

[56] *Burton v. Denman* (1848) 2 Exch. 167; *Sinclair v. Broughton and Government of India* (1882) 47 L.T. 170; *Walker v. Baird* [1892] A.C. 491; *Salaman v. Secretary of State for India* [1906] 1 K.B. 613; *Johnstone v. Pedlar* [1921] 2 A.C. 262; *Commercial & Estates Co. of Egypt v. Board of Trade* [1925] 1 K.B. 271; *Nissan v. Att.-Gen.* [1970] A.C. 179.

[57] *Netz v. Ede* [1946] Ch. 224; *R. v. Bottrill, ex p. Kuechenmeister* [1947] K.B. 41.

[58] See *Nissan v. Att.-Gen.* [1970] A.C. 179.

[59] See Collier [1968] C.L.J. 102; [1969] C.L.J. 166; de Smith (1969) 32 M.L.R. 427.

[60] *Bennett v. Bayes* (1860) 5 H. & N. 391.

[61] *Swift v. Jewsbury & Goddard* (1874) L.R. 9 Q.B. 301. See Article 93.

[62] *Arnot v. Briscoe* (1748) 1 Ves. 95; *Clark v. Hoskins* (1867) 36 L.J.Ch. 689.

[63] *Johnson v. Emerson & Sparrow* (1871) L.R. 6 Ex. 329. And see *Stevens v. Midland Counties Ry. Co.* (1854) 10 Exch. 352.

copyright, is liable, as well as his employers, for penalties for the infringement. [64]

(6) A bailiff, employed to levy a distress, illegally distrains a lodger's goods. He is personally liable under the Law of Distress Amendment Act 1908. [65]

(7) A ship is fitted with pumps which are an infringement of a patent. An injunction may be granted against the master, restraining his from using the pumps, or otherwise infringing the patent. [66] But where a custom-house agent merely passed through the custom-house an article infringing a patent, and obtained permission for landing and storing it in magazines belonging to the principals, who were the importers, it was held that the acts of the agent did not amount to an exercise or user of the patent, and that therefore no action could be maintained against him in respect of the infringement. [67]

(8) An agent converts goods of a third person to his principal's use. He is liable to the true owner for their value, even if he acted in good faith and in the belief that his principal was the owner. [68] If, in such a case, the owner elects to adopt the transaction and proceed against the agent for an account, the agent is only liable to account for so much of the proceeds of the converted property as still remains in his hands, and not for what he has duly handed over in the course of his agency to the principal. [69]

(9) An agent of an executor *de son tort* collects assets, and pays them over to his principal. The agent is personally liable to account for the assets to the right executor or administrator, or to the beneficiaries. [70] But an agent who acts by the authority of an executor (even before probate) or of a person who is subsequently granted letters of administration is not liable to account as an executor *de son tort*, because the title of the executor dates from, and that of the administrator relates back to, the time of the death. [71]

---

[64] *Baschet v. London Illustrated Standard Co.* [1900] 1 Ch. 73. *cf. Kelly's Directories Ltd v. Gavin & Lloyds* [1902] 1 Ch. 631.

[65] s. 2; *Lowe v. Dorling* [1906] 2 K.B. 772; affirming [1905] 2 K.B. 501, decided under the Lodgers Goods Protection Act 1871. See also *Interoven Stove Co. Ltd v. Hibbard etc.* [1946] 1 All E.R. 263.

[66] *Adair v. Young* (1879) 12 Ch.D. 13.

[67] *Nobel's Explosives Co. v. Jones & Co.* (1882) 8 App.Cas. 5.

[68] *Stephens v. Elwall* (1815) 4 M. & S. 259; *Hollins v. Fowler* (1874) L.R. 7 H.L. 757; *Wilson v. New Brighton Panelbeaters* [1989] 1 N.Z.L.R. 74. But see Article 116.

[69] *Re Ely, ex p. Trustee* (1900) 48 W.R. 693. See Article 113.

[70] *Sharland v. Mildon* (1846) 5 Hare 468; *Hill v. Curtis* (1865) L.R. 1 Eq. 90. See also *Padget v. Priest* (1787) 2 T.R. 97; Williams, Mortimer and Sunnucks, *Executors, Administrators and Probate* (1993), pp. 97–98.

[71] *Sykes v. Sykes* (1870) L.R. 5 C.P. 113. See Williams, Mortimer and Sunnucks, *op. cit.* n. 76 above.

(10)   An agent, on behalf of his principal, but without the principal's authority, distrains the goods of a third person. The principal ratifies the distress, which is justifiable at his instance. The agent ceases to be liable, his act being justified by the ratification.[72]

(11)   A solicitor, being retained to sue for a debt, by mistake and without malice takes all the proceedings to judgment and execution against another person of the same name as the debtor; or, having obtained judgment against the debtor, by mistake and without malice issues execution against another person of the same name. The solicitor is not liable, for the tort of wrongful process of law requires malice.[73] But liability in trespass is strict. So where a solicitor directs the seizure of particular goods, so as to make the seizure his act rather than one done as part of a public duty,[74] he is personally liable if the seizure turns out to be wrongful.[75] So, where a solicitor directs or personally takes part in the execution of a warrant for arrest, he is liable in an action for false imprisonment if the warrant is illegal.[76]

(12)   Owners of ship's provisions agree with a company to store their goods in a warehouse which is owned by the managing director of the company but leased to the company. The contract is entered into by a director on behalf of the company; but a confirming letter from the managing director and an invoice indicate that the managing director is treating the storage of the goods as his own venture. Because of negligence in supervising the refrigeration the goods are damaged. The managing director is personally liable in negligence, though there is no contract with him and he is not bailee of the goods.[77]

(13)   In a matrimonial dispute, solicitors for the husband agree to hold the husband's passport to the order of the court. With the agreement of the wife they allow it to be lodged with the embassy of the husband's country, but negligently fail to inform her of facts creating risks that the husband will obtain it, and they also fail to take practicable steps to prevent this. The husband does obtain it, kidnaps the children and takes them abroad: the wife is injured in the kidnapping. The solicitors are liable to the wife in tort.[78]

---

[72] *Hull v. Pickersgill* (1819) 1 B. & B. 282.

[73] *Davies v. Jenkins* (1843) 11 M. & W. 745. *cf. Clissold v. Cratchley* [1910] 2 K.B. 244.

[74] See *Wilson v. Tunman and Fretson* (1843) 6 M. & W. 236; *Smith v. Keal* (1882) 9 Q.B.D. 340; *Morris v. Salberg* (1889) 22 Q.B.D. 614.

[75] *Rowles v. Senior* (1846) 8 Q.B. 677; *Davies v. Jenkins,* n. 73 above; *Clissold v. Cratchley,* n. 73 above.

[76] *Green v. Elgie* (1843) 5 Q.B. 99; *Codrington v. Lloyd* (1838) 8 A. & E. 449.

[77] *Fairline Shipping Corp. v. Adamson* [1975] Q.B. 180. See also *C. Evans & Sons Ltd v. Spritebrand Ltd* [1985] 2 All E.R. 415 (liability of director for breach of copyright). *cf. Trevor Ivory Ltd v. Anderson* [1992] 2 N.Z.L.R. 517. But the *Fairline* case was doubted in *Mitsui & Co. Ltd v. Novorossiysk Shipping Co. Ltd (The Kilmun)* [1993] 1 Lloyd's Rep. 311, 328.

[78] *Al-Kandari v. J.R. Brown & Co.* [1988] Q.B. 665.

(14) Solicitors for a borrower on the security of a yacht certify to the lender that an instrument of security is fully binding on the borrower and that there are no charges on the yacht. In fact the yacht does not belong to the borrower but is being purchased by a company of which he is a shareholder, and the money was not intended to be used to enable the borrower to purchase the yacht. The solicitors knew this. They are liable to the lender.[79]

(15) Solicitors for vendors of an underlease negligently and incorrectly answer questions as to the terms of a superior lease. They are not liable to the purchaser who suffered loss thereby.[80]

(16) Brokers acting for the seller of a vessel make representations which are not true. They are not parties to the contract and cannot be sued under section 2(1) of the Misrepresentation Act 1967.[81]

Article 116

CONVERSION BY INNOCENT AGENT

(1) Where an agent holds possession or control of goods for his principal, and   **9–120**

   (a) sells and delivers or otherwise deals with the possession of and assumes to deal with the property in the goods without the authority of the true owner[82]; or

   (b) refuses without qualification to deliver possession to the true owner on demand[83]; or

   (c) transfers possession to his principal or any other person except the true owner, with notice of the claim of the true owner,[84]

he is liable in conversion to the true owner for the value of the goods, even if he obtained possession from his principal, reasonably believing that such principal owned the goods or had the right to dispose of them, and acted in good faith on the authority of such principal.

---

[79] *Allied Finance and Investments Ltd v. Haddow & Co.* [1983] N.Z.L.R. 22.

[80] *Gran Gelato Ltd v. Richcliff (Group) Ltd* [1992] Ch. 560; but see Cane, (1991) 108 L.Q.R. 539.

[81] *Resolute Maritime Inc. v. Nippon Kaiji Kyokai (The Skopas)* [1983] 1 W.L.R. 857.

[82] Illustrations 1 to 4.

[83] Illustration 7 and cases cited.

[84] Illustration 5; *Powell v. Hoyland* (1851) 6 Exch. 67; *Union Credit Bank v. Mersey Docks & Harbour Board* [1899] 2 Q.B. 205. As to agent's right to interplead, see Article 72.

(2) But an agent is not guilty of conversion who in good faith merely

(a) receives or holds goods on behalf of his principal without dealing with them[85];

(b) refuses to deliver to the true owner goods which he holds for his principal in such terms that the refusal does not amount to a repudiation of the title of the true owner[86];

(c) contracts on behalf of his principal to sell goods of which he has neither possession nor control[87];

(d) by the authority of his principal, and without notice of the claim of the true owner, deals with the possession of, without assuming to deal with the property in, the goods.[88]

Comment

9–121   The tort of conversion raises special problems in connection with agents and so requires special treatment.

9–122   **Rule (1).** Conversion may be called "an act or complex series of acts of wilful interference, without lawful justification, with any chattel in a manner inconsistent with the right of another, whereby that other is deprived of the use and possession of it."[89] It is a tort of strict liability, and, as stated in Article 115, the authority of the principal cannot provide immunity from liability for a tort committed by an agent against a third party. Therefore any act performed by an agent which amounts to a conversion is actionable against him, and it is no defence to the agent to prove that he was authorised to perform the act by a person who appeared to be the owner, or to have the authority to perform, or authorise the performance of, such acts.[90]

It is not clear whether or not this rule applies to acts done in good faith, and without notice of the claim of the true owner, on the authority of a mercantile agent, or of a buyer or seller, in possession of the goods or of the documents of title thereto with the consent of the

---

[85] *Caxton Publishing Co. v. Sutherland Publishing Co.* [1939] A.C. 178, 202.

[86] Illustration 7 and cases cited.

[87] See Comment. And see in general Clerk and Lindsell, *Torts* (16th ed.), §§ 22–68—22–75.

[88] Illustration 6.

[89] Salmond and Heuston, *Torts* (20th ed.), p. 101. See in general *ibid.*, pp. 107–109. And see *Restatement*, Appendix, reporter's note to § 349; 18th Report of Law Reform Committee (on Conversion and Detinue), Cmnd. 4774 (1971), esp. pp. 14–18.

[90] See Article 115, Illustration 8; *Consolidated Co. v. Curtis & Son* [1892] 1 Q.B. 495, Illustration 1.

true owner within the meaning of the Factors Act. The authorities are conflicting.[91] But the relevant sections refer only to the validity of the disposition made by the mercantile agent himself and do not seem, on their wording, to legalise what would otherwise be conversions by persons assisting in the making of such dispositions.

Rule (2). Merely to hold goods is no conversion unless there is refusal   **9–123** to deliver up, or a dealing with the goods inconsistent with the owner's right.[92] And an agent may refuse to deliver goods while he makes reasonable inquiries, without rendering himself liable in conversion.[93] Further, there are some cases where, although there is a dealing with the goods to which the agent is a party, he is said to have acted as a mere conduit pipe[94] and therefore not to have performed any act amounting to a conversion. Thus an agent who negotiates a sale of goods of which he has neither possession nor control between two persons who contract directly does not himself interfere with the goods and so cannot be held liable for conversion.[95] So also an agent who performs acts with relation to goods, authorised by his principal, which are no more than a bailee or finder of goods could lawfully authorise, does not commit acts of conversion,[96] *e.g.* where he merely stores or carries goods,[97] transfers them to another agent,[98] or, not knowing of any adverse claim, returns them to his principal.[99] It is also probable that he does not convert if he performs acts in a transaction that actually transfers the title, provided that he does not know that such a transaction is involved: and even if he does know of it, there is authority that he does not commit conversion provided that he does not himself participate in the transaction, but acts only ministerially.[1]

---

[91] See *Waddington & Sons v. Neale & Sons* (1907) 96 L.T. 786; *Shenstone & Co. v. Hilton* [1894] 2 Q.B. 452; (but see as to this case Murdoch, *Law of Estate Agency and Auctions* (3rd ed.), p. 326); Article 89.

[92] See above, n. 85.

[93] Illustration 7 and cases cited.

[94] *Barker v. Furlong* [1891] 2 Ch. 172, 181, 183; *Consolidated Co. v. Curtis & Son* [1892] 1 Q.B. 495, 502; *Greenway v. Fisher* (1824) 1 C. & P. 190, 192.

[95] *Turner v. Hockey* (1887) 56 L.J.Q.B. 301, as explained in *Barker v. Furlong*, n. 94 above, and *Consolidated Co. v. Curtis*, n. 90 above; *Cochrane v. Rymill* (1879) 40 L.T. 744, 746. *Turner v. Hockey* was, however, doubted by the Court of Appeal in *R.H. Willis & Son v. British Car Auctions Ltd* [1978] 1 W.L.R. 438.

[96] *Hollins v. Fowler* (1875) L.R. 7 H.L. 757, 766–767.

[97] *Union Credit Bank v. Mersey Docks & Harbour Board* [1899] 2 Q.B. 205, 216; *Barker v. Furlong*, n. 94 above, at p. 182 (carriers and packing agents "merely purport to change the position of the goods and not the property in them"). And see *Greenway v. Fisher* (1824) 1 C. & P. 190 (packer).

[98] *Re Samuel (No. 2)* [1945] Ch. 408, Illustration 8.

[99] *Union Credit Bank v. Mersey Docks & Harbour Board*, n. 97 above; *cf.* Illustration 5.

[1] *National Mercantile Bank v. Rymill* (1881) 44 L.T. 767, Illustration 6; queried by Salmond and Heuston, *Torts* (20th ed.), p. 109, in view of the opinion of Blackburn J. in

—cont. on next page

9–124   **Cheques.** In principle, a bank which collects for a customer a cheque to which the customer has no title commits conversion.[2] But banks have statutory protection. By section 4 of the Cheques Act 1957, where a banker in good faith and without negligence[3] receives payment for a customer of a cheque,[4] or, having credited a customer's account with the amount of a cheque, receives payment thereof for himself, and the customer has no title, or a defective title, to the cheque, the banker does not incur any liability to the true owner of the cheque by reason only of having received payment thereof. This provision extends to uncrossed cheques the protection previously afforded to bankers in respect of crossed cheques.[5] It seems possible that the Law Reform (Contributory Negligence) Act 1945 may apply in this context,[6] though it is not applicable to the tort of conversion.[7]

Illustrations

9–125   (1)   An auctioneer was instructed to sell by auction furniture which the possessor and apparent owner had assigned by bill of sale to a third person. The auctioneer, who had no notice of the assignment, sold the furniture at the residence of the assignor, and, in the ordinary course of business, delivered it to the purchaser. Held, that the auctioneer was liable to the asignee for the value of the furniture.[8]

(2)   A obtained certain goods by fraud. B, a broker, bought the goods in his own name from A, thinking that they would suit C, a customer of his. B, having sold the goods to C at the same price at which he had bought them from A, merely charging the usual commission, took delivery and conveyed the goods to the railway

---

—cont. from previous page

Hollins v. Fowler, n. 96 above and *Stephens v. Elwall* (1815) 4 M. & S. 259. The case was approved in *Consolidated Co. v. Curtis & Son* [1892] 1 Q.B. 495, where it was pointed out at p. 501 that the decision is "a long step in the direction which Brett J. invited the House of Lords to take in *Hollins v. Fowler*"; but doubted by the Court of Appeal in *R.H. Willis & Son v. British Car Auctions Ltd* [1978] 1 W.L.R. 438. See also *Wilson v. New Brighton Panelbeaters* [1989] 1 N.Z.L.R. 74.

[2] *Arnold v. Cheque Bank* (1876) 1 C.P.D. 578.

[3] On good faith, see Bills of Exchange Act 1882, s. 90. On negligence, see Cheques Act 1957, s. 4(3); *Thackwell v. Barclays Bank Plc* [1986] 1 All E.R. 676. See in general Byles, *Bills of Exchange* (26th ed.), Chap. 22; Chalmers and Guest *Bills of Exchange* (14th ed.), pp. 519–520, 680–681; Paget, *Law of Banking* (10th ed.), Chap. 28.

[4] The protection is not in fact limited to cheques, but applies to certain other instruments: see Cheques Act 1957, s. 4(2).

[5] Bills of Exchange Act 1882, s. 82, as amended by Bills of Exchange (Crossed Cheques) Act 1906, both repealed by Cheques Act 1957.

[6] *Lumsden & Co. v. London Trustee Savings Bank* [1971] 1 Lloyd's Rep. 114.

[7] Torts (Interference with Goods) Act 1977, s. 11(1).

[8] *Consolidated Co. v. Curtis & Son* [1892] 1 Q.B. 405; *Barker v. Furlong* [1891] 2 Ch. 172; *Brown v. Hickinbotham* (1881) 50 L.J.Q.B. 426.

station, whence they were conveyed to C. The jury found that B bought the goods merely as an agent, in the ordinary course of his business. Held, that B was liable to the true owner for the value of the goods.[9]

(3)   A hired cabs from B, and obtained advances on them from an auctioneer. The auctioneer, on A's instructions, and without notice of B's title, in good faith sold the cabs, and after deducting the advances and his expenses, paid the proceeds to A. Held, that the auctioneer was liable to B for the value of the cabs, having had control of them, and having sold them in such a way as to pass the property in them. It would be otherwise, if he had not had possession or control of the cabs, and had merely contracted to sell, without delivering them.[10]

(4)   An insurance broker effected a policy on behalf of A. A became bankrupt, and after the adjudication instructed the broker to collect money due under the policy and pay it to him. The broker, without notice of the bankruptcy, collected the money and paid it to A. Held, that the broker was liable to the trustee in bankruptcy for the amount.[11]

(5)   A husband entrusted goods, which were the property of his wife, to an auctioneer for sale. The auctioneer received notice of the wife's claim, but nevertheless subsequently sold a portion of the goods, and permitted the husband to remove the remainder. Held, that the auctioneer was liable to the wife for the value of the goods removed by the husband, as well as of those which had been sold.[12]

(6)   A held a bill of sale over horses in the possession of B. B took the horses to C's repository for sale by auction, and they were entered in the catalogue for sale. Before the sale took place, B sold the horses by private contract in C's yard. The price was paid to C, who deducted his commission and charges, and handed the balance to B, and the horses, on B's instructions, were delivered by C to the purchaser. Held, that C, having merely delivered the horses according to B's orders, and not having himself sold or otherwise assumed to deal with the property in them, was not guilty of a conversion.[13]

(7)   An agent in possession of goods by the authority of his principal, on demand by the true owner refuses to deliver them up without an order from the principal, or requires a reasonable time to ascertain whether the person demanding the goods is the true owner. Such a

---

[9] *Hollins v. Fowler* (1872) L.R. 7 Q.B. 616; affd. L.R. 7 H.L. 757; *Union Transport Finance Ltd v. British Car Auctions Ltd* [1978] 2 All E.R. 385; *R.H. Willis & Son v. British Car Auctions Ltd* [1978] 1 W.L.R. 438 (where a "provisional bid" procedure was used).

[10] *Cochrane v. Rymill* (1879) 40 L.T. 744.

[11] *McEntire v. Potter & Co.* (1889) 22 Q.B.D. 438.

[12] *Davis v. Artingstall* (1880) 49 L.J.Ch. 609. See also *Winter v. Bancks* (1901) 84 L.T. 504.

[13] *National Mercantile Bank v. Rymill* (1881) 44 L.T. 767. But this case was doubted by the Court of Appeal in *R.H. Willis & Son v. British Car Auctions Ltd* [1978] 1 W.L.R. 438. See Clerk and Lindsell, *Torts* (16th ed.), §§ 22–74—22–75.

qualified refusal is not a conversion. It is otherwise, where the refusal is absolute, or amounts to a setting-up of the principal's title to the goods. [14]

(8) The solicitor of a bankrupt receives after-acquired property on behalf of his client and on his client's instruction transfers it to another agent, knowing that that agent has been instructed to sell it and use the proceeds to educate the bankrupt's son. The solicitor is not liable in conversion. [15]

4.—EQUITY

Article 117

KNOWING RECEIPT AND ACCESSORY LIABILITY

9–126   (1) Where an agent receives money or property with notice that it is subject to a trust or fiduciary obligation, he is liable to account as a constructive trustee to the person for whom it is held in trust or to whom the fiduciary obligation is owed:

(a) if he receives that money or property with knowledge or notice that it has been transferred to him in breach of trust or fiduciary obligation; or

(b) deals with that money or property in a manner or for purposes inconsistent with the trust or obligation.

(2) An agent is also liable as a constructive trustee if he dishonestly procures or assists in a breach by his principal of a trust or fiduciary obligation affecting money or property under the principal's control.

(3) But an agent who has no notice that a breach of fiduciary obligation is being committed is not liable merely because he acts as agent in the transaction which constitutes such a breach. [16]

Comment

9–127   **Knowing receipt and accessory liability.** This Article makes brief reference to a highly controversial area of equity, and possibly restitution, which can sometimes come into question in connection with

---

[14] *Alexander v. Southey* (1821) 5 B. & A. 247; *Wilson v. Anderton* (1830) 1 B. & Ad. 450; *Lee v. Bayes and Robinson* (1856) 18 C.B. 599; *Pillott v. Wilkinson* (1864) 3 H. & C. 345.

[15] *Re Samuel (No. 2)* [1945] Ch. 408.

[16] See Comment; Hanbury and Martin, *Equity* (14th ed.), pp. 300–310; Harpum, (1986) 102 L.Q.R. 114, 267; Birks, [1993] L.M.C.L.Q. 218; Harpum, "The Basis of Equitable Liability", in *The Frontiers of Liability* (Birks ed., 1994), Vol. 1, p. 9.

the activities of some of those who may be called agents or to whom the law of agency or parts of it may be applied. They may as agents become involved in the improper activities of their principals and may sometimes be liable in this respect.

Tracing. It may be useful first to distinguish from these liabilities the 9–128 rules of tracing. An agent may acquire money or property which is subject to a trust interest, whether by way of express trust or because it comes from a fiduciary in circumstances where such an interest arises; or it may also be so as representing money or property held on trust. If he takes it with actual or constructive notice of the trust interest and its terms, or as a volunteer, he takes subject to it. But on orthodox doctrine he is not liable to account for profits beyond the value traceable; and if he parts with the money or property innocently without recognisable proceeds he ceases to be liable.[17]

Knowing receipt. The significance of the special rule as to knowing 9–129 receipt referred to in this Article is that in some circumstances the agent may be liable to account as *constructive trustee*, though by way of personal action, if he receives the money or property for his own use with knowledge or notice of the trust, and that the transfer to him was in breach of trust; or becomes aware of this later and deals in a manner inconsistent with the trust. In such cases he would be liable for profits made, in the first situation from the time of receipt and in the second from the time he acquired knowledge or notice; and he would remain liable though he had parted with the property.[18]

Such liability for knowing receipt seems to be based on the idea of knowledge or notice; but it is not clear what these notions mean in the context, nor even if they should be regarded as separate notions. In *Baden Delvaux v. Société Générale, etc., S.A.*[19] Peter Gibson J. formulated the possible degrees of knowledge for the purposes of the operation of equity as follows:

"(i) Actual knowledge; (ii) wilfully shutting one's eyes to the obvious; (iii) wilfully and recklessly failing to make such inquiries as an honest and reasonable man would make; (iv) knowledge of circumstances which would indicate the facts to an honest and reasonable man; (v) knowledge of circumstances which would put an honest and reasonable man on inquiry."

---

[17] See Article 90.
[18] *Metall und Rohstoff A.G. v. Donaldson Lufkin & Jenrette Inc.* [1990] 1 Q.B. 391, 474; *Agip (Africa) Ltd v. Jackson* [1990] Ch. 265, 291 (affd. without reference to this point [1991] Ch. 547).
[19] [1983] B.C.L.C. 325, 407 (affd. [1985] B.C.L.C. 258).

Although the meticulous discriminations of this passage have been criticised,[20] and it may well be that the categories are not exhaustive, and although it may sometimes be difficult in practice to determine which verbal formula is appropriate to a particular fact situation, it is submitted that the ground-clearing secured by these distinctions provides a useful starting point. It seems, first, that the constructive notice of conveyancers, whereby a person is deemed to have notice of property interests in respect of which he ought to have made inquiry, and which would take in all five categories, would plainly be inappropriate in the present context. Beyond this, the current trend seems to be to merge the difference between constructive notice in this sense and more general reasoning based on the idea of knowledge into a looser principle that a person has knowledge or notice of whatever a reasonable person would have discovered in the situation in question.[21] The label of "constructive notice" is still often used for this looser doctrine. On this basis a person engaged in commerce would be held to a less strict duty of inquiry than a conveyancer; but it would be knowledge or notice along these lines that creates liability for knowing receipt.

However, another view is that for the imposition of this liability there must be something further than mere knowledge or notice, however the matter is put: there must actually be some dishonesty, or at least want of probity, involving actual knowledge or wilful blindness[22], as in the case of accessory liability discussed below. The matter remains uncertain; indeed, the two notions may merge.[23] "It may well be that the underlying broad principle which runs through the authorities regarding commercial transactions is that the court will impute knowledge, on the basis of what a reasonable person would have learnt, to a person who is guilty of commercially unacceptable conduct in the particular context involved."[24]

---

[20] *Jacobs' Law of Trusts in Australia* (5th ed., ed. Meagher and Gummow), s. 1334; *Agip (Africa) Ltd v. Jackson* [1990] Ch. 265, 293. In *Royal Brunei Airlines Sdn. Bhd. v. Tan*, n. 33 below, Lord Nicholls of Birkenhead said that in the context of accessory liability (below, para. 9–130) "the *Baden* scale of knowledge is best forgotten" (at p. 761). This remark seems, however, to be addressed to knowledge in the context of that liability, where it is no longer to be relevant. The question still arises in the case of knowing receipt.

[21] *Baden Delvaux v. Société Générale, etc., S.A.*, n. 19 above, at p. 414; *Eagle Trust Plc v. S.B.C. Securities Ltd* [1992] 4 All E.R. 488, 507–509; *El Ajou v. Dollar Land Holdings Plc* [1993] 3 All E.R. 717, 739; decision revsd. [1994] 2 All E.R. 685; *Macmillan Inc. v. Bishopsgate Investment Trust* [1995] 1 W.L.R. 978, 1000. And see in general *Thomson v. Clydesdale Bank* [1893] A.C. 282.

[22] *Re Montagu's S.T.* [1987] Ch. 264, 285; see also *Barclay's Bank Plc v. Quincecare Ltd* (1988) [1992] 4 All E.R. 363; *Cowan de Groot Properties Ltd v. Eagle Trust Plc* [1992] 4 All E.R. 700, 754 *et seq.*; *Eagle Trust Plc v. SBC Securities Ltd* [1995] BCC 231. But *cf.* the Rt Hon. Lord Justice Millett, (1991) 107 L.Q.R. 71, 81 ("profoundly mistaken").

[23] On the whole issue see Moriarty, *Pressing Problems in the Law* (S.P.T.L. seminars, 1994), pp. 24–33.

[24] *Cowan de Groot Properties Ltd*, n. 21 above at p. 761 *per* Knox J.

A further possibility is that the duty to account as constructive trustee is based squarely on no more than receipt. If this is correct, the agent remains liable though he has parted with the property in circumstances in which its proceeds cannot be traced, subject only to defences of bona fide purchaser and more generally change of position.[25] These would be developments in equity which could be seen as paralleling current developments in restitutionary liability at common law.[26] Although this may seem extreme, there is some support for it in the *Royal Brunei Airlines* case referred to below.[27]

On any explanation it can also be argued, on the analogy of cases on innocent handling in the law of conversion,[28] that an agent who acts *only* as such does no more than carry out instructions and should not be liable for "receipt" at all.[29] It is, however, difficult to maintain this view where the agent receives property with actual or constructive notice of a trust, and it is in general doubtful whether the parallel can be sustained.[30] It is also much less necessary to seek such an exception if the narrower view of constructive trust liability discussed above is adopted, with its requirement of something akin to dishonesty, bearing in mind also the availability of the accessory liability category next discussed.

Accessory liability. Here the agent does not receive trust property, or if he does, the receipt is irrelevant. The liability is imposed on persons who assist in the wrongful designs of fiduciaries, and was formerly taken to require that those designs be "dishonest and fraudulent",[31] a requirement which does not appear in the "knowing receipt" category. Such situations are even more clearly based on liability *in personam*, for the agent may never hold property at all. Former cases tended to use property reasoning and the notion of constructive notice:[32] the liability

9–130

---

[25] As established in *Lipkin Gorman v. Karpnale Ltd* [1991] 2 A.C. 548: see Goff and Jones, *Law of Restitution* (4th ed.), Chap. 40; Burrows, *Law of Restitution* (1993), Chap. 15.

[26] See Birks, *Introduction to the Law of Restitution* (1985), pp. 439 *et seq.*; the Rt. Hon. Lord Justice Millett, (1991) 107 L.Q.R. 71, 81–82.

[27] Para. 9–130; see esp. at pp. 70 ("recipient liability is restitution-based"); 71 ("strict liability"). See also *El Ajou*, n. 21 above, [1993] 3 All E.R. at pp. 736, 738.

[28] See Article 116.

[29] See *Agip (Africa) Ltd v. Jackson*, n. 25 above, at pp. 291–292; *Karak Rubber Co. Ltd v. Burden (No. 2)* [1972] 1 W.L.R. 602, 633; *International Sales and Agencies Ltd v. Marcus* [1982] 3 All E.R. 551, 558; *Westpac Banking Corp. v. Savin* [1985] 2 N.Z.L.R. 41, 60, 70; see also *Mara v. Browne* [1896] 1 Ch. 199 as explained in *Williams-Ashman v. Price & Williams* [1942] Ch. 219.

[30] See Tan [1991] L.M.C.L.Q. 357.

[31] *Belmont Finance Corp. v. Williams Furniture Ltd* [1979] Ch. 250; *Agip (Africa) Ltd v. Jackson*, n. 20 above at p. 293.

[32] *Selangor United Rubber Estates Ltd v. Cradock (No. 3)* [1968] 1 W.L.R. 1555; *Karak Rubber Co. Ltd v. Burden (No. 2)* [1972] 1 W.L.R. 602; *Rowlandson v. National Westminster Bank Ltd* [1978] 1 W.L.R. 798.

was described as one for "knowing assistance", and there was much discussion of the degree of knowledge required. It has now however been decided by the Privy Council in *Royal Brunei Airlines Sdn. Bhd. v. Tan*[33] that the designs need not be dishonest or fraudulent: the liability is simply as accessory to a breach of trust; and that the state of mind required is one of dishonesty, objectively determined in accordance with criteria (in a commercial context) of what is unacceptable conduct.[34] Contrary to earlier dicta[35], it is said that the underlying rationale is the same as that governing the tort of inducement of breach of contract.[36] There may however be different nuances in other jurisdictions.[37]

9–131   **Solicitors.**[38] These questions have arisen in connection with solicitors: a solicitor may become a constructive trustee, *e.g.* by improperly applying trust funds[39] or by paying such funds to one trustee only.[40] On the other hand, a solicitor who does not intermeddle and who acts as agent only may sometimes be free of liability. Thus a solicitor was held not liable when he invested trust funds, on the instructions of the trustee, in unauthorised mortgages: he was acting as agent only.[41] Similar reasoning applies to solicitors acting in connection with fiduciaries. But these cases may require reassessment in the light of the recent developments referred to above.

9–132   **Banks.**[42] The question has also arisen in connection with banks, who may become constructive trustees, for example by seeking to apply trust

---

[33] [1995] 2 W.L.R. 64.
[34] At pp. 73, 74; adopting in this context the dictum of Knox J. in the *Cowan de Groot* case, n. 21 above.
[35] *Metall und Rohstoff A.G. v. Donaldson Lufkin & Jenrette Inc.* [1990] 1 Q.B. 391, 474; *Wickstead v. Browne* (1992) 30 N.S.W.L.R. 1, 17.
[36] At p. 76.
[37] See *Consul Development Pty Ltd v. DPC Estates Pty Ltd* (1975) 132 C.L.R. 373; *Westpac Banking Corp. v. Savin* [1985] 2 N.Z.L.R. 41; *Powell v. Thompson* [1991] 1 N.Z.L.R. 597, 611–615; *cf. Equiticorp Industries Group Ltd v. Hawkins* [1991] 3 N.Z.L.R. 700, 727–728; *Marshall Futures Ltd v. Marshall* [1992] 1 N.Z.L.R. 316, 326; *Nimmo v. Westpac Banking Corp.* [1993] 3 N.Z.L.R. 218; *Springfield Acres Ltd v. Abacus (Hong Kong) Ltd* [1994] 3 N.Z.L.R. 502.
[38] See Cordery, *Solicitors* (8th ed.), pp. 96–98, 101–102.
[39] See *Att.-Gen. v. Leicester Corp.* (1844) 7 Beav. 176 (town clerk); *Morgan v. Stephens* (1861) 3 Giff. 226; *Haray v. Caley* (1864) 33 Beav. 365; *Blyth v. Fladgate* [1891] 1 Ch. 337; *Soar v. Ashwell* [1893] 2 Q.B. 390, Illustration 5; *Cooper v. Stoneham* [1893] 68 L.T. 18. See also Illustration 3.
[40] *Lee v. Sankey* (1873) L.R. 15 Eq. 204. See also *Bank of New South Wales v. Adams* [1982] 2 N.S.W.L.R. 659. As to the liability of the partner of such a solicitor, see *Re Bell's Indenture* [1980] 1 W.L.R. 1217.
[41] *Mara v. Browne* [1986] 1 Ch. 199 as explained in *Williams-Ashman v. Price and Williams* [1942] Ch. 219; Illustration 3; Illustration 4.
[42] See Ellinger, (1994) 9 Banking and Financial L.Rev. 111.

money to a fiduciary's personal overdraft,[43] transferring money deposited with them to the personal account of the trustee, honouring cheques drawn on trust accounts for improper purposes, or by facilitating a transaction whereby a company uses its money to purchase its own shares. Unless the account is overdrawn, they are not easily regarded as "receiving" money as agents for their customers; but they can of course be on risk for "accessory" liability. The duties of bankers in such cases are difficult to define. They have an obligation to comply with their customers' instructions in relation to moneys in their customers' accounts.[44] On the other hand they have responsibilities to prevent misuse of trust funds, and evasion of the statutory provisions which prevent companies from buying their own shares.[45] They are often therefore the subject of conflicting duties.[46] Older dicta can be cited to the effect that a banker was not liable unless he was privy to the breach of trust,[47] or where an element of personal benefit was involved.[48] But other authority has placed a stricter duty on banks.[49] A proper analysis of the cases on this point is beyond the scope of this book;[50] and in any case these decisions also may require reassessment.

Illustrations

(1)   An agent of an executor applies a fund, which he knows to be   **9–133** part of the estate of the testator, in satisfaction of advances made to the executor for his own business. He is personally liable to account for the fund to the beneficiaries under the will.[51]

(2)   A director is passively involved in transactions arranged by a stranger who purchased the majority of the company's shares, whereby the company's money is used to finance the purchase. The director is liable as constructive trustee.[52]

---

[43] *cf. Neste Oy v. Lloyd's Bank Plc.* [1983] 2 Lloyd's Rep. 658, 666; approved in *Kingscroft Ins. Co. Ltd v. H.S. Weavers (Underwriting Agencies) Ltd* [1992] 1 Lloyd's Rep. 187, 195.

[44] *Baden Delvaux v. Société Génerale, etc., S.A.* [1983] B.C.L.C. 325, 419 (affd. [1985] B.C.L.C. 258).

[45] See Companies Act 1985, Part V, Chap. VII, as amended by Companies Act 1989.

[46] *Gray v. Johnston* (1868) L.R. 3 H.L. 1, 11.

[47] *Gray v. Johnston,* above.

[48] *Foxton v. Manchester and Liverpool District Banking Co.* (1881) 44 L.T. 406; *cf. Coleman v. Bucks and Oxon Union Bank* [1897] 2 Ch. 243.

[49] See *Selangor United Rubber Estates Ltd v. Cradock (No. 3)* [1968] 1 W.L.R. 1555; *Karak Rubber Co. Ltd v. Burden (No. 2)* [1972] 1 W.L.R. 602; *Belmont Finance Corp. v. Williams Furniture Ltd (No. 2)* [1980] 1 All E.R. 393; (1981) 44 M.L.R. 107; *Baden Delvaux v. Société Génerale, etc., S.A.,* n. 44 above (authorities reviewed); and in general cases cited at Illustration 6.

[50] See Paget, *Law of Banking* (10th ed.), pp. 231 *et seq.* Scott, *Trusts* (4th ed.), § 324.

[51] *Wilson v. Moore* (1834) 1 Myl. & K. 126; *ibid.* 337.

[52] *Selangor United Rubber Estates Ltd v. Cradock (No. 3),* n. 49 above, see also *Belmont Finance Corp. v. Williams (No. 2),* n. 49 above.

(3)   A trustee allows his solicitor to retain costs out of the trust estate. The solicitor has notice that the trustee has secretly bought for himself part of the trust estate. The solicitor is not a trustee of the sums received out of the estate.[53]

(4)   A solicitor receives money from a client in respect of costs and expenses in defending an action under which a third party is claiming that the client is constructive trustee of all the client's assets. The solicitor is not liable as a constructive trustee.[54]

(5)   The solicitor to a trust invests trust money mixed with moneys of other trusts, in an equitable mortgage. When the mortgage is redeemed he distributes half the proceeds to beneficiaries who have by that time become absolutely entitled to the same. He retains the other half, to which others are entitled. He holds the retained money on constructive trust.[55]

(6)   A bank transfers trust money from a trust account to the personal account of the trustees or otherwise participates in a transfer of trust money in circumstances which would put a reasonable bank on inquiry as to the nature of the transaction being conducted. The bank is liable on the beneficiaries for the amount so transferred, whether it acquired a personal benefit from the transaction or not.[56] It would be otherwise, if the bank had no notice that it was trust money, or, if it knew this, had no notice of the breach of trust.[57]

---

[53] *Re Blundell, Blundell v. Blundell* (1888) 40 Ch.D. 370; *Williams v. Williams* (1881) 17 Ch.D. 437; *Competitive Insurance Co. Ltd v. Davies Investments Ltd* [1975] 1 W.L.R. 1240 (liquidator); *cf. Blyth v. Fladgate* [1891] 1 Ch. 337.

[54] *Carl Zeiss Stiftung v. Herbert Smith & Co. (No. 2)* [1969] 2 Ch. 276.

[55] *Soar v. Ashwell* [1893] 2 Q.B. 390. See also *Gathergood v. Blundell & Brown Ltd* [1992] 3 N.Z.L.R. 643; *Nimmo v. Westpac Banking Corp.* [1993] 3 N.Z.L.R. 218.

[56] See *Baden Delvaux v. Société Génerale Etc., S.A.*, n. 44 above; *Selangor United Rubber Estates Ltd v. Cradock (No. 3)* [1968] 1 W.L.R. 1555; *Karak Rubber Co. Ltd v. Burden (No. 2)* [1972] 1 W.L.R. 602. See also *Rowlandson v. National Westminster Bank Ltd* [1978] 1 W.L.R. 798; *Westpac Banking Corp. v. Savin* [1985] 2 N.Z.L.R. 41; *Lankshear v. A.N.Z. Banking Group (New Zealand) Ltd* [1993] 1 N.Z.L.R. 481. See further *Bodenham v. Hoskyns* (1852) 12 De G.M. & G. 903; *Gray v. Lewis* (1869) L.R. 8 Eq. 526; *Ex p. Adair, re Gross* (1871) 24 L.T. 198, affd. *sub nom. Ex p. Kingston, re Gross* (1871) L.R. 6 Ch.App. 632; *Backhouse v. Charlton* (1878) 8 Ch.D. 444; *Foxton v. Manchester and Liverpool District Banking Co.* (1881) 44 L.T. 406; *Magnus v. Queensland National Bank* (1888) 37 Ch.D. 466; *John v. Dodwell & Co. Ltd* [1918] A.C. 563; *British America Elevator Co. v. British Bank of North America* [1919] A.C. 658; *Imperial Bank of Canada v. Begley* [1936] 2 All E.R. 367; *Warren Metals Ltd v. Colonial Catering Co.* [1975] 1 N.Z.L.R. 273.

[57] See *Keane v. Robarts* (1819) 4 Madd. 332; *Gray v. Johnston* (1868) L.R. 3 H.L. 1; *Thomson v. Clydesdale Bank* [1893] A.C. 282; *Coleman v. Bucks and Oxon Union Bank* [1897] 2 Ch. 243; *Union Bank of Australia v. Murray-Aynsley* [1898] A.C. 693; *Shields v. Bank of Ireland* [1901] 1 I.R. 222; *Bank of New South Wales v. Goulburn Valley Butter Co. Pty.* [1902] A.C. 543; *Barclays Bank Plc. v. Quincecare Ltd* (1988) [1992] 4 All E.R. 363.

Article 118

AGENT NOT LIABLE FOR WRONGS OF CO-AGENTS OR SUB-AGENTS WORKING FOR PRINCIPAL

An agent is not liable as such to any third person for loss or injury   **9–134**
caused by the wrongful act or omission of a co-agent not being a
partner, or of a sub-agent in privity of contract with the principal,
unless he authorised or was otherwise party or privy to such
wrongful act or omission.[58]

Comment

The relationship of employer and employee or of principal and agent   **9–135**
does not exist between co-agents: therefore an agent is not, as such,
liable to third parties for wrongs committed by co-agents acting as
such.[59] Nor is an agent liable for a sub-agent whom he appointed to act
for the principal, creating privity of contract between them[60]: indeed
such a sub-agent might, but for the fact that he often holds a position of
lower status than the appointing agent, be called a co-agent. Thus in
Stone v. Cartwright[61] the manager of a colliery was held not liable for
the negligence of a colliery employee. But an agent could be liable in
accordance with normal principles for the wrongs of a sub-agent whom
he himself employs, and who has privity of contract with him alone.[62]
And the agent is of course liable for his own personal negligence;
delegation to another agent may be evidence of such negligence.[63]

---

[58] See Comment.

[59] *Cargill v. Bower* (1878) 10 Ch.D. 502; *Re Denham & Co.* (1883) 25 Ch.D. 752; *cf. Dovey v. Cory* [1901] A.C. 477 (cases on directors: but as to the liability of directors for statements in prospectuses, see Companies Act 1985, ss. 67–69).

[60] See Chap. 5.

[61] (1795) 6 T.R. 411. See also *Bear v. Stevenson* (1874) 30 L.T. 177; *Weir v. Bell* (1878) 3 Ex.D. 238 (directors not liable for torts committed by persons working for the company).

[62] This is the more normal position of a sub-agent: see Article 37.

[63] See *Re City Equitable Fire Insurance Co.* [1925] Ch. 407; *cf. Dovey v. Cory*, n. 59 above and Article 37.

CHAPTER 10

TERMINATION OF AUTHORITY

Introductory Note

10–001   The propositions collected in this chapter, like those in Chapter 3, straddle the three main aspects of agency, the relations between principal and agent, principal and third party, and agent and third party. Therefore careful attention should be paid to determining which aspects of an agency situations is affected by each rule. Thus the termination of authority between principal and agent may not affect a third party who has no notice of such termination: Article 123 (which deals with apparent authority where actual authority is determined) must be regarded as qualifying some of the earlier Articles in the Chapter. And although a termination of authority may as between principal and agent be operative in some respects, *e.g.* in making further actions by the agent on the principal's behalf ineffective, and terminating his right to remuneration or indemnity, it may also be wrongful as a breach of contract and give rise to a right to damages: see Article 125. Furthermore, the fiduciary obligation and in some cases that as to commission may continue.

Article 119

TERMINATION OF ACTUAL AUTHORITY

10–002   (1) The actual authority of an agent is terminated

   (a) by agreement between principal and agent;
   (b) if given for a particular transaction, by the completion of that transaction[1];
   (c) if given for a limited period, by the expiration of that period, or in any case after the elapsing of a period which is reasonable in all the circumstances[2];
   (d) by the happening of any event upon the happening of which it is agreed between the principal and the agent that the authority shall terminate,[3] or upon the happening of which the agent should reasonably infer that the

---

[1] Illustrations 1–4; *Restatement*, § 106.
[2] Illustration 5; *Danby v. Coutts & Co.* (1885) 29 Ch.D. 550. Illustration 1 to Article 24; *Restatement*, § 105.
[3] See *Restatement*, § 107.

principal does not or would not wish the authority to continue[4];

(e) by the destruction of the subject-matter of the agency[5];

(f) by the happening of any event rendering the agency or its objects unlawful, impossible or otherwise frustrating the agency or its objects.[6]

(2) The actual authority of an agent is also terminated, unless it is irrevocable in accordance with the provisions of Article 120—

(a) by the death, mental incapacity or (in some situations) insolvency of the principal or the agent; or where the principal or agent is a body corporate, by its winding up or dissolution[7];

(b) by notice of revocation given, whether or not in breach of contract, by the principal to the agent[8];

(c) by notice of renunciation given, whether or not in breach of contract, by the agent to the principal and accepted by the principal.[8]

Comment

Rule (1). The circumstances stated in Rule (1) above are relevant to   **10–003** the agreement, whether contractual or not, between principal and agent, and relate to implied (or express) terms of it. It should be noted therefore that the third party may still be able to rely in some cases on the doctrine of apparent authority: see Article 123. The propositions contained in (a) to (c) are self-evident. The second part of (d) is derived from a suggestion in the *Restatement*[9] that if, for example, P authorises A to contract to sell Blackacre for a sum representing its appropriate value, and the price obtainable for Blackacre subsequently, unknown to P, triples because of the discovery of oil nearby, A might not have authority to sell at the original price even though he had received no further instructions. Where however the agent is in reasonable doubt as to whether his authority persists, his actions are to be treated as authorised if reasonable in the circumstances.[10] Rule (1)(e) is again self-evident for cases where a subject-matter can be readily identified, though here the correct analysis of the contractual position, and hence

---

[4] See Comment.

[5] *Rhodes v. Forwood* (1876) 1 App.Cas. 256, Illustration 1 to Article 125; *Northey v. Trevillion* (1902) 7 Com.Cas. 201; *Restatement*, § 110. See Article 125.

[6] See Comment.

[7] Article 121. The dissolution of a partnership may have the same effect: *ibid.*

[8] Article 122.

[9] See Comment to § 108.

[10] *cf.* Articles 26, 40.

whether the principal is liable to the agent, is open to much argument. [11] In both these cases it is a matter of interpretation whether the actual authority ends on the happening of the event or on the agent's receiving notice of the happening of the event.

Rule 1(f) involves a more general application of the doctrine of frustration to agency contracts and agreements. An agent's authority has been held to terminate when the operation of Military Service Acts made it illegal or impossible for him to perform his duties. [12] Where the contract of agency may require intercourse with the enemy during a war, the agency is normally terminated by the outbreak of war. [13] Thus the retainer of a solicitor ceases when his client becomes an alien enemy, [14] though it has been held that while the solicitor remains on the record, service upon him of an application to strike out the statement of claim is sufficient. [15] It has also been held that a purportedly irrevocable power of attorney to sell land and give a receipt for the purchase-money was not avoided by the donor subsequently becoming an alien enemy. [16] This case has however been criticised, and should at least be regarded as turning on special facts: ordinarily the relationship of principal and agent necessitates communication between the parties, [17] which would not be possible in such a situation. But the occurrence of war does not of itself determine the authority of an enemy alien resident in this country who acts for a principal also resident in this country. [18] In general each case of this type must turn on its facts: "the general grounds of abrogation are, broadly speaking, the danger of intercourse and the desire not to enhance, but to cripple, the resources of the enemy." [19]

---

[11] See Article 125.

[12] *Marshall v. Glanvill* [1917] 2 K.B. 87; and see *Morgan v. Manser* [1948] 1 K.B. 184.

[13] *Sovfracht, etc. v. Van Udens, etc.* [1943] A.C. 203, 253–255; *Hugh Stevenson & Sons Ltd v. Aktiengesellschaft für Cartonnagen Industrie* [1918] A.C. 239; *Nordisk Insulin-laboratorium v. Gorgate Products Ltd* [1953] Ch. 430 (in all of which the principal became an enemy); *Kuenigl v. Donnersmarck* [1955] 1 Q.B. 515 (where the agent became an enemy). See also *Daimler Co. Ltd v. Continental Tyre & Rubber Co. Ltd* [1916] 2 A.C. 307; Webber, *Effect of War on Contracts* (2nd ed.); McNair, *Legal Effects of War* (4th ed.); *Restatement*, §§ 115, 116.

[14] *Sovfracht, etc. v. Van Udens, etc.*, n. 13 above.

[15] *Eichengruen v. Mond* [1940] Ch. 785 (claim frivolous and vexatious).

[16] *Tingley v. Müller* [1917] 2 Ch. 144.

[17] See *Sovfracht, etc. v. Van Udens, etc.* [1943] A.C. 203, 236, 254; *Hangkam Kwingtong Woo v. Liu Lan Fong* [1951] A.C. 707, 720. But *cf. Perpetual Trustee Co. Ltd v. Aroney* (1944) 44 S.R.(N.S.W.) 313.

[18] *Nordman v. Rayner and Sturges* (1916) 33 T.L.R. 87 (where the alien was actually interned for a short period); *Schostall v. Johnson* (1919) 36 T.L.R. 75.

[19] *Hangkam Kwingtong Woo v. Liu Lan Fong*, n. 17 above at p. 179, *per* Lord Simonds (a case where the principal was in a country allied to the United Kingdom and the agent in Japanese-occupied Hong Kong). See also *Ottoman Bank v. Jebara* [1928] A.C. 269; *Sovfracht, etc. v. Van Udens*, n. 13 above.

Rule (2). The circumstances stated in Rule (2) have a different **10–004** operation. Those in (a) relate to the capacity of the principal to have an agent at all, or of the agent to act as such, and therefore the doctrines of ratification, agency of necessity and of apparent authority do not necessarily operate to protect the agent or third parties where the agent's authority has ceased.[20] There are however certain protections provided by statute.[21] Renunciation by either party, referred to in (b) and (c), terminates authority because as a matter of policy such a rule seems appropriate to the relationship[22]: but there may be repercussions both between principal and agent (where the renunciation may be a breach of contract) and as regards third parties (who may be able to rely on the doctrine of apparent authority if they had no notice of the renunciation).[23]

For the authority to be terminated, a revocation by the principal does not require to be accepted by the agent. But where there is a contract between them, on general principles a repudiatory breach is ineffective unless accepted by the innocent party. Thus any *contract* may in some respects be regarded as subsisting, even though the authority is revoked, if the revocation is a breach by the principal and is not accepted by the agent.[24] Even where it is accepted, some contractual duties operating beyond the end of the contract service may continue, as may fiduciary duties.[25] On the other hand, since the conferring or withdrawal of authority is within the power of the principal, a renunciation by the *agent* does not terminate his authority (quite apart from the question of the contractual position between them) unless the principal indicates that it should. It may, however, release the principal from the duty to give notice of the termination of authority.

Illustrations

(1) A broker is employed to sell goods. Immediately the contract of **10–005** sale is completed, he is *functus officio*, and cannot subsequently alter the terms of the contract without fresh authority from the principal.[26]

(2) A solicitor is retained to conduct an action. His authority to act for the client prima facie ceases at the judgment, though it may be

---

[20] But see Article 123.
[21] See below, para. 10–018; Article 124.
[22] Article 122.
[23] Articles 123, 124.
[24] See *Atlantic Underwriting Agencies Ltd v. Cia. di Assicurazione di Milano S.p.A.* [1979] 2 Lloyd's Rep. 240; Treitel, *Law of Contract* (9th ed.), pp. 757 *et seq.*
[25] *Thomas Marshall (Exports) Ltd v. Guinlé* [1979] Ch. 227; as to fiduciary duties see Article 45.
[26] *Blackburn v. Scholes* (1810) 2 Camp. 341.

renewed by any act showing the client's intention that the solicitor shall continue to act.[27]

(3)   An auctioneer is authorised to sell property. He has no authority to sign a memorandum of the sale a week after the sale.[28]

(4)   An estate agent was employed to let or sell a house. Having let the house, he negotiated for a sale, and subsequently found a purchaser. Held, that he had no authority to sell after having let the house, and that he was not entitled to commission on the sale.[29]

(5)   A broker is authorised to sell goods. It may be shown that by the custom of the particular trade such an authority expires with the expiration of the day on which it is given.[30]

Article 120

WHEN AUTHORITY CANNOT BE TERMINATED (IRREVOCABLE AUTHORITY)

10–006

(1)   Where the authority of an agent is given by deed,[31] or for valuable consideration,[32] for the purpose of effectuating any security, or of protecting or securing an interest of the agent, it is irrevocable during the subsistence of such security or interest.[33] But authority is not irrevocable merely because the agent would be prejudiced by its revocation,[34] or has a special property in, or lien for advances upon, the subject-matter of it,[35] the authority not being given expressly for the purpose of securing such interest or advances.

(2)   Where a power of attorney, whenever created, is expressed to be irrevocable and is given to secure a proprietary interest of the donee of the power, or the performance of an obligation owed to the donee,[36] then, so long as the donee has that

---

[27] *Butler v. Knight* (1867) L.R. 2 Ex 109; but *cf. Re Newen, Carruthers v. Newen* [1903] 1 Ch. 812. No doubt it covers matters ancillary to the judgment. See in general Cordery, *Solicitors* (8th ed.), Chap. 4.
[28] *Bell v. Balls* [1897] 1 Ch. 663. The situation could not now arise in exactly this form because of the effect of the Law of Property (Miscellaneous Provisions) Act 1989, s. 2.
[29] *Gillow & Co. v. Lord Aberdare* (1892) 9 T.L.R. 12.
[30] *Dickinson v. Lilwall* (1815) 4 Camp. 279.
[31] Illustration 1; *Walsh v. Whitcomb* (1797) 2 Esp. 565.
[32] Illustrations 2–4.
[33] See Illustrations. See also *Slatter v. Railway Commissioners (New South Wales)* (1931) 45 C.L.R. 68; *Griffin v. Clark* (1940) 40 S.R.(N.S.W.) 409; *Re Hartt Group and Land Securities Ltd* (1984) 7 D.L.R. (4th) 89 (landlord's right to re-enter and take custody as agent of tenant). Revocation may be restrained by injunction: *Knight v. Bulkeley* (1859) 5 Jur.(N.S.) 817.
[34] Illustrations 3, 5; *Clerk v. Laurie* (1857) 2 H. & N. 199, 200; *Frith v. Frith* [1906] A.C. 254. See also *Restatement*, §§ 138, 139.
[35] Illustration 5; below para. 10–010.
[36] See Comment.

interest, or the obligation remains undischarged, the power is irrevocable.[37]

(3) Authority expressed by this Article to be irrevocable is not determined by the death,[38] mental incapacity or insolvency[39] of the principal, nor, where the principal is a body corporate, by its winding up or dissolution, and cannot be revoked by the principal without the consent of the agent.[40]

(4) An enduring power of attorney as defined in the Enduring Powers of Attorney Act 1985 is not revoked by the subsequent mental incapacity of the donor, and is exercisable thereafter in accordance with the provisions of that Act.[41]

Comment

Irrevocability at common law. The dominant assumption in the cases is that a grant of authority is of its nature revocable. The mere fact that a power is declared in the instrument granting it to be irrevocable does not make it so, even if that instrument is a deed under seal. Authority can be irrevocable; but this is only where the notion of agency is employed as a legal device for a different purpose from that of normal agency, to confer a property or security interest on the "agent". In such a case it is intended that the agent use the authority not for the benefit of his principal but for his own benefit, to achieve the objects of the arrangement. The circumstances in which authority is thus irrevocable at common law are, however, difficult to define.[42] Authority is normally only irrevocable where it *is* the security or proprietary interest, or a part of it or means of achieving it, or where it secures an obligation owed by principal to agent.[43] The first notion is comparatively easy to understand: an example is the power of attorney normally taken by the mortgagee of a ship. The second is more difficult. The standard example is that of a share underwriting agreement, which confers irrevocable authority on the issuer to apply on the underwriter's behalf for shares left with him.[44] This seems a sort of guarantee. But the authority does

10–007

---

[37] Powers of Attorney Act 1971, s. 4(1). Such a power may be given to the person entitled to the interest and persons deriving title under him to that interest: s. 4(2). See in general Law Com. No. 30, Cmnd. 4473 (1970).

[38] See *Lepard v. Vernon* (1813) 2 V. & B. 51; *Spooner v. Sandilands* (1842) 1 Y. & C.Ch.Cas. 390; *Carter v. White* (1883) 25 Ch.D. 666 (completion of blanks in bill of exchange after death of drawer).

[39] *Alley v. Hotson* (1815) 4 Camp. 325; *cf. Bristow and Porter v. Taylor* (1817) 2 Stark. 50.

[40] See also Powers of Attorney Act 1971, s. 4(1).

[41] See Comment.

[42] "Perhaps the subject-matter is one not permitting completely lucid definition": Mechem *Outlines of Agency* (4th ed.), p. 179.

[43] *Smart v. Sandars* (1848) 5 C.B. 895, 917.

[44] See Illustration 4.

not become irrevocable merely because the agent will suffer loss if the principal revokes, for example because he wishes to earn commission or has committed himself to others on the basis that his authority will continue.

Such a power is referred to as a "power coupled with an interest". Normal agency involves the notion of an agent acting under the direction of and in the interests of his principal. In the case discussed here, the agent is empowered to act in his own interests. Agency is here in effect a device for conferring a property interest (a power of attorney to sue on another's behalf is a primitive form of assignment) or to give what is in effect a guarantee. Its creation should be regarded as such, rather than as a conferring of authority. Thus the *Restatement*[45] uses the phrase "power given as security", which is defined as "a power to affect the legal relations of another, created in the form of an agency authority, but held for the benefit of the power holder or a third person, and given to secure the performance of a duty or to protect a title, either legal or equitable, such power being given when the duty or title is created or given for consideration."

Although the interest protected will normally be that of the donee of the power, it has been said that at common law a power can be given as security when exercised by another on behalf of the person entitled to the security, for example, a receiver appointed by debenture holders. "The receiver's power is given to him only for the protection of the debenture holders and why should it be revoked by circumstances that do not affect a power given to them direct"?[46] This view is put forward in the wording of this Article. It is clear however that the mere right to earn commission is not an interest rendering a grant of authority irrevocable[47]; nor is an agent's lien.[48] The fact that the agent subsequently acquires an interest in the property is irrelevant: to be irrevocable, the authority must be *conferred as* protection of the agent's interest.[49]

10–008   **Statute: powers of attorney.** Special provisions as to the irrevocability of powers of attorney in like situations (for which they might well be used) are laid down in the Powers of Attorney Act 1971, s.4, and the general effect of this provision is reproduced in Rules (2) and (3) of this Article. It may be that the Act aims to declare the common law in this

---

[45] § 138.

[46] *Sowman v. David Samuel Trust Ltd* [1978] 1 W.L.R. 22, 31 *per* Goulding J.: followed in *Re Leslie Homes (Aust.) Pty Ltd* (1984) 8 A.C.L.R. 1020; and see Millett (1977) 41 Conv. 83. *Contra, Barrows v. Chief Land Registrar*, Ch.Div., October 18, 1977.

[47] *Doward, Dickson & Co. v. Williams & Co.* (1890) 6 T.L.R. 316; *Frith v. Frith* [1906] A.C. 254.

[48] Illustration 5; below, para. 10–010.

[49] *Smart v. Sandars*, n. 43 above.

respect. But it should be noted that, to be irrevocable, a power of attorney must actually be expressed to be so: this is not true at common law. Further, it has been suggested above that at common law, in the case of a grant of authority coupled with an interest, the interest need not be that of the donee of the power: but the statutory wording seems to exclude this possibility.[50] The Act also contains protection for third parties where the power was expressed to be given by way of security but was in fact not so given,[51] protection which might be difficult to establish at common law.

Enduring powers of attorney.[52] The Enduring Powers of Attorney   **10–009**
Act 1985 seeks to deal with the situation where a person who has granted a power of attorney which is not irrevocable within the above provisions becomes mentally incapable. In such a case the automatic revocation of authority, even with the statutory protection of third parties in some cases, was extremely inconvenient, since the power might have been granted, for example by an elderly person, specifically with such a contingency in mind. It appears that attorneys often continued to act in such circumstances, at risk to themselves and third parties; and use of the Court of Protection for such situations would place an excessive strain on its resources. The Act therefore permits a person to create, subject to restrictions, a power of attorney which survives such incapacity.

The Act is silent as to the degree of capacity required by the person executing such a power, and it might be thought that on general principles that person must at the time of execution have capacity to do all the acts which the attorney is being authorised to do. This would, however, mean that the Act effected little change over the previous situation, since a person in full possession of his or her faculties might be unwilling to execute such a power, but might agree to do so when aware of failing powers. It has been held, therefore, that the person concerned must understand the nature and effect of the juristic act by which the power is conferred, but need not at that time be capable of managing his or her own affairs.[53] This result is convenient, but has been powerfully criticised as contrary to basic agency theory.[54]

---

[50] But see Millett, *op. cit.* n. 46 above at p. 86.

[51] See Article 124.

[52] See Cretney, *Enduring Powers of Attorney* (3rd ed.); and as to the purposes of the legislation Law Com. No. 122 (1983). Law Com. No. 231 (1995), n. 66 below, makes extensive proposals for reform of the law in this area, which proposals would involve the replacement of the entire 1985 Act. Proposals involving the amendment of the 1985 Act appear in Law Com. No. 220, "Delegation by Individual Trustees" (1994).

[53] *Re K (Enduring Power of Attorney)* [1988] Ch. 310.

[54] Munday, (1989) 13 N.Z.U.L.R. 253.

The power, which may be general or specific or subject to particular restrictions,[55] must be in a prescribed form and contain prescribed explanatory information.[56] Such a power is not revoked by the donor's subsequent mental incapacity[57]: but where such incapacity supervenes, the donee's powers are very limited prior to registration,[58] though he and third parties are protected when acting in good faith.[59] When the donee has reason to believe that the donor is or is becoming mentally incapable (defined as incapable of managing and administering his property and affairs[60]) he must notify the donor and specified persons[61] and apply to the court for registration of the power.[62] Objections can be raised to registration[63]; but if the court registers the power, it can no longer be specifically revoked unless this is confirmed by the court[64] nor disclaimed without notice to the court.[65] Where general authority is conferred, this is widely defined[66]; and the donee also acquires specified powers, which may include a power to execute trusts[67] and to benefit himself and persons other than the donor[68]; but it seems that though under fiduciary obligations he has no actual duty to act.[69] The power is terminated by bankruptcy of the donee[70] or by the court.[71] There is statutory protection for the donee and third parties acting in good faith

---

[55] ss. 3(1)–(3).

[56] s. 2(1)–(4); and as to the form required see S.I. 1990 No. 1376, replacing S.I. 1986 No. 120 and S.I. 1987 No. 1612. Execution by the attorney is required, which is not true of ordinary powers.

[57] s. 1(1)(a).

[58] ss. 1(1)(b); 1(2); see below. The court also has powers at this time: s. 5.

[59] ss. 1(1)(b)(c); 1(3). See below.

[60] s. 13(1)(2).

[61] Sched. 1. There is power to dispense with notification: s. 6(3).

[62] s. 4.

[63] s. 6.

[64] s. 7(1)(a).

[65] s. 7(1)(b). A disclaimer before registration requires notice to the donor: s. 1(12).

[66] s. 3(2). In Victoria, legislation has been passed to make clear (in connection with a statute using such wording: see Instruments Act 1958, s. 117) that a grant of general powers does not authorise the attorney to make a decision about medical treatment for the donor of the power: but also creating a new type of Power of Attorney which does: see Medical Treatment (Enduring Power of Attorney) Act 1990 (Vic.). This and associated questions are under consideration in England: see Law Com.C.P.No.119, "Mentally Incapacitated Adults and Decision-Making: an Overview" (1991); C.P. No. 128, "Mentally Incapacitated Adults and Decision-Making: a New Jurisdiction" (1993); Law Com. No. 231, "Mental Incapacity" (1995).

[67] s. 3(3). This was apparently inserted to deal with the problem raised by *Walia v. Michael Naughton Ltd* [1985] 1 W.L.R. 115. But it goes further than this: see Cretney, *op. cit.* n. 52 above pp. 50–51.

[68] s. 3(4)(5) (including seasonable and charitable gifts).

[69] Cretney, *op. cit.* n. 52 above, p. 14.

[70] s. 2(10).

[71] s. 8. The court can give directions, but only as to administrative matters, not as to the making of gifts under moral obligation: *Re R (Enduring Power of Attorney)* [1990] Ch. 647.

for acts done before registration[72]; for acts done under instruments which do not create enduring powers of attorney[73]; and where an instrument which did not create a valid power of attorney has actually been registered.[74] In principle, a power which fails as an enduring power (*e.g.* because not executed by the attorney[75]) can be valid under the rules for ordinary powers; but there may be difficulties where only the short form prescribed in the 1985 Act is used.[76]

Reference to irrevocable authority in other contexts. Where in the   **10–010** execution of his authority the agent incurs a personal liability to a third party, such that he would be entitled to reimbursement or indemnity in respect of it, the principal cannot, by purporting to revoke the agent's authority to discharge it, destroy that right. Thus where in the pursuance of his authority the agent incurs contractual liability to pay money to a third party, he is entitled to reimbursement in respect of payments which he makes even though the principal has subsequently forbidden them.[77] The principle applies also where the agent incurs a liability in respect of an authorised transaction which it is proper for him to discharge even though it could not be legally enforced, *e.g.* a liability to pay wagering debts,[78] or barrister's fees.[79] It may also be that this principle extends to the agent's right to take positive action, *e.g.* initiate proceedings, in respect of matters occurring while he had authority, even though again, the principal forbids such action.[80] It would not, however, extend to prevent revocation merely because the agent has

---

[72] s. 1(1)(c) (applying s. 5 of the Powers of Attorney Act 1971); s. 1(3).
[73] Sched. 2.
[74] s. 9.
[75] See above, n. 56.
[76] Oerton, (1987) 131 S.J. 16.
[77] *e.g. Chappell v. Bray* (1860) 6 H. & N. 145; *Warlow v. Harrison* (1859) 1 E. & E. 309. See in general Article 64. Where the principal indemnifies the agent in advance, the same rule applies: *Yates v. Hoppe* (1850) 9 C.B. 541.
[78] *Read v. Anderson* (1884) 13 Q.B.D. 779; and see *Seymour v. Bridge* (1885) 14 Q.B.D. 460.
[79] *Rhodes v. Fielder* (1919) 89 L.J.K.B. 15.
[80] See *Daly v. Lime Street Underwriting Agencies Ltd* [1987] 2 F.T.L.R. 277, where a former member of a Lloyd's syndicate failed in an action for a declaration that there was no authority to continue an action brought by the managing agents of his syndicate, in respect of matters occurring while he was a member. The power of the agent was described in the agreement conferring it as "irrevocable", but there is no discussion whether there was any proprietary interest, or (more likely in the circumstances) obligation, to protect. There had, however, been no attempt to revoke the authority before it was exercised, and this may be the best explanation. Another possible example is the auctioneer's authority to sign a memorandum of sale of land, which was said to be irrevocable after the sale: see *Van Praagh v. Everidge* [1902] 2 Ch. 266; *Phillips v. Butler* [1945] Ch. 358; Article 30, Illustration 7. See also the *Yasuda* case [1995] Q.B. 174.

incurred other liabilities, for example given a personal undertaking that he would have authority at a certain time in the future.

These propositions are sometimes expressed as propositions relating to irrevocable authority.[81] But they do not relate to authority in the sense of the power of an agent to affect the legal position of his principal[82]: their relevance is to authority in the context of the rule that the right to reimbursement and indemnity does not extend to unauthorised acts.[83] The rules as to reimbursement and indemnity, however, are not confined to agents at all, and the common use of the term "authority" in this context can be confusing. Therefore it is submitted that the rule in question is better expressed as in the above paragraph, and without reference to any idea of irrevocable authority.[84] Similar reasoning may apply to cases where the agent is entitled to remuneration: the principal may not, by purporting to revoke authority, deprive the agent of the right to remuneration earned but not yet paid.[85]

Such propositions are sometimes also cited in connection with a supposed general rule that authority cannot be revoked once acted on. This is true in the sense that once the act authorised has been done, a purported revocation of authority to do it is *ex hypothesi* ineffective to prevent the agent carrying it through, and to obtain reimbursement, indemnity and if appropriate, remuneration in respect of it. As regards authority the proposition can go no further.

In another group of cases, where an agent holds money for his principal, and the principal directs him to pay it to a third party, and the agent notifies the third party that he holds the money for the third party, the agent becomes liable to the third party in restitution, and the principal becomes unable to cancel his instructions: the principal's trustee in bankruptcy is in the same position.[86] Here again it can be said that the authority is irrevocable. But these cases seem really to depend on the idea of attornment of money, the irrevocability being like that of a property disposition: the agent is authorised to participate in such a disposition in favour of a third party, and once he has done so it cannot be recalled.[87]

A further rule which can be expressed in terms of revocation of authority is that which provides that where an agent who contracts

---

[81] *e.g. Chappell v. Bray* (1860) 6 H. & N. 145, 162; and early editions of this book.

[82] See Article 1.

[83] Article 65.

[84] See *Warlow v. Harrison* (1859) 1 E. & E. 309, 317; *Read v. Anderson* (1884) 13 Q.B.D. 779 (Bowen L.J.); Powell, p. 395.

[85] See Articles 58–60.

[86] See, *e.g. Walker v. Rostron* (1842) 9 M. & W. 441; *Griffin v. Weatherby* (1868) L.R. 3 Q.B. 753.

[87] The cases are fully discussed under Article 114.

personally has an unsatisfied lien on the subject-matter of a contract, payment to and set-off against him is normally a discharge to the third party to the extent of the lien.[88] In such cases it can be said that the principal to this extent cannot revoke the authority to receive payment.[89] But this is a rule as to performance of contract, relating to payment to or settlement with an agent, whereby the right of the principal to intervene and require payment to himself is inapplicable to the extent to which the agent has a lien. A lien, which constitutes the agent a secured creditor, obviously cannot be unilaterally terminated by the principal, even by his bankruptcy,[90] but this is not a rule as to revocation of authority.

The idea of irrevocable authority can also be used to explain cases more properly to be considered in connection with the rule in *Milroy v. Lord*,[91] which relates to the perfection of gifts. Indeed the whole subject touches the fringes of assignment of choses in action and transfer of property generally, and many of the old cases date from a time when no proper method of assignment had been evolved, and powers of attorney and the like were used to effect what would now be an assignment.

Finally, it is arguable (though it is submitted, wrongly) that equity may intervene to restrain a revocation of authority which is in breach of contract. This point is considered under Article 122.

Illustrations

(1) A, being indebted to B, gives him a power of attorney to sell **10–011** certain land and discharge his debt out of the purchase-money. The power is irrevocable.[92]

(2) Goods are consigned to a factor for sale, and he later makes advances to the principal on the credit of them. Subsequently, the principal instructs the factor not to sell. The factor's authority is revocable, not being given for valuable consideration.[93]

(3) Goods are consigned to a factor for sale. He makes advances, in consideration of an agreement by the principal that his authority to sell shall be irrevocable. The authority is irrevocable.[94] It is a question of

---

[88] See above, para. 9–009.
[89] See *Drinkwater v. Goodwin* (1775) 1 Cowp. 251; *Robson v. Kemp* (1802) 4 Esp. 233.
[90] See Article 69. And see above, paras. 8–108, 9–009, 9–021.
[91] (1862) 4 De G.F. & J. 264; see Snell, *Equity* (29th ed.), pp. 121 *et seq.* See, *e.g.* *Kiddill v. Farnell* (1857) 3 Sn. & G. 428; *Re Williams, Williams v. Ball* [1917] 1 Ch. 1.
[92] *Gaussen v. Morton* (1830) 10 B. & C. 731. See also *Re Rose, ex p. Hasluck & Garrard* (1894) 1 Manson 218.
[93] *Smart v. Sandars* (1848) 5 C.B. 895; *Raleigh v. Atkinson* (1840) 6 M. & W. 670.
[94] See *Smart v. Sandars*, above; *De Comas v. Prost* (1865) 3 Moo.P.C.(N.S.) 158.

fact whether such an agreement was made, and it may be inferred from the circumstances.[95] In the absence of such an agreement for valuable consideration, the authority of a factor to sell does not become irrevocable by the failure of the principal duly to repay advances made on the security of the goods.[96]

(4)   A signs and addresses to B an underwriting letter by which he agrees, in consideration of a commission, to subscribe for a certain number of shares in a company, and authorises B to apply for the shares in his name and on his behalf. B, being a vendor to the company, and therefore having an interest in the raising of the capital, by letter accepts the terms of A's agreement. The authority given to B to apply for the shares is irrevocable, and A is bound to take the shares applied for and allotted in pursuance of the underwriting letter, although in the meantime he has given notice to B and to the company repudiating the agreement.[97]

(5)   An auctioneer was authorised to sell goods, and after he had incurred expenses in respect of them, the principal revoked his authority. Held, that the authority of the auctioneer was not irrevocable merely by reason of his special property in the goods and his lien on them for advances, and that he was liable to the principal in trespass for going to the premises to sell the goods after notice of the revocation.[98]

Article 121

TERMINATION OF AUTHORITY BY DEATH, MENTAL INCAPACITY OR INSOLVENCY

10–012   Subject to the provisions of Articles 124 and 125, the authority of an agent, whether conferred by deed or not and whether expressed to be irrevocable or not, is determined by the death[99] or supervening mental incapacity[1] of either the principal or the agent: or, where the principal or agent is a body corporate, by its winding up or dissolution.[2]

---

[95] *De Comas v. Prost*, above.
[96] *Smart v. Sandars*, n. 94 above.
[97] *Re Hannan's Empress Gold Mining & Development Co., Carmichael's Case* [1896] 2 Ch. 643; *Re Olympic Reinsurance Co., Pole's Case* [1920] 2 Ch. 341. *Cf. Re Consort Deep Level Gold Mines Ltd, ex p. Stark* [1897] 1 Ch. 575; *Re Bultfontein Sun Diamond Mine Ltd, ex p. Cox, Hughes and Norman* (1897) 75 L.T. 669.
[98] *Taplin v. Florence* (1851) 10 C.B. 744.
[99] Illustrations 1 to 3; *Houstoun v. Robertson* (1816) 6 Taunt. 448; *Carr v. Levingston* (1865) 35 Beav. 41; *Farrow v. Wilson* (1860) L.R. 4 C.P. 744; *Phillips v. Jones* (1888) 4 T.L.R. 401; *Restatement*, §§ 120–123.
[1] *Drew v. Nunn* (1879) 4 Q.B.D. 661; *Yonge v. Toynbee* [1910] 1 K.B. 215. As to mental incapacity, see Articles 4, 5.
[2] *Salton v. New Beeston Cycle Co.* [1900] 1 Ch. 43, Illustration 4; *Selfe v. Colonial Ice Co.* (1894) 10 W.N.(N.S.W.) 153. As regards partnerships, see Comment.

Comment

Death. The death of the agent obviously terminates his authority, for **10–013** the relationship is a highly personal one.[3] And the death of the principal deprives the agent of anyone for whom he can act.[4] Therefore on the principal's death the actual authority terminates unless it is irrevocable[5]; not only can the agent not sue for remuneration, reimbursement or indemnity in respect of acts committed after his principal dies,[6] but he may, if he continues to act, be liable for loss caused to the estate.[7] It is also probable that the principal's estate cannot be bound under the doctrine of apparent authority[8]; and that the agent may consequently be liable to the third party for breach of warranty of authority.[9] The rule if correct has the effect of protecting the estate at the expense of commerce. There is some statutory protection in the case of powers of attorney.[10] It has been suggested that it might be possible for the agent to take a special term in his agency agreement that he is to be protected against personal liability arising after the principal's death,[11] but there is no authority on the validity of such an arrangement, which would in any case only operate *inter partes*. The *Restatement*[12] enters a *caveat*:

> "No inference is to be drawn from the rule stated ... that an agent does not have the power to bind the estate of a deceased principal in transactions dependent upon a special relation between the agent and the principal, such as trustee and beneficiary, or in transactions in which special rules are applicable, as in dealings with negotiable instruments."[13]

Ratification. It is not clear whether the executors or administrators of **10–014** the deceased can ratify a contract made on behalf of the deceased: it seems that in the case usually cited for the proposition that they can, the

---

[3] See *Farrow v. Wilson*, n. 99 above, at p. 746. As regards joint agents, see *Adams v. Buckland* (1705) 2 Vern. 514; *Friend v. Young* [1897] 2 Ch. 421 and Article 11. The termination of authority may affect the position of sub-agents: see Chap. 5. Commission may continue payable after the death of the agent: see *Wilson v. Harper, Son & Co.* [1908] 2 Ch. 370; above, para. 7–041.

[4] See *Drew v. Nunn*, n. 1 above, at p. 666.

[5] Article 120.

[6] Illustration 3.

[7] Illustration 2.

[8] See Comment to Article 123.

[9] *Yonge v. Toynbee* [1910] 1 K.B. 215; Article 107. But see Article 124 as to powers of attorney.

[10] See Article 124. See also Seavey (1930) 44 Harv.L.Rev. 265.

[11] Powell, p. 389. As to the possibility of deliberately creating authority which does not terminate on the death of the principal, see Wolff (1946) 62 L.Q.R. 272; Fitzgerald (1946) 13 Solicitor 224 (which should be read now in the light of the provisions dealt with in Article 124).

[12] § 120.

[13] *cf.* Bills of Exchange Act 1882, s. 75(2), relating to payment of cheques by bankers.

contract was made on behalf of the administrators.[14] A person who purported to contract with a person who is, unknown to him, already dead, might well not have been willing to contract with the personal representatives, and the permissibility of ratification therefore seems doubtful.[15] The third party may, of course, make a fresh contract with the executors or administrators.

10–015   **Companies.** The actual dissolution of a company is obviously equivalent to the death of a non-corporate principal or agent and arguments similar to those above are applicable. But certain consequences, in some respects analogous to bankruptcy, may flow from the commencement of the winding-up.[16] Special consequences also follow the appointment of receivers and managers; or of an administrator. Reference should be made to specialised works.[17]

10–016   **Partnerships.** The rule stated in this Article also applies to cases where the principal[18] or agent[19] is a partnership, and there is by death or retirement a change in the partnership, which thereby technically becomes a new partnership.[20] If the contract is regarded as personal to the particular partners—and an agency contract usually is so regarded[21]—the agency is frustrated. *A fortiori* the same rule applies where the partnership is dissolved.[22]

10–017   **Mental incapacity.** Mental incapacity in this context means inability to appreciate the nature and quality of the act done.[23] The agent's actual authority determines where the principal becomes mentally incapable,[24] provided again that there is no irrevocable authority.[25] It would seem

---

[14] *Foster v. Bates* (1843) 12 M. & W. 226. See also Powell, p. 388, n. 7.
[15] But see *Alexander Ward & Co. Ltd v. Samyang Navigation Ltd* [1975] 1 W.L.R. 673 (liquidator: not a contract case, however).
[16] Companies Act 1985, ss. 580(2), 591(2) (notification must be given: see in general *ibid.*, s. 42); *Re Oriental Bank Corp., ex p. Guillemin* (1884) 28 Ch.D. 634. The appointment of a receiver may have a similar effect.
[17] See, *e.g.* Gower, *Modern Company Law* (5th ed.); Pennington, *Corporate Insolvency Law* (1991); Kerr, *Receivers and Administrators* (17th ed.); Picarda, *Law Relating to Receivers, Managers and Administrators* (2nd ed.).
[18] *Tasker v. Shepherd* (1861) 6 H. & N. 575; *Brace v. Calder* [1895] 2 Q.B. 253.
[19] *Friend v. Young* [1897] 2 Ch. 421.
[20] Lindley and Banks, *Partnership* (17th ed.), §§ 3–36—3–38.
[21] See cases cited at nn. 18 and 19, above.
[22] See *Bovine Ltd v. Dent & Wilkinson* (1904) 21 T.L.R. 82. But there may in the case of dissolution or retirement be liability for breach of contract: see *Bovine Ltd v. Dent & Wilkinson*, above; *Brace v. Calder*, n. 18 above; Article 60; Lindley and Banks, *op. cit.* n. 20 above, § 3–39.
[23] *Boughton v. Knight* (1873) L.R. 3 P. & D. 64, 72.
[24] *Drew v. Nunn* (1874) 4 Q.B.D. 661; *Yonge v. Toynbee* [1910] 1 K.B. 215; *Re Coleman* (1929) 24 Tas. L.R. 77 (power of attorney).
[25] Article 120. See also Article 4 as to capacity; as to mental incapacity of agent, Article 5.

that any transaction is void as being unauthorised, rather than voidable at the instance of the mentally incapable person, as would be the case if it were directly entered into.[26] Doubtless such a transaction could however be ratified like any unauthorised contract if the principal recovered his capacity.[27] But here it seems that the doctrine of apparent authority may apply to protect third parties, even though if has been held that the agent is liable for breach of warranty of authority in such a case. This involves difficulties which are discussed under Article 123. The agent's authority may, however, continue if the provisions of the Enduring Powers of Attorney Act 1985 are applicable and complied with.[28] When it is the agent who becomes mentally incapable, the authority would doubtless cease on the basis that the agent was not competent to act.[29]

Insolvency.[30] In some respects, insolvency of a sole principal is like   **10–018** his death or mental incapacity,[31] and should revoke agency authority unless it is irrevocable as being coupled with an interest.[32] Once a person is adjudicated bankrupt, dispositions of his estate between the date of the presentation of the petition and the taking effect of the appointment of a trustee are void,[33] with exceptions in favour of a bona fide purchaser.[34] When the appointment of the trustee in bankruptcy takes effect the property vests in him[35]: "property" is defined to include things in action and obligations.[36] Therefore an agent of the bankrupt cannot in general,[37] unless authorised by the trustee, dispose of the bankrupt's property; and if he receives property he receives it for the trustee, who may claim[38] or disclaim[39] it. Similar reasoning applies to

---

[26] *Imperial Loan Co. v. Stone* [1892] 1 Q.B. 599.

[27] See Articles 13–20.

[28] See above, para. 10–009.

[29] See Article 5.

[30] See Chitty, *Contracts* (27th ed.), Vol. 1, Chap. 20; *Muir Hunter on Personal Insolvency* (1987).

[31] See Story, *Agency* (6th ed.), s. 482.

[32] Article 120.

[33] Insolvency Act 1986, s. 284(1).

[34] *ibid.*, s. 284(4).

[35] *ibid.*, s. 306.

[36] *ibid.*, s. 436. If a trustee seeks to ratify an act done on behalf of the bankrupt, it might seem that he cannot, for the same reason as the executors or administrators of a deceased person cannot ratify: above, para. 10–014. But the wide wording of s. 436 may pass the power to ratify. For an example of ratification see *Alexander Ward & Co. Ltd v. Samyang Navigation Ltd* [1975] 1 W.L.R. 673.

[37] There are exceptions to what the bankrupt's estate includes: s. 283.

[38] *ibid.*, s. 307: with exceptions for bona fide purchasers, s. 307(4).

[39] *ibid.*, s. 315.

contracts. He can enter into a contract on behalf of the principal in cases where the principal can contract himself: but some contracts may be claimed or disclaimed by the trustee. The bankruptcy does not however of itself frustrate or constitute a repudiatory breach of any agency contract, though it sometimes may have this effect. Likewise the bankruptcy of the agent may or may not frustrate or constitute a repudiation or grounds for termination of any agency contract.[40]

Illustrations

10–019   (1)   A undertakes to pay B £100 if B succeeds in selling a picture at a certain price—"no sale, no pay." B endeavours to sell the picture, and after A's death succeeds in doing so. The representatives of A's estate are not bound by the contract of sale,[41] but they may ratify it if they think fit, at any rate if it purported to be made on their behalf.[42] Even if the representatives ratify the sale, they are not liable to pay B the £100 unless they ratify his contract with A, but they are liable to pay him a reasonable sum for the services performed.[43]

(2)   A stockbroker had a continuation account open with a client. The client died, and the broker, failing to get instructions from his representatives, carried over the transactions instead of closing them on or before settling day, and ultimately sold the shares at a loss. It was held that the representatives were entitled to stand by the carrying-over sale on the first settling day after the death, and that the broker was liable for the subsequent loss.[44]

(3)   A solicitor is retained to conduct a divorce suit. The retainer ceases on the death of the client pending the proceedings, and the solicitor cannot recover costs subsequently incurred, even when he had no knowledge of his client's death.[45]

(4)   While an action against a company was pending, the company was dissolved under the Companies Acts. Held, that the authority of the company's solicitor was determined by the dissolution, though he had no knowledge of it.[46]

---

[40] See *McCall v. Australian Meat Co. Ltd* (1870) 19 W.R. 188; *Hudson v. Granger* (1821) 5 B. & A. 27; *Restatement*, s. 113. But an enduring power of attorney is revoked by the insolvency of the attorney: Enduring Powers of Attorney Act 1985, s. 2(10).

[41] *Blades v. Free* (1829) 9 B. & C. 167.

[42] *Foster v. Bates* (1843) 12 M. & W. 226.

[43] *Campanari v. Woodburn* (1854) 15 C.B. 400.

[44] *Re Overweg, Haas v. Durant* [1900] 1 Ch. 209, referring of course to former practices.

[45] *Pool v. Pool* (1889) 58 L.J.P. 67; *Whitehead v. Lord* (1852) 7 Exch. 691.

[46] *Salton v. New Beeston Cycle Co.* [1900] 1 Ch. 43.

Article 122

TERMINATION OF AUTHORITY BY NOTICE OF REVOCATION OR RENUNCIATION

Subject to the provisions of Articles 120 and 124, the authority of **10–020** an agent, whether conferred by deed or not, and whether expressed to be irrevocable or not, is terminated by the principal giving to the agent notice of revocation at any time before the authority has been completely exercised,[47] or by the agent giving to the principal notice of renunciation accepted by the principal[48]; but without prejudice to any claims for damages that the principal or agent may have against the other for breach of any contract between them.[49]

Comment

General rule. The general rule, which is perhaps not widely **10–021** understood, is that the authority of an agent, whether given by power of attorney,[50] or informally, even if for consideration,[51] and whether or not expressed to be irrevocable,[52] is revocable, without prejudice to the fact that such revocation may be wrongful as between principal and agent. The revocation may be oral whether or not the authority was conferred in writing.[53] There is a power to revoke: but there is not necessarily a privilege to exercise the power—there may indeed be a duty not to do so, with the result that the revocation is a breach of contract. This is subject to the rules as to irrevocable authority set out in Article 120.

The rule is based on policy, and is the same as that relating to dismissal of persons working under contracts of service: "the proper conduct of the affairs of life necessitates that this should be so."[54] It is reinforced by the separate rule that a contract of agency will not usually be enforced by a decree of specific performance.[55] Frequently, of course, the revocation or renunciation constitutes the acceptance of a repudiatory breach by the other party.

---

[47] See Illustrations.
[48] See above, para. 10–004.
[49] Article 125; *Restatement*, §§ 118, 119.
[50] *Walsh v. Whitcomb* (1797) 2 Esp. 565; *Frith v. Frith* [1906] A.C. 254; *Sinfra Aktiengesellschaft v. Sinfra Ltd* [1939] 2 All E.R. 675.
[51] *Doward, Dickson & Co. v. Williams & Co.* (1889) 6 T.L.R. 316.
[52] See *Vynior's Case* (1609) 8 Co.Rep. 81b.
[53] *The Margaret Mitchell* (1858) Sw. 382; *R. v. Wait* (1823) 11 Price 518.
[54] *Frith v. Frith*, n. 50 above at p. 259, *per* Lord Atkinson. See also, in the sphere of public law, *Huth v. Clarke* (1890) 25 Q.B.D. 391, 394 ("delegation does not imply a denudation of power and authority"); followed in *Manton v. Brighton Corp.* [1951] 2 All E.R. 101.
[55] See Article 61.

10–022   **Effect of equity.** It is possible then to argue that there is a similarity here with the rules relating to licences to enter upon land. Such a licence, not being a property interest, may be revoked at will, even in breach of contract, and revocation makes the licensee a trespasser at common law. However, in appropriate cases equity will intervene and restrain wrongful revocation by injunction: and since there may be an entitlement to this remedy the parties' rights on such a purported revocation may be decided on the basis that equitable relief would be available, with the result that the licensee cannot be treated as a trespasser.[56] There is, however, no authority for the operation of such reasoning in agency law and it is submitted that it should not be adopted. The confidential nature of the agency relationship, whereby one person may put himself effectively in the power of another, requires a rule stronger for authority than that applicable to trespass to land.[57]

10–022A   **Reliance.** Finally, it may be said that when the agent has foreseeably relied on an assurance that the authority would not be revoked, the principal may be restrained from revoking where revocation would be inequitable or unconscionable. There are certainly dicta which if quoted out of context suggest that there is a rule to this effect.[58] They relate, however, to agents who have done exactly what was authorised and who seek no more than reimbursement or indemnity.[59] The significance of estoppel reasoning such as this in general contract law is undoubtedly increasing. But this reasoning should on principle only operate between the parties: it should not affect the authority of the agent where the only reliance is that of the agent. Where there is reliance by the third party, the doctrine of apparent authority will give such protection as is appropriate.

10–023   **Notice.** As between principal and agent, the agent's authority does not cease until he receives notice of the revocation[60]: but there may be implied revocation by an act inconsistent with the continuation of the agency, coming to the notice of the agent,[61] and in some cases the agent may be employed on the basis that no notice of revocation is required.[64]

---

[56] See *Hurst v. Picture Theatres Ltd* [1915] 1 K.B. 1; *Winter Garden Theatre (London) Ltd v. Millenium Productions Ltd* [1948] A.C. 173; Hanbury and Maudsley, *Modern Equity* (13th ed.), Chap. 27.
[57] See Mechem, *Outlines of Agency* (1952), § 262 *cf.* Article 61.
[58] *e.g. Read v. Anderson* (1884) 13 Q.B.D. 779, 781.
[59] Above, para. 10–010.
[60] See *Re Oriental Bank Corp., ex p. Guillemin* (1884) 28 Ch.D. 634, 640. This problem should not be confused with the question whether the agent can or cannot be dismissed without notice, under the terms of his contract: see Article 125.
[61] See *Smith v. Jenning's Case* (1610) Lane 97.
[62] *e.g.* an estate agent: *E.P. Nelson & Co. v. Rolfe* [1950] 1 K.B. 139. But in some cases the proper explanation may be that agency never arises, since what is revoked is the offer to appoint an agent. See Comment to Article 125.

It is suggested in the *Restatement*[65] that a repudiatory breach of his duties by the agent, as by taking a bribe, would terminate his authority automatically; but in England at any rate it seems that the better view is that this would entitle the principal to terminate the authority and no more. As regards third parties, however, revocation should be effective to remove actual authority even if unknown to the agent; but apparent authority will continue until the third party has notice.[64]

Joint principals and joint agents. Where the authority is conferred by two or more principals jointly, it is sufficient if the notice is given by or to any one of the principals,[65] and the same rule presumably applies in respect of notice given to one agent where co-agents are appointed to act jointly.[66]   10–023A

Illustrations

(1) An indenture of lease provided that an agent named in it should   10–024
have authority to receive the rent on behalf of the lessor, and that his receipt should be a sufficient discharge, during the term thereby granted. Held, that the lessor might revoke the authority during the term, the agent having no interest in the rent.[67]

(2) An auctioneer is authorised to sell certain goods by auction. His authority may be revoked by the principal at any time before the goods are knocked down to a purchaser, though the auctioneer may be liable to a bidder in consequence of withdrawing the goods.[68]

(3) Money is deposited with A, to be applied for the use of the poor. The authority may be countermanded at any time before the application of the money, and the money recovered by the principal from A.[69]

(4) Money is deposited with a stakeholder, to be paid to the winner of a wager. The authority of the stakeholder may be revoked at any time before he has actually paid over the money to the winner, and if he pays it over after notice of revocation he is personally liable to the depositor for the amount.[70]

---

[63] Comment to § 112.

[64] In *Robert Simpson Co. v. Godson* [1937] 1 D.L.R. 454 it was held that notice to a third party, but not to the agent, did not terminate the agent's *actual* authority. The decision was criticised by Wright (1937) 15 Can.B.R. 196.

[65] *Bristow and Porter v. Taylor* (1817) 2 Stark. 50.

[66] See Article 11.

[67] *Venning v. Bray* (1862) 2 B. & S. 502; and see *Doward & Co. v. Williams & Co.* (1890) 6 T.L.R. 316; *Frith v. Frith* [1906] A.C. 254.

[68] *Warlow v. Harrison* (1859) 1 E. & E. 309.

[69] *Taylor v. Lendey* (1807) 9 East 49.

[70] *Hampden v. Walsh* (1876) 1 Q.B.D. 189; *Diggle v. Higgs* (1877) 2 Ex.D. 422; *Trimble v. Hill* (1879) 5 App.Cas. 342. These cases are not affected by the Gaming Act 1892: *O'Sullivan v. Thomas* [1895] 1 Q.B. 698; *Burge v. Ashley & Smith Ltd* [1900] 1 Q.B. 744; *Re Futures Index Ltd* Ch.D., October 5, 1984.

(5) A authorised his banker to hold £20 at the disposal of B. The authority of the banker may be countermanded, provided that he has not paid the money to B, nor attorned to him to hold it on his behalf. [71]

Article 123

Apparent Authority where Actual Authority Terminated

10–025   Where a principal, by words or conduct, represents or permits it to be represented that an agent is authorised to act on his behalf, he is bound by the acts of the agent, notwithstanding the termination of authority otherwise than by the death or insolvency of the principal, to the same extent as he would have been if the authority had not been terminated, with respect to any third party dealing with the agent on the faith of any such representation, without notice of the termination of his authority. [72]

Comment

10–026   This is an application of the doctrine of apparent authority in the specific context of revocation. It has earlier been pointed out that the doctrine of apparent authority covers two types of case: situations where there is some specific representation, and cases where the representation arises only from the agent's being permitted to assume a position carrying with it a usual authority. [73] Similar ideas operate where the principal holds the agent out as owner. [74] The question whether apparent authority persists where the principal gives the agent instructions limited to a particular period, or unexpectedly revokes his instructions, has not yet been fully worked out, because most apparent authority cases refer to the extent of authority rather than its duration. [75] In the case of specific representations, the matter will turn on the length of time indicated by the representation. [76] In the case of

---

[71] *Gibson v. Minet* (1824) 9 Moo.C.P. 31; *Brummell v. M'Pherson* (1828) 5 Russ. 263. See Article 114(3).

[72] See Illustrations 1–4; *Pole v. Leask* (1862) 33 L.J.Ch. 155, 162–163; *Ryan v. Sams* (1848) 12 Q.B. 460; *Aste v. Montague* (1858) 1 F. & F. 264; *Staveley v. Uzielli* (1860) 2 F. & F. 30; *Curlewis v. Birkbeck* (1863) 3 F. & F. 894; *Debenham v. Mellon* (1880) 6 App.Cas. 24, 33; *Scarf v. Jardine* (1882) 7 App.Cas. 345, 349; *Willis, Faber & Co. Ltd v. Joyce* (1911) L.T. 576; *Morgan v. Lifetime Building Supplies Ltd* (1967) 61 D.L.R. (2d) 178; *Restatement*, §§ 124A–134, 135–136; *cf.* Partnership Act 1890, ss. 36, 8; Factors Act 1889, s. 2(2); Articles 21, 74.

[73] See Comments to Articles 22, 74.

[74] *Curlewis v. Birkbeck* (1863) 3 F. & F. 894. See Article 86.

[75] Stoljar, pp. 166–168.

[76] See *Pole v. Leask* (1862) 33 L.J.Ch. 155, 162.

usual authority it is submitted that the principal must take the risk if he did not notify the third party of the limitation or revocation.[77] This is supported by a decision of the Supreme Court of Canada[78] which specifically rejects an argument that it is necessary to look to the time of the transaction in question to determine whether there was an operative representation of authority, and takes the view that a usual authority may be deemed to continue unless there is notice that it does not. Thus where a broker is asked to sell on a particular day and sells on another, he may bind his principal. Some old cases may suggest the contrary,[79] but they date from a time when the possibility of apparent authority was not properly appreciated, and should probably, if correct, be confined to the relationship between principal and agent.

Application to cases of death or incapacity. Special problems may   **10–027** arise in cases of incapacity. Where the principal dies, it is arguable on a purely theoretical basis that no apparent authority can continue, for "How can a valid act be done in the name of a dead man?"[80] A similar argument can be put forward in insolvency situations, for by the insolvency the property is vested in a new principal, the trustee in bankruptcy.[81] It can also be put forward, though perhaps less strongly, in cases of mental incapacity, for the principal becomes incapable of continuing his consent to the relation, or of making or continuing representations to the third party.

In *Drew v. Nunn,*[82] however, a strong Court of Appeal decided that a principal who became mentally incapable could be bound under the doctrine of apparent authority, provided his initial representations were made while he was capable. The decision is clearly based on the desirability of protecting third parties: "insanity is not a privilege, but a misfortune which must not be allowed to injure innocent persons."[83] One judgment contains suggestions that the reasoning should be extended also to cases of the principal's death.[84] The decision is said to be inconsistent with *Yonge v. Toynbee,*[85] in which a solicitor who took steps in litigation on behalf of a defendant client who had unknown to

---

[77] Powell, pp. 399–402. See Comment to Article 22.
[78] *Rockland Industries Ltd v. Amerada Minerals Corp. of Canada* [1980] 2 S.C.R. 2, (1980) 108 D.L.R. (3d) 513, Illustration 4. See also *Willis, Faber & Co. Ltd v. Joyce* (1911) 104 L.T. 576.
[79] *Dickinson v. Lilwall* (1815) 4 Camp. 279; *Blackburn v. Scholes* (1810) 2 Camp. 341; *Manser v. Back* (1848) 6 Hare 443.
[80] *Watson v. King* (1815) 4 Camp. 272, 274, *per* Lord Ellenborough.
[81] Above, para. 10–018.
[82] (1879) 4 Q.B.D. 661. See also *Re Parks* (1956) 8 D.L.R. (2d) 155 (adopting a test of constructive notice).
[83] *Per* Bramwell L.J. at p. 668; see also Brett L.J. at pp. 667–668.
[84] See Brett L.J. at p. 668.
[85] [1910] 1 K.B. 215.

him become mentally incapable was held liable to pay costs incurred by the plaintiff: it is argued that if the solicitor had apparent authority there would be no loss to the third party.[86] It is, however, difficult to see how the doctrine of apparent authority could have helped the plaintiff in that case, who seems to have acted reasonably in discontinuing the action after negotiations regarding the appointment of a guardian *ad litem* had fallen through.[87] The case is in any case one on the court's summary jurisdiction over solicitors.[88] There is authority therefore that the doctrine may protect the contracts of the agent of a principal who subsequently becomes mentally incapable; and possibly one who dies. It seems right that the decision should be based on policy rather than on theory, and it is arguable that there is actually a stronger case for the application of the doctrine in the case of death than in the case of mental incapacity, for in the latter case there may be a legitimate interest in protecting the mentally incapable.[89] The question of insolvency is more complex, as it is regulated by statute; but statute in fact confers protection on third parties.[90]

The normal view nevertheless, reflected in the wording of the Article, is that where the principal dies there can be no apparent authority, even though the situation will plainly give rise to hardship[91]: there is statutory protection in the case of powers of attorney.[92] As regards insolvency, there is, as already stated, fairly extensive statutory protection afforded by insolvency law[93] as well as that covering powers of attorney.[94] In the case of mental incapacity, however, *Drew v. Nunn* holds that there can be apparent authority. It is submitted that in such a case if the third party had known of the incapacity, the transaction would have been void for lack of authority rather than voidable by the

---

[86] Powell, p. 390; Treitel, *Law of Contract*, (9th ed.), p. 666, n. 78.

[87] See Higgins (1961) 1 U.Tas.L.Rev. 569. *Drew v. Nunn* was not cited to the court in *Yonge v. Toynbee*. It seems in fact to have been an early case on apparent authority as we know it now, and was cited with approval in this connection by the Court of Appeal in *Republic of Chili v. London and River Plate Bank* (1894) 10 T.L.R. 658 and by Scrutton J. in *Willis, Faber & Co. v. Joyce* (1911) 104 L.T. 576.

[88] Indeed it is difficult to see how an implied contract of warranty of authority could arise in such a case: see above, para. 2–087.

[89] See Müller-Frienfels in *Civil Law in the Modern World* (Yiannopoulos ed., 1965) 77, 111–115 (citing comparative material); (1957) 6 Am.J.Comp.L. 165, 184–185.

[90] Above, para. 10–018.

[91] See *Blades v. Free* (1829) 9 B. & C. 167, Illustration 5 (though apparent authority was not adverted to at this time); Partnership Act 1890, s. 14(2); *Restatement*, § 120, comments *a* and *c* and Appendix, Reporter's Note to § 120; (1933) 11 Proc.Am. Law Inst. pp. 85 *et seq.* ("shocking result"); Seavey (1921) 29 Yale L.J. 859, 893–895 ("shockingly inequitable").

[92] Article 124.

[93] Above, para. 10–018.

[94] Article 124.

principal under the rule in *Imperial Loan Co. v. Stone*,[95] which applies to contracts with the principal directly.[96] Where the principal's property is, under the Mental Health Act 1983, under the control of the court, the analogy seems rather to be with bankruptcy: but the matter is too specialised for consideration here. There is again statutory protection in the case of powers of attorney.[97]

Illustrations

(1) A authorises B to purchase goods on his credit, and holds him **10–028** out to C as his agent for that purpose. C supplies goods to B, on A's credit, after revocation by A of B's authority to act on his behalf, C having had no notice of such revocation. A is liable to C for the price of the goods, even if B contracted on his own behalf, and did not intend to bind A.[98]

(2) A husband holds out his wife as having authority to pledge his credit, and subsequently becomes mentally incapable. A tradesman, on the faith of such holding out, supplies goods to the orders of the wife, without notice of the husband's incapacity. The husband is liable for the price of the goods.[99]

(3) A policy was effected through the local agent of an insurance company and notice of a loss was given to him after the branch of business concerned had been transferred to another company. The agent in fact reported the loss to the other company. Held, that that was notice to "a known agent of the company" within the meaning of the policy, the assured having no knowledge of the change of company.[1]

(4) A manager has general authority to make sales. He negotiates for a substantial contract. His superior decides that higher approval is needed for a particular transaction into which the manager would previously have been authorised to enter. This restriction is not communicated to the third party and the manager subsequently ends a telephone conversation "we have a deal." His company is bound.[2]

---

[95] [1892] 1 Q.B. 599. See Comment to Article 4.
[96] Hudson (1959) 37 Can.B.R. 497; *cf. Daily Telegraph Newspaper Co. Ltd v. McLaughlin* (1904) 1 C.L.R. 243, affd. [1904] A.C. 776. Dicta in *Taylor v. Walker* [1958] 1 Lloyd's Rep. are *contra*, but the matter was not argued. See also Powell pp. 390–391; Ashley (1928) 3 Wash.L.Rev. 133; Thomson (1951) 25 Tulane L.Rev. 249; McCormick (1960) 22 Mont.L.Rev. 74.
[97] Article 124.
[98] *Trueman v. Loder* (1840) 11 A. & E. 589; *Summers v. Solomon* (1857) 7 E. & B. 879.
[99] *Drew v. Nunn* (1879) 4 Q.B.D. 661. But see Comment; above, paras. 3–039 *et seq.*
[1] *Marsden v. City and County Ass. Co.* (1865) L.R. 1 C.P. 232. See also Article 21.
[2] *Rockland Industries Inc. v. Amerada Minerals Corp. of Canada Ltd* [1980] 2 S.C.R. 2, (1980) 108 D.L.R. (3d) 513 (approving the formulation in this Article).

(5) A woman lived with a man as his wife for some years and ordered necessaries from a tradesman to whom she had been held out by the man as having authority to pledge his credit. The man went abroad and died there, the woman continuing to order necessaries for herself and children, the tradesman having had no notice of the death. Held, that the woman had the same authority as a wife to bind the man, but that his estate was not liable for the price of the goods.[3]

Article 124

STATUTORY PROTECTION OF THIRD PARTIES AND AGENTS IN RESPECT OF ACTS DONE UNDER POWERS OF ATTORNEY

10–029

(1) Where a power of attorney has been revoked and a person, without knowledge of the revocation, deals with the donee of the power, the transaction between them is, in favour of that person, as valid as if the power had then been in existence.[4]

(2) Where a power of attorney is expressed in the instrument creating it to be irrevocable and to be given by way of security, then, unless the person dealing with the donee knows that it was not in fact given by way of security, he is entitled to assume that the power is incapable of revocation except by the donor acting with the consent of the donee, and will accordingly be treated for the purposes of Rule (1) above as having knowledge of the revocation only if he knows that it has been revoked in that manner.[5]

(3) Where the interest of a purchaser depends on whether a transaction between the donee of a power of attorney and another person was valid by virtue of Rule (1) above, it will be conclusively presumed in favour of the purchaser that that person did not at the material time know of the revocation of the power if—(a) the transaction between that person and the donee was completed within twelve months of the date on which the power came into operation, or (b) that person makes a statutory declaration, before or within three months after the completion of the purchase, that he did not at the material time know of the revocation of the power.[6]

(4) A donee of a power of attorney who acts in pursuance of the power at a time when it has been revoked does not, by reason

---

[3] *Blades v. Free* (1829) 9 B. & C. 167. But see Comment.
[4] Powers of Attorney Act 1971, s. 5(2). Further protection in respect of Stock Exchange transactions is given by s. 6.
[5] *ibid.* s. 5(3).
[6] *ibid.* s. 5(4).

of the revocation, incur any liability (either to the donor or to any other person) if at that time he did not know that the power had been revoked.[7]

Comment

This Article paraphrases the provisions of section 5(1) to (4) of the Powers of Attorney Act 1971,[8] which protect third parties and the donee of the power where the power has, unknown to them, been revoked.[9] The 1971 provisions replace sections 124, 127 and 128 of the Law of Property Act 1925, which were directed towards achieving the same sort of protection, but which were notoriously obscure and unsatisfactory. Rules (1), (2) and (3) therefore represent statutory formulations, in their particular context, of the doctrine of apparent authority. Rule (4) affects the doctrine of warranty of authority.   **10–030**

Revocation. It seems clear that revocation includes not only express or implied revocation but also death, mental incapacity and insolvency: for by section 5(5) it is provided that knowledge of the revocation of the power includes knowledge of the occurrence of any event (such as the death of the donor) which has the effect of revoking the power.[10]   **10–031**

Enduring powers of attorney. These provisions also apply to enduring powers of attorney governed by the Enduring Powers of Attorney Act 1985, with special variants.[11] That Act also contains provisions protecting the attorney and bona fide third parties in the case of transactions under instruments which did not create valid powers of attorney but have nevertheless been registered[12]; there are presumptions similar to those of the 1971 Act.[13] There are also provisions protecting those dealing with attorneys who purport to act as authorised by the statute after an application for registration has been made[14]; and where the instrument framed in the prescribed form is not a valid enduring power of attorney and hence is revoked by the incapacity of the donor.[15]   **10–032**

---

[7] *ibid.* s. 5(1).
[8] See in general Law Com. No. 30, Cmnd. 4473 (1970); (1971) 121 New L.J. 746, 751, 764, 771, 795; (1971) 115 S.J. 596; (1971) 35 Conv.(N.S.) 310; (1971) 68 L.S.Gaz. 434, 437; Land Registration (Powers of Attorney) Rules 1986 (S.I. 1986 No. 1537).
[9] The section applies whenever the power was created, but only to acts and transactions after the commencement of the Act: s. 5(7).
[10] As to revocation, see in general Article 119.
[11] s. 1(c); 9(5) (concerning the knowledge of the third party).
[12] s. 9.
[13] s. 9(4).
[14] ss. 1(1)(c), 1(3).
[15] s. 9(6) and Sched. 2. See in general Cretney, *Enduring Powers of Attorney* (3rd ed.), Chap. 8.

Article 125

COMPENSATION AT COMMON LAW ON TERMINATION OF AUTHORITY

10–033   The termination of the authority of an agent, while valid as such—

(1) may entitle the agent to compensation in accordance with the requirements of statute or delegated legislation; or

(2) may constitute a breach by the principal of the express terms of any contract of agency or of implied terms or contractual promises, in respect of any of which the principal may be liable in damages or subject to other remedies.[16]

Comment

10–034   The question whether a principal is liable to an agent for terminating his authority turns on the type of contract or other arrangement under which the agent is employed.

10–035   **Agent an employee.** If the agent is an employee he may be entitled to compensation for unfair dismissal or redundancy in accordance with the relevant statutory provisions of employment law.[17] He may also be entitled to damages at common law for wrongful dismissal, *viz.* dismissal in breach of contract.[18]

10–036   **Agent a commercial agent.** Where the agent is a commercial agent as defined by the Commercial Agents (Council Directive) Regulations 1993, the circumstances in which he may be dismissed and the compensation payable on dismissal are regulated by statutory instrument. Then provisions are discussed in Chapter 11.[19]

10–037   **Agent engaged under bilateral contract for services.** If the agent is engaged, not as an employee but as an independent intermediary, his rights will turn on whether he acts under a bilateral contract or under a unilateral one. If he himself undertakes duties towards his principal, *e.g.*

---

[16] See Comment: Powell, pp. 380–385. As to continuing commission and repayment of overpaid commission see above, paras. 7–025, 7–041.

[17] See *e.g. Harvey on Industrial Relations and Employment Law*; Chitty, *Contracts* (27th ed.), Vol. 2, Chap. 37. Special considerations apply when a company alters its articles. See *Southern Foundries Ltd v. Shirlaw* [1940] A.C. 701; *Shindler v. Northern Raincoat Co. Ltd* [1960] 1 W.L.R. 1038; Gower, *Modern Company Law* (5th ed.), pp. 153–158, 545–546; Davenport, (1993) 109 L.Q.R. 553. See also *Micklefield v. S.A.C. Technology Ltd* [1990] 1 W.L.R. 1002.

[18] See Chitty, n. 17 above, §§ 37–141 *et seq.*

[19] See esp. below, paras. 11–045 *et seq.*

to use his best endeavours, as seems to be a normal implication of a sole or exclusive agency,[20] his contract is a bilateral one involving reciprocal obligations. Usually such contracts make their own provision for termination[21]; but unless carefully drafted these may not always be as efficacious as might have been hoped.[22] Questions regarding the termination of such a contract depend on whether it has or has not a time limit specified in it.

(1) No time limit.[23] If there is no time limit referred to in the contract, three interpretations are possible as to termination.

A. TERMINABLE AT WILL. Decisions[24] and dicta[25] can be found suggesting that the confidential nature of the contract of agency means that where there are no provisions relating to termination such a contract can be terminated at will by the principal. The authority for this approach mostly derives however from unilateral contract cases, where it is the *offer* which is terminated[26]; and there is sometimes confusion with the proposition that the termination of authority is *effective* whether a breach of contract or not. It is submitted that such an approach will rarely if ever be appropriate for a binding bilateral contract, which of its nature involves the likely expenditure of time and effort by the agent.

B. NOT TERMINABLE AT ALL. Conversely, dicta can also be produced for the proposition that such a contract is (in the absence of special provision for termination) not terminable at all (other than on breach or frustration), at least if the express terms provide any support for such a construction.[27] It is submitted however that although there are cases where there is in effect the grant of a perpetual benefit in return for

---

[20] See above, para. 7–036. *Contra*, Murdoch (1975) 91 L.Q.R. 357, 373–375, who treats this as involving the offer of a unilateral contract also. See also McConnell (1983) 265 E.G. 547.

[21] *e.g. Christie & Vesey Ltd v. Maatschappij, etc., Helvetia N.V. (The Helvetia-S)* [1960] 1 Lloyd's Rep. 540. See also *Sport International Bussum B.V. v. Inter-Footwear Ltd* [1984] 1 W.L.R. 776.

[22] *e.g. Wickman Machine Tool Sales Ltd v. L. Schuler A.G.* [1974] A.C. 235, where the use of the word "condition" was not sufficient.

[23] See Carnegie (1969) 85 L.Q.R. 392; Lücke, (1973) 5 Adelaide L.Rev. 32, 48 *et seq.*

[24] *e.g. Alexander v. Davis & Son* (1885) 2 T.L.R. 142 (where the contract appears bilateral); followed in *Henry v. Lowson, ibid.* 199.

[25] *e.g. Martin-Baker Aircraft Co. Ltd v. Canadian Flight Equipment Ltd* [1955] 2 Q.B. 556, 582.

[26] *e.g. Motion v. Michaud* (1892) 8 T.L.R. 253; affd. *ibid.* 447: see below.

[27] *e.g. Llanelly Ry. and Dock Co. v. L. & N.W. Ry. Co.* (1873) L.R. 8 Ch.App. 942, 949; (1873) L.R. 7 H.L. 550, 567.

consideration,[28] in the commercial situation of representation such an interpretation would rarely be appropriate.[29]

C. TERMINABLE ON NOTICE. The third and most likely possibility is that the parties are interpreted as having at the time of the contract intended that the contract is terminable on reasonable notice, taking into account the expenditure and time incurred by the agent, the desirability of a period for readjustment of business and so forth.[30] This is so even where the contract itself makes other provision for termination,[31] unless such provision can be treated as exclusive.[32] The matter is sometimes said to turn on whether the contract is similar to an employment contract.[33] It is submitted that this interpretation will nearly always be appropriate in bilateral contract cases.

(2) Time limit. If there is a time limit contained in the contract, as where the contract provides for the agent to act for a specified period of years, it might be thought that the agent was by such a term entitled to continue to act for that period unless the contract was discharged by frustration, and that if his authority was terminated before the end of the period he would be entitled to damages. There are however many cases which hold that the principal may terminate without breach by simply going out of business[34] or disposing of the subject-matter of the

---

[28] See explanation of the *Llanelly* case by Goff L.J. in *Staffordshire Area Health Authority v. South Staffordshire Waterworks Co.* [1978] 1 W.L.R. 1387, 1402.
[29] See *Martin-Baker Aircraft Co. Ltd v. Canadian Flight Equipment Ltd* [1955] 2 Q.B. 556, 577. See also *Tower Hamlets L.B.C. v. British Gas Corp., The Times*, December 14, 1984 (no implication of reasonable duration).
[30] *e.g. Bauman v. Hulton Press Ltd* [1952] 2 All E.R. 1121 (six months); *Martin-Baker* case, n. 29 above (12 months: one contract a licence to manufacture); *Decro-Wall International S.A. v. Practitioners in Marketing Ltd* [1971] 1 W.L.R. 361 (distributorship: 12 months); *Crawford Fitting Co. v. Sydney Valve and Fittings Pty Ltd* (1988) 14 N.S.W.L.R. 438 (stressing in a distributorship contract the notion that "the relationship of the parties should continue long enough to enable the distributor to recoup extraordinary expenditure or effort"; particularly when that was incurred "with the actual or tacit authority of the principal'). "Reasonableness" is ascertained at the time of the notice given: *ibid.*; and see in general the *Staffordshire Area Health Authority* case, n. 28 above.
[31] As it did in the *Martin-Baker* case, n. 29 above (see esp. p. 573).
[32] As in *Re Berker Sportcraft Ltd's Agreements* (1947) 177 L.T. 420.
[33] *e.g.* the *Martin-Baker* case, n. 29 above at p. 582; see also *Paper Sales Corp. Ltd v. Miller Bros. Co. Ltd* (1975) 55 D.L.R. (3d) 492; *Knight v. Calderlodge Developments* (1978) 238 E.G. 117.
[34] *Ex p. Maclure* (1870) L.R. 5 Ch.App. 737; *Rhodes v. Forwood* (1876) 1 App.Cas. 256, Illustration 1 (even though the contract itself provided for termination); *Hamlyn & Co. v. Wood & Co.* [1891] 2 Q.B. 488 (sale contract); *Northey v. Trevillion* (1902) 7 Com.Cas. 201; *Lazarus v. Cairn Line Ltd* (1912) 106 L.T. 378; *In re R.S. Newman Ltd* [1916] 2 Ch. 309; *Leak v. Charles & Sons Ltd* (1948) 92 S.J. 154. As to changes in partnerships see *Tasker v. Shepherd* (1861) 6 H. & N. 575; *Cowasjee Nanabhoy v. Llallbhoy Vullubhoy* (1876) L.R. 3 Ind.App. 200; *Brace v. Calder* [1895] 2 Q.B. 253; Lindley and Banks, *Partnership* (16th ed.), § 3–39.

agency.[35] The reasoning is that the promise is only conditional on the business being carried on, which itself is not promised[36]; or that "a person is entitled to deal with his property as he chooses, and a person is entitled either to carry on his business or to give up carrying on his business, as he wishes."[37]

Other cases however hold that the principal may not do so and that there is a right to serve for a particular period,[38] sometimes explained as a right to a "continuing benefit."[39] These cases make very fine distinctions.[40] They are often explained as turning on the existence or non-existence of an implied term,[41] which is in general rarely found by the courts unless necessary to give business efficacy to the contract.[42] But in truth the question of implication of a term does not arise until the initial promise has been interpreted as absolute or non-absolute.[43] Thus in one such case[44] one member of a divided Court of Appeal posed the question whether there was any indication that a two-year contract could be ended in less than two years, and another whether there was a term that the business would be continued for two years.[45] All this emphasises the need for careful drafting of such contracts in order to avoid disputes.

The question may arise whether, if the principal is entitled to cease business, he must nevertheless give the agent reasonable notice. On the whole this seems unlikely: a cancellation of authority "from today" has been held valid.[46] The agent will however doubtless be entitled to a reasonable packing-up period before, *e.g.* he becomes a trespasser.[47]

---

[35] *Lazarus v. Cairn Line Ltd,* n. 34 above; *L. French & Co. Ltd v. Leeston Shipping Co. Ltd* [1922] 1 A.C. 451, Illustration 2 to Article 60; *Howard Houlder & Partners Ltd v. Manx Islands SS Co.* [1923] 1 K.B. 110 (all cases on ships); *Shackleton Aviation Ltd v. Maitland Drewery Aviation Ltd* [1964] 1 Lloyd's Rep. 293 (aircraft).

[36] *Warren & Co. v. Agdeshman* (1922) 38 T.L.R. 588, 590.

[37] *Alpha Trading Ltd v. Dunnshaw-Patten* [1981] Q.B. 290, 304 *per* Brandon L.J. See also *Lazarus v. Cairn Line Ltd* (1912) 106 L.T. 378, 380 (Scrutton L.J.).

[38] *Re London & Colonial Co., ex p. Clark* (1869) L.R. 7 Eq. 550; *Re Patent Floor Cloth Co. Ltd* (1872) 26 L.T. 467; *Turner v. Goldsmith* [1891] 1 Q.B. 544, Illustration 2; *Mutzenbecher v. La Aseguradora Española S.A.* [1906] 1 K.B. 254; *Reigate v. Union Manufacturing Co. (Ramsbottom) Ltd* [1918] 1 K.B. 592; *General Publicity Services Ltd v. Best's Brewery Co. Ltd* [1951] 2 T.L.R. 875; *Re Premier Products Ltd* [1965] N.Z.L.R. 50 (full analysis of case law: partly distributorship contract).

[39] *Lazarus v. Cairn Line Ltd,* n. 37 above at p. 380.

[40] *Bauman v. Hulton Press Ltd* [1952] 2 All E.R. 1121, 1124; Burrows (1968) 31 M.L.R. 390, 399.

[41] *e.g. Mutzenbecher v. La Aseguradora Española S.A.* [1906] 1 Q.B. 254; *Alpha Trading Ltd v. Dunnshaw-Patten Ltd* [1981] Q.B. 290.

[42] *cf. The Moorcock* (1889) 14 P.D. 64; above, para. 7–001.

[43] See *Re Premier Products Ltd* [1965] N.Z.L.R. 50.

[44] *Brace v. Calder* [1895] 2 Q.B. 253; see Burrows, *op. cit.* n. 40 above.

[45] See pp. 262, 259.

[46] *Lazarus v. Cairn Line Ltd* (1912) 106 L.T. 378.

[47] See *Winter Garden Theatre (London) Ltd v. Millenium Productions Ltd* [1948] A.C. 173.

This whole question interlocks very considerably with the question whether the principal is in breach of contract if he prevents the agent from earning commission. Such prevention may of course occur during the course of the agency arrangement (as when he sells himself or through another agent, or refuses to complete a negotiated transaction,[48]) as well as by complete termination of it. Reference should therefore be made also to the discussion of prevention of earning of commission under Article 60.[49]

10–038   **Agent's rights derive only from offer of unilateral contract.** In some cases the rights of an agent will be based only on a single or continuing offer by the principal to pay commission, which is best interpreted as an offer of a unilateral contract, under which the agent is not obliged to do anything but simply qualifies for commission if he does. It has been submitted elsewhere[50] that this is the best explanation of the estate agent's contractual position where he is not a sole or exclusive agent[51] and the same will be true of other canvassing agents.[52] In such a case the question of termination of authority depends on the rules for the revocation of contractual offers;[53] and although the courts have sometimes sought to answer the questions by considering the implication of a *term* it is submitted that the question is here better put as one whether there is an implied *contract* not to revoke the offer.[54] The principal might promise not to withdraw the offer in consideration of the agent commencing or maintaining activities within a reasonable time.[55] Put this way, it is obvious that such a promise will rarely be detected, and that the offer can normally be withdrawn without warning. This seems the true explanation of cases holding that an agent's authority may be withdrawn summarily.[56] This is now the accepted explanation of the position of an estate agent who is not a sole agent, unless he succeeds in securing other terms.[57] Wide dicta regarding the irrevocability of offers in such situations should be treated with caution.[58]

---

[48] *e.g. Alpha Trading Ltd v. Dunnshaw-Patten Ltd* [1981] Q.B. 290, Illustration 3 to Article 60.
[49] See also Article 61 on specific performance.
[50] See Comment to Article 60; *Luxor (Eastbourne) Ltd v. Cooper* [1941] A.C. 108, esp. at pp. 124–125; Murdoch (1975) 91 L.Q.R. 357.
[51] Murdoch, *op. cit.* above, treats sole agencies on the same basis.
[52] As to canvassing agents, see above, para. 1–017.
[53] See *Luxor (Eastbourne) Ltd v. Cooper*, n. 50 above at pp. 128–129.
[54] But see Treitel, *Law of Contract* (9th ed.), pp. 36–39.
[55] *cf. Errington v. Errington* [1952] 1 K.B. 290.
[56] *e.g. Motion v. Michaud* (1892) 8 T.L.R. 253; affd. *ibid.* 447; *Joynson v. Hunt & Son* (1905) 93 L.T. 470; *Levy v. Goldhill* [1917] 2 Ch. 297. See also *Keshen v. S. Lipsky Co. Ltd* (1956) 3 D.L.R. (2d) 438; *Lowe v. Rutherford Thompson McRae Ltd* (1970) 14 D.L.R. (3d) 772.
[57] Above, paras. 7–035—7–036.
[58] *e.g.* that of Goff L.J. in *Daulia Ltd v. Millbank Nominees Ltd* [1978] Ch. 231, 239.

Gratuitous agency. An agent who has no contractual relationship, 10–039
actual or potential, with his principal can be dismissed without liability
on the principal's part, except in so far as he has rights under the law of
restitution.

Remedies for wrongful termination. In principle a wrongful termina- 10–040
tion of authority will not terminate the contract also unless the agent
accepts the breach as doing so.[59] The usual remedy for wrongful
termination will however (apart from the statutory provisions of
employment law and the regulations governing commercial agents) be
an action for damages; though there may be cases where an injunction
or a declaration can be obtained.[60] The damages will normally be
calculated by reference to what would have been earned by way of
commission if the term of the agency had run its full course,[61] or if
reasonable notice had been given,[62] as appropriate in the circumstances,
less expenses which would have been incurred, and subject to the duty
to mitigate damages.[63]

Illustrations

(1) A and B agree that for seven years or so long as A shall 10–041
continue to carry on a business at the town of Liverpool, A shall be sole
agent at Liverpool for the sale of B's coals. After four years B sells his
colliery. He is not liable to A, for the contract does not bind him to
keep the colliery, nor to send coals to Liverpool.[64]

(2) A shirt manufacturer agreed with the plaintiff to employ him as
"agent canvasser and traveller" for five years. After two years the
manufacturer's shirt factory burnt down. The business was closed down
and he ceased to employ the plaintiff. Held, the plaintiff was entitled to
substantial damages, it being an implied term of the particular contract
in question that in employing the plaintiff for five years, the
manufacturer must be taken to have agreed to continue to send him
samples so that he could earn his commission.[65]

---

[59] *Atlantic Underwriting Agencies Ltd v. Cia. di Assicurazione di Milano S.p.A.* [1979] 2
Lloyd's Rep. 240, following *Thomas Marshall (Exports) Ltd v. Guinlé* [1979] Ch. 227.

[60] Article 61.

[61] *e.g. Reigate v. Union Manufacturing Co. (Ramsbottom Ltd)* [1918] 1 K.B. 592.

[62] *e.g. Bauman v. Hilton Press Ltd* [1952] 2 All E.R. 1121; *Roberts v. Elwells Engineers
Ltd* [1972] 2 Q.B. 586 (account not an appropriate remedy).

[63] Account must be taken of the probabilities of a sale taking place: *Hampton & Sons
Ltd v. George* [1939] 3 All E.R. 627; and see also *G. Trollope & Sons v. Caplan* [1936] 2
K.B. 382 (overruled on another point in *Luxor (Eastbourne) Ltd v. Cooper* [1941] A.C.
108). See in general McGregor, *Damages* (15th ed.), §§ 1189–1191.

[64] *Rhodes v. Forwood* (1876) 1 App.Cas. 256. See also Article 60, Illustration 2; *Groves
v. Stirling Bonding Co.* [1935] 3 D.L.R. 481.

[65] *Turner v. Goldsmith* [1891] 1 Q.B. 544. See also *Comet Group Plc v. British Sky
Broadcasting Ltd* Q.B.D., *The Times*, April 26, 1991.

CHAPTER 11

COMMERCIAL AGENTS

1.—INTRODUCTION

11–001 **Background.** In continental European countries agents are often placed in named categories which are the subject of special rules. These may require particular qualifications in the agent, and sometimes registration as a person authorised to conduct the commercial activity concerned. It has also been the case that certain categories of agent have been regarded as requiring protection against their principals, in a manner not unlike that in which employees are often, and nowadays in developed countries usually, regarded as requiring protection against their employers. In particular, it has in some countries been made legally requisite for a principal who wishes to terminate the services of an agent in certain categories to, in effect, buy him out by the payment of a sum which can be justified on the basis of the expense he has incurred and/or customer connection which he has generated—a notion often referred to by the French phrase *indemnité de clientèle*. It is thought that there is a danger that after the agent has built up a market for his principal the principal may intervene and deal direct with the customers before the agent has recovered his outlay and legitimate profit. Agents are also perceived as requiring, and have been given, protection against their principals in other ways, for example as regards the supply of information as to transactions entered into as a result of the agency and (a related question) as to payment of commission.

A directive seeking to generalise and harmonise among the E.C. countries the effect of such legislation, so far as it is applied to commercial agents, a category generally understood in civil law countries, has been in the offing since 1976. For many countries such legislation was of a familiar type and the need was only to harmonise details. For the common law countries in the E.C., however, the category, and indeed (with some exceptions) the categorisation of agents in general did not exist; and the type of legal control introduced was of a completely new type. The common law rules as to the relationship between any principal and any agent are based on the assumption that freedom of contract prevails. In so far as any protection has been perceived as necessary, it was protection of the principal against misuse of his powers by the agent, as by taking bribes, making a secret profit and in general assuming a position in which his own interests or those of others for whom he acts are adverse to those of his principal.[1] It was against the context of such perceived dangers that the fiduciary duties of the agent have developed. Their potential breadth is related to the breadth of the common law of agency itself, which does not in general utilise categories, and applies to many types of representative, some of which (*e.g.* solicitors) would not be regarded in other countries as within the law of agency at all. Where detailed control of types of agent has been introduced, as in the case of estate agents,[2] this has been done in the interest of protecting the principal against the agent, not the reverse; or even (as in the case of insurance brokers[3] and financial intermediaries) in the interest of protecting the public.

Thus it was perhaps not surprising that the Law Commission in 1977 reported rather hysterically that the proposed EEC directive on this topic "in many respects offend[s] against basic principles of the English law of agency"[4]: but this was not so. It also stated that it was "unable to identify such a social group [as commercial agents] in England"[5]: a claim that was speedily rebutted in the press at the time. A more measured report of a committee of the House of Lords assessed the proposal as one to introduce detailed regulation in an area in which it did not exist in the United Kingdom,[6] and this was correct. It may also be true that in the United Kingdom agents of the type regulated by the directive are less frequently used as instruments of market penetration than in some other countries.

The E.C. directive. The Council Directive on the Co-ordination of the **11–002** Laws of the Member States Relating to Self-Employed Commercial Agents[7] was adopted in 1986, but the United Kingdom and Ireland were given more time to bring it into force, on the (rather dubious) grounds, stated in the preamble to the directive, that "a particular effort" had to be made in those countries. Time was also granted to Italy, where such protection of the agent existed, but was in fact more elaborate and complex than elsewhere. The directive has considerable

---

[1] See Articles 45 *et seq.*
[2] See, *e.g.*, above, paras. 7–020, 7–037.
[3] See Insurance Brokers (Registration) Act 1977.
[4] Law Com. No. 84 (1977), p. 32.
[5] *Ibid.*, p. 6. See further Lando, Rabels Z., 1980, 1; Thuesen (1981) 6 E.L.Rev. 427.
[6] Select Committee on the European Communities, 51st Report, Session 1976–1977.
[7] Dir. 86/653, [1986] O.J. L382/17.

similarities with German law,[8] and reference to German law in particular may therefore sometimes assist in elucidating its likely intention, though it is obviously not to be presumed that the directive simply intended to generalise the results obtained in any one national system of law.

2.—THE COMMERCIAL AGENTS REGULATIONS

11-003   **The Commercial Agents (Council Directive) Regulations 1993.** The directive was implemented in Great Britain by regulations, the Commercial Agents (Council Directive) Regulations 1993,[9] made under section 2(2) of the European Communities Act 1972. These came into effect on January 1, 1994. They are not confined to contracts made after that date, and hence contracts of agency whenever made are subject to them, save in respect of rights and liabilities accrued before that date.[10]

11-004   **Interpretation.** On general principles of E.C. law the regulations must be interpreted against the background of the directive itself.[11] Since the wording of the regulations follows the directive extremely closely, the directive is relevant not only as to general purpose but also as to matters of detail. As will be seen, however, the directive, and hence the regulations, contain many obscurities and uncertainties. Some of these derive from the structure of the directive itself: for example, the extent to which particular provisions are *ius cogens*, *i.e.* cannot be derogated from, as opposed to *ius dispositivum*, *i.e.* provisions which only apply in the absence of other agreement, is far from clear.[12] Other problems derive from words selected by translators.[13] It should also be noted that the individual regulations are preceded by headings. These do not (apart from the chapter headings) appear in the directive itself. While instructive as to the beliefs of the English draftsman, therefore, they

---

[8] For a brief account of the relevant German law in English see Baumgarte, (1994) 5 E.B.L.Rev. 144. See further the bibliography at para. 11–054, below.

[9] S.I. 1993 No. 3053, as amended by Commercial Agents (Council Directive) (Amendment) Regulations 1993 (S.I. 1993 No. 3173). Effect was given to the directive in Northern Ireland by the Commercial Agents (Council Directive) Regulations (Northern Ireland) 1993 (S.I. 1993 No. 483), which was effective on a different date, January 13, 1994. See Schrire, (1994) 15 B.L.R. 171; Hodgkinson, (1994) 5 E.B.L.Rev. 119; Singleton, [1994] Tr. L. 26; Bell and O'Toole, (1994) 138 S.J. 10; Davis, (1994) 144 N.L.J. 388. The regulations are printed as an Appendix to this book: see below, pp. 722 *et seq.*

[10] Reg. 23.

[11] See, *e.g.*, Case 14/83, *Von Colson v. Land Nordrhein-Westfalen*: [1984] E.C.R. 1891, [1986] 2 C.M.L.R. 430; *Lister v. Forth Dry Dock & Engineering Co. Ltd* [1990] 1 A.C. 546; Case C-106/89, *Marleasing v. La Comercial Internacional de Alimentacion S.A.*: [1990] I E.C.R. 3313, [1992] 1 C.M.L.R. 305.

[12] See, *e.g.*, below, paras. 11–032, 11–034, 11–040.

[13] See, *e.g.*, below, paras. 11–031, 11–045.

provide no certain guide to the intentions of the directive. Standard English methods of statutory interpretation will in many cases of dispute be not at all appropriate. Many problems will eventually require resolution, in the last resort by the European Court of Justice.

3.—APPLICATION OF THE REGULATIONS

Transactions covered. By regulation 1(2) the regulations cover the relations between commercial agents and their principals. They therefore apply only to the internal agency relationship between principal and agent. They do not affect the external authority of the agents, nor the result of transactions entered into by him.

11–005

Conflict of laws: general rule. Regulation 1(2) also states that the regulations "apply in relation to the activities of commercial agents in Great Britain"; and by regulation 1(3) they do not apply "where the parties have agreed that the agency contract is to be governed by the law of another member State."[14] On general grounds this should mean that, subject to the exception mentioned, they apply to any commercial agent within the definition in so far as he conducts activities in Great Britain, *i.e.* England, Wales and Scotland (Northern Ireland being separately provided for[15]). Therefore a commercial agent working in Great Britain for a British principal is entitled to the benefit of the regulations; as is a French commercial agent working in Great Britain for a French principal, unless (in either case, the second obviously being more likely) the contract of agency is specified as being governed by the law of France or of another Member State. Thus the French agent is entitled instead to the protection of his own law if this is the law governing his contract of agency.

11–006

Agent of British principal working in E.C. country. This technique of application also, and more surprisingly, seems to mean that an agent of an English principal working in, for example, France is not affected by the regulations. This could be expected if his contract contains a choice of French law, which will provide its own protection under the directive. But it seems to be so even if the contract is governed by English law. In such a situation he should of course be entitled to the benefit of corresponding French legislation: but this will depend on its scope, and will in any case create a split in the applicable law, which may itself cause difficulties. The English agent will also be denied the protection of his own law, which the French agent who acts in Great Britain under a contract governed by French law has. It might be thought that the

11–007

---

[14] As to the meaning of these words see below para. 11–010.
[15] Above, n. 9.

regulations should apply wherever English (or Scots) law applies to the contract between principal and agent, but it is difficult to find support for this in the wording.

11–008   **Agent of non-E.C. foreign principal working in Great Britain.** More controversially, it seems on the wording of the regulations that the agent in England of (for example) an Australian principal, whether the agent be Australian, English or of any other nationality or residence, is entitled to their benefit, not only if the contract of agency contains a choice of English law but also if it is specified as governed by (for example) the law of New South Wales, so long as there is no choice for the law of another Member State (as it might be if the agent was French and covered France as well as the United Kingdom). For there is in the wording of the regulations no restriction to agents of principals in Member States, and it is at least arguable therefore that the regulations are an example of overriding forum policy, applicable to the activities of commercial agents in England, which an English court will apply whatever law governs the contract of agency, under Article 7(2) of the Rome Convention on the Law Applicable to Contractual Obligations,[16] which has statutory effect under the Contracts (Applicable Law) Act 1990.[17] This refers to "rules of law of the forum in a situation in which they are mandatory irrespective of the law otherwise applicable to the contract."

As against this it can be said that the regulations must be read subject to the directive, which in its preamble makes clear that the mischief was perceived as occurring "where principal and commercial agent are domiciled in different Member States", and that this policy does not require the same protection to be given to agents from non-Member States. Since there is no wording (for example, giving the regulations the "force of law"[18]) indicating that the regulations are intended to be mandatory in the sense referred to by Article 7(2), the second view may be better; but it does depend on suppositions as to the intention of the directive. The problem is similar to that concerning the applicability of the E.C. Convention rules on jurisdiction to cases which can be said to have no E.C. element.[19] Once exceptions to the rule as apparently laid down are made on this ill-defined ground of assumed purpose, problems as to how far the exceptions go will arise. The wording of the regulations seems to concentrate on pure territorial application.

---

[16] See Dicey and Morris, *Conflict of Laws* (12th ed.), Vol. 2, Rule 177.

[17] This, however, only applies to contracts entered into after April 1, 1991. In so far as the regulations, on the other hand, apply to all contracts, the application of overriding forum policy to a contract of agency entered into before that time would depend on the former rules of the common law.

[18] On this phrase see *The Hollandia* [1983] 1 A.C. 565.

[19] As in *Re Harrods (Buenos Aires) Ltd* [1992] Ch. 72.

Agent of E.C. principal working in Great Britain. Finally, the **11–009** position of the agent who is working in England on behalf of a principal in another Member State must be noted. If the agent works under a contract containing a choice of law for the law of the country of his principal, the English regulations do not protect him. The law of the country of his principal may. But if that country has applied the directive in a similar way to the English regulations, *i.e.* confining the protection to activities in its own country, the agent may be unprotected. Whether, therefore, in applying the directive only to activities in Great Britain, the right policy was selected for facilitating the application of the directive throughout the E.C., and to what extent this form of implementation complies with Community obligations, is seriously open to doubt. Had the regulations applied wherever a contract to be performed in the E.C. was governed by English law, the objectives of the directive might have been better achieved.

Contract "agreed ... to be governed by the law of another Member **11–010** **State".** There is uncertainty as to what this exclusion means. In the discussion above, the problem has been avoided by postulating in each case an express choice of law, which would certainly come within the words. The Rome Convention on the Law Applicable to Contractual Obligations provides in Article 3(1) that a contract is governed by "the law chosen by the parties". It is controversial to what degree these words extend to situations of implied and imputed choice: the text, and the accompanying Giuliano/Lagarde Report, give some guidance but leave much in the air.[20] The wording of this directive and regulations are somewhat different, and there is no further guidance given. It is uncertain therefore how far the exclusion in favour of the law of another Member State goes beyond situations where there is an express choice of law. Where however the applicable law is determined as that of a Member State by use of Article 4 of the Convention, which applies in the absence of choice and uses the notion of close connection accompanied by presumptions, it would seem that the regulations are not excluded, for this cannot be said to involve an agreement on choice of law. Where the contract is potentially governed by the law of a *non-*E.C. country, however, as in the case of the Australian principal mentioned above, the regulations are inapplicable and the rules of the Convention must apply.

Activities. Problems will also arise as to the word "activities", and **11–011** where the activities of an agent who operates from one country in another by means of fax, telex or telephone are to be regarded as taking place.

---

[20] See Dicey and Morris, *Conflict of Laws* (12th ed.), Vol. 2, pp. 1223–1229.

11–012   **What is a commercial agent?** The term "commercial agent" is, as stated above, unknown to the common law; and the definition in the regulations is therefore crucial. Such an agent is defined in regulation 2(1) as "a self-employed intermediary who has continuing authority to negotiate the sale or purchase of goods on behalf of another person (the 'principal'), or to negotiate and conclude the sale or purchase of goods on behalf of and in the name of that principal." There are specific exceptions which are dealt with below. It is, however, clear that the directive and regulations refer to an *agent*. A *distributor* of goods, though often described as an "agent", buys for resale and, unlike an agent, takes a financial risk.[21] Although in some countries distributors and sometimes franchisees are entitled to protections similar to those afforded to agents, the directive and regulations are not intended to cover distributors.[22] There is no definition of "goods"; the main problem regularly arising in this connection in the modern context is whether computer software is "goods". Contracts relating to such software are often, however, drafted in other ways, in particular as licences, and this raises special problems.

11–013   **Self-employed.** This phrase to a common lawyer contains echoes of employment law. An employee must be a natural person; hence it might be thought that the reference to self-employment carried the same implication. It seems clear that in this context that is a wrong inference and that the reference is rather to what at common law might be called an independent contractor. Hence it seems clear that a company or partnership can be a commercial agent.

11–014   **Sale or purchase of goods.** It is convenient next to note that the protection only applies to agents who act in connection with sale and purchase of goods, and does not cover agents whose principal activity lies in the provision of services, though similar legislation in other countries (*e.g.* Germany[23]) does so. The fact, however, that an agent for sale provides ancillary servicing facilities does not prevent his being a commercial agent. But when it is the selling which is subsidiary, this activity could rank as merely "secondary" under another provision of the Regulations, and they would not then apply.[24]

---

[21] Above, para. 1–029.

[22] Guidance as to the difference is afforded by Commission Notice of December 12, 1962 on Exclusive Dealing Contracts with Commercial Agents, which gives the opinion that such agents do not fall under the prohibition of Article 85(1) E.C. and distinguishes them from independent traders on the basis that independent traders hold stock as their own property, organise service to customers free of charge and determine prices or terms of business.

[23] See Baumgarte, (1994) 5 E.B.L.Rev. 144.

[24] See below, para. 11–018.

Continuing authority. The authority must be continuing; an agent **11–015**
appointed for a single transaction or a designated group of transactions
would not be covered.

Negotiate the sale and purchase of goods: canvassing agents. These **11–016**
words cover agents who are entrusted with negotiations, even though
they are not authorised to enter into the final contract itself. It may be
questioned whether it also covers agents who simply introduce business
and leave the principal to negotiate, as in the case (outside the contract
of sale of goods and hence outside this context) of estate agents. The
category is referred to in this book as one of "canvassing" or
"introducing agents".[25] Since in both cases the agent negotiates on
behalf of another it is arguable on the wording that the regulations
ought to apply. But some such intermediaries would not be regarded as
a commercial agent in continental European countries accepting the
notion,[26] and of course an estate agent is not likely to be classified as a
commercial agent either, quite apart from the fact that he acts in
connection with land and not goods. It seems likely that the key lies in
the requirement of continuing authority referred to above. A canvassing
agent who holds himself out as available to anyone would not be a
commercial agent; but one who canvasses on what one could call a
"retained" basis could, at least unless he is actually forbidden to solicit
contractual offers. Where it can be said that he has no duty to act,
problems may arise as to whether he has a *contract* of agency at all.[27]

Negotiate and conclude the sale or purchase of goods on behalf of **11–017**
and in the name of the principal. This obviously covers agents who are
actually authorised to contract on behalf of their principals. The
addition of a requirement that the agent do so "in the name of" the
principal raises problems, as this phrase can be used in civil law but
(although it was sometimes used in nineteenth century cases, usually to
differentiate undisclosed principals) has little meaning in common law.
    The three categories which require consideration are agents acting for
named principals, agents acting for unnamed principals, and agents
acting for undisclosed principals.[28] Clearly, an agent acting for a named
principal can be said to act in the principal's name. At common law it
is, however, possible that such an agent undertakes personal liability on
the contract as well as his principal.[29] Should the agent do this, civil law
parallels suggest that he should not be regarded as acting in his own

---

[25] Above, para. 1–017. The term "marketing agent" is also used.
[26] Where such an intermediary may be called "courtier" "makler" "mediatore", etc.
[27] Above, para. 7–016.
[28] For indications of the meaning of these terms see Article 2.
[29] See Article 100.

name for the purpose of these regulations in those cases where the agent's liability is upon the same contract; *i.e.* the words "acts in the name of the principal" should be taken as referring only to an agent who, to use the traditional words, "drops out" of the transaction. More difficult is the case of the agent acting for an unnamed principal, for he is more likely (though far from certain) to be regarded at common law as undertaking personal liability.[30] The best view seems to be that here again, if he undertakes no personal liability, but the third party deals solely with the principal, whoever he is, the agent acts in his principal's name: but if the agent undertakes personal liability on the same contract also, it is arguable that he does not act in the name of the principal. The nature of any liability undertaken by the agent may therefore be crucial.[31]

It is, however, difficult to see that an agent acting for an *undisclosed* principal ever acts in the principal's name, for he clearly acts in his own; and indeed the doctrine of the undisclosed principal is a difficult doctrine of common law which the draftsmen of the directive are not likely to have had fully in mind.

11–018   **Commercial agency a secondary activity.** The regulations do not apply to persons whose activities as commercial agents are to be considered secondary.[32] The meaning of this notion is elaborated for Great Britain[33] by an extensive schedule to the regulations which in effect gives further elucidation to the notion of commercial agency and states that where it may reasonably be taken that the primary purpose of the arrangement with the principal is *other* than as set out, the activities of the commercial agent as such are to be considered secondary only. The indications in this schedule are so important to a legal system that has no category of commercial agent that they require to be set out almost in full. They are as follows:

"(a)   the business of the principal is the sale, or as the case may be purchase, of goods of a particular kind; and
(b)   the goods concerned are such that—

(i)   transactions are normally individually negotiated and concluded on a commercial basis, and
(ii)   procuring a transaction on one occasion is likely to lead to a further transaction in those goods with that customer on future occasions, or to transactions in those goods with other customers in the same geographical area or among the same group of customers and

---

[30] Above, para. 9–014.
[31] *cf.* above, para. 9–006.
[32] Reg. 2(4).
[33] As authorised by Article 2(2) of the directive.

that accordingly it is in the commercial interests of the principal in developing the market in those goods to appoint a representative to such customers with a view to the representative devoting effort, skill and expenditure from his own resources to that end."

There follow indications that an arrangement falls within the above criteria, the absence of any of which is an indication that it does not. The first is that:

"(a) the principal is the manufacturer, importer or distributor of the goods;
(b) the goods are specifically identified with the principal in the market in question rather than, or to a greater extent than, with any other person;
(c) the agent devotes substantially the whole of his time to representative activities (whether for one principal or a number of principals whose interests are not conflicting);
(d) the goods are not normally available in the market in question other than by means of the agent;
(e) the arrangement is described as one of commercial agency."

Two points may be noted. First, the title or label used by the parties is relevant but not conclusive.[34] Secondly, the method of remuneration used is not one of features mentioned as relevant,[35] though it plainly is not irrelevant inasmuch as such agents are typically remunerated by commission.

Indications that commercial agency is not involved at all or is *secondary* are that

"(a) promotional material is supplied direct to potential customers;
(b) persons are granted agencies without reference to existing agents in a particular area or in relation to a particular group;
(c) customers normally select the goods for themselves and merely place their orders through the agent."

Specific exceptions. The activities of mail order catalogue agents for **11–019** consumer goods and consumer credit agents are presumed, unless the contrary is established, not to be within the definition of commercial agency. The term "commercial agent" excludes officers of companies or associations who are authorised to bind the company or organisation, partners authorised to bind their partners and persons acting as insolvency practitioners as defined in the Insolvency Act 1986[36] or its

---

[34] *cf.* above, para. 1–030.
[35] And indeed, regulation 6(3) envisages that a commercial agent need not be remunerated by commission: see below, para. 11–023.
[36] s. 388.

equivalent in other jurisdictions. [37] Nor does it apply to commercial agents whose activities are unpaid, commercial agents where they operate on commodity exchanges or in the commodity market, or the Crown Agents. [38]

4.—Relations between Agent and Principal

11–020   **Duties of agent to principal.** The regulations then turn to the mutual duties of principal and agent. By regulation 3(1) a commercial agent must "in performing his activities look after the interests of his principal and act dutifully and in good faith." In particular he must "(a) make proper efforts to negotiate and where appropriate conclude the transactions he is instructed to take care of; (b) communicate to his principal all the necessary information available to him;" and "(c) comply with reasonable instructions given by his principal." These duties are by regulation 5(1) non-derogatable, and the consequences of their breach are by regulation 5(2) governed by the normal principles of the law applicable to the contract between principal and agent, which for the purposes of this book is assumed to be English law. Although the terminology of the general duties is different from that which a common lawyer would use, such duties already exist at common law or in equity. [39] They will be remediable by actions for damages, sometimes proprietary claims and injunctions; and sometimes a breach will entitle the principal to terminate the contract. They call for no special comment, save that whereas there is controversy as to the extent to which such duties may at common law or in equity be modified or excluded, [40] the duties here laid down for commercial agents plainly may not.

11–021   **Duties of principal to agent.** The common law contains, however, no general law on the implied duties of principal to agent, and here therefore the regulations break a certain amount of new ground. Regulation 4(1) which, like regulation 3, is by virtue of regulation 5(1) non-derogatable, requires that the principal in his relations with the agent in his turn act "dutifully and in good faith." The notion of good faith has been little developed in the common law, and a principal is not normally regarded as owing fiduciary duties to his agent. [41] There is scope here therefore for the development of implied terms of fair

---

[37] Reg. 2(1)(i)(ii)(iii). In respect of (iii) the directive (Art. 1.3) uses the words "a receiver, a receiver and manager, a liquidator or a trustee in bankruptcy".
[38] Reg. 2(2).
[39] See Articles 38 *et seq.*
[40] Above paras. 6–051 *et seq.*
[41] But see above, para. 7–001.

treatment, co-operation and disclosure of relevant information; and contract terms in which the principal retains the right to act in a manner contrary to these requirements will not be valid. Decisions in France[42] and Italy[43] respectively concern a principal who sends another person to solicit offers into the area where the agent is sole representative and one who systematically refuses to conclude the contracts negotiated by the agent.

The duty is to some extent filled out with specific indications by regulation 4(2) and (3). A principal must "provide [the] agent with the necessary documentation relating to the goods concerned", "obtain for his commercial agent the information necessary for the performance of the agency contract, and in particular notify the commercial agent within a reasonable period once he anticipates that the volume of commercial transactions will be significantly lower than that which the commercial agent could normally have expected" and "inform the commercial agent within a reasonable period of his acceptance or refusal of, and of any non-execution by him of, a commercial transaction which the commercial agent has procured for him."[44] The second requirement in particular, in its reference to notification of change of volume of transactions, may involve more than some principals would be in the habit of doing. Again, the consequences of breach of duty are covered by the normal principles of law applicable to the contract, which for the purposes of this book is assumed to be English law.

Right to written statement of terms of contract. By regulation 13, **11–022** which appears in the section entitled "Conclusion and Termination of the Agency Contract", each party is "entitled to receive from the other, on request, a signed written document setting out the terms of the agency contract including any terms subsequently agreed."[45] Any purported waiver of this right is void. It is, however, not clear what the remedy is for failure to comply with the duty to supply such a document. In principle, there must be a right to damages; but loss arising from breach of the duty might not be easy to prove, and this is in any case too much of a common law approach. In labour law in the United Kingdom, there are similar requirements to supply a statement of terms of the contract of employment, but breach of this duty is cognisable in industrial tribunals. A mandatory injunction, an order of the court or a declaration would seem to be necessary. A party who

---

[42] Court of Appeal, Rennes, December 1, 1993, *Dalloz* 1994, *informations rapides*, 127.

[43] Corte di cassazione, December 18, 1985, n. 6475, Giur.it. 1986, I, 1, note de Loreto.

[44] Reg. 22 makes provision as to how a "notice, statement or other document" is to be given or supplied. It is not clear that it covers merely "informing."

[45] Provisions as to how the giving or supply of such documents is to be effected are to be found in regulation 22.

does not receive such a document may perhaps refuse to commence performance; but at least on the side of the agent this may not always be prudent.

5.—REMUNERATION AND COMMISSION

11–023 **Cases where no agreement on remuneration.** Part III of the regulations deals with remuneration. Regulation 6 provides that where no remuneration is agreed, the agent shall be entitled to "the remuneration that commercial agents appointed for the goods forming the subject-matter of his agency contract are customarily allowed in the place where he carries on his activities", and in the absence of such practice "reasonable remuneration taking into account all the aspects of the transaction." This seems straightforward and there is no reason to think that reasoning such as that already employed at common law[46] will not be equally valid under the regulations. The provision is excludable in that remuneration can be agreed and so prevent its application; and if it is agreed that there shall be no remuneration, the person concerned is not a commercial agent at all.[47] However, the regulations, and the directive, appear also to assume that a commercial agent need not be remunerated by commission, for by regulation 6(3), regulations 7 to 12 do not apply "where a commercial agent is not remunerated (wholly or in part) by commission"—an odd way of putting it, which is rendered in the enactments of some other countries in positive form, *i.e.* that the following rules apply where the agent *is* remunerated by commission. Either way, remuneration by commission is not part of the definition of commercial agents, as has already been pointed out.[48] There is a danger here that a commercial agent remunerated by salary may in some situations and/or countries be regarded as an employee and not a commercial agent at all.

11–024 **Commission.** The remainder of Part III deals with the agent's commission, defined in regulation 2(1) as "any part of the remuneration of a commercial agent which varies with the number or value of business transactions." It seeks to protect the agents against situations which have been perceived as unfair to him. As will be seen, the regulations distinguish between *entitlement* to commission, when commission is *due*, when commission shall be *paid*, and *right* to commission: though the last phrase may be an oversight of a translator and hence equivalent to "entitlement".[49]

---

[46] See Article 57.
[47] Reg. 2(2); above, para. 11–019.
[48] Above, para. 11–018.
[49] Below, para. 11–031.

Entitlement to commission. Under regulation 7(1) the agent is **11–025** "entitled to commission" on "commercial transactions concluded during the period covered by the agency contract—(a) when the transaction has been concluded as a result of his action." In considering this provision it should be borne in mind that the term "commercial agent" covers not only one who concludes transactions, but also one who negotiates them.[50] Where he actually *concludes* them there is no difficulty in seeing that he is entitled to commission. Where he merely *negotiates* them, the reference to the transaction being concluded as the result of his action will give something very like (but not necessarily the same as) the existing "effective cause" rule of English law.[51] There is nothing in the regulations which would render ineffective an entitlement to commission at an earlier stage, as for example when a customer is introduced: unlike the English estate agent cases, the concern is not about agents providing that they are entitled to commission when there is no sale, but for agents failing to obtain commission despite there having been a sale. Furthermore, it would seem that, subject to the requirement of good faith,[52] the principal can deprive the agent of commission by refusing to conclude a transaction negotiated by the agent. Existing English cases would allow the agent to protect himself against this if the clause is sufficiently clear.[53] Some of such clauses may now perhaps be contrary to the good faith requirement.

Repeat orders. By regulation 7(1)(b) the agent is entitled to **11–026** commission "where the transaction is concluded with a third party **–027** whom he has previously acquired as a customer for transactions of the same kind", *i.e.* on what is sometimes called a "repeat order" placed without the further intervention of the agent. This is an area where the English law is far from clear.[54]

Geographical zone or customer group. Finally, by regulation 7(2) the **11–028** agent is entitled to commission on transactions concluded during the period of the contract "where he has an exclusive right to a specific geographical area or to a specific group of customers and where the transaction has been entered into with a customer belonging to that area or group." Here there is even less of anything corresponding to a requirement of "effective cause" for the particular transaction: the

---

[50] Above, para. 11–016.
[51] Article 59. This rule has largely been developed in connection with estate agents, who are certainly not commercial agents, and other "canvassing agents" (above, para. 1–017) who probably are not either (above, para. 11–016).
[52] Above, para. 11–021.
[53] See Article 60.
[54] See above, para. 7–041.

entitlement is to commission on transactions which do no more than emanate from the agent's area or customer group.

11–029 **Commission on transactions after agency contract terminated.** Regulation 8 deals with this problem, on which English law is again not clear.[55] It provides that the agent is "entitled to commission" in such cases if

> "(a) the transaction is mainly attributable to his efforts during the period covered by the agency contract and if the transaction was entered into within a reasonable period after that contract terminated; or
> (b) in accordance with the conditions mentioned in regulation 7 above, the order of the third party reached the principal or the commercial agent before the agency contract terminated."

The requirements of (a) are somewhat imprecise and may give rise to difficulties. Regulation 9 then deals with situations where an agent claims under regulation 7 and commission is payable to his predecessor by virtue of regulation 8: the later agent does not qualify for commission "unless it is equitable because of the circumstances for the commission to be shared between the commercial agents"—a provision which could require adjudication if there was a dispute under it.

11–030 **When commission due and date for payment.** By regulation 10(1) a further refinement is introduced. Commission is actually *due*[56] in one of three situations: when the principal has "executed" the transaction (which presumably means performed it), or according to his agreement with the third party ought to have done so, or the third party has executed the transaction. The first two provisions are facultative only in the sense that other arrangements may be made. But the third provides a final limit which cannot, by paragraph (4), be derogated from to the detriment of the agent. This provides that commission becomes due *at the latest* when "(2) the third party has executed his part of the transaction or should have done so if the principal had executed his part of the transaction as he should have." Paragraph (3), also non-derogatable, provides that commission shall be *paid* "not later than on the last day of the month following the quarter in which it became due." There follows a provision for determining quarter periods, which may be varied by agreement. Paragraph (2) may raise problems of application when there is no time set for the principal to perform the contract.

---

[55] See above, para. 7–041.
[56] French "acquise".

"Right" to commission. The effect of the above provisions is **11–031** reinforced by regulation 11(1), which provides that "the *right* to commission can be extinguished only if and to the extent that it is established that (a) the contract between the third party and the principal will not be performed; and (b) that fact is due to a reason for which the principal is not to blame."[57] This provision cannot be derogated from to the detriment of the commercial agent.[58] It seems unlikely that any special significance is to be attached to the word "right" as opposed to "entitlement" in regulations 7, 8 and 9, as the same French word ("droit") appears in all these provisions in the French text of the directive. The overall result is that the agent only actually earns commission on business which he introduces if he either concludes the contract or it is concluded as a result of his action, and the contract is in fact performed, or not performed for reasons not attributable to the principal—unless of course the contract gives him a more generous entitlement, which it may. The contract cannot, however, reduce this entitlement, for instance by entitling him to commission only if the principal decides to perform (as opposed to enter into) the transaction (a provision which would again be possible but unlikely under the existing English law[59]).

It should be noted also that the reference is actually to non-performance for a reason for which the principal is not to *blame*. At common law a principal can be liable for non-performance even where no blame attaches to him, if the circumstances are such that he is to be regarded as having undertaken responsibility for them. It might seem therefore that the wording imports some notion of negligence which is foreign to the common law. But the French text of the directive uses the word "imputable" and other foreign texts are similar: the variation seems to arise in translation only and not to be intended to convey any effect substantially different from that which would occur under English law.[60] Hence the word "attributable", used in the previous paragraph, is probably correct. Problems may occur as to whether the principal's bankruptcy comes under this wording.

If the principal sues the third party for non-performance, the agent should normally be entitled to commission. Problems could arise if the principal refuses or fails to do so. This could lead to the inference that it

---

[57] Emphasis supplied. The agent must in such cases refund any commission he has received: reg.11(2).

[58] Reg. 11(3).

[59] See Article 60.

[60] A leading German commentary uses the words "alles was in die Risikosphäre des Unternehmers fällt" ("anything that happens within the principal's sphere of risk"): D. Brüeggeman in Staub-Brüggeman, Grosskommentar z. HGB (4th ed., Berlin, 1982), s. 87a, n. 31. In reg. 18(a), where the same word appears in the French text of the directive, the English word is this time "attributable."

is not established that the third party will not perform; or be a breach of the principal's duty of good faith. In some such situations the third party might be liable to the agent.[60a]

11–032 **Modification by contract terms.** There is certainly nothing in the regulations preventing an entitlement to commission at an *earlier* stage than they prescribe: the prohibitions on derogation are on derogation to the detriment of the agent. The question whether the provisions as to remuneration may be modified or in some respect altogether excluded, in particular as regards commission on what may loosely be called repeat orders, or where business is done simply for a person in the agent's geographical zone or group of customers, or where a transaction is concluded after the end of the agency contract, is more difficult.

The obvious answer might appear to be that they may, since only some of the provisions of regulation 10, those as to the time at which commission is due and must be paid, and of regulation 11, as to extinction of the right to commission if the contract will not be executed for reasons not attributable to the principal, are specifically made non-derogatable to the agent's detriment. If this interpretation is correct, it can be argued that as regulations 7 and 8 are not, as are other provisions, specifically made unexcludable, the entitlements which they prescribe are merely *ius dispositivum* and only operate if there are no contract terms providing otherwise. Such seems to be the understanding in, for example, Germany and France. On this basis it is possible to exclude the other situations of entitlement to commission and provide that commission only arises on transactions actually concluded as a result of the agent's actions. It would be difficult (but perhaps not impossible) to go further and reduce the right to commission on *concluded* transactions, for an attempt to postpone payment beyond a certain point would be caught by regulation 11, and if it is provided that no commission at all is due on such sales, the agency would be gratuitous and not covered by the regulations at all. On the other hand, as already pointed out, it is apparently contemplated that the agent may not be remunerated by commission at all, but rather by salary.

As against this it may be said that it is odd to provide in such firm terms when the entitlement to commission arises, if the rules only operate where there is no provision to the contrary. Further, the general wording of regulation 11(1), quoted above, which provides that the "right to commission" is extinguished "only if and to the extent that" certain circumstances connected with non-performance of the contract occur, and which cannot be derogated from to the detriment of the agent, could be taken to suggest that where a contract is concluded in the circumstances indicated in regulation 7, commission must be due

---

[60a] *cf.* above, para. 7–018, n. 76.

unless the contract is not carried out in accordance with what is prescribed in regulation 11. More generally, it is difficult to see why there should be an unexcludable right to commission in all situations where contracts are not performed bar specific exceptions, while the actual initial entitlement to commission in respect of contracts can itself be modified.

It may be that the original intention of the directive was for a complete mandatory regime, and that at some point this was modified, with the unsatisfactory results that we now have. This second interpretation, under which the main provisions as to commission are non-excludable, may be more in accord with the spirit of the directive. But it has already been pointed out that the difference between "entitlement" and "right" to commission seems likely to be accidental; and from the overall arrangement of the directive as it has actually emerged the first interpretation seems more likely to be correct. It can be justified on the basis that rights in respect of repeat orders, to an exclusive area or group or to commission on transactions after the end of the agency need not be granted; but that if they are, the accrual of commission under them cannot be restricted as to time beyond a certain point.[61] On either view, however, there should be no objection to rates of commission which vary in accordance with the effort expended, for example reduced commission on repeat and/or unsolicited orders.

Supply of information. Regulation 12 deals with the supply of information by principal to agent with a view to the calculation of commission earned. The background is plainly, like that of the previous regulation, a perception that the agent is in danger of not getting all the commission to which he is entitled. It provides in paragraphs (1) and (2) that the principal shall supply the agent with a statement of the commission due not later than the last day of the month following the quarter in which the commission has become due, setting out the main components used in calculating it; and that the agent "shall be entitled to demand that he be provided with all the information (and in particular an extract from the books) which is available to his principal and which he needs in order to check the amount of the commission due to him."[62] In this case an agreement to derogate from these provisions is by paragraph (3) stated to be void. This is without prejudice to other enactments or rules of law permitting agents to inspect their principals' books.[63]

11–033

---

[61] One may wonder, for example, what the result would be if the contract provided for commission only on every third transaction.

[62] Regulation 22 makes provision for how such statements are to be supplied.

[63] Reg. 12(4). The right to information does not require that it be given where disclosure would be contrary to public policy: reg. 21.

It is, however, not clear how the duty is to be enforced. An action for damages, which seems the most obvious remedy at common law, would seem to be of limited utility. Some sort of order of the court, for instance a mandatory injunction, or a declaration, would be required.[64]

6.—TERMINATION OF THE AGENCY

11–034   **Fixed period contract which continues to be performed.** Where there is an agency contract for a fixed period, and it continues to be performed by both parties after the expiry of the period, regulation 14 provides that it "shall be deemed to be converted" into an agency contract for an indefinite period. It then attracts the provisions for the termination of agency contracts concluded for indefinite periods, which follow in regulation 15. While this is reasonable, there is obviously here a danger for principals who allow what may be intended to be only a slight run-over, or allow a run-over by inadvertence.

Argument is possible that this provision is not mandatory, and that the result prescribed can be avoided by an appropriate term in the original contract.[65] It is true that there is no express indication that the regulation can not be derogated from, whereas non-derogation provisions appear in various forms in respect of regulations 13, 15, 17, and 18.[66] On the other hand the wording of the regulations appears to the English reader firm. Perhaps the best solution is that a contract for a fixed period containing a clause providing for what happens if the parties continue performance at the end of the period is not, at any rate at the moment when the clause first comes into operation, for the purposes of the regulations, a contract for a fixed period.[67]

11–035   **Termination of contract concluded for an indefinite period.** The regulations here provide for a situation on which English law has not been at all clear.[68] Under regulation 15(1) in all such situations the agent may terminate the contract by notice: this for English law avoids possible arguments that the contract is not terminable at all.[69] The minimum period of notice is one month for the first year of the contract, two months "for the second year commenced", and three

---

[64] The Access to Medical Reports Act 1988 confers a right to inspect such reports in certain circumstances: but here a special power is by s. 8 given to the court to order compliance.

[65] See (on the French legislation) Leloup, "Agent Commercial," *Enc. Dalloz, Répertoire de droit commercial* (Paris, 1994) at s. 71.

[66] See regs. 13(2), 15(2), 19(2).

[67] *cf.* Baldi, *Il contratto di agenzia* (5th ed., Milano, 1992) p. 534.

[68] See Article 125.

[69] Provisions as to how the giving of notice is to be effected are to be found in reg. 22.

months "for the third year commenced and for the subsequent years." Presumably this means that the two-month period becomes necessary as soon as the agent has commenced his second year of operation under the contract. The parties may agree on longer but not on shorter periods. Unless otherwise agreed, "the end of the period of notice must coincide with the end of a calendar month", which may add nearly a further month to the period of notice. Where a fixed period contract is converted into an indefinite period contract under regulation 14, discussed above, the fixed period must be taken into account in calculating the period of notice; since this refers back to unexcludable entitlements, it may be assumed that this rule is unexcludable also.

Savings for the general law. By regulation 16 the regulations do not **11–036** "affect the application of any enactment or rule of law which provides for immediate termination of the agency contract — (a) because of the failure of one party to carry out all or part of his obligations under that contract; or (b) where exceptional circumstances arise." This regulation appears to be intended to preserve the normal rules of law regarding what a common lawyer would call discharge of contract by breach, and frustration. Paragraph (a) could in fact refer to the operation of both doctrines; paragraph (b) no doubt refers to frustration, though a common lawyer would not express himself in this way. The wording of (a) could also refer to the termination of the contract by the operation of contract clauses which limit the obligations of the parties: sometimes a contract may terminate on its terms without breach or frustration, as where a party is excused from performance by a contract term but there is no breach and the circumstances are not such as to bring the doctrine of frustration into operation. An example is provided by some operations of a *force majeure* clause.[70]

Entitlement to indemnity or compensation. The most significant **11–037** provision in this part of the regulations, and indeed, from the common law point of view, in the regulations as a whole, is regulation 17, which together with regulation 18 seeks to secure that on termination of his agency the commercial agent is entitled to be "indemnified ... or compensated for damage" (regulation 17(1)). As has been explained above, this idea results from a perception that an agent may establish a market and goodwill for a principal, and then be deprived of the benefit of his investment, both in money and in labour, by termination of his authority by a principal who may then seek to deal direct with customers, or perhaps use the services of another agent at a cheaper

---

[70] See Treitel, *Frustration and Force Majeure* (1994); for a different example (outside the context of agency) see *The Kanchenjunga* [1990] 1 Lloyd's Rep. 391.

rate of commission. The agent is therefore in effect to be "bought out", as is sometimes the case in employment law.

11–038 **Provisions cannot be derogated from.** The provisions of regulations 17 and 18 cannot, by virtue of regulation 19, be derogated from to the detriment of the agent "before the agency contract expires." The provision against derogation is not difficult to understand. It may, however, be asked why derogation may nevertheless be permitted after the expiry of the contract. This seems to be because after such expiry the principal's power to exercise pressure on the agent may be assumed to be no longer operative.[71]

11–039 **When does the entitlement arise? Indefinite period contracts.** Assuming that no breach of contract by principal or agent is involved, the obvious case of entitlement occurs where a contract for an indefinite period is terminated by the principal. It is in a case such as this that an abrupt termination, even though notice is given with the minimum periods specified, may deprive the agent of expected benefits. Although English law has not recognised any rights in the agent in such circumstances, the object of the directive plainly requires it. Perhaps more surprising, however, is the fact that regulation 17(8) provides that the right to indemnity or compensation also arises where the agent dies, and regulation 18(b)(ii) assumes that it exists also where he himself terminates the agency contract "on grounds of the age, infirmity or illness of the commercial agent in consequence of which he cannot reasonably be required to continue his activities." This transfers the risk of those events to the principal, but seems in accordance with the objects of the directive as recompensing the agent (or his estate) for connections built up. Where the infirmity was foreseeable the entitlement may seem on the generous side: one might think that the agent should at the time of contracting have taken into account the fact that he might be prevented from continuing.

Problems may arise if the agent does a wrongful act which entitles the principal to terminate the contract and then dies. The common law analysis is that the contract is not terminated for breach till the innocent party to the breach elects to exercise the power to do so. Hence the right to compensation may be said to have accrued before the innocent party can terminate, though if the parties had agreed for an indemnity it might be possible to say that the payment of it was not (in whole or in part) "equitable" in accordance with regulation 17(3)(b). Otherwise, it might sometimes be possible to argue that the agent had by his

---

[71] cf. HGB para. 89b(IV); BGHZ 51, 184, 188 et seq.; BGHZ 53, Neue Juristische Wochenschrift, 1989, 35.

(wrongful) conduct terminated the contract himself, though this argument, sometimes used in employment law, is not usually very attractive.

Fixed period contracts. In the case of agency for a fixed period, **11–040** however, one might expect that (unless the agency is allowed to run on after the period), just as the periods of notice are inapplicable, so also is the requirement of payment of indemnity or compensation, for here the agent has taken on a fixed period contract and in doing so might be expected to have calculated whether or not he would receive adequate recompense for his outlay; though perhaps there should be a provision for termination before the end of the period by death, illness, etc., of the agent. Such an interpretation receives some support from the wording of the British regulations, which refers to entitlement on "termination" of the agency contract;[72] though the terminology used in the versions in other languages does not seem to give guidance here. The word "terminate" is used elsewhere in law of a voluntary act of termination, and one might argue that it does not apply where the contract simply *expires*, which is the word used in regulation 14 in connection with fixed terms. Further, even if the idea of *indemnity* on expiry of a fixed term contract might be accepted, it is not easy to see why *damage* should follow the (pre-arranged) expiry of a fixed term contract. In this sense, the wording of Regulation 17(6), which refers to "the damage he suffers as a result of the termination of his relations with his principal" is not easy to understand: if the contract ends by the expiry of time, it might be thought that damage is not suffered thereby, but (if at all) by the agent's wrong estimation of the period of contract needed to recover his outlay. Without further background, therefore, a common lawyer might come to the conclusion that there was nothing due on the regular expiry of a fixed term contract.

The general background of the directive, however, and the way in which it is understood, and similar forms of legislation have been understood, in other European countries suggests almost conclusively that not only indemnity, if otherwise available, but also compensation, where there is no indemnity, should be available in this case. For a start, one might say that although the agent regarded himself as needing a longer period of contract to recover his outlay, he might not have been able to negotiate this: hence he requires some sort of protection against the results of failure to do so. It could also be said that a fixed term contract can be renewed: when the principal fails to renew such a contract he is doing something very similar to termination, which is only not termination because he has been prudent or commercially strong

---

[72] Reg. 17(1).

enough to secure a short-term renewable contract. Both these arguments are suggestive of a notion of good faith in the exercise of the power to terminate or not to renew. There are analogies in United Kingdom labour law.[73] Finally, the thinking that entitles the agent to compensation on death or retirement suggests that there should be a right on termination of a fixed term contract. This preferred interpretation requires, however, a special meaning to be attributed to the phrase "compensation for damage", and this is discussed below.

11–041   **Indemnity.** In some countries an indemnity is payable as a matter of course. The directive in its final form, however, allowed countries to choose between indemnity and compensation; and for Great Britain, regulation 17(2) provides that "Except where the agency contract otherwise provides, the commercial agent shall be entitled to be compensated rather than idemnified." Bearing in mind, therefore, that the principal does not have to agree to such an arrangement, we proceed to the calculation of the indemnity. Regulation (3) provides that:

> "The commercial agent shall be entitled to an indemnity *if and to the extent that* —
>
> (a)   he has brought the principal new customers or has significantly increased the volume of business with existing customers and the principal continues to derive substantial benefits from the business with such customers; and
>
> (b)   the payment of this indemnity is equitable having regard to all the circumstances and, in particular, the commission lost by the commercial agent on the business transactions with such customers."[74]

This indemnity has been described for German law (where it is called "Ausgleich") as "capitalised remuneration for the continued performance".[75] Regulation 17(4) limits it to "a figure equivalent to an

---

[73] There are also analogies in land law. At common law a yearly tenant was entitled to emblements provided that the determination of the tenancy was not caused by his own act: see Megarry and Wade, *Law of Real Property* (5th ed.), p. 703.

[74] Emphasis supplied.

[75] Schmidt, *Handelsrecht* (4th ed., Berlin, 1994), p. 752; see also Joerges (ed.), *Franchising and the Law* (Baden-Baden, 1991), pp. 11 *et seq*, esp. at p. 41. According to Hopt, *Handelsvertreterrecht* (München, 1992), pp. 124–125, the claim for the indemnity is "kein reiner Vergütungsanspruch" ("not a pure claim for loss of remuneration") given the fact that payment of the indemnity is due only if it is equitable in consideration of all the circumstances (*HGB*, para. 89b(I) n. 3), and that the agent's right to indemnity is lost if he himself terminates the agency contract, unless the termination is justified by circumstances attributable to the principal, or on grounds of old age, or illness (*HGB*, para. 89b(II) n. 1).

indemnity for one year calculated from the commercial agent's annual remuneration over the preceding five years and if the contract goes back less than five years the indemnity shall be calculated on the average for the period in question." This limit, which is in substantial accord with German law,[76] gives the principal some advantage in use of the indemnity, and it is not necessarily true that principals would be best advised not to agree specifically to such an arrangement. The essence of the indemnity arrangement may therefore be regarded as a buy-out on one year's remuneration, but only "if and to the extent that" the agent has brought the business, and on an equitable basis.

The view has been taken that the two requirements of (a) and (b) above are not cumulative but alternative: this approach has been put into effect in Italy[77]; while in Germany equitable considerations may displace the rule denying the right to indemnity where the agent's behaviour would justify immediate dismissal.[78] It is however difficult to extract such possibilities from the English regulations, and equally from at least the English version of the directive itself, with which the regulations are identical at this point save for a slight difference in punctuation.

Non-derogation. The indemnity is not compulsory. But the provision **11–042** against derogation in regulation 19[79] seems to mean that if an indemnity is adopted to the exclusion of compensation it must be adopted as specified in the regulations, or under a scheme more favourable to the agent.

Time limit. By virtue of regulation 17(9) the agent loses his **11–043** entitlement "if within one year following termination of his agency contract he has not notified his principal that he intends pursuing his entitlement."

Damages. But by regulation 17(5) "the grant of an indemnity . . . shall **11–044** not prevent the commercial agent from seeking damages": these would be over and above the indemnity, and granted in respect of a breach of contract, where there was one.

Compensation. In Great Britain the indemnity is a voluntary **11–045** arrangement. If, however, there is no indemnity provided for, the agent has, as stated above, a right to be what is called "compensated for

---

[76] See *HGB*, para. 89b(II).
[77] Italian civil code, Art. 1751.
[78] See *HGB*, para. 89b.
[79] Above, para. 11–038.

damage", a right which again by regulation 19 cannot be derogated from to the agent's detriment. As stated below this seems to be *instead of* the common law right to damages. The question then arises as to what this "compensation" is and how far it is different from ordinary damages for wrongful termination of the contract. It seems clear that it is different, for in accordance with the arguments above, it appears to arise where there is no breach of the contract at all; and further, paragraphs (5) and (6) of regulation 17 seem to imply a distinction between "damages" (para. (5)) and "compensation for the damage he suffers as a result of the termination of his relations with his principal" (para. (6)). The French text of the directive uses, indeed, a different word here — "réparation" — from that used in Article 17(5) (equivalent to regulation 17(6))— "dommages-interêts": though the German text uses the same ("Schadenersatz"). This notion of compensation under the directive seems therefore a special one, in effect compensation which is payable even though no breach of contract may have occurred. It may be that there is at present no exact parallel to it[80] (as opposed to the indemnity) in the domestic law of any European country, and that special rules will need to be worked out (under the eventual guidance of the European Court of Justice).

---

[80] Though the similarity seems to be with French law; German law, which adopts the indemnity technique, is quite different. Indeed, the alternative between indemnity and compensation which is left open by Art. 17 of the directive was adopted to avoid the clash between the German and the French approach to this issue. Cp. J.-M. Leloup, *La loi du 25 juin 1991 relative aux rapports entre les agents commerciaux et leurs mandants ou le triomphe de l'intérêt commun*, J.C.P., ed. E, 1992, 105, s. 43: "L'article 17 de la directive offre aux Etats membres le choix entre deux systèmes d'indemnisation de l'agent en fin de contrat, celui de l'article 17–2, copié sur le modèle de la loi allemande, celui de l'article 17–3, inspiré par le décret de 1958 et la pratique française.". French law before the enactment of the directive stressed the wrongful nature of the termination of the contract by the principal. It gave the agent damages on this basis. It did not award compensation in case of expiration of fixed term contracts, nor in the case of termination of the contract by the death of the agent. French law after the directive is changed on these points. French jurists now face similar problems to those which arise in the interpretation of the British regulation concerning compensation for damage caused to the agent by the termination of his relations with his principal. See, *e.g.* J.-M. Leloup, *op. cit.* above, s. 40: "Ce n'est donc plus une indemnité de rupture ... c'est une indemnité de cessation de contrat." D. Ferrier, *Commentaire de la loi du 25 juin 1991 sur l'agence commerciale*, Cah. dr. entr., 1991, no. 6, p. 30, s. 34: "Cette nouvelle solution [*i.e.*, compensation for the termination of a fixed term contract] ne nous parait conforme au fondement de l'indemnité. Peut-on évoquer un prejudice subi par l'agent lorsque le contrat devient caduc ou arrive à son terme normal?" French lawyers, however, are agreed that the new law did not change the measure of damages which was usually awarded to the agent under the previous regime: see Hanine, *Agents Commerciaux, Juris Classeur, Contrats Distribution*, fasc. 1250, ss. 86 *et seq.*; J.-M. Leloup, *op. cit.* above s. 43. In most cases, for the termination of indefinite period contracts, French courts assess damages in the measure of two years of commission. This is higher than the indemnity which a German agent gets on the basis of *HGB* para. 89b(II).

Calculation. Regulation 17(7) provides that: **11–046**

"For the purpose of these Regulations such damage shall be deemed to occur *particularly* when the termination takes place in either or both of the following circumstances, namely circumstances which —

(a) deprive the commercial agent of the commission which proper performance of the agency contract would have procured for him whilst providing his principal with substantial benefits linked to the activities of the commercial agent; or

(b) have not enabled the commercial agent to amortize the costs and expenses that he had incurred in the performance of the agency contract on the advice of his principal."[81]

First method. The notion of termination depriving the agent of **11–047** commission which *proper* performance of the agency contract would have earned him seems at first glance to refer to termination by the principal in breach of contract, for the word "proper" can be taken to suggest that full performance was improperly prevented by him, as by a breach of contract. The corresponding word in the French and German texts of the directive is "normal". This does not perhaps carry the same implication of improper conduct by the principal. But it does not solve all problems, for a contract terminated with appropriate notice or expiring at the end of a fixed period would not "normally" continue. The point was, however, already been made above that the right to compensation seems not to be intended to be limited to cases of breach. Unless violence is to be done to the wording, however, it may be that this method of calculation, which involves loss of profits, should perhaps be limited to such breaches and that loss of expected profits, which are of course the main subject-matter of the indemnity, should not otherwise be recoverable under this head. On the other hand where goodwill has been established which exceeds the potential loss of commission (for example, because the agency has not yet yielded much commission but the agent has established a good network), it may be that an award should be made in respect of that.

Second method. The second method of calculation, however, relates **11–048** to actual losses by inability to amortise outlay. One may wonder how much significance is to be attributed to the principal's *advice*. The agent would often make the outlay on his own initiative to facilitate the earning of commission. The word "advice" smacks of tort, and it may be that it is intended to link the compensation with expense required or suggested by the principal and provide a way of excluding recompense

---

[81] Emphasis supplied.

713

for extravagant and unnecessary expense incurred by use of the agent's own judgment.

11–049   **Rudimentary indemnity.** All these losses, as opposed to expected profits, are recoverable even though the termination involves no breach of contract. Taking into account all the considerations above, and the fact that the word "particularly" implies that the criteria listed are not exclusive, the award of compensation can be regarded as in some sense a "rudimentary indemnity."[82]

There are nevertheless other differences between the compensation here referred to and the indemnity. First, regulation 2(a), relating to the indemnity, is initially expressed in positive form, as referring to benefits brought to the principal, though it is true that it goes on to refer to commission lost by the agent. Regulation 3, on compensation, though its criteria are not exclusive, is negative throughout, referring entirely to loss of commission and failure to amortise outlay. Secondly, the award of compensation must include damages for breach: there is no provision corresponding to regulation 17(5), referred to above, which preserves the right to damages over and above the indemnity. Thirdly, it may be that compensation requires proof of loss, and, a related point, its calculation is not to be based, as is the indemnity, on what is "equitable", but rather on principles of causation.

11–050   **Non-derogation.** As has been stated, regulation 19 provides that the parties may not derogate from the compensation provisions before the agency contract expires.[83]

11–051   **Time limit.** Like the indemnity, the right to compensation is by virtue of regulation 17(9) lost if the agent does not notify his principal within one year that he intends pursuing the entitlement.

11–052   **Relevance of general contract doctrines.** Regulation 16, which preserves the effect of general contract doctrines, has already been mentioned.[84] The fact that under such doctrine a party may be released by the other party's breach, by the terms of the contract, or by frustration,[85] does not necessarily affect the right to indemnity or compensation. Thus the agent may terminate the contract for a repudiatory breach by the principal, but remain entitled to indemnity or

---

[82] I owe this phrase to Professor Klaus Hopt, for whose advice on the meaning of the directive I am most grateful.

[83] Above, para. 11–038.

[84] Above, para. 11–036.

[85] See above, para. 11–036.

compensation; he may be similarly entitled if the contract comes to an end without breach or frustration; he may probably also do so if the contract is frustrated. This is certainly true where it is frustrated by his death or illness. In such a case the agent would be entitled by virtue of the indemnity or compensation provisions, whichever is applicable, to a sum calculated in a way different and usually more favourable to the agent, from that to which he might be entitled under the Law Reform (Frustrated Contracts) Act 1943.[86] The provisions of that Act are also excludable, which is not true of some of the provisions of regulations 17 and 18. Where it is the agent who is in repudiatory breach, however, there may be no entitlement to compensation, as is explained in the next paragraph.

Cases where no indemnity or compensation due. Regulation 18   **11–053**
provides that the indemnity or[87] compensation is not payable where

(a) the principal has terminated the agency contract because of default attributable to the commercial agent which would justify immediate termination of the agency contract pursuant to regulation 16 above."

This is not difficult to understand: the agent loses the right to these benefits if he commits a breach entitling the principal in effect to dismiss him. The phrase "attributable to the agent" is far preferable for a common lawyer to the reference to "blame" in regulation 11(1), though as already stated it is doubtful whether any distinction was intended, the word "imputable" appearing in both contexts of the French text of the directive.[88] Equally it obviously will not apply if the commercial agent has himself terminated the contract without justification. Regulation 18(b) provides that indemnity or compensation are not payable where

"the commercial agent has himself terminated the agency contract, unless such termination is justified

(i) by circumstances attributable to the principal, or
(ii) on grounds of age, infirmity or illness of the commercial agent in consequence of which he cannot reasonably be required to continue his activities."

Sub-paragraph (i) is not surprising: if the principal commits a repudiatory breach entitling the agent to terminate the contract, the agent remains entitled to indemnity or compensation. Sub-paragraph (ii)

---

[86] See Treitel, *op. cit.* above, n. 70 pp. 569—573. As to death or illness, see above, para. 11–039.
[87] These words, which appear in the directive, seem to have been omitted in error and were added to the regulations by S.I. 1993 No. 3173 (above, n. 8).
[88] Above, para. 11–031.

has already been referred to,[89] and is perhaps surprising in that it entitles the agent in effect to force his own retirement, and consequent right to the relevant payments, on the principal even in the absence of circumstances that would frustrate the contract.

Lastly, under sub-paragraph (iii), the right to indemnity or compensation is excluded

"if the agent, with the agreement of his principal, assigns his rights and duties under the agency contract to another person."

The assumption seems to be that in such a case the agent has obtained the value of the goodwill and so forth in the purchase price of his business; or has given it to another, for example a son or daughter.[90]

11–054 **Restraint of trade clauses.** A restraint of trade clause is defined as "an agreement restricting the business activities of a commercial agent following termination of the agency contract."[91] Such clauses are dealt with in regulation 20, under which a restraint of trade clause is valid:

"only if and to the extent that:

(a) it is concluded in writing; and
(b) it relates to the geographical area or the group of customers and the geographical area entrusted to the commercial agent and to the kind of goods covered by his agency under the contract."

By paragraph (2) it shall be valid for not more than two years after termination of the agency contract.

This provision probably adds little to the common law on contracts in restraint of trade, except for the requirement of writing. There is no such requirement at common law, but it does not seem likely that an agreement of this nature, which requires some precision in its drafting, would easily be entered into orally. The restriction to two years is a fixed limit, but it may be that restrictions on agents of this type for longer than two years might not easily be held reasonable at common law. The restrictions to certain types of customers and goods are likewise broadly in accord with the common law rules, though differences of detail could well occur.[92] Paragraph (3) preserves the effect of domestic enactments or rules of law which restrict the enforceability of restraint of trade clauses to a greater extent than the regulations or enables the court to reduce the obligations on the parties resulting from such clauses. It is in fact conceivable that the common

---

[89] Above, para. 11–039.
[90] See Leloup, *op. cit.* above, n. 65, ss. 88, 89.
[91] Reg. 2(1).
[92] As to the common law on contracts in restraint of trade see Chitty, *Contracts* (27th ed.), Vol. 1, ss. 16–066 *et seq.*; Treitel, *Law of Contract* (9th ed.), pp. 412 *et seq.*

law rules would operate more strictly than this regulation in some instances. The English courts have, however, no specific power to reduce the obligations under such contracts; but the power to sever invalid portions of contracts, which they have, can also come under the words.

Since reference to foreign law on this topic may be necessary it may be useful to give a brief selective bibliography.

General

A. de Theux, *Le droit de la représentation commerciale* (Brussels, 3 vols., 1975–1981); A. de Theux, *Le statut européen de l'agent commercial. Approche critique de droit comparé* (Brussels, 1992); A. de Theux, *Aperçu comparatif du statut des représentants de commerce salariés dans les Etats membres de la CE* (Brussels, 1993); G. Bogaert and U. Lohmann (eds.), *Commercial Agency and Distribution Agreements: Law and Practice in the Member States of the EC and EFTA* (2nd ed., London, 1993).

France

F. Collart Dutilleul and P. Delbecque, *Contrats civils et commerciaux* (2nd ed., Paris, 1993); J.-M. Leloup, "Agent commercial", *Encyclopédie Dalloz, Repertoire de Droit Commercial* (Paris 1994); J.-M. Leloup, *Les agents commerciaux; statuts juridiques, strategies professionelles* (3rd ed., Paris, 1995).

Germany

K. J. Hopt, *Handelsvertreterrecht* (München, 1992); K. Schmidt, *Handelsrecht* (4th ed., Köln, Berlin, 1994).

Italy

R. Baldi, *Il contratto di agenzia* (5th ed., Milano, 1992); G. Trioni, *Il contratto di agenzia* (Padova, 1994).

Spain

H. Llobregat, *El contrato de agencia mercantil* (Pamplona, 1994).

CHAPTER 12

A NOTE ON THE CONFLICT OF LAWS

12–001   In a general work on a particular topic, such as this book, it might be expected that there would be a chapter on the rules of the conflict of laws as applied to that topic. The reasons why this does not seem appropriate to provide one must therefore be stated. They may be summarised in two main points.

The first is the fact that the law of agency in common law countries is of a generalised nature means that it deploys a very wide range of legal techniques. In this book are to be found application of not only principles of contract, but also of tort, restitution and property; and also principles of equity, which may or may not be assimilatable into the above categories. There are also principles of evidence; and an uneasy interface with those of company law. The conflict of laws has separate techniques for most of these categories.

The second is that the approach to agency problems in at any rate some civil law countries appears to be significantly different from that in common law countries in many respects. Although general notions of representation are stated (often at rather an abstract level), civil law systems are apt to isolate types of agent and develop specific rules appropriate to their functions: an example is the commercial agent referred to in the previous chapter. Also, the law of agency being not so generalised, many figures, at least some of whose functions would be discussed under the law of agency in a common law country, would not be associated with that topic at all in civil law countries: an example is the solicitor. Conversely, other matters (*e.g.*, representation of minors) may be solved by agency notions in civil law countries when a common lawyer would have recourse to other techniques such as the trust.

This means that when a question of the application of foreign law arises in what a common lawyer would describe as an agency context, it may be found that the potentially relevant systems of foreign law analyse the situation quite differently, thus raising serious problems of categorisation. This is a problem of interaction between common law and civil law: it obviously will not be nearly so serious if the other potentially relevant laws are those of common law countries.

It is possible to approach the question by making an initial distinction between internal questions arising between agent and principal and external questions arising between principal and third party and agent and third party. This is a fundamental division of agency law in civil law countries and though it does not form such a central part of common law analysis, it is understood by a common lawyer without difficulty,[1] even if it is sometimes applied with more difficulty.[2] Questions of the former type are probably best dealt with by the law governing the contract between agent and principal; questions of the latter type, by the law governing the contract between principal and third party, or perhaps the law of the place where the agent had his business establishment or (which need not be be the same) acted. The division is, in pure contractual situations, a useful starting point; and the few English cases that can be used to establish the basic approaches to these two situations are well discussed in the leading English book on the conflict of laws.[3] Such an approach is also taken by an international convention on the subject, the Hague Convention on the Law Applicable to Agency of 1978.[4] As regards contract issues, this convention involves some possibility of conflict with the Rome Convention on the Law Applicable to Contractual Obligations,[5] which excludes from its scope some agency matters (the external question whether an agent is able to bind a principal[6]) but by no means all. But the Hague Convention has not been adopted in the United Kingdom.

However, starting from this point and even confining oneself to contract questions, it is not long before serious problems arise. The relationship between principal and agent need not involve a contract at all. When it does not, it may raise issues of tort, of fiduciary law, and, in some situations, of bailment.[7] What law governs any one of these questions, particularly where a foreign system approaches these topics quite differently, as for example by seeing a contract where common law would not? When on any analysis a contract must be involved, what law governs the validity and effect of an act alleged to be a ratification?[8] What law governs questions of what in common law is called apparent authority? The theory behind this type of liability varies from country to country. If it is based on estoppel, the answer may be different to that which would be given if it is based on an objective interpretation of the

12–002

---

[1] *cf.* above, para. 1–016.

[2] See Dicey and Morris, *Conflict of Laws* (12th ed.), Vol. 2, pp. 1454–1455 (on the Rome Convention, below).

[3] Dicey and Morris, *op. cit.* above, Vol. 2, Rules 198, 199.

[4] There is also a Unidroit Convention on Agency in the International Sale of Goods of 1983, which contains *substantive* rules of agency law. See Bonell (1984) 32 Am.J.Comp.L. 717; Evans, [1984] Uniform L.Rev. 73.

[5] Operative in the United Kingdom under the Contracts (Applicable Law) Act 1990.

[6] Article 1.2(f). The scope of this exclusion is not clear: see Dicey and Morris, *op. cit.* above, Vol. 2, pp. 1453–1457.

[7] See Article 56.

[8] See *Presentaciones Musicales S.A. v. Secunda* [1994] Ch 271.

contract itself, for it is arguable that estoppel is procedural.[9] But in other countries, yet further types of reasoning can be employed.

Next, the possibility of the intervention of an undisclosed principal raises problems of particular difficulty, for the basis of this intervention is not settled even in common law[10] and where anything similar is allowed in civil law systems at all it may be by the use of completely different reasoning, for example by third party rights on contracts, by assignment or *action directe* or *oblique*; and legal systems allowing such intervention may shield the principal from liability.[11] Going further, some contract decisions can at common law be explained as based on reasoning at least analogous to that governing vicarious liability in tort.[12] Any liability of an agent towards a third party on an authorised contract made for his principal is explicable in various ways.[13] The liability of an *un*authorised agent to the third party rests at common law on a separate contract between them: other systems may take different views, as indeed did English law at an earlier stage.[14] Finally, questions of powers of attorney, especially as to their revocability, may require special treatment in any system.

All in all, nowhere is it truer than in the area of agency that

"The comparative lawyer often discovers that an institution which he takes for granted in his own legal system almost as if it were part of the natural order of things is really no more than a contingent product of historical and sociological conditions which, much to his surprise and edification, is unknown in other systems and unregretted at that."[15]

12–003   If we then go beyond the above we see that in this book appear not only propositions based on the law of contract, including questions of contracts for the benefit of others and of damages recoverable for the loss of others; but also propositions on the law of tort, including questions of assumption of responsibility, which might in some systems be regarded as contractual; on restitution, which raise questions of possible proprietary claims, with their impact on insolvency law and on problems as to the recovery of profits, as well as claims *in personam*; and in general on trusts and equity, which almost always raise

---

[9] See *Janred Properties Ltd v. Ente Nazionale Italiano per il Turismo* [1987] 2 F.T.L.R. 179; affd. [1989] 2 All E.R. 444.

[10] See Article 78.

[11] See Zweigert and Kötz, *Introduction to Comparative Law* (2nd ed.), Vol. 2, pp. 113 *et seq.* But Articles 7.420 and 421 of the new Dutch Civil Code are nearer to the doctrine of undisclosed principal than are the laws of some other countries: see also Italian CC Arts. 1705–1707; Swiss Federal Code of Obligations, Arts. 32(2), 401.

[12] See above, para. 1–024.

[13] See Article 100.

[14] See Articles 107, 109, 110.

[15] Zweigert and Kötz, *op. cit.* above, Vol. 2, at p. 117.

difficulties in the conflict of laws when a civil law regime is involved and in any case raise their own problems of categorisation — for example, the extent to which particular notions and rules are substantive or remedial — in a common law system.[16] There is some discussion also of company law. The extent to which company law requires the use of agency notions is controversial: obviously some legal systems may not see a company law issue as requiring the use of general agency concepts at all, and even common law does not always treat such issues in this way.[17] The book also considers questions of bills of exchange and cheques, liens, and in general of transfer of movable property, tangible and intangible, *inter vivos*. Some of the propositions here discussed relate to the idea of notice (in varying contexts) or are matters of the law of evidence; and there may be disputes as to whether rules are substantive or procedural. Sometimes agency reasoning has even been deployed in public law, which is a separate topic.

A proper analysis of the conflict of laws implications of all the matters discussed in this book would require a second volume. An introductory analysis distinguishing between the internal and external relationships, confined to the law of contract and citing much relevant material is already to be found in the leading work on the conflict of laws[18] and need not be reformulated here. Only in respect of the Commercial Agents Directive, therefore, is there in this book discussion of the conflict of laws[19]: this seems appropriate because of the limited nature of its intervention into agency law.

Beyond this context it seems that the best function which this book can perform in relation to the conflict of laws is to draw attention to the juristic nature, or possible juristic natures, of the common law (in the widest sense) agency doctrines which it discusses. The reader confronted with a conflict of laws problem can then proceed to specialist works on the conflict of laws with a proper analysis, or at any rate the possible analyses, of the relevant English rules in mind. In such situations he or she should then remember that the appropriate analysis of the facts in other systems may, particularly if they are civil law systems, be quite different.[20]

---

[16] The Recognition of Trusts Act 1987, which provides for the application of the Hague Convention on the Law Applicable to Trusts extends, by virtue of s. 1(2), to some cases of express trusts.

[17] Such problems are excluded from the Rome Convention: Article 1.2(f).

[18] *Dicey and Morris, op. cit.* above.

[19] See Chap. 11, above.

[20] There is much useful discussion, even if now somewhat outdated, in the Hague Conference on Private International Law, *Actes et documents de la treizième session*, 1976, Vol. IV, *Agency* (1979). For a more modern coverage see Verhagen, *Agency in Private International Law* (Martinus Nijhoff/T.M.C. Asser Instituut, 1995).

1993 No. 3053

COMMERCIAL AGENTS

The Commercial Agents (Council Directive) Regulations 1993

Made	*7th December 1993*
Laid before Parliament	*8th December 1993*
Coming into Force	*1st January 1994*

ARRANGEMENT OF REGULATIONS

PART I

General

PART IV

Conclusion and Termination of the Agency Contract

PART V

Miscellaneous and Supplemental

The Secretary of State, being a Minister designated(**a**) for the purposes of section 2(2) of the European Communities Act 1972(**b**) in relation to measures relating to relations between commercial agents and their

---

(**a**) S.I. 1989/1327.
(**b**) 1972 c.68.

principals, in the exercise of the powers conferred by him by that section, hereby makes the following Regulations:

PART I

GENERAL

Citation, commencement and applicable law

1.—(1) These Regulations may be cited as the Commercial Agents (Council Directive) Regulations 1993 and shall come into force on 1st January 1994.

(2) These Regulations govern the relations between commercial agents and their principals and, subject to paragraph (3), apply in relation to the activities of commercial agents in Great Britain.

(3) Regulations 3 to 22 do not apply where the parties have agreed that the agency contract is to be governed by the law of another member State.

Interpretation, application and extent

2.—(1) In these Regulations—

"commercial agent" means a self-employed intermediary who has continuing authority to negotiate the sale or purchase of goods on behalf of another person (the "principal"), or to negotiate and conclude the sale or purchase of goods on behalf of and in the name of that principal; but shall be understood as not including in particular:

   (i) a person who, in his capacity as an officer of a company or association, is empowered to enter into commitments binding on that company or association;

   (ii) a partner who is lawfully authorised to enter into commitments binding on his partners;

   (iii) a person who acts as an insolvency practitioner (as that expression is defined in section 388 of the Insolvency Act 1986(**c**)) or the equivalent in any other jurisdiction;

"commission" means any part of the remuneration of a commercial agent which varies with the number or value of business transactions;

"restraint of trade clause" means an agreement restricting the business activities of a commercial agent following termination of the agency contract.

(**c**) 1986 c.45.

(2) These Regulations do not apply to—

   (a)   commercial agents whose activities are unpaid;

   (b)   commercial agents when they operate on commodity exchanges or in the commodity market;

   (c)   the Crown Agents for Overseas Governments and Administrations, as set up under the Crown Agents Act 1979(**d**), or its subsidiaries.

(3) The provisions of the Schedule to these Regulations have effect for the purpose of determining the persons whose activities as commercial agents are to be considered secondary.

(4) These Regulations shall not apply to the persons referred to in paragraph (3) above.

(5) These Regulations do not extend to Northern Ireland.[1]

PART II

RIGHTS AND OBLIGATIONS

Duties of a commercial agent to his principal

3.—(1) In performing his activities a commercial agent must look after the interests of his principal and act dutifully and in good faith.

(2) In particular, a commercial agent must—

   (a)   make proper efforts to negotiate and, where appropriate, conclude the transactions he is instructed to take care of;

   (b)   communicate to his principal all the necessary information available to him;

   (c)   comply with reasonable instructions given by his principal.

Duties of a principal to his commercial agent

4.—(1) In his relations with his commercial agent a principal must act dutifully and in good faith.

(2) In particular, a principal must—

   (a)   provide his commercial agent with the necessary documentation relating to the goods concerned;

   (b)   obtain for his commercial agent the information necessary for the performance of the agency contract, and in particular notify his commercial agent within a reasonable period once he

---

(**d**) 1979 c.43.
1 But similar regulations apply there; above, para. 11–003.

anticipates that the volume of commercial transactions will be significantly lower than that which the commercial agent could normally have expected.

(3) A principal shall, in addition, inform his commercial agent within a reasonable period of his acceptance or refusal of, and of any non-execution by him of, a commercial transaction which the commercial agent has procured for him.

Prohibition on derogation from regulations 3 and 4 and consequence of breach

5.—(1) The parties may not derogate from regulations 3 and 4 above.

(2) The law applicable to the contract shall govern the consequence of breach of the rights and obligations under regulations 3 and 4 above.

PART III

REMUNERATION

Form and amount of remuneration in absence of agreement

6.—(1) In the absence of any agreement as to remuneration between the parties, a commercial agent shall be entitled to the remuneration that commercial agents appointed for the goods forming the subject of his agency contract are customarily allowed in the place where he carries on his activities and, if there is no such customary practice, a commercial agent shall be entitled to reasonable remuneration taking into account all the aspects of the transaction.

(2) This regulation is without prejudice to the application of any enactment or rule of law concerning the level of remuneration.

(3) Where a commercial agent is not remunerated (wholly or in part) by commission, regulations 7 to 12 below shall not apply.

Entitlement to commission on transactions concluded during agency contract

7.—(1) A commercial agent shall be entitled to commission on commercial transactions concluded during the period covered by the agency contract—

(a) where the transaction has been concluded as a result of his action; or

(b) where the transaction is concluded with a third party whom he has previously acquired as a customer for transactions of the same kind.

(2) A commercial agent shall also be entitled to commission on transactions concluded during the period covered by the agency contract where he has an exclusive right to a specific geographical area or to a specific group of customers and where the transaction has been entered into with a customer belonging to that area or group.

Entitlement to commission on transactions concluded after agency contract has terminated

8. Subject to regulation 9 below, a commercial agent shall be entitled to commission on commercial transactions concluded after the agency contract has terminated if—

    (a)   the transaction is mainly attributable to his efforts during the period covered by the agency contract and if the transaction was entered into within a reasonable period after that contract terminated; or

    (b)   in accordance with the conditions mentioned in regulation 7 above, the order of the third party reached the principal or the commercial agent before the agency contract terminated.

Apportionment of commission between new and previous commercial agents

9.—(1) A commercial agent shall not be entitled to the commission referred to in regulation 7 above if that commission is payable, by virtue of regulation 8 above, to the previous commercial agent, unless it is equitable because of the circumstances for the commission to be shared between the commercial agents.

(2) The principal shall be liable for any sum due under paragraph (1) above to the person entitled to it in accordance with that paragraph, and any sum which the other commercial agent receives to which he is not entitled shall be refunded to the principal.

When commission due and date for payment

10.—(1) Commission shall become due as soon as, and to the extent that, one of the following circumstances occurs:

    (a)   the principal has executed the transaction; or

    (b)   the principal should, according to his agreement with the third party, have executed the transaction; or

    (c)   the third party has executed the transaction.

(2) Commission shall become due at the latest when the third party has executed his part of the transaction or should have done so if the principal had executed his part of the transaction, as he should have.

(3) The commission shall be paid not later than on the last day of the month following the quarter in which it became due, and, for the purposes of these Regulations, unless otherwise agreed between the parties, the first quarter period shall run from the date the agency contract takes effect, and subsequent periods shall run from that date in the third month thereafter or the beginning of the fourth month, whichever is the sooner.

(4) Any agreement to derogate from paragraphs (2) and (3) above to the detriment of the commercial agent shall be void.

Extinction of right to commission

11.—(1) The right to commission can be extinguished only if and to the extent that—

(a) it is established that the contract between the third party and the principal will not be executed; and

(b) that fact is due to a reason for which the principal is not to blame.

(2) Any commission which the commercial agent has already received shall be refunded if the right to it is extinguished.

(3) Any agreement to derogate from paragraph (1) above to the detriment of the commercial agent shall be void.

Periodic supply of information as to commission due and right of inspection of principal's books

12.—(1) The principal shall supply his commercial agent with a statement of the commission due, not later than the last day of the month following the quarter in which the commission has become due, and such statement shall set out the main components used in calculating the amount of the commission.

(2) A commercial agent shall be entitled to demand that he be provided with all the information (and in particular an extract from the books) which is available to his principal and which he needs in order to check the amount of the commission due to him.

(3) Any agreement to derogate from paragraphs (1) and (2) above shall be void.

(4) Nothing in this regulation shall remove or restrict the effect of, or prevent reliance upon, any enactment or rule of law which recognises the right of an agent to inspect the books of a principal.

PART IV

CONCLUSION AND TERMINATION OF THE AGENCY CONTRACT

Right to signed written statement of terms of agency contract

13.—(1) The commercial agent and principal shall each be entitled to receive from the other, on request, a signed written document setting out the terms of the agency contract including any terms subsequently agreed.

(2) Any purported waiver of the right referred to in paragraph (1) above shall be void.

Conversion of agency contract after expiry of fixed period

14. An agency contract for a fixed period which continues to be performed by both parties after that period has expired shall be deemed to be converted into an agency contract for an indefinite period.

Minimum periods of notice for termination of agency contract

15.—(1) Where an agency contract is concluded for an indefinite period either party may terminate it by notice.

(2) The period of notice shall be—

    (a)   1 month for the first year of the contract;
    (b)   2 months for the second year commenced;
    (c)   3 months for the third year commenced and for the subsequent years;

and the parties may not agree on any shorter periods of notice.

(3) If the parties agree on longer periods than those laid down in paragraph (2) above, the period of notice to be observed by the principal must not be shorter than that to be observed by the commercial agent.

(4) Unless otherwise agreed by the parties, the end of the period of notice must coincide with the end of a calendar month.

(5) The provisions of this regulation shall also apply to an agency contract for a fixed period where it is converted under regulation 14 above into an agency contract for an indefinite period subject to the proviso that the earlier fixed period must be taken into account in the calculation of the period of notice.

Savings with regard to immediate termination

16. These Regulations shall not affect the application of any enactment or rule of law which provides for the immediate termination of the agency contract—

    (a) because of the failure of one party to carry out all or part of his obligations under that contract; or

    (b) where exceptional circumstances arise.

Entitlement of commercial agent to indemnity or compensation on termination of agency contract

17.—(1) This regulation has effect for the purpose of ensuring that the commercial agent is, after termination of the agency contract, indemnified in accordance with paragraphs (3) to (5) below or compensated for damage in accordance with paragraphs (6) and (7) below.

(2) Except where the agency contact otherwise provides, the commercial agent shall be entitled to be compensated rather than indemnified.

(3) Subject to paragraph (9) and to regulation 18 below, the commercial agent shall be entitled to an indemnity if and to the extent that—

    (a) he has brought the principal new customers or has significantly increased the volume of business with existing customers and the principal continues to derive substantial benefits from the business with such customers; and

    (b) the payment of this indemnity is equitable having regard to all the circumstances and, in particular, the commission lost by the commercial agent on the business transacted with such customers.

(4) The amount of the indemnity shall not exceed a figure equivalent to an indemnity for one year calculated from the commercial agent's average annual remuneration over the preceding five years and if the contract goes back less than five years the indemnity shall be calculated on the average for the period in question.

(5) The grant of an indemnity as mentioned above shall not prevent the commercial agent from seeking damages.

(6) Subject to paragraph (9) and to regulation 18 below, the commercial agent shall be entitled to compensation for the damage he suffers as a result of the termination of his relations with his principal.

(7) For the purpose of these Regulations such damage shall be deemed to occur particularly when the termination takes place in either or both of the following circumstances, namely circumstances which—

(a) deprive the commercial agent of the commission which proper performance of the agency contract would have procured for him whilst providing his principal with substantial benefits linked to the activities of the commercial agent; or

(b) have not enabled the commercial agent to amortize the costs and expenses that he had incurred in the performance of the agency contract on the advice of his principal.

(8) Entitlement to the indemnity or compensation for damage as provided for under paragraphs (2) to (7) above shall also arise where the agency contract is terminated as a result of the death of the commercial agent.

(9) The commercial agent shall lose his entitlement to the indemnity or compensation for damage in the instances provided for in paragraphs (2) to (8) above if within one year following termination of his agency contract he has not notified his principal that he intends pursuing his entitlement.

Grounds for excluding payment of indemnity or compensation under regulation 17

18. The indemnity or* compensation referred to in regulation 17 above shall not be payable to the commercial agent where—

(a) the principal has terminated the agency contract because of default attributable to the commercial agent which would justify immediate termination of the agency contract pursuant to regulation 16 above; or

(b) the commercial agent has himself terminated the agency contract, unless such termination is justified—

  (i) by circumstances attributable to the principal, or
  (ii) on grounds of the age, infirmity or illness of the commercial agent in consequence of which he cannot reasonably be required to continue his activities; or

(c) the commercial agent, with the agreement of his principal, assigns his rights and duties under the agency contract to another person.

---

* These words were inserted by Commercial Agents (Council Directive) (Amendment) Regulations 1993 (S.I. 1993 No. 3173).

Prohibition on derogation from regulations 17 and 18

19. The parties may not derogate from regulations 17 and 18 to the detriment of the commercial agent before the agency contract expires.

Restraint of trade clauses

20.—(1) A restraint of trade clause shall be valid only if and to the extent that—

(a) it is concluded in writing; and
(b) it relates to the geographical area or the group of customers and the geographical area entrusted to the commercial agent and to the kind of goods covered by his agency under the contract.

(2) A retraint of trade clause shall be valid for not more than two years after termination of the agency contract.

(3) Nothing in this regulation shall affect any enactment or rule of law which imposes other restrictions on the validity or enforceability of restraint of trade clauses or which enables a court to reduce the obligations on the parties resulting from such clauses.

PART V

MISCELLANEOUS AND SUPPLEMENTAL

Disclosure of information

21. Nothing in these Regulations shall require information to be given where such disclosure would be contrary to public policy.

Service of notice etc

22.—(1) Any notice, statement or other document to be given or supplied to a commercial agent or to be given or supplied to the principal under these Regulations may be so given or supplied:

(a) by delivering it to him;
(b) by leaving it at his proper address addressed to him by name;
(c) by sending it by post to him addressed either to his registered address or to the address of his registered or principal office;

or by any other means provided for in the agency contract.

(2) Any such notice, statement or document may—

(a) in the case of a body corporate, be given or served on the secretary or clerk of that body;

(b) in the case of a partnership, be given to or served on any partner or on any person having the control or management of the partnership business.

Transitional provisions

23.—(1) Notwithstanding any provision in an agency contract made before 1st January 1994, these Regulations shall apply to that contract after that date and, accordingly any provision which is inconsistent with these Regulations shall have effect subject to them.

(2) Nothing in these Regulations shall affect the rights and liabilities of a commercial agent or a principal which have accrued before 1st January 1994.

7th December 1993 *Strathclyde*
Parliamentary Under-Secretary of State
Department of Trade and Industry

THE SCHEDULE Regulation 2(3)

1. The activities of a person as a commercial agent are to be considered secondary where it may reasonably be taken that the primary purpose of the arrangement with his principal is other than as set out in paragraph 2 below.

2. An arrangement falls within this paragraph if—

(a) the business of the principal is the sale, or as the case may be purchase, of goods of a particular kind; and

(b) the goods concerned are such that—

(i) transactions are normally individually negotiated and concluded on a commercial basis, and

(ii) procuring a transaction on one occasion is likely to lead to further transactions in those goods with that customer on future occasions, or to transactions in those goods with other customers in the same geographical area or among the same group of customers and

that accordingly it is in the commercial interests of the principal in developing the market in those goods to appoint a representative to such customers with a view to the representative devoting effort, skill and expenditure from his own resources to that end.

3. The following are indications that an arrangement falls within paragraph 2 above, and the absence of any of them is an indication to the contrary—

(a) the principal is the manufacturer, importer or distributor of the goods;

(b)   the goods are specifically identified with the principal in the market in question rather than, or to a greater extent than, with any other person;

(c)   the agent devotes substantially the whole of his time to representative activities (whether for one principal or for a number of principals whose interests are not conflicting);

(d)   the goods are not normally available in the market in question other than by means of the agent;

(e)   the arrangement is described as one of commercial agency.

4.   The following are indications that an arrangement does not fall within paragraph 2 above—

(a)   promotional material is supplied direct to potential customers;

(b)   persons are granted agencies without reference to existing agents in a particular area or in relation to a particular group;

(c)   customers normally select the goods for themselves and merely place their orders through the agent.

5.   The activities of the following categories of persons are presumed, unless the contrary is established, not to fall within paragraph 2 above—

Mail order catalogue agents for consumer goods

Consumer credit agents.

INDEX

735

AUTHORITY—*cont.*

breach of warranty of. *See* BREACH OF WARRANTY OF AUTHORITY.

cannot exceed powers of principal, 3–008, 3–009

contract, does not require, 1–005, 2–027, 2–028

course of employment and, 8–029, 8–173, 8–177. *See also* USUAL AUTHORITY.

defined, 1–001

delegation of. *See* DELEGATION BY AGENT.

doubt as to whether persisting, 10–003

express actual,
ambiguous terms, 3–010, 3–015—3–017, 6–010, 6–011
not under seal, 3–013—3–015
powers of attorney, 3–010—3–012
warrant, to, 3–015

fraudulent agent, 8–063—8–065

implied actual,
course of dealing, from, 3–037—3–038
credit, to sell on, 3–022
customary, 3–003, 3–030—3–036A. *See also* CUSTOM.
delegate, to, 5–001—5–007
disclose agency, to, 3–026
distrain, to, 3–020
incidental, 3–003, 3–018—3–020
receive deposit, to, 3–029
payment, to, 3–020, 3–021—3–023, 8–107, 8–108, 8–112
not in cash, 3–021—3–023
sign memorandum, to, 3–020. *See also* MEMORANDUM; LAND.
usual, 3–006, 3–024—3–026, 3–027—3–029. *See also* USUAL AUTHORITY.
warrant, to, 3–015, 3–020, 3–029, 3–036

irrevocable, 10–006—10–011

joint, 2–042, 2–043

lack of, notice of, 8–008, 8–051—8–062A

necessity, of, 3–007, 3–019. *See also* AGENCY OF NECESSITY.

negligent statement as to, 9–058, 9–112

ostensible. *See* APPARENT AUTHORITY.

power, distinguished from, 1–011

presumed, 3–039—3–051
cohabitation, from, 3–040—3–051
distinguished from implied, 3–040

AUTHORITY—*cont.*

principal,
bound by acts within, 8–001—8–050, 8–063—8–065, 8–069—8–083, 8–125—8–127
not bound by acts outside, 8–051—8–062, 8–066—8–068

property, disposition of, 8–125—8–156A

ratification of act without. *See* RATIFICATION.

representation by agent as to. *See* APPARENT AUTHORITY.

revocation of. *See* TERMINATION OF AUTHORITY.

several, 2–042, 2–043

termination. *See* TERMINATION OF AUTHORITY.

types of, 3–001—3–007

unilateral manifestation of will, arising from, 1–005, 2–032

usual. *See* USUAL AUTHORITY.

wife, of. *See* MARRIED WOMAN.

BAD DEBTS,
remuneration in respect of, 7–012

BAGSHOT HEATH,
course of robbery on, 7–005n

BAILEE,
agent as, estoppel, 6–111—6–113
agent of necessity, as, 4–005, 4–008, 4–012
authority of, 1–027, 3–020
damages recoverable by, 9–010
distinguished from agent, 1–027
lien created by, 1–027, 3–020

BAILIFF,
authority of, 3–029
fees of, liability for, 9–003
liability of, in tort, 9–119
money, liability to repay, 9–103
tender to, 3–029. *See also* DISTRESS.

BALTIC EXCHANGE,
broker on, 9–043

BANK MANAGER,
apparent authority of, 3–026, 8–046, 8–068
deceit, liability in, 9–119
documentary credits manager, 8–046
misappropriation by, 8–197
misrepresentation as to credit, 8–194, 9–119

BANKER,
accessory liability, 9–132, 9–133
collecting cheque, liability, 9–124

741

COMPANY—*cont.*
  dissolved, agency of necessity for,
    4–005
  foreign, service of writ on, 2–026
  indoor management rule, 8–035, 8–041,
    8–049
  interrogatories, answering, 8–203
  liquidation. *See* winding up.
  loan to, unauthorised, 8–199, 8–200
  manager, authority of. *See* MANAGER.
  meeting, ratification of notice of, 2–096
  memorandum signed by agent, 2–023,
    2–035
  misrepresentations as to credit, 8–194
  money received by, 8–200
  notice to, 8–210, 8–212
  organ of, 1–022, 8–185, 8–194, 8–210,
    8–212
  power of attorney by, 8–049
  pre-incorporation contract, 2–060,
    2–064, 9–078—9–081. *See also*
    NON-EXISTENT PRINCIPAL.
  primary representatives of, 1–022,
    8–185, 8–194, 8–210, 8–212
  promoters,
    authority of agents of, 8–047
    breach of warranty of authority,
      9–062
    contracts by, 9–081
    director, sale to, 6–087
    ratification of acts of, 2–060, 2–064
    secret profit by, 6–080
  public documents, constructive notice,
    8–037, 8–038
  ratification by. *See* RATIFICATION.
  receiver. *See* RECEIVER.
  sale to, by director, 6–062
  seal, unauthorised use of, 8–043
  secretary,
    admission by, 8–203
    assistant, signature, 8–194
    authority of, 3–027, 8–049, 8–068,
      8–203
    bribery of, 6–087
    clerk of, notification to, 8–212
    forgery by, 8–200
    fraud of, 8–068, 8–200
    knowledge of, 8–213
    ratification of act of, 2–096
    representation by, 2–096
    signing promissory note, 9–053
  shares, application for, 8–047
  signature of, 1–022, 8–194, 9–035,
    9–052, 9–079, 9–081
  subsidiary, as agent, 1–031

COMPANY—*cont.*
  torts of agent, liability for, 1–024
  two agents decide differently, 8–046
  ultra vires acts. *See* ULTRA VIRES
    DOCTRINE.
  vice-president, authority of, 8–068
  winding up, liquidation, dissolution,
    7–085, 7–088, 9–060, 10–002,
    10–006, 10–012, 10–015
  wrongs of agents, liability for, 8–185
COMMISSIONNAIRE, 1–018
COMPENSATION,
  on termination of authority,
    10–033—10–041. *See also*
    COMMERCIAL AGENT.
COMPULSORY PURCHASE,
  commission on, 7–031
CONCESSIONNAIRE. *See* DISTRIBUTOR.
CONFIDENTIAL INFORMATION,
  agent profiting from, 6–056, 6–076,
    6–077
  canvasser, used by, 6–077
  consent to use of, 6–075
  property, as, 6–076
  remedies, 6–076, 6–077
  solicitor, used by, 6–081
  when no longer confidential, 6–076.
    See also PROPERTY; SECRET
      PROFIT.
CONFIRMING HOUSE,
  functions of, 9–019, 9–032
  lien, 7–081
CONFLICT OF LAWS, 12–001—12–003. *See*
  also COMMERCIAL AGENT.
CONSENT,
  conditional instructions, 8–047
  to agency relationship,
    of agent, 2–032
    of principal, 2–031
CONSIGNEE,
  lien for advances, 8–154
CONSOLIDATOR,
  lien, 7–081
CONSTRUCTIVE TRUST. *See* TRUSTEE;
  ACCESSORY LIABILITY; KNOWING
  RECEIPT
CONSUMER CREDIT AGENT,
  not commercial agent, 11–019
CONTINUING BENEFIT,
  right to, 10–037
CONTRACT OF AGENCY. *See* AGENCY,
  contract of.
CONTRACTS OF AGENT,
  agent, rights and liabilities of,
    9–004—9–043

PRINCIPAL—*cont.*
  admissions binding on. *See*
    ADMISSIONS.
  agent,
    suing for, 9–010, 9–011
    who is, 9–082—9–091
  alien enemy as, 2–010, 6–071
  bankruptcy of. *See* BANKRUPTCY.
  bills of exchange, liability on. *See*
    BILLS OF EXCHANGE.
  bribery of agent, rights on. *See* BRIBE;
    BRIBERY.
  capacity to act as, 2–006—2–010
  confidential information of. *See*
    CONFIDENTIAL INFORMATION.
  consent to agency relationship, 1–004,
    1–005, 2–031
  contracts of agent. *See* CONTRACTS OF
    AGENT.
  co-operation, duties of, 7–001, 7–040
  credit given to. *See* CREDIT;
    ELECTION.
  death of. *See* DEATH.
  deeds, liability on. *See* DEED.
  defences to action by or against. *See*
    CONTRACTS OF AGENT.
  defined, 1–001
  disclosed. *See* DISCLOSED PRINCIPAL.
  duties of agent to, 6–001 *et seq.*, 11–020
  duty to account to, 6–092—6–096
  duties towards agent, 7–001 *et seq.*,
    11–021
  election to sue. *See* ELECTION.
  evidence as to disbelieved, 9–086
  fictitious. *See* NON-EXISTENT
    PRINCIPAL.
  fiduciary, as, 7–001, 11–021
  foreign. *See* FOREIGN PRINCIPAL.
  foreign sovereign as, 9–101
  gifts to agent, 6–069
  identified. *See* named.
  indemnity from agent, 8–187
  interrogatories as to, 9–013, 9–015
  joint, 2–044, 2–045, 6–098
  judgment against. *See* JUDGMENT.
  knowledge of. *See* NOTICE.
  money applied for benefit of,
    8–198—8–200
  named, 1–033
  non-existent. *See* NON-EXISTENT
    PRINCIPAL.
  notice to through agent. *See* NOTICE.
  payment over to by agent, 9–095,
    9–101, 9–103

PRINCIPAL—*cont.*
  preventing earning of commission. *See*
    REMUNERATION.
  property acquired for, 6–108—6–110,
    8–166—8–172
  property, disposition of. *See*
    PROPERTY.
  quasi-contract. *See* RESTITUTION.
  ratification by. *See* RATIFICATION.
  remedies against agent,
    personal 6–043, 6–054, 6–085,
      6–089
    proprietary, 6–042—6–044. *See also*
      TRACING.
  report to, as admission, 8–201, 8–203
  restitution. *See* RESTITUTION.
  revocation of authority by. *See*
    TERMINATION OF AUTHORITY.
  settling with agent. *See* SETTLEMENT.
  sub-agent, relations with. *See* SUB-
    AGENT.
  termination of authority by. *See*
    TERMINATION OF AUTHORITY.
  title of, estoppel as to. *See* ESTOPPEL.
  tort, liability to agent in, 7–001
  tracing by. *See* TRACING.
  undisclosed. *See* UNDISCLOSED
    PRINCIPAL.
  unidentified. *See* unnamed.
  unilateral manifestation of will, 1–005,
    2–032
  unnamed. *See* UNNAMED PRINCIPAL.
  who can be, 2–006—2–010
  wrongs of agent, liability for,
    8–173—8–200. *See also* WRONGS
    OF AGENT.
PRINTER,
  infringement of copyright, 9–119
PROFESSIONAL AGENT. *See* AGENT.
PROFIT. *See* SECRET PROFIT.
PROKURA, 1–023
PROMISSARY NOTE. *See* BILL OF
    EXCHANGE.
PROMOTER. *See* COMPANY.
PROPERTY,
  agent, of, bought by principal. *See*
    AGENT, selling to principal.
  confidential information as, 6–076
  passing of, between principal and
    agent, 7–099—7–101
  principal, of,
    agent profiting from, 6–074, 6–075,
      6–077. *See also* SECRET PROFIT.
    bought by agent. *See* AGENT,
      purchasing from principal,

PROPERTY—*cont.*
  principal, of—*cont.*
    disposition of by agent,
      8–125—8–165. *See also*
      APPARENT AUTHORITY;
      APPARENT OWNERSHIP;
      FACTORS ACT 1889; MARKET
      OVERT; MONEY; TITLE DEEDS.
    distress against, 8–163, 8–165
    duty to keep separate, 6–088, 6–091
    order for preservation, 6–042
    received for principal by agent,
      6–108—6–110, 7–100, 7–101,
      8–166—8–172
    reserved by principal. *See* ROMALPA
      CLAUSES.
    title denied by agent, 6–111—6–113
    tracing of. *See* TRACING.
    trustee of, agent as. *See* TRUSTEE.
  third party, of, misappropriated by
    agent, 8–195—8–197
PROPERTY ADVISER, 6–073
PROXY. *See* SIGNATURE.
PUBLIC HOUSE,
  manager of, 8–068
  tenant of, 8–045. *See also* HOTEL.
PUBLIC SERVANT,
  bribery of, 6–081
PURCHASE, READY, WILLING AND ABLE
  TO, 7–019, 7–020. *See also* ESTATE
  AGENT.
PURCHASER,
  introduction of, 7–018. *See also*
  BUYER.

QUANTITY SURVEYOR,
  production of documents, 6–091
  suing for fees, 3–029
QUANTUM MERUIT,
  contractual, 7–009n., 7–010, 7–012,
    7–024, 7–040
  estate agent claiming, 7–024
  excluded by contract, 7–004, 7–010,
    7–012, 7–013, 7–024, 7–031
  meaning, 7–009n., 7–024n.
  restitutionary, 7–003, 7–009, 7–050
QUASI-CONTRACT. *See* RESTITUTION.

RAILWAY INSPECTOR,
  admission by, 8–203
RATIFICATION, 1–006, 2–046—2–095
  acquiescence, by, 2–068, 2–072
  Act of State, 2–050

RATIFICATION—*cont.*
  acts capable of, 2–051—2–056
    constituting, 2–068—2–078
  administrator, by, 2–064, 10–014
  advance, in, 2–048, 3–012
  affirmance and, 2–068n.
  agent, by, 2–075
    intends to act for self, 2–059, 2–064
  agent's
    inner intentions irrelevant, 2–059,
      2–064
    liability to principal where, 2–092,
      2–096, 6–004
  alien enemy, by, 2–062, 2–064
  apparent authority and, 8–031
  assault, of, 2–057
  breach of warranty of authority and,
    9–066
  communicated, need not be, 2–049
  company, 8–185
    directors, by, 2–076, 2–079, 2–096
    notice of meeting of, 2–096
    proceedings by, defect in, 2–057
    promoters, acts of, 2–060, 2–064
    shareholders, by, 2–076, 2–096
    ultra vires acts, 2–054
  conduct, by, 2–068, 2–072
  contract, of, 2–051, 2–052, 2–069,
    2–072, 2–078, 2–079, 2–080, 2–083,
    2–084, 2–085, 2–087, 2–088, 2–090,
    2–092, 2–095, 2–096
    voidable, of, 2–052
  contract subject to, 2–080, 2–083,
    2–084, 9–079
  conversion, of, 2–052A, 2–057, 2–067,
    2–079
  Crown, by, 2–050, 2–096
  debt, payment of, 2–084
  deed, of, 2–068, 2–078
  defence of action, of, 2–096
  delegation, of, 5–004
  deposit, of, 2–079
  distress, of, 2–052A, 2–057, 2–064,
    2–067, 2–079, 2–084, 2–096, 9–119
  divesting interest, 2–086, 2–091, 2–093
  doctrine not anomalous, 2–047
  does not confer authority, 2–047,
    2–091, 2–094
  effect of, 2–047, 2–091—2–095, 6–004
  election, whether, 2–047, 2–049
  estate agent, of act of, 2–067, 2–079
  estoppel as to, 2–073
  events not preventing, 2–080—2–083

ULTRA VIRES DOCTRINE—*cont.*
Crown, agent of, 8–044
lien, effect on, 7–088
reduction of significance, 8–033, 8–038
UNDERWRITER,
authority of, 8–065
commission paid to broker, 6–087
duty of broker to, 6–019
fraudulent, 8–065
notification to solicitor of, 8–212
set-off by, 9–027
settlement with broker, 3–023, 3–036A
when broker agent of, 2–015
UNDISCLOSED PRINCIPAL, 1–007,
8–069—8–083
agent as trustee for, 8–070, 9–011
agent of,
attornment to, 8–166, 8–169, 8–170,
8–172
damages recoverable by, 9–011
disposition of property to, 8–166,
8–169—8–172
fraudulent, 8–064
liability on contract, 8–069, 8–098,
9–103
right to sue on contract, 8–070, 9–012
assignment, relevance of, 8–070, 8–080,
8–083
authority of agent of, 8–071
basis of doctrine, 8–070
bills of exchange, 8–090—8–094
capacity of agent, 8–075
circuity of action, doctrine avoiding,
8–070
contract in writing, 8–076, 8–079
deeds, 8–082
defences to action by, 8–070, 8–109
defined, 1–033, 8–072, 8–074
discovery, 8–081
doubts as to doctrine, 8–070
election as to suing. *See* ELECTION.
estoppel, relevance of, 8–109, 8–111
evidence as to existence of, 8–069,
8–079, 8–083
excluded by contract, 8–069, 8–080,
8–083, 8–169
Factors Act, 8–153
fraud of, 8–080, 8–097
fraudulent agent, 8–064
indirect agency and, 8–072
insurance policy, 8–080, 8–083
intention of agent, relevance of, 8–073
interrogatories as to, 9–013
intervenes subject to equities, 8–069,
8–098, 8–109, 8–111, 8–169, 9–012

UNDISCLOSED PRINCIPAL—*cont.*
judgment against agent. *See*
JUDGMENT.
land, purchasing, 6–109, 8–076, 8–083,
8–169
liability of, 8–069, 8–083, 8–114, 9–012
Lord Blackburn, views on, 8–070
merger. *See* JUDGMENT.
misrepresentation to, 8–099
payment to, defence against agent,
9–012
ratification by, 2–059, 2–064, 8–071,
8–078. *See also* RATIFICATION.
right to sue, 8–069, 8–083, 9–012
superior to that of agent, 9–012
scope and origin of doctrine, 8–070,
9–014
set-off against agent of, 8–107—8–112
settlement with agent of, 8–107—8–112
settling with agent, 8–100, 8–103,
8–104, 8–105
Statute of Frauds, 8–003, 8–076, 8–079
sub-agent's lien and, 7–097
theatre ticket, and, 8–080, 8–083
third party, degree of knowledge,
8–074, 8–110, 8–213
unnamed principal,
confused with, 1–035, 8–074, 8–105,
8–111, 8–114
distinguished from, 1–035
usual authority, 3–006, 8–069, 8–078,
8–083
variation of contract of, 8–109
UNDUE INFLUENCE,
presumption of, 6–036, 6–073
settled accounts, reopening of, 6–096
UNFAIR CONTRACT TERMS ACT,
fiduciary duties and, 6–052
UNINCORPORATED ASSOCIATION,
agent of, contract by,
liability, 9–079, 9–081
right to sue, 9–079
apparent authority, 8–045
breach of warranty of authority, 9–062,
9–070, 9–079
committee of, liability, 8–045, 9–081
ratification by members, 2–064
UNNAMED PRINCIPAL,
agent's
liability as, 9–086
right to sue as, 9–089
defined, 1–033
confused with undisclosed principal,
1–035, 8–074, 8–105, 8–111, 8–114,
8–117